I0821550

Reading Koine Greek

Reading Koine Greek

An Introduction and Integrated Workbook

Rodney J. Decker

Baker Academic
a division of Baker Publishing Group
Grand Rapids, Michigan

Published by Baker Academic
a division of Baker Publishing Group
P.O. Box 6287, Grand Rapids, MI 49516-6287
www.bakeracademic.com

Printed in the United States of America

Library of Congress Cataloging-in-Publication Data
Decker, Rodney J., 1952–2014.
Reading Koine Greek : an introduction and integrated workbook / Rodney J. Decker.
pages ; cm
Includes bibliographical references and index.
ISBN 978-0-8010-3928-7 (cloth)
1. Greek language, Biblical—Grammar. 2. Greek language, Biblical—Grammar—Problems, exercises, etc. I. Title.
PA817.D38 2014
487′.4—dc23 2014013739

Unless otherwise indicated, all Scripture quotations are the author's translation.

Baker Publishing Group publications use paper produced from sustainable forestry practices and postconsumer waste whenever possible.

25 26 27 28 29 30 12 11 10 9 8 7

To my Greek teachers

Robert J. Williams

William E. Arp

†Kenneth I. Brown

W. Edward Glenny

Contents

Expanded Table of Contents

Acknowledgments

I have dedicated this book to my formal Greek teachers. "Doc" Williams introduced a college sophomore to the language. Dr. Bill Arp, who is now my colleague and friend, taught the undergrad junior and senior Greek classes. Dr. Ken Brown, my ThM adviser, captivated me with textual criticism—and told me that I might be able to write someday. Years later my *Doctorvater*, Ed Glenny, assigned me Porter's *Verbal Aspect* in his Advanced Greek Grammar seminar—and I found not only my dissertation topic in those dense pages but also a love for grammar. Without the tutelage of these four men, I would not have the foundation to attempt my own grammar.

One other prof deserves mention. Though he was not one of my language teachers, Dr. Richard Engle was one of the chief reasons why I persevered in Greek. He came to the classroom after ten years of pastoral ministry. In his theology and Bible classes, I saw a blend of the biblical languages, theology, and ministry, which convinced me that if I was serious about Scripture, I had to be serious about the biblical languages. Dick's example guided my attempt at a similar integration for the dozen years I spent in the pastorate and is the vision that I now try to communicate to my students who aspire to pastoral ministry.

My other academic and linguistic debts are in printed form. No one can ever catalog (or even remember) the wide-ranging influence of the books and articles, lectures and sermons, that have shaped their thinking. From that constellation two deserve mention in the context of this book. Moisés Silva's *God, Language and Scripture* transformed my understanding of and approach to the biblical languages. I read it when it was first published, my last year in the pastorate. My beginning attempts to teach Greek the following fall were quite different from what they would otherwise have been. It is a relatively slender volume, but some "things on earth are small, yet they are extremely wise" (Prov. 30:24 NIV). The other is the work of D. A. Carson. Whether with his explicitly linguistic works on exegesis and accents or his deft handling of Scripture in his commentaries, he has modeled a capable and responsible approach to the text. The method of these two scholars is what I have come to describe as *grammatical minimalism* in contrast to a maximal, "golden nuggets" approach. That is, the most appropriate way to handle the interpretation of an ancient text (or a modern one, for that matter) is to place the least weight on the individual grammatical pieces and the greatest weight on statements in their context.

My students, too many to list, deserve my thanks. I have learned a great deal about Greek from answering the questions of hundreds of students over the years. A special thanks to those students in the last few years who spotted errata, clumsy explanations, and missing pieces as this book took shape for publication. My teaching assistant (TA) and PhD student Mark Mills has been exceptionally helpful in revising, clarifying, and proofing the manuscript. Dan Fabricatore has given valuable help and feedback while teaching my online Greek course with this material for a number of years and was my TA when he was a PhD student. Another of my former doctoral students, Neal Cushman of Northland International University, facilitated the use of this book in manuscript form for the past three years as a pilot project. The feedback that I have received from Bryan Blazosky and his TAs at Northland has helped shape the structure of the book and shown me where other instructors may not understand how or why I have done certain things. Rodney Whitacre, Stephen Carlson, Moisés Silva, Jay Smith, and Bill Combs read all or significant parts of the manuscript at various stages and provided many helpful suggestions and comments. Carl Conrad has been generous with his help over the years as we have corresponded about a great many of the grammatical matters included in this book. Any deficiencies, errors, or peculiarities that remain are certainly not due to the abundance of help that I have received; I accept the responsibility for such matters.

I would be remiss if I did not also acknowledge with gratitude the provisions of my dean, Mike Stallard, and provost, Jim Lytle. They have been generous in adjusting my teaching load and other responsibilities so that I could have time to study and write. At the beginning of my teaching career, Don Urey, then academic dean and later president of Calvary Bible College, took a chance on a young pastor who thought that he wanted to teach. Although I have taught many classes in the quarter century since he opened academia's doors to me, by choice I have always taught first-year Greek.

The editorial team at Baker Academic has been a great help in a very technical project. With James Ernest's recruiting efforts and his continuing encouragement, interaction, and critique; the superb copyediting by Amy Donaldson; and Wells Turner's skillful editing and coordination of the design and production, it has been a joy to work with their team.

Not a mere formality, I owe heartfelt thanks to my wife, Linda, for creating a home environment where I can write. Even on those long days when I spend many hours in my study, she understands. The winter when circumstances largely restricted my writing to a chair by the fire created considerable extra work for her; I am grateful. She has gone above and beyond in caring for not only me and our home but also our aging and sometimes invalid parents over the years, now having several times shared her home with one of them in their final years.

The map in the introduction is based on an outline map created by Joy A. Miller of Five J's (http://fivejs.com) and is used by permission. The "Greek Alphabet Song" in chapter 1 was written by Ben McGrew and is used with his permission; the score was converted to digital form by Alex Morris from the handwritten original. The illustrations in chapter 9 and at the end of chapter 23 were drawn by Levi Schooley and Cynthia Taylor respectively.

Photos included are used by permission of their owners:

Figure I.1 Mycenaean, Linear B Greek Tablet, National Archaeological Museum, Athens. Photo courtesy of John S. Y. Lee, Hong Kong

Figure I.2 Archaic Athenian Inscription, L. H. Jeffery Archive, Centre for the Study of Ancient Documents, Oxford

Figure 1.4 $\mathfrak{P}^{52}$, The John Rylands University Library, University of Manchester

Figure 1.5 Manuscript GA 545, Special Collections Library, University of Michigan; photo provided by the Center for the Study of NT Manuscripts

Figure 15.1 $\mathfrak{P}^{21}$ (POxy 1227), Robert C. Horn Papyri Collection, Trexler Library, Muhlenberg College, Allentown, Pennsylvania

Soli Deo gloria

Rodney J. Decker
Baptist Bible Seminary
Clarks Summit, Pennsylvania

Preface

This text is titled *Reading Koine Greek*, in part to indicate that it covers not just NT Greek but also the wider range of Bible-related Greek, especially the Septuagint (LXX) and to some extent the Pseudepigrapha and the Apostolic Fathers. The Greek of all these texts is very similar. Before you plunge in, either as a student or as a teacher, it is worth taking the time to orient yourself to the task before you and how this book is designed to help you accomplish your goals.

Why Learn Koine Greek?

Students will encounter the textbook (and Koine Greek) for a variety of reasons. Some will enroll in a Greek class because it is required in their major. Others will take such a class because it fits their schedule—and they might be curious about Greek. Others will be classics majors who are interested in the ancient world; they may have already studied Classical Greek or Latin, or this might be their first exposure to one of the classical languages. Some may be linguistics students or language majors seeking to add another language to their comparative stock. Still others will be religion or ministry students (either undergraduate, graduate, or seminary) who are interested in the Koine corpus covered by this textbook due to their interest in the content of such writings (i.e., primarily the Septuagint and New Testament but perhaps also the Pseudepigrapha or Apostolic Fathers). Some in this group may approach these texts as repositories of ancient religious thought and nothing more. Others will view the NT and LXX as canonical texts containing divine revelation.[1] Any of these interests (and variations of them) may be well served by studying Koine Greek with this textbook.

1. Most (but not all) Christians do not accept the LXX as "canonical Scripture," but it is an extremely important early translation of the Hebrew Scriptures (the first such translation of the entire Hebrew Bible in any language) that all Christians acknowledge. The LXX is also a major form of those Scriptures used by Jesus, the apostles, and the early church.

You deserve to know that I write as a Christian who accepts Scripture as an authoritative text. I teach in a theological seminary where the primary goal is to prepare students for pastoral ministry in churches that acknowledge the authority of Scripture. I have not, however, made this a theology book. It is first and foremost a language textbook. At times you may notice (or think you do!) my theological perspective. Although I would be pleased if all of you shared my perspective, I realize that will not be the case—even other Christians would surely disagree with some of my theological understanding, though I would be surprised if such matters were conspicuous in this book. I will be quite content if this book helps you learn to read a significant body of literature. You will need to come to your own conclusions as to the significance of that literature's content. In learning Koine Greek, you will be gaining the ability to interact with important texts firsthand. No longer will you be totally dependent on secondhand or thirdhand translations and commentaries. Direct access to such literary works is a crucial ability, whether you seek to understand some of these texts as authoritative divine revelation that you will then proclaim to a congregation, or whether your goal is an accurate understanding of the ancient world. The scholarship essential for either of these goals mandates that you be able to read the relevant primary source materials.

A Word to Students

Why include the LXX in a book like this? Don't most introductory textbooks intended to teach Koine Greek focus on only the NT? Yes, they do. There is, however, value in reading a wider corpus in your initial study. There is value in reading the LXX (as well as the Pseudepigrapha and the Apostolic Fathers) in Greek for the content of these other texts, even if your primary interest is in the NT. The broader scope provided by the additional texts helps you understand the thought world in which the NT was written. Likewise, if you read only the NT, you can easily end up with a fragmented view of Koine Greek as a language, since you will have isolated it from the cultural context in which the language was used.

There is a key pedagogical value as well: you are probably not as familiar with these other Koine texts outside the NT and do not have passages from them memorized, as you may for parts of the NT. That means that you have to be able to actually read the text, not just figure out enough to know what the verse is supposed to say. You will discover that the initial examples in each section are almost always from the NT, with material from other texts appearing later. If your teacher decides to use only the NT examples (and there is adequate material to do just that), you can later return to the other examples as a means of extending your abilities.

The workbook sections of this text (all the two-column examples) have been deliberately designed in parallel columns so that you can use a piece of paper to cover the right-hand column where English equivalents are given. Do *not* just read the right-hand column! Study the Greek text carefully in light of the previous discussion. See how much you can figure out from the left-hand column before removing the paper to reveal the right-hand column. If you make a habit of doing this, you will learn the relevant principles more quickly. The blank space to the right in some sections is not intended as a place to write an English translation (though some teachers may want you to do that). Rather it is where you ought to make notes or jot questions about the meaning of the Greek text. Producing an English translation is not the primary goal; the goal is rather understanding the Greek text and how it communicates meaning. Sections in which I have given a parallel English translation are intended to help you identify the construction or grammatical form involved despite the fact that you may not recognize all the other forms or the vocabulary in the text cited.

The pronunciation of Greek in its various historical stages is debated by scholars. Several proposals have been made. This textbook provides two choices. One is a form of what is called Erasmian pronunciation. This is usually selected for its pedagogical value, not for historical purposes. Some form of Erasmian pronunciation is fairly standard in academic circles. It is *not* what Greek sounded like in the Koine of the first century, but it has the pedagogical advantage of distinguishing vowel sounds, many of which have similar pronunciations in other systems. Some people think Modern Greek pronunciation should be used to teach Greek, but that is anachronistic and certainly not accurate, though it may be closer to Koine than Erasmian. Others have proposed what is probably a fairly accurate reconstruction of first-century Koine. One of the better-known proposals is Randall Buth's "Reconstructed Koine" (for further information on this system, including audio material, see http://www.biblicallanguagecenter.com). That would be a better option than the modern system, and your teacher may prefer that you use it. If so, see the alternate pronunciation given in chapter 1 along with whatever supplemental materials your teacher may provide.

For students learning to read Koine Greek for academic or ministry purposes, pronunciation is mostly (but not entirely) a convenience. Personally I use a traditional Erasmian system, freely acknowledging that it is not an accurate

---

Danker's *Concise Lexicon* (*CL*) is a standard reference tool assumed to be used in conjunction with this textbook, though the book can be used with either an unabridged lexicon such as BDAG or with other smaller lexicons. *A lexicon is essential for using this textbook.*[a]

Although a glossary appears as an appendix of this textbook, it is not intended to take the place of a standard lexicon. It lists only assigned vocabulary words, but one major purpose of a lexicon is to enable the user to understand the use of words not so assigned. As such, Danker's *Concise Lexicon* is an ideal choice, since it is more affordable than BDAG (the standard reference work) and also includes actual definitions of Greek words. Most other lexicons give only selected glosses—brief examples of ways in which a Greek word might be translated into English in some contexts—but that is only a partial step toward understanding the meaning of a Greek word in a particular context.

Words from non-NT texts that do not appear in *CL* may be identified from the parallel English text (when given) or from brief notes immediately below each such reference.

The use of a Greek NT or a printed LXX text is not required to use the textbook, since all Greek texts are cited as necessary. Many teachers, however, will require at least a Greek NT at some point in the curriculum. In my own teaching I do so for the second half of the book. Your teacher will tell you what their requirements are and which printed edition is preferred.

[a] If a current lexicon such as *CL* is not economically feasible, the best lexicon freely available online in pdf form is Abbott-Smith's *Manual Greek Lexicon of the New Testament.* It is old (1936) but serviceable; it does not, however, provide definitions for Greek words, only translation glosses.

---

representation of exactly what Jesus and Paul sounded like when they spoke Greek. If you were learning to *speak* Greek (either Koine or modern), then pronunciation would obviously be far more important.

A Word to Teachers

More depends on the teacher than on the textbook when teaching an ancient language. Good teachers can accomplish their purpose with just about any textbook, but a good textbook certainly helps. I think you will find that this one offers some advantages over other choices that are available, but in the end, it will come down to your making the language come alive for your students.[2]

There has been a fair bit of discussion in recent years about how Koine Greek ought to be taught. Since I am stretching some traditional models, let me sketch for you the way it has been done, how some propose that it ought to be done, and where my approach falls among those models. The traditional approach (by which I refer to the typical approaches used in the twentieth century, though it runs back into the nineteenth century and earlier as well) has been very deductive: a set of charts giving grammatical forms to be memorized, some brief explanations of them, a list of vocabulary to memorize, and then a set of exercises. This final section typically consisted of "made up" Greek sentences intended to be simplified examples of what the student knew to that point. As a result, there were many sentences of this sort: "the angels chased the demons down the road"—not exactly the sort of Greek that you will read in real texts such as the NT or LXX. There also were frequently English-to-Greek exercises (of similar syntactical profundity) that resulted in students producing very mechanical Greek quite unlike what any native Greek speaker would have thought to say. When students had mastered such a textbook, they could read the examples given, but they had read little real Greek. That made a Greek NT or a LXX a puzzling experience.

In the second half of the twentieth century, one of the key developments that has impacted both the study and teaching of Greek is the rise of modern linguistics.[3] Several introductory Greek grammars have appropriated some features from this study. The first was Goetchius, *The Language of the New Testament*, an insightful text but too complicated for the average student (and the average teacher too).

One outcome of this linguistic study has been a push in some circles for the use of second-language learning techniques, that is, to teach Koine Greek the way modern languages are taught—which has also been part of linguistic study. The goal then becomes oral fluency. There are certainly some advantages of this approach. If Greek could be taught as a spoken language, and if it reached the level of oral comprehension, then there would be greater facility in dealing with

2. For several helpful discussions of matters related to teaching Greek, see Porter and O'Donnell, *Linguist as Pedagogue*.

3. This is far too large a subject for me to summarize here. For a superb introduction to this study and its relevance for biblical studies in both Testaments, see Silva, *God, Language and Scripture*.

written texts as well. A drawback of this approach is that it requires a total-immersion environment to reach a level adequate for a realistic payoff. Those who could afford (both time and money) to learn in such a setting would certainly benefit. If they could then figure out how to maintain that skill level when they return to a normal environment, this could even have long-term benefit. That, of course, is the rub. Since most students learning Greek do so in college, university, or seminary, there are some obvious limitations in terms of environment and curriculum. An oral-fluency approach requires far more instruction hours than is possible in the curricular offerings of most colleges and seminaries. Unless a program is designed to be a major in Koine Greek alone, I do not think it is possible to provide sufficient instruction to reach the level of oral fluency within the limits of an undergraduate major or a seminary MDiv intended for ministry preparation. Were an oral approach attempted within the usual majors where Greek has traditionally been taught, such an approach might produce a level of proficiency seen in a year or two of a modern language in high school or college—with about as much retained use several years later.

At the opposite end of the spectrum of approaches to teaching and learning Greek are those who advocate the use of technology. Now, I have no objection to an appropriate use of technology—I use a fair bit of it in my own teaching.[4] But adapting various technologies is not what some have in mind. Rather they propose that since we have such powerful Bible study software programs available that identify and parse everything in the text, we ought to be teaching students how to use this software and explaining what the various bits of information mean. Once again, I can hardly object to the use of the major Bible study programs. This grammar would have been impossible without extensive use of such software. Students do need to learn to make effective use of such tools. The question, however, is whether the most appropriate goal is to teach software for accessing information about Greek *or* to teach Greek, which may be studied with software tools. I have concluded that the better approach is to teach Greek first. Apart from a working knowledge of the language, there will not be an adequate framework for properly understanding the bits of information provided by software—and no ability to interact with the Greek text apart from the software. There will be a constant temptation toward an unjustified grammatical maximalism, a "golden nuggets" approach to the text that does not reflect sensitivity to how the text as a whole communicates meaning. There is considerable difference between having access to large quantities of data and having knowledge.

As a result, this grammar has more in common with the traditional approach than with other methods. It does, however, attempt to benefit from linguistic study. I have also adopted a more inductive, reading-based approach in which the student is reading real Greek from the very beginning rather than chasing demons down the grammatical road. This is not a purely inductive approach, but it embeds inductive elements in a deductive framework that introduces material progressively. Rather than a separate workbook, this text includes numerous

4. See my essay "Adapting Technology to Teach Koine Greek," in Porter and O'Donnell, *Linguist as Pedagogue*, 25–42.

examples in each section of each chapter with various degrees of explanation provided in a graduated fashion.[5] Each chapter ends with an extended passage of real Greek text.

These features mean that this book may seem larger than some other introductory texts, since it is in essence two volumes in one: textbook and workbook/reader. You should not feel obligated to discuss in the classroom all the material in every chapter. Chapter 6 is a good example; it is long, but you can safely omit some large sections of it and leave the rest for reference when it is needed later. The abundant examples are intended to provide students with adequate material to explore the language after they leave your classroom. I do not emphasize translation as such (though there will inevitably be some of that), but I try to enable students to understand meaning—and *how* that meaning is communicated grammatically in the text.

Another reason for the somewhat larger size of this grammar is that more intermediate Greek material has been included than is sometimes customary for introductory texts. That material is typically in the notes or in separate sections titled "Advanced Information for Reference"; this can be skipped when teaching at the introductory level. The reason it is provided is simple: I have found that students repeatedly and habitually turn to their first-year grammar in later years when they need help with a perplexity in a text. Though the answer might in many cases be found in the more advanced grammars, having some introduction in the first book for which they reach has its advantages, especially if the question concerns not just a syntactical issue but is related to the forms of the language (often not included in intermediate or advanced texts).

The examples and texts included are drawn primarily from the NT and LXX, though with some scattered examples from other Koine texts. The title, *Reading Koine Greek*, is not intended to suggest that it encompasses all Koine texts. It is rather focused on two of the major Koine corpuses related to the Bible. In the example sections that have a parallel English translation, there will often be words or forms that the student has not yet learned. Many of these are not glossed, either because they can be identified easily enough with a lexicon (e.g., the nominative form of a third-declension word) or because the English parallel makes it obvious what they must be. In other words, the student can usually figure out what it says even if they do not understand why certain forms are spelled the way they are. That is not a problem, and you need not think that you must explain every detail. So long as they can understand the construction in question, that is sufficient. Students will pick up a great deal of Greek without realizing it by reading these examples, so that when they later meet a particular construction it will already seem familiar to them.

5. Some of the examples have been slightly simplified by omitting various constituents of the sentence, whether modifiers, unnecessary phrases, and so on. Some sentence-initial conjunctions have been omitted as well, especially καί in narrative text. Punctuation and some accents may vary slightly from published texts as a result of these omissions, most of which have *not* been marked with ellipses. None of these changes are textual judgments; they are strictly pedagogical, to enable students to focus on the elements they know or are learning. Interpreting any of these texts should always be based on full, credible editions of the work in question, read in context.

Vocabulary assignments are included in almost every chapter in fifteen-word groups, a total of 465 words. The selection initially favors NT usage, though LXX frequency is increasingly weighted toward the end of the book. I have not given simply a list of English glosses—a traditional approach that, I think, tends to give students a false confidence of what words "mean." Instead I have provided definitions along with the glosses. These definitions are not intended to be original lexical contributions or to represent fully a word's semantic field. (For that, an unabridged lexicon is needed.) I have highlighted the major and most frequent uses based on NT usage, though with an eye on LXX data as well. I have prepared these definitions on the basis of the standard lexicons, particularly those that provide actual definitions: BDAG, Danker's more recent *CL*, Louw and Nida's pioneering work in this area (LN), and for the LXX, Muraoka's lexicon (MLS).[6] At times I have tried to simplify definitions; other times I have incorporated phraseology that appears in one (and sometimes several) of these lexicons. Occasionally I have used a definition as it stands in one of them. My intention is not that students memorize these definitions (heaven forbid!) but that they read the definitions carefully as they learn the vocabulary.

A note regarding frequency figures: At a number of places in this book, including the vocabulary lists, figures are given for the frequency of particular words, grammatical forms, or constructions as found in the NT or the LXX (and occasionally other Koine literature). These are not intended as exact statistics upon which specific conclusions can be based. Their purpose is rather to give students some idea of how often they will see these phenomena. The figures used (which are sometimes rounded) are based on the tagging in the various text modules in Accordance.[7] Since there are sometimes multiple editions (especially of the NT) available as well as minor changes in later editions of these texts, the numbers may not match exactly what you find by doing a similar search, whether in Accordance or in one of the other Bible programs. The figures given, however, should be sufficiently reliable for their intended purpose.

You will soon discover that this book is written primarily for the student's benefit. I have in mind students who are not at a given moment seated in your classroom and who do not have a teacher or teaching assistant present. It is in these homework settings that a textbook is most needed. In the classroom a bare-bones book with little explanation may suffice since it will be supplemented by the teacher's art. The challenge is to provide the help needed when the teacher is

6. From time to time I have also used other lexicons, such as Abbott-Smith, Liddell and Scott, and for the LXX, Lust, Eynikel, and Hauspie (LEH) as well as Chamberlain's recent work *Greek of the Septuagint*.

7. The current version of Accordance, a superb Bible software package from OakTree Software, is v. 10.4 (2014). I have used nearly every version almost from the program's inception; consequently there might be minor discrepancies due to differing versions of the search software or the underlying databases. Such differences are insignificant for pedagogical purposes. Originally I used the GNT module, which was the Accordance implementation of the GRAMCORD tagged NT, the most recent version of which was v. 3.6 (2001). More recently I have used the GNT-T, a tagged NT text based on NA[27] developed by William Mounce and Rex Koivisto (2003; the current version is v. 4.0, 2009), as well as NA27-T (v. 1.0, 2009) and UBS4-T (v. 1.0, 2011), both of which use the same Mounce/Koivisto tagging.

not present to explain or answer questions. This perspective is also true of online courses, where the teacher is one step removed from student access. Though not primarily intended for independent study, the additional explanation may prove useful in that setting as well.

The student focus also accounts for the inclusion of English grammar discussions in many chapters. This is not because Greek is to be understood on the basis of English, but it is to enable students to understand the categories that are employed in describing Greek. Some of these features are nearly identical between the two languages (e.g., grammatical number), but others have significant differences or involve altogether new categories that do not even exist in English (e.g., the middle voice). This enables students to learn by comparing and contrasting the two language systems, relating new material to similar or contrasting elements in their own language.

A word on inclusive language: In areas of English where there has been significant and long-term change in the use of gender language, I have generally used language that reflects contemporary usage. An area where this is more complicated in a first-year grammar is the translation of Greek examples. Where a Greek sentence is best understood as referring to both men and women, I have tried to reflect that in the parallel English translation. But to avoid confusing the beginning student, I have refrained from gender-inclusive translations where it would have required rearranging or rewording the text. In such cases, I have used more formal equivalents and also generic *he* when there were no easy alternatives. This is most noticeable in the early lessons; as the lessons progress, I gradually introduce more alternatives, including singular *they*. But even in later lessons, some examples simply required too much "adjustment" for the translation to be helpful to a first-year student. In my own classes, I discuss the issues involved in gender language fairly extensively with my second-year students, but it is too much to address directly in a primer. You are welcome to depart from the translations I have provided as your own preferences dictate.

Other emphases not commonly found in traditional textbooks include a focus on the aspectual value and function of the Greek verb, the incorporation of current study of the voice system (e.g., the traditional, Latin-based system of deponency is not found here), and lexical semantics. Although there is not complete agreement on some of these issues, there is a general consensus that we now have a more accurate understanding of the language in several key areas. I have indicated my conclusions on such matters but have also attempted to indicate some of the unresolved questions so that teachers can adapt my presentation to fit their own emphases and conclusions. I have not included documentation for many such discussions (the bibliography is voluminous), but occasionally I note a key book or article.

More information on these and related subjects is provided in the Teacher's Packet that supplements this textbook. That resource also provides numerous other teaching materials that you can adapt for your own use in the classroom. See the textbook website, http://www.bakeracademic.com/readingkoinegreek, or contact the publisher for further information about this resource.

Abbreviations

Symbols

*	When prefixed to a Greek word/form, it identifies a root form
▸	Indicates either a sequence of words in a particular order *or* a Greek word/form derived from another
◂	Points to a preceding word modified (i.e., a head word) *or* a sequence of words in a particular order
!	When following a parenthetical translation gloss, marks an imperative-mood verb (i.e., a command)
×	"times" (indicates how frequently a word or form occurs, e.g., 72×)
≠	not, is not the same as

General and Bibliographic

adj.	adjective
adv.	adverb
alt.	alternate
app.	appendix
aug.	augment
BDAG	Bauer, W., F. W. Danker, W. F. Arndt, and F. W. Gingrich. *A Greek-English Lexicon of the New Testament and Other Early Christian Literature*. 3rd ed. Chicago: University of Chicago Press, 2000.
ca.	*circa,* approximately
CEB	Common English Bible
cf.	*confer*, compare
chap.	chapter
CL	Danker, F. W., with K. Krug. *The Concise Greek-English Lexicon of the New Testament*. Chicago: University of Chicago Press, 2009.
conj.	conjunction

ctr.	contrast (as a verb)
c.v.	connecting vowel
dbl.	double
decl.	declension
d.o.	direct object
ed.	editor, edition, edited by
e.g.	*exempli gratia*, for example
Eng.	English (often when a verse reference differs from MT and/or LXX)
ESV	English Standard Version
fig.	figure
f.m.	form marker (also known as tense suffix/morpheme)
gend.	gender
GNT	Good News Translation
GTJ	*Grace Theological Journal*
GW	GOD'S WORD Translation
HCSB	Holman Christian Standard Bible
i.e.	*id est*, that is
interj.	interjection
interrog.	interrogative
i.o.	indirect object
ISV	International Standard Version
KJV	King James Version
LEH	Lust, J., E. Eynikel, and K. Hauspie. *Greek-English Lexicon of the Septuagint*. Rev. ed. Stuttgart: Deutsche Bibelgesellschaft, 2003.
LN	Louw, J. P., and E. A. Nida. *Greek-English Lexicon of the New Testament Based on Semantic Domains*. 2nd ed. 2 vols. New York: United Bible Societies, 1989.
LSJ	Liddell, H. G., R. Scott, and H. S. Jones. *A Greek-English Lexicon*. 9th ed. with rev. supplement. Oxford: Clarendon, 1968.
LXX	Septuagint or Old Greek (not differentiated in this book)
MBG	Mounce, W. D. *The Morphology of Biblical Greek*. Grand Rapids: Zondervan, 1994.
MHT	Moulton, J. H., W. F. Howard, and N. Turner. *A Grammar of New Testament Greek*. 4 vols. Edinburgh: T&T Clark, 1908–76.
MLS	Muraoka, T. *A Greek-English Lexicon of the Septuagint*. Louvain: Peeters, 2009.
M-M	Moulton, J. H., and G. Milligan. *Vocabulary of the Greek New Testament*. 1930. Reprint, Peabody, MA: Hendrickson, 1997.
MT	Masoretic Text (often when a verse reference differs from English and/or LXX)
NA	Nestle, E., B. and K. Aland, et al. *Novum Testamentum Graece*. 28th ed. Stuttgart: Deutsche Bibelgesellschaft, 2012.
NASB	New American Standard Bible
NCV	New Century Version
NET	The NET Bible (New English Translation)
NETS	New English Translation of the Septuagint

NIV	New International Version
NJB	The New Jerusalem Bible
NLT	New Living Translation (2nd ed.)
NRSV	New Revised Standard Version
NT	New Testament
orig.	original, originally
p(p).	page(s)
p.e.	personal ending
PG	Patrologia graeca, edited by J.-P. Migne, 162 vols. Paris, 1857–86.
PGM	*Papyri graecae magicae: Die griechischen Zauberpapyri*. Edited by K. Preisendanz. 3 vols. Leipzig and Berlin: Teubner, 1928–41.
prep.	preposition
pron.	pronoun
REB	Revised English Bible
redup.	reduplication
RSV	Revised Standard Version
subst.	substantival, substantive
s.v.	*sub verbo* ("under the word"), refers to a specific entry in a lexicon under the word that follows the abbreviation
UBS	Aland, B., et al. *The Greek New Testament*. 4th rev. ed. New York: United Bible Societies, 1994.
v(v).	verse(s), version
v.l.	*varia lectio* ("variant reading," i.e., a textual variant)
vs.	versus

Old Testament

Gen.	Genesis
Exod.	Exodus
Lev.	Leviticus
Num.	Numbers
Deut.	Deuteronomy
Josh.	Joshua
Judg.	Judges
Ruth	Ruth
1–2 Sam.	1–2 Samuel
1–2 Kings	1–2 Kings
1–2 Chron.	1–2 Chronicles
Ezra	Ezra
Neh.	Nehemiah
Esther	Esther
Job	Job
Ps(s).	Psalm(s)
Prov.	Proverbs
Eccles.	Ecclesiastes
Song	Song of Songs/Solomon
Isa.	Isaiah
Jer.	Jeremiah
Lam.	Lamentations
Ezek.	Ezekiel
Dan.	Daniel
Hosea	Hosea
Joel	Joel
Amos	Amos
Obad.	Obadiah
Jon.	Jonah
Mic.	Micah
Nah.	Nahum
Hab.	Habakkuk
Zeph.	Zephaniah
Hag.	Haggai
Zech.	Zechariah
Mal.	Malachi

New Testament

Matt.	Matthew	1–2 Thess.	1–2 Thessalonians
Mark	Mark	1–2 Tim.	1–2 Timothy
Luke	Luke	Titus	Titus
John	John	Philem.	Philemon
Acts	Acts	Heb.	Hebrews
Rom.	Romans	James	James
1–2 Cor.	1–2 Corinthians	1–2 Pet.	1–2 Peter
Gal.	Galatians	1–3 John	1–3 John
Eph.	Ephesians	Jude	Jude
Phil.	Philippians	Rev.	Revelation
Col.	Colossians		

Old Testament Apocrypha and Septuagint

Bar.	Baruch
1–2 Esd.	1–2 Esdras (2 Esdras = Ezra, Nehemiah)
Jdt.	Judith
1–4 Kgdms.	1–4 Kingdoms (= 1–2 Samuel, 1–2 Kings)
Let. Jer.	Letter of Jeremiah (= Baruch 6)
1–4 Macc.	1–4 Maccabees
Sir.	Sirach
Wis.	Wisdom of Solomon

Apostolic Fathers

Barn.	*Barnabas*
1–2 Clem.	*1–2 Clement*
Did.	*Didache*
Herm. Sim.	*Shepherd of Hermas, Similitude(s)*
Ign. *Eph.*	Ignatius, *To the Ephesians*
Ign. *Magn.*	Ignatius, *To the Magnesians*
Ign. *Phld.*	Ignatius, *To the Philadelphians*
Trad. Elders	*Tradition of the Elders*

Old Testament Pseudepigrapha

Apoc. Sedr.	*Apocalypse of Sedrach*
1 En.	*1 Enoch*
Gk. Apoc. Ezra	*Greek Apocalypse of Ezra*
Let. Aris.	*Letter of Aristeas*
Pss. Sol.	*Psalms of Solomon*

T. Ab.	*Testament of Abraham* (rev. B)
T. Ash.	*Testament of Asher*
T. Benj.	*Testament of Benjamin*
T. Levi	*Testament of Levi*
T. Naph.	*Testament of Naphtali*

Josephus

Ag. Ap.	*Against Apion*
Ant.	*Jewish Antiquities*
J.W.	*Jewish War*
Life	*The Life*

Parsing Categories and Abbreviations

Category	Abbreviation	Meaning	Short Form[a]
Person	1st 2nd 3rd	first, second, third	1 2 3
Number	sg. pl.	singular, plural	S P
Tense-Form	aor. pres. impf. pf. plpf. fut.[b]	aorist, present, imperfect, perfect, pluperfect, future	A P I R L F
Voice	act. mid. pass.	active, middle, passive	A M P
Mood	ind. impv. subj. opt. inf. ptc.	indicative, imperative, subjunctive, optative, infinitive, participle	I M S O N P
Gender	masc. fem. neut.	masculine, feminine, neuter	M F N
Case	nom. gen. dat. acc. voc.	nominative, genitive, dative, accusative, vocative	N G D A V

[a] In some charts and reference sections, the short-form abbreviations are used. See the explanation of the short-form parsing system for verbs at the end of chap. 13.

[b] A superscript 1 or 2 before a tense-form means "first" or "second" (e.g., [1]aor. = first aorist; [2]R = second perfect).

INTRODUCTION

THE LANGUAGE OF KOINE GREEK

I.1. The language that you will study in this book has one of the longest histories of any known language. We can trace it backward well beyond 2000 BC, and in its various forms and transformations Greek has continued as a language to the modern form spoken in Greece today. The Koine Greek of the NT and the LXX is but one narrow slice of a much larger history. What you will learn in this book will not enable you to read or understand the oldest forms of the language, which used a totally different writing system. Nor will it enable you to communicate with people who speak Modern Greek (even if you were to learn Koine using Modern Greek pronunciation). The following summary, and it is only that, will help you understand how the narrow slice of Koine fits into the larger picture of the Greek language.[1]

The Pre-Koine History of the Greek Language

I.2. Before 2000 BC a people group who came to be called *Hellenes* (οἱ Ἕλληνες) came to reside in and around the Aegean. The region in which they settled was designated *Hellas* (ἡ Ἑλλάς), and their language the *Hellenic language* (ἡ Ἑλληνικὴ γλῶσσα). From where they came and exactly when remains somewhat of a mystery. The designation *Greek* comes from the Latin word *Graeci*, which the Romans used to describe these people.

The oldest known written texts in Greek, dating from the thirteenth century BC, use a form of the Greek language that is called *Mycenaean Greek*. They were written, not in the Greek alphabet that we know and use today, but in a script called *Linear B*. This was not even an alphabetic script but used glyphs

1. This summary generally follows Horrocks, *Greek: A History of the Language and Its Speakers*. See also Buck, *Greek Dialects*; and Palmer, *Greek Language*.

representing syllables rather than individual letters—a syllabary rather than an alphabet. An inscription using this form can be seen in figure I.1.

National Archaeological Museum, Athens. Photo courtesy of John S. Y. Lee

Figure I.1. Mycenaean, Linear B Greek Tablet (TA709)

I.3. Another ancient form of writing Greek is described as being written in boustrophedon style. In this format the lines of text run alternately from left to right, then right to left. This is the origin of the term *boustrophedon*, which means "as the ox plows the field." The first part of the word comes from βοῦς and means "ox"; the second part comes from στρέφειν, which means "to turn." (After the ox drags the plow the length of the field, he turns and begins a new furrow in the opposite direction.) The oldest such writing known is from the eighth century BC. You can see a sample of this form of writing in figure I.2. The actual artifact is just over three inches square.

Courtesy of the L. H. Jeffery Archive, Centre for the Study of Ancient Documents, Oxford

Figure I.2. Fragmentary Archaic Athenian Inscription, IG I3 1418

I.4. Following the collapse of the Mycenaean civilization, the Greek language disappeared into a dark tunnel; though it did not cease to exist, there are scarcely any written remains of the language in this period. When it finally emerged from the "Greek Dark Ages" (eleventh–ninth centuries BC), we find evidence of a multitude of dialectical variations in existence in the eighth century BC. Although the details remain unclear (and disputed), it appears that during those centuries (and perhaps earlier) a range of Greek dialects spread across the area then known as Greece (the Greek mainland, Thessaly, Macedonia, the Peloponnesus, the Aegean Islands, the western edge of Asia Minor, Crete, and Cyprus). The evidence is sketchy, but as best we can determine, there were two main forms of Greek in use in the eighth century, each with multiple subdivisions, as can be seen in the following table.[2]

West Greek		East Greek	
Peloponnesian Doric	*Northwest Greek*	*Attic-Ionic*	*Arcado-Cypriot*
Doric	Aeolic	Ionic	Arcadian
Megarian	Boeothian	Attic	Cypriot
	Thessalian		

The approximate locations in which these dialects were spoken are shown in figure I.3.

Figure I.3. Dialects of Ancient Greece. Key: **bold** = dialects; *italics* = place names

2. There is some disagreement as to these groupings and even the geographical distribution shown in the map (fig. I.3). The data summarized here follows Horrocks, *Greek*, 13–42.

I.5. These diverse forms of the language persisted for several centuries on more or less equal footing. It was not until the seventh to fifth centuries BC that some of the dialects began to acquire a "panhellenic" status as a result of the literature written in them. The first and perhaps most important literary works in Greek are the Homeric works the *Iliad* and *Odyssey*. We know very little of their author or dates (scholars propose a wide range from the twelfth to the seventh centuries BC), but these epic poems as we know them are composed in an archaic eastern Ionic dialect with an added sprinkling of Aeolic elements for metrical purposes. The Greek epic tradition (which probably began as an oral form) culminated in the Homeric texts in the eighth century. They achieved a literary prestige that provided the foundation for widespread imitation and the beginning of some standardization favoring the Ionic dialect in the seventh century and following.[3]

The sixth and fifth centuries BC represent the flowering of Classical Greek civilization and with it the beginnings of Greek prose literature of a philosophical and scientific nature. Here we meet writers such as Thales, Anaximander, Anaximenes, Heraclitus, and Herodotus, all of whom wrote in Ionic prose. Their achievements established Ionic as the prestige language for prose writing as of the fifth century. Ultimately, however, Attic, a sister dialect to Ionic, became the standard form of Classical Greek. This was due to several factors. Politically, in the fifth century Persia conquered Asia Minor, including Ionia on the western coast, greatly diminishing the influence of the major Ionic-speaking area. Athens was a key force in stopping Persian expansion westward, developing into a major maritime power at this time. Athens was also becoming an intellectual, cultural, and commercial center. Greek rhetoric originated in Athens about this time, producing noted orators such as Thucydides and Isocrates. This was the time of the great philosophers Socrates and Plato. The net result was the rise of Athens and its dialect, Attic, to become the gold standard of Classical Greek, albeit with the adoption of a number of formerly Ionic features. This change brought about the great influence and prestige of Attic Greek, which would last for centuries.[4]

Koine Greek

I.6. Language is always embedded in and affected by history and culture. Nowhere is that more clearly seen than in the development of Koine Greek.

Development of Koine

In the fourth century BC, Macedonia rose to power and came to dominate the Greek mainland under the leadership of Philip II. It is disputed whether the language of Macedonia should be considered a Greek dialect (if so, it was characterized by greater divergence from Attic than any of the other Greek dialects) or was another Indo-European language closely related to Greek. To provide a

3. On these matters see Horrocks, *Greek*, 9–59.
4. Horrocks, *Greek*, 60–78.

basis for political power in Greece, however, Philip's administration adopted Attic as the language of government and education. This was the natural culmination of the growing Hellenization (or perhaps better, Atticization) of Macedonian culture, a process that had begun in the fifth century.[5]

I.7. Building on his father's power base in Greece, Alexander III (356–323 BC), best known as Alexander the Great, accomplished a spectacular conquest of the ancient world: Asia Minor, Syria, Palestine, Egypt, Persia, and the frontiers of India. In accomplishing this, the young military and political genius spread Greek language and culture over a vast area. The language in use as this triumph began was standard Attic. The process of assimilating many other cultures (as well as large numbers of foreign troops into the ranks of the Greek army) had a deep impact on the language, becoming Koine Greek (κοινὴ διάλεκτος, "the common dialect"), the lingua franca of the Alexandrian Empire. "For the first time the notion of 'Greek,' which hitherto had unified the dialects only as an abstraction, acquired a more or less concrete instantiation in the form of the standard written, and increasingly spoken, Koine."[6]

The language changed as it spread, absorbing some non-Attic features and being simplified grammatically. Learning this language became imperative for indigenous populations, whether to enable military or civil service in the new regime or simply to do business with their new neighbors and masters. Koine, which was imposed top-down by the Greek rulers in the administrative centers of the empire, served a unifying function "by cementing in place the idea of a common Greek culture based on a common intellectual heritage expressed in a common Greek language."[7] Even through the political and military maneuvering of the second and first centuries BC, in which Rome emerged as the new world power, having defeated all the various divisions of Alexander's empire, Koine Greek remained the lingua franca despite the formal position of Latin as the language of Rome. Greek language (and to a lesser extent Greek culture) remained the de facto standard for most areas of life under Roman rule for several centuries. The Greek language as spoken by the Jews is sometimes called *Hellenistic Greek*, but this language is no different from Koine, and many scholars use the term for all Greek of the Hellenistic period.

Characteristics of Koine

I.8. Three major characteristics distinguish Koine Greek from Classical Greek.[8] The first is semantic change. Languages change continually; new words are created or borrowed, and old words take on new meaning or disappear altogether. This is evident in Koine. To note only a few examples: In Classical λαλέω meant

5. Horrocks, *Greek*, 79–80.
6. Horrocks, *Greek*, 87.
7. Horrocks, *Greek*, 88.
8. The discussion in this section will not be clear to you until you have mastered a good bit of this book, but it is important information for you to have as your study progresses. For now, be content with knowing that there are distinctions between various forms of the language.

"I babble," but in Koine it becomes the usual verb used to refer to normal speaking. Βάλλω could formerly refer to a somewhat violent throwing, "I hurl." This meaning is toned down in Koine, in which the word means simply "I throw," or even "I put" or "I send." The careful Classical distinction between εἰς and ἐν is giving way in Koine, where εἰς begins to encroach on the semantic territory of ἐν. Likewise with conjunctions, ἵνα, which in Classical always indicated purpose, is broadened in the Koine and used for content, purpose, result, or temporal reference.

I.9. Second, the grammar is also simplified in Koine. Although Classical Greek had many conjunctions, Koine uses relatively few, the most common of which is καί. Word formation is simplified. Older μι verbs are replaced with ω forms. Irregular formations of both verbs and nouns are regularized; for example, the second singular of οἶδα was formerly spelled οἶσθα, but in Koine it follows the regular endings and is spelled οἶδας. Attic verbs spelled with γιγ- are simplified to γι- (e.g., γίγνομαι and γιγνώσκω become γίνομαι and γινώσκω). Forms with θη begin to replace the usual aorist middle forms -σαμην and -ομην, serving as dual-voice aorist middle/passive forms. The Attic preference for -ως as the ending for some second-declension masculine nouns shifts to -ος. Some forms either disappear altogether or are used much less frequently. For example, the use of three grammatical numbers (singular, plural, and dual) is simplified to two (singular and plural). Use of the optative and the future participle falls off significantly.

I.10. Third, there is an increased explicitness and clarity in Koine, probably a reflection of the lack of intuitive understanding of bilingual, second-language users and the consequent need to spell out matters that native speakers assumed. As a result compound verbs become more common. Pronouns are supplied more frequently as subjects of verbs. Prepositions are used more frequently where formerly case alone was considered adequate for use by native speakers. The dative case in particular occurs less frequently on its own, being supplanted by various prepositional phrases. Direct discourse is now more common than indirect discourse. Redundancy in the language increases—for example, using the equivalents of "the very same" and "each and every."

Later Forms of the Greek Language

I.11. The later forms of the Greek language will not be considered in any detail here.[9] Following the Koine period is Byzantine Greek, from the fourth century AD to the fall of Byzantium/Constantinople in AD 1453. The Roman Empire divided into East and West during this period (AD 395), with the East retaining Greek as the common language but the West turning increasingly to Latin. It is during this period that by far the largest number of extant NT manuscripts were copied, most of them in Byzantium, using the new minuscule handwriting style that was invented in the ninth century (see chap. 1).

9. Those interested should consult Horrocks, *Greek*, parts 2 and 3, pp. 189–470. A summary of the characteristics of Byzantine Greek is given on pp. 226–27, 272, and in more detail, 284–322.

After 1453 the language is called *Modern Greek*. In the earlier history of Modern Greek there were two dialects: *Katharevousa* (καθαρεύουσα), the official language of government, education, and church; and *Demotic* (δημοτική), the common, spoken language of every day. These reflect an attempt to restore a form of the language based on ancient Attic on the one hand (Katharevousa) and the continued developments in the Koine on the other (Demotic).[10] In 1976 the Demotic form was legislated as the official language of Greece and is now referred to as *Standard Modern Greek*.[11] An additional change was implemented in 1982, when the previous system of multiple diacritics was abandoned for a simpler, monotonic system. The older, polytonic Greek employed three accents, two breathing marks, and a diaeresis. Standard Modern Greek is now written with only one accent (the *tonos*), an occasional diaeresis, and no breathing marks. To note a few of the differences in Standard Modern Greek when compared with the Koine, there are now only three main cases: nominative, genitive, and accusative; the dative has disappeared except in a few set expressions. The perfect and future tense forms have been dropped, their function being replaced by the use of auxiliary verbs. The optative mood, infinitives, and μι verb forms have been eliminated. Only a past participle remains.

Nature of the Greek of the New Testament

I.12. How are the "anomalies" of the Greek found in the NT to be explained, since they differ from Classical Greek at many points? The answer to that question is evident in light of the preceding discussion, but the question was debated prior to the twentieth century. It is worth noting here so that you can read older works with some understanding of their limitations. Formerly, three common explanations were offered. The Hebraists argued that the unusual constructions found in the NT (when compared with Classical Greek) were due to Hebrew influence. The purists insisted that the anomalies were really good, Classical Greek, so the goal was to search for Classical parallels to such constructions (even if such parallels are rare and sometimes forced). The third proposal was Holy Spirit Greek: scholars such as Cremer and Thayer suggested that the Holy Spirit *changed* the language of any people who received a divine revelation so that it would be adequate to communicate divine revelation. Thayer, for example, listed hundreds of unique NT words that were necessary to express the message exactly. Since Thayer's time, however, almost all these words have been found in earlier Greek literature. His work was prepared before the discovery of a wide range of biblical papyri, so he had no knowledge of

10. The use of a Katharevousa Greek ("corrected" by Attic norms) dates to the mid-nineteenth century and continued until 1976.

11. An extremely contentious, politicized debate throughout the twentieth century culminated in this decision. For the historical, political, cultural, and linguistic background of the controversy, see Horrocks, *Greek*, 438–66.

the vast quantity of material that would be published shortly after his lexicon came off the press.[12]

I.13. In the twentieth century it was argued that the NT was written in standard Koine Greek. This was the conclusion of scholars such as Deissmann and Moulton, who initially studied the papyri. Two scholars have more recently suggested qualifications or refinements to the Deissmann-Moulton judgment. Rydbeck compares the NT to the *Fachprosa*, the technical prose writers of the Koine period.[13] He contends that in the first century AD there was an intermediate level of Koine Greek between that of popular Greek and the literary. He appeals to the technical, scientific prose writers of the early imperial era such as Theophrastus and Dioscurides, arguing that their style is neither that of the popular, spoken language of the time nor that of the literary writings. This was the language of the scientist as well as government.

Wallace has argued that the language of the NT should be understood as conversational Greek.[14] That is, Koine Greek has within it a range of expression, ranging from the "high" literary Greek of a writer like Polybius or Plutarch to the speech of illiterate people on the street (see fig. I.4). Between these two extremes is the conversational Greek of educated people—essentially Rydbeck's *Fachprosa*. There is a full range of options along this spectrum, and the NT writers (as do the LXX translators) take their places in the central area. Some texts such as Luke-Acts, James, and 1 Peter lie toward the right side of the conversational portion of the spectrum. Toward the left end of this span are the books with simpler Greek such as Mark and John. The Pauline writings and Matthew sit squarely in the middle. There are perhaps, as Wallace suggests, three overlapping factors necessary to account for the Greek of the NT. The *vocabulary* is largely shared with the vernacular Greek of the day. The *grammar and syntax*, however, are closer to the literary Koine. Also relevant is the *style*, which in the case of the NT (and LXX even more so due to its nature as a translation) is Semitic.

Figure I.4. Nature of Koine Greek

12. Even in the twentieth century some similar suggestions were made. It was proposed that the NT was a unique dialect of Koine (Turner and Gehman) or that parts of the NT were translation Greek, either from Aramaic (Torrey, Black) or Hebrew (Segal, Manson). For classic essays by these writers, see the collection by Porter, ed., *Language of the New Testament*.

13. Rydbeck, "On the Question of Linguistic Levels."

14. Wallace, *Greek Grammar*, 17–30.

Lessons

1

ALPHABET

Getting Started

1.1. This is where it all begins. This chapter will introduce you to the alphabet and to some basic concepts as to how meaning is communicated in Greek. Not all languages are structured in the same way; the structure of Greek is quite different from English.

Alphabet and Pronunciation

1.2. Until you learn the alphabet well, there is not much else that you can do. It is difficult to learn pronunciation from a book, so teachers will supplement this material to help you learn to pronounce the letters and words of the language. Their pronunciation should be followed even if it differs from what is given here, so that you can understand each other.

The Greek Alphabet

1.3. We will start with the alphabet. There are twenty-four letters, one of which has two forms. Just like English (but not like all languages), the Greek alphabet also has both uppercase and lowercase letters.[1]

α β γ δ ε ζ η θ ι κ λ μ ν ξ ο π ρ σ/ς τ υ φ χ ψ ω

Α Β Γ Δ Ε Ζ Η Θ Ι Κ Λ Μ Ν Ξ Ο Π Ρ Σ Τ Υ Φ Χ Ψ Ω

1. Greek has not always had uppercase and lowercase letters. When the literature of Koine Greek was written, there was only one case. The origin of two distinct cases, *upper* and *lower*, as we call them in English, can be traced to the ninth century AD.

Each of these letters also has a name. In English, an *a* is an *a* is an *a*, and there is not much more we can say about that letter in terms of identifying it.[2] But in Greek, the letter α has the name *alpha* (ἄλφα). See the table below under "Pronunciation" for the name of each of the Greek letters.

Writing the Letters

1.4. The handwritten forms of Greek letters are shaped slightly different compared with the printed forms above.[3] Follow the style and method for writing each letter as shown in figure 1.1. Begin each letter where the star appears. Some characters have a small arrow to indicate the direction in which you should begin the stroke. Most characters can be drawn with a single stroke, but some require two (ε, κ, λ, τ, φ, χ, ψ) or even three (π) strokes. Be careful that each lowercase letter is proportioned vertically in relation to the midline. (The uppercase letters are all written "full height.") Be sure to make the nu (ν) and upsilon (υ) distinct. The nu must always have a sharp point at the bottom, and the upsilon must always have a rounded bottom.

There are two forms of the lowercase sigma. When it occurs at the beginning or middle of a word, it is written σ, but when it comes at the end of a word (and only then), it is written ς and is called a *final sigma*. The σ is a *medial sigma*.

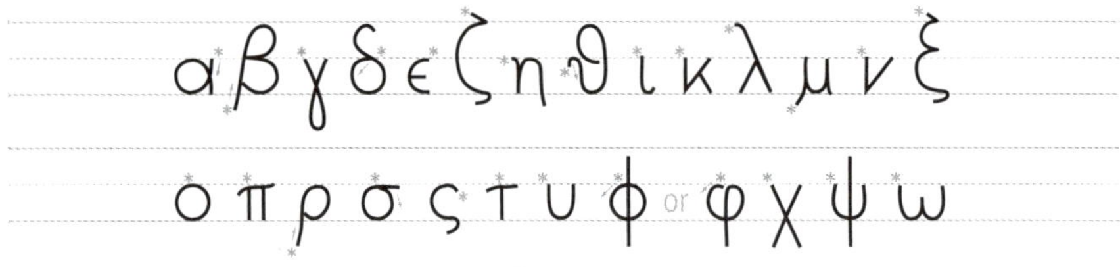

Figure 1.1

1.5. Figure 1.2 shows what the author's handwriting looks like. It is not fancy, but it is legible. It is easy to look at printed characters in a book or on screen and despair of copying them, so this shows you what your own attempts should resemble. You can surely do better, but your goal should be no less. Even if your English handwriting is atrocious, work hard at developing a neat Greek hand. It is much easier to learn Greek when you can read what you have written.

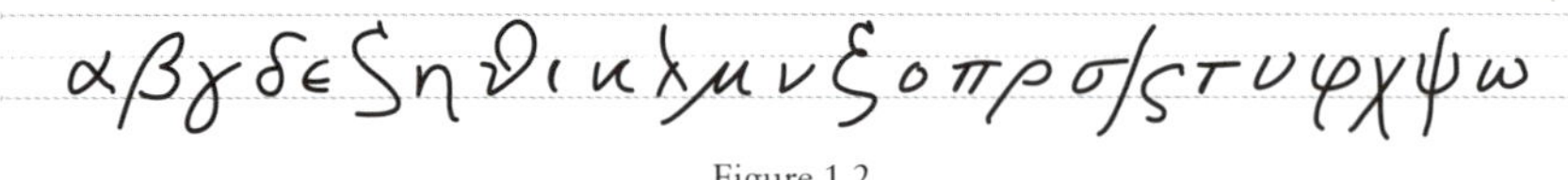

Figure 1.2

2. Technically some English letters also have names (e.g., the letter *j* can be identified as a *jay*, and *y* may be spelled out as *wye*), but these are rarely, if ever, used in common parlance.

3. There are a few variations in some of the letters. Your teacher may write a letter or two somewhat differently from what is shown here. If so, follow that pattern.

Handwriting Practice

1.6. Use the blank lines below for your initial practice. You can pretend that you are back in kindergarten or first grade.

α

Recognition

1.7. The following passage from the Greek NT contains every letter of the Greek alphabet. Can you identify all twenty-five forms? (Remember that there are twenty-four letters, but one of them has two forms.)

ἐν ᾧ καὶ τοῖς ἐν φυλακῇ πνεύμασιν πορευθεὶς ἐκήρυξεν, ἀπειθήσασίν ποτε ὅτε ἀπεξεδέχετο ἡ τοῦ θεοῦ μακροθυμία ἐν ἡμέραις Νῶε κατασκευαζομένης κιβωτοῦ εἰς ἣν ὀλίγοι, τοῦτ᾽ ἔστιν ὀκτὼ ψυχαί, διεσώθησαν δι᾽ ὕδατος. (1 Pet. 3:19–20)

Pronunciation

1.8. Here is a pronunciation key for each letter. The sound each letter makes in a word is similar to the italicized English letter(s) in the fourth (or fifth) column.[4]

Lowercase	Name	Uppercase	Pronunciation	Alternate Pronunciation[a]
α	alpha	Α	*a*lms	
β	beta	Β	*b*ook	*v*oice
γ	gamma	Γ	*g*oat	*y*ield (before ι, ε, η)
δ	delta	Δ	*d*og	*th*is
ε	epsilon	Ε	*e*pic	
ζ	zeta	Ζ	a*dz*e, ku*dz*u	*z*oo
η	eta	Η	*a*pe	
θ	theta	Θ	*th*eism	
ι	iota	Ι	*i*gloo (short), sk*i* (long)	sk*i* (always)
κ	kappa	Κ	*k*ite	
λ	lambda	Λ	*l*id	
μ	mu	Μ	*m*ouse	
ν	nu	Ν	*n*ot	
ξ	xi	Ξ	a*x*	

4. The pronunciation of Greek in its various historical stages is debated by scholars. What you read in this chapter represents one form of what is called Erasmian pronunciation, though an alternate system is also given. See the explanation in the preface.

Lowercase	Name	Uppercase	Pronunciation	Alternate Pronunciation[a]
ο	omicron	Ο	*o*ptimum	*o*bey
π	pi	Π	*p*e*pp*er	
ρ	rho	Ρ	*r*ed	
σ/ς	sigma	Σ	*s*ide	
τ	tau	Τ	*t*op	
υ	upsilon	Υ	m*oo*n[b]	
φ	phi	Φ	*ph*ase	
χ	chi	Χ	lo*ch*[c]	
ψ	psi	Ψ	cu*ps*	
ω	omega	Ω	*o*bey	

[a] The last column in the chart above gives the phonetic values used in "Reconstructed Koine." Only sounds that differ are listed; all others are the same. See also the chart of the diphthongs below. You should use *only* the phonetic values in column 4 or the ones in column 5 (not both), depending on which system of pronunciation your teacher uses.

[b] The pronunciation of upsilon varies considerably among NT grammars and teachers, so you may be advised to use a different pronunciation. If you know German, the pronunciation of upsilon is often said to sound like *ü* as in über.

[c] The letter chi makes a gutteral sound pronounced in the back of your throat; it is not the more "crisp" sound of *ch* in *choir.* Follow your teacher's pronunciation.

Each letter sounds like the first sound in its name.

α sounds like the *a* in *a*lpha.
λ sounds like the *l* in *l*ambda.
φ sounds like the *ph* in *ph*i, etc.

Gamma (γ) sounds like our English g, but a double gamma (γγ) sounds like *ng*. There are a few other combinations with γ that do this also (γκ, γξ, γχ), but the double gamma is the most common. For example, ἄγγελος is pronounced *an´-ge-los* (not *ag-ge-los*).

Vowels

1.9. Vowels are the "glue" that hold consonants together, enable pronunciation (it is nearly impossible to pronounce a string of consonants with no vowels), and distinguish similar words. In Greek they also have a morphological function: they serve to join various parts of a word (e.g., a stem and an ending) and to distinguish some forms of a word from other forms.

Hint: To help remember the Greek vowels, relate them to English vowels:

English vowels: *a e i o u* (and sometimes *y* and *w*)[5]
Greek vowels: α ε ι ο υ + η and ω

5. English teachers and grammarians do not agree on whether or not to include *w* as a vowel.

The following table shows you which vowels are short and long as well as how the short ones lengthen (Greek vowels have a habit of doing that). Vowels that can be either short or long (depending on the spelling of a particular word or form) are technically pronounced differently in each case, but most people tend to be a bit sloppy in such distinctions. There are rules to determine when one of these is long or short,[6] but this need not concern us right now. You will learn the most significant variations from listening to your teacher pronounce Greek in class.

Short		Long	Either Long or Short
ε	▶	η	α, ι, υ
ο	▶	ω	

Similar Letters

Be careful not to confuse the Greek letters that look like an unrelated English letter:

eta	η	≠	n
mu	μ	≠	u
nu	ν	≠	v
rho	ρ	≠	p
chi	χ	≠	x
omega	ω	≠	w

Diphthongs

1.10. Diphthongs (sometimes called *digraphs*) are a combination of two vowels that are pronounced as a single sound. The eight diphthongs are as follows in the table below. The pronunciation of each is illustrated by the italicized English letters in the second column. The third column gives one example of a Greek word in which the diphthong occurs.

	Pronunciation	Example	Translation	Alternate Pronunciation[a]
αι	*ai*sle, *eye*	αἴρω	I lift up	*e*pic (same as ε)
ει	w*ei*ght, fr*ei*ght	εἰ	if	sk*i* (same as ι)
οι	b*oi*l	οἰκία	house	m*ew* (same as υ)
αυ	s*au*erkraut, h*ow*	αὐτός	he	*Av*e Maria[b]
ου	s*ou*p, hoop	οὐδέ	neither	
υι	s*ui*te	υἱός	son	
ευ, ηυ	f*eu*d	εὐθύς	then	*ev*er
		ηὔξαμεν	we grow	kn*av*e[c]

[a] See the table under "Pronunciation" above and the note on the "Alternate Pronunciation" column.

[b] Before the letters π, τ, κ, φ, θ, or χ, the diphthong αυ is pronounced like the *af* in *after* when using Restored Koine pronunciation.

[c] Before the letters π, τ, κ, φ, θ, or χ, the diphthong ευ is pronounced *ef* and ηυ becomes *ehf.*

6. As just one example, iota is long "when it ends a word or syllable, or forms a syllable by itself, e.g. ἐλπί-σι, ὅτι, πεδ-ί-ον; the sound of *i* in *pin*, when it is followed by a consonant in the same syllable, e.g. πρίν, κίν-δυνος" (Kühner, *Grammar of the Greek Language*, 17).

Improper diphthongs are also combinations of two vowels, but here the letter iota is written *below* the preceding letter. There are three such combinations: ᾳ, ῃ, and ῳ. An iota is not always written as a subscript when it follows another vowel. It usually happens when various endings are added to a word, and then only if the preceding vowel is a long vowel. (An iota is the only letter that can be written as a subscript, and it does so only under a long vowel: η, ω, or long α.) Here is an example: τῷ Ἠσαΐᾳ τῷ προφήτῃ. Pronunciation of these improper diphthongs is the same as that of the letters *without* the subscript: α, η, ω. The iota subscript distinguishes only the written form of the word, not its oral form.

Diphthongs are almost always long. The only exceptions are οι and αι when they come at the end of a word, in which case they are considered short for purposes of applying the accent rules (see the Advanced Information for Reference section at the end of this chapter).

Diaeresis

1.11. When two adjacent vowels are pronounced as parts of separate syllables (especially if they would normally form a diphthong), they are marked with a diaeresis: two dots written above the second vowel. (*Diaeresis* is from the word διαίρεσις, "division, separation.") The vowel so marked is almost always an iota, sometimes an upsilon. This is most common in Greek names and other words transliterated from a Semitic language. Almost all words in the LXX with a diaeresis fall into this category—for example, Σεμεϊ ("Shimei"), Κεϊλα ("Keilah"), Αμεσσαϊ ("Amasa"), and Ἰαϊρ ("Jair"). The most common such word is Μωϋσῆς ("Moses"), which occurs 80 times in the NT and more than 700 times in the LXX. Other common forms with a diaeresis include Καϊάφας ("Caiaphas"), Βηθσαϊδά ("Bethsaida"), Ἑβραϊστί ("in the Hebrew/Aramaic language"), and ἀλληλουϊά ("hallelujah"). Other Greek words with a diaeresis that are not the result of transliteration include προΐστημι, χοϊκός, διϊσχυρίζομαι, διϋλίζω, πραΰς, δηλαϊστός, and ἀΐδιος. (English makes sparing use of the same marker; it can be seen in a word like *naïve*.)

Diaeresis in Greek Manuscripts

Sometimes a diaeresis is used in a Greek manuscript that is written *scriptio continua,* that is, without spaces between words, to clarify a word division. The oldest known NT manuscript, 𝔓[52], includes such a mark in John 18:31–32, ΟΥΔΕΝΑΪΝΑΟΛ[ΟΓΟΣ]. The text reads as follows in a printed Testament: οὐδένα· ἵνα ὁ λόγος. The diaeresis marks the conjunction of the vowels alpha and iota as *not* being a diphthong. In this case the two letters are part of two different words—words that are even part of two different verses in our modern texts. A diaeresis was no longer needed for this purpose once Greek orthography developed a minuscule script that used word division, in the ninth century.

Breathing Marks

1.12. Greek uses one of two diacritic marks above the first vowel (or diphthong) in a word beginning with a vowel to indicate pronunciation. The two diacritic marks are the smooth breathing (ἀ) and the rough breathing (ἁ).

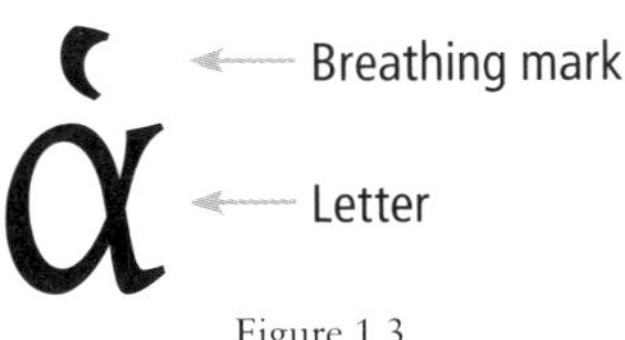

Figure 1.3

You may have noticed that the Greek alphabet does not have any equivalent of our English letter or sound *h*. This is the purpose of the breathing marks: they tell you whether or not there is to be an *h* sound at the front of a word.[7]

The smooth breathing mark means that there is no change in sound. That is, pronounce the vowel as you normally would—for example, ἀ = *ah*. The rough breathing mark adds an *h* sound in front. That is, pronounce the vowel with the *h* sound in front of it: ἁ = *hah*; ἑ = *heh*; etc.). Greek also uses a rough breathing mark (never a smooth) on all words that begin with the letter rho (ρ). This is the sound *rh*.[8] When a word begins with a diphthong, the breathing mark is placed over the second letter—for example, αἷμα.

When an iota (ι) occurs at the beginning of a word, it has a *y* sound: Ἰησοῦς is pronounced *yay-soos'*. This is common in Greek names, especially names that originated as Hebrew or Aramaic words.

Punctuation

1.13. Greek uses the following punctuation marks. Some are the same as English, some are different.

Commas and periods are the same as English: θεός, θεόν.
The Greek semicolon (or colon)[9] is a raised dot: θεός·
A question mark looks like our English semicolon: θεός;

The last mark in the list is the hardest to keep straight when you are beginning, but it will make an enormous difference in what you understand a text to say. For example, the statement ἔστιν θεός. says: "There is a god" (or perhaps, "God is" or "God exists"). But if we change the punctuation to ἔστιν θεός; then we have: "Is there a god?" (or perhaps, "Does God exist?").

7. The front of a word is the only place where Greek uses the *h* sound (although in Latin script the letter *h* is used to transliterate φ [phi] and θ [theta]). Some scholars suggest that the *h* sound was not pronounced in first-century Koine. It is, however, vocalized in academic, Erasmian pronunciation.

8. Breathing marks may also appear in some texts when there is a double rho in the middle of a word. This depends on the editor and is not a common convention in current printed texts or in BDAG.

9. Greek does not distinguish the colon from a semicolon as we do in English. The raised dot (sometimes called a *middle point* or a *mid-dot*) in Greek serves to indicate either function, though it is most commonly the equivalent of an English semicolon.

Accents

1.14. There are three accent marks in ancient Greek.[10]

acute: ά
grave: ὰ
circumflex: ῶ or ῶ

These accents were not often written at the time when the LXX and the NT were written, though they originated around 200 BC. The accents were developed to indicate not stress (as we use accents in English dictionaries today) but pitch. This reflected the way Greek was pronounced in the Classical period. The acute marked a high, rising pitch, the circumflex a pitch that rose and fell on the same syllable, and the grave a normal, low pitch.[11] Consistent use of accents does not show up in Greek manuscripts until after AD 600. This means that the accents you see in a printed edition of the LXX or NT were not originally present. Although they are later editorial conventions, they are accurate, reliable, and very helpful.

The Hazards of Pronunciation

A story is told of the fourth-century Athenian actor of tragedy Hegelochus, "who in declaiming a line of Euripides ending with γαλήν' ὁρῶ ('I see a calm') pronounced a circumflex instead of an acute, and sent the audience into roars of laughter: γαλῆν ὁρῶ = 'I see a weasel'" (MHT 2:52).

1.15. How do you know which accent to use and where to put it? Accent rules are complicated. Entire books have been written on Greek accents.[12] Some teachers expect you to learn a fair bit about these matters. Others take a more pragmatic approach and expect you to know accents only when they differentiate between two words. Unless your teacher tells you otherwise, follow these guidelines.

Know the names of the three accents.

Stress the accented syllable when you pronounce a Greek word.

Remember that a grave accent can never stand at the end of a word unless there is another Greek word immediately following it (without even a punctuation mark

Poly Who?

In Modern Greek all three accents have been replaced with a single accent mark, the *tonos* (which looks similar to an acute accent). This is why ancient Greek is described as *polytonic* (that is, it has multiple accents: *poly-*) but Modern Greek is *monotonic* (a single accent: *mono-*). Modern Greek has also dropped diacritical marks such as breathing marks and the diaeresis.

10. The accent named *grave* is pronounced *gräv* (an ä sounds like the *a* in father); some pronounce it like the English synonym for a cemetery plot: *grave* (*grāv*). The circumflex accent can be written either as a simple curve (ˆ) or in the "wiggly" tilde form (~). Many fonts and published books (including *CL*, BDAG, and the NA Greek NT) use the tilde form, but others such as the UBS Greek NT and Rahlfs's LXX use the curved form. The more usual form in handwritten text is the simpler curved shape.

11. The grave is sometimes described as a falling pitch, but "in fact it indicated a pitch maintained at the normal level, in contrast to (and therefore lower than) the acute or the circumflex" (Carson, *Greek Accents*, 16). For those who can read music, these accents are given in musical notation in MHT 2:53.

12. One of the best is Carson, *Greek Accents*.

intervening). If it does (e.g., when you cite a word out of context), the grave must *always* be changed to an acute accent.

There will be a few instances in which the accent will make a difference in the word, and in those cases I will tell you what you must learn. For Greek students who want to go a bit further in this area, see the Advanced Information for Reference section at the end of this chapter for a brief summary or Carson's book *Greek Accents* for the details.

Uppercase Letters

1.16. What about the uppercase letters? Uppercase letters are used less frequently in printed editions of Greek texts than in English. There are only three situations in which you find an uppercase letter in modern editions of Koine Greek texts:

Proper names are capitalized.

The first letter of a *paragraph* receives a capital letter (but *not* the beginning of every sentence).[13]

The first letter of a direct quote is capitalized. There are no quotation marks in Greek, so the uppercase letter is one of your clues to a quotation.

You will learn the uppercase letters as you go. Most of them are quite obvious and easy to recognize.

αΑ βΒ γΓ δΔ εΕ ζΖ ηΗ θΘ ιΙ κΚ λΛ μΜ νΝ ξΞ οΟ πΠ ρΡ σΣ τΤ υΥ φΦ χΧ ψΨ ωΩ

For practice in identifying the uppercase letters, try reading this palindrome one letter at a time.[14]

ΝΙΨΟΝΑΝΟΜΗΜΑΜΗΜΟΝΑΝΟΨΙΝ

Acute Accents "Out of Flow"

Not changing a grave accent to an acute accent when "out of flow" (the technical designation for a Greek word without another Greek word immediately following it) is one of the most common mistakes people make with Greek accents, especially when copying a word from a digital text. People who know will think that *you* know what you are doing if you always make this simple change.

For example, if in a research paper you refer to the first word in Mark 1:1, Ἀρχὴ τοῦ εὐαγγελίου Ἰησοῦ Χριστοῦ υἱοῦ θεοῦ, your statement should read *not*, "The first word in Mark's Gospel is ἀρχὴ," but, "The first word in Mark's Gospel is ἀρχή." In its original context the word ἀρχή is followed immediately by another Greek word (τοῦ), so the grave accent is correct. But when you cite that word alone, it is followed by not a Greek word but a punctuation mark or an English word.

A Greek Palindrome

A palindrome is a word or sentence that reads identically forward and backward—for example, "Do geese see God?" The palindrome inscription cited in the text, ΝΙΨΟΝΑΝΟΜΗΜΑΜΗΜΟΝΑΝΟΨΙΝ, is from the Hagia Sophia.[a] Written in modern orthography the palindrome reads, Νίψον ἀνόμημα μὴ μόναν ὄψιν, and means, "Wash your sin, not only your face." The word *palindrome* is itself from a Greek word, παλίνδρομος, a compound of πάλιν, "again," and δραμεῖν, "to run" / δρόμος, "a race, race course."

[a] In Greek, Ἁγία Σοφία is short for Ναός τῆς Ἁγίας τοῦ Θεοῦ Σοφίας, "Church of the Holy Wisdom of God." This is an Eastern Orthodox church building in Constantinople (modern Istanbul) that was constructed in the fourth century. For over a thousand years it was the Patriarchal Basilica of Constantinople. It is now a museum.

13. The NA text also uses a capital for the beginning of a "subparagraph," otherwise indicated by a wide space within the line of text.

14. Cited by Metzger, *Reminiscences of an Octogenarian*, 23. For an explanation of this text, see the sidebar "A Greek Palindrome."

Now You Try It

1.17. Identify each of the "marks" (letters, accents, breathing marks, etc.) in this portion of the NT (Mark 1:1–3).

> 1 Ἀρχὴ τοῦ εὐαγγελίου Ἰησοῦ Χριστοῦ υἱοῦ θεοῦ. 2 Καθὼς γέγραπται ἐν τῷ Ἠσαΐᾳ
> τῷ προφήτῃ, Ἰδοὺ ἀποστέλλω τὸν ἄγγελόν μου πρὸ προσώπου σου, ὃς κατα-
> σκευάσει τὴν ὁδόν σου· 3 φωνὴ βοῶντος ἐν τῇ ἐρήμῳ, Ἑτοιμάσατε τὴν ὁδὸν
> κυρίου, εὐθείας ποιεῖτε τὰς τρίβους αὐτοῦ.

The "Original" New Testament

1.18. You might be interested to know that at the time the NT was first written, *all* the letters were "uppercase"—or at least all the same case—and most of them looked similar to forms that later became uppercase letters. These letters are called uncials (or sometimes majuscules). Lowercase letters were not invented until the ninth century. Figure 1.4 is a photo of possibly the oldest known manuscript of any part of the NT. This manuscript is known as 𝔓^{52} (that is, papyrus manuscript number 52), dated to the first half of the second century AD, perhaps about AD 120. If that date is accurate, then it may be only a quarter century from the time John originally wrote the Gospel in Ephesus—hundreds of miles from where this copy was found in Egypt. The letters look quite different from the way they are written today. Also notice that there is no word division and no punctuation. Those features come much later. The text here is John 18:31–34. The actual manuscript fragment measures about 3.5″× 2.25″. It is presently located in the John Rylands University Library at the University of Manchester.

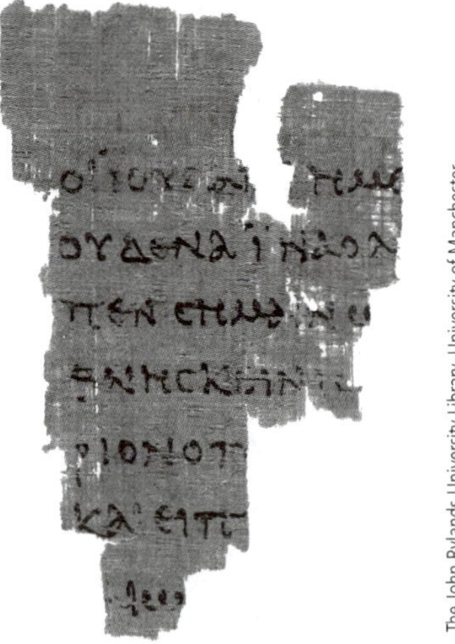

The John Rylands University Library, University of Manchester

Figure 1.4. Manuscript 𝔓^{52}

By contrast, figure 1.5 shows a much later (fifteenth century AD) manuscript, written in minuscule script, which has both uppercase and lowercase letters. In this writing style many letters are written together, and numerous ligatures are used. This is manuscript 545 and shows the beginning of Mark's Gospel. You will notice that the title of the Gospel, 'ΕΥΑΓΓ'ΕΛΙΟΝΚΑΤ'ΑΜ'ΑΡΚΟΝ (in modern orthography, Εὐαγγέλιον κατὰ Μάρκον) is still written in the older, uncial script.

Photo provided by the Center for the Study of New Testament Manuscripts

Figure 1.5. Manuscript GA 545 from the Special Collections Library, University of Michigan

The text that you see in this textbook and in a printed LXX or Greek NT is the modern form of the Greek alphabet, which was developed after the printing revolution in the fifteenth century.[15] New Testament scholars have long since worked through the questions of the proper word division and punctuation. There are a very few instances in which there is not agreement on such matters and where it does make some difference in what the text says, but those are few and far between. Unless you run across a discussion of such matters in a good commentary, you can safely trust your Greek NT as it is printed without constantly worrying as to whether or not the word division is correct.

For example, in Mark 10:40 the original would have looked something like this:

ΑΛΛΟΙΣΗΤΟΙΜΑΣΤΑΙ

15. Technically, we use the modern form of the *polytonic Greek* alphabet. Modern Greek (as spoken and written in the country of Greece today) is *monotonic* (see the explanation under "Accents" above), but that is a relatively recent change, dating from the 1960s, when a major change in Greek spelling and orthography was legislated by the Greek government.

This might be read as ἀλλ' οἷς ἡτοίμασται and translated, "but it is for those for whom it is prepared." Or it could be read as ἄλλοις ἡτοίμασται and translated, "it is prepared for others."[16] Modern translations go with the first option.

Sing the Alphabet

1.19. Music is another way to practice your developing Greek pronunciation skills. There are a number of Greek alphabet songs, but the one shown in figure 1.6 is very simple, does not require much musical skill, and uses an old, familiar tune.

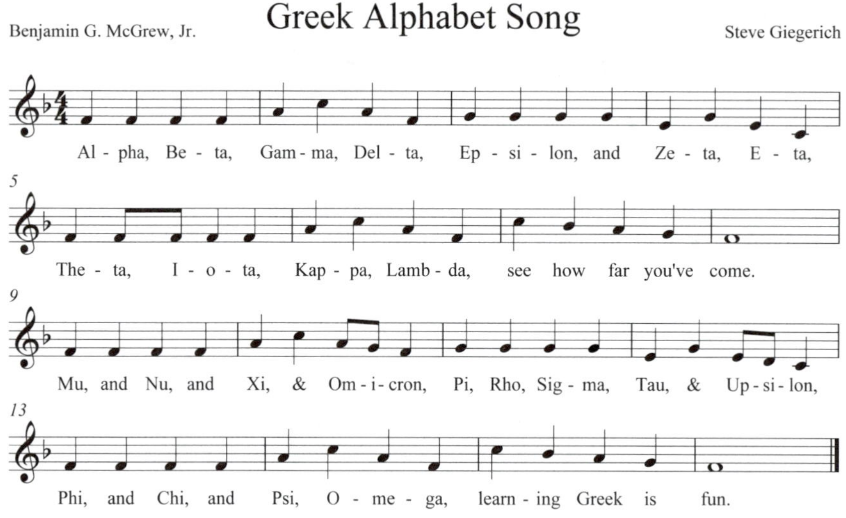

Figure 1.6

Semantics and Structure

1.20. Now that you know the alphabet and are becoming comfortable at pronouncing Greek words, we need to figure out how these basic building blocks can express meaning. The various Greek texts that you want to read and understand (probably the Greek NT and perhaps the LXX) consist of a large number of alphabetic characters grouped into segments of various sizes. This grouping is not random or mathematical, but it is deliberate and meaningful. We do not understand texts merely by recognizing the letters or by knowing the words formed from them. Words are one of the smaller groups of letters that convey information, but these words must be organized into a coherent, structured

16. You will need to read the context to make sense of this example, but the issue is that "the seats beside Jesus, then, are reserved either for certain ones who have already been designated (and these might well be the sons of Zebedee themselves), or for others (excluding the sons of Zebedee)" (Aland and Aland, *Text of the New Testament*, 277).

whole to communicate meaning. You need to understand the basic structure of language to begin comprehending this meaning.

1.21. Language consists of structured information. Although the word is one such structural unit, there are even smaller units that are meaningful. The smallest such units are sometimes called *morphemes* and consist of individual letters or syllables that modify the meaning of an individual word. For example, in English one morpheme is the letter *s* added to the end of some nouns to create plurals. The word *cat* is singular, but *cats* is plural; the difference in meaning is the one-letter morpheme *-s*. Likewise, other structural meaning units are larger than words. A verb, such as *run*, is often accompanied by several related words that compose a verb phrase—for example, *had been running*. But more is still needed to make a meaningful statement. Who or what is running? Is this a reference to a race or hunting or a boat, a fish, a disease, or a harried mother? Without context, there is only potential meaning in this phrase.

> He had been running toward the finish line when he stumbled.
> The hounds had been running the fox the whole evening.
> The yacht had been running before the wind when the storm hit.
> The salmon had been running for several days.
> Her nose had been running all day.
> She had been running all week and was exhausted.

Each of these statements provides more information that changes our understanding of the verb *run* or the verb phrase *had been running*. This additional information, however, is organized in a structured way. In English it is typical first to indicate who it is that is doing the action, then to tell what they did, and finally to give additional information about the event. An English speaker understands the pattern in which these pieces of information are recorded. If the expected pattern is not followed, communication is either hindered or prevented altogether.

> all week running she had been and exhausted was
> was she all running week exhausted had been and

Both of the examples just given have all the same words, but they do not follow English patterns. The first might sound like someone trying (not very successfully) to imitate Yoda, but the second is total nonsense.

1.22. Various languages have different patterns for forming communicative sentences. English is sometimes described as an *analytical language*. Languages of this type depend on the order of words in a sentence and various particles to indicate the relationship of the words in the sentence and thus the intended meaning. The words have a very limited range of changes to their form. Other languages can be called *agglutinative*. In cases such as these, meaning units are juxtaposed in ever-increasing-length words for which there is no limit in length.[17]

17. In Turkish, an agglutinative language, *ev* = *house*; *evler* = *houses*; *evleri* = *his houses*; *evleriden* = *from his houses*, etc. I am told that in Hawaiian, *Kananinoheaokuuhomeopuukaimanaalohilohi-*

By contrast, Greek is an inflected (sometimes called *synthetic*) language, in which meaning is indicated by various morphemes (prefixes and suffixes) added to words to indicate how they are related to other words in the sentence.[18] As a result, what we assume to be "normal" word order in an English sentence can be very different in Greek, since the inflectional endings on the words tell us which word is the subject and which the object, and so forth.

1.23. Other than word order, there are additional elements of structure in both English and Greek. One of these relates to the kinds of words that are used. Speaking somewhat broadly, we can say that some words are function words and some are content words. Content words are those that have lexical value (or more likely, values) that can be defined in terms of reference. We can define the lexical value or content of a word like χείρ; it is the body part at the end of the arm containing fingers, that is, a hand. But other words do not lend themselves to this sort of referential definition. Instead of defining their content, we can only describe how they function in a sentence. For example, to describe the word ἵνα, we can say that it is a word that normally functions to introduce a subordinate clause indicating purpose, result, content, or explanation. There is no real "content" to such a word; it does not refer to anything. In summary, remember that content words "mean," function words "do."

Sentences normally contain both content words and function words that are structured in such a way as to communicate meaning. Although there are some exceptions (e.g., short, one-word sentences such as "Fire!"), we usually expect both content and some indication of function. Take the following sentence as an example:

> This book is largely concerned with Hobbits, and from its pages a reader may discover much of their character and a little of their history.[19]

As a few samples, these are content words: *book*, *Hobbits*, *pages*, *reader*, *discover*, *character*, and *history*. Function words include *this*, *with*, *and*, *from*, *a*, and *may*. Neither of these sets of words communicates meaning on its own, not even if we put a period after them and enclose them in quotation marks.

> "Book Hobbits pages reader discover character history."
> "This with and from a may."

In the following chapters you will learn many content words that are part of Koine Greek vocabulary, words such as κύριος, οὐρανός, Ἰησοῦς, πιστεύω, γράφω, and ἀποθνῄσκω. There will also be numerous function words, such as καί, γάρ, οὖν, ἐν, ἐνώπιον, ὁ, and εἰ. More important, you will learn how these words are arranged in a structure that communicates meaning.

nokeawealamakaokaokalani, a single word consisting of sixty-three letters, means "The beautiful aroma of my home at Sparkling Diamond Hill is carried to the eyes of heaven."

18. The addition of various morphemes may seem agglutinative, but inflected languages can add only certain types of prefixes and suffixes and in fixed patterns. There are a limited number of elements that can be added to the base word, and compound words are relatively rare.

19. Tolkien, *Lord of the Rings*, Prologue, §1, "Concerning Hobbits."

Vocabulary

1.24. Vocabulary is essential to the beginning stages of learning Greek. There is nothing more frustrating than staring at a written text and not knowing what the words mean. Even if you recognize what part of speech[20] they are, you must have a basic vocabulary even to guess at the meaning of other words. Although context is always the determinative factor in meaning, if you do not know many words, there will be no meaningful context to consider.

In this textbook you will learn 465 words if you master the assigned vocabulary (15 words per chapter). These vocabulary assignments begin in the next chapter. The list of words you will learn in this book includes all the words that occur 44 times or more in the NT, many additional words that occur between 43 and 36 times in the NT and very frequently in the LXX, and a few others that occur fewer than 36 times in the NT but that are frequently used words in the LXX. From a LXX perspective you will learn all the words that occur more than 460 times in the LXX, many that occur more than 200 times, some that occur more than 100 times, and others that occur fewer than 100 times but that are frequent in the NT. This will give you a reasonable base from which to read most NT and LXX texts, though you will still need to consult your lexicon frequently. In your future study you will want to extend your vocabulary abilities further, at least to the words occurring 20 or more times in the NT (and 10 would be better). If you want to read much LXX, perhaps 100+ would be a good goal in that larger corpus.

Why Learn Vocabulary?

"There is almost never a student who can sight-read complicated Greek or Latin after a year of study. Part of the reason for this is vocabulary. Think of how many words you know in English. If you are a typical educated adult native-English speaker, you might know 30,000 or 40,000 words. Furthermore, you know words from all walks of life; you know some technical vocabulary of many fields, from auto mechanics to politics to religion. Of course, there are certain technical fields whose vocabulary is rarely recognized by anyone other than specialists, but most of us know a wide variety of words from many fields. It is very rare for a non-native speaker to gain that kind of breadth of vocabulary in a foreign tongue, ancient or modern. What you are hoping for is not that you would be able to pick up anything in Greek or Latin and read it easily. Instead, you are hoping to learn enough grammar and enough of the vocabulary of your field (whether it is religion, history, medicine, or law) that you can read material in your own field with some facility."

(Fairbairn, *Understanding Language*, 174–75)

1.25. What a student is typically expected to memorize as a reading aid are the English glosses for these common Greek words, that is, how they might be translated into English in some common contexts. You learn, λόγος, "word"; θεός, "god"; καί, "and." But what do these words actually *mean*? That is a different question. Although vocabulary cards and textbook lists typically give only a few one-word equivalents (i.e., glosses), these vocabulary words can be defined.

20. *Part of speech* is the traditional term for what is now sometimes called *word class*. Either term includes such categories as noun, verb, adjective, and so on. The vocabulary lists given at the end of each chapter are divided into these groups so that you have an idea how the Greek words you are learning are likely to function in a Greek text.

We are accustomed to our English dictionaries providing actual definitions, but Greek-English dictionaries have only recently begun providing similar help. You are not expected to memorize formal definitions for the 465 words in this textbook, but the vocabulary assignments in each chapter and the glossary in the back of the book provide a definition for each word. You should read these carefully, since they enable more accurate understanding of the words you are learning; they also will enable you to distinguish between some words that cannot be differentiated on the basis of an English gloss. If you were to learn both δεξιός and ἐξουσία as "right," you would not know which one meant "right, as in authority" and which meant "right, as opposed to left."

The definitions provided are not exhaustive. Many of these words have other, less common uses that are not included. The definitions given are based on and derived from the major lexicons, often simplified to some extent. The purpose of these definitions is to help you think in terms of *meaning* rather than simple English glosses. The lexicons should be consulted for more authoritative discussions. Although this textbook assumes the use of Danker's *Concise Lexicon* (*CL*) as a companion volume, other lexicons can be used. The only other standard lexicon that provides definitions is the third edition of Bauer, Danker, Arndt, and Gingrich (BDAG), an essential tool for serious study of the NT.[21]

It is very important that you learn the assigned words well and drill and review them constantly during this course. Begin working on the vocabulary at the same time you begin studying the material for each new chapter; do not wait until you have finished the chapter to tackle the assigned vocabulary words. Your teacher will talk about some ways to learn and review vocabulary. Not everyone learns the same way when it comes to vocabulary, so try several methods to find what works for you. The "tested and tried" system uses small paper flash cards, or you can use the newer digital flash-card systems.

— — — — — — — — — — — — — —

Advanced Information for Reference:
Greek Accents

1.26. To take the next step in learning accents, you first need to know something about syllables in Greek words. The most basic principle is that for every vowel or diphthong, there is one syllable. Single consonants go with the following vowel; double consonants (e.g., γγ) are divided.

The last three syllables of a Greek word are named, starting from the end of the word. The last syllable is called the *ultima*, the second-to-last syllable is the *penult*, and the third is the *antepenult*. Accent rules relate to these named

21. Louw and Nida's lexicon (LN) is a useful supplement, but it is not a standard lexicon and cannot serve as the only such reference work to be consulted. For LXX study there are more specialized lexicons available (LEH gives only glosses; MLS provides basic definitions).

syllables, and accents can occur only on these three syllables. A syllable is considered long or short if the vowel or diphthong in that syllable is long or short.

The accent on nouns (and related words) is said to be retentive (or persistent) in that it usually stays on the same syllable in which it is found in the lexical form (that is, the form as it is spelled in a lexicon). Verb accent, by contrast, is recessive in that it moves toward the front of the word as far as the general rules of accent allow when the ending changes. (Many infinitives, however, are not recessive.)

Here are the most basic rules of accent.

1. An acute accent can be used on any of the last three syllables of a word.
2. A circumflex accent can occur only on one of the last two syllables (ultima or penult) and only if that syllable is long.
3. A grave accent can occur only on the ultima.
4. If the ultima is long, the accent can occur only on one of the last two syllables.
    a. If the accent is on the penult, it can only be an acute.
    b. If the accent is on the ultima, it may be either acute or circumflex.
5. If the ultima is short and the penult is long, the penult must have a circumflex *if* it is accented (it may not be).
6. If there is an acute accent on the ultima and there is another accented Greek word immediately following with no intervening punctuation, the acute always changes to a grave.
7. If a word in a Greek text has a grave on the ultima, that word, if cited out of context with no other Greek text immediately following, or with a punctuation mark immediately following, or if followed by an ellipsis in the citation, must have the grave changed to an acute.

Accent Trivia

For those of you who like Greek trivia, here are some terms related to accents. The rest of you can safely ignore these terms—though if you ever encounter one of them, you can find out what they are all about right here. Each is the name for a particular syllable that has a particular accent.

Oxytone: ultima syllable with an acute accent
Paroxytone: penult with acute
Proparoxytone: antepenult with acute
Perispomenon: ultima with circumflex
Properispomenon: penult with circumflex
Barytone: a word with no accent on the ultima

An observant reader will notice that rules 1–5 do not specify which accent must be used or on which syllable. They only indicate what is and is not possible. The actual accent must be determined from the accent on the lexical form as modified by these rules when the ending on the word changes. (You will soon learn that the endings on nouns and verbs and other parts of speech often change to indicate the word's function in the sentence or to mark particular nuances of meaning.)

The above summary does not include some specific situations in which accents will change. These situations include words with a contraction (especially contract verbs) and words that are classed as enclitics or proclitics. Explanations of some of these situations will be found later in the book.

— — — — — — — — — — — — — —

Key Things to Know for Chapter 1

1.27. Each chapter will conclude with a summary section to enable you to verify that you have mastered the most important material. Some entries will be statements, others questions. The vocabulary words assigned for each chapter, beginning with chapter 2, are assumed; they will not be listed again in the "Key Things to Know" sections.

Greek alphabet: You must be able to recite it orally as well as write it.

Vowels: Do you know the seven letters that are classed as vowels?

Diphthongs: Can you pronounce each one correctly when you find it in a word?

Accents: Unless your teacher tells you otherwise, know the three items listed in §1.15. (Some teachers will want you to learn more about accents.)

Miscellanea: Do you recognize the two breathing marks and the various marks of punctuation?

Pronunciation: It will take a few weeks before you are totally comfortable reading Greek aloud, but by the time you have finished this chapter, you should be able to read clearly and accurately from a printed Greek text and be able to follow along and distinguish the words when you hear someone else read a text (though you will not know what most of them mean yet). You may read slowly at first, but keep practicing. It will come in time.

2

NOUNS: PART 1

Nominative and Accusative Cases

2.1. This chapter introduces you to Greek nouns, the grammatical terms that are used to describe them, their forms (that is, morphology), and some of their functions in Greek sentences. But first we need some linguistic background to understand why Greek nouns differ from English ones. We will also consider some basic grammatical terminology in relation to English.

Types of Languages

2.2. In the first chapter you learned that there are several different types of languages, and each type communicates meaning by certain structures. How does that affect our understanding of Greek nouns? In *analytical languages* such as English, word function is determined by word order. Consider this English sentence:

Tom hit Bill.

Who hit whom? Who is the hitter and who is the "hittee"? How do you know? Now we will change this sentence a bit. Using the same words spelled the same way, we could say:

Bill hit Tom.

What does this do to the meaning of the sentence? The change in meaning is substantial. That is because English word order normally follows the pattern:

subject ▸ verb ▸ object

We know which person did the hitting and who was hit, since English usually places the subject first, then the verb, followed by the direct object.[1]

2.3. Another type of language is called an *inflected language*. In this case, word function is *not* indicated by word order; rather, it is indicated by changes in the *form* (that is, the spelling) of the words in the sentence. Since Greek is an inflected language, this means that word order is not semantic in Greek. That is, changing the order of the words does not change the meaning as it does in English. We will take our sample sentence above and rewrite it as six variations in "Greeklish."

Word-Order Convulsions

When word order is incorrect in English, communication suffers—though the reader/hearer may laugh.

> The burglar was about 30 years old, white, 5′ 10″, with wavy hair weighing about 150 pounds.
>
> The family lawyer will read the will tomorrow at the residence of Mr. Jones, who died June 19 to accommodate his relatives.
>
> The dog was hungry and made the mistake of nipping a two-year-old who was trying to force-feed it in his ear.

Tomoς hit Billov.
Billov hit Tomoς.
Hit Billov Tomoς.
Hit Tomoς Billov.
Billov Tomoς hit.
Tomoς Billov hit.

If these were real Greek sentences, all six would say the same thing, despite the fact that the words occur in six different sequences.[2] Note that the "Greeklish" endings on the nouns stay the same from sentence to sentence, so the meaning also stays the same. The word with the ending -ος is always the subject of the sentence, and the word with the -ov ending is always the direct object. In other words, the -ος word is doing the action, and the -ov word is receiving the action. In all six instances, Tom is the one doing the hitting, and Bill is being hit.

The *forms* of the words in Greek are thus much more crucial to understanding the meaning of the statement than they are in English. It also means that you will need to pay better attention to *spelling* than some of you do in your own language. Varying a few letters in a word can change the meaning of a sentence quite drastically. If we change: "Tomoς hit Billov" to "Tomov hit Billoς," then Bill becomes the responsible agent instead of Tom.

1. If these terms are not familiar to you, the *subject* of a sentence identifies who or what performs the action described. The action word in a sentence is called the *verb*. If that action is done to someone or something, we designate that the *direct object*.

2. The emphasis might be somewhat different with differing word order, though that would also depend on the form of the verb that is used.

English Grammatical Terminology

2.4. Since Greek uses word endings and not word order to indicate syntactic relationships and thus communicate meaning, you will need to understand the various grammatical categories used in Greek more clearly than you do in your own language. In the process of learning Greek grammar, you will probably learn quite a bit of English grammar as well.

Gender

2.5. Gender is a tough category to understand correctly, especially in twenty-first-century Western, English-speaking society. The terms used here differ from what you often hear. Just remember that we are using technical grammatical terminology in this book, not the nontechnical usage of popular speech. First, gender is not the same as sex. *Sex* is a physiological category: male or female. *Gender* is a grammatical category: masculine, feminine, or neuter. Words do not possess sex; they are characterized by gender. The genders are simply groups of words that use the same inflectional endings—linguistic classifications, not biological ones. Sometimes it seems that gender and sex coincide. Such coincidences are called *natural gender*. That is, if a feminine-gender word refers to a person (or animal) of the female sex, this can be termed *natural gender*. Many English words have natural gender, but that is not as true in Greek.

English does not use the category of gender very much, certainly far less than Greek. It can indicate gender in three ways: (1) by adding or changing an ending (prince, princess; widow, widower), (2) by changing the word (boy ▸ girl; uncle ▸ aunt), or (3) by adding another word (friend ▸ boyfriend *or* girlfriend; bride ▸ bridegroom).

There are some other elements of gender in our language, though some of these conventions are changing. The English pronouns *he, she,* and *it* indicate masculine, feminine, and neuter. Ships and hurricanes were traditionally referred to as feminine (*she*) and were usually given ladies' names—though this obviously has nothing to do with sex. *Man* and *he* were formerly either masculine or generic, but current usage in some parts of our society has begun to restrict these words to male reference. This is gradually becoming "standard usage." Although the generic use of *man* is still intelligible, it may sometimes cause offense.

Gender Systems

There are many different systems of grammatical gender among the world's languages. The choice of three gender categories in Greek (masculine, feminine, and neuter) is intelligible to us even though English nouns do not usually grammaticalize these categories. Many languages that have grammatical gender have only two categories (often animate and inanimate). French has masculine and feminine, but no neuter. Other languages have more genders. Bininj Gun-Wok (an Australian language) has four genders: masculine, feminine, vegetable, and neuter. Some Niger-Congo languages have as many as twenty genders (e.g., Nigerian Fula).

Number

2.6. The category of number (singular and plural) is more familiar to us—and Greek number is very much like English number. The most common way to indicate number in English is to add the letter *s* to a noun to make it plural (dog ▸ dogs), but there are other ways to indicate the difference in number: child ▸ children; ox ▸ oxen; mouse ▸ mice. Sometimes the same word is used to indicate both singular and plural: sheep.

Case

2.7. *Case* identifies the function of a noun or pronoun in a sentence. *Function* refers to whether a word is the subject, direct object, or indirect object, and so on, in a sentence.

There are three cases in English. They are named *subjective*, *objective*, and *possessive*. (Greek uses different names and adds more cases; we will learn those a bit later.) The subjective case is used for the subject of a sentence; it identifies who is doing the action described by the verb:[3]

Pinocchio broke his nose.
He broke his nose.

The objective case is used for the direct object; it identifies who or what receives the action of the verb.

Pinocchio broke his *nose*.
Pinocchio broke *him*.[4]

The possessive case is a statement of possession:[5]

Pinocchio broke *his* nose.
Jiminy Cricket told Geppetto about *Pinocchio's* nose.
His master lost *his* puppet.

English words sometimes change their spelling when they change case, but most of the time they do not. Greek words *almost always* change their spelling when they change case.

3. It is actually a bit more complicated than this, but a simple description will do for now.

4. That may seem like an odd sentence, but it makes perfectly good sense if *him* refers to a stallion or perhaps if Pinocchio was a wrestler.

5. The possessive case in English is broader than possession or ownership, but that is perhaps one of the most common uses and the one most commonly thought of due to the designation *possessive*.

Greek Grammatical Terminology

2.8. Browse through this section first, then come back and study it more carefully. Some things that are not clear at first will fit together better once you get the big picture. Your goal in this section is not to memorize specific "Greek things" but to understand how the system works. I will tell you when you encounter material that you must memorize. In many instances below I will give you only one example, not the entire range of possibilities.

Gender

2.9. Greek nouns *always* have grammatical gender. A given word always has the same gender, and it never changes. The three gender categories in Greek are masculine, feminine, and neuter. The word λόγος ("word") is masculine. Always. Even if it is a woman speaking—or if it is emanating from the ear buds of an iPod, having been synthesized by a computer program. The word δόξα ("glory") is feminine, and the word ἱερόν ("temple") is neuter. (You will learn how to identify this information shortly—it is typically found in the ending on the word.)

Remember that this is a *grammatical* statement; it does not tell us anything about the sex of the object. The gender of some words may sound "natural" to us: υἱός, "son," for example, is masculine. That seems perfectly sensible to us. Other words, however, do not seem at all natural: κοράσιον, "little girl," is neuter (even nice little girls!); χείρ, "hand," is feminine regardless of whether it is a man's hand or a woman's hand; and ἀκροβυστία, "foreskin," is feminine! That makes no sense at all to us, but that is only because we are presupposing that gender is the same as sex. Remember that gender is a grammatical category no different than number in its associations. The category of gender tells us which endings to use on nouns and how to spell other words (such as adjectives) that are related to them.

Number

2.10. The grammatical category of number works in Greek just as it does in English. Singular and plural are the only categories for number in Koine Greek.[6] The only difference is how you know a word is singular or plural. Again, it is the *ending* on the word that indicates this. The same endings that indicate case and gender also identify the grammatical number of the word. For example, λόγος ("word") is singular and λόγοι ("words") is plural.

6. In older forms of Greek there was also a dual form. This was used for things that came in pairs—for example, ears. The same category is used in Biblical/Classical Hebrew and also in Modern Hebrew, though less frequently, since many duals from the classical period have become plurals in the modern form of the language.

Case

2.11. As in English, case identifies the function of a noun or pronoun in a Greek sentence. Greek uses five cases (only four of which are common) to indicate how words in a sentence function. Remember that word order is very flexible in Greek, so case is much more important for understanding meaning than it is in English. The Greek cases are

nominative
genitive
dative
accusative
vocative

The nominative is the case used to identify the subject of a sentence, and the accusative identifies the object. These are parallel to the subjective and objective cases in English. (We will study the other cases later.) The word ἀπόστολος means "apostle." When it is spelled with -ος at the end (ἀπόστολος), we know that the word is functioning as the *subject* of a sentence, because it is in nominative case. But if we change -ος to -ον (ἀπόστολον), we know that the word is now functioning as the *direct object* of the sentence, because it is in the accusative case. If the subject or object were plural, we would use -οι and -ους instead of -ος and -ον respectively.

For starters, the following examples use English word order. Which words are nominative and which are accusative? What is the subject and what is the direct object in each sentence? (The word γινώσκει is a verb that means "he knows"; τοὺς διαλογισμούς means "the thoughts"; the other words are in the vocabulary list for this chapter.)

κύριος γινώσκει τοὺς διαλογισμούς (1 Cor. 3:20).
θεὸς γινώσκει τοὺς διαλογισμούς.
κύριος γινώσκει Χριστόν.
Χριστὸς γινώσκει θεόν.

Unlike English, Greek word order does *not* determine the function of a word in the sentence or the meaning of the sentence. Function and meaning are determined by case. All these sentences say the same thing ("The Lord knows the thoughts"):

κύριος γινώσκει τοὺς διαλογισμούς.
γινώσκει τοὺς διαλογισμοὺς κύριος.
τοὺς διαλογισμοὺς κύριος γινώσκει.
γινώσκει κύριος τοὺς διαλογισμούς.

Declension

2.12. *Declension* refers to different ways to change the ending of a word to indicate its function in the sentence, or we could say that it is a set of endings in a fixed pattern used to indicate case and number. Various languages have varying numbers of such sets; Greek has three declensions, Latin has five. Let me illustrate this concept with "goofy English." We could say that there are three English declensions for plural.

The ***s* declension**: This declension would include all the words that form their plurals by adding an *s* to the word[7]—for example, cat ▸ cat*s*; truck ▸ truck*s*; mother ▸ mother*s*; book ▸ book*s*; window ▸ window*s*; computer ▸ computer*s*; iPod ▸ iPod*s*.

The ***en* declension**: This declension would include all the words that form their plurals by adding *en* to the word—for example, ox ▸ ox*en*; child ▸ childr*en*; brother ▸ brethr*en*.[8]

The **zero declension**: This declension would include all the words that do not change their form to create a plural. Only the context can determine whether the words in the zero declension are singular or plural[9]—for example, fish, series, deer, corps, bellows, species.

If you ask an English teacher about these declensions, you would get a puzzled look, but it may help you understand how Greek is structured. For nouns, Greek has three declensions, that is, different patterns of endings, with profound names:

first declension
second declension
third declension

That means there are three sets of endings that we will use on Greek nouns to indicate number and case. You will learn two sets of endings in this chapter and a third one later.

Stem and Ending

2.13. The stem is the word with the case ending removed. For example, the stem of the word ἀπόστολος is ἀποστολο-. *Ending* is a rather general word for

7. Or sometimes *-es* (e.g., box ▸ box*es*).

8. The normal plural for *brother* is now *brothers*. The illustration above uses the older English spelling, *brethren* (which you might recognize if you have ever used a King James Bible or read Shakespeare).

9. Remember this when you get frustrated with Greek for not having an explicit form, forcing you to judge from the context. English often does the same thing. It might be more frequent in Greek than English, or perhaps we just notice it more because we make such judgments automatically in English without even stopping to think about them.

what is appended to the stem. It is similar to a suffix. Endings can sometimes be composed of multiple parts, each of which has its own name.[10]

First and Second Noun Declensions

2.14. The endings that are used on Greek nouns to indicate case and number are shown in the following chart. Memorize this chart exactly!

First- and Second-Declension Case Endings

	2nd Decl. (M/f)	1st Decl. (F/m)	2nd Decl. (N)
NS	ος	α or η	ον
GS	ου	ας or ης	ου
DS	ῳ	ᾳ or ῃ	ῳ
AS	ον	αν or ην	ον
NP	οι	αι	α
GP	ων	ων	ων
DP	οις	αις	οις
AP	ους	ας	α

You read this kind of chart as follows: the first main column, titled "2nd Decl. (M/f)," tells you that second-declension nouns (which are *usually*—but not always—masculine)[11] use a set of eight endings to indicate the case/number indicated in the left column; first-declension nouns (which are *almost always* feminine),[12] use the endings in the center column, and so forth.

The first four rows are singular endings (S), the last four are plural (P). The N, G, D, A are the four cases: nominative, genitive, dative, and accusative. We have talked about only nominative and accusative thus far; we will study the genitive and dative cases in the next chapter. "NS" thus refers to an ending that is nominative singular. The same ending tells you two things: case and number. "AP" tells you the ending is accusative plural, and so forth.[13]

2.15. The vast majority of second-declension nouns are masculine (and so use the endings in column 1) or neuter (and so use the endings in column 3); a small number of second-declension nouns are feminine (and use the endings in column 1). The endings in columns 1 and 3 are almost identical. The second-declension

10. Each of these pieces is called, in technical terminology, a *morpheme*—the smallest meaningful unit in a word.

11. That is why you see the parentheses in the chart and the uppercase/lowercase distinction: (M/f), (F/m), (N). The last column, the neuter variation of the second declension, is *always* neuter.

12. Most first-declension masculine words are proper names. There are only a half dozen that use alpha endings that are not names, and all of them are used infrequently. In chap. 3 you will meet a few common first-declension masculine words that use eta endings.

13. In place of the single-letter abbreviations used here (i.e., N, G, D, A and S, P), some reference works will use the abbreviations nom., gen., dat., acc., sg., and pl.

neuter column is just a variation of column 1; only the nominative and accusative forms differ. First-declension nouns all follow the same pattern in the plural, but first-declension singular nouns may end with forms using alpha, eta, or a consistent hybrid pattern. In the hybrid pattern, the vowel switches from alpha to eta in the genitive and dative singular forms, resulting in the vowel pattern α η η α.[14] There is also a third declension, which you will meet in chapter 11.

Technically, the vowel on the front of the ending shown in the chart above is part of the stem, not the ending (it is called a *connecting vowel* or a *stem vowel*). This vowel determines the declension category: stems that end with an omicron are second declension; those with an alpha or eta are first declension. It is easier to memorize the endings *with* the vowel because then you can pronounce the ending as a syllable. It also enables you to distinguish a number of forms that otherwise have identical endings.[15]

Technical Case Endings

The technical endings (that is, without the connecting vowels) are as follows (see *MBG*, 165, for a detailed explanation):

	2nd Decl. (M/f)	1st Decl. (F/m)	2nd Decl. (N)
NS	ς	—	ν
GS	υ	ς	υ
DS	ι	ι	ι
AS	ν	ν	ν
NP	ι	ι	α
GP	ων	ων	ων
DP	ις	ις	ις
AP	υς	ς	α

2.16. Here is a similar chart, but with actual words instead of just the endings. The meanings of the words are as follows: λόγος, "word"; ὁδός, "road"; ὥρα, "hour"; γραφή, "writing" or "Scripture"; δόξα, "glory"; and ἔργον, "work."

First- and Second-Declension Nouns

	2nd Declension		1st Declension			2nd Declension
	M	(f)		F		N
NS	λόγος	ὁδός	ὥρα	γραφή	δόξα	ἔργον
GS	λόγου	ὁδοῦ	ὥρας	γραφῆς	δόξης	ἔργου
DS	λόγῳ	ὁδῷ	ὥρᾳ	γραφῇ	δόξῃ	ἔργῳ
AS	λόγον	ὁδόν	ὥραν	γραφήν	δόξαν	ἔργον
NP	λόγοι	ὁδοί	ὧραι	γραφαί	δόξαι	ἔργα
GP	λόγων	ὁδῶν	ὡρῶν	γραφῶν	δοξῶν	ἔργων
DP	λόγοις	ὁδοῖς	ὥραις	γραφαῖς	δόξαις	ἔργοις
AP	λόγους	ὁδούς	ὥρας	γραφάς	δόξας	ἔργα

14. There are only 36 words in the NT that do this, and only 3 are common (i.e., they occur 50 or more times in the NT: δόξα, "glory"; γλῶσσα, "tongue, language"; θάλασσα, "sea, lake"). There is a rule that tells you which words will use the hybrid pattern (Smyth, *Greek Grammar*, §217a–c). If you want a list of all these words, see *MBG*, 174. The three patterns given above are the only patterns used; no Greek word has any other pattern, such as η α α η or α η α η.

15. If you study the chart of the technical endings in the sidebar "Technical Case Endings," you will find that there are three endings with only a sigma, five with only an iota, and three with ις. Most of these are easily distinguished if you learn the endings with the connecting vowel.

Lexical Form

2.17. In an English dictionary you know that you will not find an entry for the plural form of a noun; it is always listed under the singular. There are similar conventions for Greek. To find a Greek word in a Greek-English lexicon, you need to know its "lexical form."

A term you need to remember: *lexical form* = the way a word is spelled in the dictionary/lexicon. For nouns, the lexical form is always the nominative singular form.

Parsing

2.18. To parse a Greek noun means to describe it grammatically. Use this formula for consistency and completeness:

Gender, Number, Case ▸ Lexical Form, Gloss

The *lexical form* gives the complete form found in the lexicon. A *gloss* is a simple English equivalent of the lexical form without necessarily considering the context. It is *not* a translation of the inflected form.

For example, if I were to ask you to parse λόγους, you would tell me: masculine plural accusative ▸ λόγος, ου, ὁ, "word."[16] You know this because you recognize the ending, -ους, as matching the masculine plural accusative form in the chart that you just memorized.

Declension and Gender

2.19. First-declension nouns (that is, nouns with first-declension endings) are *usually* feminine, *sometimes* masculine. Second-declension nouns are *usually* masculine or neuter, *sometimes* feminine. Remember: the M/F/N headings as you see on the charts above are *general guidelines,* not invariables; the 2/1/2 heading, however, is *always* true.[17] That is, if a word has one of the endings from the center column, it is a first-declension word. *Always.* Whether it is masculine or feminine.

Examples

2.20. Read each of the following examples aloud, and then identify all the words that you can identify as subjects or as direct objects. You do not have enough information yet to identify all the words or to figure out what these sentences

16. The "ου, ὁ" is part of the lexical form. You will learn what these pieces mean shortly.

17. The capital letters used in these headings represent the usual classification, but a lowercase letter in the same heading (e.g., M/f) is to remind you that sometimes these forms are feminine rather than the usual masculine.

mean, but you can find at least one word whose function you can identify in each sentence (sometimes two) based on what you have learned thus far. You do not have to translate these sentences.

John 3:16, ἠγάπησεν[a] ὁ θεὸς τὸν κόσμον.
Matt. 9:8, οἱ ὄχλοι ἐδόξασαν[a] τὸν θεόν.
Matt. 22:37, Ἀγαπήσεις τὸν θεόν.
Acts 2:32, τὸν [Χριστὸν] ἀνέστησεν[a] ὁ θεός.
Rom. 8:3, ὁ θεὸς τὸν υἱὸν πέμψας.
Rev. 16:21, ἐβλασφήμησαν[a] οἱ ἄνθρωποι τὸν θεόν.
Gen. 1:1, ἐποίησεν[a] ὁ θεὸς τὸν οὐρανὸν καὶ τὴν γῆν.
Gen. 2:7, ἔπλασεν[a] ὁ θεὸς τὸν ἄνθρωπον.

The words above marked with a superscript *a* end with a nu, but they are verbs, not nouns. Later you will learn how to tell the difference.

The Article

2.21. In English, the words that we call *articles* are special adjectives used mostly with nouns to indicate "definiteness" (i.e., how specific is the referent?). English has two articles: the definite article, *the* (*the* book), which identifies a specific, identifiable referent, and the indefinite article, *a* or *an* (*a* book; *an* apple), which refers to any such object in a class.

Greek has only one article. The article functions differently in Greek than it does in English in that it can do more things than the English article can, but what the English definite article does, the Greek article can do also. This means that, for starters, you can think of the Greek article as roughly similar to the English definite article, *the*, in some of its uses, even though we will expand and modify that conception in due time. There is no such thing as a definite article in Greek—only an article that may or may not express definiteness. Likewise, the lack of an article is not necessarily an expression of indefiniteness but may express a qualitative meaning or some other nuance. You will learn these other uses inductively throughout the book.[18] (There is no specific word in Greek equivalent to our English *a* or *an*.)

Frequency of the Article

The article occurs almost 20,000 times in the NT, more than 88,000 times in the LXX, and proportionately as often in other Greek literature. You must know it. Well. Backward and forward.

In Greek, the article must agree with the noun it modifies in gender, number, and case. *Always*. The Greek article always *precedes* the word it governs (e.g., ὁ θεός; *never* θεὸς ὁ), just as in English the article always precedes the word it modifies (the book, or an apple, *never* book the, or apple an). Some other words,

18. The best discussion of the article is in Wallace, *Greek Grammar*, 206–54. For those of you wanting to go further, I would encourage you to browse that section. Pay particular attention to the *qualitative* use of anarthrous forms (i.e., words without an article, 244–45), which is different from English, as well as the generic use of the article (227–31).

such as a conjunction or modifier, may intervene between the article and the word it modifies (e.g., ὁ δὲ θεός), but the article still precedes the word it modifies. If you remember these things, you will be able to identify the function of words that you do not otherwise recognize, since there is only one set of articles and they are used for everything in Greek that uses an article.

Complete Article Chart

2.22. *This chart must be memorized exactly.* Be sure to include the rough breathing marks where needed and the iota subscripts. Knowing the forms in this chart well is *very important*, and it will help you understand more sentences than you can count.

	Masc.	Fem.	Neut.
NS	ὁ	ἡ	τό
GS	τοῦ	τῆς	τοῦ
DS	τῷ	τῇ	τῷ
AS	τόν	τήν	τό
NP	οἱ	αἱ	τά
GP	τῶν	τῶν	τῶν
DP	τοῖς	ταῖς	τοῖς
AP	τούς	τάς	τά

Article "Tidbits"

2.23. *Personal names* may or may not have the article in Greek, but if they do, we omit it in English translation since English does not use the article with names. You will see both Ἰησοῦς and ὁ Ἰησοῦς in the NT, but both are translated simply "Jesus."[19] We would not say, "The Jesus died," any more than we would say, "The Robert died." Translation must communicate in proper grammar in the receptor language or it is not accurate translation.

Abstract nouns often have the article in Greek but usually do not have it in English. Abstract nouns refer to intangible, abstract entities or concepts, not physical objects you can point a finger at and say "that is x." For example,

love, ἡ ἀγάπη
truth, ἡ ἀλήθεια
holiness, ὁ ἁγιασμός
guilt, τὸ αἴτιον

In most cases, these are represented in English without an article. For example, Rom. 13:10, **ἡ ἀγάπη** τῷ πλησίον κακὸν οὐκ ἐργάζεται, means, "*Love* does not do evil to a neighbor."

19. Ἰησοῦς is nominative case (as you would guess from the article). See the explanation in the "Vocabulary Notes" at the end of chap. 3.

Basic Greek Sentence Patterns

2.24. Common sentence patterns in Greek include subject ▸ verb ▸ object (just like English), object ▸ verb ▸ subject, and verb ▸ subject ▸ object. Some of these are more common than others, but all of them occur. We will begin by learning some of the common kinds of nouns and verbs that can be used in simple sentences using these patterns. Later we will learn more complex types of sentences.

The *kernel* of a sentence consists of the main statement, stripped of all its modifiers. It typically consists of subject, verb, and direct object (or predicate nominative). Sometimes it is only a subject and a verb—and since, as you will learn later, Greek includes a subject in every verb, it may be only one word: the verb.

Lexicon or Dictionary?

You will hear both of these terms used to describe the same reference book. Some people think that *dictionary* is for English and that *lexicon* is the correct, or at least more technical, term for foreign language dictionaries. The terms are actually synonymous. The English word *lexicon* comes from Greek, λεξικόν, while *dictionary* comes from Latin, *dictionarium.* Traditionally the study of ancient Greek has favored the designation *lexicon,* and perhaps that is appropriate since it is a loanword from Greek, but *dictionary* is equally correct.[a]

[a] For beginning Greek we typically use an abridged, beginner's lexicon such as Danker's *Concise Lexicon* (*CL*) or Trenchard's *Concise Dictionary of New Testament Greek.* In due time you will move to the unabridged, full-fledged lexicon by Bauer, Danker, Arndt, and Gingrich (BDAG).

Reading Exercises

2.25. In the following texts you will find a mixture of Greek and English. Only the parts of the statement that you can recognize are in Greek. You will find reading exercises like this in the early chapters of the book; later the texts will be all Greek, with notes or explanations for the parts you do not know yet. In the parallel column you will be asked questions about the text on the left. Your answer should be first in Greek; that is, what Greek word answers the question? (Do not base your answers on English word order!) Once you know that, then you can use your lexicon to find out what it means.

Mark 2:10, ἐξουσίαν has ὁ υἱός.	Who has what? How do you know?
Mark 2:23, On the Sabbath Jesus was going through the grain fields καὶ οἱ μαθηταί were picking heads of grain.	Who was/were picking grain? Was it one person or several? How do you know?
Mark 4:15, When they hear, ὁ σατανᾶς[a] takes away τὸν λόγον that was sown.	Who does the taking away? What is taken away? How do you know?

[a] This word is a bit odd; decide how it is functioning based on the article.

Mark 11:3, If anyone says to you, "Why are you doing this?" say, Ὁ κύριος χρείαν has.	The last phrase says that someone has something. Who has what?

Mark 12:41, ὁ ὄχλος threw χαλκόν into τὸ γαζοφυλάκιον.	Who was throwing? What were they throwing? Into what were they throwing it?
Mark 13:12, Will betray ἀδελφὸς ἀδελφόν.	Two instances of the same word. What is different? How does the difference help you understand what is happening?
Mark 13:22, ψευδόχριστοι καὶ ψευδοπροφῆται will give σημεῖα.	Who is giving what?
Luke 2:35, Your τὴν ψυχήν will pierce ῥομφαία.	Who or what will do the piercing? What is pierced?
John 1:45, Found Φίλιππος τὸν Ναθαναήλ.[a]	Who did the finding? Who was found?

[a] The word Ναθαναήλ is indeclinable; that is, it does not use case endings, so it never changes its spelling. (Many Hebrew names appear this way when transliterated into Greek.) You can tell what case it is in this passage by the article.

Ruth 1:6, Has visited κύριος τὸν λαὸν his to give them ἄρτους.	Who did the visiting? Who was visited? What does the case of ἄρτους tell you about this word's function in the sentence?
Jdt. 2:17, He took καμήλους καὶ ὄνους καὶ ἡμιόνους for their τὴν ἀπαρτίαν.[a]	What did he take? What case and gender is ἀπαρτίαν?

[a] Not in NT lexicons: ἡμίονος, ου, ὁ/ἡ, "mule"; ἀπαρτία, ας, ἡ, "baggage, supplies."

Barn. 6.10, For speaks ὁ προφήτης παραβολήν.	Who speaks? What does he speak?

Reading Passage: John 1:1–8

2.26. You will not understand much of the following text. Use it for reading practice. Identify as many things in this text as you can (articles, case endings, etc.). If you have begun learning the vocabulary for this chapter, you should recognize several words from that list.

The Word Was in the Beginning

1'Εν ἀρχῇ ἦν ὁ λόγος, καὶ ὁ λόγος ἦν πρὸς τὸν θεόν, καὶ θεὸς ἦν ὁ λόγος. 2οὗτος
ἦν ἐν ἀρχῇ πρὸς τὸν θεόν. 3πάντα δι' αὐτοῦ ἐγένετο, καὶ χωρὶς αὐτοῦ ἐγένετο
οὐδὲ ἕν ὃ γέγονεν. 4ἐν αὐτῷ ζωὴ ἦν, καὶ ἡ ζωὴ ἦν τὸ φῶς τῶν ἀνθρώπων· 5καὶ
τὸ φῶς ἐν τῇ σκοτίᾳ φαίνει, καὶ ἡ σκοτία αὐτὸ οὐ κατέλαβεν.

6'Εγένετο ἄνθρωπος, ἀπεσταλμένος παρὰ θεοῦ, ὄνομα αὐτῷ Ἰωάννης· 7οὗτος
ἦλθεν εἰς μαρτυρίαν ἵνα μαρτυρήσῃ περὶ τοῦ φωτός, ἵνα πάντες πιστεύσωσιν
δι' αὐτοῦ. 8οὐκ ἦν ἐκεῖνος τὸ φῶς, ἀλλ' ἵνα μαρτυρήσῃ περὶ τοῦ φωτός.

Vocabulary for Chapter 2

2.27. The vocabulary lists in each chapter are organized first by part of speech, then roughly by NT frequency. Where related words are in the same chapter (e.g., compound forms), they are often listed together.

Part of Speech	Definition	Possible Glosses	Frequency	
Word			NT	LXX
Article				
ὁ, ἡ, τό	A diverse, multipurpose marker: (1) a defining marker, the Greek article, "the"; (2) as a demonstrative, "this one, that one"	the; this/that one	19,870	88,439
Conjunctions				
καί	A function word that marks connection or addition: (1) connective (copula), "and," joining equal words, clauses, etc. (i.e., a coordinating conjunction); (2) additive (adjunctive/adverbial), "also, even" [See the "Vocabulary Notes."]	and (conj.); even, also (adv.)	9,153	62,240
δέ	A multipurpose coordinating, postpositive[a] conjunction or narrative marker linking two grammatically equal items that have some difference in referent (subject, participant, time, place, etc.)	but, now, and	2,792	4,887
ὅτι	A conjunction that links two clauses by (1) defining, "that"; (2) introducing a subordinate clause or indirect statement; (3) introducing a direct statement = quotation marks; (4) indicating cause, "because," inference, "for," or a query, "why?"	because, that, since	1,296	4,041
γάρ	A multipurpose, postpositive[a] marker that may function as a narrative connector or as an expression of reaction or perspective, "for" (usually a subordinating conjunction): (1) explanatory; (2) astonishment; (3) causal; or (4) inferential	for	1,041	1,529
Nouns				
θεός, οῦ, ὁ	An immortal entity/deity, whether in a monotheistic or polytheistic context, may refer to a supreme being in any religion, or in a lesser sense to the devil, or even to human beings who have some special status	god, God	1,317	3,984
κύριος, ου, ὁ	Person who is in control due to possession, ownership, or position; or who is esteemed for authority or high status, whether human or divine	lord, master, sir	717	8,591
ἄνθρωπος, ου, ὁ	Human being, often used generically of men or women, either in distinction from God or in reference to a specific person	man, person, human being, mankind, humankind	550	1,430
Χριστός, οῦ, ὁ	Expected fulfiller of the hopes of Israel for an end-time deliverer; also sometimes used almost as a personal name for Jesus	Messiah, Christ	529	51

Part of Speech	Definition	Possible Glosses	Frequency	
Word			NT	LXX
υἱός, οῦ, ὁ	Male offspring (human or animal), or by extension, someone closely related (not necessarily by birth) or characterized by some quality	son, descendant, offspring, child, or (if context allows) person	377	5,190
ἀδελφός, οῦ, ὁ	Male sibling (i.e., "brother"); in an extended sense, one with common interests, community fellow	brother; compatriot, "brother(s) and/or sister(s)"	343	924
λόγος, ου, ὁ	An expression of the content of thought, whether an individual term ("word") or longer expressions (written or oral; widely varied English glosses may be used, e.g., "statement," "question," or "report"); the personified expression of God, "the Logos"	word, statement, message; Logos	330	1,238
οὐρανός, οῦ, ὁ	That part of the universe surrounding the earth, including the atmosphere ("sky") and/or the place where other cosmic bodies are located ("the heavens"); the place where God's presence is manifested ("heaven")	sky, the heavens; heaven	273	682
νόμος, ου, ὁ	A principle or standard relating to behavior, whether traditional and unwritten ("custom, norm") or written as legislation ("law") in general or a specific legal corpus ("the law," e.g., the Mosaic law)	law, principle; custom, norm	194	427
κόσμος, ου, ὁ	An orderly arrangement of things, whether the entire cosmos ("universe"), our planet ("world"), society/culture, or the human beings who live in or compose one of the above	world, universe, people	186	72

[a] A postpositive conjunction is one that never stands first in its clause. In an English equivalent, these words need to be relocated to the front of the clause even if it occurs as the second or third word (or even later) in Greek. See further the discussion of δέ in §8.9.

Vocabulary Notes

2.28. The simple conjunction καί, which occurs more than 9,000 times in the NT, is a very complex word and used in a great variety of ways. Although a beginner may often get by with the simple "and," it is worth keeping in mind the potential variety. These other uses will become more evident as your reading ability increases. BDAG explains that καί is "found most frequently by far of all Gk. particles in the NT; since it is not only used much more commonly here than in other Gk. lit. but oft. in a different sense, or rather in different circumstances, it contributes greatly to some of the distinctive coloring of the NT

About Memorizing

I attempt to keep rote memory to a minimum in this textbook, but the things that I tell you must be memorized are absolutely essential. Your teacher will tell you what is expected in your class, but in any case, the goal is not memorizing forms but learning to understand Greek. The case endings (which are also part of the article) are some of the most basic building blocks of the language. You will never learn Greek if you do not know these cold.

style. . . . The vivacious versatility of [καί] . . . can easily be depressed by the [translation] 'and,' whose repetition in a brief area of text lacks the support of arresting aspects of Gk. syntax" (494).

2.29. Key Things to Know for Chapter 2

Do you understand the function of gender, number, and case?

How do you know what word in a Greek sentence is the subject and what is the direct object?

You must be able to write from memory the chart of the first- and second-declension noun endings.

You must be able to write the chart of the Greek article letter-perfect from memory.

3

NOUNS: PART 2

Genitive and Dative Cases

3.1. In the previous chapter you learned the basics about nouns and were introduced to the first two cases (though you learned endings for all four cases). In this chapter we will study the second two cases: genitive and dative. There is one more case, the vocative, which is seldom used (see app. D). We will begin by looking at some similar features in English.

English Background

Possessive Case

3.2. In English we use the possessive case to indicate ownership (e.g., *Daniel's* computer). Actually the English possessive case is much broader than possession or ownership (though that is what most students think of when they hear the term).[1] As one English grammar explains, "we employ the possessive case of a noun or pronoun when we wish to indicate *possession* or *source*. We also use the possessive to indicate concepts involving *time, place, author,* or *doer.*" A note then explains that "in effect, we employ the possessive case to change a substantive to a modifier."[2] These half-dozen examples are given to illustrate the range of English usage:[3]

1. A number of grammatical terms used to describe either English or Greek are imprecise or even inaccurate. They have developed over many centuries, and by now the tradition is so deeply embedded that it is extremely difficult to make changes.

2. Buckler and McAvoy, *English Fundamentals*, 107 §9h.

3. Buckler and McAvoy, *English Fundamentals*, 107 §9h. I have reformatted the text and abridged the explanations given for each of these examples.

Possession: I bought the *neighbor's* car.
Authorship: The instructor assigned *Fielding's* novel.
Subject of: They unveiled *Roosevelt's* portrait.
Time: We were happy to see the *day's* end.
Place: Did they find the *trail's* end?
Doer of an action: They resented that *man's* actions.

Indirect Object

3.3. We refer to the person/thing to whom or for whom the action of the verb is done as the indirect object. This is usually one word and most commonly occurs (in English) between the verb and the direct object. For example,

Meghan threw Liam an apple.

In this sentence we say that "Liam" is the indirect object, because he receives the action (and the apple also).[4] The subject of this sentence (the doer of the action) is "Meghan." The direct object is "apple," since that is what is thrown. Consider a variation of this example:

Meghan threw an apple to Liam.

This second sentence says the exact same thing but uses a prepositional phrase ("to Liam") instead of an indirect object.[5] English does not have a separate case for the indirect object; Greek does.

Genitive Case

3.4. A genitive-case noun functions to restrict (or *modify*) another word in the sentence, usually the word directly preceding it in word order.[6] The word being modified is called the *head word*. The way in which the genitive restricts the head word varies. There is not a single "meaning" for the genitive case but a range of semantic relationships. You will see some of the most common ones in this chapter, but your understanding of the genitive will grow as you continue studying. The key is to ask in what way the genitive noun restricts the reference of the head noun. To determine that, you need to consider the context. If you were trying to express this relationship in English, you might do so by using an

4. The sentence "Meghan threw Liam" says something quite different.

5. Would you agree that English is sometimes weird? It can say the same thing two different ways with no difference in meaning. Actually, that is very normal. It is the same way in Greek. Do not try to make every little difference in Greek the basis for some special nuance—a "golden nugget." As you hear people talking about the Greek NT (whether commentators, preachers, or Bible study leaders), it is often a safe rule of thumb that their reliable knowledge of Greek is inversely proportionate to the number of "golden nuggets" that they find in the text.

6. A Greek genitive noun or pronoun may also be the object of a preposition or the direct object of some verbs. For now, do not worry about these other functions.

English prepositional phrase with the word *of.* But in other cases it may make better sense to use *from*, *for*, *by*, or *with*. In yet other instances you will use the English possessive suffix, *'s*. Sometimes you discover that we use an entirely different form to express it in English.

For example, we might refer to *the word* or *a word* (which might be Tom, Dick, or Harry's word—any old word at all), but we could be more specific by referring to *Anna's word* or to *the word of God*.[7] Or consider these two English examples:

A wife is expecting a baby in October. (Thousands of wives fit that description.)
Rob's wife is expecting a baby in October (or: *The wife of Rob* . . .).

In English we would call this second example an instance of the possessive case; in Greek it would be in the genitive case. The genitive ("Rob's") restricts the head word ("wife"). It is not just a "wife" who anticipates giving birth, but "Rob's wife" (we will call her Stephanie). Note that this is not strictly possession but relationship. (Rob does not own Stephanie.)

3.5. In Greek, the genitive is formed by adding an ending to the stem of the word. For example, the word θεός is in the nominative case. If we change the ending from -ος to the genitive ending -ου, then θεοῦ might mean (depending on the context), *of God*, *from God*, or *God's*. The usual pattern in Greek is for the word in the genitive case to *follow* the noun it modifies, though occasionally it will precede the word it modifies. Here are some examples.

βιβλίος **θεοῦ** = "book *of/from God*" or "*God's* book."
νόμοι **θεοῦ** = "laws *of/from God*" or "*God's* laws"
λόγος **θεοῦ** = "word *of/from God*" or "*God's* word"
υἱὸς **ἀνθρώπου** = "son *of man*" or "a *man's* son"
δόξα **ἡλίου** = "glory *of the sun*" or "*the sun's* glory"

Do not think of all genitives as indicating ownership or even the equivalent of the English possessive case; some are, some are not. The Greek genitive case is *not* the equivalent to possession or ownership, though it includes those meanings among its various functions. In other words, these ideas are a subset of the larger category called *genitive*, as the following examples illustrate:

τὴν παραβολὴν **τῶν ζιζανίων** = the parable *of the weeds*
This refers not to the parable *that belongs to* the weeds but to the parable *about* the weeds.

ἡμέρα **ὀργῆς** = the day *of wrath*
The day does not *belong to* wrath; it is rather the day that is *characterized by* wrath.

7. In English "of God" is a prepositional phrase, but in Greek it would be a genitive-case noun (θεοῦ). Many Greek genitives are translated with such an "of" phrase, but that is not the only way to translate a genitive.

τῷ φόβῳ **τοῦ κυρίου** = the fear *of the Lord*

This fear is not one that *belongs to* the Lord but is the fear that is *appropriately directed toward* the Lord.

All these genitives restrict the meaning of their head noun by describing it in some way.

Not all nouns use -ου as the genitive ending. You will remember from the chart of case endings that you memorized in chapter 2 that there are several possible genitive endings. Study that chart, reproduced here, and notice that there are different genitive forms for each declension as well as for singular and plural.

First- and Second-Declension Case Endings

	2nd Decl. (M/f)	1st Decl. (F/m)	2nd Decl. (N)
NS	ος	α or η	ον
GS	ου	ας or ης	ου
DS	ῳ	ᾳ or ῃ	ῳ
AS	ον	αν or ην	ον
NP	οι	αι	α
GP	ων	ων	ων
DP	οις	αις	οις
AP	ους	ας	α

Teaching Cats Greek

Bruce Metzger, a well-known NT scholar, recounts this little ditty that requires knowing some Greek to understand.[a]

There was a kind curate of Kew
Who kept a large cat in the pew,
Which he taught every week
alphabetical Greek,
But got no farther than *mu*.

Not only is mu one of the letters of the Greek alphabet (μ), but it is also the vocative form of the Greek word for "mouse": μῦς, μυός, ὁ; the vocative form is μῦ. (The vocative is the case of direct address; see app. D.) The phrase μῦς ἀρουραῖος refers to a field mouse or a hamster. The adjective ἀρουραῖος means "from the country, rural."

[a] Metzger, *Reminiscences of an Octogenarian*, 23.

3.6. *Examples of the Genitive Case*

Mark 1:3, Ἑτοιμάσατε τὴν ὁδὸν **κυρίου**. — Prepare the way *of the Lord*.

Mark 1:14, ἦλθεν ὁ Ἰησοῦς[a] εἰς τὴν Γαλιλαίαν κηρύσσων τὸ εὐαγγέλιον **τοῦ θεοῦ**. — Jesus came into Galilee preaching the good news *from God*.

[a] Did you remember the spelling of Ἰησοῦς? (It is one of the vocabulary words for this chapter.) What case is it? Check your lexicon if you are not sure. There is also a very helpful context clue in this verse.

Mark 2:10, ἐξουσίαν ἔχει ὁ υἱὸς **τοῦ ἀνθρώπου**. — The Son *of Man* has authority.

Mark 1:1, Ἀρχὴ **τοῦ εὐαγγελίου Ἰησοῦ Χριστοῦ** — The beginning *of the good news about Jesus Christ*

In this last example, two genitives appear in succession, each one modifying the word before it. The first genitive, τοῦ εὐαγγελίου, modifies ἀρχή—it is the beginning *of the good news*; the second, Ἰησοῦ Χριστοῦ, modifies τοῦ εὐαγγελίου—the good news is *about Jesus Christ.*

You might have noticed that in two of the examples above, the word εὐαγγέλιον occurs with a genitive following it. In the first example, Mark 1:14, I suggested an English gloss "good news *from God*," but in the second, Mark 1:1, the gloss is "the good news *about Jesus Christ*." This illustrates the flexible range of the genitive case. In each occurrence you must ask, What does the context suggest as the meaning or relationship between the genitive noun and the head noun? You may sometimes disagree with my judgments, and that is fine so long as you can explain from the context why you think it should be different. Sometimes it is just a different way to express the meaning in English; other times it might imply an alternate meaning.

Gen. 1:11, εἶπεν ὁ θεός, Βλαστησάτω ἡ γῆ βοτάνην **χόρτου.**

God said, "Let the earth produce pasture *of grass* [i.e., grass pastures, or pastures filled with grass]."

Gen. 2:6, πηγὴ ἐπότιζεν τὸ πρόσωπον **τῆς γῆς.**

A spring watered the surface *of the earth.*

Lexical Form

3.7. The lexical form of every noun is always given in the same format: θρόνος, ου, ὁ, "throne." The four pieces of this entry tell you the following:

The nominative singular form is θρόνος.

The ending for the genitive case is -ου, thus the genitive form is θρόνου.

The article is ὁ, which is the masculine article; therefore the word θρόνος is in the masculine gender.

The gloss for this word (a simple English equivalent) is "throne."

What is the equivalent information for these two words?

ἁμαρτία, ας, ἡ, "sin"
εὐαγγέλιον, ου, τό, "good news"

The article in the lexical entry is important. It is the only way to find out the gender of a noun. Masculine nouns will always be listed in the lexicon with the masculine singular article ὁ following the genitive ending. Feminine nouns will have the feminine singular article ἡ and neuter words have the neuter singular article τό.

The genitive ending in the lexical entry is important because some words have different patterns of endings; for example, first-declension words may have either an alpha or an eta. (This will be even more important later, especially in the third declension—another set of endings we will meet in chap. 11.) You can always tell which alternate is used by knowing the nominative and genitive forms (which is why they are included in the lexical form). First-declension forms have three possible ending patterns: all alphas (α), all etas (η), or an α-η-η-α pattern.

ἁμαρτία, ας, ἡ, "sin" ▸ ἁμαρτία, ας, ᾳ, αν, αι, ων, αις, ας
ἀρχή, ης, ἡ, "beginning" ▸ ἀρχή, ης, ῃ, ην, αι, ων, αις, ας
δόξα, ης, ἡ, "glory" ▸ δόξα, ης, ῃ, αν, αι, ων, αις, ας

Open your lexicon and look up some of the nouns in the vocabulary lists for chapters 1 and 2. Look for the consistent format in the lexicon, and notice how the article and genitive ending are listed in each instance. Then open to a random page in your lexicon, and see how many words you can identify as nouns based on the pattern shown in the lexical form. Do not worry about other things in the entries shown below that you do not understand, especially in the entry shown from BDAG; in due time you will learn what the other information means.

Shown below are images from three lexicons. Each shows the entry for the word θρόνος. Figure 3.1 shows the entry from Danker's *Concise Lexicon* (p. 141).

θρόνος, ου, ὁ [akin to θρᾶνος 'bench'; 'chair, seat'] ***throne*** (the customary gloss reflecting the status of the one for whom a chair is set aside)**—a.** of human seat of power **Lk 1:32, 52; Ac 2:30.—b.** of God's seat of power **Hb 1:8; 12:2; Rv 1:4; 7:15.** Of heaven as God's throne **Mt 5:34; 23:22; Ac 7:49.—c.** by metonymy in pl. as collective ***the enthroned*** **Col 1:16.**

Figure 3.1

3.8. Most Greek lexicons do not mark the part of speech explicitly, though it is always possible to determine the part of speech if you know the conventions used; we will learn them later. Figure 3.2 shows what the entry for θρόνος looks like in an unabridged lexicon, BDAG (p. 460). This is the standard tool for exegesis in the NT. There is far more information here than you can handle at this point, but it will hint at some of the riches that lie ahead. For now, skim the entire entry, but focus primarily on the first portion of the first line, and compare it with the other samples included here.

θρόνος, ου, ὁ (Hom.+; ins, pap, LXX, pseudepigr.; Jos., Ant. 7, 353; 8, 399; Mel., P. 83, 620 [B]; loanw. in rabb.).

❶ ***chair, seat***—ⓐ gener. ἐκάθισεν ἐπὶ τοῦ θρόνου (Mary) *sat down on her chair* GJs 11:1 (JosAs 7:1 Ἰωσὴφ ἐκάθισεν ἐπὶ θρόνου *sat on a chair*).

ⓑ specif. a chair set aside for one of high status, *throne*.

α. of human kings and rulers (Hdt. 1, 14, 3; X., Cyr. 6, 1, 6; Herodian 1, 8, 4) καθελεῖν ἀπὸ θρόνων *dethrone* **Lk 1:52.** The throne of David (2 Km 3:10; PsSol 17:6), the ancestor of the Messiah **1:32; Ac 2:30.**

β. of God (Soph., Ant. 1041; OGI 383 [ins of Antiochus of Commagene] 41f πρὸς οὐρανίους Διὸς Ὠρομάσδου θρόνους; Ps 46:9; Ezk. Trag. vs. 68 [in Eus., PE 9, 29, 5]; TestSol 13:5 C) **Hb 12:2; Rv 7:15; 12:5; 22:1, 3;** cp. **1:4; 3:21b; 4:2ff, 9; 5:1, 6f, 11, 13** al. (s. Cat. Cod. Astr. IX/2 p. 118f, notes w. lit.).—ὁ θρόνος τ. χάριτος **Hb 4:16;** τ. μεγαλωσύνης **8:1.**—Of heaven as God's throne (after Is 66:1) **Mt 5:34; 23:22; Ac 7:49;** B 16:2 (the two last pass. are direct quot. of Is 66:1.—Cp. Theosophien 56, 33f. For heaven as the throne of Zeus s. Orpheus: Hymn. 62, 2f Q. and Demosth. 25, 11).

γ. of Christ, who occupies the throne of his ancestor David (s. α above). It is a θ. δόξης αὐτοῦ **Mt 19:28a; 25:31** (PsSol; 2:19); an eternal throne **Hb 1:8** (Ps 44:7), which stands at the right hand of the Father's throne Pol 2:1 or is even identical w. it **Rv 22:1, 3;** cp. **3:21b.** His own are to share this throne w. him vs. **21a.**

δ. of the 12 apostles as judges (Philochorus [IV/III BC]: 328 fgm. 64bβ Jac. the νομοφύλακες . . . ἐπὶ θρόνων ἐκάθηντο; Plut., Mor. 807b; Paus. 2, 31, 3; Ps 121:5; Jos., Ant. 18, 107) or rulers in the time of the final consummation **Mt 19:28b** (Galen X 406 K. Θέσσαλος ἅμα τοῖς ἑαυτοῦ σοφισταῖς ἐφ' ὑψηλοῦ θρόνου καθήμενος); **Lk 22:30;** cp. **Rv 20:4.**

ε. of the 24 elders of **Rv 4:4; 11:16.**—Rv also mentions thrones of infernal powers; the throne of the dragon, which the 'beast' receives **13:2;** cp. **16:10.**—ὁ θ. τοῦ Σατανᾶ **2:13** in the letter to Pergamum is freq. (e.g. Dssm., LO 240, 8 [LAE 280, 2]; Lohmeyer ad loc.; Boll 112, 4) taken to be the famous Altar of Zeus there (cp. En 25:3 the mountain whose peak is like a throne); others (Zahn; JWeiss, RE X 551) prefer to think of the temple of Asclepius, and Bousset of Perg. as the center of the emperor-cult.—TBirt, D. Thron d. Satans: PhilologWoch 52, '32, 259–66.

❷ **supreme power over a political entity, *dominion, sovereignty,*** fig. extension of mng. 1 (a semantic component prob. present in some of the aforementioned passages, for the idea of authority is intimately associated with the chair that is reserved for an authority figure) θ. αἰώνιος of Jesus Christ 1 Cl 65:2; MPol 21.

❸ **name of a class of powerful beings, earthly or transcendent, *the enthroned,*** pl. (TestLevi 3:8; cp. the astrol. PMich 149 XVI, 23 and 24 [II AD].—Kephal. I 117, 24–26, personification of the one who sits on the throne, the judge) perh. of transcendent beings **Col 1:16** (cp. Mel., P. 83, 620; DSanger, in EDNT s.v.), but in view of the ref. to things 'seen and unseen' in the same vs. it is probable that the author thinks also of earthly rulers (s. 2 above).—B. 481. DELG. DDD 1628–31. M-M. TW.

Figure 3.2

Most lexicons use the standard system for indicating gender as illustrated in figures 3.1 and 3.2, but a few tools indicate the gender of nouns in a different way. If you were using one of the lexicons that follow this pattern, you would find not the article as a gender marker but an *m*, *f*, or *n* (for *masculine*, *feminine*, or *neuter*).

Standard Form	Alternate Form
θρόνος, ου, ὁ, "throne"	θρόνος, ου m
ἁμαρτία, ας, ἡ, "sin"	ἁμαρτία, ας f
εὐαγγέλιον, ου, τό, "good news"	εὐαγγέλιον, ου n

An example of this alternate format is found in Louw and Nida's lexicon (LN; see fig. 3.3).[8]

8. LN, 1:67, §6.112. Louw and Nida's work is a specialty lexicon, not a standard one for regular use. It does make a nice supplement to BDAG. Your teacher can tell you more about it. Another lexicon that uses this alternate pattern is Muraoka's *Greek-English Lexicon of the Septuagint*.

6.112 θρόνος[a], ου *m*: a relatively large and elaborate seat upon which a ruler sits on official occasions – 'throne.' εἶδον ἐπὶ τὴν δεξιὰν τοῦ καθημένου ἐπὶ τοῦ θρόνου βιβλίον 'I saw a book in the right hand of the one sitting on the throne' Re 5.1. In some languages 'throne' is rendered as 'the seat of judging' or 'the seat of decision-making for a ruler.'

Figure 3.3

Dative Case

3.9. The dative case is used to express various relationships within a sentence. The function of the dative case in expressing syntactical relationships is quite varied. A word in the dative case often functions as an indirect object or the object of some prepositions. It is sometimes a direct object (more on that later) and may also indicate advantage or disadvantage, instrument, means, or reference. (Do not try to memorize this list of uses; the list is intended only to give you some idea of what to expect in the examples below.) When you encounter a dative-case word in a sentence, you should think, what sort of relationship is being expressed in this context? Sometimes to put this into English, we make the dative-case noun into the object of an English preposition such as *to*, *for*, *with*, *in*, *on*, *at*, or *by*.

Like the genitive, the dative is formed by adding a special ending to the stem of the word. Review the case ending chart once again, this time focusing on the dative forms.

First- and Second-Declension Case Endings

	2nd Decl. (M/f)	1st Decl. (F/m)	2nd Decl. (N)
NS	ος	α or η	ον
GS	ου	ας or ης	ου
DS	ῳ	ᾳ or ῃ	ῳ
AS	ον	αν or ην	ον
NP	οι	αι	α
GP	ων	ων	ων
DP	οις	αις	οις
AP	ους	ας	α

There is always an iota in a dative case ending, subscripted in the singular, written on the line in the plural. Other than the nominative plural, these are the only noun endings that have an iota, so it is an important parsing clue. If a word is a noun and it has an iota subscript in the ending, it *must* be in the dative case.

3.10. *Examples of the Dative Case*

John 5:22, ὁ [θεὸς] τὴν κρίσιν δέδωκεν **τῷ υἱῷ.** — God has given *the Son* judgment (or, God has given judgment *to the Son*).

The direct object (what is given) is judgment (τὴν κρίσιν). That action—the giving of judgment (that is, the authority and responsibility to exercise judgment)—is done in relation to the Son; that is, τῷ υἱῷ is the indirect object.

Mark 6:41, κατέκλασεν τοὺς ἄρτους καὶ ἐδίδου **τοῖς μαθηταῖς** αὐτοῦ. — He broke the loaves of bread, and he gave [the pieces] *to his disciples.*

Rom. 6:2, ἀπεθάνομεν **τῇ ἁμαρτίᾳ.** — We died *to sin.*

This dative is not an indirect object, nor can it be a direct object, since the verb ἀπεθάνομεν ("we died") does not take a direct object (that is, it is intransitive). This use of the dative is sometimes called a *dative of reference*: we died *with reference to* sin.

Sin is usually taken as an abstract concept in this statement, so the article is not translated. If you thought it referred to the sinful nature, then you might translate it "we died to *the sin* [nature]"—but that is an exegetical question.

John 21:8, οἱ μαθηταὶ **τῷ πλοιαρίῳ** ἦλθον. — The disciples came *in the boat.*

Acts 12:2, ἀνεῖλεν δὲ Ἰάκωβον τὸν ἀδελφὸν Ἰωάννου **μαχαίρῃ.** — He killed James the brother of John *with a sword.*

Gen. 3:6, εἶδεν ἡ γυνὴ ὅτι καλὸν [was] τὸ ξύλον καὶ ὅτι [it was] ἀρεστὸν **τοῖς ὀφθαλμοῖς.** — The woman saw that the tree was good and that it was pleasing *to the eyes.*

Gen. 4:15, ἔθετο κύριος ὁ θεὸς σημεῖον **τῷ Κάϊν.** — The Lord God placed a sign *on Cain.*

Gen. 8:20, ᾠκοδόμησεν Νῶε θυσιαστήριον **τῷ θεῷ.** — Noah built an altar *to God.*

Reading Exercises

3.11. In the reading exercises for this chapter, since you have so few pieces of the language to work with, I have given you simple verses from the NT in English with only the words in Greek that you should know or can figure out with your lexicon. If you understand the case and function of these Greek words, they will fit into the English sentence given and make good sense. For each one, ask yourself, How is this word functioning in the sentence? Is it the subject? The object? A modifier? An indirect object? Be sure you can explain why based on the *case* of the Greek word, not on what the English says. Some of these are very familiar verses, but do not rely on what you may have memorized to explain what it means. The word order has been modified and some words omitted to make it manageable for you.

Mark 6:13, They cast out many δαιμόνια καί anointed many ἀρρώστους ἐλαίῳ.

John 1:29, Behold ὁ ἀμνὸς τοῦ θεοῦ who takes away τὴν ἁμαρτίαν τοῦ κόσμου.

John 1:51, You will see τὸν οὐρανόν opened καὶ τοὺς ἀγγέλους τοῦ θεοῦ ascending and descending on τὸν υἱὸν τοῦ ἀνθρώπου.

Rom. 2:13, οἱ ἀκροαταὶ νόμου will not be justified, ἀλλ' οἱ ποιηταὶ νόμου.

Both nominative nouns in this example from Rom. 2:13 have an unusual set of endings. When you identify them in your lexicon, they will both have a lexical form that ends with -ής, οῦ, ὁ. The nominative ending given in the lexicon, -ής (remember that all nouns are listed alphabetically in the lexicon in the nominative singular form, so this *must* be a nominative ending), does not match the chart you have learned. It *looks like* a genitive ending (first declension, eta pattern), but it is not. There are not many words that do this. The key to identifying them is the lexical entry, or for the more common words in this small group, memorizing the full entry given in the vocabulary lists. That is, do not memorize just "μαθητής, disciple" (one of the vocabulary words in this chapter), but be sure to learn "μαθητής, οῦ, ὁ, 'disciple.'" See the "Vocabulary Notes" in this chapter for more information.

Now You Try It

3.12. This time the words have been left in their original order, and for words you do not know, an English equivalent has been inserted in parentheses immediately after that word or else added in a note when it refers to word clusters. You will need to identify the function of each remaining word based on its case. *Do not guess by what you think makes sense!* If you identify the case correctly, you will be able to explain what it means. The questions appended to each statement are designed to help you test your understanding. Some sentences have been adapted and do not read exactly as they do in the original text. If you were to write out a translation, you would need to rearrange the sentence into English word order (subject ▸ verb ▸ object) to make sense.

Matt. 3:3, Ἑτοιμάσατε (Prepare!)[a] τὴν ὁδὸν κυρίου.

The subject of this verb is assumed in English, since it is an imperative; the Greek form tells you that it is a plural "you." What are they to prepare? How is ὁδόν described?

[a] In the examples given in this textbook, an exclamation mark following a parenthetical English gloss is used to indicate that the word is an imperative (a command word). Ordinarily, you would not use that mark if you were putting the statement into English.

Matt. 2:19, ἰδοὺ ἄγγελος κυρίου φαίνεται (appeared) τῷ Ἰωσήφ.

Who appeared? How do you know? What case is the last word, and how do you know? Why is it in this case?

Mark 3:3, λέγει (he said) τῷ ἀνθρώπῳ, Ἔγειρε (stand up!).

What case is ἀνθρώπῳ, and why did Mark use that case?

Mark 4:33, παραβολαῖς ἐλάλει (he spoke) αὐτοῖς τὸν λόγον.

What case is παραβολαῖς, and how would you express the meaning in English? αὐτοῖς is a pronoun that you have not learned yet, but with your lexicon you can figure it out (if you are using *CL*, see entry 2.b. under this word), or you can jump ahead to chapter 4.

1 John 2:15, Μὴ ἀγαπᾶτε[a] τὸν κόσμον. ἐάν τις ἀγαπᾷ[b] τὸν κόσμον, οὐκ ἔστιν[c] ἡ ἀγάπη τοῦ [θεοῦ] ἐν αὐτῷ.[d]

The word κόσμον occurs twice in this verse; both times it functions the same way. What is the relation between this word and the others in the same clause? In the last clause (after the comma), how does ἀγάπη function? How is this ἀγάπη described?

[a] Μὴ ἀγαπᾶτε, "Do not love!"
[b] ἐάν τις ἀγαπᾷ, "If anyone loves"
[c] οὐκ ἔστιν, "(it) is not"
[d] ἐν αὐτῷ, "in him"

Gen. 3:8, ἤκουσαν (they heard) τὴν φωνὴν κυρίου.

What did they hear? How do you know? How is φωνήν described?

Ps. 1:6, γινώσκει (he knows) κύριος ὁδὸν δικαίων.

δικαίων is actually an adjective, not a noun, but it acts like a noun here. So long as you know that it means "righteous," you can understand it. Who knows (γινώσκει)? How do *you* know that he knows (i.e., grammatically)? What does he know? How is ὁδόν described?

Gen. 9:8–9, εἶπεν (said) ὁ θεὸς τῷ Νῶε καὶ τοῖς υἱοῖς αὐτοῦ, Ἐγὼ ἰδοὺ ἀνίστημι (am establishing) τὴν διαθήκην μου ὑμῖν (with you).

Who is speaking, and to whom is the speaking directed? Why is Ἐγώ capitalized? Who is doing the "establishing," and what is being established? How is διαθήκην described? What case is ὑμῖν, and why is it in that case?

3.13. *Challenge Verse*

Mark 2:15, τελῶναι καὶ ἁμαρτωλοὶ συνανέκειντο (were reclining) τῷ Ἰησοῦ καὶ τοῖς μαθηταῖς αὐτοῦ.

What declension is τελῶναι? What gender, number, case?[a] What case is Ἰησοῦ? What context clue tells you this might not be a genitive-case noun?[b] What sort of relationship do the two dative-case nouns in this sentence express? How would you express this in English?

[a] See the "Vocabulary Notes" for this chapter; this word follows the same pattern as μαθητής.

[b] The forms of Ἰησοῦς do not follow the normal patterns; this is not uncommon with personal names. See the "Vocabulary Notes" on Ἰησοῦς at the end of this chapter for the endings.

— — — — — — — — — — — — — —

Advanced Information for Reference: Grammatical Diagramming

3.14. You will find grammatical diagrams throughout the book. They visually illustrate the grammatical relationships of the various constructions that you are learning. You will find them in each chapter where you learn a new feature that can be illustrated in this way. The first example uses a sentence that you read in "Now You Try It" above.

Matt. 2:19, ἰδοὺ ἄγγελος κυρίου φαίνεται (appeared) τῷ Ἰωσήφ.

Behold, an angel of the Lord appeared to Joseph.

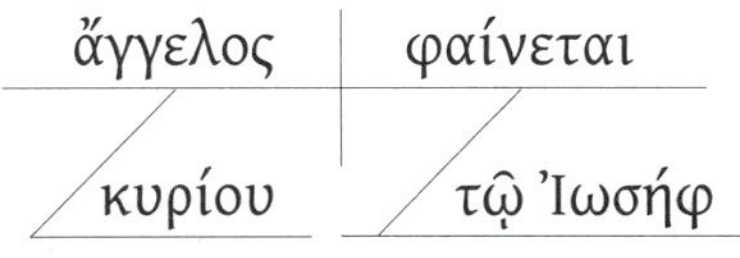

Figure 3.4

The basic structure of a grammatical diagram arranges the kernel of the sentence on a baseline, separating the subject and verb by a vertical line. Modifiers are placed on an angle bracket under the word they describe. As shown in figure 3.4, genitives that modify a noun (or pronoun) use the oblique angle bracket; datives that function as an indirect object allow the base of the angle bracket to protrude to the left.

— — — — — — — — — — — — — —

Reading Passage: John 1:1–5

3.15. In the following passage all the words or forms that you have not yet learned have been identified the first time they occur. All the other words are ones that you should be able to recognize or to identify with your lexicon. You will not understand all the nuances of this text at this point, but you already know enough to make good sense of the message communicated. (You read this passage in the last chapter; now you can understand more of it.)

The Word Was in the Beginning

1'Εν (in) ἀρχῇ ἦν (was) ὁ λόγος, καὶ ὁ λόγος ἦν πρὸς (with) τὸν θεόν, καὶ
θεὸς ἦν ὁ λόγος. 2οὗτος (he) ἦν ἐν ἀρχῇ πρὸς τὸν θεόν. 3πάντα (all things) δι'
(through) αὐτοῦ (him) ἐγένετο (came into being), καὶ χωρὶς αὐτοῦ ἐγένετο
οὐδὲ ἕν[a] ὃ (which) γέγονεν (exists). 4ἐν αὐτῷ ζωὴ ἦν, καὶ ἡ ζωὴ ἦν τὸ φῶς τῶν
ἀνθρώπων· 5καὶ τὸ φῶς ἐν τῇ σκοτίᾳ φαίνει (shines), καὶ ἡ σκοτία αὐτὸ (it) οὐ
κατέλαβεν (has overcome).

[a] οὐδὲ ἕν, "nothing"

Repeated Words

αὐτοῦ or αὐτῷ, "him"
ἐγένετο, "came into being"
ἐν, "in"
ἦν, "was"[9]
πρός, "with"

Notes and Study Questions

In verses 1–2 the verb ἦν occurs four times, and it occurs twice more in verse 4. What is its subject in each instance? How do you know?

The last instance of ἦν in verse 1 has two words in the nominative case. What grammatical feature distinguishes their function in the sentence?[10]

Which word in verse 4 is genitive, and why does John use this case?

Who or what is trying to "overcome" (κατέλαβεν) in verse 5? How do you know?

9. The word ἦν is roughly equivalent to a past tense form of our English verb "to be." It occurs very frequently in the NT and LXX, though you will not learn its grammatical form until lesson 16. It will be glossed when it occurs in examples that have no parallel English translation, but you will also quickly learn it from seeing it so frequently.

10. This example introduces a feature that we have not yet talked about. You will meet it officially in chap. 5, but if you think your way through the verse, you can figure out what it must mean. It is a construction that is also used in English.

3.16. Vocabulary for Chapter 3

Part of Speech	Definition	Possible Glosses	Frequency	
Word			NT	LXX
Conjunctions				
ἀλλά (spelled ἀλλ' before a vowel)	An adversative coordinating conjunction most often used following a negative statement to suggest a contrasting statement or view or to explain	but, yet, except	638	557
οὖν	An inferential or sequence marker (postpositive, coordinating conjunction) used to indicate a conclusion drawn from preceding information or to mark a stage of narrative development	then, therefore	499	260
Nouns				
Ἰησοῦς, οῦ, ὁ	Personal name used of various individuals, in the NT most commonly Jesus Christ [See the "Vocabulary Notes."]	Jesus, Joshua	917	272
ἡμέρα, ας, ἡ	A period of time of varying length, whether a twenty-four-hour day, the period from sunrise to sunset, or a longer period of time during which something happens	day	389	2,567
μαθητής, οῦ, ὁ	One who learns under the instruction of a teacher, whether with committed attachment ("disciple") or less formally ("student, pupil") [See the "Vocabulary Notes."]	disciple; student	261	0
γῆ, ῆς, ἡ	The earth (i.e., the planet on which we live) or figuratively of the people who live there; some part of the earth, whether a region/land, or the soil	land, earth, region, soil	250	3,154
ἄγγελος, ου, ὁ	A personal being (human or supernatural) who transmits a message on behalf of another	messenger, angel	175	350
ὄχλος, ου, ὁ	A group of people, usually consisting of a large number of such	crowd, multitude	175	55
ἁμαρτία, ας, ἡ	A volitional choice or act contrary to (usually God's) standards of uprightness, which results in liability/guilt	sin	173	545
ἔργον, ου, τό	That which is done, an activity ("work") or the result of activity ("product"); more generally, "thing, matter"	work, deed, action, task; thing, matter	169	590
δόξα, ης, ἡ	Esteem, either an intrinsic characteristic or an attribution of it; a splendid/magnificent display, seen as a visible brightness/radiance or, metaphorically, as worthy character [See the "Vocabulary Notes."]	glory, majesty, fame, brightness	166	453
βασιλεία, ας, ἡ	The act of ruling; the realm over which that rule is exercised; especially God's reign in fulfillment of promises to Israel	kingdom, kingship	162	447
Παῦλος, ου, ὁ	A personal name; in the NT usually of the apostle Paul	Paul	158	0

Part of Speech	Definition	Possible Glosses	Frequency	
Word			NT	LXX
ὥρα, ας, ἡ	Period of time as one division of a day, a term used roughly as our "hour" (both having various degrees of precision); an undefined time reference that may be relatively short; a particular time when something is to happen	hour, occasion, moment, time	106	74
γραφή, ῆς, ἡ	That which is written; in the NT used exclusively as a designation of the OT, "Scripture"; outside the NT it can refer to other written documents	writing, Scripture	50	50

Vocabulary Notes

3.17. Some of these vocabulary words are worth examining more closely.

δόξα, ης, ἡ, glory

Did you notice that the format of this entry is different when compared with the other vocabulary words on the list? The other nouns in the list have the more "usual" endings. According to the lexical entry, what is the genitive form?

The paradigm for δόξα has the hybrid α-η-η-α pattern of endings in the singular:

NS	δόξα	NP	δόξαι
GS	δόξης	GP	δοξῶν
DS	δόξῃ	DP	δόξαις
AS	δόξαν	AP	δόξας

Similar words that occur 10 or more times in the NT include the following:

δόξα, ης, ἡ, "glory" 166×
θάλασσα, ης, ἡ, "sea" 91×
γλῶσσα, ης, ἡ, "tongue" 50×
μάχαιρα, ης, ἡ, "sword" 29×
ῥίζα, ης, ἡ, "root" 17×
τράπεζα, ης, ἡ, "table" 15×
ἄκανθα, ης, ἡ, "thorn" 14×

Many other words that use this pattern are *hapax legomena* (ἅπαξ λεγόμενα, "once spoken," that is, words that occur only once in the NT or in the LXX). They are often called *hapax* for short. Many are also proper names.

μαθητής, οῦ, ὁ, disciple

3.18. The word μαθητής, "disciple," is found 261 times in the NT; it is not found in the LXX. Note the lexical form in the vocabulary list for this chapter: μαθητής, οῦ, ὁ. This is an unusual pattern of endings. You can tell from the lexical form that something strange is happening, since the nominative and genitive endings do not match any of the patterns that you have learned. This word is declined like this:

NS	μαθητής	NP	μαθητάι
GS	μαθητοῦ	GP	μαθητῶν
DS	μαθητῇ	DP	μαθηταῖς
AS	μαθητήν	AP	μαθητάς

In later chapters you will meet two more words that use this unusual pattern of endings: προφήτης (144×) and Ἰωάννης (135×). These are all *first-declension* masculine nouns. The best thing to do is just memorize them—and be sure you are memorizing the *entire* lexical form, including the genitive ending and the article. Despite their oddity, you need to learn them early since they occur so frequently in the NT. One of the most helpful parsing aids for these words is the article, since that never changes spelling from its standard forms. Not all instances of μαθητής, προφήτης, and Ἰωάννης have an article, but many do. (For μαθητής, approximately 240 of the 261 instances in the NT *do* have the article. For προφήτης it is more than 90 of 144, but for Ἰωάννης, only 33 of 135.)

Ἰησοῦς, οῦ, ὁ, Jesus, Joshua

3.19. Names sometimes have an unusual set of endings, especially those that are transliterated from Hebrew into Greek. Ἰησοῦς is one such name. It occurs 272 times in the LXX, usually as the Greek name for Joshua. In the NT it occurs 917 times, mostly (but not always) as the personal name of Jesus the Messiah (Ἰησοῦς Χριστός). The ending shown in the lexical form does not match any of the forms you have learned. It looks like an accusative plural ending, but it is, indeed, nominative. The case endings are as follows:

NS	Ἰησοῦς
GS	Ἰησοῦ
DS	Ἰησοῦ
AS	Ἰησοῦν
VS	Ἰησοῦ

There are two ways to determine whether an -οῦ ending is a genitive, a dative, or a vocative[11]: first, the article (if one is used) will always distinguish genitive from dative (there is no vocative article), or second, context. Whenever a word has "oddities" such as this, the lexicon will give you the necessary information to identify the various forms.

3.20. Key Things to Know for Chapter 3

Can you identify the Greek genitive and dative forms?
How does a genitive-case noun function in Greek?
What are the most common English equivalents for the genitive?
What word does a Greek genitive noun usually modify?
What is a "lexical form"?
How does a dative-case noun function in Greek?
What are the most common English equivalents for the dative?

11. The vocative (VS, vocative singular, in the chart above) is the case of direct address; it is not common in the NT or LXX (see app. D).

4

PRONOUNS: PART 1

Personal Pronouns

4.1. In this chapter you will meet the personal pronouns, first in their familiar English dress, then their Greek cousins. There are other types of pronouns that will be introduced later.

English Pronouns

We will start with an example that will take you way back—back to first grade. What is the pronoun in the following four-sentence cluster?

> "Look, Sally. Look, look, look! Look at the fire truck. It is red."

A pronoun is a word substitute for a noun. The pronoun in the cluster just above is "it." Pronouns are used in language for variety. Instead of a noun constantly being repeated, a pronoun is used to refer back to a noun already identified in the context. An *antecedent* is a word (or sometimes a phrase or concept) in the preceding context to which a pronoun refers. In the example above and in figure 4.1, the antecedent is "the fire truck."

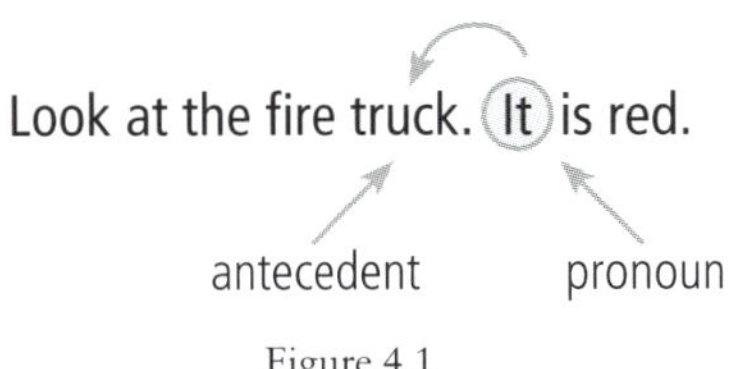

Figure 4.1

English pronouns may be described grammatically according to person, gender, number, and case. Most of these classifications are familiar, but this is the first time that we have met the grammatical category of *person*.

Person

4.2. There are three subcategories within the grammatical classification of person:

First person: *I* (sg.); *we* (pl.)
Second person: *you* (sg. or pl.)
Third person: *he, she, it* (sg.); *they* (pl.)

I (the speaker) am speaking to *you* (a second party, the hearer) about *him*, *her*, *them*, or *it* (a third party, that is, anyone or anything besides the speaker or the hearer). By the nature of their reference, first- and second-person pronouns normally occur in oral dialogue or written discourse such as a letter rather than in historical narrative. Third-person pronouns occur in any statement regardless of what the genre is.[1]

Case

4.3. We have already talked about case in connection with nouns, but we need to think about it now in relation to pronouns—one instance in which English also has distinct spellings for the same word when used in different cases.

Which pronoun is correct in each of the following sentences?

I will learn Greek. (or) *Me* will learn Greek.
Joe will teach *I*. (or) Joe will teach *me*.
Him will teach *he*. (or) *He* will teach *him*.

The correct pronoun is immediately obvious to native speakers of English, but their judgment is usually "because it sounds right." The difference, though you may not know the technical terminology from English, is one of case. *I* and *he* are subjective case in English (= nominative case in Greek); *me* and *him* are objective case (= accusative case in Greek). In English, subjects are always in the subjective case, and objects (whether direct objects, indirect objects, or the objects of prepositions) are always in the objective case.

Gender

4.4. English also distinguishes the gender of some pronouns. There is no difference in the form or spelling in first- or second-person pronouns to distinguish

1. Historical narrative may, of course, embed oral dialogue or personal letters in the narrative.

gender; we use *I* and *you* regardless of the person to whom we refer. But third-person pronouns do distinguish gender; in this case we use *he*, *she*, or *it*.

> *He* will teach Joe.
> *She* will teach Joe.
> *It* will teach Joe.

All these forms (*he*, *she*, *it*) are essentially the same word, the personal pronoun.

The pronoun uses different forms, depending on person, number, and case. The case of a pronoun is determined by its function in the sentence.

Greek Pronouns

4.5. In the material below, we will initially study the first- and second-person pronouns, and then in the following section we will examine the third-person pronoun. Greek pronouns function almost identically to English pronouns. One difference is that Greek has four cases instead of just two.[2]

First- and Second-Person Pronouns

4.6. The lexical form of the first- and second-person pronouns are ἐγώ and σύ.

	1st Person		2nd Person	
NS	ἐγώ	I	σύ	you
GS	ἐμοῦ (μου)	my	σοῦ (σου)	your
DS	ἐμοί (μοι)	(to) me	σοί (σοι)	(to) you
AS	ἐμέ (με)	me	σέ (σε)	you
NP	ἡμεῖς	we	ὑμεῖς	you
GP	ἡμῶν	our	ὑμῶν	your
DP	ἡμῖν	(to) us	ὑμῖν	(to) you
AP	ἡμᾶς	us	ὑμᾶς	you

The singular of the oblique cases (the cases other than nominative) of ἐγώ and σύ are said to be *enclitic* forms. That is, they can lose their accent to the preceding word in some situations. The first-person singular forms also drop the initial epsilon when they are enclitic; there is no difference in meaning.[3]

When a first- or second-person nominative-case pronoun is used, it always has some degree of emphasis. Every Greek verb, as you will learn in due time, has a default, built-in subject as part of the verb form itself, so there is no need

2. Pronouns do not occur in the vocative case.

3. It has traditionally been said that the accented forms are emphatic, but this is debatable. A more probable explanation relates to word order, but the details are well beyond your needs at the moment. All you need to be able to do now is to recognize either form as a pronoun.

to specify the subject with a pronoun. When a writer chooses to use a pronoun anyway, there is a certain degree of attention drawn to the subject of the statement. This emphasis is not strong; it is closer to a verbal inflection in which there is a noticeable stress on the pronoun.

4.7. Pronouns function in a sentence the same way that nouns do; they can occur in any place that a noun can. That is, nominative pronouns will function as subjects, accusatives as objects. Like a genitive noun, a genitive pronoun usually follows the word it modifies, as it does in the following example, which has three genitive pronouns:

Mark 1:2, Καθὼς γέγραπται (it is written) ἐν τῷ Ἠσαΐᾳ τῷ προφήτῃ, Ἰδοὺ ἀποστέλλω (I am sending) τὸν ἄγγελόν **μου** πρὸ προσώπου **σου**, ὃς κατασκευάσει (will prepare) τὴν ὁδόν **σου**.	As it is written in Isaiah the prophet, "Behold, I am sending *my* messenger before *your* face, who will prepare *your* way."

τὸν ἄγγελον ◂ **μου** . . . προσώπου ◂ **σου** . . . τὴν ὁδόν ◂ **σου**
my messenger . . . *your* face . . . *your* way

But a genitive pronoun may sometimes precede the noun, as in the next example.

Mark 2:5, ἰδὼν (seeing) ὁ Ἰησοῦς τὴν πίστιν αὐτῶν λέγει (he said) τῷ παραλυτικῷ, Τέκνον, ἀφίενταί (are forgiven) **σου** αἱ ἁμαρτίαι.	Jesus, seeing their faith, said to the paralytic, "Son, *your* sins are forgiven."

σου ▸ αἱ ἁμαρτίαι, *your* sins

There is no difference in meaning regardless of which pattern a writer uses.

4.8. Examples of First- and Second-Person Pronouns

Mark 1:8, **ἐγὼ** ἐβάπτισα (I baptized) **ὑμᾶς** ὕδατι.	*I* baptized *you* with water.
Mark 1:11, **Σὺ** εἶ (are) ὁ υἱός **μου**.	*You* are *my* son.
Mark 6:22, Αἴτησόν (ask!) **με** καὶ δώσω (I will give) **σοι**.	Ask *me*, and I will give [it] *to you*.
Gen. 3:13, Ὁ ὄφις ἠπάτησέν (deceived) **με**, καὶ ἔφαγον (I ate).	The snake deceived *me*, and I ate.

Exod. 2:19, εἶπαν (they said), Ἄνθρωπος Αἰγύπτιος (Egyptian) ἐρρύσατο (rescued) **ἡμᾶς** καὶ ἤντλησεν (he drew water) **ἡμῖν** καὶ ἐπότισεν (he watered) τὰ πρόβατα **ἡμῶν**.	They said, "An Egyptian man rescued *us*, and he drew water *for us*, and he watered *our* flock."

4.9. Now You Try It

Mark 3:32, λέγουσιν (they said) αὐτῷ, Ἰδοὺ ἡ μήτηρ (mother) σου καὶ οἱ ἀδελφοί σου καὶ αἱ ἀδελφαί σου ἔξω (are outside) ζητοῦσίν (they are seeking) σε.	To whom are they speaking? How much of this statement is a direct quote? What is the relationship between the people outside and the person to whom these words are spoken? Who is being sought?
John 1:49, ἀπεκρίθη (he answered) Ναθαναήλ, Ῥαββί, σὺ εἶ (are) ὁ υἱὸς τοῦ θεοῦ, σὺ βασιλεὺς (king) εἶ τοῦ Ἰσραήλ.	What case is σύ, and how is it functioning in these two clauses?
Gen. 3:14, γῆν φάγῃ (you will eat) πάσας (all) τὰς ἡμέρας τῆς ζωῆς σου.	What will "you" eat? What case is ζωῆς, and why is it in that case? Can you explain the person, number, case, and antecedent of σου?
Gen. 4:9, εἶπεν (said) ὁ θεὸς πρὸς Κάϊν, Ποῦ ἐστιν Ἄβελ ὁ ἀδελφός σου; ὁ δὲ[a] εἶπεν, Οὐ γινώσκω· μὴ φύλαξ (a guard) τοῦ ἀδελφοῦ μού εἰμι ἐγώ;	Two oral statements are quoted here. How do you know where each begins? Who is speaking in each one? How do you know? How is Κάϊν related to Ἄβελ? How does the grammar tell you this?

[a] ὁ δέ, "But he"

The Third-Person Pronoun: αὐτός

4.10. The third-person pronoun is αὐτός, αὐτή, αὐτό (= masculine, feminine, neuter). Notice that there is gender in the third-person pronouns, unlike first- and second-person pronouns, which do not distinguish gender. If you were to put the third-person pronoun into English, the masculine forms usually would be some form of "he, his, him"; the feminine, "she" or "her"; and the neuter, "it" or "its." The plural is "they," "their," or "them" regardless of gender. (See also the sidebar below on "Generic Pronouns" for additional English options.)

	Masc.	Fem.	Neut.
NS	αὐτός	αὐτή	αὐτό
GS	αὐτοῦ	αὐτῆς	αὐτοῦ
DS	αὐτῷ	αὐτῇ	αὐτῷ
AS	αὐτόν	αὐτήν	αὐτό

	Masc.	Fem.	Neut.
NP	αὐτοί	αὐταί	αὐτά
GP	αὐτῶν	αὐτῶν	αὐτῶν
DP	αὐτοῖς	αὐταῖς	αὐτοῖς
AP	αὐτούς	αὐτάς	αὐτά

This third-person pronoun occurs more than 5,200 times in the NT, so you will see it very frequently. The pronoun αὐτός agrees with its antecedent in *gender* and *number*. Its *case* is determined by the pronoun's function in the clause, just as were the first- and second-person pronouns considered earlier in this chapter.

You should not think of αὐτός as meaning "he," even when it occurs in masculine gender (though it will often be represented that way in English). Rather it is a word that refers to its antecedent: "the person or thing to which I have just referred." One of your first concerns is to determine to whom or what a particular pronoun refers. Only then do you know the "meaning" of the pronoun and what an appropriate English equivalent might be. (See the section on "Natural Gender" and the sidebar on "Generic Pronouns" below.)

Tip

The pronoun αὐτός always has a smooth breathing mark. This is important to remember, because you will later meet a similar word that is distinguished only by the breathing mark.

Examples of the Third-Person Pronoun

4.11. Do you understand this simplest use of αὐτός? If so, you should be able to understand these sentences.

Mark 1:8, ἐγὼ ἐβάπτισα (baptized) ὑμᾶς ὕδατι (with water), **αὐτὸς** δὲ βαπτίσει (will baptize) ὑμᾶς ἐν πνεύματι ἁγίῳ.	I baptized you with water, but *he* will baptize you with the Holy Spirit.
Mark 1:12, Καὶ εὐθὺς[a] τὸ πνεῦμα **αὐτὸν** ἐκβάλλει (he sent) εἰς τὴν ἔρημον.	Then the Spirit sent *him* into the wilderness.

[a] In this verse and many others from Mark's Gospel καὶ εὐθύς is translated as simply "then"; elsewhere it may be best represented in English as "so" or "now." Mark uses it to mean, "the next thing I want to tell you is. . . ." This is a unique Markan idiom; it does not mean "and immediately." For more information about this construction, see Decker, "Use of εὐθύς."

Mark 1:13, ἦν μετὰ τῶν θηρίων, καὶ οἱ ἄγγελοι διηκόνουν (they were ministering) **αὐτῷ**.	He was with the wild animals, and the angels were ministering *to him*.
Gen. 1:22, ηὐλόγησεν (blessed) **αὐτὰ** ὁ θεός.	God blessed them.

Gen. 2:18, εἶπεν (said) κύριος ὁ θεός, Οὐ καλὸν εἶναι (to be) τὸν ἄνθρωπον μόνον· ποιήσωμεν (let us make) **αὐτῷ** βοηθὸν κατ᾽ **αὐτόν**.	The Lord God said, "For the man to be alone is not good. Let us make *for him* a helper corresponding to *him*."

4.12. Now You Try It

Mark 1:20, ἐκάλεσεν (he called) αὐτούς. καὶ ἀφέντες (leaving) τὸν πατέρα[a] αὐτῶν Ζεβεδαῖον ἀπῆλθον (they departed).	What Greek word tells us who was called? How do you know? Whom did they leave? Whose father was it?

[a] πατήρ, πατρός, ὁ, "father." This is a third-declension noun; go by the article to identify the case.

Mark 1:26, σπαράξαν (it shook) αὐτὸν τὸ πνεῦμα[a] καὶ ἐξῆλθεν (it came out).	Who did the shaking? How do you know? Who or what was shaken?

[a] The reference here is to an unclean spirit, a demon.

Mark 1:37, εὗρον (they found) αὐτὸν καὶ λέγουσιν (they said) αὐτῷ . . .	Why are αὐτόν and αὐτῷ in different cases?
Gen. 2:22, ἤγαγεν (he brought) αὐτὴν πρὸς τὸν Ἀδάμ.	Who was brought? What can you tell about the antecedent *grammatically*? (The antecedent is not included in the clause cited.)
Gen. 4:8, εἶπεν (said) Κάϊν πρὸς Ἅβελ τὸν ἀδελφὸν **αὐτοῦ**, Διέλθωμεν (let us go) εἰς τὸ πεδίον.	What case is αὐτοῦ, and why is it in that case? What is the antecedent of αὐτοῦ?

Natural Gender

4.13. Since there are differences between the Greek and English use of pronouns, when translating you must use the proper English gender regardless of gender in Greek. This is not a grammatical difference but a cultural convention. The best way to explain this is with an example.

If a third-person pronoun in Greek refers to ὁ κόσμος, then it will be masculine gender in Greek, because the antecedent, ὁ κόσμος, is masculine; thus αὐτός will be used rather than αὐτή or αὐτό. But in English it should not be thought of as the equivalent of "he," but rather as "it," because English speakers do not refer to the world as "he."

We must understand pronouns in terms of natural gender in each language. Remember that what is "natural" in Greek may not be natural in English. If you were involved in an official translation project, that would be part of the translation task. If a translated text does not communicate naturally in the target language, it has done only a partial job of translation. It is no mark of distinction to produce English that sounds odd. The NT did not sound odd to its original readers, and contemporary translations should not sound odd either.

John 7:7, ὁ κόσμος cannot hate ὑμᾶς, ἐμὲ δέ it does hate, ὅτι[a] ἐγὼ μαρτυρῶ (I testify) περὶ **αὐτοῦ** ὅτι[a] τὰ ἔργα **αὐτοῦ** πονηρά ἐστιν (they are).

Can you identify the two "recipients" of the verb "hate"? (What case must both words be?) Even though both instances of αὐτοῦ are masculine, do not think of them as "he/him." How would you say it in English?

[a] The first ὅτι introduces a reason, "because"; the second tells us *what* Jesus testified, "that."

The Word αὐτοῦ

There is a lexical entry αὐτοῦ, which you should not confuse with αὐτός. The entry αὐτοῦ is an adverb of location meaning "here, there," not a pronoun. Yes, there is also a genitive form of αὐτός that is spelled the same. How do you tell the difference? Context. But there is a pretty reliable rule of thumb: When you find αὐτοῦ in a text, it is probably the genitive of αὐτός, since the adverb occurs only 4 times in the entire NT and only 8 times in the LXX.[a] By contrast, the genitive form of the pronoun αὐτός (αὐτοῦ) occurs 1,590 times in the NT and 10,465 times in the LXX.

[a] The adverb αὐτοῦ is likewise rare in other Koine literature such as Philo (5× vs. 733×). The adverb αὐτοῦ does not occur at all in Josephus (the genitive pronoun occurs 2,061×), the Apostolic Fathers (556× for the pronoun), or the Pseudepigrapha (which has the pronoun 1,688×). These figures verify that the rule of thumb works across a wide corpus of Koine writings.

Mark 11:2, καὶ λέγει αὐτοῖς, Ὑπάγετε (Go!) εἰς τὴν κώμην, καὶ εὑρήσετε (you will find) πῶλον δεδεμένον (tied)· λύσατε (Loose!) **αὐτόν.**

Why is αὐτοῖς dative? What gender is πῶλον? What is the antecedent of αὐτόν? How would you put it into English?

Matt. 16:18, οἰκοδομήσω (I will build) μου τὴν ἐκκλησίαν καὶ πύλαι ᾅδου[a] οὐ κατισχύσουσιν (they will overcome) **αὐτῆς**.[b]

Who will do the building? Whose ἐκκλησία is this? How should αὐτῆς be put into English? What pronoun would we use in our language?

[a] πύλαι ᾅδου, "gates of Hades" (probably a reference to death; see Isa. 38:10).

[b] αὐτῆς is genitive, but it is the *direct object* of κατισχύσουσιν; you will learn why later.

Generic Pronouns

The masculine forms of the pronoun αὐτός can function as generic terms. That is, they can refer either to males or to a mixed group of men and women. In older English usage, the singular was traditionally represented by "he," which was also considered to be generic. In more contemporary usage, however, the generic use of "he" has declined significantly. Though it is still comprehensible and used in some contexts, alternative expressions have become more common. Since English does not have a separate third-person singular pronoun with a generic meaning (the neuter "it" is never used for this purpose), it has become common to use as generic singulars what were formerly plural pronouns: "they, their," and so on. Not many years ago *they* and *their* were still viewed as plural pronouns, but they are increasingly listed as forms that are either singular or plural, depending on the antecedent, just as *you* is determined contextually to be singular or plural. English purists are not pleased with this development, but it is a shift that is now well documented in English usage.

Consider a couple of NT examples and how they might be put into contemporary English.

1. 1 Corinthians 2:14

ψυχικὸς δὲ **ἄνθρωπος** οὐ δέχεται τὰ τοῦ πνεύματος τοῦ θεοῦ· μωρία γὰρ **αὐτῷ**.

The statement begins with a reference to a person (the generic use of ἄνθρωπος), and it is continued with a third-person singular pronoun in the following clause (αὐτῷ). The meaning, or better, the referent, of the pronoun αὐτῷ comes from its antecedent, ἄνθρωπος. Accurately expressing the generic reference in English can be handled several ways. The traditional English pattern, which uses both "man" and "he/him" in a generic sense, is seen in the KJV:

> But the natural *man* receiveth not the things of the Spirit of God: for they are foolishness unto *him*.

More contemporary usage is reflected in the CEB:

> But *people* who are unspiritual don't accept the things from God's Spirit. They are foolishness to *them*.

2. Matthew 16:26

τί γὰρ ὠφεληθήσεται **ἄνθρωπος** ἐὰν τὸν κόσμον ὅλον κερδήσῃ τὴν δὲ ψυχὴν **αὐτοῦ** ζημιωθῇ; ἢ τί δώσει **ἄνθρωπος** ἀντάλλαγμα τῆς ψυχῆς **αὐτοῦ**;

Two translations of this verse are given below, one reflecting traditional use, the other more contemporary patterns of reference.

> For what will it profit a *man* if he gains the whole world and forfeits *his* soul? Or what shall a *man* give in return for *his* soul? (ESV)
>
> What good will it be for *someone* to gain the whole world, yet forfeit *their* soul? Or what can *anyone* give in exchange for *their* soul? (NIV)

In every such case, the crucial factor is determining the antecedent of the pronoun. It must be understood in such a way that it reflects the referent of that antecedent. Generic antecedents require generic pronouns.

— — — — — — — — — — — — — —

4.14. Advanced Information for Reference: Diagramming Pronouns

Mark 1:2, ἀποστέλλω (I am sending) τὸν ἄγγελόν μου [καὶ] κατασκευάσει (he will prepare) τὴν ὁδόν σου.

I am sending my messenger, and he will prepare your way.

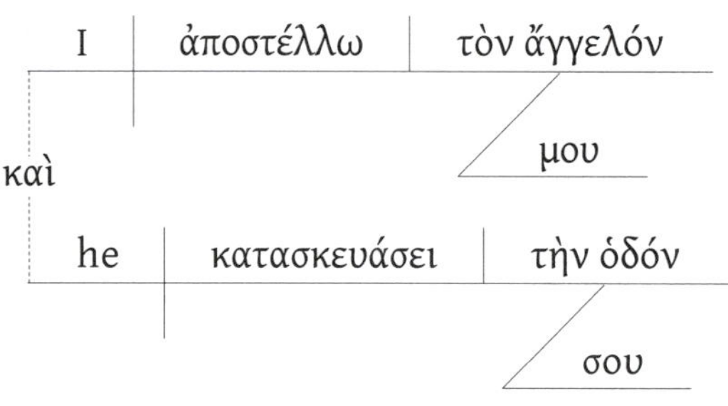

Figure 4.2

Note particularly the function of the genitive pronouns in this passage. Two coordinate clauses are joined by a vertical dashed line, and the conjunction is placed on that line.

— — — — — — — — — — — — — —

Reading Passage: John 16:1–7

4.15. The pronouns in this paragraph are marked with bold type. Words that you do not know or that you cannot easily identify with your lexicon are glossed. Verbs are identified with "v:" preceding the gloss.

The Coming of the Counselor

[1]Ταῦτα (these things) λελάληκα (v: I have spoken) **ὑμῖν** ἵνα (so that) μὴ σκαν-
δαλισθῆτε (v: you fall away). [2]ἀποσυναγώγους ποιήσουσιν (v: they will make)
ὑμᾶς· ἀλλ' ἔρχεται (v: is coming) ὥρα ἵνα πᾶς ὁ ἀποκτείνας[a] **ὑμᾶς** δόξῃ (v: will
think) λατρείαν προσφέρειν (v: to offer) τῷ θεῷ. [3]καὶ ταῦτα ποιήσουσιν ὅτι
(because) οὐκ ἔγνωσαν (v: they know) τὸν πατέρα (Father) οὐδὲ **ἐμέ**. [4]ἀλλὰ
ταῦτα λελάληκα **ὑμῖν** ἵνα ὅταν ἔλθῃ (v: it comes) ἡ ὥρα **αὐτῶν** μνημονεύητε
(v: you may remember) **αὐτῶν**[b] ὅτι **ἐγὼ** εἶπον (v: told) **ὑμῖν**.

Ταῦτα δὲ **ὑμῖν** ἐξ (from) ἀρχῆς οὐκ εἶπον, ὅτι μεθ' (with) **ὑμῶν** ἤμην (v: I
was). [5]νῦν δὲ ὑπάγω (v: I go) πρὸς (to) τὸν πέμψαντά (one who sent) **με**, καὶ
οὐδεὶς ἐξ (from/of) **ὑμῶν** ἐρωτᾷ (v: is asking) **με**, Ποῦ ὑπάγεις (v: you are
going); [6]ἀλλ' ὅτι ταῦτα λελάληκα **ὑμῖν** ἡ λύπη πεπλήρωκεν (v: fills) **ὑμῶν** τὴν
καρδίαν. [7]ἀλλ' **ἐγὼ** τὴν ἀλήθειαν λέγω (v: am speaking) **ὑμῖν**, συμφέρει (v: it
is better) **ὑμῖν** ἵνα **ἐγὼ** ἀπέλθω (v: go away). ἐὰν γὰρ μὴ ἀπέλθω, ὁ παράκλητος

οὐκ ἐλεύσεται (v: will come) πρὸς ὑμᾶς· ἐὰν δὲ πορευθῶ (v: I go), πέμψω (v: I will send) **αὐτὸν πρὸς ὑμᾶς.**

[a] πᾶς ὁ ἀποκτείνας, "everyone who kills"

[b] The genitive αὐτῶν is the direct object of the verb μνημονεύητε. Some verbs take a genitive rather than the usual accusative for their objects. You will learn more about this in §7.23.

Repeated Words

ἀπέλθω, "I go away"
εἶπον, "I tell/told"
ἵνα, "that, so that, in order that"
λελάληκα, "I have spoken"
ποιήσουσιν, "they will do/make"
πρός, "to"
ταῦτα, "these things"

4.16. Vocabulary for Chapter 4

Part of Speech	Definition	Possible Glosses	Frequency	
Word			NT	LXX
Conjunction				
ἵνα	A conjunction that normally introduces a subordinate clause indicating purpose, result, content, or explanation (governs subjunctive mood)	in order that, that	663	615
Nouns				
καρδία, ας, ἡ	The physical organ that pumps blood in the body; metaphorically (always so in the NT), the person/personhood, often with cognitive, affective, volitional, or moral overtones; middle, center	heart, mind (wide range; see lexicon)	156	963
Πέτρος, ου, ὁ	Personal name, in the NT the apostle Peter; stone (LXX, but not so used in the NT)	Peter, stone	156	13
προφήτης, ου, ὁ	A person who expounds matters transcending normal insight or awareness, known only by special revelation (in the NT almost always an OT or Christian prophet, rarely a non-Christian, polytheist; in the LXX usually a "true" prophet, but also used of "false" prophets); by metonymy, the writing of a prophet or sometimes the OT as a whole [For declension, see the "Vocabulary Notes" on μαθητής in §3.18.]	prophet; the Prophets	144	328
λαός, οῦ, ὁ	A group of humans either gathered together or identified geographically, ethnically, or with reference to their relationship to God	people	142	2,064

Part of Speech	Definition	Possible Glosses	Frequency	
Word			NT	LXX
δοῦλος, ου, ὁ	A male slave, a person who is the legal property of another whom he must obey (pl. may be generic)	slave	124	383
θάνατος, ου, ὁ	Death, either natural/physical or spiritual	death	120	362
ἀγάπη, ης, ἡ	High interest in and regard for the well-being of another, love, affection	love	116	19
οἶκος, ου, ὁ	A physical structure for habitation ("house") or a place where people live ("home"); the people who live in a house ("household, family")	house, home; household	114	2,062
Pronouns				
αὐτός, ή, ό	Pronoun: personal, third person ("he, she, it, they"); adjective [see §§6.18–25]: intensive ("-self") or identifying ("[the] same")	(1) he, she, it, they; (2) him-, her-, itself; (3) same	5,595	29,416
ὑμεῖς	Personal pronoun, second-person plural nominative of σύ	you (pl.)	1,840	3,335
ἐγώ	Personal pronoun, first-person singular nominative	I	1,725	12,529
σύ	Personal pronoun, second-person singular nominative	you (sg.)	1,069	10,692
ἡμεῖς	Personal pronoun, first-person plural nominative of ἐγώ	we	864	176
μου and ἐμοῦ	Personal pronoun, first-person singular genitive of ἐγώ	my	677	4,834

4.17. Key Things to Know for Chapter 4

Can you distinguish the three categories of grammatical person?

What is an antecedent of a pronoun?

You must be able to recognize all the forms of the pronouns in this chapter when you see them in context.

5

VERBS: PART 1

Verb Basics

5.1. This chapter does not try to introduce everything you need to know about verbs. You will learn more in later chapters about verbs. By learning the basics about verbs now, you will be able to understand more of the sentences that we read sooner than if we waited until a later chapter.

We will begin with an example. If you were reading in your Greek NT, you might read this:

> ἐγείρουσιν αὐτὸν καὶ λέγουσιν αὐτῷ· Διδάσκαλε . . . (Mark 4:38)

By checking an English translation you would discover that this means, "They woke him and said to him, 'Teacher . . .'" (ESV). From what you have already learned, you can figure out that αὐτόν is a direct object, since it is in the accusative case, and that αὐτῷ is an indirect object, because it is in the dative case. The word διδάσκαλε might look strange to you since you have not learned an ending that consists of only an epsilon, but you could probably guess from your lexicon that it is a form of the word διδάσκαλος, "teacher"—and you would be correct; this is an example of the fifth case, the vocative (used for direct address; see app. D). But what about the other two words, ἐγείρουσιν and λέγουσιν? Since you have found a direct object and an indirect object, you might suspect that they are verbs, and once again you would be right. But there is no subject—no word(s) in the nominative case. How did the translators know that it refers to something done by more than one person? Why did the translators not choose "I" or "you" or "she"?

5.2. In this chapter you will learn why the subject is "they." We need to look at these two words and figure out what is going on. Notice that both of them have the same ending—the last five letters in both ἐγείρουσιν and λέγουσιν are the same: -ουσιν. The first part of each word is different; this is the stem, which carries the lexical meaning of the word. The stem ἐγειρ- tells you that Mark is describing the action of awaking, and the stem λεγ- indicates speaking. In the lexicon, they are listed as ἐγείρω and λέγω. Both end with an omega. Why does Mark change the spelling and use -ουσιν instead of an omega? You have perhaps already figured that out by now. The -ουσιν tells you that this action is being done by more than one person. Every Greek verb has a built-in subject. Unlike English verbs, which (in most situations) require that the subject be indicated by a separate word, Greek verbs carry their own subjects in their back pocket, as it were. Sometimes there will also be a word in the nominative case to specify the subject, but even without that, there is a subject hiding in every verb. Now we need to look at the nitty-gritty of the verb and learn the grammatical terms used to describe them.

The Basics about English Verbs

5.3. This section offers a brief summary of the English verb, focusing on items that are most helpful for learning Greek. If this is not familiar territory to you, it would be wise to review an English grammar.

Most people know that a verb is defined in general terms as the word in a sentence that refers to an action or a state of being.

He *read* the book.
God *is* sovereign.
Anna *sleeps* soundly.
Levi *climbed* the tree.

In English a verb may be a single word ("She *read* the lexical entry carefully") or a phrase ("She *had been reading* the lexical entry carefully"). When other verb forms are added to a simple verb, they usually indicate differences of tense, voice, or mood.[1] Notice the changes to the same basic verb in the following examples:

He frequently *hits* the ball over the fence.
I am sure that he *will hit* the ball over the fence.
He *would hit* the ball over the fence were he to get a fast ball.
He *has been hitting* the ball over the fence in practice.
He *was hit* by the ball when it bounced off the fence.

One of the most common distinctions in English verbs is their tense, that is, how they express time—something that almost every English verb does. The basic tenses are often viewed as past, present, and future.[2]

1. These are sometimes called auxiliary or helping verbs. The most common are *do*, *have*, and *be* (and their various forms).

2. Some English grammarians include other tenses, such as the future perfect or the past perfect. Other grammarians insist that there are only two tenses in English, present and past.

Past: I ran.
Present: I run.
Future: I will run.

These statements can be modified by other words to express other nuances. The example, "I run," can also express future time if we say, "I run a marathon tomorrow."

5.4. Some verbs (either a simple verb or a verb phrase) have direct objects. That is, there is a substantive (e.g., a noun or pronoun) following the verb that indicates who or what receives the action. A verb that takes a direct object is called a *transitive verb*. Verbs that do not have a direct object are called *intransitive verbs*.

Transitive: She *drove* the *car* to the mall.
Intransitive: Her diamond *sparkled*.

We can also indicate whether a verb is complete in itself or requires something additional to complete it. The sentence "The volcano erupted" is complete in itself. Other sentences require some kind of complement: "Daniel closed" is incomplete apart from an object, such as "Daniel closed the lid." The category of complements is larger than direct objects, however. Other types of complements include indirect objects and object complements.

Indirect object: Cody gave *her* a diamond.

The indirect object ("her") indicates to or for whom the action of the verb is done.

Object complement: Bill appointed *John chairman*.

In the second example the verb, "appointed," takes two complements; one is the direct object ("John"), and the other, which renames the object, we call the *object complement* ("chairman").

Other types of verbs that we call *linking verbs* (or *state-of-being verbs*) do not take direct objects. Instead they have a predicate nominative or a predicate adjective—a substantive that renames the subject or an adjective that describes the subject. (Some English grammars call these *subjective complements*.) The most common such verb in English is *to be*.

Predicate nominative: Linda was a teacher.
Predicate adjective: Rachel is red-headed.

The Basics about Greek Verbs

5.5. The following introduction to the basic terms and definitions related to verbs will help you understand enough to read relatively simple Greek sentences.

Basic Grammar

There are many similarities between the English and Greek verbs. You may assume that all the material in the preceding summary also applies to Greek verbs except for the following.

To reflect various elements of verbal meaning, Greek changes the form of the verb. It does this by adding prefixes and suffixes to the verb. There are some constructions in which additional words are used (similar to the use of auxiliary or helping verbs in English), but these are not nearly as common as in English. The way that time is expressed also differs from English; rather than relying primarily on the tense of the verb, Greek relies more heavily on contextual descriptions to indicate or clarify the time involved.

In addition to the term *object complement*, we will refer to *double accusatives*. The full description will sound something like this: "the direct object (or, object complement) in a double-accusative, object-complement construction." The function is the same; the terminology is simply expanded.

How all these pieces actually work in Greek is what we will learn one step at a time in this and the following chapters.

5.6. *Terminology*

Stem: the basic part of a verb to which are added prefixes and suffixes; this is the part that carries the lexical meaning of the word.

Ending: a suffix added to the stem that identifies the default, built-in subject found in every verb. The ending indicates both person and number. This is sometimes called a *personal ending*.

Number: the same grammatical category as used with nouns: singular and plural.

Person: a grammatical category that distinguishes between the speaker/writer and those to whom the speaker/writer is referring. There are three values for grammatical person in both English and Greek: first, second, and third person.

- First person refers to the speaker/writer: I (sg.) or we (pl.).
- Second person refers to the person to whom one speaks: you, that is, a "second party." In English "you" can be either singular or plural; in Greek the spelling distinguishes between second-person singular and second-person plural.
- Third person refers to someone or something else, that is, neither the speaker nor the person to whom one speaks: he, she, it, or if plural, they or them.

Present Active Indicative

5.7. The simple form of the verb that you will learn in this chapter is described grammatically as a present active indicative verb. Later we will learn what each of those descriptors mean. For now you will learn a simple, default English equivalent that will enable you to understand some basic sentences. To do that we need a model verb—one that we will use each time we meet a new kind of verb. That model verb is simple in both spelling and meaning: λύω.

Meet λύω the Lion—King of the Verbs!

If you fail to get to know him,
he will *destroy* your grade
or at least *untie* your shoes!
So *loosen* your tie; we need to get to work.

Figure 5.1

All that (admittedly, a series of poor puns) to introduce you to the standard paradigm verb that we will use for almost all verb forms throughout the rest of this book. The word λύω means "I loose, untie, destroy." It may seem like an odd word to choose, but λύω is very predictable, occurs in most forms that we will study, and is a simple word, so we use it frequently.

5.8. This chapter introduces verbs that may be described grammatically in terms of their *tense-form* (or more traditionally, *tense*), *voice*, and *mood*. In particular, present *tense-form*, active *voice*, and indicative *mood*. There are other options for each of these categories, and we will learn them a few at a time. For now we will use a *common equivalent* for present active indicative verbs. By *common* we mean that this is how a verb form is often expressed in English, without any context to suggest otherwise. It is only an approximation of how that word might be expressed in English and must be examined in light of the context before it is used in any particular statement. It gives you something to start with as you work through a sentence.[3] There is no one invariant equivalent. As is true of almost any Greek word or phrase, there are multiple ways to express it accurately in English. A common equivalent for the verb λύω is "I

3. As you become more proficient with the language, you will intuitively think of somewhat different equivalents as you read. From the flow of the context, you will sense what the writer is saying and how it is best expressed in English.

am loosing." That is, since it is a first-person singular present active indicative form, a rough equivalent in English is often "I am loosing." Sometimes it will be closer to the simple "I loose."

Identifying Greek Verbs

5.9. How does one learn to identify Greek verbs? (Was that question in the back of your mind?) There are two approaches. One, which might be called the *traditional approach* since it was the typical way Greek was taught in past centuries, provides you with a large set of charts—a separate chart for just about every kind of verb in Greek. To learn a new kind of verb, memorize another chart. To be very honest, it gets rather tedious after a while unless you are one of the few people who can process large quantities of rote memory data with ease.

A second approach to learning Greek verbs attempts to reduce rote memorization as much as possible (it can never be eliminated entirely)[4] and instead teaches you a set of formulas that can be used to identify verbs as you read. There will be four basic charts to memorize (rather than several dozen) and a formula for each kind of verb. These formulas specify the various "pieces" (technically, *morphemes*) that constitute each kind of verb, including which of the four sets of endings any particular verb uses. You learn the formulas frontward and then apply them backward as you decipher each verb that you encounter in the text.

Formula

5.10. *Formula* is short for *morphological formula*: a summary of the way that a verb is formed. Here is the first one.

Formula for Present Active Indicative Verbs

stem + connecting vowel + A personal endings
Example: λυ + ο + μεν ▸ λύομεν

The *stem* is the most basic form of a verb. This is what supplies the semantic value of the word, that is, what it means. The stem λυ- refers to the action of loosing or untying or destroying something.

The *connecting vowel* is a vowel that connects the stem and the personal ending.[5] (Quite a profound name, is it not?) The connecting vowel (often abbreviated "c.v." in this textbook, especially in charts) will always be either an omicron or an epsilon (these two letters are the only letters used as connecting vowels).[6] The

4. Occasionally a student reads this statement as if it said, "eliminates rote memory." That is entirely wrong. You *must* memorize certain core data. You may think there is quite a bit of it to learn even with this second approach, but it is a whole lot less than the traditional approach.

5. Some grammars refer to this as a *theme vowel*.

6. There is a rule that tells you which it will be. You are not responsible to know this rule, but if you are curious, here it is: if the next letter is mu or nu, the connecting vowel is omicron, otherwise it is epsilon; if there is no letter following, the connecting vowel can be either omicron or epsilon.

same connecting vowels are used for all verb forms that use connecting vowels (some forms do not—that is one thing that the formula tells you, whether or not to use a connecting vowel).

The *personal ending* is a suffix that indicates the person and number of the verb form. *Person* is the same as for pronouns: first, second, or third; *number* is the familiar singular or plural. Altogether there are four sets of personal endings (often abbreviated "p.e." in this textbook, especially in charts) that you will learn; we designate them as sets A, B, C, and D and arrange them in a chart of four quadrants (for short, a four-quad chart). You will learn more about these endings in later chapters, the B endings in chapter 7, and C and D endings in chapters 14 and 16.

Personal Endings

A. Primary Active	B. Secondary Active
C. Primary Middle	D. Secondary Middle

5.11. Because Greek verbs have a personal ending that indicates person and number, there is always a default, built-in, back-pocket subject included with every verb. If there is not an expressed nominative-case subject in the sentence, you reach in the verb's back pocket and pull out the default subject. If there is a nominative-case subject, then you just leave the back-pocket subject tucked away.

Here is what the complete set of present active indicative forms looks like for λύω:

Present Active Indicative of λύω

	Form	c.v. + A p.e.	Gloss	c.v.	A p.e.
1S	λύω	ω	I am loosing	ο	–
2S	λύεις	εις	You are loosing	ε	ς
3S	λύει	ει	He/she/it is loosing	ε	ι
1P	λύομεν	ομεν	We are loosing	ο	μεν
2P	λύετε	ετε	You are loosing	ε	τε
3P	λύουσι(ν)	ουσι(ν)	They are loosing	ο	νσι(ν)

You must be able to reproduce columns 1 through 4 of this chart both mentally and on paper instantly at any time, day or night, from now on. It is that important.[7] The last two columns are to help you understand what is happening, not for you to memorize.

5.12. Notice a few things in this chart: The *stem* (λυ-) stays the same throughout. The forms listed in the "A p.e." (= set A of the personal endings) column

7. I often tell students that they must pass the "2 a.m. test" on these forms. That is, they need to have someone wake them without warning at 2 a.m. and ask, "What are the present active indicative forms of λύω?" When the student can recite them immediately and fall back asleep (or continue sleeping), they pass the test. (Yes, there is some hyperbole here, but it is intended to stress the necessity of learning these forms well.)

are the technical endings. The combination c.v. + p.e. does not always appear exactly as you might expect, since there are often changes due to the combination.[8] Thus in the second singular form, the connecting vowel epsilon lengthens to the diphthong ει when combined with the ending sigma. Likewise in the third plural the first nu drops out and the connecting vowel lengthens from omicron to the diphthong ου to compensate.

The connecting vowels are either omicron or epsilon—but note that in the first singular form the omicron lengthens to omega because there is no personal ending in the first singular (or you might say that there is a "null ending"), thus the omicron lengthens to compensate.[9] Likewise in the third plural form, the connecting vowel omicron lengthens when the nu of the ending drops out, because it gets squeezed between the connecting vowel and the following sigma.

In the third plural form, λύουσι(ν), the nu is "movable"; it may or may not be present in any given instance—that is why it is in parentheses.[10] Some prefer to learn the form with the nu present and remember that it is sometimes missing (that is what I recommend),[11] while others prefer to learn it without the nu and remember that sometimes it is there.

5.13. The column titled "Gloss" gives an English approximation of the Greek form. Exactly how any given Greek verb is best represented in English depends a great deal on the context. Do not think that the gloss listed in the chart is the only way or even the best way to put these verb forms into English. It may often work, but you must be sensitive to English idiom in each instance. The English pronoun (i.e., *I*, *you*, *he*, etc.) in the Gloss column is part of the verb. The form λύομεν does not mean just "loose" or "to loose" (that is the infinitive, λύειν) but "*we* are loosing."

How do you use this chart? The chart essentially provides a template (which follows the formula) that requires only that you recognize the different stem for different words. That is, if, instead of λύομεν, you see the form ἀκούομεν, you know that it is still a first-person plural form (because the -ομεν is the first plural ending) but that the word is not λύω but ἀκούω. So a common English equivalent would be "we are hearing" rather than "we are loosing."

Parsing

5.14. *Parsing* a verb means to describe all its grammatical pieces that collectively tell us what a particular grammatical form means. The pattern used in this textbook to parse verbs is as follows:

person, number, tense-form, voice, mood ▸ lexical form, gloss

8. There are other ways to explain some of these combinations. What is given here is simplified for pedagogical purposes.

9. This is sometimes called *compensatory lengthening*.

10. When a word ends with a vowel and the following word begins with a vowel, the letter nu is usually added to make it easier to pronounce. (You will see it both ways in the NT.) We do something very similar in English: we say, "a critter," but "an animal." (The English rule is that if a word begins with a vowel, the indefinite article is *an*, otherwise it is *a*.)

11. One reason for this is that the nu is far more often present on third plural verbs in the NT than absent, and that in a ratio of nearly 70 to 1. The LXX also uses the nu far more often than not.

For example, if you were asked to parse λύει, you would respond, "third singular present active indicative ▸ λύω, 'I loose.'" Or, in abbreviated form: "3rd sg. pres. act. ind. ▸ λύω, 'I loose.'" For now, all the verbs you see will be present active indicative verbs. All you need to identify is the person and number.

Tip

Remember that the standard lexical forms always end with omega (the first-person singular ending)—for example, λύω. To figure out another form of a verb, take the personal ending off and put an omega in its place; that will be the way it is listed in the lexicon.

5.15. *Examples*

Mark 1:2, Ἰδοὺ **ἀποστέλλω** τὸν ἄγγελον. — Behold, *I am sending*[a] the messenger.

[a] In the context, this would most naturally be translated with the English future, "I will send"; the "default" translation has been retained here since you are just beginning to learn about verbs.

Mark 8:24, **Βλέπω** τοὺς ἀνθρώπους. — *I see* people.

John 2:3, **λέγει**, Οἶνον οὐκ[a] **ἔχουσιν**. — *She*[b] *said*, "*They do* not *have* wine."

[a] The word οὐκ is a form of the negative οὐ, "no, not." When the following word begins with a vowel, οὐ changes to οὐκ; the meaning is unchanged.

[b] The context indicates that a woman is speaking.

Gen. 15:12, ἰδοὺ φόβος σκοτεινὸς μέγας **ἐπιπίπτει** αὐτῷ. — Behold a great dark fear *fell* on him.

Gen. 27:2, εἶπεν, Οὐ **γινώσκω** τὴν ἡμέραν τῆς τελευτῆς μου. — He said, "*I do* not *know* the day of my death."

5.16. *Now You Try It*

John 1:45, εὑρίσκει Φίλιππος τὸν Ναθαναήλ. — What action is described? Who performed the action? Upon whom was it performed? How do you know in each instance?

John 5:34, ἐγὼ δὲ οὐ τὴν μαρτυρίαν λαμβάνω. — Which word is the verb? Who is doing the action? What receives the action? How does οὐ affect the meaning of the statement?

John 5:38, τὸν λόγον αὐτοῦ οὐκ ἔχετε. — Which word is the verb? Can you parse it? Who is doing the action? How do you know? What receives the action? How do you know? What case is αὐτοῦ, and why is it in that case?

Gen. 49:18, τὴν σωτηρίαν περιμένω κυρίου. — What does περιμένω mean? What is the subject and the direct object? What case is κυρίου, and why is it in that case?

Gen. 21:7, θηλάζει παιδίον Σάρρα.	Which word is the verb? Can you parse it? Who is doing the action? How do you know? What receives the action? How do you know?
Num. 20:19, λέγουσιν αὐτῷ οἱ υἱοὶ Ἰσραήλ.	Who is acting? Ἰσραήλ is an indeclinable form; what case must it be here? What are they doing? What is the indirect object?

The Forms of εἰμί

5.17. The equivalent of our English verb "to be" or "I am" or "he/she/it is," and so forth, in Greek is some form of the word εἰμί.[12] This is called by various names: *linking verb*, *being verb*, *auxiliary verb*, *copulative verb*, or just *copula*. This verb functions differently from an ordinary verb in that it can never take a direct object in the accusative case. Instead it takes a second nominative-case substantive (i.e., noun, adjective, or another form functioning as a noun), called a *predicate nominative*, which further identifies the subject. Some grammars call this a *subject complement*.

The two nominatives refer to things that are approximately equal. For example, "Rob is a teacher." The subject is "Rob," and the linking verb "is" connects the subject with the predicate nominative, "teacher." The larger category is normally the predicate nominative, and the subject usually identifies one part of the larger category. That is, in the example just given, the larger category is "teacher," since there are other teachers than Rob.

Whenever you see some form of the Greek verb εἰμί, you should look for two nominatives: a subject and a predicate nominative. Sometimes the subject is the back-pocket subject in the verb, so if you find only one nominative with εἰμί, it is probably the predicate nominative.

The spellings of the various forms of the linking verb do not follow the usual patterns in Greek—these verbs are typically irregular in formation in most languages. So it is simplest just to memorize the forms. The following chart does not include all the forms of this word; we will meet the others later.

Present [Active] Indicative of εἰμί

	Form	Gloss
1S	εἰμί	I am
2S	εἶ	You are
3S	ἐστί(ν)	He/she/it is
1P	ἐσμέν	We are
2P	ἐστέ	You are
3P	εἰσί(ν)	They are

12. In addition to εἰμί there are several other linking verbs in Greek, including γίνομαι and ὑπάρχω.

5.18. Just as with the verb λύω, a separate pronoun is not needed, because the verb already indicates the grammatical person. That is, ἐστέ does not mean just "are" (with "you" supplied to make better English); it means "you are."

The second singular form includes both a breathing mark and an accent. This is one of the forms that is distinguished from other words only by the accent and breathing mark. For example, the word εἰ is a different word from εἶ even though they have the same two letters and are pronounced the same. The word εἰ means "if," but εἶ means "you are."

This verb is an enclitic. That means it will usually not have an accent when you see it in a text, since the accent shifts to the previous word (which will then usually have two accents). The only form that is not an enclitic is the second singular form, which will always appear with the accent and breathing mark that you see in the chart above.

Both third-person forms of εἰμί have a movable nu. You will see both ἐστί and ἐστίν, εἰσί and εἰσίν. The nu (ν) is in parentheses in the chart to indicate that sometimes it is used and sometimes it "moves" (that is, it is omitted). In the NT the nu is far more frequently included than omitted.

Most grammars list this form as simply the "present indicative" of εἰμί because there are no other forms in the present. That is, there is no present middle or present passive of εἰμί. At that point calling it an active does not mean very much. On the other hand, the endings used are A-quad endings (though irregular). Most students seem to find it easier to keep the parsing consistent with other verb forms and include "active" in the parsing. Your teacher may prefer that you do it differently, so follow their advice.

5.19. *Examples of εἰμί*

John 9:24, ὁ ἄνθρωπος ἁμαρτωλός **ἐστιν**.	The man *is* a sinner.
John 17:17, ὁ λόγος ὁ σὸς ἀλήθειά **ἐστιν**.	Your word *is* truth.

The word σός is an adjective that modifies λόγος. You will learn soon that one place an adjective can occur when modifying a noun is in the following pattern: article ▸ noun ▸ article ▸ adjective. Thus ὁ λόγος ὁ σός means "your word."

Mark 12:35, Πῶς λέγουσιν οἱ γραμματεῖς ὅτι ὁ Χριστὸς υἱὸς Δαυίδ **ἐστιν**;	How do the scribes say that the Messiah *is* the son of David?

This is a question rather than a statement. The first part is included so you can make sense of the last clause, which contains the linking verb. The subject of the first clause is οἱ γραμματεῖς, for which you can use the article to figure out the case (the ending is from the third declension, which you have not learned yet).

Mark 3:29, ἔνοχός **ἐστιν** αἰωνίου ἁμαρτήματος.	*He is* guilty of an eternal sin.

In this example there is only one nominative, the adjective ἔνοχος. The subject is the default third-person subject from the verb. When an adjective functions as a predicate nominative, it is called a *predicate adjective*.

1 Macc. 7:18, Οὐκ **ἔστιν** αὐτοῖς ἀλήθεια. *There is* not truth in them.

This is an example of εἰμί used with the meaning "there is"—sometimes called the *existential use* of εἰμί. One clue to this meaning in modern texts is that it is usually accented as ἔστιν instead of ἐστίν when it has this meaning.[13]

5.20. *Now You Try It*

Mark 14:34, Περίλυπός **ἐστιν** ἡ ψυχή μου.

Mark 2:28, κύριός **ἐστιν** ὁ υἱὸς τοῦ ἀνθρώπου.

Notice that the word order is reversed in these examples: the predicate nominative comes first, and the subject follows the linking verb. In Mark 2:28 we know that ὁ υἱός is the subject, since it has an article and κύριος does not. There are two accents on κύριός; the second one belongs to ἐστιν. This is called an *enclitic form*, in which the accent from one word shifts back to the preceding word. In such situations, the two words are pronounced together as if they were a single word.

Gen. 3:10, γυμνός **εἰμι**.

Gen. 4:9, εἶπεν (said) ὁ θεὸς πρὸς Κάϊν, Ποῦ **ἐστιν** Ἅβελ ὁ ἀδελφός σου;

— — — — — — — — — — — — — —

5.21. Advanced Information for Reference: Diagramming εἰμί

John 12:50, ἡ ἐντολὴ αὐτοῦ ζωὴ αἰώνιός **ἐστιν**. His command *is* eternal life.

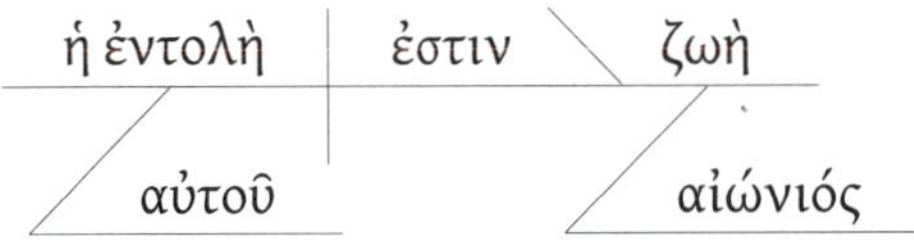

Figure 5.2

13. The accent pattern ἔστιν does not always indicate the existential use; the same pattern also occurs when ἔστιν occurs at the beginning of a sentence.

Sentences whose main verb is a form of εἰμί typically have a predicate nominative or a predicate adjective. These predicate words are diagrammed with a back-slanting line following the linking verb.

— — — — — — — — — — — — — —

Present Active Infinitives

5.22. In English, an infinitive is a verb preceded by the word *to*. It simply names an action without identifying the subject; the infinitive itself does not say "who done it." For example, "*To read* is my greatest enjoyment," or "I began *to tremble* when I saw her coming down the aisle."

The Greek infinitive is one of the simplest forms in the verbal system. It does not require a separate preposition as English does (*to*) but just attaches a single suffix to the verb stem. The present active infinitive of λύω is λύειν, "to loose." There are other infinitives that you will learn later—for example, aorist infinitives—but there is only one form for the present active infinitive.

A common English gloss for the infinitive is simply "to" plus the verb; thus λύειν can be represented in English as "to loose." The Greek infinitive can be used like an English infinitive, but the Greek infinitive has additional uses and traits as well, most of which we will study later.

Unlike other verbs, the infinitive never has a nominative-case subject. Finite verbs have such subjects; non-finite verbs, such as infinitives, do not. If it is necessary to specify who is doing the action described by the infinitive, the word is placed in the accusative case, which we call the *accusative subject* of the infinitive. Infinitives can have direct objects in the accusative. They can also have *both* an accusative subject *and* an accusative object. In most cases it will be obvious from the context which is the subject; often it is the first accusative in word order in the clause. The infinitive can also take an article, though not all do. The article is always neuter singular and most commonly accusative, though it can occur in any case.[14] We will discuss the infinitive in more detail in chapter 22.

Examples of the Present Active Infinitive

5.23. Most of the following examples are not complete sentences but only short phrases to help you understand how infinitives express meaning.

Mark 2:12, **δοξάζειν** τὸν θεόν	*To glorify* God
Mark 3:15, **ἔχειν** ἐξουσίαν **ἐκβάλλειν** τὰ δαιμόνια	*To have* authority *to cast out* demons [two infinitives]
Luke 5:1, **ἀκούειν** τὸν λόγον τοῦ θεοῦ	*To hear* the word of God

14. In the NT, there are 98 accusative articles with infinitives, 67 genitives, 48 datives, and only 9 nominatives. In the LXX, the genitive case dominates (1,494 of 2,215 total).

John 5:26, ζωὴν **ἔχειν**	*To have* life
2 Kgdms. (2 Sam.) 14:17, **τοῦ ἀκούειν** τὸ ἀγαθὸν καὶ τὸ πονηρόν	*To hear* the good and the evil
Eccles. 11:7, ἀγαθὸν τοῖς ὀφθαλμοῖς τοῦ **βλέπειν** τὸν ἥλιον.	It is good for the eyes *to see* the sun.

The first clause assumes ἐστίν and uses the built-in subject, "it"; ἀγαθόν is the predicate nominative (remember that -ον can be nominative case in neuter).

Reading Exercises

5.24. The following examples have a parallel English equivalent given on the right, and some words or phrases in the verse are given in English to simplify the sentence for you. Some statements have been modified slightly to use forms you know. Cover the right-hand column and figure out what the verse in the left column says. Words you do not recognize are ones that you can identify with the use of your lexicon. You should be able to identify the endings on these words. When you are satisfied (or totally stumped), slip your cover sheet down to see if you are correct. If the right-hand column says something quite different from what you thought the left-hand column said, then study that verse some more to figure out why.

Mark 1:30, ἡ δὲ πενθερά of Simon was sick, καὶ εὐθὺς[a] λέγουσιν αὐτῷ concerning her.	*Now the mother-in-law* of Simon was sick, *so they spoke to him* concerning her.

[a] καὶ εὐθύς in this statement is represented in English as "so." See the note on Mark 1:12 in §4.11.

Mark 4:9, The one who ἔχει ears ἀκούειν let him hear.	The one who *has* ears *to hear*, let him hear (or, had better listen).
Mark 4:20, ἀκούουσιν τὸν λόγον καί they welcome it καὶ καρποφοροῦσιν.	*They hear the word and* they welcome it, *and they produce fruit.*
Mark 6:18, Said γὰρ ὁ Ἰωάννης τῷ Ἡρῴδῃ ὅτι[a] Οὐκ it is lawful for you ἔχειν the wife τοῦ ἀδελφοῦ σου.	*For John* said *to Herod*, "It is *not* lawful for you *to have* the wife *of your brother*."

[a] The conjunction ὅτι is often used to introduce a direct quote; it is the equivalent of our English quotation marks.

Mark 13:28, Learn τὴν παραβολήν· When the fig tree puts out its leaves γινώσκετε ὅτι ἐγγὺς τὸ θέρος ἐστίν.	Learn *the parable*: When the fig tree puts out its leaves, *you know that summer is near.*

5.25. *Now You Try It*

John 9:27, I told ὑμῖν ἤδη καὶ οὐκ [ἀκούετε]· Why πάλιν θέλετε ἀκούειν;

Who did not hear? How do you know? What did they desire?

Rom. 11:8, καθὼς γέγραπται (it is written), Ἔδωκεν (he gave) αὐτοῖς ὁ θεὸς πνεῦμα κατανύξεως,[a] ὀφθαλμοὺς τοῦ μὴ βλέπειν καὶ ὦτα (ears) τοῦ μὴ ἀκούειν.

[a] πνεῦμα κατανύξεως, "a spirit of stupor"

Who gave this "spirit"? How do you know? How is the "spirit of stupor" explained? What does it mean?

Deut. 29:3, καὶ οὐκ ἔδωκεν κύριος ὁ θεὸς ὑμῖν καρδίαν εἰδέναι (to understand) καὶ ὀφθαλμοὺς βλέπειν καὶ ὦτα ἀκούειν.

What is the subject and main verb in this sentence? What did God *not* do? What do the infinitives tell you?

Deuteronomy 29:3 is one of the two verses that Paul combines and paraphrases in his quotation in Rom. 11:8. (This is Deut. 29:4 in English; the other verse Paul includes is Isa. 29:10.) See the previous example for some of the vocabulary here.

Reading Passage: John 15:1–8

5.26. This passage includes a number of present active verb forms, both indicatives and infinitives; they have been marked in the text. You should be able to recognize and parse each of these forms. You will also see multiple forms of two key verbs in this passage. In due time you will learn why they are different and what these differences mean. You may be able to figure out some of them now from the context of each use. These words are φέρω, "I bear, produce" (which occurs in this passage as φέρον, φέρῃ, φέρειν, φέρει, and φέρητε) and μένω, "I remain" (which occurs as μείνατε, μένῃ, μένητε, μένων, μείνητε, and μείνῃ). There are also some third-declension noun forms included. If they are nominative singular forms that you can identify with your lexicon, they are not marked. (The genitive form in the lexicon will not match any patterns you have learned yet.) Some repeated words that you have not had yet are listed below the reading passage.

The Vine and the Branches

1 Ἐγώ **εἰμι** ἡ ἄμπελος ἡ ἀληθινὴ (true) καὶ ὁ πατήρ μου ὁ γεωργός **ἐστιν**. 2 πᾶν
(every) κλῆμα (branch) ἐν (in) ἐμοὶ μὴ φέρον (producing) καρπὸν **αἴρει** αὐτό,
καὶ πᾶν τὸ καρπὸν φέρον **καθαίρει** αὐτὸ ἵνα (so that) καρπὸν πλείονα (more)
φέρῃ (it may produce). 3 ἤδη ὑμεῖς καθαροί **ἐστε** διὰ (because of) τὸν λόγον
ὃν (which) λελάληκα (I have spoken) ὑμῖν· 4 μείνατε (remain!) ἐν ἐμοί, κἀγὼ
ἐν ὑμῖν. καθὼς τὸ κλῆμα οὐ δύναται (is able) καρπὸν **φέρειν** ἀφ' (from) ἑαυτοῦ
(itself) ἐὰν μὴ[a] μένῃ (it remains) ἐν τῇ ἀμπέλῳ, οὕτως οὐδὲ ὑμεῖς ἐὰν μὴ[a] ἐν
ἐμοὶ μένητε (you remain). 5 ἐγώ **εἰμι** ἡ ἄμπελος, ὑμεῖς τὰ κλήματα (branches).
ὁ μένων (one who remains) ἐν ἐμοὶ κἀγὼ ἐν αὐτῷ οὗτος (he) **φέρει** καρπὸν

πολύν (much), ὅτι (because) χωρὶς ἐμοῦ οὐ δύνασθε (you are able) **ποιεῖν** οὐδέν.[b] [6]ἐὰν μή[a] τις (anyone) μένῃ ἐν ἐμοί, ἐβλήθη (he will be thrown) ἔξω ὡς τὸ κλῆμα καὶ ἐξηράνθη (he will wither) καὶ **συνάγουσιν** αὐτὰ καὶ εἰς (into) τὸ πῦρ **βάλλουσιν** καὶ καίεται (it will be burned). [7]ἐὰν (if) μείνητε (you remain) ἐν ἐμοὶ καὶ τὰ ῥήματά (words) μου ἐν ὑμῖν μείνῃ (remain), ὃ ἐὰν[c] θέλητε (you want) αἰτήσασθε (ask!), καὶ γενήσεται (it will become/happen) ὑμῖν. [8]ἐν τούτῳ ἐδοξάσθη (is glorified) ὁ πατήρ μου, ἵνα (that) καρπὸν πολὺν φέρητε (you may produce) καὶ γένησθε (you may be) ἐμοὶ μαθηταί.

[a] ἐὰν μή, "except"

[b] Verse 5 contains a double negative: οὐ followed a few words later by οὐδέν (a compound form of οὐ). In English a double negative produces a positive meaning, but in Greek a double negative serves to emphasize the negation. Thus "You are not able to do nothing" in English means "You are able to do something." But οὐ δύνασθε ποιεῖν οὐδέν means "you are able to do nothing at all."

[c] ὃ ἐάν, "whatever"

Repeated Words

ἐν, "in"

κλῆμα, "branch"

οὐδέ, οὐδέν, a negative; use "no, nothing, no one, etc." as context and English idiom suggest

πᾶν, "every"

πολύν, "much"

φέρον, "bearing, producing"

5.27. Vocabulary for Chapter 5

Part of Speech	Definition	Possible Glosses	Frequency	
Word			NT	LXX
Adverbs				
οὐ, οὐκ, οὐχ, οὐχί	Particle of negation, usually used adverbially to negate an indicative-mood verb (spelling variations depend on the next word; meaning is unchanged) [See "The Negatives" in §§6.32–35.]	no, not	1,606	6,077
μή	Particle of negation, usually used adverbially to negate a non-indicative verb or non-finite verbal	no, not, lest	1,042	3,179
Verbs				
εἰμί	The Greek "being/linking/copula/auxiliary" verb, roughly equivalent to the English "to be" (English requires a broad range of translations)	I am, exist, live, am present	2,460	6,947
ἐστίν	An inflected verb form: 3rd sg. pres. (act.) ind. of εἰμί	he/she/it is	896	1,863

Part of Speech	Definition	Possible Glosses	Frequency	
Word			NT	LXX
εἰσίν	An inflected verb form: 3rd pl. pres. (act.) ind. of εἰμί	they are	157	261
λέγω	To make a statement or utterance, either oral or written, for which English often has specific words appropriate to various contexts ("say, speak, tell, declare, report, call," etc.)	I say, speak	2,354	4,610
ἔχω	To possess; to bear/carry on one's person; to be in a position to do something; etc. (a very diverse semantic range)	I have, hold	708	497
ἀκούω	To receive information via the ear; to heed or understand what is said	I hear; I obey, understand	428	1,069
γινώσκω	To be in receipt of information that results in understanding; to form a judgment	I know, learn; I understand	222	746
θέλω	To have a desire for something	I wish, desire, will	208	148
γράφω	To inscribe letters or symbols on a writing surface; to compose a written text; to write	I write	191	304
εὑρίσκω	To find or locate something (intentionally or coincidentally)	I find	176	613
ἐσθίω	To consume food (various metaphorical uses are also common)	I eat	158	686
βλέπω	To use one's eyes for sensory perception (various metaphorical uses are also common)	I see, look at	133	133
λύω	To undo something that is used to tie up or constrain something; to do away with; to reduce something to ruin by tearing down or breaking to pieces	I loose, set free, untie; I bring to an end, abolish; I destroy, tear down, break up	42	29

5.28. Key Things to Know for Chapter 5

You must be able to reproduce the present active indicative forms of λύω and εἰμί exactly and with no hesitation. (Can you pass the "2 a.m. test"?)

What is a connecting vowel, and what vowels can be used in that role?

What is a movable nu?

What is the present active infinitive form of λύω?

How does an infinitive differ from a "normal" verb like λύω?

6

MODIFIERS

Adjectives and Adverbs

6.1. Now that we have learned some of the most basic building blocks in the language, nouns and verbs, we need to add some variety. Language would be pretty boring if all we ever said was "Sally saw the train," "The dog chased the cat," or "George sneezed." One of the ways we can add that variety is by using words that describe these basic building blocks. To describe nouns we use words called *adjectives*, and to describe verbs we use *adverbs*.

Adjectives

6.2. An adjective is a word that modifies a substantive by describing, qualifying, limiting, or restricting it. Yet that definition does not help if you do not know what a substantive is, so we need to start there. A substantive is any word or group of words that functions as a noun. In English a substantive may be a noun, a pronoun, a gerund, a phrase, or a clause. For example, not only is *dirge* a noun, but so is *the wailing*—which is a gerund (a verb that acts like a noun). Thus both *dirge* and *the wailing* can be described as substantives. In Greek there are additional options that we will meet in due time.

English Adjectives

6.3. Adjectives may function one of three ways in English. First, an adjective may modify a noun (or other substantive). We can say, for example, "He is a *good* dog." The adjective "good" tells us what kind of dog we are talking about. Adjectives that function this way usually precede the noun they modify and are called *attributive adjectives*—that is, they attribute a quality to a noun.

The second function is similar, but more indirect. Instead of referring directly to "the good dog," we can make a statement about the dog—for example, "The dog is *bad*." In this case we use a linking verb ("is") and append an adjective. This is often called a *predicate adjective*, which is nothing more than an adjective functioning as a predicate nominative.

The third function of adjectives in English is to take the place of a noun. These are called *substantival adjectives*. Even though a word is technically an adjective, we sometimes use it like a noun. In the two following examples the adjectives *good*, *bad*, and *dead* are used in noun slots.

Both the *good* and the *bad* are here.
The *dead* will rise.

Contrast similar statements using nouns.

Both dogs and cats are here.
The flag will rise.

A Note on Terminology

The noun modified by an adjective is called a *head word*.

He is a	good	dog.
	↕ adjective	↕ head word
ἐστὶν	καλὸν	κυνάριον.

A word modified by a genitive noun is also called a *head word*.

Preach	the word	of God.
	↕ head word	↕ gen. noun
κήρυξον	τὸν λόγον	θεοῦ.

Greek Adjectives

6.4. Greek adjectives function much like English adjectives. There are a few differences in position, and so forth, partly because Greek adjectives change form (that is, the way they are spelled), whereas English adjectives are always spelled the same way. The following sections tell you what you need to know.

Form of the Adjective

6.5. The most important thing to know about adjectives is that when modifying a noun, adjectives agree with that noun in gender, number, and case. An adjective does not have any gender of its own; it may be used to modify a noun in any gender. It does that by adding an ending that matches the noun in gender, number, and case. Since adjectives use the same case endings as nouns, that means there are no new endings to learn. The only difference is that these same endings now identify *gender*, not declension. Study the following examples, and notice that adjectives have the same endings that nouns have. The endings that you learned as second-declension endings for nouns (ος, ου, ῳ, ον, οι, ων, οις, ους) function as the endings on all masculine adjectives. Likewise, the first-declension endings (α/η, ας/ης, ᾳ/ῃ, αν/ην, αι, ων, αις, ας) become the feminine endings for adjectives, and the neuter variation of the second declension (ον, ου, ῳ, ον, α, ων, οις, α) provides the endings used on neuter adjectives.

	Masc.	Fem.		Neut.
NS	ἀγαθός	ἀγαθή	πονηρά	ἀγαθόν
GS	ἀγαθοῦ	ἀγαθῆς	πονηρᾶς	ἀγαθοῦ
DS	ἀγαθῷ	ἀγαθῇ	πονηρᾷ	ἀγαθῷ
AS	ἀγαθόν	ἀγαθήν	πονηράν	ἀγαθόν
NP	ἀγαθοί	ἀγαθαί	πονηραί	ἀγαθά
GP	ἀγαθῶν	ἀγαθῶν	πονηρῶν	ἀγαθῶν
DP	ἀγαθοῖς	ἀγαθαῖς	πονηραῖς	ἀγαθοῖς
AP	ἀγαθούς	ἀγαθάς	πονηράς	ἀγαθά

6.6. You will notice that a feminine adjective may use either alpha endings or eta endings.[1] Which one it uses depends on the spelling of the adjective, and each adjective always uses the same pattern. (You do not have to know why, just be able to recognize them.) In the chart above, πονηρά ("bad") has been added so that you can see a feminine form that uses alpha endings.

T. Benj. 4.2, ὁ **ἀγαθὸς** ἄνθρωπος οὐκ ἔχει **σκοτεινὸν** ὀφθαλμόν.	The *good* person does not have a *dark* eye.
Mark 14:12, τῇ **πρώτῃ** ἡμέρᾳ τῶν ἀζύμων λέγουσιν αὐτῷ οἱ μαθηταὶ αὐτοῦ, . . .	On the *first* day of Unleavened Bread his disciples said to him, . . .

In a lexicon, an adjective entry will look like this: ἀγαθός, ή, όν, *good*. This gives the masculine, feminine, and neuter endings; the entry does *not* use the same pattern as nouns. (You will remember that in a lexicon a noun entry gives the nominative singular form followed by the genitive singular ending and the article.) Adjectives will always be listed alphabetically in a lexicon according to the *masculine nominative singular* spelling, with the feminine and neuter endings added; there is no genitive ending listed and no article.

Remember that when modifying a noun, adjectives agree with that noun in gender, number, and case. This does not mean the endings will be spelled the same. Sometimes they will, but an adjective may have alpha endings when modifying a noun that uses eta endings (and vice versa). For example, "a bad commandment" could be written in Greek as πονηρὰ ἐντολή. Both words are feminine nominative singular, even though πονηρά uses the alpha endings and ἐντολή uses eta endings. Likewise, first-declension masculine words (or second-declension

1. There are only three adjectives in the NT that use the mixed α/η feminine endings: πᾶς ("all"), ἅπας ("whole"), and μέλας ("black"). For example, the feminine forms of πᾶς are as follows: πᾶσα, πάσης, πάσῃ, πᾶσαν, πᾶσαι, πασῶν, πάσαις, πάσας. All other feminine adjectives will have either α-pure or η-pure endings.

feminine words) will not usually match the spelling of the case endings of their adjectives.[2]

1 Tim. 6:15, ὁ **μακάριος** καὶ **μόνος** δυνάστης	the *blessed* and *only* Sovereign
1 Clem. 34.1, Ὁ **ἀγαθὸς** ἐργάτης λαμβάνει τὸν ἄρτον τοῦ ἔργου αὐτοῦ.	The *good* worker receives the bread of his work.

Two-Form Adjectives

6.7. Some adjectives use the same endings for masculine and feminine; these are usually the masculine endings above.[3] They will be listed in the lexicon like this: ἔρημος, ον, *desolate*. They decline in the following pattern:

	Masc./Fem.	Neut.
NS	ἔρημος	ἔρημον
GS	ἐρήμου	ἐρήμου
DS	ἐρήμῳ	ἐρήμῳ
AS	ἔρημον	ἔρημον
NP	ἔρημοι	ἔρημα
GP	ἐρήμων	ἐρήμων
DP	ἐρήμοις	ἐρήμοις
AP	ἐρήμους	ἔρημα

There are only a half-dozen such words that are common in the NT; you will learn them as part of the vocabulary in later chapters.[4] There are more adjectives that follow this pattern; most such words occur infrequently in the NT, but they occur often enough that you need to understand what is going on when you find one in the text.

2. In the same way, if either the adjective or noun is indeclinable, the endings will not be spelled the same; for example, Josephus refers to ταῖς ἐννέα πύλαις ("the nine gates") of Solomon's temple (*J.W.* 5.5.3 §205). The adjective ἐννέα ("nine") does not decline.

3. Some two-form adjectives use third-declension endings, for which see chap. 12.

4. In addition to ἔρημος, ον ("desolate"; occurs 48× in the NT and 65× in the LXX), other frequent adjectives with this pattern of endings are αἰώνιος, ον ("eternal," 71× NT/153× LXX; more on this adjective below); ἁμαρτωλός, όν ("sinful," 47×/179×); and διάβολος, ον ("slanderous," 37×/22×). There are also two third-declension adjectives (both numbers) that are common: τρεῖς, τρία ("three," 68×/352×) and τέσσαρες, α ("four," 41×/224×). Less common (and not part of the vocabulary of this textbook) are words such as ἀληθής, ές ("true," 26×/20×) and ἀσθενής, ές ("weak, sick," 26×/21×); see app. A for their forms. There are over four hundred two-ending adjectives, but most of these occur only a few times in the NT.

The adjective αἰώνιος, ον is *usually* a two-form adjective, but rarely it uses a separate form for feminine (only 2× in the NT). This is a more common pattern in the LXX, where 12 of the 60 occurrences of the feminine form use alpha endings. As a result, some lexicons (including *CL*, but not BDAG) list this word as αἰώνιος, α, ον.

6.8. Examples of Two-Form Adjectives

John 17:3, αὕτη δέ ἐστιν ἡ **αἰώνιος** ζωή. — Now this is *eternal* life.

Gal. 3:1, Ὦ **ἀνόητοι**[a] Γαλάται.[b] — O *foolish* Galatians!

[a] ἀνόητος, ον, "foolish, dull-witted"
[b] Γαλάτης, ου, ὁ, "an inhabitant of Galatia, a Galatian"

Bar. 4:29, ἐπάξει ὑμῖν τὴν **αἰώνιον** εὐφροσύνην. — He will bring you *everlasting* rejoicing.

Functions of Adjectives

6.9. Greek adjectives, like English ones, may function attributively (modify a noun), predicatively (as part of the predicate in a sentence, they describe the subject), or substantivally (substitute for a noun). When modifying a noun (attributive and predicate adjectives), adjectives agree with that noun in gender, number, and case.

Attributive Adjectives

6.10. Attributive adjectives are typically a direct description of a noun: τὸν **πρῶτον** λόγον ("the *first* word") or τοῖς **κενοῖς** λόγοις ("the *empty* words") or **πιστοῦ** λόγου ("a *faithful/dependable* word"). Predicate adjectives make a statement about the noun: οἱ λόγοι **ἀληθινοί** εἰσιν ("the words are *true*").

An adjective that modifies an articular noun will always have an article in front of the adjective. This is called the *attributive position.* Two attributive patterns may occur; there is no difference in meaning.

first attributive position	article ▸ *adjective* ▸ noun ὁ **ἅγιος** θεός, "the *holy* God"
second attributive position	article ▸ noun ▸ article ▸ *adjective* ὁ θεὸς ὁ **ἅγιος**, "the *holy* God"

All the adjective examples thus far in this chapter have been in first attributive position; the word order is the same as English. Next is an example of an adjective in second attributive position.

Luke 5:37, ῥήξει ὁ οἶνος ὁ **νέος** τοὺς ἀσκούς. — The *new* wine will break the wineskins.

Whenever an attributive adjective follows the noun, the article must be repeated before the adjective. This is different from English, which does not use the second attributive position.

Predicate Adjectives

6.11. When no article precedes an adjective used with an articular noun, the adjective is said to be in predicate position and is translated as a predicate adjective,[5] supplying the verb *is*/*are*. In Greek (but not in English) a noun and an adjective can thus form a complete sentence all by themselves—for example, οἱ λόγοι ἀληθινοί, "The words are true." A separate verb is not needed. Two patterns may occur; there is no difference in meaning.[6]

first predicate position	adjective ▶ article ▶ noun **ἅγιος** ὁ θεός, "God is *holy*"
second predicate position	article ▶ noun ▶ adjective ὁ θεὸς **ἅγιος**, "God is *holy*"

Here are two examples of adjectives in predicate position, one in each of the two possible predicate positions.

Matt. 13:16, ὑμῶν **μακάριοι** οἱ ὀφθαλμοί.	Your eyes are *blessed*.
Rom. 11:16, εἰ δὲ ἡ ἀπαρχὴ **ἁγία**, καὶ τὸ φύραμα·[a] καὶ εἰ ἡ ῥίζα **ἁγία**, καὶ οἱ κλάδοι.	But if the firstfruits offering[b] is *holy*, also the batch of dough, and if the root is *holy*, also the branches.

[a] φύραμα, ατος, τό, "batch of dough." This is a third-declension noun; go by the article.

[b] The firstfruits offering in this instance consisted of a piece of dough pinched off from the full batch of dough.

Adjectives with Anarthrous Nouns

6.12. What about nouns without articles (*anarthrous* nouns)? I am glad you asked, since this is the situation approximately 2,400 times in the NT—a quarter of all adjective-noun constructions, so you will see it fairly often. Here the rule is . . . CONTEXT! In such situations the adjective can be either attributive or predicate. Both ἀγαθὸς ἄνθρωπος and ἄνθρωπος ἀγαθός can mean either "a good man," or "A man *is* good." Only context can tell which one the writer intended. The most helpful context clue that distinguishes many such instances is the presence of another verb in the clause. In this case the adjective must be attributive since there cannot be two verbs in the same clause.[7]

5. You may be familiar with the term *subject complement* instead of *predicate adjective*. They refer to the same thing: an adjective functioning as a subject complement.

6. The second predicate position is not as common in the NT as the first predicate position.

7. There can be a compound predicate in which two (or more) verbs are connected by καί.

— — — — — — — — — — — — — —

6.13. Advanced Information for Reference: Diagramming Attributive Adjectives

John 20:3, Ἐξῆλθεν ὁ Πέτρος καὶ ὁ **ἄλλος** μαθητής.	Peter and the *other* disciple went out.

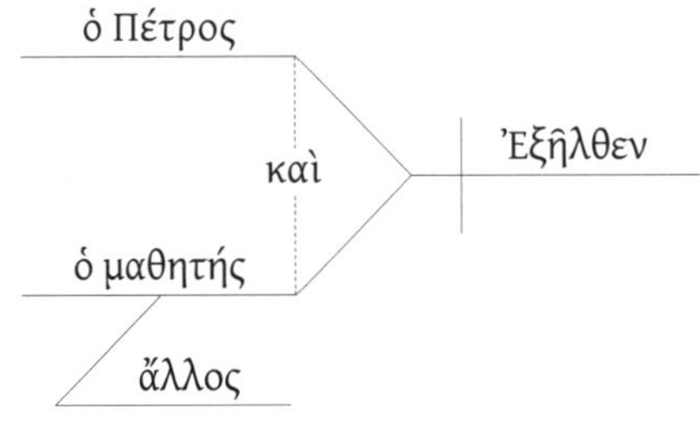

Figure 6.1

— — — — — — — — — — — — — —

Substantival Adjectives

6.14. Substantival adjectives take the place of a noun. Even though they are adjectives, in a sentence they act just like a noun. When they do, they usually have an article (but not always) and take the case appropriate to their function in the sentence; gender and number will agree with the noun for which they substitute. If an adjective functions as the subject of a sentence, it will be in the nominative case (e.g., ὁ διάβολος, "the adversary, the devil"); if it functions as an indirect object, it will be in the dative case (e.g., τῷ παραλυτικῷ, "to the paralytic"); and so on.[8]

Matt. 13:39, ὁ **ἐχθρός** ἐστιν ὁ **διάβολος**.	The *enemy* is the *devil.*
Mark 10:21, δὸς (give!) **τοῖς πτωχοῖς**.	Give *to the poor.*
Matt. 12:35, ὁ ἀγαθὸς ἄνθρωπος ἐκβάλλει **ἀγαθά**, καὶ ὁ πονηρὸς ἄνθρωπος ἐκβάλλει **πονηρά**.	The good person brings out *good things*, and the evil person brings out *evil things.*

— — — — — — — — — — — — — —

6.15. Advanced Information for Reference: Diagramming Substantival Adjectives

Matt. 13:43, **οἱ δίκαιοι** ἐκλάμψουσιν ὡς ὁ ἥλιος.	*The righteous* will shine as the sun.

8. διάβολος, ον, "slanderous," is most commonly used substantivally as "the slanderer/adversary"; παραλυτικός, ή, όν, "paralyzed," is commonly "paralyzed person."

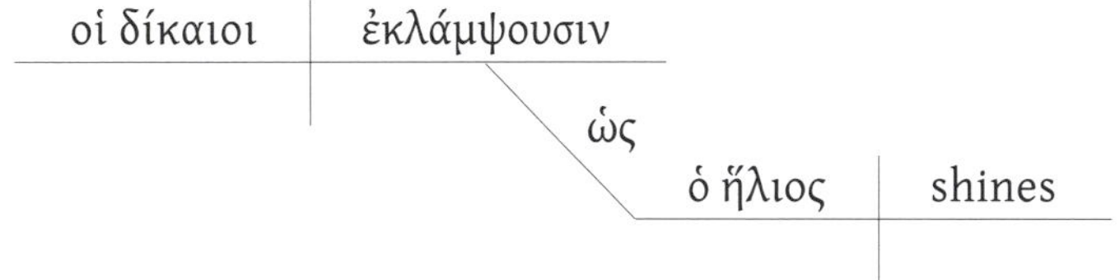

Figure 6.2

A substantival adjective is diagrammed as if it were a noun. Words that are assumed in Greek may be supplied in English, such as "shines" in the example above. Other diagramming conventions supply "x" as a placeholder for these words or would insert the assumed Greek form in square brackets.

— — — — — — — — — — — — — —

Examples of Adjectives

6.16. Now, that is a lot of information with only a few examples, so we need to look at some Greek texts that use adjectives.

Mark 1:24, εἶ **ὁ ἅγιος** τοῦ θεοῦ.	You are *the Holy One* of God.
John 4:23, οἱ **ἀληθινοὶ** προσκυνηταὶ προσκυνήσουσιν (will worship) τῷ πατρί.	The *true* worshipers will worship the Father.
Rom. 7:12, ὁ νόμος **ἅγιος** καὶ ἡ ἐντολὴ **ἁγία** καὶ **δικαία** καὶ **ἀγαθή**.	The law is *holy*, and the commandment is *holy* and *righteous* and *good*.
Mark 1:26, σπαράξαν (it convulsed) αὐτὸν τὸ πνεῦμα τὸ **ἀκάθαρτον** καὶ φωνῆσαν (crying out) φωνῇ **μεγάλῃ** ἐξῆλθεν (it came out) ἐξ (out) αὐτοῦ.[a]	The *unclean* spirit convulsed him, and crying out with a *loud* voice, it came out of him.

[a] The repetition of ἐξ (the preposition ἐκ, "out") as a prefix on the verb and as a separate preposition following the verb is redundant in English but is common in Greek and is even a mark of good style. "Out" is used only once in an English equivalent.

Luke 1:49, **ἅγιον** τὸ ὄνομα αὐτοῦ.	His name is *holy*.
2 Tim. 2:11, **πιστὸς** ὁ λόγος· εἰ γὰρ συναπεθάνομεν, καὶ συζήσομεν.[a]	The saying is *trustworthy*: For if we died with [him], also we will live together with [him].

[a] The verb συζήσομεν is a compound form: σύν + ζάω. A nu on the end of a preposition often drops off when prefixed to a verb that begins with a consonant. The previous verb in this clause, συναπεθάνομεν, did not drop the nu because the stem began with a vowel. See your lexicon for the meaning of both verbs (συναποθνῄσκω and συζάω). They are forms you have not yet learned to identify; the first is an aorist, and the second a future tense-form.

T. Benj. 6.5, ἡ **ἀγαθὴ** διάνοια οὐκ ἔχει δύο γλώσσας.	The *good* mind does not have two tongues.

Gen. 1:2, ἡ δὲ γῆ ἦν **ἀόρατος** καὶ **ἀκατασκεύαστος.**

Now the earth was *unseen* and *unformed.*

Gen. 13:13, οἱ δὲ ἄνθρωποι οἱ ἐν Σοδόμοις[a] **πονηροὶ** καὶ **ἁμαρτωλοί.**

Now the men in Sodom were *evil* and *sinful.*

[a] οἱ ἐν Σοδόμοις, "the ones in Sodom"

Now You Try It

6.17. Many words that you have not learned yet are glossed parenthetically in the following examples. Any that are not glossed either you should know from your vocabulary or you can identify by using your lexicon.

John 6:40, ἀναστήσω (I will raise) αὐτὸν ἐγὼ τῇ **ἐσχάτῃ** ἡμέρᾳ.

Who is raising whom? (Give the Greek word, and tell how you know.) Why is ἡμέρᾳ in the dative case? (It is *not* the indirect object.) How is ἡμέρᾳ described?

John 3:16, Οὕτως ἠγάπησεν (he loved) ὁ θεὸς τὸν κόσμον, ὥστε τὸν υἱὸν τὸν **μονογενῆ**[a] ἔδωκεν (he gave).[b]

Who loved whom? Who gave whom? What does ὥστε indicate? How is υἱόν described?

[a] The adjective μονογενῆ is a two-form adjective (μονογενής, ές) that follows an uncommon pattern of endings. In this text you can tell that it must be masculine singular accusative because of the article. See app. A for the full set of forms; μονογενής follows the same pattern as ἀληθής.

[b] Since the Son is clearly related to God as Son to Father in Johannine theology (see, e.g., John 1:14; 3:35), you can understand the article in τὸν υἱόν as "his," even though it is not a pronoun by form. This use of the article as a pronoun is common.

1 Cor. 1:9, **πιστὸς** ὁ θεός.

Identify the subject, verb, and predicate in this statement.

John 5:30, ἡ κρίσις ἡ **ἐμὴ δικαία** ἐστίν.

There are two adjectives, and each is functioning differently. Explain each one.

John 5:25, ἀμὴν ἀμὴν λέγω ὑμῖν ὅτι ἔρχεται (it is coming) ὥρα (an hour) καὶ νῦν ἐστιν ὅτε **οἱ νεκροὶ** ἀκούσουσιν (they will hear).

How is the adjective functioning in this verse? What case is ὑμῖν and why is it in that case? ("Why" relates to how it is functioning in the sentence, not how you know what case it is.)

Rev. 22:6, εἶπέν (he said) μοι, Οὗτοι[a] οἱ λόγοι **πιστοὶ** καὶ **ἀληθινοί.**

Why is μοι in the dative case? How are οἱ λόγοι described, in addition to οὗτοι? There is no verb in the quotation; what would you need to add if you were to put it into English? How is that addition justified?

[a] οὗτοι ("these") is a pronoun modifying οἱ λόγοι; even though it is in predicate position, you do not add a form of *is* as you do with adjectives in this position.

Ruth 2:10, ἐγώ εἰμι ξένη.[a]

[a] The adjective ξένη often has an article when used substantivally (see your lexicon), but it is not necessary (as here).

This is part of Ruth's response to the kindness shown to her by Boaz.

1 Kgdms. (1 Sam.) 2:2, οὐκ[a] ἔστιν **ἅγιος** ὡς κύριος, καὶ οὐκ ἔστιν **δίκαιος** ὡς ὁ θεὸς ἡμῶν· οὐκ ἔστιν **ἅγιος** πλὴν σοῦ.

Is πλήν functioning as a conjunction or a preposition in this verse? (See your lexicon.) Why is σοῦ in the genitive case?

[a] The negative οὐκ negates the verb ἔστιν, "there is" (note the accent; see §5.19), and the adjective functions substantivally: "There is not one who is holy." All three phrases are similar.

This is Hannah's prayer ascribing greatness to God.

αὐτός as an Adjective

6.18. You met the word αὐτός in chapter 4. In the vast majority of instances, this word is the third-person pronoun ("he, she, it"). In some instances, it can also function as an adjective, with two different meanings.

αὐτός = Identification, "Same"

6.19. The first use of αὐτός as an adjective is called the *adjectival identifying use*. In this situation αὐτός functions, not as a pronoun, but as an adjective modifying another word in the same gender, number, and case. It is usually in *attributive* position: it will be preceded by an article (usually first attributive position, but occasionally second). In this instance it means "same." This identifies or particularizes the noun.

Examples of the Adjectival Identifying Use of αὐτός

6.20. In first attributive position:

Mark 14:39, καὶ πάλιν ἀπελθὼν προσηύξατο τὸν **αὐτὸν** λόγον.[a]

And again after going away he prayed the *same* thing.

[a] λόγος can mean not only "word" but also "thing"—which makes better sense here. "He prayed the same word" communicates only in an awkward fashion in English; it is *not* more "literal" or accurate, only more clumsy and amateurish.

1 Cor. 15:39, οὐ πᾶσα σὰρξ ἡ **αὐτὴ** σάρξ.

Not all flesh is the *same* flesh.

2 Cor. 4:13, ἔχοντες τὸ **αὐτὸ** πνεῦμα τῆς πίστεως, καὶ ἡμεῖς πιστεύομεν.

But having the *same* spirit of faith, we also believe.

1 Clem. 20.8, ὠκεανὸς[a] καὶ οἱ μετ' αὐτὸν[b] κόσμοι ταῖς **αὐταῖς** ταγαῖς τοῦ δεσπότου διευθύνονται.[c]

The ocean and the lands beyond it by the *same* decrees of the Master are governed.

[a] ὠκεανός, οῦ, ὁ, "ocean"

[b] μετ' αὐτόν, "beyond it" (first attributive position)

[c] διευθύνω, "I guide, direct, govern"

6.21. In second attributive position (rare in NT):

Heb. 11:9, Πίστει (by faith) παρῴκησεν[a] εἰς γῆν τῆς ἐπαγγελίας ὡς ἀλλοτρίαν ἐν σκηναῖς κατοικήσας[b] μετὰ Ἰσαὰκ καὶ Ἰακὼβ τῶν συγκληρονόμων τῆς ἐπαγγελίας τῆς **αὐτῆς**.

By faith he lived in the land of promise as an alien, dwelling in tents with Isaac and Jacob, joint heirs of the *same* promise.

[a] An aorist form you will learn later: παροικέω, "I live."

[b] Another aorist form like παροικέω, "living, dwelling, residing." It is a participle, so there is no subject; it modifies παρῴκησεν.

Herm. Sim. 66.1, Μετὰ ἡμέρας ὀλίγας εἶδον (I saw) αὐτὸν εἰς τὸ πεδίον[a] τὸ **αὐτὸ** ὅπου καὶ τοὺς ποιμένας ἑωράκειν (I had seen).

After a few days I saw him in the *same* plain where I had also seen the shepherds.

[a] πεδίον, ου, τό, "plain, field"

2 Macc. 3:33, οἱ **αὐτοὶ** νεανίαι πάλιν ἐφάνησαν τῷ Ἡλιοδώρῳ.

The *same* young men appeared again to Heliodorus.

6.22. The following examples show the less common adjectival identifying function of αὐτός when it is in predicate position (αὐτός ▸ article ▸ noun). Only context can determine this. Normally when αὐτός is in predicate position it will be the intensive use (see below), but sometimes that makes no sense, in which case we conclude that it is identifying rather than emphasizing. (This situation is not common.)

Luke 13:31, Ἐν **αὐτῇ** τῇ ὥρᾳ προσῆλθάν τινες Φαρισαῖοι.

In the *same* hour (or, *that very* hour) some Pharisees came.

2 Esd. (Ezra) 5:3, ἐν **αὐτῷ** τῷ καιρῷ ἦλθεν (he came) ἐπ' αὐτοὺς Θανθαναϊ ἔπαρχος[a] πέραν τοῦ ποταμοῦ καὶ Σαθαρβουζανὰ καὶ οἱ σύνδουλοι αὐτῶν.

At the *same* time (or, *that very* day) Thanthanai, the commander beyond the River, came to them, and Satharbouzana and their fellow slaves.

[a] ἔπαρχος, ου, ὁ, "commanding officer"

6.23. If αὐτός has an article, but it does *not* modify another word, it may be substantival: "the same one/thing."

Ps. 101:28 (102:27 Eng.), σὺ δὲ **ὁ αὐτὸς** εἶ.	But you are *the same*.
1 Cor. 1:10, Παρακαλῶ (I exhort) δὲ ὑμᾶς, ἀδελφοί,[a] διὰ τοῦ ὀνόματος τοῦ κυρίου ἡμῶν Ἰησοῦ Χριστοῦ, ἵνα **τὸ αὐτὸ** λέγητε πάντες (all).[b]	But I exhort you, brothers and sisters, in the name of our Lord Jesus Christ, that you all speak *the same thing*.

[a] See the sidebar in §6.25, "ἀδελφός as 'Brother or Sister.'"

[b] πάντες is the nominative subject (it is a third-declension form you have not learned yet), and τὸ αὐτό is the accusative direct object.

Phil. 3:1, Τὸ λοιπόν, ἀδελφοί μου, χαίρετε (rejoice!) ἐν κυρίῳ. **τὰ αὐτὰ** γράφειν ὑμῖν ἐμοὶ μὲν οὐκ ὀκνηρόν, ὑμῖν δὲ ἀσφαλές.	Finally, my brothers and sisters, rejoice in the Lord. For me to write *the same things* to you is not troublesome, but for you it is safe [i.e., a safe course of action].

αὐτός = Intensification, "-self"

6.24. The second use of αὐτός as an adjective does not identify but indicates emphasis. This was one of the linguistic tools that speakers and writers had to indicate what was most prominent in their discourse. In English this is often equivalent to the use of *himself* (or *herself*, *itself*, *themselves*, etc.). When it is used to indicate emphasis, αὐτός modifies another word with which it agrees in gender, number, and case (just like any other adjective), but it is usually *not* preceded by an article (predicate position; see §6.11). It is almost always in the nominative case (239× of 243× in the NT), and it usually modifies the subject of the sentence.[9]

6.25. Examples of the Adjectival Intensifying Use of αὐτός

John 4:2, Ἰησοῦς **αὐτὸς** οὐκ ἐβάπτιζεν ἀλλ' οἱ μαθηταὶ αὐτοῦ.	Jesus *himself* was not baptizing, but his disciples [were baptizing].

In this passage, αὐτός modifies a noun with which it agrees in gender, number, and case. As usual, it is in the nominative case modifying the subject, and it is apparently in predicate position.[10] But what about αὐτοῦ? Why is

9. The subject that is modified by αὐτός functioning as an adjective does not have to be third person. It may modify a second-person pronoun: σὺ αὐτὸς λέγεις τῷ ἀδελφῷ σου ("You *yourself* speak to your brother"). Or the subject may come from the verb (i.e., there may not be a separate word in the sentence that serves as the subject): αὐτὸς λέγεις τῷ ἀδελφῷ σου ("You *yourself* speak to your brother"). Both of these sentences are intensive statements, but the first gives greater prominence to the statement by using the explicit second-person pronoun as the subject along with the intensive use of αὐτός.

10. Without an article it is not possible to determine this grammatically, but it makes good sense as such here.

it not translated "themselves" in this verse? (The answer is in the footnote, but try to figure it out for yourself before you check.)[11]

John 5:36, **αὐτὰ** τὰ ἔργα ἃ ποιῶ μαρτυρεῖ περὶ ἐμοῦ.	The works *themselves* which I am doing testify concerning me.
Mark 12:36, **αὐτὸς** Δαυὶδ εἶπεν ἐν τῷ πνεύματι τῷ ἁγίῳ.	David *himself* spoke by the Holy Spirit.
Josh. 4:9, ἔστησεν (set up) δὲ Ἰησοῦς καὶ ἄλλους δώδεκα λίθους ἐν **αὐτῷ** τῷ Ἰορδάνῃ.	Now Joshua also set up twelve other stones in the Jordan [River] *itself.*

ἀδελφός as "Brother or Sister"

In lesson 2 you learned that the vocabulary word ἀδελφός means "male sibling (i.e., 'brother'); in an extended sense, one with common interests, community fellow." The common translation glosses listed were "brother; compatriot, 'brother(s) and/or sister(s).'" The example in 1 Cor. 1:10 is the first time you have seen this word used with reference to both men and women—fellow believers. In contemporary English, *brother(s)* is a gender-specific term for males, but in Koine Greek, ἀδελφός could be used as an inclusive term, "brother or sister" or "brothers and sisters." The original context must determine whether a gender-inclusive or a gender-specific reference is intended. Not every use is gender-inclusive (see, e.g., Acts 2:37, where ἀδελφοί refers only to men), but some clearly refer to both men and women, such as the example given from 1 Cor. 1:10 (for the singular, see James 4:11). Sometimes "fellow believer" or "fellow Christian" is a suitable way to express the meaning. Some recent English Bible translations reflect current English usage, either in the text (e.g., NIV, NLT, CEB) or in a footnote (e.g., ESV, but only for ἀδελφοί); a few translations (e.g., HCSB) retain the traditional "brother," regardless of the referent.

Now You Try It

6.26. These examples include several different uses of αὐτός. They are not marked, so you must decide how each one is functioning.

John 14:11, πιστεύετέ μοι ὅτι ἐγὼ ἐν τῷ πατρὶ καὶ ὁ πατὴρ ἐν ἐμοί· εἰ δὲ μή, διὰ τὰ ἔργα αὐτὰ πιστεύετε.	

This sentence introduces a grammatical pattern that you have not seen yet. In the first clause the pronoun μοι is in the dative case, but it functions as the *direct* object of the verb πιστεύετε, not the indirect object. The disciples are

11. Αὐτοῦ does not agree with a noun; οἱ μαθηταί is nominative plural, but αὐτοῦ is genitive singular.

to believe Jesus when he describes his relationship to the Father (the dative indicates the object of their faith, and the ὅτι clause the content). Some verbs customarily or optionally may take their direct object in the dative or genitive case rather than the usual accusative. See the fuller explanation in the next chapter ("Objects in Genitive or Dative Cases").

Matt. 17:8, ἐπάραντες (when they raised) δὲ τοὺς ὀφθαλμοὺς αὐτῶν οὐδένα[a] εἶδον (they saw) εἰ μὴ αὐτὸν Ἰησοῦν μόνον.

[a] The lexical form of οὐδένα is οὐδείς. See the paradigm in §12.25.

John 2:23–24, πολλοὶ ἐπίστευσαν εἰς τὸ ὄνομα αὐτοῦ θεωροῦντες (because they saw) αὐτοῦ τὰ σημεῖα ἃ ἐποίει (he did)· αὐτὸς δὲ Ἰησοῦς οὐκ ἐπίστευεν (entrust) αὐτὸν αὐτοῖς διὰ τὸ αὐτὸν[a] γινώσκειν[b] πάντας.

[a] αὐτόν, even though it is accusative, is the *subject* of the infinitive (γινώσκειν). You will understand why after we study infinitives in chap. 22.

[b] διὰ τό + infinitive (γινώσκειν) forms a causal statement, "because . . ."

Adverbs

6.27. Thus far in this chapter we have studied words that modify nouns, that is, adjectives. Now it is time to look at one of the ways a writer or speaker can add a little variety to verbs. The words that modify or describe verbs are called *adverbs.*

Most English speakers studying Greek can define an adverb as a word that modifies a verb. Some will also recognize that adverbs can modify other words such as other adverbs, adjectives, prepositions, or larger word units. Greek adverbs are similar in function, and like English adverbs, they do not decline. That is, in contrast to the adjectives earlier in this chapter, adverbs have only one ending rather than a set of endings. The most common ending for Greek adverbs is -ως (similar to the English *-ly* suffix).[12] This ending is added to an adjective to create the adverb.[13] Thus in English we have the

Summary of αὐτός

Function	Usual Position	English Equivalent
Pronoun	—	he, she, it
Adjective: identifying	attributive	same
Adjective: intensive	predicate	self

12. The most common way to form an adverb in English is to add an *-ly* suffix to an adjective, but not all adverbs in English have such a suffix (e.g., *then, downward*). Nor are all English words ending with *-ly* adverbs (e.g., *manly, fly*), and neither are all Greek words that end with -ως (e.g., αἰδώς, "respect"—a noun; Ἀμώς, "Amos"—a proper noun; γέλως, "laughter"—a noun; and εἰδώς, "knowing"—a participle).

13. There will be some apparent spelling anomalies at the end of the stem, but that is usually the case with adverbs formed from third-declension adjectives. Technically, the ending is added to the genitive plural form of the adjective.

adjective *nice* and the adverb *nicely*. So in Greek we have similar formations, which include the following:

Adjective		Adverb
ἁγνός, "pure"	▶	ἁγνῶς, "purely"
ἄδικος, "unjust"	▶	ἀδίκως, "unjustly"
βραδύς, "slow"	▶	βραδέως, "slowly"
δίκαιος, "just, righteous"	▶	δικαίως, "justly, righteously"
ἔσχατος, "last"	▶	ἐσχάτως, "lastly, finally"
ἕτερος, "other, different"	▶	ἑτέρως, "otherwise, differently"
ἰσχυρός, "strong"	▶	ἰσχυρῶς, "strongly"
καινός, "new"	▶	καινῶς, "newly"
κακός, "bad, evil, wicked"	▶	κακῶς, "badly, evilly, wickedly"
μέγας, "large, great"	▶	μεγάλως, "greatly"
μωρός, "foolish"	▶	μωρῶς, "foolishly"
ὅλος, "whole, complete"	▶	ὅλως, "wholly, completely"
ὅμοιος, "like, similar"	▶	ὁμοίως, "likewise, similarly"
ταχύς, "quick"	▶	ταχέως, "quickly"
φανερός, "clear, plain"	▶	φανερῶς, "clearly, plainly"

6.28. Many of these -ως adverbs describe the manner in which the action of the verb is performed. Other suffixes that are also used to create adverbs might express time (-οτε), source (-θεν), position (-ω), or frequency (-ις),[14] and others have no distinctive suffix at all. The best way to identify an adverb is through learning the most common ones and by using the lexicon for the others. The syntax of adverbs is flexible, but it is common for adverbs of time to precede the word modified, while adverbs of place typically follow the word modified. Other types of adverbs can be found in either position.

The most common word in Koine texts (other than the article), the conjunction καί, can also be used as an adverb. As a conjunction, καί is most commonly equivalent to the English "and" or "but"; it always joins two equal grammatical pieces (two nouns, two verbs, two phrases, two clauses, etc.). When the elements standing on either side of καί are *not* grammatically equal, then καί is being used adverbially and means "even" or "also."

Adverbs can also be used substantivally (as a noun). In these instances an article is used as a *nominalizer* to indicate that the adverb is being used as a noun. For example, the adverb ἄνω, "up, above," can be used as a noun: **τὰ ἄνω** ζητεῖτε ("Seek *the things above*," Col. 3:1); the neuter plural article tells us that it is to

14. Examples of these include τότε, "then" (time); ἄνωθεν, "from above" (source); ὄπισω, "behind" (position); and δίς, "twice" (frequency).

"the things" that are above that the writer refers. Or in Luke 1:48, ἀπὸ **τοῦ νῦν** μακαριοῦσίν με means "from *the present time* they will bless me" (the adverb νῦν means "now," thus "the now time," or "the present time").

6.29. *Examples of Adverbs*

Mark 1:45, ἤρχοντο πρὸς αὐτὸν **πάντοθεν**.	They came to him *from everywhere*.
Mark 2:25, λέγει αὐτοῖς, **Οὐδέποτε** ἀνέγνωτε τί ἐποίησεν Δαυίδ;	He said to them, "Have you *never* read what David did?"
Mark 3:1, εἰσῆλθεν **πάλιν** εἰς τὴν συναγωγήν.	He entered *again* into the synagogue.
Mark 7:6, **Καλῶς** ἐπροφήτευσεν Ἠσαΐας περὶ ὑμῶν τῶν ὑποκριτῶν.	Isaiah prophesied *well* [i.e., *correctly*] concerning you hypocrites.
Gen. 7:4, **ἔτι** γὰρ ἡμερῶν ἑπτὰ ἐγὼ ἐπάγω ὑετὸν ἐπὶ τὴν γῆν.	For *yet* seven days [and] I will bring rain on the earth [i.e., *within* seven days, I will bring . . .].

6.30. *Now You Try It*

Matt. 4:8, **Πάλιν** παραλαμβάνει αὐτὸν ὁ διάβολος εἰς ὄρος ὑψηλὸν **λίαν**.

There are two adverbs in this sentence; the first modifies the verb, the second an adjective.

Mark 16:2, **λίαν πρωῒ** ἔρχονται ἐπὶ τὸ μνημεῖον.

The adverb λίαν modifies another adverb, πρωΐ, which in turn modifies the verb, ἔρχονται ("they came").

Rom. 1:9, **ἀδιαλείπτως** μνείαν ὑμῶν ποιοῦμαι (I am making).

Matt. 26:71, λέγει **τοῖς ἐκεῖ**, Οὗτος ἦν (he was) μετὰ Ἰησοῦ τοῦ Ναζωραίου.

Exod. 2:13, Διὰ τί[a] σὺ τύπτεις τὸν **πλησίον**;

[a] Διὰ τί, "why?"

6.31. Advanced Information for Reference: Diagramming Adverbs

Rom. 3:21, **Νυνὶ** δὲ χωρὶς νόμου δικαιοσύνη θεοῦ πεφανέρωται.

But the righteousness of God is *now* revealed apart from the law.

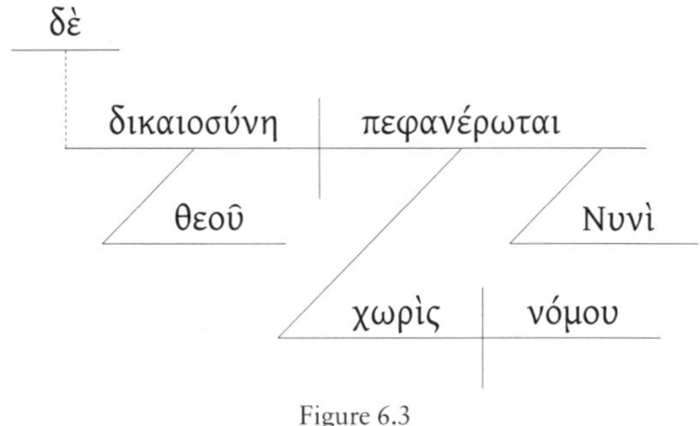

Figure 6.3

The Negatives

6.32. Greek has a number of ways of expressing negation, but the most common is the use of a negative adverb, either οὐ or μή. There are multiple forms of these two basic words. In the case of οὐ, the spelling will change depending on the following word. If the following word begins with a vowel with a smooth breathing, it takes the form οὐκ; before a word with a rough breathing, it is οὐχ. (This difference is simply for euphony; it does not affect the meaning.) There are also compound forms such as οὐδείς/μηδείς, οὔπω/μήπω, οὐδέπω/μηδέπω, and οὐθείς/μηθείς. (See your lexicon for these forms.)

The words οὐ and μή are synonymous in meaning, but they are typically used in different contexts. Most verbs are negated with the negative adverb οὐ, but some kinds of verbs require μή.[15] All you need to know now is that both οὐ and μή negate the statement in which they occur. Remember that these words are adverbs, so they will normally negate verbs (not nouns).

6.33. There is one additional use of the negative in rhetorical questions that is important to remember. If speakers want to imply a particular answer to a yes or no question, they can do so by their choice of negatives. In questions phrased in the indicative mood, using οὐ implies a positive/yes answer, but using μή implies a negative/no answer. For example, if I were to ask you about your preparation for a Greek exam, I could phrase my question one of two ways in English: "You studied for this exam, didn't you?" or "You didn't study for this exam, did you?" The first implies a positive answer—I am assuming that you did study (your exam score demonstrated it). The second question also makes an

15. You will learn later what the difference is. If you are dying to know now, indicative-mood verbs normally take οὐ, but all other moods (e.g., subjunctive, imperative, etc.) use μή.

assumption: it assumes, based on your score, that you did not study. The word order in the English sentences implies the answer.

Greek can make this same distinction, but word order is not useful in this case, since word order is not generally semantic in Greek. Instead, οὐ is used in questions in which the speaker wants to imply a positive answer, but μή is selected to imply a negative answer.[16] (The various forms of οὐ and μή carry the same implications.) The negative will often (though not always) stand at the beginning of such a rhetorical question.

Consider the following examples and notice the implications of the choice of οὐ or μή in each case. You will want to check the context of each of these (use an English Bible) to understand the implications of the speaker's choice of negatives.[17]

6.34. Examples of Negatives in Questions

John 9:40, **Μὴ** καὶ ἡμεῖς τυφλοί ἐσμεν;	"We are *not* blind also, are we?"

The implication of the question with μή in this verse could be paraphrased, "You can't mean, can you, that we are also blind?!"

Mark 6:3, **οὐχ** οὗτός ἐστιν ὁ τέκτων, ὁ υἱὸς τῆς Μαρίας καὶ ἀδελφὸς Ἰακώβου καὶ Ἰωσῆτος καὶ Ἰούδα καὶ Σίμωνος; καὶ **οὐκ** εἰσὶν αἱ ἀδελφαὶ αὐτοῦ ὧδε πρὸς ἡμᾶς;	"This is the carpenter, is*n't* it? The son of Mary and the brother of James and Joses and Jude and Simon? And his sisters are here with us, are*n't* they?
Gen. 37:13, εἶπεν Ἰσραὴλ πρὸς Ἰωσήφ, **Οὐχ** οἱ ἀδελφοί σου ποιμαίνουσιν ἐν Συχέμ; δεῦρο ἀποστείλω σε πρὸς αὐτούς.	Israel said to Joseph, "Your brothers are pasturing [the flocks] in Shechem, are*n't* they? Come, I will send you to them."

6.35. Now You Try It

Luke 17:17, ὁ Ἰησοῦς εἶπεν (said), **Οὐχὶ** οἱ δέκα ἐκαθαρίσθησαν (were cleansed); οἱ δὲ ἐννέα ποῦ;	
1 Cor. 12:29–30, **μὴ** πάντες[a] ἀπόστολοι;[b] **μὴ** πάντες προφῆται; **μὴ** πάντες διδάσκαλοι; **μὴ** πάντες δυνάμεις;[c] **μὴ** πάντες χαρίσματα[c] ἔχουσιν ἰαμάτων;[c] **μὴ** πάντες γλώσσαις λαλοῦσιν; **μὴ** πάντες διερμηνεύουσιν;[d]	

[a] πάντες, "all" (masc. pl. nom.)

[b] Each verbless clause (a form of the verb εἰμί must be supplied) in these two verses contains two nominatives: one a substantival adjective, and the other a noun. The first nominative in word order is the subject, and the second is the predicate nominative (see §14.13.3).

16. This is one situation in which the negative μή can be used with an indicative verb.

17. The parallel English equivalents given in this section deliberately use a translation that makes the meaning unambiguous. Simpler English equivalents may often be satisfactory.

[c] These words are all third-declension nouns that you will learn later: δυνάμεις, fem. pl. nom. ▶ δύναμις, εως, ἡ, "deed of power" (i.e., one of the words for "miracle" in the NT); χαρίσματα, neut. pl. acc. ▶ χάρισμα, ατος, τό, "gift"; ἰαμάτων, neut. pl. gen. ▶ ἴαμα, ατος, τό, "healing."

[d] A long string of negative rhetorical questions such as this sounds very stilted if translated with the implications spelled out explicitly as above, so standard translations often simplify the questions; e.g., "Are all apostles? Are all prophets? Are all teachers? Do all work miracles? Do all possess gifts of healing? Do all speak with tongues? Do all interpret?" (ESV; cf. NIV; ctr. NASB, NET, which retain the negative implications).

— — — — — — — — — — — — — —

Advanced Information for Reference: Comparative and Superlative Adjectives and Adverbs

6.36. The following material is supplemental, and many instructors will not take time to cover it in class with you. It is provided here as a resource for when you encounter other forms of adjectives. These are not nearly as common as the regular adjectives, but it is important to understand them when you do discover one in your reading. You should at least skim through this material so that you know what is here. Someday you will need it.

Comparative and Superlative Adjectives

6.37. An adjective can have three degrees: positive, comparative, or superlative. The positive degree is the usual, uncompared form of the adjective: "large" (μέγας). The comparative degree denotes the greater of two items: "larger" (μείζων). The superlative degree describes the greatest, or a comparison of three or more: "largest" (μέγιστος). Not all such forms are created the same way, but one common formation is the use of specific suffixes, one set of which is -τερος, -τερα, -τερον (masc., fem., neut.) for comparative and -τατος, -τατη, -τατον for superlative. Another pattern uses -ων, -ιστος for comparative and superlative, respectively. Some words have substitute forms for the comparative and superlative instead of modifying the positive form (see ἀγαθός in the following list; it has two sets of forms). The most common words of these types in both the NT and LXX are listed below. Masculine singular nominative forms are shown.[18]

ἀγαθός ▶ κρείττων ▶ κράτιστος ("strong, stronger, strongest" *or* "good, better, best")[19]

ἀγαθός ▶ βελτίων ▶ βέλτιστα ("good, better, best")

ἐλαχύς ▶ ἐλάσσων ▶ ἐλάχιστος ("little, less, least")

κάλος ▶ κάλλιστος ▶ καλλίστατος ("good, better, best")

18. Not all forms of each word listed here occur in the NT or LXX.

19. The adjective ἀγαθός has several sets of comparatives. The two most commonly used in Koine are listed; there were others in Classical Greek. The κρείττων/κράτιστος set is typically used when the comparison involves strength or force, but βελτίων/βέλτιστα when the comparison involves moral qualities (see further Smyth, *Greek Grammar*, §319).

μέγας ▸ μείζων ▸ μέγιστος ("large, larger, largest" *or* "great, greater, greatest")[20]
μικρός ▸ μικρότερος ▸ μικρότατος ("small, smaller, smallest")
πολύς ▸ πλείων ▸ πλεῖστος ("many, more, most")[21]
πρέσβυς ▸ πρεσβύτερος ▸ πρεσβύτατος ("old, older, oldest")
ὕψος ▸ ὑψηλός ▸ ὕψιστος ("high, higher, highest")

These comparative and superlative forms are declined like the usual adjective forms. The -ος ending in -τερος and -τατος forms is the masculine singular nominative ending. Three sample paradigms of comparative forms are shown to illustrate the ending patterns. One gives the irregular comparative formation using -ων, a second the common comparative -τερος formation. The third is a superlative using -τατος. Only masculine forms are shown here, though the full set of forms for all genders may be used.

Comparative and Superlative Adjectives

	Comparative		Superlative
	μέγας, "great"	ἄξιος, "worthy"	
NS	μείζων	ἀξιώτερος	ἀξιώτατος
GS	μείζονος	ἀξιωτέρου	ἀξιωτάτου
DS	μείζονι	ἀξιωτέρῳ	ἀξιωτάτῳ
AS	μείζονα	ἀξιώτερον	ἀξιώτατον
NP	μείζονες	ἀξιώτεροι	ἀξιώτατοι
GP	μειζόνων	ἀξιωτέρων	ἀξιωτάτων
DP	μείζοσι(ν)	ἀξιωτέροις	ἀξιωτάτοις
AP	μείζονας	ἀξιωτέρους	ἀξιωτάτους

In Koine Greek the superlative degree was dying out, its function being assumed by the comparative. For example, someone might use μείζων when context requires us to understand it as if it were μέγιστος. Most superlative forms have an elative sense, that is, instead of "greatest," the elative sense would be "very great." As usual, context is the key in understanding the meaning of any given statement. A good lexicon will tell you what you need to know about these forms and the variations that are possible.[22]

20. Μέγας is unusual in having two comparative forms. The original comparative was μείζων, but that word had begun to lose its comparative force and was slowly being replaced by μειζότερος, a process only beginning in NT times. Μειζότερος does not occur at all in the LXX and only once in the NT.

21. The full paradigm of the comparative form πλείων is given in app. A.

22. Most comparative and superlative forms appear in the lexicon under the positive form, though a few have their own listing. If you do not find a form in one place, check the other.

Comparative and Superlative Adverbs

6.38. Comparative adverbs use the same comparative morphemes as do comparative adjectives. The most common ending is -τερως (the usual adverb ending -ως replacing the case ending on the comparative adjective ending -τερος)—for example, περισσοτέρως, "even more." Also common is the use of the neuter singular accusative form of the comparative adjective as a comparative adverb; for example, ὕστερον, "later," is the neuter form of ὕστερος, α, ον, "last." To create a superlative, the plural form may be used instead of the singular; for example, βέλτιστα (neut. pl. acc.), "best," functions as the superlative of ἀγαθός. Thus we have σοφῶς (positive, "wisely"), σοφώτερον (comparative, "more wisely"), and σοφώτατα (superlative, "most wisely").

Many comparative and superlative adverbs, however, use nonstandard formations that must be learned or identified with the lexicon. These adverb forms will usually be listed in the lexicon under the adjective. The most common superlative adverb in the NT is μάλιστα, "most of all, especially," and it occurs there only 12 times.[23] The positive form is μάλα ("very"), and the comparative is μᾶλλον ("more"). Other forms include the adverb εὖ, "well," which uses βέλτιον, "better," as the comparative form. Likewise the adverb ἐγγύς, "near," uses either ἐγγύτερον or ἆσσον, "nearer," as the comparative and ἔγγιστα, "nearest," as the superlative.

Forms of μέγας and πολύς

6.39. The adjectives μέγας ("great, large") and πολύς ("much, many") have a few oddities. Both follow the same pattern, which is (mostly) second declension for masculine and neuter and first declension (eta endings) for feminine. The nominative and accusative singular in both masculine and neuter, however, appear to use third-declension endings (which you will learn later). Their forms are as follows:

	Masc.	Fem.	Neut.	Masc.	Fem.	Neut.
NS	πολύς	πολλή	πολύ	μέγας	μεγάλη	μέγα
GS	πολλοῦ	πολλῆς	πολλοῦ	μεγάλου	μεγάλης	μεγάλου
DS	πολλῷ	πολλῇ	πολλῷ	μεγάλῳ	μεγάλῃ	μεγάλῳ
AS	πολύν	πολλήν	πολύ	μέγαν	μεγάλην	μέγα
NP	πολλοί	πολλαί	πολλά	μεγάλοι	μεγάλαι	μεγάλα
GP	πολλῶν	πολλῶν	πολλῶν	μεγάλων	μεγάλων	μεγάλων
DP	πολλοῖς	πολλαῖς	πολλοῖς	μεγάλοις	μεγάλαις	μεγάλοις
AP	πολλούς	πολλάς	πολλά	μεγάλους	μεγάλας	μεγάλα

23. The superlative form μάλιστα occurs only 6 times in the LXX, but 31 times in the Pseudepigrapha, 303 times in Josephus, 259 times in Philo, and 14 times in the Apostolic Fathers.

6.40. Examples of Comparative and Superlative Adjectives

2 Tim. 4:13, φέρε (bring!) τὰ βιβλία **μάλιστα** τὰς μεμβράνας.	Bring the books, *especially* the parchments.
Gal. 4:13, εὐηγγελισάμην ὑμῖν τὸ **πρότερον**.[a]	I preached to you *first*.

[a] The adverb πρότερον often has an article; the meaning is unaffected.

Acts 26:5, τὴν **ἀκριβεστάτην**[a] αἵρεσιν τῆς ἡμετέρας θρησκείας	The *strictest* party of our religion

[a] The superlative suffix can take regular adjective endings; here it is a fem. sg. acc., -τάτην, instead of -τάτος.

Mark 12:31, **μείζων** τούτων[a] ἄλλη ἐντολὴ οὐκ ἔστιν.	There is no other commandment *greater* than these.

[a] With comparative forms (either adjectives or adverbs), it is common to use a genitive-case noun or pronoun to indicate what is being compared. This is called a "genitive of comparison," and the word *than* is supplied with the genitive in translation. Thus μείζων τούτων means "greater than these."

1 Cor. 7:9, **κρεῖττόν** ἐστιν γαμῆσαι ἢ[a] πυροῦσθαι.[b]	It is *better* to marry than to burn [i.e., with sexual desire].

[a] For the word ἤ, see your lexicon; in this instance, it means "than" instead of "or."

[b] Both γαμῆσαι and πυροῦσθαι are infinitive forms that you have not learned yet. In the translation they are "to marry" and "to burn."

Gen. 47:6, ἰδοὺ ἡ γῆ Αἰγύπτου ἐναντίον σού ἐστιν· ἐν τῇ **βελτίστῃ**[a] γῇ κατοίκισον (settle!) τὸν πατέρα (father) σου καὶ τοὺς ἀδελφούς σου.	Behold, the land of Egypt is before you. Settle your father and your brothers in the *best* land.

[a] βέλτιστα (neut. pl. acc.) functions as the superlative adjective of ἀγαθός. Here the form βελτίστῃ is the fem. sg. dat. form to agree with τῇ γῇ (first attributive position).

6.41. Now You Try It

John 4:1, ἤκουσαν (heard) οἱ φαρισαῖοι ὅτι Ἰησοῦς **πλείονας** μαθητὰς ποιεῖ καὶ βαπτίζει ἢ Ἰωάννης.	Who heard? What did they hear? Who is doing the action of βαπτίζει? Who is receiving the action? What word does the adjective πλείονας modify?
Heb. 4:12, ὁ λόγος τοῦ θεοῦ [is] ἐνεργὴς καὶ **τομώτερος** ὑπὲρ πᾶσαν μάχαιραν δίστομον.	What is the subject? How is it restricted? What two equal things does καί connect?

Heb. 7:22, **κρείττονος** διαθήκης γέγονεν[a] ἔγγυος Ἰησοῦς.

What is the subject and the predicate nominative of the linking verb? What is an ἔγγυος, and how is the word described? How is διαθήκης described?

[a] γέγονεν is a linking verb similar to εἰμί, "is."

1 Clem. 13.1, **μάλιστα** μεμνημένοι (remembering) τῶν λόγων τοῦ κυρίου Ἰησοῦ

Let. Aris. 296, ἄξιοι θαυμασμοῦ κατεφαίνοντό (they appeared) μοι καὶ τοῖς παροῦσι (ones present), **μάλιστα** δὲ τοῖς φιλοσόφοις.

— — — — — — — — — — — — — —

6.42. Reading Passage: John 5:39–47

Adjective forms in the reading passage are marked with bold.

How Can You Believe?

39ἐραυνᾶτε (you are searching) τὰς γραφάς, ὅτι (because) ὑμεῖς δοκεῖτε ἐν (in)
αὐταῖς ζωὴν **αἰώνιον** ἔχειν· καὶ ἐκεῖναί εἰσιν αἱ μαρτυροῦσαι (ones that testify)
περὶ (concerning) ἐμοῦ· 40καὶ οὐ θέλετε ἐλθεῖν (to come) πρός με ἵνα (that)
ζωὴν ἔχητε (you should have).

41Δόξαν παρὰ (from) ἀνθρώπων οὐ λαμβάνω, 42ἀλλὰ ἔγνωκα (I know) ὑμᾶς
ὅτι (that) τὴν ἀγάπην τοῦ θεοῦ οὐκ ἔχετε ἐν ἑαυτοῖς. 43ἐγὼ ἐλήλυθα (have
come) ἐν τῷ ὀνόματι (name) τοῦ πατρός (Father) μου, καὶ οὐ λαμβάνετέ με·
ἐὰν (if) **ἄλλος** ἔλθῃ (should come) ἐν τῷ ὀνόματι τῷ **ἰδίῳ**, ἐκεῖνον λήμψεσθε
(you will receive). 44πῶς δύνασθε (are able) ὑμεῖς πιστεῦσαι (to believe) δόξαν
παρὰ ἀλλήλων λαμβάνοντες (when you receive), καὶ τὴν δόξαν τὴν παρὰ[a] τοῦ
μόνου θεοῦ οὐ ζητεῖτε; 45μὴ δοκεῖτε (think!) ὅτι (that) ἐγὼ κατηγορήσω (will
accuse) ὑμῶν πρὸς (to/before) τὸν πατέρα (Father)· ἔστιν ὁ κατηγορῶν (one
who accuses) ὑμῶν[b] Μωϋσῆς, εἰς ὃν[c] ὑμεῖς ἠλπίκατε (hope). 46εἰ γὰρ ἐπιστεύετε
(you had believed) Μωϋσεῖ, ἐπιστεύετε (you would have believed) ἂν[d] ἐμοί·[e]
περὶ (concerning) γὰρ ἐμοῦ ἐκεῖνος (he) ἔγραψεν (wrote). 47εἰ δὲ τοῖς ἐκείνου
(his) γράμμασιν (writings, NPD) οὐ πιστεύετε, πῶς τοῖς **ἐμοῖς** ῥήμασιν (words,
NPD) πιστεύσετε (you will believe);

[a] τὴν παρά, "which is from"

[b] For an explanation of the genitive case of ὑμῶν, see §7.23.

[c] εἰς ὅν, "in whom"

[d] The word ἄν ("then") is in a postpositive position, so in an English equivalent it would be understood before the preceding verb, ἐπιστεύετε.

[e] For an explanation of the dative case of ἐμοί, see §7.23.

6.43. Vocabulary for Chapter 6

Part of Speech	Definition	Possible Glosses	Frequency	
Word			NT	LXX
Adjectives				
ἅγιος, α, ον	Set apart for deity	holy (adj.); God's people, saints (subst.)	233	832
Ἰουδαῖος, αία, αῖον	Jewish/Judean either by birth/ethnicity or by practice (adj.); Jew/Judean (subst.)	Jewish/Judean (adj.); Jew/Judean (subst.)	195	207
ἄλλος, η, ο	That which is distinct from another entity	other, another	155	108
πρῶτος, η, ον	Having primary position in a sequence, either temporally, numerically, or in prominence	first, earlier	155	223
νεκρός, ά, όν	Without life, "dead" (adj.); one who is dead, "corpse" (subst.) (both adj. and noun may refer to physical or spiritual/moral death)[a]	dead (adj.); dead body, corpse (subst.)	128	83
ἴδιος, α, ον	Belonging to oneself	one's own	114	79
μόνος, η, ον	The only entity in a class or the only such entity that is present	only, alone	114	164
δίκαιος, α, ον	In accord with standards for acceptable behavior, that which is obligatory in view of certain requirements of justice; conforming to the laws of God, being in a right relationship with God; substantivally, one who has been declared right before God	upright, fair; righteous, just	79	435
δυνατός, ή, όν	Having power or competence; capable of being realized, to be possible	able, capable, powerful; it is possible (neut.)	32	185
Adverbs				
οὕτως	A particle that introduces a description of the manner or way in which something is done	in this manner, thus, so	208	852
καθώς	A marker of similarity or manner	as, even as, just as	182	279
τότε	A temporal adverb that specifies sequence (A then B) or refers to a specific time (either past or future)	then, at that time, when	160	293
νῦν	A temporal adverb that indicates present time	now (adv.); the present (subst.)	147	701
πάλιν	An adverb that indicates repetition or additional occurrence	again, once more	141	88
ἐκεῖ	An adverb of place indicating a location in contrast to "here"	there, in that place	105	798

[a] *CL* lists νεκρός as two separate entries, one an adjective (νεκρός, ά, όν), the other a noun (νεκρός, ου, ὁ). BDAG has a single listing under the adjective form with two divisions, adjective and noun.

6.44. Key Things to Know for Chapter 6

What is the most important thing to know about Greek adjectives?

What endings do adjectives use?

When using a lexicon, how can you distinguish nouns from adjectives?

What are the four positions of adjectives, and how does that affect their meaning?

Do you understand and can you distinguish the two uses of αὐτός as an adjective?

What is the most common way to create an adverb in Greek?

When does καί function as an adverb, and what does it mean in that situation?

How can a Greek speaker/writer imply a yes or no answer to a question?

7

VERBS: PART 2

Simple Aorist Verbs

7.1. You have already met one of the basic verb forms in Greek, the present active indicative. This chapter will introduce you to another important form, the aorist active indicative. It is the most common verb form in the NT and in the LXX.[1]

First Aorist Active Indicative Verbs

7.2. The aorist tense-form functions as the main story-line verb in narrative. When recounting a story in Greek, writers typically sketch the main events by using aorist verbs. Observe how this works in Mark 6. Aorist indicative forms are in bold.

Verbal Forms in Mark 6:39–44

He commanded them all to sit down in groups on the green grass.
So **they sat down** in groups, by hundreds and by fifties.
    And having taken the five loaves and the two fish,
    looking up to heaven
he blessed
and **broke** the loaves
    and gave them to his disciples to set before them.
And **he divided** the two fish among all [of them].

1. The aorist active indicative form accounts for 4,409 of 9,939 active indicative verbs in the NT (44%) and 24,607 of 43,372 in the LXX (57%). For comparison, the next most common in the NT is the present active indicative with 3,141 (32%) and the future active indicative in the LXX, 8,057 (19%).

And **they** all **ate**
and **were satisfied.**
And **they took up** twelve baskets full of broken pieces and of the fish.
And the ones who ate the loaves were five thousand men.

The aorist tense-form is, in many ways, the default verb form—one that writers use when they do not want to say anything in particular about a situation, only that it occurs (or has occurred or will occur). Sometimes students think the aorist is quite esoteric and significant. This is often because we do not have an aorist form in English, so it sounds a bit magical. You may even hear people say things like "It's an aorist, therefore . . . ," as if the aorist were particularly important. That is a bit ironic since it is the least significant of all the tense-forms; it is the normal form one uses when the nuances of the other tense-forms are not important. We will talk more about this in a later chapter. In the example from Mark 6 above, it is the normal way to tell a story. So, we need to learn what this form looks like.

Aorist Morphology

7.3. Greek has two ways to create an aorist tense-form. They are called *first aorist* and *second aorist*. For this chapter we will be concerned with only the first aorist; we will study the second aorist in chapter 18.

Formula for First Aorist Active Indicative Verbs

augment + stem + form marker σα + B personal endings

Augment

7.4. An *augment* is the letter epsilon prefixed to the front of a word as part of the formula to indicate the tense-form of the verb and to specify that secondary endings are to be used rather than primary.[2] Only indicative-mood verbs have augments.[3] The various tense-forms of the indicative are classed in two groups depending on whether or not an augment is used.

Primary Forms (*do not* have augment)	Secondary Forms (*do* have augment)
present	imperfect
future	aorist
perfect	pluperfect

2. It is often said that the augment is a past-time marker. It is true that many verbs that have augments do refer to past time, but that is because the verb forms that have augments as part of their spelling are typically used in statements that refer to the past (e.g., historical narrative).

3. Outside the indicative mood the secondary endings are not normally used. For example, the aorist subjunctive has no augment and uses primary endings even though aorist indicatives always use secondary endings.

Stem and Form Marker

7.5. The *stem* of a first aorist verb is the same as the lexical form; that is, the base part of the verb will be spelled just as it is in the lexicon. A *form marker* is a syllable (technically, a morpheme) added to the end of the stem of a verb to identify it as being a particular tense-form.[4] Not all tense-forms use form markers, and there are several different form markers for the various tense-forms. If you compare the formula you learned for the present active indicative verbs in chapter 5 with this new formula for first aorist active indicative verbs, you will notice that the first aorist tense-form has no connecting vowel. The first aorist form does not need another vowel to connect the stem and ending, since the form marker (σα) already has its own vowel.

The first aorist is one of the easiest verb forms to recognize: if there is a σα between the stem and the ending of a verb, it must be an aorist. Other aorist forms also use the same σα form marker (e.g., the aorist infinitive, which you will meet later in this chapter), but the σα is still a distinctive marker for an aorist (and more specifically, for a first aorist form).

Personal Endings: The Four-Quad Chart

7.6. As you will recall from chapter 5, there are four basic sets of endings that are used on verbs. These endings indicate person and number. We designate these sets of endings as A, B, C, and D. The four-quad chart is structured very deliberately. On the left side of the chart are those endings that do not use augments. In the indicative these are classed as *primary forms*. The endings on the right side of the chart do use augments and are designated *secondary forms* in the indicative. The two top quadrants consist of endings that normally occur on active-voice forms in contrast to the bottom quadrants, which are usually middle voice. (We have not talked about all these grammatical categories yet, but we will in due time. At this point you need to understand only that there is logical layout in the four quadrants.)

Personal Endings

A. Primary Active	B. Secondary Active
C. Primary Middle	D. Secondary Middle

7.7. You first met the A endings in chapter 5. We are now ready for a new set. The aorist active indicative forms use the B endings. The following chart shows what the B endings look like when used on a first aorist active indicative verb.

4. This morpheme goes by several names. In various grammars you will find it referred to as a tense morpheme, tense suffix, tense formative, aspect morpheme, and so forth.

(First) Aorist Active Indicative of λύω

	Form	f.m. + B p.e.	Gloss	p.e.
1S	ἔλυσα	σα	I loosed	[ν][a]
2S	ἔλυσας	σας	You loosed	ς
3S	ἔλυσε(ν)	σε(ν)	He/she/it loosed	(ν)
1P	ἐλύσαμεν	σαμεν	We loosed	μεν
2P	ἐλύσατε	σατε	You loosed	τε
3P	ἔλυσαν	σαν	They loosed	ν

[a] Most verb forms that use the B endings have a nu in the first singular, but it drops off in the first aorist active indicative. It is nothing you need to worry about now. We will talk about this again in chaps. 15 and 16.

The center column in the table ("f.m. + B p.e.") shows the aorist form marker σα combined with the personal ending. The actual personal endings are shown in the last column ("p.e."). In the third singular form in the table, the nu is placed in parentheses to indicate that it is a movable nu—sometimes it is omitted. The key column that you must memorize is the "Form" column, which begins with ἔλυσα; this set of forms includes the augment, stem, form marker σα, and personal endings as they actually appear in a Greek text.

Meaning

7.8. We will study the aorist tense-form in more detail in later chapters. For now it is enough to know that it can often be represented in English with a simple tense, usually a simple past ("I loosed"), though sometimes a simple present or future will best suit the context ("I loose" or "I will loose"). The aorist simply refers to a situation in summary without indicating anything further about the action.

7.9. *Examples of First Aorist Active Indicative Verbs*

John 8:30, πολλοὶ **ἐπίστευσαν** εἰς αὐτόν.	Many *believed* in him.

Notice how the aorist verb is formed: ἐπίστευσαν is composed of the augment epsilon + the verb stem πίστευ- (from the lexical form πιστεύω) + the aorist form marker σα + the third plural ending nu. If you compare the paradigm form of λύω above, you will discover that the only thing that is different is the stem. Observe the same pattern in the following examples.

Rom. 4:3, τί ἡ γραφὴ λέγει; **Ἐπίστευσεν** δὲ Ἀβραὰμ τῷ θεῷ.	What does Scripture say? "Now Abraham *believed* God."

The dative τῷ θεῷ is functioning as the direct object. For an explanation as to why it is not in the customary accusative case, see "Objects in Genitive or Dative Cases" (§7.23).

2 Kgdms. (2 Sam.) 2:11, Δαυὶδ **ἐβασίλευσεν** ἐν Χεβρὼν ἐπὶ τὸν οἶκον Ἰούδα, ἑπτὰ ἔτη (years) καὶ ἓξ μῆνας (months).	David *reigned* in Hebron over the house of Judah seven years and six months.
Jer. 3:4, οὐχ οἶκόν με **ἐκάλεσας** καὶ πατέρα καὶ ἀρχηγὸν τῆς παρθενίας σου;	Did *you* not *call* me Home and Father and Guide of your youth?[a]

[a] In this context παρθενία probably means "youth," though it could be "virginity" (i.e., when one was young and still a virgin). The Hebrew word translated here by παρθενία is the word for "youth," not "virgin." Read the context of this very metaphorical passage in your English Bible.

7.10. *Now You Try It*

Mark 1:20, καὶ εὐθὺς[a] **ἐκάλεσεν** αὐτούς.

[a] For καὶ εὐθύς, see the note on Mark 1:12 in §4.11.

Gen. 2:8, **ἐφύτευσεν** κύριος ὁ θεὸς παράδεισον ἐν Ἐδέμ.

Isa. 42:6, ἐγὼ κύριος ὁ θεὸς **ἐκάλεσά** σε ἐν δικαιοσύνῃ.

Aorist Active Infinitives

7.11. You will remember that in English, an infinitive is a verb preceded by the word *to*. It simply names an action—for example, "to study." We met present infinitives in chapter 5, and we will talk about their various functions in chapter 22. For now, here is the form of the (first) aorist active infinitive: λῦσαι. You will notice that its formula is quite simple:

Formula for First Aorist Active Infinitives

stem + aorist infinitive marker σαι

The aorist infinitive marker includes the aorist form marker σα. There is no augment; only indicatives have augments.[5] Although there are other uses for the infinitive, for now, just think of it as a simple English infinitive; for example, λῦσαι may be represented in English as "to loose." This is the same as the present infinitive that you met in chapter 5. Since English has only one infinitive, it is not possible to distinguish the various tense-forms of the infinitive in English.

5. Remember that the augment is a marker for secondary personal endings (the B and D quadrants). Non-finite forms (i.e., infinitives and participles) do not use personal endings. Other non-indicative finite forms do not use secondary endings (e.g., the subjunctive mood, which you will learn later), so they do not use augments either.

7.12. *Examples of the Aorist Active Infinitive*

Mark 1:7, οὐκ εἰμὶ ἱκανὸς **λῦσαι** τὸν ἱμάντα τῶν ὑποδημάτων αὐτοῦ. — I am not worthy *to untie* the thong of his sandals.

Matt. 12:10, Εἰ[a] ἔξεστιν τοῖς σάββασιν[b] **θεραπεῦσαι**; — Is it lawful *to heal* on the Sabbath?

[a] The particle εἰ can be used to introduce a question, but it is not represented by a specific word in English.
[b] The plural τοῖς σάββασιν is idiomatic; it is equivalent to the English "Sabbath."

Judg. 14:15, ἦ[a] **πτωχεῦσαι** ἐκαλέσατε ἡμᾶς; — Did you really invite us *to be beggars*?

[a] Watch the accent carefully on this word; it is an adverb, not the comparative particle "or."

7.13. *Now You Try It*

Luke 5:32, οὐκ ἐλήλυθα (I have come) **καλέσαι** δικαίους ἀλλὰ ἁμαρτωλοὺς εἰς μετάνοιαν.

Mark 10:40, τὸ **καθίσαι** ἐκ δεξιῶν μου

7.14. Advanced Information for Reference: Diagramming Infinitives

Deut. 4:26, ὑμεῖς διαβαίνετε τὸν Ἰορδάνην ἐκεῖ **κληρονομῆσαι** αὐτήν. — You are crossing the Jordan *to inherit* it there.

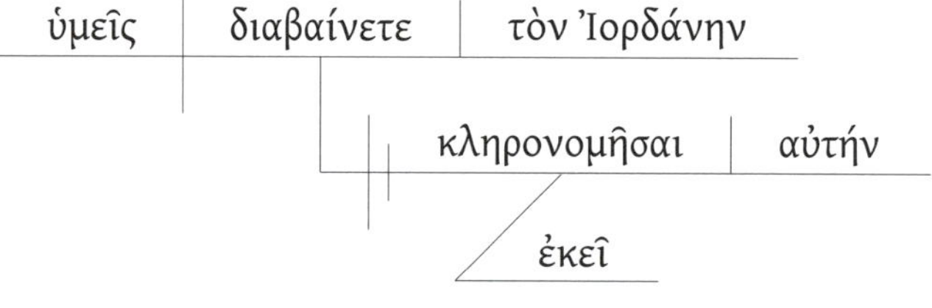

Figure 7.1

Infinitives are diagrammed with a double vertical line in front of the infinitive. Its connection to the rest of the diagram depends on how the infinitive functions. In chapter 22 we will study infinitives and their various functions (and how they are diagrammed) in more detail.

Augment Variations

7.15. The standard form of the augment is the letter epsilon prefixed to the verb stem, but not all augments are standard. Verbs that begin with a short vowel do not use the standard epsilon augment. Instead, the augment lengthens the vowel. Here are the more common patterns that you will see.[6]

α, ε ▸ η
ο ▸ ω

There are also some other augment variations that you will meet in chapter 16. The ones illustrated here are the most common.

Ablaut

The technical term used to describe vowel changes is *ablaut.* This term may be used to describe any vowel that changes its length, either from a long vowel to a short vowel, or (more commonly) from a short vowel to a long vowel or a diphthong. It can also describe a vowel that contracts (two vowels that combine to form a diphthong), or one that drops out (more technically called *elision*), or two vowels being transposed (more technically, *metathesis).* A synonym used in some reference works is *vowel gradation.*

7.16. *Examples of Augment Variations*

Mark 14:64, **ἠκούσατε** τῆς βλασφημίας. — *You heard* the blasphemy!

The genitive τῆς βλασφημίας is functioning as the direct object. For an explanation as to why it is not in the customary accusative case, see "Objects in Genitive or Dative Cases" (§7.23).

Jer. 32:36 (25:36 MT/Eng.), **ὠλέθρευσεν**[a] κύριος τὰ βοσκήματα (pastures) αὐτῶν. — The Lord *laid waste* their pastures.

[a] ὀλεθρεύω, "I destroy, lay waste"

7.17. *Now You Try It*

Mark 11:18, καὶ **ἤκουσαν** οἱ ἀρχιερεῖς καὶ οἱ γραμματεῖς καὶ ἐζήτουν [they were seeking] πῶς αὐτὸν ἀπολέσωσιν [they might destroy].

Gen. 39:19, **ἤκουσεν** ὁ κύριος αὐτοῦ τὰ ῥήματα (words) τῆς γυναικὸς (wife) αὐτοῦ.

6. This also happens sometimes when a word begins with a diphthong (e.g., αι, ει ▸ η). Other times the diphthong remains unchanged.

Aorist Contract Verbs

7.18. By now you have probably seen enough Greek examples to understand that changes from the usual patterns often happen to make words easier or more pleasant to pronounce. Such changes are sometimes described as *euphonic* (εὐ + φωνή, "good sound"). The examples that you have just seen with augments on the front of aorist verbs whose stems begin with a vowel are of just this sort. There is another change like this that takes place at the end of some aorist verbs. Instead of a stem that begins with a vowel, these verbs have stems that end with a short vowel (ε, ο, α). They are called *contract verbs*, and the vowel affected is called the *stem vowel*. In these verbs, when a form marker is added to the stem, the stem vowel lengthens. Just as with augments on the front of the stem, alpha and epsilon lengthen to eta, and an omicron lengthens to omega.

α, ε ▸ η
ο ▸ ω

The principle is not difficult, and it is easy to spot these words. For example, the lexical form γεννάω becomes ἐγέννησα in the first-person singular aorist active indicative form (see fig. 7.2). In this case the stem vowel alpha lengthens to eta when the aorist form marker σα is added.

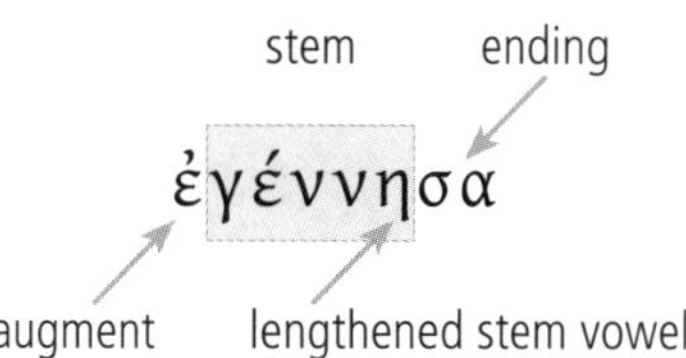

Figure 7.2. Contract Morphology

7.19. The most common aorist form like this in the NT is ἐγέννησεν (third singular). It would look like this in a sentence: Ἀβραὰμ **ἐγέννησεν** τὸν Ἰσαάκ ("Abraham *begat* Isaac," Matt. 1:2). Other examples that are common include the following:

ποιέω ▸ ἐποίησεν (3rd sg.) ▸ ἐποίησαν (3rd pl.)
λαλέω ▸ ἐλάλησα (1st sg.) ▸ ἐλάλησεν (3rd sg.)

And yes, some words can have changes on both ends of the stem. For example, the word ἀγαπάω looks like this in the third singular aorist: ἠγάπησεν. You would read, for example, in John 3:19, **ἠγάπησαν** οἱ ἄνθρωποι τὸ σκότος ("people *loved* darkness").

7.20. *Examples of Aorist Contract Verbs*

Matt. 13:26, ὁ χόρτος καρπὸν **ἐποίησεν**.[a] — The plant *produced* a crop.

[a] ποιέω, "I make, produce"

Matt. 13:34, **ἐλάλησεν**[a] ὁ Ἰησοῦς ἐν παραβολαῖς τοῖς ὄχλοις. — Jesus *spoke* in parables to the crowds.

[a] λαλέω, "I speak"

Matt. 14:3, Ὁ Ἡρῴδης τὸν Ἰωάννην **ἔδησεν**.[a] — Herod *bound* John.

[a] δέω, "I bind"

Mark 15:25, **ἐσταύρωσαν**[a] αὐτόν. — *They crucified* him.

[a] σταυρόω, "I crucify"

Gen. 3:6, εἶδεν (saw) ἡ γυνὴ ὅτι καλὸν τὸ ξύλον καὶ ὅτι ἀρεστὸν τοῖς ὀφθαλμοῖς καὶ ὡραῖόν ἐστιν τοῦ **κατανοῆσαι**.[a] — The woman saw that the tree was good and that (it was) pleasing to the eyes and it was beautiful *to contemplate*.

[a] κατανοέω, "I observe, consider, contemplate"

7.21. *Now You Try It*

Matt. 22:2, **ἐποίησεν** γάμους τῷ υἱῷ αὐτοῦ. — What is the main verb? Is there a subject and or a direct object? How is the dative-case noun functioning?

Mark 6:17, Αὐτὸς γὰρ ὁ Ἡρῴδης **ἐκράτησεν**[a] τὸν Ἰωάννην καὶ **ἔδησεν**[b] αὐτὸν ἐν φυλακῇ. — Can you explain the vowel changes in both verbs? Who seized whom? How is αὐτός functioning? Who bound whom?

[a] κρατέω, "I seize"
[b] δέω, "I bind"

Mark 9:35, **ἐφώνησεν** τοὺς δώδεκα καὶ λέγει αὐτοῖς . . . — Who/what is the subject of the sentence? What is the direct object? Why is αὐτοῖς dative?

Luke 7:5, τὴν συναγωγὴν αὐτὸς **ᾠκοδόμησεν** ἡμῖν. — Who/what is the subject of the sentence? Can you explain the omega with iota subscript on the front of the verb? (What is the lexical form?) What is the direct object? Is ἡμῖν first person or second? What case is ἡμῖν? How would you express that in English?

Luke 9:11, οἱ ὄχλοι **ἠκολούθησαν** αὐτῷ. — How do you parse ἠκολούθησαν? Who is doing the action? Why is αὐτῷ in the dative case?

Gen. 24:23, εἰ ἔστιν τόπος ἡμῖν **καταλῦσαι;**

What is the case of τόπος, and how is it functioning in the sentence? Why is ἡμῖν in the dative case? Which of the meanings for καταλύω best fits this context? (You may need to check the larger context in an English Bible.)

Remember that εἰ may be used to introduce a question (see the note at Matt. 12:10 in §7.12). The subject comes from the verb.

Examples of the Aorist

7.22. The following examples include some of each of the various forms of the aorist that you met in this chapter. These forms are not in boldface as in the earlier examples, so that you can practice identifying them.

John 19:10, λέγει οὖν αὐτῷ ὁ Πιλᾶτος, Ἐμοὶ οὐ λαλεῖς; ἐξουσίαν ἔχω ἀπολῦσαί σε καὶ ἐξουσίαν ἔχω σταυρῶσαί σε.

Titus 1:3, ἐφανέρωσεν δὲ καιροῖς ἰδίοις τὸν λόγον αὐτοῦ.

Heb. 11:20, εὐλόγησεν Ἰσαὰκ τὸν Ἰακὼβ καὶ τὸν Ἠσαῦ.

Heb. 13:7, ἐλάλησαν ὑμῖν τὸν λόγον τοῦ θεοῦ.

1 John 2:7, Ἀγαπητοί, οὐκ ἐντολὴν καινὴν γράφω ὑμῖν ἀλλ᾽ ἐντολὴν παλαιάν· ἡ ἐντολὴ ἡ παλαιά ἐστιν ὁ λόγος ὃν[a] ἠκούσατε.

[a] ὅν, "which"

Rev. 3:10, ἐτήρησας τὸν λόγον τῆς ὑπομονῆς μου.

Rom. 15:27, ὀφείλουσιν λειτουργῆσαι αὐτοῖς.

In the following verses an English equivalent has been provided, since these non-NT texts may not be as familiar. Cover the verses in the English column as you work on each passage. Use the English only to check your work after you think you understand each verse.

Gen. 1:1, Ἐν ἀρχῇ ἐποίησεν ὁ θεὸς τὸν οὐρανὸν καὶ τὴν γῆν.	In the beginning God made the heaven and the earth.
Gen. 2:3, ηὐλόγησεν ὁ θεὸς τὴν ἡμέραν τὴν ἑβδόμην.	God blessed the seventh day.
Ps. 44:8 (45:7 Eng.), ἠγάπησας δικαιοσύνην καὶ ἐμίσησας ἀνομίαν·	You loved righteousness and hated lawlessness.

Objects in Genitive or Dative Cases

7.23. The normal case for a direct object is, as you have already learned, the accusative. Some verbs, however, may take their object in the genitive or dative case. This depends on conventional usage with specific verbs.[7] For example, it is common for verbs that refer to sense perception to take their direct objects in the genitive case. Thus ἀκούω may have either an accusative or a genitive object. The standard Greek lexicon, BDAG, will indicate such usage; shorter lexicons usually do not. There were two examples earlier in this chapter, one with a genitive object (Mark 14:64) and one a dative (Rom. 4:3). Additional examples follow.

Matt. 9:25, ἐκράτησεν **τῆς χειρὸς** αὐτῆς.	He took her *hand*.
Rev. 16:1, ἤκουσα μεγάλης **φωνῆς**.	I heard a loud *voice*.
Luke 1:20, οὐκ ἐπίστευσας **τοῖς λόγοις** μου.	You did not believe my *words*.
1 Cor. 1:4, Εὐχαριστῶ **τῷ θεῷ** μου πάντοτε.	I always thank my *God*.

Subjects

7.24. There are several situations in which you should pay particular attention to the subject of a sentence or instances in which the subject might not be the form you expect.

Personal Pronouns as Subjects

7.25. If every Greek verb has a pronoun built in, then why does Greek even have pronouns? And what difference does it make if a verb has both a built-in pronoun/subject and a separate nominative-case pronoun?

7. Some such conventions may be simply idiomatic; others may have some semantic association. The reasons go well beyond the needs of first-year study. When you want to pursue the question further, see Wallace, *Greek Grammar*, 131–34, 171–73; Blass, Debrunner, and Funk, *Greek Grammar*, §§169–78, 202.

First, pronouns can be used for other things in a sentence besides subjects, so Greek would need pronouns anyway. But what about sentences like this one from Mark?

Mark 14:58, **Ἡμεῖς** ἠκούσαμεν αὐτοῦ λέγοντος (saying) ὅτι **Ἐγὼ** καταλύσω (I will destroy) τὸν ναὸν τοῦτον.	*We* heard him saying, "*I* will destroy this temple."

Wouldn't the following sentence say the same thing?

ἠκούσαμεν αὐτοῦ λέγοντος ὅτι Καταλύσω τὸν ναὸν τοῦτον.

In one sense, yes, the two sentences are semantically identical. Nothing changes in regard to the action and the subject. There is, however, some subtle emphasis when the pronoun is added. It is not the level of shouting, but the speaker does focus attention more particularly on the subject by adding what is otherwise a superfluous pronoun. This is usually the case with first- and second-person pronouns.

7.26. In the example above from Mark 14 you can almost hear the statement: *We* heard him say, "*I* will destroy this temple." The speakers are witnesses in a court case, emphasizing the reliability of their testimony—which focuses on the legal charge: *we* heard *him* say this.

The third person is less distinctive—unless it is functioning as an identifying or intensive pronoun, or if the context suggests emphasis. For example, it is possible to indicate a contrast by the use of ἀλλά or δέ with a pronoun in two coordinated clauses. The contrast comes, not from the occurrence of αὐτός, but from the contrasted clauses. For an example in which αὐτός probably *is* somewhat emphatic, consider a statement that you saw in chapter 4.

Mark 1:8, **ἐγὼ** ἐβάπτισα (baptized) ὑμᾶς ὕδατι (with water), **αὐτὸς** δὲ βαπτίσει (will baptize) ὑμᾶς ἐν πνεύματι ἁγίῳ.	*I* baptized you with water, but *he* will baptize you with the Holy Spirit.

Sometimes it may be appropriate to try to represent this subtle emphasis in English (perhaps with italics or a vocal inflection), but often it is not necessary—and doing so would frequently sound stilted. Do, however, remember the emphasis as you interpret the text; it will sometimes help you get a better feel for what is being said.

Neuter Plural Subjects with Singular Verbs

7.27. Here is a situation that you will want to remember: A neuter plural subject *may* (and usually does) take a singular verb. The best way to understand this is to look at some examples.

John 7:7, **τὰ ἔργα** αὐτοῦ πονηρά **ἐστιν.** — Its *works are* evil.

Although the verb in this sentence (ἐστιν) is singular, the subject (τὰ ἔργα) is plural. In these cases we translate following the number of the subject (that is, translate as if the verb were plural): "Its works are evil" (not "its work is evil"). The antecedent of αὐτοῦ is ὁ κόσμος in verse 7a (not included here), so translate "its," not "his."

John 6:63, **τὰ ῥήματα** πνεῦμά **ἐστιν.** — *The words are* spirit.

John 10:3, **τὰ πρόβατα**[a] τῆς φωνῆς αὐτοῦ **ἀκούει.**[b] — *The sheep hear* his voice.

[a] neut. pl. nom. ▶ πρόβατον, ου, τό, "sheep"

[b] "he/she/it hears"; ἀκούω takes its direct object in the genitive case rather than the usual accusative.

1 John 4:1, δοκιμάζετε (2P, "test!") τὰ πνεύματα εἰ ἐκ τοῦ θεοῦ **ἐστιν** (3S). — Test the spirits [to see] if *they are* from God.

In this example the neuter plural noun is the direct object of the plural verb δοκιμάζετε. The verb in the second clause, ἐστιν, is singular even though it refers to the plural antecedent in the first clause.

Mark 4:4, καὶ **ἦλθεν**[a] **τὰ πετεινὰ**[b] καὶ **κατέφαγεν**[c] αὐτό (it [i.e., the seed]). — The birds *came* and *gobbled* it up.

[a] 3rd sg., "he/she/it came"

[b] neut. pl. nom. ▶ πετεινόν, οῦ, τό, "bird"

[c] 3rd sg., "he/she/it ate" (φάγω [ἐσθίω] = "I eat," but with the intensive κατά prefix = "I gobble up")

The plural subject in the examples above is probably being viewed collectively.[8] Not every neuter plural subject has a singular verb, however. Here is an example of one with a plural verb.

James 2:19, τὰ δαιμόνια **πιστεύουσιν** καὶ **φρίσσουσιν.** — The demons *believe*, and *they shudder.*

Reading Passage: John 18:19–24

7.28. In this passage the aorist verbs you should be able to identify are bold; other aorist forms you have not learned yet are underlined. Five of these forms are numbered and will be explained below.

8. If you want to pursue this further, see Wallace, *Greek Grammar*, 399–400, who says that "since the neuter usually refers to impersonal things (including animals), the singular verb regards the plural subject as a *collective* whole. It is appropriate to translate the subject as a plural as well as the verb, rather than translate both as singulars."

Jesus Interrogated by the High Priest

19 Ὁ οὖν ἀρχιερεὺς (high priest) (1) **ἠρώτησεν** τὸν Ἰησοῦν περὶ (about) τῶν
μαθητῶν αὐτοῦ καὶ περὶ τῆς διδαχῆς αὐτοῦ. 20 (2) ἀπεκρίθη (answered) αὐτῷ
Ἰησοῦς, ⟦Ἐγὼ παρρησίᾳ λελάληκα (have spoken) τῷ κόσμῳ, ἐγὼ πάντοτε
ἐδίδαξα (taught) ἐν (in) συναγωγῇ καὶ ἐν τῷ ἱερῷ, ὅπου πάντες (all) οἱ Ἰουδαῖοι
συνέρχονται (assemble), καὶ ἐν κρυπτῷ **ἐλάλησα** οὐδέν (nothing). 21 τί με ἐρωτᾷς
(are you asking); ἐρώτησον (ask!) τοὺς ἀκηκοότας (ones who heard) τί **ἐλάλησα**
αὐτοῖς· ἴδε οὗτοι (they) οἴδασιν ἃ εἶπον[a] ἐγώ.⟧ 22 ταῦτα δὲ αὐτοῦ εἰπόντος εἷς
παρεστηκὼς τῶν ὑπηρετῶν (3) ἔδωκεν[b] ῥάπισμα τῷ Ἰησοῦ εἰπών (saying),
⟦Οὕτως ἀποκρίνῃ (you answer) τῷ ἀρχιερεῖ (high priest);⟧ 23 (4) ἀπεκρίθη
(answered) αὐτῷ Ἰησοῦς, ⟦Εἰ κακῶς **ἐλάλησα**, μαρτύρησον (testify!) περὶ τοῦ
κακοῦ· εἰ δὲ καλῶς, τί με δέρεις;⟧ 24 (5) ἀπέστειλεν (sent) οὖν αὐτὸν ὁ Ἅννας
δεδεμένον (bound) πρὸς (to) Καϊάφαν τὸν ἀρχιερέα (high priest).

[a] οἴδασιν ἃ εἶπον, "they know what I said"

[b] ταῦτα δὲ αὐτοῦ εἰπόντος εἷς παρεστηκὼς τῶν ὑπηρετῶν ἔδωκεν, "when he said these things, one of the officers standing there gave"

Notice how the five numbered aorist forms function to sketch the basic story line of the narrative. Embedded within the story, in double brackets, are three instances of direct discourse (words quoted directly); these are not part of the story line, but the verbs that introduce them are.

1. The high priest *asked* . . .
2. Jesus answered . . . ⟦Direct discourse⟧
3. He gave . . . saying ⟦Direct discourse⟧
4. Jesus answered . . . ⟦Direct discourse⟧
5. Annas sent . . .

7.29. Vocabulary for Chapter 7

Part of Speech	Definition	Possible Glosses	Frequency	
Word			NT	LXX
Nouns				
φωνή, ῆς, ἡ	Any type of sound or auditory effect; the ability to produce a sound	sound, noise, voice	139	633
ζωή, ῆς, ἡ	Life, that which distinguishes plants and animals from inanimate things; the period between birth and death	life	135	289
Ἰωάννης, ου, ὁ	Personal name of a number of people in the NT and Apocrypha, in the NT most frequently John the Baptizer or John the apostle	John	135	16
ἐκκλησία, ας, ἡ	A gathering of people with common interests, in the LXX with reference to the assembled nation of Israel, in the NT primarily of a group of Christians in an area or of all Christians	assembly, church	114	103

Part of Speech	Definition	Possible Glosses	Frequency	
Word			NT	LXX
ἀλήθεια, ας, ἡ	That which is really so or what actually happened	truth	109	206
Verbs				
ποιέω	To produce something material; to bring about a state or condition	I make, create; I do, perform	568	3,390
πιστεύω	To have confidence in the reliability of something or that something will be granted	I believe, trust, have faith in	241	88
ἀγαπάω	To have an interest in another person to the extent that one determines to contribute to that person's well-being [Often synonymous with φιλέω; see LN §25.43.]	I love	143	283
εἶ	An inflected verb form: 2nd sg. pres. (act.) ind. of εἰμί	you are	92	255
ἐσμέν	An inflected verb form: 1st pl. pres. (act.) ind. of εἰμί	we are	52	46
ἐστέ	An inflected verb form: 2nd pl. pres. (act.) ind. of εἰμί	you are	92	41
δέω	To restrain someone or something (usually) by physical means (may also be metaphorical, e.g., a legal restraint); to fasten objects together	I bind; I tie	43	69
ἐπικαλέω	To give a name to someone or address someone by a name; to call upon someone, to invoke; legal term: to appeal (a ruling), to call a witness	I name, give a name; I call upon, call out; I appeal to (mid.)	30	188
ἰσχύω	To have the necessary resources and capacity to accomplish something; to be in control	I am able/strong, have power, am competent	28	106
προφητεύω	To reveal hidden information (in Scripture this is typically through divine revelation, but it can refer to other agency); to foretell the future	I prophesy, foretell	28	117

7.30. Key Things to Know for Chapter 7

What is an augment?

Can you give the formula for aorist active indicative from memory?

What is the form marker for aorist verbs?

The aorist active indicative forms of λύω must be learned letter-perfect.

What is the aorist active infinitive of λύω?

What happens to an augment when a word begins with a short vowel?

What happens when a form marker is added to a verb stem that ends with a short vowel?

How may a neuter plural subject affect the verb in the sentence?

8

SYNTAX: PART 1

CONJUNCTIONS

8.1. You have learned quite a few grammatical pieces of the Greek language by now, and you have also figured out quite a bit of syntax just by the examples that you have been reading. Now it is time to sketch out more systematically some principles of syntax—the way in which a language organizes the various words into phrases, clauses, statements, and larger units.

Function Words and Content Words

8.2. You will remember from chapter 1 (§1.23) that languages typically contain two types of words, both of which are necessary to communicate meaning. Often it is the *content words* that receive the most attention, because they identify things, actions, and so on. These are words like the nouns and verbs that seem to have fairly specific meaning or a fairly limited range of meanings. Thus we think of English words such as *ball* or *throw* or Greek words such as λόγος and κηρύσσω in somewhat narrow terms. These are the sort of words that are typically the focus of word studies and that some commentaries talk about the most. Other words, however, seem more ambiguous in terms of their meaning. What does our English word *an* mean? Or *was*? What about ὁ or καί or ἐν?[1] These words are called *function words*. They are the seemingly insignificant words that tie

1. You have probably not heard many word studies on these words. There is a story told of a famous (or perhaps, infamous!) sermon preached in the chapel service of a well-known seminary in which the visiting preacher spent much of his time expounding the significance of the Greek word *yap*. That is not a wise thing for a preacher to do when speaking to an audience composed of students and professors who know Greek. (Can you identify the preacher's error? If not, consider the list of conjunctions discussed below.)

all the other words in a sentence together in a systematic, organized whole. If all we had were content words, no meaning would be expressed. For example, what does this word string mean?

worship Zeus provide connection population city

Regardless of what context you might imagine, this string of words has no meaning (except perhaps in a spelling bee), because we do not know the relationship between the words. This example, picked at random from a journal lying on my desk at the moment, needs structure. That is exactly what the full sentence provides.

The worship of Zeus provided a particular connection with the Hellenistic population of the city.

Now that we know how the words relate to each other, we can talk about meaning. The same would be true if we had a string of only function words.

The of a with the of the

Without content words, there is nothing for function words to do. It would be somewhat like tying your shoes without the laces. The knot is what holds things together, but "knot" (a function word in my analogy) is a meaningless concept apart from laces (content words).

Clues to Sentence Structure

8.3. Every language has certain patterns that enable a reader to decode the meaning of a sentence. This involves the patterns of how content words are connected by function words, but also other things such as inflection and word order. There are two equally important things to learn when studying a new language: the meaning of the most common words and the structural clues used by that language.

Sometimes students try to learn Greek just by learning vocabulary (or looking up words in a lexicon) and then guessing at the meaning of a sentence for which they know many of the words. Unfortunately, such guesses are often wrong because they are based on how an *English* sentence might put those words together. Instead you must learn the structural clues for Greek. For example, if you saw the sentence τινὰς ἀνθρώπους βάλλει ὁ ἀπόστολος (a made-up example) and recognized only the lexical meaning of the three content words (ἀνθρώπους, βάλλει, ἀπόστολος; man, throw, apostle), you might conclude that the sentence says, "The man was throwing the apostle." You would be basing your conclusion on English structure. As you have already learned, Greek word order is much more flexible, since meaning is determined not by word order (e.g., subject ▸ verb ▸ object) but by other structural markers. In this case, it is the inflection of the words and the function words that tell you what this sentence actually says: "The apostle was throwing some men."[2] This is quite different from "The man was throwing the apostle." We can tell the difference because of the endings on the words (these inflections include the third-person singular ending on βάλλει, the nominative singular ending on ἀπόστολος along with a matching article, and the accusative plural ending on ἀνθρώπους) and the accusative plural function word τινάς.

You have already learned some of the structural principles, and you will learn more as you continue your study, but for now, we need to examine some of the ways that words are put together and some of the more common types of function words used to mark their relationship.

Phrases, Clauses, and Sentences

8.4. We will start with phrases, clauses, and sentences. We use these terms a lot, but often sloppily and without understanding what they mean. A *clause* is a group of related words that contains a subject and a predicate; that is, it says something (a predicate) about something (a subject). If this clause stands alone (or could stand alone) and forms a complete thought, it is called a *sentence* (i.e., all sentences are also clauses, but the reverse is not necessarily true). By contrast, a *phrase* is a group of related words that does *not* contain both a subject and predicate. The most common distinguishing feature is the lack of a verb (which a clause must have in order to have a predicate),[3] though a phrase may also lack a subject.[4]

Examples of phrases:

into the woods
the valuable book
an especially cold winter day
will be prudently avoided

Examples of clauses (these are also sentences):

Weston ran into the woods.
Sherry shoveled the sidewalk.
Audrey poked the big bug with a stick.
They wanted to name him Tanker.

Main and Subordinate Clauses

8.5. Clauses that can stand alone and that form a complete sentence are called *main clauses* (or *independent clauses*, or *primary clauses*). A *subordinate clause*

2. Yes, I know, that sounds like an odd sentence. Think of a wrestling match.

3. In Greek (less commonly in English) a linking verb may be omitted but implied in a clause. This is called a verbless clause.

4. Since Greek finite verbs have a "back pocket" subject in the personal ending, phrases missing a subject will typically have infinitives or participles, or no verbal form at all.

(also called a *dependent clause* or a *secondary clause*) is a group of related words containing a subject and verb that cannot stand alone, since it does not express a complete thought. Subordinate clauses are usually introduced by a subordinating conjunction.[5] The most common (used more than 100× in the NT) subordinating and coordinating conjunctions in Greek are discussed in detail later in this chapter.

English Examples

8.6. The main/independent clause in each example below is in normal type; subordinate clauses are italicized, and the subordinating conjunction that introduces each dependent clause is in bold. The word in brackets at the end of each sentence classifies the semantic value of the subordinate clause in that sentence (i.e., what sort of information does the subordinate clause add to the sentence?).

If *I go home*, I will eat dinner [conditional].
I will go home **because** *I want to eat dinner* [causal].
I will go home **in order to** *eat dinner* [purpose].
Because *my wife has supper ready*, I am going home [causal].
When *my wife has supper ready*, I will go home immediately, **because** *I am hungry* [temporal; causal].
My wife's supper, **which** *is ready to eat*, is superb [relative].

Conjunctions

8.7. One means that Greek has of marking the relationship between various words, phrases, and clauses is the conjunction. There are function words that connect equal elements (coordinating conjunctions) and others that connect sentence parts that are not equal (subordinating conjunctions). The most common coordinating conjunctions in Greek are καί, δέ, ἀλλά, οὖν, ἤ, and τέ. The most common subordinating conjunctions are ὅτι, ἵνα, εἰ, ἐάν, γάρ, ὡς, καθώς, ὅταν, and ὅτε. Some of these conjunctions (those occurring 500 or more times in the NT and proportionately as often in the LXX) are discussed below. You will meet the others in the course of your study in later lessons. You will notice that the conjunctions do not have a lot of specific meaning, and each one may be used in a wide variety of contexts. It is the context that enables us to identify their meaning and function in each instance.

Because this section has many divisions, there will not be separately titled "Now You Try It" examples, but there will often be one such example with each conjunction below.

5. In Greek there are some other options, such as some participles or participial phrases that translate as subordinate clauses in English.

καί

8.8. Καί, which occurs in the NT more than 8,000 times and in the LXX more than 57,700 times, functions as a connective—an indicator of continuity between clauses or words—but it does not, in itself, tell the reader how the two elements are connected other than that they function equally. This is the default, unmarked coordinating conjunction in Greek. In English this is often expressed by "and," but the context might suggest that it could be "but" (if there is a contrast evident), "then," or some other English word.[6] The elements connected might be two nouns, two verbs, two phrases, and so on.

Connecting Nouns

2 Pet. 1:1, Συμεὼν Πέτρος **δοῦλος καὶ ἀπόστολος** Ἰησοῦ Χριστοῦ	Simon Peter, *a slave and apostle* of Jesus Christ
2 Cor. 1:3, Εὐλογητὸς **ὁ θεὸς καὶ πατὴρ** τοῦ κυρίου ἡμῶν Ἰησοῦ Χριστοῦ.	

Connecting Verbs

Matt. 11:4, ἀπαγγείλατε (Tell!) Ἰωάννῃ ἃ (what) **ἀκούετε καὶ βλέπετε.**	Tell John what you *hear and see.*
1 Kgdms. (1 Sam.) 2:7, κύριος **πτωχίζει**[a] **καὶ πλουτίζει.**	

[a] πτωχίζω, "I make poor"

Connecting Phrases

Mark 3:7–8, ἀπὸ τῆς Γαλιλαίας **καὶ** ἀπὸ τῆς Ἰουδαίας **καὶ** ἀπὸ Ἱεροσολύμων **καὶ** ἀπὸ τῆς Ἰδουμαίας **καὶ** πέραν τοῦ Ἰορδάνου **καὶ** περὶ Τύρον καὶ Σιδῶνα	from Galilee *and* from Judea *and* from Jerusalem *and* from Idumea *and* beyond the Jordan *and* around Tyre and Sidon

This example contains a number of prepositions that you will study in the next chapter. You can figure out easily enough what they must mean from the parallel text. In English, we would generally use a series of commas for all constructions such as are found here. The last καί connects two nouns.

6. Sometimes καί is not a conjunction at all but functions as an adverb: "even, also." You can usually tell these two uses apart by whether or not the two linked elements are grammatically equal (or if there *are* two elements). If they are not equal or there are not two elements, then καί is probably being used adverbially. Here is an example: Mark 4:41, Τίς ἄρα οὗτός ἐστιν ὅτι **καὶ** ὁ ἄνεμος καὶ ἡ θάλασσα ὑπακούει αὐτῷ; ("Who, then, is this that *even* the wind and the sea obey him?") Note that the second καί in this example is a coordinating conjunction ("and").

Connecting Clauses

Mark 1:13, ἦν (he was) μετὰ τῶν θηρίων, **καὶ** οἱ ἄγγελοι διηκόνουν (they were ministering) αὐτῷ.	He was with the wild animals *and* the angels were ministering to him.
Exod. 18:16, διακρίνω ἕκαστον **καὶ** συμβιβάζω αὐτοὺς τὰ προστάγματα τοῦ θεοῦ **καὶ** τὸν νόμον αὐτοῦ.	I judge each one, *and* I teach them the commands of God *and* his law.

The first καί joins two clauses, the second two nouns.

Gen. 5:2, ἄρσεν **καὶ** θῆλυ ἐποίησεν αὐτοὺς **καὶ** εὐλόγησεν αὐτούς.

The first καί connects a compound complement; the second connects two clauses.

Apposition

Greek often uses a construction called *apposition* to explain words. In this construction a substantive (a noun or any other word that functions as a noun)[a] that explains a preceding word is placed in the same case and closely follows the word that it is explaining. You can see this in the example from 2 Cor. 1:3 in §8.8. After mentioning τοῦ κυρίου ἡμῶν, Paul clarifies that he is referring to Jesus by placing Ἰησοῦ Χριστοῦ immediately after that phrase: "our Lord, Jesus Christ." Ἰησοῦ Χριστοῦ is in the genitive case because τοῦ κυρίου ἡμῶν is in the genitive. Not all genitive words, of course, are in apposition; contrast the occurrence of the same genitive phrase Ἰησοῦ Χριστοῦ in the 2 Pet. 1:1 example. There Ἰησοῦ Χριστοῦ does not explain the preceding nominative, ἀπόστολος (Ἰησοῦ Χριστοῦ is not the same as ἀπόστολος), but restricts its reference by indicating whose apostle Paul is: "an apostle of Jesus Christ."

Other examples of apposition include Πιλάτῳ τῷ ἡγεμόνι ("Pilate, the governor," Matt. 27:2) and τῷ θεῷ τῷ σωτῆρί μου ("God, my Savior," Luke 1:47). Sometimes other words intervene between the two items in apposition: ἐν ᾧ ἔχομεν τὴν ἀπολύτρωσιν διὰ τοῦ αἵματος αὐτοῦ, τὴν ἄφεσιν τῶν παραπτωμάτων ("in whom we have redemption through his blood, the forgiveness of sins," Eph. 1:7). In this example, the accusative noun τὴν ἄφεσιν ("forgiveness," a third-declension form you will learn in lesson 11) is in apposition to the preceding accusative, τὴν ἀπολύτρωσιν ("redemption," another third-declension word), even though it is separated by an intervening phrase. Paul explains that redemption consists of this forgiveness.

[a] For the use of an infinitive as a noun in apposition to another noun, see §22.29.c.

δέ

8.9. Δέ is also a coordinating conjunction, like καί, so it also links equal elements; it occurs approximately 2,800 times in the NT and nearly 5,000 times in the LXX. It differs from καί in that there is usually some discontinuity, something different in the two items linked. The difference may be a shift of grammatical subject or of participant, time, or place. This difference sometimes is expressed in English by the word "but" (if a contrast is implied by the context); other times "now" or simply "and" is more suitable. Δέ links phrases and clauses rather than individual words. An unusual feature of δέ is that it is postpositive; that is, it never stands first in its clause.[7] From an English perspective you might view it as a bashful word that tries to hide behind other words. When such a statement is put into English, the conjunction must be moved back to the head of the clause, since English does not use *and* or *but* in a postpositive position.[8]

Mark 5:35–36, [Some people said,] Ἡ θυγάτηρ σου ἀπέθανεν (she died). ὁ **δὲ** Ἰησοῦς λέγει τῷ ἀρχισυναγώγῳ, Μὴ φοβοῦ (be afraid!), μόνον πίστευε (believe!).	Some people said, "Your daughter died." *But* Jesus said to the ruler of the synagogue, "Do not be afraid, only believe."
Gk. Apoc. Ezra 3.4, διὰ σέ, προφῆτά μου, εἶπόν σοι τὴν ἡμέραν, τὴν **δὲ** ὥραν οὐκ εἶπόν σοι.	Because of you, my prophet, I have told you the day, *but* the hour I have not told you.
John 2:23–24, πολλοὶ ἐπίστευσαν εἰς τὸ ὄνομα αὐτοῦ· αὐτὸς **δὲ** Ἰησοῦς οὐκ ἐπίστευεν αὐτὸν αὐτοῖς.	

ὅτι

8.10. Ὅτι occurs nearly 1,300 times in the NT and about 3,800 times in the LXX. This subordinating conjunction has three main functions. First, it may explain what caused something to happen, the reason for the statement in the main clause. This function is often called a *causal* ὅτι and introduces an adverbial clause; it is represented in English as

Direct Discourse and ὅτι

Direct discourse introduced with ὅτι should never use both "that" and quotation marks in English. To do so is redundant; only quotation marks should be used. Indirect discourse should never be represented with quotation marks, since in English these indicate a direct quote; use only "that" in such instances.

7. The word δέ typically is the second or third word in its clause, but it can occur later as well; for example, in 1 John 2:2 it is the fifth word: καὶ αὐτὸς ἱλασμός ἐστιν περὶ τῶν ἁμαρτιῶν ἡμῶν, οὐ περὶ τῶν ἡμετέρων δὲ μόνον ἀλλὰ καὶ περὶ ὅλου τοῦ κόσμου.

8. Similar to δέ, the English conjunction *however* may occur in a postpositive position. For example, in Bilbo's birthday speech he says, "The banquet was very splendid, *however*, though I had a bad cold at the time, I remember, and could only say 'thag you very buch'" (Tolkien, *Lord of the Rings*, book 1, chap. 1).

"because." Second, it may introduce an entire clause that functions as a noun—the clause acts as (takes the place of) a noun. This is sometimes called a *content* ὅτι. In this case the English representation is typically "that." Third, ὅτι can introduce words that have been spoken or thought; this is called a *recitative* ὅτι. Sometimes these are direct quotes; other times they report what was said or thought (but do not quote the words verbatim). In the first case we call the statement *direct discourse* and represent ὅτι with quotation marks; the second is *indirect discourse*, which we introduce with the word "that." Examples of each of these follow:

Acts 10:38, διῆλθεν (he went about) εὐεργετῶν (doing good), **ὅτι ὁ θεὸς ἦν μετ' αὐτοῦ.**	He went about doing good, *because* God was with him. [causal]
1 John 1:5, ἔστιν αὕτη ἡ ἀγγελία, **ὅτι ὁ** θεὸς φῶς ἐστιν.	This is the message, *that* God is light. [content]
Mark 1:37, λέγουσιν αὐτῷ **ὅτι** Πάντες ζητοῦσίν σε.	They said to him, "Everyone is seeking you." [recitative, direct discourse]
John 5:15, ὁ ἄνθρωπος ἀνήγγειλεν (he announced) τοῖς Ἰουδαίοις **ὅτι** Ἰησοῦς ἐστιν ὁ ποιήσας (one who made) αὐτὸν ὑγιῆ.	The man announced to the Jews *that* Jesus was the one who made him well.

The original statement may have been the equivalent of "Jesus made me well." Or this may simply be a summary statement of what he said. Note that this cannot be direct discourse, because the man would not have said, "Jesus is the one who made *him* well." (Do you see how the difference between "me" and "him" helps distinguish direct discourse from indirect discourse?) See chapter 31 for more information.

γάρ

8.11. Γάρ is a subordinating conjunction that typically introduces a clause that explains or gives a reason for what precedes. It clues the reader that the following statement will introduce information that is not in the story line (in narrative) or part of the main argument (in exposition) but is intended to help the reader understand the preceding statement. It is most commonly represented in English as "for," but sometimes "since" or "then" will be best suited to the context in English. Like δέ, it is also a postpositive word. It occurs over 1,000 times in the NT, much more frequently in the Epistles where an argument is being developed than in narrative portions.[9] It is proportionately less common in the LXX, where it occurs only about 1,500 times.

9. In the Gospels and Acts, γάρ occurs about 4 times per thousand words. In Romans through Galatians, the average is about 14 times per thousand words, with the technical argument of Romans representing the high end, with almost 17 instances per thousand.

Mark 14:70, Ἀληθῶς ἐξ αὐτῶν εἶ, καὶ **γὰρ** Γαλιλαῖος εἶ.

Surely you are from them [i.e., one of Jesus' disciples], *for* you also are a Galilean.

John 3:19, ἠγάπησαν οἱ ἄνθρωποι μᾶλλον[a] τὸ σκότος ἢ τὸ φῶς· ἦν **γὰρ** αὐτῶν πονηρὰ τὰ ἔργα.[b]

People loved the darkness rather than the light, *for* their deeds were evil.

[a] μᾶλλον . . . ἤ ("rather than") presents a comparison between τὸ σκότος and τὸ φῶς. (The word φῶς is a third-declension noun you will meet later; it means "light.")

[b] In the last clause there is a linking verb (ἦν, "it was") with two nominatives. The subject is identified by the article (τὰ ἔργα); the other nominative (πονηρά) is the predicate nominative (or, more technically, a predicate adjective). Did you remember that neuter plural nouns usually take a singular verb?

Rom. 1:19, τὸ γνωστὸν τοῦ θεοῦ φανερόν ἐστιν ἐν αὐτοῖς· ὁ θεὸς **γὰρ** αὐτοῖς ἐφανέρωσεν.

Isa. 13:6, ὀλολύζετε (cry out!), ἐγγὺς **γὰρ** ἡ ἡμέρα κυρίου.

ἵνα

8.12. The conjunction ἵνα is used 663 times in the NT and 615 times in the LXX. It is used much more frequently in Koine than in Classical Greek and with a wider range of function. It is almost always used with a subjunctive-mood verb[10] and usually introduces subordinate clauses that indicate a variety of possible relationships to the main clause, most of which relate to the intention of the speaker/writer in some way. The more common relationships are purpose (often translated "in order to"), result ("so that"), or content ("that").

ἵνα Indicating Purpose

Mark 3:14, ἐποίησεν δώδεκα **ἵνα** ἀποστέλλῃ (he might send) αὐτοὺς κηρύσσειν.

He appointed twelve *in order that* he might send them to preach.

Mark 15:20, ἐξάγουσιν αὐτὸν **ἵνα** σταυρώσωσιν (they might crucify) αὐτόν.

John 5:34, ταῦτα λέγω **ἵνα** ὑμεῖς σωθῆτε (may be saved).

10. You will not meet subjunctive-mood verbs until chap. 28. Any that are found in examples before then will be indicated for you, usually by an English gloss or a note. When you read ἵνα in a text, you will need to assess the options above in light of the context; just realize that you probably will not understand the morphology of the following verb.

ἵνα Indicating Result

John 7:23, εἰ περιτομὴν λαμβάνει ἄνθρωπος ἐν σαββάτῳ **ἵνα** μὴ λυθῇ (should be broken) ὁ νόμος Μωϋσέως . . .

If a man receives circumcision on the Sabbath *with the result that* the Law of Moses should not be broken . . .[a]

[a] The NIV gives more natural English (and adding the rest of the verse for context): "Now if a boy can be circumcised on the Sabbath so that the law of Moses may not be broken, why are you angry with me for healing a man's whole body on the Sabbath?" You will notice that ἄνθρωπος, normally a generic word for a person, is understood in the context as referring to a boy (it is normally boys, not men or people in general, who are circumcised).

ἵνα Indicating Content

Mark 6:25, Θέλω **ἵνα** ἐξαυτῆς δῷς (you should give) μοι τὴν κεφαλὴν Ἰωάννου τοῦ βαπτιστοῦ.

I want *that* immediately you should give me the head of John the Baptizer.

Phil. 1:9, προσεύχομαι, (I am praying) **ἵνα** ἡ ἀγάπη ὑμῶν ἔτι μᾶλλον καὶ μᾶλλον περισσεύῃ (may abound).

I am praying *that* your love yet more and more may abound.

1 Cor. 14:5, θέλω δὲ ὑμᾶς λαλεῖν γλώσσαις, μᾶλλον δὲ **ἵνα** προφητεύητε (you may prophesy).

ἀλλά

8.13. The coordinating conjunction ἀλλά (used over 600 times in the NT, but only about 550 times in the LXX) indicates contrast between two sentence elements (or between two sentences). Often there is a negative element in the preceding statement, for which ἀλλά introduces a contrasting positive statement. Most commonly this word becomes "but" in English, or sometimes "rather" or "on the contrary." Since ἀλλά ends with a vowel, this vowel is sometimes replaced with an apostrophe when the following word begins with a vowel (see the first example below).

John 4:2, Ἰησοῦς αὐτὸς οὐκ ἐβάπτιζεν **ἀλλ'** οἱ μαθηταὶ αὐτοῦ.

Jesus himself was not baptizing, *but* his disciples [were baptizing].

Gen. 40:15, οὐκ ἐποίησα οὐδέν,[a] **ἀλλ'** ἐνέβαλόν με εἰς τὸν λάκκον τοῦτον.

I did nothing, *but* they threw me into this pit.

[a] On double negatives in Greek, see §5.26, note b.

Mark 2:22, οὐδεὶς βάλλει οἶνον νέον εἰς ἀσκοὺς παλαιούς· **ἀλλὰ** οἶνον νέον εἰς ἀσκοὺς καινούς.

The Longest Words in Greek

This chapter contains some of the shortest words in Greek. By contrast, the longest word in the NT is the twenty-letter participle προκεχειροτονημένοις in Acts 10:41. That is longer than some entire verses in the NT. Including the article τοῖς, it means "to the ones who are chosen." In the LXX there is a twenty-four-letter word in Num. 32:30, συγκατακληρονομηθήσονται, "they shall inherit together with."

If you were to search Greek texts outside the NT, you would find such monstrosities as ἀστραποβροντοξαλαζορειθροδᾳμαστός (33 letters, or 34 if you count the iota subscript), a genitive feminine singular adjective meaning "dominated by lightning, thunder, hail, and flood" (*Basilius* [Basil the Great], *Letters* 365 [= PG 32:1109A]). Beyond "serious literature" there are even longer words. In the subliterary magical papyri you could find κεραυνομεγακλονοζηνπερατοκοσμολαμπροβελοπλουτοδότα—fifty letters (*PGM* 12.175). I have no idea what it means.

οὖν

8.14. The coordinating conjunction οὖν serves to draw inferences from previous statements (in narrative often introducing direct discourse as people respond to various events or the statements of others) or to resume discussion of a topic that has been interrupted. Unlike a γάρ clause, the statement introduced by οὖν is part of the story line (in narrative) or argument (in exposition). In English it might be represented as "now," "then," "therefore," or "thus." It occurs nearly 500 times in the NT, of which 200 are found in John's Gospel and over 100 in Paul. The LXX has fewer than half this number (about 250). This is another postpositive conjunction.

John 4:7, 9, λέγει αὐτῇ ὁ Ἰησοῦς, Δός (Give!) μοι πεῖν.[a] λέγει **οὖν** αὐτῷ ἡ γυνὴ ἡ Σαμαρῖτις . . .

Jesus said to her, "Give me [something] to drink." *Then* the Samaritan woman said to him . . .

[a] You will recognize πεῖν as an infinitive, but the lexical form may be puzzling. It is from πίνω; you will understand why in chap. 21.

Rom. 5:1, Δικαιωθέντες **οὖν** ἐκ πίστεως εἰρήνην ἔχομεν πρὸς τὸν θεὸν διὰ τοῦ κυρίου ἡμῶν Ἰησοῦ Χριστοῦ.

Therefore being justified by faith, we have peace with God through our Lord Jesus Christ.

The inference that Paul draws in Rom. 5:1 is based on the argument of the preceding four chapters, most specifically chapter 4, in which he has explained and illustrated justification in the experience of Abraham. (The first word in this sentence is a participle, "being justified." Some of the other words are also new, but you can follow the argument of the verse if you compare the two columns.)

Gen. 40:8, εἶπεν δὲ αὐτοῖς Ἰωσήφ, Οὐχὶ διὰ τοῦ θεοῦ ἡ διασάφησις αὐτῶν[a] ἐστιν; διηγήσασθε (recount!) **οὖν** μοι.

So Joseph said to them, "Is not their explanation through God? *So then,* recount [the dreams] to me."

[a] The antecedent of αὐτῶν is the dreams of Pharaoh's cupbearer and baker. In the last clause the direct object (which also refers to these dreams) is assumed.

8.15. Advanced Information for Reference: Diagramming Main and Subordinate Clauses

John 13:13, ὑμεῖς φωνεῖτέ με Ὁ διδάσκαλος καὶ Ὁ κύριος, **καὶ** καλῶς λέγετε, εἰμὶ **γάρ**.

You call me Teacher and Lord, *and* you speak correctly, *for* I am [Teacher and Lord].

This example shows two main clauses connected by καί and one subordinate clause introduced with the postpositive conjunction γάρ, which, you will notice, is the *last* word in a sentence.

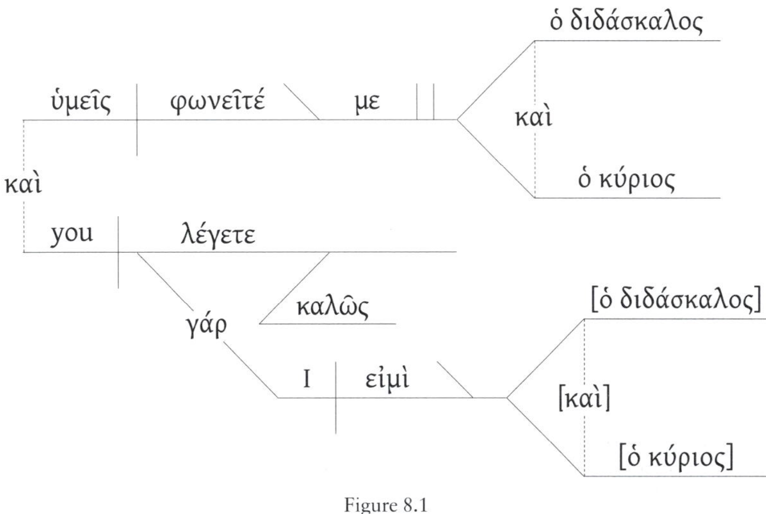

Figure 8.1

Reading Passages

8.16. In the following texts pay particular attention to the function of the conjunctions (marked with boldface in the Greek and italics in the translation) and the clauses. There will be a number of words that you do not recognize; that is OK, since you do not have to understand everything that is included, just enough to track the function of the conjunctions and the division of the sentences into phrases and clauses.

Mark 2:1–5

8.17. The first example comes from Mark, who has a habit of overusing the conjunction καί, perhaps due to the influence of the Semitic conjunction *waw* in his native language.[11] This paragraph consists of a series of short sentences, most of which are linked by καί. In the translation provided below, you will notice that a number of instances of καί are not translated for reasons of English style, and an ampersand (&) marks the omission.

Jesus Heals a Paralytic

1**Καὶ** εἰσελθὼν (coming) πάλιν εἰς Καφαρναοὺμ δι᾽ ἡμερῶν[a] ἠκούσθη (it was heard) **ὅτι** ἐν οἴκῳ ἐστίν. 2**καὶ** συνήχθησαν (they gathered) πολλοὶ **ὥστε** μηκέτι χωρεῖν μηδὲ τὰ πρὸς τὴν θύραν,[b] **καὶ** ἐλάλει (he was speaking/teaching) αὐτοῖς τὸν λόγον. 3**καὶ** ἔρχονται φέροντες (carrying) πρὸς αὐτὸν παραλυτικὸν αἰρόμενον (carried) ὑπὸ τεσσάρων. 4**καὶ** μὴ δυνάμενοι προσενέγκαι[c] αὐτῷ διὰ τὸν ὄχλον ἀπεστέγασαν (they unroofed) τὴν στέγην ὅπου ἦν, **καὶ** ἐξορύξαντες (having dug) χαλῶσι (they lowered) τὸν κράβαττον ὅπου ὁ παραλυτικὸς κατέκειτο (was lying). 5**καὶ** ἰδὼν (seeing) ὁ Ἰησοῦς τὴν πίστιν αὐτῶν λέγει τῷ παραλυτικῷ, Τέκνον, ἀφίενταί (they are forgiven) σου αἱ ἁμαρτίαι.

a δι᾽ ἡμερῶν, "after several days"

b The first half of v. 2 is complicated; see the translation below, and do not worry about the details now.

c δυνάμενοι προσενέγκαι, "able to bring"

Translation

1(&)When [Jesus] entered Capernaum again after several days, it was heard *that* he was home. 2(&)Many people gathered *so that* there was no longer any room [at the house], not even near the doorway, *and* he was teaching them the word. 3(&)Some people came, bringing a paralyzed man to him, carried by four [people], 4*and* since they were not able to bring [him] to [Jesus] because of the crowd, they unroofed the roof where he was. (&) Having dug through [the roof], they lowered the mat on which the paralyzed man was lying. 5(&)Seeing their faith, Jesus said to the paralyzed man, "Son, your sins are forgiven."

Romans 5:12–14a

8.18. In contrast to Mark's style, Paul writes much longer sentences, connecting the clauses with a complex web of subordinating conjunctions. The following text is one long sentence, which uses καί twice, followed by γάρ, δέ, and ἀλλά.

Sin and Death Enter the World

12Διὰ τοῦτο ὥσπερ δι᾽ ἑνὸς ἀνθρώπου ἡ ἁμαρτία εἰς τὸν κόσμον εἰσῆλθεν (entered) **καὶ** διὰ τῆς ἁμαρτίας ὁ θάνατος, **καὶ** οὕτως εἰς πάντας ἀνθρώπους ὁ θάνατος διῆλθεν (it passed), ἐφ᾽ ᾧ[a] πάντες (all) ἥμαρτον (sinned)· 13ἄχρι **γὰρ** νόμου ἁμαρτία ἦν ἐν κόσμῳ, ἁμαρτία **δὲ** οὐκ ἐλλογεῖται (it was reckoned) μὴ ὄντος (being) νόμου, 14**ἀλλὰ** ἐβασίλευσεν ὁ θάνατος ἀπὸ (from) Ἀδὰμ μέχρι (until) Μωϋσέως.

a ἐφ᾽ ᾧ, "because"

11. In Mark, more than 60 percent of the sentences begin with καί. By contrast, in Matthew the figure is only 30 percent.

Translation

[12]Therefore, just as through one man sin came into the world, *and* death through sin, *and* so death spread to all people because all sinned—[13]*for* until the law, sin was in the world, *but* sin is not reckoned where there is no law, [14]*yet* death reigned from Adam to Moses.

Genesis 27:39–40 LXX

8.19. This selection is mostly poetic verse. As is characteristic of the LXX, the usual conjunction is καί, reflecting the Hebrew *waw*, though δέ also occurs, along with ἡνίκα ἐάν.

Esau's "Blessing"

[39]ἀποκριθεὶς (answering) **δὲ** Ἰσαὰκ ὁ πατὴρ αὐτοῦ εἶπεν αὐτῷ,
Ἰδοὺ ἀπὸ τῆς πιότητος τῆς γῆς ἔσται ἡ κατοίκησίς σου
καὶ ἀπὸ τῆς δρόσου τοῦ οὐρανοῦ ἄνωθεν·
[40]**καὶ** ἐπὶ τῇ μαχαίρῃ σου ζήσῃ (you will live)
καὶ τῷ ἀδελφῷ σου δουλεύσεις (you will be subject)·
ἔσται **δὲ ἡνίκα ἐὰν**[a] καθέλῃς (you bring down/destroy),
καὶ ἐκλύσεις (you will loose) τὸν ζυγὸν αὐτοῦ ἀπὸ τοῦ τραχήλου σου.

[a] ἡνίκα ἐάν, a conjunctive phrase, "when"

Translation

[39]*Then* answering, Isaac his father said to him,
"See, away from the abundance of the earth will be your dwelling,
and away from the dew of heaven above.
[40]*And* by your sword you will live,
and you will be subject to your brother,
but it will be *when* you overpower [him],
then you will loose his yoke from your neck."

LXX Syntax

Roughly speaking, it is true to say that in the Greek of the LXX there is no syntax, only parataxis. The whole is one great scheme of clauses connected by καί, and we have to trust to the sense to tell us which is to be so emphasized as to make it into the apodosis [i.e., which are subordinate clauses]. (Conybeare and Stock, *Grammar of Septuagint Greek,* §40)

A related characteristic of LXX syntax is beginning a sentence with καὶ ἐγένετο followed by a subordinate clause introduced by καί, e.g., Num. 21:9, **καὶ ἐγένετο** ὅταν ἔδακνεν ὄφις ἄνθρωπον, καὶ ἐπέβλεψεν ἐπὶ τὸν ὄφιν τὸν χαλκοῦν **καὶ** ἔζη ("*and it came to be* when a snake bit a person and they looked on the bronze snake, *then* they lived").

— — — — — — — — — — — — — —

Advanced Information for Reference:
Sentence Patterns

8.20. Not all instructors will take the time to cover this section in class. There is nothing here that you are intended to memorize. It is designed to help you understand the concepts involved in Greek syntax—how sentences are constructed. I recommend that you read through this material, seeking to understand the patterns that are used. If you learn nothing else than that Greek sentences have widely varied patterns of word order (especially when compared with English), you will have understood the most important principle in this section.

In earlier chapters, you learned a few basic sentence patterns. Now that you have learned more of the basics of the language, we can extend our study a bit further. Various Greek verbs take a variety of complements; some have none, others may have one or two complements of various kinds and in various cases.[12] In this textbook, *verbal complement* refers to the categories commonly called *direct object* (usually accusative, sometimes genitive or dative) and *indirect object* (dative case). Verbs that take two such complements will typically have a direct object and an indirect object, or a direct object with a double accusative. Verbs with only one complement may have either a direct object or, if it is a linking verb such as εἰμί, a predicate nominative (or subject complement).

8.21. Greek arranges these elements in several basic sentence patterns. We will list them here and then illustrate the variety involved. Note that this initial list of sentence types *does not indicate word order*; it indicates only the constituent elements included.[13] In the illustrations below, the variety of word order used for each sentence type will be illustrated.

Sentence Types

1. Subject–Verb
2. Subject–Verb–Predicate Nominative
3. Subject–Verb–Direct Object
4. Subject–Verb–Indirect Object–Direct Object
5. Subject–Verb–Direct Object–Object Complement

Since Greek is an inflected language, the possible sequences of these complements are more varied than they are in English, which relies on fairly consistent word order to communicate meaning. English sentences almost always follow Subject–Verb–Complement order. The exceptions are specific constructions such as questions that place the verb ahead of the subject.

12. Technically all Greek verbs have at least one complement, since the subject is considered a complement. Since all Greek verbs have a default, back-pocket subject, it is not particularly helpful to think of the subject as a complement. Later you will learn that verbs can also take adjuncts in addition to complements.

13. The five sentence types are based on Funk, *Beginning-Intermediate Grammar*, 2:377–91, §§500–523.

8.22. The following examples of the five sentence types in Greek also illustrate some of the word-order patterns involving the various verbal complements. As you read more and more Greek texts, you will discover that some of these patterns are more common than others, but you need to realize that all are acceptable Greek style and all communicate the writer's meaning accurately.[14] In many instances the English equivalent must be reordered so as to correctly communicate the meaning in English.

Do not try to translate all the Greek in the many examples listed below. Use the English equivalent in the right-hand column to pick your way quickly through the Greek text, observing the case endings you know that identify the function of the various words and the verbs that you are learning thus far. *Some of the words included use grammatical forms that you have not yet learned.* You will understand more of these examples later, and they will serve you well for reference purposes.

In the patterns below, "Verb/Subject" refers to the back-pocket subject in the verb; there is not a separate nominative-case word for the subject.

Type 1 Sentences: Subject–Verb

8.23. These sentences are built around an *intransitive verb* (one that does not require a direct object to complete the thought).

Verb/Subject

This is a complete, one-word sentence.

Mark 4:3, Ἀκούετε.[a]	Listen!

[a] ἀκούω, "I hear"; the form here is a second-person plural imperative.

Rom. 3:9, προεχόμεθα;[a]	Are we better? (or, Do we have an advantage?)

[a] προέχω, "I have an advantage"; this form is first plural.

Subject ▸ Verb

1 Cor. 8:1, ἡ ἀγάπη οἰκοδομεῖ.	Love builds up.
1 Cor. 13:4, Ἡ ἀγάπη μακροθυμεῖ.	Love is patient.
James 2:19, τὰ δαιμόνια πιστεύουσιν.	The demons believe.

14. Scholars debate whether or not there is any significance to these variations, but the arguments are not yet definitive despite some assertions. It is possible that some patterns may suggest a focus on a particular part of the statement, but that should not be extrapolated to conclude that this involves heavy emphasis. The *meaning* of a statement does not change if word order changes, though the focus might.

Type 2 Sentences: Subject–Verb–Predicate Nominative

8.24. Sentences involving predicate nominatives (sometimes called *subject complements*) must have a linking verb, the most common of which are εἰμί and γίνομαι.

Predicate Nominative ▸ [Verb] ▸ Subject (or the Reverse)

By placing *verb* in brackets, I indicate a verbless clause, in which a form of εἰμί must be supplied.

John 4:24, πνεῦμα[a] ὁ θεός. — God is spirit.

[a] This is a third-declension noun, nominative singular, "spirit."

Mark 5:9, Λεγιὼν ὄνομά μοι. — Legion is my name.

Verb/Subject ▸ Predicate Nominative (or the Reverse)

Matt. 3:11, οὐκ εἰμὶ ἱκανός. — I am not worthy.

Matt. 4:3, υἱὸς εἶ τοῦ θεοῦ. — You are the Son of God.

Mark 3:29, ἔνοχός ἐστιν. — He is guilty.

Subject ▸ Verb ▸ Predicate Nominative

Matt. 13:38, ὁ ἀγρός ἐστιν ὁ κόσμος. — The field is the world.

1 Tim. 1:5, τὸ τέλος τῆς παραγγελίας ἐστὶν ἀγάπη. — The goal of [our] command is love.

Subject ▸ Predicate Nominative ▸ Verb

Matt. 13:39, ὁ θερισμὸς συντέλεια αἰῶνός (of the age) ἐστιν, οἱ δὲ θερισταὶ ἄγγελοί εἰσιν. — The harvest is the end of the age, and the reapers are angels.

Mark 12:35, ὁ Χριστὸς υἱὸς Δαυίδ ἐστιν. — The Messiah is the son of David.

Verb ▸ Subject ▸ Predicate Nominative

Matt. 5:48, Ἔσεσθε[a] ὑμεῖς τέλειοι. — You must be perfect.

[a] Second plural; this is a future form functioning as an imperative.

Rom. 14:17, ἐστὶν ἡ βασιλεία τοῦ θεοῦ δικαιοσύνη.	The kingdom of God is righteousness.
Gen. 42:11, οὐκ εἰσὶν οἱ παῖδές σου κατάσκοποι.	Your servants are not spies.

Verb ▸ Predicate Nominative ▸ Subject

Acts 10:34, οὐκ ἔστιν προσωπολήμπτης ὁ θεός.	God is not one who shows favoritism.

Predicate Nominative ▸ Subject ▸ Verb

Isa. 30:18, κριτὴς κύριος ὁ θεὸς ἡμῶν ἐστιν.	The Lord our God is judge.

Predicate Nominative ▸ Verb ▸ Subject

Mark 2:28, κύριός ἐστιν ὁ υἱὸς τοῦ ἀνθρώπου.	The Son of Man is lord.
John 4:19, προφήτης εἶ σύ.	You are a prophet.
4 Macc. 2:7, κύριός ἐστιν τῶν παθῶν ὁ λογισμός.	Reason is master of the passions.
1 Chron. 28:3, ἄνθρωπος πολεμιστὴς εἶ σύ.	You are a man—a warrior.

Type 3 Sentences: Subject–Verb–Direct Object

8.25. The verbal complements in all the examples of type 3 sentences listed here are accusative direct objects. As explained in §7.23, the direct object could also be in the genitive or dative case.

Verb/Subject ▸ Verbal Complement

Mark 1:2, Ἰδοὺ ἀποστέλλω τὸν ἄγγελον.	Behold, I am sending the messenger.
Mark 8:24, Βλέπω τοὺς ἀνθρώπους.	I see people.

Subject ▸ Verb ▸ Verbal Complement

Mark 12:41, ὁ ὄχλος βάλλει χαλκόν.	The crowd threw money.
John 7:51, ὁ νόμος κρίνει τὸν ἄνθρωπον;	Does the law judge a person?

Verb ▸ Verbal Complement ▸ Subject

John 2:9, φωνεῖ τὸν νυμφίον ὁ ἀρχιτρίκλινος.	The head waiter called the bridegroom.
Rev. 9:3, ἔχουσιν ἐξουσίαν οἱ σκορπίοι.	The scorpions have authority.
Gen. 21:7, θηλάζει παιδίον Σάρρα.	Sarah is nursing a child.

Verb ▸ Subject ▸ Verbal Complement

John 1:45, εὑρίσκει Φίλιππος τὸν Ναθαναήλ.	Philip found Nathaniel.
Mark 9:2, παραλαμβάνει ὁ Ἰησοῦς τὸν Πέτρον.	Jesus took Peter.
1 Esd. 4:23, λαμβάνει ἄνθρωπος τὴν ῥομφαίαν.	A man takes the sword.

Verbal Complement ▸ Verb ▸ Subject

Mark 2:10, ἐξουσίαν ἔχει ὁ υἱός.	The Son has authority.
John 7:23, περιτομὴν λαμβάνει ἄνθρωπος.	A man receives circumcision (i.e., a man is circumcised).
1 Chron. 28:9, καρδίας ἐτάζει[a] κύριος.	The Lord examines the heart.

[a] ἐτάζω, "I test, examine"

Subject ▸ Verbal Complement ▸ Verb

Mark 11:3, Ὁ κύριος χρείαν ἔχει.	The Lord has a need.
Luke 5:24, ὁ υἱὸς ἐξουσίαν ἔχει.	The Son has authority.

Compare Luke 5:24 with Mark 2:10 in the examples just above and notice that the same statement can be made with more than one word order.

Verbal Complement ▸ Subject ▸ Verb

This pattern is rare, but it does occur.

1 Kgdms. (1 Sam.) 25:28, πόλεμον ὁ κύριος πολεμεῖ.	The Lord fights the battle.

Type 4 Sentences: Subject–Verb –Indirect Object–Direct Object

8.26. All the examples given for type 4 and 5 sentences have verb/subject (i.e., "back pocket" subjects), but the same type sentences could also have subject ▸ verb order.

Verb ▸ Verbal Complement (Acc. D.O.) ▸ Verbal Complement (Dat. I.O.),
or
Verb ▸ Verbal Complement (Dat. I.O.) ▸ Verbal Complement (Acc. D.O.)

1 Kgdms. (1 Sam.) 1:28, κιχρῶ αὐτὸν τῷ κυρίῳ.	I lend him to the Lord.
Prov. 10:10, συνάγει [ἀνθρώποις] λύπας.	He gathers people grief (or, he gathers grief for people).

8.27. Type 5 Sentences: Subject–Verb –Direct Object–Object Complement

Verb ▸ Verbal Complement (Acc. D.O.) ▸ Object Complement (Dbl. Acc.)

Luke 11:46, φορτίζετε τοὺς ἀνθρώπους φορτία.	You burden people with burdens.

— — — — — — — — — — — — — —

8.28. Vocabulary for Chapter 8

Part of Speech	Definition	Possible Glosses	Frequency	
Word			NT	LXX
Conjunctions				
ἐάν	Conditional particle that introduces the "if" part of a conditional statement; sometimes used as a subordinating temporal conjunction, "when" (governs subjunctive mood)	if; when	351	1,343
ἕως	Subordinating conjunction indicating a temporal limit ("until"); or used as a preposition with the genitive, either spatially or temporally ("as far as" or "until")	until (conj.); as far as, until (prep. + gen.)	146	1,565
οὐδέ, οὔτε	A coordinating conjunction that negates a clause and links it to a preceding negative clause	and not, not even, neither, nor	143	614
ὥστε	A conjunction that introduces a result clause, either coordinate or subordinate; sometimes "intended result" = purpose	for this reason, therefore; so that, that; in order that	83	182
διό	A subordinating conjunction that introduces an inference from the preceding statement	wherefore, therefore, for this reason	53	24

Part of Speech	Definition	Possible Glosses	Frequency	
Word			NT	LXX
ὅπως	A subordinating conjunction indicating purpose (governs subjunctive mood)	in order that, that, how	53	264
Nouns				
ψυχή, ῆς, ἡ	The quality of physical life without which a body cannot function, that which animates a body; that which is integral to being a person, the seat and center of the inner human life	life; soul, (inner) self	103	976
ἐξουσία, ας, ἡ	The right to speak or act without first obtaining approval, freedom of choice or action; the right to control or govern, power exercised by rulers or others in high position by virtue of their office	authority, right, power, control	102	79
ὁδός, οῦ, ἡ	A route for traveling; metaphorically, way of life; the lifestyle and beliefs of Christianity ("the Way")	road, way, highway; the Way	101	891
ὀφθαλμός, οῦ, ὁ	Sensory organ of sight; metaphorically of moral/spiritual understanding	eye, sight	100	678
τέκνον, ου, τό	An offspring of human parents without specific reference to sex or age; plural may refer collectively to descendants from a common ancestor; one who is dear to another (not related genetically)	child, descendant	99	314
Φαρισαῖος, ου, ὁ	A member of a religious and political Jewish party at the time of Jesus characterized by strict observance of the Mosaic law as understood by the scribes	Pharisee	98	0
ἄρτος, ου, ὁ	A baked cake or loaf made from a cereal grain (barley, wheat, etc.); food in general	bread, loaf; food	97	307
οἰκία, ας, ἡ	A physical structure in which people live; a group of people who live in that structure	house, home; household, family	93	268
ἀπόστολος, ου, ὁ	One who is sent on a mission; in the NT, usually the Twelve, who were Jesus' official messengers	apostle, envoy, messenger	80	0

8.29. Key Things to Know for Chapter 8

What is the difference between a function word and a content word?

How can you distinguish a subordinate clause from an independent clause?

The function of conjunctions is essential to communication, and Greek has a full collection of conjunctions that specify the relationships between various sentences and often the parts of the sentences. You need to learn the most common conjunctions as vocabulary items, but it is just as important to understand how they function. Be sure all the examples given in this chapter make good sense to you.

9

SYNTAX: PART 2

PREPOSITIONS

9.1. In this second part of our study of Greek syntax, we will look at several additional topics, including prepositions and the use of the article as a function marker.

Prepositions and Prepositional Phrases

Prepositions are a key part of both English and Greek. We will begin with a look at English prepositions and then compare the function of prepositions and prepositional phrases in Greek. Some aspects of Greek prepositions are very similar to English, others quite different.

English Prepositions

9.2. A preposition is a function word that combines with a noun or pronoun to form a modifying phrase. Remember that *function words* indicate relationships between words in a clause, so we could say, in general terms, that prepositions are words that indicate relationships between words in a sentence.

Using the sentence and the list of words following figure 9.1, notice how the meaning changes when you insert into the blank the various words, all of which are English prepositions.

Figure 9.1

The man ran _______ the woods.

in	through	to	under	above
from	into	out (of)	beside	around

Not all prepositions can be illustrated in this "woodsy" way; not all express a spatial relationship. For example, the preposition *before* can indicate a spatial relationship but is more often a temporal relationship; *until* is only temporal, never spatial.

The noun or pronoun with which the preposition combines is always in the objective case and is referred to as the *object* of the preposition. The phrase that consists of a preposition and its object is called a *prepositional phrase.*

The man	**ran**	**into**	**the woods.**
subject	verb	preposition	object of the preposition
		prepositional phrase	

Greek Prepositions

9.3. You will quickly discover that Greek prepositions function very much like English ones. If we were to rewrite the sentence above in Greek, we would be able to pick from the following list to describe the same set of relationships between the word *ran* (which would be a form of τρέχω) and the word *woods* (a form of ὕλη) as depicted in figure 9.1.

ἐν	διά	πρός	ὑπό	ἄνω
ἀπό	εἰς	ἐκ	παρά	περί

Although there is a significant (and very helpful) overlap in the function of prepositions between English and Greek, we can be more specific in regard to Greek prepositions since Greek is an inflected language. A Greek preposition is a function word that combines with a noun or pronoun in a particular case to form a modifying phrase that clarifies the meaning of that case. Frequently case alone is adequate to indicate the function of a noun or pronoun in a sentence, but for greater clarity a preposition may be added to make it less ambiguous. Compare the following examples, which make similar statements, one using just a dative case, the others with a preposition and the accusative or dative case.

Acts 18:8, Κρίσπος δὲ ἐπίστευσεν **τῷ κυρίῳ.**	Now Crispus believed *in the Lord.*
Acts 11:17, ἡμῖν πιστεύσασιν **ἐπὶ** τὸν κύριον Ἰησοῦν Χριστόν	To us who believed *in* the Lord Jesus Christ
Ps. 77:22 (78:22 Eng.), οὐκ ἐπίστευσαν **ἐν** τῷ θεῷ.	They did not believe *in* God.

Syntax and Meaning of Greek Prepositions

9.4. Prepositional phrases usually modify the verb. For example, in Mark 7:6, Jesus says, ἐπροφήτευσεν Ἠσαΐας περὶ ὑμῶν. The prepositional phrase, περὶ ὑμῶν, modifies the verb, ἐπροφήτευσεν: "Isaiah prophesied concerning you"; it does not modify the noun adjacent to the preposition—it was not the "concerning-you-Isaiah" who prophesied. For now, think of prepositional phrases as adverbial modifiers. Later in this chapter you will learn how to identify prepositional phrases that function adjectivally.

The meaning of a Greek preposition depends on the case of its object. The preposition does not have any case of its own (it is indeclinable); it is incorrect to say that a preposition is in the genitive case. A preposition is said to *govern* a case (or, *take* a case), but that case is the case of its object, not the case of the preposition. Some prepositions always govern the same case and therefore always have the same meaning (e.g., ἐν always governs the dative case and means "in"). Other prepositions may take their object in two or three cases and so may have two or three different meanings. The following table illustrates this with prepositions that govern one, two, or three cases.

	ἐν	διά	πρός
Genitive	—	through	for
Dative	in	—	at
Accusative	—	on account of	to

For example, if you encounter a sentence in which the preposition πρός is used, you must check the case of its object before you can determine correctly what it means. If its object is in the dative case, you would understand it to mean "at," rather than "for" or "to."

Sometimes the various meanings of a preposition are fairly close, even if used with a different case; other times the difference in case makes a significant difference in meaning. Although the table above shows only a single meaning for each combination of preposition and case, you should conceptualize the meanings of prepositions *not* as illustrated in figure 9.2 (narrow, distinct meanings) but as seen in figure 9.3 (broad, overlapping areas of meaning).[1]

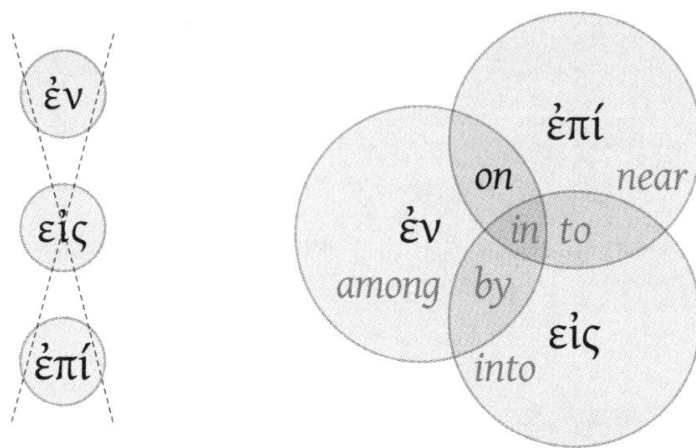

Figure 9.2 Figure 9.3

9.5. What you learn as vocabulary glosses of a preposition are only the more common uses of that preposition. If you were to look up each preposition in a basic lexicon, you would find a much broader range of translation options (and a full-fledged lexicon such as BDAG would give you even more). The *context* is the determining factor in selecting which English word best represents the sense of the Greek statement. For now, learn the basic glosses given in the vocabulary list, and remember that they are only general guidelines.

When you first learned the basics of the cases, you learned that a preposition was often used to help represent the meaning of the genitive and dative cases in English. When there is already an explicit preposition in Greek, however, you do not need to add another one in English to represent the meaning of the case. The explicit preposition makes the statement even more specific.

ὁ λόγος θεοῦ = the word of God
But: ὁ λόγος ἀπὸ θεοῦ = the word from God [*not*: the word from of God]

In this example the addition of ἀπό makes the statement more explicit than the simple genitive-case noun by itself. Although ὁ λόγος θεοῦ *could* mean "the word from God" in an appropriate context, there is no ambiguity in the second statement.

1. This is not unique to Greek. English prepositions are also very flexible in meaning. Only the context can determine the particular meaning in each situation. Note these English examples, which illustrate how flexible and diverse is the meaning of a simple English preposition, *with* (Goetchius, *Language of the New Testament*, 147).

He fought *with* the Japanese.	(i.e., *against* them)
He fought *with* the A.E.F.	(i.e., *together with* it)
He fought *with* a machine gun.	(i.e., *by means of* it)
He fought *with* courage.	(i.e., *in a* courageous *manner*)

Form of Greek Prepositions

9.6. The *form* of a preposition does not decline. That is, prepositions do not use case endings; they are not inflected. There are, however, some minor changes in their spelling from time to time. Prepositions that end with a vowel *may* drop that vowel or change the spelling slightly.[2] This change is for euphony—to make it easier to pronounce. The two most common spelling changes are π ▸ φ and τ ▸ θ. You do not have to know the rules as to why these changes occur,[3] nor do you need to memorize the list of examples below; just be able to recognize the abbreviated forms. They are quite obvious.

ἀπό	▸	ἀπ' or ἀφ'
ὑπό	▸	ὑπ' or ὑφ'
ἐπί	▸	ἐπ' or ἐφ'
μετά	▸	μετ' or μεθ'
κατά	▸	κατ' or καθ'
ἀντί	▸	ἀντ' or ἀνθ'
παρά	▸	παρ'
ἀνά	▸	ἀν'[a]
διά	▸	δι'
ἐκ	▸	ἐξ

[a]The shortening of ἀνά to ἀν' is very rare in Koine (never in the NT or LXX), though it was common in Classical Greek.

Changes of this sort may be seen scattered throughout the examples given below.

Prepositions for Clarity

The use of prepositions to make a statement more explicit is one of the characteristics of Koine Greek in contrast to the older, Classical Greek. Prior to the development of Koine in the fourth century BC, more prepositions were used in the language, each with a fairly narrow range of meaning. In Koine, however, the number of prepositions is reduced, but they are used much more frequently for purposes of clarity. This is due to Koine being a learned, second language for many speakers who did not have the native, intuitive sense for the fine distinctions of the Classical prepositions or of the probable meaning expressed by the case alone. As a result, the number of options was simplified, but the result of using fewer prepositions more frequently was that the language became more explicit.

2. These changes usually occur but occasionally do not. For example, both κατὰ εἷς (Mark 14:19) and καθ' εἷς (John 8:9) occur in the NT (though only once each). Likewise, both ἐπὶ ἔθνος (Matt. 24:7) and ἐπ' ἔθνος (Mark 13:8) occur. Even in parallel passages the spelling may differ. Mark 9:2 has μετὰ ἡμέρας ἕξ; the same statement in Matt. 17:1 has μεθ' ἡμέρας ἕξ. Greek writers in both the Classical and Koine periods were notoriously inconsistent in such spellings; there were general patterns but no standardization in this regard.

3. For those who are curious about such things (or for those whose goal is to do Greek composition), the final vowel of a preposition drops off if the next word begins with a vowel. If the vowel at the beginning of the next word has a rough breathing mark, then prepositions that end with pi, kappa, or tau (after dropping a final vowel) change to phi, chi, and theta (respectively). Likewise ἐκ becomes ἐξ when the following word begins with a vowel (regardless of the breathing mark used). A few prepositions that end with a vowel never drop that vowel—for example, περί and πρό.

A Visual Representation of Prepositions

9.7. To help you visualize the meanings of prepositions that express a spatial relationship, study the illustration of the apple that is riddled with "wormy prepositions" in figure 9.4.[4]

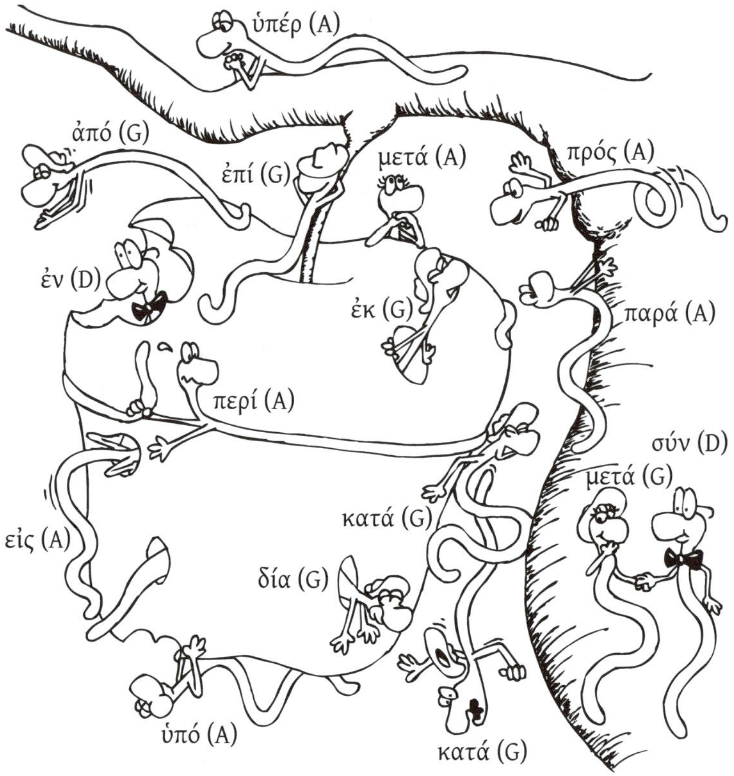

Figure 9.4

9.8. *Examples of Prepositions*

Mark 1:23, ἦν[a] **ἐν** τῇ συναγωγῇ αὐτῶν ἄνθρωπος.	A man was *in* their synagogue.

[a] ἦν is a form of εἰμί, "he/she/it was."

Mark 5:21, ἦν **παρὰ** τὴν θάλασσαν.	He was *alongside* (or, near) the lake.
Matt. 19:26, ὁ Ἰησοῦς εἶπεν αὐτοῖς, **Παρὰ** ἀνθρώποις τοῦτο ἀδύνατόν ἐστιν, **παρὰ** δὲ θεῷ πάντα δυνατά.	Jesus said to them, "*With* people this is impossible, but *with* God all things are possible."

4. If you are sharp, you will be able to figure out how each worm tells you which case is used as its object.

Gen. 36:33, ἀπέθανεν (he died) δὲ Βάλακ, καὶ ἐβασίλευσεν **ἀντ'** αὐτοῦ Ἰωβὰβ υἱὸς Ζάρα **ἐκ** Βοσόρρας.

Now Balak died, and Jobab, the son of Zerah *from* Bozrah, reigned *instead of* him.

9.9. *Now You Try It*

Mark 2:27, Τὸ σάββατον **διὰ** τὸν ἄνθρωπον ἐγένετο (was made) καὶ οὐχ ὁ ἄνθρωπος **διὰ** τὸ σάββατον.

What is the verb for the second clause? How does each of the prepositional phrases function in the sentence? What do they modify? What case is the object of διά? What would be different if the sentence had τοῦ ἀνθρώπου instead of τὸν ἄνθρωπον?

John 4:39, πολλοί (many) ἐπίστευσαν **εἰς** αὐτὸν τῶν Σαμαριτῶν[a] **διὰ** τὸν λόγον τῆς γυναικός.[b]

What case is the object of διά? *Why* did many of the Samaritans believe? How is the "word" (λόγον) described?

[a] τῶν Σαμαριτῶν modifies πολλοί. This use of the genitive is called a partitive genitive; it specifies the larger group of which the head word is a part. That is, the larger group is "the Samaritans," and the part is the "many." It is not common for a genitive to be separated this far from its head word, but it does happen.

[b] "woman" (go by the article); this is a third-declension form that you will learn later.

Rom. 5:14, ἐβασίλευσεν ὁ θάνατος **ἀπὸ** Ἀδὰμ **μέχρι** Μωϋσέως.

How do you parse ἐβασίλευσεν? Two prepositions are paired here; check your lexicon for the meanings of the prepositions.

2 Chron. 1:1, ἐνίσχυσεν[a] Σαλωμὼν υἱὸς[b] Δαυὶδ **ἐπὶ** τὴν βασιλείαν αὐτοῦ, καὶ κύριος ὁ θεὸς αὐτοῦ **μετ'** αὐτοῦ καὶ ἐμεγάλυνεν[c] αὐτὸν **εἰς** ὕψος.[d]

[a] The aorist form of ἐνισχύω does not lengthen the initial epsilon as you would expect to reflect the augment; this is called an *implicit augment*. In this context, "I establish" would be a good way to express the meaning in English.

[b] Apposition; see the sidebar near §8.8.

[c] μεγαλύνω, "I make great, exalt"; the aorist form marker you expect is missing (you will learn why in chap. 21).

[d] εἰς ὕψος, idiom, "greatly" (Yes, ὕψος is an accusative-case noun [third declension, see chap. 11]; prepositions are not used with nominative-case objects.)

Prepositions Used with Adverbs

9.10. Most instances of prepositions occur with a substantive (noun, pronoun, etc.) as the object, and that by a very wide margin. Prepositions can, however, take an adverb as an object. This is unusual in that adverbs do not have case. Many of these instances are used in set phrases (idioms). Consider the following examples.

Mark 14:54, ὁ Πέτρος **ἀπὸ μακρόθεν** ἠκολούθησεν αὐτῷ. — Peter followed him *from a distance*.

Luke 16:16, Ὁ νόμος καὶ οἱ προφῆται μέχρι Ἰωάννου· **ἀπὸ τότε** ἡ βασιλεία τοῦ θεοῦ εὐαγγελίζεται. — The Law and the Prophets [were preached][a] until John; *from then*[b] the kingdom of God is being preached.

[a] The first half of the verse is a verbless clause, so a verb must be supplied. Most such instances take some form of the verb εἰμί, but here the parallel with the second clause suggests that we should understand the verb εὐαγγελίζω.
[b] ἀπὸ τότε is formally translated "from then," but in idiomatic English it means "since that time."

John 14:7, **ἀπ' ἄρτι** γινώσκετε αὐτόν. — *From now on* you know him.

1 Kgdms. (1 Sam.) 7:12, **Ἕως ἐνταῦθα** ἐβοήθησεν ἡμῖν κύριος. — *Until now* the Lord has helped us.

3 Kgdms. (1 Kings) 1:4, ἡ νεᾶνις καλὴ **ἕως σφόδρα**. — The girl was beautiful *to the extreme* [i.e., The girl was very beautiful].

Prefixed Prepositions

9.11. Prepositions may be prefixed to verbs and nouns to form compound words.[5] Thus you will find forms such as ἐκβάλλω (ἐκ + βάλλω) and εἴσοδος (εἰς + ὁδός). Occasionally two prepositions are prefixed—for example, ἐπισυνάγω (ἐπί + σύν + ἄγω). When a preposition ending with a vowel is prefixed to a word that begins with a vowel, the final vowel of the preposition is typically elided; thus δία + ἐγείρω becomes διεγείρω. If the word to which the preposition is attached begins with a rough breathing mark, the spelling of some prepositions may change slightly; thus ἀπό + ὁρίζω becomes ἀφορίζω.[6] Other prepositions may have a different spelling when prefixed to a word beginning with certain consonants. This is for purposes of pronunciation (euphony). For example, σύν may be spelled συμ-, συλ-, or συγ-, and ἐν is typically ἐμ- in such compounds.

The effect of the preposition on the meaning of the word with which it is compounded is generally unpredictable. Some such compounds have no effect at all; both ἐνδοξάζω and δοξάζω mean "I bless." In other instances the combination is transparent in that the common meanings of both elements can be seen (e.g., ἐκπέμπω, "I send out"). In other cases there is a significant change of meaning, though *how* the meaning changes is not predictable based only on the typical meaning of the preposition. For example, ἀναστρέφω does not mean "I turn up" (ἀνά, "up" + στρέφω, "I turn"). Depending on the context, it may mean "I turn upside down" or "I turn back, return." Some prepositions may give the verb to which they are joined a durative (e.g., διαμένω) or intensive (e.g., κατακρίνω) meaning. The only sure way to determine such things is to consult a good lexicon; *CL*, BDAG, and LN will all provide the necessary

5. Some prepositions are never used this way; they are called improper prepositions—those that cannot be prefixed to another word. These include words such as ἐνώπιον, ἄχρι, and ὀπίσω.
6. These changes are the same as those listed earlier in the chapter.

information. If you do not find any indication in the lexicon of what might seem to be the obvious meaning, then you should not base your understanding on a presumed etymology.

The Article as a Function Marker

9.12. The article can be used not only with a noun or adjective but also as a function marker. In these situations an article can be used to change the function of another part of speech or a phrase to make it function like an adjective or a noun. The most common example of this use of the article is found with prepositional phrases, though the article can be used similarly with other constructions as well. The illustrations here use prepositions.

The Article as an Adjective Marker

9.13. An article can govern not only a noun (ὁ λόγος) or an adjective (ὁ καλός) but also a prepositional phrase—for example, τοῖς ἐν τῇ οἰκίᾳ. Remember that most prepositional phrases are adverbial (they modify the verb). The normal way to indicate that a prepositional phrase is modifying a *noun* is to add the article *in front of* the preposition.

For example, the two following statements say something quite different.[7]

ὁ ἵππος (horse) ἐν τῇ κώμῃ (village) ἐστὶν μικρός.
ὁ ἵππος ὁ ἐν τῇ κώμῃ ἐστὶν μικρός.

Although we might represent both of them in English as, "The horse in the village is small," that is somewhat ambiguous in English (though from what we know of the world and how things are, we would likely make the correct assumption). Does the English statement mean that the horse is small when he is in the village (but large when he is not), or that the horse, which is in the village, is a small horse? Greek makes this distinction explicit. The first sentence asserts that the horse is small when he is in the village. Since prepositional phrases are normally adverbial, the phrase ἐν τῇ κώμῃ ("in the village") modifies the verb ἐστίν. The second statement, however, adds something to clarify the meaning. Note that the article is added on the front of the prepositional phrase, indicating that the reference is to "the horse that is in the village."

9.14. This is the first time that you have seen an article used with something other than a noun or a substantival adjective. (There are other options you will meet in due time, but do not worry about them now.) What the article does in this situation is essentially convert the prepositional phrase into an adjective; it tells the reader that the prepositional phrase ἐν τῇ κώμῃ modifies not the verb but the *noun*.[8] Which noun? And can you identify the adjective position that is used?

7. This sample sentence comes from Voelz, *Fundamental Greek Grammar*, 77–78.
8. The article in this usage is technically called an *adjectivizer.*

ὁ ἵππος ὁ ἐν τῇ κώμῃ = article ▸ noun ▸ article ▸ modifier

This is the second attributive position, and in this instance the modifier is a prepositional phrase rather than a simple adjective. When the prepositional phrase functions as an adjective, the article will always agree with the noun it modifies in gender, number, and case. In the examples that follow, the relative phrase "which is" is supplied for clarity; it may often be omitted if the adjectival nature of the prepositional phrase is clear without it.

John 5:44, τὴν δόξαν **τὴν παρὰ τοῦ θεοῦ**	The glory *which is from God*
Luke 6:41, Τί δὲ βλέπεις τὸ κάρφος **τὸ ἐν τῷ ὀφθαλμῷ** τοῦ ἀδελφοῦ σου, τὴν δὲ δοκὸν **τὴν ἐν τῷ ἰδίῳ ὀφθαλμῷ** οὐ κατανοεῖς;	Why do you see the speck *which is in* your fellow believer's *eye* but do not notice the log *which is in your own eye*?
Gen. 37:22, ἐμβάλετε (throw!) αὐτὸν εἰς τὸν λάκκον τοῦτον **τὸν ἐν τῇ ἐρήμῳ.**	Throw him in this pit *which is in the wilderness.*

A prepositional phrase may also occur in the first attributive position.

2 Cor. 7:10, **ἡ κατὰ θεὸν** λύπη . . . ἡ δὲ τοῦ κόσμου λύπη	The "*according to God*" grief . . . but the "of the world" grief (or in better English, *godly grief* . . . but worldly grief)

In this example the first phrase illustrates an article governing a prepositional phrase (κατὰ θεόν), but in the second phrase the article governs a genitive noun phrase (τοῦ κόσμου). Both function the same way: to describe the noun λύπη.

Adjectival Phrases without Articles

Although use of the article is the normal way of indicating that a prepositional phrase is functioning adjectivally, it is possible for an anarthrous phrase to function the same way. Normally if you find a prepositional phrase without an article, you should assume that it is adverbial (that is by far the most common situation), but if the context just does not make sense, you will need to consider the possibility that it is adjectival, as, for example, in Mark 1:23: ἄνθρωπος ἐν πνεύματι ἀκαθάρτῳ ("a man with an evil spirit"). In the following example, the prepositional phrase ἀντὶ πολλῶν is probably best taken as adjectival, modifying the noun λύτρον, rather than as adverbial, modifying the infinitive δοῦναι: Mark 10:45, ὁ υἱὸς τοῦ ἀνθρώπου ἦλθεν (came) δοῦναι (to give) τὴν ψυχὴν αὐτοῦ λύτρον **ἀντὶ πολλῶν** ("the Son of Man came to give his life as a ransom *for many*"). See also Mark 5:2 (2×); 12:25.

The Article as a Noun Marker

9.15. Other times the article converts the prepositional phrase, not into an adjective, but into a noun. It functions like a substantival adjective, taking the place of a noun.[9] For example, in Acts 1:3 we are told that during his postresurrection ministry, Jesus was speaking **τὰ** περὶ τῆς βασιλείας τοῦ θεοῦ ("*the things* concerning the kingdom of God"). The entire prepositional phrase functions as the direct object of the verb "speaking."[10] The neuter plural article in this instance means "the things," and it is accusative since it functions as the object. When a prepositional phrase functions as a noun, the article will always be in the case appropriate to its function in the sentence (subjects are nominative, objects are accusative, etc.).

Rom. 9:6, **οἱ** ἐξ Ἰσραήλ	*The ones* from Israel
Rom. 4:14, **οἱ** ἐκ νόμου	*The ones* from the law (= the ones who live by/follow the law)
1 Cor. 9:20, **τοὺς** ὑπὸ νόμον	*The ones* under the law
Gen. 7:23, κατελείφθη (he was left) μόνος Νῶε καὶ **οἱ** μετ᾽ αὐτοῦ ἐν τῇ κιβωτῷ.	Only Noah was left and *the ones* with him in the ark.[a]

[a] For smoother English we could translate with a compound subject and the verb as a plural: "Only Noah and the ones with him in the ark were left."

Examples of the Article as a Function Marker

9.16. Many of the examples in the next two sections are not complete sentences. (Watch for the period or lack of it at the end of each example.) Instances of the article used as a function marker both as adjective and noun are included here.

Matt. 6:9, Πάτερ ἡμῶν **ὁ** ἐν τοῖς οὐρανοῖς	Our Father *who* is in heaven

So long as I tell you that πάτερ is a vocative noun,[11] you can understand that the prepositional phrase modifies πάτερ ("Father"). In sentences like this it is sometimes helpful to translate the article as a relative pronoun: "who," "which/that," and so on—for example, "Our Father *who* is in heaven" (traditionally, "Our Father *which* art in heaven").

Mark 3:22, οἱ γραμματεῖς **οἱ** ἀπὸ Ἱεροσολύμων	The scribes from Jerusalem

9. The article in this usage is technically called a *nominalizer.*

10. Technically, "speaking" is a participle, but it still takes an object.

11. Vocative is the case used for direct address; see app. D. This noun, πατήρ, πατρός, ὁ, is in the third declension (do not worry about the form now—we will figure that out later).

Mark 15:43, Ἰωσὴφ **ὁ** ἀπὸ Ἁριμαθαίας	Joseph *who was* from Arimathea (traditionally translated "Joseph of Arimathea")
John 15:25, ὁ λόγος **ὁ** ἐν τῷ νόμῳ	The word *which is* [written] in the Law
Exod. 3:7, εἶπεν (he said) δὲ κύριος πρὸς Μωϋσῆν, Εἶδον (I have seen) τὴν κάκωσιν (oppression) τοῦ λαοῦ μου **τοῦ** ἐν Αἰγύπτῳ.	But the Lord said to Moses, "I have seen the oppression of my people *who are* in Egypt."

9.17. *Now You Try It*

Rom. 7:10, ἡ ἐντολὴ **ἡ** εἰς ζωήν	
Rom. 8:39, τῆς ἀγάπης τοῦ θεοῦ **τῆς** ἐν Χριστῷ Ἰησοῦ τῷ κυρίῳ ἡμῶν	
Acts 8:14, **οἱ** ἐν Ἱεροσολύμοις ἀπόστολοι	
Rom. 10:5, Μωϋσῆς γὰρ γράφει τὴν δικαιοσύνην **τὴν** ἐκ τοῦ νόμου.	
Gen. 3:1, τῶν θηρίων **τῶν** ἐπὶ τῆς γῆς	
Gen. 13:13, οἱ δὲ ἄνθρωποι **οἱ** ἐν Σοδόμοις πονηροὶ καὶ ἁμαρτωλοὶ ἐναντίον τοῦ θεοῦ σφόδρα.	You will have to supply a form of εἰμί in this sentence. What is the subject and what is the predicate nominative? How is the second οἱ functioning in this sentence?

— — — — — — — — — — — — — —

Advanced Information for Reference:
Special Uses Involving Prepositions

9.18. There are some particular instances involving prepositions that are important to recognize. Many of these are idiomatic in nature; that is, you would not be able to predict the meaning simply from recognizing the individual words. Only a catalog-style list is given here with one example for each, but it is sufficient to alert you to the type of meanings involved and give you a place to check them later when you encounter them in a text.

ἀνὰ μέσον (a compound preposition): "among, between, in the midst of"

Matt. 13:25, ἦλθεν αὐτοῦ ὁ ἐχθρὸς καὶ ἐπέσπειρεν ζιζάνια **ἀνὰ μέσον** τοῦ σίτου.	His enemy came and sowed weed seed *among* the grain.

διὰ τοῦτο: "because of this, on account of this"

John 15:19, **διὰ τοῦτο** μισεῖ ὑμᾶς ὁ κόσμος.	*On account of this* the world will hate you.

ἐπί + genitive: in a temporal context usually refers to a *point* of time

Luke 4:27, πολλοὶ λεπροὶ ἦσαν (there were) ἐν τῷ Ἰσραὴλ **ἐπὶ Ἐλισαίου** τοῦ προφήτου.

There were many lepers in Israel *at the time of Elisha* the prophet.

ἐπί + dative: in a temporal context usually implies the time *during* which something happens

Eph. 4:26, ὁ ἥλιος μὴ ἐπιδυέτω (let it go down) **ἐπὶ τῷ παροργισμῷ** ὑμῶν.

Do not let the sun go down *during* your *wrath* [i.e., while you are angry].

ἐπί + accusative: in a temporal context usually references an *extent* of time

Luke 4:25, πολλαὶ χῆραι ἦσαν ἐν ταῖς ἡμέραις Ἠλίου ἐν τῷ Ἰσραήλ, ὅτε ἐκλείσθη ὁ οὐρανὸς **ἐπὶ ἔτη τρία καὶ μῆνας ἕξ.**

There were many widows in the days of Elijah in Israel, when the sky was shut up *for three years and six months.*

— — — — — — — — — — — — — —

— — — — — — — — — — — — — —

9.19. Advanced Information for Reference: Diagramming Prepositional Phrases

John 1:1, **Ἐν ἀρχῇ** ἦν ὁ λόγος, καὶ ὁ λόγος ἦν **πρὸς τὸν θεόν**, καὶ θεὸς ἦν ὁ λόγος.

The Word was *in the beginning*, and the Word was *with God*, and the Word was God.

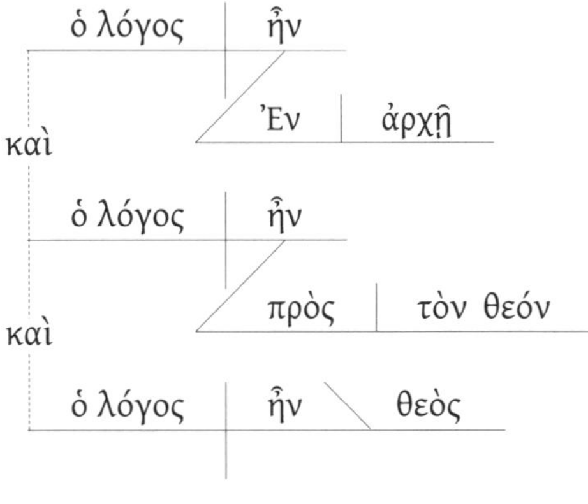

Figure 9.5

— — — — — — — — — — — — — —

9.20. Reading Passage: Colossians 1:1–8

Paul's Thanksgiving

1Παῦλος ἀπόστολος Χριστοῦ Ἰησοῦ **διὰ** θελήματος (will) θεοῦ καὶ Τιμόθεος ὁ
ἀδελφὸς 2τοῖς **ἐν** Κολοσσαῖς ἁγίοις καὶ πιστοῖς ἀδελφοῖς **ἐν** Χριστῷ, χάρις ὑμῖν
καὶ εἰρήνη **ἀπὸ** θεοῦ πατρὸς (Father) ἡμῶν.
3Εὐχαριστοῦμεν τῷ θεῷ πατρὶ (Father) τοῦ κυρίου ἡμῶν Ἰησοῦ Χριστοῦ
πάντοτε **περὶ** ὑμῶν προσευχόμενοι (praying), 4ἀκούσαντες (having heard)
τὴν πίστιν (faith) ὑμῶν **ἐν** Χριστῷ Ἰησοῦ καὶ τὴν ἀγάπην ἣν (which) ἔχετε **εἰς**
πάντας τοὺς ἁγίους 5**διὰ** τὴν ἐλπίδα (hope) τὴν ἀποκειμένην (reserved) ὑμῖν **ἐν**
τοῖς οὐρανοῖς, ἣν προηκούσατε **ἐν** τῷ λόγῳ τῆς ἀληθείας τοῦ εὐαγγελίου 6τοῦ
παρόντος (which has come) **εἰς** ὑμᾶς, καθὼς καὶ **ἐν** παντὶ (all) τῷ κόσμῳ ἐστὶν
καρποφορούμενον (producing fruit) καὶ αὐξανόμενον (growing) καθὼς καὶ **ἐν**
ὑμῖν, **ἀφ'** ἧς ἡμέρας ἠκούσατε καὶ ἐπέγνωτε (you understood) τὴν χάριν (grace)
τοῦ θεοῦ **ἐν** ἀληθείᾳ· 7καθὼς ἐμάθετε (you learned) **ἀπὸ** Ἐπαφρᾶ τοῦ ἀγαπητοῦ
συνδούλου ἡμῶν, ὅς (who) ἐστιν πιστὸς **ὑπὲρ** ὑμῶν διάκονος τοῦ Χριστοῦ,
8ὁ καὶ δηλώσας (who declared) ἡμῖν τὴν ὑμῶν ἀγάπην **ἐν** πνεύματι (Spirit).

Vocabulary for Chapter 9

9.21. You may need to plan a bit more time than usual to learn the vocabulary for this chapter. The most common prepositions are included in this list to enable you to compare and contrast their range of meaning. Although this facilitates understanding the concepts involved, it may be a bit more difficult to learn a list with a number of short, sometimes similar words.

Part of Speech	Definition	Possible Glosses	Frequency	
Word			NT	LXX
Adjectives				
ὅλος, η, ον	Being complete in extent	whole, complete (adj.); entirely (adv.)	109	272
ἀγαθός, ή, όν	Achieving a high standard of excellence, positive moral qualities	good, useful, beneficial, helpful	102	599
καλός, ή, όν	Of high quality and therefore satisfying; a positive moral quality that is favorably valued; attractive in outward form; fitting	good, beautiful	100	235
ἕτερος, α, ον	Distinct from another item, sometimes indicating dissimilarity [often synonymous with ἄλλος]; one's neighbor	other, another, different; neighbor	98	258
Noun				
βιβλίον, ου, τό	Written document regardless of size (one or multiple sheets or pages) or format (loose sheet, scroll, or codex form)	book, scroll; document	34	186
Prepositions				
ἐν	A preposition used with the dative case that generally refers to position within, but usage is quite varied with many possible English equivalents, depending on the context	(prep. + dat.) in, on, among	2,752	14,275

Part of Speech	Definition	Possible Glosses	Frequency	
Word			NT	LXX
εἰς	A preposition used with the accusative case that generally refers to entrance into, direction, or limit (these can be spatial or temporal), but usage is quite varied with many possible English equivalents, depending on the context; in Koine, often overlaps with ἐν in meaning [Note the smooth breathing: this is not εἷς.]	(prep. + acc.) into, in, among; until	1,768	7,438
ἐκ, ἐξ	A preposition used with the genitive case that generally refers to separation or derivation, but usage is quite varied with many possible English equivalents, depending on the context	(prep. + gen.) out of, from	914	3,823
ἐπί	A preposition used with any of three cases that generally refers to location ("on" or "over") or time ("at" or "in"); some English equivalents are usable with all three cases, others are appropriate for only one of the cases [see *CL* or BDAG]	(prep. + gen.) on, over, when; (prep. + dat.) on the basis of, at; (prep. + acc.) on, to, against	890	7,297
πρός	A preposition most commonly used with the accusative case to indicate destination or goal ("to, toward"), but occasionally with the genitive ("in the interest of") or dative ("at, near") case	(prep. + acc.) to, toward, with; (prep. + gen.) in the interest of; (prep. + dat.) at, near	700	3,338
διά	A preposition used with the genitive (spatial, temporal, instrumental) and accusative cases (spatial or causal)	(prep. + gen.) through, during; (prep. + acc.) because of, on account of	667	1,427
ἀπό	A preposition used with the genitive case that generally indicates separation or source, sometimes temporal or causal	(prep. + gen.) from	646	4,150
κατά	A preposition used most commonly with the accusative case (sometimes with the genitive), expressing measure in terms of extension or correspondence	(prep. + acc.) according to, throughout, during; (prep. + gen.) down, against	473	2,140
μετά	A preposition used with the genitive case to indicate association or accompaniment, or with the accusative case to indicate position or sequence (either temporal or spatial)	(prep. + gen.) with; (prep. + acc.) after	469	2,534
περί	A preposition used with the genitive and accusative cases that describes various aspects of being near or related to something (spatial, temporal, logical)	(prep. + gen.) about, concerning; (prep. + acc.) around	333	852

9.22. Key Things to Know for Chapter 9

What do prepositional phrases usually modify?

Can you explain the relationship between prepositions and case?

What is the usual way of indicating that a prepositional phrase modifies a noun or takes the place of a noun?

10

PRONOUNS: PART 2

Other Types of Pronouns

10.1. In chapter 4 you met the personal pronouns: first, second, and third person. The words ἐγώ/ἡμεῖς, σύ/ὑμεῖς, and αὐτός/αὐτή/αὐτό should all be very familiar by now. In this chapter, you will meet several other types of pronouns.

Demonstrative Pronouns

The English demonstratives are *this/these* and *that/those*. These words may be used as pronouns, in which case we call them *demonstrative pronouns*:

This is what I am going to do.
Those must be painted.

The same words may also be used as adjectives; in this instance they modify nouns and are called *demonstrative adjectives*:

This course is a piece of cake!
These cookies are as hard as rocks.

The words *this* and *these* are called *near demonstratives*; *that* and *those* are named *far demonstratives*. This is not a spatial relationship but refers to what is uppermost in the speaker's mind ("near") or more remote conceptually ("far").

Greek demonstratives function much like English demonstratives.

Near Demonstrative Forms

10.2. The forms of the demonstratives are easy, since they are little more than two new vocabulary words to learn. They use the same set of case endings that you already know, and they occur in each of the three genders. Here is what they look like. Do the bold portions of these words look familiar? Compare them to the forms on the article chart.

Near Demonstrative Pronoun

	Masc.	Fem.	Neut.
NS	οὗτος	αὕτη	τοῦτο
GS	τούτ**ου**	ταύτ**ης**	τούτ**ου**
DS	τούτ**ῳ**	ταύτ**ῃ**	τούτ**ῳ**
AS	τοῦτ**ον**	ταύτ**ην**	τοῦτ**ο**
NP	οὗτ**οι**	αὗτ**αι**	ταῦτ**α**
GP	τούτ**ων**	τούτ**ων**	τούτ**ων**
DP	τούτ**οις**	ταύτ**αις**	τούτ**οις**
AP	τούτ**ους**	ταύτ**ας**	ταῦτ**α**

One tricky thing to remember about the demonstratives is that the nominative forms do not look like the other case forms. In the lexicon this word is listed alphabetically under οὗτος (that is, the masculine singular nominative form), but when you shift to any of the oblique cases, the rough breathing drops off and is replaced by a tau. The nominative plural retains the rough breathing. Likewise, the feminine forms follow the same pattern. The tau is present throughout in the neuter. Do notice that the genitive plural form in the feminine has omicron as the second letter rather than the characteristic alpha. This means that the genitive plural form by itself does not distinguish gender.

The Importance of Breathing Marks

Demonstratives always have a *rough* breathing mark or a tau (τ). This enables you to distinguish them from the feminine forms of αὐτός such as αὐτή.

Far Demonstrative Forms

10.3. The far demonstrative is very consistent; it has none of the morphological variations of its near cousins.

Far Demonstrative Pronoun

	Masc.	Fem.	Neut.
NS	ἐκεῖνος	ἐκείνη	ἐκεῖνο
GS	ἐκείνου	ἐκείνης	ἐκείνου
DS	ἐκείνῳ	ἐκείνῃ	ἐκείνῳ
AS	ἐκεῖνον	ἐκείνην	ἐκεῖνο

NP	ἐκεῖνοι	ἐκεῖναι	ἐκεῖνα
GP	ἐκείνων	ἐκείνων	ἐκείνων
DP	ἐκείνοις	ἐκείναις	ἐκείνοις
AP	ἐκείνους	ἐκείνας	ἐκεῖνα

Although the article does not show up on the end of the far demonstrative like it does in the near demonstratives, the same case endings are used here—and you already know them from their use on nouns and adjectives.

The Use of Demonstratives

Demonstratives as Substantives

10.4. The demonstratives may be used substantivally:

This person/thing (*or* this one/man/woman)
That person/thing (*or* that one/man/woman)

Follow natural gender in translating; translate masculine forms with an English phrase that implies reference to someone of the male sex (or, if the context suggests, a generic form that may refer to either sex), translate feminine forms in such a way as to represent female sex, and so forth. Word meanings and the referent of the pronoun may suggest otherwise in some cases, and English may have conventions that differ from Greek at this point.

John 1:34, **οὗτός** ἐστιν ὁ υἱὸς τοῦ θεοῦ.	*This one* is the Son of God.
Mark 4:15–16, **οὗτοι** δέ εἰσιν οἱ παρὰ τὴν ὁδόν· καὶ **οὗτοί** εἰσιν οἱ ἐπὶ τὰ πετρώδη.	Now *these* are the ones along the road; and *these* are the ones on the rocky ground.
John 9:28, Σὺ μαθητὴς εἶ **ἐκείνου**, ἡμεῖς δὲ τοῦ Μωϋσέως ἐσμὲν μαθηταί.	You are a disciple of *that one*, but we are disciples of Moses.
Hab. 2:13, οὐ **ταῦτά** ἐστιν παρὰ κυρίου παντοκράτορος;	Are not *these things* from the Lord Almighty?

Demonstratives as Adjectives

10.5. A demonstrative can also be used as an adjective (*this/that x*). It will be in predicate position to the noun that it modifies (that is, there will not be an article in front of it), but do not supply a verb. Both ὁ ἄνθρωπος οὗτος (this second predicate position is more common in the NT) and οὗτος ὁ ἄνθρωπος (the less common first predicate position) mean "this man."[1]

1. The far demonstrative occurs only in predicate position in the NT. Attributive position—either first attributive (ὁ ἐκεῖνος ἄνθρωπος) or second attributive (ὁ ἄνθρωπος ὁ ἐκεῖνος)—is possible but

Mark 14:71, Οὐκ οἶδα τὸν ἄνθρωπον **τοῦτον.**	I do not know *this* man.
Mark 15:39, Ἀληθῶς **οὗτος** ὁ ἄνθρωπος υἱὸς θεοῦ ἦν.	Truly *this* man was the Son of God.
Prov. 1:19, **αὗται** αἱ ὁδοί εἰσιν πάντων τῶν συντελούντων τὰ ἄνομα· τῇ γὰρ ἀσεβείᾳ τὴν ἑαυτῶν ψυχὴν ἀφαιροῦνται.	*These* are the ways of all who perpetrate lawless deeds, for by unrighteousness they take away their own life.

A common adjectival use of the far demonstrative is in expressions of time.

Mark 4:35, λέγει αὐτοῖς **ἐν ἐκείνῃ τῇ ἡμέρᾳ.**	He said to them *in that day.*
Mark 8:1, **Ἐν ἐκείναις ταῖς ἡμέραις** πάλιν [there was] πολλοῦ ὄχλου.	*In those days* there was a large crowd.
Num. 9:6, οὐκ ἠδύναντο (they were able) ποιῆσαι τὸ πάσχα **ἐν τῇ ἡμέρᾳ ἐκείνῃ,** καὶ προσῆλθον (they came) ἐναντίον Μωϋσῆ καὶ Ἀαρὼν **ἐν ἐκείνῃ τῇ ἡμέρᾳ.**	They were not able to observe the Passover *in that day*, and so they came before Moses and Aaron *in that day.*

Demonstratives as Personal Pronouns

10.6. Sometimes you can represent a demonstrative in English simply as a personal pronoun: *he/she/it*. This is what is sometimes referred to as a *weakened demonstrative*. Of course the beginning student's question is, How do I know when this is the case? To which the standard answer is forthcoming: "context"![2] One of the context clues is to ask if there is any sort of contrast implied in the context: does the writer intend you to think about *this person* as opposed to some other person? Or is the writer simply referring to an individual "on his (or her) own"? A contrast should usually be maintained with *this/that*, but if there is no contrast, a simple English *he/she/it* is probably adequate.

Here are two examples of demonstratives that appear to have the weakened force of a personal pronoun:

Luke 1:32, **οὗτος** ἔσται (will be) μέγας καὶ υἱὸς ὑψίστου (of the highest) κληθήσεται (he will be called).	*He* will be great, and he will be called the Son of the Highest.

It would be possible to translate this sentence as "*This one* will be great"—but that is somewhat clumsy English, and the context does not suggest any particular reason to specify "this one" as opposed to "that one."[3]

---

occurs rarely in Koine. It is not found at all in the NT, and second attributive occurs only a few times in the LXX (e.g., Exod. 2:11). A first attributive example occurs in *T. Ab.* 7.9.

2. That seems to be the answer to a great many questions like this, but that is language—there typically is no set of rules for such things.

3. Read some of the contemporary translations that pay close attention to both English and Greek to see how this works (e.g., NIV or HCSB); you might find that the NASB too often mechanically

John 1:8, οὐκ ἦν **ἐκεῖνος** τὸ φῶς.

He was not the light.

Gen. 10:9, **οὗτος** ἦν γίγας κυνηγὸς ἐναντίον κυρίου τοῦ θεοῦ· διὰ τοῦτο[a] ἐροῦσιν (they will say), Ὡς Νεβρὼδ γίγας κυνηγὸς ἐναντίον κυρίου.

He was a mighty hunter before the Lord God; on account of this they will say, "Like Nimrod, a mighty hunter before the Lord."

[a] διὰ τοῦτο; see §9.18.

10.7. *Now You Try It*

Mark 9:7, **Οὗτός** ἐστιν ὁ υἱός μου ὁ ἀγαπητός.

John 21:7, λέγει οὖν ὁ μαθητὴς **ἐκεῖνος** τῷ Πέτρῳ, Ὁ κύριός ἐστιν.

John 1:2, **οὗτος** ἦν (was) ἐν ἀρχῇ πρὸς τὸν θεόν.

John 1:19, **αὕτη** ἐστὶν ἡ μαρτυρία τοῦ Ἰωάννου.

John 1:41, εὑρίσκει **οὗτος** πρῶτον τὸν ἀδελφὸν τὸν ἴδιον Σίμωνα καὶ λέγει αὐτῷ, Εὑρήκαμεν (we have found) τὸν Μεσσίαν.

John 20:13, λέγουσιν αὐτῇ **ἐκεῖνοι**, Γύναι,[a] τί κλαίεις;

[a] Vocative case; see app. D.

Gen. 31:43, τί ποιήσω[a] **ταύταις**[b] σήμερον ἢ τοῖς τέκνοις αὐτῶν;

[a] "What shall I do?" (τί is an interrogative pronoun; see §12.13).

[b] Be sure you notice the gender of this pronoun. To whom does it refer?

Jon. 4:2, προσεύξατο (he prayed) πρὸς κύριον καὶ εἶπεν (he said), Ὦ κύριε,[a] οὐχ **οὗτοι** οἱ λόγοι μου ἔτι ὄντος μου[b] ἐν τῇ γῇ μου;

[a] Vocative case; see app. D.

[b] ἔτι ὄντος μου, "while I was still living" (This is a genitive absolute construction, which you will learn about in chap. 27.)

---

leaves weakened demonstratives as *this/that* and as a result comes across as rather clumsy English (though in Luke 1:32 it is correct).

10.8. *Challenge Verse*

Mark 4:20, **ἐκεῖνοί** εἰσιν οἱ[a] ἐπὶ τὴν γῆν τὴν καλὴν σπαρέντες (sown).

[a] The article οἱ governs σπαρέντες ("the ones sown"), not the prepositional phrase, which modifies σπαρέντες in first attributive position.

An Implied Gesture

Sometimes a demonstrative implies a physical gesture. In the following example you can almost see Peter pointing to the six men who stood with him as he explained to the church in Jerusalem why he had been so bold as to enter the home of a Gentile and eat with him: *these* ☞ six brothers are my witnesses.

Acts 11:12, ἦλθον δὲ σὺν ἐμοὶ καὶ ☞ **οἱ ἓξ ἀδελφοὶ οὗτοι** καὶ εἰσήλθομεν εἰς τὸν οἶκον τοῦ ἀνδρός.	[The Spirit told me to have no hesitation about going with them.] *These six brothers* also went with me, and we entered the man's house. (NIV)

Relative Pronouns

10.9. In addition to demonstrative pronouns, Greek also has what is called a *relative pronoun*. Since English also has a relative pronoun that functions very much like its older Greek cousin, we will begin with English and then compare Greek usage. English usage is more important than usual here, since relative pronouns are used in such diverse ways in our own language. How one translates a Greek relative pronoun (and the relative clause that it introduces) is largely a matter of English grammar. The syntactical form functions similarly in both languages; relative clauses in Greek are almost always translated by the same formal structure in English.

English Relative Pronouns

10.10. The relative pronouns in English include such words as *who* (or the objective and possessive forms: *whom, whose*), *which*, *what*, and *that*.[4] *Relative clause* refers to the relative pronoun and the clause that it introduces. In the following sentence the relative clause is italicized.

The boy *who is driving the tractor* is my grandson Cody.

4. The word *that* is not always a relative pronoun in English, but it may be (e.g., "The book that you are reading . . ."). It may also be an adverb ("I'll go that far, but no farther") or a conjunction ("I believe that Jesus is God"). In English there has been a technical distinction between *which* and *that*—a distinction that students (and teachers) sometimes have trouble remembering. The rules of English usage are beginning to blur that distinction so you can ignore them for our purposes.

Relative clauses can function as a unit in a sentence and can take the place of a noun (or sometimes an adjective). Compare the following sentence pairs, and note how the italicized words function syntactically in each sentence.

I eat *clams.*	"Clams" is the direct object of the sentence.
I eat *what is served me.*	The relative clause functions in the sentence as the direct object the same way that "clams" does in the previous sentence.
Ryan is not against me.	"Ryan" is the subject.
Whoever is with me is not against me.	The relative clause is the subject.
Give the Bible to *Audrey.*	"Audrey" is the object of the preposition.
Give the Bible to *whoever asks for it.*	The relative clause is the object of the preposition.

10.11. In the examples just cited, the relative clause functions the same as the simple noun. Other times the antecedent of a relative pronoun is an entire clause, in which case the relative introduces an adjectival clause.

We are going to study Greek tonight, *which* is the wise thing to do.

The relative pronouns *which* and *what* (and their indefinite forms, *whichever* and *whatever*) can be used as adjectives, in which case they are often called *pronominal adjectives*, that is, pronouns functioning as adjectives. In the following two examples, the relative pronoun modifies the noun "book":

I know *which* book I am going to order: BDAG!
Whatever books you buy, you need to get BDAG.

Greek Relative Pronouns

10.12. The relative pronoun in Greek functions very much as it does in English. We will first learn what the relative pronouns look like, then consider some principles as to how they function in sentences, and finally look at a number of examples.

Forms of the Greek Relative Pronoun

10.13. Compare the forms on the chart below with similar forms that you have already learned.

Greek Relative Pronouns

	Masc.	Fem.	Neut.	English Equivalent
NS	ὅς	ἥ	ὅ	who, which, that
GS	οὗ	ἧς	οὗ	whose, of whom
DS	ᾧ	ᾗ	ᾧ	to whom, which
AS	ὅν	ἥν	ὅ	whom, which, that
NP	οἵ	αἵ	ἅ	who, which, that
GP	ὧν	ὧν	ὧν	whose, of whom
DP	οἷς	αἷς	οἷς	to whom, which
AP	οὕς	ἅς	ἅ	whom, which, that

ὁ, ἡ, οἱ, αἱ are all forms of the article. To keep the article and the relative pronoun distinct, remember that the relative pronoun *always* has a rough breathing mark *and* an accent mark. The article has only a rough breathing mark. In many cases the basic difference between the article and relative pronoun is that the article begins with a tau but the relative pronoun uses a rough breathing mark instead. The word ἦν, with a smooth breathing and circumflex accent, is a form of εἰμί, "he/she/it was" (you will learn this form in chap. 16), whereas the relative pronoun is ἥν, with a rough breathing and an acute accent.

The Relative Pronoun in the LXX

One of the most salient characteristics of LXX Greek is the repetition of the pronoun after the relative, as though in English, instead of saying "the land which they possessed," we were to say habitually "the land which they possessed it," and so in all similar cases. This anomaly is due to the literal following of the Hebrew text. Now in Hebrew the relative is indeclinable. Its meaning therefore is not complete until a pronoun has been added to determine it. But the relative in Greek being declinable, the translator was forced to assign to it gender, number, and case, which rendered the addition of the pronoun after it unnecessary. Nevertheless the pronoun was retained out of regard for the sacred text.[a]

For example, Num. 35:25, ὁ ἱερεὺς ὁ μέγας, **ὃν** ἔχρισαν **αὐτὸν** τῷ ἐλαίῳ τῷ ἁγίῳ, "the high priest, *whom* they anointed *him* with holy oil."

[a] Conybeare and Stock, *Grammar of Septuagint Greek*, §69.

Grammar of the Relative Pronoun

10.14. Relative pronouns most commonly relate a clause (called a *relative clause*) to a previous statement.[5] The word in the previous statement to which the relative pronoun refers is the antecedent, just as with other pronouns. The number and gender of a relative pronoun are determined by its antecedent (just like a personal pronoun). The case of a relative pronoun is determined by its function in its own clause. Most relative pronouns stand at the head of the relative clause. The most common exception to that principle is when the relative pronoun is the object of a preposition, in which case it follows the preposition.

5. Although it is not common, occasionally a relative pronoun has no antecedent. In such situations the clause is called a *headless relative clause*. For example, 1 John begins with the words "That which was from the beginning." The English "that which" translates a relative pronoun (ὅ) that cannot have an antecedent, since it is the first word in the book of 1 John.

Mark 1:2, ἀποστέλλω **τὸν ἄγγελόν** μου, **ὃς** κατασκευάσει τὴν ὁδόν σου. | I will send my *messenger*, *who* will prepare your way.

In this example, the relative pronoun, ὅς, is nominative because it functions as the subject of the verb κατασκευάσει (will prepare). It is masculine singular to agree with its antecedent, τὸν ἄγγελον, in the preceding clause.

The relative clause is always a *subordinate* clause. That is, it never expresses the main idea of the sentence. In the example just above, the main idea is "I will send my messenger." The subordinate, relative clause then tells us something further about that statement—in this case, what the messenger is going to do.

10.15. If a relative pronoun does not have an antecedent, it is often translated as "the one who" or "the ones who" or "that which." There are other viable English equivalents that may sound better in various contexts: "he who," "those whom," and so on.[6] In these instances the relative clause is functioning substantivally, taking the place of a noun.

Mark 3:13, ἀναβαίνει (he ascended) εἰς τὸ ὄρος καὶ προσκαλεῖται (he summoned) **οὓς** ἤθελεν (he desired) αὐτός. | He ascended the mountain[a] and summoned *those whom* he desired.

[a] We do not say "he ascended *into* a mountain" in English, so the preposition εἰς is omitted in translation.

Here the relative pronoun is in the accusative case because it is functioning as the direct object of the verb ἤθελεν (he desired); the subject of the clause is αὐτός. There is no antecedent for the pronoun in this example. The entire relative clause (**οὓς** ἤθελεν αὐτός) functions as the object of the main verb, προσκαλεῖται. He summoned not Grant, or Meghan, or the townspeople, but "those whom he desired."

10.16. When a relative pronoun is combined with ἄν or ἐάν, the phrase expresses an indefinite idea.[7] Instead of translating as *who*, *whom*, *which*, and so forth, the indefinite form is *whoever*, *whomever*, *whichever*. Instead of referring to a specific person or thing, the indefinite is a general reference to anyone or anything that fits the description. These indefinite forms are used with a specific verb form that you have not yet learned, the subjunctive. Even though you will not understand why the verb is spelled the way it is in the examples that follow, you can still make good sense of the statements, using the parallel English text.

Mark 3:35, **ὃς ἂν** ποιήσῃ τὸ θέλημα τοῦ θεοῦ, οὗτος ἀδελφός μου καὶ ἀδελφὴ καὶ μήτηρ ἐστίν. | *Whoever* does the will of God, this one is my brother and sister and mother.

The relative pronoun ὅς is nominative because it is the subject of ποιήσῃ, "he/she/it does."

6. Remember that *who* is subjective (nominative) case in English and *whom* is objective (accusative) case, so the correct English form must be selected, depending on the pronoun's function in its own clause.

7. There is also a specific form called the *indefinite relative pronoun*, ὅστις, a compound formed from the relative pronoun and the indefinite pronoun. Both parts of this word decline, so you will see not only ὅστις but also forms such as αἵτινες and ὅτου. See chap. 12 for details and app. A for a complete set of these forms.

Mark 8:35, **ὃς ἐὰν** θέλῃ (desires) τὴν ψυχὴν αὐτοῦ σῶσαι (to save) ἀπολέσει (will lose) αὐτήν.

Whoever desires to save their life will lose it.

The subject of the main verb, ἀπολέσει, is the entire relative clause (ὃς ἐὰν θέλῃ τὴν ψυχὴν αὐτοῦ σῶσαι). ὅς is nominative since it is the subject of the verb θέλῃ in the relative clause. The reference of the entire verse is to "whoever" (ὃς ἐάν), so the translation uses singular *they* for αὐτοῦ (some might prefer the older generic *he*).

1 Macc. 2:41, ἐβουλεύσαντο (they decided) τῇ ἡμέρᾳ ἐκείνῃ λέγοντες (saying), Πᾶς ἄνθρωπος, **ὃς ἐὰν** ἔλθῃ (should come) ἐφ' ἡμᾶς εἰς πόλεμον τῇ ἡμέρᾳ τῶν σαββάτων,[a] πολεμήσωμεν (let us fight) κατέναντι αὐτοῦ.

They decided on that day saying, "Every person, whoever should come against us in battle on the Sabbath, let us fight against him."

[a] τῇ ἡμέρᾳ τῶν σαββάτων, i.e., "on the Sabbath" (Σάββατον is customarily plural even if only one day is intended.)

Attraction of Case

The normal practice is that the case of the relative pronoun (as any other pronoun) is determined by its function in its own clause. Despite this pattern, language is often untidy, and the relative pronoun sometimes matches the case of its antecedent in the main clause rather than its function in its own clause. There are some general patterns for why this happens, but you do not need to worry about that now.[a]

Mark 7:13, ἀκυροῦντες (nullifying) τὸν λόγον τοῦ θεοῦ τῇ παραδόσει ὑμῶν **ᾗ** παρεδώκατε (you hand down).

[This is] nullifying the Word of God by your tradition, *which* you hand down.

The relative pronoun (ᾗ) is in the dative case to agree with its antecedent, τῇ παραδόσει, even though we would normally expect it to be accusative as the direct object of the verb in the relative clause, παρεδώκατε.

[a] If you are curious regarding the explanation, see Wallace, *Greek Grammar*, 337–39.

10.17. Now You Try It

Mark 10:39, ὁ Ἰησοῦς εἶπεν (said) αὐτοῖς, Τὸ ποτήριον **ὃ** ἐγὼ πίνω πίεσθε (you will drink).

Mark 6:16, ὁ Ἡρῴδης ἔλεγεν (said), **Ὃν** ἐγὼ ἀπεκεφάλισα (beheaded) Ἰωάννην, οὗτος ἠγέρθη (is raised).

John 2:22, ἐπίστευσαν τῇ γραφῇ καὶ τῷ λόγῳ **ὃν** εἶπεν (he spoke) ὁ Ἰησοῦς.

3 Kgdms. (1 Kings) 2:11, αἱ ἡμέραι, **ἃς** ἐβασίλευσεν Δαυὶδ ἐπὶ τὸν Ἰσραήλ, τεσσαράκοντα ἔτη· ἐν Χεβρὼν ἐβασίλευσεν ἔτη ἑπτὰ καὶ ἐν Ἰερουσαλὴμ τριάκοντα τρία ἔτη.

Dan. 3:96 (3:29 Eng.), νῦν ἐγὼ κρίνω ἵνα πᾶν ἔθνος καὶ πᾶσαι φυλαὶ καὶ πᾶσαι γλῶσσαι, **ὃς ἂν** βλασφημήσῃ (should blaspheme) εἰς τὸν κύριον τὸν θεὸν Σεδράχ, Μισάχ, Ἀβδεναγώ, διαμελισθήσεται (he will be dismembered) καὶ ἡ οἰκία αὐτοῦ δημευθήσεται (will be confiscated), διότι οὐκ ἔστιν θεὸς ἕτερος **ὃς** δυνήσεται ἐξελέσθαι[a] οὕτως.

[a] δυνήσεται ἐξελέσθαι, "he is able to deliver"

John 6:9, Ἔστιν παιδάριον ὧδε **ὃς** ἔχει πέντε ἄρτους.

In this example the relative pronoun does not agree in gender with its antecedent. The pronoun ὅς is masculine, but the antecedent, παιδάριον, is neuter. This is an instance of natural gender—the neuter παιδάριον refers to a boy in this instance, so the pronoun is masculine.

Reflexive Pronouns

10.18. A reflexive pronoun is used when the object (either a direct object or the object of a preposition) refers back to the subject of the sentence. These words are usually the equivalent of the English compound pronouns *myself*, *yourself*, *himself*, *herself*, *itself*, *ourselves*, *yourselves*, *themselves*. In some contexts the simple English pronoun is more appropriate. These words occur only in the oblique cases since they are never used as subjects. In the lexicon, they will appear as three separate entries (one for each person), listed under the genitive spelling:

1. ἐμαυτοῦ, ῆς, "myself": This is the first-person reflexive pronoun. The lexical entry gives the masculine singular genitive and the feminine singular genitive forms. The chart below gives the complete set of these forms, although there are no feminine forms in the NT and only three each in the LXX[8] and Josephus; neuter forms do not occur at all.

8. E.g., in 3 Kgdms. (1 Kings) 17:12 the widow of Zerapath says, Ἐγὼ συλλέγω δύο ξυλάρια καὶ εἰσελεύσομαι καὶ ποιήσω αὐτὸ ἐμαυτῇ καὶ τοῖς τέκνοις μου ("I am gathering two sticks, and I will go in and prepare it [i.e., the remaining handful of flour] *for myself* and my children").

2. σεαυτοῦ, ῆς, "yourself": This entry gives the masculine and feminine genitive forms of the second-person reflexive pronouns. There are no feminine forms in the NT but 21 in the LXX;[9] neuter forms do not occur at all.
3. ἑαυτοῦ, ῆς, οῦ, "himself, herself, itself": The three forms listed in the lexicon are masculine, feminine, and neuter (singular, genitive).

Forms of Reflexive Pronouns

	1st Person		2nd Person	
	Masc.	Fem.	Masc.	Fem.
NS	—	—	—	—
GS	ἐμαυτοῦ	ἐμαυτῆς	σεαυτοῦ	σεαυτῆς
DS	ἐμαυτῷ	ἐμαυτῇ	σεαυτῷ	σεαυτῇ
AS	ἐμαυτόν	ἐμαυτήν	σεαυτόν	σεαυτήν

	3rd Person		
	Masc.	Fem.	Neut.
NS	—	—	—
GS	ἑαυτοῦ	ἑαυτῆς	ἑαυτοῦ
DS	ἑαυτῷ	ἑαυτῇ	ἑαυτῷ
AS	ἑαυτόν	ἑαυτήν	ἑαυτό
NP	—	—	—
GP	ἑαυτῶν	ἑαυτῶν	ἑαυτῶν
DP	ἑαυτοῖς	ἑαυταῖς	ἑαυτοῖς
AP	ἑαυτούς	ἑαυτάς	ἑαυτά

The first- and second-person reflexive pronouns have only singular forms. The plural forms of the third-person ἑαυτοῦ also function as plurals for the first and second person. Context must determine if first or second person is intended. See ἑαυτά in 1 John 5:21 (§10.20) for an example of the plural used for second person.

10.19. *Examples of Reflexive Pronouns*

John 5:31, Ἐὰν ἐγὼ μαρτυρῶ περὶ **ἐμαυτοῦ**, ἡ μαρτυρία μου οὐκ ἔστιν ἀληθής.

If I testify concerning *myself*, my testimony is not true.

John 17:19, ὑπὲρ αὐτῶν ἐγὼ ἁγιάζω (I set apart) **ἐμαυτόν**.

On their behalf I set *myself* apart.

9. Josephus has four feminine forms, but three are an alternate formation: σαυτῆς, σαυτῇ, σαυτήν; Philo's usage is similar.

Matt. 15:30, προσῆλθον αὐτῷ ὄχλοι πολλοὶ ἔχοντες μεθ' **ἑαυτῶν** χωλούς, τυφλούς, κυλλούς, κωφούς, καὶ ἑτέρους πολλούς.

Many crowds came to him having with *them*[a] the lame, blind, crippled, mute, and many others.

[a] Here the simple pronoun is necessary in English; reading this as "themselves" would be very awkward.

Zech. 12:12–14, κόψεται (it will mourn) ἡ γῆ κατὰ φυλὰς φυλάς,[a]	The land will mourn tribes by tribes,
φυλὴ καθ' **ἑαυτὴν** καὶ αἱ γυναῖκες αὐτῶν καθ' **ἑαυτάς**,	a tribe by *itself* and their wives by *themselves*,
φυλὴ οἴκου Δαυὶδ καθ' **ἑαυτὴν** καὶ αἱ γυναῖκες αὐτῶν καθ' **ἑαυτάς**,	the tribe of the house of David by *itself* and their wives by *themselves*,
φυλὴ οἴκου Νάθαν καθ' **ἑαυτὴν** καὶ αἱ γυναῖκες αὐτῶν καθ' **ἑαυτάς**,	the tribe of Nathan by *itself* and their wives by *themselves*,
φυλὴ οἴκου Λευὶ καθ' **ἑαυτὴν** καὶ αἱ γυναῖκες αὐτῶν καθ' **ἑαυτάς**,	the tribe of Levi by *itself* and their wives by *themselves*,
φυλὴ τοῦ Συμεὼν καθ' **ἑαυτὴν** καὶ αἱ γυναῖκες αὐτῶν καθ' **ἑαυτάς**,	the tribe of Simeon by *itself* and their wives by *themselves*,
πᾶσαι αἱ φυλαὶ αἱ ὑπολελειμμέναι φυλὴ καθ' **ἑαυτὴν** καὶ αἱ γυναῖκες αὐτῶν καθ' **ἑαυτάς**.	all the tribes that are left, a tribe by *itself* and their wives by *themselves*.

[a] The English parallel gives a formal equivalent that reflects the fact that φυλάς is plural; idiomatically we would say, "each tribe by itself."

This text is interesting in the repetition of the reflexive pronouns in a formulaic manner. Each section is formatted here to begin on a new line so that you can see the parallels more easily. The preposition κατά (spelled καθ' before a vowel with rough breathing) is used in a distributive sense.

10.20. *Now You Try It*

Mark 4:17, οὐκ ἔχουσιν ῥίζαν ἐν **ἑαυτοῖς**.

Mark 5:5, ἦν κατακόπτων[a] **ἑαυτὸν** λίθοις.

[a] ἦν κατακόπτων, "he was cutting"

Mark 12:31, Ἀγαπήσεις (Love!) τὸν πλησίον σου ὡς **σεαυτόν**.

1 John 5:21, Τεκνία, φυλάξατε (guard!) **ἑαυτὰ** ἀπὸ τῶν εἰδώλων.

Apoc. Sedr. 1.11, ψεύστης ἐστὶν καὶ **ἑαυτὸν** φρεναπατᾷ.[a]

[a] This is a contract verb; you will learn why the ending changes from -ει to -ᾳ in chap. 21. It is the 3rd sg. pres. act. ind. of φρεναπατάω.

1 Clem. 17.3–4, Ἰὼβ ἦν (was) δίκαιος καὶ ἄμεμπτος, ἀληθινός, θεοσεβής. ἀλλ' αὐτὸς **ἑαυτοῦ** κατηγορεῖ,[a] Οὐδεὶς καθαρὸς ἀπὸ ῥύπου.

[a] When κατηγορέω (a technical legal term: "I bring charges in court") is used with a genitive, the word in the genitive identifies against whom the charge is brought.

Reciprocal Pronouns

10.21. When a speaker wants to refer to a relationship involving two parties equally in a give-and-take relationship (which may include the speaker or may be two other parties), the reciprocal pronoun can be used: ἀλλήλων, "one another." Since there are always two (or more) parties involved, this word only occurs in the plural. Only masculine forms are found in the NT, but both feminine and neuter forms are found in the LXX and other Koine writings.[10] Due to the nature of the relationship, a reciprocal pronoun cannot be the subject of a sentence, so no nominative forms occur.

Forms of Reciprocal Pronouns

	Masc.	Fem.	Neut.
NP	—	—	—
GP	ἀλλήλων	ἀλλήλων	ἀλλήλων
DP	ἀλλήλοις	ἀλλήλαις	ἀλλήλοις
AP	ἀλλήλους	ἀλλήλας	ἄλληλα

10.22. *Examples of Reciprocal Pronouns*

Eph. 4:25, ἐσμὲν **ἀλλήλων** μέλη.

We are members of *one another*.

1 John 1:7, κοινωνίαν ἔχομεν μετ' **ἀλλήλων**.

We have fellowship with *one another*.

John 13:14, εἰ οὖν ἐγὼ ἔνιψα (I washed) ὑμῶν τοὺς πόδας (feet) ὁ κύριος καὶ ὁ διδάσκαλος, καὶ ὑμεῖς ὀφείλετε **ἀλλήλων** νίπτειν (to wash) τοὺς πόδας.

Therefore if I, Lord and Teacher, washed your feet, you also ought to wash *one another's* feet.

10. The parties need not be personal, though they most commonly are (and always are in the NT); inanimate objects can also be related in various ways to "one another," whether ships, pages, furniture parts, and so on.

Amos 4:1, 3, Ἀκούσατε τὸν λόγον τοῦτον, δαμάλεις τῆς Βασανίτιδος· Ἐξενεχθήσεσθε γυμναὶ κατέναντι **ἀλλήλων**[a] καὶ ἀπορριφήσεσθε εἰς τὸ ὄρος τὸ Ῥεμμάν, λέγει κύριος ὁ θεός.

Hear this word, heifers of Bashan: "You will be carried out naked before *one another* and cast out on Mount Remman," says the Lord God.

[a] ἀλλήλων is feminine since it refers to the "heifers" (δάμαλις), which in this context is probably a figurative reference to wealthy women.

10.23. *Now You Try It*

Gal. 5:13, διὰ τῆς ἀγάπης δουλεύετε (serve!) **ἀλλήλοις**.

1 Thess. 4:9, ὑμεῖς θεοδίδακτοί ("God-taught") ἐστε εἰς τὸ ἀγαπᾶν[a] **ἀλλήλους**.

[a] εἰς τὸ ἀγαπᾶν, "to love" (an infinitive construction you will learn in chap. 22).

Exod. 25:20, οἱ χερουβὶμ will have τὰ πρόσωπα αὐτῶν εἰς **ἄλληλα**.[a]

[a] The neuter ἄλληλα is used to agree with πρόσωπα.

Possessive Adjectives

10.24. Although the genitive form of the personal pronoun may be used to indicate possession (e.g., ὁ λόγος τοῦ θεοῦ, "the Word of God"), Greek also has a class of adjectives that can be used (though less commonly) for this purpose.[11] These are called *possessive adjectives*. These include the singular forms ἐμός, ή, όν ("my, mine") and σός, ή, όν ("your"), and the plural forms ἡμέτερος, α, ον ("our") and ὑμέτερος, α, ον ("your"). All these forms decline using the same endings as a regular adjective, function in sentences like any other adjective in both position and meaning, and will agree with the noun they modify in gender, number, and case.

Plural Forms of Singular Pronouns?

Although it might initially seem confusing, there are *plural forms* of the singular pronouns ἐμός and σός, as well as *singular forms* of the plural pronouns ἡμέτερος and ὑμέτερος. Pronouns must match their antecedent. When referring to one person, the singular ἐμός or σός is used, but if the antecedent is plural, then the plural ἡμέτερος or ὑμέτερος is used. Yet they must also *agree in form* with the noun they modify. Thus if the noun modified is singular, both the singular and plural pronouns will use a singular ending. For example, a speaker might use ὁ ἐμὸς λόγος ("my word") when referring to what he or she says but ὁ ἡμέτερος λόγος ("our word") when referring to a group.

11. Some reference tools class these words as *possessive adjectives*, others as *possessive pronouns*.

Forms of Possessive Adjectives

10.25. The first-person singular form, ἐμός, "my," the possessive adjective form of ἐγώ, is used 76 times in the NT and 104 times in the LXX. The first-person plural, ἡμέτερος, "our," occurs only 7 times in the NT and 22 times in the LXX. These words are declined below. There is no need to memorize these charts; you already know the endings, so all that is necessary is to recognize the word with its various endings. Not all of the forms shown in the following tables occur in the NT, though most of them do occur in the LXX or in other Koine texts. (The same is true of the second-person forms below.)

First-Person Singular Possessive Adjective

	Masc.	Fem.	Neut.
NS	ἐμός	ἐμή	ἐμόν
GS	ἐμοῦ	ἐμῆς	ἐμοῦ
DS	ἐμῷ	ἐμῇ	ἐμῷ
AS	ἐμόν	ἐμήν	ἐμόν
NP	ἐμοί	ἐμαί	ἐμά
GP	ἐμῶν	ἐμῶν	ἐμῶν
DP	ἐμοῖς	ἐμαῖς	ἐμοῖς
AP	ἐμούς	ἐμάς	ἐμά

First-Person Plural Possessive Adjective

	Masc.	Fem.	Neut.
NS	ἡμέτερος	ἡμετέρα	ἡμέτερον
GS	ἡμετέρου	ἡμετέρας	ἡμετέρου
DS	ἡμετέρῳ	ἡμετέρᾳ	ἡμετέρῳ
AS	ἡμέτερον	ἡμετέραν	ἡμέτερον
NP	ἡμέτεροι	ἡμέτεραι	ἡμέτερα
GP	ἡμετέρων	ἡμετέρων	ἡμετέρων
DP	ἡμετέροις	ἡμετέραις	ἡμετέροις
AP	ἡμετέρους	ἡμετέρας	ἡμέτερα

The second-person singular form, σός, "your," the possessive form of σύ, is used 25 times in the NT and 135 times in the LXX. The second-person plural, ὑμέτερος, "your," which occurs only 11 times in the NT and 4 times in the LXX, is not common in Koine. These terms decline as follows. As with the first-person forms, there is no need to memorize this chart, since you already know the endings.

Second-Person Singular Possessive Adjective

	Masc.	Fem.	Neut.
NS	σός	σή	σόν
GS	σοῦ	σῆς	σοῦ
DS	σῷ	σῇ	σῷ
AS	σόν	σήν	σόν
NP	σοί	σαί	σά
GP	σῶν	σῶν	σῶν
DP	σοῖς	σαῖς	σοῖς
AP	σούς	σάς	σά

Second-Person Plural Possessive Adjective

	Masc.	Fem.	Neut.
NS	ὑμέτερος	ὑμετέρα	ὑμέτερον
GS	ὑμετέρου	ὑμετέρας	ὑμετέρου
DS	ὑμετέρῳ	ὑμετέρᾳ	ὑμετέρῳ
AS	ὑμέτερον	ὑμετέραν	ὑμέτερον
NP	ὑμέτεροι	ὑμέτεραι	ὑμέτερα
GP	ὑμετέρων	ὑμετέρων	ὑμετέρων
DP	ὑμετέροις	ὑμετέραις	ὑμετέροις
AP	ὑμετέρους	ὑμετέρας	ὑμέτερα

10.26. *Examples of Possessive Adjectives*

John 5:30, ἡ κρίσις ἡ **ἐμὴ** δικαία ἐστίν.

My judgment is righteous.

John 7:8, ἐγὼ οὐκ ἀναβαίνω εἰς τὴν ἑορτὴν ταύτην, ὅτι ὁ **ἐμὸς** καιρὸς οὔπω πεπλήρωται (is come).

I am not going up to this feast because *my* time is not yet come.

Mark 2:18, Διὰ τί[a] οἱ μαθηταὶ Ἰωάννου καὶ οἱ μαθηταὶ τῶν Φαρισαίων νηστεύουσιν, οἱ δὲ **σοὶ**[b] μαθηταὶ οὐ νηστεύουσιν;

"Why do John's disciples and the Pharisees' disciples fast, but *your* disciples do not fast?"

[a] Διὰ τί, "Why?"

[b] You may have noticed that the masc. pl. nom. form of the possessive adjective σός is identical to the accented form of the dative singular second-person personal pronoun σοί (§4.6). You can distinguish them in this example because the possessive adjective occurs where you would expect to find a modifier: first attributive position.

John 4:42, τῇ τε γυναικὶ[a] ἔλεγον (they said) ὅτι Οὐκέτι διὰ τὴν **σὴν** λαλιὰν πιστεύομεν.

They said to the woman, "We no longer believe because of *your* word."

[a] τῇ γυναικί, "to the woman" (dative, third declension)

Matt. 20:14, ἆρον (take!) τὸ **σὸν** καὶ ὕπαγε (go!).

Take what is *yours* and go.

This example shows the substantival use of the pronoun with the article functioning as a nominalizer.

Bar. 4:24, νῦν ἑωράκασιν (they see) αἱ πάροικοι Σιὼν τὴν **ὑμετέραν** αἰχμαλωσίαν.

The neighbors of Zion now see *your* captivity.

Prov. 1:13, τὴν κτῆσιν αὐτοῦ τὴν πολυτελῆ καταλαβώμεθα (let us take), πλήσωμεν (let us fill) δὲ οἴκους **ἡμετέρους** σκύλων.

Let us take his expensive possessions, and let us fill *our* houses with plunder.

10.27. *Now You Try It*

John 7:6, λέγει αὐτοῖς ὁ Ἰησοῦς, Ὁ καιρὸς **ὁ ἐμὸς** οὔπω πάρεστιν (is come), ὁ δὲ καιρὸς **ὁ ὑμέτερος** πάντοτέ ἐστιν ἕτοιμος.

John 8:17, ἐν τῷ νόμῳ δὲ **τῷ ὑμετέρῳ** γέγραπται ὅτι δύο ἀνθρώπων ἡ μαρτυρία ἀληθής ἐστιν.

John 14:27, εἰρήνην τὴν **ἐμὴν** δίδωμι (I give) ὑμῖν.

1 John 1:3, ἡ κοινωνία ἡ **ἡμετέρα** μετὰ τοῦ πατρὸς (Father) καὶ μετὰ τοῦ υἱοῦ αὐτοῦ Ἰησοῦ Χριστοῦ.

Gen. 30:27, εἶπεν (he said) αὐτῷ Λαβάν, Εὐλόγησέν με ὁ θεὸς τῇ **σῇ** εἰσόδῳ.

10.28. Advanced Information for Reference: Diagramming Relative Pronouns

John 4:50, ἐπίστευσεν ὁ ἄνθρωπος τῷ λόγῳ **ὃν** εἶπεν (he spoke) αὐτῷ ὁ Ἰησοῦς.

The man believed the word *which* Jesus spoke to him.

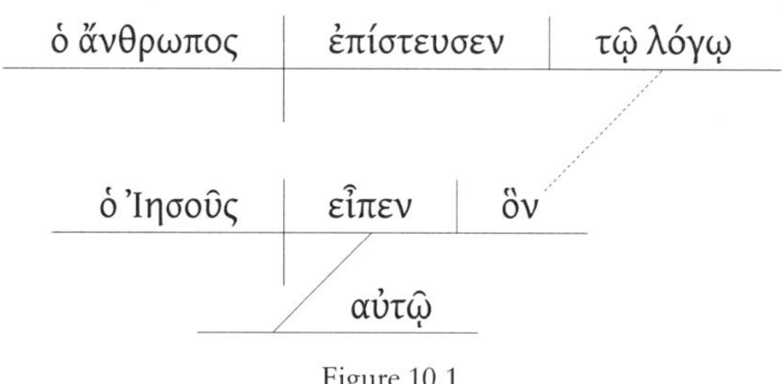

Figure 10.1

Relative clauses are subordinate clauses, so they are diagrammed below the main clause. A dotted line connects the relative pronoun to its antecedent in the main clause.

Reading Passage: 1 John 2:18–27

10.29. There are a number of repeated forms in this passage that you have not yet learned. They are glossed or explained the first time each one occurs but not in their later occurrences.

Many Antichrists Have Come

18Παιδία, ἐσχάτη ὥρα ἐστίν, καὶ καθὼς ἠκούσατε ὅτι ἀντίχριστος ἔρχεται (is
coming), καὶ νῦν ἀντίχριστοι πολλοὶ γεγόνασιν (have come), ὅθεν γινώσκομεν
ὅτι ἐσχάτη ὥρα ἐστίν. 19ἐξ ἡμῶν ἐξῆλθαν (they went out) ἀλλ' οὐκ ἦσαν (they
were) ἐξ ἡμῶν· εἰ γὰρ ἐξ ἡμῶν ἦσαν, μεμενήκεισαν (they would remain) ἂν
μεθ' ἡμῶν· ἀλλ' ἵνα φανερωθῶσιν (it should be evident) ὅτι οὐκ εἰσὶν πάντες[a]
ἐξ ἡμῶν. 20καὶ ὑμεῖς χρῖσμα ἔχετε ἀπὸ τοῦ ἁγίου καὶ οἴδατε (you know) πάντες.[a]
21οὐκ ἔγραψα ὑμῖν ὅτι οὐκ οἴδατε τὴν ἀλήθειαν ἀλλ' ὅτι οἴδατε αὐτὴν καὶ ὅτι
πᾶν (every) ψεῦδος ἐκ τῆς ἀληθείας οὐκ ἔστιν.[b] 22Τίς (who?) ἐστιν ὁ ψεύστης
εἰ μὴ ὁ ἀρνούμενος (one who denies) ὅτι[c] Ἰησοῦς οὐκ ἔστιν ὁ Χριστός; **οὗτός**
ἐστιν ὁ ἀντίχριστος, ὁ ἀρνούμενος τὸν πατέρα (Father) καὶ τὸν υἱόν. 23πᾶς ὁ[d]
ἀρνούμενος τὸν υἱὸν οὐδὲ τὸν πατέρα ἔχει, ὁ ὁμολογῶν (one who confesses)
τὸν υἱὸν καὶ τὸν πατέρα ἔχει. 24ὑμεῖς **ὃ** ἠκούσατε ἀπ' ἀρχῆς, ἐν ὑμῖν μενέτω (let
it remain). ἐὰν ἐν ὑμῖν μείνῃ (it remains) **ὃ** ἀπ' ἀρχῆς ἠκούσατε, καὶ ὑμεῖς ἐν
τῷ υἱῷ καὶ ἐν τῷ πατρὶ (Father) μενεῖτε (you will remain).[e] 25καὶ **αὕτη** ἐστὶν
ἡ ἐπαγγελία **ἣν** αὐτὸς ἐπηγγείλατο (promised) ἡμῖν, τὴν ζωὴν τὴν αἰώνιον.

26**Ταῦτα** ἔγραψα ὑμῖν περὶ τῶν πλανώντων (ones who deceive) ὑμᾶς. 27καὶ
ὑμεῖς τὸ χρῖσμα **ὃ** ἐλάβετε (you received) ἀπ' αὐτοῦ, μένει ἐν ὑμῖν καὶ οὐ χρείαν

ἔχετε ἵνα τις (anyone) διδάσκῃ (should teach) ὑμᾶς, ἀλλ᾽ ὡς τὸ αὐτοῦ χρῖσμα διδάσκει ὑμᾶς περὶ πάντων (all things) καὶ ἀληθές ἐστιν καὶ οὐκ ἔστιν ψεῦδος, καὶ καθὼς ἐδίδαξεν ὑμᾶς, μένετε (remain!) ἐν αὐτῷ.

[a] πάντες is a third-declension adjective (see chap. 12), masc. pl. nom. In v. 19 it is a substantival adjective functioning as the subject of the sentence. In v. 20 it modifies the back-pocket subject of the verb οἴδατε, thus "all of you know/have knowledge."

[b] πᾶν . . . οὐκ ἔστιν, formally, "every lie is not from the truth," but we would say more naturally in English, "no lie is from the truth."

[c] This is a "recitative" ὅτι that introduces discourse; it is not a content statement. The meaning expressed by a discourse statement ("the one who denies [saying], "Jesus is not the Messiah") is consistent with John's Christology elsewhere in 1 John, but taking ὅτι as content ("the one who denies that Jesus is not the Messiah") would amount to a double negative in English (the *liar* would be affirming that "Jesus is the Messiah") and contradict John's teaching. Can you distinguish the two different statements?

[d] πᾶς ὁ, "everyone who"

[e] Watch the punctuation carefully in v. 24. There are two instances of καί, and they function differently. The comma will help clarify the meaning.

10.30. Vocabulary for Chapter 10

Part of Speech	Definition	Possible Glosses	Frequency	
Word			NT	LXX
Adjectives				
πτωχός, ή, όν	In a needy, impoverished condition; deficient in quality or worn out	poor; shabby; beggar (subst.)	34	124
καθαρός, ά, όν	Free from contamination, whether ceremonial or physical; free from guilt or moral impurity	clean, cleansed, pure; innocent	27	160
Prepositions				
ὑπό	A preposition used with the genitive to indicate agent or cause, or with the accusative to indicate a lower position	(prep. + gen.) by; (prep. + acc.) under, below	220	498
παρά	A preposition used with three cases, all referring to some sort of association: with the genitive, a point of origin or source; with the dative, a close connection; and with the accusative, nearness	(prep. + gen.) from; (prep. + dat.) with, beside, near, in the presence of; (prep. + acc.) alongside, by	194	879
ὑπέρ	A preposition used with either the genitive (benefit, replacement, cause, or interest) or accusative (extent beyond) cases	(prep. + gen.) in behalf of, for, in place of, because of, about; (prep. + acc.) above, beyond, over	150	427
σύν	A preposition used with the dative to indicate association or connection	(prep. + dat.) with	128	233
ἐνώπιον	A preposition used with the genitive to indicate being in the sight of someone	(prep. + gen.) before, in front of, in the sight of	94	558
Pronouns				
οὗτος, αὕτη, τοῦτο	A near demonstrative pronoun referring to the person or thing comparatively near at hand ("this" as opposed to ἐκεῖνος/"that")	this, this one, these; he, she, it, they	1,388	4,411

Part of Speech	Definition	Possible Glosses	Frequency	
Word			NT	LXX
ὅς, ἥ, ὅ	Relative pronoun that usually refers to another noun earlier in the sentence or discourse, introducing a clause that further describes that noun	who, which, that	1,365	4,886
ἑαυτοῦ, ῆς, οῦ	A pronoun that makes a reflexive reference to a person or thing (third person; never occurs in nominative case, so lexical form is genitive; cf. first person, ἐμαυτοῦ; second person, σεαυτοῦ)	himself, herself, itself; themselves	319	662
ἐκεῖνος, η, ο	Far demonstrative pronoun referring to the person or thing that is comparatively remote ("that" as opposed to οὗτος/"this")	that, that one/man/woman/thing; those	265	739
ἀλλήλων	A pronoun that refers to a reciprocal relationship between two or more people (or rarely, things); never occurs in nominative or in singular, so genitive plural is used for lexical form	one another	100	42
ἐμός, ή, όν (pl. ἡμέτερος)	A pronoun that refers to something pertaining to the speaker, often a possessive or responsible relationship	my, mine; our	76	112
σεαυτοῦ, ῆς	A pronoun that makes a reflexive, second-person reference to a person; a reflexive pronoun (second person; never occurs in nominative case or in neuter, so lexical form is genitive; cf. first person, ἐμαυτοῦ; third person, ἑαυτοῦ)	yourself	43	218
ἐμαυτοῦ, ῆς	A pronoun that makes a reflexive, first-person reference to the speaker; a reflexive pronoun (first person; never occurs in nominative case, in plural, or in neuter, so lexical form is genitive; cf. second person, σεαυτοῦ; third person, ἑαυτοῦ)	myself	37	59

10.31. Key Things to Know for Chapter 10

The pronouns in this chapter are learned as vocabulary items, *not* charts to memorize. They use regular case endings, so you need only to recognize the word. Can you do that?

The near demonstrative οὗτος can be puzzling if you do not remember that most forms are spelled τουτ- instead of οὗτ-. Remember that they will always have a rough breathing mark or a tau on the front of the word.

Relative pronouns always have a rough breathing mark *and* an accent placed over what looks like just a case ending. Do not confuse this with the article, which begins with either a tau or a rough breathing mark *without* an accent.

The *number* and *gender* of a relative pronoun are determined by its antecedent, but its *case* is determined by its function in the sentence.

Remember that a relative clause is a *subordinate* clause, so the main idea of the sentence will not be found in that clause.

11

THIRD DECLENSION: PART 1

NOUNS

11.1. By now you are very comfortable with nouns and adjectives of the first and second declensions. Although you once thought them to be strange creatures (compared with English), they have become familiar friends. There is also a third declension, used for both nouns and adjectives, which we will learn in this chapter. Before you begin, you might want to review the two earlier chapters on nouns (chaps. 2 and 3).

Third-Declension Nouns

11.2. If you can pronounce the following nonsense phrase and drill it into your head, you will have most of what you need to know for third-declension nouns:

Saucy a, S own sin os

Repeat it enough times to make it second nature. It may sound like an "applesauce" recipe or perhaps even flippant, but it works. Now we need to make the leap to Greek. The nonsense phrase above is simply a mnemonic device to help you remember the basic third-declension endings:

ς ος ι α, ες ων σιν ας

Third-declension nouns do not use connecting vowels, so the stem ends with an unbuffered consonant. In the first and second declensions there is always an omicron or an epsilon connecting vowel, even if it sometimes lengthens to omega or eta. You learned the first sets of noun endings *with the connecting vowel*, since that made each ending easier to pronounce and thus easier to memorize. But the third-declension endings are harder to pronounce as individual morphemes, since several of them are not complete syllables, because they do not include a vowel. That is why it is easier to learn them as a continuous phrase, since you can now pronounce syllables rather than hissing and grunting.

Complete Case Ending Chart

11.3. Do not worry—you are not going to memorize the chart below in the form in which you see it here. It looks more complicated than the noun ending chart you worked with earlier, but follow the notes below, and you will do just fine. This chart shows the technical endings for first and second declensions in the shaded columns.

Decl.	2		1		2		3	3
Gend.	(M/f)		(F/m)		N		M/F	N
NS	ος	ς	α/η	—	ον	ν	ς	—
GS	ου	υ	ας/ης	ς	ου	υ	ος	ος
DS	ῳ	ι	ᾳ/ῃ	ι	ῳ	ι	ι	ι
AS	ον	ν	αν/ην	ν	ον	ν	α/ν	—
NP	οι	ι	αι	ι	α	α	ες	α
GP	ων	ν	ων	ν	ων	ν	ων	ων
DP	οις	ις	αις	ις	οις	ις	σι(ν)	σι(ν)
AP	ους	υς	ας	ς	α	α	ας	α

In the third declension both masculine and feminine nouns use the same set of endings, which is why there is only one column marked "M/F." Third-declension neuter nouns use the same basic set of endings, though there are a few variations.

For the third-declension endings as a group, compare them with the first- and second-declension endings in the left columns for similarities; if you focus on the technical endings (shaded columns), there will be more-obvious similarities than if you think in terms of the entire ending. Notice that there are no connecting vowels used with third-declension endings. These endings are, indeed, slightly different from the first and second declensions, but if you learn the nonsense, "applesauce" phrase above, you will have the basic endings in good shape. Just remember that there are some variations in the neuter as well as in some of the masculine and feminine forms. The nu at the end of the dative plural is movable; it is usually present but may drop out in some situations. You do not need to know when or why; just be able to recognize either one as a dative plural ending.

You will want to remember that for third-declension nouns, the *genitive singular* ending is usually -ος. This can be easily mistaken for a second-declension *nominative singular* ending. You can distinguish these two forms on one of two bases (sometimes either or both; sometimes only the second). First, the article will be your best friend, since the forms of the article do not change. Thus even an odd-looking third-declension noun, if it has an article, will be easily identifiable. Of course, not all nouns have articles. So, second, the lexical form is crucial. If the lexical form ends with "-ος, ου + article," it is a second-declension noun, and an -ος ending is, of course, nominative; if the lexical form ends with a consonant (other than the sigma in -ος), it is third declension, and an -ος ending on a word indicates genitive case.[1]

Third-Declension Noun Patterns

11.4. Here are several third-declension nouns. Look up each one in your lexicon, and study the entry. The same pattern of information is given in the lexical form as for other nouns that you have already learned. What information does the lexicon give for each of these words?

ἰχθύς, "fish"
στάχυς, "head of grain"
ἰσχύς, "strength"
ὗς, "sow" (i.e., adult female pig)

What is the nominative and genitive case form for each word? What gender?

If we were to list a complete set of forms, they would look like this example:

ἰχθύς, ἰχθύος, ἰχθύϊ, ἰχθύν, ἰχθύες, ἰχθύων, ἰχθύσιν, ἰχθύας

The pattern in the next three examples (which you should also look up in your lexicon) will be slightly different. There is no sigma for the nominative singular ending. For the first one, πῦρ, this is because it is neuter, so that is expected. The second two, however, are not neuter. Some masculine or feminine third-declension nouns do not have a sigma in the nominative singular; they *appear* to be using the nominative neuter singular ending ("blank" or "null").[2]

πῦρ, "fire"
χείρ, "hand"
αἰών, "age"

Variations in Third-Declension Nouns

11.5. The examples given above evidence a fairly regular pattern of endings, but the morphology of the third declension is far more varied than that of the first two declensions. *Most* third-declension nouns do not have such a simple pattern of endings. There is diversity of opinion among Greek teachers as to how much time (and memorization) is appropriate here. This textbook follows a more minimalist approach. That means that you may not be able to identify every detail of every odd third-declension form, but if you learn the basics well

1. There are some third-declension nouns whose lexical form ends with -ος, such as ὄρος ("mountain"), but the genitive ending given makes it obvious that it is third declension: ὄρος, ους, τό.

2. As you will learn below, there are other reasons for this. There are specific situations in which the sigma ending drops off and leaves the nominative consisting of just the stem.

(especially the standard set of endings), you will be able to identify most of the more frequent ones. The trade-off for having less grunt work in the memorization department is that you will need to look up the less-common forms. (A fairly complete set of forms is given in app. A.) But you *must* master the basics—well!

The Square of Stops

11.6. The primary reason for the variation in the third declension is the absence of a connecting vowel. As a result, there are some clashing combinations of consonants that are difficult to pronounce. To avoid such combinations, Greek modifies the spelling of third-declension nouns when certain combinations of consonants occur.[3] These changes may be summarized in a table called the *square of stops*.

Square of Stops

				+ σ =
Labials	π	β	φ	ψ
Velars	κ	γ	χ	ξ
Dentals	τ	δ	θ	σ

The name for this table comes from two factors. First, the nine key letters are arranged deliberately in a *square*. Second, these nine letters are classified by linguists as *stops*. This refers to how the flow of air is stopped in your mouth as the sound is produced.[4] When a stop is followed by an *s* sound (in Greek that is the sigma), the two letters are combined to produce the letter in the far right-hand column. The table reads horizontally. For example, a pi, beta, or phi, when combined with a sigma, results in a psi.[5]

The square of stops is a very important tool that is necessary to understand third-declension nouns. We will also use it repeatedly in later chapters for verbs. *It is important that you memorize it exactly*, including the exact sequence of letters in each row, since we will later use this table vertically as well as horizontally.[6] The point of the chart—*which we will use and reuse throughout the remainder of the book* in multiple contexts—is that certain kinds of letters act in a certain, predictable way.

The following examples are intended to help you understand the principle involved as it is applied in third-declension nouns. Do not be discouraged by the

3. These modifications may be described as euphonic, that is, to make it sound better. The opposite of euphony is cacophony.

4. Labials are letters that are pronounced by the flow of air being stopped by the lips, the velars by the soft palate and tongue, and the dentals by touching the tongue to the teeth.

5. Since it is the sigma that introduces the change, this chart is primarily relevant in the nominative singular and dative plural forms of the third declension. Whatever happens in the nominative singular also happens in the dative plural because the ending begins with a sigma in both instances (sigma alone in nominative, -σιν in dative). E.g., σάρξ, σαρκός, ἡ, "flesh," in the nominative is *σαρκ + σ = σάρξ, and in the dative is *σαρκ + σιν = σαρξίν.

6. You do not need to memorize the labels for each row (labials, velars, dentals) unless your teacher tells you to do so.

seemingly endless mass of data in the following paragraphs. You do *not* need to memorize the explanations or be able to explain every such change whenever you encounter a third-declension noun, but if you grasp the gist of these examples, you will not be frustrated when you see similar changes elsewhere.

Labials + σ ▸ ψ

11.7. When a sigma is added to a *labial* (π, β, φ), the result is the combination/compound letter psi. Here is an example of how this works. (This is only for illustration; you need not memorize the specifics.)

λαῖλαψ, λαίλαπος, ἡ, "storm"
stem = λαιλαπ- + σ = λαῖλαψ

The lexical form for the Greek equivalent of our English word *storm* is λαῖλαψ, λαίλαπος, ἡ, "storm." The stem for this word is λαιλαπ-. Note that the last letter of the stem is a labial (pi). The feminine singular nominative ending in the third declension is sigma. The square of stops tells us that when the letter pi is followed by a sigma, the result is the compound letter psi (π + σ = ψ); thus the feminine singular nominative form of the word is λαῖλαψ (not λαῖλαπς). In the genitive, however, the sigma is not adjacent to the labial, because the ending is ος—the omicron separates the two consonants—so the form is λαίλαπος.

> **Identifying Noun Stems**
>
> How do you know/find the stem of a noun? Here is the rule (which you should remember): *To determine the stem of any noun, start with the genitive singular form and drop the ending; what is left is the stem.* (You now know one more reason why the genitive form is listed in the lexicon.) This does not work consistently with any other case; you must use the genitive singular form. This rule is not noun-specific; it also works for adjectives. In this case use the masculine singular genitive form. There may be a few instances in which this rule does not appear to work, but that is usually due to historical changes that are no longer evident in the lexical form of the verb.

Luke 8:23, κατέβη (it descended) **λαῖλαψ** ἀνέμου εἰς τὴν λίμνην.	A wind*storm*[a] descended on the lake.

[a] Formally: "*a storm* of wind"

Without the detailed explanation (which is fairly obvious if you follow the same pattern as for λαῖλαψ above), the following paragraphs show what happens in some other instances.

Velars + σ ▸ ξ

11.8. When a sigma is added to a *velar* (κ, γ, χ), the result is the combination/compound letter xi. For example:

σάρξ, σαρκός, ἡ, flesh
stem = σαρκ- + σ = σάρξ

John 1:14, ὁ λόγος **σὰρξ** ἐγένετο (he became) καὶ ἐσκήνωσεν ἐν ἡμῖν.	The Word became *flesh* and lived among us.

Dentals + σ ▸ σ

11.9. When a sigma is added to a *dental* (τ, δ, θ), the result is the letter sigma. For example:

ἐλπίς, ἐλπίδος, ἡ, hope
stem = ἐλπιδ- + σ = ἐλπίς

2 Cor. 1:7, ἡ **ἐλπὶς** ἡμῶν βεβαία (it is secure) ὑπὲρ ὑμῶν. — Our *hope* for you is secure.

Double Change

11.10. Some letter combinations undergo more than one change. For example, the word *night* (νύξ, νυκτός, ἡ) is formed as follows:

stem = νυκτ- + σ [τ + σ] = σ ▸ νυκς (an "intermediate form" that never appears in a Greek text),
then κ + σ = ξ ▸ νύξ (the spelling always found in Greek)

Matt. 4:2, νηστεύσας ἡμέρας τεσσεράκοντα (forty) καὶ **νύκτας** τεσσεράκοντα. — He fasted forty days and forty *nights*.

Liquid Nouns

11.11. First, a definition: a *liquid* is any word whose *stem* ends with either λ, μ, ν, or ρ.[7] This type of word is not limited to nouns; we will later meet liquid verbs. All liquid nouns, however, are third declension by definition, since the stem ends with a consonant.

There are two key things to remember about liquids.

A sigma will not stand after a liquid; it will drop out.

In a liquid, short vowels that occur between a pair of final consonants in the stem usually drop out or lengthen.

Below are two examples of liquid nouns.

1. ποιμήν, -ποιμένος, ὁ, *shepherd, pastor.* To find the stem, start with the singular genitive form, ποιμένος. Drop the case ending (ος); the stem is thus ποιμεν-, so you know this is a liquid noun, since the last letter of the stem is a nu, one of the liquids. In the singular nominative form, the ending sigma is dropped after the nu, and the epsilon is lengthened to eta since the short vowel, epsilon, is sandwiched between the two consonants, mu and nu, thus ποιμήν.

stem = ποιμεν- + σ [ν + σ] = ν and μεν ▸ μην ▸ ποιμήν

7. Technically the liquids are λ and ρ; μ and ν are nasals. It is somewhat standard practice, however, to simply group all four together as liquids, at least for purposes of first-year Greek.

Matt. 25:32, **ὁ ποιμὴν** ἀφορίζει τὰ πρόβατα ἀπὸ τῶν ἐρίφων.

The shepherd separates the sheep from the goats.

John 10:14, Ἐγώ εἰμι **ὁ ποιμὴν** ὁ καλὸς καὶ γινώσκω τὰ ἐμὰ καὶ γινώσκουσί με τὰ ἐμά.[a]

I am *the* good *shepherd*, and I know my own, and my own know me.

[a] For τὰ ἐμά, see ἐμός in §10.25; with the neuter plural article, it means "the things of me," or "my own things." In this context, it refers to the shepherd's sheep. "My own" is a good option for an English equivalent.

Job 1:16, Πῦρ ἔπεσεν (it fell) ἐκ τοῦ οὐρανοῦ καὶ κατέκαυσεν (it burned) τὰ πρόβατα καὶ **τοὺς ποιμένας** κατέφαγεν (it consumed) ὁμοίως.

Fire fell from heaven and burned the sheep, and it consumed *the shepherds* likewise.

2. πατήρ, πατρός, ὁ, *father*. The word πατήρ undergoes multiple changes in the creation of the various case forms, most of which you need not worry about.[8] To find the stem, start with the singular genitive form, πατρός, and drop the case ending (ος), thus πατρ- (or as it appears in some cases, πατερ-). The singular nominative ending sigma drops off after rho, and the epsilon (which drops out in the genitive singular as well as in both dative forms), lengthens between the consonants tau and rho. The full set of forms is as follows: πατήρ, πατρός, πατρί, πατέρα, πατέρες, πατέρων, πατράσιν, πατέρας.

stem = πατ[ε]ρ + σ[ρ + σ] = ρ and τ[ε]ρ ▸ τηρ ▸ πατήρ

Mark 9:24, **ὁ πατὴρ** τοῦ παιδίου ἔλεγεν, Πιστεύω.

The father of the child said, "I believe."

Mark 8:38, ὁ υἱὸς τοῦ ἀνθρώπου ἔλθῃ (he will come) ἐν τῇ δόξῃ **τοῦ πατρὸς** αὐτοῦ μετὰ τῶν ἀγγέλων τῶν ἁγίων.

The Son of Man will come in the glory *of* his *father* with the holy angels.

2 Clem. 20.5, Τῷ μόνῳ θεῷ ἀοράτῳ, **πατρὶ** τῆς ἀληθείας, τῷ ἐξαποστεί-λαντι (one who sent) ἡμῖν τὸν σωτῆρα καὶ ἀρχηγὸν τῆς ἀφθαρσίας, δι' οὗ καὶ ἐφανέρωσεν ἡμῖν τὴν ἀλήθειαν καὶ τὴν ἐπουράνιον ζωήν, αὐτῷ ἡ δόξα εἰς τοὺς αἰῶνας τῶν αἰώνων.[a] ἀμήν.

To the only God, invisible, *Father* of truth, to the one who sent to us the Savior and Founder of immortality, through whom also he revealed to us truth and heavenly life, to him be glory forever. Amen.

[a] αἰών, ῶνος, ὁ is also a third-declension word; the complete paradigm is given in app. A. The phrase εἰς τοὺς αἰῶνας τῶν αἰώνων is formally, "unto the ages of the ages," but is best communicated in English as "forever."

8. The curious can find the details in *MBG*, 209–10.

Six Key, Representative Paradigms

11.12. There are a number of changes similar to those described above that take place in third-declension words, mostly because the stem ends with a consonant and there is no connecting vowel. As a consequence some consonant combinations result in spelling changes. There are also some third-declension words whose stem does not *appear* to end in a consonant. This is often because historically the stem once ended in a digamma (e.g., βασιλεύς) or a consonantal iota (e.g., πόλις and πίστις).[9] Both of these letters are archaic in Koine, though the changes they produced in earlier stages of the language are still visible. (See app. E for more information on these archaic letters.)

The easiest way to identify the gender, number, and case of a third-declension noun is to look for the article. If there is an article, then identifying the form is easy, since the article will always match the chart that you learned in chapter 2. Many third-declension nouns will have an article.

For those nouns without an article, a helpful approach is to study several representative words that illustrate the most common changes. Familiarity, without having to memorize more forms, will often provide enough clues to point you in the right direction. In using the following paradigms, if you can match the nominative and genitive form of a word to one of those given here, you can tell what the rest of the forms will be. A larger set of third-declension noun paradigms is given for reference in appendix A.

	σάρξ, σαρκός, ἡ, **flesh**	ὄνομα, ατος, τό, **name**	ἄρχων, οντος, ὁ, **ruler**
NS	σάρξ	ὄνομα	ἄρχων
GS	σαρκός	ὀνόματος	ἄρχοντος
DS	σαρκί	ὀνόματι	ἄρχοντι
AS	σάρκα	ὄνομα	ἄρχοντα
NP	σάρκες	ὀνόματα	ἄρχοντες
GP	σαρκῶν	ὀνομάτων	ἀρχόντων
DP	σαρξί(ν)	ὀνόμασι(ν)	ἄρχουσι(ν)
AP	σάρκας	ὀνόματα	ἄρχοντας

	ἔθνος, ους, τό, **nation**	βασιλεύς, έως, ὁ, **king**	πόλις, εως, ἡ, **city**
NS	ἔθνος	βασιλεύς	πόλις
GS	ἔθνους	βασιλέως	πόλεως
DS	ἔθνει	βασιλεῖ	πόλει
AS	ἔθνος	βασιλέα	πόλιν

9. For more information on these types of words, including a complete list for the NT, see *MBG*, 202–6.

	ἔθνος, ους, τό, nation	βασιλεύς, έως, ὁ, king	πόλις, εως, ἡ, city
NP	ἔθνη	βασιλεῖς	πόλεις
GP	ἐθνῶν	βασιλέων	πόλεων
DP	ἔθνεσι(ν)	βασιλεῦσι(ν)	πόλεσι(ν)
AP	ἔθνη	βασιλεῖς	πόλεις

Other frequent third-declension words (used more than 50 times in the NT) include γυνή, χάρις, ἐλπίς, ὕδωρ, φῶς, αἰών, ἀνήρ, πατήρ, and μήτηρ.

11.13. *Examples of Third-Declension Nouns*

Rom. 11:13, εἰμὶ ἐγὼ **ἐθνῶν** ἀπόστολος.	I am an apostle *of the Gentiles*.
Rom. 5:1, Δικαιωθέντες (being justified) οὖν ἐκ **πίστεως** εἰρήνην ἔχομεν πρὸς τὸν θεὸν διὰ τοῦ κυρίου ἡμῶν Ἰησοῦ Χριστοῦ.	Therefore being justified by *faith*, we have peace with God through our Lord Jesus Christ.
Mark 6:14, ἤκουσεν ὁ **βασιλεὺς** Ἡρῴδης, φανερὸν γὰρ ἐγένετο τὸ **ὄνομα**[a] αὐτοῦ.	*King* Herod heard [this], for his *name* had become well known.

[a] ὄνομα, ατος, τό, "name," here refers to Jesus' *reputation*.

Mark 14:38, τὸ μὲν **πνεῦμα** πρόθυμον ἡ δὲ **σὰρξ** ἀσθενής.[a]	On the one hand, the *spirit* is willing, but on the other hand, the *flesh* is weak.[b]

[a] A published translation would not likely make the μέν . . . δέ contrast explicit, since it makes for somewhat clumsy English.

[b] You will need to supply a verb in this sentence.

Heb. 4:16, προσερχώμεθα οὖν μετὰ παρρησίας τῷ θρόνῳ τῆς **χάριτος**, ἵνα λάβωμεν **ἔλεος**[a] καὶ **χάριν** εὕρωμεν εἰς εὔκαιρον βοήθειαν.	Therefore let us approach with confidence the throne of *grace* in order that we may receive *mercy* and find *grace* in time of need.

[a] ἔλεος, ους, τό, "mercy," follows the same pattern of endings as ἔθνος, for which see above.

Ezek. 48:31, αἱ πύλαι τῆς **πόλεως** ἐπ' **ὀνόμασιν** φυλῶν τοῦ Ἰσραήλ.	The gates of the *city* [will be named] after *the names* of the tribes of Israel.

11.14. *Now You Try It*

John 4:17, ἀπεκρίθη (answered) ἡ **γυνὴ** καὶ εἶπεν (said) αὐτῷ, Οὐκ ἔχω **ἄνδρα**. λέγει αὐτῇ ὁ Ἰησοῦς, Καλῶς εἶπας (you have said) ὅτι **Ἄνδρα** οὐκ ἔχω.	Who is speaking in the first sentence? In the second sentence? To whom are these people speaking? How do you know? What is said? What case is ἄνδρα (both times), and why is that case used here?

Eph. 5:25, Οἱ **ἄνδρες**, ἀγαπᾶτε (love!) τὰς **γυναῖκας**, καθὼς καὶ ὁ Χριστὸς ἠγάπησεν (loved) τὴν ἐκκλησίαν καὶ ἑαυτὸν παρέδωκεν (gave) ὑπὲρ αὐτῆς.

How would ἄνδρες and γυναῖκας be represented in English? (It is not the usual gloss; check your lexicon.) What gender is αὐτῆς, and why is it that gender? How could you say it in English?

Mark 3:22, οἱ **γραμματεῖς** οἱ ἀπὸ Ἱεροσολύμων ἔλεγον (were saying) ὅτι Βεελζεβοὺλ ἔχει καὶ ὅτι ἐν τῷ **ἄρχοντι** τῶν δαιμονίων ἐκβάλλει τὰ δαιμόνια.

How is the second instance of οἱ functioning? What information do the two instances of ὅτι supply? What is καί linking?

Luke 1:33, βασιλεύσει (he will reign) ἐπὶ τὸν οἶκον Ἰακὼβ εἰς τοὺς **αἰῶνας**[a] καὶ τῆς βασιλείας αὐτοῦ οὐκ ἔσται (there will be) τέλος.

[a] εἰς τοὺς αἰῶνας is an idiom: "forever."

T. Ash. 7.7, ἐπισυνάξει (he will gather) ὑμᾶς κύριος ἐν **πίστει** δι᾽ **ἐλπίδα** εὐσπλαγχνίας[a] αὐτοῦ, διὰ[b] Ἀβραὰμ καὶ Ἰσαὰκ καὶ Ἰακώβ.

[a] εὐσπλαγχνία, ας, ἡ, "tenderheartedness, tender mercy, benevolence"

[b] The preposition διά may be used with either the genitive or accusative case, but in this text all three objects are indeclinable forms. The context of the statement suggests that we should understand these forms to be accusative.

Ign. *Eph.* 17.1, μὴ ἀλείφεσθε[a] (be besmeared!) δυσωδίαν[b] τῆς διδασκαλίας τοῦ **ἄρχοντος** τοῦ **αἰῶνος** τούτου.

[a] An accusative with the verb ἀλείφω may identify either what/who is anointed or besmeared, or it may identify the material with which the action is performed.

[b] δυσωδία, ας, ἡ, "filth"

Reading Passage: Luke 5:2–11

11.15. Third-declension forms are marked in bold.

Jesus' First Disciples

2εἶδεν (he saw) δύο πλοῖα ἑστῶτα (which were anchored) παρὰ τὴν λίμνην· οἱ
δὲ **ἁλιεῖς** ἀπ᾽ αὐτῶν ἀποβάντες (having disembarked) ἔπλυνον (were washing)
τὰ δίκτυα. 3ἐμβὰς (having embarked) δὲ εἰς ἓν (one) τῶν πλοίων, ὃ ἦν (was)
Σίμωνος, ἠρώτησεν αὐτὸν ἀπὸ τῆς γῆς ἐπαναγαγεῖν (to put out) ὀλίγον, καθίσας
(having sat down) δὲ ἐκ τοῦ πλοίου ἐδίδασκεν (he was teaching) τοὺς ὄχλους.
4ὡς δὲ ἐπαύσατο (he finished) λαλῶν (speaking), εἶπεν (he said) πρὸς τὸν
Σίμωνα, Ἐπανάγαγε (put out!) εἰς τὸ **βάθος** καὶ χαλάσατε (let down!) τὰ δίκτυα
ὑμῶν εἰς ἄγραν. 5καὶ ἀποκριθεὶς (answering) **Σίμων** εἶπεν (said), Ἐπιστάτα,[a] δι᾽
ὅλης **νυκτὸς** κοπιάσαντες (having worked) οὐδὲν ἐλάβομεν (we have caught)·

ἐπὶ δὲ τῷ **ῥήματί** σου χαλάσω (I will let down) τὰ δίκτυα. 6καὶ τοῦτο ποιήσαντες
(having done) συνέκλεισαν[b] (they were filled) **πλῆθος ἰχθύων** πολύ,[c] διερρήσσετο
(were breaking) δὲ τὰ δίκτυα αὐτῶν. 7καὶ κατένευσαν τοῖς μετόχοις ἐν τῷ ἑτέρῳ
πλοίῳ τοῦ ἐλθόντας (coming) συλλαβέσθαι[d] αὐτοῖς· καὶ ἦλθον (they came)
καὶ ἔπλησαν (they filled) ἀμφότερα τὰ πλοῖα ὥστε βυθίζεσθαι (to sink) αὐτά.
8ἰδὼν (seeing) δὲ **Σίμων** Πέτρος προσέπεσεν (fell before) τοῖς **γόνασιν** Ἰησοῦ
λέγων (saying), Ἔξελθε (depart!) ἀπ᾽ ἐμοῦ, ὅτι **ἀνὴρ** ἁμαρτωλός εἰμι, κύριε.[e]
9**θάμβος** γὰρ περιέσχεν (had seized) αὐτὸν καὶ **πάντας** τοὺς σὺν αὐτῷ ἐπὶ τῇ ἄγρᾳ
τῶν **ἰχθύων** ὧν συνέλαβον (they had caught), 10ὁμοίως δὲ καὶ Ἰάκωβον καὶ
Ἰωάννην υἱοὺς Ζεβεδαίου, οἳ ἦσαν (were) κοινωνοὶ τῷ **Σίμωνι**. καὶ εἶπεν (said)
πρὸς τὸν **Σίμωνα** ὁ Ἰησοῦς, Μὴ φοβοῦ (be afraid!)· ἀπὸ τοῦ νῦν ἀνθρώπους ἔσῃ
ζωγρῶν.[f] 11καὶ καταγαγόντες (having brought) τὰ πλοῖα ἐπὶ τὴν γῆν ἀφέντες
(having left) πάντα (all) ἠκολούθησαν αὐτῷ.

a "Master," vocative case (see app. D).

b συνέκλεισαν ▶ συγκλείω. When the preposition συν is prefixed to the verb κλείω, the combination ν + κ becomes γκ for euphony. In the aorist form συνέκλεισαν the augment separates these two consonants, so the nu does not change to gamma.

c The form πολύ here uses partial third-declension endings. See the forms of this word in chapter 6.

d τοῦ . . . συλλαβέσθαι, "to help"

e "Lord," vocative case (see app. D).

f ἔσῃ ζωγρῶν, "you will catch alive"

11.16. Vocabulary for Chapter 11

Part of Speech	Definition	Possible Glosses	Frequency	
Word			NT	LXX
Nouns				
πατήρ, πατρός, ὁ	A male parent or ancestor; metaphorically of someone esteemed; God as Father (of Jesus or a believer)	father	413	1,451
πνεῦμα, ατος, τό	Air in motion ("wind"); one aspect of a human's immaterial being (ctr. σῶμα, "body"); an attitude or disposition; a divine person, the third member of the godhead (in orthodox Christian theology); an incorporeal, supernatural being (e.g., an angel)	wind, breeze; spirit; Spirit	379	382
πίστις, εως, ἡ	Confidence based on the reliability of the one trusted; that which is believed; a characteristic of someone in whom confidence can be placed	faith, belief; the faith; faithfulness	243	59
ὄνομα, ατος, τό	A designation used to identify, either specifically (i.e., a proper name) or generally (referring to a category)	name, reputation	231	1,045
ἀνήρ, ἀνδρός, ὁ	An adult human male; a specific man as related to a woman (i.e., a husband)[a]	man, male; husband	216	1,918
γυνή, αικός, ἡ	An adult human female; a specific woman as related to a man (i.e., a wife)	woman; wife	215	1,074

Part of Speech	Definition	Possible Glosses	Frequency	
Word			NT	LXX
χείρ, χειρός, ἡ	The body part at the end of the arm containing fingers ("hand"; occasionally of an animal, e.g., a dog's paw); one component of that part (i.e., "finger") or occasionally the entire member, arm as a whole; that which may be produced with the hand ("handwriting"; numerous metaphorical uses, esp. in the LXX)	hand, finger; handwriting	177	1,943
ἔθνος, ους, τό	A group of people viewed as an entity on the basis of kinship, geography, or custom; in the plural often refers to non-Jews, i.e., Gentiles	nation; Gentiles (pl.)	162	1,003
πόλις, εως, ἡ	A population center of varying size and population; by metonymy it may refer to the people who live in that place	city, town	162	1,576
χάρις, ιτος, ἡ	A disposition marked by generosity, frequently unmotivated by the worth of the recipient; a response to such generosity; with reference to God, divine favor or work for the benefit of others at no cost to them	grace, favor, kindness; thanks, gratitude	155	164
σάρξ, σαρκός, ἡ	The material that covers the bones of a human or animal body ("flesh"); the physical body; a living being with a physical body; humans as physical beings; an immaterial aspect of a person viewed as a source of or subject to sinful desires (ethical use)	flesh, body; sinful nature	147	215
σῶμα, ατος, τό	A structured physical unit viewed as a whole, whether human, animal, plant, etc.; a unified group of people, in the NT often Christian believers as a whole, both living, dead, and yet to be	body	142	136
αἰών, ῶνος, ὁ	A long period of time, in either the past or the future; a segment of time as a particular unit of history; eternity (if context suggests no end)	age, eternity	122	750
βασιλεύς, έως, ὁ	A man who is the supreme ruler in a country by right of succession to the throne; God as the supreme ruler of everything that exists by right of being the Creator	king	115	3,476
κρίμα, ατος, τό	The evaluation of conduct by a court of law; the legal decision as a result of such evaluation; the process of bringing a legal claim before a court of law	judging, judgment; decision, verdict; lawsuit	27	255

[a] In the LXX ἀνήρ is often used as a distributive pronoun with the same meaning as ἕκαστος. This is a very formal translation of the Hebrew idiom; it is not at all a native Greek idiom. For example, Judg. 16:5, ἡμεῖς δώσομέν σοι ἀνὴρ χιλίους καὶ ἑκατὸν ἀργυρίου, "we will *each* give you 1,100 pieces of silver."

11.17. Key Things to Know for Chapter 11

Know the third-declension endings.

Third-declension nouns do not have a connecting vowel.

What is the square of stops, and why is it important?

Be familiar with, but do not try to memorize, the six key representative paradigms for third-declension nouns. Study their forms, and review them frequently.

12

THIRD DECLENSION: PART 2

Adjectives and Pronouns

12.1. You learned third-declension nouns in the previous chapter. We will now add adjective and pronoun forms that also use third-declension endings. You will also learn how to steal chickens!

Third-Declension Adjectives

12.2. Third-declension adjectives use the same endings as third-declension nouns and have all the same variations. The most common such adjective is πᾶς, "each, all, every." The lexical entry reads πᾶς, πᾶσα, πᾶν.[1] Since this is an adjective, three nominative forms are given, first masculine, then feminine, and finally the neuter form. This word uses third-declension endings in the masculine and neuter but first-declension endings in feminine. For this reason it is sometimes referred to as a 3/1/3 adjective.

Decl. Gend.	3 Masc.	1 Fem.	3 Neut.
NS	πᾶς	πᾶσα	πᾶν
GS	παντός	πάσης	παντός
DS	παντί	πάσῃ	παντί
AS	πάντα	πᾶσαν	πᾶν
NP	πάντες	πᾶσαι	πάντα
GP	πάντων	πασῶν	πάντων
DP	πᾶσι(ν)	πάσαις	πᾶσι(ν)
AP	πάντας	πάσας	πάντα

1. Some lexicons will also give the genitive forms: παντός, πάσης, παντός.

Πᾶς illustrates two features of third-declension words. First, it is an example of the most common word in which a tau cannot stand at the end of a word and will drop off. In the neuter nominative singular form, the stem, παντ-, + case ending – (i.e., "blank") results in παντ, but since tau cannot stand at the end of a word, the tau drops off, so the final spelling is πᾶν.

Second, the consonant pair ντ drops out when followed by a sigma. (The ντ acts like a stop even though only the tau is part of the square of stops). That explains why most forms are spelled with παντ, but the nominative singular and dative plural have πᾶς or πασ-.

*παντ + ς = πᾶς in nominative masculine singular

12.3. When πᾶς modifies a noun, it is almost always in predicate position, but it functions the same as other adjectives in attributive position. That is, the phrase **πάσας** τὰς βασιλείας τοῦ κόσμου (Matt. 4:8) means "*all* the kingdoms of the world." Likewise **πᾶσα** ἡ πόλις (Matt. 8:34) means "the *whole* town." The uncommon use of πᾶς in attributive position functions the same way: ὁ γὰρ **πᾶς** νόμος (Gal. 5:14) means "the *whole* law" and τὴν **πᾶσαν** κακίαν ταύτην (1 Kgdms. [1 Sam.] 12:20), "*all* this evil." With an anarthrous noun, **πᾶν** δένδρον ἀγαθὸν καρποὺς καλοὺς ποιεῖ (Matt. 7:17) means "*every* good tree produces good fruit."

In Classical Greek there was a fairly consistent pattern of usage with the word πᾶς. In the singular, when modifying an articular noun, πᾶς had a collective meaning (e.g., **πᾶσα** ἡ πόλις, "*all* the city"), but when modifying an anarthrous noun, it had a distributive sense (e.g., **πᾶσα** πόλις, "*every* city"). Likewise when πᾶς occurred in attributive position (it is usually in predicate position), it was emphatic. These patterns are no longer reliable guides in Koine, though the context sometimes justifies such an understanding. Especially in the LXX, but also in the NT, the syntactical distinctions have been blurred.[2]

Tip

The form πάντα can be parsed one of three ways (study the chart until you find all three). Context will determine whether any given instance is nominative or accusative and whether masculine or neuter.

Two-Form Adjectives of the Third Declension

12.4. Although most two-form adjectives use second-declension endings (see §6.7), some use a third-declension pattern. As with the second-declension forms, these adjectives use the same set of endings for both masculine and feminine. Most of these words are declined like ἀληθής. Some use the less common pattern of ἄφρων.

2. See Conybeare and Stock, *Grammar of Septuagint Greek*, §63.

	Masc./Fem.	Neut.	Masc./Fem.	Neut.
NS	ἀληθής	ἀληθές	ἄφρων	ἄφρον
GS	ἀληθοῦς	ἀληθοῦς	ἄφρονος	ἄφρονος
DS	ἀληθεῖ	ἀληθεῖ	ἄφρονι	ἄφρονι
AS	ἀληθῆ	ἀληθές	ἄφρονα	ἄφρον
NP	ἀληθεῖς	ἀληθῆ	ἄφρονες	ἄφρονα
GP	ἀληθῶν	ἀληθῶν	ἀφρόνων	ἀφρόνων
DP	ἀληθέσι(ν)	ἀληθέσι(ν)	ἄφροσι(ν)	ἄφροσι(ν)
AP	ἀληθεῖς	ἀληθῆ	ἄφρονας	ἄφρονα

Words that follow this pattern include ἀληθής ("true"), ἀσθενής ("weak"), πλήρης ("full"), and ψευδής ("false").

Numerical Adjectives and Adverbs

12.5. The adjectives that express quantitative numerical values are called *cardinal numbers* (*one*, *two*, etc.). Those that express sequence are *ordinals* (*first*, *second*, etc.). There are also adverbs that express frequency (*once*, *twice*, etc.), as well as numerals.[3]

Cardinal Numbers

12.6. Of the cardinals, εἷς, "one," is a 3/1/3 form like πᾶς; that is, it uses third-declension endings in masculine and neuter, but first-declension forms are used for feminine. The lexical entry is εἷς, μία, ἕν. The adjective δύο, "two," has only a single set of forms for all three genders. Τρεῖς, "three," is a two-form adjective that follows the same pattern of endings as ἀληθής. Τέσσαρες, "four," is a two-form adjective with standard third-declension endings. These are largely third-declension forms. Numbers "five" (πέντε), "six" (ἕξ), "seven" (ἑπτά), "eight" (ὀκτώ), "nine" (ἐννέα), and "ten" (δέκα) are indeclinable.

Cardinal Number Forms

	εἷς			δύο		τρεῖς		τέσσαρες	
	M	F	N	M/F/N		M/F	N	M/F	N
NS	εἷς	μία	ἕν	NP	δύο	τρεῖς	τρία	τέσσαρες	τέσσαρα[c]
GS	ἑνός	μιᾶς	ἑνός	GP	δύο	τριῶν	τριῶν	τεσσάρων	τεσσάρων
DS	ἑνί	μιᾷ	ἑνί	DP	δυσί(ν)[a]	τρισί(ν)	τρισί(ν)	τέσσαρσιν	τέσσαρσιν
AS	ἕνα	μίαν	ἕν	AP	δύο	τρεῖς	τρία	τέσσαρας[b]	τέσσαρα[c]

[a] In the LXX δύο is sometimes treated as an indeclinable form, so it may also be used as a dative. Occasionally the dative form is spelled δυεῖν in the LXX.

[b] Or τέσσαρες

[c] Or τέσσερα

3. In the LXX there are also some instances of noun forms: τετράς, αδος, ἡ, "four, the fourth day (of the week or month)"; εἰκάς, άδος, ἡ, "twenty, twentieth day (of the month)"; and τριάκας, αδος, ἡ, "thirty, thirtieth day (of the month)." These do not occur in the NT.

There are two compound forms that include εἷς, μία, ἕν. Both οὐδείς, οὐδεμία, οὐδέν and μηδείς, μηδεμία, μηδέν mean "no one." The etymology is transparent: the negative οὐ or μή + δέ + the word εἷς, μία, ἕν. The endings of these words follow the same pattern as shown in the chart above. In the LXX the older spellings οὐθείς and μηθείς also occur frequently; there is no difference in meaning.[4]

In the LXX (and occasionally in the NT) εἷς may function as the equivalent of the English indefinite article.[5]

2 Kgdms. (2 Sam.) 2:18, Ἀσαὴλ κοῦφος τοῖς ποσὶν αὐτοῦ ὡσεὶ **μία** δορκὰς ἐν ἀγρῷ.	Asael was swift on his feet as *a* gazelle in the field.
Matt. 8:19, **εἷς** γραμματεὺς εἶπεν αὐτῷ, Διδάσκαλε . . .	*A* scribe said to him, "Teacher . . ."

Stealing Chickens

If you want a mnemonic for remembering the word εἷς, try this silly phrase: "Steal me a chicken!" Or perhaps, "Steal me *one* chicken!" That is: εἷς, μία, ἕν . . . (Yes, I know, εἷς is not exactly "heist," but it is close enough for a mnemonic device.)

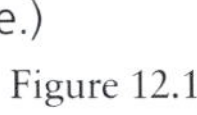

Figure 12.1

Ordinal Numbers

12.7. The ordinals are formed as first- and second-declension adjectives. The forms follow the same patterns as other adjectives. "First" through "tenth" are as follows.

Ordinal Number Forms

		Frequency	
		NT	LXX
πρῶτος, η, ον	first	155	226
δεύτερος, α, ον	second	43	217
τρίτος, η, ον	third	56	167
τέταρτος, η, ον	fourth	10	94
πέμπτος, η, ον	fifth	4	94
ἕκτος, η, ον	sixth	14	61
ἕβδομος, η, ον	seventh	9	129
ὄγδοος, η, ον	eighth	5	45
ἔνατος, η, ον	ninth	10	32
δέκατος, η, ον	tenth	7	98

4. In the NT there are a few instances of the spelling οὐθείς, none of μηθείς.

5. See further, Conybeare and Stock, *Grammar of Septuagint Greek*, §2; MLS, s.v. εἷς, 197.c; and BDAG, s.v. εἷς, 292.3.b.

Numerical Adverbs

12.8. Numerical adverbs express frequency: "once," "twice," and so forth. They are most commonly spelled with the adverb suffix -ακις. As with other adverbs that you learned in chapter 6, these forms do not decline. The forms from "once" through "seven times" are as follows ("eight," "nine," and "ten times" do not occur in the NT or the LXX).

Numerical Adverbs

		Frequency	
		NT	LXX
ἅπαξ	once	14	42
δίς	twice	6	17
τρίς	three times	12	12
τετράκις	four times	—	—
πεντάκις	five times	1	1
ἑξάκις	six times	—	3
ἑπτάκις	seven times	4	24

Numerals

12.9. Greek numerals (i.e., numerical signs/symbols) are not used in the text of the NT. Unlike English, Greek did not have separate symbols for numerals. Where English uses 1, 2, 3, and so on, Greek uses the alphabetical symbols, but appends a number sign: α´, β´, γ´. The only place where you will see them in a Greek NT or in a LXX text is in the titles of paired books such as ΠΡΟΣ ΚΟΡΙΝΘΙΟΥΣ Α´ and Β´ or ΒΑΣΙΛΕΙΩΝ Α´, Β´, Γ´, and Δ´ and to number the Psalms. For a fuller discussion of Greek numerals, see appendix E.

Examples of Third-Declension Adjectives

12.10. In the following examples all third-declension forms are marked, both nouns and adjectives.

Rev. 1:7, ὄψεται αὐτὸν **πᾶς** ὀφθαλμός.	*Every* eye will see him.
Gal. 5:14, ὁ γὰρ **πᾶς** νόμος ἐν **ἑνὶ** λόγῳ πεπλήρωται (is fulfilled), ἐν τῷ[a] Ἀγαπήσεις (Love!) τὸν πλησίον σου ὡς σεαυτόν.	For the *whole* law is fulfilled in *one* word, in this: "Love your neighbor as yourself."

[a] The article τῷ functions here as a nominalizer to introduce the quotation that follows, from Lev. 19:18. In essence the entire quote functions as a noun that is the object of the preposition ἐν.

Matt. 4:8, Πάλιν παραλαμβάνει αὐτὸν ὁ διάβολος εἰς **ὄρος** ὑψηλὸν λίαν καὶ δείκνυσιν (he showed) αὐτῷ **πάσας** τὰς βασιλείας τοῦ κόσμου καὶ τὴν δόξαν αὐτῶν.

Again the devil took him to a very high *mountain* and showed him *all* the kingdoms of the world and their glory.

John 1:16, ὅτι ἐκ τοῦ **πληρώματος** αὐτοῦ ἡμεῖς **πάντες** ἐλάβομεν καὶ **χάριν** ἀντὶ **χάριτος**.

For out of his *fullness* we *all* have also received *grace* in place of *grace*.

John 1:16 is an interesting verse in a number of ways. It is very terse and may seem almost cryptic. The repeated **χάρις** is not identified explicitly in this verse. What "grace" is this? The keys are probably the preposition **ἀντί** and the context. The preposition expresses substitution ("in place of"). Then verse 17 explains verse 16: **ὅτι ὁ νόμος διὰ Μωϋσέως ἐδόθη, ἡ χάρις καὶ ἡ ἀλήθεια διὰ Ἰησοῦ Χριστοῦ ἐγένετο** ("for the Law was given through Moses; grace and truth came through Jesus Christ"). The conjunction **ὅτι** is probably causal, "for, because." The reference may be to God's gracious gift of the old covenant (the Mosaic law) being replaced by the new (and better) gracious gift of the new covenant (summarized by grace and truth).

Mark 9:5, ὁ Πέτρος λέγει τῷ Ἰησοῦ, Ῥαββί, καλόν ἐστιν ἡμᾶς ὧδε εἶναι, καὶ ποιήσωμεν (let us make) τρεῖς σκηνάς, σοὶ **μίαν** καὶ Μωϋσεῖ **μίαν** καὶ Ἠλίᾳ **μίαν**.

Peter said to Jesus, "Rabbi, for us to be here is good, so let us make three tents, *one* for you, *one* for Moses, and *one* for Elijah."

Gen. 9:19, **τρεῖς** οὗτοί εἰσιν οἱ υἱοὶ Νῶε· ἀπὸ τούτων διεσπάρησαν (they were scattered) ἐπὶ **πᾶσαν** τὴν γῆν.

These *three* are the sons of Noah; from these they were scattered over *all* the earth.

12.11. *Now You Try It*

Matt. 18:5, ὃς ἐὰν δέξηται (welcomes) **ἓν** παιδίον τοιοῦτο ἐπὶ **τῷ ὀνόματί** μου, ἐμὲ δέχεται (welcomes).

Mark 11:29, ὁ δὲ Ἰησοῦς εἶπεν (said) αὐτοῖς, Ἐπερωτήσω (I will ask) ὑμᾶς **ἕνα** λόγον.

Mark 10:27, **πάντα** δυνατὰ παρὰ τῷ θεῷ.[a]

[a] You will need to supply a linking verb. The form πάντα can be parsed one of three ways. Which is it here?

Exod. 10:22, ἐξέτεινεν δὲ Μωυσῆς τὴν χεῖρα εἰς τὸν οὐρανόν, καὶ ἐγένετο (there was) σκότος γνόφος θύελλα ἐπὶ **πᾶσαν** γῆν Αἰγύπτου **τρεῖς** ἡμέρας.

Did. 10.5, μνήσθητι (remember!), κύριε, τῆς ἐκκλησίας σου, τοῦ ῥύσασθαι[a] αὐτὴν ἀπὸ **παντὸς** πονηροῦ καὶ τελειῶσαι αὐτὴν ἐν τῇ ἀγάπῃ σου, καὶ σύναξον (gather!) αὐτὴν ἀπὸ τῶν **τεσσάρων** ἀνέμων εἰς τὴν σὴν βασιλείαν, ὅτι σοῦ ἐστιν ἡ δύναμις καὶ ἡ δόξα εἰς τοὺς **αἰῶνας**.

[a] τοῦ ῥύσασθαι is an articular infinitive form that you have not learned yet; it expresses purpose: "to deliver."

Tip

Here is another reason for learning the full lexical entry, including the article: it will enable you to figure out which adjective is modifying which head word in some sentences. For example, in James 3:5, does the adjective μικρόν modify the noun in front of it (γλῶσσα) or the noun after it (μέλος)?

James 3:5, ἡ γλῶσσα **μικρὸν** μέλος ἐστίν.

What *gender* are the nouns and the adjective? This statement uses a third-declension noun, so be sure to check your lexicon to identify the forms correctly. This statement says, "The tongue is a little member" (*not*: "the little tongue is a member"), because the adjective is neuter, agreeing with μέλος, not γλῶσσα (which is feminine). A similar situation involves φθαρτοῦ in Rom. 1:23.

Third-Declension Pronouns

12.12. Several pronouns use the same set of third-declension endings that you have learned for nouns and adjectives. These are the indefinite and interrogative pronouns as well as the indefinite relative pronoun.

Indefinite and Interrogative Pronouns

12.13. Interrogative pronouns are those that ask a question regarding someone or something—for example, *who* or *what*. Indefinite pronouns are used with reference to unspecified persons or things—for example, *someone* or *anything*—rather than a specific person or thing. These two forms are spelled identically in Greek; only the accent distinguishes the forms. This is one instance in which you must be able to identify the word on the basis of the accent.

To distinguish these two pronouns, watch the accents and the punctuation in the clause in which the word is used. An interrogative pronoun, which is usually at the beginning of the clause, *always* has an acute accent on the front of the word and will have a question mark at the end of the clause. The indefinite pronoun will have either no accent (usually) or an accent at the end of the word (sometimes).[6] The presence of a question mark is the easiest way to identify most interrogative pronouns, even if you cannot remember the accent patterns.

	Indefinite Pronoun		Interrogative Pronoun	
	M/F	N	M/F	N
NS	τις	τι	τίς	τί
GS	τινός	τινός	τίνος	τίνος
DS	τινί	τινί	τίνι	τίνι
AS	τινά	τι	τίνα	τί
NP	τινές	τινά	τίνες	τίνα
GP	τινῶν	τινῶν	τίνων	τίνων
DP	τισί(ν)	τισί(ν)	τίσι(ν)	τίσι(ν)
AP	τινάς	τινά	τίνας	τίνα

The indefinite form is an *enclitic*: a word that is pronounced together with the preceding word and shares the accent of that word, having none of its own. This means that the accent will vary from what is shown above when it is used in context. Most such forms do not have an accent at all; if they do, it will be on the syllable shown with the acute in the chart above, but in these cases it will almost always be a grave accent rather than acute.

Remember that the original text had *no accents*, so these are editorial decisions based on context—as are all punctuation marks. But the accents are reliable, and they will save you a lot of time figuring out each one when you run across them in the text. There might be a tiny handful in the NT that could be read either way, but that is rare. At this point in your studies you should trust the editors and read the text as it is printed in this regard.

12.14. Examples of Indefinite and Interrogative Pronouns

3 John 9, Ἔγραψά (I wrote) **τι** τῇ ἐκκλησίᾳ.	I wrote *something* to the church.
Mark 5:9, ἐπηρώτα (he asked) αὐτόν, **Τί** ὄνομά σοι; καὶ λέγει αὐτῷ, Λεγιὼν ὄνομά μοι, ὅτι πολλοί ἐσμεν.	He asked him, "*What* is your name?" And he said to him, "My name is Legion, because we are many."
Mark 10:18, ὁ δὲ Ἰησοῦς εἶπεν (said) αὐτῷ, **Τί** με λέγεις ἀγαθόν; οὐδεὶς ἀγαθὸς εἰ μὴ εἷς ὁ θεός.	Jesus said to him, "*Why* do you call me good? No one is good except one: God."
Heb. 3:4, πᾶς γὰρ οἶκος κατασκευάζεται ὑπό **τινος**.	For every house is built by *someone*.

6. The indefinite pronoun in the NT has no accent more than 460 times out of about 530 occurrences (about 87 percent). In the LXX approximately 230 of 260 have no accent (89 percent).

Gen. 13:16, εἰ δύναταί **τις** ἐξαριθμῆσαι τὴν ἄμμον τῆς γῆς, καὶ τὸ σπέρμα σου ἐξαριθμηθήσεται.

If *anyone* is able to count the sand of the earth, then your seed will be counted.

Gen. 18:13, εἶπεν κύριος πρὸς Ἀβραάμ, **Τί** ὅτι ἐγέλασεν Σάρρα;

The Lord said to Abraham, "*Why* is it that Sarah laughed?"

12.15. Now You Try It

Luke 6:2, **τινὲς** δὲ τῶν Φαρισαίων εἶπαν, **Τί** ποιεῖτε ὃ οὐκ ἔξεστιν τοῖς σάββασιν;

John 6:64, ἀλλ' εἰσὶν ἐξ ὑμῶν **τινες** οἳ οὐ πιστεύουσιν.

Gal. 6:15, οὔτε γὰρ περιτομή **τί** ἐστιν οὔτε ἀκροβυστία ἀλλὰ καινὴ κτίσις.

Gen. 19:12, Εἶπαν (they said) δὲ οἱ ἄνδρες πρὸς Λώτ, Ἔστιν **τίς** σοι ὧδε, γαμβροὶ[a] ἢ υἱοὶ ἢ θυγατέρες;

[a] γαμβρός, οῦ, ὁ, "in-law," either "son-in-law" or "father-in-law"

Gen. 24:65, εἶπεν (she said) τῷ παιδί, **Τίς** ἐστιν ὁ ἄνθρωπος ἐκεῖνος;

Indefinite Pronouns as Adjectives

12.16. The indefinite pronoun can also function as an adjective. (The interrogative pronoun occasionally functions the same way.) In this instance the pronoun occurs close to the noun it modifies; it may precede or follow the noun. For example, νεανίσκος τις means "a certain young man" (Mark 14:51).

12.17. Examples of Indefinite Pronouns as Adjectives

Luke 8:27, ὑπήντησεν ἀνήρ **τις** ἐκ τῆς πόλεως.

A *certain* man from the town met [him].

Mark 14:47, εἷς δέ **τις** ἔπαισεν τὸν δοῦλον τοῦ ἀρχιερέως.

But a *certain* one struck the slave of the high priest.

Acts 5:1, Ἀνὴρ δέ **τις** Ἁνανίας ὀνόματι σὺν Σαπφίρῃ τῇ γυναικὶ αὐτοῦ ἐπώλησεν κτῆμα.

Now a *certain* man named Ananias with Sapphira his wife sold a piece of property.

Job 1:1, Ἄνθρωπός **τις** ἦν ἐν χώρᾳ τῇ Αὐσίτιδι, ᾧ ὄνομα Ἰώβ, καὶ ἦν ὁ ἄνθρωπος ἐκεῖνος ἀληθινός, ἄμεμπτος, δίκαιος, θεοσεβής.

There was a *certain* man in the country of Ausitis whose name was Job, and that man was true, blameless, righteous, [and] devout.

12.18. Now You Try It

Acts 18:24, Ἰουδαῖος δέ **τις** Ἀπολλῶς ὀνόματι, Ἀλεξανδρεὺς τῷ γένει, ἀνὴρ λόγιος, κατήντησεν εἰς Ἔφεσον.

1 Cor. 7:12–13, εἴ **τις** ἀδελφὸς γυναῖκα ἔχει ἄπιστον καὶ αὕτη συνευδοκεῖ οἰκεῖν μετ' αὐτοῦ, μὴ ἀφιέτω (he must divorce) αὐτήν· καὶ γυνὴ εἴ **τις** ἔχει ἄνδρα ἄπιστον καὶ οὗτος συνευδοκεῖ οἰκεῖν μετ' αὐτῆς, μὴ ἀφιέτω τὸν ἄνδρα.

T. Naph. 5.4, νεανίας **τις** ἐπιδίδωσιν (gave) αὐτῷ βάια φοινίκων δώδεκα.

Indefinite Relative Pronoun

12.19. There is also an indefinite relative pronoun in Greek, ὅστις, which is a combination of the relative pronoun with the indefinite pronoun τις. Both parts of the word decline, and for the most part do so the same way each part declines separately. Most of the forms in the chart below do not occur in the NT. The vast majority of NT forms are nominative case. (You do *not* need to learn this chart. It is provided simply for reference.)

	Masc.	Fem.	Neut.
NS	ὅστις	ἥτις	ὅ τι (ὅτι)
GS	οὗτινος	ἧστινος	ὅτου
DS	ᾧτινι	ᾗτινι	ᾧτινι
AS	ὅντινα	ἥντινα	ὅτι (ὅ τι)
NP	οἵτινες	αἵτινες	ἅτινα
GP	ὧντινων	ὧντινων	ὧντινων
DP	οἷστισι(ν)	αἷστισι(ν)	οἷστισι(ν)
AP	οὕστινας	ἅστινας	ἅτινα

The neuter singular nominative form is usually written as two words (ὅ τι) in modern texts, but you will sometimes find it written as a single word.[7] It is then, of course, the same spelling as the conjunction ὅτι. Context must determine which form it is; the conjunction is far more common than the pronoun.

The indefinite relative pronoun ὅστις functions just like a regular relative pronoun but sometimes (not always) has the "ever" idea, that is, not just "who" but "whoever." The regular relative pronoun is more definite; "who" refers to "the one who," but the indefinite relative does not specify, it is just "whoever."

7. The older Greek texts published by Westcott and Hort and by Tischendorf are examples where this form is printed as a single word, ὅτι.

In Koine Greek, however, the indefinite relative has begun to be used in places where you would normally expect the regular relative, so if the "ever" idea does not seem to fit the context, consider the possibility that it might be the more definite idea that is present. Most of the examples below are equivalent to regular relative pronouns; there is no indefinite sense at all. That is particularly obvious when the reference is to a particular person identified in the context—for example, John 8:53 and Rom. 16:12.

An Idiom

An idiomatic usage found in both the NT and LXX is the expression ἕως ὅτου, a temporal expression meaning "until" or "while." In this case ἕως, which normally functions as a conjunction, serves as a preposition governing a genitive-case object.

12.20. Examples of Indefinite Relative Pronouns

Mark 6:23, ὤμοσεν αὐτῇ, Ὅ τι ἐάν με αἰτήσῃς δώσω σοι.	He swore to her, "*Whatever* you ask I will give you."
Mark 12:18, ἔρχονται Σαδδουκαῖοι πρὸς αὐτόν, **οἵτινες** λέγουσιν ἀνάστασιν μὴ εἶναι.	Sadducees came to him, *who* say a resurrection is not to be (or in better English, that there is no resurrection).
1 Kgdms. (1 Sam.) 30:4, ἦρεν (he raised) Δαυὶδ καὶ οἱ ἄνδρες αὐτοῦ τὴν φωνὴν αὐτῶν καὶ ἔκλαυσαν (they wept), ἕως **ὅτου** οὐκ ἦν ἐν αὐτοῖς ἰσχὺς ἔτι κλαίειν.	David and his men raised their voices and wept *until* there was not in them strength to weep any longer.
Ign. *Phld.* 3.1, Ἀπέχεσθε τῶν κακῶν βοτανῶν, **ἅστινας**[a] οὐ γεωργεῖ Ἰησοῦς Χριστός.	Stay away from evil plants, *which* Jesus Christ does not cultivate.[b]

[a] ἅστινας is accusative because it is the direct object of γεωργεῖ; it is feminine plural to agree with its antecedent, βοτανῶν.

[b] This odd-sounding exhortation occurs in the midst of a series of varied metaphors (wolves, races, sheep, shepherds, and agriculture).

12.21. Now You Try It

Rom. 9:4, **οἵτινές** εἰσιν Ἰσραηλῖται, ὧν ἡ υἱοθεσία καὶ ἡ δόξα καὶ αἱ διαθῆκαι καὶ ἡ νομοθεσία καὶ ἡ λατρεία καὶ αἱ ἐπαγγελίαι.	
Rom. 16:12, ἀσπάσασθε (Greet!) Τρύφαιναν[a] καὶ Τρυφῶσαν τὰς κοπιώσας[b] ἐν κυρίῳ. ἀσπάσασθε Περσίδα τὴν ἀγαπητήν, **ἥτις** πολλὰ ἐκοπίασεν ἐν κυρίῳ.	

[a] The three names, Τρύφαιναν, Τρυφῶσαν, and Περσίδα are all women's names—note the feminine endings.

[b] τὰς κοπιώσας is a participle that describes the three women: "who labored."

John 8:53, μὴ σὺ μείζων εἶ τοῦ πατρὸς ἡμῶν Ἀβραάμ, **ὅστις** ἀπέθανεν; καὶ οἱ προφῆται ἀπέθανον. τίνα σεαυτὸν ποιεῖς;

Exod. 20:2, Ἐγώ εἰμι κύριος ὁ θεός σου, **ὅστις** ἐξήγαγόν (I brought) σε ἐκ γῆς Αἰγύπτου ἐξ οἴκου δουλείας.

Relative pronouns do not have person (i.e., first-, second-, or third-person forms). In the nominative case (as in this example) the relative pronoun most commonly occurs with third-person verbs, but the verb agrees in person and number with the *antecedent* of the relative pronoun. Here the first-person singular verb ἐξήγαγόν agrees with ἐγώ, the antecedent of ὅστις.[8] In English we would express ὅστις ἐξήγαγόν σε as "who brought you out."

ὅστις in Romans 6:2

Rom. 6:1–2, Τί οὖν ἐροῦμεν; ἐπιμένωμεν τῇ ἁμαρτίᾳ, ἵνα ἡ χάρις πλεονάσῃ; μὴ γένοιτο. οἵτινες ἀπεθάνομεν τῇ ἁμαρτίᾳ, πῶς ἔτι ζήσομεν ἐν αὐτῇ;

What shall we say, then? Shall we continue in sin that grace may abound? Absolutely not! How shall those who died to sin still live in it?

The word ὅστις is an example in which distinctions formerly followed carefully in Classical Greek have broken down in the Koine. Most NT uses of ὅστις are essentially equivalent to the normal relative pronoun ὅς. Only a few NT examples contain some of the former qualitative or indefinite sense of the Classical use.[a]

Romans 6:2 is an example in which ὅστις seems to retain something of its former qualitative nature. Moo explains that "the indefinite relative pronoun οἵτινες is often equivalent in the NT to the simple relative pronoun (ὅς), but it is used deliberately here with a 'qualitative' nuance: 'we who are of such a nature that. . . .'"[b]

[a] Moule, *Idiom Book*, 123–25.
[b] Moo, *Romans*, 357n24.

8. See Smyth, *Greek Grammar*, §2501.b. The use of a nominative relative pronoun with a first-person verb is rare. In the NT and LXX I know of only two other instances: Lev. 20:24, ἐγὼ κύριος ὁ θεὸς ὑμῶν, ὃς διώρισα ὑμᾶς ἀπὸ πάντων τῶν ἐθνῶν, and 1 Cor. 15:9, Ἐγὼ γάρ εἰμι ὁ ἐλάχιστος τῶν ἀποστόλων ὃς οὐκ εἰμὶ ἱκανὸς καλεῖσθαι ἀπόστολος.

— — — — — — — — — — — — — —

12.22. Advanced Information for Reference: Diagramming Interrogative Pronouns

John 1:22, εἶπαν οὖν αὐτῷ, **Τίς** εἶ; **τί** λέγεις περὶ σεαυτοῦ;

Therefore they said to him, "*Who* are you? *What* do you say about yourself?"

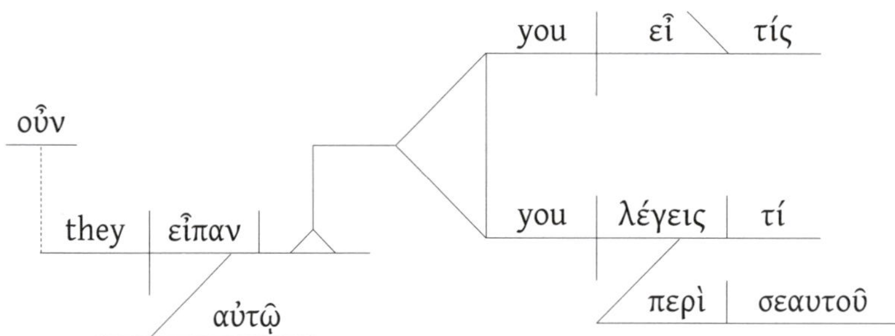

Figure 12.2

This example not only shows interrogative pronouns but also illustrates how direct discourse is diagrammed. The section of the diagram that is on stilts functions as a unit: what they said is the object complement (direct object) of the verb εἶπαν ("they said").

— — — — — — — — — — — — — —

12.23. Reading Passage: John 7:19–27

Reaction to Jesus' Teaching

[19]οὐ Μωϋσῆς δέδωκεν (he gave) ὑμῖν τὸν νόμον; καὶ **οὐδεὶς** ἐξ ὑμῶν ποιεῖ τὸν νόμον. **τί** με ζητεῖτε ἀποκτεῖναι (to kill); [20]ἀπεκρίθη (answered) ὁ ὄχλος, Δαιμόνιον ἔχεις· **τίς** σε ζητεῖ ἀποκτεῖναι; [21]ἀπεκρίθη Ἰησοῦς καὶ εἶπεν (said) αὐτοῖς, **Ἓν** ἔργον ἐποίησα καὶ **πάντες** θαυμάζετε. [22]διὰ τοῦτο Μωϋσῆς δέδωκεν ὑμῖν τὴν περιτομὴν καὶ ἐν σαββάτῳ περιτέμνετε ἄνθρωπον· [23]εἰ περιτομὴν λαμβάνει ἄνθρωπος ἐν σαββάτῳ ἵνα μὴ λυθῇ (should be broken) ὁ νόμος Μωϋσέως, ἐμοὶ χολᾶτε[a] ὅτι ὅλον ἄνθρωπον ὑγιῆ ἐποίησα ἐν σαββάτῳ; [24]μὴ κρίνετε (judge!) κατ' ὄψιν,[b] ἀλλὰ τὴν δικαίαν κρίσιν κρίνετε (judge!).

[25]Ἔλεγον (they said) οὖν **τινες** ἐκ τῶν Ἱεροσολυμιτῶν, Οὐχ οὗτός ἐστιν ὃν ζητοῦσιν ἀποκτεῖναι; [26]καὶ ἴδε παρρησίᾳ[c] λαλεῖ καὶ **οὐδὲν** αὐτῷ λέγουσιν. μήποτε ἀληθῶς ἔγνωσαν (they know) οἱ ἄρχοντες ὅτι οὗτός ἐστιν ὁ Χριστός; [27]ἀλλὰ τοῦτον οἴδαμεν (we know) πόθεν ἐστίν· ὁ δὲ Χριστὸς ὅταν ἔρχηται (he comes) **οὐδεὶς** γινώσκει πόθεν ἐστίν.

[a] χολᾶτε ▶ χολάω, an alpha contract verb in which the alpha at the end of the stem contracts with the usual connecting vowel: α + ε = α

[b] This phrase is an idiom. It does not say "do not judge according to the face" (which is what the individual words mean), but as BDAG (s.v. ὄψις, 746.2) explains, "κατ' ὄψιν κρίνειν judge by the outward appearance."

[c] The dative παρρησίᾳ (▶ παρρησία, ας, ἡ, "plainness, openness to the public") is formally, "in public," but it functions very much like an adverb, "openly, publicly."

12.24. Vocabulary for Chapter 12

Part of Speech	Definition	Possible Glosses	Frequency	
Word			NT	LXX
Adjectives				
πᾶς, πᾶσα, πᾶν	An adjective denoting comprehensiveness, either as an aggregate ("all, whole") or with reference to the components of the whole ("each, every")	all, whole; each, every	1,244	6,833
εἷς, μία, ἕν	The number one [rough breathing, not εἰς]	one, 1	344	1,052
δύο	The number two	two, 2	135	645
τρεῖς, τρία	The number three	three, 3	68	376
τέσσαρες, α	The number four	four, 4	41	224
πέντε	The number five (indeclinable)	five, 5	38	278
ἕξ	The number six (indeclinable)	six, 6	13	134
ἑπτά	The number seven (indeclinable)	seven, 7	88	377
δέκα	The number ten (indeclinable)	ten, 10	25	326
οὐδείς, οὐδεμία, οὐδέν	A marker of negation typically used with indicative-mood verbs	no one, nothing	234	270
μηδείς, μηδεμία, μηδέν	A marker of negation typically used with non-indicative-mood verbs	no one, nothing	114	67
ἅπας, ασα, αν	The totality of something (intensive form of the adj. πᾶς)	all, the whole (with articular noun); all, everybody, everything (subst.)	34	78
Pronouns				
τίς, τί	A pronoun that introduces a question (an interrogative pronoun)	who? what? which? why?	555	1,530
τις, τι	A pronoun that refers to an unspecified person or thing (an indefinite pronoun, enclitic)	someone, anyone; something, anything (neut.)	525	319
ὅστις, ἥτις, ὅτι	Relative pronoun that usually refers to another noun earlier in the sentence or discourse, introducing a clause that further describes that noun (originally an indefinite relative pronoun, but not usually distinguished from ὅς in Koine Greek)	who, which (sometimes indefinite: whoever, whatever, whichever)	153	135

Vocabulary Notes

12.25. The adjective οὐδείς is a compound form: οὐ + δέ + εἷς ("no one, nothing"). The word occurs only in the singular, due to its meaning. It declines the same as εἷς, using third-declension endings.

masc.: οὐδείς, οὐδενός, οὐδενί, οὐδένα
fem.: οὐδεμία, οὐδεμιᾶς, οὐδεμιᾷ, οὐδεμίαν
neut.: οὐδέν, οὐδενός, οὐδενί, οὐδέν

12.26. Key Things to Know for Chapter 12

The adjective πᾶς—remember that the stem is παντ-.
How many chickens can you steal in third declension?
Can you count to four in Greek?
What does the designation "indefinite" mean in connection with pronouns (either the "indefinite pronoun" or the "indefinite relative pronoun")?
What is the easiest way to identify most interrogative pronouns and distinguish them from the indefinite pronoun?

13

VERBS: PART 3

Verbal Semantics

13.1. We have already met some basic verbs in chapters 5 and 7, but we did not discuss any of the intricacies of the various semantic nuances communicated by verbs. The verb system in Greek is more complex than in English, so it is important to understand the various categories by which verbs are described. This chapter will help you develop a conceptual framework to understand verbs.

The material in this chapter is more detailed and technical than in other chapters, and you may not grasp the significance of all the content the first time through it. As you progress to later chapters on the verb you can return to this chapter for clarification or further study as needed. For now, your goal should be to grasp the framework of the verbal system. Do not be surprised if some of it seems a bit muddy (or even a bit obtuse) right now. It will become clearer as you press on into subsequent chapters.

The heart of the Greek language is the verb. Thus far we have not focused on verbs, though you have seen and read many of them. You actually know quite a bit about verbs and how they work already, much of which you have absorbed unconsciously as you have seen them in context with other forms we have studied. We will begin with a review of the basics of English verbs and then move to Greek verbs—which are much easier than English verbs. Though there may be more forms and seemingly more details due to the morphology of verbs (since Greek is an inflected language), that makes Greek verbs much more regular and explicit than English ones. English can be infuriating for non-native speakers to learn, due to all the exceptions we have in our language, especially for verbs.

English Grammar

13.2. Verbs may be described grammatically in several categories, some of which we have already studied, since they are also used with nouns, adjectives, or pronouns. These categories should be familiar to you (if not, review the discussion in earlier chapters):

Person: first (*I*, *we*), second (*you*), third (*he*, *she*, *it*, *they*)
Number: singular, plural

Verbs must agree with their subjects in person and number. You know this, but perhaps unconsciously, in that certain sentences sound right and others do not because you learned such principles by hearing correct English spoken rather than by learning a rule regarding grammatical agreement.

Correct: "It *is* not our part to master all the tides of the world, but to do what *is* in us for the succor of those years wherein we *are* set."[1]

In this sentence the singular form of the verb "is" agrees with the singular subject in its clause, "it" and "what"; the plural verb "are" agrees with the plural subject "we." To exchange the singular and plural forms destroys the grammatical agreement between subject and verb, as can be seen in the following example.

Incorrect: It *are* not our part to master all the tides of the world, but to do what *are* in us for the succor of those years wherein we *is* set.

13.3. English verbs do not usually change spelling to indicate a change in person or number. Singular or plural is marked in the *subject* of an English sentence, not in the verb in many cases. (The verb *to be* is unusual in this regard.) Notice that in the following sentences the verb does not change spelling even though the subject changes from singular to plural.

I *studied* Greek thoughtfully last night.
He *studied* Greek thoughtfully last night.
They *studied* Greek thoughtfully last night.

Some English verbs do add a suffix to indicate number, though this is restricted to third-person singular, in which an "*s*-form" is used for the singular.

I/we *study* Greek every Saturday.
She/he *studies* Greek every day.
They *study* Greek every morning.

1. Gandalf, in Tolkien, *Lord of the Rings*, book 5, chap. 9.

Voice is another grammatical category we use to describe English verbs. In English there are two voices: active and passive. This is a description of the relation between the grammatical subject of a sentence and the situation referenced by the verb. If the subject is performing the action, we call it *active voice*: "Aiden *hit* the ball." By contrast, if the action described by the verb is done, not by, but to the subject, we call it *passive voice*: "Aiden *was hit* by the ball."

Mood (sometimes called *mode* or *attitude*) is said to describe the relationship between the statement and reality. That is not a particularly helpful definition, is it? Here is how one English grammar describes it; note especially the final sentence.

> Mood . . . is that property of a verb which indicates how the verbal idea is to be regarded—whether as a statement of fact; a command; a supposition, a doubt, or impossibility. The three moods generally recognized are the indicative, the imperative, and the subjunctive. But neither in form nor in meaning are these three moods sharply distinguished from one another in modern English.[2]

The subjunctive is less common in English than it once was (we will talk more about it in chap. 28), so for now the difference between an indicative (an assertion, a statement of fact) and an imperative (a command) is adequate.

> Indicative: Liam hit the ball.
> Imperative: Hit the ball! (Or, since imperatives do not have subjects, add a vocative: Liam, hit the ball!)

13.4. *Tense* is "a grammatical category referring to the location of a situation in time."[3] We usually think of tense as being composed of three categories: past, present, and future. Some English grammars, however, list only two (past and present). Other grammars have six tenses, and some twelve.[4] In addition to the basic three (which are sometimes called the *simple tenses*), the six-tense advocates add three more *perfect tenses*: present perfect, past perfect, and future perfect. Since Greek does not use these same tenses, we do not need to spend a lot of time here, and you could get by nicely by thinking only of the three simple tenses for our purposes. But here is an example of each in case you are interested. Each tense-form actually has more than one use in relation to time;[5] only the most common use of each tense is illustrated here.

2. Pence and Emery, *Grammar of Present-Day English*, 256.

3. Greenbaum, *Oxford English Grammar*, 253, §5.20.

4. Two tenses: Greenbaum, *Oxford English Grammar*, 253, §5.20; Huddleston and Pullum, *English Grammar*, 56; and Huddleston and Pullum, *Cambridge Grammar of the English Language*, 208–12; three tenses: Kaplan, *English Grammar*, 187–90; six tenses: Pence and Emery, *Grammar of Present-Day English*, 261–67; and twelve: Fairbairn, *Understanding Language*, 117.

5. English can use the present tense, for example, to indicate not only present time but also past time (the historical present) or future time—and there is even variation within the category of present time. Many English grammars give examples of these uses; see, for example, Greenbaum, *Oxford English Grammar*, 254–66, §§5.21–24; Huddleston and Pullum, *English Grammar*, 30–31, 44–48. This last grammar explicitly states that "by a **past** tense we mean one whose most central use is to indicate past time. . . . It is important to be aware that preterite [i.e., past] tense does not

Simple Tenses

Present: He *is living* in the country.	He is living there presently.
Past: He *lived* in the country.	In the past he lived there, but may not be doing so presently.
Future: He *will live* in the country.	He will live there in the future.

Perfect Tenses

Present perfect: He *has lived* in the country since 2003.

Past perfect: He *had lived* in the country when he was a child.

Future perfect: He *will have lived* in the country for ten years as of [some future date].

English also expresses what is called *verbal aspect*, although that terminology is not commonly used.[6] For example, what is the difference between these two statements?

I read Tolkien last week.
I was reading Tolkien last week.

The first sentence merely says that an event occurred last week. It does not tell us the nature of your reading other than that it happened. It views the action as a *simple* event. Linguists call this *perfective aspect*: action viewed as a whole.[7] The English phrasing in the first example does not require that you read the entire Tolkien corpus last week. (That is feasible if you are a fast reader, but you would get very little else done that week.) It might mean that, or it might mean that you read one of his many writings (perhaps *The Children of Húron*), or it might just mean that you read a few sentences from *The Silmarillion*.

We typically add an *-ed* to English verbs to indicate perfective aspect, though there are other ways to do it. In English, perfective aspect often refers to events in the past ("I studied," "I ate"), but it can also be used for present time ("I study," "I eat").

The second statement, "I was reading Tolkien last week," pictures the action of reading as an ongoing action that took place over a period of time. We still do not know how long you read or whether you finished. If you were reading *The Lord of the Rings*, you would have read for quite some time if you read all of it. But the same statement would be equally true if you read only the words

always signal past time" (30–31). An equivalent statement is made concerning the present tense in the next paragraph (31).

6. More technical English grammars do, indeed, discuss aspect, and some use the same technical terms *perfective* and *imperfective* that are used here for Greek (e.g., Huddleston and Pullum, *English Grammar*, 51–53; see also Huddleston and Pullum, *Cambridge Grammar of the English Language*, 124).

7. I am using technical linguistic terms here (*perfective*, *imperfective*). In more common English grammar parlance, this is what is sometimes described as the difference between the simple and progressive tenses.

"The Road goes ever on and on."[8] The way the action is viewed in the second statement is what a linguist might call *imperfective aspect*: action viewed as a process. In English we typically use a helping verb and append *-ing* to the end of the verb to indicate this. In English, imperfective aspect is often used of events in the present ("I am reading," "I am eating"), but it can also be used to refer to past time ("I was reading," "I was eating").

This difference between perfective (a simple event) and imperfective (a process) is what we mean by *verbal aspect* in English. Greek will be similar, but there are some significant differences in how the verb functions and what meanings it conveys.

Greek Grammar

13.5. The Greek verb is, in many ways, quite similar to English in that most of the grammatical categories summarized above still apply in Greek. Some of them are expanded in that they have more subcategories, but the basic concepts will be familiar.

Grammatical Agreement

13.6. Grammatical agreement in Greek is the same principle as in English: subject and verb must agree in person and number. Since Greek is an inflected language, this agreement is more evident than it is in English. Greek uses personal endings to indicate person and number, both of which must match between subject and verb. (Remember that English verbs usually do not change spelling to reflect grammatical person.) These endings are suffixes that are appended to every verb, much like the case endings that are added to nouns and adjectives. For each verb form there are six endings: first-, second-, and third-person singular, and first-, second-, and third-person plural. (There were eight case/number endings for nouns.) Here is a typical set of verb forms for the verb βάλλω, "I throw." You will recognize them as the same forms that you learned in chapter 5 when you first met present active indicative verbs.

1S	βάλλω	I am throwing
2S	βάλλεις	You are throwing
3S	βάλλει	He/she/it is throwing
1P	βάλλομεν	We are throwing
2P	βάλλετε	You are throwing
3P	βάλλουσι(ν)	They are throwing

The stem of this word is βαλλ-. In each case a suffix is added to indicate the subject, whether first, second, or third person, singular or plural.[9] In other words,

8. Tolkien, *Lord of the Rings*, book 1, chap. 3.

9. A stem is never used alone. It must always have a personal ending added. You will never see βαλλ in a sentence. It will always be one of the forms in the chart above (or another similar form you have not met yet).

every Greek verb has a built-in, default subject. This is not like English. If I say just "throw" in English, I have no idea who is doing the throwing.[10] I must have an explicit word for the subject—for example, "I throw" or "they throw." In Greek we can have a complete sentence with just one word, since all verbs have this built-in subject. Thus βάλλει does not mean just "throw," but "he (*or* she *or* it) is throwing."

Tense-Form

13.7. In English, *tense* refers primarily to the *time* when the action of the verb takes place[11] and secondarily to the verb's *aspect*. If you are studying Greek right now, then the verb is in the *present tense* ("I am studying"). If you are planning on doing it tomorrow, then the verb is in the *future tense* ("I will study"). If you did it last night (I am sure that you did!), then the verb is in the *past tense* ("I studied"). In other words, in English the terms *tense* and *time* largely refer to the same thing: *when* the subject of the verb performs the action.[12]

The traditional term *tense* has a somewhat different meaning in Greek than it does in English. When we use *tense* in Greek, our natural inclination is to think "time," because that is the primary meaning of *tense* in English. Since there is some pragmatic overlap (as you will soon see), you might be tempted to use *tense* and *time* synonymously in Greek as well, but it is more complex than that.

In Greek a verb tense-form expresses primarily the grammatical meaning of *aspect*; it is not synonymous with nor primarily focused on where a situation is located in time. The *aorist tense-form*, to pick just one form as an example, refers to the way the verb is formed/spelled (to be technical, we could say that it refers to the morphology): the grammatical form that identifies perfective aspect. In itself it does not tell us *when* an event occurred. An aorist form usually refers to a situation located in the past but may sometimes be used in reference to the present or the future, or to a situation for which time is not relevant. The same principle is basically true of the other tense-forms as well: present, imperfect, perfect, and pluperfect.[13] Each has common uses in reference to the location of a situation in time as well as some less common ones.

13.8. The complicating factor is that traditional Greek grammars have used the same name for the *form* of the Greek verb as English does for the *time* of the action: *tense*. In this grammar the term *tense-form* refers only to the morphological *form* of the verb. For example, *present tense-form* refers to a specific morphological pattern, not to the fact that the form is often used to refer to events

10. You do not even know if this word is a verb. It could also be a noun: "The throw to home plate was too late."

11. Technically, we would say that in English *tense* refers to the grammaticalized location of an event in time.

12. As noted above, English is not absolute in this regard. Present tense-form verbs can sometimes refer to the future, and so forth.

13. Some of the other tense-forms do not have the full range that is evident in the aorist form, but the principle is true: the form does not in itself identify invariably a particular time relationship; context must always be considered. Even older grammars acknowledge this since they recognize that context can indicate what they view as exceptions to standard usage.

located in present time. *Tense-form* in and of itself primarily communicates aspect. Of course, in a specific context verbs also have some temporal reference, though that is not the primary point. It might be better if we could jettison the term *tense* altogether and just refer to the *form* of the verb, but the tradition is so well entrenched that we are probably stuck with a term that is not ideal.[14] Do not confuse *tense* (as it is used in Greek) with *time* (*tense* in English). This grammar uses the hyphenated term *tense-form* to distinguish the Greek category from English tense yet still maintain some connection with traditional terminology.[15]

A logical question to ask next would be: if the Greek tense-form (the morphological form of the verb) does not have an invariable, fixed time reference in and of itself, then how do we know for sure to what time a writer refers? There are common patterns, but they cannot be automatically assumed to be the situation every time; we need to verify the time reference from the context. Greek uses various temporal indicators in the context, which, along with other contextual factors (e.g., genre), help us verify the writer's intended time reference.[16] That may seem subjective to us, but it is only because "English verbs, whatever else they do, always seem to indicate time reference, [but] a rather large number of languages around the world manage quite nicely, thank you, with verbs that do not by themselves have that reference."[17]

Aspect

13.9. Because aspect in English is not as prominent as it is in Greek, it may seem to be more complicated than it really is. Aspect is the category that tells us how the author portrays the situation (as a whole, as a process, or as a state).[18] It is a subjective category in that a writer may chose to portray the same situation *either* as a complete event *or* as a process *or* as a state. The examples used earlier show you that English can also make similar distinctions.

I *read* Tolkien last week.
I *was reading* Tolkien last week.

Greek can describe the same situation from different viewpoints. In Mark 12:41 this statement is made about Jesus: ἐθεώρει πῶς ὁ ὄχλος βάλλει χαλκὸν

14. Robertson made this same observation a century ago: "The term tense . . . is a misnomer and a hindrance to the understanding of this aspect of the verb-form. . . . We must therefore dismiss time from our minds in the study of the forms of the tenses as well as in the matter of syntax. It is too late to get a new name, however" (*Grammar*, 343–44).

15. These distinctions are most clear in the non-indicative verbs, but they apply to the indicative also. Many grammarians would not agree with the emphasis expressed here, arguing that time is still a factor even in the indicative.

16. The study of how contextual factors affect our understanding of a particular verb form and in particular the statement in which it is used is called *pragmatics*.

17. Silva, *God, Language and Scripture*, 112.

18. Aspect is not wholly unrelated to temporal considerations, but it does not relate to when an event takes place (its location in time). The difference between perfective and imperfective aspect can be viewed in temporal terms: imperfective aspect views a situation as being extended in time (though just how long that may be varies enormously); perfective aspect views a situation as a whole without reference to any extent of time that may be included in the actual situation.

εἰς τὸ γαζοφυλάκιον ("He was observing how the crowd *was throwing* money into the offering box"). This statement uses imperfective aspect to describe the actions of the crowd in terms of a process. Yet a few verses later (v. 44), referring to the same event, we are told that πάντες ἐκ τοῦ περισσεύοντος αὐτοῖς ἔβαλον ("All out of their abundance *threw* [money into the offering box]"). The second statement uses perfective aspect, which views the action as a whole. We would be foolish to insist that two different kinds of actions are being described just because one verse uses βάλλει and the other ἔβαλον.[19]

Tense and Aspect

Perhaps no feature of the biblical languages is the source of more confusion and fanciful interpretation than the verbal "tenses." Beginning Greek students, upon being confronted with the term *aorist* (which is normally not used in English grammar), tend to inject quasi-mysterious associations into it. After all, they are first taught that it is roughly equivalent to the simple past tense (preterite) in English, only to find out, a few weeks later, that the Greek imperative can have an aorist as well as a present form. How can one request a person today to do something yesterday? And when the teacher informs the students that the aorist does not really indicate time, they become ripe either for experiencing total bewilderment or for developing preposterous exegesis. . . .

Surely the first step out of this mire is to appreciate that there is nothing peculiar about verbs that indicate *aspect* (= how is the action presented by the speaker) rather than *time* (= when does the action take place). In English, for example, the difference between *John wrote a letter* and *John was writing a letter* is not one of temporal reference: both verbal constructions could be used when referring to the *one* event that took place, say, last Monday evening. Rather, the distinction is an aspectual one: the second expression indicates progressive action (to use a traditional category), while the first one does not. Moreover, English has the lexical means to express a wide variety of aspectual distinctions: *used to write; kept on writing; started to write.*

There are indeed some differences between English and the biblical languages, and it is those differences that create confusion. Whereas English verbs, whatever else they do, always seem to indicate time reference, a rather large number of languages around the world manage quite nicely, thank you, with verbs that do not by themselves have that reference. The speakers of these languages, of course, can indicate the time through lexical and other means (*yesterday, tomorrow,* the context of the utterance, etc.), but the verbal form itself gives no hint.

—Silva, *God, Language and Scripture*, 111–13

13.10. The category of aspect is expressed in Greek by the *tense-form* of the verb. How the verb is spelled (stem, endings, etc.) tells us how the writer has chosen to portray/view the situation. In Greek there are three aspects.

Imperfective aspect: verbs that describe a situation as a process

19. The same verb, βάλλω, is used seven times in Mark 12:41–44. Each time it describes people putting money into the offering box, but three different tense-forms are used: twice present, once an imperfect, and the others aorist.

Perfective aspect: verbs that describe a situation as a complete event, without commenting on whether or not it is a process[20]

Stative aspect: verbs that describe a state of affairs (a condition) that exists, with no reference to any progress, and that involves no change

If we use this third aspect in a sentence similar to the examples given above, we might say: "I *have read* Tolkien."[21] The point of this statement is not the action that took place, and not that it was either a process or a complete event, but the *state of affairs that exists*: I have read, and therefore I know something. The fact that you spent time doing something (reading) at some particular location in time (presumably in the past) is not particularly relevant to the statement (though sometimes it can be inferred from the context).[22] The focus is on the "read state" in which you now find yourself. English has no exact equivalent to stative aspect. It will often be communicated as a simple present tense in English ("I am read" in the sense that "I know") or sometimes as an English perfect ("I have read"). A biblical example is Jesus' statement from the cross: τετέλεσται, "It is finished" (John 19:30). This cry declared that his work on the cross was now in a state of completion.[23] Although there certainly was a preceding event that brought about this state, that is not the writer's focus in this statement. You will not encounter stative aspect verbs until a later chapter. We will talk more about them then.

13.11. The three aspects that we have just described can be identified by the verb forms that are used. The following table lists the tense-forms with their aspects.[24] The aspect of a tense-form does not change. That is, aorist forms always express perfective aspect, present forms always express imperfective aspect, and so on. (That does not mean that they will always be expressed the same way in English or that other contextual factors may not affect the meaning; we will say more about these differences later.)

Perfective aspect	aorist tense-form
Imperfective aspect	present and imperfect tense-forms
Stative aspect	perfect and pluperfect tense-forms

20. Perfective aspect is defined as a *complete* event, not as a complet*ed* one—there is a significant difference. The most significant difference is that if we say "complet*ed*" we have implied past time, but perfective aspect does not require reference to past time. It often does refer to past time, but that is not invariable.

21. Although more clumsy English, "I am read" would be closer to what is expressed by the Greek stative aspect. We might use this phrasing in a statement such as "He is well read on the lore of Middle-Earth."

22. Frequently you will hear some well-intentioned person who misses the point of the stative aspect and finds great exegetical ore in the fact that this state is the result of a past, completed act. Although there may well be such an act in the past (few states are eternal) that gave rise to the present state ("results"), it is invalid to prove it from the simple fact that the Greek verb has stative aspect.

23. Although it is true that this state came about as a result of a previous action and that it will have effects that continue into the future, that is not what *this verb* says. Jesus' only point is to describe the state that pertained at the time.

24. The future tense-form is not listed here since scholars are not agreed about whether it expresses aspect. See the discussion in chap. 19.

Here is an illustration of the three aspects using two words that are basically synonymous (τελέω and τελειόω); all three refer to the cross.

> Luke 12:50, I have a baptism to undergo, and how distressed I am until *it is completed*! (aorist tense-form = perfective aspect)
>
> Luke 13:32, Go tell that fox, "I will drive out demons and heal people today and tomorrow, and on the third day *I will reach my goal*." (present tense-form = imperfective aspect)
>
> John 19:30, When he had received the drink, Jesus said, "*It is finished*." With that, he bowed his head and gave up his spirit. (perfect tense-form = stative aspect)

Note that you cannot distinguish these aspects in English. That is why you are learning Greek.

There are some general patterns that will facilitate our beginning efforts at understanding the meaning of verbs. We will use a common English equivalent for each verb form in the paradigm charts. This will be an expression that often works in English, but you must realize that there are many variations that may also be legitimate. The common equivalents are only for pedagogical purposes as we are learning verbs and are not absolutes that must be used every time in every context.

Aktionsart

13.12. In Greek, aspect must be distinguished from another category called *Aktionsart*. Both of these categories relate to the type of action that is involved. *Aktionsart* is a more objective statement of the *actual nature* of the action/situation. This is based not on the tense-form of the verb (the tense-form specifies aspect) but on a combination of lexis (what the word means) and context. Though the terminology is not always used, and though the meaning is often attributed (incorrectly) to the tense rather than lexis and context, this is what many intermediate and advanced Greek grammars and some commentaries are discussing when they talk about such categories as iterative, customary, tendential, gnomic, and so on. There is not much discussion of *Aktionsart* in this textbook; that is left for more advanced study at a later time. You should, however, be aware that it is a valid category and that it is neither synonymous with aspect nor based on the tense-form of the verb.

Voice

13.13. The grammatical category of voice in Greek refers to the same basic concept as in English: the relation between the subject and the verb. Greek, however, describes this relationship somewhat differently and introduces a third category that is not present in English.

The Greek voice system consists primarily of contrasting situation-focused and subject-focused verbs (see fig. 13.1). The first of these, *situation-focused verbs*, refers to verbs that are in the active voice. The primary focus of these verbs is on that which is described by the verb itself. When we say that these verbs are "active," we mean that the subject performs or causes the action, or, in the case of a state, the subject is the focus of the state. Although such verbs obviously include reference to a subject,[25] no particular emphasis on that subject is intended by the voice of the verb.

The second category of voice includes verbs that are *subject-focused*.[26] This category draws particular attention to the role/relationship of the subject in the situation.[27] Verbs that are subject-focused shift attention from the situation itself to the role of the subject. "Its specific feature is the *affectedness* of the subject of the verb in, or by, the event denoted by the verb."[28]

In the subject-focused category, there is a further choice between *passive voice*, in which the subject receives the action, and *middle voice*, in which the subject performs the action but with a self-interest nuance. In both these situations the speaker/writer deliberately chooses to formulate the statement to focus attention on the subject in a way that a situation-focused, active-voice verb does not.

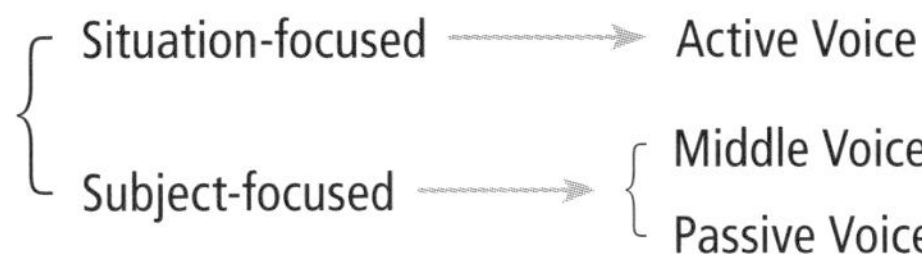

Figure 13.1. Voice Morphology

13.14. As you will discover in the next few chapters, there are usually two basic sets of *forms*: one set for active and another for middle or passive.[29] The middle forms can *function* as either middle or passive. This dual-purpose form usually functions as a middle but may function as a passive if the context indicates that meaning.[30]

When we say that a form *functions* actively, we mean that the subject is performing the action described in the verb and that the focus is on the action (e.g., "I hit the ball"). When we refer instead to a middle form, we mean that the subject is performing the action described in the verb *but that the focus is on the subject* rather than on the action itself (e.g., "*I* hit the ball").[31] When we describe the

25. You will remember that all finite verb forms in Greek have an inherent, back-pocket subject in the personal ending, and they may have a separate subject specified in the sentence as well.

26. See Conrad, "New Observations on Voice," 7. The terminology "subject-focused" is Conrad's; the parallel term "situation-focused" is my own coinage.

27. A subject may be emphasized in ways other than by the voice of the verb; for example, a first- or second-person pronoun may serve to emphasize the subject.

28. Bakker, "Voice, Aspect and Aktionsart," 24.

29. In a few tense-forms the middle voice and the passive voice are distinguished morphologically; that is, they are spelled differently.

30. These dual-purpose forms are sometimes called *middle/passive forms* or *mediopassives*.

31. Notice that in this English example we must use a typographical feature to focus attention on the subject (italic) since English has no means to do this grammatically.

form as passive, we mean that the subject is receiving the action described by the verb and that this action is performed by someone other than the subject (e.g., "I was hit by the ball").

Mood

13.15. In Greek, *mood* is defined the same as in English: a grammatical category that describes how the verb is to be viewed in relationship to reality. Greek, however, has categories of mood not used in English.

Initially we will study the indicative mood. Verbs in this mood make an assertion about reality—they portray a situation as "real." Such verbs might be used in a statement ("I love learning Greek") or a question ("Do you enjoy learning Greek as much as I do?") and may relate to an action ("I studied Greek for three hours last night") or a state ("I understand Greek"). This is by far the most common mood in both English and Greek.

The other moods that we will meet later are as follows. The *subjunctive* is the mood of potential. That is, it is not "real," but it could be—for example, "If you would study Greek with me, I'd buy supper." You are not studying with me now, but you could. The potential situation is only conceptualized in the speaker's (or writer's) mind. The *imperative* is the mood of command—for example, "Study your Greek tonight!" This assumes you are not studying now, but you know what I want you to do tonight. The *optative* is the mood of wish—for example, "May you study Greek all night." (This, of course, is a prayer of blessing.) We will talk more about mood when we get to chapters 28 and 29, which deal with these three additional moods.

Can Lies Be True?

Do not confuse the category of *reality* as it describes the indicative mood with that of *truth*. Lies are usually told in the indicative mood. When Sarah denied to God that she had laughed (Gen. 18:15), her statement, "I did not laugh," is presented in the LXX with an indicative-mood verb.

Verb Morphology

13.16. Verbs consist of two major parts: stem and ending.[32] The ending, in turn, is typically composed of two parts: connecting vowel and personal ending.[33]

Stem	Ending	
	Connecting Vowel	Personal Ending

32. There are potentially more parts to a verb form. The explanation above gives only the major parts that every verb must have. In due time you will learn that there are several things we can prefix to the front of a word (e.g., a preposition, an augment, or reduplication) as well as insert between the stem and the ending (e.g., infixes called *form markers*).

33. The two component parts of the ending are optional in some verb forms (though all have one or the other and most have both); some have no connecting vowel, and others may appear to have no personal ending in some person/number forms.

The verb stem carries the lexis—the basic meaning of the word. (Remember that nouns have stems also.) The ending is the suffix added to the stem to indicate person and number. The ending consists of the technical personal ending that marks person and number as well as the connecting vowel—which serves a phonological, morphological function: it makes it easier to pronounce the stem and ending together.

For example, in the word βάλλομεν (see fig. 13.2), the stem is βαλλ- (it tells you that this word refers to the action of throwing), the connecting vowel is omicron (which makes it easier to pronounce), and the personal ending is -μεν (which tells you who is doing the action: first-person plural, "we").

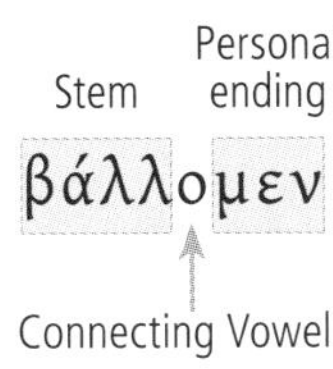

Figure 13.2

Parsing

13.17. *Parsing* a verb means to describe all its grammatical pieces that collectively tell us what a particular grammatical form means. The pattern used in this textbook to parse finite[34] verbs is as follows:[35]

person, number, tense-form, voice, mood ▸ lexical form, gloss

For example, λύει = third singular present active indicative ▸ λύω, "I loose." In abbreviated form: 3rd sg. pres. act. ind. ▸ λύω, "I loose."

The symbol ▸ means "from" and identifies the lexical form of the verb being parsed.[36] The *gloss* (= a common English equivalent) represents the lexical form, not the inflected form (for which you need context to represent accurately).

34. A finite verb is one that has grammatical person, that is, it is limited to a particular subject doing the action. Later we will meet other kinds of verbs (technically, "verbals") that do not have grammatical person. We call these forms *non-finite forms*; there are two of them: the participle and the infinitive.

35. The short-form abbreviation would be: 3SPAI ▸ λύω, "I loose." (In this textbook the short forms are used in some charts and reference sections.) There are other abbreviation systems in use; some are variations on what is shown here, others are much more technical. Some teachers will prefer that you use a different pattern, but it will include the same information, just in a different order. If your teacher tells you to parse following a different pattern, then follow those instructions. It is very helpful to learn to parse in the same pattern each time, since it saves you from forgetting any of the pieces.

36. When you are writing by hand or typing a parsing formula, you can use a simple arrow: >.

Parsing Abbreviations

Category	Abbreviation	Meaning	Short Form
Person	1st 2nd 3rd	first, second, third	1 2 3
Number	sg. pl.	singular, plural	S P
Tense-Form	aor. pres. impf. pf. plpf. fut.[a]	aorist, present, imperfect, perfect, pluperfect, future	A P I R L F
Voice	act. mid. pass.	active, middle, passive	A M P
Mood	ind. impv. subj. opt. inf. ptc.	indicative, imperative, subjunctive, optative, infinitive, participle	I M S O N P
Gender	masc. fem. neut.	masculine, feminine, neuter	M F N
Case	nom. gen. dat. acc. voc.	nominative, genitive, dative, accusative, vocative	N G D A V

[a] A superscript 1 or 2 before a tense-form means "first" or "second" (e.g., ¹aor. = first aorist; ²R = second perfect).

Non-finite verbal forms are parsed in a slightly different pattern since the grammatical information they contain differs from finite forms. The infinitive displays only tense-form, voice, and "mood"[37] (e.g., λύειν = present active infinitive ▸ λύω, I loose; in short form: PAN ▸ λύω, I loose). The participle includes tense-form, voice, "mood," gender, number, and case (e.g., λύων = present active participle masculine singular nominative ▸ λύω, I loose; in short form: PAPMSN ▸ λύω, I loose). The last two rows of this chart—gender and case—are used *only* for participles.

The short-form system[38] shown in the last column is a lot faster to write and is much more compact, but if you use this system, the letters must always be in exactly the same order as the formula above. That is necessary since several of these abbreviations mean different things in different positions. For example, "P" can mean either plural (if it is in second position), or present (if it is in third position), or passive (if it is in fourth position), or participle (if it is in fifth position).

Optional Reading Passage: Genesis 1:1–10

13.18. For words that are glossed, the gloss appears with only the first occurrence of the word and is not repeated later in the passage.

37. Technically, neither infinitive nor participle is a mood; the name of their grammatical category is simply placed in the "mood" slot when parsing.

38. The single-letter abbreviations originated many years ago with the Gramcord database and are widely used, especially in Bible software programs.

Creation

1Ἐν ἀρχῇ ἐποίησεν ὁ θεὸς τὸν οὐρανὸν καὶ τὴν γῆν. 2ἡ δὲ γῆ ἦν (was) ἀόρατος καὶ ἀκατασκεύαστος,[a] καὶ σκότος ἐπάνω τῆς ἀβύσσου, καὶ πνεῦμα θεοῦ
ἐπεφέρετο (was moving/rushing) ἐπάνω τοῦ ὕδατος. 3καὶ εἶπεν (said) ὁ θεός,
Γενηθήτω (let there be!) φῶς. καὶ ἐγένετο (came to be) φῶς. 4καὶ εἶδεν (saw)
ὁ θεὸς τὸ φῶς ὅτι καλόν. καὶ διεχώρισεν (divided) ὁ θεὸς ἀνὰ μέσον[b] τοῦ
φωτὸς καὶ ἀνὰ μέσον[b] τοῦ σκότους. 5καὶ ἐκάλεσεν ὁ θεὸς τὸ φῶς ἡμέραν καὶ
τὸ σκότος ἐκάλεσεν νύκτα. καὶ ἐγένετο ἑσπέρα καὶ ἐγένετο πρωί, ἡμέρα μία.
6Καὶ εἶπεν ὁ θεός, Γενηθήτω στερέωμα ἐν μέσῳ τοῦ ὕδατος καὶ ἔστω διαχωρίζον[c] ἀνὰ μέσον[b] ὕδατος καὶ ὕδατος. καὶ ἐγένετο οὕτως. 7καὶ ἐποίησεν ὁ
θεὸς τὸ στερέωμα, καὶ διεχώρισεν ὁ θεὸς ἀνὰ μέσον[b] τοῦ ὕδατος, ὃ ἦν ὑποκάτω
τοῦ στερεώματος, καὶ ἀνὰ μέσον[b] τοῦ ὕδατος τοῦ ἐπάνω τοῦ στερεώματος.[d]
8καὶ ἐκάλεσεν ὁ θεὸς τὸ στερέωμα οὐρανόν. καὶ εἶδεν ὁ θεὸς ὅτι καλόν. καὶ
ἐγένετο ἑσπέρα καὶ ἐγένετο πρωί, ἡμέρα δευτέρα.
9Καὶ εἶπεν ὁ θεός, Συναχθήτω (let it be gathered together!) τὸ ὕδωρ τὸ
ὑποκάτω τοῦ οὐρανοῦ[e] εἰς συναγωγὴν μίαν, καὶ ὀφθήτω (let it appear!) ἡ
ξηρά. καὶ ἐγένετο οὕτως. καὶ συνήχθη (it
was gathered together) τὸ ὕδωρ τὸ ὑποκάτω
τοῦ οὐρανοῦ[e] εἰς τὰς συναγωγὰς αὐτῶν, καὶ
ὤφθη (it appeared) ἡ ξηρά. 10καὶ ἐκάλεσεν
ὁ θεὸς τὴν ξηρὰν γῆν καὶ τὰ συστήματα[f] τῶν
ὑδάτων ἐκάλεσεν θαλάσσας. καὶ εἶδεν ὁ θεὸς
ὅτι καλόν.

[a] ἀκατασκεύαστος, ον (a two-form adjective, not found in NT and only here in LXX), "unformed, incomplete" (LEH, 20)

[b] ἀνὰ μέσον, "between"

[c] ἔστω διαχωρίζον, "let it divide!"

[d] τοῦ ἐπάνω τοῦ στερεώματος, "which was above the firmament"

[e] τὸ ὑποκάτω τοῦ οὐρανοῦ, "which was under the sky"

[f] σύστημα, ατος, τό, "a whole that has accumulated" (MLS, 542), "gathering"

Does It Sound Complicated?

You need not yet have complete mastery of all the Greek grammatical terminology introduced in this chapter. Each of the items introduced in this chapter will be developed in some detail, piece by piece, in the following chapters. You should, however, have sufficient understanding to see how Greek and English differ. You will probably want to return to this chapter for clarification as each of these grammatical terms is encountered in future chapters.

Vocabulary for Chapter 13

13.19. There is no vocabulary for chapter 13.

13.20. Key Things to Know for Chapter 13

The key to this chapter is understanding the various grammatical categories that are discussed.

At this point you should understand very well all the terms in the section "English Grammar."

14

VERBS: PART 4

Present (Imperfective) Indicative Verbs

14.1. We have previously met both present and aorist active indicative verbs, in chapters 5 and 7, but we did not spend much time on their specific meaning. Now that we have discussed the various elements of meaning expressed by the verb, it is time to revisit the verbs you have learned and integrate the new information.

Present Active Indicative

14.2. You have already learned the following forms of the present active indicative verb.

Present Active Indicative of λύω

	Form	c.v. + A p.e.	Gloss	c.v.	A p.e.
1S	λύω	ω	I am loosing	ο	–
2S	λύεις	εις	You are loosing	ε	ς
3S	λύει	ει	He/she/it is loosing	ε	ι
1P	λύομεν	ομεν	We are loosing	ο	μεν
2P	λύετε	ετε	You are loosing	ε	τε
3P	λύουσι(ν)	ουσι(ν)	They are loosing	ο	νσι(ν)

The *present tense-form* is a grammatical category that indicates imperfective aspect. That is, when you see a verb in the present tense-form, you know immediately that the writer has chosen to view the situation as a process.

In the indicative mood, present tense-form verbs often refer to a situation in present time, but the tense-form of a verb does not directly mean present time.

The present tense-form indicates imperfective aspect. The time to which such a verb refers may be any of several references, depending on the context.

The category *active voice* tells you that the grammatical subject of the sentence performs the action described by the verb. This is in contrast to passive-voice verbs, in which the subject receives the action of the verb.

Indicative mood tells us that the writer is making a statement about reality (as opposed to a command or a wish). All the verbs that you will study for several chapters will be indicative verbs.

Reading Exercises

14.3. You have already read quite a few sentences that use present active indicative tense-forms, but now that we have extended our grammatical description of this form, think through each of the following examples, and ask yourself how this additional information affects your understanding of the verb forms in these passages. Notice that normal English usage does not always use the default *-ing* form to represent a Greek imperfective form (e.g., John 1:29, below). Some such forms sound like a perfective form in English, but this is due to English idiom, not Greek.

John 1:25, Τί **βαπτίζεις** εἰ σὺ οὐκ εἶ ὁ Χριστὸς οὐδὲ Ἠλίας οὐδὲ ὁ προφήτης;	Why *are you baptizing* if you are neither the Messiah nor Elijah nor the Prophet?
John 1:29, Τῇ ἐπαύριον **βλέπει** τὸν Ἰησοῦν ἐρχόμενον (coming) πρὸς αὐτὸν καὶ **λέγει**, Ἴδε ὁ ἀμνὸς τοῦ θεοῦ ὁ αἴρων (one who takes away) τὴν ἁμαρτίαν τοῦ κόσμου.	The next day he [i.e., John] *saw* Jesus coming to him, and *he said*, "Behold, the lamb of God who takes away the sin of the world."
John 13:33, τεκνία, ἔτι μικρὸν μεθ' ὑμῶν εἰμι· ὅπου ἐγὼ **ὑπάγω** ὑμεῖς οὐ δύνασθε ἐλθεῖν.[a]	Little children, I will be with you a little while yet; where *I am going* you are not able to come.
Ezek. 2:3, εἶπεν (he said) πρός με, Υἱὲ ἀνθρώπου, **ἐξαποστέλλω** ἐγώ σε πρὸς τὸν οἶκον τοῦ Ἰσραήλ.	He said to me, "Son of Man, *I am sending* you to the house of Israel."

[a] δύνασθε ἐλθεῖν, "you are able to come"

Present Middle Indicative

14.4. Now we need to extend our knowledge of present indicative verbs from those in the active voice to a new form, the present middle indicative. English has only two voices, active and passive, which might make it difficult to think of any other kind of "voice." Greek, however, has not two but three voices: active, middle, and passive. All the verbs you have seen thus far have been in the active voice. That is, the subject is doing the action expressed by the verb, and the focus has been on the situation, on the action (or state) itself. This section introduces the middle voice; we will meet the Greek passive voice in the next chapter.

Forms of the Present Middle Indicative

14.5. The middle voice uses a new set of forms that are different from the active forms you have already learned. We will have more to say about the meaning and use of these verbs a bit later, but for now, we need to see what they look like.

Formula for Present Middle Indicative Verbs

stem + connecting vowel + C personal endings
Example: λυ + ο + μαι ▸ λύομαι

Present Middle Indicative of λύω

	Form	c.v. + C p.e.	Gloss	c.v.	p.e.
1S	λύομαι	ομαι	I am loosing	ο	μαι
2S	λύῃ	ῃ	You are loosing	ε	σαι
3S	λύεται	εται	He/she/it is loosing	ε	ται
1P	λυόμεθα	ομεθα	We are loosing	ο	μεθα
2P	λύεσθε	εσθε	You are loosing	ε	σθε
3P	λύονται	ονται	They are loosing	ο	νται

The major difference from the active voice is that middle-voice verbs use a different set of endings: -ομαι, -ῃ, -εται, -ομεθα, -εσθε, -ονται. We refer to them as the *C endings* as a convenience.[1] These are primary endings, which means that there is never an augment on the front of a word that uses these endings, and they *usually* appear on middle-voice verbs.

The second singular form is a bit odd; the actual, technical ending (see last column) is σαι, but here is what happens (you *do not* need to memorize this): λυ + ε + σαι. First, the sigma drops out between two vowels, then ε + α contract to eta, and finally the iota becomes a subscript, since it now follows eta, which is a long vowel. So the final result is λύῃ. Since it *always* does this, it is much simpler to just learn the ending as ῃ rather than σαι.[2]

You do *not* need to memorize the last two columns in the chart above.

1. Some grammars call these *primary middle endings*. See the four-quad chart at §14.11.

2. Did I say, "It *always* does this"? Well, most of the time it does (and always in the present middle indicative). But one set of forms that you will meet later does not use a connecting vowel, so in that case the ending will be σαι. The forms that use the technical ending σαι are much less common than the ones that use the contracted form ῃ.

Meaning of Present Middle Indicative Verbs

14.6. The *aspect* of these verbs is imperfective, the same as present active, because they are still present tense-forms. Likewise, the *time* will often be present time. A typical English equivalent (one you might think of without any context to suggest otherwise) for a present middle indicative verb is "I am loosing." Does that sound just like a present active indicative verb? In English translation it is not usually possible to distinguish the Greek active voice from the middle voice for the simple reason that English does not have a middle voice. Since a Greek middle-voice verb indicates that the subject is performing the action, it *must* be represented as an English active-voice verb; we have no other choice in English.

The middle voice is used in Greek to describe a wide range of situations. There are not neat, tidy categories of usage; instead, Greek speakers associated a range of ideas with the middle voice. You will learn more about these various nuances later, but the following diagram may help you conceptualize the ideas that are frequently expressed with the middle voice in Greek.[3]

Middle Forms That Differ in Meaning

Although most Greek verbs will sound the same in both active and middle voice when put into English, some middle-voice verbs have meanings that can be distinguished. An example of this may be seen in the verb λούω (note that this is not the standard paradigm verb λύω). In the active voice λούω means "I wash (something or someone)," but in the middle voice it means "I bathe (myself)." Your lexicon will point out any such distinctions that you need to know.

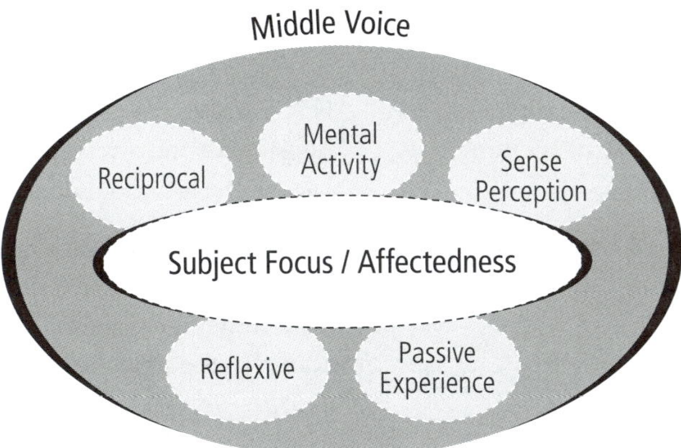

Figure 14.1

14.7. Although in English the meaning of a middle-voice verb sounds the same as an active-voice verb, the focus is different. You should remember from

3. You will note that the diagram deliberately uses dashed lines for the various ideas since they are not distinct categories. Other concepts could be added, but the basics illustrated here are adequate to give you the idea. Also observe that the idea clouds overlap; that is because they are not always clearly delineated from other, similar ideas.

the last chapter that active verbs focus on the situation—the action or state described by the verb. By contrast, middle-voice verbs are subject-focused: they focus attention on the grammatical *subject*. That is, the speaker or writer is more concerned with the subject who does the action than with the action itself. (That is an oversimplified explanation, but it will do for now.)

Here are a few examples in English (slightly paraphrased) of verses that use a Greek middle-voice verb. They are not categorized with various names as if there were different kinds of middles, though you will find different associations with the subject focus in these examples.

Languages with Middle Voice

Languages that have a middle voice include not only Greek but also Proto-Indo-European, Sanskrit, Icelandic, Russian, Fulfulde, Somali, Bengali, Temiar, Tamil, and Albanian. Some languages have *more* than three voices. Classical Mongolian has five: active, passive, causative, reciprocal, and cooperative.

Matt. 27:5, Judas went out and *hanged himself.*	Here is a classic example of an action performed by the subject that has obvious impact on the subject himself. There is no separate word for "himself"—that comes from the middle voice, the meaning of the word translated "hanged," and the context.
Matt. 27:24, Pilate *washed* his hands.	This is a typical example of the subject doing something to himself. Statements of dressing, grooming, washing, and so on, are often expressed with the middle voice.
Acts 12:21, Herod, *having put on* his royal clothes, was speaking to them.	This instance is a participle and shows the "self-interest/involvement" of the middle voice—one is seldom dressed by another.
John 9:22, The Jews had already *agreed together.*	This middle verb shows how the voice functions in a collective setting—the group together makes a decision; "deciding" is a particularly subject-focused action.
Acts 1:18, Judas *purchased* a field.	It would be overtranslated to say "he purchased it for himself"—but that reflects the gist of the context: he bought his own burial plot.
Acts 5:2, Ananias *kept back* some of the price.	A statement that he gave the money to someone else would be active, but here the middle is appropriate since he keeps it *for himself.*

2 Tim. 2:13, He is not able *to deny* himself.

This example includes an uncommon construction; it uses *both* a middle-voice verb *and* a reflexive pronoun to focus attention on the subject.

James 1:21, *Receive* the implanted word.

Receiving something, especially the Word, is something you can do only for yourself. Others may receive you, and you may receive others, but you can never receive something in this sense *for someone else*. (Even if you receive, for example, a package on someone else's behalf, the middle voice would focus on your reception of the package.)

14.8. *Examples of Present Middle Indicative Verbs*

Matt. 2:13, ἰδοὺ ἄγγελος κυρίου **φαίνεται** κατ' ὄναρ[a] τῷ Ἰωσήφ.

Behold an angel from the Lord *appeared* to Joseph in a dream.

[a] κατ' ὄναρ, "in a dream"

Mark 14:41, λέγει αὐτοῖς, **Ἀναπαύεσθε;**[a] ἀπέχει· ἦλθεν[b] ἡ ὥρα.

He said to them, "*Are you resting*? Enough! The hour has come."

[a] ἀναπαύω, "I rest." There are differences of punctuation at this point among the various editions of the Greek NT and among English translations. The verse can be read several different ways. Since there was no punctuation in the original Greek text, these differences merely reflect differing editorial decisions.

[b] ἦλθεν, "it has come"

Mark 3:13, ἀναβαίνει εἰς τὸ ὄρος καὶ **προσκαλεῖται** οὓς ἤθελεν αὐτός.

He ascended[a] the mountain and *summoned* those whom he desired.

[a] The English idiom does not require that εἰς be translated by a separate word; the collocation of "ascended" and "the mountain" communicates the same idea that ἀναβαίνει εἰς τὸ ὄρος does in Greek. We do not say "he ascended into a mountain" in English.

In this example, you will notice that the ending in the verb προσκαλεῖται is slightly different from what you might expect. Instead of -εται, it is spelled -εῖται. The only slight difference is that the connecting vowel (epsilon) has lengthened to the diphthong ει. This is because the verb stem ends with an epsilon (προσκαλε-), and the two epsilons (the stem vowel and the connecting vowel) contract to ει to make it easier to pronounce. (Try pronouncing two epsilons side by side in a word!) Verbs whose stem ends with a short vowel, you will remember, are called *contract verbs* (see chapter 7 if you need a review). These minor differences do not change any meaning; it is strictly for pronunciation purposes. There is a more detailed discussion of contract verbs in chapter 21 to illustrate the range of possible changes. Most of them involve epsilons and omicrons.

Exod. 17:2, εἶπεν αὐτοῖς Μωϋσῆς, Τί **λοιδορεῖσθέ** μοι, καὶ τί πειράζετε κύριον;

Moses said to them, "Why are *you reviling* me, and why are you testing the Lord?"

Gen. 32:12, ἐξελοῦ (deliver!) με ἐκ χειρὸς τοῦ ἀδελφοῦ μου Ἠσαῦ, ὅτι **φοβοῦμαι** ἐγὼ αὐτόν.

Deliver me from the hand of my brother Esau, because *I am afraid* of him.

14.9. *Now You Try It*

Matt. 15:2, οὐ **νίπτονται** τὰς χεῖρας αὐτῶν ὅταν ἄρτον ἐσθίωσιν (they eat).

Who is washing what? Is someone having their hands washed? Or are they washing their own hands? Or something else? Can you identify the subordinate clause and explain how it affects the meaning of the main clause?

John 7:52, Μὴ καὶ σὺ[a] ἐκ τῆς Γαλιλαίας **εἶ**; ἐραύνησον (search!) καὶ ἴδε (see!) ὅτι ἐκ τῆς Γαλιλαίας προφήτης οὐκ **ἐγείρεται.**

What case is προφήτης? (Are you sure? Check the lexical form.) What word does the prepositional phrase modify?

[a] σύ, "you," refers to Nicodemus, not Jesus.

You will remember (§6.33) that when rhetorical questions are asked in the indicative mood with the verb negated using μή, a *negative* answer is implied. In the example from John 7:52, the questioners (Jewish religious leaders) know that Nicodemus is *not* from Galilee. We could understand their question this way: "You are not from Galilee too, are you?!" This has a different tone than simply, "Are you from Galilee too?"

Matt. 20:22, ἀποκριθεὶς (answering) δὲ ὁ Ἰησοῦς εἶπεν, Οὐκ οἴδατε τί[a] **αἰτεῖσθε.**[b]

Is the subject of both verbs in Jesus' statement the same or different? How do you know? What case is τί, nom. or acc.? How do you know? (The form is the same.)

[a] The pronoun τί might seem tricky at this point. There is no question mark at the end of this sentence, so you might assume that it is an indefinite pronoun. But there is an implied (or indirect) question here: "You are asking what?" So it is an interrogative pronoun, not an indefinite one.

[b] αἰτεῖσθε is a contract verb; see above.

Ps. 9:24 (10:3 MT/Eng.), **ἐπαινεῖται** ὁ ἁμαρτωλὸς ἐν ταῖς ἐπιθυμίαις τῆς ψυχῆς αὐτοῦ, καὶ ὁ ἀδικῶν **ἐνευλογεῖται.**

How will you express the idea of the middle voice in the two occurrences in this verse? Who is praising and blessing whom? What is their "basis" for doing so?

Challenge Verses

14.10. These verses will make you think carefully, but there is nothing here that you have not had or cannot easily identify with your lexicon. The goal is not to be able to produce a polished translation but to understand how each word contributes to the meaning of these statements.

Rom. 1:8–9, Πρῶτον μὲν εὐχαριστῶ τῷ θεῷ μου διὰ Ἰησοῦ Χριστοῦ περὶ πάντων ὑμῶν ὅτι ἡ πίστις ὑμῶν καταγγέλλεται (it is being reported) ἐν ὅλῳ τῷ κόσμῳ. μάρτυς γάρ μού ἐστιν ὁ θεός, ᾧ λατρεύω ἐν τῷ πνεύματί μου ἐν τῷ εὐαγγελίῳ τοῦ υἱοῦ αὐτοῦ, ὡς ἀδιαλείπτως μνείαν ὑμῶν **ποιοῦμαι.**[a]

[a] The verb ποιοῦμαι is another contract verb; ε + ο = ου.

The Four-Quad Chart

14.11. You have now met three of the four sets of endings that you need to memorize. For perspective, here is the four-quad chart with the pieces filled in that you have already learned. (Quadrant B looks a bit different since you first saw it with aorist verbs that do not use a connecting vowel; we will come back to this quadrant of the chart in chaps. 16 and 17 and explain the differences.)

A	ω	ον	B
	εις	ες	
	ει	ε(ν)	
	ομεν	ομεν	
	ετε	ετε	
	ουσι(ν)	ον	
C	ομαι		D
	ῃ		
	εται		
	ομεθα		
	εσθε		
	ονται		

"Grace Alone" and the Middle Voice

In the second verse of "Grace Alone"[a] the words read,

Every loving word we say
Every tear we wipe away
Every sorrow turned to praise
Is only by His grace.

The phrase "we wipe away," if written in Greek, would indicate whether the authors intended to refer to wiping away someone else's tears or one's own tears. Wiping away someone else's tears would be represented by the active voice (perhaps ἐξαλείφομεν πᾶν δάκρυον), but if the reference were to wiping away the tears from one's own eyes, it would be phrased with the middle voice (perhaps ἐξαλειφόμεθα πᾶν δάκρυον).

[a] "Grace Alone" was written by Scott Wesley Brown and Jeff Nelson. ©1998, Maranatha! Music.

There is a simple logic to the structure of this chart. If you split it horizontally, the top of the chart (quadrants A and B) contains typically active-voice endings, and the bottom of the chart (quadrants C and D) contains middle-voice endings, also used by most passive forms. (This is not absolute, since one set of passive forms uses quadrant B.) If you split the chart vertically, the left side (quadrants A and C) contains primary endings, and the right side (quadrants B and D) contains secondary endings. The difference between primary and secondary forms is morphological: secondary forms have an augment, which serves as a marker for secondary endings; primary forms do not have an augment.[4]

— — — — — — — — — — — — — —

Advanced Information for Reference: Determining the Subject

14.12. How does one determine the subject of a sentence when a linking verb occurs with two nominatives? Here is what you need to know to figure that out.[5] First, some definitions. The *linking verbs* (also known as *equative verbs*, *copulative verbs*, or *being verbs*) in Greek are εἰμί, γίνομαι, and ὑπάρχω.[6] A *predicate nominative* is a second substantive used with a linking verb that restates, defines, or in some way further explains or categorizes the subject of the sentence. This relationship is approximate; it is not the same as a mathematical formula A = B. Often the predicate nominative describes a category of which the subject is a part—for example, "Laura is a girl" (there are other persons who belong to the category "girl" besides Laura) and "God is love" (love is not identical with God).

A *substantive* is a noun or any other word or group of words that functions as a noun (e.g., pronouns, adjectives, infinitives, participles, prepositional phrases, and entire clauses can all function as nouns).

The Hierarchy of Rules

14.13. When a linking verb, most commonly εἰμί, is accompanied by two nominative substantives, several rules apply:

1. If one of the nominatives is a pronoun, it is always the subject. Sometimes this pronoun is the default/built-in subject of the verb, which means that a linking verb may have only one explicit nominative substantive.

2a. If one is a proper noun (a name) and the other a common noun, the proper noun is the subject.

4. This holds true in other moods as well. In moods such as the subjunctive that never have augments (augments are an indicative thing), the tense-forms that use secondary endings in the indicative change to primary endings.

5. For more detail, see Wallace, *Greek Grammar*, 40–48, on which this summary is based; and McGaughy, *Descriptive Analysis of Εἶναι*, 23–65.

6. In addition to the three primary linking verbs listed above, there are a few others that sometimes take a predicate nominative. These include the passive forms of καλέω and εὑρίσκω, also λέγω, and sometimes μένω.

2b. If one nominative has an article and the other does not, the one with the article is the subject.
3. If *both* nominatives have one of the "tags" from 2a–b (that is, a proper noun or an article) or if *neither* has such a tag, then the first in word order is the subject. This statement is also known as a *convertible proposition* (see below), but it may still be important in the context to specify the correct subject.

These rules are hierarchical; the higher rule always prevails (rule 1 being the highest), except for 2a and 2b, which hold equal rank (hence the numbering). A convertible proposition (3) is a statement in which the subject and predicate nominative can be reversed with no change in meaning. This is an important category; if you forget it or confuse it, the meaning of some texts can be badly mangled. For example, if you thought that 1 John 1:5 was a convertible proposition (ὁ θεὸς φῶς ἐστιν), you would be making a first-century Jewish-Christian writer into a pantheist—an anomalous conclusion indeed.

14.14. Examples

Rule 1

Matt. 16:18, σὺ εἶ Πέτρος.	You are Peter.
Luke 1:18, ἐγώ εἰμι πρεσβύτης.	I am an old man.
Luke 7:12, αὐτὴ ἦν χήρα.	She was a widow.

Rule 2a

James 5:17, Ἠλίας ἄνθρωπος ἦν.	Elijah was a man.

Rule 2b

John 4:24, πνεῦμα ὁ θεός.	God is spirit. (The verb εἰμί is understood.)

Rule 3

Matt. 13:38, ὁ δὲ ἀγρός ἐστιν ὁ κόσμος.	The field is the world.
John 8:39, Ὁ πατὴρ ἡμῶν Ἀβραάμ ἐστιν.	Our father is Abraham.
John 15:1, ὁ πατήρ μου ὁ γεωργός ἐστιν.	My Father is the vinedresser.

Other Guidelines

14.15. There are two additional guidelines that, though not as commonly needed as the hierarchy of rules, are crucial in some situations:

First, if one of the substantives does not have case (e.g., an adverb, an anarthrous prepositional phrase, etc.), the nominative substantive is always the subject. Often one of the formal rules will make this relationship clear also.

Matt. 26:18, Ὁ καιρός μου ἐγγύς ἐστιν.	My time is near.
1 John 2:4, ἐν τούτῳ ἡ ἀλήθεια οὐκ ἔστιν.	The truth is not in this one.

Second, the subject must always agree with the verb in person and number.[7] This may at times help distinguish the subject. Most examples are first- or second-person pronouns (and thus the first rule applies), but some situations with the third person occur. In the example from Rom. 2:14 below, the word νόμος cannot be the subject, since it is singular and εἰσιν is plural (3PPAI); the subject must therefore come from the verb. If you were to miss this point, you might try to make the verse say, "A law was for them."

Rom. 2:14, ἑαυτοῖς **εἰσιν νόμος**.	*They are a law* to themselves.
Matt. 26:22, **ἤρξαντο** λέγειν αὐτῷ **εἷς** ἕκαστος.	*They began* to say to him *one* after another.
Luke 12:53, **διαμερισθήσονται πατὴρ** ἐπὶ υἱῷ.	*They will be divided, a father* against a son.
John 10:16, **γενήσονται** μία **ποίμνη**, εἷς ποιμήν.	*There will be* one *flock*, one shepherd.

14.16. Examples

Heb. 1:10, ἔργα τῶν χειρῶν σού **εἰσιν οἱ οὐρανοί**.	*The heavens are* the works of your hands.
Mark 2:28, ὥστε κύριός **ἐστιν ὁ υἱὸς** τοῦ ἀνθρώπου καὶ τοῦ σαββάτου.	So then, *the Son* of Man *is* Lord, even of the Sabbath.

The word καί is to be understood in this example as an adverb ("even") rather than as a conjunction. The sentence does *not* say, "the Son of Man and of the Sabbath is Lord." Since one cannot be the "son of the Sabbath" in the same sense that one can be the "Son of Man," καί is not a coordinating conjunction in this statement.

Matt. 11:14, **αὐτός ἐστιν** Ἠλίας.	*He is* Elijah.
Luke 7:25, **οἱ** ἐν ἱματισμῷ ἐνδόξῳ ἐν τοῖς βασιλείοις **εἰσίν**.	*Those* in fancy clothes *are* in the royal palaces.

The article οἱ is a noun marker indicating that the prepositional phrase, ἐν ἱματισμῷ ἐνδόξῳ, functions as a nominative noun in the sentence.

7. Except, of course, for the situation that a neuter plural subject may take a singular verb.

14.17. Now You Try It

1 John 4:8, ὁ θεὸς ἀγάπη ἐστίν.

What is the subject? What is the predicate nominative? How do you know?

John 20:31, Ἰησοῦς ἐστιν ὁ Χριστός.

What is different about this example compared with the previous one? What kind of statement is it?

John 1:1, Ἐν ἀρχῇ ἦν[a] ὁ λόγος, καὶ ὁ λόγος ἦν πρὸς τὸν θεόν, καὶ θεὸς ἦν ὁ λόγος.

[a] ἦν, "he/she/it was"

This example combines both prepositions and the question of the subject. In the third clause, what is the subject? Why?

1 John 4:15, ὃς ἐὰν ὁμολογήσῃ[a] ὅτι Ἰησοῦς ἐστιν ὁ υἱὸς τοῦ θεοῦ, ὁ θεὸς ἐν αὐτῷ μένει καὶ αὐτὸς ἐν τῷ θεῷ.

What is the subject of the ὅτι clause? What is the verb for the last clause (the last four words)?

[a] ὃς ἐὰν ὁμολογήσῃ = "whoever confesses"; the ὅτι clause gives the content of the confession.

Gen. 25:27, Ἰακὼβ δὲ ἦν (was) ἄνθρωπος ἄπλαστος.[a]

[a] ἄπλαστος, ος, ον, might be glossed either of two different ways: "natural, unaffected, simple" (LEH, 48), or a character that is "not fully formed and set" (MLS, 69).

14.18. Reading Passage: 1 Corinthians 16:5–11, 19–24

Paul's Plans and Greetings

5 Ἐλεύσομαι (I will come) δὲ πρὸς ὑμᾶς ὅταν Μακεδονίαν διέλθω (I pass
through)· Μακεδονίαν γὰρ **διέρχομαι**, 6 πρὸς ὑμᾶς δὲ τυχὸν (perhaps) παρα-
μενῶ (I will stay) ἢ καὶ παραχειμάσω (I will spend the winter), ἵνα ὑμεῖς με
προπέμψητε (may send on the way) οὗ ἐὰν[a] πορεύωμαι (I should go). 7 οὐ θέλω
γὰρ ὑμᾶς ἄρτι ἐν παρόδῳ ἰδεῖν (to see), ἐλπίζω γὰρ χρόνον τινὰ ἐπιμεῖναι (to
spend) πρὸς ὑμᾶς ἐὰν ὁ κύριος ἐπιτρέψῃ (permits). 8 ἐπιμενῶ (I will remain)
δὲ ἐν Ἐφέσῳ ἕως τῆς πεντηκοστῆς· 9 θύρα γάρ μοι ἀνέῳγεν (is open) μεγάλη
καὶ ἐνεργής, καὶ ἀντικείμενοι (adversaries) πολλοί.

10 Ἐὰν δὲ ἔλθῃ (he comes) Τιμόθεος, βλέπετε (see to it!), ἵνα ἀφόβως γένηται
(he may be) πρὸς ὑμᾶς· τὸ γὰρ ἔργον κυρίου **ἐργάζεται** ὡς κἀγώ· 11 μή τις οὖν αὐτὸν
ἐξουθενήσῃ (despise). προπέμψατε (send on the way!) δὲ αὐτὸν ἐν εἰρήνῃ, ἵνα
ἔλθῃ (he may come) πρός με· **ἐκδέχομαι** γὰρ αὐτὸν μετὰ τῶν ἀδελφῶν.

19 **Ἀσπάζονται** ὑμᾶς αἱ ἐκκλησίαι τῆς Ἀσίας. **ἀσπάζεται** ὑμᾶς ἐν κυρίῳ πολλὰ
Ἀκύλας καὶ Πρίσκα σὺν τῇ κατ' οἶκον αὐτῶν ἐκκλησίᾳ. 20 **ἀσπάζονται** ὑμᾶς οἱ
ἀδελφοὶ πάντες. Ἀσπάσασθε (greet!) ἀλλήλους ἐν φιλήματι ἁγίῳ.

21 Ὁ ἀσπασμὸς τῇ ἐμῇ χειρὶ Παύλου. 22 εἴ τις οὐ φιλεῖ τὸν κύριον, ἤτω (let him
be) ἀνάθεμα. Μαράνα θά. 23 ἡ χάρις τοῦ κυρίου Ἰησοῦ μεθ' ὑμῶν. 24 ἡ ἀγάπη μου
μετὰ πάντων ὑμῶν ἐν Χριστῷ Ἰησοῦ.

[a] οὗ ἐάν, "wherever"

14.19. Vocabulary for Chapter 14

Part of Speech	Definition	Possible Glosses	Frequency	
Word			NT	LXX
Crasis Form				
κἀγώ	A crasis form of καί + ἐγώ (κἀμοί, dat.; κἀμέ, acc.); a personal affirmation adding to or confirming a previous statement	and I, but I; I also; I in particular	84	94
Verbs				
καλέω	To express something aloud; to request the presence or response of someone ("invite," social or soteric); to call authoritatively ("summon"); to assign a name	I call, say; I invite; I summon, call; I name	148	512
διδάσκω	To provide instruction in a formal or informal setting; to tell someone what to do	I teach, instruct; I tell (what to do)	97	107
πίπτω	To move downward from a higher to a lower level, typically rapidly and freely without control; to drop deliberately to the ground as a sign of humility before a high-ranking person or before God; metaphorically, to experience destruction or ruin, either physically or morally	I fall (down); I am destroyed	90	424
πέμπω	To cause someone or something to depart for a particular purpose	I send	79	22
ὑπάγω	To proceed from a position, be on the move in a particular direction; to leave someone's presence	I go; I depart, go away, leave	79	2
ἀνοίγω	To move or change something from a shut or closed position to enable access or function	I open	77	182
βαπτίζω	To dip, plunge, or immerse in water or another liquid, to drown [see LSJ and M-M]; in the LXX, to dip in water, to wash; in the NT it designates one of several actions, including a Jewish cleansing ritual using water, John's ceremony for confession of sin in the Jordan River, a similar ceremony authorized by Jesus, the Christian water ceremony of confession of faith,[a] a metaphorical reference to a work involving the Spirit uniting people with Christ and his Body at conversion, and various other metaphorical uses	I dip, immerse, baptize	77	4
ἄγω	To direct the movement of an object from one position to another; metaphorically, to direct the intellectual or moral life of another	I lead, bring	67	274
ἀπολύω	To set free from a condition or obligation (legal or medical, etc.); to cause to depart from a place; to terminate a marriage	I release, set free, deliver; I dismiss, send away; I divorce	66	27
δοξάζω	To enhance or exalt the esteem or reputation of another by word or action; to attribute high status to someone	I glorify, praise, honor	61	143

Part of Speech	Definition	Possible Glosses	Frequency	
Word			NT	LXX
θεραπεύω	Generally, to offer helpful service; specifically, to care for or treat medically, thus to cause someone to recover health	I heal, restore; I help out, serve	43	24
πάσχω	Generally to experience something, whether positive or negative, but in the NT almost always negative; to undergo a painful experience, to be subject to difficult circumstances; also in the LXX, to grieve over	I suffer, endure/undergo (something)	42	19
ἐνδύω	To provide covering, to put clothing on someone (act.); to clothe oneself, put on, wear (mid.)	I dress, clothe (act.); I put on, wear (mid.)	27	118
ὀμνύω	To take an oath affirming the truthfulness of what one says	I swear, take an oath	26	188

[a] Christians differ as to the mode of the confessional ceremony; some think the unmarked meaning is to be preserved (i.e., baptism by immersion); others allow other modes (pouring, sprinkling), so they transliterate the word as "I baptize."

14.20. Key Things to Know for Chapter 14

The present active indicative forms should be familiar already; if you have not learned them cold, do so before you go further.

Learn the formula for present middle indicative verbs.

You need to learn the new set of endings, the C endings, which are used for the present middle indicative tense-form.

How do present middle indicative verbs differ in meaning from present active indicative verbs?

What happens when a connecting vowel is added to a verb stem that ends with an epsilon or omicron?

15

VERBS: PART 5

PASSIVE VOICE AND MIDDLE-ONLY VERBS

15.1. Picture in your mind the following event. You are at a track and field tournament. The current event is the hammer throw. You have just witnessed a throw of over 260 feet. The woman who threw that distance may have set a world record. Describe what you saw by creating two different sentences that include the following grammatical elements:

1. Subject: "woman" Object: "hammer"
2. Subject: "hammer" Object (of preposition): "woman"

What is the *grammatical* difference between the two sentences that you just created?[1] It is the *voice* of the verb: active voice versus passive voice.

Active:	*threw*	The subject, "woman," is *doing* the action.
Passive:	*was thrown*	The subject, "hammer," is *receiving* the action rather than doing it. The doer of the action is expressed by the prepositional phrase "by the woman."

In contemporary English the passive voice is often denigrated as a sign of weak writing—but the passive is still alive and well, even in good English. It is even more common in Greek.

1. I am assuming that you came up with these two sentences: (1) The woman *threw* the hammer. (2) The hammer *was thrown* by the woman.

Present Passive Indicative

15.2. You will remember from chapter 13 that passive voice means that the grammatical subject of the sentence is *receiving the action* described by the verb; the subject is not *doing* the action of the verb. The verbs in this section will be present tense-form, passive voice, and indicative mood. The aspect is imperfective, the same as present active indicative verbs and present middle indicative verbs. The time will often be present time. A common way to express this in English is "he is being loosed." The passive voice uses the same set of endings as the present middle indicative verbs that you learned in chapter 14 (set C).

Formula for Present Passive Indicative Verbs

stem + connecting vowel + C personal endings
Example: λυ + ο + μαι ▸ λύομαι

Present Passive Indicative of λύω

	Form	c.v. + C p.e.	Gloss	c.v.	p.e.
1S	λύομαι	ομαι	I am being loosed	ο	μαι
2S	λύῃ	ῃ	You are being loosed	ε	σαι
3S	λύεται	εται	He/she/it is being loosed	ε	ται
1P	λυόμεθα	ομεθα	We are being loosed	ο	μεθα
2P	λύεσθε	εσθε	You are being loosed	ε	σθε
3P	λύονται	ονται	They are being loosed	ο	νται

Notice that the *form* of the passive is identical to the middle. The same formula and endings are used. The English gloss, however, is quite different. Remember: you must always keep *form* and *function* distinct. The *form* for passive voice is the same as middle, but the *function* of the passive is different.

Since English does have a passive form (in contrast to the middle voice, which is not used in English), we can express this fairly directly in the English language. You will remember from our earlier discussions that a passive verb describes a situation in which the grammatical subject of the sentence is not *doing* the action but rather is the *recipient* of the action—the action of the verb is being performed upon the subject. The focus is on the subject, not on the action per se. In our paradigm verb, λύω, the subject ("I") is no longer performing the action of the verb ("untying," e.g., someone's shoes). Rather, someone else (from the verb alone we do not know who) is performing the action *to* or *on* the subject—which we express in English, using a helping verb, as "I am *being* untied/loosed."

Examples of the Present Passive Indicative

15.3. Here are several sample passive sentences to get you started. For the moment, do not worry about how we know they are passive rather than middle.

Just take my word for it now, and try to understand what meaning is being communicated by the use of the passive voice. In the next section, we will come to the question of how we know they are passive.

Mark 10:38, ἐγὼ **βαπτίζομαι.**	I *am being baptized.*
Mark 4:15, οὗτοί εἰσιν οἱ παρὰ τὴν ὁδόν· ὅπου **σπείρεται** ὁ λόγος.	These are the ones along the road where the word *is sown.*
Mark 12:25, ὅταν γὰρ ἐκ νεκρῶν ἀναστῶσιν οὔτε γαμοῦσιν οὔτε **γαμίζονται,** ἀλλ' εἰσὶν ὡς ἄγγελοι ἐν τοῖς οὐρανοῖς.	For when they rise from the dead they will neither marry nor *be given in marriage*, but they will be like angels in heaven.
Gen. 43:18, Διὰ τὸ ἀργύριον ἐν τοῖς μαρσίπποις ἡμῶν ἡμεῖς **εἰσαγόμεθα.**	Because of the money in our bags we *are being brought in.*

How to Distinguish Passive from Middle

15.4. The logical question, then, is this: How can you tell middle and passive verbs apart if the forms are the same? The answer is, once again: Context! There are two key context clues that will often help you resolve this question. The first—and by far the most common and clear clue—is a statement of agency in the sentence *other than the subject.*

1. Often a passive verb in Greek has the equivalent of *by* following it to specify "who done it" ("Elementary, my dear Watson!"). This is called an *agent construction.* In Greek this is most often expressed by the preposition ὑπό, which, when used with a genitive-case object of the preposition, tells us who the personal agent is who performs the action referenced by the verb.

2 Cor. 1:4, παρακαλούμεθα[a] αὐτοὶ **ὑπὸ τοῦ θεοῦ.**	We ourselves are being comforted *by God.*

[a] παρακαλούμεθα is a contract verb; ε + ο = ου.

Isa. 45:17, Ἰσραὴλ σῴζεται **ὑπὸ κυρίου.**	Israel will be saved *by the Lord.*

There are other possibilities for indicating the agent, but they are less common. One is a dative substantive alone that expresses the agent. In this case it is not usually a person but rather an impersonal instrument that is said to perform the action.

Matt. 13:40, τὰ ζιζάνια **πυρὶ** κατακαίεται.	The tares are burned *with fire.*
Prov. 6:2, παγὶς γὰρ ἰσχυρὰ ἀνδρὶ τὰ ἴδια χείλη, καὶ ἁλίσκεται[a] **χείλεσιν**[b] ἰδίου στόματος.	His own lips are a strong snare to a man, and he is caught *by the lips* of his own mouth.

[a] ἁλίσκεται ▸ ἁλίσκομαι, "I am caught"
[b] χείλεσιν, neut. pl. dat. ▸ χεῖλος, ους, τό, "lip"

Or you may find ἀπό + genitive.

James 1:13, **Ἀπὸ θεοῦ** πειράζομαι.	I am being tempted *by God*.[a]

[a] This is only part of the verse. Read the rest in a Greek NT or an English Bible before you draw too many conclusions.

Or διά + genitive may be used, often indicating intermediate agency.

1 Tim. 4:5, ἁγιάζεται γὰρ **διὰ λόγου** θεοῦ καὶ **ἐντεύξεως**.	It is made holy *through the word* of God and *prayer*.

There are also a few other less common agent markers, including παρά + genitive, ἐν + dative, and ἐκ + genitive.

2. The second context clue is if there is a direct object in the sentence. If so, the verb is *probably* middle. Passive verbs do not usually have direct objects.[2] For example, in the following statement ἐντέλλομαι is not a passive verb, since it has a direct object, ταῦτα.

John 15:17, ταῦτα **ἐντέλλομαι** ὑμῖν.	*I am commanding* you these things.

Middle voice verbs do not *require* a direct object; it is possible to have an intransitive middle verb that does not take an object.

Passives without an Agent Marker

15.5. There are some instances where there is no specific contextual marker for a passive other than common sense and a knowledge of the real world as to how things happen. Be careful, however, not to appeal to this explanation too quickly; middle voice is more common than passive.

Rev. 8:11, καὶ τὸ ὄνομα τοῦ ἀστέρος **λέγεται** ὁ Ἄψινθος (Wormwood).	The name of the star *is*[a] Wormwood.

[a] Formally λέγεται would be glossed "is named," but to say that "the name is named" is redundant in English.

Matt. 2:4, ἐπυνθάνετο (he inquired) παρ' αὐτῶν ποῦ ὁ Χριστὸς **γεννᾶται**.[a]	He inquired from them where the Messiah *was to be born*.

[a] γεννᾶται is a contract verb; α + ε = α.

2. *Advanced information for reference*: About the only time a passive verb will have a direct object is if the equivalent statement in active voice uses a double accusative. For example, active: Bill taught *him Greek*; passive: *He* was taught *Greek* by Bill. As a possible Greek example, see Heb. 5:1, Πᾶς ἀρχιερεὺς καθίσταται τὰ πρὸς τὸν θεόν ("Every high priest is put in charge of the things relating to God"). In the active this might be phrased, "He put the high priest in charge of the things relating to God"; both "high priest" and "the things" would be accusative. Wallace (*Greek Grammar*, 438–39) lists a number of examples, but they all use passive forms that you have not learned yet.

Context!

You have noticed by now that the word *context* shows up quite frequently in this textbook (over 200 times, if you are curious). Perhaps you have begun to think that Greek is unique in this regard—that it is the only language that requires so much attention to context to decide what something means. Greek is actually quite normal in this regard. We do not notice it in our own language, because we do it intuitively without even realizing that we are making such decisions. Here are a few examples to help you understand how important such contextual decisions are in English.

> The bandage was wound around the wound.
> The dump was so full that it had to refuse more refuse.
> Since there is no time like the present, he thought it was time to present the present.
> After a number of Novocain injections, my jaw got number.
> How can I intimate this to my most intimate friend?

Yes, these are all homonyms. But how does an English speaker disambiguate forms with different meanings, especially when many of them involve different parts of speech? How do we know that a given word is a noun rather than a verb? Or which meaning of a noun is intended? Context!

15.6. *Now You Try It*

1 Cor. 2:15, ὁ δὲ πνευματικὸς ἀνακρίνει τὰ πάντα, αὐτὸς δὲ **ὑπ'** οὐδενὸς **ἀνακρίνεται.**

Note the contrast between active and passive forms of the same verb in this verse.

Heb. 7:7, χωρὶς δὲ πάσης ἀντιλογίας τὸ ἔλαττον **ὑπὸ** τοῦ κρείττονος **εὐλογεῖται.**[a]

What is the subject? Is χωρίς functioning as an adverb or preposition? What case are πάσης and ἀντιλογίας? Why?

[a] εὐλογεῖται is a contract verb.

Heb. 9:22, **ἐν** αἵματι πάντα **καθαρίζεται** κατὰ τὸν νόμον.

Is there an explicit, nominative-case subject in this verse?

Exod. 3:2, ὤφθη (he appeared) δὲ αὐτῷ ἄγγελος κυρίου ἐν φλογὶ πυρὸς ἐκ τοῦ βάτου, καὶ ὁρᾷ (he observed) ὅτι ὁ βάτος **καίεται πυρί,** ὁ δὲ βάτος οὐ κατεκαίετο[a] (it was not consumed).

[a] καίω, "I burn," but κατακαίω, "I burn up, consume"

Who appeared? *How* did he appear? *Where* did he appear? What does ὅτι tell you? What is being burned? What case is πυρί, and why is it that case?

Do You Understand?

15.7. Is the boldface form in each verse below functioning as a middle- or a passive-voice verb? How do you know? (They are listed in NT order, and several examples are given of each voice.)

Mark 10:38, ὁ δὲ Ἰησοῦς εἶπεν (he said) αὐτοῖς, Οὐκ οἴδατε[a] τί **αἰτεῖσθε**.[b]

[a] οἶδα, "I know"
[b] αἰτέω, "I ask"

Mark 15:24, σταυροῦσιν[a] αὐτὸν καὶ **διαμερίζονται**[b] τὰ ἱμάτια αὐτοῦ.

[a] σταυρόω, "I crucify"
[b] διαμερίζω, "I divide"

Rom. 8:14, ὅσοι γὰρ πνεύματι θεοῦ **ἄγονται**,[a] οὗτοι υἱοὶ θεοῦ εἰσιν.

[a] ἄγω, "I lead"

Heb. 3:4, πᾶς γὰρ οἶκος **κατασκευάζεται**[a] ὑπό τινος.

[a] κατασκευάζω, "I build"

James 1:14, ἕκαστος δὲ **πειράζεται**[a] ὑπὸ τῆς ἰδίας ἐπιθυμίας.

[a] πειράζω, "I tempt"

In the example from Gal. 3:3 below, *be careful:* not every dative indicates the *agent* of a passive verb. In this example, *who* is finishing? The flesh (the dative), or the Galatians?

Gal. 3:3, οὕτως ἀνόητοί[a] ἐστε, ἐναρξάμενοι (having begun) πνεύματι νῦν σαρκὶ **ἐπιτελεῖσθε**;[b]

[a] ἀνόητος, ον, "foolish" (adj.)
[b] ἐπιτελέω, "I finish"

The verb that is parallel to ἐπιτελεῖσθε is a participle (ἐναρξάμενοι) and can *only* be middle, never passive, since in aorist there are separate forms for middle and passive, in contrast to the present forms we are working with now, which use the same form for both voices.

Middle-Only Verbs

15.8. Here is something a bit different. Parse this word: ἔρχονται. Would you suggest a third plural present middle indicative form of ἔρχω? I thought so. At least at this point in your exposure to Greek, that would be the expected answer. But now look up ἔρχω in your lexicon. (Do this before reading further.)

An Ancient New Testament Manuscript

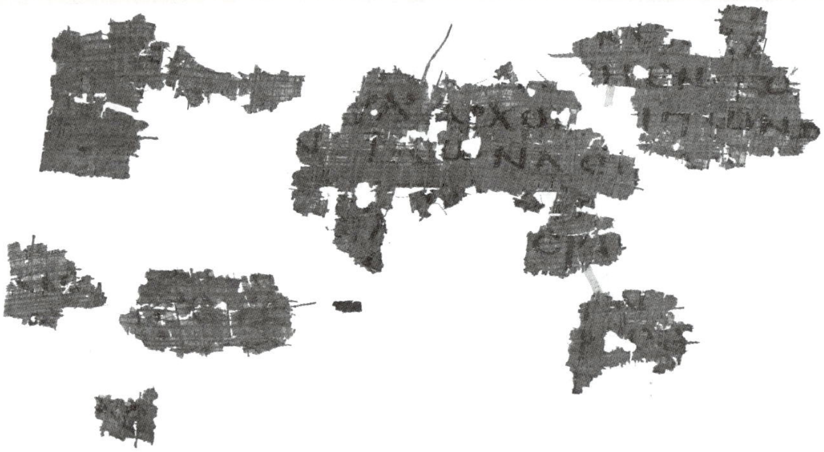

Robert C. Horn Papyri Collection, Trexler Library, Muhlenberg College, Allentown, Pennsylvania

Figure 15.1. 𝔓[21] (POxy 1227), a Fifth-Century Papyrus Fragment with Matthew 12:24–26

You did not find it, did you? (And if you did not look it up, then shame on you! Go look it up anyway, just to see for yourself that it really is not there. Do not take my word for it—besides, it is good practice.) What you *will* find is the form ἔρχομαι, not ἔρχω. Note the different ending. The stem is the same, but instead of having the usual first singular ending from set A (an omega), in the lexicon it has the first singular ending from set C (-ομαι).

15.9. There are some verbs that *always* occur in the middle form; they use only the C personal endings, never the A set. These verbs *do not have an active form*. That is, you will never see them with active personal endings (set A). For this reason they are called *middle-only verbs*.

This is a set of verbs that typically has an inherent middle meaning in the very lexis of the word itself. That is, the meaning of the word makes the subject focus of the middle form very natural. For example, think about the meanings of these words. Can you envision it being done to someone other than the subject?

μασάομαι, "I bite my lips or tongue" (Rev. 16:10)
κτάομαι, "I get, acquire" (Acts 22:28)[3]

3. Greek would not use the verb κτάομαι to mean "I acquire/buy for someone else"; that would probably be expressed by ἀγοράζω.

γεύομαι, "I taste" (John 2:9)[4]
κοιμάομαι, "I fall asleep, die" (Acts 12:6)
δέχομαι, "I welcome" (Mark 6:11)

When a verb does not use active endings, the lexical form ends with -ομαι rather than the usual omega. For example, λέγω is a regular verb in that it has active endings (as well as middle), but ἔρχομαι never uses active endings. Any time you find a lexical form with this -ομαι ending, you know that it is a middle-only verb and never has the A set of endings. Most such verbs that have an -ομαι ending in the lexical form are middle voice, though they may sometimes be used as passives. (This depends on the context; look for the passive clues given above.)

These verbs are parsed like any other verb. The only difference is that the lexical form that you list in your parsing will have an -ομαι ending. For example, if I asked you to parse ἔρχεσθε, you would tell me: second plural present middle indicative from ἔρχομαι, "I come." Or, if you are parsing a word in context and there is a passive marker, then it is parsed as passive.

15.10. *Examples of Middle-Only Verbs*

Mark 1:7, ἐκήρυσσεν λέγων (saying), **Ἔρχεται** ὁ ἰσχυρότερός μου ὀπίσω μου.

He preached, saying, "The one stronger than me *is coming* behind me."

Mark 2:18, οἱ μαθηταὶ Ἰωάννου καὶ οἱ Φαρισαῖοι **ἔρχονται** καὶ λέγουσιν αὐτῷ, Διὰ τί οἱ μαθηταὶ Ἰωάννου καὶ οἱ μαθηταὶ τῶν Φαρισαίων νηστεύουσιν, οἱ δὲ σοὶ μαθηταὶ οὐ νηστεύουσιν;

The disciples of John and the Pharisees *came* and said to him, "Why are the disciples of John and the disciples of the Pharisees fasting, but your disciples are not fasting?"

Mark 8:1–2, λέγει αὐτοῖς, **Σπλαγχνίζομαι** ἐπὶ τὸν ὄχλον.

He said to them, "*I have compassion* on the crowd."

Gen. 2:10, ποταμὸς δὲ **ἐκπορεύεται** ἐξ Ἐδὲμ ποτίζειν τὸν παράδεισον.

Now a river *went out* from Eden to water the garden.

2 Esd. 16:6 (Neh. 6:6 Eng.), Ἐν ἔθνεσιν ἠκούσθη (it was heard) ὅτι σὺ καὶ οἱ Ἰουδαῖοι **λογίζεσθε** ἀποστατῆσαι,[a] διὰ τοῦτο σὺ οἰκοδομεῖς τὸ τεῖχος,[b] καὶ σὺ γίνῃ (would become) αὐτοῖς εἰς βασιλέα.

Among the nations it was heard that you and the Judeans *intend* to rebel, (that) for this reason you are building the wall, and (that) you would become their king.

[a] ἀποστατέω, "I revolt, rebel"
[b] τεῖχος, ους, τό, "wall"

4. There is a rare active form of this verb (never used in the NT and only once in LXX) that means "I give someone else a taste of something."

15.11. *Now You Try It*

John 5:17, ὁ δὲ Ἰησοῦς ἀπεκρίνατο[a] αὐτοῖς, Ὁ πατήρ μου ἕως ἄρτι **ἐργάζεται** κἀγὼ **ἐργάζομαι**·

[a] ἀποκρίνομαι often means "I answer," but it sometimes refers to a response to a situation where no question is in view. In these instances "I respond" is often a good English equivalent.

John 10:4, ἔμπροσθεν αὐτῶν **πορεύεται**, καὶ τὰ πρόβατα αὐτῷ ἀκολουθεῖ, ὅτι οἴδασιν (they know) τὴν φωνὴν αὐτοῦ.

Rom. 1:16, Οὐ γὰρ **ἐπαισχύνομαι** τὸ εὐαγγέλιον, δύναμις γὰρ θεοῦ ἐστιν εἰς σωτηρίαν.

Rom. 7:22, **συνήδομαι** γὰρ τῷ νόμῳ τοῦ θεοῦ κατὰ τὸν ἔσω ἄνθρωπον.

Gen. 31:35, εἶπεν τῷ πατρὶ αὐτῆς, Μὴ βαρέως φέρε,[a] κύριε· οὐ **δύναμαι**[b] ἀναστῆναι[c] ἐνώπιόν σου.

[a] μὴ βαρέως φέρε, "do not be annoyed/upset"

[b] See the vocabulary list for this chapter.

[c] aor. act. inf. ▶ ἀνίστημι, "I rise"

1 Clem. 8.2, λέγει κύριος, οὐ **βούλομαι** τὸν θάνατον τοῦ ἁμαρτωλοῦ.

15.12. *Challenge Verses*

Rom. 1:18–20, **Ἀποκαλύπτεται** γὰρ ὀργὴ θεοῦ ἀπ' οὐρανοῦ ἐπὶ πᾶσαν ἀσέβειαν καὶ ἀδικίαν ἀνθρώπων τῶν τὴν ἀλήθειαν ἐν ἀδικίᾳ κατεχόντων (ones who suppress), διότι τὸ γνωστὸν τοῦ θεοῦ φανερόν ἐστιν ἐν αὐτοῖς· ὁ θεὸς γὰρ αὐτοῖς ἐφανέρωσεν. τὰ γὰρ ἀόρατα αὐτοῦ ἀπὸ κτίσεως κόσμου τοῖς ποιήμασιν νοούμενα (being understood) **καθορᾶται**,[a] ἥ τε ἀΐδιος αὐτοῦ δύναμις καὶ θειότης, εἰς τὸ εἶναι[b] αὐτοὺς ἀναπολογήτους.

[a] καθοράω is a contract verb; α + ε = α.

[b] One way that Greek can indicate a statement of purpose is to use εἰς τό + an infinitive, here εἰς τὸ εἶναι.

— — — — — — — — — — — — — —

15.13. Advanced Information for Reference: Diagramming Passive Verbs

2 Cor. 1:4, παρακαλούμεθα αὐτοὶ **ὑπὸ τοῦ θεοῦ.** — We ourselves are being comforted *by God.*

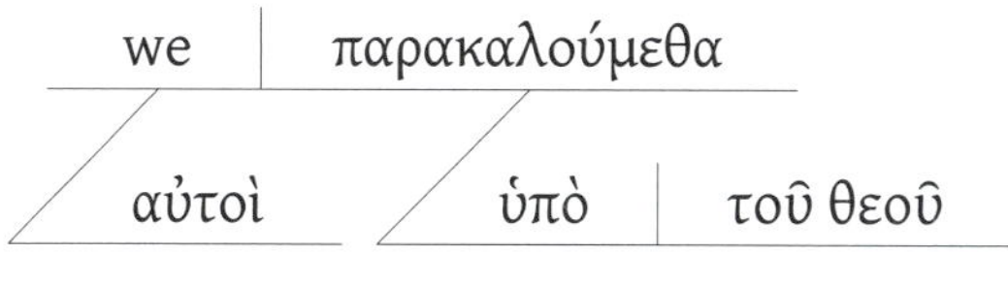

Figure 15.2

The agent marker in a passive construction is diagrammed as a modifier. The usual agent marker, ὑπό with the genitive, is diagrammed as any other prepositional phrase. Do you remember why αὐτοί cannot be the subject in this statement?

— — — — — — — — — — — — — —

15.14. Reading Passage: 1 Corinthians 15:35–44

How Are the Dead Raised?

[35]Ἀλλὰ ἐρεῖ (will ask) τις, Πῶς **ἐγείρονται** οἱ νεκροί; ποίῳ δὲ σώματι **ἔρχονται;**
[36]ἄφρων, σὺ ὃ σπείρεις, οὐ **ζῳοποιεῖται** ἐὰν μὴ ἀποθάνῃ (it should die)· [37]καὶ ὃ
σπείρεις, οὐ τὸ σῶμα τὸ γενησόμενον (which will be) σπείρεις ἀλλὰ γυμνὸν
κόκκον εἰ τύχοι[a] σίτου ἤ τινος τῶν λοιπῶν· [38]ὁ δὲ θεὸς δίδωσιν (gives) αὐτῷ
σῶμα καθὼς ἠθέλησεν, καὶ ἑκάστῳ τῶν σπερμάτων ἴδιον σῶμα. [39]οὐ πᾶσα
σὰρξ ἡ αὐτὴ σὰρξ ἀλλὰ ἄλλη μὲν ἀνθρώπων, ἄλλη δὲ σὰρξ κτηνῶν, ἄλλη δὲ
σὰρξ πτηνῶν, ἄλλη δὲ ἰχθύων. [40]καὶ σώματα ἐπουράνια, καὶ σώματα ἐπίγεια·
ἀλλὰ ἑτέρα μὲν ἡ τῶν ἐπουρανίων δόξα, ἑτέρα δὲ ἡ τῶν ἐπιγείων. [41]ἄλλη δόξα
ἡλίου, καὶ ἄλλη δόξα σελήνης, καὶ ἄλλη δόξα ἀστέρων· ἀστὴρ γὰρ ἀστέρος
διαφέρει ἐν δόξῃ.

[42]Οὕτως καὶ ἡ ἀνάστασις τῶν νεκρῶν. **σπείρεται** ἐν φθορᾷ, **ἐγείρεται** ἐν
ἀφθαρσίᾳ· [43]**σπείρεται** ἐν ἀτιμίᾳ, **ἐγείρεται** ἐν δόξῃ· **σπείρεται** ἐν ἀσθενείᾳ, **ἐγείρεται** ἐν δυνάμει· [44]**σπείρεται** σῶμα ψυχικόν, **ἐγείρεται** σῶμα πνευματικόν. εἰ ἔστιν
σῶμα ψυχικόν, ἔστιν καὶ πνευματικόν.

[a] εἰ τύχοι, "perhaps"

15.15. Vocabulary for Chapter 15

Part of Speech	Definition	Possible Glosses	Frequency	
Word			NT	LXX
Adjectives				
πονηρός, ά, όν	Morally or socially worthless, by either social or divine standards; deficient in quality so as to be worthless (of physical goods); unhealthy	evil, wicked, bad; worthless; sick	78	381
αἰώνιος, ον	Describing a period of time as being a long time ago or as being without boundaries or interruption or as of unending duration	long ago; eternal	71	153
Verbs				
ἔρχομαι	To move from one point to another (geographical or temporal), which may be described from the perspective of either the origin or destination ("come" is the usual equivalent; "go" is less common in Koine)	I come, arrive; I go	634	1,054
ἐξέρχομαι	To move away from a location	I go/come out/away	218	742
εἰσέρχομαι	To enter into a space or into an event or state	I come/go in(to), enter	194	700
ἀπέρχομαι	To depart from a place	I go away, depart	117	229
προσέρχομαι	To approach a person, move toward someone/something; to approach a deity in worship, fellowship, or prayer	I come/go to, approach	86	113
διέρχομαι	To travel/move in or through an area	I go/pass (through); I come, arrive	43	146
δύναμαι	To be capable of doing something (used with an infinitive to specify what is done) [See the "Vocabulary Notes."]	I am able	210	332
κάθημαι	To be in a seated position; to take a seated position; metaphorically, to be a resident in a place	I sit; I sit down, take a seat; I live, reside (metaphorical)	91	180
προσεύχομαι	To address a deity in prayer (a general term for presenting requests, worship, etc.)	I pray	85	107
ἀσπάζομαι	To address someone hospitably, either in person (whether arriving or departing) or in correspondence	I greet, welcome, say good-bye	59	10
δέχομαι	To accept the presence of a person or the arrival of a thing, often with connotations of enthusiasm or joy; to readily receive information and to regard it as true	I receive, welcome, take; I accept, receive readily	56	62
ἐργάζομαι	To engage in activity that involves effort; to do or accomplish something through work (the result of the activity)	I work; I do, accomplish, carry out	41	122
λογίζομαι	To engage in numerical calculation, determine by mathematical process; metaphorically of mental activity in general: to give careful thought to a matter	I reckon, account, calculate; I think about, consider, ponder	40	121

Vocabulary Notes

15.16. The verb δύναμαι, "I am able," has a set of endings that may initially look irregular. It does not use connecting vowels, since its stem ends with alpha. The endings are normal; just think of the alpha as taking the place of the usual connecting vowel. It is declined as shown below. This verb will always have an infinitive with it to specify what it is that is able or possible. We call this a *complementary infinitive*, since it complements (i.e., completes) the meaning of the main verb.

1S	δύναμαι	1P	δυνάμεθα
2S	δύνασαι (or δύνῃ)	2P	δύνασθε
3S	δύναται	3P	δύνανται

15.17. Key Things to Know for Chapter 15

How does the passive voice differ in meaning from the active and middle voices?

Learn the formula for present passive indicative verbs.

If the passive voice is identical to the middle voice in spelling, how can you tell them apart? (Be specific.)

What is a "middle-only" verb?

16

VERBS: PART 6

Imperfect (Remote Imperfective) Indicative Verbs

16.1. We will first do a short review of verbs, and then we will meet a new tense-form, the imperfect.

Verb Review

Aspect is a grammatical description of how the speaker/writer views a situation. This may be either imperfective (in which the situation is viewed as a process), perfective (the situation is viewed as a whole with no reference to a process—even if there *is* process involved), or stative (the situation is viewed as a state or condition with no reference to action, change, or energy involved). These three aspects might be illustrated in English with reference to eating a meal as "I was eating," "I ate," and "I have eaten, [and thus] I am full."

The tense-form of a verb refers to the spelling of a verb that identifies which of the verbal aspects the writer intends. There are three major tense-forms and two minor ones. The present tense-form expresses imperfective aspect, the aorist encodes perfective aspect, and the perfect has stative aspect. The minor tense-forms are imperfect (with imperfective aspect like the present) and pluperfect (stative aspect).[1] These minor tense-forms are distinguished from their major counterparts, not by their aspect, but by their function in the language. (We will talk more about this later.)

The tense-form of the verb in Greek does not express time the way it does in English. Time is a property of statements, not individual verbs, and it is determined by looking at the tense and the context. We can describe various

1. There is also a future tense-form, but scholars are not agreed about whether this expresses aspect. See the discussion in chap. 19.

statements with categories similar to what we use in English, such as past, present, future, or unrestricted.[2]

Introduction to the Imperfect

16.2. This chapter introduces a new form: the imperfect. And no, it is not "defective." The name refers to its aspect, not its quality. The aspect of the imperfect form is imperfective, in which a situation is viewed as a process.[3] Imperfect verbs are most often used in past-time statements, but they are sometimes found in statements that do not focus on the past. They may have relevance to present time (from the perspective of the writer) or, in statements that do not refer to any particular time, they may be temporally unrestricted. (Imperfect verbs are not used in future-time statements.) Here are some examples of statements in the NT that use imperfect verbs.

> "Why *were you seeking* me?" (Luke 2:49). Jesus is speaking to his mother regarding the search over the past three days.
>
> "*I wish* to be present with you now" (Gal. 4:20). This is not a past desire but Paul's present desire as he writes to the Galatians.
>
> "*It is necessary* to do these things" (Matt. 23:23). This is a temporally unrestricted statement that refers to an ongoing duty. In the context the Pharisees have not done these things (justice, mercy, and faithfulness), but Jesus' point is that the obligation to do so is always binding.

Since the imperfect is most commonly used in past-referring statements, a common English equivalent is a past progressive.

> Imperfect active or middle indicative of λύω: "I was loosing"
> Imperfect passive indicative of λύω: "I was being loosed"

Typical equivalents such as this are intended only to give you some means of conceptualizing the meaning of the verb until you can sort out the entire statement. Sometimes you have a pretty good idea of what it says by the time you have read as far as the verb in a given statement; other times you need to read further and then make a mental adjustment as you discover new information. It is not always necessary that a Greek imperfect verb be represented with an *-ing* form in English, though that is often appropriate. Some statements are better left as simple verb forms in English due to English idiom. This does not change the aspect or meaning of the Greek verb but affects only its English representation.

2. *Unrestricted* refers to statements in which time is not relevant or those that relate to all times.

3. Be careful to keep these two words straight: *imperfect* refers to the tense-form (i.e., how the verb is spelled), but *imperfective* identifies the aspect. Remember that the present tense-form also expresses imperfective aspect.

Forms of the Imperfect

16.3. The formulas for imperfect indicative verbs are as follows. A chart with both sets of forms is found below.

Formula for Imperfect Active Indicative Verbs

augment + stem + connecting vowel + B personal endings

Formula for Imperfect Middle Indicative Verbs

augment + stem + connecting vowel + D personal endings

You met the B personal endings in chapter 7. They will look slightly different here. That is because the aorist tense-form used σα as a form marker and did not use a connecting vowel. The actual endings are the same (though the first aorist does not use the nu in the first singular form).[4]

B Personal Endings

1S	ον
2S	ες
3S	ε(ν)
1P	ομεν
2P	ετε
3P	ον

This is the first tense-form you have met that uses the D set of endings. They are as follows, including the connecting vowel.

D Personal Endings

1S	ομην
2S	ου
3S	ετο
1P	ομεθα
2P	εσθε
3P	οντο

16.4. You will remember from chapter 7 that an augment is the letter epsilon prefixed to a verb stem as part of the formula to indicate the tense-form and to specify that secondary endings are to be used rather than primary. The various tense-forms of the indicative are classed in two groups, depending on whether or not an augment is used.

4. If we keep the alpha from the form marker, the aorist uses B endings that look like this: α, ας, εν, αμεν, ατε, αν. If you compare the B endings as used in the imperfect, the similarity is obvious so long as you replace the alpha from the form marker with the omicron or epsilon connecting vowel: ον, ες, εν, ομεν, ετε, ον.

Primary Forms *do not* have an augment	**Secondary Forms** *do* have an augment
present	imperfect
future	aorist
perfect	pluperfect

16.5. The imperfect is the second set of forms that we have met that use secondary endings. Altogether, you have now learned four sets of endings. You already know the primary endings. With this last set (D), you know all the endings you need to memorize for indicative verbs. All the other indicative forms that we will meet will use one of these four sets. It is helpful to visualize them in a four-quad chart.

Personal Endings

A. Primary Active	B. Secondary Active
C. Primary Middle	D. Secondary Middle

If you split this chart vertically, the two left quadrants are the primary endings and the right quadrants are the secondary endings. If you split the chart horizontally, the top portion is active, and the bottom is middle. We call the bottom sets *middle* even though they are sometimes used for passive-voice verbs.[5] The same is also true of the top section: they are traditionally called *active endings* but are sometimes (though less commonly) used on passive verbs.

The following is what the entire four-quad chart looks like if we fill in an actual verb and list the endings as well. The table shows the present and imperfect forms of λύω so you can see not only the endings but also a complete verb. Other tense-forms will use the same endings; for example, the perfect uses primary (A/C) endings, and the aorist uses secondary (B/D). Remember that the endings shown *include* the connecting vowels.

5. The form is technically middle. The passive voice is distinguished not morphologically but contextually. When middle forms are accompanied by passive markers in the context, we call them *passive*. Some prefer to call the endings *middle/passive* as a reminder of this dual function.

The Complete Four-Quad Verb Chart

		A. Primary		B. Secondary	
Active	1S	λύω	ω	ἔλυον	ον
	2S	λύεις	εις	ἔλυες	ες
	3S	λύει	ει	ἔλυε(ν)	ε(ν)
	1P	λύομεν	ομεν	ἐλύομεν	ομεν
	2P	λύετε	ετε	ἐλύετε	ετε
	3P	λύουσι(ν)	ουσι(ν)	ἔλυον	ον
		C. Primary		D. Secondary	
Middle	1S	λύομαι	ομαι	ἐλυόμην	ομην
	2S	λύῃ	ῃ/εσαι[a]	ἐλύου	ου
	3S	λύεται	εται	ἐλύετο	ετο
	1P	λυόμεθα	ομεθα	ἐλυόμεθα	ομεθα
	2P	λύεσθε	εσθε	ἐλύεσθε	εσθε
	3P	λύονται	ονται	ἐλύοντο	οντο

[a] The technical second singular primary middle ending is -σαι (with ε as the connecting vowel), but this *always* changes to -ῃ (the σ drops out when squeezed between two vowels, then the ε lengthens and the iota becomes subscript). Learn this ending as ῃ. The *only* time you will see the full -σαι ending is one form you will meet later that does not use a connecting vowel. We will sort that one out when we find it. By far the largest number of such forms in the NT and LXX use -ῃ, not -σαι.

16.6. The following tables show the forms of the imperfect tense-form in each of the three voices: active, middle, and passive.

Imperfect Active Indicative of λύω

	Form	c.v. + B p.e.	Gloss	c.v.	p.e.
1S	ἔλυον	ον	I was loosing	ο	ν
2S	ἔλυες	ες	You were loosing	ε	ς
3S	ἔλυε(ν)	ε(ν)	He/she/it was loosing	ε	(ν)
1P	ἐλύομεν	ομεν	We were loosing	ο	μεν
2P	ἐλύετε	ετε	You were loosing	ε	τε
3P	ἔλυον	ον	They were loosing	ο	ν

Imperfect Middle Indicative of λύω

	Form	c.v. + D p.e.	Gloss	c.v.	p.e.
1S	ἐλυόμην	ομην	I was loosing	ο	μην
2S	ἐλύου	ου[a]	You were loosing	ε	σο [ου]
3S	ἐλύετο	ετο	He/she/it was loosing	ε	το
1P	ἐλυόμεθα	ομεθα	We were loosing	ο	μεθα
2P	ἐλύεσθε	εσθε	You were loosing	ε	σθε
3P	ἐλύοντο	οντο	They were loosing	ο	ντο

[a] Technically, the ending is -σο, but the σ drops out when squeezed between the connecting vowel (ε) and the omicron. As a result, ε + ο lengthens to -ου. (Just learn it as -ου and do not worry about the rest—it is always -ου.)

Imperfect Passive Indicative of λύω[a]

	Form	c.v. + D p.e.	Gloss	c.v.	p.e.
1S	ἐλυόμην	ομην	I was being loosed	ο	μην
2S	ἐλύου	ου[b]	You were being loosed	ε	σο [ου]
3S	ἐλύετο	ετο	He/she/it was being loosed	ε	το
1P	ἐλυόμεθα	ομεθα	We were being loosed	ο	μεθα
2P	ἐλύεσθε	εσθε	You were being loosed	ε	σθε
3P	ἐλύοντο	οντο	They were being loosed	ο	ντο

[a] These forms, which are identical to the imperfect middle indicative forms, should be parsed as passive only if there is an agent marker in the context that indicates passive rather than middle.

[b] See the note on the Imperfect Middle Indicative chart above. The second singular ending is -σο, but the σ drops out, and ε + ο lengthens to -ου.

Function of the Imperfect

16.7. The substantive difference between the present and imperfect forms is *remoteness*. The imperfect is used in statements that are more remote than statements using the present. The imperfect may be logically, temporally, physically, or focally remote compared to the present tense-form. The imperfect often has a *discourse function* in narrative: it supplies background information or sometimes introduces dialogue or summary statements.

Here is an illustration from a short passage in Mark. The clauses containing the main story-line verbs are marked in bold type (these sketch the basic events of the story), and the background details (the imperfect forms) are in italics. (Since we have not studied all the forms yet, we will not distinguish other forms in this example.)

Verbal Forms in Mark 2:1–4

When he had come back to Capernaum several days later,
it was heard
that he was at home.
Many were gathered together,
so that there was no longer room, even near the door;
he was speaking the word to them.
They came,
bringing to him a paralytic,
carried by four men.
Being unable to get to him because of the crowd,
they removed the roof
where he was,
and when they had dug an opening,
they let down the pallet
on which the paralytic was lying.

Can you see how the *imperfects* are working here? The first tells us what Jesus was doing when the paralytic arrived: he was teaching. This is not the main point of the story, but it helps you understand the setting—it is background information. The second imperfect fills in some more background information. The reader might assume that the paralytic was still on the pallet, so it is not necessary to say so, but Mark tucks it in with the more remote imperfect form for clarity.

16.8. When this discourse function of backgrounding is recognized, it is not necessary to insist on the traditional equivalent, "I was loosing" (for ἔλυον). Doing so avoids two potential problems. First, in English it is often more natural to use a simple "I loosed." This is the same as a common aorist equivalent. Doing so precludes guessing the tense-form from the translation, but that is always precarious business anyway. Second, it avoids confusing the semantics of verbal aspect with considerations that are more properly connected with *Aktionsart*. Too often it is assumed that an imperfect tense-form intends to describe an action that is extended in time. Although that is sometimes true, that may not be the point a Greek writer is making by selecting the remote imperfective aspect. It is true that imperfective aspect views a situation as a process, but by itself that says nothing about the actual nature of the situation. If instead we focus on the function of the tense-form, then we can ask, How is that said most naturally in English? If a writer intends a focus on the inceptive or ongoing nature of an action, then lexis and context are necessary adjuncts to communicate this.

16.9. Examples of Imperfects

Mark 1:21, εἰσπορεύονται εἰς Καφαρναούμ· καὶ εὐθὺς[a] τοῖς σάββασιν εἰσελθὼν (having entered) εἰς τὴν συναγωγὴν **ἐδίδασκεν**.	They went to Capernaum, then on the Sabbath, having entered the synagogue, *he was teaching*.

[a] For καὶ εὐθύς, see the note on Mark 1:12 in §4.11.

Mark 2:24, οἱ Φαρισαῖοι **ἔλεγον** αὐτῷ, Ἴδε τί ποιοῦσιν τοῖς σάββασιν ὃ οὐκ ἔξεστιν;	The Pharisees *said* to him, "Look, why are they doing on the Sabbath what is not lawful?"
Acts 8:3, Σαῦλος **ἐλυμαίνετο** τὴν ἐκκλησίαν.	Saul *was wreaking havoc on* the church.
Acts 8:12, ὅτε δὲ ἐπίστευσαν τῷ Φιλίππῳ εὐαγγελιζομένῳ περὶ τῆς βασιλείας τοῦ θεοῦ καὶ τοῦ ὀνόματος Ἰησοῦ Χριστοῦ, **ἐβαπτίζοντο** ἄνδρες τε καὶ γυναῖκες.	But when they believed Philip, who was proclaiming the good news concerning the kingdom of God and the name of Jesus Christ, *they were baptized*, both men and women.
Gen. 2:6, πηγὴ δὲ **ἐπότιζεν** πᾶν τὸ πρόσωπον τῆς γῆς.	A spring *watered* all the surface of the ground.

Imperfect Forms of εἰμί

16.10. You *must* be able to recognize the following forms of εἰμί when you see them. They are not hard if you stop and evaluate how these forms are created. Most are the normal B-quad endings added to a stem that consists of only ε—which lengthens to η because of the augment (see explanation of the lengthening below). The two odd forms are the first singular and the third plural. The first singular appears to use a D ending, and the third plural uses an alternate secondary ending (that you will see again in the aorist passive). The nu in the third singular ending is *not* movable; it will always be present.

Imperfect [Active] Indicative of εἰμί

	Form	Frequency NT/LXX	Gloss	Alternate Forms (NT/LXX)
1S	ἤμην	15/45	I was	
2S	ἦς	56/3	You were	or ἦσθα (2/16)
3S	ἦν	413/853	He was	
1P	ἦμεν	8/5	We were	or ἤμεθα (5/2)
2P	ἦτε	19/12	You were	
3P	ἦσαν	95/272	They were	

The numbers following the form indicate the number of times that form occurs in the NT/LXX. As you can tell, there is one (third singular) that is far more common than any of the rest, and only one other (third plural) that is somewhat common. The last column lists two alternate forms that are sometimes used.

Many grammars list this form as simply the "imperfect indicative" of εἰμί because there are no other forms in the imperfect.[6] That is, there is no imperfect middle or imperfect passive of εἰμί, so calling it an active does not mean very much. On the other hand, the endings used are B-quad endings (though irregular). Most students seem to find it easier to keep the parsing consistent with other verb forms and include "active" in the parsing. Your teacher may prefer that you do it differently, so follow their advice.

Caution!

The third singular imperfect form of εἰμί can be easily confused with the relative pronoun, since it looks very much like the feminine singular accusative form of that pronoun. The difference is only the accent and the breathing mark. If it has a circumflex and smooth breathing, it is a form of εἰμί (ἦν), but if it has an acute or grave accent and rough breathing, it is the relative pronoun, ἥν (which, in context, often appears with the grave accent, ἣν).

6. It has also been referred to as the *augmented form* of εἰμί in contrast to the *unaugmented form* (i.e., what this book calls the present [active] indicative).

16.11. Examples of Imperfect Forms of εἰμί

Mark 4:36, ἀφέντες τὸν ὄχλον παραλαμβάνουσιν αὐτὸν ὡς **ἦν** ἐν τῷ πλοίῳ, καὶ ἄλλα πλοῖα **ἦν** μετ' αὐτοῦ.

Leaving the crowd, they took him as *he was* in the boat, and other boats *were* with him.

John 11:21, εἶπεν (she said) οὖν ἡ Μάρθα πρὸς τὸν Ἰησοῦν, Κύριε, εἰ **ἦς** ὧδε οὐκ ἄν[a] ἀπέθανεν (he died) ὁ ἀδελφός μου.

Therefore Martha said to Jesus, "Lord, if *you were* here,[b] then my brother would not have died."

[a] The paired words εἰ . . . ἄν tell you that this statement is assumed not to be true. We will study this construction in chap. 30.

[b] In more formal English, we would say "if you had been here." The less formal use has been retained here for continuity with the typical glosses for the imperfect of εἰμί as given in the preceding section.

Mark 14:67, αὐτῷ λέγει, Καὶ σὺ μετὰ τοῦ Ναζαρηνοῦ **ἦσθα**[a] τοῦ Ἰησοῦ.

She said to him, "You also *were* with the Nazarene, Jesus."

[a] Notice the alternate form of εἰμί that is used.

Gen. 2:25, **ἦσαν** οἱ δύο γυμνοί, ὅ τε Ἀδὰμ καὶ ἡ γυνὴ αὐτοῦ, καὶ οὐκ ᾐσχύνοντο.[a]

The two *were* naked, both Adam and his wife, and they were not ashamed.

[a] Notice also the imperfect form of αἰσχύνω.

Augment Variations

16.12. The augment used on secondary forms is always an epsilon on the front of the verb stem, but it does not always look exactly like that. There are some situations in which it lengthens or is not the first letter. (You saw some of these variations when you studied the aorist forms in chap. 7, so some of this is review, but other similar changes will be new. The examples below include both imperfect and aorist forms.)

In words beginning with a vowel, the augment lengthens the vowel. Both alpha and epsilon lengthen to an eta.

ἀκούω ▸ ἤκουον
ἔρχομαι ▸ ἠρχόμην
εὑρίσκω ▸ ηὕρισκον[7]

Mark 12:37, ὁ πολὺς ὄχλος **ἤκουεν** αὐτοῦ ἡδέως.

The large crowd *heard* him gladly.

Mark 2:13, πᾶς ὁ ὄχλος **ἤρχετο** πρὸς αὐτόν, καὶ ἐδίδασκεν αὐτούς.

All the crowd *came* to him, and he taught them.

7. Sometimes εὑρίσκω does not lengthen the initial vowel, so you will occasionally see εὕρισκον.

Acts 7:11, οὐχ **ηὕρισκον** χορτάσματα οἱ πατέρες ἡμῶν.	Our fathers [i.e., ancestors] did not *find* food.

An omicron lengthens to omega.

ὀνειδίζω ("I reproach") ▸ ὠνείδιζον

Mark 15:32, οἱ συνεσταυρωμένοι (being crucified together) σὺν αὐτῷ **ὠνείδιζον** αὐτόν.	Those being crucified with him *were mocking* him.

16.13. The diphthongs αι and οι follow the same pattern, lengthening to ῃ and ῳ respectively. The iota becomes subscript when the initial vowel lengthens.[8]

αι ▸ ῃ
οι ▸ ῳ

Acts 12:20, **ᾐτοῦντο**[a] εἰρήνην.	*They asked for* peace.

[a] ᾐτοῦντο ▸ αἰτέω, an ε contract verb, "I ask"

Luke 17:28, ὁμοίως καθὼς ἐγένετο ἐν ταῖς ἡμέραις Λώτ· ἤσθιον, ἔπινον, ἠγόραζον, ἐπώλουν, ἐφύτευον, **ᾠκοδόμουν.**[a]	Likewise as it was in the days of Lot: they were eating, drinking, buying, selling, planting, [and] *building*.

[a] There are six imperfect verbs in this verse, including a form of οἰκοδομέω, "I build."

Words beginning with the long vowels iota and upsilon or with a diphthong such as ευ do not change to indicate the presence of an augment—since they are already long, they cannot lengthen any further.[9] These verbs are said to have an *implicit augment*. The only way you know the verb is augmented is because it has a secondary ending.

Mark 5:4, οὐδεὶς **ἴσχυεν**[a] αὐτὸν δαμάσαι.	No one *was strong enough* to bind him.

[a] ἰσχύω, "I am strong"

Acts 16:25, Παῦλος καὶ Σιλᾶς **ὕμνουν**[a] τὸν θεόν.	Paul and Silas *were singing praise to* God.

[a] ὑμνέω, an ε contract verb, "I sing in praise of/to"

Mark 6:31, οὐδὲ φαγεῖν **εὐκαίρουν.**	They did not *have time* to eat.

8. There are also a few instances in which ει lengthens to η, but that is only with internal augments in compound forms of εἰμί (e.g., ἀπῄεσαν)—but those are odd forms anyway. (See the explanation in the text regarding augments that occur within a word.)

9. One of the more common verbs that begin with ευ is εὑρίσκω, but most of the augmented forms of this verb that occur in the NT and LXX are ones that you have not learned yet.

16.14. In compound verbs, the augment appears *between* the preposition and stem. This is sometimes called an *internal augment*. Some prefixed prepositions change their spelling slightly when the augment is inserted on the front of the stem. These are the same changes that you learned in §9.6, so they should be easy to identify.

προσδέχομαι ▸ προσεδεχόμην
ἀποθνῄσκω ▸ ἀπέθνῃσκον
ἐκβάλλω ▸ ἐξέβαλλον

Luke 23:51, ὃς **προσεδέχετο**[a] τὴν βασιλείαν τοῦ θεοῦ — Who *was waiting for* the kingdom of God

[a] προσεδέχετο ▸ προσδέχομαι, "I wait for"

Luke 8:42, θυγάτηρ μονογενὴς καὶ αὐτὴ **ἀπέθνῃσκεν**[a] — An only daughter, and *she was dying*

[a] ἀπέθνῃσκεν ▸ ἀποθνῄσκω, "I die"

Mark 6:13, δαιμόνια πολλὰ **ἐξέβαλλον**.[a] — *They cast out* many demons.

[a] ἐξέβαλλον ▸ ἐκβάλλω, "I throw out"

Compound augmented verbs that prefix a preposition ending with a vowel *usually* drop the vowel; the augment takes its place.

καταβαίνω ▸ κατέβαινον
ὑποστέλλω ▸ ὑπέστελλον

Luke 10:30, ὁ Ἰησοῦς εἶπεν, Ἄνθρωπός τις **κατέβαινεν**[a] ἀπὸ Ἰερουσαλὴμ εἰς Ἰεριχώ. — Jesus said, "A certain man *was going down* from Jerusalem to Jericho."

[a] κατέβαινεν ▸ καταβαίνω, "I go down"

Gal. 2:12, ὅτε δὲ ἦλθον, **ὑπέστελλεν**[a] καὶ ἀφώριζεν ἑαυτόν. — But when they came, *he drew back* and separated himself.

[a] ὑπέστελλεν ▸ ὑποστέλλω, "I draw back"

16.15. Now You Try It

Mark 3:11, τὰ πνεύματα τὰ ἀκάθαρτα **προσέπιπτον** αὐτῷ καὶ **ἔκραζον** ὅτι Σὺ εἶ ὁ υἱὸς τοῦ θεοῦ.

Mark 14:49, καθ' ἡμέραν **ἤμην** πρὸς ὑμᾶς ἐν τῷ ἱερῷ.

John 4:6, **ἦν** δὲ ἐκεῖ πηγὴ τοῦ Ἰακώβ. ὁ οὖν Ἰησοῦς κεκοπιακὼς (being weary) ἐκ τῆς ὁδοιπορίας **ἐκαθέζετο** οὕτως ἐπὶ τῇ πηγῇ· ὥρα **ἦν** ὡς ἕκτη.

Acts 3:2, καί τις ἀνὴρ χωλὸς ἐκ κοιλίας μητρὸς αὐτοῦ **ἐβαστάζετο**.

Acts 12:24, Ὁ δὲ λόγος τοῦ θεοῦ **ηὔξανεν** καὶ **ἐπληθύνετο**.

Gen. 41:2, ἰδοὺ ὥσπερ ἐκ τοῦ ποταμοῦ **ἀνέβαινον** ἑπτὰ βόες καλαὶ τῷ εἴδει καὶ ἐκλεκταὶ ταῖς σαρξὶν καὶ **ἐβόσκοντο** ἐν τῷ ἄχει (grass).

1 Clem. 50.5, μακάριοί ἐσμεν, ἀγαπητοί, εἰ τὰ προστάγματα τοῦ θεοῦ **ἐποιοῦμεν** ἐν ὁμονοίᾳ[a] ἀγάπης.

[a] ὁμόνοια, ας, ἡ, "oneness of mind, unanimity, concord, harmony"

16.16. Challenge Verse

1 En. 14.8, ἐμοὶ ἐφ' ὁράσει οὕτως ἐδείχθη (it was shown)· ἰδοὺ νεφέλαι ἐν τῇ ὁράσει **ἐκάλουν** καὶ ὁμίχλαι με **ἐφώνουν**, καὶ διαδρομαὶ τῶν ἀστέρων καὶ διαστραπαί[a] με **κατεσπούδαζον**[b] καὶ **ἐθορύβαζόν** με, καὶ ἄνεμοι ἐν τῇ ὁράσει μου ἐξεπέτασάν (they stunned) με.

[a] διαστραπή, ῆς, ἡ, "lightning"
[b] κατασπουδάζω, "I am troubled or bothered"

Reading Passage: Mark 6:2–6

16.17. Notes have been provided to help you with forms you do not know yet. All the rest you should be able to figure out. Use your lexicon as needed. Pay particular attention to the ways in which the six imperfect tense-forms *function* in this paragraph. There are more in this short text than you will usually find in similar-length paragraphs.

A Prophet without Honor

[2]γενομένου σαββάτου[a] ἤρξατο (he began) διδάσκειν ἐν τῇ συναγωγῇ, καὶ πολλοὶ ἀκούοντες (hearing) **ἐξεπλήσσοντο** λέγοντες (saying), Πόθεν τούτῳ ταῦτα, καὶ τίς ἡ σοφία ἡ δοθεῖσα (which has been given) τούτῳ, καὶ αἱ δυνάμεις τοιαῦται διὰ τῶν χειρῶν αὐτοῦ γινόμεναι (are happening); [3]οὐχ οὗτός ἐστιν ὁ τέκτων, ὁ υἱὸς τῆς Μαρίας καὶ ἀδελφὸς Ἰακώβου καὶ Ἰωσῆτος καὶ Ἰούδα καὶ Σίμωνος; καὶ οὐκ εἰσὶν αἱ ἀδελφαὶ αὐτοῦ ὧδε πρὸς ἡμᾶς; καὶ **ἐσκανδαλίζοντο** ἐν αὐτῷ. [4]καὶ **ἔλεγεν** αὐτοῖς ὁ Ἰησοῦς ὅτι Οὐκ ἔστιν προφήτης ἄτιμος εἰ μὴ ἐν τῇ πατρίδι αὐτοῦ καὶ ἐν τοῖς συγγενεῦσιν αὐτοῦ καὶ ἐν τῇ οἰκίᾳ αὐτοῦ. [5]καὶ οὐκ **ἐδύνατο**[b] ἐκεῖ ποιῆσαι (to do) οὐδεμίαν δύναμιν, εἰ μὴ ὀλίγοις ἀρρώστοις ἐπιθεὶς (placing) τὰς χεῖρας ἐθεράπευσεν. [6]καὶ **ἐθαύμαζεν** διὰ τὴν ἀπιστίαν αὐτῶν. Καὶ **περιῆγεν** τὰς κώμας κύκλῳ διδάσκων (teaching).

[a] γενομένου σαββάτου, "when it was the Sabbath" (a genitive absolute construction, which you will learn in chap. 27)

[b] Compare the forms of δύναμαι given at the end of chap. 15.

16.18. Vocabulary for Chapter 16

Part of Speech	Definition	Possible Glosses	Frequency	
Word			NT	LXX
Adjectives				
ἕκαστος, η, ον	An individual person or thing, each one of an aggregate in an individual sense; can also be used as a substantive	each, every; each one, everyone	82	356
πιστός, ή, όν	Worthy of trust, of dependable character; characterized by trust, "believing"; one who confesses the Christian faith, "believer" (subst.) [cf. the noun πίστις]	faithful, dependable, trustworthy; believing; believer	67	75
ἀγαπητός, ή, όν	To be in a special relationship with another, to be loved/esteemed	beloved, dear, esteemed	61	24
Adverbs				
πῶς	An interrogative adverb that inquires as to the manner or way in which something is by requesting information or clarification, expressing surprise, criticism, or deliberation; an exclamatory marker	how? how!	103	129
ἔτι	A function word indicating continuation (or with a negative, lack of it) or addition (ctr. ἤδη, "already")	still, yet; (not) anymore, any longer	93	549
Foreign Word				
ἀμήν	A transliterated Hebrew word expressing strong affirmation of what is stated, often used by Jesus and later by Christians in a worshipful context	amen, truly, verily, "so let it be"	129	10

Part of Speech	Definition	Possible Glosses	Frequency	
Word			NT	LXX
Interjection				
ἰδού	A demonstrative particle that draws attention to what follows or marks strong emphasis	behold! see! look! (or just "!")	200	1,145
Nouns				
τόπος, ου, ὁ	A spatial area, whether a specific named locality or a general reference; the location for an object or activity, etc.	place, location, space	94	613
δικαιοσύνη, ης, ἡ	A state that is in accord with standards for acceptable behavior; being in a right relationship with God, either declaratively (the result of justification) or practically (living in such a way as to reflect the judicial reality)	uprightness, righteousness	92	351
εἰρήνη, ης, ἡ	A state of concord or harmony in personal or political relationships; a state of well-being (used as a greeting)	peace	92	294
θάλασσα, ης, ἡ	A large body of salt water; a large inland body of fresh water	sea; lake	91	450
Verbs				
ἦν	An inflected verb form: 3rd sg. impf. (act.) ind. of εἰμί	he/she/it was	413	1,297
δεῖ	An impersonal verb expressing what is necessary, compulsory, or fitting	it is necessary; one must; it had to be	101	50
ὑπάρχω	To be present; to come into being; what belongs to someone (subst. neut. ptc.)	I am, exist; property, holdings, possessions (subst.)	60	157
συνάγω	To bring together as a group (either people or things)	I gather/call together, assemble	59	377

16.19. Key Things to Know for Chapter 16

What is the aspect of the imperfect tense-form?

Be sure that you keep the terms *imperfect* and *imperfective* distinct in your thinking.

The formulas for imperfect active indicative and imperfect middle indicative verbs.

You should know the standard B and D endings. (You first learned the B endings when you met the aorist, but they looked slightly different there due to the form marker σα.)

Remember that the endings given in the four-quad chart *include* the connecting vowels to make them easier to pronounce and therefore easier to memorize.

Since both the present and the imperfect tense-forms express imperfective aspect, how do they differ?

Can you recognize an augment even if it occurs in one of the variations discussed in this chapter?

17

VERBS: PART 7

Aorist (Perfective) Indicative Verbs

17.1. You have previously met some of the most common aorist tense-forms, the first aorist active indicatives and the aorist active infinitive. In this chapter we will review those forms and meet some new forms of the aorist.

Meaning of the Aorist

17.2. You have already learned (chap. 7) that the aorist simply refers to a situation in summary without indicating anything further about the action. In chapter 13 we studied *verbal aspect* and learned that it refers to the way in which a speaker or writer chooses to view a situation. The aorist tense-form identifies that perspective as perfective aspect; it describes a complete situation, referring to it as a whole without commenting on whether or not it involves a process. You have already seen many aorist verbs used in various contexts, so now it is time to learn some new forms and discover how they are used to communicate meaning in a wider variety of settings.

Forms of the Aorist

17.3. You already know the aorist active infinitive, λῦσαι, and the aorist active indicative forms. We will review them first and then add the aorist middle and aorist passive forms.

Formula for First Aorist Active Indicative Verbs

augment + stem + form marker σα + B personal endings

(First) Aorist Active Indicative of λύω

	Form	f.m. + B p.e.	Gloss	p.e.
1S	ἔλυσα	σα	I loosed	-[ν]
2S	ἔλυσας	σας	You loosed	ς
3S	ἔλυσε(ν)	σε(ν)	He/she/it loosed	-(ν)
1P	ἐλύσαμεν	σαμεν	We loosed	μεν
2P	ἐλύσατε	σατε	You loosed	τε
3P	ἔλυσαν	σαν	They loosed	ν

17.4. *Review Verses*

Rom. 5:14, ἀλλὰ **ἐβασίλευσεν** ὁ θάνατος ἀπὸ Ἀδὰμ μέχρι Μωϋσέως.

Rom. 13:11, νῦν γὰρ ἐγγύτερον[a] ἡμῶν ἡ σωτηρία ἢ ὅτε **ἐπιστεύσαμεν.**

[a] ἐγγύτερον is a comparative form of ἐγγύς (see §6.38).

John 19:10, λέγει οὖν αὐτῷ ὁ Πιλᾶτος, Ἐξουσίαν ἔχω **ἀπολῦσαί** σε.

Gen. 2:8, **ἐφύτευσεν** κύριος ὁ θεὸς παράδεισον ἐν Ἐδέμ.

Gen. 15:6, **ἐπίστευσεν** Ἀβράμ τῷ θεῷ.

Gen. 37:27, **ἤκουσαν** δὲ οἱ ἀδελφοὶ αὐτοῦ.

Perfective versus Punctiliar

You should not confuse the Greek perfective aspect with the English description *punctiliar*. *Punctiliar* describes a momentary action as occurring in a single point of time. Just because the Greek perfective aspect describes something as a whole in summary fashion does not mean that it happens in a punctiliar way. The perfective aspect *can* be used to describe a punctiliar action (e.g., "he fell dead"). However, a verb that refers to a punctiliar action is punctiliar not because of the aspect of the Greek verb but because of the context and the meaning of the words. That is, we know that "fell dead" happens only once—and quickly at that (punctiliar)—because of the combination of the two words "fell" and "dead." The same verb ("die") could also be used to portray the same situation as a process by using the imperfective form ("he was dying") or a state of affairs ("he is dead").

First Aorist Middle Indicative

17.5. The (first) aorist middle indicative follows the same pattern as the aorist active indicative except that it uses the D set of endings. You have already seen all these pieces used in other forms, so the only thing you need to remember is the formula to identify this combination.

Formula for Aorist Middle Indicative Verbs

augment + stem + form marker σα + D personal endings

The forms will look like this. The last column in the chart below ("IMI endings") gives the standard D endings as seen with the connecting vowel in the imperfect middle indicative; when added to the aorist form marker σα, the D endings produce the forms in the second column. Since the aorist form marker ends with a vowel, there is no need for a separate connecting vowel, so it is omitted.

Aorist Middle Indicative of λύω

	Form	f.m. + D p.e.	Gloss	p.e.	IMI endings
1S	ἐλυσάμην	σαμην	I loosed	μην	ομην
2S	ἐλύσω	σω	You loosed	σο[a]	ου
3S	ἐλύσατο	σατο	He/she/it loosed	το	ετο
1P	ἐλυσάμεθα	σαμεθα	We loosed	μεθα	ομεθα
2P	ἐλύσασθε	σασθε	You loosed	σθε	εσθε
3P	ἐλύσαντο	σαντο	They loosed	ντο	οντο

[a] The technical ending for second singular is -σο, but when it is added to the form marker σα, the sigma in the ending drops out when squeezed between two vowels, and the alpha from the form marker and the omicron in the ending contract to form omega. This is slightly different from what occurs in the imperfect, where the resulting form is -ου. The second person singular aorist middle form is not common in the NT or the LXX.

17.6. *Examples of Aorist Middle Indicative*

Luke 14:4, **ἰάσατο** αὐτόν.	He *healed* him.
Acts 1:11, **ἐθεάσασθε** αὐτὸν πορευόμενον (going) εἰς τὸν οὐρανόν.	You *saw* him going into heaven.
Acts 2:26, διὰ τοῦτο **ηὐφράνθη**... **ἠγαλλιάσατο** ἡ γλῶσσά μου.	On account of this my tongue *rejoices*.
Gal. 3:27, ὅσοι γὰρ εἰς Χριστὸν ἐβαπτίσθητε (you have been baptized), Χριστὸν **ἐνεδύσασθε**.	For as many of you as have been baptized into Christ *have put on* Christ.
Gen. 24:18–19, ἐπότισεν αὐτόν, ἕως **ἐπαύσατο** πίνων.	She gave him a drink until *he stopped* drinking.[a]

[a] This passage refers to Rebecca serving Abraham's servant.

17.7. *Now You Try It*

1 Pet. 2:2–3, ὡς βρέφη τὸ γάλα ἐπιποθήσατε (desire!), εἰ **ἐγεύσασθε** ὅτι χρηστὸς ὁ κύριος.

What is the subject of ἐγεύσασθε? What does the ὅτι clause tell you? What verb must you supply in the ὅτι clause?

John 11:53, **ἐβουλεύσαντο** ἵνα ἀποκτείνωσιν (they should kill) αὐτόν.

What is the subject of ἐβουλεύσαντο? What does the ἵνα clause tell you? How does αὐτόν relate to the other words in the sentence?

John 12:10, **ἐβουλεύσαντο** δὲ οἱ ἀρχιερεῖς (chief priests) ἵνα καὶ τὸν Λάζαρον ἀποκτείνωσιν.

What is the subject of ἐβουλεύσαντο? What nuance does καί add to the second clause?

Gen. 11:8, **ἐπαύσαντο** οἰκοδομοῦντες (building) τὴν πόλιν καὶ τὸν πύργον.

Who is doing the action? How do you know? What is the function of καί?

Gen. 12:8, **ἐπεκαλέσατο** ἐπὶ τῷ ὀνόματι (name) κυρίου.

Gen. 26:22, ὤρυξεν[a] φρέαρ[b] ἕτερον, καὶ οὐκ **ἐμαχέσαντο** περὶ αὐτοῦ.

[a] ὀρύσσω, "I dig"

[b] φρέαρ, ατος, τό, "a water well"

Minor Aorist Variations

17.8. As you have already seen in previous chapters, there are sometimes some minor variations from what the formula predicts. Many aorist middle forms reflect one or both of the minor variations described below or are second aorist forms (described in chap. 18).

See if you can figure out some of these variations on your own *before* reading the explanation. The examples below are mostly aorist active forms, though the same patterns hold for aorist middle forms as well.

Think . . .

What is different about the next two aorist verb forms from what you might have expected?

The third singular aorist active indicative form of ζητέω is ἐζήτησεν.

The third plural aorist active indicative form of πληρόω is ἐπλήρωσαν.

Contract Verbs

17.9. We have already seen contract verbs in earlier chapters (for aorist contracts, see §7.18), and we will talk about them in more detail in chapter 21. For now all you need to know is that when a verb stem ends with an epsilon, omicron, or alpha, that stem vowel lengthens when a form marker is added. They lengthen as follows:

ε ▸ η
ο ▸ ω
α ▸ η

It does not matter which form marker is used. In the case of an aorist, the lengthening takes place when the form marker σα is added, but it will happen in other forms that use different form markers. Thus the aorist of ἀγαπάω is ἠγάπησα (not ἠγάπασα), ζητέω becomes ἐζήτησα, and πληρόω becomes ἐπλήρωσα.

17.10. Examples

Mark 1:11, φωνὴ ἐγένετο (came) ἐκ τῶν οὐρανῶν, Σὺ εἶ ὁ υἱός μου ὁ ἀγαπητός, ἐν σοὶ **εὐδόκησα.**	A voice came from heaven: "You are my beloved Son, with you *I am pleased.*"
Luke 20:19, Καὶ **ἐζήτησαν** οἱ γραμματεῖς καὶ οἱ ἀρχιερεῖς ἐπιβαλεῖν ἐπ' αὐτὸν τὰς χεῖρας.	The scribes and the chief priests *sought* to lay hands on him [i.e., to arrest him].
Acts 5:3, εἶπεν δὲ ὁ Πέτρος, Ἀνανία, διὰ τί **ἐπλήρωσεν** ὁ Σατανᾶς τὴν καρδίαν σου ψεύσασθαι (to lie).	Peter said, "Ananias, why has Satan *filled* your heart to lie?"
Rom. 1:19, διότι τὸ γνωστὸν τοῦ θεοῦ φανερόν ἐστιν ἐν αὐτοῖς· ὁ θεὸς γὰρ αὐτοῖς **ἐφανέρωσεν.**	Because what is known about God is plain in them, for God *has made it plain* in them.
Gen. 1:5, **ἐκάλεσεν** ὁ θεὸς τὸ φῶς ἡμέραν καὶ τὸ σκότος **ἐκάλεσεν** νύκτα.	God *called* the light "day," and the darkness *he called* "night."

There are a few contract verbs in which the stem vowel does *not* lengthen; καλέω is one of the most common such verbs (see also Gen. 12:8 in the previous section).

17.11. Now You Try It

John 3:16, Οὕτως γὰρ **ἠγάπησεν** ὁ θεὸς τὸν κόσμον.	What is the subject, verb, and object in this statement?
Mark 15:43, Ἰωσὴφ ὁ ἀπὸ Ἁριμαθαίας[a] εἰσῆλθεν (he came) πρὸς τὸν Πιλᾶτον καὶ **ᾐτήσατο** τὸ σῶμα τοῦ Ἰησοῦ.	Can you figure out what happened to the augment on ᾐτήσατο? What case must σῶμα be, nom. or acc.? (Remember neuter nouns have the same form in both cases.) How do you know?

[a] Ἰωσὴφ ὁ ἀπὸ Ἁριμαθαίας, "Joseph, the one from Arimathea," or simply "Joseph of Arimathea"

Rom. 9:13, καθὼς γέγραπται (it is written), Τὸν Ἰακὼβ **ἠγάπησα**, τὸν δὲ Ἠσαῦ **ἐμίσησα**.

Gen. 1:1, Ἐν ἀρχῇ **ἐποίησεν** ὁ θεὸς τὸν οὐρανὸν καὶ τὴν γῆν.

1 Clem. 8.1, Οἱ λειτουργοὶ τῆς χάριτος τοῦ θεοῦ διὰ πνεύματος ἁγίου περὶ μετανοίας **ἐλάλησαν**.

17.12. *Think . . .*

What is different about the following aorist verb forms from what you might have expected? Do you recognize a consistent pattern of changes? (These are *not* contract verbs.)

The first singular aorist active indicative form of γράφω is ἔγραψα.

The third singular aorist middle indicative form of γράφω is ἐγράψατο.

The second singular aorist active indicative form of διδάσκω is ἐδίδαξας.

The third plural aorist active indicative form of διδάσκω is ἐδίδαξαν.

The Square of Stops

17.13. Do you remember the square of stops? You first met this phenomenon in connection with third-declension nouns in which certain letters combined with a sigma to produce a related hybrid letter. This time the sigma comes from the form marker σα, which is added to the stem. Whenever such a sigma is added to a stem that ends with one of the nine consonants that form the square of stops, it combines exactly the same as it did in the third declension.

			+ σ =
π	β	φ	ψ
κ	γ	χ	ξ
τ	δ	θ	σ

Thus βλέπω + σα results in ἔβλεψα (not ἔβλεπσα), because π + σ = ψ. You can see these changes in the following examples. A verb whose stem ends in -ιζω or -αζω also acts like a square-of-stops form. Such verbs follow the pattern of the third row.[1]

17.14. Examples

1 Cor. 5:9, **Ἔγραψα** ὑμῖν ἐν τῇ ἐπιστολῇ. — *I wrote* to you in the letter.

1. Though you do not need to know why, if you are curious, it is often because the actual verb root ends with a delta.

John 7:28, **ἔκραξεν** οὖν ἐν τῷ ἱερῷ ὁ Ἰησοῦς, Κἀμὲ οἴδατε καὶ οἴδατε πόθεν εἰμί.

Therefore Jesus *cried out* in the temple, "You know me, and you know from where I am."

Mark 10:20, Διδάσκαλε, ταῦτα πάντα **ἐφυλαξάμην** ἐκ νεότητός μου.

"Teacher, all these things *I have kept* from my youth."

Mark 14:6, ὁ δὲ Ἰησοῦς εἶπεν, Καλὸν ἔργον **ἠργάσατο**[a] ἐν ἐμοί.

But Jesus said, "*She has done* a good deed for me."

[a] ἐργάζομαι; the subject of the verb is a woman.

Ign. *Phld.* 10.2, ὡς καὶ[a] αἱ ἔγγιστα ἐκκλησίαι **ἔπεμψαν** ἐπισκόπους, αἱ δὲ πρεσβυτέρους καὶ διακόνους.[b]

Indeed the neighboring churches *sent* overseers, and the [other churches sent] elders and deacons.

[a] ὡς καί introduces a decisive reason, represented in English here as "indeed."

[b] Ignatius has requested that the church at Philadelphia send a deacon as a messenger to the church in Syrian Antioch. This statement is part of his "encouragement" for them to do so, suggesting that if other churches have already done so, surely they could do the same.

17.15. Now You Try It

Luke 11:1, Ἰωάννης **ἐδίδαξεν** τοὺς μαθητὰς αὐτοῦ.

What is the subject and object of ἐδίδαξεν? What is unusual about the *form* of the subject?

John 19:19, **ἔγραψεν** δὲ καὶ τίτλον ὁ Πιλᾶτος καὶ ἔθηκεν (he placed [it]) ἐπὶ τοῦ σταυροῦ.

Who did the writing? Where did he place the τίτλον?

John 13:12, **ἔνιψεν** τοὺς πόδας[a] αὐτῶν.

To what was ἔνιψεν done?

[a] πόδας ▸ ποῦς (a third-declension form; go by the article to identify the case)

1 Cor. 15:1, Γνωρίζω δὲ ὑμῖν, ἀδελφοί, τὸ εὐαγγέλιον ὃ **εὐηγγελισάμην** ὑμῖν.

Gen. 14:8, **παρετάξαντο**[a] αὐτοῖς εἰς πόλεμον ἐν τῇ κοιλάδι[b] τῇ ἁλυκῇ.

[a] παρατάσσω, "I draw up in battle array"

[b] κοιλάς, άδος, ἡ, "valley"

Trad. Elders 2, Ποῦ οὖν ἐτέθη (he was placed) ὁ πρῶτος ἄνθρωπος; ἐν τῷ παραδείσῳ[a] δηλονότι,[b] καθὼς γέγραπται (it is written)· Καὶ **ἐφύτευσεν** ὁ θεὸς παράδεισον ἐν Ἐδέμ.[c]

[a] παράδεισος, ου, ὁ, "garden"

[b] δηλονότι, "clearly" (adv.)

[c] This text is sometimes cited as Papias 28.1 (some electronic editions), though it cannot be linked to Papias. It is cited here from Holmes, *Apostolic Fathers*, 768.

— — — — — — — — — — — — — —

Advanced Information for Reference:
Homonyms

17.16. Here is a tidbit worth knowing. Some verbs have a *different lexical meaning* in active and middle voice. It is possible that these are actually homonyms, two different words that are spelled the same. They came to be viewed as a single word since by convention one was used only in the active voice, the other only in middle. Most Greek lexicons list them as a single entry. This is not frequent, but at least one word for which this is true is a fairly common word, ἄρχω. Another is ἅπτω, "I kindle (a fire)" and ἅπτομαι, "I touch." The lexicon will tell you anything you need to know in regard to any other such words. Figure 17.1 shows the entry for ἄρχω in BDAG.[2]

ἄρχω fut. ἄρξω; 1 aor. ἦρξα LXX. Mid.: fut. ἄρξομαι; 1 aor. ἠρξάμην; pf. ἦργμαι (Hom.+) lit. *be first.*

❶ **to rule or govern, w. implication of special status,** ***rule*** act. w. gen. *over someth.* or *someone* (Hom., Hdt. et al.; UPZ 81 col. 2, 18 [II BC] as an epithet of Isis: τῶν ἐν τῷ κόσμῳ ἄρχουσα; En 9:7; EpArist 190; Demetr.: 722 fgm. 1, 12 Jac.; Philo, Congr. Erud. Gr. 6; Just., D. 90, 4; 111, 1) τῶν ἐθνῶν **Mk 10:42; Ro 15:12** (Is 11:10). εἰς πόλιν ἄρχουσαν δύσεως *into the city that rules over the West* ApcPt Rainer 15f. τῶν θηρίων τ. γῆς B 6:12 (cp. Gen 1:26, 28). τῆς περὶ τὴν γῆν διακοσμήσεως ἔδωκεν ἄ. (angels) *authority to govern the earth* Papias (4).

❷ **to initiate an action, process, or state of being,** ***begin*** mid., except for GMary s. 2aα.—ⓐ w. pres. inf. (DHesseling, Z. Syntax v. ἄρχομαι: ByzZ 20, 1911, 147–64; JKleist, Mk '36, 154–61 Marcan ἤρξατο; GReichenkron, Die Umschreibung m. occipere, incipere u. coepisse: Syntactica u. Stilistica, Festschr. EGamillscheg '57, 473–75; MReiser, Syntax u. Stil (Mk), '84, 43–45).

Figure 17.1. ἄρχω in BDAG

In the case of ἄρχω, which occurs 86 times in the NT, it usually occurs as an aorist middle indicative verb (60 of the 86 instances in the NT). It occurs in the NT only once as a present middle indicative. In the middle voice ἄρχω means "I begin" (84 times), but there are two instances in the NT of the active voice, which means "I rule." In the LXX the middle is also the most common, though the proportion is not so one-sided; the middle is used 99 times, and the active 48.

2. In this case, possibly through an oversight, *CL* omits the note that meaning 2 is for middle voice. If you are using *CL* as your lexicon, you will want to add a note in the margin to indicate this.

17.17. Examples of ἄρχω

Mark 4:1, πάλιν **ἤρξατο** διδάσκειν παρὰ τὴν θάλασσαν.

Again *he began* to teach beside the lake.

Gen. 45:26, ἀνήγγειλαν (they reported) αὐτῷ λέγοντες (saying) ὅτι Ὁ υἱός σου Ἰωσὴφ ζῇ (is alive), καὶ αὐτὸς **ἄρχει** πάσης γῆς Αἰγύπτου.

They reported to him, saying, "Your son Joseph is alive, and he *is ruling* all the land of Egypt."

17.18. Now You Try It

Acts 2:4, **ἤρξαντο** λαλεῖν ἑτέραις γλώσσαις.

Gen. 1:17–18, ἔθετο (he set) αὐτοὺς ὁ θεὸς ἐν τῷ στερεώματι (firmament) τοῦ οὐρανοῦ ὥστε φαίνειν ἐπὶ τῆς γῆς καὶ **ἄρχειν** τῆς ἡμέρας καὶ τῆς νυκτός.

— — — — — — — — — — — — — —

Aorist Passive Indicative Verbs

17.19. The aorist passive forms introduce two new features. First, a new form marker, θη, and second, the use of B personal endings with passive forms (which normally use C or D endings). The formula looks like this:

Formula for Aorist Passive Indicative Verbs

augment + stem[3] + form marker θη + B personal endings

As you study this formula and the chart below, you will notice that there is no connecting vowel. That is because the form marker θη ends with a vowel (eta), so another vowel is not needed to add the personal ending. The last column in the chart below shows the standard set of B endings (including the connecting vowel) for comparison. The θη form marker is used only for aorist passive forms.[4]

3. The stem used for aorist passive forms is usually the same as the present stem. That is, the stem will be spelled the same as you find it listed in the lexicon. There are some words for which the stem of the aorist passive forms changes spelling. The change is often relatively minor. Your best friend here will be your lexicon, which will note any significant changes. You can also check the catalog of verb forms in app. B of this textbook.

4. This statement will be qualified in the Advanced Information for Reference section at the end of this chapter. Although these forms have traditionally been designated as passive forms, they can sometimes be middle. They are introduced here as simply passive because that is their most common use.

Aorist Passive Indicative of λύω

	Form	(f.m.) + B p.e.[a]	Gloss	c.v. + p.e.
1S	ἐλύθην	ην	I was loosed	ον
2S	ἐλύθης	ης	You were loosed	ες
3S	ἐλύθη	η	He/she/it was loosed	ε(ν)
1P	ἐλύθημεν	ημεν	We were loosed	ομεν
2P	ἐλύθητε	ητε	You were loosed	ετε
3P	ἐλύθησαν	ησαν	They were loosed	ον

[a] This column gives the vowel from the end of the form marker with the B personal ending.

The third plural ending is -σαν. This is a variant ending used in place of the usual -ον. This verb form looks like it has two form markers: θη and σα. Technically it does not, but it may help you remember this form. (You might think of it as if the σα tells you aorist, and the θη before it tells you aorist passive.)

17.20. *Examples of Aorist Passive Indicative*

Mark 9:2, μετὰ ἡμέρας ἓξ παραλαμβάνει ὁ Ἰησοῦς τὸν Πέτρον καὶ τὸν Ἰάκωβον καὶ τὸν Ἰωάννην καὶ ἀναφέρει αὐτοὺς εἰς ὄρος ὑψηλὸν κατ᾽ ἰδίαν μόνους. καὶ **μετεμορφώθη** ἔμπροσθεν αὐτῶν.

After six days Jesus took Peter and James and John and led them up a high mountain by themselves alone; and *he was transformed* before them.

Mark 4:41, **ἐφοβήθησαν** φόβον μέγαν[a] καὶ ἔλεγον πρὸς ἀλλήλους, Τίς ἄρα οὗτός ἐστιν ὅτι καὶ ὁ ἄνεμος καὶ ἡ θάλασσα ὑπακούει αὐτῷ;

They were terrified and said to one another, "Who, then, is this that even the wind and the lake obey him?!"

[a] ἐφοβήθησαν φόβον μέγαν is called a *cognate accusative* construction, in which the noun form of the verb follows in the accusative case. It is a very emphatic way of saying they were afraid; formally, "they were afraid with a great fear," or in normal English, "they were terrified." (Although Hebrew has a similar idiom, this is a native Greek construction.)

17.21. *Now You Try It*

Rom. 3:2, **ἐπιστεύθησαν** τὰ λόγια τοῦ θεοῦ.

In this verse πιστεύω does not mean "I believe." See your lexicon for other options.

Heb. 11:2, ἐν ταύτῃ γὰρ **ἐμαρτυρήθησαν** οἱ πρεσβύτεροι.

You will need to check your lexicon for translation options in this verse; two words do not have their simplest meaning that you have learned for vocabulary purposes.

Josephus, *Ant.* 13.419, Τιγράνης[a] [invaded] εἰς τὴν Συρίαν καί τοῦτο **ἐφόβησε**[b] τὴν βασίλισσαν[c] καὶ τὸ ἔθνος.

[a] This is the name of an Armenian king.

[b] This verb is *not* an aorist passive; it illustrates the active meaning of φοβέω: "I cause someone else to be afraid." (In the NT φοβέω is always passive; in the LXX only 2 of 435 instances are in active voice.)

[c] Check the spelling of this word carefully in your lexicon.

Expanding the Square of Stops

17.22. With the aorist passive form marker come a few additional changes in some verbs. You will remember the square of stops from your earlier study. In all previous instances in which we used that chart it was the addition of a sigma that triggered changes in the spelling of some words. The theta in the aorist passive can result in similar changes. Here is the chart with a new column added on the right.

			+ σ	+ θ
π	β	φ	ψ	φθ
κ	γ	χ	ξ	χθ
τ	δ	θ	σ	σθ

For example, for the word διδάσκω, the stem ends with a kappa, which changes to a chi when the aorist passive form marker is added: ἐδιδάχθητε.[5] (This is the second plural form seen in the example from 2 Thess. 2:15 below.) All the changes you are used to seeing with the square of stops are relevant here also; it is just a new column. Remember that these changes affect the *root* of the word rather than the present stem seen in the lexical form. Thus the verb βαπτίζω forms its aorist passive from the root *βαπτιδ, and it is the delta that is the stop, not the zeta that appears in the lexical form. So as before, remember that verbs whose lexical form has a stem ending in zeta also act like a square-of-stops form.

17.23. Examples

Mark 1:9, ἦλθεν (he came) Ἰησοῦς ἀπὸ Ναζαρὲτ τῆς Γαλιλαίας καὶ **ἐβαπτίσθη** εἰς τὸν Ἰορδάνην ὑπὸ Ἰωάννου.

Jesus came from Nazareth in Galilee and *was baptized* in the Jordan by John.

Mark 6:50, πάντες γὰρ αὐτὸν εἶδον (they saw) καὶ **ἐταράχθησαν**.

For everyone saw him, and *they were afraid*.

Gen. 3:7, **διηνοίχθησαν** οἱ ὀφθαλμοὶ τῶν δύο, καὶ ἔγνωσαν (they knew) ὅτι γυμνοὶ ἦσαν.

The eyes of the two *were opened*, and they knew that they were naked.

5. For those who are curious, the root of διδάσκω is *δακ, and the aorist passive stem is διδασκ- (formed with "iota reduplication" and the addition of σκ; the kappa from the root drops out when σκ is added). In the aorist passive form ἐδιδάχθητε, not only does the kappa combine with theta, but the sigma also drops out.

17.24. Now You Try It

Mark 1:42, καὶ εὐθὺς ἀπῆλθεν (it left) ἀπ' αὐτοῦ ἡ λέπρα, καὶ **ἐκαθαρίσθη**.

2 Thess. 2:15, ἄρα οὖν, ἀδελφοί, στήκετε (stand firm!), καὶ κρατεῖτε (hold!) τὰς παραδόσεις ἃς **ἐδιδάχθητε** εἴτε διὰ λόγου εἴτε δι' ἐπιστολῆς ἡμῶν.

— — — — — — — — — — — — — —

Advanced Information for Reference: θη-Middle Forms

17.25. Most verb forms that contain the form marker θη and follow the aorist passive formula (augment + stem + form marker θη + B personal endings) are, indeed, aorist passive forms. This is actually a dual-voice form similar to present and imperfect forms that are usually middle voice but that may function as passives if there is an agent marker in the context. Here the proportion is reversed, in that the middle voice is less common. When the context or the meaning of the word makes it clear that passive voice makes no sense, we call the form a **θη-*middle***. A number of these are intransitive middles. A few examples will make this clear. Each of the forms marked in the following examples should be parsed as middle voice, not passive, despite the θη form marker.

Mark 2:2, **συνήχθησαν**[a] πολλοὶ καὶ ἐλάλει αὐτοῖς τὸν λόγον.	*Many gathered*, and he spoke the word to them.

[a] συνήχθησαν ▶ συνάγω; internal augment, square of stops form (γ + θ = χθ)

In this example, the people were not gathered by someone else; they assembled of their own volition.

Jude 11, τῇ ὁδῷ τοῦ Κάϊν **ἐπορεύθησαν**.	*They have traveled* in the way of Cain.
1 Cor. 3:1, Κἀγώ, ἀδελφοί, οὐκ **ἠδυνήθην**[a] λαλῆσαι ὑμῖν ὡς πνευματικοῖς ἀλλ' ὡς σαρκίνοις, ὡς νηπίοις ἐν Χριστῷ.	And I, brothers, *was* not *able* to speak to you as to spiritual people, but as to fleshy people, as to babies in Christ.

[a] This is the verb δύναμαι, which you learned in chap. 15. It typically has an irregular augment with an eta rather than the usual epsilon.

Matt. 1:19, Ἰωσὴφ δὲ ὁ ἀνὴρ αὐτῆς, δίκαιος ὢν (being) καὶ μὴ θέλων (wanting) αὐτὴν δειγματίσαι, **ἐβουλήθη** λάθρᾳ ἀπολῦσαι αὐτήν.	But Joseph her husband, being righteous and not wanting to disgrace her, *determined* to divorce her quietly.

Gen. 6:5, **ἐπληθύνθησαν** αἱ κακίαι τῶν ἀνθρώπων ἐπὶ τῆς γῆς.	The wicked actions of people *multiplied* on the earth.

— — — — — — — — — — — — — —

Reading Passage: Revelation 9:1–6, 12–21

17.26. This passage is the longest you have had a chance to read thus far; it is not difficult. There will be many words that you do not know, but they are easy enough to identify with your lexicon. All aorist forms that you should know are marked. Any verb forms that you have not yet learned are glossed in parentheses. There are also notes on some forms explaining a few new features of forms that you have seen or that are very similar to ones you already know.

Angels with Trumpets

1Καὶ ὁ πέμπτος ἄγγελος **ἐσάλπισεν**· καὶ εἶδον (I saw) ἀστέρα ἐκ τοῦ οὐρανοῦ πε-
πτωκότα (fallen) εἰς τὴν γῆν, καὶ **ἐδόθη**[a] αὐτῷ ἡ κλεὶς τοῦ φρέατος τῆς ἀβύσσου
2καὶ **ἤνοιξεν** τὸ φρέαρ τῆς ἀβύσσου, καὶ ἀνέβη (it went up) καπνὸς ἐκ τοῦ φρέατος ὡς καπνὸς καμίνου μεγάλης, καὶ **ἐσκοτώθη** ὁ ἥλιος καὶ ὁ ἀὴρ ἐκ τοῦ καπνοῦ
τοῦ φρέατος. 3καὶ ἐκ τοῦ καπνοῦ ἐξῆλθον (they went out) ἀκρίδες εἰς τὴν γῆν,
καὶ **ἐδόθη**[a] αὐταῖς ἐξουσία ὡς ἔχουσιν ἐξουσίαν οἱ σκορπίοι τῆς γῆς. 4καὶ ἐρρέθη[b]
(it was told) αὐταῖς ἵνα μὴ ἀδικήσουσιν[c] τὸν χόρτον τῆς γῆς οὐδὲ πᾶν χλωρὸν
οὐδὲ πᾶν δένδρον, εἰ μὴ τοὺς ἀνθρώπους οἵτινες οὐκ ἔχουσι τὴν σφραγῖδα τοῦ
θεοῦ ἐπὶ τῶν μετώπων. 5καὶ **ἐδόθη**[a] αὐτοῖς ἵνα μὴ ἀποκτείνωσιν (they should
kill) αὐτούς, ἀλλ' ἵνα βασανισθήσονται (they should be tormented)[d] μῆνας
πέντε, καὶ ὁ βασανισμὸς αὐτῶν ὡς βασανισμὸς σκορπίου ὅταν παίσῃ (it stings)
ἄνθρωπον. 6καὶ ἐν ταῖς ἡμέραις ἐκείναις ζητήσουσιν[c] οἱ ἄνθρωποι τὸν θάνατον
καὶ οὐ μὴ εὑρήσουσιν (they will find) αὐτόν, καὶ ἐπιθυμήσουσιν[c] ἀποθανεῖν καὶ
φεύγει ὁ θάνατος ἀπ' αὐτῶν. . . .

12Ἡ οὐαὶ ἡ μία ἀπῆλθεν (has passed)· ἰδοὺ ἔρχεται ἔτι δύο οὐαὶ μετὰ ταῦτα.

13Καὶ ὁ ἕκτος ἄγγελος **ἐσάλπισεν**· καὶ **ἤκουσα** φωνὴν μίαν ἐκ τῶν τεσσάρων
κεράτων τοῦ θυσιαστηρίου τοῦ χρυσοῦ τοῦ ἐνώπιον τοῦ θεοῦ, 14λέγοντα (saying)
τῷ ἕκτῳ ἀγγέλῳ, ὁ ἔχων (one who had) τὴν σάλπιγγα, Λῦσον (Release!) τοὺς
τέσσαρας ἀγγέλους τοὺς δεδεμένους (ones who are bound) ἐπὶ τῷ ποταμῷ
τῷ μεγάλῳ Εὐφράτῃ. 15καὶ **ἐλύθησαν** οἱ τέσσαρες ἄγγελοι οἱ ἡτοιμασμένοι (ones
prepared) εἰς τὴν ὥραν καὶ ἡμέραν καὶ μῆνα καὶ ἐνιαυτόν, ἵνα ἀποκτείνωσιν
(they should kill) τὸ τρίτον τῶν ἀνθρώπων. 16καὶ ὁ ἀριθμὸς τῶν στρατευμάτων
τοῦ ἱππικοῦ δισμυριάδες μυριάδων, **ἤκουσα** τὸν ἀριθμὸν αὐτῶν. 17καὶ οὕτως
εἶδον (I saw) τοὺς ἵππους ἐν τῇ ὁράσει καὶ τοὺς καθημένους (ones who sat) ἐπ'
αὐτῶν, ἔχοντας (having) θώρακας πυρίνους καὶ ὑακινθίνους καὶ θειώδεις, καὶ
αἱ κεφαλαὶ τῶν ἵππων ὡς κεφαλαὶ λεόντων, καὶ ἐκ τῶν στομάτων αὐτῶν ἐκπορεύεται πῦρ καὶ καπνὸς καὶ θεῖον. 18ἀπὸ τῶν τριῶν πληγῶν τούτων **ἀπεκτάνθησαν**[e] τὸ τρίτον τῶν ἀνθρώπων, ἐκ τοῦ πυρὸς καὶ τοῦ καπνοῦ καὶ τοῦ θείου τοῦ
ἐκπορευομένου (which came) ἐκ τῶν στομάτων αὐτῶν. 19ἡ γὰρ ἐξουσία τῶν
ἵππων ἐν τῷ στόματι αὐτῶν ἐστιν καὶ ἐν ταῖς οὐραῖς αὐτῶν, αἱ γὰρ οὐραὶ αὐτῶν
ὅμοιαι ὄφεσιν, ἔχουσαι (having) κεφαλὰς καὶ ἐν αὐταῖς ἀδικοῦσιν.

[20]Καὶ οἱ λοιποὶ τῶν ἀνθρώπων, οἳ οὐκ **ἀπεκτάνθησαν**[e] ἐν ταῖς πληγαῖς ταύταις, οὐδὲ **μετενόησαν** ἐκ τῶν ἔργων τῶν χειρῶν αὐτῶν, ἵνα μὴ προσκυνήσουσιν[c] τὰ δαιμόνια καὶ τὰ εἴδωλα τὰ χρυσᾶ καὶ τὰ ἀργυρᾶ καὶ τὰ χαλκᾶ καὶ τὰ λίθινα καὶ τὰ ξύλινα, ἃ οὔτε βλέπειν δύνανται οὔτε ἀκούειν οὔτε περιπατεῖν, [21]καὶ οὐ **μετενόησαν** ἐκ τῶν φόνων αὐτῶν οὔτε ἐκ τῶν φαρμάκων αὐτῶν οὔτε ἐκ τῆς πορνείας αὐτῶν οὔτε ἐκ τῶν κλεμμάτων αὐτῶν.

[a] ἐδόθη is a form you have not seen yet, but so long as you know that the stem is δο- and the lexical form is δίδωμι, you can identify it easily enough.

[b] ἐρρέθη is an aorist passive form, as you can tell from the form marker, but it is a second aorist (see chap. 18). Notice the ending, and do not worry about the stem for now.

[c] This is a form you have not had yet; if you omitted the second sigma from the end, how would you parse it? Once you have done that, then that sigma form marker tells you it is a future tense-form, not a present. Remember that any form marker will cause a short vowel at the end of the stem to lengthen.

[d] The verb βασανισθήσονται could be understood either as a θη-middle form ("they will suffer torment") or as a passive ("they will be tormented").

[e] The stem of ἀπεκτάνθησαν is a liquid (ends with nu), and the last vowel (a diphthong, actually) in the stem changes slightly in this form.

17.27. Vocabulary for Chapter 17

Part of Speech	Definition	Possible Glosses	Frequency	
Word			NT	LXX
Adverbs				
οὔτε	A negative adverbial particle (actually οὐ τέ) that dismisses an activity or thing that follows, most often occurring in multiples	and not, neither . . . nor	87	123
ὅπου	An adverb of place indicating location	where; wherever (with subjunctive)	82	22
μᾶλλον	A comparative adverb indicating increase or addition, or marking a change in procedure	(much) more, all the more; rather, instead	81	52
ἔξω	Formally, an adverb of place indicating a position beyond a limit or boundary, but it can also be used as an adjective, that which does not belong; a preposition used with the genitive to indicate movement away from; a substantive (with the article), those who are not part of the referenced group	without (adv.); outer, foreign (adj.); outside (prep. + gen.); outsiders (subst. with article)	63	104
Particles				
ὡς	A particle used in very diverse ways (adverb, conjunction, comparative particle), typically indicating some similarity or comparison (see BDAG or *CL* for details)	as, like; when, after, while; (so) that, how; in order to; about, approximately (with numerals)	504	1,965
εἰ	A conditional particle that marks a contingency of some sort (mostly used with the indicative mood)	if, whether	503	805

Part of Speech	Definition	Possible Glosses	Frequency	
Word			NT	LXX
ἤ	A particle indicating either an alternative or a series of alternatives (disjunctive, "or"), or a comparison ("than")	or, either . . . or; than, rather than	343	934
τέ	An enclitic particle that marks a close relationship between sequential states or events, or between coordinate nonsequential items (often combined with other particles or conjunctions; see *CL*)	and (so), so, and likewise	215	277
μέν	A postpositive particle marking emphasis, typically used with other particles or conjunctions (e.g., μέν . . . δέ) to contrast opposing statements or sometimes to emphasize a parallel[a]	on the one hand, indeed	179	222
ἄν	A particle with diverse uses, most of which nuance the verb with some element of contingency or generalization, often translated as a part of the verbal phrase rather than as a discrete element	then, would, ever, might	167	619
ὅταν	A temporal conjunction (or particle) that refers to a conditional or possible action, one that is sometimes repeated ("whenever"); mostly used with the subjunctive mood	when, at the time that; whenever	123	210
ὅτε	A temporal conjunction (or particle) that links two events either in terms of when they both occur or in terms of the temporal extent of both	when; as long as, while	103	173
Verbs				
ἄρχω	(1) To rule or govern (act.; only twice in the NT, more common in the LXX); (2) to initiate an action, process, or state (mid.) [probably homonyms]	(1) I rule (act.); (2) I begin (mid.)	86	231
εὐαγγελίζω	To pass on information that is good news to the recipient; to spread the good news of God's provision of salvation in Jesus Christ (usually mid., sometimes pass.; rarely act.)	I announce/bring good news/the gospel	54	23
πείθω	Generally, to persuade, but this verb evidences the affects of voice and tense-form on meaning more than many verbs and may consist of conflated homonyms: to cause someone to come to a particular point of view or course of action (act.); to submit to, comply, conform to, follow, obey (mid.); to be persuaded or convinced by someone else (focus on the process) (pass.); to believe/trust, be confident, having been convinced (focus on the state of confidence) (pf. act. and mid.)	I persuade, appeal to, urge (act.); I submit (mid.); I am persuaded (pass.); I believe (pf. act./mid.)	52	184

[a] The paired use of μέν . . . δέ ("on the one hand . . . on the other hand"), so common in the NT (as in Classical Greek), is rare in the LXX.

17.28. Key Things to Know for Chapter 17

Know the formulas for aorist active indicative, aorist middle indicative, and aorist passive indicative verbs.

What happens to the aorist middle indicative form of a contract verb?

Do you remember the square of stops? How is it relevant to aorist tense-form verbs? What new feature is added to the chart in the aorist passive?

18

VERBS: PART 8

Second Aorist (Perfective) Indicative Verbs

18.1. We will begin with an analogy.[1] English creates the past tense in two different ways. Notice how this works with the verbs *study* and *eat*.

English present: "*I study* all the time" (or: *I am studying*).
English past: "*I studied* last night." Here we add *-ed* to form the past tense.

English present: "*I eat* breakfast every day."
English past: "*I ate* breakfast yesterday." In this instance we change the stem to form the past tense.

From this simple example you will notice that English can form the past tense in either of these two different ways. Which pattern is followed depends on the verb in question; some use *-ed* (*study* ▸ *studied*), and others change the stem (*eat* ▸ *ate;* cf. *go* ▸ *went*). There is no difference in meaning in English regardless of how the past tense is created.

Greek does something very similar in that there are two ways to create the tense-form of the verb that expresses perfective aspect, the aorist tense-form. They are called by the imaginative names *first aorist* and *second aorist* (abbreviated: "aor." and "²aor.").[2] There is *no difference in meaning* between first and second aorist forms. Usually we say simply *aorist* when talking about either

1. Remember that it is only an analogy; do not think because of this illustration that the aorist is equivalent to the English past tense.

2. If it is important to indicate that a form is a first aorist form, the abbreviation "¹aor." can be used. These forms go by a variety of names. In some grammars the second aorist is called a *strong aorist* in contrast to a *weak aorist* (i.e., first aorist). In others this pair may be called *irregular aorist* (i.e., second aorist) and *regular* or *sigmatic aorist*.

one unless it is important or helpful to know which pattern was used. A Greek verb normally will have *either* a first aorist *or* a second aorist form/spelling, but not both.[3]

Second Aorist Active Forms

18.2. From the review in the previous chapter, you will remember that the formula for the first aorist active indicative tense-form was *augment* + *stem* + *form marker* σα + *B personal endings*. You will also remember that the formula for the imperfect active indicative tense-form was *augment* + *stem* + *connecting vowel* + *B personal endings*. Compare these formulas with the following second aorist active indicative formula.

Formula for Second Aorist Active Indicative Verbs

augment + *aorist stem* + connecting vowel + B personal endings

This formula is identical to the imperfect active indicative except for one piece: the stem. You can tell the two apart because the imperfect always uses the same stem as the present tense-form, but the second aorist form will use a *different stem*. Or we could say that the imperfect will have a stem that is spelled the same as the lexical form, but the second aorist will have a different spelling of the stem from what is given as the main entry in the lexicon.[4]

To examine a sample second aorist form, we will need to use a different verb from what we normally use, because λύω does not have a second aorist form. We will instead use λαμβάνω, "I take, receive."

Formulas and Stems

In the verb formulas used in this book, a formula listed with just "stem" uses a stem that is spelled just like the lexical form. Whenever there is a *change* in the stem that occurs regularly (and only then), it will be identified in the formula. For example, the second aorist form specifies "aorist stem" because the verb stem in these forms is never spelled the same as the lexical form.

3. A few verbs have both a first and second aorist form, but these are rare.

4. Technically, it is not the present stem that is being changed, but it is a different form of the root. The *root* of a verb is the simplest form of the verb from which all the various tense stems are created. In each tense-form the base form of the verb is called the *stem*. Many times the root is unchanged from stem to stem (i.e., the stem that you see in the lexicon never changes regardless of whether the tense-form is a present or an aorist or any other form). If any of the stems change the spelling of the root, it is more likely to be the present that changes rather than the aorist. That may seem counterintuitive, but it is only because we have traditionally listed the present tense-form as the main, alphabetical entry in the lexicon (and therefore what you learn as a vocabulary word), so it seems to be the more normal form. Determining the root and the various stems is not obvious in many instances and is a subject that goes well beyond the needs of a first-year student. Lexicons such as BDAG or *CL* will usually give you the information that you need to identify the various forms. Likewise the morphology catalog in app. B of this textbook will point you in the right direction. If you need more detail than these tools provide, the best recourse is an advanced reference tool such as *MBG*. Though very helpful in some specialized situations, it is not a tool that most students will use very often.

Lexical form: λαμβάνω (= present active indicative)
Root: *λαβ
Present stem: λαμβαν
Aorist stem: λαβ

18.3. The last column on the chart below lists the imperfect active indicative form for comparison with the second aorist form.

Second Aorist Active Indicative of λαμβάνω

	Form	c.v. + B p.e.	Gloss	Impf. Act. Ind.
1S	ἔλαβον	ον	I took	ἐλάμβανον
2S	ἔλαβες	ες	You took	ἐλάμβανες
3S	ἔλαβε(ν)	ε(ν)	He/she/it took	ἐλάμβανε(ν)
1P	ἐλάβομεν	ομεν	We took	ἐλαμβάνομεν
2P	ἐλάβετε	ετε	You took	ἐλαμβάνετε
3P	ἔλαβον	ον	They took	ἐλάμβανον

Compare the second aorist forms (first Greek column) with the imperfect active indicative (last column) of the same word (λαμβάνω).[5] The only difference is that the second aorist form uses a stem (λαβ-) that is different from the stem of the lexical form (λαμβαν-).

18.4. *Examples of Aorist Forms of λαμβάνω*

Matt. 8:17, Αὐτὸς τὰς ἀσθενείας ἡμῶν **ἔλαβεν** καὶ τὰς νόσους ἐβάστασεν.

He *took* our sicknesses and bore (our) diseases.

John 1:16, ἐκ τοῦ πληρώματος αὐτοῦ ἡμεῖς πάντες **ἐλάβομεν** καὶ[a] χάριν ἀντὶ χάριτος.

From his fullness we all *received* grace in place of grace.

[a] The word καί has not been translated since it would be clumsy in English. It should probably be understood adverbially: "we all received *even* grace in place of grace."

1 Cor. 4:7, τί δὲ ἔχεις ὃ οὐκ **ἔλαβες**;

What do you have that *you did* not *receive*?

Gen. 2:15, **ἔλαβεν** κύριος ὁ θεὸς τὸν ἄνθρωπον, ὃν ἔπλασεν, καὶ ἔθετο (he placed) αὐτὸν ἐν τῷ παραδείσῳ φυλάσσειν αὐτόν.

The Lord God *took* the man whom he had made and placed him in the garden to guard it.

5. You will rarely see the imperfect of λαμβάνω; it occurs only one time in the NT (Acts 8:17). Even in the much larger corpus of the LXX, it occurs only 14 times (8 of which are the third singular form). The aorist of λαμβάνω, however, is very common, occurring 185 times in the NT (of which 68 are aorist active indicatives) and 895 times in the LXX (of which 520 are aorist active indicatives).

18.5. *Now You Try It*

Luke 7:16, **ἔλαβεν** φόβος πάντας καὶ ἐδόξαζον τὸν θεόν.

Rom. 5:11, We are rejoicing ἐν τῷ θεῷ διὰ τοῦ κυρίου ἡμῶν Ἰησοῦ Χριστοῦ δι' οὗ νῦν τὴν καταλλαγὴν **ἐλάβομεν**.

Gal. 3:2, τοῦτο μόνον θέλω μαθεῖν ἀφ' ὑμῶν· ἐξ ἔργων νόμου τὸ πνεῦμα **ἐλάβετε** ἢ ἐξ ἀκοῆς πίστεως;

Deut. 3:4, ἐκρατήσαμεν πασῶν τῶν πόλεων αὐτοῦ ἐν τῷ καιρῷ ἐκείνῳ, οὐκ ἦν πόλις, ἣν οὐκ **ἐλάβομεν** παρ' αὐτῶν.

Second Aorist Forms with the "Wrong" Endings

Although almost all second aorist forms use the endings shown above, occasionally a *first aorist ending* appears. That is, instead of the usual forms that use omicron or epsilon as the connecting vowel, the ending is spelled with an alpha. In essence this is a first aorist ending, retaining the alpha from the form marker in place of the connecting vowel. Thus in addition to **εἶπον** (3rd pl. ²aor. act. ind. ▸ λέγω) you will also see **εἶπαν** both in the NT and LXX. Since you already recognize that spelling from the first aorist, you may not even realize that it is different. The meaning is the same; it is just an alternate spelling.

Stem Changes

18.6. The change in stem that identifies a second aorist is usually quite simple. Most commonly, double consonants in the lexical form (the present stem) become single consonants, and vowels/diphthongs may undergo ablaut.[6] Sometimes the present stem modifies the root by adding a letter or syllable, but the aorist retains the same spelling as the root. Here are examples of each of the most common types of changes.

Lexical Form	Root	Present Stem	Aorist Stem
βάλλω	*βαλ	βαλλ-	βαλ-
φεύγω	*φυγ	φευγ-	φυγ-
λαμβάνω	*λαβ	λαμβαν-	λαβ-
πίνω	*πι	πιν-	πι-
γινώσκω	*γνω	γινωσκ-	γνω-

6. If you need a refresher on the term *ablaut*, see the sidebar "Ablaut" in chap. 7.

John 19:24, ἐπὶ τὸν ἱματισμόν μου **ἔβαλον** κλῆρον.	For my garment *they cast* lots.
Mark 16:8, **ἔφυγον** ἀπὸ τοῦ μνημείου.	*They fled* from the tomb.
Col. 4:10, Ἀσπάζεται ὑμᾶς Ἀρίσταρχος ὁ συναιχμάλωτός μου καὶ Μᾶρκος ὁ ἀνεψιὸς Βαρναβᾶ (περὶ οὗ **ἐλάβετε** ἐντολάς).	Aristarchus my fellow prisoner greets you, and [so does] Mark the cousin of Barnabas (concerning whom *you received* instructions).
Mark 14:23, **ἔπιον** ἐξ αὐτοῦ πάντες.	Everyone *drank* from it.
Rom. 3:17, ὁδὸν εἰρήνης οὐκ **ἔγνωσαν**.	*They do not know* the way of peace.

Different Roots

18.7. Sometimes the apparent change in a second aorist stem is radical. This is usually the case when the aorist stem is formed from a totally different root than the present stem. For example, ἐσθίω is the present tense-form of the verb "I eat," but the second aorist is ἔφαγον. Compare the present, imperfect, and aorist forms (respectively) of this verb in the following examples.

Mark 7:28, τὰ κυνάρια ὑποκάτω τῆς τραπέζης **ἐσθίουσιν** ἀπὸ τῶν ψιχίων τῶν παιδίων.	The dogs under the table *are eating* from the crumbs of the children.
Exod. 16:3, **ἠσθίομεν** ἄρτους εἰς πλησμονήν.	*We were eating* bread to the full.
Mark 2:26, τοὺς ἄρτους τῆς προθέσεως **ἔφαγεν**.	*He ate* the Bread of the Presence.

Verbs may have different *roots* in different forms. You recognize the word λέγω (present), but the aorist form of this word is εἶπον. Why is there such a drastic difference in the spelling of these forms? Why does ἐσθίω become ἔφαγον and λέγω become εἶπον in the aorist? It is probable that many of these were originally different words with synonymous (or very similar) meanings. Each was conventionally used only in certain tense-forms, some in present, others in aorist. Eventually they came to be used as if they were different forms of the same word.[7]

The same thing happens in English. The word *go* (present tense) and *went* (past tense) are not etymologically related. English formerly had a past tense of *go* (*eode*, Anglo-Saxon; *yode* in Middle English). It also had a present tense of *went*, the form *wend*. This last word still occurs in English, though rarely.

7. Verbs that use different roots may be called *defective verbs* (the individual roots do not occur in all tense-forms) or *suppletive forms* (the various roots supplement each other to enable a full range of tense-forms). Both *defective* and *suppletive* are larger category terms that may refer to items other than verbs having multiple roots.

You will sometimes read it in poetry where it enables the poet to maintain the rhyme (notice *wend* — *end* in the sidebar). We now use *go* and *went* as if they are present and past tenses of the same word even though they are unrelated etymologically.

Underwoods, *by Robert Louis Stevenson*

Book 1, Scene III—The Canoe Speaks

On the great streams the ships may go
About men's business to and fro.
But I, the egg-shell pinnace, sleep
On crystal waters ankle-deep:
. . . .
My dipping paddle scarcely shakes
The berry in the bramble-brakes;
Still forth on my green way I ***wend***
Beside the cottage garden-***end***;
And by the nested angler fare,
And take the lovers unaware.

Greek Verbs with Different Roots

18.8. All the Greek verbs that have different roots in Koine are given below.[8] You have not yet learned all the forms listed here. Do not be concerned to understand how all of them are formed or why they are spelled the way they are. Instead look for the similarities in the root forms and the specific tense-forms built on those roots. You will understand more of this later, and then you can refer back to these lists.

Common Verbs with Multiple Roots

Lexical Form	Root	Present	Future	Aorist	Perfect
λέγω, "I say"	*λεγ	λέγω			
	*ϝερ/*ϝρη[a]		ἐρῶ	ἐρρέθην (aor. pass.)	εἴρηκα
	*ϝεπ			εἶπον[b] (aor. act.)	
ἔρχομαι, "I come"	*ἐρχ	ἔρχομαι			
	*ἐλευθ/*ἐλθ		ἐλεύσομαι	ἦλθον	ἐλήλυθα
ἐσθίω, "I eat"	*ἐσθι	ἐσθίω			
	*φαγ		φάγομαι	ἔφαγον	
ὁράω, "I see"	*ϝορα	ὁράω			ἑώρακα
	*οπ		ὄψομαι	ὠψάμην (aor. mid.) ὤφθην (aor. pass.)	
	*ϝιδ			εἶδον (aor. act.) ἰδεῖν (aor. act. inf.)	
φέρω, "I carry"	*φερ	φέρω			
	*οι		οἴσω		
	*ενεκ			ἤνεγκα/ἤνεγκον (aor. act.) ἠνέχθην (aor. pass.)	ἐνήνοχα

[a] Note the obsolete letter digamma (ϝ) in this root and several others in this list; see app. E.

[b] The epsilon in the root undergoes ablaut to ει when the digamma drops out and an augment is added.

8. The convention used here is to identify a root with a prefixed asterisk. You will never see any Greek text that is marked in this way appearing as a separate word; there will always be prefixes or suffixes added, and many times there will also be vowel ablaut (sometimes called *vowel gradation*) as well.

Digamma

The letter digamma appears in some of the roots discussed in this chapter. This is an obsolete letter that is no longer used in Koine. It is written ϝ and had a *w* sound. See appendix E for more information about this letter and several other obsolete characters in Greek.

Less Common Verbs with Multiple Roots

Lexical Form	Root	Present	Future	Aorist	Perfect
αἱρέω, "I choose"[a]	*αιρε	αἱρέω	αἱρήσομαι	ᾑρέθην (aor. pass.)	ᾕρημαι (pf. mid.)
	*ϝελ/*ϝαλ			εἱλόμην/εἱλάμην (aor. act.)	
πάσχω, "I suffer"	*παθ	πάσχω		ἔπαθον	
	*πενθ		πείσομαι		πέπονθα
πίνω, "I drink"	*πι	πίνω	πίομαι	ἔπιον	
	*πο				πέπωκα
τρέχω, "I run"	*θρεχ	τρέχω			
	*δραμ/*δρομ		δραμοῦμαι	ἔδραμον	δεδράμηκα

[a] Watch the breathing mark and accent of this word carefully; it is not the word αἴρω.

18.9. Examples of Greek Verbs with Different Roots

1 Cor. 11:24, ἔκλασεν καὶ **εἶπεν**, Τοῦτό μού ἐστιν τὸ σῶμα τὸ ὑπὲρ ὑμῶν.

He broke it and *said*, "This is my body, which is for you."

Gal. 1:21, ἔπειτα **ἦλθον** εἰς τὰ κλίματα τῆς Συρίας καὶ τῆς Κιλικίας.

Then *I went* into the regions of Syria and Cilicia.

Gal. 1:19, ἕτερον δὲ τῶν ἀποστόλων οὐκ **εἶδον** εἰ μὴ Ἰάκωβον τὸν ἀδελφὸν τοῦ κυρίου.

But *I did* not *see* another of the apostles except James the Lord's brother.

The translation given above is a formal equivalent to help you understand the structure of the verse. In more idiomatic English we would probably express the first part of this statement as, "But I saw none of the other apostles."

John 4:33, ἔλεγον οὖν οἱ μαθηταὶ πρὸς ἀλλήλους, Μή τις **ἤνεγκεν** αὐτῷ φαγεῖν;

Then the disciples said to one another, "No one *has brought* him [anything] to eat, have they?" (or, "It's not that anyone *has brought* him food, is it?")

Gen. 24:54, **ἔφαγον** καὶ **ἔπιον**, αὐτὸς καὶ οἱ ἄνδρες οἱ μετ' αὐτοῦ.

They ate and *drank*, he and the men who were with him.

1 Kgdms. (1 Sam.) 4:12, **ἔδραμεν** ἀνὴρ Ἰεμιναῖος ἐκ τῆς παρατάξεως[a] καὶ **ἦλθεν** εἰς Σηλὼμ ἐν τῇ ἡμέρᾳ ἐκείνῃ, καὶ τὰ ἱμάτια αὐτοῦ διερρηγότα, καὶ γῆ ἐπὶ τῆς κεφαλῆς αὐτοῦ.

[a] παράταξις, εως, ἡ, "battle line, place of battle"

A man, a Benjamite, *ran* from the battle line and *came* to Shiloh in that day, and his garments were torn, and there was dirt on his head.

Recognizing Second Aorist Forms

18.10. How do you identify the stem of a second aorist verb? What is its lexical form? Many of these different stems are close in spelling to the lexical form and fairly obvious. Remember the common kinds of changes (see above). You would do well to learn the most common verbs that have divergent stems. In vocabulary lists for each chapter, ask yourself, Is this form close enough that I will be able to remember the lexical form? If not, memorize the aorist stem along with the definition.[9] For example, when you learn that the second aorist form of ἀποθνῄσκω is ἀπέθανον, you will need to ask yourself if that is the sort of change you will be able to figure out when you encounter it in a text. The same applies for the second aorist of ἔρχομαι, which is ἦλθον. Every person is different, so your decision may be different from your neighbor's.

When you are stumped by an odd form, try looking it up in your lexicon just the way it is spelled. If you encounter ἤγαγεν and have no idea what it is, then try looking it up under eta in your lexicon (even though you suspect that the eta might be an augment). What you will find in Danker's *Concise Lexicon* is this:

ἤγαγον 2 aor. act. ind. of ἄγω

Likewise, for ἐφάγομεν you will find:

ἔφαγον 2 aor. act. ind. of ἐσθίω

Note that you will find only first singular forms, not second or third singular forms, nor first, second, or third plural forms. In other words, aorist forms listed alphabetically will always end with -ον (or sometimes αμην if it is a middle-only form).

18.11. If none of these suggestions help, check the lexicon under the word that you *think* it is. Lexicons will typically list the aorist form if a word has a second aorist.[10] The most complete listing of this sort of information in a lexicon is found in BDAG. That is just one of the reasons why that particular tool is indispensable

9. You do not need to do this for every verb, but the vocabulary in this textbook assigns only the most frequent words, so memorizing any unusual second aorist forms of these words has a significant payoff in terms of the frequency with which you will see such forms.

10. Danker's *Concise Lexicon* is an exception; it gives no such morphological information under the main entry, though it does list most of these alphabetically under the inflected form. If you do not find a matching form in the lexicon, then consult the morphology catalog in app. B of this textbook. First aorist forms are usually not listed in lexicons, since they use the same stem as the lexical form, though if a particular verb uses both first and second aorist spellings, then both may be given.

for serious exegesis. For example, perhaps you are reading 2 Tim. 4:20, Τρόφιμον δὲ ἀπέλιπον ἐν Μιλήτῳ, and you do not recognize the verb ἀπέλιπον. Glancing at your lexicon shows that there is no verb that begins απελιπ- or απολιπ-. Since vowels often undergo ablaut in the various verb stems, you might wonder, "Is ἀπέλιπον from ἀπολείπω?" That would be a good guess. If you look under ἀπολείπω you will often find a note that its second aorist form is ἀπέλιπον.[11] The present stem is λειπ-, but the aorist stem is λιπ-. The first part of the entry in BDAG reads as follows.

> ἀπολείπω impf. ἀπέλειπον; fut. ἀπολείψω; 1 aor. ἀπέλειψα LXX; 2 aor. ἀπέλιπον, mid. ἀπελιπόμην, 3 sg. pass. ἀπελείφθη LXX (Hom.+).
> 1. to cause or permit to remain in a place upon going away, *leave behind* . . .

With compound verbs another thing you might try is to look up the word without the prepositional prefix. Sometimes the lexicon will give the aorist form of the base word but not the compound form.

18.12. Another resource is one that you have as appendix B in this textbook: the "Morphology Catalog of Common Koine Verbs." This gives a variety of forms (including the second aorist forms) of the most common verbs in the NT and in the LXX. If you were wondering if a particular form, perhaps ἔπαθεν, was from πάσχω, you could turn to the verb catalog in appendix B and find this info:

> πάσχω (NT 42): 3SFAI παθεῖται; 3PFAI παθοῦνται; ²AAI ἔπαθον; ²RAI πέπονθα; 3PLAI ἐπεπόνθεισαν; ²RAP πεπονθώς

The catalog uses the short-form parsing abbreviations for verbs due to the large quantity of information included. See the explanation at the end of chapter 13. In the example cited here, "3SFAI" means "third singular future active indicative."

Try these various tips in the following examples. If one does not help, try one of the other options until you can identify the second aorist verbs in these verses. The first few have an English equivalent to get you started.

18.13. Examples

Mark 10:18, ὁ Ἰησοῦς **εἶπεν** αὐτῷ, Τί με λέγεις ἀγαθόν; οὐδεὶς ἀγαθὸς εἰ μὴ εἷς ὁ θεός.	Jesus *said* to him, "Why do you call me good? No one is good except one: God."
Mark 1:35, **ἐξῆλθεν** καὶ **ἀπῆλθεν** εἰς ἔρημον τόπον κἀκεῖ προσηύχετο.	*He went out* and *departed* to a deserted place, and there he prayed.
Mark 1:37, **εὗρον** αὐτὸν καὶ λέγουσιν αὐτῷ ὅτι Πάντες ζητοῦσίν σε.	*They found* him and said to him, "Everyone is looking for you."[a]

[a] Formally, "all are seeking you," but English idiom prefers the collective singular, "everyone," even though that requires changing the Greek plural verb to a singular. The meaning is unchanged.

11. BDAG also tells you that in the LXX there is a first aorist form, ἀπέλειψα, but this does not occur in the NT.

Gen. 2:22, ᾠκοδόμησεν κύριος ὁ θεὸς τὴν πλευράν, ἣν **ἔλαβεν** ἀπὸ τοῦ Ἀδάμ, εἰς γυναῖκα καὶ **ἤγαγεν** αὐτὴν πρὸς τὸν Ἀδάμ.

The Lord God fashioned the rib which *he had taken* from Adam into a woman, and *he brought* her to Adam.

18.14. Now You Try It

Mark 4:4, ὃ μὲν[a] **ἔπεσεν** παρὰ τὴν ὁδόν, καὶ **ἦλθεν** τὰ πετεινὰ καὶ **κατέφαγεν** αὐτό.

[a] ὃ μέν, "some"; introduces a series that is continued in the verses that follow.

Rev. 10:10, **ἔλαβον** τὸ βιβλαρίδιον ἐκ τῆς χειρὸς τοῦ ἀγγέλου καὶ **κατέφαγον** αὐτό.

1 Macc. 9:65, **ἀπέλιπεν**[a] Ἰωναθὰν Σίμωνα τὸν ἀδελφὸν αὐτοῦ ἐν τῇ πόλει καὶ **ἐξῆλθεν** εἰς τὴν χώραν καὶ **ἦλθεν** ἐν ἀριθμῷ.[b]

[a] You will have to distinguish the subject and object of the first verb by context since both are indeclinable forms.

[b] ἐν ἀριθμῷ is formally, "in/with a number," but the sense of the context is that this is "with a [small] number." The setting is a military encounter in which those mentioned here defeat a much larger army.

Aorist Active Indicative of γινώσκω

18.15. The root and aorist stem of γινώσκω is *γνω. The paradigm is a bit unusual; it is a second aorist form. The stem vowel, omega, combines with the connecting vowel, omicron, to form omega as a result of the ablaut. All but the third plural form are standard second aorist forms. The third singular does not use the movable nu. The third plural uses the second aorist stem but appears to add the first aorist form marker. This one is a bit tricky, but you will want to remember it since it occurs frequently in the NT (213 times, of which 89 are the third singular form) and the LXX (207 times, of which 88 are the third singular form).

Second Aorist Active Indicative of γινώσκω

1S	ἔγνων
2S	ἔγνως
3S	ἔγνω
1P	ἔγνωμεν
2P	ἔγνωτε
3P	ἔγνωσαν

18.16. Examples of the Aorist Active Indicative of γινώσκω

Mark 12:12, ἐζήτουν αὐτὸν κρατῆσαι, **ἔγνωσαν** γὰρ ὅτι πρὸς αὐτοὺς τὴν παραβολὴν εἶπεν.	They sought to seize him, for *they knew* that he had spoken the parable against them.
John 1:10, ἐν τῷ κόσμῳ ἦν, καὶ ὁ κόσμος δι' αὐτοῦ ἐγένετο, καὶ ὁ κόσμος αὐτὸν οὐκ **ἔγνω**.	He was in the world, and the world came into being through him, and the world did not *know* him.

18.17. Now You Try It

John 17:25, πάτερ δίκαιε,[a] καὶ ὁ κόσμος σε οὐκ **ἔγνω**, ἐγὼ δέ σε **ἔγνων**, καὶ οὗτοι **ἔγνωσαν** ὅτι σύ με ἀπέστειλας.

a For πάτερ and δίκαιε see app. D.

Gen. 20:6, εἶπεν δὲ αὐτῷ ὁ θεὸς καθ' ὕπνον, Κἀγὼ **ἔγνων** ὅτι ἐν καθαρᾷ καρδίᾳ ἐποίησας τοῦτο.

Josephus, *Life* 182, ὁ δὲ βασιλεὺς Ἀγρίππας ὡς **ἔγνω** ψευδῆ[a] τὴν περὶ Φιλίππου φήμην ἔπεμψεν ἱππεῖς τοὺς παραπέμψοντας[b] τὸν Φίλιππον.

a ψευδῆ is a two-form adjective, ψευδής, ές. It follows the same pattern of endings as does ἀληθής (see chap. 12).
b ἱππεῖς τοὺς παραπέμψοντας, "a cavalry which would escort"

This text will make you think; Josephus is not the easiest Greek writer to read. Here he places an attributive adjective in predicate position.

Second Aorist Middle Indicative Forms

18.18. Everything that you have learned thus far in this chapter regarding the aorist active indicative form also applies to the aorist middle indicative. All you need is the appropriate formula.

Formula for Second Aorist Middle Indicative Verbs

augment + *aorist stem* + connecting vowel + D personal endings

The only difference from the aorist active is that the D endings are used. (These forms are always aorist *middle*; there is a distinct form for aorist passive, which you will learn later.) If we use the verb γίνομαι as an example, the aorist middle forms will look like this:

Second Aorist Middle Indicative of γίνομαι

	Form	c.v. + D p.e.	Gloss
1S	ἐγενόμην	ομην	I became
2S	ἐγένου	ου	You became
3S	ἐγένετο	ετο	He/she/it became
1P	ἐγενόμεθα	ομεθα	We became
2P	ἐγένεσθε	εσθε	You became
3P	ἐγένοντο	οντο	They became

18.19. *Examples of Second Aorist Middle Indicative Verbs*

Matt. 6:29, λέγω ὑμῖν ὅτι οὐδὲ Σολομὼν ἐν πάσῃ τῇ δόξῃ αὐτοῦ **περιεβάλετο** ὡς ἓν τούτων.

I say to you that not even Solomon in all his glory *was clothed* as one of these.

Acts 7:10, **ἐξείλατο**[a] αὐτὸν ἐκ πασῶν τῶν θλίψεων αὐτοῦ καὶ ἔδωκεν (he gave) αὐτῷ χάριν καὶ σοφίαν ἐναντίον Φαραὼ βασιλέως Αἰγύπτου.

[a] ἐξείλατο ▶ ἐξαιρέω

He rescued him from all his troubles and gave him grace and wisdom before Pharaoh, king of Egypt.

Gen. 4:3–4, καὶ **ἐγένετο** μεθ' ἡμέρας ἤνεγκεν Κάϊν ἀπὸ τῶν καρπῶν τῆς γῆς θυσίαν τῷ κυρίῳ, καὶ Ἅβελ ἤνεγκεν καὶ αὐτὸς ἀπὸ τῶν πρωτοτόκων τῶν προβάτων αὐτοῦ.

This example shows the most common second aorist middle indicative verb. This specific form, ἐγένετο, occurs 202 times in the NT, and other person/number combinations of the same word bring the total to 233. (There are only 30 other second aorist middle indicative forms in the entire NT.) The same form occurs 793 times in the LXX, often as καὶ ἐγένετο to introduce a new pericope in the narrative.

18.20. *Now You Try It*

Mark 1:11, φωνὴ **ἐγένετο** ἐκ τῶν οὐρανῶν, Σὺ εἶ ὁ υἱός μου ὁ ἀγαπητός.

Acts 12:11, ὁ Πέτρος εἶπεν, Νῦν οἶδα ἀληθῶς ὅτι ἐξαπέστειλεν ὁ κύριος τὸν ἄγγελον αὐτοῦ καὶ **ἐξείλατό** με ἐκ χειρὸς Ἡρῴδου.

Rom. 15:7, Διὸ προσλαμβάνεσθε (welcome!) ἀλλήλους, καθὼς καὶ ὁ Χριστὸς **προσελάβετο** ὑμᾶς εἰς δόξαν τοῦ θεοῦ.

Wis. 7:10, ὑπὲρ ὑγίειαν καὶ εὐμορφίαν ἠγάπησα αὐτὴν καὶ **προειλόμην** αὐτὴν ἀντὶ φωτὸς ἔχειν.

Frequent Second Aorist Forms

18.21. The following list gives the eleven most important verbs for which you should be able to recognize the second aorist forms. Some are obvious enough to recognize if you know the lexical form, especially words that have a common root but have ablaut or other changes to the root for the aorist stem. Others must simply be memorized as another vocabulary word, especially verbs whose aorist is formed from a different root than the lexical form, which uses the present stem.[12]

Under each main form are listed the compound forms of that verb. If you know the main entry, you can also identify the second aorist form of the other words with no additional memorization. That is, once you know that the second aorist of λέγω is εἶπον, then it is easy to identify προεῖπον as the second aorist of προλέγω. The second aorist of the main forms in this list occur a total of 1,605 times in the NT—not bad for learning 11 forms. But you can leverage these 11 forms by their compounds to recognize a total of 2,041 NT forms and nearly 1,600 more in the LXX.[13] (If other moods were included, the numbers would be considerably higher.) Now that is a real payoff for learning 11 basic forms!

18.22. The format of these entries is as follows:

lexical form ▸ second aorist form (*root), "gloss" (occurrences of this lexical form in the NT) [total of all forms including compounds]

λέγω ▸ εἶπον (*ϝεπ/*ϝερ), "I say, speak, tell" (775) [779]
  προλέγω, "I say ahead of time; I foretell" (3)
  συλλέγω, "I gather, collect, glean" (1)

ἔρχομαι ▸ ἦλθον (*ελευθ/*ελθ), "I come, go" (171) [456]
  ἀνέρχομαι, "I go up, return, enter" (3)

12. If the second aorist stem changes from a different root or due to ablaut, and so forth, it is listed after the root to show the spelling of the second aorist form, often with a note to explain the formation. There will be a few anomalies from time to time. For example, the second aorist of λέγω sometimes uses a first aorist ending instead of the usual second (see the sidebar "Second Aorist Forms with the 'Wrong' Endings" earlier in this lesson).

13. The number 1,605 is the total of figures in parentheses in this list; the number 2,041 is the total of figures in brackets. The entry for θνήσκω is calculated slightly differently from the others due to the fact that there are no instances of an aorist of θνήσκω in the NT (only perfects), so the main NT form, ἀποθνήσκω, was used for the total in parentheses instead.

ἀντιπαρέρχομαι, "I come upon, surprise, pass by on the other side" (2)
ἀπέρχομαι, "I go away, depart" (61)
διέρχομαι, "I pass through" (7)
εἰσέρχομαι, "I enter" (60)
ἐξέρχομαι, "I come out, go out" (103)
ἐπέρχομαι, "I come upon, am at hand" (1)
κατέρχομαι, "I come down, go down, return" (8)
παρεισέρχομαι, "I enter" (2)
παρέρχομαι, "I pass by, pass away" (3)
περιέρχομαι, "I travel about" (1)
προέρχομαι, "I go before" (2)
προσέρχομαι, "I come to" (25)
συνεισέρχομαι, "I go in with" (2)
συνέρχομαι, "I come/go together" (5)

γίνομαι ▸ ἐγενόμην (*γεν),[14] "I become, am, am born, am created" (233) [244]
παραγίνομαι, "I come, appear" (11)

ὁράω ▸ εἶδον (*ϝιδ), "I see" (146) [147]
ἐφοράω, "I watch over, observe" (1)

λαμβάνω ▸ ἔλαβον (*λαβ),[15] "I take, receive, choose" (68) [104]
ἀναλαμβάνω, "I take up, raise, undertake" (1)
ἀντιλαμβάνω, "I take hold of together, support, take part in" (1)
ἀπολαμβάνω, "I receive" (2)
ἐπιλαμβάνομαι, "I take hold of" (2)
καταλαμβάνω, "I take, overtake, reach" (3)
παραλαμβάνω, "I take" (17)
προλαμβάνω, "I do ahead of time; I am surprised" (1)
προσλαμβάνω, "I increase; I receive, accept" (5)
συλλαμβάνω, "I seize" (3)
ὑπολαμβάνω, "I suppose; I lift up; I reply" (1)

πίπτω ▸ ἔπεσα (*πετ),[16] "I fall" (45) [73]
ἀναπίπτω, "I fall down, recline, sit down" (6)
ἀποπίπτω, "I fall" (1)
ἐκπίπτω, "I fall" (4)

14. The root (and aorist stem) is *γεν, but for the present stem this undergoes ablaut and becomes γιν-.

15. The root (and aorist stem) is *λαβ, but the present stem adds both μ and αν ▸ λαμβαν-.

16. In the aorist form the tau drops out when the sigma is added, and the stem reduplicates by prefixing πι- (similar to iota reduplication in the μι verbs, which you will learn later).

ἐπιπίπτω, "I fall, fall upon, attack" (8)
καταπίπτω, "I fall down" (1)
περιπίπτω, "I strike; I fall among; I embrace" (1)
προσπίπτω, "I fall upon; I fall down before" (6)
συμπίπτω, "I collapse, fall together" (1)

βάλλω ▸ ἔβαλον (*βαλ), "I throw, put" (30) [61]
ἀναβάλλω, "I lay on, throw on; I defer" (1)
ἐκβάλλω, "I cast/send out" (13)
ἐπιβάλλω, "I lay hands on, throw" (8)
παραβάλλω, "I throw aside; I am attentive; I arrive" (1)
περιβάλλω, "I put on, clothe" (6)
συμβάλλω, "I meet, consider, compare" (1)
ὑποβάλλω, "I subject, submit; I substitute" (1)

εὑρίσκω ▸ εὗρον (*ευρ),[17] "I find" (54) [55]
ἀνευρίσκω, "I discover, seek" (1)

ἄγω ▸ ἤγαγον (*αγ),[18] "I bring, lead, go, celebrate" (23) [55]
ἀνάγω, "I lead/bring up; I bring before; I offer up" (3)
ἀπάγω, "I lead away" (7)
εἰσάγω, "I bring in" (6)
ἐξάγω, "I lead away, bring out" (5)
κατάγω, "I bring down, lead down" (2)
προάγω, "I go before" (1)
συνάγω, "I gather, bring together" (8)

θνῄσκω, [ἔθανον] (*θαν), "I die" (0) [51]
ἀποθνῄσκω ▸ ἀπέθανον, "I die" (48)
συναποθνῄσκω, "I die with" (3)

ἔχω ▸ ἔσχον (*σεχ ▸ σχ), "I have" (12) [18]
ἀνέχω, "I lift, esteem, hinder, stop, bear, suffer" (1)
ἐπέχω, "I hold, hold back; I notice, give close attention to" (1)
μετέχω, "I partake" (1)
παρέχω, "I provide, cause, grant, present" (1)
περιέχω, "I surround, seize, contain, say" (1)
συνέχω, "I surround, control, constrain" (1)

17. The root *ευρ has the suffix -ισκ- added to form the present stem.
18. The root *αγ is reduplicated to form the aorist stem, αγαγ-, then the first alpha of the stem is lengthened by the augment, ἠγαγ-.

Second Aorist Passive Indicative Verbs

18.23. You have already learned that the formula for an aorist passive indicative verb is *augment + stem + form marker* θη *+ B personal endings.* All you need to know about *second* aorist passive verbs is that the second aorist passive sometimes uses a different stem, and the theta may drop out of the form marker. Some of these forms do both (use a different stem and drop the theta); others do one or the other. When a second aorist passive form drops the theta, the form marker looks like it is just an eta. In any case, you *do not need to know* if it is first or second aorist, just that it is aorist.[19]

Formula for Second Aorist Passive Indicative Verbs

augment + stem[20] + form marker η + B personal endings

The second aorist passive forms of χαίρω ("I rejoice") appear below. It is the most common second aorist passive verb in the NT (yet it occurs only 13 times). The stem has changed (ablaut) from χαιρ- to just χαρ-.

Second Aorist Passive Indicative of χαίρω

1S	ἐχάρην
2S	ἐχάρης
3S	ἐχάρη
1P	ἐχάρημεν
2P	ἐχάρητε
3P	ἐχάρησαν

The next most common second aorist passive verbs in the NT are the following:

ἀνοίγω, most commonly third singular (ἠνοίγη) or third plural (ἠνεῴχθησαν)[21]
φαίνω, usually seen in third singular (ἐφάνη)
ὑποτάσσω (first singular, ὑπετάγη; third plural, ὑπετάγησαν)

In all the forms cited as examples, the stem changes from the lexical form, and the form marker is almost always just eta rather than θη. Some second aorist

19. Some grammars use the term *second aorist* only for forms that have a different stem, not for those with the same stem but no theta. This grammar uses it for forms that have either characteristic.

20. The stem for second aorist passive indicative verbs is *usually* the same as the lexical form, but it can change. If it does change, it may be the same as the second aorist active stem, or it may be different altogether. (The verb λαμβάνω, e.g., has a second aorist active ἔλαβον but a second aorist passive ἐλήμφθην.) If it does change, the lexicon or morphology catalog (app. B) will tell you what you need to know.

21. The verb ἀνοίγω shows the variation that is possible in the aorist passive. (Most verbs consistently follow the same pattern; to have three different patterns in one verb as does ἀνοίγω is unusual.) It sometimes appears with a stem that is different from the lexical form and uses the full θη form marker: ἠνεῴχθην. Other times it uses the same stem as the lexical form with the θη form marker: ἠνοίχθην. Still other times it uses the same stem but drops the theta from the form marker: ἠνοίγην. There are also verbs that use a different stem *and* drop the theta (e.g., θάπτω, which appears as ἐτάφην in aorist passive).

passive verbs, however, do not change the stem. For example, γράφω appears as ἐγράφην.

18.24. *Examples of Second Aorist Passive Indicative Verbs*

Matt. 1:20, ἄγγελος κυρίου κατ' ὄναρ **ἐφάνη** αὐτῷ.

An angel of the Lord *appeared* to him in a dream.

Matt. 3:16, **ἠνεῴχθησαν** αὐτῷ οἱ οὐρανοί, καὶ εἶδεν τὸ πνεῦμα τοῦ θεοῦ.

The heavens *were opened* to him, and he saw the Spirit of God.

Gen. 45:16, διεβοήθη[a] ἡ φωνὴ εἰς τὸν οἶκον Φαραώ, Ἥκασιν (they have come) οἱ ἀδελφοὶ Ἰωσήφ. **ἐχάρη** δὲ Φαραὼ καὶ ἡ θεραπεία αὐτοῦ.

The message was announced in Pharaoh's house, "Joseph's brothers have come." And Pharaoh and his household staff *rejoiced*.

[a] διαβοάω, "I announce abroad, proclaim"

18.25. *Now You Try It*

Mark 14:11, **ἐχάρησαν** καὶ ἐπηγγείλαντο αὐτῷ ἀργύριον δοῦναι (to give).

Rom. 8:20, τῇ ματαιότητι ἡ κτίσις **ὑπετάγη**.

Rev. 11:19, **ἠνοίγη** ὁ ναὸς τοῦ θεοῦ ὁ ἐν τῷ οὐρανῷ καὶ **ὤφθη** ἡ κιβωτὸς τῆς διαθήκης αὐτοῦ ἐν τῷ ναῷ αὐτοῦ.

Num. 23:4, **ἐφάνη** ὁ θεὸς τῷ Βαλαάμ, καὶ εἶπεν πρὸς αὐτὸν Βαλαάμ, Τοὺς ἑπτὰ βωμοὺς ἡτοίμασα καὶ ἀνεβίβασα[a] μόσχον καὶ κριὸν[b] ἐπὶ τὸν βωμόν.

[a] ἀναβιβάζω has a wider range of meaning in the LXX than in the NT. The only NT use (Matt. 13:48) means "I draw up" a net onto the shore. In the LXX it can be used to mean "I offer (a sacrifice)," that is, to raise it up and place it on the altar.

[b] κριός, οῦ, ὁ, "ram, male sheep"

18.26. *Challenge Verse*

Rev. 20:12, εἶδον τοὺς νεκρούς, τοὺς μεγάλους καὶ τοὺς μικρούς, ἑστῶτας (standing) ἐνώπιον τοῦ θρόνου. καὶ βιβλία **ἠνοίχθησαν**, καὶ ἄλλο βιβλίον **ἠνοίχθη**, ὅ ἐστιν τῆς ζωῆς, καὶ ἐκρίθησαν οἱ νεκροὶ ἐκ τῶν γεγραμμένων (things written) ἐν τοῖς βιβλίοις κατὰ τὰ ἔργα αὐτῶν.

θη-Middle Forms

18.27. You will remember from chapter 17 that some θη forms are not passive in meaning but (at least in English) seem idiomatic. They are called **θη**-*middle forms* and are translated just like any other middle form. These aorist θη forms are essentially *aorist intransitive* forms, in contrast to the aorist middle (i.e., a form created with a σα form marker), which is typically transitive.

Transitive *takes* a direct object	Intransitive *does not take* a direct object
"I answered the question."	"I answered."

Some of the aorist passive examples above may be considered θη-middle forms even if the theta has dropped out. See, for example, the intransitive forms in Matt. 1:20; Mark 14:11; Gen. 45:16; and Num. 23:4.

Examples of θη-Middle Forms

18.28. The aorist middle form ἀπεκρινάμην[22] is usually transitive, that is, it has an object. The lexical form is ἀποκρίνομαι, "I answer"; the -ομαι ending tells us that this is a middle-only form. Notice that in both of the following examples there is an accusative direct object.

Matt. 27:12, οὐδεν **ἀπεκρίνατο.**	He [Jesus] answered nothing.
Mark 14:61, ὁ δὲ οὐκ **ἀπεκρίνατο** οὐδέν.[a]	But he did not answer him anything at all.

[a] The double negative is an emphatic statement; see the note on John 15:5 in §5.26.

Although there are not active forms of ἀποκρίνομαι, there are θη forms. The aorist form ἀπεκρίθη, "he/she answered," is an intransitive θη-middle form.

Mark 7:28, ἡ δὲ **ἀπεκρίθη** καὶ λέγει αὐτῷ, Κύριε, . . .	But she *answered* and said to him, "Lord, . . ."

You do *not* translate this example as "she was answered" (that is, by someone else), because ἀπεκρίθη is not passive despite the θη. It is a θη-middle form in which the subject performs the action.

22. Yes, ἀπεκρινάμην is an aorist middle. You would have expected -σαμην, but this is a liquid verb in which the sigma drops out following a liquid. (Do you remember liquid nouns from chap. 11?) We will study liquid verbs in chap. 21.

ἀποκρίνομαι and the LXX

Some of the usage of ἀποκρίνομαι may reflect the influence of the LXX, where ἀπεκρίθη (aorist passive indicative, 133× in LXX; 82× in NT) is the "normal" form, but ἀπεκρίνατο (aorist middle indicative, only 4× in LXX and 7× in NT) is used in solemn, legal, or poetic statements. Some of these variations may also be idiolectical ("that is just the way he says it") or genre related. The aorist passive indicative form occurs 104 times in Matthew through Acts and Revelation (and 82 of those are the 3rd sg. form, ἀπεκρίθη); by contrast, in Romans through Jude these forms do not occur at all. Likewise with the aorist middle indicative form—it is used 7 times in Matthew through Acts, in contrast to no uses in Romans through Jude.

18.29. Reading Passage: John 19:16–30

The Crucifixion of Jesus

16 τότε οὖν παρέδωκεν (he delivered) αὐτὸν αὐτοῖς ἵνα σταυρωθῇ (he should
be crucified).

Παρέλαβον οὖν τὸν Ἰησοῦν, 17 καὶ βαστάζων (carrying) ἑαυτῷ τὸν σταυρὸν
ἐξῆλθεν εἰς τὸν Κρανίου Τόπον, ὃ λέγεται Ἑβραϊστὶ Γολγοθᾶ, 18 ὅπου αὐτὸν
ἐσταύρωσαν, καὶ μετ᾽ αὐτοῦ ἄλλους δύο ἐντεῦθεν καὶ ἐντεῦθεν,[a] μέσον δὲ τὸν
Ἰησοῦν. 19 ἔγραψεν δὲ καὶ τίτλον ὁ Πιλᾶτος καὶ ἔθηκεν (he placed) ἐπὶ τοῦ σταυ-
ροῦ· ἦν δὲ γεγραμμένον (written), Ἰησοῦς ὁ Ναζωραῖος ὁ βασιλεὺς τῶν Ἰουδαίων.
20 τοῦτον οὖν τὸν τίτλον πολλοὶ **ἀνέγνωσαν** τῶν Ἰουδαίων, ὅτι ἐγγὺς ἦν ὁ τόπος
τῆς πόλεως ὅπου ἐσταυρώθη ὁ Ἰησοῦς· καὶ ἦν γεγραμμένον (written) Ἑβραϊστί,
Ῥωμαϊστί, Ἑλληνιστί. 21 ἔλεγον οὖν τῷ Πιλάτῳ οἱ ἀρχιερεῖς τῶν Ἰουδαίων, Μὴ
γράφε (write!), Ὁ βασιλεὺς τῶν Ἰουδαίων, ἀλλ᾽ ὅτι ἐκεῖνος εἶπεν, Βασιλεύς εἰμι
τῶν Ἰουδαίων. 22 **ἀπεκρίθη** ὁ Πιλᾶτος, Ὃ γέγραφα (I have written), γέγραφα.

23 Οἱ οὖν στρατιῶται, ὅτε ἐσταύρωσαν τὸν Ἰησοῦν, **ἔλαβον** τὰ ἱμάτια αὐτοῦ
καὶ ἐποίησαν τέσσαρα μέρη,[b] ἑκάστῳ στρατιώτῃ μέρος, καὶ τὸν χιτῶνα. ἦν δὲ
ὁ χιτὼν ἄραφος, ἐκ τῶν ἄνωθεν ὑφαντὸς δι᾽ ὅλου.[c] 24 **εἶπαν** οὖν πρὸς ἀλλήλους,
Μὴ σχίσωμεν (let's tear) αὐτόν, ἀλλὰ λάχωμεν (let's cast lots) περὶ αὐτοῦ
τίνος ἔσται·[d] ἵνα ἡ γραφὴ πληρωθῇ (may be fulfilled) ἡ λέγουσα (which says),
Διεμερίσαντο τὰ ἱμάτιά μου ἑαυτοῖς καὶ ἐπὶ τὸν ἱματισμόν μου **ἔβαλον** κλῆρον.[e]
Οἱ μὲν οὖν στρατιῶται ταῦτα ἐποίησαν. 25 εἱστήκεισαν (they stood) δὲ παρὰ τῷ
σταυρῷ τοῦ Ἰησοῦ ἡ μήτηρ αὐτοῦ καὶ ἡ ἀδελφὴ τῆς μητρὸς αὐτοῦ, Μαρία ἡ
τοῦ Κλωπᾶ καὶ Μαρία ἡ Μαγδαληνή. 26 Ἰησοῦς οὖν λέγει τῇ μητρί, Γύναι,[f] ἴδε
ὁ υἱός σου. 27 εἶτα λέγει τῷ μαθητῇ, Ἴδε ἡ μήτηρ σου. καὶ ἀπ᾽ ἐκείνης τῆς ὥρας
ἔλαβεν ὁ μαθητὴς αὐτὴν εἰς τὰ ἴδια.

28 Μετὰ τοῦτο εἰδὼς (knowing) ὁ Ἰησοῦς ὅτι ἤδη πάντα τετέλεσται (were
complete), ἵνα τελειωθῇ (should be fulfilled) ἡ γραφή, λέγει, Διψῶ. 29 σκεῦος
ἔκειτο[g] ὄξους μεστόν· σπόγγον οὖν μεστὸν τοῦ ὄξους ὑσσώπῳ περιθέντες (putting) **προσήνεγκαν** αὐτοῦ τῷ στόματι. 30 ὅτε οὖν **ἔλαβεν** τὸ ὄξος ὁ Ἰησοῦς **εἶπεν**,
Τετέλεσται (it is finished), καὶ κλίνας (bowing) τὴν κεφαλὴν παρέδωκεν (he
gave up) τὸ πνεῦμα.

a ἐντεῦθεν, "from here" (adv.); ἐντεῦθεν καὶ ἐντεῦθεν, formally, "from here and from there" = "on each side"

[b] μέρη may perplex you at first. It is from μέρος, ους, τό, a third-declension noun that follows a less common pattern of endings. See the paradigm for ἔθνος, ους, τό, in app. A ("Six Key, Representative Paradigms").

[c] ἐκ τῶν ἄνωθεν ὑφαντὸς δι' ὅλου, "from above woven through all" = "woven in one piece from top to bottom"

[d] περὶ αὐτοῦ τίνος ἔσται, "concerning it whose it will be" = "to see who will get it" (τίνος, interrogative pronoun in an indirect question; ἔσται, future form of εἰμί). The soldiers' statement stops at this point. The following statement, beginning with ἵνα, is the author's editorial comment explaining the significance of their actions.

[e] Διεμερίσαντο . . . κλῆρον is quoted from Ps. 21:19 (22:18 Eng.).

[f] Γύναι, vocative form of γυνή (a third-declension noun)

[g] ἔκειτο, 3rd sg. impf. mid. ind. ▶ κεῖμαι, "I lie"; the clause σκεῦος ἔκειτο ὄξους μεστόν means "a jar full of sour wine was sitting there."

18.30. Vocabulary for Chapter 18

Part of Speech	Definition	Possible Glosses	Frequency	
Word			NT	LXX
Adjective				
δώδεκα	The number twelve (indeclinable); when used as a noun in the NT this refers to the group of Jesus' disciples (even if not all twelve are present)	twelve, 12; the Twelve	75	100
Adverbs				
ἤδη	A temporal adverb most commonly expressing completion or referring to a previous situation (ctr. ἔτι, "still")	already, now	61	64
ὧδε	Adverb of place with reference to relative nearness; can also have temporal implications referring to a present circumstance	here, in this place; in this case	61	89
Conjunction				
διότι	A subordinating conjunction that gives a reason for the preceding statement or that draws an inference from it	because, for; therefore	24	341
Idiom				
εἰ μή	An idiomatic expression specifying an exception	except	86	93
Nouns				
καιρός, οῦ, ὁ	A point of time or a period of time, general or specific (wide variety of uses, depending on contextual adjuncts)	time, period	85	487
σημεῖον, ου, τό	A distinctive indication or confirmation by which something is known (in the NT this word often refers to a miracle, but it should not usually be translated as such) [cf. δύναμις and τέρας]	sign, indication; (miraculous) sign, portent	77	120

Part of Speech	Definition	Possible Glosses	Frequency	
Word			NT	LXX
Verbs				
γίνομαι	Generally, to transfer from one state or condition to another; to come into being by birth, production, or manufacture; to occur; to enter a new condition; to change location; etc. [Read the summary in *CL*!]	I become, I am/exist; I am born/produced; I come about, take place	669	2,174
εἶπον	To express a thought, opinion, or idea in spoken words (used as the ²aor. of λέγω)	I said, told	62	4,608
εἶπεν	Very common inflected verb form: 3rd sg. ²aor. act. ind. of εἶπον (λέγω)	he/she/it said/told	613	2,758
λαμβάνω	To get hold of something; to take possession of; to take away; to receive a person or thing; to be a receiver (in a passive sense)	I take, grasp; I acquire; I take away, remove; I accept; I receive	258	1,335
παραλαμβάνω	To take into close association; to gain control of	I take (to myself), take with/along; I take over; I accept	49	38
πορεύω	To cause to go, to carry (act.; not in the NT or LXX); to move or travel from one place to another (mid. and pass.)	I go, proceed (mid. and pass.)	153	1,263
ἀπεκρίθη	Very common inflected verb form (a θη-middle form): 3rd sg. aor. pass. ind. of ἀποκρίνω; to make a response, to either a specific question, a statement, or a situation	he/she/it answered	82	95
εἶδον	To perceive by seeing with the eyes; to become aware of or notice something (used as ²aor. of ὁράω) [see chap. 21]	I saw, perceived; I noticed	76	207

18.31. Key Things to Know for Chapter 18

How does a second aorist form differ from a first aorist form in spelling? (That is another way of saying you need to know the three formulas for second aorist indicative forms: active, middle, and passive.)

There is no difference in meaning between a first and a second aorist form; both express perfective aspect.

Can you identify the most common types of stem changes that occur in second aorist verbs?

What is the difference between a verb stem and a verb root?

What is meant when we say that a verb may have more than one root?

19

VERBS: PART 9

Future Indicative Verbs

19.1. This is a relatively straightforward chapter. The future tense-form in Greek is closer in meaning and usage to the future tense in English than most other Greek tense-forms are to the English tenses with similar names, though there are some differences as well. The future tense-form expresses expectation, which is most commonly rendered in English as future time. The Greek future tense-form is actually more closely related to the category of mood than of tense.[1] It has an unusual history in the language, and scholars have puzzled over it for a long time, but that is a far more technical issue than we want to tackle in the first year.

Uses of the Future Tense-Form

19.2. The future tense-form in Greek is used in a somewhat broader range of contexts than its namesake in English. We can illustrate some of the different ways it is used with the following examples. In each sentence the italicized words are the translation of a Greek future tense-form verb.

> *Prospective* contexts (future referring): Matt. 7:22, "Many *will say* to me in that day . . ."

1. It is possible that the English future should also be considered a mood rather than a tense. This is the analysis of Huddleston, *Grammar of English*, 133, 174; see also Huddleston and Pullum, *English Grammar*, 56.

This use is the most like English and represents the most common use of the future in both Greek and English.

Commanding contexts (functions as an imperative): 1 Pet. 1:16, "*Be holy,* because I am holy."[2]

An imperative statement, if obeyed, will of necessity be in the future, but this is quite different from a predictive statement, since the speaker is expressing a desire, not predicting a future situation.

Deliberative contexts: Matt. 21:37, "They *will respect* my son."

This is not a prediction but the vineyard owner thinking to himself—deliberating on the consequences of his contemplated action.

Temporally unrestricted contexts: Gal. 6:16, "As for all who *walk* by this rule, peace and mercy be upon them" (ESV); "Peace and mercy to all who *follow* this rule" (NIV).

This is not a statement true only of the future. It is equally true of the present. Most English translations do not translate the verb in Gal. 6:16 as a future tense in English but instead use a simple English present—entirely appropriate to the use of the future in this context (RSV, NIV, ESV, REB, NJB, CEB, HCSB, NLT, GNT, GW, NCV, ISV). A few translations do use an English future tense at this point (NASB, NRSV, NET).

Grammar of the Future Tense-Form

19.3. The Greek future tense-form is probably best viewed as aspectually vague. That is, from the form alone it is not possible to say that the writer is viewing the situation either as a process, as a complete event, or as a state.[3]

The future tense-form almost always refers to future time in some way; it is never used in a statement that is limited to past or present, but it may sometimes be temporally unrestricted.[4] This is the one form that is *almost* always related to a particular time; it is very different from the present and aorist tense-forms in that regard.

A common English equivalent of the standard paradigm verb λύω is the simple English future tense: "I will loose." If you discover that the context makes clear,

2. This statement is quoted from the LXX, where it appears in Lev. 11:44, 45; 19:2; and 20:7.

3. The terminology *aspectually vague* is Porter's (*Verbal Aspect*, 410); Fanning (*Verbal Aspect*, 122–23) describes it as "non-aspectual." There is some disagreement among scholars regarding the aspect of the future, even among scholars who have worked in the area of Greek verbal aspect. The explanation given here represents one approach. An alternative is to define the future tense-form as having perfective aspect (i.e., its aspect may be similar to that of the aorist; cf. Campbell, *Verbal Aspect*, 139, 159). The real difference at the functional level is minimal.

4. Temporally unrestricted forms are those that do not relate directly to time, either because a statement is true at different times ("God *loves* a cheerful giver") or because a statement is one for which time is irrelevant ("God *is* love").

for example, an imperatival force, then you will need to tweak your understanding of the form in that instance.

The Future Active and Middle Indicative Forms

19.4. This section will introduce you to both the active- and middle-voice forms of the future. There is a distinct form for the future passive, which you will meet later in this chapter.

Formation of the Future

The future is EASY! There are *no new endings* to learn. To make a future form, we just add the letter sigma as a form marker between the stem and the connecting vowel. (You will remember that the first aorist tense-form used σα as a form marker.) Compare the following future formulas with the ones you already know for other tense-forms.

Formula for Future Active Indicative Verbs

stem + form marker σ + connecting vowel + A personal endings

Formula for Future Middle Indicative Verbs

stem + form marker σ + connecting vowel + C personal endings

Note that the second formula is *only* middle voice, never passive. There is a separate form for the future passive that uses a different form marker. Many verbs used in the future middle form do not have active forms; they are middle-only forms. For now, the future active indicative stem will be the same as the present active indicative stem. In similar contexts English equivalents for the future active and future middle will be identical (since English does not have a middle voice). The meaning of the middle voice (subject focus) in the future tense-form is the same as it is in present middle indicative verbs.

19.5. *Forms of the Future Active Indicative*

Future Active Indicative of λύω

	Form	c.v. + A p.e.	Gloss
1S	λύσω	ω	I will loose
2S	λύσεις	εις	You will loose
3S	λύσει	ει	He/she/it will loose
1P	λύσομεν	ομεν	We will loose
2P	λύσετε	ετε	You will loose
3P	λύσουσι(ν)	ουσι(ν)	They will loose

19.6. *Examples of the Future Active Indicative*

Luke 1:33, **βασιλεύσει** ἐπὶ τὸν οἶκον Ἰακὼβ εἰς τοὺς αἰῶνας.

He will reign over the house of Jacob forever.

Matt. 8:7, λέγει αὐτῷ, Ἐγὼ **θεραπεύσω** αὐτόν.

He said to him, "I *will heal* him."

Rev. 5:10, **βασιλεύσουσιν** ἐπὶ τῆς γῆς.

They will reign on the earth.

Gen. 5:29, ἐπωνόμασεν τὸ ὄνομα αὐτοῦ Νῶε λέγων (saying), Οὗτος **διαναπαύσει**[a] ἡμᾶς ἀπὸ τῶν ἔργων ἡμῶν καὶ ἀπὸ τῶν λυπῶν τῶν χειρῶν ἡμῶν καὶ ἀπὸ τῆς γῆς, ἧς κατηράσατο κύριος ὁ θεός.

[a] διαναπαύω, "I allow to rest a while"

They named him Noah, saying, "He *will give* us *rest* from our labors and from the grief of our hands and from the ground that the Lord God cursed."

19.7. *Forms of the Future Middle Indicative*

Future Middle Indicative of λύω

	Form	c.v. + C p.e.	Gloss
1S	λύσομαι	ομαι	I will loose
2S	λύσῃ	ῃ	You will loose
3S	λύσεται	εται	He/she/it will loose
1P	λυσόμεθα	ομεθα	We will loose
2P	λύσεσθε	εσθε	You will loose
3P	λύσονται	ονται	They will loose

19.8. *Examples of the Future Middle Indicative*

Acts 28:28, τοῖς ἔθνεσιν ἀπεστάλη (it has been sent) τοῦτο τὸ σωτήριον τοῦ θεοῦ· αὐτοὶ καὶ **ἀκούσονται**.

This salvation from God has been sent to the Gentiles; they *will* also *listen*.

Luke 15:18, **πορεύσομαι** πρὸς τὸν πατέρα μου καὶ ἐρῶ (I will say) αὐτῷ, Πάτερ, ἥμαρτον εἰς τὸν οὐρανὸν καὶ ἐνώπιόν σου.

I will go to my father, and I will say to him, "Father, I sinned against heaven and before you."

Gen. 24:19, εἶπεν, Καὶ ταῖς καμήλοις σου **ὑδρεύσομαι**,[a] ἕως ἂν[b] πᾶσαι πίωσιν (they have drunk).

[a] ὑδρεύω, "I draw or carry water"

[b] ἕως ἄν, "until"

She said, "For your camels also *I will draw water* until they have all drunk."

19.9. *Examples of Future Active and Middle Indicative Verbs*

Matt. 1:23, **καλέσουσιν** τὸ ὄνομα αὐτοῦ Ἐμμανουήλ.	*They will name* him Emmanuel.

The expression καλέσουσιν τὸ ὄνομα αὐτοῦ sounds odd to us if it is translated formally in English, since we do not say it this way ("to call someone a name" is derogatory in English); we would say simply, "They will name him Emmanuel." This idiom occurs in several other examples in this chapter.

The next verse is a bit tricky (but not too bad). I have given you an English equivalent, but try to figure it out for yourself before you read it.

John 3:12, εἰ τὰ ἐπίγεια[a] εἶπον ὑμῖν καὶ οὐ πιστεύετε, πῶς ἐὰν εἴπω (I speak) ὑμῖν τὰ ἐπουράνια[a] **πιστεύσετε;**	If I spoke to you [about] earthly things and you did not believe, how *will you believe* if I speak to you [about] heavenly things?

[a] The phrases τὰ ἐπίγεια and τὰ ἐπουράνια are both similar uses of the article: "the things on earth/heaven" = "the earthly/heavenly things."

Gen. 24:39, Μήποτε οὐ **πορεύσεται** ἡ γυνὴ μετ' ἐμοῦ.	Perhaps the woman *will* not *go* with me.

19.10. *Now You Try It*

Matt. 27:42, βασιλεὺς Ἰσραήλ ἐστιν,[a] καταβάτω[b] νῦν ἀπὸ τοῦ σταυροῦ καὶ **πιστεύσομεν** ἐπ' αὐτόν.

[a] The first phrase is sarcastic. Read the context in your English Bible.
[b] "Let him come down!"

Acts 17:32, Ἀκούσαντες (having heard of) δὲ ἀνάστασιν νεκρῶν οἱ μὲν[a] ἐχλεύαζον,[b] οἱ δὲ εἶπαν, **Ἀκουσόμεθά** σου περὶ τούτου καὶ πάλιν.

[a] The use of μέν . . . δέ introduces a series of alternatives: "on the one hand . . . on the other hand." In this verse, as used with the article οἱ, it means "some mocked, but others said."
[b] χλευάζω, "I mock"

Exod. 6:6, Ἐγὼ κύριος καὶ **ῥύσομαι** ὑμᾶς ἐκ τῆς δουλείας.

Exod. 24:7, καὶ λαβὼν (taking) τὸ βιβλίον τῆς διαθήκης ἀνέγνω εἰς τὰ ὦτα τοῦ λαοῦ, καὶ εἶπαν, Πάντα, ὅσα ἐλάλησεν κύριος, ποιήσομεν καὶ **ἀκουσόμεθα.**

Contract Verbs in the Future Tense-Form

19.11. The stem vowel of a contract verb usually lengthens when a form marker (in this case sigma) is added.[5] Remember that a contract verb is one whose stem ends with one of the three short vowels, ε, ο, α, which lengthen to η, ω, η respectively. The normal pattern looks like this first plural example: ἀγαπήσομεν (i.e., rather than ἀγαπάσομεν). There are a few less-common instances in which the stem vowel of some verbs does not lengthen. The first singular future form of καλέω is καλέσω, not καλήσω (see the example in Luke 1:13 below).[6]

Future Active and Middle Indicative of ἀγαπάω

	Active	Middle
1S	ἀγαπήσω	ἀγαπήσομαι
2S	ἀγαπήσεις	ἀγαπήσῃ
3S	ἀγαπήσει	ἀγαπήσεται
1P	ἀγαπήσομεν	ἀγαπησόμεθα
2P	ἀγαπήσετε	ἀγαπήσεσθε
3P	ἀγαπήσουσι(ν)	ἀγαπήσονται

19.12. *Examples of Future Contract Verbs*

Matt. 4:19, λέγει αὐτοῖς, Δεῦτε (follow!) ὀπίσω μου, καὶ **ποιήσω**[a] ὑμᾶς ἁλιεῖς ἀνθρώπων.

[a] ποιέω = ε ▸ η

He said to them, "Follow me and *I will make* you fishers of people."

Matt. 9:18, Come and place τὴν χεῖρά σου ἐπ᾽ αὐτήν, καὶ **ζήσεται.**[a]

[a] ζάω = α ▸ η

Come and place your hand on her, and *she will live.*

Matt. 11:16, Τίνι δὲ **ὁμοιώσω**[a] τὴν γενεὰν ταύτην;

[a] ὁμοιόω = ο ▸ ω

To what *shall I compare* this generation?

19.13. *Now You Try It*

Luke 1:13, ἡ γυνή σου Ἐλισάβετ **γεννήσει** υἱόν σοι καὶ **καλέσεις** τὸ ὄνομα αὐτοῦ Ἰωάννην.

5. This is true whenever a form marker is added in other forms also—for example, aorist forms that add σα as a form marker or perfect forms that use κα.

6. This is distinctive of particular words. Any given word will follow the same pattern, either always lengthening the connecting vowel (which most words do) or not.

John 14:23, ἀπεκρίθη Ἰησοῦς καὶ εἶπεν αὐτῷ, Ἐάν τις ἀγαπᾷ (loves) με τὸν λόγον μου **τηρήσει**, καὶ ὁ πατήρ μου **ἀγαπήσει** αὐτὸν καὶ πρὸς αὐτὸν ἐλευσόμεθα (we will come) καὶ μονὴν παρ᾽ αὐτῷ **ποιησόμεθα**.

Exod. 34:20, πρωτότοκον ὑποζυγίου **λυτρώσῃ** προβάτῳ. πᾶν πρωτότοκον τῶν υἱῶν σου **λυτρώσῃ**. οὐκ ὀφθήσῃ ἐνώπιόν μου κενός.

The Square of Stops and the Future Tense-Form

19.14. Now here is a perplexity for you to think about:

The future of βλέπω is βλέψω.
The future of ἔχω is ἕξω.[7]
The future of πείθω is πείσω.

Why? Why are these forms not spelled ἔχσω, βλέπσω, and πείθσω? Is that not what the formula specifies? Do you remember the square of stops? Of course you do, and the heading for this section was a helpful reminder, wasn't it? When a sigma (the future form marker) is added to a verb stem ending in a *stop*, they will combine. This functions the same as did similar combinations in third-declension nouns and in aorist verb forms.

Square of Stops

			+ σ =
π	β	φ	ψ
κ	γ	χ	ξ
τ	δ	θ	σ

19.15. *Examples*

Luke 20:13, εἶπεν ὁ κύριος τοῦ ἀμπελῶνος (vineyard), **Πέμψω** τὸν υἱόν μου τὸν ἀγαπητόν.

The owner of the vineyard said, "*I will send* my beloved son."

Mark 14:28, μετὰ τὸ ἐγερθῆναί με[a] **προάξω** ὑμᾶς εἰς τὴν Γαλιλαίαν.

[a] μετὰ τὸ ἐγερθῆναί με, "after I have been raised"

After I have been raised *I will go* before you into Galilee.

7. Yes, the rough breathing mark on the future is correct. This word used to be spelled σέχω, and the rough breathing mark compensates for the sigma that dropped out. If you really want to know all the gory details about this form (and its compounds), see *MBG*, 260n10.

19.16. *Now You Try It*

Matt. 1:23, Ἰδοὺ ἡ παρθένος ἐν γαστρὶ **ἕξει**[a] καὶ **τέξεται**[b] υἱόν, καὶ καλέσουσιν τὸ ὄνομα αὐτοῦ Ἐμμανουήλ.

[a] ἐν γαστρὶ ἕξει is an idiom: "she will have in belly" = "she will be pregnant."

[b] The formation of τέξεται from τίκτω is really complicated (see *MBG*, 262nn6–8). For now, be content that the xi is a form marker affected by the square of stops. If you are *really* curious (you do not have to know this), the root is *τκ, which uses iota reduplication to form the present stem, τιτκ-, which then undergoes metathesis (reversal of letters) to form τικτ-, and thus the present is τίκτω. The future form is built from the root *τκ, which experiences vowel gradation with the insertion of ε (thus τεκ-), and κ + σ = ξ, so the future form is τέξομαι.

Matt. 12:19, οὐκ **ἐρίσει** οὐδὲ **κραυγάσει**, οὐδὲ **ἀκούσει** τις ἐν ταῖς πλατείαις τὴν φωνὴν αὐτοῦ.

Verbs that end in -ιζω or -αζω also act like square-of-stops forms in the future just as they did in the aorist—and for the same reason: their stems typically end in a delta. Two of the three futures in this verse are formed this way.

Pss. Sol. 13.6, ὅτι δεινὴ[a] ἡ καταστροφὴ τοῦ ἁμαρτωλοῦ, καὶ οὐχ **ἅψεται**[b] δικαίου οὐδὲν[c] ἐκ πάντων τούτων.

[a] δεινή is from δεινός, ή, όν, not δεῖνα.

[b] ἅπτω can take a genitive direct object.

[c] Since οὐδέν is a neuter form, it could be either nominative or accusative; here it is nominative.

This verse can serve as a good test of how well you understand the grammar and syntax you have been learning, since it is from a book that you have probably never read and almost certainly have never memorized. The *Psalms of Solomon* are part of the OT Pseudepigrapha (not the Apocrypha). You will need your lexicon handy. You will have to supply a verb in the first clause.

The Future of εἰμί

19.17. You also need to know the future forms of εἰμί—they occur nearly 200 times in the NT (191 to be precise) and far more than that in the LXX (1,726 times). These are the only future forms of εἰμί. They are parsed as middle voice because they use the C set of personal endings, but since there is no alternate choice (there is no future active form of εἰμί), the fact that these forms are middle is not significant.[8]

8. Some grammars list the future of εἰμί as simply "future indicative of εἰμί" rather than specifying the voice. The voice is included here for consistency in identifying the form, but your teacher may prefer that you describe it differently.

Future [Middle] Indicative Forms of εἰμί

1S	ἔσομαι	I will be
2S	ἔσῃ	You will be
3S	ἔσται	He/she/it will be
1P	ἐσόμεθα	We will be
2P	ἔσεσθε	You will be
3P	ἔσονται	They will be

You need to be able to *recognize* these forms, but you do not necessarily need to memorize the paradigm. They are not hard to recognize: whenever you see what appears to be a personal ending with a sigma form marker and all there is for a stem is the letter epsilon, you are almost certainly dealing with a future form of εἰμί. The third singular is by far the most common: 118 of the 186 total occurrences of future forms of εἰμί in the NT, and 1,263 of the 1,726 total occurrences of future forms of εἰμί in the LXX; the third plural is next with only 31 NT and 242 LXX forms. Here is a sample of each of the six forms in context.

A Tricky Form

How would you parse this form?

ζητήσεις

Given that this chapter is about future tense-forms, you would probably say, "future." In some contexts you would be correct, but in other contexts, the identical form would not even be a verb. There is a third-declension pattern that can look just like a future. Compare these two verses:

Titus 3:9, μωρὰς δὲ **ζητήσεις** καὶ γενεαλογίας καὶ ἔρεις καὶ μάχας νομικὰς περιΐστασο (avoid!).	But avoid foolish *controversies*, genealogies, dissensions, and quarrels about the law.
Sir. 33:33, ἐν ποίᾳ ὁδῷ **ζητήσεις** αὐτόν;	On what road *will you seek* him?

If you did not recognize that ζητήσεις could be a feminine plural accusative noun from ζήτησις, εως, ἡ, "debate, controversy," you might initially be very puzzled by the Titus passage, thinking that Paul was encouraging (or perhaps predicting) foolish controversy. See the pattern of endings used on πόλις in §11.12 or in app. A, §A.4.

19.18. *Examples of the Future of εἰμί*

2 Cor. 6:18, **ἔσομαι** ὑμῖν εἰς πατέρα καὶ ὑμεῖς **ἔσεσθέ** μοι εἰς υἱοὺς καὶ θυγατέρας, λέγει κύριος παντοκράτωρ.	"*I will be* your Father, and you *will be* my sons and daughters," says the Lord Almighty.

Mark 13:4, Εἰπόν (tell!) ἡμῖν, πότε ταῦτα **ἔσται**;	Tell us, when *will* these things *happen*?
Gen. 12:2, ποιήσω σε εἰς ἔθνος μέγα καὶ εὐλογήσω σε καὶ μεγαλυνῶ τὸ ὄνομά σου, καὶ **ἔσῃ** εὐλογητός.	I will make you a great nation, and I will bless you, and I will make your name great, and *you will be* blessed.
Jdt. 5:21, **ἐσόμεθα** εἰς ὀνειδισμὸν ἐναντίον πάσης τῆς γῆς.	*We will be* a disgrace before all the earth [i.e., before everybody].

19.19. *Now You Try It*

Mark 10:8, **ἔσονται** οἱ δύο εἰς σάρκα μίαν.

1 Tim. 4:6, καλὸς **ἔσῃ** διάκονος Χριστοῦ Ἰησοῦ.

1 John 3:2, Ἀγαπητοί, νῦν τέκνα θεοῦ ἐσμεν, καὶ οὔπω ἐφανερώθη (it has appeared) τί **ἐσόμεθα**. οἴδαμεν ὅτι ἐὰν φανερωθῇ (he appears), ὅμοιοι αὐτῷ **ἐσόμεθα**, ὅτι ὀψόμεθα (we will see) αὐτὸν καθώς ἐστιν.

Exod. 4:16, αὐτός σοι προσλαλήσει πρὸς τὸν λαόν, καὶ αὐτὸς **ἔσται** σου στόμα, σὺ δὲ αὐτῷ **ἔσῃ** τὰ πρὸς τὸν θεόν.[a]

[a] τὰ πρὸς τὸν θεόν, "the things pertaining to God" (This is an odd phrase that does not reflect the Hebrew text well.)

Gen. 26:3, **ἔσομαι** μετὰ σοῦ καὶ εὐλογήσω σε· σοὶ γὰρ καὶ τῷ σπέρματί σου δώσω[a] πᾶσαν τὴν γῆν ταύτην.

[a] δώσω, "I will give" (1st sg. fut. act. ind. ▶ δίδωμι, stem δο-). You will study μι *verbs* in chaps. 32–33, but if you know the stem for δίδωμι, you can easily identify the future form.

Future Passive Indicative

19.20. The future passive has a form distinct from the future middle. This is unlike the present and imperfect tense-forms, in which the middle form can also be passive if there is an agent marker in the context. The future passive tense-form follows the same pattern as the aorist passive; whatever the aorist passive does in terms of stem and form marker, the future passive follows suit.

Formula for Future Passive Indicative Verbs

aor. pass. stem + form marker θησ + connecting vowel + C personal endings

There is no augment, because this is a primary form, not secondary. You might think of the θησ form marker as the aorist passive form marker *and* the future active form marker combined. (It is not, but it may help you remember it.) The endings are the C set of personal endings. The stem of a future passive will always be identical to the aorist passive stem. While this is often the same as the present stem, if it does change in the aorist passive, it will use the same stem in the future passive. Both a form marker and a connecting vowel are used, because the form marker ends with a consonant (sigma), thus another vowel is needed to connect the personal ending.

Future Passive Indicative of λύω

	Form	c.v. + C p.e.	Gloss
1S	λυθήσομαι	ομαι	I will be loosed
2S	λυθήσῃ	ῃ	You will be loosed
3S	λυθήσεται	εται	He/she/it will be loosed
1P	λυθησόμεθα	ομεθα	We will be loosed
2P	λυθήσεσθε	εσθε	You will be loosed
3P	λυθήσονται	ονται	They will be loosed

19.21. *Examples of the Future Passive Indicative*

Mark 5:28, ἔλεγεν γὰρ ὅτι Ἐὰν ἅψωμαι[a] τῶν ἱματίων αὐτοῦ **σωθήσομαι**. — For she said, "If I touch his cloak, *I will be healed*."

[a] ἅψωμαι ▶ ἅπτομαι, "I touch" (This is a woman speaking in reference to Jesus.)

Mark 9:49, πᾶς γὰρ πυρὶ **ἁλισθήσεται**.[a] — For everyone *will be salted* with fire.

[a] ἁλίζω, "I salt." This is one of Jesus' most enigmatic statements. It is not difficult to understand what the words say, but it is most puzzling to interpret.

Gen. 2:23, εἶπεν Ἀδάμ, Τοῦτο νῦν ὀστοῦν ἐκ τῶν ὀστέων μου καὶ σὰρξ ἐκ τῆς σαρκός μου· αὕτη **κληθήσεται** γυνή, ὅτι ἐκ τοῦ ἀνδρὸς αὐτῆς ἐλήμφθη αὕτη. — Adam said, "This is now bone of my bones and flesh of my flesh; she *will be called* 'woman' because she was taken from her husband."

19.22. *Now You Try It*

Col. 3:4, ὑμεῖς σὺν αὐτῷ **φανερωθήσεσθε** ἐν δόξῃ.

Matt. 24:14, **κηρυχθήσεται** τοῦτο τὸ εὐαγγέλιον τῆς βασιλείας ἐν ὅλῃ τῇ οἰκουμένῃ.

In this example, the verb is κηρύσσω, and the stem is κηρυγ-. A good lexicon such as BDAG will help you with many forms that may otherwise puzzle you. Unfortunately, *CL* does not provide any help on this particular form. (If you do not find the help you need in your lexicon, check the morphology catalog in app. B.) The first part of the entry for κηρύσσω in BDAG reads like this:

κηρύσσω impf. ἐκήρυσσον; fut. κηρύξω; 1 aor. ἐκήρυξα, inf. κηρύξαι . . . ; pf. inf. κεκηρυχέναι . . . pass.: 1 fut. κηρυχθήσομαι; 1 aor. ἐκηρύχθην; pf. κεκήρυγμαι . . .

1. **to make an official announcement,** ***announce, make known,*** by an official herald or one who functions as such . . .

2. **to make public declarations,** ***proclaim aloud***

Gen. 2:24, ἕνεκεν τούτου[a] καταλείψει ἄνθρωπος τὸν πατέρα αὐτοῦ καὶ τὴν μητέρα αὐτοῦ καὶ **προσκολληθήσεται** πρὸς τὴν γυναῖκα αὐτοῦ, καὶ ἔσονται οἱ δύο εἰς σάρκα μίαν.

[a] ἕνεκεν τούτου, "for this reason"

A Deceptive Form

19.23. Watch out for forms like ἐγεννήθησαν and ἐφοβήθησαν in the next two examples. Check the endings carefully (which quadrant are they: A, B, C, or D?) as well as the first letter of the word. Are these two verbs future passive forms? They do have θησ in front of an ending.

John 1:12–13, ὅσοι ἔλαβον αὐτόν, ἔδωκεν (he gave) αὐτοῖς ἐξουσίαν τέκνα θεοῦ γενέσθαι (to be), τοῖς πιστεύουσιν (ones who believe) εἰς τὸ ὄνομα αὐτοῦ, οἳ οὐκ ἐξ αἱμάτων οὐδὲ ἐκ θελήματος σαρκὸς οὐδὲ ἐκ θελήματος ἀνδρὸς ἀλλ' ἐκ θεοῦ **ἐγεννήθησαν**.

All who received him, to them he gave the capability to be children of God, to the ones who believe on his name, who *were begotten,* not out of bloods, neither out of the will of the flesh, nor out of the will of man, but from God.[a]

[a] A fairly formal English equivalent has been given for John 1:13. There are some idiomatic expressions here that would communicate more effectively if a functionally equivalent expression were used. See NIV and NET for some ways to do this.

John 6:19, θεωροῦσιν τὸν Ἰησοῦν περιπατοῦντα (walking) ἐπὶ τῆς θαλάσσης, καὶ **ἐφοβήθησαν**.

They saw Jesus walking on the lake, and *they were afraid*.

These verbs are third plural *aorist* passive forms, *not* future passive. This aorist passive ending is the only time that a θησ following a verb stem is *not* a future passive form marker. The aorist passive form marker is still only θη; the sigma is part of the personal ending. Watch for the augment as a reminder that it is an aorist (there is no augment on the future form). Also watch for the *ending*: -σαν and -αν are secondary endings; the third plural C ending (which the future would have) is -ονται.

19.24. *Now You Try It*

Mark 2:2, **συνήχθησαν** πολλοί, καὶ ἐλάλει αὐτοῖς τὸν λόγον.

Think through the parsing of συνήχθησαν step by step, following these questions.

Is θησ the future passive form marker?
What is the ending?
Is there an augment?

If you answer those questions correctly, you should realize that this is an *aorist* passive with a third plural ending. So we would parse it as a third plural aorist passive indicative, but of what word? Does the pattern συν-ηχ-θη-σαν tell us that this is a form of συνέχω? That sounds reasonable, but it is always wise to verify your conclusion with the lexicon. In this case, if you look up συνέχω in BDAG or in the morphology catalog in appendix B of this book, you would find that the aorist active form is συνέσχον—and though a separate aorist passive form is not listed, the spelling of the aorist active form ought to be sufficiently different to give you pause. Remember the square of stops? The χ is formed from κ, γ, or χ. Check your lexicon just as it is spelled: συνήχθησαν. You will not find the third plural form, but you will probably find the first singular, συνήχθην. For example, if you are looking at *CL*, you would find this entry:

συνήχθην 1 aor. pass. ind. of συνάγω

Here is what you would find in BDAG:

συνάγω fut. συνάξω; 1 aor. συνῆξα (. . .), inf. συνάξαι **Lk 3:17 v.l.** (. . .); 2 aor. συνήγαγον. Pass.: 1 fut. συναχθήσομαι; 1 aor. συνήχθην; pf. 3 sg. συνῆκται LXX (Hom. et al.)

1. to cause to come together, *gather (in)*—a. things: . . . **b.** of persons *bring* or *call together, gather* a number of persons . . .—Pass., either in the passive sense *be gathered* or *brought together* . . . ; or w. act. force *gather, come together, assemble* . . .

2. to effect renewed relations, *bring together, reconcile* . . .

3. to bring together with, *lead* or *bring (to)* . . .

4. to extend a welcome to, *invite/receive as a guest* . . .

5. intr. . . . **to move to another position, *advance, move* . . .**—M-M.

19.25. Watch the punctuation in BDAG (and other lexicons) carefully. Periods, semicolons, and commas all have significance and divide the entry into discrete sections. Here the designation "pass.:" (in the first paragraph that gives the morphology) governs *all the forms that follow*. That is, the listings "1 fut. συναχθήσομαι; 1 aor. συνήχθην; pf. 3 sg. συνῆκται" are all passive forms: first future passive indicative, first aorist passive indicative, and perfect passive indicative.

Also note that there is a separate listing for the meaning of this word when it is used in the passive voice (1.b.). It need not have an actual passive meaning in that there may not be someone or something that is doing the gathering. Even though the form is morphologically "passive" (i.e., it has a θη form marker), it may have a meaning that BDAG designates as active ("w. act. force"). A "θη-middle" designation would be a better description in this instance.

As long as we are looking at BDAG, let me point out a few other things. The information in parentheses at the end of the first paragraph indicates the range of usage for this word: the oldest known use is found in Homer (= Hom.), and it is found regularly from that time onward. The various forms are fairly self-explanatory. The abbreviation *v.l.* after "Lk 3:17" indicates a textual variant (*varia lectio*) in which the aorist infinitive is found. The "(. . .)" portion of the entry immediately following the *v.l.* (elided in the excerpt above) contains bibliographical information on this variant reading. At the end of the entry, the "M-M" note tells you that this word is listed in Moulton and Milligan's specialized lexicon of the papyri (*Vocabulary of the Greek New Testament*)—this is helpful since M-M does not list every word; with BDAG's help you know that it is worth consulting M-M.

Second Future Passive Indicative Forms

19.26. All you need to know about second future passives is that the theta drops out, so the form marker appears to be ησ instead of θησ. You *do not have to know* if it is a first or second future, just that it is future. There are not many of these forms; only 17 words have second future passive forms in the NT, occurring a total of only 30 times. The LXX has a greater number of such forms, but only one verb is particularly common, στρέφω, and its compound forms occur about 60 times.[9]

19.27. Examples of Second Future Passive Indicative Forms

Matt. 7:7, κρούετε (knock!) καὶ **ἀνοιγήσεται** ὑμῖν.	Knock, and *it will be opened* for you.
Matt. 21:37, ὕστερον ἀπέστειλεν πρὸς αὐτοὺς τὸν υἱὸν αὐτοῦ λέγων, **Ἐντραπήσονται** τὸν υἱόν μου.	Last of all he sent his son to them, saying, "*They will respect* my son."
Sir. 50:28, μακάριος ὃς ἐν τούτοις **ἀναστραφήσεται**, καὶ θεὶς (placing) αὐτὰ ἐπὶ καρδίαν αὐτοῦ[a] σοφισθήσεται.	Blessed is the one who *will live* by these things, and placing them on his heart he will be wise.

[a] The expression θεὶς αὐτὰ ἐπὶ καρδίαν αὐτοῦ has the idea that might be expressed by a similar English idiom: "taking them to heart." The participle θείς might be temporal ("when he takes them to heart") or conditional ("if he takes them to heart"). We will study participle options like this in chaps. 23 and 24.

9. The single most common form is ἀποστρέφω, with 27 instances in the LXX. Other forms of στρέφω are compounds with ἀνα-, δια-, ἐκανα-, ἐπι-, κατα-, μετα-, and περι-. The only other words that have second future forms occurring more than 10 times in the LXX are compounds of τρίβω (20×) and κρύπτω (14×).

19.28. Now You Try It

1 Cor. 15:51, πάντες οὐ κοιμηθησόμεθα, πάντες δὲ **ἀλλαγησόμεθα**.[a]

[a] This form may puzzle you at first. Remember that the future passive follows the same pattern as the aorist passive. If the stem changes in the aorist passive, the future passive will do the same thing. The lexicons do not usually list a form with the ἀλλαγ- stem, but you will find the help you need in the morphology catalog (see the "Odd Forms" section) in app. B. Can you figure it out from there?

Num. 22:34, καὶ νῦν εἰ μή σοι ἀρέσκει, **ἀποστραφήσομαι**.

Ps. 33:21 (34:20 Eng.), κύριος φυλάσσει πάντα τὰ ὀστᾶ[a] αὐτῶν, ἓν ἐξ αὐτῶν οὐ **συντριβήσεται**.

[a] ὀστᾶ, neut. pl. acc. ▸ ὀστέον, ου, τό, "bone"; the paradigm is irregular (see BDAG for details).

1 Kgdms. (1 Sam.) 20:5, εἶπεν Δαυὶδ πρὸς Ἰωναθάν, Ἰδοὺ δὴ νεομηνία αὔριον, καὶ ἐγὼ οὐ καθήσομαι μετὰ τοῦ βασιλέως φαγεῖν, καὶ ἐξαποστελεῖς με, καὶ **κρυβήσομαι** ἐν τῷ πεδίῳ ἕως δείλης.[a]

[a] δείλη, ης, ἡ, "late afternoon, evening"

Imperatival Futures

19.29. As illustrated earlier in the chapter (see "Uses of the Future Tense-Form"), the future can be used in place of an imperative form. For example, in 1 Pet. 1:16 you would read διότι γέγραπται ὅτι Ἅγιοι **ἔσεσθε**, ὅτι ἐγὼ ἅγιός εἰμι, which English translations give as: "for it is written: '*Be* holy, because I am holy'" (NIV). Or in Matt. 22:37 you read, ὁ δὲ ἔφη (he said) αὐτῷ, **Ἀγαπήσεις** κύριον τὸν θεόν σου ἐν ὅλῃ τῇ καρδίᾳ σου καὶ ἐν ὅλῃ τῇ ψυχῇ σου καὶ ἐν ὅλῃ τῇ διανοίᾳ σου. That is not a prediction. Instead it is a command: "He said to him, '*Love* the Lord your God with all your heart, with all your soul, and with all your mind'" (HCSB). Although this may seem surprising to you, we *do* use the future this way in English, though rarely. For example, when a mother or father says to a son or daughter, "You *will* clean your room tonight!" the form is future, but the meaning is clearly imperatival, not predictive.

In the NT the imperatival use of the future tense-form is most common in Matthew, but it is also found elsewhere. The NT frequency is due largely to the influence of the OT, mediated through the LXX, where this usage is quite common. The first example above (1 Pet. 1:16) is quoted from Lev. 19:2, and the second (Matt. 22:37) is from Deut. 6:5. This usage is not common outside the NT, but it is a recognized Greek usage.[10]

10. See Goodwin, *Syntax*, §§69–70; and Smyth, *Greek Grammar*, §§1917–19. These are Classical Greek grammars, and they cite examples from that corpus.

19.30. *Examples of Future Active and Middle Indicative Verbs*

Mark 9:35, Εἴ τις θέλει πρῶτος εἶναι, **ἔσται** πάντων ἔσχατος καὶ πάντων διάκονος.

If anyone desires to be first, *he must be* last of all and servant of all.

Luke 1:31, **καλέσεις** τὸ ὄνομα αὐτοῦ Ἰησοῦν.

You are to name him Jesus.

Matt. 19:18, λέγει αὐτῷ, Ποίας; ὁ δὲ Ἰησοῦς εἶπεν, Τό[a] Οὐ **φονεύσεις**, Οὐ **μοιχεύσεις**, Οὐ **κλέψεις**, Οὐ **ψευδομαρτυρήσεις**.

He said to him, "Which ones?" And Jesus answered, "*Do* not *murder*, *do* not *commit adultery*, *do* not *steal*, *do* not *bear false witness.*"

[a] The article τό probably looks odd to you since it is followed by a series of negated verbs. This article functions as a nominalizer, indicating that the entire series of verbs that follows serves as the content of what Jesus said and the direct object of the verb εἶπεν.

Acts 18:15, **ὄψεσθε** αὐτοί·[a] κριτὴς ἐγὼ τούτων οὐ βούλομαι εἶναι.

See to it yourselves. I don't want to be a judge of such things. (HCSB)

[a] Did you remember the function of αὐτός in this construction? You will want to read the context of this statement in an English Bible to make sense of it.

19.31. *Now You Try It*

Matt. 6:5, οὐκ **ἔσεσθε** ὡς οἱ ὑποκριταί.

Gal. 5:14, **Ἀγαπήσεις** τὸν πλησίον σου ὡς σεαυτόν.

Gen. 24:38, εἰς τὸν οἶκον τοῦ πατρός μου **πορεύσῃ** καὶ εἰς τὴν φυλήν μου καὶ λήμψῃ[a] γυναῖκα τῷ υἱῷ μου ἐκεῖθεν.

[a] 2nd sg. fut. mid. ind. ▸ λαμβάνω (root *λαβ; the α lengthens to η, a μ is added, and the square of stops β + σ = ψ produces the future stem, λημψ-); this is a middle-only form in the future.

Exod. 18:19, **ἀνοίσεις**[a] τοὺς λόγους αὐτῶν πρὸς τὸν θεόν.

[a] From ἀναφέρω, second future stem ἀνοι-, root *οι. This is one of the verbs with multiple roots; see §18.8.

Exod. 20:3–5, 7, οὐκ **ἔσονταί** σοι θεοὶ ἕτεροι πλὴν ἐμοῦ. οὐ **ποιήσεις** σεαυτῷ εἴδωλον. οὐ **προσκυνήσεις** αὐτοῖς οὐδὲ μὴ λατρεύσῃς[a] αὐτοῖς· ἐγὼ γάρ εἰμι κύριος ὁ θεός σου. οὐ **λήμψῃ** τὸ ὄνομα κυρίου τοῦ θεοῦ σου ἐπὶ ματαίῳ.

[a] οὐδὲ μὴ λατρεύσῃς, "neither serve" (double negative)

Reading Passages

19.32. *John 5:25–29*

A Time Is Coming

25ἀμὴν ἀμὴν λέγω ὑμῖν ὅτι ἔρχεται[a] ὥρα καὶ νῦν ἐστιν ὅτε οἱ νεκροὶ ἀκούσουσιν
τῆς φωνῆς τοῦ υἱοῦ τοῦ θεοῦ καὶ οἱ ἀκούσαντες (ones who hear) ζήσουσιν.
26ὥσπερ γὰρ ὁ πατὴρ ἔχει ζωὴν ἐν ἑαυτῷ, οὕτως καὶ τῷ υἱῷ ἔδωκεν (he gave)
ζωὴν ἔχειν (to have) ἐν ἑαυτῷ. 27καὶ ἐξουσίαν ἔδωκεν (he gave) αὐτῷ κρίσιν
ποιεῖν, ὅτι υἱὸς ἀνθρώπου ἐστίν. 28μὴ θαυμάζετε[b] τοῦτο,[c] ὅτι ἔρχεται ὥρα ἐν ᾗ
πάντες οἱ ἐν τοῖς μνημείοις ἀκούσουσιν τῆς φωνῆς αὐτοῦ 29καὶ ἐκπορεύσονται
οἱ[d] τὰ ἀγαθὰ ποιήσαντες (who have done) εἰς ἀνάστασιν ζωῆς, οἱ[d] δὲ τὰ φαῦλα
πράξαντες (who have done) εἰς ἀνάστασιν κρίσεως.

[a] Notice the future use of the present form; it recurs again later in the paragraph.

[b] This is actually an imperative form (the μή is one clue; indicative verbs normally use οὐ), so you would say: "Do not be amazed."

[c] To make good English here we have to supply "at"—"*at* this."

[d] Both articles marked above govern a verbal form several words later in the clause with the verb's object intervening: οἱ ποιήσαντες and οἱ πράξαντες. (The verbal forms are both participles, but with the article they act like nouns. You will learn this construction in chap. 25.) The article tells you how they are functioning in the sentence.

19.33. *Matthew 24:20–31*

There are fifteen future forms in this passage. See if you can identify all of them before you begin reading. Three of the fifteen future forms you have not met yet; they are underlined and translated for you.

The Coming of the Son of Man

20προσεύχεσθε (pray!) δὲ ἵνα μὴ γένηται (it should not be) ἡ φυγὴ ὑμῶν
χειμῶνος μηδὲ σαββάτῳ. 21ἔσται γὰρ τότε θλῖψις μεγάλη οἵα οὐ γέγονεν (has
been) ἀπ' ἀρχῆς κόσμου ἕως τοῦ νῦν οὐδ' οὐ μὴ γένηται (it will be). 22καὶ εἰ
μὴ ἐκολοβώθησαν αἱ ἡμέραι ἐκεῖναι, οὐκ ἂν ἐσώθη πᾶσα σάρξ· διὰ δὲ τοὺς
ἐκλεκτοὺς κολοβωθήσονται αἱ ἡμέραι ἐκεῖναι. 23τότε ἐάν τις ὑμῖν εἴπῃ (should
say), Ἰδοὺ ὧδε ὁ Χριστός, ἤ, Ὧδε, μὴ πιστεύσητε (you believe)· 24ἐγερθήσονται
γὰρ ψευδόχριστοι καὶ ψευδοπροφῆται καὶ <u>δώσουσιν</u> (they will do/perform)
σημεῖα μεγάλα καὶ τέρατα ὥστε πλανῆσαι, εἰ δυνατόν, καὶ τοὺς ἐκλεκτούς. 25ἰδοὺ
προείρηκα (I have told in advance) ὑμῖν. 26ἐὰν οὖν εἴπωσιν (they should say)
ὑμῖν, Ἰδοὺ ἐν τῇ ἐρήμῳ ἐστίν, μὴ ἐξέλθητε (you go out)· Ἰδοὺ ἐν τοῖς ταμείοις,
μὴ πιστεύσητε (you believe)· 27ὥσπερ γὰρ ἡ ἀστραπὴ ἐξέρχεται ἀπὸ ἀνατολῶν
καὶ φαίνεται ἕως δυσμῶν, οὕτως ἔσται ἡ παρουσία τοῦ υἱοῦ τοῦ ἀνθρώπου·
28ὅπου ἐὰν ᾖ (it should be) τὸ πτῶμα, ἐκεῖ συναχθήσονται οἱ ἀετοί.
29Εὐθέως δὲ μετὰ τὴν θλῖψιν τῶν ἡμερῶν ἐκείνων

ὁ ἥλιος σκοτισθήσεται,
    καὶ ἡ σελήνη οὐ <u>δώσει</u> (it will give) τὸ φέγγος αὐτῆς,
καὶ οἱ ἀστέρες πεσοῦνται ἀπὸ τοῦ οὐρανοῦ,
    καὶ αἱ δυνάμεις τῶν οὐρανῶν σαλευθήσονται.

[30]καὶ τότε φανήσεται τὸ σημεῖον τοῦ υἱοῦ τοῦ ἀνθρώπου ἐν οὐρανῷ, καὶ τότε
κόψονται πᾶσαι αἱ φυλαὶ τῆς γῆς καὶ ὄψονται τὸν υἱὸν τοῦ ἀνθρώπου ἐρχόμενον (coming) ἐπὶ τῶν νεφελῶν τοῦ οὐρανοῦ μετὰ δυνάμεως καὶ δόξης πολλῆς·
[31]καὶ ἀποστελεῖ (he will send)[a] τοὺς ἀγγέλους αὐτοῦ μετὰ σάλπιγγος μεγάλης,
καὶ ἐπισυνάξουσιν τοὺς ἐκλεκτοὺς αὐτοῦ ἐκ τῶν τεσσάρων ἀνέμων ἀπ' ἄκρων
οὐρανῶν ἕως τῶν ἄκρων αὐτῶν.

[a] 3rd sg. fut. act. ind. ▸ ἀποστέλλω. This is a form you have not met yet; one lambda and the sigma form marker both drop out. You will learn why in chap. 21.

19.34. Vocabulary for Chapter 19

Part of Speech	Definition	Possible Glosses	Frequency	
Word			NT	LXX
Nouns				
μέρος, ους, τό	A piece or part of a whole (wide usage depending on context: body part, geographical area, party, etc.)	part, member; region; party	42	139
χιλιάς, άδος, ἡ	A group of one thousand (collective noun)	(group of) a thousand	23	340
σκηνή, ῆς, ἡ	A temporary, movable shelter	tent, hut, booth, tabernacle	20	434
Preposition				
ἀντί	A preposition used with the genitive case indicating correspondence in which one thing is to be replaced by or substituted with or for another	(prep. + gen.) instead of, for, in behalf of	21	391
Verbs				
(1) ἅπτω; (2) ἅπτομαι	(1) To cause to burn or give light (act.); (2) to make contact with something (for various purposes) [1 and 2 are homonyms, but 2 is a middle-only verb]	(1) I kindle, ignite (act.); (2) I touch, take hold of, cling to (mid.)	39	134
δικαιόω	To render a favorable verdict, pronounce innocent; in Pauline theology, a judicial act in which God declares the believing sinner righteous	I justify, vindicate	39	51
περισσεύω	(1) Intransitive: to be in abundance (number, amount, quality, etc.); to be wealthy; (2) transitive: to cause something to exist in abundance	(1) I abound, am rich, have an abundance; (2) I cause to abound	39	9
πλανάω	To cause someone to go astray, lead them from the right path (act.); to depart from the right path (mid.); to be misled, deceived (pass.)	I lead astray, deceive (act.); I go astray (mid.); I am misled, deceived (pass.)	39	126
ἀσθενέω	To experience physical weakness as a result of sickness or some other incapacity; to lack capacity for something whether physical or otherwise	I am weak/sick; I am deficient	33	77

Part of Speech	Definition	Possible Glosses	Frequency	
Word			NT	LXX
ἐλπίζω	To have confidence of something positive coming to pass	I hope, hope for; I expect	31	117
φεύγω	To seek safety by fleeing from a place or situation; to avoid something due to danger	I flee, escape; I avoid, shun	29	250
καταλείπω	To leave someone or something behind by departure or death; to depart from a place	I leave behind, leave alone; I leave, depart	24	289
μιμνῄσκω	To remind someone of something (act.); to recall information from one's own memory (mid.); to be reminded (pass.) (never act. in the NT or LXX; often listed as μιμνῄσκομαι)	I remind (act.); I remember, mention (mid.); I am reminded (pass.)	23	262
βασιλεύω	To exercise royal authority as king; to become king	I am king, I rule/reign as king; I become king	21	402
ἐντέλλω	To give authoritative instructions	I command, order	15	424

19.35. Key Things to Know for Chapter 19

Can you list more than one way in which the future tense-form is used, that is, more than as a simple temporal, predictive statement regarding the future?

What are the *two* future form markers, and for which forms are they used?

What are the *formulas* for the three future indicative forms in this chapter (active, middle, and passive)?

What happens to the spelling of a contract verb when a form marker is added in the future? How is this similar to an aorist verb?

Can you still reproduce the square of stops from memory? If not, you should review it.

Do you recognize future forms of εἰμί when you spot them in a text?

In what one case is a θησ *not* a future form marker? What are your clues to remember this form?

What is different about a second future passive?

20

VERBS: PART 10

Perfect and Pluperfect (Stative) Indicative Verbs

20.1. Thus far you have met those tense-forms that express perfective (aorist) and imperfective aspect (present and imperfect). There is a third aspect that we have mentioned but not yet discussed: stative aspect.[1] This is expressed by two tense-forms: the perfect and the pluperfect. Both are used much less frequently than the other forms you have studied. The pluperfect was dying out in the Koine, and only a handful of examples are found in the NT.

Perfect Indicative Verbs

20.2. This is the last indicative form to learn. The perfect is one of the easiest of all the forms to identify. English does not have an exact equivalent of the Greek perfect tense-form. There is a form called *perfect* in English, but it is quite different from the form called by the same name in Greek. Do not confuse the two. Some of the confusion regarding the meaning of the Greek perfect tense-form has likely resulted from assuming that it is equivalent to the English perfect tense.[2]

1. *Stative* can also be used as a description of a verb's *Aktionsart*, but when so used it is not an aspect statement. Both are similar categories, but they are determined differently (aspect is based on tense-form, *Aktionsart* on a verb's lexis and the context).

2. There are actually three perfect tenses in English. The present perfect tense (sometimes called simply the *perfect tense*) may be illustrated as "I have come" or "I have been coming"; the past perfect tense (sometimes called the *pluperfect*) is "I had come" or "I had been coming"; and the future perfect tense is "I shall have come" or very rarely, "I shall have been coming."

Meaning of the Perfect Tense-Form

20.3. The aspect of the perfect is stative: it describes a state/condition rather than an action—a situation described with no reference to change or expenditure of energy.[3] This "state" refers to the state of the grammatical subject of the sentence, not the object. Comparing the following common English glosses of each of the tense-forms will give you an idea of some of the differences between these forms. (Third singular forms are used in these examples.)[4]

	λύω	γράφω
Present	He is loosing	He is writing
Aorist	She loosed	She wrote
Imperfect	He was loosing	He was writing
Future	She will loose	She will write
Perfect	He is loose	It is written

You will notice in these examples that the first four all describe an *action*: writing or loosing. The perfect tense-form, however, does *not* describe an action. There is a significant difference between, say, "he is writing" or "she wrote" and "it is written." The perfect describes a particular *condition*. With γράφω it is a "written condition"; a book can be described as "written" in contrast to an author's current work ("she *is writing* a book") or a book that someone envisions but has not yet written ("he *will write* another book next year"). It is true that this condition ("it is written") is likely the result of a previous action. We could not describe a book as "written" unless an author previously wrote it. The perfect tense-form, however, does not focus on the previous action; it describes only the condition. Any reference to or conclusions regarding *how* the condition came to be must be gleaned from the context. Nor does the statement say anything about the continuation of the state beyond the time referred to by the verb.[5]

Representing the Perfect in English

20.4. An equivalent of the perfect in English is a bit difficult, because we have no exact equivalent. The best we can do in most cases is to think in terms of a simple present form in English.[6]

3. This is disputed by grammarians, and not all are agreed on the best way to explain the perfect. "The semantic nature of the perfect and pluperfect tense-forms is one of the great puzzles in Greek linguistics" (Campbell, *Basics of Verbal Aspect*, 46).

4. The perfect of γράφω uses "it" instead of "he" or "she" since it is difficult to think of an appropriate context in which a third singular form of γράφω would have a personal reference. In both the NT and LXX this form always refers to an existing written record (usually Scripture), never to the act of writing or to a person who writes.

5. It is probably best not to describe the perfect form as "completed action with continuing results" (a traditional definition), though that is tempting when the antecedent action is very obvious in the context.

6. Remember that the Greek present tense-form is usually the rough equivalent of a continuous present in English (e.g., "I am loosing").

Perfect active: I am loose.
Perfect passive: I am loosed.

If the context emphasizes the antecedent action that has resulted in the subsequent state of affairs, then it may sometimes be helpful to think of the perfect as "I have been loosed," though "I am loose" is still often preferable in such situations. If the simple present makes good sense in English, then do not conceive of the meaning in terms of the English helping verb *have*. Some statements, however, make good sense in English only as "I have been x," but this is a matter of English idiom, not a reflection of the meaning of the Greek statement.

For example, the perfect of γράφω is often given as "it is written" when referring to quotations of the OT in the NT, as seen in Rom. 1:17 (NIV): "For in the gospel the righteousness of God is revealed—a righteousness that is by faith from first to last, just as *it is written*: 'The righteous will live by faith.'" This could also be expressed in English as "it stands written." To say "it has been written" (a traditional translation of the perfect) would focus the attention on the *past action* rather than on the *condition* being described.

Significance of the Perfect

20.5. The perfect tense-form is almost always significant when it is used. This is the exact opposite of the significance of the aorist—the default tense-form. Though it is certainly not a mechanical indicator, writers may use the perfect to highlight particular points, and sometimes the perfect is used to summarize the main point of a particular pericope in narrative. When you find a perfect tense-form, ask yourself, does this passage make sense if I understand this statement to be a key point in the narrative or argument? Sometimes it does, but do not force this interpretation if the context does not justify such a conclusion.

Perfect Active Indicative

20.6. But now that we have talked about what it means, what does the perfect tense-form look like? We first need to learn a new term: *reduplication*. This is the duplication of an initial consonant plus an epsilon at the front of a verb stem. For example, λύω with reduplication looks like this: λελυ-. The first letter of the stem is lambda, so it is duplicated and added to the front of the stem along with the letter epsilon (always in that order).

Formula for Perfect Active Indicative Verbs

reduplication + stem[7] + form marker κα + A personal endings
Example: λε + λυ + κα + μεν ▸ λελύκαμεν

7. The stem is usually the same as that of the present, but it can sometimes change. If it changes, it will sometimes be the same as the aorist stem, or it may be an entirely different stem.

Perfect Active Indicative of λύω

	Form	f.m. + A p.e.	Gloss	A p.e.	B p.e.	aor. f.m. + B p.e.
1S	λέλυκα	κα	I am loose	—	ν	σα
2S	λέλυκας	κας	You are loose	ς	ς	σας
3S	λέλυκε(ν)	κε(ν)	He/she/it is loose	ι	—	σε(ν)
1P	λελύκαμεν	καμεν	We are loose	μεν	μεν	σαμεν
2P	λελύκατε	κατε	You are loose	τε	τε	σατε
3P	λελύκασι(ν)	κασι(ν)	They are loose	νσι(ν)	ν	σαν

The second Greek column shows the primary A-quad endings used by the perfect together with the perfect form marker (κα). The columns on the right show both A and B endings (the technical endings without connecting vowels). You might be surprised how much alike these endings can look. The key variable is the connecting vowel or the vowel that forms part of the form marker. The perfect endings might look superficially like the first aorist endings (last column), but that is due to the common alpha in the form marker, not the endings. That the perfect does use A endings is evident from the first singular and third plural forms. The third singular form does not follow the standard A endings but substitutes a movable nu for the iota (at that point it is similar to the B endings).

20.7. Examples of the Perfect Active Indicative

John 8:33, ἀπεκρίθησαν πρὸς αὐτόν, Σπέρμα Ἀβραάμ ἐσμεν καὶ οὐδενὶ **δεδουλεύκαμεν** πώποτε.

They answered him, "We are the descendants of Abraham and *we have* never *been enslaved* to anyone.

This example refers to a past condition (which they assert is still true at the time they speak), as indicated by the word πώποτε. The fact that their claim is patently untrue does not change the grammatical meaning of the statement that they make.[8]

Luke 24:29, Μεῖνον (Remain!) μεθ' ἡμῶν, ὅτι πρὸς ἑσπέραν ἐστὶν καὶ **κέκλικεν** ἤδη ἡ ἡμέρα.

Remain with us, because it is already evening, and the day *is* already *far spent*.

Mark 5:34, ὁ δὲ εἶπεν αὐτῇ, Θυγάτηρ, ἡ πίστις σου **σέσωκέν** σε.

But he said to her, "Daughter, your faith *has healed* you."

The example in Mark 5:34 illustrates a perfect that is probably best translated with the helping verb ("has healed"), though that is mostly a matter of English idiom. The point is that she is presently healthy.

8. They conveniently ignore the Assyrian and Babylonian captivities, to say nothing of their former domination by the Greek Empire (and its successors) and the contemporary Roman rule of Palestine.

20.8. Now You Try It

John 6:69, ἡμεῖς **πεπιστεύκαμεν** ὅτι σὺ εἶ ὁ ἅγιος τοῦ θεοῦ.

Num. 12:2, εἶπαν, Μὴ Μωϋσῇ μόνῳ **λελάληκεν** κύριος; οὐχὶ καὶ ἡμῖν ἐλάλησεν;

Note the significance of the use of μή in this statement.

Num. 23:11, εἶπεν Βαλὰκ πρὸς Βαλαάμ, Τί **πεποίηκάς** μοι; εἰς κατάρασιν ἐχθρῶν μου **κέκληκά** σε, καὶ ἰδοὺ **εὐλόγηκας**[a] εὐλογίαν.[b]

[a] This is a perfect form. The seeming lack of reduplication is explained in the next section.

[b] εὐλόγηκας εὐλογίαν reflects a typical Hebrew expression in which cognate forms are used. Formally the text reads, "you have blessed with blessing"; idiomatically, "you have surely blessed him." (Can you hear Balak's exasperation with Balaam?)

Perfect Variations

20.9. Since that was almost too easy, there must be more to it, right? Well, not much, but there are a few variations that you will see from time to time.

If a word begins with a vowel, it reduplicates by *lengthening.* This is called *vocalic reduplication.* As a result, it may look like an augment. You can tell that it is not an aorist or an imperfect from the form marker κα. Having two clear markers (reduplication and a distinctive form marker) is very helpful. Even if one gets fuzzy, the other one is still there.

2 Cor. 11:21, κατὰ ἀτιμίαν λέγω, ὡς ὅτι ἡμεῖς **ἠσθενήκαμεν**.[a]

To [my] shame I say that we *are weak*.[b]

[a] ἠσθενήκαμεν ▸ ἀσθενέω, "I am weak"

[b] The ὡς is not expressed directly in English idiom. NET makes this a parenthetical statement and translates, "To my disgrace I must say that we were too weak for that!" Read the context in your English Bible. This is not the easiest sentence, so if you don't get all of it, that is OK.

Matt. 4:17, Ἀπὸ τότε ἤρξατο (began) ὁ Ἰησοῦς κηρύσσειν καὶ λέγειν, Μετανοεῖτε (Repent!)· **ἤγγικεν**[a] γὰρ ἡ βασιλεία τῶν οὐρανῶν.

[a] ἤγγικεν ▸ ἐγγίζω, perfect stem = ἐγγι-

20.10. The stem vowel of a contract verb lengthens when the form marker κα is added, just as it does with σα, or θη, or any other form marker.

John 1:34, κἀγὼ **μεμαρτύρηκα** ὅτι οὗτός ἐστιν ὁ υἱὸς τοῦ θεοῦ.

John 2:10, σὺ **τετήρηκας** τὸν καλὸν οἶνον ἕως ἄρτι.

This perfect is traditionally translated as "you have kept," but "you keep" may be adequate.

Words beginning with φ, χ, θ (the square of stops again) reduplicate as πεφ-, κεχ-, τεθ-. Note the relationship of the relevant columns in the chart: verbs beginning with a letter in the third column reduplicate using the letters in the first column. This is one of the reasons you were told that you must learn the square of stops in the correct column order.[9]

π	β	φ
κ	γ	χ
τ	δ	θ

Mark 15:44, ὁ δὲ Πιλᾶτος ἐθαύμασεν εἰ ἤδη **τέθνηκεν.**[a]

But Pilate was amazed that *he was* already *dead.*

[a] τέθνηκεν ▶ θνῄσκω, perfect stem = θνη-

John 16:27, αὐτὸς γὰρ ὁ πατὴρ φιλεῖ ὑμᾶς, ὅτι ὑμεῖς ἐμὲ **πεφιλήκατε** καὶ πεπιστεύκατε ὅτι ἐγὼ παρὰ τοῦ θεοῦ ἐξῆλθον.

If a word begins with a diphthong, it may lengthen or may remain as is. In John 1:41 εὑρίσκω does not lengthen, though the form marker κα makes it obvious that it is a perfect.

John 1:41, **Εὑρήκαμεν** τὸν Μεσσίαν.

We have found the Messiah.

20.11. If a word (or perfect stem) begins with two consonants, it usually prefixes just an epsilon. For example, the perfect stem of γινώσκω is γνω-.

John 8:52, εἶπον οὖν αὐτῷ οἱ Ἰουδαῖοι, Νῦν **ἐγνώκαμεν** ὅτι δαιμόνιον ἔχεις.

Therefore the Jews said to him, "Now *we know* that you have a demon."

Compound verbs reduplicate between the preposition and the stem (this characteristic is the same as verbs with augments).

9. The names of the columns (which you *don't* need to memorize) are *unvoiced* (π, κ, τ), *voiced* (β, γ, δ), and *aspirates* (φ, χ, θ). What that means in regard to reduplication is that perfect verbs that begin with an aspirate reduplicate with the equivalent unvoiced consonant.

Acts 13:33, ταύτην ὁ θεὸς **ἐκπεπλήρωκεν.** — God *has fulfilled* this.

1 John 3:14, ἡμεῖς οἴδαμεν ὅτι **μεταβεβήκαμεν**[a] ἐκ τοῦ θανάτου εἰς τὴν ζωήν, ὅτι ἀγαπῶμεν τοὺς ἀδελφούς.

[a] μεταβεβήκαμεν ▸ μεταβαίνω, "I pass," perfect stem = μεταβη-

A dental (τ, δ, or θ) at the end of a verb stem will usually drop out when a kappa is added to the stem. (This is like adding a sigma in the future and aorist tense-forms). This is the same with stems that end with -ιζω or -αζω; the zeta in the lexical form appears to drop out, but the form is usually a perfect stem ending in a delta.

1 Tim. 4:10, **ἠλπίκαμεν**[a] ἐπὶ θεῷ ζῶντι, ὅς ἐστιν σωτὴρ πάντων ἀνθρώπων. — *We hope* in the living God, who is the Savior of all people.

[a] ἠλπίκαμεν ▸ ἐλπίζω, perfect stem = ἐλπιδ-

Perfect Middle Indicative

20.12. Everything that you have learned about the perfect active is also true of the perfect middle indicative. Like the present and imperfect, this form can also function as a passive if there is a passive marker in the context. The same context clues apply that you met in chapter 15.

Formula for Perfect Middle Indicative Verbs

reduplication + stem[10] + C personal endings
Example: λε + λυ + μαι ▸ λέλυμαι

There is *no form marker* and *no connecting vowel* in the perfect middle. This is the only form in which a personal ending is added directly to the stem. It is also the only form in which the second singular ending shows up in its original spelling: σαι. When you first met the C personal endings, you learned the second singular ending, not as σαι, but as ῃ. That change was because the sigma, when squeezed between two vowels (connecting vowel and the alpha of the ending), dropped out. As a result, the alpha lengthened to an eta, and the iota became subscript. Every other set of forms with C endings has a connecting vowel, but the perfect middle does not. As a result, the sigma does not drop out, since it is not squeezed between two vowels. I told you when you learned these endings that you would one day see the "real ending" show up. This is where it happens—and it is the only time it does.

10. The stem is usually the same as the lexical form, but it may change in some words.

Perfect Middle Indicative of λύω

	Form	C p.e.	Middle Gloss	Passive Gloss[a]
1S	λέλυμαι	μαι	I am loose	I am loosed
2S	λέλυσαι	σαι	You are loose	You are loosed
3S	λέλυται	ται	He/she/it is loose	He/she/it is loosed
1P	λελύμεθα	μεθα	We are loose	We are loosed
2P	λέλυσθε	σθε	You are loose	You are loosed
3P	λέλυνται[b]	νται	They are loose	They are loosed

[a] Remember that you can use a passive equivalent in English only if the context marks the form as passive in some way (e.g., with an agent marker). If there is no passive indication, then these forms should be treated as middle voice.

[b] *Advanced information for reference*: Certain verbs whose stem ends in a consonant do not use the form shown above. Instead they use an alternate means of expressing the same meaning. For example, the verb γράφω does not use γέγραφνται but instead uses γεγραμμένοι εἰσίν (e.g., 1 Chron. 29:29). See also τεταγμέναι εἰσίν (Rom. 13:1, τάσσω). Such two-word forms, composed of a participle and a form of εἰμί, are called *periphrastics* and will be explained in chap. 27. These forms do not occur frequently.

20.13. Examples of the Perfect Middle Indicative

Mark 1:15, **Πεπλήρωται** ὁ καιρὸς καὶ ἤγγικεν ἡ βασιλεία τοῦ θεοῦ.

The time *is fulfilled*, and the kingdom of God is near.

Mark 16:4, θεωροῦσιν ὅτι **ἀποκεκύλισται** ὁ λίθος.

They saw that the stone *was rolled away*.

Matt. 4:7, ἔφη (he said) αὐτῷ ὁ Ἰησοῦς, Πάλιν **γέγραπται**, Οὐκ ἐκπειράσεις (test!) κύριον τὸν θεόν σου.

Jesus said to him, "Again, *it is written*: 'Do not test the Lord your God.'"

Acts 27:24, ἰδοὺ **κεχάρισταί**[a] σοι ὁ θεὸς πάντας τοὺς πλέοντας[b] μετὰ σοῦ.

Behold, God *has graciously given* to you all the ones who sail with you.

[a] χαρίζομαι, "I give as a gracious gift"

[b] τοὺς πλέοντας (▶ πλέω), "the ones who sail"

This is a statement made to Paul by an angel just before his shipwreck on the island of Malta while en route to Rome.

20.14. Now You Try It

Mark 1:2, Καθὼς **γέγραπται** ἐν τῷ Ἠσαΐᾳ τῷ προφήτῃ . . .

Acts 25:12, Καίσαρα **ἐπικέκλησαι**, ἐπὶ Καίσαρα πορεύσῃ.

2 Tim. 4:7, τὸν καλὸν ἀγῶνα **ἠγώνισμαι**.

Exod. 5:3, λέγουσιν αὐτῷ, Ὁ θεὸς τῶν Ἑβραίων **προσκέκληται** ἡμᾶς· πορευσόμεθα οὖν ὁδὸν τριῶν ἡμερῶν εἰς τὴν ἔρημον, ὅπως θύσωμεν (we may sacrifice) τῷ θεῷ ἡμῶν.

Second Perfects

20.15. What would you expect to happen in a second perfect form based on what you know about other "second" forms, such as the second future passive, second aorist passive, and second aorist active? The second perfects' nickname tells all: κ-less perfects. The form marker is not κα but just an alpha.[11] There are not many words in the NT that have a second perfect form (see *MBG*, §45.5b for a list)—fewer than twenty. The most common are as follows.[12]

Lexical Form	Perfect Form	Parsing	Frequency in NT
γίνομαι	(all perfect forms)		47×
	γέγονεν[b]	3rd sg. ²pf. act. ind.	31×
ἔρχομαι	(all perfect forms)		17×
	ἐλήλυθεν[b]	3rd sg.	8×
ἀκούω	(all perfect forms)		9×
	ἀκηκόαμεν[c]	1st pl.	6×
πείθω[a]	(all perfect forms)		12×
	πέποιθα[b]	1st sg. ²pf. act. ind.	2×
	πέπεισμαι	1st sg. ²pf. mid. ind.	4×

[a] The active form πείθω has a causative sense, "to win over, to make (someone) trust." The middle, πείθομαι, has an inherent middle sense (subject focus), "to trust, have confidence, obey."

[b] The second perfect form of this word is listed in BDAG alphabetically just as it is spelled, but it is *not* in *CL*.

[c] This form is *not* listed in BDAG, but it *is* in *CL*.

There are a few other common verbs that have second perfect forms, but they occur only two times each; all are listed in *CL* and BDAG.

ἀνοίγω ▸ ἀνέῳγεν
γράφω ▸ γέγραφα

11. The category of "second perfect" applies only to perfect active forms, since the perfect middle does not have a form marker.

12. As would be expected from a larger corpus, the LXX has a wider range of these forms. Of those listed in the text from the NT, ἀκούω and πείθω have a full set of active forms. The verb ἀκούω occurs 33 times as perfect active indicative: ἀκήκοα, ἀκήκοας, ἀκήκοεν, ἀκηκόαμεν, ἀκηκόατε, ἀκηκόασιν. Likewise πείθω occurs 32 times: πέποιθα, πέποιθας, πέποιθεν, πεποίθαμεν, πεποίθατε, πεποίθασιν (and once as πέποιθαν). More numerous, but missing the second plural, is γίνομαι, 60 times: γέγονα, γέγονας, γέγονεν, γεγόναμεν, [γεγόνατε], γεγόνασιν.

πάσχω ▸ πεπόνθασιν

προσέρχομαι ▸ προσεληλύθατε

20.16. Examples of Second Perfects

Matt. 27:43, **πέποιθεν**[a] ἐπὶ τὸν θεόν· εἶπεν γὰρ ὅτι Θεοῦ εἰμι υἱός.

He trusts in God, for he said, "I am the Son of God."

[a] πέποιθεν ▸ πείθω; the statement describes not an action but Jesus' attitude, his state of trust in God.

Luke 14:22, εἶπεν ὁ δοῦλος, Κύριε, **γέγονεν**[a] ὃ ἐπέταξας.[b]

The slave said, "Sir, what you commanded *has been done*."

[a] γέγονεν ▸ γίνομαι
[b] ἐπέταξας, 2nd sg. aor. act. ind. ▸ ἐπιτάσσω, "I command"

John 3:19, αὕτη δέ ἐστιν ἡ κρίσις ὅτι τὸ φῶς **ἐλήλυθεν** εἰς τὸν κόσμον καὶ ἠγάπησαν οἱ ἄνθρωποι μᾶλλον τὸ σκότος ἢ τὸ φῶς· ἦν γὰρ αὐτῶν πονηρὰ τὰ ἔργα.

But this is the judgment: light *is* (or, *has*) *come* into the world, and people loved the darkness rather than the light, for their deeds were evil.

20.17. Now You Try It

1 John 1:5, Καὶ ἔστιν αὕτη ἡ ἀγγελία ἣν **ἀκηκόαμεν** ἀπ' αὐτοῦ καὶ ἀναγγέλλομεν ὑμῖν, ὅτι ὁ θεὸς φῶς ἐστιν καὶ σκοτία ἐν αὐτῷ οὐκ ἔστιν οὐδεμία.

Phil. 2:24, **πέποιθα** δὲ ἐν κυρίῳ ὅτι καὶ αὐτὸς ταχέως ἐλεύσομαι.

2 Tim. 1:12, οἶδα γὰρ ᾧ πεπίστευκα καὶ **πέπεισμαι** ὅτι δυνατός ἐστιν τὴν παραθήκην μου φυλάξαι εἰς ἐκείνην τὴν ἡμέραν.

Gen. 3:22, εἶπεν ὁ θεός, Ἰδοὺ Ἀδὰμ **γέγονεν** ὡς εἷς ἐξ ἡμῶν τοῦ γινώσκειν καλὸν καὶ πονηρόν.

Exod. 2:20, ὁ δὲ εἶπεν ταῖς θυγατράσιν αὐτοῦ, Καὶ ποῦ ἐστι; καὶ ἵνα τί[a] οὕτως **καταλελοίπατε** τὸν ἄνθρωπον; καλέσατε οὖν αὐτόν, ὅπως φάγῃ (he might eat) ἄρτον.

[a] ἵνα τί, "why?"

οἶδα

20.18. The most common form that is technically a second perfect is οἶδα, which occurs 210 times in the NT and 221 times in the LXX.[13] Most grammars and lexicons just call it a *perfect* (not *second perfect*), since it is so common. There is no visible reduplication, since the stem begins with a diphthong, and the kappa has dropped out of the form marker κα, leaving only the alpha.

	Form	Frequency	
		NT	LXX
1S	οἶδα	56	41
2S	οἶδας	17	27
3S	οἶδε(ν)	22	38
1P	οἴδαμεν	43	11
2P	οἴδατε	64	14
3P	οἴδασι(ν)	8	13

The word οἶδα is almost always best translated as a simple English present: "I know" (just like most other perfects). It does not function as if it were a present or have present meaning, as some grammars suggest. It is true that this word does not have a complete set of forms; it occurs only in perfect and pluperfect.[14] The missing forms, however, are supplied by γινώσκω (which seldom occurs in the perfect, only 19 of more than 200 instances). Together the complementary forms of οἶδα and γινώσκω function almost as if they were a single word, with no significant difference in meaning.

20.19. Examples of οἶδα

Mark 10:38, ὁ δὲ Ἰησοῦς εἶπεν αὐτοῖς, Οὐκ **οἴδατε** τί αἰτεῖσθε.

But Jesus said to them, "*You do* not *know* what you ask."

Matt. 20:25, ὁ δὲ Ἰησοῦς εἶπεν, **Οἴδατε** ὅτι οἱ ἄρχοντες (rulers) τῶν ἐθνῶν κατακυριεύουσιν αὐτῶν καὶ οἱ μεγάλοι κατεξουσιάζουσιν αὐτῶν.

But Jesus said, "*You know* that the rulers of the Gentiles are lording it over them, and the great ones are lording it over them [i.e., over the rulers]."

20.20. Now You Try It

John 3:2, οὗτος ἦλθεν πρὸς αὐτὸν νυκτὸς καὶ εἶπεν αὐτῷ, Ῥαββί, **οἴδαμεν** ὅτι ἀπὸ θεοῦ ἐλήλυθας διδάσκαλος.

13. Technically, οἶδα is an irregular μι verb that at one time was spelled ἴδοιμι. You will learn μι verbs in chaps. 32–33.

14. There is one future form, εἰδήσουσιν (Heb. 8:11; cf. Jer. 38:34 [31:34 Eng.]), and the aorist active infinitive, εἰδῆσαι, appears twice in the LXX (Deut. 4:35; Jdt. 9:14).

Gen. 31:6, αὐταὶ[a] δὲ **οἴδατε** ὅτι ἐν πάσῃ τῇ ἰσχύι μου δεδούλευκα τῷ πατρὶ ὑμῶν.

[a] Do you remember the use of αὐτός that is evident here?

— — — — — — — — — — — — — —

Advanced Information for Reference: The Pluperfect

20.21. The pluperfect was a dying form in Koine Greek.[15] It was a long, morphologically cumbersome form and did not have sufficient distinctiveness to justify its continued use, especially by the non-native speakers of Koine. There are only 86 examples in the NT. Even the LXX has relatively few, evidencing 206 in a much larger literary corpus. There are 63 in the OT Pseudepigrapha and only 36 in the Apostolic Fathers.

Meaning of the Pluperfect

20.22. The pluperfect tense-form is, as the name implies, related to the perfect tense-form. Its relationship is similar to the present/imperfect relationship. Both express the same aspect, but the paired form is more remote than the primary one. The present expresses imperfective aspect, as does the remote, imperfect form. The perfect tense-form encodes stative aspect, as does its remote paired form, the pluperfect. The pluperfect, however, is even more remote than the imperfect—expressing heightened remoteness. The imperfect is often used to sketch background information in narrative, but the pluperfect references the background of the background.

Expressing the pluperfect in English is usually best done with a simple English present or a simple past tense, very similar to the perfect. The differences seen in the examples below are largely due to English idiom.

Form of the Pluperfect

20.23. The pluperfect is built on the perfect stem and shares a number of common elements with the perfect form.

Formula for Pluperfect Active Indicative Verbs

augment + reduplication + perfect stem + form marker κ
+ connecting vowel/diphthong ει + B personal endings

The augment is often missing in Koine usage of the pluperfect. There is also a "second pluperfect," which is formed the same as the "first" form except that

15. Your teacher may elect to skip this section, since it is a form rarely used in the NT.

there is no form marker. There is only one instance of a second pluperfect in the NT: ἐπεποίθει, 3rd sg. ²plpf. act. ind. ▸ πείθω.

Formula for Pluperfect Middle Indicative Verbs

augment + reduplication + perfect stem + D endings

This form can also be a passive if there is an agent marker in the context; it functions like the present and perfect middle forms in this regard.

Pluperfect Active and Middle Indicative of λύω

	Active	Middle
1S	ἐλελύκειν	ἐλελύμην
2S	ἐλελύκεις	ἐλέλυσο
3S	ἐλελύκει(ν)	ἐλέλυτο
1P	ἐλελύκειμεν	ἐλελύμεθα
2P	ἐλελύκειτε	ἐλέλυσθε
3P	ἐλελύκεισαν	ἐλέλυντο[a]

[a] The third plural form, like the perfect, is often formed periphrastically.

20.24. There are only 32 different pluperfect forms in the NT, and the list of these plus all those used more than once in the LXX totals only 52. They are listed below for reference. Compare the formulas above. Many are easily recognizable, particularly the ones that do have both an augment and a reduplication. The most common word used in the pluperfect is οἶδα. A few of the forms in the following list are μι verbs, which you will learn later. The parsings in the following reference list use the short-form abbreviations explained at the end of chapter 13 (e.g., "3SLAI" means "third singular pluperfect active indicative").

ἀνθειστήκει, 3SLAI ▸ ἀνθίστημι
ἀπεληλύθεισαν, 3PLAI ▸ ἀπέρχομαι
γεγόνει, 3SLAI ▸ γίνομαι
δεδώκει, 3SLAI ▸ δίδωμι
δεδώκεισαν, 3PLAI ▸ δίδωμι
διεγνώκει, 3SLAI ▸ διαγινώσκω
ἐβέβλητο, 3SLMI ▸ βάλλω
ἐγεγόνει, 3SLAI ▸ γίνομαι
ἐγέγραπτο, 3SLPI ▸ γράφω
ἐγνώκειτε, 2PLAI ▸ γινώσκω
ἐδεδοίκειν, 1SLAI ▸ δείδω
ἐζήλωκα, 1SLAI ▸ ζηλόω
εἰρήκει, 3SLAI ▸ λέγω
εἱστήκει, 3SLAI ▸ ἵστημι
εἱστήκειν, 1SLAI ▸ ἵστημι
εἱστήκεισαν, 3PLAI ▸ ἵστημι
εἰώθει, 3SLAI ▸ εἴωθα
ἐκβεβλήκει, 3SLAI ▸ ἐκβάλλω
ἐληλύθει, 3SLAI ▸ ἔρχομαι
ἐληλύθεισαν, 3PLAI ▸ ἔρχομαι
ἐνεδεδύκει, 3SLAI ▸ ἐνδύω
ἐξεληλύθει, 3SLAI ▸ ἐξέρχομαι
ἐπεγέγραπτο, 3SLMI ▸ ἐπιγράφω
ἐπεκέκλητο, 3SLMI ▸ ἐπικαλέω
ἐπεπλήρωτο, 3SLPI ▸ πληρόω
ἐπεποίθεις, 2SLAI ▸ πείθω
ἐπεποίθει, 3SLAI ▸ πείθω
ἐπεποίθεισαν, 3PLAI ▸ πείθω

ἐπεστήρικτο, 3SLPI ▸ ἐπιστηρίζω
ἐφειστήκει, 3SLAI ▸ ἐφίστημι
ἑωράκει, 3SLAI ▸ ὁράω
ᾔδει, 3SLAI ▸ οἶδα
ᾔδειμεν, 1PLAI ▸ οἶδα
ᾔδειν, 1SLAI ▸ οἶδα
ᾔδεις, 2SLAI ▸ οἶδα
ᾔδεισαν, 3PLAI ▸ οἶδα
ᾔδειτε, 2PLAI ▸ οἶδα
καθειστήκεισαν, 3PLAI ▸ καθίστημι
κεκρίκει, 3SLAI ▸ κρίνω
μεμενήκεισαν, 3PLAI ▸ μένω
παραδεδώκεισαν, 3PLAI ▸ παραδίδωμι
παρειστήκει, 3SLAI ▸ παρίστημι
παρειστήκεισαν, 3PLAI ▸ παρίστημι
παρεμβεβλήκεισαν, 3PLAI ▸ παρεμβάλλω
πεπιστεύκεισαν, 3PLAI ▸ πιστεύω
πεποιήκεισαν, 3PLAI ▸ ποιέω
περιεδέδετο, 3SLMI ▸ περιδέω
συνεληλύθεισαν, 3PLAI ▸ συνέρχομαι
συνετέθειντο, 3PLMI ▸ συντίθημι
συνηρπάκει, 3SLAI ▸ συναρπάζω
τεθεμελίωτο, 3SLMI ▸ θεμελιόω
ᾠκοδόμητο, 3SLMI ▸ οἰκοδομέω

20.25. Examples

John 2:9, ὡς δὲ ἐγεύσατο ὁ ἀρχιτρίκλινος τὸ ὕδωρ οἶνον γεγενημένον καὶ οὐκ **ᾔδει** πόθεν ἐστίν, οἱ δὲ διάκονοι **ᾔδεισαν** οἱ ἠντληκότες τὸ ὕδωρ, φωνεῖ τὸν νυμφίον ὁ ἀρχιτρίκλινος.

But when the head waiter tasted the water which had become wine—now, *he did* not *know* where it was from, but the servants who drew the water *knew*—the head waiter summoned the bridegroom.

The syntax is a bit clumsy here with the subject repeated twice, likely due to the parenthetical explanation in the middle of the sentence. The remote, background function of the pluperfect can be readily seen in this example.

John 4:8, οἱ γὰρ μαθηταὶ αὐτοῦ **ἀπεληλύθεισαν** εἰς τὴν πόλιν ἵνα τροφὰς ἀγοράσωσιν.

For his disciples *had gone* into the town in order to buy food.

Again, notice the background nature of the explanation—this verse is often punctuated as a parenthetical statement in English translations. Also note both the augment and the reduplication in this form of ἀπέρχομαι.

John 6:17, σκοτία ἤδη **ἐγεγόνει** καὶ οὔπω **ἐληλύθει** πρὸς αὐτοὺς ὁ Ἰησοῦς.

It had already *become* dark, and Jesus *had* not yet *come* to them.

Gen. 28:16, ἐξηγέρθη Ἰακὼβ ἀπὸ τοῦ ὕπνου αὐτοῦ καὶ εἶπεν ὅτι Ἔστιν κύριος ἐν τῷ τόπῳ τούτῳ, ἐγὼ δὲ οὐκ **ᾔδειν**.

Jacob awoke from his sleep and said, "The Lord is in this place, but *I did* not *know* [it]."

20.26. Reading Passage: John 16:25–33

You May Have Peace

[25]Ταῦτα ἐν παροιμίαις **λελάληκα** ὑμῖν· ἔρχεται ὥρα ὅτε οὐκέτι ἐν παροιμίαις
λαλήσω ὑμῖν, ἀλλὰ παρρησίᾳ περὶ τοῦ πατρὸς ἀπαγγελῶ ὑμῖν. [26]ἐν ἐκείνῃ τῇ
ἡμέρᾳ ἐν τῷ ὀνόματί μου αἰτήσεσθε, καὶ οὐ λέγω ὑμῖν ὅτι ἐγὼ ἐρωτήσω τὸν
πατέρα περὶ ὑμῶν· [27]αὐτὸς γὰρ ὁ πατὴρ φιλεῖ ὑμᾶς, ὅτι ὑμεῖς ἐμὲ **πεφιλήκατε** καὶ
πεπιστεύκατε ὅτι ἐγὼ παρὰ τοῦ θεοῦ ἐξῆλθον. [28]ἐξῆλθον παρὰ τοῦ πατρὸς καὶ
ἐλήλυθα εἰς τὸν κόσμον· πάλιν ἀφίημι (I am leaving) τὸν κόσμον καὶ πορεύομαι
πρὸς τὸν πατέρα. [29]Λέγουσιν οἱ μαθηταὶ αὐτοῦ, Ἴδε νῦν ἐν παρρησίᾳ λαλεῖς καὶ
παροιμίαν οὐδεμίαν λέγεις. [30]νῦν **οἴδαμεν** ὅτι **οἶδας** πάντα καὶ οὐ χρείαν ἔχεις
ἵνα τίς σε ἐρωτᾷ (should ask)· ἐν τούτῳ πιστεύομεν ὅτι ἀπὸ θεοῦ ἐξῆλθες.
[31]ἀπεκρίθη αὐτοῖς Ἰησοῦς, Ἄρτι πιστεύετε; [32]ἰδοὺ ἔρχεται ὥρα καὶ **ἐλήλυθεν** ἵνα
σκορπισθῆτε (you will be scattered) ἕκαστος εἰς τὰ ἴδια κἀμὲ μόνον ἀφῆτε (you
will leave)· καὶ οὐκ εἰμὶ μόνος, ὅτι ὁ πατὴρ μετ' ἐμοῦ ἐστιν. [33]ταῦτα **λελάληκα**
ὑμῖν ἵνα ἐν ἐμοὶ εἰρήνην ἔχητε (you may have)· ἐν τῷ κόσμῳ θλῖψιν ἔχετε·
ἀλλὰ θαρσεῖτε (take heart!), ἐγὼ **νενίκηκα** τὸν κόσμον.

20.27. Vocabulary for Chapter 20

Part of Speech	Definition	Possible Glosses	Frequency	
Word			NT	LXX
Adjectives				
ἄξιος, ία, ον	Deemed to correspond to an expectation of worth; deserving, worthy of (reward or punishment)	worthy, fit, deserving	41	40
ὀλίγος, η, ον	Being relatively small in number or extent; quickly, a little (neut. used as adv.)	few; little, small, short	40	101
Adverbs				
πάντοτε	A temporal adverb expressing continuation	always, at all times	41	2
σήμερον	A temporal adverb indicating reference to the present day (though day is not necessarily defined in strict, twenty-four-hour terms)	today	41	290
χωρίς	An adverb that indicates a situation occurs by itself, separately from other factors; also used as a preposition with the genitive	separately, apart, by itself (adv.); without, apart from (prep. + gen.)	41	20
Nouns				
Ἱεροσόλυμα, ἡ	Usually the proper name of the main city in Israel or its inhabitants (also spelled Ἰερουσαλήμ; either spelling may have smooth or rough breathing)	Jerusalem	139	881
τιμή, ῆς, ἡ	The amount at which something is valued; a high level of respect	price, value; honor, esteem	41	77
μνημεῖον, ου, τό	A memorial structure to recall a past event; a place for depositing the remains of a deceased person	monument, memorial; grave, tomb	40	16

Part of Speech	Definition	Possible Glosses	Frequency	
Word			NT	LXX
τέλος, ους, τό	A point of time that marks the end of a period or process; the goal toward which something is being directed; the name for an indirect revenue tax, either a toll or custom duties	end, termination; goal, outcome; tax, (customs) duty	40	165
θύρα, ας, ἡ	An object used to open or close an entranceway; a passageway providing entrance to a place	door; entrance, gateway, doorway	39	239
πρόβατον, ου, τό	A grass-eating animal with a thick, wool coat and cared for by a shepherd (i.e., a sheep); metaphorically, people under the care of a leader, such as a king or pastor	sheep	39	296
Particle				
ἄρα	A postpositive particle that introduces an inference or result from what precedes; may also add a sense of tentativeness to a statement (ctr. ἀρά, "curse"; and the interrogative ἆρα)	then, so, consequently, as a result; perhaps, conceivably	49	77
Verbs				
οἶδα	To find out, have information about; to grasp the meaning of something	I know, understand	318	283
ἑτοιμάζω	To put in a state of readiness	I prepare, make ready	40	173
κλαίω	To express grief or sorrow aloud (ctr. δακρύω, which may refer to a more silent expression of grief)	I weep, cry, sob	40	168

20.28. Key Things to Know for Chapter 20

Know the distinction between Greek and English perfect tenses.

What is reduplication, and what is its significance?

Know the formula for perfect active indicative.

How does the square of stops affect reduplication in the perfect tense-form?

What is a "second perfect," and what is its nickname?

21

VERBS: PART 11

Contract and Liquid Verbs

21.1. You have already seen contract verbs in several chapters, but it will be helpful to pull all the related information together here. Liquid verbs (which are not wet!) are a new topic. Both contract and liquid verbs are variations on forms you already know.

Contract Verbs

21.2. The key to contract verbs is this: a verb stem that ends with a short vowel (ε, ο, α) will *contract* with the connecting vowel according to the following (abbreviated) chart.[1] The left column is the *stem vowel* and the top row is the first letter (or diphthong) of the ending.

	ε	ει	η	ῃ	ο	ου	ω
ε	ει	ει	η	ῃ	ου	ου	ω
ο	ου	οι	ω	οι	ου	ου	ω
α	α	ᾳ	α	ᾳ	ω	ω	ω

The Form of ζάω

Ζάω ("I live, am alive") is *not* an alpha contract verb, despite the usual lexical listing. The lexical form is ζῶ, as shown in *CL* (and implied in BDAG). This word appears to act like a contract verb (alpha lengthening to eta), but either the eta comes from the original root, ζη-ι̯ω (not a lengthened alpha), *or* this is a rare example of an *eta contract* verb, which acts much like an alpha contract except that the contraction of η + ε = η and the contraction of η + ει = ῃ, thus: ζῶ, ζῇς, ζῇ, ζῶμεν, ζῆτε, ζῶσι(ν); the infinitive is ζῆν.

1. The full chart of all possible contractions is much larger. Some textbooks show a full-page chart. The abbreviated charts given here are adequate for the vast majority of such situations.

Here are three examples to show you how this works. All are present active indicative forms.

The first singular of φιλέω = φιλε + ω = φιλῶ, *not* φιλέω, because ε + ω = ω.
The first plural of φιλέω = φιλε + ομεν = φιλοῦμεν, *not* φιλέομεν, because ε + ο = ου.
The second singular of φιλέω = φιλε + εις = φιλεῖς *not* φιλέεις, because ε + ει = ει.

The form ending with -εω is the lexical form, but you will *never* see φιλέω in the NT (or other Greek texts); the first singular will *always* be φιλῶ in written texts. Why, then, does the lexicon print a form that never occurs? This lexical form shows what the stem vowel is before it contracts. All contract verbs appear this way. It also enables us to identify various groups of contract verbs. These are referred to as epsilon contracts, omicron contracts, or alpha contracts, based on the stem vowel.

21.3. Contraction in this way happens only in the present and imperfect tense-forms, since these are the only tenses in which a stem vowel and a connecting vowel come together. In forms that use a form marker, the vowels are separated and do not contract. (Remember, though, that whenever a form marker is added to a contract verb, the stem vowel will lengthen.)

Common Epsilon Contract Verbs:
αἰτέω, "I ask"
ζητέω, "I seek"
καλέω, "I call, summon"
κληρονομέω, "I inherit"
λαλέω, "I speak"
μετανοέω, "I repent"
οἰκοδομέω, "I build"
ποιέω, "I do, make"
τηρέω, "I keep"
φιλέω, "I love"
φωνέω, "I call/cry out"

Common Omicron Contract Verbs:
δικαιόω, "I declare righteous"
ζηλόω, "I am zealous"
θανατόω, "I put to death"
κοινόω, "I defile"
ὁμοιόω, "I become like"
πληρόω, "I fill"
σταυρόω, "I crucify"
ταπεινόω, "I humble"
τελειόω, "I finish"
ὑψόω, "I lift up"
φανερόω, "I make known"

Common Alpha Contract Verbs:
ἀγαπάω, "I love"
γεννάω, "I beget"
ἐπερωτάω, "I ask"
ἐπιτιμάω, "I rebuke"
ἐρωτάω, "I ask"
κοπιάω, "I become weary"
νικάω, "I conquer"
ὁράω, "I see"
πεινάω, I am hungry"
πλανάω, "I deceive"
τιμάω, "I honor"

Contract Verb Rules

21.4. Some textbooks give long lists of rules for contract verbs. Some settle for the abridged chart of contractions that you saw above. Others provide a very large chart of the possible contract combinations of both single vowels and diphthongs. I am sure these approaches are all valid, but I do not think that most students find it helpful to memorize such lists and charts. You could—for a quiz. But you will not remember them very long. So do not worry about memorizing a long set of rules and big charts. Instead, do it the quick and dirty way. There are only three things you need to remember to identify *most* contracts.

1. Know this very brief chart:

	ε	ο
ε	ει	ου
ο	ου	ου

   This is another way to say that ει and ου are signs of lengthened vowels. The largest number of contracts in the NT involve just these two vowels (ε, ο). That makes sense, since those are the two connecting vowels, and they are also the most common of the contract verb stem vowels.
2. Remember this key principle: the personal endings on contract verbs are almost identical to the standard endings you have already learned, though the connecting vowels may differ from the standard paradigm charts.
3. Knowing your vocabulary well is the biggest single help for identifying contract verbs.

Taking this minimalist approach will not enable you to immediately identify every contract verb or to explain precisely what is happening and why. But if you grasp the principle of how contract verbs work (and know your vocabulary well), you will probably be able to guess accurately that a particular form is a contract verb and deduce what it must be. When you are stuck, you may just have to look up a few tricky ones—but you would likely have to do that for some contract verbs anyway.

Contract Verb Forms

21.5. The following charts are for reference. I do not intend for you to memorize these charts. Study them to see the pattern of changes. When you are puzzled by a form that you think might be a contract verb, check these charts for verification. The most common contract verbs are the epsilon contracts—and that by a wide margin.[2] The most troublesome are the alpha contracts. Shown here are the most common verbs for each kind of contract verb: ποιέω, πληρόω, and

2. To illustrate with figures from the NT, there are 364 epsilon contract verbs, which occur a total of 3,951 times. By contrast, there are only 112 omicron contract verbs, occurring 611 times. There are only 102 alpha contract verbs, but these are more commonly used words, occurring 1,484 times.

ἀγαπάω. The present active infinitive is also shown, since the same contraction occurs in that form. Pay special attention to the present active infinitive form of the omicron and alpha contracts, since it varies the most from what you expect.

21.6. *Present Active Indicative*

Present Active Indicative

	Non-Contract	ε Contract	ο Contract	α Contract
	λύω	ποιέω	πληρόω	ἀγαπάω
1S	λύω	ποιῶ	πληρῶ	ἀγαπῶ
2S	λύεις	ποιεῖς	πληροῖς	ἀγαπᾷς
3S	λύει	ποιεῖ	πληροῖ	ἀγαπᾷ
1P	λύομεν	ποιοῦμεν	πληροῦμεν	ἀγαπῶμεν
2P	λύετε	ποιεῖτε	πληροῦτε	ἀγαπᾶτε
3P	λύουσι(ν)	ποιοῦσι(ν)	πληροῦσι(ν)	ἀγαπῶσι(ν)
Inf.	λύειν	ποιεῖν	πληροῦν	ἀγαπᾶν

21.7. Examples of Present Active Contracts

Mark 2:24, οἱ Φαρισαῖοι ἔλεγον αὐτῷ, Ἴδε τί **ποιοῦσιν** τοῖς σάββασιν ὃ οὐκ ἔξεστιν;

The Pharisees said to him, "See here! Why *are they doing* on the Sabbath what is not lawful?"

Matt. 19:17, ὁ δὲ εἶπεν αὐτῷ, Τί με **ἐρωτᾷς** περὶ τοῦ ἀγαθοῦ;

So he said to him, "Why do *you ask* me concerning the good?"

Gal. 3:8, ἐκ πίστεως **δικαιοῖ** τὰ ἔθνη ὁ θεός.

God *justifies* the Gentiles by faith.

Gen. 4:10, εἶπεν ὁ θεός, Φωνὴ αἵματος τοῦ ἀδελφοῦ σου **βοᾷ** πρός με ἐκ τῆς γῆς.

God said, "The voice of your brother's blood *is crying out* to me from the ground."

Gen. 24:37, ὥρκισέν με ὁ κύριός μου λέγων, Οὐ λήμψῃ γυναῖκα τῷ υἱῷ μου ἀπὸ τῶν θυγατέρων τῶν Χαναναίων, ἐν οἷς ἐγὼ **παροικῶ** ἐν τῇ γῇ αὐτῶν.[a]

My master made me swear an oath, saying, "Do not take a wife for my son from the daughters of the Canaanites, among whom *I live* in their land."

[a] The pronoun αὐτῶν is redundant in Greek (and English) in light of οἷς earlier in the clause, though it reflects a fairly formal equivalent of the Hebrew text being translated. We would say simply, "in whose land I live."

21.8. Now You Try It

1 John 3:22, τὰς ἐντολὰς αὐτοῦ **τηροῦμεν** καὶ τὰ ἀρεστὰ ἐνώπιον αὐτοῦ **ποιοῦμεν**.

Luke 7:5, **ἀγαπᾷ** γὰρ τὸ ἔθνος ἡμῶν καὶ τὴν συναγωγὴν αὐτὸς ᾠκοδόμησεν ἡμῖν.

Luke 9:31, ἔλεγον τὴν ἔξοδον αὐτοῦ, ἣν ἤμελλεν **πληροῦν** ἐν Ἰερουσαλήμ.

1 John 4:11, Ἀγαπητοί, εἰ οὕτως ὁ θεὸς ἠγάπησεν ἡμᾶς, καὶ ἡμεῖς ὀφείλομεν ἀλλήλους **ἀγαπᾶν**.

Exod. 5:15, οἱ γραμματεῖς[a] τῶν υἱῶν Ἰσραὴλ κατεβόησαν πρὸς Φαραώ, Ἵνα τί[b] οὕτως **ποιεῖς** τοῖς σοῖς οἰκέταις;

[a] For γραμματεύς, έως, ὁ, do not think of the usual NT "scribes." The context makes it clear that these are Jewish men appointed by the Egyptians to supervise and coordinate their fellows' slave labor. Perhaps "foreman" would be a suitable equivalent in this context.

[b] Ἵνα τί, "why?"

21.9. *Present Middle Indicative*

Present Middle Indicative[a]

	Non-Contract	ε Contract	ο Contract	α Contract
	λύω	ποιέω	πληρόω	ἀγαπάω
1S	λύομαι	ποιοῦμαι	πληροῦμαι	ἀγαπῶμαι
2S	λύῃ	ποιῇ	πληροῖ	ἀγαπᾷ
3S	λύεται	ποιεῖται	πληροῦται	ἀγαπᾶται
1P	λυόμεθα	ποιούμεθα	πληρούμεθα	ἀγαπώμεθα
2P	λύεσθε	ποιεῖσθε	πληροῦσθε	ἀγαπᾶσθε
3P	λύονται	ποιοῦνται	πληροῦνται	ἀγαπῶνται
Inf.	λύεσθαι	ποιεῖσθαι	πληροῦσθαι	ἀγαπᾶσθαι

[a] These forms can also function as passives if there is a passive marker in the context.

21.10. Examples of Present Middle Contracts

Matt. 20:22, ἀποκριθεὶς δὲ ὁ Ἰησοῦς εἶπεν, Οὐκ οἴδατε τί **αἰτεῖσθε**.

But Jesus, answering, said, "You do not know what *you are asking*."

Rom. 1:9, μάρτυς γάρ μού ἐστιν ὁ θεός, ᾧ λατρεύω ἐν τῷ πνεύματί μου ἐν τῷ εὐαγγελίῳ τοῦ υἱοῦ αὐτοῦ, ὡς ἀδιαλείπτως μνείαν ὑμῶν **ποιοῦμαι**.

For God is my witness, whom I serve in my spirit in the gospel of his Son, as unceasingly *I make* mention of you (or, I mention you [i.e., in prayer]).

Gen. 32:12, ἐξελοῦ (deliver!) με ἐκ χειρὸς τοῦ ἀδελφοῦ μου Ἠσαῦ, ὅτι **φοβοῦμαι** ἐγὼ αὐτόν.

Deliver me from the hand of my brother Esau, because *I am afraid* of him.

21.11. Now You Try It

1 Cor. 14:17, σὺ μὲν γὰρ καλῶς εὐχαριστεῖς ἀλλ' ὁ ἕτερος οὐκ **οἰκοδομεῖται**.

Luke 13:32, εἶπεν αὐτοῖς, Εἴπατε (tell!) τῇ ἀλώπεκι ταύτῃ, Ἰδοὺ ἐκβάλλω δαιμόνια καὶ ἰάσεις ἀποτελῶ σήμερον καὶ αὔριον καὶ τῇ τρίτῃ **τελειοῦμαι**.[a]

[a] You will want to read the context of this statement in an English Bible and also study your lexicon carefully.

Matt. 22:29, ἀποκριθεὶς δὲ ὁ Ἰησοῦς εἶπεν αὐτοῖς, **Πλανᾶσθε** μὴ εἰδότες (knowing) τὰς γραφὰς μηδὲ τὴν δύναμιν τοῦ θεοῦ.

Exod. 32:11, ἐδεήθη (he prayed) Μωϋσῆς ἔναντι κυρίου τοῦ θεοῦ καὶ εἶπεν, Ἵνα τί, κύριε, **θυμοῖ** ὀργῇ εἰς τὸν λαόν σου;

1 Esd. 4:20, ἄνθρωπος τὸν ἑαυτοῦ πατέρα ἐγκαταλείπει, ὃς ἐξέθρεψεν[a] αὐτόν, καὶ τὴν ἰδίαν χώραν καὶ πρὸς τὴν ἰδίαν γυναῖκα **κολλᾶται**.

[a] ἐξέθρεψεν ▶ ἐκτρέφω

21.12. *Imperfect Active Indicative*

Imperfect Active Indicative

	Non-Contract	ε Contract	ο Contract	α Contract
	λύω	ποιέω	πληρόω	ἀγαπάω
1S	ἔλυον	ἐποίουν	ἐπλήρουν	ἠγάπων
2S	ἔλυες	ἐποίεις	ἐπλήρους	ἠγάπας
3S	ἔλυε(ν)[a]	ἐποίει	ἐπλήρου	ἠγάπα
1P	ἐλύομεν	ἐποιοῦμεν	ἐπληροῦμεν	ἠγαπῶμεν
2P	ἐλύετε	ἐποιεῖτε	ἐπληροῦτε	ἠγαπᾶτε
3P	ἔλυον	ἐποίουν	ἐπλήρουν	ἠγάπων

[a] Contract verbs never take the movable nu in the third singular imperfect active indicative.

21.13. Examples of Imperfect Active Indicative Contracts

Mark 4:34, χωρὶς δὲ παραβολῆς οὐκ **ἐλάλει** αὐτοῖς, κατ' ἰδίαν δὲ τοῖς ἰδίοις μαθηταῖς ἐπέλυεν πάντα.

So without a parable *he did* not *speak* to them, but alone with his own disciples he explained everything.

Acts 13:25, ὡς δὲ **ἐπλήρου** Ἰωάννης τὸν δρόμον,[a] ἔλεγεν . . .

But as John *was completing* the course, he said . . .

[a] δρόμος, "(race) course, course of life, mission"

Gen. 11:30, ἦν Σάρα στεῖρα καὶ οὐκ **ἐτεκνοποίει.**

Sarah was barren and *was* not *bearing children.*

21.14. Now You Try It

Mark 7:17, Καὶ ὅτε εἰσῆλθεν εἰς οἶκον ἀπὸ τοῦ ὄχλου, **ἐπηρώτων** αὐτὸν οἱ μαθηταὶ αὐτοῦ τὴν παραβολήν.

Gen. 25:28, ἠγάπησεν δὲ Ἰσαὰκ τὸν Ἠσαῦ, ὅτι ἡ θήρα αὐτοῦ βρῶσις αὐτῷ· Ῥεβέκκα δὲ **ἠγάπα** τὸν Ἰακώβ.

1 Macc. 6:45, ἐπέδραμεν αὐτῷ θράσει[a] εἰς μέσον τῆς φάλαγγος[b] καὶ **ἐθανάτου** δεξιὰ καὶ εὐώνυμα, καὶ ἐσχίζοντο ἀπ' αὐτοῦ ἔνθα καὶ ἔνθα.[c]

[a] θράσος, ους, τό, "courage, boldness"
[b] φάλαγξ, αγγος, ἡ, "battle line, phalanx"
[c] ἔνθα, adv., "there"; ἔνθα καὶ ἔνθα, "on each side"

21.15. *Imperfect Middle Indicative*

Imperfect Middle Indicative

	Non-Contract	ε Contract	ο Contract	α Contract
	λύω	ποιέω	πληρόω	ἀγαπάω
1S	ἐλυόμην	ἐποιούμην	ἐπληρούμην	ἠγαπώμην
2S	ἐλύου	ἐποιοῦ	ἐπληροῦ	ἠγαπῶ
3S	ἐλύετο	ἐποιεῖτο	ἐπληροῦτο	ἠγαπᾶτο
1P	ἐλυόμεθα	ἐποιούμεθα	ἐπληρούμεθα	ἠγαπώμεθα
2P	ἐλύεσθε	ἐποιεῖσθε	ἐπληροῦσθε	ἠγαπᾶσθε
3P	ἐλύοντο	ἐποιοῦντο	ἐπληροῦντο	ἠγαπῶντο

21.16. Examples of Imperfect Middle Indicative Contracts

Mark 16:8, οὐδενὶ οὐδὲν εἶπαν· **ἐφοβοῦντο** γάρ.

They said nothing to anyone, for *they were awed.*[a]

[a] Traditionally ἐφοβοῦντο has been translated "afraid" in this verse. That is appropriate if you think the women were scared silly (as if they had seen a ghost), but if you think the context reflects the awesome impact that a resurrection had on these witnesses, then "were awed" may make better sense. Read the context and decide for yourself.

Acts 13:52, οἵ τε μαθηταὶ **ἐπληροῦντο** χαρᾶς καὶ πνεύματος ἁγίου.

Now the disciples *were filled* with joy and with the Holy Spirit.

1 Macc. 1:57, ὅπου εὑρίσκετο παρά τινι βιβλίον διαθήκης, καὶ εἴ τις συνευδόκει τῷ νόμῳ, τὸ σύγκριμα[a] τοῦ βασιλέως **ἐθανάτου** αὐτόν.

Where a Book of the Covenant was found with someone [i.e., in their possession], and if anyone was giving approval to the Law, the decree of the king *put* him *to death*.

[a] σύγκριμα, -ατος, τό, "decree"

21.17. Now You Try It

Luke 10:40, ἡ δὲ Μάρθα **περιεσπᾶτο**[a] περὶ πολλὴν διακονίαν.

[a] περισπάω, "I am distracted, busy"

Exod. 1:21, ἐπειδὴ **ἐφοβοῦντο** αἱ μαῖαι[a] τὸν θεόν, ἐποίησαν ἑαυταῖς οἰκίας.

[a] μαῖα, ας, ἡ, "midwife"

3 Macc. 1:25, οἱ δὲ περὶ τὸν βασιλέα πρεσβύτεροι πολλαχῶς (in many ways) **ἐπειρῶντο** τὸν ἀγέρωχον[a] αὐτοῦ νοῦν ἐξιστάνειν[b] τῆς ἐντεθυμημένης[c] ἐπιβουλῆς.

[a] ἀγέρωχος, ος, ον, "arrogant"

[b] ἐξίστημι/ἐξιστάνω does not have the meaning here that you will find in a NT lexicon. In this context it means "I divert from."

[c] ἐντεθυμημένης functions as an adjective, "contemplated."

Perfect Middle Indicative Contracts

21.18. There is only one other matter related to contract verbs that needs to be mentioned. You would probably figure it out just fine, but for clarity, the forms of the perfect middle tense-form are shown below. Remember that this form does not use either a connecting vowel or a form marker, yet the stem vowel in contract verbs still lengthens. The omicron contract verb πληρόω is shown here, but all contracts follow the same pattern. (These forms do not occur frequently in the NT.)

Perfect Middle Indicative

	Non-Contract	ο Contract
	λύω	πληρόω
1S	λέλυμαι	πεπλήρωμαι
2S	λέλυσαι	πεπλήρωσαι
3S	λέλυται	πεπλήρωται

	Non-Contract	ο Contract
	λύω	πληρόω
1P	λελύμεθα	πεπληρώμεθα
2P	λέλυσθε	πεπλήρωσθε
3P	λέλυνται	πεπλήρωνται

21.19. Examples of Perfect Middle Indicative Contracts

Luke 4:21, ἤρξατο δὲ λέγειν πρὸς αὐτοὺς ὅτι Σήμερον **πεπλήρωται** ἡ γραφὴ αὕτη ἐν τοῖς ὠσὶν ὑμῶν.

So he began to say to them, "Today this Scripture *is fulfilled* in your hearing."

John 7:47, ἀπεκρίθησαν οὖν αὐτοῖς οἱ Φαρισαῖοι, Μὴ καὶ ὑμεῖς **πεπλάνησθε;**

Therefore the Pharisees answered them, "You haven't *been deceived* too, have you?"

Gen. 43:3, εἶπεν δὲ αὐτῷ Ἰούδας, Διαμαρτυρίᾳ[a] **διαμεμαρτύρηται**[b] ἡμῖν ὁ ἄνθρωπος, Οὐκ ὄψεσθε τὸ πρόσωπόν μου, ἐὰν μὴ ὁ ἀδελφὸς ὑμῶν ὁ νεώτερος μεθ' ὑμῶν ᾖ (is).

Judah said to him, "With a solemn declaration the man *has solemnly declared* to us, 'You shall not see my face unless your younger brother is with you.'"

[a] διαμαρτυρία, ας, ἡ, "solemn declaration, testimony"

[b] διαμαρτύρομαι, "I affirm/declare solemnly" (though a middle-only form, it is an ε contract verb)

21.20. Now You Try It

John 3:29, ὁ δὲ φίλος τοῦ νυμφίου χαίρει διὰ τὴν φωνὴν τοῦ νυμφίου. αὕτη οὖν ἡ χαρὰ ἡ ἐμὴ **πεπλήρωται.**

Acts 16:10, **προσκέκληται** ἡμᾶς ὁ θεὸς εὐαγγελίσασθαι αὐτούς.

1 Cor. 7:27, **δέδεσαι** γυναικί, μὴ ζήτει λύσιν· λέλυσαι ἀπὸ γυναικός, μὴ ζήτει γυναῖκα.[a]

[a] This verse can be translated in at least two ways. As it is punctuated in the Greek NT, it is composed of two statements. Most modern English versions, however, translate the first and third clauses as questions. One version that follows the punctuation as given above is NET. Once you think you have it figured out, compare several English versions to see how they may differ.

John 11:11, ταῦτα εἶπεν, καὶ μετὰ τοῦτο λέγει αὐτοῖς, Λάζαρος ὁ φίλος ἡμῶν **κεκοίμηται·** ἀλλὰ πορεύομαι ἵνα ἐξυπνίσω (I may awaken) αὐτόν.

Zeph. 3:15, περιεῖλεν[a] κύριος τὰ ἀδικήματά σου, **λελύτρωταί** σε ἐκ χειρὸς ἐχθρῶν σου· βασιλεὺς Ἰσραὴλ κύριος ἐν μέσῳ σου.

[a] περιεῖλεν ▶ περιαιρέω

Job 30:14, βέλεσιν αὐτοῦ κατηκόντισέν[a] με, **κέχρηταί**[b] μοι ὡς βούλεται, ἐν ὀδύναις πέφυρμαι.[c]

[a] κατακοντίζω, "I shoot down"
[b] χράω, "I use, treat, deal with"
[c] φύρω, "I am steeped/soaked with"

Liquid Verbs

21.21. Liquid verbs have a liquid consonant as the last letter of the stem. The consonants classed as liquids, you will remember, are λ, μ, ν, and ρ. You first met them in connection with third-declension nouns in chapter 11. Below are some common liquid verbs:

Stems ending in lambda: βάλλω ("I throw"), ὀφείλω ("I ought"—only LXX as future), ἀποστέλλω ("I send"), and other compound forms of -στελλω and -τελλω.

Stems ending in nu: ἀποκτείνω ("I kill"), κρίνω ("I judge"), κατακρίνω ("I condemn"), μένω ("I remain"), ποιμαίνω ("I shepherd"), φαίνω ("I shine"), and other compound forms of -τεινω.

Stems ending in rho: αἴρω ("I take up"), ἐγείρω ("I raise"), φθείρω ("I corrupt").

Liquid Futures

21.22. Here is what you need to know about liquid futures.

A sigma will never stand after a liquid; the sigma will drop out.

Some futures do not have a sigma.[3]

Futures without a sigma usually have a circumflex accent over the ending.

There may be minor spelling changes in the stem (e.g., some double consonants may simplify, vowels may undergo ablaut).

Study the forms below, and compare the three columns of Greek forms. The middle Greek column, "Present (Liquid)," is the normal present active indicative form of a liquid verb. It is not different from a non-liquid verb. The last

3. Technically, liquid futures add εσ as a form marker, the σ drops out, and ε contracts with the connecting vowel (*MBG*, 92).

column shows what happens to the accent on an *epsilon contract* verb, ποιέω. This textbook has paid relatively little attention to accents, but this is one point where such detail can be useful. You end up with a circumflex over the connecting vowel (or diphthong if it contracts to one). What is important to remember here is that if you see a circumflex in this position *on a liquid verb,* it is almost certainly a future form—which is what is shown in the first Greek column in this chart. If the stem is an epsilon contract verb, the circumflex indicates not a future but a present form, so you must be able to identify a verb as either a liquid or a contract based on the lexical form.

Future Active Indicative of Liquid Verbs

	Future (Liquid)	Present (Liquid)	Present (Contract)
	κρίνω	κρίνω	ποιέω
1S	κρινῶ	κρίνω	ποιῶ
2S	κρινεῖς	κρίνεις	ποιεῖς
3S	κρινεῖ	κρίνει	ποιεῖ
1P	κρινοῦμεν	κρίνομεν	ποιοῦμεν
2P	κρινεῖτε	κρίνετε	ποιεῖτε
3P	κρινοῦσι(ν)	κρίνουσι(ν)	ποιοῦσι(ν)

Take time to study this chart (and the one below, of the future middle), and compare them with the charts of the regular future forms in chapter 19. You do not have to memorize these charts, but review them carefully enough so that you are familiar with them.

Future Middle Indicative of Liquid Verbs

	Future (Liquid)	Present (Liquid)	Present (Contract)
	κρίνω	κρίνω	ποιέω
1S	κρινοῦμαι	κρίνομαι	ποιοῦμαι
2S	κρινῇ	κρίνῃ	ποιῇ
3S	κρινεῖται	κρίνεται	ποιεῖται
1P	κρινούμεθα	κρινόμεθα	ποιούμεθα
2P	κρινεῖσθε	κρίνεσθε	ποιεῖσθε
3P	κρινοῦνται	κρίνονται	ποιοῦνται

21.23. Examples of Liquid Future Verbs

Luke 12:58, ὁ πράκτωρ σε **βαλεῖ** εἰς φυλακήν.	The constable *will throw* you into prison.

Mark 9:31, Ὁ υἱὸς τοῦ ἀνθρώπου παραδίδοται (will be delivered)[a] εἰς χεῖρας ἀνθρώπων, καὶ **ἀποκτενοῦσιν** αὐτόν.

The Son of Man will be delivered into the hands of men, and *they will kill* him.

[a] Note that there is a present and a future verb in parallel in this verse, both referring to future time.

Deut. 16:19, οὐκ **ἐκκλινοῦσιν** κρίσιν, οὐκ ἐπιγνώσονται πρόσωπον[a] οὐδὲ λήμψονται δῶρον· τὰ γὰρ δῶρα ἐκτυφλοῖ ὀφθαλμοὺς σοφῶν καὶ ἐξαίρει λόγους δικαίων.[b]

They shall not *turn aside* justice, they shall not show partiality, neither shall they take a bribe, for bribes blind wise eyes and carry off righteous words.

[a] ἐπιγνώσονται πρόσωπον, an idiom meaning to "show partiality"

[b] The translation above takes σοφῶν and δικαίων as attributive genitives (see Wallace, *Grammar,* 86–88). These two adjectives might also be taken as substantival: "eyes of the wise" and "words of the righteous."

Jdt. 14:3, οὗτοι πορεύσονται εἰς τὴν παρεμβολὴν αὐτῶν καὶ **ἐγεροῦσι** τοὺς στρατηγοὺς τῆς δυνάμεως[a] Ἀσσούρ· καὶ συνδραμοῦνται ἐπὶ τὴν σκηνὴν Ὀλοφέρνου καὶ οὐχ εὑρήσουσιν αὐτόν, καὶ ἐπιπεσεῖται ἐπ᾽ αὐτοὺς φόβος, καὶ φεύξονται ἀπὸ προσώπου ὑμῶν.

They will go into their camp and *will rouse* the commanders of the Assyrian army; they will run to the tent of Holofernes, and they will not find him, and fear will fall upon them, and they will flee from before you.

[a] δύναμις, εως, ἡ, "power" in the sense of "military power," i.e., "an army"; it is not used with this meaning in the NT, but it is in the LXX.

21.24. Now You Try It

John 12:48, ὁ λόγος **κρινεῖ** αὐτὸν ἐν τῇ ἐσχάτῃ ἡμέρᾳ.

John 2:20, εἶπαν οὖν οἱ Ἰουδαῖοι, Ὁ ναὸς οὗτος [has been under construction for forty-six years],[a] καὶ σὺ ἐν τρισὶν ἡμέραις **ἐγερεῖς** αὐτόν;

[a] English has been supplied here for two reasons: the verb form used is one you have not yet learned, and there is an exegetical question regarding the meaning. The English cited follows NET. See the commentaries and the NET note.

Jer. 13:9, Τάδε λέγει κύριος, Οὕτω **φθερῶ** τὴν ὕβριν Ἰούδα καὶ τὴν ὕβριν Ἰερουσαλήμ.

Num. 1:50, αὐτοὶ **ἀροῦσιν** τὴν σκηνὴν καὶ πάντα τὰ σκεύη αὐτῆς, καὶ αὐτοὶ λειτουργήσουσιν ἐν αὐτῇ καὶ κύκλῳ τῆς σκηνῆς παρεμβαλοῦσιν.[a]

[a] παρεμβάλλω, "I surround," here in the sense, "I encamp around"

Attic Futures

21.25. Similar to the liquid future is a form known as an *Attic future*. These are forms in which the form marker sigma has dropped out. They will look like the liquid future forms shown above, but they do not have stems ending in a liquid. They are most commonly verbs ending in -ιζω (the actual stem of which often ends with a delta). Some verbs will occur in both the usual future form and the Attic future formation. For example, καθίζω may occur either with a sigma form marker, καθίσω, or without, καθιῶ.[4]

Isa. 11:10 = Rom. 15:12, ἐπ' αὐτῷ ἔθνη **ἐλπιοῦσιν.**[a]	In him the Gentiles *will hope.*

[a] 3rd pl. fut. act. ind. ▸ ἐλπίζω

See also ποτιῶ in Gen. 24:46 below.

Liquid Aorists

21.26. What is similar in the formation of future and aorist that may be relevant to the category of liquid aorist? Correct! The form marker begins with sigma, so liquid aorists follow the same patterns. You do not need to learn another formula for liquid aorists; just remember that if the sigma drops out, then the form marker will show up as just an alpha. Here is what they will look like.

Liquid Aorist Forms

	Active	Middle
	μένω	κρίνω
1S	ἔμεινα	ἐκρινάμην
2S	ἔμεινας	ἐκρίνω
3S	ἔμεινε(ν)	ἐκρίνατο
1P	ἐμείναμεν	ἐκρινάμεθα
2P	ἐμείνατε	ἐκρίνασθε
3P	ἔμειναν	ἐκρίναντο
Inf	μεῖναι	κρίνασθαι

Remember that there may be minor spelling changes in the stem of a liquid. As with the future liquids, some double consonants may simplify, and some vowels may undergo ablaut. In the case of μένω, the vowel in the stem underwent ablaut to become the diphthong ει. The aorist infinitive is also affected by a liquid stem. You have learned that the usual aorist active infinitive form is λῦσαι. When a liquid verb is involved—for example, μένω—the sigma drops out, leaving the

4. Although not common in the NT, according to Conybeare and Stock, Attic futures are more common in the LXX than they were in Attic Greek (*Grammar of Septuagint Greek*, §21 with a list of LXX examples). For a complete list of Attic futures in the NT, see *MBG*, 96, §43.7b.

infinitive form as μεῖναι. Notice that in this case the epsilon in the stem has also lengthened to the diphthong ει.

The most common liquid aorist forms in the NT are from αἴρω, ἀπαγγέλλω, ἀποκτείνω, ἀποστέλλω, ἐγείρω, μένω, and πίνω. Two specific liquid aorist forms each occur more than 20 times in the NT (both are 3S): ἀπέστειλεν (36×) and ἤγειρεν (21×). There are some verbs that you might assume are liquids based on their lexical form but that are not liquids, since they use a different stem in the future and aorist. For example, βάλλω is not a liquid in the aorist (it is a liquid in the future active), since the aorist stem is βλη-.[5] Other words in this category include βαίνω and its many compounds, the aorist stem of which is βα-. Also second aorist forms are not part of the liquid category, since they do not use σα as a form marker.

21.27. Examples of Liquid Aorists

Mark 8:26, **ἀπέστειλεν** αὐτὸν εἰς οἶκον αὐτοῦ.	*He sent* him to his house.
Mark 9:27, ὁ δὲ Ἰησοῦς **ἤγειρεν** αὐτόν.	But Jesus *raised* him.
Mark 10:3, ὁ δὲ ἀποκριθεὶς εἶπεν αὐτοῖς, Τί ὑμῖν **ἐνετείλατο** Μωϋσῆς;	But answering he said to them, "What *did* Moses *command* you?"
Gen. 24:46, εἶπεν, Πίε (drink!) σύ, καὶ τὰς καμήλους σου ποτιῶ.[a] καὶ **ἔπιον**, καὶ τὰς καμήλους μου ἐπότισεν.	She said, "You drink, and I will water your camels." And *I drank*, and she watered my camels.

[a] An Attic future (see the explanation earlier in this chapter).

2 Macc. 5:1, Περὶ δὲ τὸν καιρὸν τοῦτον τὴν δευτέραν ἔφοδον[a] ὁ Ἀντίοχος εἰς Αἴγυπτον **ἐστείλατο**.[b]	But about this time Antiochus *prepared for* his second entrance into Egypt.

[a] ἔφοδος, ου, ἡ, "approach, entrance; attempt"; here the entrance into Egypt is an attempt at military conquest, so it could be translated as "invasion" (so NETS).

[b] στέλλω has a wide range of usage; here it probably means either "I prepare myself for" or perhaps "I go, journey."

21.28. Now You Try It

John 4:40, **ἔμεινεν** ἐκεῖ δύο ἡμέρας.	
John 12:17, τὸν Λάζαρον ἐφώνησεν ἐκ τοῦ μνημείου καὶ **ἤγειρεν** αὐτὸν ἐκ νεκρῶν.	

5. The explanation given here is slightly oversimplified; there are other possible ways to explain the formation of the aorist stem of βάλλω. If you are curious, see *MBG*, 301n5.

Num. 11:27, ὁ νεανίσκος **ἀπήγγειλεν** Μωϋσῇ, Ἐλδὰδ καὶ Μωδὰδ προφητεύουσιν ἐν τῇ παρεμβολῇ.

1 Kgdms. (1 Sam.) 11:4, ἔρχονται οἱ ἄγγελοι εἰς Γαβαὰ πρὸς Σαοὺλ καὶ λαλοῦσιν τοὺς λόγους εἰς τὰ ὦτα τοῦ λαοῦ, καὶ **ἦραν** πᾶς ὁ λαὸς τὴν φωνὴν αὐτῶν καὶ ἔκλαυσαν.

Reading Passage: Matthew 24:4–20

21.29. This passage contains not only a number of liquid and contract verbs but also quite a few future passive forms, which will prove to be a good review.

Troubles That Come before the End

4ἀποκριθεὶς ὁ Ἰησοῦς εἶπεν αὐτοῖς, Βλέπετε (watch out!) μή τις ὑμᾶς πλανήσῃ
(should deceive)· 5πολλοὶ γὰρ ἐλεύσονται ἐπὶ τῷ ὀνόματί μου λέγοντες (saying),
Ἐγώ εἰμι ὁ Χριστός, καὶ πολλοὺς **πλανήσουσιν.** 6**μελλήσετε**[a] δὲ ἀκούειν πολέμους
καὶ ἀκοὰς πολέμων· ὁρᾶτε (see to it!) μὴ θροεῖσθε (don’t be alarmed!)· δεῖ γὰρ
γενέσθαι (to be), ἀλλ’ οὔπω ἐστὶν τὸ τέλος. 7ἐγερθήσεται γὰρ ἔθνος ἐπὶ ἔθνος
καὶ βασιλεία ἐπὶ βασιλείαν καὶ ἔσονται λιμοὶ καὶ σεισμοὶ κατὰ τόπους·[b] 8πάντα
δὲ ταῦτα ἀρχὴ ὠδίνων. 9τότε παραδώσουσιν (they will deliver up) ὑμᾶς εἰς
θλῖψιν καὶ **ἀποκτενοῦσιν** ὑμᾶς, καὶ ἔσεσθε μισούμενοι (hated) ὑπὸ πάντων τῶν
ἐθνῶν διὰ τὸ ὄνομά μου. 10καὶ τότε σκανδαλισθήσονται πολλοὶ καὶ ἀλλήλους
παραδώσουσιν καὶ **μισήσουσιν** ἀλλήλους· 11καὶ πολλοὶ ψευδοπροφῆται ἐγερ-
θήσονται καὶ **πλανήσουσιν** πολλούς· 12καὶ διὰ τὸ πληθυνθῆναι[c] τὴν ἀνομίαν
ψυγήσεται ἡ ἀγάπη τῶν πολλῶν. 13ὁ δὲ ὑπομείνας (who endures) εἰς τέλος
οὗτος σωθήσεται. 14καὶ κηρυχθήσεται τοῦτο τὸ εὐαγγέλιον τῆς βασιλείας ἐν
ὅλῃ τῇ οἰκουμένῃ εἰς μαρτύριον πᾶσιν τοῖς ἔθνεσιν, καὶ τότε ἥξει τὸ τέλος.
15Ὅταν οὖν ἴδητε (you see) τὸ βδέλυγμα τῆς ἐρημώσεως τὸ ῥηθὲν (which
was spoken) διὰ Δανιὴλ τοῦ προφήτου ἑστὸς (standing) ἐν τόπῳ ἁγίῳ, ὁ
ἀναγινώσκων (reader) νοείτω (let him understand!), 16τότε οἱ ἐν τῇ Ἰου-
δαίᾳ φευγέτωσαν (must flee!) εἰς τὰ ὄρη, 17ὁ ἐπὶ τοῦ δώματος μὴ καταβάτω
(must not come down!) **ἆραι** τὰ ἐκ τῆς οἰκίας αὐτοῦ, 18καὶ ὁ ἐν τῷ ἀγρῷ μὴ
ἐπιστρεψάτω (must not go back!) ὀπίσω **ἆραι** τὸ ἱμάτιον αὐτοῦ. 19οὐαὶ δὲ ταῖς
ἐν γαστρὶ ἐχούσαις (ones who have)[d] καὶ ταῖς θηλαζούσαις (nursing mothers)
ἐν ἐκείναις ταῖς ἡμέραις. 20προσεύχεσθε (pray!) δὲ ἵνα μὴ γένηται (it should
not be) ἡ φυγὴ ὑμῶν χειμῶνος μηδὲ σαββάτῳ.

[a] μελλήσετε appears in the lexicon as a liquid stem, μέλλω, but the future has retained an old form of the stem, which originally ended with an epsilon: μελλε-. That means that in the future μέλλω is a contract verb, not a liquid.

[b] κατὰ τόπους, “in various places”

[c] διὰ τὸ πληθυνθῆναι τὴν ἀνομίαν, “because lawlessness will increase.” In the next lesson, you will learn that διὰ τό with an infinitive (πληθυνθῆναι) is a causal statement.

[d] ταῖς ἐν γαστρὶ ἐχούσαις, formally, “to the ones who have in belly”—an idiom for “those who are pregnant”

21.30. Vocabulary for Chapter 21

Part of Speech	Definition	Possible Glosses	Frequency	
Word			NT	LXX
Verbs				
ὁράω	To perceive with the eye or the mind; to understand; to be alert or to accept responsibility for something (hortatory or imperatival)	I see, notice; I perceive; See to it!	454	1,539
λαλέω	To make a sound; to utter words so as to make a statement	I make sounds; I speak, say, tell	296	1,189
κρίνω	To make a distinction between items or situations so as to come to a conclusion; may be used in a variety of contexts, both positive and negative, whether of a legal judgment or sentence, of pressing legal charges, or seeing that justice is done (esp. LXX); or of personal matters in which a decision is made	I prefer, select; I judge, condemn, press charges; I judge justly, see that justice is done; I decide, think, consider	114	271
ἀποκρίνω	To make a response, to either a specific question, a statement, or a situation (never act. in NT, once in LXX; act. appears more often in other Koine literature; often listed as ἀποκρίνομαι)	I answer, reply, say in response/reaction to	231	277
ἐγείρω	To move from an inert state or position, the nature of which depends on the context, whether from sitting, lying, sleeping, sickness, death, inertia, or obscurity	I rise, get/raise/lift up; I awake, rouse	144	57
ζῶ (usually listed as ζάω)[a]	To be alive physically or spiritually; to conduct oneself in a certain manner	I live, am alive; I live	140	554
ἀποστέλλω	To send someone or something from one place to another	I send, send away	132	691
μένω	To remain in a place, condition, or position for a period of time	I remain, stay, continue; I live (in a place)	118	89
ζητέω	To search for something (not necessarily something lost), whether an object, information, or some action	I seek, look for; I investigate, deliberate	117	320
μέλλω	To take place in the future, whether an expected event or one intended or determined, whether imminent or distant	I am about to; I intend, propose; I have determined	109	43
παρακαλέω	To summon someone into one's presence; to urge or request strongly; to exhort someone to have courage or joy	I invite, call; I exhort, urge; I encourage, comfort	109	139
αἴρω	To raise something to a higher position; to move from one place to another [≠ αἱρέω]	I lift/take/pick up; I remove, take/carry away	101	289
ἀπαγγέλλω	To give an account of something (usually oral); to make something known publicly	I announce, report, tell; I proclaim	45	254
μισέω	To have a strong aversion to or dislike for someone or something; to consider unworthy of notice [The English word "hate" is sometimes too strong and may have wrong connotations.]	I hate; I disregard, disdain	40	182

Part of Speech	Definition	Possible Glosses	Frequency	
Word			NT	LXX
φιλέω	To have a special interest in and high regard and affection for someone or something; to indicate that affection by a kiss [Originally the more common word in older forms of Greek, but in Koine is often replaced by and synonymous with ἀγαπάω; see LN §25.43; BDAG, 1056.]	I love, like; I kiss	25	32

[a] ζάω is not an alpha contract verb; the lexical form is ζῶ; see the sidebar earlier in this chapter.

21.31. Key Things to Know for Chapter 21

How do you identify contract and liquid verbs by their lexical form?

Do you understand what happens in present and imperfect tense-form contract verbs?

Know the three contract verb rules, including the corresponding chart.

What are the four liquids? (The answer is *not* "water, Pepsi, ice tea, and milk.")

22

NON-FINITE VERBS: PART 1

INFINITIVES

22.1. We are now moving into non-finite verb forms. Although you have already met several common infinitive forms, most of the verbs that we have studied have been indicative-mood verbs. All indicatives are finite forms: verbs that have person and number and therefore have a default, built-in, back-pocket subject (and can therefore also take a subject in the nominative case). Both infinitives and participles are *non-finite* forms. The infinitive has no explicit subject. That is why we call it an *in*finitive. The *finite* forms (such as the indicative-mood verbs) are *limited* by their built-in subjects.

The Nature of the Infinitive

22.2. In English, an infinitive is a verb preceded by the word *to*. It simply names an action—for example, "Frodo began *to climb* the Winding Stair." In Greek, the infinitive is a single-word form morphologically; it does not use a preposition as does the English infinitive. Functionally it is a compound form in that it has characteristics like that of two other parts of speech: the noun and the verb. We can think of the infinitive as a verbal noun.

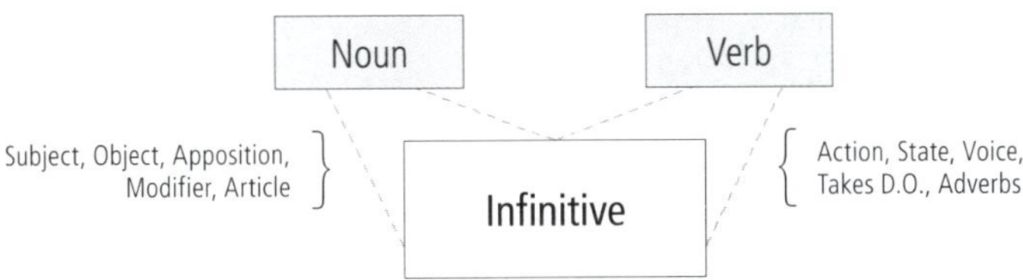

Figure 22.1. The Hybrid Nature of the Infinitive

Due to its hybrid nature (see fig. 22.1), the infinitive, like a noun, can function as a subject or an object, it can be used in apposition or as a modifier, it can take an article, and so on. But since it is also part verb, it may describe an action or state, it has voice, it can take an object, it can be modified by an adverb, and it has tense/aspect.

Forms of the Infinitive

22.3. The forms of the infinitive are easier than many other verbal forms in that they do not have a full set of forms to keep track of. There is only one form for each tense-form/voice combination. In the chart, note the usual form markers. The four forms emphasized in the chart below are the most common[1] and, with the infinitive of εἰμί (see below), are the most important ones to remember. For the others it is enough at this point to be able to recognize that any form with a -σθαι or -ναι ending is an infinitive. From there the form markers σα and θη (which you already know) will be enough to get you in the right ballpark even if you cannot write this entire chart from memory.

Present and Aorist Infinitives

	Lexical Form	Active	Middle	Passive
Present	λύω	λύειν	λύεσθαι	
First Aorist	λύω	λῦσαι	λύσασθαι	λυθῆναι
Second Aorist	βάλλω	βαλεῖν	βαλέσθαι	βληθῆναι[a]

[a] A few verbs drop the theta from the aorist passive form marker, so the ending is just -ηναι; these forms are not common.

You will notice that none of the aorist infinitives have augments. Only indicatives have augments. The augment is a marker for secondary endings, which are used only in the indicative mood.[2]

22.4. Second aorist forms have a similar pattern to what you saw with second aorist indicative verbs: the second aorist infinitive looks identical to the present infinitive *except for the stem* (just as the second aorist active indicative looked the same as the imperfect active indicative except for the stem). Only the second aorist stem tells you that it is an aorist form.

There are also some future (only 5 in NT, 75 in LXX) and perfect (49 NT, 101 LXX) infinitives, but their relatively small number means you will not see

1. There are 1,242 aorist infinitives and 996 present infinitives in the NT. Of the aorist forms, 849 are first aorist (612 active, 66 middle, and 171 passive) and 393 are second aorist (347 active, 46 middle). In the LXX the pattern is as follows: 4,523 aorist infinitives (3,367 active, 416 middle, and 470 passive) and 2,208 present infinitives (1,690 active, 429 middle, and 89 passive). These statistics are more than trivia; they can help you envision what forms you will see most often.

2. This is a general principle that will be true even in other forms that we have not yet met. In the subjunctive mood, for example, both the aorist and present tense-forms use primary endings. In the participle, no personal endings are used, since it, like the infinitive, is a non-finite form.

them very often.[3] The familiar form markers and reduplication tell you all you need to know to be able to identify these forms when you do encounter them.

Future and Perfect Infinitive of λύω

	Active	Middle	Passive
Future	λύσειν	λύσεσθαι	—
Perfect	λελυκέναι	λελύσθαι	

Infinitive of εἰμί

22.5. The present active infinitive of εἰμί is εἶναι. There are only a very few future middle infinitives, ἔσεσθαι (4 in the NT and 6 in the LXX).

22.6. *Examples of the Infinitive*

Mark 7:27, οὐκ ἔστιν καλὸν **λαβεῖν** τὸν ἄρτον τῶν τέκνων καὶ τοῖς κυναρίοις **βαλεῖν**.	It is not good *to take* the children's bread and *throw* it to the dogs.
Exod. 29:46, γνώσονται ὅτι ἐγώ εἰμι κύριος ὁ θεὸς αὐτῶν ὁ ἐξαγαγὼν αὐτοὺς ἐκ γῆς Αἰγύπτου **ἐπικληθῆναι** αὐτοῖς καὶ θεὸς **εἶναι** αὐτῶν.	They will know that I am the Lord their God who brought them out of the land of Egypt *to be invoked* by them and *to be* their God.

22.7. *Now You Try It*

Matt. 4:17, Ἀπὸ τότε ἤρξατο ὁ Ἰησοῦς **κηρύσσειν** καὶ **λέγειν**, Μετανοεῖτε (repent!)· ἤγγικεν γὰρ ἡ βασιλεία τῶν οὐρανῶν.	
Gen. 2:5, ἄνθρωπος οὐκ ἦν **ἐργάζεσθαι** τὴν γῆν.	

Contract Forms of the Infinitive

22.8. Only present infinitives are impacted by the changes seen in contract verbs. The same sort of contractions take place in the infinitive as you saw in the indicative mood. Specifically, the infinitive ending -ειν contracts with the stem vowel. Examples of each class of contracts are as follows.

3. The future infinitive was being replaced in Koine by μέλλω with the present infinitive.

Present Infinitive Contracts

	Active	Middle
ποιέω	ποιεῖν	ποιεῖσθαι
πληρόω	πληροῦν	πληροῦσθαι
ἀγαπάω	ἀγαπᾶν	ἀγαπᾶσθαι

Although not a contraction, the addition of the aorist infinitive ending to a contract verb causes the stem vowel to lengthen just as it did in the first aorist indicative. For example, the aorist infinitive of ποιέω is ποιῆσαι.

22.9. Examples of Contract Infinitives

Matt. 12:2, οἱ δὲ Φαρισαῖοι εἶπαν αὐτῷ, Ἰδοὺ οἱ μαθηταί σου ποιοῦσιν ὃ οὐκ ἔξεστιν **ποιεῖν** ἐν σαββάτῳ.	But the Pharisees said to him, "Look here! Your disciples are doing what is not lawful *to do* on the Sabbath."
Rom. 13:3, θέλεις μὴ **φοβεῖσθαι** τὴν ἐξουσίαν; τὸ ἀγαθὸν ποίει.	Do you desire not *to fear* the authorities? Do what is good.
1 Tim. 2:1, Παρακαλῶ οὖν πρῶτον πάντων **ποιεῖσθαι** δεήσεις προσευχὰς ἐντεύξεις εὐχαριστίας ὑπὲρ πάντων ἀνθρώπων.	Wherefore I exhort [you] first of all, *to make* requests, prayers, intercessions, and thanksgivings for all people.

22.10. Now You Try It

Luke 9:31, ἔλεγον τὴν ἔξοδον αὐτοῦ, ἣν ἤμελλεν **πληροῦν**[a] ἐν Ἰερουσαλήμ.

[a] This is the only instance of a present infinitive of πληρόω in the NT, but it serves as a pattern for other omicron contract forms.

Eph. 5:28, οὕτως ὀφείλουσιν καὶ οἱ ἄνδρες **ἀγαπᾶν** τὰς ἑαυτῶν γυναῖκας ὡς τὰ ἑαυτῶν σώματα.

Gen. 18:7, εἰς τὰς βόας ἔδραμεν Ἀβραὰμ καὶ ἔλαβεν μοσχάριον[a] ἁπαλὸν καὶ καλὸν καὶ ἔδωκεν (he gave) τῷ παιδί, καὶ ἐτάχυνεν[b] τοῦ **ποιῆσαι** αὐτό.

[a] μοσχάριον, ου, τό, "young calf" (diminutive form of μόσχος)
[b] ταχύνω, "I hasten, hurry"

Meaning and Aspect of the Infinitive

22.11. A common English equivalent for all forms of the infinitive is "to" plus the verb, thus "to loose" (active and middle) or "to be loosed" (passive). It is not possible to distinguish a present infinitive from an aorist infinitive when expressing it in English since there is only one English infinitive form. Many infinitives, however, will not sound like an English infinitive, since they are used to express other ideas and relationships (see below). In other words, Greek infinitives have a much broader range of functions than do their English cousins and as a result often cannot be represented with a formal equivalent in English.

The aspect of the infinitive is the same as other tense-forms. The present has imperfective aspect, the aorist has perfective, and the perfect is stative. These distinctions cannot be represented in English due, once again, to the limitations of English. That is one of the reasons you are learning Greek.

The Accusative with an Infinitive

Determining which of two accusatives is the subject of an infinitive is a debated matter. There are two different situations, each of which must be evaluated separately. When it involves a linking verb (e.g., εἶναι), the same principles apply as when there are two nominatives with a finite form of εἰμί (see the hierarchy of rules in §14.13). When the infinitive is a regular, transitive verb, the decision about which accusative is the subject is based mostly on context, but there is a 70+ percent likelihood that the first in word order is the subject.[a]

[a]For a summary of several of the major studies on this question, see Wallace's *Greek Grammar*, which lists a number of examples (192–97). Most of the examples cited there show the less common situation, in which the second accusative is the subject.

Grammar of the Infinitive

22.12. The Greek infinitive, unlike an English infinitive, can take an article: τὸ γράφειν ("to write"). It can also have an accusative-case object: ἰδεῖν σημεῖον ("to see a sign"). The infinitive can be modified by an adverb or phrase: λαλῆσαι οὕτως ("to speak in this way").

Technically, the infinitive never has a subject. Finite verbs have subjects; non-finite verbs such as infinitives do not. If it is necessary to specify who is doing the action of the infinitive, an *accusative*-case substantive is used, a construction that we call the *accusative subject of the infinitive*.[4] These accusative subjects are most commonly pronouns.

Examples of Accusative Subjects of the Infinitive

22.13. In some of the following examples you will see the infinitive used in ways that we have not discussed yet. For now, focus on the accusative substantive that is functioning as the subject of the infinitive. The explanation for the various uses of the infinitive follows in a later section in this chapter.

1 Cor. 14:5, θέλω **ὑμᾶς** λαλεῖν.	I want *you* to speak.

The accusative ὑμᾶς is the subject of the infinitive, indicating who is to speak; it is not the direct object of θέλω.

4. Some grammarians have a delightful, though rather clumsy, name for these accusative subjects: *the accusative of general reference, the so-called subject of the infinitive*.

Matt. 15:31, ὥστε **τὸν ὄχλον** θαυμάσαι	So that *the crowd* marveled
Rom. 15:13, εἰς τὸ περισσεύειν **ὑμᾶς** ἐν τῇ ἐλπίδι	In order that *you* may abound in hope

22.14. *Now You Try It*

Acts 9:3, **αὐτὸν** ἐγγίζειν τῇ Δαμασκῷ	
Mark 2:23, Καὶ ἐγένετο **αὐτὸν** ἐν τοῖς σάββασιν παραπορεύεσθαι διὰ τῶν σπορίμων, καὶ οἱ μαθηταὶ αὐτοῦ ἤρξαντο ὁδὸν ποιεῖν τίλλοντες (picking) τοὺς στάχυας.[a]	

[a] Work out the meaning of the example above before you read the rest of this note. A very formal English equivalent might read, "And it came to be that on the Sabbath he *was going through* the grain fields, and his disciples began *to make* a way, picking heads of grain." A more functional equivalent is given in the NIV: "One Sabbath Jesus was going through the grainfields, and as his disciples walked along, they began to pick some heads of grain." This is just as accurate and is how we would say it in English. The subject has been supplied for clarity, since Jesus has not yet been mentioned in this paragraph.

Not every accusative used with an infinitive is the subject. Infinitives can have objects in the accusative as well. They can also have both an accusative subject and an accusative object. In most cases it will be obvious from the context which is the subject. Often it is the first accusative in word order in the clause, but there are many exceptions.

22.15. *Examples of Accusative Objects of the Infinitive*

John 2:24, διὰ τὸ **αὐτὸν** γινώσκειν **πάντας**	Because *he* knew *everyone*
Acts 4:2, διαπονούμενοι διὰ τὸ διδάσκειν **αὐτοὺς τὸν λαόν**	Being annoyed because *they* were teaching *the people*

22.16. *Now You Try It*

Mark 3:15, ἔχειν **ἐξουσίαν** ἐκβάλλειν **τὰ δαιμόνια**	To have *authority* to cast out *demons*

Both infinitives in the example above have accusative objects.

Gen. 9:14, ἔσται ἐν τῷ συννεφεῖν[a] **με νεφέλας** ἐπὶ τὴν γῆν ὀφθήσεται τὸ τόξον[b] μου ἐν τῇ νεφέλῃ.	

[a] συννεφέω, "I let/cause clouds to gather"; for ἐν τῷ + infinitive, see §22.26.d.

[b] τόξον, ου, τό, "bow" is not here an archer's bow (the only definition given in *CL*) but a rainbow.

Gen. 22:10, ἐξέτεινεν Ἀβραὰμ τὴν χεῖρα αὐτοῦ λαβεῖν **τὴν μάχαιραν** σφάξαι **τὸν υἱὸν** αὐτοῦ.	

The Infinitive with a Predicate Nominative

22.17. When a linking verb (εἰμί or γίνομαι) is used in the infinitive form (εἶναι or γενέσθαι), it can have a predicate *nominative.* This is the only time a nominative is used with an infinitive, since subjects and objects of the infinitive (when they are expressed) are in the *accusative* case.

Gal. 2:9, Ἰάκωβος καὶ Κηφᾶς καὶ Ἰωάννης, οἱ δοκοῦντες **στῦλοι εἶναι**	James and Cephas and John, the ones perceived *to be pillars*
Acts 17:18, Ξένων δαιμονίων δοκεῖ **καταγγελεὺς εἶναι.**	He seems *to be a preacher* of strange gods.
1 Tim. 1:6–7, ἐξετράπησαν εἰς ματαιολογίαν θέλοντες **εἶναι νομοδιδάσκαλοι.**	They have wandered into vain talking, desiring *to be teachers of the Law.*

A few other verbs also take a predicate nominative with an infinitive. These are the same verbs that do so with finite forms—for example, καλέω.

Luke 15:19, οὐκέτι εἰμὶ ἄξιος **κληθῆναι υἱός** σου.	I am no longer worthy *to be called* your *son.*

22.18. *Now You Try It*

John 9:27, μὴ καὶ ὑμεῖς θέλετε αὐτοῦ **μαθηταὶ γενέσθαι;**	
Rom. 9:3, ηὐχόμην[a] γὰρ **ἀνάθεμα εἶναι** αὐτὸς **ἐγὼ**[b] ἀπὸ τοῦ Χριστοῦ[c] ὑπὲρ τῶν ἀδελφῶν μου.	For I could wish [that] *I* myself *were accursed,* [cut off] from Christ for the sake of my brothers.

[a] This imperfect form of εὔχομαι means "I could wish."

[b] The nominative subject of the infinitive εἶναι is ἐγώ; the nominative αὐτός is the adjectival intensive use of αὐτός (§6.24) that modifies ἐγώ, "I myself."

[c] The prepositional phrase with ἀπό indicates separation from Christ—the result of being accursed. This is made more clear in English if "cut off" is supplied in a translation.

1 Kgdms. (1 Sam.) 3:21, ἐπιστεύθη Σαμουὴλ **προφήτης γενέσθαι** τῷ κυρίῳ εἰς πάντα Ἰσραήλ.	

The Infinitive with a Predicate Accusative

22.19. It is also possible for linking verbs to follow the usual infinitive pattern and take an accusative subject or a predicate accusative (or both) with an infinitive, as the following examples show.

Luke 20:41, Εἶπεν πρὸς αὐτούς, Πῶς λέγουσιν **τὸν Χριστὸν εἶναι** Δαυὶδ **υἱόν**;	He said to them, "How do they say that *the Messiah is* David's *son*?"
1 Tim. 6:5, νομιζόντων **πορισμὸν εἶναι τὴν εὐσέβειαν**	Imagining *godliness to be gain*[a]

[a] Notice that the "subject" of the infinitive is determined by the same hierarchy of rules as it was with finite forms. In this example, the article indicates that τὴν εὐσέβειαν is the accusative subject of the infinitive εἶναι, and πορισμόν is the predicate accusative.

Gen. 38:15, Ἰούδας ἔδοξεν **αὐτὴν πόρνην εἶναι.**	Judah thought *her to be a prostitute.*

22.20. *Now You Try It*

Rom. 15:8, λέγω γὰρ **Χριστὸν διάκονον γεγενῆσθαι** περιτομῆς ὑπὲρ ἀληθείας θεοῦ.	
1 Macc. 3:44, ἠθροίσθη ἡ συναγωγὴ **τοῦ εἶναι ἑτοίμους** εἰς πόλεμον καὶ τοῦ προσεύξασθαι καὶ αἰτῆσαι ἔλεος καὶ οἰκτιρμούς.	

The Infinitive with an Article or Preposition

22.21. The infinitive may be used with or without the article. If an article is present, it is most commonly the neuter singular article τό, which can be nominative or accusative. Next most common is the neuter singular genitive τοῦ. The article usually immediately precedes the infinitive. There are some specific patterns in which the article is used with the infinitive to express a particular meaning (see "Advanced Information for Reference: Uses of the Infinitive" below) or to indicate the case of the infinitive when it is functioning as a noun. See the examples above from John 2:24; Rom. 15:13; and Acts 4:2.

When an infinitive is preceded by a preposition, there are specific, idiomatic nuances of meaning that a Greek speaker/writer assumes. It is important to know these in order to understand the sentence correctly. Each of these is illustrated in the following Advanced Information for Reference section. When used with a preposition, the infinitive has an article; the case of the article is determined by the preposition.[5]

5. In the NT the infinitive always has the article when used with a preposition, though this is not the situation in other Koine texts outside the NT. For example, 2 Esd. 22:24 (Neh. 12:24 Eng.),

— — — — — — — — — — — — — —

Advanced Information for Reference:
Uses of the Infinitive

22.22. The Greek infinitive is used in quite a wide variety of ways. The following examples are representative and cover the vast majority of instances. Grammatical diagrams have been included to help you understand how the infinitive functions in the sentence. Notice particularly what word the infinitive modifies—something that a grammatical diagram illustrates nicely. The symbol used to indicate an infinitive in a grammatical diagram is ǂ. Not all words from the verse have been included in the diagrams below. Some words that are included will be forms you have not yet learned, but you can read enough of the sentence with the help of the parallel English equivalent to make sense of the infinitive. A "Now You Try It" section follows the catalog of uses and includes at least one example of each category.

These categories are summaries of the type of context in which infinitives are used; they do not describe different kinds of infinitives. Referring to an "infinitive of purpose" is a shorthand expression for "an infinitive used in a context that expresses purpose."

1. Infinitives Used in Purpose Statements

22.23. The infinitive alone (that is, without one of the more specific prepositional markers noted below) can indicate the purpose for which the action of the main verb[6] was done; in this instance, it is normally used without an article. (About 200 of 250 purpose infinitives in the NT are anarthrous.) Other ways to express purpose with an infinitive are to use an article or an article with a preposition (εἰς or πρός). Although ὥστε + an infinitive usually indicates result, it sometimes indicates purpose. In English, purpose can sometimes be expressed with a simple English infinitive, though "in order to x" is more explicit.

a. Infinitive without an Article (Anarthrous)

Luke 3:12, ἦλθον τελῶναι[a] **βαπτισθῆναι.**	Tax collectors came *in order to be baptized.*

[a] Note that τελῶναι is not an infinitive; it is a noun with a nominative feminine plural ending (the nu preceding the ending is part of the stem).

οἱ ἀδελφοὶ αὐτῶν κατεναντίον αὐτῶν **εἰς ὑμνεῖν καὶ αἰνεῖν** ἐν ἐντολῇ Δαυίδ, "their brothers were opposite them *to sing and praise* by the command of David." See also Sir. 38:27.

6. Here and in the following sections, "main verb" refers to the verb that the infinitive modifies, which may be a finite verb in the main clause or in a subordinate clause, a participle, or another infinitive.

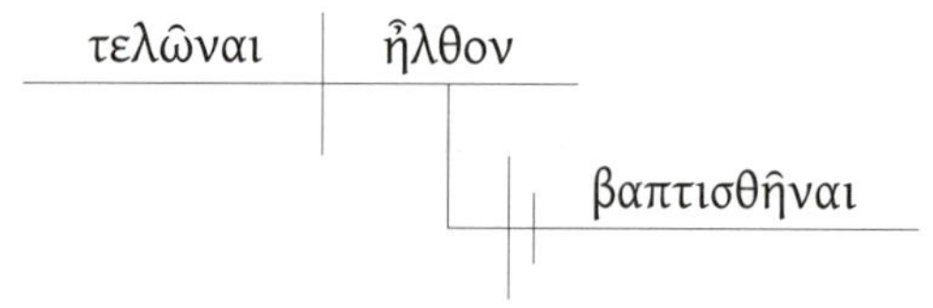

Figure 22.2

Matt. 2:2, εἴδομεν αὐτοῦ τὸν ἀστέρα ἐν τῇ ἀνατολῇ καὶ ἤλθομεν **προσκυνῆσαι** αὐτῷ.

We saw his star in the east, and we have come *to worship* him.

b. Infinitive with an Article (Articular)

When an infinitive expressing purpose has an article (but not a preposition), the article is normally τοῦ.

Luke 8:5, Ἐξῆλθεν ὁ σπείρων (sower) **τοῦ σπεῖραι** τὸν σπόρον αὐτοῦ.

The sower went out *in order to sow* his seed.

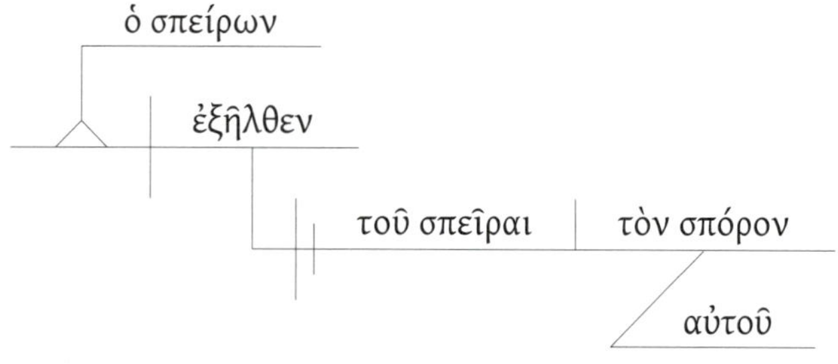

Figure 22.3

Matt. 11:1, ὁ Ἰησοῦς μετέβη[a] ἐκεῖθεν **τοῦ διδάσκειν καὶ κηρύσσειν** ἐν ταῖς πόλεσιν αὐτῶν.

Jesus moved on from there *in order to teach and preach* in their villages.

[a] μετέβη is a second aorist form of μεταβαίνω.

c. Infinitive with Preposition + Article

Eph. 6:11, ἐνδύσασθε (Put on!) τὴν πανοπλίαν τοῦ θεοῦ **πρὸς τὸ δύνασθαι** ὑμᾶς στῆναι.[a]

Put on the armor of God *in order that* you *may be able* to stand.

[a] The infinitive στῆναι is complementary to the preceding infinitive.

Rom. 3:25–26, ὃν προέθετο ὁ θεὸς ἱλαστήριον **εἰς τὸ εἶναι** αὐτὸν δίκαιον

Whom God displayed publicly as a satisfactory sacrifice *in order that* he [i.e., God] *might be* righteous

d. Infinitive with ὥστε

Gen. 1:17, ἔθετο (he set) αὐτοὺς ὁ θεὸς ἐν τῷ στερεώματι (firmament) τοῦ οὐρανοῦ **ὥστε φαίνειν** ἐπὶ τῆς γῆς.

God set them in the firmament of the heaven *in order to shine* on the earth.

Matt. 10:1, προσκαλεσάμενος τοὺς δώδεκα μαθητὰς αὐτοῦ ἔδωκεν αὐτοῖς ἐξουσίαν πνευμάτων ἀκαθάρτων **ὥστε ἐκβάλλειν** αὐτὰ καὶ **θεραπεύειν** πᾶσαν νόσον καὶ πᾶσαν μαλακίαν.

Summoning his twelve disciples, he gave them authority over unclean spirits *to cast* them *out* and *to heal* every disease and every sickness.

2. Infinitives Used in Result Statements

22.24. When an infinitive is used to indicate the result of the action described by the main verb, the clause often begins with ὥστε. Other result constructions include the article τοῦ with the infinitive, an anarthrous infinitive, or εἰς τό + infinitive. This concept is often expressed in English with the phrase "so that." Purpose and result are very similar ideas—thus the similar structures used. If the statement in its context seems to focus on the *intent* of the action, it is purpose; if on the *outcome*, then it is result.

a. Result Indicated with ὥστε

Matt. 15:30–31, ἐθεράπευσεν αὐτούς· **ὥστε** τὸν ὄχλον **θαυμάσαι**.

He healed them, *so that* the crowd *marveled*.

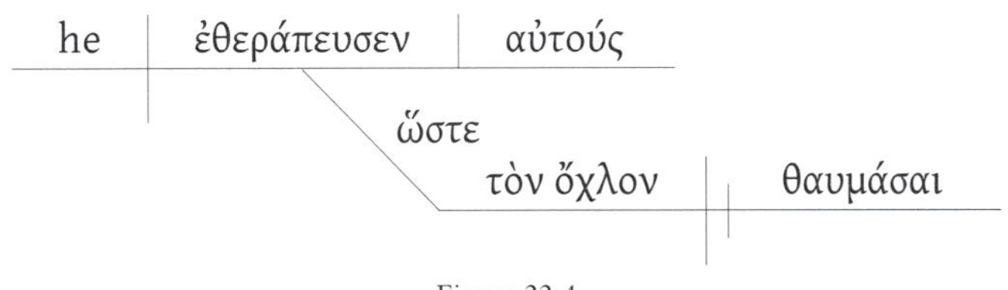

Figure 22.4

In the diagram, the conjunction ὥστε introduces a subordinate clause, so it is placed on a shelf with a right-slanting line (modifiers use left-slanting lines). Also notice how the accusative subject of the infinitive is indicated.

b. Result Indicated with τοῦ + Infinitive

Lev. 4:3, ἐὰν μὲν ὁ ἀρχιερεὺς ἁμάρτῃ **τοῦ** τὸν λαὸν **ἁμαρτεῖν**, καὶ προσάξει περὶ τῆς ἁμαρτίας αὐτοῦ μόσχον ἐκ βοῶν ἄμωμον τῷ κυρίῳ περὶ τῆς ἁμαρτίας αὐτοῦ.

If, then, the high priest should sin *so that* the people *sin*, then he shall offer concerning his sin an unblemished calf from the cattle to the Lord for his sin.

c. Result Indicated with Only an Infinitive

Rev. 5:5, ἰδοὺ ἐνίκησεν ὁ λέων ὁ ἐκ τῆς φυλῆς Ἰούδα, ἡ ῥίζα Δαυίδ, **ἀνοῖξαι** τὸ βιβλίον.

Behold, the Lion of the tribe of Judah, the root of David, has conquered, *so that he may open* the book.

d. Result Indicated with εἰς τό + Infinitive

Rom. 4:18, ἐπίστευσεν **εἰς τὸ γενέσθαι αὐτὸν** πατέρα πολλῶν ἐθνῶν.

[Abram] believed, *with the result that he became* a father of many nations.

3. Infinitives Used in Causal Statements

22.25. An infinitive may be used in a statement that explains what caused the action in the main verb. This is most commonly expressed by using διὰ τό + infinitive, though occasionally τοῦ + infinitive occurs. This use should be distinguished from purpose (what was the *intent* of the subject in doing something?) and result (what happened as a result of the action described by the verb?).

Acts 4:1–3, οἱ ἱερεῖς, διαπονούμενοι **διὰ τὸ διδάσκειν** αὐτοὺς τὸν λαόν, ἐπέβαλον αὐτοῖς τὰς χεῖρας.[a]

The priests, being disturbed *because* they *were teaching* the people, seized them.

[a] In a more formal translation, the last phrase might be worded "they laid hands on them," but the English connotation of that phrase is quite different from what the Greek means. The translation above ("seized them") communicates more accurately.

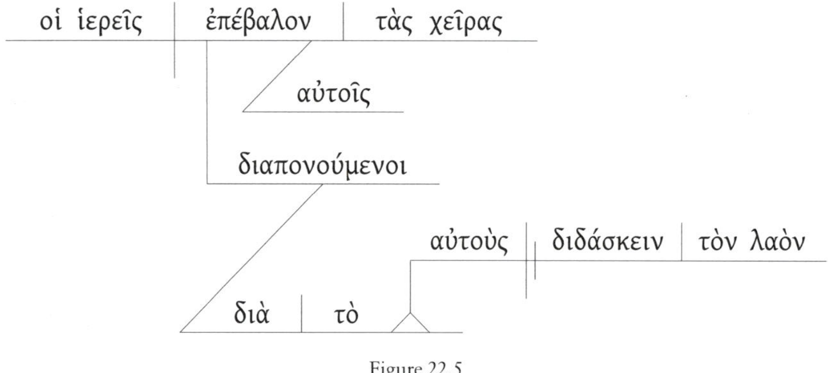

Figure 22.5

Gen. 39:23, πάντα ἦν διὰ χειρὸς Ἰωσὴφ **διὰ τὸ** τὸν κύριον μετ' αὐτοῦ **εἶναι**.

Everything was [done] through the hand of Joseph *because* the Lord *was* with him.

In this example the infinitive and its article are separated much further than is usually the case: διὰ τό . . . εἶναι includes both an accusative subject of the infinitive and a modifying prepositional phrase in first attributive position. The phrase at the beginning of the sentence, πάντα ἦν διὰ χειρὸς Ἰωσήφ, has been represented fairly formally in the translation above. More functionally the idiom says that "everything was under Joseph's control."

4. Infinitives Used in Temporal Statements

22.26. An infinitive can be used to express various temporal relationships through the use of several prepositions or conjunctions. The nature of the time reference depends on the meaning of the preposition, sometimes in combination with the aspect of the tense-form.[7]

a. πρό

Gal. 3:23, **Πρὸ τοῦ** δὲ **ἐλθεῖν** τὴν πίστιν[a] ὑπὸ νόμον ἐφρουρούμεθα.

But *before* faith *came* we were held captive under the law.

[a] Notice the accusative subject of the infinitive.

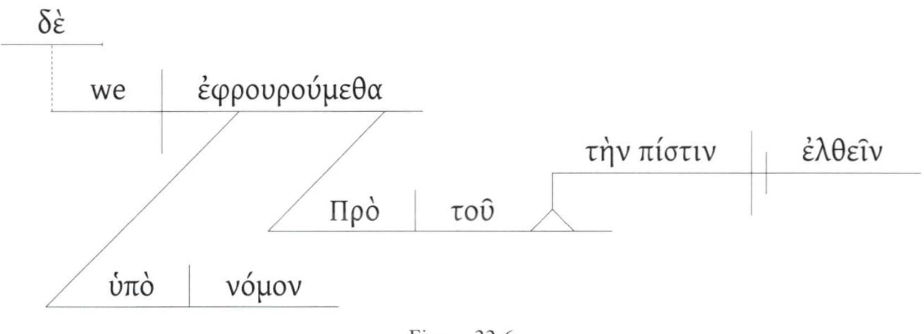

Figure 22.6

b. ἕως τοῦ[8]

Acts 8:40, Φίλιππος εὐηγγελίζετο τὰς πόλεις πάσας **ἕως τοῦ ἐλθεῖν** αὐτὸν εἰς Καισάρειαν.

Philip was evangelizing all the cities *until* he *came* to Caesarea.

7. A grammatical diagram is shown for only the first example, since all the infinitive constructions used to express time follow the same pattern.

8. The NT uses ἕως with an infinitive only once, though it is more common in the LXX. Although ἕως τοῦ is usually a temporal expression, ἕως + an infinitive (without an article) can be either spatial (e.g., Gen. 13:10, ὡς ὁ παράδεισος τοῦ θεοῦ καὶ ὡς ἡ γῆ Αἰγύπτου **ἕως ἐλθεῖν** εἰς Ζόγορα, "like the garden of God and like the land of Egypt *until one comes* to Zoar") or temporal (e.g., 3 Kgdms. 2:35c [1 Kings 3:1 MT/Eng.], ἔλαβεν τὴν θυγατέρα Φαραὼ καὶ εἰσήγαγεν αὐτὴν εἰς τὴν πόλιν Δαυὶδ **ἕως συντελέσαι** αὐτὸν τὸν οἶκον αὐτοῦ καὶ τὸν οἶκον κυρίου, "he took the daughter of Pharaoh and brought her into the city of David *until he first finished* his house and the house of the Lord").

c. μετά

Acts 1:3, οἷς καὶ παρέστησεν ἑαυτὸν ζῶντα (alive) **μετὰ τὸ παθεῖν** αὐτόν

To whom also he showed himself alive *after* he *suffered*

d. ἐν τῷ

The use of ἐν τῷ + present infinitive is often "while," and ἐν τῷ + aorist infinitive can be "after," but other times "when" or "as" is more appropriate as a general time reference. Context, as always, is the determining factor. (Not all uses of ἐν with an infinitive are temporal, but many are.)

Luke 24:51, **ἐν τῷ εὐλογεῖν** αὐτὸν αὐτοὺς διέστη ἀπ' αὐτῶν καὶ ἀνεφέρετο εἰς τὸν οὐρανόν.

While he *was blessing* them, he parted from them and ascended into heaven.[a]

[a] This translation assumes that ἀνεφέρετο is middle voice; many translations make it passive, but there is no passive indication in the context.

Gen. 11:2, **ἐν τῷ κινῆσαι** αὐτοὺς ἀπὸ ἀνατολῶν εὗρον πεδίον ἐν γῇ Σενναὰρ καὶ κατῴκησαν ἐκεῖ.

When they *moved* from the east, they found a plain in the land of Shinar, and they settled there.

e. πρὶν ἤ (or Simply πρίν)

This word usually appears with an aorist infinitive and is glossed as "before."

Matt. 1:18, Τοῦ δὲ Ἰησοῦ Χριστοῦ ἡ γένεσις οὕτως ἦν. μνηστευθείσης[a] τῆς μητρὸς αὐτοῦ Μαρίας τῷ Ἰωσήφ, **πρὶν ἢ συνελθεῖν** αὐτοὺς εὑρέθη ἐν γαστρὶ ἔχουσα ἐκ πνεύματος ἁγίου.

But the birth of Jesus Christ was this way: Mary his mother had been engaged to Joseph, [but] *before* they *came together*, she was found to be pregnant by the Holy Spirit.[b]

[a] The phrase μνηστευθείσης . . . Μαρίας is called a genitive absolute (see lesson 27). The genitive phrase τῆς μητρὸς αὐτοῦ Μαρίας acts as the subject of the genitive participle μνηστευθείσης, which in this context is translated as part of a temporal statement: "when Mary had been engaged . . ."

[b] The phrase ἐν γαστρὶ ἔχουσα (formally, "in belly having") is an idiom for "to be pregnant"; Mary was thus "found/discovered to be pregnant" *before* they "came together" (συνελθεῖν ▶ συνέρχομαι, i.e., a euphemism for "had sexual intercourse").

5. Infinitives Used in Complementary Statements

22.27. A complementary infinitive *completes* the idea of another verb (it does not "pay it a compl<u>i</u>ment").[9] Some verbs, such as ἔξεστιν, μέλλω, δύναμαι, and ἄρχομαι, always take a complementary infinitive, and θέλω, κελεύω, and

9. If spelling is not your strong point, then note that *complement* and *compliment* are two different words. Your spouse (or friend) gets the compliments, but Greek verbs get the complements.

ὀφείλω often do. (There are a number of other verbs that occasionally have a complementary infinitive as well.)[10]

Mark 4:1, πάλιν ἤρξατο **διδάσκειν** παρὰ τὴν θάλασσαν.	Again he began *to teach* beside the lake.

The verb ἄρχομαι (ἤρξατο, 3rd sg. aor. mid. ind.) does not seem complete by itself. In the example above, what did he begin? Although English might get by in some rare instance using "he began" without a complement, Greek never does. The verb ἄρχομαι is always followed by an infinitive that completes the meaning. The verb and the infinitive function together as if they were a single word.

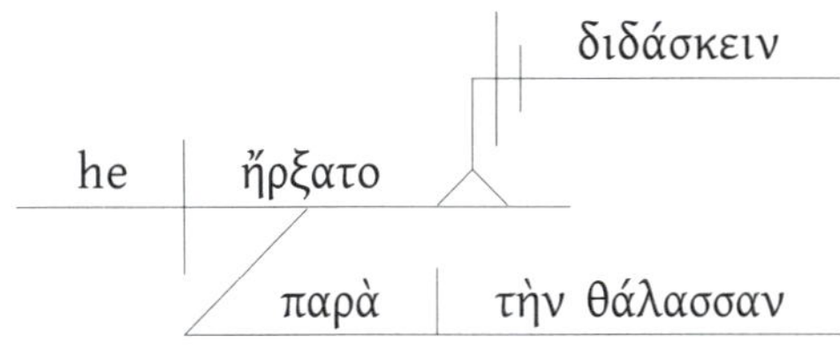

Figure 22.7

Rom. 15:22, ἐνεκοπτόμην[a] **τοῦ ἐλθεῖν** πρὸς ὑμᾶς.	I was prevented *from coming* to you.

[a] ἐνεκοπτόμην, 1st sg. impf. pass. ind. ▶ ἐγκόπτω, "I hinder"

6. Infinitives Used in Indirect Discourse

22.28. First a word about the category of discourse. *Direct discourse* is the reporting of someone's statement (or sometimes, thought) with some indication that the words are exactly as originally spoken. *Indirect discourse* is the reporting of someone's statement or thought in such a way that the content is preserved, but the exact words are not recorded. We will discuss this in more detail in chapter 31.

One way to express indirect discourse in Greek is to use an infinitive that functions as the direct object of a verb of *saying*, *wishing*, or *thinking* (e.g., λέγω, θέλω, λογίζομαι). Since the infinitive functions as a noun, it could be viewed as a subcategory under the next heading. In this situation, the person referring to the previous statement represents the main/finite verb of the original statement with an infinitive form of the same verb. (Not all instances of indirect discourse use an infinitive; the speaker has several options, of which this is one.)

10. This list sometimes includes δεῖ, but when this word occurs with an infinitive, it usually functions as the subject of δεῖ rather than as its complement. See the discussion below and Wallace, *Greek Grammar*, 601.

Acts 28:6, ἔλεγον αὐτὸν **εἶναι** θεόν. They were saying that he *was* a god.

The original statement would have been "He is a god"—perhaps something like αὐτὸς θεός ἐστιν.[11] If we put this into English, we would almost always use a finite verb as the most natural English equivalent. (Rendering the Greek infinitive with an English infinitive in this construction is sometimes possible, but uncommon.)

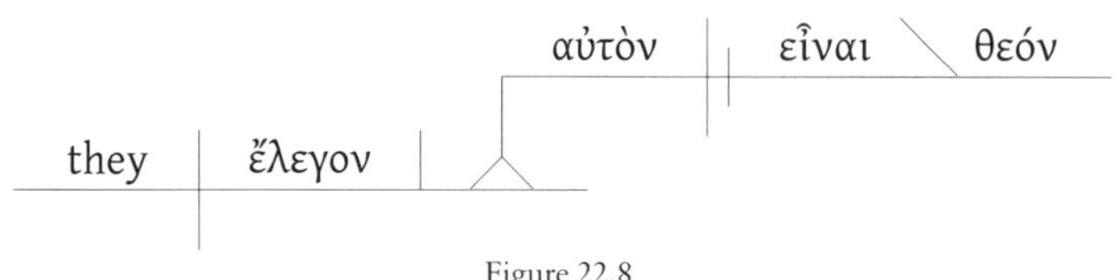

Figure 22.8

Acts 23:8, Σαδδουκαῖοι γὰρ λέγουσιν μὴ **εἶναι** ἀνάστασιν μήτε ἄγγελον μήτε πνεῦμα. For the Sadducees say *there is* neither resurrection, nor angel, nor spirit.

The original statement could have been, ἀνάστασις οὐκ ἔστιν οὔτε ἄγγελος οὔτε πνεῦμα, "There is neither resurrection, nor angel, nor spirit."[12]

7. The Infinitive Used as a Noun

22.29. Infinitives often function like nouns. As such, an infinitive or infinitive phrase can take the place of just about any noun in a sentence, whether the subject or object or some other noun. It may be used with or without an article. When the article is used, it is often to clarify the function of the infinitive in the sentence. It may, for example, indicate that the infinitive is the subject rather than the predicate nominative (see the example from Phil. 1:21 below).

a. Object

An infinitive used as an object is not as common a use as a subject, but the example given here is perhaps a bit easier to grasp than the examples in 7.b.

Mark 12:12, ἐζήτουν αὐτὸν **κρατῆσαι**. They were seeking *to seize* him.

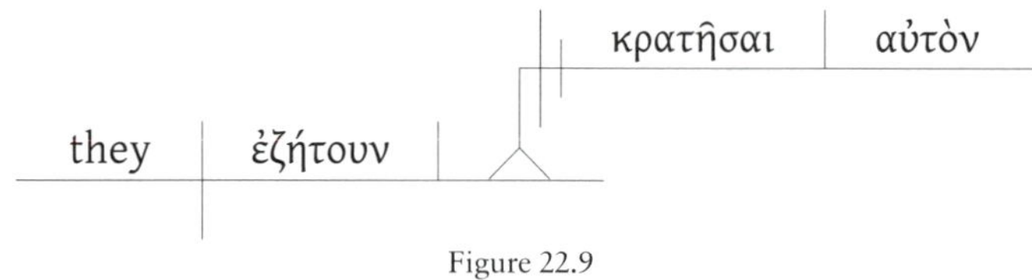

Figure 22.9

11. This is the phrase in Josh. 24:17, though there the context makes it clear that a definite reference rather than an indefinite, "a god," is intended. Here in Acts 28:6, the context is clearly a polytheistic reference.

12. Cf. the statement of some of the Corinthians that Paul quotes using direct discourse: 1 Cor. 15:12, πῶς λέγουσιν ἐν ὑμῖν τινες ὅτι ἀνάστασις νεκρῶν οὐκ ἔστιν;

Phil. 4:10, ἀνεθάλετε[a] τὸ ὑπὲρ ἐμοῦ **φρονεῖν**. — You renewed *caring* about me.

[a] ἀνεθάλετε, 2nd pl. aor. act. ind. ▶ ἀναθάλλω, "I renew"

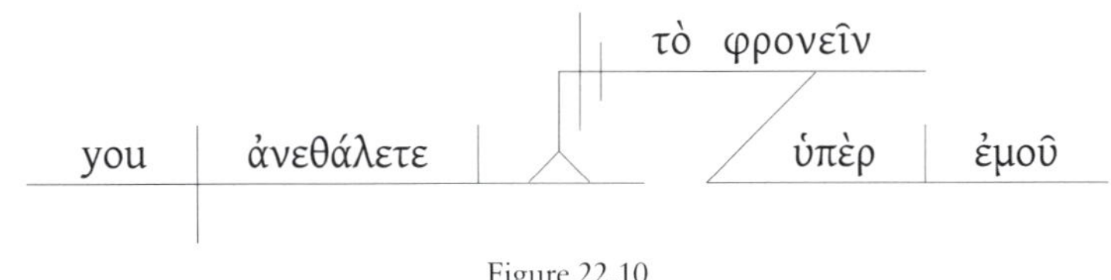

Figure 22.10

John 5:26, ὁ πατὴρ . . . τῷ υἱῷ ἔδωκεν (he gave) ζωὴν **ἔχειν** ἐν ἑαυτῷ. — The Father gave to the Son *to have* life in himself.

b. Subject

An infinitive phrase can function as the subject of a finite verb. This is a fairly common use of the infinitive (more common than the use of an infinitive as an object).

Eph. 6:20, δεῖ με **λαλῆσαι**. — It is necessary for me *to speak*.

Or, "I must *speak*"; or, to make the subject function clearer (though we would not say it this way in English), "For me *to speak* is necessary." Note that δεῖ is an impersonal verb that does not take a personal subject. See the diagram.

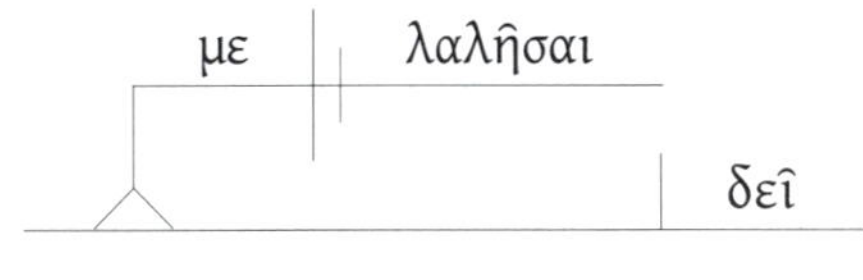

Figure 22.11

Phil. 1:21, ἐμοὶ γὰρ **τὸ ζῆν**[a] Χριστὸς καὶ **τὸ ἀποθανεῖν** κέρδος. — For me *to live* is Christ and *to die* is gain.

[a] ζῆν is the infinitive of ζῶ (ζάω); see the discussion of this form in the sidebar in chapter 21.

In this example the article with both infinitives marks them as the subject rather than the predicate nominative in their own clause. Without this indication in the first clause, we would normally take Χριστός as the subject, since it is a proper name.

c. Apposition

This differs from the epexegetical infinitive in that the epexegetical use explains a noun (or adjective)—it tells something about it—whereas an appositional infinitive *defines* a noun.[13]

1 Thess. 4:3, τοῦτό ἐστιν θέλημα τοῦ θεοῦ, ὁ ἁγιασμὸς ὑμῶν, **ἀπέχεσθαι** ὑμᾶς ἀπὸ τῆς πορνείας.

This is the will of God, your sanctification, that you *abstain* from immorality.

This sentence consists of three phrases in apposition; each one explains the previous one in a more specific way. (When diagramming, an equals sign is used to indicate apposition.)

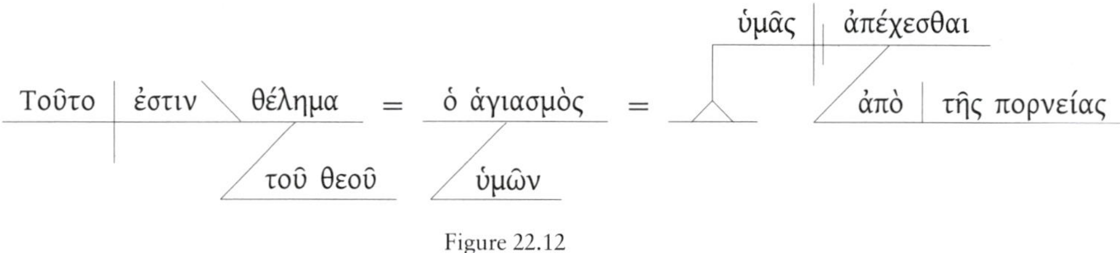

Figure 22.12

Acts 26:16, εἰς τοῦτο γὰρ ὤφθην σοι, **προχειρίσασθαί** σε ὑπηρέτην καὶ μάρτυρα.

For this reason I appeared to you, *to appoint* you a servant and witness.

The infinitive προχειρίσασθαι is in apposition to the demonstrative pronoun τοῦτο. The phrase εἰς τοῦτο, "unto this," means "for this reason." The infinitive προχειρίσασθαι defines the reason (τοῦτο).

8. Infinitives Used in Epexegetical (Explanatory) Statements

22.30. When an infinitive is used to *explain* a noun or an adjective (rather than a verb) in the sentence, it is called an epexegetical infinitive. In one sense, many types of infinitives explain other words in the sentence. The epexegetical category is used when a more specific use is not appropriate. Compare the appositional use of the infinitive (see §22.29.c), which *defines* a noun, with the epexegetical use, which *explains* a noun.

a. Epexegetical without an Article

Rev. 5:9, Ἄξιος εἶ **λαβεῖν** τὸ βιβλίον.

You are worthy *to take* the book.

13. Apposition is a grammatical relationship that is normally between two adjacent substantives in the same case that define each other (see the sidebar near §8.8). Since the infinitive can function as a noun, it can also appear in apposition to a noun even though it does not have a case.

Here the infinitive explains in what way the subject (the Lamb, Jesus) is worthy. He is not said to be worthy of praise or worthy of receiving an award. Nor is this a purpose statement: he is not worthy *in order to* open the book (he is worthy, book or not). Rather, the point of this statement is that the Lamb is worthy *to take the book*.

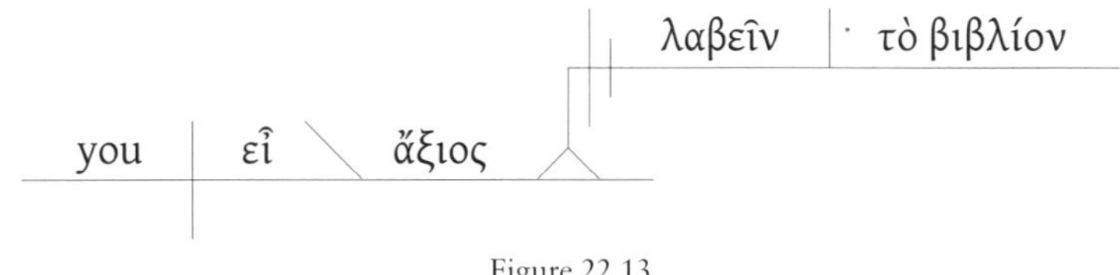

Figure 22.13

b. Epexegetical with an Article

Acts 14:9, ἔχει πίστιν **τοῦ σωθῆναι.** — He has faith *to be saved*.

The infinitive describes faith: it is a "to-be-saved" kind of faith.

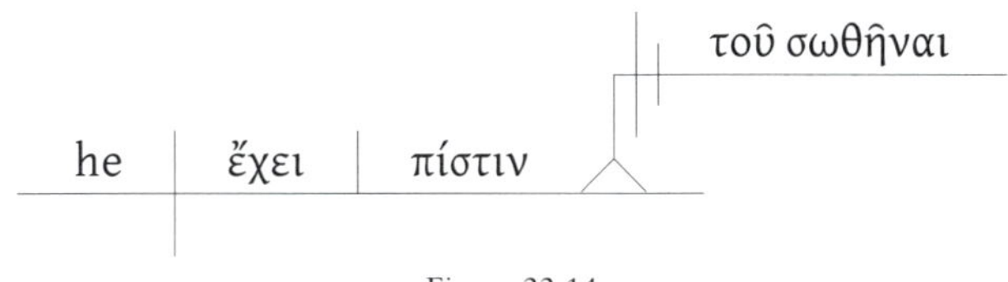

Figure 22.14

Luke 10:19, ἰδοὺ δέδωκα ὑμῖν τὴν ἐξουσίαν **τοῦ πατεῖν** ἐπάνω ὄφεων καὶ σκορπίων. — Behold, I have given you the authority *to walk* on snakes and scorpions.

22.31. Now You Try It

John 1:33, ὁ πέμψας (one who sent) με **βαπτίζειν** ἐν ὕδατι ἐκεῖνός μοι εἶπεν . . .

Luke 11:31, βασίλισσα νότου ἦλθεν ἐκ τῶν περάτων τῆς γῆς **ἀκοῦσαι** τὴν σοφίαν Σολομῶνος, καὶ ἰδοὺ πλεῖον Σολομῶνος ὧδε.

Matt. 8:24, καὶ ἰδοὺ σεισμὸς μέγας ἐγένετο ἐν τῇ θαλάσσῃ, **ὥστε** τὸ πλοῖον **καλύπτεσθαι** ὑπὸ τῶν κυμάτων, αὐτὸς δὲ ἐκάθευδεν.

Mark 1:27, ἐθαμβήθησαν ἅπαντες **ὥστε συζητεῖν** πρὸς ἑαυτοὺς λέγοντας, Τί ἐστιν τοῦτο; διδαχὴ καινὴ κατ' ἐξουσίαν· καὶ τοῖς πνεύμασι τοῖς ἀκαθάρτοις ἐπιτάσσει, καὶ ὑπακούουσιν αὐτῷ.

Matt. 5:17, Μὴ νομίσητε[a] ὅτι ἦλθον **καταλῦσαι** τὸν νόμον ἢ τοὺς προφήτας· οὐκ ἦλθον **καταλῦσαι** ἀλλὰ **πληρῶσαι.**

[a] Μὴ νομίσητε is an aorist subjunctive of prohibition; it means, "Don't think."

Mark 14:55, οἱ δὲ ἀρχιερεῖς καὶ ὅλον τὸ συνέδριον ἐζήτουν κατὰ τοῦ Ἰησοῦ μαρτυρίαν **εἰς τὸ θανατῶσαι** αὐτόν, καὶ οὐχ ηὕρισκον.

Acts 16:26, ἄφνω δὲ σεισμὸς ἐγένετο μέγας **ὥστε σαλευθῆναι** τὰ θεμέλια τοῦ δεσμωτηρίου.

Heb. 10:9 = Ps. 39:8–9 (40:7–8 Eng.), Ἰδοὺ ἥκω **τοῦ ποιῆσαι** τὸ θέλημά σου.

Dan. 8:15, καὶ ἐγένετο ἐν τῷ θεωρεῖν με, ἐγὼ Δανιήλ, τὸ ὅραμα ἐζήτουν **διανοηθῆναι.**

2 Cor. 9:1, περισσόν μοί ἐστιν **τὸ γράφειν** ὑμῖν.

What is the main verb? What is the subject? How is the nominative case indicated, and how is the subject distinguished from the predicate nominative? What is the predicate nominative? (In this case it is technically a predicate adjective.)

— — — — — — — — — — — — — —

Reading Passage: Philippians 4:10–12

22.32. The following three-verse paragraph contains a number of infinitives. Study it carefully, using the notes below when you are really stuck. (It is wise to cover the notes as you begin reading and discipline yourself not to look for help until you have exhausted your resources, which includes your lexicon.) There are new words here and some idiomatic expressions. The first verse is the hardest.

Rejoicing and Contentment

10Ἐχάρην[a] δὲ ἐν κυρίῳ μεγάλως[b] ὅτι ἤδη ποτὲ[c] ἀνεθάλετε[d] **τὸ**[e] ὑπὲρ ἐμοῦ **φρονεῖν**,
ἐφ' ᾧ[f] καὶ ἐφρονεῖτε,[g] ἠκαιρεῖσθε[h] δέ.[i] 11οὐχ ὅτι καθ' ὑστέρησιν λέγω, ἐγὼ γὰρ
ἔμαθον[j] ἐν οἷς εἰμι αὐτάρκης **εἶναι.** 12οἶδα καὶ **ταπεινοῦσθαι**, οἶδα καὶ **περισσεύειν**·

ἐν παντὶ καὶ ἐν πᾶσιν[k] μεμύημαι,[l] καὶ[m] **χορτάζεσθαι** καὶ **πεινᾶν** καὶ **περισσεύειν** καὶ **ὑστερεῖσθαι**.

[a] Ἐχάρην is a second aorist passive; can you parse it?

[b] Do you recognize the ending -ως on μεγάλως? It is a common marker for a particular part of speech.

[c] ἤδη ποτέ, "now at last"

[d] ἀναθάλλω, "I renew"

[e] The article τό governs the infinitive φρονεῖν with a prepositional phrase, ὑπὲρ ἐμοῦ, functioning as a modifier in first attributive position. The article in accusative case tells us here that the infinitive is functioning as the direct object of ἀνεθάλετε.

[f] ἐφ' ᾧ refers back to Paul (the antecedent is ἐμοῦ); "You were indeed [καί] concerned *for me*" (ESV).

[g] In this context φρονέω means not just "I think" but "I am concerned."

[h] Do you recognize the formation of ἠκαιρεῖσθε? Alpha privative[14] + a verb form of καιρός, "time" (which does not occur in Greek as a separate word, presumably καιρέω) = ἀκαιρέομαι, "I have no opportunity." The alpha has been lengthened; what does that tell you?

[i] If it looks odd to have δέ at the end of a sentence, remember that it is postpositive, and in a two-word clause it *must* come last.

[j] ἔμαθον, a second aorist form of μανθάνω

[k] παντί and πᾶσιν differ in only one way; what is it? (The expression is somewhat idiomatic; after you have identified the grammatical difference, compare several English translations to see how they have distinguished these words.)

[l] μεμύημαι—to identify this form, note each of the pieces on both the beginning and end of the word, identify the stem, and note that a *stem* vowel has been lengthened (it is not a connecting vowel as it first appears).

[m] The string of four καί's in the last clause of the verse sets up a series of alternatives that is described by four infinitives.

22.33. Reading Passage: 1 Thessalonians 4:1–12

Living to Please God

1Λοιπὸν οὖν, ἀδελφοί, ἐρωτῶμεν ὑμᾶς καὶ παρακαλοῦμεν ἐν κυρίῳ Ἰησοῦ,
ἵνα καθὼς παρελάβετε παρ' ἡμῶν τὸ πῶς δεῖ ὑμᾶς **περιπατεῖν** καὶ **ἀρέσκειν** θεῷ,
καθὼς καὶ περιπατεῖτε, ἵνα περισσεύητε (you should abound) μᾶλλον.[a] 2οἴδατε
γὰρ τίνας παραγγελίας ἐδώκαμεν (we gave) ὑμῖν διὰ τοῦ κυρίου Ἰησοῦ. 3τοῦτο
γάρ ἐστιν θέλημα τοῦ θεοῦ, ὁ ἁγιασμὸς ὑμῶν, **ἀπέχεσθαι** ὑμᾶς ἀπὸ τῆς πορνείας,
4**εἰδέναι**[b] ἕκαστον ὑμῶν τὸ ἑαυτοῦ σκεῦος **κτᾶσθαι**[c] ἐν ἁγιασμῷ καὶ τιμῇ, 5μὴ ἐν
πάθει ἐπιθυμίας καθάπερ καὶ τὰ ἔθνη τὰ μὴ εἰδότα (who know) τὸν θεόν, 6τὸ
μὴ **ὑπερβαίνειν** καὶ **πλεονεκτεῖν** ἐν τῷ πράγματι τὸν ἀδελφὸν αὐτοῦ, διότι ἔκδικος
κύριος περὶ πάντων τούτων, καθὼς καὶ προείπαμεν ὑμῖν καὶ διεμαρτυράμεθα.
7οὐ γὰρ ἐκάλεσεν ἡμᾶς ὁ θεὸς ἐπὶ ἀκαθαρσίᾳ ἀλλ' ἐν ἁγιασμῷ. 8τοιγαροῦν ὁ
ἀθετῶν (one who rejects) οὐκ ἄνθρωπον ἀθετεῖ ἀλλὰ τὸν θεὸν τὸν καὶ διδόντα
(one who gave) τὸ πνεῦμα αὐτοῦ τὸ ἅγιον εἰς ὑμᾶς.

9Περὶ δὲ τῆς φιλαδελφίας οὐ χρείαν ἔχετε **γράφειν**[d] ὑμῖν, αὐτοὶ γὰρ ὑμεῖς
θεοδίδακτοί ἐστε εἰς τὸ **ἀγαπᾶν** ἀλλήλους, 10καὶ γὰρ ποιεῖτε αὐτὸ εἰς πάντας
τοὺς ἀδελφοὺς τοὺς ἐν ὅλῃ τῇ Μακεδονίᾳ. παρακαλοῦμεν δὲ ὑμᾶς, ἀδελφοί,
περισσεύειν μᾶλλον 11καὶ **φιλοτιμεῖσθαι** ἡσυχάζειν καὶ **πράσσειν** τὰ ἴδια καὶ

14. An *alpha privative* is the use of an alpha prefixed to the front of a Greek word to negate it; cf. "un-" in English. For example: *unhelpful* ▸ *helpful*; ἄγαμος, "unmarried" ▸ γάμος, "married."

ἐργάζεσθαι ταῖς ἰδίαις χερσὶν ὑμῶν, καθὼς ὑμῖν παρηγγείλαμεν, 12ἵνα περιπατῆτε[e] εὐσχημόνως πρὸς τοὺς ἔξω καὶ μηδενὸς χρείαν ἔχητε.[e]

[a] Verse 1 is not at all in English word order—but then, it is Greek, not English. You have learned all the forms in this verse except one, though as you read through the verse it will seem awkward. Compare several English translations to see how they have adjusted the punctuation, word order, and even clause order so as to communicate in good English. In some translations you will wonder if you are reading the same verse, due to the extensive changes. NET, NRSV, ESV, and HCSB provide formal equivalent translations that are readable; NIV has made more extensive changes to the verse structure to produce more natural English.

[b] Perfect active infinitive of οἶδα

[c] This is an alpha contract, middle-only verb.

[d] This is a somewhat elliptical phrase; to make it intelligible in English, you will need to supply a subject for the infinitive and translate it like a finite verb. Some translations supply "anyone," others use "me" (i.e., Paul).

[e] ἵνα περιπατῆτε καί ἔχητε, "so that you may walk and have" (ἵνα governs both verbs).

22.34. Vocabulary for Chapter 22

Part of Speech	Definition	Possible Glosses	Frequency	
Word			NT	LXX
Adjectives				
πολύς, πολλή, πολύ	Extensive in scope, whether with reference to number, quantity, measure, or quality; comparative form: πλείων; superlative: πλεῖστος (many possible equivalents in English, depending on referent and context)	much (sg.), many (pl.); large, great, big	416	822
μέγας, μεγάλη, μέγα	A large quantity in terms of extent, scale, space, number, time, status, importance, intensity, etc.; comparative form: μείζων; superlative: μέγιστος (many possible equivalents in English, depending on referent and context)	great, large, big, long	243	916
Nouns				
ἀρχιερεύς, έως, ὁ	The person who serves as the head priest in a religious system; in plural, collective for priests of high rank	high priest; chief priests	122	44
δύναμις, εως, ἡ	The capacity to function adequately in a particular situation; a deed that demonstrates this capacity [This word often refers to a miracle in the NT, but it should not be translated as such; cf. σημεῖον and τέρας.]	ability, capability, strength, power; deed of power (NT); armed military force (LXX)	119	590
αἷμα, ατος, τό	The red, oxygen-bearing liquid circulating in the bodies of humans and animals; any dark-red liquid; descent, parentage; metaphorically, a person's life (to take, shed, or give blood is to kill/die)	blood; descent, parentage; lifeblood; murder, killing, death	97	401
πούς, ποδός, ὁ	The body part at the end of the leg (sometimes the reference is to the entire leg); the equivalent part of an animal; the supporting piece of an object (e.g., the bottom part of a table leg, or sometimes the entire leg); a measure of distance	foot	93	301

μήτηρ, μητρός, ἡ	A female parent; numerous metaphorical uses with an analogical meaning	mother	83	338
Μωϋσῆς, έως, ὁ	A personal name, in the LXX and NT the name of Israel's leader at the time of the exodus; the books of the OT written by him	Moses	80	819
στόμα, ατος, τό	The body part used for eating and speaking/creating sounds (either human or animal); the opening (or edge) of an object analogous to the body part	mouth, jaws; edge	78	489
Prepositions				
ἄχρι, ἄχρις	A preposition used with the genitive (sometimes as a conjunction) to indicate an extent of time up to a specified event, mostly used of time, occasionally of situations [The spelling ἄχρις is not common; it is sometimes used before words beginning with a vowel.]	until (prep. + gen., or conj.); as far as	49	3
ἔμπροσθεν	A preposition used with the genitive to indicate position in front of something; occasionally used in its older adverbial sense of place in front	before, in front of (prep. + gen.); in front, ahead (adv.)	48	162
Pronoun				
ὅσος, η, ον	A relative pronoun indicating quantity or number (in the LXX never a correlative as in Classical Greek; NT only rarely correlative)	all who, all that, as many as, as much as	110	615
Verbs				
σῴζω	To rescue from a hazardous situation, from sickness, or from spiritual/eternal death	I save, deliver, heal	106	363
ἐκπορεύομαι	To move from one place to another, usually of people, but various other uses such as water flowing from a place	I come/go (out), proceed	33	172
καθαρίζω	To make clean by removing dirt or impure substance; to cleanse ritually by meeting ceremonial requirements; to heal someone of disease; to cleanse from sin	I make clean, cleanse; I heal; I purify	31	125

22.35. Key Things to Know for Chapter 22

Why are infinitives classified as non-finite forms?

Know the forms (endings) of present and aorist infinitives.

What is the infinitive form of εἰμί?

What is important to remember about the accusative case when used with an infinitive?

Know the various uses of the infinitive.

23

NON-FINITE VERBS: PART 2

IMPERFECTIVE ADVERBIAL PARTICIPLES

23.1. The next chapters are your first foray into the world of participles, an exciting and important aspect of Greek grammar with considerable interpretive importance. Perhaps it would be helpful if you saw one example before we begin. Here is the text of Eph. 2:1–7. You will not understand all the Greek; use the English column as your primary text and pick out what you can of the Greek.

NASB

1And you were dead in your trespasses and sins,
2in which you formerly walked according to the
course of this world, according to the prince of
the power of the air, of the spirit that is now
working in the sons of disobedience. 3Among
them we too all formerly lived in the lusts of
our flesh, indulging the desires of the flesh and
of the mind, and were by nature children of
wrath, even as the rest. 4But God, being rich in
mercy, because of His great love with which He
loved us, 5even when we were dead in our trans-
gressions, made us alive together with Christ
(by grace you have been saved), 6and raised us
up with Him, and seated us with Him in the
heavenly places in Christ Jesus, 7so that in the
ages to come He might show the surpassing
riches of His grace in kindness toward us in
Christ Jesus.

Greek

1Καὶ ὑμᾶς ὄντας νεκροὺς τοῖς παραπτώμα-
σιν καὶ ταῖς ἁμαρτίαις ὑμῶν, 2ἐν αἷς ποτε
περιεπατήσατε κατὰ τὸν αἰῶνα τοῦ κόσμου
τούτου, κατὰ τὸν ἄρχοντα τῆς ἐξουσίας τοῦ
ἀέρος, τοῦ πνεύματος τοῦ νῦν ἐνεργοῦντος
ἐν τοῖς υἱοῖς τῆς ἀπειθείας· 3ἐν οἷς καὶ
ἡμεῖς πάντες ἀνεστράφημέν ποτε ἐν ταῖς
ἐπιθυμίαις τῆς σαρκὸς ἡμῶν ποιοῦντες τὰ
θελήματα τῆς σαρκὸς καὶ τῶν διανοιῶν, καὶ
ἤμεθα τέκνα φύσει ὀργῆς ὡς καὶ οἱ λοιποί·
4ὁ δὲ θεὸς πλούσιος ὢν ἐν ἐλέει, διὰ τὴν
πολλὴν ἀγάπην αὐτοῦ ἣν ἠγάπησεν ἡμᾶς,
5καὶ ὄντας ἡμᾶς νεκροὺς τοῖς παραπτώμα-
σιν συνεζωοποίησεν τῷ Χριστῷ,—χάριτί
ἐστε σεσῳσμένοι—6καὶ συνήγειρεν καὶ
συνεκάθισεν ἐν τοῖς ἐπουρανίοις ἐν Χριστῷ
Ἰησοῦ, 7ἵνα ἐνδείξηται ἐν τοῖς αἰῶσιν τοῖς
ἐπερχομένοις τὸ ὑπερβάλλον πλοῦτος τῆς
χάριτος αὐτοῦ ἐν χρηστότητι ἐφ' ἡμᾶς ἐν
Χριστῷ Ἰησοῦ.

Reading just the NASB English text above, you would assume that there was a subject ("you") and a main verb ("were dead") in 2:1. The classic KJV takes a different approach in verse 1a: "And you hath he quickened, who were dead," but there is no word for "quickened" (i.e., "made alive") in the Greek text of verse 1. If you were limited to an English translation for your study, you might base your understanding of this text on the assumption that there is a main statement in verse 1. But if you read your Greek text, you will discover that there is not a main verb in verse 1, or in verses 2, or 3, or 4. It is not until you get to verse 5 that you will find the main verb.

23.2. A more formal equivalent of verse 1 would be "And you, being dead." The text then goes on for several verses describing that dead state—but not yet getting to Paul's main point (the statement containing the main verb). In verse 4 Paul starts in that direction with his statement, "But God, being rich in mercy" (and here the NASB does translate the verbal form as a participle). But notice that there is a new subject now (not "you" but "God"), but there still is not a main verb. That elusive verb finally shows up in verse 5 (and it goes with the subject from v. 4): "But God . . . made us alive together with Christ" (ὁ δὲ θεός . . . συνεζωοποίησεν τῷ Χριστῷ). This, by the way, is the phrase that the KJV moves all the way back to verse 1 (and repeats in v. 5) in an attempt to make an intelligible sentence that is not seven verses long.

To make a long story short, the point is that you might misread Paul's major point here unless you can tell that the first four verses are built on two participles ("*being* dead," **ὄντας** νεκρούς [v. 1], and "*being* rich," πλούσιος **ὤν** [v. 4]). Those are important points, but they are subordinate to the main statement in this seven-verse sentence: "But God . . . made us alive . . . and raised us up . . . and seated us" (ὁ δὲ θεός . . . συνεζωοποίησεν . . . καὶ συνήγειρεν καὶ συνεκάθισεν [vv. 4–6]). Your understanding of the text should reflect the emphasis the author has communicated by the grammatical structure and syntax of the text. To do that you need to understand participles.

Introduction to Participles

23.3. As you have already learned, there are two kinds of verbal forms: finite and non-finite. Finite verbs have person and number: a default, built-in subject. Participles (and infinitives) are not finite verbs, so we call them *non-finite* forms, which means that they do not have grammatical person. That is, there is no default, built-in, back-pocket subject as with regular verbs. Non-finite forms simply describe an action without telling us who did it, or they apply a verbal description to a noun. You met the first of the non-finite forms, the infinitive, in the last chapter. In this chapter you will meet the second of these non-finite verbals: the participle.

We will begin with English participles—a subject that is often rather vague in the minds of English speakers.

English Participles

23.4. Participles in English are verbs that have *-ing* endings but no subject and no helping verb[1] and that modify a noun; they act like adjectives.

23.5. English Examples

The car *sitting* in the parking lot has a flat tire.
Leaping to his feet, he hurled the rock.
Listening to a new song on my phone, I studied for my Greek exam.
Snarling cats will often scratch.
The prophet had a fire *burning* in his bones.

The following examples have *-ing* forms, but they are not participles.

I will be *heading* to bed right after the game. (This verbal form has a subject, so it is not a finite verb.)
I like *teaching* Greek. (This is an English gerund, an *-ing* form of a verb used as a noun.)

An English participle functions as an adjective. In Greek, participles may modify either nouns (adjectival) or verbs (adverbial). The italicized words in the following examples would all be participles if they were written *in Greek*.

After eating the freshly baked pie, my Greek teacher gave us an easy quiz.[2]
The puppy *chewing* on the table leg must learn to behave!

"After eating" tells us something about "gave": when the teacher gave the quiz; it functions adverbially. "Chewing" tells us something about that "puppy" (which puppy is causing trouble), so it functions adjectivally.

The participle and its modifiers constitute a *participial phrase*. Consider this sentence.

The car *sitting* in the parking lot has a flat tire.

Here the words "*sitting* in the parking lot" compose a participial phrase; the prepositional phrase, "in the parking lot," is part of the larger participial phrase.

Diagramming Participles

23.6. Although this textbook does not attempt to teach you how to diagram Greek sentences, seeing the differences in how adjectival and adverbial participles

1. This is the English present active participle; there are a few other less frequent participle forms in English, including past and perfect participles. We will simplify for our purposes and pretend that the English present participle is all there is.

2. In English, "eating" is a gerund functioning as the object of a preposition, not a participle, but in Greek a participle would likely be used here.

are diagrammed may help you understand how they function differently. Two of the examples above are diagrammed in figures 23.1 and 23.2 *as if they were Greek sentences*. Not every word in each sentence is included.

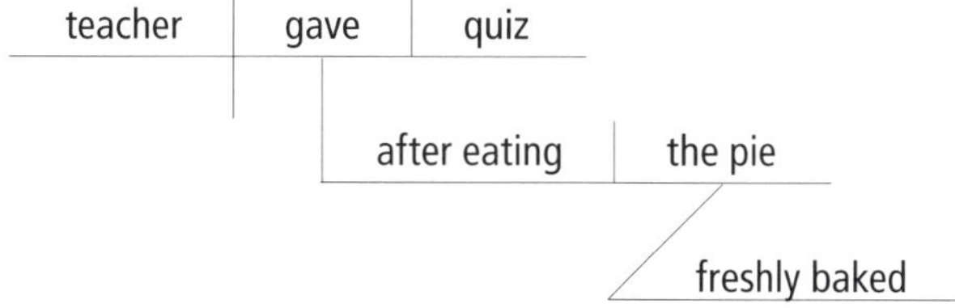

Figure 23.1. The Adverbial Participle

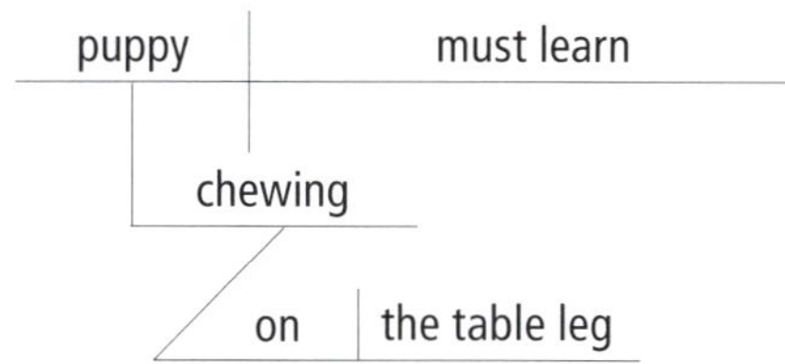

Figure 23.2. The Adjectival Participle

Greek Participles

23.7. Now that we have surveyed English participles, it is time to turn our attention to Greek participles.

Frequency of Participles in the New Testament

Total number of verses in the NT with participles:	4,277
Total number of participles in the NT:	6,662

These figures show a ratio of 1.6 participles per verse in the NT. That is, on average, in every two verses you will find three participles. That tells you how important it is to understand and be able to recognize a participle. Or to illustrate it a different way, the total number of verbal forms in the NT is 28,110. That includes finite verbs (indicatives, subjunctives, optatives, and imperatives) and non-finite forms (participles and infinitives). There are 6,662 participles, or 23.7 percent of all verbal forms.

The participles of the following verbs constitute most of the participles in the NT; you will recognize them as very common words. The number beside each verb indicates how many times participial forms of the verb occur in the NT (frequency in the LXX is similar).

λέγω	515
ἔχω	240
εἰμί	160
ἔρχομαι	158
ἀκούω	136
γίνομαι	136
ὁράω/εἶδον	117
ἀποκρίνομαι	103
ποιέω	99

Of these, the most common inflected forms are λέγων (179×), λέγοντες (151×) (both are present tense-forms of λέγω), ἀποκριθείς (an aorist form of ἀποκρίνομαι; 91×), and ἔχων (86×). As long as we are looking at statistics, here are a few more figures to give you some idea of what is coming.

Total Number of Participles in the NT:	**6,662**
Imperfective (Present)	3,687
Perfective (Aorist)	2,289 (including 819 second aorist forms)
Stative (Perfect)	673
Future	13

The Nature of Participles

23.8. Participles are a hybrid form, part verb and part adjective (see fig. 23.3). This is similar to the infinitive, which is a hybrid of verb and noun.

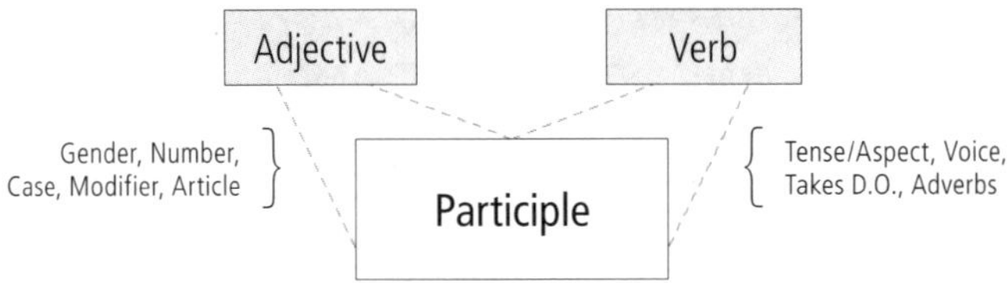

Figure 23.3. The Hybrid Nature of the Participle

The participle, being a hybrid form, has characteristics of both the adjective and the verb. Like an adjective, it has gender, number, and case; it functions as a modifier in any way that an adjective can (including functioning substantivally); it can take an article; and so forth. But since it is also part verb, that means that it also has tense/aspect and voice; it can take a direct object, be modified by an adverb, and so on. In addition to this grammatical analogy, the participle, like the mule, is a real workhorse in the language. Greek writers use participles for many different things, and it would be hard to imagine the language without them.

Basic Grammar of the Greek Participle

23.9. All participles are formed from a verb, which means that the lexical form of every participle is a verb. This is very important to remember. When you parse a participle, you cannot use a noun as the lexical form; it must be a verb. Participles are *not* finite verbs (so we call them *non-finite forms*)—which means that they do not have personal endings. There is no default, built-in, back-pocket subject like finite verbs have. Participles (and infinitives) are sometimes called *verbals* to distinguish them from regular/finite verbs.

The key to a participle's *form* is *verbal aspect*. Each aspect has an associated participle:

imperfective (present tense-form participles)
perfective (aorist tense-form participles)
stative (perfect tense-form participles)

There are no imperfect participles in Greek. A few future participles occur, but they are rare: only a dozen in the NT and less than six dozen (out of 14,500 participles) in the LXX.

The usual "verb things" that you have already learned also apply to participles: voice, number, and so on. Participles may have modifiers (objects, prepositions, adjectives, genitive nouns, adverbs). They are almost always negated by μή rather than οὐ.[3]

Participles *never* have a nominative-case subject. Not only do they not have a built-in subject like finite verbs, but they cannot take a nominative-case subject either. So, how do you know "who done it"? For adverbial participles (which we will talk about below), *the same agent as the main verb is assumed*. If you want to know who is doing the action described by the participle, ask: who is performing the action of the main verb? For an active- or middle-voice participle, this will be the subject of the sentence. For a passive participle, the agent indicated by the agent marker in the context is assumed to be performing the action described by the participle.

The Greek Mule

A good analogy for understanding the Greek participle is to call it the *Greek mule*. That term comes from Robertson's massive grammar. In discussing "The Double Aspect of the Participle," he explains that "the very name participle (*pars, capio*) indicates this fact. The word is part adjective, part verb. Voss calls it *mules,* which is part horse and part ass."[a] In case your Latin is a bit rusty: *pars* = "a part" and *capio* = "I take"; that is, the participle "takes a part" of the meaning of both verb and adjective. And if your zoology is rusty, mules were bred as work animals. A mule is a crossbreed from mating a female horse (a mare) with a male donkey (a jack).

[a] Robertson, *Grammar*, 1101. Voss, whom Robertson cites from Farrar's 1876 *Greek Syntax,* was a major classical grammarian from the Netherlands, Gerardus Vossius (1577–1649).

23.10. There are two basic kinds of participles: adverbial and adjectival.[4] These are descriptions of how the participle functions in the sentence. Some participles

3. The general principle is that οὐ negates only indicative verbs. I have found only 21 participles in the NT that are negated by οὐ (out of 6,662): Matt. 12:4; 22:11; Luke 6:42; John 10:12; Acts 7:5; Rom. 9:25; 2 Cor. 3:3; 4:8 (2×), 9 (2×); 12:1, 4; Gal. 4:8, 27 (2×); Col. 2:19; Heb. 11:1, 35; 1 Pet. 1:8; 2 Pet. 1:16.

4. Adverbial participles are sometimes called *circumstantial* participles because they describe circumstances in/under which the action of the main verb occurs.

act like adjectives and modify a substantive or take the place of a substantive. Other participles modify a verb. Here is an example of each kind.

Adjectival: τοῦ **φαινομένου** ἀστέρος ("the *shining* star"), Matt. 2:7
Adverbial: ἀπῆλθεν **λυπούμενος** ("he went away *grieving*"), Matt. 19:22

Adjectival participles, when modifying a noun, agree with that noun in gender, number, and case, just like adjectives. They occur in the same grammatical

---

The Importance of the Case of Participles

Why do some translations of Jude 22b sound so different? In the classic KJV, Jude 21–23 reads as follows.

> [21]Keep yourselves in the love of God, looking for the mercy of our Lord Jesus Christ unto eternal life. [22]And of some have compassion, *making a difference:* [23]And others save with fear, pulling them out of the fire; hating even the garment spotted by the flesh.

By contrast, most modern translations read something like this:

> [21]Keep yourselves in God's love as you wait for the mercy of our Lord Jesus Christ to bring you to eternal life. [22]Be merciful *to those who doubt;* [23]save others by snatching them from the fire; to others show mercy, mixed with fear—hating even the clothing stained by corrupted flesh. (NIV)

The translations "making a difference" and "to those who doubt" sound like they are saying very different things. This does involve a textual variant, seemingly a very tiny one—only two or three letters. It is the same word in both variants, but the textual choice is between two different case endings. Here is the Greek text in question.

καὶ οὓς μὲν ἐλεᾶτε **διακριν[ομένους/όμενοι**?]

If the text reads διακρινόμενοι, then the participle is nominative, an adverbial participle modifying the verb ἐλεᾶτε, referring to how that action is performed.[a] This is the reading that lies behind the KJV. But if the text reads διακρινομένους, then the participle is accusative, an adjectival substantival participle that functions as the direct object. This is the reading that lies behind modern translations (e.g., NIV). For now, just note the significance of the example and the difference it can make in translation. After you have worked through the next few chapters and have learned more about participles, come back to this example and work out the meaning on your own.[b]

[a] We have not yet learned how participles are formed. For now it is enough if you know that they use the regular case endings that you learned very early in your study of Greek.

[b] This example also illustrates how words may have different meanings, depending on how they function in a sentence. A lexicon will list several meanings for διακρίνω, but which one makes sense sometimes depends on whether the word is functioning as part of the subject or of the object of a sentence. (The older KJV translation "making a difference" would be expressed in contemporary English as "distinguishing" or "evaluating." It does not have the meaning of our current idiom "to make a difference.")

---

positions in which an adjective may occur. When taking the place of a noun (i.e., a substantival adjectival participle, functioning like a substantival adjective), their case is determined by their function in the sentence.

Adverbial participles, since they modify the verb and therefore assume the same actor as the nominative-case subject, occur only in the nominative case.[5] There are two exceptions to this general rule, which you will meet later.

These principles help identify who is doing the action expressed by the participle. Greek decides such questions based, not on word order (as would English), but on grammatical *agreement*. The gender, number, and case of a participle enables us to determine who is doing what, regardless of word order.

Imperfective (Present) Participles

23.11. After what may have seemed like a very long introduction, we are now ready to look at the forms of the participles. Just like the finite verbs that we studied in the previous chapters, we will learn the participles, not by memorizing chart after chart of forms, but by learning a simple formula—one very similar to the verb formulas you already know. The pieces will be very similar, though we will use two new elements: participle markers and *case endings*. This reflects the hybrid nature of the participle, which is part verb and part adjective. Its verb "parent" brings along the verb stem, connecting vowels, and form markers. The adjective "parent" contributes the case endings.

Forms of the Imperfective (Present) Participle

23.12. The first of the participle formulas is for imperfective participles. You will notice that this formula is generic for all imperfective participles. It does not distinguish voice or gender. Those variations are identified by the specific participle marker that is used (see below).

Formula for Imperfective (Present) Participles

stem + connecting vowel + participle marker + case endings

Along with this formula you also need to learn three participle markers. We will reuse them in the subsequent participle forms as well (aorist and perfect). On the same chart we can also include the case endings; different participles use different declension endings.

5. This is not a universal consensus among grammarians, but *at the very least* it is a general rule with a very high degree of reliability. The *English translation* of some participles may make it sound like some oblique-case participles are adverbial, but the point is not how they are translated but how they function in Greek. On this, see the important article by Culy, "Clue Is in the Case."

Voice	Gender	Participle Marker	Declension Endings
Active	m/n	ντ	3
	f	ουσ[a]	1
Middle/passive	m/f/n	μεν	2/1/2

[a] What is listed here as the active participle marker in the feminine is the connecting vowel *and* participle marker together (ουσ). The participle marker is actually ντ, just like the masculine and neuter forms. You don't really want to know what happened to it. Trust me, you don't. But if you are desperately curious for morphological trivia, see *MBG*, 152n2, §91.1. It is simpler (*much* simpler) just to think of ουσ as the connecting vowel and participle marker for feminine.

You need to know *both* the formula *and* the three participle markers. The following charts show the forms of the imperfective (present) participle. You do not need to memorize these charts. If you understand the formula and participle marker chart above, you will be able to identify these forms easily. Each of the pieces is listed here in a separate column so that you can see how the participle is formed.

23.13. Forms of the Present Active Participle

Present Active Participle of λύω

	Masc.			Fem.			Neut.		
NS	λύ	ων	–	λύ	ουσ	α	λῦ	ον	—
GS	λύ	οντ	ος	λυ	ούσ	ης	λύ	οντ	ος
DS	λύ	οντ	ι	λυ	ούσ	ῃ	λύ	οντ	ι
AS	λύ	οντ	α	λύ	ουσ	αν	λῦ	ον	—
NP	λύ	οντ	ες	λύ	ουσ	αι	λύ	οντ	α
GP	λυ	όντ	ων	λυ	ουσ	ῶν	λυ	όντ	ων
DP	λύ	ου	σι(ν)	λυ	ούσ	αις	λύ	ου	σι(ν)
AP	λύ	οντ	ας	λυ	ούσ	ας	λύ	οντ	α

Compare each of these forms with the imperfective (present) participle formula. The first Greek column in each section is the verb stem, λυ-. The next column is the connecting vowel combined with the participle marker. (The connecting vowel for all participles is omicron, though it sometimes undergoes ablaut.) The third column is the case ending.

There are only two unexpected variations—though both of them follow familiar patterns. The first is the nominative singular form in masculine and neuter. Since this form uses third-declension endings, and specifically the variation of third declension that uses a blank (or null) ending for the nominative singular (rather than the more common sigma), the tau drops off. (You might remember from an earlier chapter that a tau cannot stand at the end of a word.) When the tau drops off, the connecting vowel, omicron, lengthens to compensate. Thus instead of the expected -οντ, we have the form λύων. Since this is the most common form of all participles in the NT, you will want to remember it. In the neuter, the same thing happens, except that the connecting vowel does not lengthen, which enables you to distinguish masculine from neuter forms, which would otherwise be identical.

The second variation is the dative plural form in masculine and neuter (and here both genders are identical). The complicating factor here is the sigma on the ending. You will probably remember that a sigma caused complications in third-declension nouns from time to time. When the sigma is added, the ντ participle marker drops out, and the omicron connecting vowel lengthens to the diphthong ου.

The feminine forms are perfectly regular. That is helpful, since they occur much less frequently than the masculine forms.

Examples of Present Active Participles

23.14. These examples are all present active participles, nominative singular—one of each gender. Since we have not yet talked about the meaning of participles, focus on identifying the forms, and do not be concerned about how they came to be translated as they are here.

Mark 1:14, ἦλθεν ὁ Ἰησοῦς εἰς τὴν Γαλιλαίαν **κηρύσσων** τὸ εὐαγγέλιον τοῦ θεοῦ.	Jesus came into Galilee, *preaching* the good news from God.
1 Pet. 3:6, Σάρρα ὑπήκουσεν τῷ Ἀβραὰμ κύριον αὐτὸν **καλοῦσα**.	Sarah obeyed Abraham, *calling* him lord.
Acts 20:23, τὸ πνεῦμα τὸ ἅγιον κατὰ πόλιν διαμαρτύρεταί μοι **λέγον** ὅτι δεσμὰ καὶ θλίψεις με μένουσιν.	The Holy Spirit testifies to me in every city, *saying* that bonds and hardships await me.

23.15. Forms of the Present Middle Participle

Present Middle Participle of λύω

	Masc.			Fem.			Neut.		
NS	λυ	όμεν	ος	λυ	ομέν	η	λυ	όμεν	ον
GS	λυ	ομέν	ου	λυ	ομέν	ης	λυ	ομέν	ου
DS	λυ	ομέν	ῳ	λυ	ομέν	ῃ	λυ	ομέν	ῳ
AS	λυ	όμεν	ον	λυ	ομέν	ην	λυ	όμεν	ον
NP	λυ	όμεν	οι	λυ	όμεν	αι	λυ	όμεν	α
GP	λυ	ομέν	ων	λυ	ομέν	ων	λυ	ομέν	ων
DP	λυ	ομέν	οις	λυ	ομέν	αις	λυ	ομέν	οις
AP	λυ	ομέν	ους	λυ	ομέν	ας	λυ	όμεν	α

These forms are properly middle voice, but as with present middle indicative verbs, they sometimes function as passives. The passive participle is identified the same way that present passive indicative verbs were identified: a middle form with an agent marker in the context. In context, middle forms must always be identified as either middle or passive. You cannot parse them as "mid./pass." Generally you should assume that such a form is middle unless there is some indication in the context to suggest passive.

These middle (and passive) participles are perhaps the easiest to recognize. They all have -ομεν- between the stem and ending (i.e., a connecting vowel and a participle marker). There are no unexpected variations—a student's dream form.

Examples of Present Middle Participles

23.16. The following examples are all imperfective (present) middle or passive participles, nominative singular or plural. We have not yet talked about the meaning of participles; for now, focus on identifying the forms.

Matt. 6:7, **Προσευχόμενοι** δὲ μὴ βατταλογήσητε (you babble) ὥσπερ οἱ ἐθνικοί.	But *when you pray*, do not babble like the pagans.
Mark 1:13, ἦν ἐν τῇ ἐρήμῳ τεσσεράκοντα ἡμέρας **πειραζόμενος** ὑπὸ τοῦ Σατανᾶ.	He was in the wilderness forty days, *being tempted* by Satan.
Mark 4:19, αἱ μέριμναι τοῦ αἰῶνος **εἰσπορευόμεναι** συμπνίγουσιν τὸν λόγον.	The cares of the age choke the word *when they enter.*
Rom. 3:21, δικαιοσύνη θεοῦ πεφανέρωται **μαρτυρουμένη** ὑπὸ τοῦ νόμου καὶ τῶν προφητῶν.	The righteousness of God has been revealed, *being testified* by the Law and the Prophets.
2 Cor. 3:14, τὸ κάλυμμα ἐπὶ τῇ ἀναγνώσει τῆς παλαιᾶς διαθήκης μένει, μὴ **ἀνακαλυπτόμενον**.	The veil remains upon the reading of the old covenant, not *being unveiled* [i.e., when the old covenant is read].

How to Parse Participles

23.17. Participles are parsed very much like finite verbs, but the pieces are slightly different. Here is what you need to include to describe a participle:

tense-form, voice, "mood,"[6] gender, number, case ▸ lexical form, gloss
Example: λύων = pres. act. ptc. masc. sg. nom. ▸ λύω, "I loose"

6. "Participle" is not technically a mood (it is a part of speech parallel to "verb"), but it performs a similar function in terms of a parsing description.

Meaning of Imperfective (Present) Participles

23.18. The key to the meaning of a participle is *verbal aspect*. Present participles convey imperfective aspect; aorist participles convey perfective aspect. As you will remember from earlier chapters, imperfective aspect is a means of expressing the writer's view of the situation as a process. Likewise, perfective aspect views a situation in summary as a whole event. The same situation may be viewed from either perspective. It is not always easy or possible to reflect such aspectual distinctions in English since English participles do not express these same distinctions. If it is possible to communicate the aspect of the Greek participle in good English, then do so. If the result is awkward English, then do not force it. You should, however, *always* remember aspect in exegesis. Before we can develop this further, we need to talk about the function of participles.

Function of Imperfective (Present) Participles

23.19. As you learned earlier in this chapter, participles have two major functions: adverbial and adjectival. In this chapter and the next we will focus on adverbial participles. Adjectival participles will follow these two chapters.

Adverbial participles (which will be in the nominative case) will usually be represented as an English *adverbial clause* that modifies the verb. Some such participles will be adequately expressed as a simple participle in English: a formal equivalent consisting of just the verb with an *-ing* ending and no subject. Most adverbial participles, however, will require more than that. Various relationships are possible. *These relationships depend entirely on the context.* You must ask: What is the relationship between the verb and the participle? In what sort of context is this participle used? If the context makes clear what is intended, then you *should* make this explicit in English. The most common of these relationships are the following four. We will look at different types of relationships in the next chapter.[7] These categories are summaries of the types of contexts in which the participles are used; they do not describe different kinds of participles. Referring to a "causal participle" is just a shorthand expression for "an adverbial participle used in a context where the participle is clearly related to the main verb in a causal way."

23.20. Adverbial participles may be used in contexts that express cause, purpose, means, or temporality. Only one example of each is given here, but the later section of examples provides many more, as will the next chapter.

7. There is a flow chart in app. C that will help you conceptualize the various uses of the participle as well as the options for adverbial participles. Most of that chart will not make a lot of sense yet, but it will in time. If you look at it now, pay most attention to the section in the lower right portion of the chart, which includes the four categories discussed in the text here along with other similar options.

1. Participles Used in Causal Statements

Causal participles are used in statements that answer these questions: Why has the action of the main verb been done? What has caused it? In the following example, from Acts 2, what caused David to speak? It is *because* he was a prophet.

Acts 2:30–31, προφήτης οὖν **ὑπάρχων** ἐλάλησεν περὶ τῆς ἀναστάσεως τοῦ Χριστοῦ.	Therefore *because he was* a prophet he spoke concerning the resurrection of Christ.[a]

[a] The participle is a form of ὑπάρχω, "I am"—a synonym for εἰμί.

In this situation you might get by with an English participle, "*Being* a prophet," but since the context makes it clear that the participle explains *why* David spoke, it is better to use the more explicit expression, "Because he was." Yes, that uses an English finite verb rather than an English participle. That is not only acceptable but very often necessary, since English participles do not always function in exactly the same way Greek participles do.

2. Participles Used in Purpose Statements

Participles of purpose are used to focus attention on the *motive* for which the action of the main verb has been done. Why has the subject done that? Participles in purpose constructions can often be represented with the phrase "in order to."

John 12:33, τοῦτο δὲ ἔλεγεν **σημαίνων** ποίῳ θανάτῳ ἤμελλεν ἀποθνῄσκειν.	He said this *in order to indicate* by what sort of death he was about to die.

In this example from John 12, *why* does Jesus speak? He says this (τοῦτο ἔλεγεν) *for the purpose of* indicating particular information.

3. Participles Used in Statements of Means

The participle of means defines or *explains the means by which* the action of the main verb has been accomplished.[8] In the following verse, how does Paul say that the apostles have labored? What are the *means* employed?

1 Cor. 4:12, κοπιῶμεν **ἐργαζόμενοι** ταῖς ἰδίαις χερσίν.	We labor, *working* (or, *by working*) with our own hands.

4. Participles Used in Temporal Statements

The primary function of a *temporal participle* is to explain when the action of the main verb has occurred. When participles are used in temporal expressions,

8. If the participle describes the emotion or attitude connected with the action, it is called a *participle of manner*, not means. See the discussion in the next chapter.

it is *relative* time that is in view—relative to the main verb. We express that with terms such as *while, after, before, when, since, as*.

Mark 2:14, **παράγων** εἶδεν Λευίν. *As he was passing by* he saw Levi.

23.21. We need to say a bit more about the category of "temporal participle." It is last in this list since almost any participle *can* be understood with a temporal nuance, but that does not mean that is what the author intended. We need to explore that a bit. First, there is no time expressed by the *tense-form* of the participle. Any time reference for the participle must come from the context, just as was true of a finite verb. An imperfective (present) participle tells you only that it conveys imperfective aspect and that it uses the present stem to create the form. The stem of a present participle will be spelled the same as the stem of a present indicative form of the same verb.

Second, the time of an adverbial participle is *relative* to the time of the verbal form it modifies. It describes an event that occurs antecedent to, simultaneous with, or subsequent to the situation/action described by the main verbal form. This is true not only of temporal adverbial participles but of all adverbial participles. The action of the participle has some relationship to the verbal form that it modifies. Logically, there is almost always some temporal relationship between any two situations. One must always be antecedent to, simultaneous with, or subsequent to the other.

Third, imperfective participles *often* (not always) describe events/situations happening simultaneously with the main verb. This relates to imperfective aspect being a view of the action as a process, making it a natural way to say that one action *is going on* at the same time as another. Perfective participles *often* (not always) describe events/situations happening antecedent to the main verb.[9] This also relates to the aspectual viewpoint, since it is natural to refer to an antecedent action as a whole rather than as in progress. You must examine each participle in its context to determine the temporal relationship. Do not lock into one fixed time for each form, since doing so could twist your understanding of a passage.

In summary, you should use the category of "temporal adverbial participle" as a last resort and only when the context makes it clear that the main point being communicated by the participle is the time relationship to the main verb.

The extra words in the translations above (e.g., "because," "by") are added to express the logical relationship between the two actions (the action of the verb and that of the participle) that is made clear by the context. There are no separate words in the Greek sentence for these English words. Other instances may take more (sometimes considerably more) words in English to express what a Greek reader would have assumed automatically from the context. In most of these instances we supply a subject in English (it comes from the main verb and

9. This area is not yet resolved in grammar; a number of proposals have been offered. Some think that word order plays a role here also. Take all such claims with caution, and test every participle against the context to see if the assumed temporal reference actually makes sense. The context is a more reliable guide than any rule.

its subject) and translate the participle as if it were a finite verb. The result is a subordinate adverbial clause. This is necessary, since English expresses these relationships differently from Greek.

Participle of εἰμί

Forms of the Participle of εἰμί

23.22. The linking verb εἰμί has only one significant set of participle forms, a present active participle.[10]

Present Active Participle of εἰμί

	Masc.	Fem.	Neut.
NS	ὤν	οὖσα	ὄν
GS	ὄντος	οὔσης	ὄντος
DS	ὄντι	οὔσῃ	ὄντι
AS	ὄντα	οὖσαν	ὄν
NP	ὄντες	οὖσαι	ὄντα
GP	ὄντων	οὐσῶν	ὄντων
DP	οὖσι(ν)	οὔσαις	οὖσι(ν)
AP	ὄντας	οὔσας	ὄντα

Does this chart look familiar? It ought to. Compare it with the imperfective (present) active participle chart earlier in this chapter. It is identical to the participle of λύω, *but with no stem*. The participle of εἰμί consists of just the connecting vowel, participle marker, and case ending. The following are the only forms that occur more than 10 times in the NT: ὤν (42×), ὄντες (26×), ὄντα (12×), ὄντος (14×), and ὄντας (11×). Distribution in the LXX is similar.

Examples of the Participle of εἰμί

John 10:33, ἀπεκρίθησαν αὐτῷ οἱ Ἰουδαῖοι, Περὶ καλοῦ ἔργου οὐ λιθάζομέν σε ἀλλὰ περὶ βλασφημίας, καὶ ὅτι σὺ ἄνθρωπος **ὢν** ποιεῖς σεαυτὸν θεόν.

The Jews answered him, "We are not stoning you for a good work but for blasphemy, and because you, *being* a man, make yourself God."

Rom. 5:10, εἰ γὰρ ἐχθροὶ **ὄντες** κατηλλάγημεν τῷ θεῷ διὰ τοῦ θανάτου τοῦ υἱοῦ αὐτοῦ . . .

For if *while we were* enemies we were reconciled to God through the death of his Son . . .

10. There is one other participle of εἰμί in the NT, and it occurs only once: ἐσόμενον is a future middle participle neuter singular accusative (Luke 22:49). There are also eleven instances of the future middle participle of εἰμί in the LXX, the most common of which is ἐσόμενα (neuter plural accusative; e.g., Dan. 2:45). These can be identified by the future form marker following the stem (which is only an epsilon), preceding the connecting vowel and participle marker.

The nominatives ἄνθρωπος and ἐχθροί in these two examples are predicate nominatives, not the subject. Remember: participles do not take nominative-case subjects.

Participles of Contract Verbs

Forms of Contract Verb Participles

23.23. As you might suspect, contract verbs can cause some minor changes in the spelling of participle forms. They are the same changes that you have already seen in finite verbs. They affect only the present participle, both active and middle forms. A few examples are given here, but a full set of forms may be found in appendix A.

The most common change in epsilon and omicron contract participles is the lengthening of the connecting vowel from omicron to ου (ε/ο + ο = ου). The most common such forms in the NT and LXX are masculine plural nominative forms such as λαλοῦντες and masculine plural accusative forms such as κατοικοῦντας. (Compare the non-contract forms λύοντες and λύοντας.) Also common are masculine singular nominative forms like λαλῶν (from λαλέω; the uncontracted form would have been λαλεων).

Alpha contracts will look a bit different; instead of seeing ου in place of an omicron, you will see an omega (α + ο = ω). The most frequently occurring form in the NT and LXX is ἀγαπῶν, a masculine singular nominative participle of ἀγαπάω.[11]

23.24. Examples of Contract Verb Participles

The examples below include each kind of contract. The lexical forms used are λαλέω, περιπατέω, δολόω, and προσδοκάω.

Acts 6:13, Ὁ ἄνθρωπος οὗτος οὐ παύεται **λαλῶν** ῥήματα κατὰ τοῦ τόπου τοῦ ἁγίου τούτου καὶ τοῦ νόμου.	This man does not stop *speaking* words against this holy place and the law.
2 Cor. 4:2, ἀπειπάμεθα τὰ κρυπτὰ τῆς αἰσχύνης, μὴ **περιπατοῦντες** ἐν πανουργίᾳ μηδὲ **δολοῦντες** τὸν λόγον τοῦ θεοῦ.	We have renounced the secret things of shame, not *walking* [i.e., living] by trickery or *distorting* the Word of God.
Acts 3:5, ὁ δὲ ἐπεῖχεν αὐτοῖς **προσδοκῶν** τι παρ' αὐτῶν λαβεῖν.	But he paid close attention to them *because he expected* to receive something from them.

11. Forms of ζῶ (ζάω) *appear* to be alpha contracts, but they are not (see the sidebar in chap. 21): ζῶντος (masculine or neuter singular genitive), ζῶντι (masculine singular dative), ζῶντες (masculine plural nominative), ζώντων (masculine plural genitive).

Summary

23.25. Perhaps all this detail seems complicated. *Don't let those participles get you down!* Participles are one of the most fascinating—and profitable—parts of the Greek language. Your understanding of many passages will be clarified significantly when you understand the participle. One thing to remember in this regard is that a participle will never be the main verb in a sentence—even though they may show up in standard English translations looking and sounding like finite verbs.[12] They are always modifiers of some sort, subordinate to the main idea expressed by the finite verb form.

Figure 23.4

Now You Try It

23.26. At this point, the best thing you can do is read, read, read. The more participles you see in sentences, the better off you will be. It is well worth it. In the examples that follow, ask yourself:

What is the main idea—the kernel—of the sentence?
How does the participle relate to the main verb?

Mark 1:10, καὶ εὐθὺς **ἀναβαίνων** ἐκ τοῦ ὕδατος εἶδεν τοὺς οὐρανούς.

Mark 1:16, **παράγων** παρὰ τὴν θάλασσαν τῆς Γαλιλαίας εἶδεν Σίμωνα καὶ Ἀνδρέαν.

12. Modern English translations often use finite verbs to represent participles when they try to simplify long, complex Greek sentences into shorter English ones. Even formal equivalent translations (sometimes called "literal" translations) do this. That is fine for purposes of English style, but always base your study on the Greek text; do not depend on the secondhand perspective of a translation, which must also balance other factors, such as readability and style.

Mark 3:11, τὰ πνεύματα τὰ ἀκάθαρτα, ὅταν αὐτὸν ἐθεώρουν, προσέπιπτον αὐτῷ καὶ ἔκραζον **λέγοντες** ὅτι Σὺ εἶ ὁ υἱὸς τοῦ θεοῦ.

Mark 6:48, ἔρχεται πρὸς αὐτοὺς **περιπατῶν** ἐπὶ τῆς θαλάσσης.

Mark 8:11, ἐξῆλθον οἱ Φαρισαῖοι καὶ ἤρξαντο συζητεῖν αὐτῷ, **ζητοῦντες** παρ' αὐτοῦ σημεῖον ἀπὸ τοῦ οὐρανοῦ, **πειράζοντες** αὐτόν.

Mark 15:29, ἐβλασφήμουν αὐτὸν **κινοῦντες** τὰς κεφαλὰς αὐτῶν καὶ **λέγοντες** . . .

Gen. 3:5, διανοιχθήσονται ὑμῶν οἱ ὀφθαλμοί, καὶ ἔσεσθε ὡς θεοὶ **γινώσκοντες** καλὸν καὶ πονηρόν.

Gen. 25:29, ἦλθεν Ἠσαῦ ἐκ τοῦ πεδίου[a] **ἐκλείπων.**[b]

[a] πεδίον, ου, τό, "level place, plain, field"

[b] ἐκλείπω, "I am faint" (NT contexts do not offer a parallel for this use of the word; there the basic meaning is "I fail," but it is used of money or life, not hunger.)

Gen. 37:35, Καταβήσομαι πρὸς τὸν υἱόν μου **πενθῶν** εἰς ᾅδου.

Gen. 43:7, οἱ δὲ εἶπαν, **Ἐρωτῶν** ἐπηρώτησεν ἡμᾶς ὁ ἄνθρωπος καὶ τὴν γενεὰν ἡμῶν **λέγων,** Εἰ ἔτι ὁ πατὴρ ὑμῶν ζῇ; εἰ ἔστιν ὑμῖν ἀδελφός;

Num. 10:17, καθελοῦσιν[a] τὴν σκηνὴν καὶ ἐξαροῦσιν[b] οἱ υἱοὶ Γεδσὼν καὶ οἱ υἱοὶ Μεραρὶ **αἴροντες** τὴν σκηνήν.

[a] καθαιρέω; see καθελῶ in the morphology catalog (under "Odd Forms") in app. B.

[b] ἐξαίρω, "I break off/strike/move camp" (not used with this meaning in the NT).

— — — — — — — — — — — — — —

23.27. Advanced Information for Reference: Diagramming Participles

Mark 1:10, καὶ εὐθὺς **ἀναβαίνων** ἐκ τοῦ ὕδατος εἶδεν τοὺς οὐρανούς.

Then, coming up out of the water, he saw the heavens.

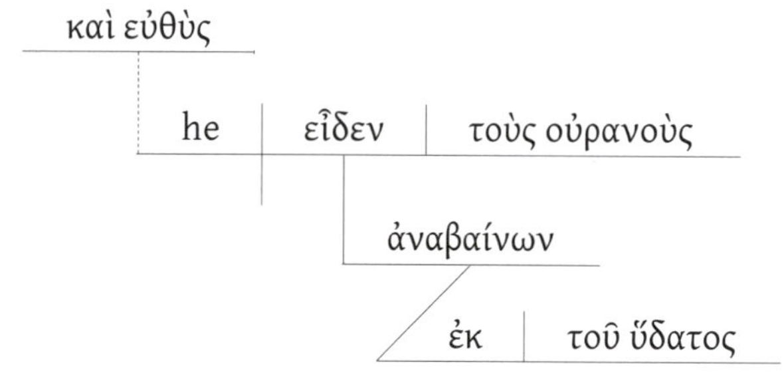

Figure 23.5

Adverbial participles are diagrammed as modifiers and placed under the verb they describe. To distinguish the fact that they are verbal forms, a right-angle bracket is used instead of the angled brackets used for adverbs, prepositional phrases, and similar non-verbal modifiers.

— — — — — — — — — — — — — —

Reading Passage: 1 Thessalonians 2:5–12

23.28. Before you begin the following paragraph, identify all the participles. You should find nine imperfective participles.[13]

Paul's Ministry

5οὔτε γάρ ποτε ἐν λόγῳ κολακείας ἐγενήθημεν, καθὼς οἴδατε, οὔτε ἐν
προφάσει πλεονεξίας, θεὸς μάρτυς, 6οὔτε ζητοῦντες ἐξ ἀνθρώπων δόξαν οὔτε
ἀφ' ὑμῶν οὔτε ἀπ' ἄλλων, 7δυνάμενοι ἐν βάρει εἶναι ὡς Χριστοῦ ἀπόστολοι.
ἀλλὰ ἐγενήθημεν νήπιοι ἐν μέσῳ ὑμῶν, ὡς ἐὰν τροφὸς θάλπῃ (she cares) τὰ
ἑαυτῆς τέκνα, 8οὕτως ὁμειρόμενοι ὑμῶν εὐδοκοῦμεν μεταδοῦναι (to share)
ὑμῖν οὐ μόνον τὸ εὐαγγέλιον τοῦ θεοῦ ἀλλὰ καὶ τὰς ἑαυτῶν ψυχάς, διότι
ἀγαπητοὶ ἡμῖν ἐγενήθητε. 9μνημονεύετε γάρ, ἀδελφοί, τὸν κόπον ἡμῶν καὶ
τὸν μόχθον· νυκτὸς καὶ ἡμέρας ἐργαζόμενοι πρὸς τὸ μὴ ἐπιβαρῆσαί τινα ὑμῶν
ἐκηρύξαμεν εἰς ὑμᾶς τὸ εὐαγγέλιον τοῦ θεοῦ. 10ὑμεῖς μάρτυρες καὶ ὁ θεός,
ὡς ὁσίως καὶ δικαίως καὶ ἀμέμπτως ὑμῖν τοῖς πιστεύουσιν (ones who believe) ἐγενήθημεν, 11καθάπερ οἴδατε, ὡς ἕνα ἕκαστον ὑμῶν ὡς πατὴρ τέκνα

13. Here is the answer (but do not read this until you have tried it yourself first): there is one each in verses 6–10 and four more in verse 12 (ζητοῦντες, δυνάμενοι, ὁμειρόμενοι, ἐργαζόμενοι, πιστεύουσιν, παρακαλοῦντες, παραμυθούμενοι, μαρτυρόμενοι, and καλοῦντος). In this list, two of the participles function adjectivally (τοῖς πιστεύουσιν, "to those who believe" [v. 10], and τοῦ καλοῦντος, "the one who called" [v. 12]).

ἑαυτοῦ [12]παρακαλοῦντες ὑμᾶς καὶ παραμυθούμενοι καὶ μαρτυρόμενοι εἰς τὸ περιπατεῖν ὑμᾶς ἀξίως τοῦ θεοῦ τοῦ καλοῦντος (one who called) ὑμᾶς εἰς τὴν ἑαυτοῦ βασιλείαν καὶ δόξαν.

23.29. Vocabulary for Chapter 23

Part of Speech	Definition	Possible Glosses	Frequency	
Word			NT	LXX
Adverb				
εὐθύς	A temporal adverb referring to a short period of time, either the time before something takes place or the rapidity with which it happens; in a few instances the context makes it clear that there is little if any time interval; a "weakened" sense occurs with καὶ εὐθύς in Mark, where it functions as a conjunction, "then, next" [The more common word is εὐθέως, "immediately"; do not confuse with the adj. εὐθύς, εῖα, ύ, "straight."]	quickly, promptly, at once; immediately; then, next	51	66
Nouns				
εὐαγγέλιον, ου, τό	An announcement or message containing good news; the content of the NT message of God's good news—the provision of salvation in Jesus Christ; reward for good news (LXX) [The later use as a title of a written work about Jesus' life and teaching is not found in the NT text.]	good news, gospel; reward for good news (LXX)	76	1
πρόσωπον, ου, τό	The front part of the head; personal presence (many idiomatic uses, especially with prepositions; see the lexicon); the outer surface of something	face, appearance; person; surface, countenance	76	1,297
ὕδωρ, ὕδατος, τό	The liquid we know as water; a body of water; metaphorically of life-giving salvation	water	76	675
κεφαλή, ῆς, ἡ	The part of the body that contains the brain (human or animal); authority due to rank; the uppermost part, extremity of something	head; extremity	75	433
Σίμων, ωνος, ὁ	A personal name of multiple people in both the OT and NT, most commonly in the NT of the apostle Simon Peter	Simon	75	80
φῶς, φωτός, τό	The physical agent that stimulates the sense of sight to make things visible ("light"); a source of light; metaphorically of various situations that can be illustrated with illumination	light	73	176
πῦρ, πυρός, τό	Combustion that produces light and heat	fire	71	540
Ἰσραήλ, ὁ	An indeclinable personal name, in Scripture the patriarch Jacob; Jacob/Israel's descendants, the twelve tribes composing the nation of Israel	Israel	68	2,748

Part of Speech	Definition	Possible Glosses	Frequency	
Word			NT	LXX
ῥῆμα, ατος, τό	That which is said (typically oral instead of written, ctr. λόγος; many English variations possible due to context); that which can be spoken about	word, saying; a matter, thing, event	68	548
γραμματεύς, έως, ὁ	A government official charged with record keeping; a specialist in the law of Moses	secretary (of state), clerk; scribe, legal scholar	63	85
ὄρος, ὄρους, τό	A geographical elevation that is higher than a βοῦνος ("small hill"); a region characterized by this feature [As in English, "hill" and "mountain" are relative terms and locale specific.]	mountain, hill; mountainous region, hilly area	63	680
θέλημα, ατος, τό	That which one wishes to happen [≠ legal "last will and testament"]	will, desire, what is willed or desired	62	51
νύξ, νυκτός, ἡ	The chronological span from sunset to sunrise; a symbol of intellectual, moral, and spiritual ignorance and darkness	night	61	294
ἐλπίς, ίδος, ἡ	The state of looking forward to something with confidence regarding its realization; that which is the basis for such a hope; that for which one hopes	hope, expectation	53	116

23.30. Key Things to Know for Chapter 23

Know the various participle markers (including the connecting vowel or form marker if there is one).

How do you know who is doing the action of an adverbial participle?

What are the two basic kinds of participles?

In what case is an adverbial participle?

Know the formula for imperfective participles.

Can you list the four basic uses of adverbial participles?

24

NON-FINITE VERBS: PART 3

Perfective Adverbial Participles

24.1. This chapter discusses participles that function the same way and in the same sort of contexts as do the imperfective (present) participles in the last chapter. The only difference here is that these participles express perfective aspect (aorist tense-form) instead of imperfective.

Perfective (Aorist) Participles

24.2. Good news! Although "perfective participle" sounds like something else new to learn, you already know everything you need to know to identify these forms. (Well, almost.) Would you like some evidence that you know more than you think you do? Parse the following forms of λύω. Evaluate each word, and identify the pieces you recognize.

λυσάντων
λυσαμένοις
λυθέντι

If you have worked thoughtfully and combined things that you already know, you have hopefully noted the aorist form marker (σα), two participle markers (ντ and μεν), and familiar case endings. The θε in the third form might be puzzling at first, but you should remember a form very similar to this. (Do you remember that vowels often change their length?) Check your answers with the parsings given in the footnote.[1] Did you get them all right? Or if not, when you checked the answers, did they made good sense?

1. Answers: λυσάντων, aor. act. ptc. masc. pl. gen.; λυσαμένοις, aor. mid. ptc. masc. pl. dat.; and λυθέντι, aor. pass. ptc. masc. sg. dat. Each of these three forms could also be neuter.

Grammar and Form of Perfective (Aorist) Participles

24.3. All the information in the "Introduction to Participles" section in the last chapter is still relevant. We need to add only a few details to clarify the grammar of aorist participles. First, the aspect of aorist participles is *perfective*: the situation is viewed as a whole. Second, as to the time reference of an aorist participle, remember that participles are described in terms of relative time. Aorist participles can technically refer to any time, but they are most often *prior to* or *simultaneous with* the action of the main verb. Third, these forms will sound the same when put into English as did present participles in the preceding chapter. Seldom can we distinguish between an aorist and a present participle on the basis of its English translation.

Formula for Perfective (Aorist) Participles

stem + aorist form marker + participle marker + case endings

The only difference between this formula and the one for the imperfective participle is that the aorist form marker is inserted—and since both such markers end with vowels (σα and θη), the connecting vowel is no longer needed. You are used to seeing θη in the aorist passive indicative; the difference here is only that the vowel is shortened from eta to epsilon, so the aorist form marker appears as θε in the participle. The participle markers are the same ones that you have already learned for the imperfective participles: ντ and μεν. So long as you recognize the individual pieces, you can easily identify an aorist participle. For example, an aorist active participle will have the aorist form marker σα and the active participle marker ντ.

24.4. Forms of the Aorist Active Participle

Aorist Active Participle of λύω

	Masc.			Fem.			Neut.		
NS	λύ	σα	ς	λύ	σασ	α	λῦ	σαν	–
GS	λύ	σαντ	ος	λυ	σάσ	ης	λύ	σαντ	ος
DS	λύ	σαντ	ι	λυ	σάσ	ῃ	λύ	σαντ	ι
AS	λύ	σαντ	α	λύ	σασ	αν	λῦ	σαν	–
NP	λύ	σαντ	ες	λύ	σασ	αι	λύ	σαντ	α
GP	λυ	σάντ	ων	λυ	σασ	ῶν	λυ	σάντ	ων
DP	λύ	σα	σι(ν)	λυ	σάσ	αις	λύ	σα	σι(ν)
AP	λύ	σαντ	ας	λυ	σάσ	ας	λύ	σαντ	α

The identification keys here are the σαντ for masculine and neuter forms (aorist form marker and participle marker) and σασ for the feminine (form marker σα takes the place of the ου in ουσ). Just as with the imperfective participle, there are a couple of forms that initially look unusual, and again they are the same ones: nominative singular and dative plural in masculine and neuter. The reasons are the same also—it is that sigma again. It causes the ντ to drop out in the nominative singular and the dative plural masculine. In the neuter the same thing happens in the dative plural, but in the nominative singular the blank/null ending causes only the tau to drop. The feminine forms use just a sigma for the participle marker, which, with the aorist form marker, produces the characteristic σασ.[2]

24.5. Examples of the Aorist Active Participle

John 7:40, οὖν **ἀκούσαντες** τῶν λόγων τούτων ἔλεγον, Οὗτός ἐστιν ἀληθῶς ὁ προφήτης.	Therefore *having heard* these words, they said, "This one truly is the Prophet!"
Eph. 1:15–16, Διὰ τοῦτο κἀγὼ **ἀκούσας** τὴν ἀγάπην τὴν εἰς πάντας τοὺς ἁγίους[a] οὐ παύομαι εὐχαριστῶν ὑπὲρ ὑμῶν.	For this reason I also, *when*[b] *I heard about* [your] love for all God's people, have not ceased giving thanks for you.

[a] Be sure to check a recent lexicon (e.g., *CL* or BDAG) for translation options for ἅγιος when used as an articular plural referring to people.

[b] Or possibly, "because I have heard" (cf. NET, ESV), but even a temporal meaning such as "when" implies a causal relationship in English.

Gen. 12:18, **καλέσας** δὲ Φαραὼ τὸν Ἀβρὰμ εἶπεν, Τί τοῦτο ἐποίησάς μοι, ὅτι οὐκ ἀπήγγειλάς μοι ὅτι γυνή σού ἐστιν;	Pharaoh, *having summoned* Abram, said, "What is this you have done to me, that you did not tell me that she was your wife?"

The square of stops may affect the spelling of any of the aorist participle forms that use σα as a form marker. The same changes that you saw in the indicative mood (see chap. 17) also occur here. In the example following, the lexical form is ἀναβλέπω. The stop is the pi at the end of the stem, which combines with the aorist form marker σα to form ψα: ἀναβλέψας.

Gen. 13:14, Ὁ δὲ θεὸς εἶπεν τῷ Ἀβρὰμ μετὰ τὸ διαχωρισθῆναι τὸν Λὼτ ἀπ' αὐτοῦ, **Ἀναβλέψας** τοῖς ὀφθαλμοῖς σου ἰδὲ ἀπὸ τοῦ τόπου, οὗ νῦν σὺ εἶ, πρὸς βορρᾶν καὶ λίβα καὶ ἀνατολὰς καὶ θάλασσαν.	So God said to Abram after Lot separated from him, "*Looking up* with your eyes, look from the place where you are now toward the north and south and east and the sea."

2. The feminine participle marker listed above as σασ was actually ντ originally. You do not need to know what happened to it. But if you are desperately curious for morphological trivia, see *MBG*, 155n2, §93.1. It is much simpler just to think of σασ as the aorist form marker and participle marker for feminine. If this sounds similar to ουσ in the present participle, you are right.

24.6. Forms of the Aorist Middle Participle

Aorist Middle Participle of λύω

	Masc.			Fem.			Neut.		
NS	λυ	σάμεν	ος	λυ	σαμέν	η	λυ	σάμεν	ον
GS	λυ	σαμέν	ου	λυ	σαμέν	ης	λυ	σαμέν	ου
DS	λυ	σαμέν	ῳ	λυ	σαμέν	ῃ	λυ	σαμέν	ῳ
AS	λυ	σάμεν	ον	λυ	σαμέν	ην	λυ	σάμεν	ον
NP	λυ	σάμεν	οι	λυ	σάμεν	αι	λυ	σάμεν	α
GP	λυ	σαμέν	ων	λυ	σαμέν	ων	λυ	σαμέν	ων
DP	λυ	σαμέν	οις	λυ	σαμέν	αις	λυ	σαμέν	οις
AP	λυ	σαμέν	ους	λυ	σαμέν	ας	λυ	σάμεν	α

The perfective (aorist) middle participle is delightfully regular, just the aorist form marker σα and the participle marker μεν—and it is the same for all genders; only the endings distinguish which is which. This form is only middle; there is a separate form for the aorist passive.

24.7. Examples of the Aorist Middle Participle

Mark 3:23, **προσκαλεσάμενος** αὐτοὺς ἐν παραβολαῖς ἔλεγεν αὐτοῖς.

Having summoned them, he spoke to them in parables.

Mark 3:5, **περιβλεψάμενος** αὐτοὺς μετ᾽ ὀργῆς, συλλυπούμενος ἐπὶ τῇ πωρώσει τῆς καρδίας αὐτῶν λέγει τῷ ἀνθρώπῳ, Ἔκτεινον (stretch out!) τὴν χεῖρα.

After looking around at them in anger, being grieved at the hardness of their hearts, he said to the man, "Stretch out your hand."

Exod. 2:12, **περιβλεψάμενος** δὲ ὧδε καὶ ὧδε οὐχ ὁρᾷ οὐδένα καὶ πατάξας τὸν Αἰγύπτιον ἔκρυψεν αὐτὸν ἐν τῇ ἄμμῳ.

Now *looking around* this way and that, he did not see anyone, so having struck the Egyptian, he hid him in the sand.

24.8. Forms of the Aorist Passive Participle

Aorist Passive Participle of λύω

	Masc.			Fem.			Neut.		
NS	λυ	θεί	ς	λυ	θεῖσ	α	λυ	θέν	–
GS	λυ	θέντ	ος	λυ	θείσ	ης	λυ	θέντ	ος
DS	λυ	θέντ	ι	λυ	θείσ	ῃ	λυ	θέντ	ι
AS	λυ	θέντ	α	λυ	θεῖσ	αν	λυ	θέν	–
NP	λυ	θέντ	ες	λυ	θεῖσ	αι	λυ	θέντ	α
GP	λυ	θέντ	ων	λυ	θεισ	ῶν	λυ	θέντ	ων
DP	λυ	θεῖ	σι(ν)	λυ	θείσ	αις	λυ	θεῖ	σι(ν)
AP	λυ	θέντ	ας	λυ	θείσ	ας	λυ	θέντ	α

The aorist passive participle uses the same form marker as did the aorist passive indicative except that the eta has been shortened to epsilon. Thus the standard combination is θεντ (or θεισ for feminine). Again the nominative singular and dative plural forms have slight differences—but they should be familiar by now. (If you do not remember what happens, reread the explanations in the previous sections.)

24.9. Examples of the Aorist Passive Participle

Matt. 2:12, **χρηματισθέντες** κατ᾽ ὄναρ μὴ ἀνακάμψαι πρὸς Ἡρῴδην, δι᾽ ἄλλης ὁδοῦ ἀνεχώρησαν εἰς τὴν χώραν αὐτῶν.

Having been warned in a dream not to return to Herod, by another way they returned to their country.

Acts 4:23, **Ἀπολυθέντες** δὲ ἦλθον πρὸς τοὺς ἰδίους καὶ ἀπήγγειλαν ὅσα πρὸς αὐτοὺς οἱ ἀρχιερεῖς καὶ οἱ πρεσβύτεροι εἶπαν.

Now *having been released*, they went to their own [people] and reported what the chief priests and the elders had said to them.

Rom. 5:1, **Δικαιωθέντες** οὖν ἐκ πίστεως εἰρήνην ἔχομεν πρὸς τὸν θεὸν διὰ τοῦ κυρίου ἡμῶν Ἰησοῦ Χριστοῦ.

Therefore *having been justified* by faith, we have peace with God through our Lord Jesus Christ.

1 Esd. 9:2, **αὐλισθεὶς** ἐκεῖ ἄρτου οὐκ ἐγεύσατο οὐδὲ ὕδωρ ἔπιεν πενθῶν ὑπὲρ τῶν ἀνομιῶν τῶν μεγάλων τοῦ πλήθους.

Having spent the night there, he did not taste food, nor did he drink water, mourning for the great lawlessness of the people.

24.10. θη-Middle Intransitive Participles

As you learned in chapter 17, some verbal forms that have a θη form marker are not passives but rather θη-middle intransitive forms. This is also common in participles, as the following examples illustrate. Some of the most common verbs used with aorist "passive" participle forms are actually middle voice, not passive.

Mark 8:29, **ἀποκριθεὶς** ὁ Πέτρος λέγει αὐτῷ, Σὺ εἶ ὁ Χριστός.

Answering, Peter said to him, "You are the Messiah."

The participle ἀποκριθείς is the most common aorist passive participle form in the NT, occurring nearly 100 times (though much less frequently in the LXX). It is a liquid form, ἀποκρίνω, the nu dropping out when the form marker is added. It does not mean "being answered" (by someone else) as the category "passive" would imply. When used with a finite verb of speaking, as it is here, it is redundant in English even though considered normal style in Greek.

Matt. 22:15, Τότε **πορευθέντες** οἱ Φαρισαῖοι συμβούλιον ἔλαβον ὅπως αὐτὸν παγιδεύσωσιν (they might entrap) ἐν λόγῳ.

Then *after they had gone out*, the Pharisees took counsel how they might entrap him in a word [i.e., in something he said].

Matt. 2:21, ὁ δὲ **ἐγερθεὶς** παρέλαβεν τὸ παιδίον καὶ τὴν μητέρα αὐτοῦ καὶ εἰσῆλθεν εἰς γῆν Ἰσραήλ.

But he, *having risen*, took the child and his mother and went to the land of Israel.

The participle ἐγερθείς is from ἐγείρω; note that the stem begins with an epsilon—participles do not have augments. Although this appears to be aorist passive in form, it is most likely a θη-middle intransitive form, not passive in meaning. That is, the verse does not say, "have been aroused" (i.e., by the angel), but refers only to the fact that Joseph got up from sleep and obeyed the command he had received.

Gen. 18:9, Εἶπεν δὲ πρὸς αὐτόν, Ποῦ Σάρρα ἡ γυνή σου; ὁ δὲ **ἀποκριθεὶς** εἶπεν, Ἰδοὺ ἐν τῇ σκηνῇ.

Then he said to him, "Where is Sarah your wife?" And *answering* he said, "There in the tent."

Second Aorist Participles

24.11. If the indicative form of a verb uses the second aorist pattern, the perfective participle will also be a second aorist form. This aorist participle acts similar to the indicative in this instance, using an aorist stem[3] and no form marker. The key to identifying this as an aorist rather than a present participle is the stem; otherwise the participle will look identical to a present participle. Here are the formulas for three participle forms, one new form and two that are familiar; compare and contrast them so that you understand how they differ from one another.

Formula for Imperfective (Present) Participles

stem + connecting vowel + participle marker + case endings

Formula for Perfective (Second Aorist) Participles

aorist stem + connecting vowel + participle marker + case endings

Formula for Perfective (First Aorist) Participles

stem + aorist form marker + participle marker + case endings

Compare the following forms of βάλλω to see these differences. Pay particular attention to the stem: the present stem of βάλλω has a double lambda, the aorist stem only a single lambda.

3. The aorist stem will always be spelled differently from the present stem, which appears in the lexical form.

βάλλω	1st sg. pres. act. ind. (lexical form)
ἔβαλλον	1st sg. impf. act. ind.
ἔβαλον	1st sg. ²aor. act. ind.
βάλλοντος	pres. act. ptc. masc. sg. gen.
βαλόντος	²aor. act. ptc. masc. sg. gen.
βληθείς	²aor. pass. ptc. masc. sg. nom.[a]

[a] The aorist passive stem is βλη-. It is technically the same as the other second aorist forms (βαλ-), but there have been some changes (if you are the curious type, see *MBG*, §v-2d1 for the details). It is perhaps easiest to learn to recognize βλη- as another stem for βάλλω. It is used by aorist passive, future passive, and perfect active forms.

Forms of the Second Aorist Active Participle

24.12. Here is what the second aorist form of the participle looks like for ἔρχομαι, one of the most common verbs using this pattern. The aorist stem for this verb, you will remember, is ἐλθ-, though you may remember it best in the form ἦλθον (1st sg. aor. act. ind. ▸ ἔρχομαι). Only indicatives have augments, so instead of the eta, you see the original epsilon in the participle.

Second Aorist Active Participle of ἔρχομαι

	Masc.			Fem.			Neut.		
NS	ἐλθ	ών	–	ἐλθ	οῦσ	α	ἐλθ	όν	–
GS	ἐλθ	όντ	ος	ἐλθ	ούσ	ης	ἐλθ	όντ	ος
DS	ἐλθ	όντ	ι	ἐλθ	ούσ	ῃ	ἐλθ	όντ	ι
AS	ἐλθ	όντ	α	ἐλθ	οῦσ	αν	ἐλθ	όν	–
NP	ἐλθ	όντ	ες	ἐλθ	οῦσ	αι	ἐλθ	όντ	α
GP	ἐλθ	όντ	ων	ἐλθ	ουσ	ῶν	ἐλθ	όντ	ων
DP	ἐλθ	οῦ	σι(ν)	ἐλθ	ούσ	αις	ἐλθ	οῦ	σι(ν)
AP	ἐλθ	όντ	ας	ἐλθ	ούσ	ας	ἐλθ	όντ	α

24.13. Examples of Second Aorist Active Participles

Mark 1:21, καὶ εὐθὺς[a] τοῖς σάββασιν **εἰσελθὼν**[b] εἰς τὴν συναγωγὴν ἐδίδασκεν.

Then on the Sabbath, *having entered* the synagogue, he was teaching.

[a] For καὶ εὐθύς see the note on Mark 1:12 in chap. 4 under "Examples of the Third-Person Pronoun."
[b] εἰσελθών ▸ εἰσέρχομαι

John 19:26, Ἰησοῦς οὖν **ἰδὼν**[a] τὴν μητέρα καὶ τὸν μαθητήν, λέγει τῇ μητρί, Γύναι, ἴδε ὁ υἱός σου.

Therefore Jesus, *having looked at* [his] mother and the disciple [i.e., John], said to [his] mother, "Woman, here is your son."[b]

[a] ἰδών ▸ ὁράω
[b] Traditionally ἴδε has been translated in this verse as "Behold!" (e.g., KJV, NASB, ESV), but see BDAG, 466.3, "to indicate a place or individual, *here is (are)*," followed by NIV, NRSV, NET, HCSB, and CEB.

Mark 6:41, **λαβὼν**[a] τοὺς πέντε ἄρτους καὶ τοὺς δύο ἰχθύας ἀναβλέψας εἰς τὸν οὐρανὸν εὐλόγησεν καὶ κατέκλασεν τοὺς ἄρτους.

Having taken the five loaves and the two fish, [and] having looked up to heaven, he blessed and broke the loaves.

[a] λαβών ▶ λαμβάνω

Gen. 6:2, **ἰδόντες**[a] δὲ οἱ υἱοὶ τοῦ θεοῦ τὰς θυγατέρας τῶν ἀνθρώπων ὅτι καλαί εἰσιν, ἔλαβον ἑαυτοῖς γυναῖκας ἀπὸ πασῶν, ὧν ἐξελέξαντο.

Now the sons of God, *because they saw* the daughters of men, that they were beautiful,[b] took for themselves wives from all whom they chose.

[a] ἰδόντες ▶ ὁράω

[b] In English we would structure this statement differently. We would say, "because they saw that the daughters of men were beautiful." The translation given above is quite formal, following the Greek syntax.

Forms of the Second Aorist Middle Participle

24.14. The most common verb that uses a second aorist pattern in the aorist middle form is γίνομαι, the aorist stem of which is γεν-.

Second Aorist Middle Participle of γίνομαι

	Masc.			Fem.			Neut.		
NS	γεν	όμεν	ος	γεν	ομέν	η	γεν	όμεν	ον
GS	γεν	ομέν	ου	γεν	ομέν	ης	γεν	ομέν	ου
DS	γεν	ομέν	ῳ	γεν	ομέν	ῃ	γεν	ομέν	ῳ
AS	γεν	όμεν	ον	γεν	ομέν	ην	γεν	όμεν	ον
NP	γεν	όμεν	οι	γεν	όμεν	αι	γεν	όμεν	α
GP	γεν	ομέν	ων	γεν	ομέν	ων	γεν	ομέν	ων
DP	γεν	ομέν	οις	γεν	ομέν	αις	γεν	ομέν	οις
AP	γεν	ομέν	ους	γεν	ομέν	ας	γεν	όμεν	α

24.15. Examples of Second Aorist Middle Participles

Mark 8:23, **ἐπιλαβόμενος**[a] τῆς χειρὸς τοῦ τυφλοῦ ἐξήνεγκεν αὐτὸν ἔξω τῆς κώμης.

Having taken the hand of the blind man, he led him outside the village.

[a] ἐπιλαβόμενος ▶ ἐπιλαμβάνω

Gal. 3:13, Χριστὸς ἡμᾶς ἐξηγόρασεν ἐκ τῆς κατάρας τοῦ νόμου **γενόμενος**[a] ὑπὲρ ἡμῶν κατάρα.

Christ has redeemed us from the curse of the law *by becoming* a curse for us.

[a] γενόμενος ▶ γίνομαι

Gen. 38:14, **περιελομένη**[a] τὰ ἱμάτια τῆς χηρεύσεως[b] ἀφ᾽ ἑαυτῆς περιεβάλετο θέριστρον.[c]

Having taken off from herself the garments of widowhood, she dressed in light summer clothes.

[a] περιελομένη ▶ περιαιρέω

[b] χήρευσις, εως, ἡ, "widowhood"

[c] θέριστρον, ου, τό, "light summer garment"

Forms of the Second Aorist Passive Participle

24.16. There are a very few second aorist passive forms in the NT. They are distinct in that they do not have a theta in the aorist passive form marker.[4] (Remember that the theta also dropped out of the form marker in the second aorist passive indicative.) Almost all of these forms occur only once; two occur three or four times. Only στρέφω occurs more frequently than that, with ten NT examples, most of which are στραφείς (²aor. pass. ptc. masc. sg. nom.). This may initially look like a second singular present active indicative form, but the stem tells you something is different.[5]

The oblique forms (genitive, dative, and accusative cases) will have εντ instead of θεντ as the form marker/participle marker combination. In the nominative, however, since the case ending is a sigma, the ντ drops out and the epsilon lengthens to ει, resulting in a form like στραφείς. For completeness, here are the forms of στρέφω.[6]

Aorist Participle of γινώσκω

The participle of γινώσκω has a few apparent irregularities. In the aorist active participle the masculine singular nominative form is γνούς. The aorist stem is γνω-. The ντ participle marker has dropped out due to the sigma that follows (the case ending for nominative singular in third declension). As a result the stem vowel undergoes ablaut to become ου. The same thing happens in the dative plural. You will find a compound form of γινώσκω as a participle in the "Reading Passage" below (see §24.21, Mark 2:8).

Second Aorist Passive Participle of στρέφω

	Masc.			Fem.			Neut.		
NS	στραφ	εί	ς	στραφ	εῖσ	α	στραφ	έν	–
GS	στραφ	έντ	ος	στραφ	είσ	ης	στραφ	έντ	ος
DS	στραφ	έντ	ι	στραφ	είσ	ῃ	στραφ	έντ	ι
AS	στραφ	έντ	α	στραφ	εῖσ	αν	στραφ	έν	–
NP	στραφ	έντ	ες	στραφ	εῖσ	αι	στραφ	έντ	α
GP	στραφ	έντ	ων	στραφ	εισ	ῶν	στραφ	έντ	ων
DP	στραφ	εῖ	σι(ν)	στραφ	είσ	αις	στραφ	εῖ	σι(ν)
AP	στραφ	έντ	ας	στραφ	είσ	ας	στραφ	έντ	α

4. There are only sixteen such forms in the NT: ἀποσταλέντι, ἁρπαγέντα, διασπαρέντες, διαταγείς, ἐμπλακέντες, ἐπιστραφείς, καταλλαγέντες, σπαρείς, σπαρέντες, στραφείς, στραφεῖσα, στραφέντες, συμφυεῖσαι, συνταφέντες, ὑποταγέντων, and φυέν.

5. The 2nd sg. pres. act. ind. form of στρέφω would be στρέφεις—the stem is unchanged from the lexical form.

6. Less than a half dozen of these forms occur in Koine Greek texts related to the NT, but seeing the overall pattern will help you understand the forms better.

24.17. Examples of Second Aorist Passive Participles

Rom. 5:10, εἰ γὰρ ἐχθροὶ ὄντες κατηλλάγημεν τῷ θεῷ διὰ τοῦ θανάτου τοῦ υἱοῦ αὐτοῦ, πολλῷ μᾶλλον **καταλλαγέντες**[a] σωθησόμεθα ἐν τῇ ζωῇ αὐτοῦ.

For if while we were enemies we were reconciled to God through the death of his Son, much more rather *having been reconciled*, we will be saved by his life.

[a] καταλλαγέντες ▸ καταλλάσσω. The verb καταλλάσσω is a compound form: κατά + ἀλλάσσω. The root (as well as the aorist stem) is *αλλαγ; the present stem becomes αλλασσ- (γ + ι̯ = σσ). In the second aorist, the theta drops out, leaving only ντ as the form marker. Although καταλλάσσω does not occur frequently, it is an important word in NT theology. All the forms of καταλλάσσω that occur in the NT and LXX are listed in the morphology catalog in app. B.

Luke 7:44, **στραφεὶς**[a] πρὸς τὴν γυναῖκα τῷ Σίμωνι ἔφη, Βλέπεις ταύτην τὴν γυναῖκα;

Having turned to the woman, he said to Simon, "Do you see this woman?"

[a] στραφείς ▸ στρέφω is a θη-middle intransitive form (see the discussion earlier in this chapter). The context here makes it obvious that Jesus is not being turned by someone else.

T. Ab. 12.3, **στραφεὶς** λέγει Ἀβραὰμ πρὸς Μιχαήλ, Θεωρεῖς τὴν ἁμαρτίαν ταύτην; ἀλλά, κύριε,[a] πέμψον (send!) πῦρ ἐξ οὐρανοῦ, ἵνα καταφάγῃ (it may destroy) αὐτούς.

Having turned, Abraham said to Michael, "Do you see this sin? But, sir, send fire from heaven in order that it may destroy them."

[a] In the context, it is not certain whether Abraham is addressing Michael (in which case κύριε is translated as "sir" or "lord") or whether his request is addressed directly to God, which would suggest the translation "Lord." The first seems more likely.

Now You Try It

24.18. The following texts have examples of all the various aorist participles discussed in this chapter.

Mark 1:43, **ἐμβριμησάμενος** αὐτῷ εὐθὺς ἐξέβαλεν αὐτόν.

Rom. 15:28, τοῦτο οὖν **ἐπιτελέσας** καὶ **σφραγισάμενος** αὐτοῖς τὸν καρπὸν τοῦτον, ἀπελεύσομαι δι' ὑμῶν εἰς Σπανίαν.

Phil. 2:6–8, ὃς ἐν μορφῇ θεοῦ ὑπάρχων οὐχ ἁρπαγμὸν ἡγήσατο τὸ εἶναι ἴσα θεῷ, ἀλλὰ ἑαυτὸν ἐκένωσεν μορφὴν δούλου **λαβών**, ἐν ὁμοιώματι ἀνθρώπων **γενόμενος**· καὶ σχήματι **εὑρεθεὶς** ὡς ἄνθρωπος ἐταπείνωσεν ἑαυτὸν **γενόμενος** ὑπήκοος μέχρι θανάτου, θανάτου δὲ σταυροῦ.

Col. 2:15, **ἀπεκδυσάμενος** τὰς ἀρχὰς καὶ τὰς ἐξουσίας ἐδειγμάτισεν ἐν παρρησίᾳ, **θριαμβεύσας** αὐτοὺς ἐν αὐτῷ.

1 Clem. 5.4, Πέτρον, ὃς διὰ ζῆλον ἄδικον οὐχ ἕνα οὐδὲ δύο ἀλλὰ πλείονας ὑπήνεγκεν πόνους, καὶ οὕτω **μαρτυρήσας** ἐπορεύθη εἰς τὸν τόπον τῆς δόξης.

2 Clem. 8.4, ὥστε, ἀδελφοί, **ποιήσαντες** τὸ θέλημα τοῦ πατρὸς καὶ τὴν σάρκα ἁγνὴν **τηρήσαντες** καὶ τὰς ἐντολὰς τοῦ κυρίου **φυλάξαντες** ληψόμεθα ζωὴν αἰώνιον.

Ign. *Magn.* 1.3, ἐν ᾧ ὑπομένοντες τὴν πᾶσαν ἐπήρειαν τοῦ ἄρχοντος τοῦ αἰῶνος τούτου καὶ **διαφυγόντες** θεοῦ τευξόμεθα.

Challenge Passage

24.19. There are nine participles in the following passage, both aorist and present; active, middle, and passive. They are not marked. It is a good test of how well you understand the participles we have studied thus far. One of the nine is a use of the participle you have not learned yet, but you should still be able to parse it correctly. An answer key is given at the end of the chapter, but do your best before looking at it.

1 Clem. 5.6–7, ἑπτάκις δεσμὰ φορέσας, φυγαδευθείς, λιθασθείς, κῆρυξ γενόμενος ἔν τε τῇ ἀνατολῇ καὶ ἐν τῇ δύσει, τὸ γενναῖον τῆς πίστεως αὐτοῦ κλέος ἔλαβεν, δικαιοσύνην διδάξας ὅλον τὸν κόσμον καὶ ἐπὶ τὸ τέρμα[a] τῆς δύσεως ἐλθών· καὶ μαρτυρήσας ἐπὶ τῶν ἡγουμένων, οὕτως ἀπηλλάγη τοῦ κόσμου καὶ εἰς τὸν ἅγιον τόπον ἐπορεύθη, ὑπομονῆς γενόμενος μέγιστος ὑπογραμμός.

[a] τέρμα, ατος, τό, "end, limit, boundary"

— — — — — — — — — — — — — —

Advanced Information for Reference: Additional Examples of Adverbial Participles[7]

24.20. The following section illustrates the range of contexts in which adverbial participles are used beyond the four most common categories listed in the last chapter (which are included again here so you have a complete list). Remember that these are not different *kinds* of participles but participles used in various *contexts*.

1. Participles Used in Statements of Manner

A participle of manner describes the *emotion* or *attitude* in which the main verb has been done (contrast the participle of means). These can often be translated with a simple English participle.

Matt. 19:22, ἀπῆλθεν **λυπούμενος**.	He went away *grieving*.
Acts 5:41, ἐπορεύοντο **χαίροντες**.	They went on their way *rejoicing*.

2. Participles Used in Statements of Means

This participle describes the *method* by which the action of the main verb has been accomplished (contrast the participle of manner).

Acts 9:22, Σαῦλος συνέχυννεν τοὺς Ἰουδαίους **συμβιβάζων** ὅτι οὗτός ἐστιν ὁ Χριστός.	Saul confounded the Jews *by proving* that this One [i.e., Jesus] was the Messiah.
Matt. 27:4, Ἥμαρτον **παραδοὺς**[a] αἷμα ἀθῷον.	I have sinned *by betraying* innocent blood.

[a] The form παραδούς is a nominative; this is the aor. act. ptc. masc. sg. nom. form of a μι verb, which you have not yet learned. It may look like an accusative ending, but the stem is δο-, and the stem vowel omicron lengthens to ου when the ντ participle marker drops out due to the addition of the case ending sigma.

3. Participles Used in Causal Statements

A causal participle describes the *cause* or *reason* for the action of the main verb.

John 4:6, ὁ Ἰησοῦς **κεκοπιακὼς**[a] ἐκ τῆς ὁδοιπορίας ἐκαθέζετο οὕτως ἐπὶ τῇ πηγῇ.	Jesus, *because he was weary* from the journey, sat thus on the well.

[a] κεκοπιακώς, pf. act. ptc. masc. sg. nom. ▶ κοπιάω. You will learn this form in chap. 26.

7. See further Wallace, *Greek Grammar*, 622–50. See also the participle chart in app. C.

Matt. 1:19, Ἰωσὴφ ὁ ἀνὴρ αὐτῆς, δίκαιος **ὢν** καὶ μὴ **θέλων** αὐτὴν δειγματίσαι, ἐβουλήθη λάθρᾳ ἀπολῦσαι αὐτήν.

Joseph her husband, *because he was* righteous and *because he was* not *willing* to shame her, decided to divorce her secretly.

4. Participles Used in Conditional Statements

Conditional participles describe the *conditions* on which the action of the main verb is dependent.

Gal. 6:9, καιρῷ γὰρ ἰδίῳ θερίσομεν μὴ **ἐκλυόμενοι.**

For in due time we will reap *if we do* not *lose heart*.

1 Tim. 4:4, οὐδὲν ἀπόβλητον μετὰ εὐχαριστίας **λαμβανόμενον.**

Nothing is to be rejected *if it is received* with thanksgiving.

5. Participles Used in Concessive Statements

Concessive participles describe an apparent anomaly: the main verb has "happened" *even though* the situation in the participle was such as it was.

John 9:25, ἓν οἶδα ὅτι τυφλὸς **ὢν** ἄρτι βλέπω.

I know one thing: *although I was* blind, now I see.

The participle could be represented with an English participle ("being blind"), but the concessive translation makes the meaning much clearer; ὅτι is represented as a colon.

Rom. 1:21, **γνόντες** τὸν θεὸν οὐχ ὡς θεὸν ἐδόξασαν.

Although they knew God, they did not glorify him as God.

1 Pet. 1:8, ὃν οὐκ **ἰδόντες** ἀγαπᾶτε.

Whom, not *seeing*, you love (or, Whom, *although you do* not *see him*, you love).

6. Participles Used in Purpose Statements

A purpose participle describes *why* the action of the main verb has been done: what was the *intention* of the actor? These are often best represented as an infinitive in English.

John 6:6, τοῦτο ἔλεγεν **πειράζων** αὐτόν· αὐτὸς γὰρ ᾔδει (he knew) τί ἔμελλεν ποιεῖν.

He said this *to test* him, for he knew what he would do.

Luke 13:7, Ἰδοὺ τρία ἔτη ἀφ' οὗ ἔρχομαι **ζητῶν** καρπὸν ἐν τῇ συκῇ ταύτῃ καὶ οὐχ εὑρίσκω.

Look, for three years I have come *seeking* (or, *to seek*) fruit from this fig tree, and I have not found [any].

7. Participles Used in Result Statements

A participle of result describes the *actual outcome* of the action of the main verb. "The participle of result is not necessarily opposed to the participle of purpose. Indeed, many result participles describe the result of an action *that was also intended*. The difference between the two, therefore, is primarily one of emphasis."[8]

Mark 9:7, ἐγένετο νεφέλη **ἐπισκιάζουσα** αὐτοῖς.	A cloud came *covering* them [i.e., with the result that it covered them].
Luke 4:15, αὐτὸς ἐδίδασκεν ἐν ταῖς συναγωγαῖς αὐτῶν **δοξαζόμενος** ὑπὸ πάντων.	He was teaching in their synagogues, *being glorified* by everyone [i.e., with the result that he was glorified by everyone].

8. Participles Used in Statements of Attendant Circumstance

Attendant circumstance participles describe an action or situation that is parallel with, but subordinate to, the main verb. Most attendant circumstance participles have the following characteristics. The tense-form of the (1) participle and the (2) main verb are usually aorist, and (3) the mood of the main verb is imperative or indicative. (4) The participle usually precedes the main verb both in word order and time of event. (5) They are most frequent in narrative literature, infrequent elsewhere.[9]

Mark 6:17, Αὐτὸς γὰρ ὁ Ἡρῴδης **ἀποστείλας** ἐκράτησεν τὸν Ἰωάννην καὶ ἔδησεν αὐτὸν ἐν φυλακῇ.	For Herod himself *sent* and seized John and bound him in prison.
Mark 9:26, **κράξας** καὶ πολλὰ **σπαράξας** ἐξῆλθεν.	[The demon] *cried out* and *convulsed* [the boy] severely and came out.
Matt. 2:13, **Ἐγερθεὶς** παράλαβε (take!) τὸ παιδίον καὶ τὴν μητέρα αὐτοῦ καὶ φεῦγε (flee!) εἰς Αἴγυπτον.	*Get up*, and take the child and his mother and flee to Egypt.

In this example the action described by the participle is parallel to the main verb (the imperative παράλαβε, "take!"). An attendant circumstance participle takes on the same mood as the finite verb with which it is parallel.

9. Participles Used in Temporal Statements

Just about any adverbial participle can be translated so as to make sense as a temporal participle (since any two related events must of necessity have some

8. Wallace, *Greek Grammar*, 637, see also 638.
9. Wallace, *Greek Grammar*, 642.

temporal relationship), but this is a last-resort classification if the context does not substantiate a more specific description. Although the temporal relationship is not relevant in some statements, in some others the participle does serve primarily to describe the temporal relationship between various events.

John 16:8, **ἐλθὼν** ἐκεῖνος ἐλέγξει τὸν κόσμον περὶ ἁμαρτίας καὶ περὶ δικαιοσύνης καὶ περὶ κρίσεως.

Coming (or, *when he comes/has come*), he will convict the world concerning sin, righteousness, and judgment.

Mark 9:15, πᾶς ὁ ὄχλος **ἰδόντες** αὐτὸν ἐξεθαμβήθησαν.

When all the crowd *saw* him they were amazed.

This could be translated as an attendant circumstance participle ("all the crowd saw him *and* they were amazed"), but the writer's point in this context does not seem to be on two separate events; rather, the writer is telling us *when* the action of the main verb has occurred: "when [they] saw."

Rev. 19:20, τὸ θηρίον καὶ ὁ ψευδοπροφήτης . . . · **ζῶντες** ἐβλήθησαν οἱ δύο εἰς τὴν λίμνην τοῦ πυρός.

The beast and the false prophet . . . ; *while they were [still] living* the two were cast into the lake of fire.

A Disputed Text

Acts 23:27, ἐξειλάμην **μαθὼν** ὅτι Ῥωμαῖός ἐστιν.

I rescued [him], *learning* [subsequently] that he was a Roman [citizen].

This example raises exegetical questions. Some commentators accuse the Roman tribune of twisting the truth, assuming that we are to understand him to say: "Having learned that he was a Roman, I rescued him." To arrive at this conclusion, the commentator assumes that an aorist participle (in this case, μαθών) must always refer to *antecedent* action in relation to the main verb, but perhaps the tribune reports to his superior exactly what happened as the previous account clearly records: Paul is rescued, and then the tribune learns that Paul is a Roman. Either option is grammatically possible.

— — — — — — — — — — — — — —

Reading Passage: Mark 2:1–12

24.21. Before you begin reading this passage, skim through the text and identify all the participles. You should find eleven: five aorist and six present. The answers are in the note, but do not look until you have worked through the passage for yourself.[10]

10. Aorist participles: εἰσελθών, ἐξορύξαντες, ἰδών, ἐπιγνούς, ἄρας; and present: φέροντες, αἰρόμενον, δυνάμενοι, καθήμενοι, διαλογιζόμενοι, λέγοντας.

Jesus Forgives a Paralytic

1Καὶ εἰσελθὼν πάλιν εἰς Καφαρναοὺμ δι᾽ ἡμερῶν ἠκούσθη ὅτι ἐν οἴκῳ ἐστίν. 2καὶ
συνήχθησαν πολλοὶ ὥστε μηκέτι χωρεῖν μηδὲ τὰ πρὸς τὴν θύραν,[a] καὶ ἐλάλει
αὐτοῖς τὸν λόγον. 3καὶ ἔρχονται φέροντες πρὸς αὐτὸν παραλυτικὸν αἰρόμενον
ὑπὸ τεσσάρων. 4καὶ μὴ δυνάμενοι προσενέγκαι αὐτῷ διὰ τὸν ὄχλον ἀπεστέγασαν
τὴν στέγην ὅπου ἦν, καὶ ἐξορύξαντες χαλῶσι τὸν κράβαττον ὅπου ὁ παραλυτικὸς κατέκειτο. 5καὶ ἰδὼν ὁ Ἰησοῦς τὴν πίστιν αὐτῶν λέγει τῷ παραλυτικῷ,
Τέκνον, ἀφίενταί (they are forgiven) σου αἱ ἁμαρτίαι. 6ἦσαν δέ τινες τῶν γραμματέων ἐκεῖ καθήμενοι καὶ διαλογιζόμενοι ἐν ταῖς καρδίαις αὐτῶν, 7Τί οὗτος
οὕτως λαλεῖ; βλασφημεῖ· τίς δύναται ἀφιέναι (to forgive) ἁμαρτίας εἰ μὴ εἷς ὁ
θεός; 8καὶ εὐθὺς ἐπιγνοὺς ὁ Ἰησοῦς τῷ πνεύματι αὐτοῦ ὅτι οὕτως διαλογίζον-
ται ἐν ἑαυτοῖς λέγει αὐτοῖς, Τί ταῦτα διαλογίζεσθε ἐν ταῖς καρδίαις ὑμῶν; 9τί
ἐστιν εὐκοπώτερον, εἰπεῖν τῷ παραλυτικῷ, Ἀφίενταί (they are forgiven) σου
αἱ ἁμαρτίαι, ἢ εἰπεῖν, Ἔγειρε (get up!) καὶ ἆρον (pick up!) τὸν κράβαττόν σου
καὶ περιπάτει (walk!); 10ἵνα δὲ εἰδῆτε (you may know) ὅτι ἐξουσίαν ἔχει ὁ υἱὸς
τοῦ ἀνθρώπου ἀφιέναι (to forgive) ἁμαρτίας ἐπὶ τῆς γῆς—λέγει τῷ παραλυτικῷ, 11Σοὶ λέγω, ἔγειρε (get up!) ἆρον (pick up!) τὸν κράβαττόν σου καὶ ὕπαγε
(go!) εἰς τὸν οἶκόν σου. 12καὶ ἠγέρθη καὶ εὐθὺς ἄρας τὸν κράβαττον ἐξῆλθεν
ἔμπροσθεν πάντων, ὥστε ἐξίστασθαι πάντας καὶ δοξάζειν τὸν θεὸν λέγοντας[b]
ὅτι Οὕτως οὐδέποτε εἴδομεν.

[a] The expression τὰ πρὸς τὴν θύραν is idiomatic. The article is a nominalizer that changes the function of the prepositional phrase to a substantive. Formally it reads, "the things/places by the door" (i.e., the space in front of the door). Many English translations say "outside the door" or something similar.

[b] λέγοντας is in the accusative case (rather than nominative, as you have seen elsewhere in this chapter) because it modifies the *infinitive*, δοξάζειν. You will remember that the subject of an infinitive is always in the accusative case, so it should make sense that an adverbial participle modifying an infinitive would also be accusative.

24.22. Vocabulary for Chapter 24

Part of Speech	Definition	Possible Glosses	Frequency	
Word			NT	LXX
Adjective				
πρεσβύτερος, α, ον	Older in age; usually substantival: older person (relatively); an old person (absolutely); a recognized leader in either Jewish or Christian contexts; used temporally of one's progenitors, either individually or corporately	older, elder; ancestors	66	206
Nouns				
Ἀβραάμ, ὁ	An indeclinable personal name, in the LXX and NT the father of the Jewish nation through Isaac (and other people groups through Ishmael), formerly named Ἀβράμ	Abraham	73	210

Part of Speech	Definition	Possible Glosses	Frequency	
Word			NT	LXX
ἱερόν, οῦ, τό	A building dedicated to the service and worship of a god or gods, in the LXX and NT usually of the temple in Jerusalem, including the entire complex with its various courts	temple	71	116
ναός, οῦ, ὁ	A building dedicated to the service and worship of a god or gods, in the LXX and NT usually of the temple proper in Jerusalem composed of the Holy Place and the Most Holy Place, located at the center of the larger temple complex (ἱερόν), though sometimes referring to the entire complex	temple	45	118
πλοῖον, ου, τό	A vessel for traveling on water, ranging in size from a small fishing boat to a large seagoing ship	boat, ship	68	41
σάββατον, ου, τό	The seventh day of the week in Israel's calendar ("Sabbath"); the period of seven days divided by the Sabbath (usually pl.) ("week")	Sabbath; week	68	130
ἐντολή, ῆς, ἡ	An authoritative directive for action; the Mosaic covenant as a whole, the law	command, commandment, law; the law (of Moses)	67	240
καρπός, οῦ, ὁ	The product of a plant (whether tree, vine, bush, vegetable, etc.), agricultural produce; the offspring of a person; metaphorically of the result or outcome of an action or attitude	fruit, produce (subst.), crop, harvest; offspring; result, product (metaphorical)	66	125
δαιμόνιον, ου, τό	An evil, incorporeal, supernatural being often identified as a fallen/sinful angel	demon	63	17
Δαυίδ, ὁ	An indeclinable personal name, in the LXX and NT refers to Israel's great king	David	59	1,090
διδάσκαλος, ου, ὁ	A person who provides instruction by giving information or by showing or explaining how to do something	teacher, instructor, tutor	59	2
λίθος, ου, ὁ	A piece of rock, whether naturally formed or in a fabricated shape; a precious stone, jewel	stone	59	306
Particles				
εἴτε	A function word indicating a direct or indirect question suggesting alternatives, usually paired (εἴτε . . . εἴτε) [crasis form: εἰ + τέ]	if, whether (if x or if y; whether x or y)	65	9
μηδέ, μήτε	A negative particle indicating disjunction as part of a series	and not, but not, nor, not even, don't even	56	139
Preposition				
πρό	A preposition used with the genitive case that indicates either a spatial position in front of something or a temporal location earlier than another point	(prep. + gen.) before, in front of; earlier than, before	47	251

24.23. Challenge Passage Answer Key

1 Clem. 5.6–7, ἑπτάκις δεσμὰ **φορέσας**, **φυγαδευθείς**, **λιθασθείς**, κῆρυξ **γενόμενος** ἔν τε τῇ ἀνατολῇ καὶ ἐν τῇ δύσει, τὸ γενναῖον τῆς πίστεως αὐτοῦ κλέος ἔλαβεν, δικαιοσύνην **διδάξας** ὅλον τὸν κόσμον καὶ ἐπὶ τὸ τέρμα[a] τῆς δύσεως **ἐλθών**· καὶ **μαρτυρήσας** ἐπὶ τῶν **ἡγουμένων**,[b] οὕτως ἀπηλλάγη τοῦ κόσμου καὶ εἰς τὸν ἅγιον τόπον ἐπορεύθη, ὑπομονῆς **γενόμενος** μέγιστος ὑπογραμμός.

Seven times *having worn* chains, *having been driven into exile*, *having been stoned*, *having been* a preacher both in the east and the west, he received genuine fame for his faith, *having taught* righteousness in all the world and *having come* to the boundary of the west. And *having testified* before *rulers* he thus departed from the world and went to the holy place, *having become* a great example of patience.

[a] τέρμα, ατος, τό, "end, limit, boundary" (The expression ἐπὶ τὸ τέρμα τῆς δύσεως ἐλθών has significance for Pauline chronology.)

[b] τῶν ἡγουμένων: you should recognize this as a participle, but it is a use that you will not learn until chap. 25. Here the participle acts like a noun instead of an adverb: "the ones who rule, rulers."

Participle parsings:

φορέσας, AAPMSN ▸ φορέω
φυγαδευθείς, APPMSN ▸ φυγαδεύω
λιθασθείς, APPMSN ▸ λιθάζω
γενόμενος, [2]AMPMSN ▸ γίνομαι
διδάξας, AAPMSN ▸ διδάσκω
ἐλθών, [2]AAPMSN ▸ ἔρχομαι
μαρτυρήσας, AAPMSN ▸ μαρτυρέω
ἡγουμένων, PMPMPG ▸ ἡγέομαι
γενόμενος, [2]AMPMSN ▸ γίνομαι

24.24. Key Things to Know for Chapter 24

Know the formulas for perfective participles.

Know the various formulas for all participles.

How does the form of a second aorist participle (active and middle) differ from a first aorist?

What is unique about the form marker for a second aorist passive participle?

If your teacher has covered the material in §24.20, then you should also know the additional uses of the adverbial participle; review the participle chart in appendix C.

25

NON-FINITE VERBS: PART 4

Adjectival Participles

25.1. There are no new forms to learn in this chapter. Instead we will study a new use of the participle forms that you have just learned. The two previous chapters introduced you to adverbial participles. This chapter shows you how the same forms can be used adjectivally.

Adjectival Participle Basics

25.2. This is a good news section: there are no new forms to learn. Even better news is that there is not any bad news to offset the good news. Adjectival participles are just a *different use* of the *same forms*. Remember the difference between *form* and *function*. A language can use the same form for different functions; the same form can communicate different things in different contexts. Just as the simple word καί normally functions as a coordinating conjunction, the exact same form can also function as an adverb in a different context.[1]

Participles, as you learned in chapter 23, are part verb and part adjective. *Adverbial* participles act more like *verbs*, but *adjectival* participles act more like *adjectives.* A participle can do anything an adjective can. Just as an adjective can modify a noun (the *red* barn) or substitute for a noun (I saw *red*), so can Greek participles. English grammar handles this situation differently. The adjectival use is classed as a participle (the *weeping* student), but English defines another part of speech when a verbal form functions substantivally: the gerund (the *weeping* stopped). Greek does not have gerunds; an infinitive is more commonly used for that purpose.

1. You will remember that to function as a conjunction, καί must have two equal grammatical units on either side of it (i.e., it can connect two nouns, two verbs, two phrases, two clauses, etc.). When this situation is not present, καί is most likely an adverb and is often equivalent to "even" or "also" in English.

All the participles that we have studied in the last two chapters have been adverbial participles and have therefore always modified verbs. In this section, we meet adjectival participles for the first time. There are no new forms involved; we are simply using the same imperfective and perfective participles we already know, but in a different way.

Adjectival Participle Functions

25.3. How can you tell if a participle is functioning adjectivally or adverbially? Here are the key principles to remember:

A participle with the article ("articular") must be an adjectival participle; it cannot be an adverbial participle.

A participle without an article ("anarthrous") is usually an adverbial participle, but it may be adjectival in some contexts.

Any participle in one of the oblique cases (genitive, dative, and accusative) is almost certainly adjectival. This is because an adverbial participle assumes the same subject as the main verb and so must be nominative to agree with the subject of that verb.[2]

A nominative participle, however, may be adverbial or adjectival. Nominative-case participles may modify the verb or another word in nominative case, or they may take the place of a nominative-case noun either as a subject or as a predicate nominative.

Compare the functions of the two participles in the following examples, and note how their case is determined. This is visualized in the grammatical diagrams that accompany each example.

Adverbial Participle: Nominative Case

Mark 1:14, ἦλθεν ὁ Ἰησοῦς εἰς τὴν Γαλιλαίαν **κηρύσσων** τὸ εὐαγγέλιον τοῦ θεοῦ.

Jesus came into Galilee *preaching* the good news from God.

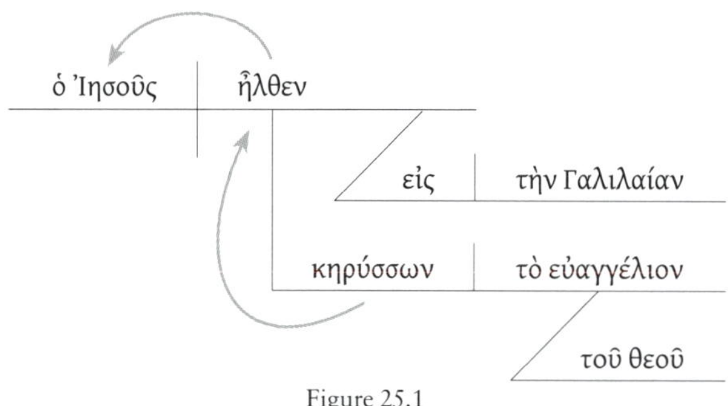

Figure 25.1

2. There are some exceptions to this rule, but it holds in the vast majority of instances. Not all grammarians are willing to state the principle as bluntly as it is above, but all would agree that it is certainly a general principle. Most such exceptions are a recognized construction (the genitive absolute) that you will meet later.

Adjectival Participle: Genitive Case

Matt. 16:16, Σὺ εἶ ὁ Χριστὸς ὁ υἱὸς τοῦ θεοῦ **τοῦ ζῶντος**. — You are the Messiah, the Son of the *living* God.

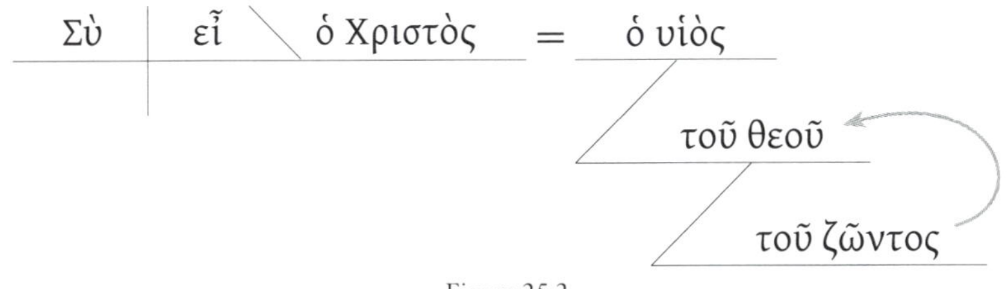

Figure 25.2

Adjectival Participle Grammar

25.4. In Greek, the usual way to indicate that a participle is functioning adjectivally is to use the article. We will explore this use with the verb λέγω, "I say," a finite verb with a built-in, back-pocket subject. The present active participle is λέγων, "saying," and the second aorist participle is εἰπών. Remember that adjectives can function either to modify a noun (attributive) or to take the place of a noun (substantival). When used with an adjectival participle, the article can often be represented as a relative pronoun in English (the "who" in the examples below).

Here is an example of an *adjectival attributive* use of the participle:

2 Cor. 4:6, ὅτι ὁ θεὸς **ὁ εἰπών**, Ἐκ σκότους φῶς λάμψει — For God, *who said*, "Let light shine out of darkness"[a]

[a] The finite verb in this example, λάμψει (▸ λάμπω), is a future tense-form used as an imperative.

Notice that the participle (εἰπών) agrees with the noun it modifies (ὁ θεός) in gender, number, and case. Attributive participles can be used as a modifier in either first or second attributive position; that is, either (1) article ▸ modifier ▸ noun, or (2) article ▸ noun ▸ article ▸ modifier. The example just above shows second attributive position, but the subject phrase could also have been written as ὁ εἰπὼν θεός.

25.5. If there is no noun with which an articular participle agrees in gender, number, and case, then it is *substantival* and is taking the place of a noun. For example, ὁ λέγων means "the one who is saying"; the participle functions just like a substantival adjective. Here is an example of that phrase in a sentence:

1 John 2:4, **ὁ λέγων** ὅτι Ἔγνωκα αὐτὸν **καὶ** τὰς ἐντολὰς αὐτοῦ μὴ **τηρῶν**, ψεύστης ἐστίν. — *The one who says*, "I know him," *and does* not *keep* his commands, is a liar.

The second participle in this verse functions the same way and is governed by the same article, connected by καί: "the one who says and keeps."

Matt. 7:21, Οὐ πᾶς **ὁ λέγων** μοι, Κύριε κύριε, εἰσελεύσεται εἰς τὴν βασιλείαν τῶν οὐρανῶν.

Not everyone *who says* to me, "Lord, Lord," will enter into the kingdom of heaven.

In this example ὁ λέγων is modified by the adjective πᾶς, so "the one who says" becomes "everyone who says."

A substantival participle will be in whatever gender, number, and case is appropriate to its function in the sentence. If it functions as the subject, it will be in nominative case; if it functions as the object, it will be accusative. Substantival participles will usually follow natural gender; for example, if the reference is to a man (or is generic), the participle will be masculine. A substantival participle can function anyplace in a sentence that a noun can function.

If there is an oblique-case participle that agrees in gender, number, and case with a noun in the same clause, it is almost always an attributive participle.

An adjectival participle need not have an article. Without an article a participle can function as either an attributive or a substantival adjectival participle. Remember: *with* an article, it must be adjectival; *without* an article, it *may* be adjectival (but is more often adverbial).

Examples of Adjectival Participles

Simple Examples from the New Testament

25.6. The following examples show both of the attributive positions and a substantival participle; there is one of each of the oblique cases.

Matt. 16:16, Σίμων Πέτρος εἶπεν, Σὺ εἶ ὁ Χριστὸς ὁ υἱὸς τοῦ θεοῦ **τοῦ ζῶντος**. (second attributive)

Simon Peter said, "You are the Messiah, the Son of the *living* God."

Acts 16:13, καθίσαντες ἐλαλοῦμεν ταῖς **συνελθούσαις**[a] γυναιξίν.[b] (first attributive)

Sitting down, we spoke to the women *who had gathered.*

[a] συνελθούσαις, ²aor. act. ptc. ▶ συνέρχομαι, "I gather together"
[b] γυναιξίν, fem. pl. dat. ▶ γυνή, αικός, ἡ, "woman"

Rev. 20:11, εἶδον θρόνον μέγαν λευκὸν καὶ **τὸν καθήμενον** ἐπ᾽ αὐτόν. (substantival)

I saw a large white throne and *the one who was seated* on it.

Mark 5:31, ἔλεγον αὐτῷ οἱ μαθηταὶ αὐτοῦ, Βλέπεις τὸν ὄχλον **συνθλίβοντά** σε καὶ λέγεις, Τίς μου ἥψατο; (attributive anarthrous)

His disciples said to him, "You see the crowd *which is pressing* you, and you ask, 'Who touched me?!'"

Mark 1:3, φωνὴ **βοῶντος** ἐν τῇ ἐρήμῳ, Ἑτοιμάσατε (Prepare!) τὴν ὁδὸν κυρίου. (substantival anarthrous)

A voice *of one who is calling* in the desert, "Prepare the way of the Lord."

Since the participle βοῶντος is genitive, it must be adjectival, but since it does *not* agree with the noun φωνή, it cannot be attributive. It must therefore be substantival.

Additional Examples from the New Testament

25.7. The following examples, drawn mostly from the early chapters of Mark's Gospel, include a broader range of forms and cover the full range of uses. The last few examples mix in some adverbial forms to give you some practice in distinguishing the two types of participles.

Mark 1:32, ἔφερον πρὸς αὐτὸν πάντας **τοὺς** κακῶς **ἔχοντας** καὶ **τοὺς δαιμονιζομένους**.

Mark 2:14, εἶδεν Λευὶν τὸν τοῦ Ἁλφαίου **καθήμενον** ἐπὶ τὸ τελώνιον.

Be careful here; the article τόν does *not* govern the participle, even though it agrees with it in gender, number, and case. Rather, τόν functions as a nominalizer, turning the following genitive phrase into an accusative-case noun, which functions in apposition to the direct object (Λευίν) of εἶδεν. The appositional phrase, τὸν τοῦ Ἁλφαίου, tells us who Levi is: the son of Alphaeus.

Mark 5:15, ἔρχονται πρὸς τὸν Ἰησοῦν καὶ θεωροῦσιν **τὸν δαιμονιζόμενον καθήμενον ἱματισμένον**[a] καὶ **σωφρονοῦντα**, καὶ ἐφοβήθησαν.

[a] ἱματισμένον, pf. mid. ptc. masc. sg. acc. ▶ ἱματίζω, "I clothe"

Mark 1:10, καὶ εὐθὺς[a] **ἀναβαίνων** ἐκ τοῦ ὕδατος εἶδεν **σχιζομένους** τοὺς οὐρανοὺς καὶ τὸ πνεῦμα ὡς περιστερὰν **καταβαῖνον** εἰς αὐτόν.

[a] For καὶ εὐθύς see the note on Mark 1:12 in chap. 4 under "Examples of the Third-Person Pronoun."

Mark 1:19, προβὰς[a] ὀλίγον εἶδεν Ἰάκωβον τὸν τοῦ Ζεβεδαίου καὶ Ἰωάννην τὸν ἀδελφὸν αὐτοῦ καὶ αὐτοὺς ἐν τῷ πλοίῳ **καταρτίζοντας** τὰ δίκτυα.

[a] This form is ²aor. act. ptc. masc. sg. nom. ▶ προβαίνω, "I go ahead," though it does not follow the usual pattern. Verbs formed from βαίνω use the μι verb formation for the second aorist instead of the usual ω verb forms (Smyth, *Greek Grammar*, §687). You will learn μι verb participles in chaps. 32–33. For now, just accept the participle and focus on understanding how the participle functions in this statement.

Mark 2:3, ἔρχονται **φέροντες** πρὸς αὐτὸν παραλυτικὸν **αἰρόμενον** ὑπὸ τεσσάρων.

Matt. 13:47, Πάλιν ὁμοία ἐστὶν ἡ βασιλεία τῶν οὐρανῶν σαγήνῃ **βληθείσῃ**[a] εἰς τὴν θάλασσαν.

[a] βληθείσῃ ▶ βάλλω

25.8. *Examples from the Septuagint*

Judg. 1:9, μετὰ ταῦτα κατέβησαν οἱ υἱοὶ Ἰούδα πολεμῆσαι ἐν τῷ Χαναναίῳ τῷ **κατοικοῦντι** τὴν ὀρεινὴν καὶ τὸν νότον καὶ τὴν πεδινήν.

Judg. 1:16, ἀνέβησαν ἐκ τῆς πόλεως τῶν φοινίκων πρὸς τοὺς υἱοὺς Ἰούδα εἰς τὴν ἔρημον τὴν **οὖσαν** ἐν τῷ νότῳ ἐπὶ καταβάσεως Ἀράδ.

Judg. 1:24, εἶδον οἱ **φυλάσσοντες** ἄνδρα **ἐκπορευόμενον** ἐκ τῆς πόλεως καὶ ἔλαβαν αὐτὸν καὶ εἶπον αὐτῷ, Δεῖξον (show!) ἡμῖν τὴν εἴσοδον τῆς πόλεως, καὶ ποιήσομεν μετὰ σοῦ ἔλεος.

Judg. 2:2, ὑμεῖς οὐ διαθήσεσθε (you will make) διαθήκην τοῖς **ἐγκαθημένοις**[a] εἰς τὴν γῆν ταύτην.

[a] ἐγκάθημαι, "I reside, dwell, live"

Judg. 2:12, ἐγκατέλιπον τὸν κύριον θεὸν τῶν πατέρων αὐτῶν τὸν **ἐξαγαγόντα** αὐτοὺς ἐκ γῆς Αἰγύπτου καὶ ἐπορεύθησαν ὀπίσω θεῶν ἑτέρων ἀπὸ τῶν θεῶν τῶν λαῶν τῶν περικύκλῳ[a] αὐτῶν καὶ προσεκύνησαν αὐτοῖς καὶ παρώργισαν τὸν κύριον.

[a] περικύκλῳ (adv.), "round about"

Judg. 2:16, ἤγειρεν αὐτοῖς κύριος κριτὰς καὶ ἔσωσεν αὐτοὺς ἐκ χειρὸς τῶν **προνομευόντων**[a] αὐτούς.

[a] προνομεύω, "I plunder, spoil, capture"

The Importance of Case

Acts 3:26, ὁ θεὸς ἀπέστειλεν αὐτὸν **εὐλογοῦντα** ὑμᾶς. — God sent him *who blesses* you.

Εὐλογοῦντα is an adjectival participle modifying αὐτόν—note that it is in the accusative case. It refers to Jesus as God's Servant who blesses his people. This verse is often cited as an example of an adverbial participle of purpose (it is translated that way in most English versions, e.g., NIV, NRSV, ESV), but that classification cannot explain why the participle is accusative. The full verse says, ὑμῖν πρῶτον ἀναστήσας ὁ θεὸς τὸν παῖδα αὐτοῦ ἀπέστειλεν αὐτὸν εὐλογοῦντα ὑμᾶς ἐν τῷ ἀποστρέφειν ἕκαστον ἀπὸ τῶν πονηριῶν ὑμῶν. In a fairly formal equivalent translation (so you can follow the wording more easily) this says, "To you first, God, having raised his Servant, sent him who blesses you by turning each [of you] from your evil ways." The infinitive phrase, ἐν τῷ ἀποστρέφειν, specifies the means by which Jesus blesses his people.

Reading Passage: John 6:35–51

25.9. You can read almost this entire selection without help. The few words that you have not yet learned are glossed for you in parentheses. *After* you have finished your work on this passage, check your understanding against a standard English translation.

The Bread of Life

[35]εἶπεν αὐτοῖς ὁ Ἰησοῦς, Ἐγώ εἰμι ὁ ἄρτος τῆς ζωῆς· ὁ ἐρχόμενος πρὸς ἐμὲ οὐ μὴ
πεινάσῃ (will be hungry), καὶ ὁ πιστεύων εἰς ἐμὲ οὐ μὴ διψήσει (will be thirsty)
πώποτε. [36]ἀλλ' εἶπον ὑμῖν ὅτι καὶ ἑωράκατέ (you see) με καὶ οὐ πιστεύετε. [37]Πᾶν
ὃ δίδωσίν (gives) μοι ὁ πατὴρ πρὸς ἐμὲ ἥξει, καὶ τὸν ἐρχόμενον πρὸς ἐμὲ οὐ μὴ
ἐκβάλω (I will cast out) ἔξω, [38]ὅτι καταβέβηκα ἀπὸ τοῦ οὐρανοῦ οὐχ ἵνα ποιῶ
(I should do) τὸ θέλημα τὸ ἐμὸν ἀλλὰ τὸ θέλημα τοῦ πέμψαντός με. [39]τοῦτο
δέ ἐστιν τὸ θέλημα τοῦ πέμψαντός με, ἵνα πᾶν ὃ δέδωκέν (he has given) μοι
μὴ ἀπολέσω (I should lose) ἐξ αὐτοῦ, ἀλλὰ ἀναστήσω (I should raise) αὐτὸ
ἐν τῇ ἐσχάτῃ ἡμέρᾳ. [40]τοῦτο γάρ ἐστιν τὸ θέλημα τοῦ πατρός μου, ἵνα πᾶς ὁ
θεωρῶν τὸν υἱὸν καὶ πιστεύων εἰς αὐτὸν ἔχῃ (should have) ζωὴν αἰώνιον, καὶ
ἀναστήσω (I should raise) αὐτὸν ἐγὼ ἐν τῇ ἐσχάτῃ ἡμέρᾳ.

[41]Ἐγόγγυζον οὖν οἱ Ἰουδαῖοι περὶ αὐτοῦ ὅτι εἶπεν, Ἐγώ εἰμι ὁ ἄρτος ὁ
καταβὰς ἐκ τοῦ οὐρανοῦ, [42]καὶ ἔλεγον, Οὐχ οὗτός ἐστιν Ἰησοῦς ὁ υἱὸς Ἰωσήφ,
οὗ ἡμεῖς οἴδαμεν τὸν πατέρα καὶ τὴν μητέρα; πῶς νῦν λέγει ὅτι Ἐκ τοῦ
οὐρανοῦ καταβέβηκα; [43]ἀπεκρίθη Ἰησοῦς καὶ εἶπεν αὐτοῖς, Μὴ γογγύζετε
(grumble!) μετ' ἀλλήλων. [44]οὐδεὶς δύναται ἐλθεῖν πρός με ἐὰν μὴ ὁ πατὴρ
ὁ πέμψας με ἑλκύσῃ (should draw) αὐτόν, κἀγὼ ἀναστήσω αὐτὸν ἐν τῇ
ἐσχάτῃ ἡμέρᾳ. [45]ἔστιν γεγραμμένον[a] ἐν τοῖς προφήταις. Καὶ ἔσονται πάντες
διδακτοὶ θεοῦ· πᾶς ὁ ἀκούσας παρὰ τοῦ πατρὸς καὶ μαθὼν ἔρχεται πρὸς ἐμέ.
[46]οὐχ ὅτι τὸν πατέρα ἑώρακέν τις εἰ μὴ ὁ ὢν παρὰ τοῦ θεοῦ, οὗτος ἑώρακεν
τὸν πατέρα. [47]ἀμὴν ἀμὴν λέγω ὑμῖν, ὁ πιστεύων ἔχει ζωὴν αἰώνιον. [48]ἐγώ
εἰμι ὁ ἄρτος τῆς ζωῆς. [49]οἱ πατέρες ὑμῶν ἔφαγον ἐν τῇ ἐρήμῳ τὸ μάννα καὶ

ἀπέθανον· [50]οὗτός ἐστιν ὁ ἄρτος ὁ ἐκ τοῦ οὐρανοῦ καταβαίνων, ἵνα τις ἐξ αὐτοῦ φάγῃ (may eat) καὶ μὴ ἀποθάνῃ (may die). [51]ἐγώ εἰμι ὁ ἄρτος ὁ ζῶν ὁ ἐκ τοῦ οὐρανοῦ καταβάς.

[a] ἔστιν γεγραμμένον, "it is written" (a construction you will learn in the next chapter). Though you have not learned this form yet, can you identify the second word as a perfect participle? What two parsing clues can you identify?

25.10. Vocabulary for Chapter 25

Part of Speech	Definition	Possible Glosses	Frequency	
Word			NT	LXX
Verbs				
βάλλω	To cause to move from one location to another, with either a forceful or more subdued motion (English equivalents will depend largely on the object moved and other contextual factors.)	I throw, hurl; I put, place, lay	122	59
ἐκβάλλω	To cause to move away from a place or condition (English idiom varies considerably, depending on various contextual factors.)	I put out, cast out, throw out, take out, send out	81	101
ἀποθνῄσκω	To stop living	I die	111	600
γεννάω	To cause something to come into existence, usually of the human father's role in the conception of a child, but also of childbirth by the mother or occasionally of animal procreation; to cause something to happen	I beget, father, procreate; I bear (a child), give birth to; I bring forth, produce	97	253
περιπατέω	To move about by walking, be a pedestrian; metaphorically, to engage in a course of action, conduct one's life	I walk, walk/go about; I live, behave (metaphorical)	95	34
ἀκολουθέω	To follow in the footsteps of someone; to follow as a disciple	I follow, accompany, go along with	90	13
πληρόω	To increase the contents of something to maximum capacity; to bring an event, period of time, or prophecy to completion	I fill, fill up; I fulfill, complete, finish	86	112
ἀναβαίνω[a]	To be in motion, usually upward; to get into a boat; to emerge, make an appearance; "to enter the heart" (idiom = "to think about")	I go up, ascend, come up; I embark; I appear; I think	82	614
καταβαίνω	To be in motion downward, descend from a higher to a lower place	I go down, come down	81	349
μαρτυρέω	To attest to something based on personal knowledge, bear witness	I bear witness, testify	76	13
ἀποκτείνω	To forcibly end the life of someone or something	I kill	74	212
φανερόω	To cause to be in a condition that makes observation or knowledge possible	I reveal, disclose, make known/visible	49	1

Part of Speech	Definition	Possible Glosses	Frequency	
Word			NT	LXX
πράσσω	To engage in activity so as to accomplish something (often equivalent to ποιέω); to behave in a certain way	I do, accomplish; I act, behave	39	37
εὐχαριστέω	To express appreciation for benefit received, express gratitude to	I give thanks; I thank	38	6
πειράζω	To make an effort to determine the nature or character of someone or something; to entice to commit sin; to attempt to trap someone by a malicious query or offer	I test, try, make trial of, put to the test; I tempt	38	62

[a] The base word of this compound, βαίνω ("I go, walk, tread, stand"), does not occur in the NT alone (and only a few times in the LXX), but it is worth remembering since there are many compound verbs built on this base, including ἀνα-, ἀπο-, δια-, ἐκ-, ἐν-/ἐμ-, ἐπι-, κατα-, μετα-, παρα-, προ-, προσ-, συν-/συγ-/συμ-, and ὑπερ-.

25.11. Key Things to Know for Chapter 25

How do you distinguish if a participle is functioning adjectivally or adverbially? (Know the key principles.)

In what two ways are adjectival participles used?

How are these two uses of adjectival participles identified?

26

NON-FINITE VERBS: PART 5

Stative and Future Participles

26.1. There are two more sets of participles to learn, the perfect and future participles. There are not nearly as many stative participles in the language as imperfective and perfective forms, and even fewer of the future. Here are the figures for the participle in the NT and LXX.

Participle Distribution

	NT	LXX
Imperfective	3,687	9,041
Perfective	2,289	3,109
Stative	673	2,291
Future	13	69
Total	6,662	14,510

As you can tell from these figures, you will not see nearly as many of the stative and future participles in the NT as other participles, but enough so that you need to be able to recognize them.

Stative (Perfect) Participles

26.2. The aspect of the perfect participle is the same as perfect forms in the indicative: stative. It is used to describe states or conditions rather than actions.

With no new information, parse these words (answers are at the end of the chapter). Pay attention to the pieces that you recognize; there are many pieces reused from earlier chapters. With what you already know and some shrewd guesses, you can probably parse all of these forms.

1. γεγεννημένον
2. γεγεννηκότος
3. διαμεμενηκότες
4. πεποιηκόσιν
5. ἠλπικότες
6. παρηκολουθηκότι
7. ἐγνωκότες
8. βεβλημένος
9. ἠγαπημένων
10. ἀπεσταλμέναις

From the heading you know that these are stative (perfect) participles, but can you figure out *why* from the morphology of each of the forms in this list? Four of the examples above (5, 6, 9, 10) have vocalic reduplication. The only thing that is new in some of these forms is the morpheme οτ. Can you figure out what it must be?

Stative (Perfect) Active Participles

26.3. Except for the perfect participle markers, everything else will be familiar: reduplication, stem, form marker, and endings.

Formula for Stative (Perfect) Active Participles

reduplication + stem + form marker κ + participle marker οτ/υι + case endings

You do not have to memorize the following chart—just know the formula above, and be able to recognize the pieces.

Perfect Active Participle of λύω

	Masc.			Fem.			Neut.		
NS	λελυ	κώ	ς	λελυ	κυῖ	α	λελυ	κό	ς
GS	λελυ	κότ	ος	λελυ	κυί	ας	λελυ	κότ	ος
DS	λελυ	κότ	ι	λελυ	κυί	ᾳ	λελυ	κότ	ι
AS	λελυ	κότ	α	λελυ	κυῖ	αν	λελυ	κό	ς
NP	λελυ	κότ	ες	λελυ	κυῖ	αι	λελυ	κότ	α
GP	λελυ	κότ	ων	λελυ	κυι	ῶν	λελυ	κότ	ων
DP	λελυ	κό	σι(ν)	λελυ	κυί	αις	λελυ	κό	σι(ν)
AP	λελυ	κότ	ας	λελυ	κυί	ας	λελυ	κότ	α

The participle marker for masculine and neuter is οτ, and for feminine it is υι. The masculine and neuter forms use third-declension endings; feminine uses the first declension. There are only 12 feminine perfect active participles in the

NT. The large majority will be masculine (181), with some neuter forms (31). As should be a familiar pattern by now, there are a couple of forms in this chart that don't seem to follow the regular case endings—the nominative singular and dative plural in masculine and neuter. It is once again the sigma in the case ending that causes these changes.

Most perfect participles are adjectival in function; there are few adverbial perfect participles.

26.4. Examples of the Stative (Perfect) Active Participle

John 7:15, ἐθαύμαζον οὖν οἱ Ἰουδαῖοι λέγοντες, Πῶς οὗτος γράμματα οἶδεν μὴ **μεμαθηκώς**;	Therefore the Jews marveled, saying, "How does he know letters *since he is* not *educated?*"[a]

[a] The translation given above is quite formal, but the contextual implications may give it a different tone. Compare several English translations (especially NET and HCSB) and the commentaries.

Matt. 21:5, Ἰδοὺ ὁ βασιλεύς σου ἔρχεταί σοι πραῢς καὶ **ἐπιβεβηκὼς** ἐπὶ ὄνον καὶ ἐπὶ πῶλον υἱὸν ὑποζυγίου.	Look! Your king is coming to you, gentle and *mounted* on a donkey, even on a colt, the foal of a donkey.
Gen. 32:2, Ἰακὼβ ἀπῆλθεν εἰς τὴν ἑαυτοῦ ὁδόν. καὶ ἀναβλέψας εἶδεν παρεμβολὴν θεοῦ **παρεμβεβληκυῖαν**, καὶ συνήντησαν αὐτῷ οἱ ἄγγελοι τοῦ θεοῦ.	Jacob departed his own way. And looking up he saw an encampment of God *encamped*, and the angels of God met him.
1 Clem. 43.5, εὑρέθη ἡ ῥάβδος Ἀαρὼν οὐ μόνον **βεβλαστηκυῖα**, ἀλλὰ καὶ καρπὸν ἔχουσα.	The rod of Aaron was found, not only *budded*, but also having fruit.

26.5. Now You Try It

John 4:6, ἦν δὲ ἐκεῖ πηγὴ τοῦ Ἰακώβ. ὁ οὖν Ἰησοῦς **κεκοπιακὼς** ἐκ τῆς ὁδοιπορίας ἐκαθέζετο οὕτως ἐπὶ τῇ πηγῇ.	
John 8:31, Ἔλεγεν οὖν ὁ Ἰησοῦς πρὸς **τοὺς πεπιστευκότας** αὐτῷ Ἰουδαίους, Ἐὰν ὑμεῖς μείνητε (remain) ἐν τῷ λόγῳ τῷ ἐμῷ, ἀληθῶς μαθηταί μού ἐστε.	
2 Tim. 4:8, λοιπὸν[a] ἀπόκειταί μοι ὁ τῆς δικαιοσύνης στέφανος, ὃν ἀποδώσει[b] μοι ὁ κύριος ἐν ἐκείνῃ τῇ ἡμέρᾳ, ὁ δίκαιος κριτής, οὐ μόνον δὲ ἐμοὶ ἀλλὰ καὶ πᾶσι **τοῖς ἠγαπηκόσι** τὴν ἐπιφάνειαν αὐτοῦ.	

[a] Read the entire entry in your lexicon carefully.

[b] This is a kind of verb you have not met yet, but so long as you know that the verb stem is δο-, you can parse it easily. The lexical form is ἀποδίδωμι. You will meet this form in chap. 32.

Ruth 2:20, εἶπεν Νωεμὶν τῇ νύμφῃ αὐτῆς, Εὐλογητός ἐστιν τῷ κυρίῳ, ὅτι οὐκ ἐγκατέλιπεν τὸ ἔλεος αὐτοῦ μετὰ τῶν ζώντων καὶ μετὰ τῶν **τεθνηκότων**. καὶ εἶπεν αὐτῇ Νωεμίν, Ἐγγίζει ἡμῖν ὁ ἀνήρ, ἐκ τῶν ἀγχιστευόντων[a] ἡμᾶς ἐστιν.

[a] ἀγχιστεύω, "to be next of kin . . . ; to exercise the rights and responsibilities of a kinsman, to redeem" (LEH, 7)

Stative (Perfect) Middle Participles

26.6. As with perfect indicative forms, the perfect has a set of middle participles that can also, if there are appropriate context indicators, function as perfect passive participles.

Formula for Stative (Perfect) Middle Participles

reduplication + stem + participle marker μεν + case endings

The participle marker is the same as always for middle forms (μεν). There is no connecting vowel and no perfect form marker (remember that the perfect middle indicative also omitted both of these morphemes), so the only clue that the form is a perfect is the reduplication. With these two markers, however, the form is easy to spot: reduplication on the front of the stem tells you that it is perfect; μεν added to the end of stem tells you it is a middle participle.

Perfect Middle Participle of λύω

	Masc.			Fem.			Neut.		
NS	λελυ	μέν	ος	λελυ	μέν	η	λελυ	μέν	ον
GS	λελυ	μέν	ου	λελυ	μέν	ης	λελυ	μέν	ου
DS	λελυ	μέν	ῳ	λελυ	μέν	ῃ	λελυ	μέν	ῳ
AS	λελυ	μέν	ον	λελυ	μέν	ην	λελυ	μέν	ον
NP	λελυ	μέν	οι	λελυ	μέν	αι	λελυ	μέν	α
GP	λελυ	μέν	ων	λελυ	μέν	ων	λελυ	μέν	ων
DP	λελυ	μέν	οις	λελυ	μέν	αις	λελυ	μέν	οις
AP	λελυ	μέν	ους	λελυ	μέν	ας	λελυ	μέν	α

26.7. Examples of the Stative (Perfect) Middle Participle

Rom. 4:19, μὴ ἀσθενήσας τῇ πίστει κατενόησεν τὸ ἑαυτοῦ σῶμα ἤδη **νενεκρωμένον**.

Not being weak in faith, he considered his own body already *dead*.

Rev. 10:1, εἶδον ἄλλον ἄγγελον ἰσχυρὸν καταβαίνοντα ἐκ τοῦ οὐρανοῦ **περιβεβλημένον** νεφέλην, καὶ ἡ ἶρις ἐπὶ τῆς κεφαλῆς αὐτοῦ καὶ τὸ πρόσωπον αὐτοῦ ὡς ὁ ἥλιος καὶ οἱ πόδες αὐτοῦ ὡς στῦλοι πυρός.

I saw another strong angel coming down out of heaven, *who was clothed with* a cloud and the rainbow above his head and his face like the sun and his legs as pillars of fire.

Mark 15:32, **οἱ συνεσταυρωμένοι** σὺν αὐτῷ ὠνείδιζον αὐτόν.

The ones who were crucified with him mocked him.

1 Esd. 5:40, εἶπεν αὐτοῖς Νεεμίας καὶ Ἀτθαρίας μὴ μετέχειν[a] τῶν ἁγίων αὐτούς, ἕως ἀναστῇ ἀρχιερεὺς **ἐνδεδυμένος** τὴν δήλωσιν[b] καὶ τὴν ἀλήθειαν.

Nehemiah (and Attharias)[c] told them that they were not to partake of the holy things until a priest *wearing* the Revelation and Truth should arise.

[a] The infinitive is used in indirect discourse.

[b] The phrase τὴν δήλωσιν καὶ τὴν ἀλήθειαν refers to what has traditionally been called the Urim and Thummim; "δήλωσις, εως, ἡ, *revelation, manifestation* . . . ; *interpretation* . . . ; *symbol of revelation* (semit., transl. of the Urim . . .)" (LEH, 134).

[c] The singular verb with a compound subject is not unusual; it is seen in the Gospels with reference to Jesus and the disciples (e.g., Mark 8:27, ἐξῆλθεν ὁ Ἰησοῦς καὶ οἱ μαθηταὶ αὐτοῦ). It may imply that the verb agrees with the first named subject as the primary referent, with whom the second party is associated but is not the primary or most significant speaker. In the example above the second party is placed in parentheses to suggest this.

1 Clem. title and salutation, Κλημεντος Προς Κορινθιους Α΄. Ἡ ἐκκλησία τοῦ θεοῦ ἡ παροικοῦσα Ῥώμην τῇ ἐκκλησίᾳ τοῦ θεοῦ τῇ παροικούσῃ Κόρινθον, κλητοῖς **ἡγιασμένοις** ἐν θελήματι θεοῦ διὰ τοῦ κυρίου ἡμῶν Ἰησοῦ Χριστοῦ. Χάρις ὑμῖν καὶ εἰρήνη ἀπὸ παντοκράτορος θεοῦ διὰ Ἰησοῦ Χριστοῦ πληθυνθείη.[a]

Clement to the Corinthians 1. The church of God which resides at Rome to the church of God which resides at Corinth, to those who are called, *sanctified* by the will of God through our Lord Jesus Christ. May grace and peace from Almighty God through Jesus Christ be yours in ever greater measure.

[a] πληθυνθείη, "may it be increased"; this verb is in the optative mood and expresses a wish, here a prayer of blessing. The translation given above combines ὑμῖν with πληθυνθείη, "may [it] be yours in ever greater measure."

26.8. Now You Try It

Matt. 11:28, Δεῦτε (Come!) πρός με πάντες οἱ κοπιῶντες καὶ **πεφορτισμένοι**, κἀγὼ ἀναπαύσω ὑμᾶς.

Mark 3:1, εἰσῆλθεν πάλιν εἰς τὴν συναγωγήν. καὶ ἦν ἐκεῖ ἄνθρωπος **ἐξηραμμένην** ἔχων τὴν χεῖρα.

How do you know that ἐξηραμμένην is a perfect participle? What is its lexical form? (This one is a bit tricky. It *looks* like there is a preposition on the front of the verb stem.) What word does it modify? How do you know?

Mark 16:5, εἰσελθοῦσαι εἰς τὸ μνημεῖον εἶδον νεανίσκον καθήμενον ἐν τοῖς δεξιοῖς **περιβεβλημένον** στολὴν λευκήν, καὶ ἐξεθαμβήθησαν.

1 Cor. 1:2, τῇ ἐκκλησίᾳ τοῦ θεοῦ τῇ οὔσῃ ἐν Κορίνθῳ, **ἡγιασμένοις** ἐν Χριστῷ Ἰησοῦ, κλητοῖς ἁγίοις, σὺν πᾶσιν τοῖς ἐπικαλουμένοις τὸ ὄνομα τοῦ κυρίου ἡμῶν Ἰησοῦ Χριστοῦ ἐν παντὶ τόπῳ, αὐτῶν καὶ ἡμῶν.

Gen. 25:26, μετὰ τοῦτο ἐξῆλθεν ὁ ἀδελφὸς αὐτοῦ, καὶ ἡ χεὶρ αὐτοῦ **ἐπειλημμένη** τῆς πτέρνης Ἠσαῦ· καὶ ἐκάλεσεν τὸ ὄνομα αὐτοῦ Ἰακώβ.

Ps. 102:17–18 (103:17–18 Eng.), τὸ δὲ ἔλεος τοῦ κυρίου ἀπὸ τοῦ αἰῶνος καὶ ἕως τοῦ αἰῶνος ἐπὶ τοὺς φοβουμένους αὐτόν, καὶ ἡ δικαιοσύνη αὐτοῦ ἐπὶ υἱοὺς υἱῶν τοῖς φυλάσσουσιν τὴν διαθήκην αὐτοῦ καὶ **μεμνημένοις** τῶν ἐντολῶν αὐτοῦ τοῦ ποιῆσαι αὐτάς.

Did. 2.5, οὐκ ἔσται ὁ λόγος σου ψευδής, οὐ κενός, ἀλλὰ **μεμεστωμένος** πράξει.

Stative (Perfect) Passive Participles

26.9. As with other perfect forms, a participle that is middle in form may function as a passive participle if there is indication in the context that someone other than the grammatical subject is the agent. This concept should be familiar by now, so all that is needed are some examples.

26.10. Examples of the Stative (Perfect) Passive Participle

Acts 10:17, οἱ ἄνδρες **οἱ ἀπεσταλμένοι** ὑπὸ τοῦ Κορνηλίου ἐπέστησαν (stood) ἐπὶ τὸν πυλῶνα.

The men *who had been sent* by Cornelius stood at the gate.

Acts 10:33, νῦν οὖν πάντες ἡμεῖς ἐνώπιον τοῦ θεοῦ πάρεσμεν ἀκοῦσαι πάντα **τὰ προστεταγμένα** σοι ὑπὸ τοῦ κυρίου.

Therefore we are all now here in the presence of God to hear all *the things commanded* you by the Lord.

Acts 10:40–41, τοῦτον ὁ θεὸς ἤγειρεν ἐν τῇ τρίτῃ ἡμέρᾳ καὶ ἔδωκεν (he gave) αὐτὸν ἐμφανῆ γενέσθαι, οὐ παντὶ τῷ λαῷ, ἀλλὰ μάρτυσιν **τοῖς προκεχειροτονημένοις** ὑπὸ τοῦ θεου.

God raised him on the third day and caused him to be seen, not by all the people, but by witnesses *who were chosen* by God.

1 Cor. 7:25, γνώμην δίδωμι (I give) ὡς **ἠλεημένος** ὑπὸ κυρίου πιστὸς εἶναι.

I give a judgment as *one who has been shown mercy* by the Lord to be trustworthy.

In this example the participle is adjectival, used substantivally, even though it does not have the article. The lexical form is ἐλεέω.

Gen. 14:19, ηὐλόγησεν τὸν Ἀβρὰμ καὶ εἶπεν, **Εὐλογημένος** Ἀβρὰμ τῷ θεῷ τῷ ὑψίστῳ, ὃς ἔκτισεν τὸν οὐρανὸν καὶ τὴν γῆν.

He blessed Abram and said, "Blessed be Abram by God Most High, who created the heaven and the earth."

1 Kgdms. 21:10 (1 Sam. 21:9 Eng.), εἶπεν ὁ ἱερεύς, Ἰδοὺ ἡ ῥομφαία Γολιὰθ τοῦ ἀλλοφύλου, ὃν ἐπάταξας ἐν τῇ κοιλάδι Ἠλά, καὶ αὐτὴ **ἐνειλημένη** ἐν ἱματίῳ.

The priest said, "Look, the sword of Goliath the foreigner [i.e., Philistine], whom you killed in the Valley of Elah, and it is *wrapped* in a garment."

26.11. Now You Try It

1 Thess. 1:4, εἰδότες, ἀδελφοὶ **ἠγαπημένοι** ὑπὸ τοῦ θεοῦ, τὴν ἐκλογὴν ὑμῶν

2 Thess. 2:13, Ἡμεῖς δὲ ὀφείλομεν εὐχαριστεῖν τῷ θεῷ πάντοτε περὶ ὑμῶν, ἀδελφοὶ **ἠγαπημένοι** ὑπὸ κυρίου, ὅτι εἵλατο ὑμᾶς ὁ θεός.

Jude 17, Ὑμεῖς δέ, ἀγαπητοί, μνήσθητε (remember!) τῶν ῥημάτων **τῶν προειρημένων** ὑπὸ τῶν ἀποστόλων τοῦ κυρίου ἡμῶν Ἰησοῦ Χριστοῦ.

2 Esd. (Ezra) 4:7, ἐν ἡμέραις Ἀρθασασθὰ ἔγραψεν ἐν εἰρήνῃ Μιθραδάτῃ πρὸς Ἀρθασασθά, βασιλέα Περσῶν·[a] ἔγραψεν ὁ φορολόγος[b] γραφὴν Συριστὶ[c] καὶ **ἡρμηνευμένην.**

[a] Πέρσης, ου, ὁ, "Persian"

[b] φορολόγος, ου, ὁ, "tax collector"

[c] Συριστί, adv., "in Aramaic"

3 Kgdms. (1 Kings) 2:3, φυλάξεις τὴν φυλακὴν κυρίου τοῦ θεοῦ σου τοῦ πορεύεσθαι ἐν ταῖς ὁδοῖς αὐτοῦ φυλάσσειν τὰς ἐντολὰς αὐτοῦ καὶ τὰ δικαιώματα καὶ τὰ κρίματα τὰ **γεγραμμένα** ἐν νόμῳ Μωϋσέως.

Challenge Verse

26.12. The word order in this verse is not at all like English, but if you pay attention to the cases and grammatical agreement, you can figure it out. You will need to look up several words, but none of the forms used are unusually difficult. The trickiest part is the article ὁ. What word does it govern? What is the kernel of the sentence?

Gal. 3:17, τοῦτο δὲ λέγω· διαθήκην **προκεκυρωμένην** ὑπὸ τοῦ θεοῦ ὁ μετὰ τετρακόσια καὶ τριάκοντα ἔτη **γεγονὼς** νόμος οὐκ ἀκυροῖ εἰς τὸ καταργῆσαι τὴν ἐπαγγελίαν.

Second Perfect Participles

26.13. Second perfect participles do not occur frequently, but there are two verbs worth attention. The verbs οἶδα and γίνομαι have second perfect forms in which the kappa disappears from the form marker. In the NT and LXX only the masculine and neuter forms appear more than a few times.

Second Perfect Active Participle

	οἶδα	γίνομαι	
	Masc.	Masc.	Neut.
NS	εἰδώς	γεγονώς	γεγονός
GS	εἰδότος	γεγονότος	γεγονότος
DS	εἰδότι	γεγονότι	γεγονότι
AS	εἰδότα	γεγονότας	γεγονός
NP	εἰδότες	γεγονότες	γεγονότα
GP	εἰδότων	γεγονότων	γεγονότων
DP	εἰδόσι(ν)	γεγονόσι(ν)	γεγονόσι(ν)
AP	εἰδότας	γεγονότας	γεγονότα

There are only a few instances of a feminine form of γίνομαι, which follows the pattern γεγονυῖα, γεγονυῖας, and so on. The middle/passive participle of γίνομαι is regular (e.g., γεγενημένος).

Mark 12:15, ὁ δὲ **εἰδὼς** αὐτῶν τὴν ὑπόκρισιν εἶπεν αὐτοῖς, Τί με πειράζετε; φέρετέ (bring!) μοι δηνάριον ἵνα ἴδω (I may look [at it]).

But he, *knowing* their hypocrisy, said to them, "Why are you testing me? Bring me a denarius so that I may look at it."

Rom 5:3, καυχώμεθα ἐν ταῖς θλίψεσιν, **εἰδότες** ὅτι ἡ θλῖψις ὑπομονὴν κατεργάζεται.

We rejoice in afflictions, *knowing* that affliction produces patience.

Luke 8:34, **ἰδόντες** δὲ οἱ βόσκοντες τὸ γεγονὸς ἔφυγον καὶ ἀπήγγειλαν εἰς τὴν πόλιν καὶ εἰς τοὺς ἀγρούς.

But the herdsmen, *seeing* what had happened, fled and announced [it] in the city and in the countryside.

Future Participles

26.14. There are very few future participles used in either the NT or the LXX, only 13 and 64 respectively. They are sufficiently infrequent that your teacher may choose to skip this section altogether and leave it for your reference as needed. The forms of the future participle are not at all difficult, and they function the same ways as the other participles that you have already learned.

Forms of the Future Participle

26.15. The forms of the future participle are similar to the imperfective (present) participle: just insert the usual future form markers: σ or θησ.

Formula for Future Participles

stem + form marker σ + connecting vowel + participle marker + case endings

The same participle markers are used as for the imperfective participle: ντ, ουσ, and μεν. Most of the forms shown in the following tables do not occur in the NT (almost all NT forms are active voice); more of them are found in the LXX. Seeing the complete charts, however, enables you to grasp the patterns more easily.

Future Active Participle of λύω

	Masc.				Fem.				Neut.			
NS	λύ	σ	ων	–	λύ	σ	ουσ	α	λῦ	σ	ον	–
GS	λύ	σ	οντ	ος	λυ	σ	ούσ	ης	λύ	σ	οντ	ος
DS	λύ	σ	οντ	ι	λυ	σ	ούσ	ῃ	λύ	σ	οντ	ι
AS	λύ	σ	οντ	α	λύ	σ	ουσ	αν	λῦ	σ	ον	–
NP	λύ	σ	οντ	ες	λύ	σ	ουσ	αι	λύ	σ	οντ	α
GP	λυ	σ	όντ	ων	λυ	σ	ουσ	ῶν	λυ	σ	όντ	ων
DP	λύ	σ	ου	σι(ν)	λυ	σ	ούσ	αις	λύ	σ	ου	σι(ν)
AP	λύ	σ	οντ	ας	λυ	σ	ούσ	ας	λύ	σ	οντ	α

Future Middle Participle of λύω

	Masc.				Fem.				Neut.			
NS	λυ	σ	όμεν	ος	λυ	σ	ομέν	η	λυ	σ	όμεν	ον
GS	λυ	σ	ομέν	ου	λυ	σ	ομέν	ης	λυ	σ	ομέν	ου
DS	λυ	σ	ομέν	ῳ	λυ	σ	ομέν	ῃ	λυ	σ	ομέν	ῳ
AS	λυ	σ	όμεν	ον	λυ	σ	ομέν	ην	λυ	σ	όμεν	ον
NP	λυ	σ	όμεν	οι	λυ	σ	όμεν	αι	λυ	σ	όμεν	α
GP	λυ	σ	ομέν	ων	λυ	σ	ομέν	ων	λυ	σ	ομέν	ων
DP	λυ	σ	ομέν	οις	λυ	σ	ομέν	αις	λυ	σ	ομέν	οις
AP	λυ	σ	ομέν	ους	λυ	σ	ομέν	ας	λυ	σ	όμεν	α

Future Passive Participle of λύω

	Masc.				Fem.				Neut.			
NS	λυ	θησ	όμεν	ος	λυ	θησ	ομέν	η	λυ	θησ	όμεν	ον
GS	λυ	θησ	ομέν	ου	λυ	θησ	ομέν	ης	λυ	θησ	ομέν	ου
DS	λυ	θησ	ομέν	ῳ	λυ	θησ	ομέν	ῃ	λυ	θησ	ομέν	ῳ
AS	λυ	θησ	όμεν	ον	λυ	θησ	ομέν	ην	λυ	θησ	όμεν	ον
NP	λυ	θησ	όμεν	οι	λυ	θησ	όμεν	αι	λυ	θησ	όμεν	α
GP	λυ	θησ	ομέν	ων	λυ	θησ	ομέν	ων	λυ	θησ	ομέν	ων
DP	λυ	θησ	ομέν	οις	λυ	θησ	ομέν	αις	λυ	θησ	ομέν	οις
AP	λυ	θησ	ομέν	ους	λυ	θησ	ομέν	ας	λυ	θησ	όμεν	α

Future Middle Participle of εἰμί

	Masc.	Fem.	Neut.
NS	ἐσόμενος	ἐσομένη	ἐσόμενον
GS	ἐσομένου	ἐσομένης	ἐσομένου
DS	ἐσομένῳ	ἐσομένῃ	ἐσομένῳ
AS	ἐσόμενον	ἐσομένην	ἐσόμενον
NP	ἐσόμενοι	ἐσόμεναι	ἐσόμενα
GP	ἐσομένων	ἐσομένων	ἐσομένων
DP	ἐσομένοις	ἐσομέναις	ἐσομένοις
AP	ἐσομένους	ἐσομένας	ἐσόμενα

The usual patterns found with contract verbs (κακόω ▸ κακώσων), square of stops (ἄγω ▸ ἄξων), and liquids (κατακρίνω ▸ κατακρινῶν; ἀποτίνω ▸ ἀποτείσων) apply to future participles, the changes being triggered by the addition of sigma as the form marker. Some verbs have a different stem in the future, which also shows in the participle (λαμβάνω ▸ λημψόμενος). One specific form worthy of comment is the participle of γίνομαι, which is built on the stem γεν- with the addition of an eta. In the NT you will see the form γενησόμενον in 1 Cor.

15:37. In the LXX the same form occurs in Eccles. 1:9, and in 1:11 you will find γενησομένων.

As you will see in some of the examples below, future participles are often used to express purpose. When this makes good sense in the context, it can be represented in English as "to x" or "in order to x."

26.16. *Examples of Future Participles*

1 Cor. 15:37, οὐ τὸ σῶμα **τὸ γενησόμενον** σπείρεις ἀλλὰ γυμνὸν κόκκον.	You do not sow the body *which will be*, but a bare seed.
Heb. 3:5, Μωϋσῆς μὲν πιστὸς ἐν ὅλῳ τῷ οἴκῳ αὐτοῦ ὡς θεράπων εἰς μαρτύριον **τῶν λαληθησομένων**.	Moses indeed [was] faithful in all his house as a servant in order to testify *of the things that would be spoken* [i.e., in the future].
1 Pet. 3:13, τίς **ὁ κακώσων** ὑμᾶς ἐὰν τοῦ ἀγαθοῦ ζηλωταὶ γένησθε (you are);	Who [is] *the one who will do evil* to you if you are devoted to the good?
Rom. 8:34, τίς **ὁ κατακρινῶν**; Χριστὸς Ἰησοῦς ὁ ἀποθανών, μᾶλλον δὲ ἐγερθείς, ὃς καί ἐστιν ἐν δεξιᾷ τοῦ θεοῦ, ὃς καὶ ἐντυγχάνει ὑπὲρ ἡμῶν.	Who [is] *the one who will condemn*? Christ Jesus [is] the one who died, and more than that has been raised, who is also at the right hand of God, who also intercedes on our behalf.
Jdt. 12:14, εἶπεν πρὸς αὐτὸν Ἰουδίθ, Καὶ τίς εἰμι ἐγὼ **ἀντεροῦσα**[a] τῷ κυρίῳ μου; [a] ἀντεῖπον, "I speak against"	Judith said to him, "Who, then, am I, *who would speak against* my lord?"
1 Macc. 15:28, ἀπέστειλεν πρὸς αὐτὸν Ἀθηνόβιον ἕνα τῶν φίλων αὐτοῦ **κοινολογησόμενον** αὐτῷ.	He sent Athenobius to him, one of his friends, *to negotiate with* him.
2 Macc. 9:13, ηὔχετο δὲ ὁ μιαρὸς πρὸς **τὸν** οὐκέτι αὐτὸν **ἐλεήσοντα** δεσπότην.	But the vile person made a vow to *the one who would* no longer *have mercy on* him—the Lord.
2 Macc. 11:32, πέπομφα[a] δὲ καὶ τὸν Μενέλαον **παρακαλέσοντα** ὑμᾶς. [a] 1st sg. pf. act. ind. ▶ πέμπω	And I have also sent Menelaus *to encourage* you.
Ps. 21:32 (22:31 Eng.), ἀναγγελοῦσιν τὴν δικαιοσύνην αὐτοῦ λαῷ **τῷ τεχθησομένῳ**,[a] ὅτι ἐποίησεν ὁ κύριος. [a] τεχθησομένῳ ▶ τίκτω	They will announce his righteousness to the people *who will be born*, because the Lord has done [it].

26.17. *Challenge Verses*

Psalm 77:5–7 (78:5–7 Eng.)

5ἀνέστησεν (he established) μαρτύριον ἐν Ἰακὼβ
καὶ νόμον ἔθετο (he placed) ἐν Ἰσραήλ,
ὅσα ἐνετείλατο τοῖς πατράσιν ἡμῶν
τοῦ γνωρίσαι αὐτὰ τοῖς υἱοῖς αὐτῶν,
6ὅπως ἂν γνῷ (they should know) γενεὰ ἑτέρα,
υἱοὶ **οἱ τεχθησόμενοι**,
καὶ ἀναστήσονται καὶ ἀπαγγελοῦσιν αὐτὰ τοῖς υἱοῖς αὐτῶν,
7ἵνα θῶνται (they would set) ἐπὶ τὸν θεὸν τὴν ἐλπίδα αὐτῶν
καὶ μὴ ἐπιλάθωνται (they should forget) τῶν ἔργων τοῦ θεοῦ
καὶ τὰς ἐντολὰς αὐτοῦ ἐκζητήσουσιν.

26.18. Reading Passage: Revelation 20:7–15

After the Thousand Years

7Καὶ ὅταν τελεσθῇ (it is finished) τὰ χίλια ἔτη,[a] λυθήσεται ὁ Σατανᾶς ἐκ τῆς
φυλακῆς αὐτοῦ 8καὶ ἐξελεύσεται πλανῆσαι τὰ ἔθνη τὰ ἐν ταῖς τέσσαρσιν γωνίαις
τῆς γῆς, τὸν Γὼγ καὶ Μαγώγ, συναγαγεῖν αὐτοὺς εἰς τὸν πόλεμον, ὧν ὁ ἀριθμὸς
αὐτῶν[b] ὡς ἡ ἄμμος τῆς θαλάσσης. 9καὶ ἀνέβησαν ἐπὶ τὸ πλάτος τῆς γῆς καὶ
ἐκύκλευσαν τὴν παρεμβολὴν τῶν ἁγίων καὶ τὴν πόλιν τὴν **ἠγαπημένην**, καὶ
κατέβη πῦρ ἐκ τοῦ οὐρανοῦ καὶ κατέφαγεν αὐτούς. 10καὶ ὁ διάβολος ὁ πλανῶν
αὐτοὺς ἐβλήθη εἰς τὴν λίμνην τοῦ πυρὸς καὶ θείου ὅπου καὶ τὸ θηρίον καὶ ὁ
ψευδοπροφήτης, καὶ βασανισθήσονται ἡμέρας καὶ νυκτὸς εἰς τοὺς αἰῶνας τῶν
αἰώνων.

11Καὶ εἶδον θρόνον μέγαν λευκὸν καὶ τὸν καθήμενον ἐπ᾽ αὐτόν, οὗ ἀπὸ
τοῦ προσώπου ἔφυγεν ἡ γῆ καὶ ὁ οὐρανὸς καὶ τόπος οὐχ εὑρέθη αὐτοῖς. 12καὶ
εἶδον τοὺς νεκρούς, τοὺς μεγάλους καὶ τοὺς μικρούς, **ἑστῶτας**[c] ἐνώπιον τοῦ
θρόνου. καὶ βιβλία ἠνοίχθησαν, καὶ ἄλλο βιβλίον ἠνοίχθη, ὅ ἐστιν τῆς ζωῆς,
καὶ ἐκρίθησαν οἱ νεκροὶ ἐκ τῶν **γεγραμμένων** ἐν τοῖς βιβλίοις κατὰ τὰ ἔργα
αὐτῶν. 13καὶ ἔδωκεν (it gave) ἡ θάλασσα τοὺς νεκροὺς τοὺς ἐν αὐτῇ καὶ ὁ
θάνατος καὶ ὁ ᾅδης ἔδωκαν (they gave) τοὺς νεκροὺς τοὺς ἐν αὐτοῖς, καὶ
ἐκρίθησαν ἕκαστος κατὰ τὰ ἔργα αὐτῶν. 14καὶ ὁ θάνατος καὶ ὁ ᾅδης ἐβλήθησαν εἰς τὴν λίμνην τοῦ πυρός. οὗτος ὁ θάνατος ὁ δεύτερός ἐστιν, ἡ λίμνη τοῦ
πυρός. 15καὶ εἴ τις οὐχ εὑρέθη ἐν τῇ βίβλῳ τῆς ζωῆς **γεγραμμένος**, ἐβλήθη εἰς
τὴν λίμνην τοῦ πυρός.

[a] Did you remember that a neuter plural subject can take a singular verb?

[b] ὧν ὁ ἀριθμὸς αὐτῶν, formally, "of whom the number of them." The second genitive is redundant, so in English we would say simply, "their number."

[c] ἑστῶτας is a μι verb that you have not learned yet. The stem is στα-, pf. act. ptc. masc. pl. acc. ▸ ἵστημι, "I stand."

26.19. Vocabulary for Chapter 26

Part of Speech / Word	Definition	Possible Glosses	Frequency NT	Frequency LXX
Adjectives				
ἱκανός, ή, όν	Characterized by sufficient extent, quantity, or degree; extensive in extent or degree (with no reference to sufficiency)	sufficient, adequate, competent, qualified, able; considerable, many, quite a few	39	46
διάβολος, ον	Characterized by intent to slander, oppose, or otherwise harm someone's reputation or interests; in the NT usually substantival, διάβολος, ου, ὁ, referring to the devil	slanderous, accusing falsely; devil, adversary (subst.)	37	22
Adverb				
ἐκεῖθεν	An adverb of place indicating source as from a particular place	from there	37	150
Nouns				
ἐπιθυμία, ας, ἡ	A strong desire for something, whether good or bad	desire, longing, craving, lust	38	85
ἀγρός, οῦ, ὁ	An area of land outside settled/residential areas, typically for agricultural use	field, land, countryside, open country	36	246
ὀργή, ῆς, ἡ	Strong displeasure with the conduct of another; strong displeasure directed toward retribution for offensive behavior	wrath, anger	36	305
οὖς, ὠτός, τό	The organ of hearing (ctr. ὠτάριον, which refers to the outer ear); the mental ability to understand or perceive	ear; hearing	36	190
προσευχή, ῆς, ἡ	A petition addressed to deity; a place where such petitions are regularly offered (in the NT usually a synagogue, though also informal locations)	prayer; place of prayer	36	115
Verbs				
χαίρω	To experience joy or contentment in a particular circumstance or event; to express a polite social greeting upon meeting someone or at the beginning of a letter (impv. or inf.)	I rejoice, am glad/cheerful; Greetings! Hello!	74	87
πίνω	To swallow a liquid; to take in or absorb a liquid	I drink	73	297
αἰτέω	To ask for something; to ask that something be given or that an action be performed; to present a petition to deity, make a request in prayer; to demand [This is a somewhat stronger word for asking than ἐρωτάω, sometimes implying a claim or expectation; though it can be used anyplace that ἐρωτάω is used, the reverse is not necessarily true.]	I ask, request; I petition, pray; I demand, insist on	70	94

Part of Speech	Definition	Possible Glosses	Frequency	
Word			NT	LXX
ἐρωτάω	To ask for/seek information, ask a question; to ask that something be given or that an action be performed; to invite [This is a more generic word for asking, in contrast to αἰτέω.]	I ask, inquire; I ask for, request; I invite	63	70
ἐπερωτάω	To ask a question [not distinguishable from ἐρωτάω]	I ask, inquire; I ask for, request	56	75
βούλομαι	To desire to have/experience something; to plan a course of action on the basis of deliberation	I wish, desire; I intend, plan, determine	37	128
παραγίνομαι	To come to be in a place (either generally or with focus on the public nature of the place)	I arrive, come, draw near, am present; I appear	37	178

26.20. Answers to Parsing at the Beginning of This Chapter

1. γεγεννημένον	pf. mid. ptc. neut. sg. nom. ▶ γεννάω
2. γεγεννηκότος	pf. act. ptc. masc. sg. gen. ▶ γεννάω
3. διαμεμενηκότες	pf. act. ptc. masc. pl. nom. ▶ διαμένω
4. πεποιηκόσιν	pf. act. ptc. masc. pl. dat. ▶ ποιέω
5. ἠλπικότες	pf. act. ptc. masc. pl. nom. ▶ ἐλπίζω
6. παρηκολουθηκότι	pf. act. ptc. masc. sg. dat. ▶ παρακολουθέω
7. ἐγνωκότες	pf. act. ptc. masc. pl. nom. ▶ γινώσκω
8. βεβλημένος	pf. mid. ptc. masc. sg. nom. ▶ βάλλω
9. ἠγαπημένων	pf. mid. ptc. masc. pl. gen. ▶ ἀγαπάω[a]
10. ἀπεσταλμέναις	pf. mid. ptc. fem. pl. dat. ▶ ἀποστέλλω

[a] This form could also be feminine or neuter.

26.21. Key Things to Know for Chapter 26

Can you give the formulas for the following?

Stative active participles

Stative middle participles

Future participles

27

NON-FINITE VERBS: PART 6

Genitive Absolutes and Periphrastics

27.1. This chapter introduces two new functions of participles, the genitive absolute construction and the periphrastic. There are no new forms in this chapter, just two new ways in which participles are used.

Genitive Absolutes

27.2. Genitive absolutes are an interesting solution to a problem posed by the grammar of the participle. If you remember that an adverbial participle modifies the verb and assumes the same subject, how could you use an adverbial participle that refers to someone other than that subject? Of course you might reply, Why do you need to use a participle at all? Is it not possible to make two separate statements, one referring to each person? Yes, you could, but the point of using a participle for this purpose is to indicate the writer's focus. Which of the two actions is primary, and which is secondary? By using a participle, the writer can tell the reader that its action is less prominent and that the main subject and verb is the primary focus. Study this illustration.[1]

θεραπεύων τοὺς ἀσθενεῖς ὁ μαθητὴς κηρύσσει τὸ εὐαγγέλιον.	Healing the sick, the disciple is preaching the gospel.

In this sentence the main point is that the disciple is preaching. Along with that, presumably as a simultaneous temporal adverbial participle, he is also

1. This illustration is adapted from Voelz, *Fundamental Greek Grammar*, 149–50. The sentence used is not from any Koine text; it is an artificial, but very helpful, example.

healing the sick. The same person, the disciple, is doing both the preaching and the healing, but the healing is secondary to the main statement.

27.3. What if we wanted to indicate that someone else, perhaps Jesus, was doing the healing but still keep the focus on the disciple's preaching? We cannot just add Ἰησοῦς to the first clause (Ἰησοῦς θεραπεύων τοὺς ἀσθενεῖς ὁ μαθητὴς κηρύσσει τὸ εὐαγγέλιον), because participles cannot take a subject in the nominative case. We could make this into two sentences, but then the two actions (healing and preaching) would be equal. We could also use a subordinate clause for the healing (e.g., ὁ μαθητὴς κηρύσσει τὸ εὐαγγέλιον ὅταν Ἰησοῦς ἐθεράπευεν τοὺς ἀσθενεῖς), but this is only one option. Greek has a way to do this with a participle.

> θεραπεύοντος τοῦ Ἰησοῦ τοὺς ἀσθενεῖς ὁ μαθητὴς κηρύσσει τὸ εὐαγγέλιον.

Notice what has stayed the same and what has changed. There is still only one finite verb with the same subject (ὁ μαθητὴς κηρύσσει), but the participle has become a genitive (θεραπεύοντος instead of θεραπεύων), and a genitive-case substantive has been added (τοῦ Ἰησοῦ). This construction is called a *genitive absolute*. It would be represented in English something like this:

> While Jesus is healing the sick, the disciple is preaching the gospel.

27.4. Most genitive absolutes are temporal (their primary function is to describe an event that is related in time to the main verb), but they can express any of the relationships that could be expressed by adverbial participles alone. Most such constructions occur at the beginning of the sentence. The second most common position is at the end. Genitive absolutes in the middle of a clause are unusual, but possible.[2]

There are normally four elements in a genitive absolute:

1. A substantive (usually a noun or pronoun) in genitive case
2. An anarthrous[3] participle in genitive case
3. No grammatical connection with the rest of the sentence (This is another way of saying that the subject of the participle is not the same as the subject of the main verb; i.e., someone different is doing the two actions.)[4]

What Is Absolute?

The name *genitive absolute* comes from the fact that this construction "stands alone," apart from the syntax of the rest of the sentence. This is the use of *absolute* that you would find defined in an English dictionary as "viewed or existing independently and not in relation to other things."[a] English once used absolute constructions, but they are rare in our contemporary language. For example, "The day being rainy, Camden did not go for a run." Today we would almost always say, "Since the day was rainy, Camden did not go for a run."[b]

[a] *New Oxford American Dictionary*, 3rd ed., s.v. "absolute."

[b] The English example is from Fairbairn, *Understanding Language*, 160.

2. In John 13:2 *two* genitive absolutes occur together at the beginning of the sentence.
3. You will remember that *anarthrous* means without an article.
4. In most (but not all) cases the genitive subject of the participle is not referenced at all in the main statement, not even as the object.

4. A thought connection with the sentence (The actions of the participle and the main verb are related in some way; they are not irrelevant to each other.)

There are some examples that may not have all four of these elements, but the norm is for all four elements to be present. The most common item that is sometimes missing is the third. This is sometimes because there is an overlap of subjects.

Mark 11:12, τῇ ἐπαύριον **ἐξελθόντων αὐτῶν** ἀπὸ Βηθανίας ἐπείνασεν.

On the next day *as they were leaving* Bethany, he was hungry.

Here αὐτῶν refers to Jesus and the Twelve. The third singular subject of ἐπείνασεν is Jesus—even though he is also included in the plural pronoun reference of αὐτῶν in the genitive absolute.

Other times a pronoun in the main statement refers to the same person as the subject of the genitive absolute.

Mark 13:1, **ἐκπορευομένου αὐτοῦ** ἐκ τοῦ ἱεροῦ λέγει αὐτῷ εἷς τῶν μαθητῶν αὐτοῦ.

As he was leaving the temple, one of his disciples said to him.

In this instance, the genitive subject of the participle, αὐτοῦ, is the same as the referent of the pronoun αὐτῷ, the indirect object in the main clause.

The function of the participle is to change the reference of the subject,[5] and in this situation, the subject of the genitive absolute is rarely the subject of the main clause. The focus shifts from one party in the genitive absolute to a different party that is the subject of the verb in the main clause.

27.5. *Examples of Genitive Absolutes*

Mark 5:2, **ἐξελθόντος αὐτοῦ** ἐκ τοῦ πλοίου εὐθὺς ὑπήντησεν αὐτῷ ἐκ τῶν μνημείων ἄνθρωπος ἐν πνεύματι ἀκαθάρτῳ.

As he was getting out of the boat, immediately a man from the tombs with an unclean spirit met him.

Two people are mentioned in this sentence. The main subject is the demon-possessed man; the secondary focus is on Jesus, who is getting out of the boat.

Rom. 5:6, ἔτι γὰρ Χριστὸς **ὄντων ἡμῶν** ἀσθενῶν ἔτι κατὰ καιρὸν ὑπὲρ ἀσεβῶν ἀπέθανεν.

For *while we were* yet powerless, at just the right time Christ died for the ungodly.

5. This is sometimes described as a "switch reference device."

The word order in this sentence is tricky; the subject stands at the beginning, and the main verb at the end. This shows the less common situation of a genitive absolute occurring in the middle of a sentence. The word order probably accounts for the repetition of ἔτι, which is needed only once in English. This sentence can be expressed several different ways in English, depending largely on how the phrases are arranged; compare various English translations to see some of the alternatives.

Gal. 3:25, **ἐλθούσης** δὲ **τῆς πίστεως** οὐκέτι ὑπὸ παιδαγωγόν ἐσμεν.

Because faith came we are no longer under a tutor.

The translation given above takes the genitive absolute as a causal expression. It could also be understood temporally: "*Now that this faith has come*" (NIV and most English translations).

Heb. 2:3–4, τηλικαύτης σωτηρίας εἰς ἡμᾶς ἐβεβαιώθη, **συνεπιμαρτυροῦντος τοῦ θεοῦ** σημείοις τε καὶ τέρασιν καὶ ποικίλαις δυνάμεσιν.

Such a great salvation was confirmed to us, *God bearing witness* by both signs and wonders and various deeds of power.

1 Clem. 40.1, Προδήλων οὖν ἡμῖν **ὄντων τούτων** καὶ ἐγκεκυφότες εἰς τὰ βάθη τῆς θείας γνώσεως, πάντα τάξει ποιεῖν ὀφείλομεν ὅσα ὁ δεσπότης ἐπιτελεῖν ἐκέλευσεν κατὰ καιροὺς τεταγμένους.

Therefore *these things being* clear to us, and having searched into the depths of the divine knowledge, we ought to do all things in order which the Master commanded [us] to do at the appointed time.

27.6. *Now You Try It*

Mark 5:18, **ἐμβαίνοντος αὐτοῦ** εἰς τὸ πλοῖον παρεκάλει αὐτὸν ὁ δαιμονισθεὶς ἵνα μετ' αὐτοῦ ᾖ.[a]

[a] ᾖ is a form you have not yet learned; it is a subjunctive form of εἰμί and is translated here as "he might be."

John 2:3, **ὑστερήσαντος οἴνου** λέγει ἡ μήτηρ τοῦ Ἰησοῦ πρὸς αὐτόν, Οἶνον οὐκ ἔχουσιν.

Mark 14:43, ἔτι **αὐτοῦ λαλοῦντος** παραγίνεται Ἰούδας εἷς τῶν δώδεκα καὶ μετ' αὐτοῦ ὄχλος μετὰ μαχαιρῶν καὶ ξύλων παρὰ τῶν ἀρχιερέων καὶ τῶν γραμματέων καὶ τῶν πρεσβυτέρων.

1 Pet. 5:4, **φανερωθέντος τοῦ ἀρχιποίμενος** κομιεῖσθε[a] τὸν ἀμαράντινον τῆς δόξης στέφανον.

[a] This is an Attic future form (see chap. 21): 2nd pl. fut. mid. ind. ▶ κομίζω, "I receive"

Josh. 4:22–23, Ἐπὶ ξηρᾶς διέβη[a] Ἰσραὴλ τὸν Ἰορδάνην **ἀποξηράναντος**[b] **κυρίου τοῦ θεοῦ ἡμῶν** τὸ ὕδωρ τοῦ Ἰορδάνου ἐκ τοῦ ἔμπροσθεν αὐτῶν μέχρι οὗ διέβησαν, καθάπερ ἐποίησεν κύριος ὁ θεὸς ἡμῶν τὴν ἐρυθρὰν θάλασσαν, ἣν ἀπεξήρανεν κύριος ὁ θεὸς ἡμῶν ἔμπροσθεν ἡμῶν ἕως παρήλθομεν.

[a] 3rd sg. aor. act. ind. ▶ διαβαίνω, "I go through" (See also διέβησαν later in the sentence.)

[b] ἀποξηραίνω, "I dry up." This is a liquid verb. What changes have taken place? The same verb shows up again later in the sentence.

— — — — — — — — — — — — — —

27.7. Advanced Information for Reference: Diagramming Genitive Absolutes

Gal. 3:25, **ἐλθούσης** δὲ **τῆς πίστεως** οὐκέτι ὑπὸ παιδαγωγόν ἐσμεν.

Because faith came we are no longer under a tutor.

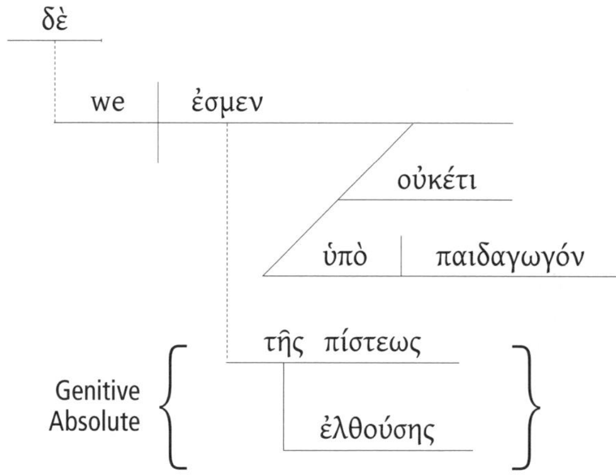

Figure 27.1

Genitive absolutes are placed below the main clause, bracketed, labeled, and connected to the baseline by a dotted line. The participle is on a right-angle bracket under the genitive subject.

— — — — — — — — — — — — — —

Periphrastics

27.8. A periphrastic is a grammatical circumlocution: a roundabout way of saying something that could be said more directly.[6] The periphrastic construction uses a linking verb (usually a form of εἰμί) and a participle together instead of a finite verb alone. The two elements can be in either order, but the most common is for the verb to precede the participle (about 70 percent of the time in the NT), which will always be anarthrous and nominative. There is no difference in meaning between the equivalent finite verb and the periphrastic; it is just another way to say it. Although periphrastic use is very common in language in general,[7] it is not nearly as common in Greek.

For example, the one-word sentence ἐδίδασκεν uses the usual finite verb form. By contrast, the following expression says the exact same thing but uses a circumlocution to say it: ἦν διδάσκων. Both have the same meaning: "he was teaching." In most periphrastic constructions the form of εἰμί supplies person, number, and mood, while the participle supplies aspect, voice, and lexis.[8] In this example, ἦν is third person, singular number, indicative mood, and the participle διδάσκων is imperfective aspect (present tense-form), active voice, from διδάσκω ("I teach"). The resulting form thus functions as a third singular present active indicative of διδάσκω.

27.9. To understand the meaning of the most common periphrastic constructions,[9] parse the equivalent single-verb form by using the person, number, and mood of the linking verb and the tense-form, voice, and lexis of the participle, then interpret accordingly. For example, ἦν ἐνδεδυμένος (Mark 1:6) is evaluated as follows. The linking verb ἦν is a third singular imperfect active indicative of εἰμί, and it supplies these semantics: third person, singular number, and indicative mood. The participle ἐνδεδυμένος is a perfect middle participle masculine singular nominative of ἐνδύω, and it supplies these semantics: perfect tense-form, middle voice, and the lexical form ἐνδύω, "I put on, clothe." The periphrastic thus *functions* as a third singular perfect middle indicative of ἐνδύω, "he was clothed."

6. The English word *periphrastic* = περί, "around" + φράσις, "speech, a way/style of speaking."

7. Some languages, such as English, use the periphrastic construction as the predominant verb form. For example, the phrase "I was eating" consists of the linking verb "I was" combined with the participle "eating." And you thought that "periphrastics" were some strange-sounding phenomenon unique to Greek—you have been using them in English for years without knowing it!

8. *Lexis*, you will remember, is what the word means; it is shorthand for "the lexical meaning of the word." In a periphrastic, this comes from the participle, not the linking verb.

9. This basic parsing system accounts for all imperfective periphrastics (the most common forms) and rare perfective periphrastics. For stative periphrastics with an imperfect or future form of εἰμί, see the table in the text.

The complete parsing system for periphrastics may be summarized in the following table.

Aspect of the Periphrastic	Tense-Form of the Participle	Tense-Form of εἰμί	Finite Tense-Form Equivalent
Imperfective	Present	Present	Present
		Imperfect	Imperfect
		Future	Future
Stative	Perfect	Present	Perfect
		Imperfect	Pluperfect
		Future	Future-Perfect
Perfective	Aorist	Imperfect	Aorist

You will notice that mood is not included in the table above. Although most periphrastics are indicatives, they occasionally occur in the subjunctive (e.g., John 3:27; 2 John 12) and imperative (e.g., Matt. 5:25; Luke 19:17) moods. Subjunctive forms are more common than imperatives (12 vs. 4 in the NT). The mood of the periphrastic is determined by the mood of εἰμί.

27.10. There are three situations in which a periphrastic may be used. First, some grammatical forms do not appear in the language. They have either died out (or are in the process of doing so) or may never have been used. For example, there was formerly a future-perfect form δεδήσεται ("he will be bound," 3rd sg. fut.-pf. mid. ind. ▸ δέω, "I bind"),[10] but this is extremely rare in Koine.[11] In its place a *replacement* periphrastic form is used—for example, ἔσται δεδεμένον (Matt. 16:19). Second, some periphrastic forms are used where there are existing finite forms with no discernible difference in usage. These *equivalent* form periphrastics are used for stylistic purposes. The periphrastic above, ἦν διδάσκων, is identical to ἐδίδασκεν, and both expressions occur. Third, a few periphrastics may be used to express some additional meaning not possible with a finite form, or they may express some form of emphasis. The future periphrastic is one example of the periphrastic expressing additional meaning in this category (see below). The use of ἐστε σεσωμένοι in Eph. 2:5, 8 may represent an instance where the periphrastic contributes to some degree of emphasis in the context. These *distinctive* periphrastics are often imperfective, but it should not be assumed that all imperfective periphrastics have such an emphasis, nor should they be viewed as a major point in exegeting a text.[12]

10. The future-perfect is not equivalent to a future tense-form; the compound future-perfect elements refer to a state or condition (stative aspect) that will be true in the future. In a particular context you may be able to express this idea in an English equivalent, but to say "he will be in a bound state" is very clumsy English.

11. There are at least four such forms in the LXX: κεκλήσεται (Lev. 13:45; Hosea 12:1), κεκράξομαι (9×; e.g., Ps. 21:3 [22:2 Eng.]), εἰδήσουσιν (Jer. 38:34, quoted in Heb. 8:11), and ἀνακεκράξεται (Joel 4:16).

12. A periphrastic sometimes has a "certain emphasis" (Blass, Debrunner, and Funk, *Greek Grammar*, 179, §353.1; see also BDAG, s.v. εἰμί, 286.11.e, f). In Classical Greek this "emphasis" was often a matter of duration of time, but such usage is not usually present in the Koine. There are about a dozen periphrastics that may have some emphasis in the NT, most often in Paul. For a detailed discussion, see Green, "Understanding EIMI Periphrastics in the Greek of the New Testament," 261–332.

27.11. The future periphrastic is one way to explicitly specify imperfective aspect in a context of future time.[13] This can be seen in Mark 13:13: **ἔσεσθε μισούμενοι** ὑπὸ πάντων διὰ τὸ ὄνομά μου ("*You will be hated* by everyone because of my name"). The time value comes from the future tense-form of εἰμί, whereas the imperfective aspect comes from the participle. Perfective periphrastics (i.e., those that use an aorist participle) are very rare.[14]

Not every instance of a linking verb with an anarthrous participle is a periphrastic. Scholars differ as to how this is determined and how any given instance is to be evaluated.[15] It is possible for a wide range of words to occur between the linking verb and the participle. One general principle that is often helpful is the presence of a phrase indicating location between the two elements. In such situations it is less likely that a legitimate periphrastic occurs, though there are a few apparent exceptions. Each instance will need to be evaluated in light of its context. A decision one way or the other can sometimes make an interpretive difference in a passage (see, e.g., Mark 1:13, which is probably *not* a periphrastic).

Three Uses of Periphrastics

1. **Replacement form** when an equivalent finite form is missing
2. **Equivalent form** for stylistic purposes
3. **Distinctive form** to express additional meaning or emphasis

These uses are sometimes designated more technically in the grammars as *suppletive, substitute,* and *expressive* uses of the periphrastic.

Examples of Periphrastics

27.12. In each example the functional parsing of the periphrastic is given in brackets.

Mark 1:22, ἐξεπλήσσοντο ἐπὶ τῇ διδαχῇ αὐτοῦ· **ἦν** γὰρ **διδάσκων** αὐτοὺς ὡς ἐξουσίαν ἔχων καὶ οὐχ ὡς οἱ γραμματεῖς. [3rd sg. impf. act. ind. ▸ διδάσκω]

They were amazed at his teaching, for *he was teaching* them as one who had authority and not as the scribes.

John 1:24, **ἀπεσταλμένοι ἦσαν** ἐκ τῶν Φαρισαίων. [3rd pl. plpf. pass. ind. ▸ ἀποστέλλω]

They were sent from the Pharisees.

13. An alternative is to use a present tense-form if the context makes the future reference clear.

14. See Luke 23:19, ἦν βληθείς; and 2 Cor. 5:19, ἦν θέμενος.

15. Some suggest that the only basis is "appropriateness in the context" (Fanning, *Verbal Aspect*, 311). Others propose more-specific guidelines, such as denying as periphrastics any constructions with words intervening between the verb and the participle except conjunctions and words that explicitly modify the participle (Porter, *Idioms*, 45–46; see the more extensive discussion in Porter, *Verbal Aspect*, 441–86). For a careful analysis of this question, see Green, "Periphrastics," 176–238.

Mark 9:4, ὤφθη[a] αὐτοῖς Ἠλίας σὺν Μωϋσεῖ καὶ **ἦσαν συλλαλοῦντες** τῷ Ἰησοῦ. [3rd pl. impf. act. ind. ▸ συλλαλέω]	Elijah appeared to them with Moses, and *they were talking* with Jesus.

[a] ὤφθη, 3rd sg. aor. pass. ind. ▸ ὁράω, "I see"

Mark 13:13, **ἔσεσθε μισούμενοι** ὑπὸ πάντων διὰ τὸ ὄνομά μου. [2nd pl. fut. pass. ind. ▸ μισέω, with imperfective aspect]	*You will be hated* by everyone because of my name.
Matt. 10:26, Μὴ οὖν φοβηθῆτε (fear!) αὐτούς· οὐδὲν γάρ **ἐστιν κεκαλυμμένον** ὃ οὐκ ἀποκαλυφθήσεται καὶ κρυπτὸν ὃ οὐ γνωσθήσεται. [3rd sg. pf. pass. ind. ▸ καλύπτω]	Therefore do not fear them, for nothing *is hidden* which will not be revealed and hidden which will not be made known.
Gen. 4:2, καὶ ἐγένετο Ἅβελ ποιμὴν προβάτων, Κάϊν δὲ **ἦν ἐργαζόμενος** τὴν γῆν. [3rd sg. impf. act. ind. ▸ ἐργάζομαι]	Now Abel became a shepherd of sheep, but Cain *was working* the soil.
Exod. 12:5–6, πρόβατον τέλειον ἄρσεν ἐνιαύσιον ἔσται ὑμῖν· ἀπὸ τῶν ἀρνῶν καὶ τῶν ἐρίφων λήμψεσθε. καὶ **ἔσται** ὑμῖν **διατετηρημένον**[a] ἕως τῆς τεσσαρεσκαιδεκάτης τοῦ μηνὸς τούτου, καὶ σφάξουσιν αὐτὸ πᾶν τὸ πλῆθος συναγωγῆς[b] υἱῶν Ἰσραὴλ πρὸς ἑσπέραν. [3rd sg. fut.-pf. pass. ind. ▸ διατηρέω]	You will have[c] a perfect male sheep, one year old; take it from the lambs and kids. Then *it will be kept* for you until the fourteenth of this month, and all the community of the congregation of the sons of Israel will kill it toward evening.

[a] This periphrastic is an example of the replacement future-perfect form discussed earlier in this chapter.

[b] τὸ πλῆθος συναγωγῆς, "the community of the congregation," is redundant in English; it refers to "the whole congregation."

[c] "You will have" (ἔσται ὑμῖν) is more formally, "it will be to you," but that does not communicate in English. The expression must be understood in light of the use of λαμβάνω in v. 3 to mean "I choose/select."

Now You Try It

27.13. For each periphrastic, identify the functional parsing.

Matt. 18:20, οὗ[a] γάρ **εἰσιν** δύο ἢ τρεῖς **συνηγμένοι** εἰς τὸ ἐμὸν ὄνομα, ἐκεῖ εἰμι ἐν μέσῳ αὐτῶν.	

[a] The word οὗ is the adverb "where," not a relative pronoun.

Acts 2:13, ἕτεροι δὲ διαχλευάζοντες ἔλεγον ὅτι Γλεύκους **μεμεστωμένοι εἰσίν**.	

Rom. 13:1, οὐ γὰρ ἔστιν ἐξουσία εἰ μὴ ὑπὸ θεοῦ, αἱ δὲ οὖσαι ὑπὸ θεοῦ **τεταγμέναι εἰσίν**.

2 Cor. 4:3, εἰ δὲ καὶ **ἔστιν κεκαλυμμένον** τὸ εὐαγγέλιον ἡμῶν, ἐν τοῖς ἀπολλυμένοις **ἐστὶν κεκαλυμμένον**.

Gal. 1:22, **ἤμην** δὲ **ἀγνοούμενος** τῷ προσώπῳ ταῖς ἐκκλησίαις τῆς Ἰουδαίας ταῖς ἐν Χριστῷ.

1 Kgdms. (1 Sam.) 3:1, Καὶ τὸ παιδάριον Σαμουὴλ **ἦν λειτουργῶν** τῷ κυρίῳ ἐνώπιον Ἠλὶ τοῦ ἱερέως· καὶ ῥῆμα κυρίου ἦν τίμιον[a] ἐν ταῖς ἡμέραις ἐκείναις, οὐκ **ἦν** ὅρασις **διαστέλλουσα**.[b]

[a] Your lexicon will suggest "precious" for τίμιος, but it is precious because it is rare or scarce.

[b] διαστέλλω here has the sense of "distinct" or "clear."

2 Esd. 11:4 (Neh. 1:4 Eng.), καὶ ἐγένετο ἐν τῷ ἀκοῦσαί με τοὺς λόγους τούτους ἐκάθισα καὶ ἔκλαυσα καὶ ἐπένθησα ἡμέρας καὶ **ἤμην νηστεύων καὶ προσευχόμενος** ἐνώπιον θεοῦ τοῦ οὐρανοῦ.

— — — — — — — — — — — — — —

27.14. Advanced Information for Reference: Diagramming Periphrastics

Gen. 4:2, καὶ ἐγένετο Ἅβελ ποιμὴν προβάτων, Κάϊν δὲ **ἦν ἐργαζόμενος** τὴν γῆν.

Now Abel became a shepherd of sheep, but Cain *was working* the soil.

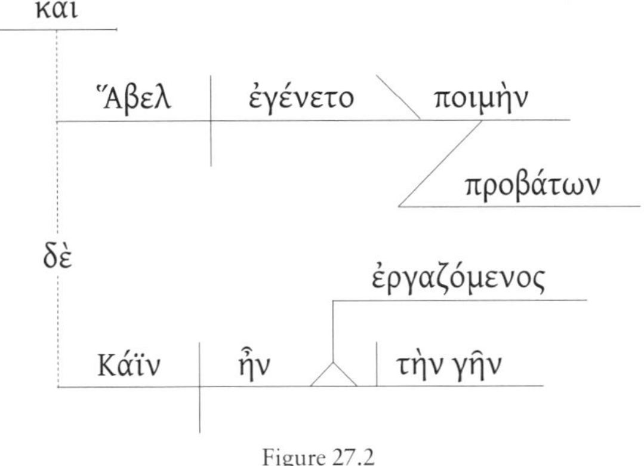

Figure 27.2

A periphrastic is diagrammed by placing the participle on stilts next to the linking verb.

— — — — — — — — — — — — — —

Reading Passage: Mark 1:1–22

27.15. Mark 1:1–22 is a very helpful review of participles. You have already read a number of verses in this pericope, so that will make it easier. You should find twenty-three participles in these verses. Included are two periphrastics, one of which is a compound construction: one form of εἰμί governs two participles.

The Beginning of Jesus' Ministry

1Ἀρχὴ τοῦ εὐαγγελίου Ἰησοῦ Χριστοῦ υἱοῦ θεοῦ.
2Καθὼς γέγραπται ἐν τῷ Ἠσαΐᾳ τῷ προφήτῃ,

Ἰδοὺ ἀποστέλλω τὸν ἄγγελόν μου πρὸ προσώπου σου,
ὃς κατασκευάσει τὴν ὁδόν σου·
3φωνὴ βοῶντος ἐν τῇ ἐρήμῳ,
Ἑτοιμάσατε (Prepare!) τὴν ὁδὸν κυρίου,
εὐθείας ποιεῖτε (make!) τὰς τρίβους αὐτοῦ,

4ἐγένετο Ἰωάννης ὁ βαπτίζων ἐν τῇ ἐρήμῳ καὶ κηρύσσων βάπτισμα μετανοίας
εἰς ἄφεσιν ἁμαρτιῶν. 5καὶ ἐξεπορεύετο πρὸς αὐτὸν πᾶσα ἡ Ἰουδαία χώρα καὶ
οἱ Ἱεροσολυμῖται πάντες, καὶ ἐβαπτίζοντο ὑπ᾽ αὐτοῦ ἐν τῷ Ἰορδάνῃ ποταμῷ
ἐξομολογούμενοι τὰς ἁμαρτίας αὐτῶν. 6καὶ ἦν ὁ Ἰωάννης ἐνδεδυμένος τρίχας
καμήλου καὶ ζώνην δερματίνην περὶ τὴν ὀσφὺν αὐτοῦ καὶ ἐσθίων ἀκρίδας καὶ
μέλι ἄγριον. 7καὶ ἐκήρυσσεν λέγων, Ἔρχεται ὁ ἰσχυρότερός μου ὀπίσω μου, οὗ
οὐκ εἰμὶ ἱκανὸς κύψας λῦσαι τὸν ἱμάντα τῶν ὑποδημάτων αὐτοῦ. 8ἐγὼ ἐβάπτισα
ὑμᾶς ὕδατι, αὐτὸς δὲ βαπτίσει ὑμᾶς ἐν πνεύματι ἁγίῳ.

9Καὶ ἐγένετο ἐν ἐκείναις ταῖς ἡμέραις ἦλθεν Ἰησοῦς ἀπὸ Ναζαρὲτ τῆς Γαλιλαίας καὶ ἐβαπτίσθη εἰς τὸν Ἰορδάνην ὑπὸ Ἰωάννου. 10καὶ εὐθὺς[a] ἀναβαίνων
ἐκ τοῦ ὕδατος εἶδεν σχιζομένους τοὺς οὐρανοὺς καὶ τὸ πνεῦμα ὡς περιστερὰν
καταβαῖνον εἰς αὐτόν· 11καὶ φωνὴ ἐγένετο ἐκ τῶν οὐρανῶν, Σὺ εἶ ὁ υἱός μου ὁ
ἀγαπητός, ἐν σοὶ εὐδόκησα.

12Καὶ εὐθὺς[a] τὸ πνεῦμα αὐτὸν ἐκβάλλει εἰς τὴν ἔρημον. 13καὶ ἦν ἐν τῇ ἐρήμῳ
τεσσεράκοντα ἡμέρας πειραζόμενος ὑπὸ τοῦ Σατανᾶ, καὶ ἦν μετὰ τῶν θηρίων,
καὶ οἱ ἄγγελοι διηκόνουν αὐτῷ.

14Μετὰ δὲ τὸ παραδοθῆναι[b] τὸν Ἰωάννην ἦλθεν ὁ Ἰησοῦς εἰς τὴν Γαλιλαίαν
κηρύσσων τὸ εὐαγγέλιον τοῦ θεοῦ 15καὶ λέγων ὅτι Πεπλήρωται ὁ καιρὸς καὶ
ἤγγικεν ἡ βασιλεία τοῦ θεοῦ· μετανοεῖτε (repent!) καὶ πιστεύετε (believe!) ἐν
τῷ εὐαγγελίῳ.

16Καὶ παράγων παρὰ τὴν θάλασσαν τῆς Γαλιλαίας εἶδεν Σίμωνα καὶ Ἀνδρέαν
τὸν ἀδελφὸν Σίμωνος ἀμφιβάλλοντας ἐν τῇ θαλάσσῃ· ἦσαν γὰρ ἁλιεῖς. 17καὶ
εἶπεν αὐτοῖς ὁ Ἰησοῦς, Δεῦτε[c] ὀπίσω μου, καὶ ποιήσω ὑμᾶς γενέσθαι ἁλιεῖς
ἀνθρώπων. 18καὶ εὐθὺς ἀφέντες (leaving)[d] τὰ δίκτυα ἠκολούθησαν αὐτῷ. 19Καὶ
προβὰς ὀλίγον εἶδεν Ἰάκωβον τὸν τοῦ Ζεβεδαίου καὶ Ἰωάννην τὸν ἀδελφὸν
αὐτοῦ καὶ αὐτοὺς ἐν τῷ πλοίῳ καταρτίζοντας τὰ δίκτυα, 20καὶ εὐθὺς ἐκάλεσεν

αὐτούς. καὶ ἀφέντες (leaving)[d] τὸν πατέρα αὐτῶν Ζεβεδαῖον ἐν τῷ πλοίῳ μετὰ
τῶν μισθωτῶν ἀπῆλθον ὀπίσω αὐτοῦ.
[21]Καὶ εἰσπορεύονται εἰς Καφαρναούμ· καὶ εὐθὺς[a] τοῖς σάββασιν εἰσελθὼν
εἰς τὴν συναγωγὴν ἐδίδασκεν. [22]καὶ ἐξεπλήσσοντο ἐπὶ τῇ διδαχῇ αὐτοῦ· ἦν γὰρ
διδάσκων αὐτοὺς ὡς ἐξουσίαν ἔχων καὶ οὐχ ὡς οἱ γραμματεῖς.

[a] Do you remember Mark's idiomatic use of καὶ εὐθύς? You have seen it a number of times already (see the note on Mark 1:12 in §4.11).

[b] This is a μι verb (stem δο-; aor. pass. inf.), "I arrest." Do you remember the significance of μετά with an articular infinitive? See chap. 22 if you do not.

[c] "Follow!" See the explanation of this same expression in Matt. 11:28 in §31.6.

[d] This form is a participle, so do not read it as the main verb in the clause.

27.16. Vocabulary for Chapter 27

Part of Speech	Definition	Possible Glosses	Frequency	
Word			NT	LXX
Adjectives				
μέσος, η, ον	A middle position (either spatial or temporal); position within or between; "the middle" (subst., τὸ μέσον)	middle, in the midst, among	58	872
τοιοῦτος, αύτη, οῦτον	Similar to some person or thing already mentioned in a context (used either as an adj., pron., or subst. and may be correlative with ὅστις, οἷος, or ὥσπερ)	such, of such a kind, such as this; such a person/thing (subst.)	57	82
τρίτος, η, ον	Third in a series; a third part of something (subst.); for the third time (adv.)	third; third part (subst.); third time, thrice (adv.)	56	179
Nouns				
θρόνος, ου, ὁ	A special chair set aside for someone of high status (e.g., a king)	throne	62	163
Γαλιλαία, ας, ἡ	A postexilic geographical area constituting the northern part of Palestine	Galilee	61	25
ἱμάτιον, ου, τό	Clothing in general; the outer garment worn over a χιτών	garment, clothing; cloak, coat, robe	60	221
συναγωγή, ῆς, ἡ	An assembly or collection of things or people; a place where people assemble; in the NT, the Jewish synagogue (where Jews assembled for worship) or a place where Christians assembled; the people who gathered in such a place (Jews or Christians)	assembly, collection; synagogue, meeting/assembly place; congregation	56	228
Verbs				
τηρέω	To maintain in a secure state by maintaining custody or by perpetuating a state or activity; to conduct oneself in obedience to instruction or law	I keep watch over, guard, preserve; I observe, keep	70	37

Part of Speech	Definition	Possible Glosses	Frequency	
Word			NT	LXX
φέρω	To move something from one place to another by either carrying it or otherwise causing it to move; metaphorically, to carry something (positive or negative); to bring about a yield, be productive (of plants) [numerous other less common uses; see BDAG and MLS]	I carry, transport, lead, bring; I endure; I produce, yield, bear	66	290
δοκέω	To consider an idea as probable; to entertain an opinion	I think, suppose, believe, regard, decide; I seem, have the appearance, think	62	64
προσκυνέω	To do obeisance to, prostrate oneself before; to express in attitude or gesture one's complete dependence on, submission to, or reverence of a high authority figure (human or divine)	I do obeisance to, prostrate myself before, welcome respectfully; I worship	60	229
θεωρέω	To observe attentively; to conclude on the basis of personal experience	I look at, observe, take notice of; I infer, perceive	58	53
σπείρω	To sow seeds, plant a field by sowing; to scatter abroad (LXX)	I sow (seeds), plant; I scatter, disperse	52	62
ὑποτάσσω	To place under/below, either under the authority of or appended in a document (LXX) (act.); to become subject to (pass.); to subject oneself to, obey (mid.)	I subject, subordinate (someone else) (act.); I append, attach (LXX) (act.); I become subject to (pass.); I submit, obey (mid.)	38	28
ἀδικέω	To act in an unjust manner by violating law; to do wrong to someone, treat unjustly; to cause damage to, mistreat	I do wrong, act unjustly; I wrong (someone); I injure, harm, mistreat	25	70

27.17. Key Things to Know for Chapter 27

What four elements are necessary to have a genitive absolute?

Can you define a periphrastic?

How do you parse the functional equivalent form of a periphrastic?

Review participles and their formulas.

28

VERBS: PART 12

Subjunctive-Mood Verbs

28.1. This chapter will use an inductive approach to introduce you to verbs in the subjunctive mood.

Introduction

We will begin with the following NT example. Read the following sentence, paying particular attention to the word ἄγωμεν. Use the notes below the verse only when you have finished your own work on this verse.

John 11:7, μετὰ τοῦτο λέγει τοῖς μαθηταῖς, Ἄγωμεν εἰς τὴν Ἰουδαίαν πάλιν.
What is the lexical form for ἄγωμεν?
What person and number is it?

You probably have identified it correctly as a form of ἄγω. But did you notice something slightly different from what you expected? The usual form for a first plural would be ἄγομεν. Notice that the connecting vowel has lengthened from omicron to omega.

Now browse the context of this passage in several standard English translations, and note how ἄγωμεν has been translated. How is it translated differently from a regular indicative-mood verb? What nuance is added? This is *not* an indicative-mood verb. It is, as I am sure you have guessed from the chapter title, a subjunctive-mood verb.

28.2. In the following passage, John 11:1–16, browse through the text, noting especially the way in which the italicized words are translated. Ask yourself in each of these instances, is this a statement of or about reality? That is, does the statement describe something that is real or that exists? Or is it only a reference to a *potential* situation that may or may not become real? (There is a fairly wide range here, so do not expect them all to be the same. We will sort that out a bit later.)

You do not have to parse every word, but do try to follow the text as best you can, using the English translation on the right (NASB) as a temporary crutch. (Be sure to notice the *periphrastic* in the first verse. Do you remember that construction from the preceding chapter?)

28.3. *Examples of the Subjunctive: John 11:1–16*

1 Ἦν δέ τις ἀσθενῶν, Λάζαρος ἀπὸ Βηθανίας, ἐκ τῆς κώμης Μαρίας καὶ Μάρθας τῆς ἀδελφῆς αὐτῆς.

Now a certain man was sick, Lazarus of Bethany, the village of Mary and her sister Martha.

2 ἦν δὲ Μαριὰμ ἡ ἀλείψασα τὸν κύριον μύρῳ καὶ ἐκμάξασα τοὺς πόδας αὐτοῦ ταῖς θριξὶν αὐτῆς, ἧς ὁ ἀδελφὸς Λάζαρος ἠσθένει.

It was the Mary who anointed the Lord with ointment, and wiped His feet with her hair, whose brother Lazarus was sick.

3 ἀπέστειλαν οὖν αἱ ἀδελφαὶ πρὸς αὐτὸν λέγουσαι, Κύριε, ἴδε ὃν φιλεῖς ἀσθενεῖ.

So the sisters sent word to Him, saying, "Lord, behold, he whom You love is sick."

4 ἀκούσας δὲ ὁ Ἰησοῦς εἶπεν, Αὕτη ἡ ἀσθένεια οὐκ ἔστιν πρὸς θάνατον ἀλλ' ὑπὲρ τῆς δόξης τοῦ θεοῦ, **ἵνα δοξασθῇ** ὁ υἱὸς τοῦ θεοῦ δι' αὐτῆς.

But when Jesus heard this, He said, "This sickness is not to end in death, but for the glory of God, *so that* the Son of God *may be glorified* by it."

5 ἠγάπα δὲ ὁ Ἰησοῦς τὴν Μάρθαν καὶ τὴν ἀδελφὴν αὐτῆς καὶ τὸν Λάζαρον.

Now Jesus loved Martha and her sister and Lazarus.

6 ὡς οὖν ἤκουσεν ὅτι ἀσθενεῖ, τότε μὲν ἔμεινεν ἐν ᾧ ἦν τόπῳ δύο ἡμέρας,

So when He heard that he was sick, He then stayed two days longer in the place where He was.

7 ἔπειτα μετὰ τοῦτο λέγει τοῖς μαθηταῖς, **Ἄγωμεν** εἰς τὴν Ἰουδαίαν πάλιν.

Then after this He said to the disciples, "*Let us go* to Judea again."

8 λέγουσιν αὐτῷ οἱ μαθηταί, Ῥαββί, νῦν ἐζήτουν σε λιθάσαι οἱ Ἰουδαῖοι, καὶ πάλιν ὑπάγεις ἐκεῖ;

The disciples said to Him, "Rabbi, the Jews were just now seeking to stone You, and are You going there again?"

9 ἀπεκρίθη Ἰησοῦς, Οὐχὶ δώδεκα ὧραί εἰσιν τῆς ἡμέρας; **ἐάν** τις **περιπατῇ** ἐν τῇ ἡμέρᾳ, οὐ προσκόπτει, ὅτι τὸ φῶς τοῦ κόσμου τούτου βλέπει·

Jesus answered, "Are there not twelve hours in the day? *If* anyone *walks* in the day, he does not stumble, because he sees the light of this world.

10 **ἐὰν** δέ τις **περιπατῇ** ἐν τῇ νυκτί, προσκόπτει, ὅτι τὸ φῶς οὐκ ἔστιν ἐν αὐτῷ.	"But *if* anyone *walks* in the night, he stumbles, because the light is not in him."
11 ταῦτα εἶπεν, καὶ μετὰ τοῦτο λέγει αὐτοῖς, Λάζαρος ὁ φίλος ἡμῶν κεκοίμηται· ἀλλὰ πορεύομαι **ἵνα ἐξυπνίσω** αὐτόν.	This He said, and after that He said to them, "Our friend Lazarus has fallen asleep; but I go, *so that I may awaken* him *out of sleep*."
12 εἶπαν οὖν οἱ μαθηταὶ αὐτῷ, Κύριε, εἰ κεκοίμηται σωθήσεται.	The disciples then said to Him, "Lord, if he has fallen asleep, he will recover."
13 εἰρήκει δὲ ὁ Ἰησοῦς περὶ τοῦ θανάτου αὐτοῦ, ἐκεῖνοι δὲ ἔδοξαν ὅτι περὶ τῆς κοιμήσεως τοῦ ὕπνου λέγει.	Now Jesus had spoken of his death, but they thought that He was speaking of literal sleep.
14 τότε οὖν εἶπεν αὐτοῖς ὁ Ἰησοῦς παρρησίᾳ, Λάζαρος ἀπέθανεν,	So Jesus then said to them plainly, "Lazarus is dead,
15 καὶ χαίρω δι' ὑμᾶς **ἵνα πιστεύσητε**, ὅτι οὐκ ἤμην ἐκεῖ· ἀλλὰ **ἄγωμεν** πρὸς αὐτόν.	and I am glad for your sakes that I was not there, *so that you may believe*; but *let us go* to him."
16 εἶπεν οὖν Θωμᾶς ὁ λεγόμενος Δίδυμος τοῖς συμμαθηταῖς, **Ἄγωμεν** καὶ ἡμεῖς **ἵνα ἀποθάνωμεν** μετ' αὐτοῦ.	Therefore Thomas, who is called Didymus, said to his fellow disciples, "*Let us* also *go*, *so that we may die* with Him."

All the subjunctive verbs found in verses 4, 11, 15a, 16b express *purpose* and use ἵνα; they are usually translated "in order that/to." The verbs in verses 7, 15b, 16a are often called *hortatory* subjunctives. They occur in first plural forms and are translated "let us." Verses 9 and 10 contain conditional statements; ἐάν with a subjunctive is translated "if."

Additional Examples of the Subjunctive

28.4. Here are some additional examples that round out the morphology and uses of the subjunctive.

Matt. 21:22, πάντα **ὅσα ἂν αἰτήσητε** ἐν τῇ προσευχῇ πιστεύοντες λήμψεσθε.	*Whatever you ask* in prayer you will receive if you believe.
1 Cor. 15:32, εἰ νεκροὶ οὐκ ἐγείρονται, **Φάγωμεν** καὶ **πίωμεν**, αὔριον γὰρ ἀποθνῄσκομεν.	If the dead do not rise, then *let us eat* and *drink*, for tomorrow we will die.

John 6:29, ἀπεκρίθη ὁ Ἰησοῦς καὶ εἶπεν αὐτοῖς, Τοῦτό ἐστιν τὸ ἔργον τοῦ θεοῦ, **ἵνα πιστεύητε** εἰς ὃν ἀπέστειλεν ἐκεῖνος.

Jesus answered and said to them, "This is the work of God, *that you should believe* in the one whom he sent.

Mark 6:24, ἐξελθοῦσα εἶπεν τῇ μητρὶ αὐτῆς, Τί **αἰτήσωμαι**; ἡ δὲ εἶπεν, Τὴν κεφαλὴν Ἰωάννου τοῦ βαπτίζοντος.

Going out she said to her mother, "What *should I request*?" And she said, "The head of John the Baptizer!"

Grammar of the Subjunctive

28.5. Now that you have some sense of what this new category involves, we will sort out the grammar a bit more systematically. The *subjunctive* is the name given to one of the grammatical categories called *mood*. This is in contrast to the indicative mood, which we have studied previously. The indicative mood is a statement of fact or reality (or a question about factuality or reality). By contrast, the subjunctive is the mood of *potential* or *possibility*. The situation to which reference is made is only conceptualized in the mind of the speaker or writer. In a later chapter you will meet the imperative mood—verbs that express the speaker's volition, often (but not always) in the form of a command. (You might want to review the preliminary discussion of mood in chap. 13.)

The English Subjunctive

28.6. There is a subjunctive mood in English, but it is less common than it once was. It has traditionally been explained by English grammars as expressing "an idea that is a supposition, a wish, or an idea that is doubtful or uncertain."[1] More recently some English grammarians have redefined the category of "subjunctive" from a characteristic of a verb to a clause-level description.[2] The traditional description of the English subjunctive is closer to the Greek subjunctive than the newer, functional explanation. Since both approaches are in use, examples of each English definition follow.

Traditional English Examples
If I were you, *I should not think* of accepting.
Would that you were in my place.
Had I been in your place, *I should have laughed*.

Functional English Examples
We insist that she *be kept* informed.
They demanded that the park *remain* open.

1. Pence and Emery, *Grammar of Present-Day English*, 257. The traditional English examples given in the text have been selected from this grammar.
2. This redefinition is most clearly articulated by Huddleston and Pullum, *Cambridge Grammar of the English Language*, 993–94. The functional examples cited are from this grammar.

The Greek Subjunctive

28.7. The subjunctive is quite common in Greek; there are 1,867 subjunctive verbs in the NT and 5,270 in the LXX. Although you might get by without knowing much about an English subjunctive, you will need to understand the Greek form well. Here are the basics that you need to master.

The Greek subjunctive occurs predominantly in the present and the aorist (there are also a few perfects: 10 in the NT, 7 in LXX). The tense-forms of the subjunctive mood say nothing about the time of the situation. Any time reference comes from the mood. Because subjunctives express potential, they usually relate to the future. The meaning of the tense-forms in the subjunctive is verbal aspect: the present expresses imperfective aspect (it describes a situation as a process), and the aorist expresses perfective aspect (it describes a situation as a whole). The aspect of the Greek subjunctive can seldom be distinguished when put into English, but it should be noted in exegesis.

If you put a Greek subjunctive into English, it should always reflect the *potential nature* of the statement. Often using the English helping verb "should" will be appropriate for this purpose. If a subjunctive verb is governed by a specific conjunction (see further details on these below), that conjunction is usually an adequate expression of potential in English, as you can see from the following examples: ἐὰν ἔρχηται, "*if* he comes"; ὅταν ἔρχηται, "*when* he comes"; and ἕως ἔρχηται, "*until* he comes."

Forms of the Subjunctive

28.8. It is not necessary to memorize a formula for each set of subjunctive forms or even for the subjunctive mood generally, but so that you can compare it with the other forms and formulas that you already know, here is what it looks like.

Formula for Subjunctive Verbs

stem + [form marker] + *lengthened connecting vowel* + A or C personal endings

The key to identifying a subjunctive-mood verb is a lengthened connecting vowel. Subjunctives always use primary endings (A or C) for both present and aorist forms. (There is no augment in the subjunctive, so we cannot use secondary endings. Remember: *only indicatives have augments.*) The aorist subjunctive adds the form marker sigma (*not* the usual σα)[3] before the lengthened connecting vowel.

The forms are listed in the chart below. *There is no need to memorize this chart*. You should be able to recognize it from what you already know, so long as you remember that it is the connecting vowel that lengthens to form

3. This is probably because the subjunctive requires the presence of the connecting vowel to identify the form, but that means that two vowels in a row (i.e., the alpha from the usual aorist form marker σα and the connecting vowel) are redundant, to say nothing of hard to pronounce. So one of them has to go—and only the alpha is dispensable if the form is to be recognized as a subjunctive.

the subjunctive. The first Greek column gives present *indicative* forms for comparison.

Subjunctive Forms

	Pres. Act. Ind.	Pres. Act. Subj.	Aor. Act. Subj.	²Aor. Act. Subj.
	λύω	λύω	λύω	λαμβάνω
1S	λύω	λύω	λύσω	λάβω
2S	λύεις	λύῃς	λύσῃς	λάβῃς
3S	λύει	λύῃ	λύσῃ	λάβῃ
1P	λύομεν	λύωμεν	λύσωμεν	λάβωμεν
2P	λύετε	λύητε	λύσητε	λάβητε
3P	λύουσι(ν)	λύωσι(ν)	λύσωσι(ν)	λάβωσι(ν)

	Pres. Mid. Ind.	Pres. Mid. Subj.	Aor. Mid. Subj.	²Aor. Mid. Subj.
1S	λύομαι	λύωμαι	λύσωμαι	γένωμαι
2S	λύῃ	λύῃ	λύσῃ	γένῃ
3S	λύεται	λύηται	λύσηται	γένηται
1P	λυόμεθα	λυώμεθα	λυσώμεθα	γενώμεθα
2P	λύεσθε	λύησθε	λύσησθε	γένησθε
3P	λύονται	λύωνται	λύσωνται	γένωνται

All three subjunctive columns use the same sets of endings (active and middle) for both present and aorist forms. The present and second aorist forms are identical except for the aorist stem. Some subjunctive forms are identical with other forms you already know, either present or future indicatives (e.g., λύω, λύῃ, λύσω); *only context can distinguish which is which.*[4] There are some specific things to look for in the context. Is the statement one about reality, or does it refer to a potential situation? Is the clause introduced with one of the conjunctions that govern the subjunctive mood? (See below for these conjunctions.)

Read back through the Greek passages at the beginning of this chapter, and compare them with the forms shown in the table above. Then try the examples below. You will find that they are easy to identify so long as you remember that it is the *lengthened connecting vowel* that is the identification key.

4. Λύω can be 1st sg. pres. act. ind. or subj.; λύῃ can be 2nd sg. pres. mid. ind. or subj., or 3rd sg. pres. act. subj.; and λύσω can be 1st sg. fut. act. ind. or aor. act. subj. If the verb is a liquid, the -ῃ ending could also indicate a 2nd sg. fut. mid. ind. (e.g., μενῇ).

28.9. *Now You Try It*

Mark 4:15, οὗτοι δέ εἰσιν οἱ παρὰ τὴν ὁδόν· ὅπου σπείρεται ὁ λόγος καὶ ὅταν **ἀκούσωσιν**, εὐθὺς ἔρχεται ὁ Σατανᾶς καὶ αἴρει τὸν λόγον τὸν ἐσπαρμένον εἰς αὐτούς.

Matt. 4:3, ὁ πειράζων εἶπεν αὐτῷ, Εἰ υἱὸς εἶ τοῦ θεοῦ, εἰπὲ (command!) ἵνα οἱ λίθοι οὗτοι ἄρτοι **γένωνται**.

Luke 9:57–58, πορευομένων αὐτῶν ἐν τῇ ὁδῷ εἶπέν τις πρὸς αὐτόν, Ἀκολουθήσω σοι ὅπου ἐὰν **ἀπέρχῃ**. καὶ εἶπεν αὐτῷ ὁ Ἰησοῦς, Αἱ ἀλώπεκες φωλεοὺς ἔχουσιν καὶ τὰ πετεινὰ τοῦ οὐρανοῦ κατασκηνώσεις, ὁ δὲ υἱὸς τοῦ ἀνθρώπου οὐκ ἔχει ποῦ τὴν κεφαλὴν **κλίνῃ**.

Gen. 4:8, εἶπεν Καϊν πρὸς Ἅβελ τὸν ἀδελφὸν αὐτοῦ, **Διέλθωμεν** εἰς τὸ πεδίον.[a]

[a] πεδίον, ου, τό, "field"

Other Subjunctive Forms

28.10. There is only one set of forms for the subjunctive of εἰμί; it looks like the regular present active subjunctive with no stem—just the ending. The aorist passive subjunctive uses theta as a form marker. The only perfect subjunctive found in the NT and LXX is the verb οἶδα.[5] These forms are shown in the following table.

Other Subjunctive Forms

	Pres. [Act.] Subj. of εἰμί	Aor. Pass. Subj. of λύω	Pf. Act. Subj. of οἶδα
1S	ὦ	λυθῶ	εἰδῶ
2S	ᾖς	λυθῇς	εἰδῇς
3S	ᾖ	λυθῇ	εἰδῇ
1P	ὦμεν	λυθῶμεν	εἰδῶμεν
2P	ἦτε	λυθῆτε	εἰδῆτε
3P	ὦσι(ν)	λυθῶσι(ν)	εἰδῶσι(ν)

5. There are ten perfect subjunctives of οἶδα in the NT and seven in the LXX. The perfect active subjunctive forms attested are 1st sg., εἰδῶ; 1st pl., εἰδῶμεν; 2nd sg., εἰδῇς; 2nd pl., εἰδῆτε; 3rd pl., εἰδῶσιν. There are also perfect subjunctive forms of ἀποκληρόω, ἐνέχω, ἐφίστημι, θνήσκω, μέλει, πυργόω, σύνοιδα, and τυγχάνω in Koine texts outside the NT, but such forms are quite rare. They are readily recognizable with reduplication and the same endings as seen on the present subjunctive in the NT.

There is also a second aorist passive form, which, like the second aorist passive indicative, omits the theta. As a result the second aorist passive subjunctive form is identical to the second aorist active subjunctive. Parsing is by context. There are only a few of these in the NT (about a dozen verbs). Most occur only once, three occur twice, and only one occurs five times. As a sample, the most common such verb is φαίνω, which has these second aorist passive forms: second singular, φανῇς; third singular, φανῇ; first plural, φανῶμεν; third plural, φανῶσιν.

Future Subjunctives?

You may be tempted to parse some aorist subjunctive forms such as **λύσωμεν** as future subjunctives because you see what *look like* two familiar parsing clues: a sigma as the future form marker and a lengthened connecting vowel as the sign of the subjunctive. Remember that in the subjunctive mood the aorist uses sigma as a form marker. ***There is no such thing as a future subjunctive!*** They do not exist. You will be reminded multiple times—and you will still forget sometimes.

Contract Verb Subjunctives

28.11. The contract verbs have their usual variations in the present subjunctive. You need not memorize the following charts, because they follow familiar patterns that you already know. Handle these contract forms the same as you have in all the other forms. Know the most common types of contractions, and know your vocabulary well. The connecting vowel is all that is affected. For reference, here are the most common contract verbs in the NT and LXX, one from each category. The epsilon contracts are the easiest to identify. The most troublesome forms are the second and third singular forms of the omicron and alpha contracts.

28.12. *Forms of Present Active Subjunctive Contracts*

Present Active Subjunctive Contracts

	ποιέω	πληρόω	ἀγαπάω
1S	ποιῶ	πληρῶ	ἀγαπῶ
2S	ποιῇς	πληροῖς	ἀγαπᾷς
3S	ποιῇ	πληροῖ	ἀγαπᾷ
1P	ποιῶμεν	πληρῶμεν	ἀγαπῶμεν
2P	ποιῆτε	πληρῶτε	ἀγαπᾶτε
3P	ποιῶσι(ν)	πληρῶσι(ν)	ἀγαπῶσι(ν)

28.13. *Examples of Present Active Subjunctive Contracts*

John 13:17, εἰ ταῦτα οἴδατε, μακάριοί ἐστε **ἐὰν ποιῆτε** αὐτά.

If you know these things, you are blessed *if you do* them.

Col. 4:17, εἴπατε[a] Ἀρχίππῳ, Βλέπε[b] τὴν διακονίαν ἣν παρέλαβες ἐν κυρίῳ, **ἵνα** αὐτὴν **πληροῖς**.

[a] impv. ▶ λέγω/εἶπον
[b] impv. ▶ βλέπω

Say to Archippus, "See to the ministry which you received in the Lord, *that you fulfill* it."

1 John 3:23, αὕτη ἐστὶν ἡ ἐντολὴ αὐτοῦ, **ἵνα πιστεύσωμεν** τῷ ὀνόματι τοῦ υἱοῦ αὐτοῦ Ἰησοῦ Χριστοῦ **καὶ ἀγαπῶμεν** ἀλλήλους.

This is his command, *that we believe* in the name of his Son Jesus Christ *and* [*that*] *we should love* one another.

Lev. 25:54, **ἐὰν** δὲ μὴ **λυτρῶται** κατὰ ταῦτα, ἐξελεύσεται ἐν τῷ ἔτει τῆς ἀφέσεως αὐτὸς καὶ τὰ παιδία αὐτοῦ μετ᾽ αὐτοῦ.

But *if he should* not *be redeemed* according to these [provisions], he will go forth [i.e., go free] in the year of forgiveness and his children with him.

In the aorist, the form marker prevents contraction of the lengthened connecting vowel, but the *stem vowel* lengthens when adding a form marker, as it normally does in such situations.

28.14. *Forms of Aorist Active Subjunctive Contracts*

Aorist Active Subjunctive Contracts

	ποιέω	πληρόω	ἀγαπάω
1S	ποιήσω	πληρώσω	ἀγαπήσω
2S	ποιήσῃς	πληρώσῃς	ἀγαπήσῃς
3S	ποιήσῃ	πληρώσῃ	ἀγαπήσῃ
1P	ποιήσωμεν	πληρώσωμεν	ἀγαπήσωμεν
2P	ποιήσητε	πληρώσητε	ἀγαπήσητε
3P	ποιήσωσι(ν)	πληρώσωσι(ν)	ἀγαπήσωσι(ν)

28.15. *Examples of Aorist Active Subjunctive Contracts*

Matt. 27:22, λέγει αὐτοῖς ὁ Πιλᾶτος, Τί οὖν **ποιήσω** Ἰησοῦν τὸν λεγόμενον Χριστόν;

Pilate said to them, "What, then, *should I do* with Jesus, the one called 'Messiah'?"

Eph. 4:10, ὁ καταβὰς αὐτός ἐστιν καὶ ὁ ἀναβὰς ὑπεράνω πάντων τῶν οὐρανῶν, **ἵνα πληρώσῃ** τὰ πάντα.

The one who descended is also the one who ascended above all the heavens *in order that he should fill* all things.

Matt. 5:46, **ἐὰν** γὰρ **ἀγαπήσητε** τοὺς ἀγαπῶντας ὑμᾶς, τίνα μισθὸν ἔχετε; οὐχὶ καὶ οἱ τελῶναι τὸ αὐτὸ ποιοῦσιν;

For *if you love* those who love you, what reward do you have? Don't even the tax collectors do the same thing?

Gen. 2:18, εἶπεν κύριος ὁ θεός, Οὐ καλὸν εἶναι τὸν ἄνθρωπον μόνον· **ποιήσωμεν** αὐτῷ βοηθὸν κατ' αὐτόν.

The Lord God said, "It is not good for the man to be alone; *let us make* him a helper corresponding to him."

Forms of αἰτέω

Compare the following forms of the verb αἰτέω (an epsilon contract verb). It is very important to remember *which vowel* lengthens to indicate the subjunctive. Otherwise, you will confuse these forms with future or aorist indicative forms.

ᾐτήσατε, 2nd pl. aor. act. ind. (The initial diphthong lengthens because of the augment, and the stem vowel lengthens when the aorist form marker σα is added.)
αἰτήσετε, 2nd pl. fut. act. ind. (The stem vowel lengthens when the future form marker sigma is added.)
αἰτήσητε, 2nd pl. aor. act. subj. (The stem vowel lengthens when aorist form marker sigma is added, *and* the connecting vowel lengthens to indicate subjunctive.)

28.16. *Forms of Present Middle Subjunctive Contracts*

Present Middle Subjunctive Contracts

	αἰτέω	λυτρόω	χαλάω
1S	αἰτῶμαι	λυτρῶμαι	χαλῶμαι
2S	αἰτῇ	λυτροῖ	χαλᾷ
3S	αἰτῆται	λυτρῶται	χαλᾶται
1P	αἰτώμεθα	λυτρώμεθα	χαλώμεθα
2P	αἰτῆσθε	λυτρῶσθε	χαλᾶσθε
3P	αἰτῶνται	λυτρῶνται	χαλῶνται

Examples of Present Middle Subjunctive Contracts

28.17. These forms are rare in both the NT and the LXX.

1 John 5:14–15, αὕτη ἐστὶν ἡ παρρησία ἣν ἔχομεν πρὸς αὐτὸν ὅτι **ἐάν** τι **αἰτώμεθα** κατὰ τὸ θέλημα αὐτοῦ ἀκούει ἡμῶν. καὶ ἐὰν οἴδαμεν ὅτι ἀκούει ἡμῶν **ὃ ἐὰν αἰτώμεθα**, οἴδαμεν ὅτι ἔχομεν τὰ αἰτήματα ἃ ᾐτήκαμεν ἀπ' αὐτοῦ.

This is the confidence which we have before him, that *if we ask* anything according to his will, he will hear us. And if we know that he hears us *whatever we ask*, we know that we have the requests which we request from him.

Lev. 27:27, **ἐὰν** δὲ μὴ **λυτρῶται**, πραθήσεται[a] κατὰ τὸ τίμημα αὐτοῦ.

But *if he does* not *redeem* [the animal], it will be sold according to its value.

[a] πραθήσεται ▶ πιπράσκω

Exod. 36:28, συνέσφιγξεν[a] τὸ λογεῖον (breastplate) ἀπὸ τῶν δακτυλίων τῶν ἐπ' αὐτοῦ εἰς τοὺς δακτυλίους τῆς ἐπωμίδος (ephod), **ἵνα** μὴ **χαλᾶται**[b] τὸ λογεῖον ἀπὸ τῆς ἐπωμίδος.

He fastened the breastplate by the rings which were attached to it to the rings of the ephod *in order that* the breastplate not *sag down* from the ephod.

[a] συσφίγγω, "I fasten"
[b] χαλάω, "I loosen, hang down"

28.18. *Forms of Aorist Middle Subjunctive Contracts*

Aorist Middle Subjunctive Contracts

	αἰτέω	λυτρόω	χράω
1S	αἰτήσωμαι	λυτρώσωμαι	χρήσωμαι
2S	αἰτήσῃ	λυτρώσῃ	χρήσῃ
3S	αἰτήσηται	λυτρώσηται	χρήσηται
1P	αἰτησώμεθα	λυτρωσώμεθα	χρησώμεθα
2P	αἰτήσησθε	λυτρώσησθε	χρήσησθε
3P	αἰτήσωνται	λυτρώσωνται	χρήσωνται

28.19. *Examples of Aorist Middle Subjunctive Contracts*

John 11:22, οἶδα ὅτι **ὅσα ἂν αἰτήσῃ** τὸν θεὸν δώσει (he will give) σοι ὁ θεός.

I know that *whatever you ask* God, God will give you.

Titus 2:14, ὃς ἔδωκεν (he gave) ἑαυτὸν ὑπὲρ ἡμῶν, **ἵνα λυτρώσηται** ἡμᾶς ἀπὸ πάσης ἀνομίας

Who gave himself for us *in order to redeem* us from all lawlessness

1 Macc. 13:46, εἶπαν, Μὴ ἡμῖν **χρήσῃ**[a] κατὰ τὰς πονηρίας ἡμῶν, ἀλλὰ κατὰ τὸ ἔλεός σου.

They said, "Do not *treat* us according to our evil deeds but according to your mercy."

[a] χράω, "I use, treat, deal with"

28.20. *Forms of Aorist Passive Subjunctive Contracts*

Aorist Passive Subjunctive Contracts

	φοβέω	πληρόω	πλανάω
1S	φοβηθῶ	πληρωθῶ	πλανηθῶ
2S	φοβηθῇς	πληρωθῇς	πλανηθῇς
3S	φοβηθῇ	πληρωθῇ	πλανηθῇ
1P	φοβηθῶμεν	πληρωθῶμεν	πλανηθῶμεν
2P	φοβηθῆτε	πληρωθῆτε	πλανηθῆτε
3P	φοβηθῶσι(ν)	πληρωθῶσι(ν)	πλανηθῶσι(ν)

The aorist passive subjunctive is not affected by contract verb rules, since the form marker separates the stem vowel from the connecting vowel, but the *stem vowel* lengthens when adding a form marker as usual. The endings look the same as those of the active subjunctives, apart from the accents. The chart and examples are given here simply to show you that these forms are perfectly regular.

28.21. *Examples of Aorist Passive Subjunctive Contracts*

Matt. 1:20, Ἰωσὴφ υἱὸς Δαυίδ, μὴ **φοβηθῇς** παραλαβεῖν Μαρίαν τὴν γυναῖκά σου.

Joseph, son of David, do not *be afraid* to take Mary as your wife.

John 15:11, Ταῦτα λελάληκα ὑμῖν **ἵνα** ἡ χαρὰ ἡ ἐμὴ ἐν ὑμῖν ᾖ **καὶ** ἡ χαρὰ ὑμῶν **πληρωθῇ**.

I have spoken these things to you *in order that* my joy may be in you *and* [*that*] your joy *may be full*.

Isa. 35:8, ἐκεῖ ἔσται ὁδὸς καθαρὰ καὶ ὁδὸς ἁγία κληθήσεται· οἱ δὲ διεσπαρμένοι πορεύσονται ἐπ᾽ αὐτῆς καὶ **οὐ μὴ πλανηθῶσιν**.

A clean highway will be there, and it will be called a holy highway, and those who have been dispersed will walk on it, and *they will not be led astray*.

28.22. *Now You Try It*

John 1:7–8, οὗτος ἦλθεν εἰς μαρτυρίαν ἵνα **μαρτυρήσῃ** περὶ τοῦ φωτός, ἵνα πάντες **πιστεύσωσιν** δι᾽ αὐτοῦ. οὐκ ἦν ἐκεῖνος τὸ φῶς, ἀλλ᾽ ἵνα **μαρτυρήσῃ** περὶ τοῦ φωτός.

John 3:3, ἀπεκρίθη Ἰησοῦς καὶ εἶπεν αὐτῷ, Ἀμὴν ἀμὴν λέγω σοι, ἐὰν μή τις **γεννηθῇ** ἄνωθεν, οὐ δύναται ἰδεῖν τὴν βασιλείαν τοῦ θεοῦ.

1 Clem. 7.3, **ἴδωμεν** τί καλὸν καὶ τί τερπνὸν καὶ τί προσδεκτὸν ἐνώπιον τοῦ ποιήσαντος ἡμᾶς.

1 En. 6.4, ἀπεκρίθησαν οὖν αὐτῷ πάντες, **Ὀμόσωμεν** ὅρκῳ πάντες καὶ **ἀναθεματίσωμεν** πάντες ἀλλήλους μὴ ἀποστρέψαι τὴν γνώμην ταύτην, μέχρις οὗ ἂν **τελέσωμεν** αὐτὴν καὶ **ποιήσωμεν** τὸ πρᾶγμα τοῦτο.

Ambiguous Contract Forms

28.23. Contract verbs can present some perplexing situations in which the same form might be parsed multiple ways. Here is an example in which *by form alone* λυτρώσῃ could be parsed any of three different ways.

Exod. 34:20, πρωτότοκον ὑποζυγίου **λυτρώσῃ** προβάτῳ· ἐὰν δὲ μὴ **λυτρώσῃ** αὐτό, τιμὴν δώσεις (you will give). πᾶν πρωτότοκον τῶν υἱῶν σου **λυτρώσῃ**.

The form λυτρώσῃ could be parsed in any of the following ways.

2nd sg. fut. mid. ind.
2nd sg. aor. mid. subj.
3rd sg. aor. act. subj.

Compare the paradigms in the preceding pages, and verify each of these parsing patterns. In these cases you must look for context clues as to which is correct. In each instance you should ask, are there any conjunctions that govern the subjunctive? If so, that rules out an indicative parsing. What about the grammatical person? Who is speaking or spoken to? What is being described? These forms are rarely ambiguous when evaluated in context.[6]

Conjunctions Governing Subjunctives

28.24. A number of key words govern the subjunctive mood. In the examples earlier in this chapter, you probably noticed that words other than just the subjunctive verb were marked. These key words include ἵνα, ἐάν, ὅταν, ἕως, and

6. In the example from Exod. 34:20, the first and third instances of λυτρώσῃ are both 2nd sg. fut. mid. ind. God is speaking to the people (εἶπεν κύριος, v. 10) giving them laws to obey; thus second-person future is appropriate (imperatival futures). In other, nonlegislative contexts, a subjunctive might be correct. The legal context, however, points to an imperatival statement: *you must*, not *you should*. The second instance is 2nd sg. aor. mid. subj., as clarified by the use of ἐάν. In English this verse would say, "The firstborn of a work animal *you shall redeem* with a sheep. But if *you do* not *redeem* it, you shall give [i.e., pay] a price. Every firstborn of your sons *you shall redeem*."

forms of ἀν (e.g., ὃς ἄν, ὅπου ἄν, and ἕως ἄν). What this means is that when you see one of these conjunctions, you should expect to find a subjunctive-mood verb following it (sometimes several).

There are some variations here in that some of these words can also be used with other moods, but their most common use is with the subjunctive. See the entries in BDAG for each of these words for more detail (*CL* is not as helpful on this point). For example, ἵνα is most commonly used with the subjunctive, but occasionally it does occur with an indicative-mood verb, usually a future indicative (only rarely with a present indicative, and then often with a textual variant that has the subjunctive).[7] The situation is similar with ἐάν and ὅταν (indicatives almost always have a textual variant with the subjunctive). With ἕως there is greater flexibility, but in this instance it is often due to the fact that ἕως can be used not only as a conjunction with the subjunctive (and occasionally with the indicative) but also as a preposition or an adverb.

Subjunctive Summary

Subjunctives occur predominantly in the present (464× in the NT; 618× in the LXX) and the aorist (1,396× in the NT; 4,648× in the LXX).

There is no such thing as a future subjunctive!!!

Subjunctives never have an augment (only indicatives have augments), so they use primary endings.

They are identified by the lengthening of the *connecting vowel* (not the stem vowel).

Do you remember that there is no such thing as a future subjunctive?

Uses of the Subjunctive

28.25. The subjunctive functions in statements that express several nuances in Greek. The examples below illustrate the most common uses. Study them carefully, and notice the variations in meaning that are possible, *depending on the context*. Some have specific context clues; others depend on the reader understanding the sense of the statement in the context. There are not different *kinds* of subjunctives, only different uses, or better, subjunctives used in different kinds of statements. That is, a *hortatory subjunctive* is not a different kind of subjunctive from the *deliberative subjunctive*. Both are just subjunctive verbs, but they are used in different contexts that convey the hortatory or deliberative ideas. The common labels should be understood as shorthand labels; for example, *hortatory subjunctive* should be understood to refer to the use of a subjunctive verb in a hortatory statement.

Subjunctives Used in Purpose Statements

28.26. To express purpose using a subjunctive verb, it is common to introduce the clause with the conjunction ἵνα. When the statement is negated (with μή, since the verb is subjunctive), the combination ἵνα μή can be represented in

7. The conjunction ἵνα can also occur with a form that is dying out in the Koine: the optative mood; though not so used in the NT, it is elsewhere in Koine Greek. There is one instance in the LXX: 4 Macc. 17:1, **ἵνα μὴ ψαύσειέν** τις τοῦ σώματος αὐτῆς, ἑαυτὴν ἔρριψε κατὰ τῆς πυρᾶς ("*So that* no one *might touch* her body, she threw herself into the fire").

English by "lest" in some contexts, though that phraseology is not as common as it once was in our language.

1 John 2:1, Τεκνία μου, ταῦτα γράφω ὑμῖν **ἵνα μὴ ἁμάρτητε.**

My little children, I am writing these things to you *in order that you do not sin.*

Mark 7:9, ἔλεγεν αὐτοῖς, Καλῶς ἀθετεῖτε τὴν ἐντολὴν τοῦ θεοῦ, **ἵνα** τὴν παράδοσιν ὑμῶν **στήσητε.**

He said to them, "You nicely set aside the command of God *in order to establish* your tradition."

This example will stretch you a bit beyond where we are just now since στήσητε is a μι verb. The stem is στα-, and the lexical form is ἵστημι. We will learn these verb forms in chapters 32 and 33. Jesus' statement recorded in Mark 7 is one of strong, biting irony. NET captures the irony implied by καλῶς this way: "You neatly reject."

1 Chron. 28:8, καὶ νῦν κατὰ πρόσωπον πάσης ἐκκλησίας κυρίου καὶ ἐν ὠσὶν[a] θεοῦ ἡμῶν φυλάξασθε (guard!) καὶ ζητήσατε (seek!) πάσας τὰς ἐντολὰς κυρίου τοῦ θεοῦ ἡμῶν, **ἵνα κληρονομήσητε** τὴν γῆν τὴν ἀγαθὴν καὶ **κατακληρονομήσητε** τοῖς υἱοῖς ὑμῶν μεθ' ὑμᾶς ἕως αἰῶνος.

And now in front of all the assembly of the Lord and in the hearing of our God, guard and seek all the commandments of the Lord our God *in order that you may inherit* the good land and *give it as a rightful possession* to your sons after you forever.

[a] οὖς, ὠτός, τό, "ear, hearing" (a tricky third-declension noun)

Subjunctives Used in Hortatory Statements

28.27. Hortatory subjunctives will be in the first-person plural and will not be introduced by one of the conjunctions that govern the subjunctive mood.[8] This is not a command but an exhortation. When Greek speakers wanted to express a direct command, they used the imperative mood. By contrast if they wanted to encourage action, they used a hortatory subjunctive. Notice that the speaker is included in the action in a hortatory subjunctive ("let us do this" or "we should do this") but not in an imperative ("[you] do this!").

Mark 4:35, λέγει αὐτοῖς, **Διέλθωμεν** εἰς τὸ πέραν.

He said to them, "*Let us go across* to the other side [of the lake]."

Rom. 13:12, ἡ νὺξ προέκοψεν, ἡ δὲ ἡμέρα ἤγγικεν. **ἀποθώμεθα**[a] οὖν τὰ ἔργα τοῦ σκότους, **ἐνδυσώμεθα** δὲ τὰ ὅπλα τοῦ φωτός.

The night is far gone, and the day is near. Wherefore *let us lay aside* the works of the darkness, and *let us put on* the armor of the light.

[a] ἀποθώμεθα is a μι verb, which you will learn in chaps. 32 and 33. The stem of this compound verb (ἀποτίθημι) is θε, which lengthens to θω in the subjunctive.

8. Just because a subjunctive verb is first plural does not mean that it *must* be a hortatory subjunctive.

Gen. 4:8, εἶπεν Κάϊν πρὸς Ἅβελ τὸν ἀδελφὸν αὐτοῦ, **Διέλθωμεν** εἰς τὸ πεδίον.

Cain said to his brother Abel, "*Let's go out* to the field."

Subjunctives Used in Conditional Statements

28.28. Conditional statements that involve a subjunctive-mood verb are introduced with ἐάν. (We will study this type of statement in more detail in a later chapter.)

Mark 5:28, ἔλεγεν ὅτι **Ἐὰν ἅψωμαι** κἂν τῶν ἱματίων αὐτοῦ σωθήσομαι.

She was saying, "*If I touch* even his garment, I will be healed."

Rom. 14:8, **ἐάν** τε γὰρ **ζῶμεν**, τῷ κυρίῳ ζῶμεν, **ἐάν** τε **ἀποθνῄσκωμεν**, τῷ κυρίῳ ἀποθνῄσκομεν. **ἐάν** τε οὖν **ζῶμεν ἐάν** τε **ἀποθνῄσκωμεν**, τοῦ κυρίου ἐσμέν.

For if *we should live*, to the Lord we live, and if *we should die*, to the Lord we die. Wherefore if *we should live*, or if *we should die*, of the Lord we are [= we belong to the Lord].

Notice that there are two identical forms in this verse (ζῶμεν). The first *is* a subjunctive, the second is an indicative. The form is the same (this is not an alpha contract verb; see the sidebar in chap. 21). The context determines the sense; the parallel construction with ἀποθνῄσκωμεν/ἀποθνῄσκομεν in the second clause is particularly helpful in this regard. As an isolated word, ζῶμεν may be parsed as either subjunctive or indicative; parsed in context, it can be only one of the two forms. The word τέ above is not common in the NT. For a simple translation, ἐάν τε may be translated together as "if."[9]

Judg. 4:8, εἶπεν πρὸς αὐτὴν Βαράκ, **Ἐὰν πορευθῇς** μετ' ἐμοῦ, πορεύσομαι, καὶ **ἐὰν** μὴ **πορευθῇς** μετ' ἐμοῦ, οὐ πορεύσομαι· ὅτι οὐκ οἶδα τὴν ἡμέραν, ἐν ᾗ εὐοδοῖ[a] κύριος τὸν ἄγγελον μετ' ἐμοῦ.

Barak said to her, "*If you go* with me, I will go, and *if you do* not *go* with me, I will not go, because I do not know the day in which the Lord will send his angel on a good journey with me."

[a] εὐοδοῖ, 3rd sg. pres. act. ind. εὐοδόω, "I send on a good journey, help on the way" (*CL* gives only the metaphorical use for the NT, "I prosper, succeed," but the LXX often uses the nonmetaphorical meaning.)

Subjunctives Used in Statements of Negation and Strong Negation

28.29. A subjunctive may be negated simply with μή or more strongly with οὐ μή and an aorist subjunctive.

9. BDAG (s.v. τέ, 993.2.b) gives the more technical, precise translation for this verse: "For just as when we live, we live to the Lord, so also when we die, we die to the Lord. . . . So, not only if we live, but also if we die (i.e. whether we live or die) we belong to the Lord."

1 Tim. 5:1–2, Πρεσβυτέρῳ **μὴ ἐπιπλήξῃς** ἀλλὰ παρακάλει ὡς πατέρα, νεωτέρους ὡς ἀδελφούς, πρεσβυτέρας ὡς μητέρας, νεωτέρας ὡς ἀδελφὰς ἐν πάσῃ ἁγνείᾳ.

Do not rebuke an older man, but exhort [him] as a father; [exhort] younger men as brothers, older women as mothers, younger women as sisters in all purity.

Although the least frequent use of the subjunctive, οὐ μή with an aorist subjunctive is the strongest way to say "no." It occurs only 5 times in Paul's Epistles, though more in the Gospels, with a total of approximately 75 times in the NT. It is more common in the LXX, occurring over 500 times.[10]

Gal. 5:16, Λέγω δέ, πνεύματι περιπατεῖτε [walk!] καὶ ἐπιθυμίαν σαρκὸς **οὐ μὴ τελέσητε.**

But I say, walk by the Spirit, and the strong desires of the flesh *you will never fulfill.*

Job 14:7, ἔστιν γὰρ δένδρῳ ἐλπίς· ἐὰν γὰρ ἐκκοπῇ, ἔτι ἐπανθήσει,[a] καὶ ὁ ῥάδαμνος[b] αὐτοῦ **οὐ μὴ ἐκλίπῃ.**[c]

[a] ἐπανθέω, "I bloom/flower/sprout"
[b] ῥάδαμνος, ου, ὁ, "sprout, twig, branch"
[c] ἐκλίπῃ, 3rd sg. aor. act. subj. ▶ ἐκλείπω, "I fail"

For there is hope in a tree; for if it should be cut down, yet it will sprout, and its branch *will not fail.*

Subjunctives Used in Indefinite Relative Statements

28.30. Subjunctives are often used with an indefinite relative pronoun (ὃς ἄν, etc.) to suggest the potential nature of a situation: "whoever should do x."

Mark 3:29, **ὃς δ᾽ ἂν βλασφημήσῃ** εἰς τὸ πνεῦμα τὸ ἅγιον, οὐκ ἔχει ἄφεσιν εἰς τὸν αἰῶνα, ἀλλὰ ἔνοχός ἐστιν αἰωνίου ἁμαρτήματος.

Whoever blasphemes the Holy Spirit will never have forgiveness but is guilty of an eternal sin.

1 Cor. 11:27, **ὃς ἂν ἐσθίῃ** τὸν ἄρτον ἢ **πίνῃ** τὸ ποτήριον τοῦ κυρίου ἀναξίως, ἔνοχος ἔσται τοῦ σώματος καὶ τοῦ αἵματος τοῦ κυρίου.

Whoever eats the bread or *drinks* the cup of the Lord unworthily will be guilty of the body and blood of the Lord.

Esther 2:4, καὶ ἡ γυνή, **ᾗ ἂν ἀρέσῃ** τῷ βασιλεῖ, βασιλεύσει ἀντὶ Ἀστίν.

Now the woman, *whoever is pleasing* to the king, will reign instead of Vashti.

This example shows a feminine relative pronoun used with ἄν.

Subjunctives Used in Temporal Statements

28.31. Several nuances are possible when using various temporal markers that govern the subjunctive mood.

10. See the note on οὐ μή in §29.15.5.

John 13:38, ἀμὴν ἀμὴν λέγω σοι, οὐ μὴ ἀλέκτωρ φωνήσῃ **ἕως οὗ**[a] **ἀρνήσῃ** με τρίς.

Truly, truly I say to you, the rooster will not crow *until you deny* me three times.

[a] The expression ἕως οὗ is elliptical; it assumes the fuller statement, ἕως τοῦ χρόνου ᾧ, "until the time in which." A simple "until" is adequate in English.

1 Cor. 15:54–55, **ὅταν** δὲ τὸ φθαρτὸν τοῦτο **ἐνδύσηται** ἀφθαρσίαν καὶ τὸ θνητὸν τοῦτο **ἐνδύσηται** ἀθανασίαν, τότε γενήσεται ὁ λόγος ὁ γεγραμμένος, Κατεπόθη[a] ὁ θάνατος εἰς νῖκος. ποῦ σου, θάνατε,[b] τὸ νῖκος; ποῦ σου, θάνατε,[b] τὸ κέντρον;

But *when* this corruptible *puts on* incorruption and this mortal *puts on* immortality, then will be the word that has been written, "Death has been swallowed up in victory. Where, O Death, is your victory? Where, O Death, is your sting?"

[a] Κατεπόθη, 3rd sg. aor. pass. ind. ▶ καταπίνω, "I swallow up"
[b] θάνατε, voc., "O Death!"

Judg. 13:17, εἶπεν Μανωὲ πρὸς τὸν ἄγγελον κυρίου, Τί ὄνομά σοι, ἵνα, **ὅταν ἔλθῃ** τὸ ῥῆμά σου, δοξάσωμέν σε;

Manoah said to the angel of the Lord, "What is your name, so that we may honor you *when* your word *comes?*"

And remember: *There is no such thing as a future subjunctive!* (Have you heard that before?)

28.32. *Now You Try It*

Acts 3:19–20, μετανοήσατε (repent!) οὖν καὶ ἐπιστρέψατε (turn back!) εἰς τὸ ἐξαλειφθῆναι ὑμῶν τὰς ἁμαρτίας, ὅπως ἂν **ἔλθωσιν** καιροὶ ἀναψύξεως ἀπὸ προσώπου τοῦ κυρίου καὶ **ἀποστείλῃ** τὸν προκεχειρισμένον ὑμῖν Χριστὸν Ἰησοῦν.

Rom. 1:13, οὐ θέλω δὲ ὑμᾶς ἀγνοεῖν, ἀδελφοί, ὅτι πολλάκις προεθέμην (I purposed) ἐλθεῖν πρὸς ὑμᾶς, καὶ ἐκωλύθην ἄχρι τοῦ δεῦρο, ἵνα τινὰ καρπὸν **σχῶ** καὶ ἐν ὑμῖν καθὼς καὶ ἐν τοῖς λοιποῖς ἔθνεσιν.

1 Cor. 1:10, Παρακαλῶ δὲ ὑμᾶς, ἀδελφοί, διὰ τοῦ ὀνόματος τοῦ κυρίου ἡμῶν Ἰησοῦ Χριστοῦ, ἵνα τὸ αὐτὸ **λέγητε** πάντες καὶ μὴ **ᾖ** ἐν ὑμῖν σχίσματα, **ἦτε** δὲ κατηρτισμένοι ἐν τῷ αὐτῷ νοῒ καὶ ἐν τῇ αὐτῇ γνώμῃ.

Num. 9:14, ἐὰν δὲ **προσέλθῃ** πρὸς ὑμᾶς προσήλυτος[a] ἐν τῇ γῇ ὑμῶν καὶ ποιήσει τὸ πάσχα κυρίῳ, κατὰ τὸν νόμον τοῦ πάσχα καὶ κατὰ τὴν σύνταξιν αὐτοῦ ποιήσει αὐτό· νόμος εἷς ἔσται ὑμῖν καὶ τῷ προσηλύτῳ καὶ τῷ αὐτόχθονι[b] τῆς γῆς.

[a] προσήλυτος in the NT refers to a proselyte to Judaism (see *CL*), but in the LXX it may also (and perhaps more commonly) refer to an immigrant or resident alien (see LEH and MLS); ctr. πάροικος, who was only a short-term resident in the land.

[b] αὐτόχθων, ον, "indigenous, native"; subst. αὐτόχθων, ονος, ὁ, "someone who is native to a particular country"

Josh. 1:9, ἰδοὺ ἐντέταλμαί σοι· ἴσχυε (be strong!) καὶ ἀνδρίζου (act like a man!), μὴ **δειλιάσῃς** μηδὲ **φοβηθῇς**, ὅτι μετὰ σοῦ κύριος ὁ θεός σου εἰς πάντα, οὗ ἐὰν **πορεύῃ**.

— — — — — — — — — — — — — —

28.33. Advanced Information for Reference: Diagramming Subjunctives

1 John 2:1, Τεκνία μου, ταῦτα γράφω ὑμῖν **ἵνα μὴ ἁμάρτητε.**

My little children, I am writing these things to you *in order that you do not sin.*

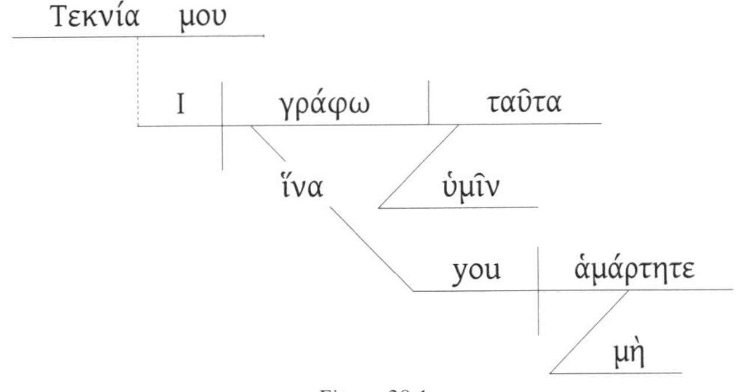

Figure 28.1

Subjunctive-mood verbs always occur in a subordinate clause, so they are diagrammed on a separate baseline, connected to the main clause with a right-slanting diagonal line that branches from the main line below the verb.

— — — — — — — — — — — — — —

28.34. Reading Passage: Matthew 5:17–30

Excerpt from the Sermon on the Mount

17Μὴ **νομίσητε** ὅτι ἦλθον καταλῦσαι τὸν νόμον ἢ τοὺς προφήτας· οὐκ ἦλθον
καταλῦσαι ἀλλὰ πληρῶσαι. 18ἀμὴν γὰρ λέγω ὑμῖν· ἕως ἂν **παρέλθῃ** ὁ οὐρανὸς καὶ
ἡ γῆ, ἰῶτα ἓν ἢ μία κεραία οὐ μὴ **παρέλθῃ** ἀπὸ τοῦ νόμου, ἕως ἂν πάντα **γένηται.**
19ὃς ἐὰν οὖν **λύσῃ** μίαν τῶν ἐντολῶν τούτων τῶν ἐλαχίστων καὶ **διδάξῃ** οὕτως
τοὺς ἀνθρώπους, ἐλάχιστος κληθήσεται ἐν τῇ βασιλείᾳ τῶν οὐρανῶν· ὃς δ᾽ ἂν
ποιήσῃ καὶ **διδάξῃ**, οὗτος μέγας κληθήσεται ἐν τῇ βασιλείᾳ τῶν οὐρανῶν. 20λέγω
γὰρ ὑμῖν ὅτι ἐὰν μὴ **περισσεύσῃ** ὑμῶν ἡ δικαιοσύνη πλεῖον τῶν γραμματέων καὶ
Φαρισαίων, οὐ μὴ **εἰσέλθητε** εἰς τὴν βασιλείαν τῶν οὐρανῶν.

21Ἠκούσατε ὅτι ἐρρέθη τοῖς ἀρχαίοις, Οὐ φονεύσεις· ὃς δ᾽ ἂν **φονεύσῃ**, ἔνοχος
ἔσται τῇ κρίσει. 22ἐγὼ δὲ λέγω ὑμῖν ὅτι πᾶς ὁ ὀργιζόμενος τῷ ἀδελφῷ αὐτοῦ
ἔνοχος ἔσται τῇ κρίσει· ὃς δ᾽ ἂν **εἴπῃ** τῷ ἀδελφῷ αὐτοῦ, Ῥακά, ἔνοχος ἔσται τῷ
συνεδρίῳ· ὃς δ᾽ ἂν **εἴπῃ**, Μωρέ, ἔνοχος ἔσται εἰς τὴν γέενναν τοῦ πυρός. 23ἐὰν οὖν
προσφέρῃς τὸ δῶρόν σου ἐπὶ τὸ θυσιαστήριον κἀκεῖ **μνησθῇς** ὅτι ὁ ἀδελφός σου
ἔχει τι κατὰ σοῦ, 24ἄφες (leave!) ἐκεῖ τὸ δῶρόν σου ἔμπροσθεν τοῦ θυσιαστηρίου
καὶ ὕπαγε (go!) πρῶτον διαλλάγηθι (be reconciled!) τῷ ἀδελφῷ σου, καὶ τότε
ἐλθὼν πρόσφερε (offer!) τὸ δῶρόν σου. 25ἴσθι (be!) εὐνοῶν τῷ ἀντιδίκῳ σου
ταχύ, ἕως ὅτου εἶ μετ᾽ αὐτοῦ ἐν τῇ ὁδῷ, μήποτέ σε **παραδῷ**[a] (should deliver
up) ὁ ἀντίδικος τῷ κριτῇ καὶ ὁ κριτὴς τῷ ὑπηρέτῃ καὶ εἰς φυλακὴν βληθήσῃ·
26ἀμὴν λέγω σοι, οὐ μὴ **ἐξέλθῃς** ἐκεῖθεν, ἕως ἂν **ἀποδῷς**[a] (you repay) τὸν ἔσχα-
τον κοδράντην.

27Ἠκούσατε ὅτι ἐρρέθη, Οὐ μοιχεύσεις. 28ἐγὼ δὲ λέγω ὑμῖν ὅτι πᾶς ὁ βλέπων
γυναῖκα πρὸς τὸ ἐπιθυμῆσαι αὐτὴν ἤδη ἐμοίχευσεν αὐτὴν ἐν τῇ καρδίᾳ αὐτοῦ.
29εἰ δὲ ὁ ὀφθαλμός σου ὁ δεξιὸς σκανδαλίζει σε, ἔξελε (remove!) αὐτὸν καὶ
βάλε (throw!) ἀπὸ σοῦ· συμφέρει γάρ σοι ἵνα **ἀπόληται** (you should lose) ἓν
τῶν μελῶν σου καὶ μὴ ὅλον τὸ σῶμά σου **βληθῇ** εἰς γέενναν. 30καὶ εἰ ἡ δεξιά
σου χεὶρ σκανδαλίζει σε, ἔκκοψον (cut off) αὐτὴν καὶ βάλε (throw!) ἀπὸ σοῦ·
συμφέρει γάρ σοι ἵνα **ἀπόληται** (you should lose) ἓν τῶν μελῶν σου καὶ μὴ
ὅλον τὸ σῶμά σου εἰς γέενναν **ἀπέλθῃ.**

[a] These verbs are both μι verb subjunctive forms, which you will learn in chap. 33.

28.35. Vocabulary for Chapter 28

Part of Speech	Definition	Possible Glosses	Frequency	
Word			NT	LXX
Adjectives				
λοιπός, ή, όν	Left and remaining out of a larger quantity; not previously included; that which/the one who remains (subst.); from now on, finally (adv.)	remaining; rest of; the rest, the other (subst.); from now on, finally (adv.)	55	120
πλείων	The comparative adjective form of πολύς ("much, large"), a quantity greater in scope than another	larger, more, greater, bigger	55	86

Part of Speech	Definition	Possible Glosses	Frequency	
Word			NT	LXX
δεξιός, ά, όν	On the right-hand side as opposed to the left in a particular frame of reference; the right hand, the right-hand side (subst.)	right (opposite of "left"; ≠ "correct"); the right hand/side	54	228
ἔσχατος, η, ον	Coming at the end or after all others, either spatially, temporally, or in rank	last, farthest; later; least, most insignificant	52	154
κακός, ή, όν	Having a harmful or injurious effect, causing harm; morally or socially reprehensible, contrary to custom or law; that which is bad/evil, one who does what is bad/evil (subst.)	harmful, dangerous; bad, evil; misfortune, a wrong, an evil deed/person	50	384
μακάριος, ία, ιον	Being in a desirable, agreeable condition, enjoying special advantage or favor	blessed, happy, fortunate, privileged	50	73
τυφλός, ή, όν	Unable to see; lacking understanding (metaphorical); a person who cannot see or understand (subst.)	blind; blind person	50	25
Nouns				
ἀρχή, ῆς, ἡ	The commencement or derivation of something; an authority figure who is preeminent [See the verb ἄρχω in chap. 17.]	beginning, start, origin; ruler, authority	55	239
Πιλᾶτος, ου, ὁ	A personal name; in the NT, the Roman prefect (πραίφεκτος/*praefectus*, Roman administrator) of Judea AD 26–36	Pilate	55	0
χρόνος, ου, ὁ	A period/span of time (time during which); a particular point of time (time at which)	period of time, time; occasion	54	141
ἐπαγγελία, ας, ἡ	That which one has committed to do for another	promise	52	8
παιδίον, ου, τό	A young human being, normally one who has not yet reached puberty, though sometimes (esp. in the LXX) used of older people (teens and young adults)	child	52	169
σοφία, ας, ἡ	Knowledge that makes possible skillful activity or performance, the capacity to understand and to act prudently as a result	wisdom, skill	51	254
γλῶσσα, ης, ἡ	The muscular organ in the mouth used for tasting, licking, swallowing, and making sounds (in humans, for speaking; "tongue"); a system of words used in communication ("language")	tongue; language	50	169
παραβολή, ῆς, ἡ	A story or pithy saying designed to illustrate a truth through comparison; something that serves as an example pointing beyond itself to a future realization	parable, illustration; type, symbol	50	45

28.36. Key Things to Know for Chapter 28

In what grammatical category does "subjunctive" belong?

What is the basic meaning of the subjunctive?

Know the subjunctive formula.

What is the one key morphological feature that distinguishes a subjunctive from an indicative?

In what tense-forms are subjunctives found? Do they ever have an augment?

Know the uses of the subjunctive (a half dozen were discussed in this chapter).

How many future subjunctives occur in the NT?

Can you list several conjunctions that usually govern the subjunctive?

29

VERBS: PART 13

Imperative- and Optative-Mood Verbs

29.1. Two moods form the focus of this chapter: the imperative and the optative moods. English has a specific kind of verb that is used to give directives: the imperative. Greek likewise has an imperative verb form that can function much like its English counterpart but that can also be used in ways different from English. Greek also has a verb form that is not found in English: the optative. It is not used frequently in the NT (only 68×), though it is more common in the LXX (590×).

The Imperative Mood

English Imperatives

29.2. We will begin with a review of English imperatives. The imperative is a different mood from the indicative or the subjunctive. Rather than making a statement or asking a question about reality, it is the mood of *directive*, which refers to "various ways of getting people to do things"; this includes requests, orders, and directions.[1] English imperatives are almost exclusively in the second person; we address a directive to a second party ("you"), either singular or plural.[2] Although the form of the verb is the same as a simple present-tense indicative verb, it is distinguished in that the subject is not usually expressed in the clause. That is, we would normally say, "Throw him overboard," or "Shut the door." We

1. Huddleston and Pullum, *English Grammar*, 32.

2. Third-person imperatives are uncommon in English (some grammarians reject the category altogether), but they may occur in statements such as "Somebody shut the door." The alternative explanation in English is that "Somebody" is a vocative and the sentence should be punctuated, "Somebody, [you] shut the door."

can include a subject for emphasis (e.g., "You throw him overboard," or "You shut the door"), but that is unusual in English.[3] There is no tense in the English imperative; we have just one form, the imperative.

When the form/spelling of an English imperative is identical to the indicative-mood verb, how do you tell the difference? The answer is context! (Did you think that it was only Greek that placed so much emphasis on context?) We look or listen specifically for such context clues as the lack of an expressed subject, the vocal tone used (when you hear it orally), and the specific situation in view.

Notice that there is no difference in the form/spelling of the verb in any of the following sentences, all of which include the same three words, "Shut the door." Only the first two are imperatives.

"Shut the door."
"The noise is becoming distracting. Tom, *shut the door.*"
"What should you do in case of fire?" "[You should] *Shut the door.*"
"What did you just do?" "[I] *Shut the door.*"
"If you *shut the door,* it will be quieter in here."
"In sales you often have people *shut the door* in your face."

Greek Imperatives

29.3. Now we need to look at Greek imperatives. The same general pattern of usage to which we are accustomed in English continues, but there are a few differences. First, both second and third person are used. Second, there are both aorist and present forms of the imperative. These tense-forms indicate aspect only. The time always relates in some sense to the future. Assuming that the imperative is realized or obeyed, it must be future from the time of speaking, since one cannot command something in the past.

The imperative forms shown here include a connecting vowel or form marker, the imperative marker τω, and the personal ending. Present imperatives use a connecting vowel; aorist forms have the usual aorist form marker σα (active and middle) or θη (for aorist passive). The imperative morpheme τω shows only in the third-person imperative. The basic form is τω, but it may appear as θω, τε, or θε due to ablaut.

Imperative Forms

	Pres. Act.	Aor. Act.	Gloss (Pres. and Aor.)
2S	λῦε	λῦσον[a]	Loose!
3S	λυέτω	λυσάτω	He/she/it must loose!
2P	λύετε[a]	λύσατε[b]	Loose!
3P	λυέτωσαν	λυσάτωσαν	They must loose!
	↑ ε = c.v.	↑ σα = f.m.	

3. In a statement like, "Tom, shut the door," the word "Tom" is not the subject of the verb; it is a vocative. There is not an explicit subject in the imperative clause.

	Pres. Mid.[c]	Aor. Mid.	Gloss (Pres. and Aor.)
2S	λύου[b]	λῦσαι[a]	Loose!
3S	λυέσθω	λυσάσθω	He/she/it must loose!
2P	λύεσθε[a]	λύσασθε[b]	Loose!
3P	λυέσθωσαν	λυσάσθωσαν	They must loose!
	↑ ε = c.v.	↑ σα = f.m.	

[a] *Identical* to another form (indicative, infinitive, or participle)

[b] *Similar* to the indicative (but no augment)

[c] These forms may also be passive if the context justifies it.

The English glosses given in the tables above may sound stilted if used without adjustment in English. They communicate the basic idea that is being conveyed by the imperative, but each instance should be communicated in natural English. See the discussions later in this chapter regarding the ways in which the imperative is used, since these can significantly affect the selection of an English equivalent.

Examples of the Imperative

29.4. The following examples show the four most common imperative forms in the NT. These are the only forms that occur more than 100 times each out of more than 1,630 imperatives.[4]

Mark 2:11, **ὕπαγε** εἰς τὸν οἶκόν σου. [2nd sg. pres. act. impv.] — *Go* to your house.

Mark 1:15, **πιστεύετε** ἐν τῷ εὐαγγελίῳ. [2nd pl. pres. act. impv.] — *Believe* in the gospel.

Mark 6:36, **ἀπόλυσον** αὐτούς. [2nd sg. aor. act. impv.] — *Send* them *away*.

Mark 11:2, **λύσατε** αὐτὸν καὶ **φέρετε**. [2nd pl. aor. act. impv. and 2nd pl. pres. act. impv.] — *Untie* it and *bring* [it to me]. (The reference is to a colt.)

Likewise, some of the most common of these imperatives in the LXX include the following:

Gen. 31:46, εἶπεν δὲ Ἰακὼβ τοῖς ἀδελφοῖς αὐτοῦ, **Συλλέγετε** λίθους. — But Jacob said to his brothers, "*Gather* stones."

4. There are 870 present imperatives in the NT (of which 602 are active voice) and 762 aorist imperatives (of which 609 are active voice). In the LXX the aorist dominates, with half of all imperatives being aorist active second-person forms (*ca*. 3,300/6,650).

Lev. 20:23, οὐχὶ **πορεύεσθε** τοῖς νομίμοις τῶν ἐθνῶν. — *Do* not *walk* by the laws of the Gentiles.

Deut. 4:1, νῦν, Ἰσραήλ, **ἄκουε** τῶν δικαιωμάτων καὶ τῶν κριμάτων, ὅσα ἐγὼ διδάσκω ὑμᾶς σήμερον ποιεῖν. — Now, Israel, *obey* the statutes and judgments which I am teaching you to do today.

Deut. 24:9, **μνήσθητι** ὅσα ἐποίησεν κύριος ὁ θεός σου τῇ Μαριὰμ ἐν τῇ ὁδῷ ἐκπορευομένων ὑμῶν ἐξ Αἰγύπτου. — *Remember* what the Lord your God did to Miriam in the way as you were coming out of Egypt.

Variations in the Form of Imperatives

29.5. The usual variations in form occur with such verbs as contracts and square-of-stops forms. With *contract verbs*, the stem vowel contracts with the connecting vowel just as you have seen repeatedly in other forms. For example, ποιέω will appear as ποιείτω in 3rd sg. pres. act. impv. (not ποιεέτω). In the aorist, when the form marker is added, the stem vowel will lengthen (e.g., ποιήσατε). Likewise the *square of stops* is relevant to aorist imperatives. This produces forms such as διωξάτω as the 3rd sg. aor. act. impv. of διώκω.

The Shortest Verse in the Bible?

Everyone knows that the shortest verse in the Bible is "Jesus wept" (John 11:35). But is it? In Greek, John 11:35 is ἐδάκρυσεν ὁ Ἰησοῦς: three words instead of two (and sixteen characters). There is a two-word verse that is shorter in Greek: 1 Thess. 5:16, Πάντοτε χαίρετε, "Rejoice always," is only fourteen characters. The next verse, 1 Thess. 5:17, is also two words, but it contains twenty-two characters: ἀδιαλείπτως προσεύχεσθε ("Pray unceasingly"). Both of these two-word verses contain imperatives.

Present Active Imperative Contracts

	ποιέω	ζηλόω	ὁράω
2S	ποίει	ζήλου	ὅρα
3S	ποιείτω	ζηλούτω	ὁράτω
2P	ποιεῖτε	ζηλοῦτε	ὁρᾶτε
3P	ποιείτωσαν	ζηλούτωσαν	ὁράτωσαν

Other Imperative Forms

29.6. Second aorist forms also follow similar patterns to other second aorist forms that you have already learned. The endings will be the same as those of the present imperative; only an aorist stem will identify the form as aorist instead of present. The forms βαλέτω and λαβέτω are the aorist imperatives of βάλλω (aorist stem βαλ-) and λαμβάνω (aorist stem λαβ-).

There are also four perfect imperatives in the NT (and 17 in the LXX), which command a certain state (e.g., Mark 4:39, πεφίμωσο, "Be still"; James 1:19 [cf. Eph. 5:5], ἴστε, "take note"; Judg. 9:15, πεποίθατε, "trust") or are part of a stereotyped greeting (e.g., Acts 15:29 [cf. 2 Macc. 11:28], ἔρρωσθε, "farewell").[5] These are identical to perfect indicative forms, so parsing is based on context.

Second Aorist Imperatives

	Active	Middle	Passive
	ἔρχομαι	λαμβάνω	ἐπιστρέφω
2S	ἐλθέ	λαβοῦ	ἐπιστράφητι
3S	ἐλθέτω	λαβέσθω	ἐπιστραφήτω
2P	ἔλθετε	λάβεσθε	ἐπιστράφητε
3P	ἐλθέτωσαν	λαβέσθωσαν	ἐπιστραφήτωσαν

The second aorist forms sometimes use first aorist endings with an alpha instead of the normal epsilon (e.g., ἐλθάτω instead of ἐλθέτω). The imperative forms of εἰμί shown below are formally present active imperatives, though these are the only forms of the imperative available for εἰμί, so the designation "present active" is not meaningful.

Aorist Passive Imperatives and the Imperative of εἰμί

	Aor. Pass.	Gloss	[Pres. Act.] of εἰμί	Gloss
2S	λύθητι	Be loosed!	ἴσθι	Be!
3S	λυθήτω	He/she/it must be loosed!	ἔστω	He/she/it must be!
2P	λύθητε[a]	Be loosed!	ἔστε	Be!
3P	λυθήτωσαν	They must be loosed!	ἔστωσαν	They must be!
	↑ θη = f.m.			

[a] *Similar* to the indicative (but no augment)

29.7. *Examples of the Imperative*

Luke 3:4, εὐθείας **ποιεῖτε** τὰς τρίβους αὐτοῦ. — *Make* his paths straight.

Matt. 3:8, **ποιήσατε** οὖν καρπὸν ἄξιον τῆς μετανοίας. — Therefore *produce* fruit worthy of repentance.

Matt. 5:37, **ἔστω** δὲ ὁ λόγος ὑμῶν ναὶ ναί, οὒ οὔ· τὸ δὲ περισσὸν τούτων ἐκ τοῦ πονηροῦ ἐστιν. — So *let* your word *be* "yes, yes" or "no, no"; and what is beyond this is from the evil one.

5. Πεφίμωσο (2nd sg. pf. mid. impv. ▸ φιμόω), ἔρρωσθε (2nd pl. pf. mid. impv. ▸ ῥώννυμι), and ἴστε (2nd pl. pf. act. impv. ▸ οἶδα). The LXX shows only two verbs with more than a single perfect imperative form. One is ἔρρωσθε (the same as the NT form), which occurs five times. The other is πεποιθέτω (3rd sg. pf. act. impv. ▸ πείθω), which occurs six times.

Mark 14:22, **Λάβετε**, τοῦτό ἐστιν τὸ σῶμά μου.	*Take* [it]; this is my body.
John 4:16, Λέγει αὐτῇ, "**Ὕπαγε φώνησον** τὸν ἄνδρα σου καὶ **ἐλθὲ** ἐνθάδε.	He said to her, "*Go*, *call* your husband, and *come* here."
Gen. 4:23, εἶπεν δὲ Λάμεχ ταῖς ἑαυτοῦ γυναιξίν Ἀδὰ καὶ Σελλά, **Ἀκούσατέ** μου τῆς φωνῆς.	Lamech said to his wives, Ada and Zellah, "*Hear* my voice!"
Gen. 6:14, **ποίησον** οὖν σεαυτῷ κιβωτὸν ἐκ ξύλων τετραγώνων.	Therefore *make* for yourself an ark out of squared lumber.

Now You Try It

29.8. This section draws from all the imperative forms.

Mark 1:25, ἐπετίμησεν αὐτῷ ὁ Ἰησοῦς λέγων, **Φιμώθητι** καὶ **ἔξελθε** ἐξ αὐτοῦ.

Acts 3:6, εἶπεν δὲ Πέτρος, Ἀργύριον καὶ χρυσίον οὐχ ὑπάρχει μοι, ὃ δὲ ἔχω τοῦτό σοι δίδωμι (I give)· ἐν τῷ ὀνόματι Ἰησοῦ Χριστοῦ τοῦ Ναζωραίου **ἔγειρε** καὶ **περιπάτει**.

Rom. 6:11, οὕτως καὶ ὑμεῖς **λογίζεσθε** ἑαυτοὺς εἶναι νεκροὺς μὲν τῇ ἁμαρτίᾳ ζῶντας δὲ τῷ θεῷ ἐν Χριστῷ Ἰησοῦ.

2 Cor. 13:12, **ἀσπάσασθε** ἀλλήλους ἐν ἁγίῳ φιλήματι. ἀσπάζονται ὑμᾶς οἱ ἅγιοι πάντες.

Eph. 5:3, πορνεία δὲ καὶ ἀκαθαρσία πᾶσα ἢ πλεονεξία μηδὲ **ὀνομαζέσθω** ἐν ὑμῖν, καθὼς πρέπει ἁγίοις.

Gen. 13:8, εἶπεν δὲ Ἀβρὰμ τῷ Λώτ, Μὴ **ἔστω** μάχη ἀνὰ μέσον ἐμοῦ καὶ σοῦ.

Gen. 37:6, εἶπεν αὐτοῖς, **Ἀκούσατε** τοῦ ἐνυπνίου τούτου.

Exod. 7:19, εἶπεν δὲ κύριος πρὸς Μωϋσῆν, **Εἰπὸν** Ἀαρὼν τῷ ἀδελφῷ σου, **Λαβὲ** τὴν ῥάβδον σου καὶ **ἔκτεινον** τὴν χεῖρά σου ἐπὶ τὰ ὕδατα Αἰγύπτου.

Exod. 32:23, λέγουσιν γάρ μοι, **Ποίησον** ἡμῖν θεούς, οἳ προπορεύσονται ἡμῶν· ὁ γὰρ Μωϋσῆς οὗτος ὁ ἄνθρωπος, ὃς ἐξήγαγεν ἡμᾶς ἐξ Αἰγύπτου, οὐκ οἴδαμεν, τί γέγονεν αὐτῷ.

Ps. 102:22 (103:22 Eng.), **εὐλογεῖτε** τὸν κύριον, πάντα τὰ ἔργα αὐτοῦ ἐν παντὶ τόπῳ τῆς δεσποτείας αὐτοῦ· **εὐλόγει**, ἡ ψυχή μου, τὸν κύριον.

Distinguishing Similar Forms

29.9. The second plural present imperatives, both active and middle, are identical to their indicative counterparts. Whether or not any such form is an imperative is usually obvious in the context. Occasionally this makes a difference in how a passage is understood. Good commentaries will usually discuss these alternatives. One clue that will sometimes help distinguish identical forms is the *negative*. Of course, not every imperative has a negative; most commands are positive. Negative imperatives use μή, not οὐ. The general principle (to which there are some exceptions) is that οὐ is the negative for the indicative mood, and μή is used with all other verbal forms.

Examples

29.10. In the following examples, read the context in an English Bible. Ask yourself, even if μή were not used, would the context make it obvious that this is an indicative or an imperative?

Mark 13:21, ἐάν τις ὑμῖν εἴπῃ, Ἴδε ὧδε ὁ Χριστός, Ἴδε ἐκεῖ, **μὴ πιστεύετε**.

If anyone should say to you, "Look! Here is the Messiah. Look! There [he is]," *do not believe* [it].

John 5:28, **μὴ θαυμάζετε** τοῦτο, ὅτι ἔρχεται ὥρα ἐν ᾗ πάντες οἱ ἐν τοῖς μνημείοις ἀκούσουσιν τῆς φωνῆς αὐτοῦ.

Do not be amazed at this, because an hour is coming in which all those in the graves will hear his voice.

Luke 2:10, εἶπεν αὐτοῖς ὁ ἄγγελος, **Μὴ φοβεῖσθε**, ἰδοὺ γὰρ εὐαγγελίζομαι ὑμῖν χαρὰν μεγάλην ἥτις ἔσται παντὶ τῷ λαῷ.

The angel said to them, "*Do not be afraid,* for look, I announce to you great joy, which is for all the people.

Matt. 6:16, Ὅταν δὲ νηστεύητε, **μὴ γίνεσθε** ὡς οἱ ὑποκριταὶ σκυθρωποί.

But when you fast, *do not be* gloomy like the hypocrites.

The following examples include some verbs that are indicative and some imperative. Can you tell which is which? (Again, use your English Bible to check the context as necessary.) In the English equivalent given in the parallel column, a blank line is used as a placeholder for the form highlighted in the Greek text.

Matt. 13:17, ἀμὴν γὰρ λέγω ὑμῖν ὅτι πολλοὶ προφῆται καὶ δίκαιοι ἐπεθύμησαν ἰδεῖν ἃ **βλέπετε** καὶ οὐκ εἶδαν, καὶ ἀκοῦσαι ἃ **ἀκούετε** καὶ οὐκ ἤκουσαν.	For truly I say to you that many prophets and righteous people have desired to see what ____ and did not see and to hear what ____ and did not hear.
Matt. 24:2, ὁ δὲ ἀποκριθεὶς εἶπεν αὐτοῖς, **Οὐ βλέπετε** ταῦτα πάντα;	But answering he said to them, "____ all these things?"
Mark 4:24, ἔλεγεν αὐτοῖς, **Βλέπετε** τί **ἀκούετε**.	He said to them, "____ what ____."
Mark 16:6, ὁ δὲ λέγει αὐταῖς, **Μὴ ἐκθαμβεῖσθε**· Ἰησοῦν **ζητεῖτε** τὸν Ναζαρηνὸν τὸν ἐσταυρωμένον· ἠγέρθη, οὐκ ἔστιν ὧδε.	So he said to them, "____.____ Jesus the Nazarene, who was crucified. He has risen; he is not here."
1 Cor. 10:31, εἴτε οὖν **ἐσθίετε** εἴτε **πίνετε** εἴτε τι **ποιεῖτε**, πάντα εἰς δόξαν θεοῦ **ποιεῖτε**.	Therefore whether ____ or whether ____ or whether ____, ____ all to the glory of God.

The Force and Uses of the Imperative

29.11. The significance of an imperative form is not always a simple matter to discern. Several factors interact in any given statement.

Force of the Imperative

The imperative often has strong force in that it expresses a command, but this is not always the case. Since it is a mood that expresses volition, some imperatives may have a weaker force in which a command seems quite inappropriate. Statements of this sort are sometimes referred to as *requests* in contrast to *commands*. Here is an example in which no sense of a command is involved.

Matt. 8:31, οἱ δὲ δαίμονες παρεκάλουν αὐτὸν λέγοντες, Εἰ ἐκβάλλεις ἡμᾶς, **ἀπόστειλον** ἡμᾶς εἰς τὴν ἀγέλην τῶν χοίρων.	So the demons begged him, saying, "If you cast us out, *send* us into the herd of pigs."

Even though the form ἀπόστειλον is clearly an imperative (2nd sg. aor. act. impv.), the demons have no ability to command Jesus to do anything. In this sort of context, the form that we identify as an imperative functions as a request. That is indicated by three factors in this context: the status of the two parties (the demons are subordinate to Jesus), the introductory word παρεκάλουν, "they begged," and the attitude already expressed in the context (see v. 29).

A weakened force for the imperative may also be observed in other types of statements that are still commands but that are introduced by a word that adds a note of politeness. That is, the speaker seeks to soften the imperative (which might otherwise be viewed as a harsh demand) by the way in which it is introduced. The following example illustrates common phrasing in Paul's writings.

1 Cor. 4:16, παρακαλῶ οὖν ὑμᾶς, μιμηταί μου **γίνεσθε**.	Therefore I exhort you, *be* imitators of me.

As in the previous example, the verb παρακαλέω is used, but since the writer stands in an authority relationship to his readers (he is an apostle), the imperative does not become a request, yet it is somewhat softened in its tone in contrast to a demand.

The use of the imperative in prayer is also an example of a weakened imperative. These are usually expressed with aorist imperatives and are to be understood as requests. The classic example is the Lord's Prayer.

Matt. 6:9–10, Οὕτως οὖν **προσεύχεσθε** ὑμεῖς·	Therefore *pray* in this manner:
Πάτερ ἡμῶν ὁ ἐν τοῖς οὐρανοῖς·	Our Father, who is in heaven,
ἁγιασθήτω τὸ ὄνομά σου·	*May* your name *be regarded as holy*,
ἐλθέτω ἡ βασιλεία σου·	*May* your kingdom *come*,
γενηθήτω τὸ θέλημά σου,	*May* your will *be done*,
ὡς ἐν οὐρανῷ καὶ ἐπὶ γῆς.	As in heaven, so on earth.

Verbal Aspect of the Imperative

29.12. In addition to contextual considerations of force, an imperative is also affected by the verbal aspect selected. Aorist imperatives express perfective aspect (= viewed as a whole); as the default imperative form, they simply state a command, often one related to a specific situation. Present imperatives express imperfective aspect (= viewed as a process); they are often used to express some additional element, whether a broader, policy command (i.e., a general command that has ongoing relevance), or sometimes a more emphatic one.

Rev. 1:11, Ὃ βλέπεις **γράψον** εἰς βιβλίον.	What you see *write* in a book.

This is an aorist imperative related to a specific situation.

1 Cor. 14:1, **Διώκετε** τὴν ἀγάπην.	*Pursue* love.

This present imperative establishes an ongoing obligation.

Assuming that the context justifies the emphasis, the use of a present imperative may convey a continuous action (as in the 1 Cor. 14 example above) or an emphatic, insistent command.

Luke 23:21, **Σταύρου σταύρου** αὐτόν.	*Crucify! Crucify* him!

Interestingly, a similar statement in John 19:6 uses a doubled aorist imperative: Σταύρωσον σταύρωσον. The parallel statement in John 19:15 reads Ἆρον ἆρον, σταύρωσον αὐτόν ("Away with him! Away with him! Crucify him!"). The doubled imperative ἆρον is an aorist. It is probably the repetition of either tense-form that produces the emphasis. In any case all such contextual factors need to be weighed when trying to decide how best to understand any given imperative form. As a general rule, think in terms of the simplest English equivalent unless there is some evidence in the context that suggests an additional connotation.

Third-Person Imperatives

29.13. Although third-person imperatives may not even exist in English,[6] they are common in Greek. In the strictest sense a third-person imperative expresses to a second party the volition of the speaker that something be done by a third person or persons. Since there is no equivalent form in English, this imperative form has traditionally been translated "*let* him/her/them [do x]." To avoid the implication that this is a statement of permission, it may be preferable to translate some such statements as "he/she/they *must* [do x]."

29.14. *Examples*

Heb. 1:6, **προσκυνησάτωσαν** αὐτῷ πάντες ἄγγελοι θεοῦ.	*Let* all the angels of God *worship* him (or, all the angels of God *must worship* him).
Gal. 1:8, ἐὰν ἡμεῖς ἢ ἄγγελος ἐξ οὐρανοῦ εὐαγγελίζηται ὑμῖν παρ' ὃ εὐηγγελισάμεθα ὑμῖν, ἀνάθεμα **ἔστω**.	If we or an angel from heaven preach a gospel to you contrary to what we preached to you, *let him be* anathema.
Deut. 4:10, εἶπεν κύριος πρός με, Ἐκκλησίασον πρός με τὸν λαόν, καὶ **ἀκουσάτωσαν** τὰ ῥήματά μου.	The Lord said to me, "Assemble the people before me, and *let them listen to* my words" (or, *they must listen to* my words).

More commonly, however, third-person imperatives *function* as indirect second-person imperatives. That is, the command, though formally stated with reference to a third party, is something that the speaker intends to be obeyed by the second party to whom the statement is addressed. This is another way by

6. See the possible example cited at the beginning of this chapter.

which the force of an imperative may be softened somewhat. You will notice that a nominative-case subject is often expressed with a third-person imperative, though it is not the agent expected to act nor the party whom the speaker is addressing.

Consider the following examples, and ask yourself, whom does the speaker expect to act? The second party, to whom the statement is addressed, or the party identified by the third-person reference?

John 14:1, Μὴ **ταρασσέσθω** ὑμῶν ἡ καρδία· πιστεύετε εἰς τὸν θεὸν καὶ εἰς ἐμὲ πιστεύετε.	*Let* not your heart *be troubled*; you believe in God, believe also in me.

The subject of the imperative is ἡ καρδία, but this third-person imperative *functions as* a second-person command addressed to Jesus' hearers. (Also note the potential ambiguity of the form πιστεύετε as well as the punctuation of the last clause.)

Matt. 5:16, οὕτως **λαμψάτω** τὸ φῶς ὑμῶν ἔμπροσθεν τῶν ἀνθρώπων, ὅπως ἴδωσιν ὑμῶν τὰ καλὰ ἔργα καὶ δοξάσωσιν τὸν πατέρα ὑμῶν τὸν ἐν τοῖς οὐρανοῖς.	In the same way *let* your light *shine* before people so that they may see your good works and glorify your Father, who is in heaven.
Matt. 27:22, λέγει αὐτοῖς ὁ Πιλᾶτος, Τί οὖν ποιήσω Ἰησοῦν τὸν λεγόμενον Χριστόν; λέγουσιν πάντες, **Σταυρωθήτω**.	Pilate said to them, "What, then, should I do with Jesus who is called Messiah?" They all shouted, "*Let him be crucified!*"

The imperative states what *Pilate* is to do.

Mark 13:14, ὁ ἀναγινώσκων **νοείτω**.	*Let* the reader *understand*.

That is, "You, reader, must understand." The intention is that the readers understand the imperative as addressed to them, even though it is phrased in third person.

How to Say "No!"

29.15. Some have said that the hardest word to say in English is *no*. Regardless of how difficult it may be, we have essentially only one option. Greek has a half dozen.

Six Ways to Say "No!" in English

Our only options in English are typographic or, in oral speech, a verbal inflection.

no No *No!* NO! NO! NOOO!!!

Six Ways to Say "No!" in Greek

1. οὐ + indicative: simple negation (Any of the spelling variants for οὐ can be used.)

   Matt. 16:23, **οὐ φρονεῖς** τὰ τοῦ θεοῦ. — *You are not thinking* the things of God.

2. μή + aorist imperative: prohibits an action (Any of the spelling variants for μή can be used.)

   Mark 13:16, ὁ εἰς τὸν ἀγρὸν **μὴ ἐπιστρεψάτω.** — *Let* the one in the field *not turn back*.

3. μή + present imperative: prohibits an action

   John 5:28, **μὴ θαυμάζετε** τοῦτο. — *Do not marvel* at this.

4. μή + aorist subjunctive: stronger negation than οὐ with the indicative

   Rev. 10:4, **μὴ** αὐτὰ **γράψῃς.** — *Do not write* these things.

5. οὐ μή + aorist subjunctive: the strongest way to say "No!"

   John 6:37, τὸν ἐρχόμενον πρὸς ἐμὲ **οὐ μὴ ἐκβάλω** ἔξω. — The one who comes to me *I will never cast* out.

In English a double negative cancels itself ("I am not not going to study" means "I *am* going to study"), but in Greek double negatives *intensify* the negation rather than cancel it.[7]

6. μή + optative mood: negative wish

   Rom. 6:2, **μὴ γένοιτο.** — *May it never come to be* (or, "God forbid!" [KJV]).

The Optative Mood

29.16. There are two grammatical forms that are rarely used in the NT; they were dying forms in the language. You have already met one of them in an earlier chapter: the pluperfect tense-form. The second is the optative mood. You will encounter this mood in the NT (though not frequently), and you may also read outside that corpus in older writings where the optative may occur more frequently. The moods studied thus far are the indicative, subjunctive, and imperative. The optative is a fourth mood. It occurs only 68 times in the NT, but 590 times in the LXX and 266 times in the Pseudepigrapha. The Apostolic Fathers use it only 50 times. In the Koine this mood was being replaced by the subjunctive.[8]

7. The strength of οὐ μή with the aorist subjunctive should not be overemphasized. See the discussion in MHT (1:187–92) and Lee ("Some Features," 18–23); a summary may be found at Mark 9:1 in Decker, *Mark*.

8. There is a later resurgence of the optative under the influence of Atticism (an artificial revival of Classical Greek modes of expression) in some of the later patristic writers such as Gregory of Nazianzus and Gregory of Nyssa (both fourth century AD).

Meaning of the Optative

29.17. Just as the indicative is the mood of "reality" and the subjunctive the mood of "potential," the optative is the mood of "wish."[9] This is not necessarily of the "wish upon a star" variety (though a Greek speaker would probably have used the optative for that sort of wish) but can include intention, prayer, potential, or desire as well. It can also be used in indirect discourse in place of an indicative or subjunctive in the original statement. As a more remote potential mood, it normally relates to the future; you would not typically use it to say "I wish I had done that yesterday."[10] Here is a basic example to get you started.

Luke 1:38, εἶπεν δὲ Μαριάμ, Ἰδοὺ ἡ δούλη κυρίου· **γένοιτό** μοι κατὰ τὸ ῥῆμά σου.	But Mary said, "Behold, the servant of the Lord; *may it be* to me according to your word."

For further discussion and classification of the various types of statements in which the optative is used, consult the grammars.[11]

Forms of the Optative

29.18. In the NT, the optative occurs only in the present and (most commonly) the aorist 23 and 45 times respectively. In the present and second aorist, the optative "mood marker" appears combined with the connecting vowel as οι and in the first aorist combined with the form marker as σαι.[12] If you remember only two things about the optative, it should be these: an οι in front of an ending marks an optative, and σαι (which you normally want to make an infinitive) *with a verb ending after it* is an optative. As you will see in the following charts, the personal endings are not exactly like any previous set that you have learned. Some look like endings of μι verbs (which you have not learned yet; see chaps. 32–33), others look like primary endings, and yet others like secondary endings (but there is no augment). The following charts will provide a reference for you to check when you run into some odd-looking forms. There are other forms of the optative (e.g., future and perfect) in Classical Greek and in other Koine writings as well.[13] If you need help with these, see the extensive charts in *MBG*, 135–43.

9. This is what the name *optative* means; it is from the Latin *opto*, "I wish."

10. In Classical Greek the optative was one means of expressing indirect discourse (which is a past-time use), but that use is rare in Koine. In the NT it occurs only a few times in Luke's writings.

11. You will find helpful discussion of the optative in Goetchius, *Language of the New Testament*, 310–13, §§383–88; Porter, *Idioms*, 59–61; Wallace, *Greek Grammar*, 480–84; and Smyth, *Greek Grammar*, 406–9, §§1814–34.

12. As you might suspect, it is more complicated than I have described above, but the simplified discussion and the charts for reference are adequate for now. For the details, see *MBG*, 135–43.

13. There are five future optatives in the LXX; they look like the present forms above with the usual future form marker (sigma). Perfect optatives are not found in the NT or LXX, but they do appear in Josephus.

Present and Second Aorist Optatives

	Pres. Act. λύω	Pres. Mid. λύω	²Aor. Act. βάλλω	²Aor. Mid. βάλλω
1S	λύοιμι	λυοίμην	βάλοιμι	βαλοίμην
2S	λύοις	λύοιο	βάλοις	βάλοιο
3S	λύοι	λύοιτο	βάλοι	βάλοιτο
1P	λύοιμεν	λυοίμεθα	βάλοιμεν	βαλοίμεθα
2P	λύοιτε	λύοισθε	βάλοιτε	βάλοισθε
3P	λύοιεν	λύοιντο	βάλοιεν	βάλοιντο

First Aorist Optative of λύω

	Active	Middle	Passive
1S	λύσαιμι	λυσαίμην	λυθείην
2S	λύσαις	λύσαιο	λυθείης
3S	λύσαι	λύσαιτο	λυθείη
1P	λύσαιμεν	λυσαίμεθα	λυθεῖμεν
2P	λύσαιτε	λύσαισθε	λυθεῖτε
3P	λύσαιεν	λύσαιντο	λυθεῖεν

The forms above are for the standard ω verbs; there are other forms for the μι verbs, but the only ones that occur in the NT are δῴη, 3rd sg. aor. act. opt. ▸ δίδωμι (4×); ὀναίμην, 1st sg. aor. mid. opt. ▸ ὀνίνημι (1×); and εἴη, 3rd sg. pres. act. opt. ▸ εἰμί (12×).

29.19. *Examples*

Mark 11:14, ἀποκριθεὶς εἶπεν αὐτῇ, Μηκέτι εἰς τὸν αἰῶνα ἐκ σοῦ μηδεὶς καρπὸν **φάγοι**. [3rd sg. ²aor. act. opt.]	Answering, he said to it [i.e., a fig tree], "*May* no one ever *eat* fruit from you again."
Rom. 6:1–2, Τί οὖν ἐροῦμεν; ἐπιμένωμεν τῇ ἁμαρτίᾳ, ἵνα ἡ χάρις πλεονάσῃ; μὴ **γένοιτο**. οἵτινες ἀπεθάνομεν τῇ ἁμαρτίᾳ, πῶς ἔτι ζήσομεν ἐν αὐτῇ; [3rd sg. ²aor. mid. opt.]	What, then, shall we say? Should we continue in sin that grace might abound? *May it* never *be*! We who died to sin, how shall we still live in it?
Acts 17:11, οἵτινες ἐδέξαντο τὸν λόγον μετὰ πάσης προθυμίας καθ' ἡμέραν ἀνακρίνοντες τὰς γραφὰς εἰ **ἔχοι** ταῦτα οὕτως [3rd sg. pres. act. opt.]	Who welcomed the word eagerly, daily searching the Scriptures [to see] if these things *might be* so

In this example, a neuter plural subject appears with a singular verb; the translation is somewhat functional. The optative verb is a form of ἔχω, but a less common use of it. Here ἔχω means "I am in some state or condition" and is used impersonally (see BDAG, 422.10.1; *CL*, 158.5.a.).

29.20. Reading Passage: 1 Timothy 6:6–21

Godliness for Ministry

6ἔστιν δὲ πορισμὸς μέγας ἡ εὐσέβεια μετὰ αὐταρκείας· 7οὐδὲν γὰρ εἰσηνέγκαμεν
εἰς τὸν κόσμον, ὅτι[a] οὐδὲ ἐξενεγκεῖν τι δυνάμεθα· 8ἔχοντες δὲ διατροφὰς καὶ
σκεπάσματα, τούτοις ἀρκεσθησόμεθα. 9οἱ δὲ βουλόμενοι πλουτεῖν ἐμπίπτουσιν
εἰς πειρασμὸν καὶ παγίδα καὶ ἐπιθυμίας πολλὰς ἀνοήτους καὶ βλαβεράς, αἵτινες βυθίζουσιν τοὺς ἀνθρώπους εἰς ὄλεθρον καὶ ἀπώλειαν. 10ῥίζα γὰρ πάντων
τῶν κακῶν ἐστιν ἡ φιλαργυρία,[b] ἧς τινες ὀρεγόμενοι ἀπεπλανήθησαν[c] ἀπὸ τῆς
πίστεως καὶ ἑαυτοὺς περιέπειραν ὀδύναις πολλαῖς.

11Σὺ δέ, ὦ ἄνθρωπε θεοῦ, ταῦτα **φεῦγε· δίωκε** δὲ δικαιοσύνην εὐσέβειαν πίστιν,
ἀγάπην ὑπομονὴν πραϋπαθίαν. 12**ἀγωνίζου** τὸν καλὸν ἀγῶνα τῆς πίστεως, **ἐπι-
λαβοῦ** τῆς αἰωνίου ζωῆς, εἰς ἣν ἐκλήθης καὶ ὡμολόγησας τὴν καλὴν ὁμολογίαν
ἐνώπιον πολλῶν μαρτύρων. 13παραγγέλλω σοι ἐνώπιον τοῦ θεοῦ τοῦ ζῳογο-
νοῦντος τὰ πάντα καὶ Χριστοῦ Ἰησοῦ τοῦ μαρτυρήσαντος ἐπὶ Ποντίου Πιλάτου
τὴν καλὴν ὁμολογίαν, 14τηρῆσαί σε τὴν ἐντολὴν ἄσπιλον ἀνεπίλημπτον μέχρι
τῆς ἐπιφανείας τοῦ κυρίου ἡμῶν Ἰησοῦ Χριστοῦ, 15ἣν καιροῖς ἰδίοις δείξει[d] ὁ
μακάριος καὶ μόνος δυνάστης, ὁ βασιλεὺς τῶν βασιλευόντων καὶ κύριος τῶν
κυριευόντων, 16ὁ μόνος ἔχων ἀθανασίαν, φῶς οἰκῶν ἀπρόσιτον, ὃν εἶδεν οὐδεὶς
ἀνθρώπων[e] οὐδὲ ἰδεῖν δύναται· ᾧ τιμὴ καὶ κράτος αἰώνιον, ἀμήν.

17Τοῖς πλουσίοις ἐν τῷ νῦν αἰῶνι **παράγγελλε** μὴ ὑψηλοφρονεῖν μηδὲ
ἠλπικέναι ἐπὶ πλούτου ἀδηλότητι ἀλλ᾽ ἐπὶ θεῷ τῷ παρέχοντι ἡμῖν πάντα
πλουσίως εἰς ἀπόλαυσιν, 18ἀγαθοεργεῖν, πλουτεῖν ἐν ἔργοις καλοῖς, εὐμετα-
δότους εἶναι, κοινωνικούς, 19ἀποθησαυρίζοντας ἑαυτοῖς θεμέλιον καλὸν εἰς
τὸ μέλλον,[f] ἵνα ἐπιλάβωνται τῆς ὄντως ζωῆς.[g]

20Ὦ Τιμόθεε, τὴν παραθήκην **φύλαξον** ἐκτρεπόμενος τὰς βεβήλους κενο-
φωνίας καὶ ἀντιθέσεις τῆς ψευδωνύμου γνώσεως, 21ἥν τινες ἐπαγγελλόμενοι
περὶ τὴν πίστιν ἠστόχησαν. Ἡ χάρις μεθ᾽ ὑμῶν.

[a] In this context the conjunction is called a "consecutive ὅτι" that indicates result: "so that." BDAG translates, "we have brought nothing into the world, so that (as a result) we can take nothing out of it" (s.v. ὅτι, 732.5.c).

[b] How do you know which of the nominatives is the subject of the first clause in v. 10?

[c] Is ἀπεπλανήθησαν a future passive or an aorist passive? How do you know? Once you have decided on the tense, does this θη form function as a passive or middle?

[d] δείξει, 3rd sg. fut. act. ind. ▸ δείκνυμι, "I make known"

[e] οὐδεὶς ἀνθρώπων, formally, "no one among humans," but for English purposes, simply "no one" is adequate. The genitive is called a "partitive genitive." In this use of the case, the genitive identifies a larger category or group of which the head word (οὐδείς) is a part.

[f] εἰς τὸ μέλλον, "for the future"; μέλλον is a participle of μέλλω.

[g] τῆς ὄντως ζωῆς, idiom, "the life that is truly life" (formally, "the truly life"—which communicates nothing helpful in English)

29.21. Vocabulary for Chapter 29

Part of Speech	Definition	Possible Glosses	Frequency	
Word			NT	LXX
Adjectives				
ἁμαρτωλός, όν	Characterized by failure to meet or neglect of moral, religious, cultural, or legal expectations; given to ἁμαρτία (usually in relation to God in the LXX and NT, but also of human expectations)	sinful, irreligious; sinner, outsider (subst.)	47	178
καινός, ή, όν	Characterized by having been in existence for only a short time, of recent origin; being new and therefore superior; not being well known previously [not distinguishable in meaning from νέος in most instances]	new, recent; unfamiliar, previously unknown	42	58
νέος, α, ον	Characterized by having been in existence for only a short time, of recent origin; being new and therefore superior; a living being who is relatively young, often the younger of two (not distinguishable in meaning from καινός in most instances)	new, recent; young, younger	23	125
Adverb				
οὐκέτι	Up to a point, but not beyond (temporal); a negative inference (logical)	no longer, no more; not, then not	47	112
Nouns				
γενεά, ᾶς, ἡ	A group of people born about the same time; a period of time in which a group of people born about the same time live; those people having common characteristics or interests; an undefined period of time	generation, contemporaries; kind (of people), race; age	43	238
σπέρμα, ατος, τό	The source from which something is propagated, both plants (seed) and animals or humans (semen); the product of propagation collectively (of animals or humans)	seed, semen; offspring, children, posterity, descendants	43	280
Verbs				
κηρύσσω	To make a public pronouncement as a herald	I preach, proclaim	61	31
ἐπιγινώσκω	To be in receipt of information that results in understanding; sometimes the context suggests the contribution of the prefixed preposition: to understand/know well/exactly/completely; to recognize based on previous knowledge (often indistinguishable from γινώσκω)	I know, understand, learn, find out; I understand/know well/exactly/completely; I recognize, acknowledge	44	145
κατοικέω	To live or stay as a resident	I live, dwell, inhabit, reside	44	685
ἁμαρτάνω	To commit a wrong by violating the standards established by God (almost always so in the NT), custom, or (human) law	I sin	43	270
ἔφη	An inflected verb form: 3rd sg. (impf. or ²aor.) act. ind. of φημί	he/she/it was saying (or said)	43	23

Part of Speech	Definition	Possible Glosses	Frequency	
Word			NT	LXX
θαυμάζω	To be extraordinarily impressed or disturbed/shocked by something	I marvel, wonder (at), am amazed, astonished, shocked	43	57
φωνέω	To utter or give out a sound intended to attract attention (human or otherwise); to summon someone to come	I call/cry (out), speak loudly; I summon, invite	43	24
ἐγγίζω	To draw closer to a reference point (either spatially or temporally)	I come/draw near, approach	42	158
εὐλογέω	To say something commendatory of someone, express high praise; to invoke God's favor on someone, ask for the granting of special favor; to bestow favor or benefit	I speak well of, praise, extol; I bless; I provide with benefits	42	516

29.22. Key Things to Know for Chapter 29

Know the grammatical person in which imperatives occur.

Know the tense-forms in which the imperative is used.

Know the key to distinguishing similar forms (e.g., second plural active/middle imperative and indicative).

The uses of the imperative: how do you distinguish a strong imperative from a weak one? What difference does this make in meaning?

In what two ways are third-person imperatives used?

Know the meaning of the optative.

30

SYNTAX: PART 3

FORMAL CONDITIONS

30.1. Conditions and statements about various conditions are a part of life. Languages have a variety of ways in which the contingent aspects of our lives may be expressed. In Greek there are both formal conditions (those defined by explicit syntactical features) and informal conditions (those understood to be conditional from the context rather than defined by specific grammatical forms). In this chapter we will study the formal conditions. Informal conditions are covered in the next chapter.

An Introduction to Formal Conditions

30.2. Conditional statements, sometimes referred to simply as *conditionals*, of various sorts play an important part in several disciplines. Computer programs use Boolean conditions to determine what action to take next. Formal logic uses statements such as "p → q" ("If p, then q"). Conditional statements are also used in geometry, insurance, law, and so forth.

In language study, a conditional statement is the use of a subordinate clause to indicate that the main clause is in some way conditioned upon the truth or falsity of the proposition in the subordinate *if* clause. English typically expresses a condition grammatically in the form "if *a*, then *b*."[1] Greek has

1. Technically, English also has several types of conditions, though the distinctions are not conscious ones to most English speakers and are not often discussed in English grammars. In English it is possible, for example, to distinguish between open conditions and closed conditions. The first leaves open the fulfillment of the condition. The second assumes lack of fulfillment: that it has not been fulfilled (a past condition), is not fulfilled (a present condition), or will not be fulfilled (a future condition). For a grammatical discussion of the English constructions, see Greenbaum

four classes of conditions, though only three of them are significant for reading the NT; all four, however, are used in the wider body of Koine literature, including the LXX.

There has been much discussion on the subject of conditional sentences in the last century. There are two schools of thought on how best to describe conditional statements; one follows the general lines of William Goodwin, and the other follows Basil Gildersleeve (both were classical scholars active in the late 1800s). The most common approach in biblical studies is that of Gildersleeve as popularized by A. T. Robertson's *Grammar* and by Blass, Debrunner, and Funk's *Greek Grammar*. In classical studies, however, the Goodwin approach may be more common (see, e.g., the standard classical reference grammar by Smyth). The discussion in this chapter uses the classification most commonly found in biblical studies as a working model.

Conditions in C

Here is a sample of a conditional statement written in C (a computer programming language):

```
if (x > 10)
  my_variable = 'foo';
else
  my_variable = 'bar';
```

Terminology

30.3. In order to facilitate a discussion of formal conditions, you need to know the technical terminology that is involved. There are two key terms: *protasis* and *apodosis*. The protasis is the "if" part of the statement and forms the subordinate clause; the apodosis is the "then" part of the statement and is the main clause in the statement. We will use this profound sentence as an example.

> If you eat all the cheese, then I won't have anything to put on the mousetrap.

The protasis is "If you eat all the cheese." The apodosis is "then I won't have anything to put on the mousetrap." These two parts can appear in either order (this is true in both English and Greek). Thus the following sentence is also possible and has the same meaning in English:[2]

> I won't have anything to put on the mousetrap if you eat all the cheese.

The *then* does not always appear explicitly in English or Greek (unless it is a second-class condition—see below). You may supply it or omit it as appropriate to make good, clear English.

(*Oxford English Grammar*, 340–41) or, in greater detail, Huddleston and Pullum (*Cambridge Grammar*, 738–65).

2. For purposes of English grammar, if the protasis precedes the apodosis, the two clauses are separated by a comma. No comma is used if the order is reversed.

Since the apodosis is the main clause, and the protasis is the subordinate clause, the apodosis goes on the baseline when diagramming a conditional statement. The English sentence used above is partially diagrammed in figure 30.1 as an example.

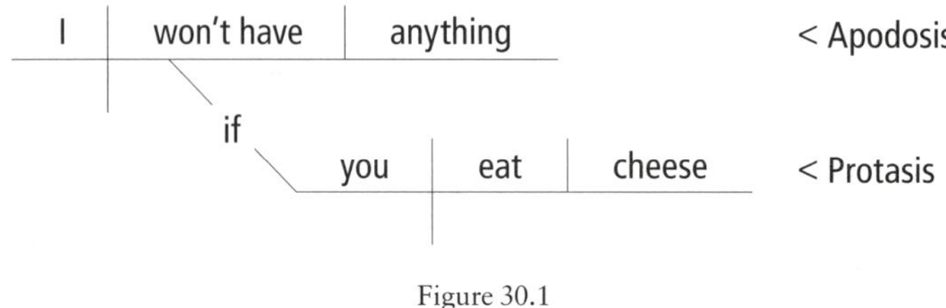

Figure 30.1

Overview of Conditional Statements

30.4. The chart below sketches the basic grammatical construction of each of the three major conditional statements.

Structure of Conditional Statements

Class	Meaning	Protasis	Apodosis
First	Simple logical connection	εἰ + indicative	any verb form
Second	Assumed to be contrary to fact	εἰ + secondary form/indicative	ἄν + secondary form/indicative
Third	Simple logical connection	ἐάν + subjunctive	any verb form

When the chart above specifies *any verb form*, it means just that: any mood or any tense-form may occur. For second-class conditions, *secondary form* refers to aorist, imperfect, or pluperfect tense-forms, which are always in the indicative mood in this type of condition. These are the tense-forms that use B or D endings and have an augment.

First-Class Conditions

30.5. There are approximately 300 first-class conditions in the NT.[3] Identifying these statements involves recognizing a statement that has a protasis with εἰ + an indicative-mood verb (other forms of εἰ may also occur; e.g., εἴπερ) and an apodosis that may have a verb in any form or mood.[4] Technically we would also

3. For further reading on first-class conditions, see Boyer, "First Class Conditions."

4. Not every instance of εἰ involves a conditional statement. One instance that may initially puzzle you is the use of εἰ to introduce either a direct or indirect question instead of a conditional statement (see *CL*, 109.2; BDAG, 277.5). This use is seen in both the NT and the LXX, perhaps more commonly in the LXX; εἰ is not used to introduce direct questions in Classical Greek.

have to specify that the apodosis is not introduced by ἄν, since second-class conditions also match the general description for a first-class condition. First-class conditions are those that cannot be more narrowly defined as second class.

Meaning

30.6. The first-class condition expresses a simple, logical connection: if the protasis is true, then the apodosis is also true. No statement is made as to whether or not the protasis is indeed true. It sometimes is true and sometimes is false. In other instances the truth or falsity of the statement is undetermined. (These judgments may be made only on the basis of the context.) It can often be said that the protasis is *assumed to be true* for purposes of argument. This does not mean that the writer believes it to be true in actuality, nor that what the writer believes to be the case is, indeed, an accurate or truthful statement.

If the context provides evidence that the protasis is indeed true, it *may* be possible to translate the particle εἰ as "since," but few (if any) such instances *should* be translated this way. The author's meaning, as evidenced from the context, almost always necessitates "if" in English to retain the rhetorical force of the statement. This is especially true if the conditional statement is the basis of an exhortation. To translate with a "since" *informs* the readers rather than *challenges* them to think. It also changes the force of a statement from what a Koine Greek reader would have understood in the first century. Then it would have been viewed simply as an "if" and not the equivalent of our "since." Using "since" retains a *logical* connection to the apodosis, but it loses the *conditional* nature of that connection.

It is *never* legitimate to argue a first-class condition backward. That is, it is always invalid to say "Because this is a first-class condition, therefore the condition must be true." You can see the problems with such an assumption in the example from Matt. 12:27 below. If you were to study all the first-class conditions in the NT and ask, based on the context of each statement, "Is the protasis actually true?" you would find something like the following.[5]

The protasis is:	% (number of occurrences)	Example
True	37% (115)	Rom. 8:9
False	12% (36)	Matt. 12:27
Undetermined	51% (155)	Rom. 8:13

The reasons why many instances are listed as undetermined vary, but typically these statements refer to repeated situations or to general truths in which the circumstances vary. In some situations with some people involved, it may be true, but with other people at a different time it may be false.

5. Boyer, "First Class Conditions," 76.

30.7. *Examples*

1 John 3:13, μὴ θαυμάζετε,[a] ἀδελφοί, **εἰ μισεῖ** ὑμᾶς ὁ κόσμος.

Do not marvel, brothers, *if* the world *hates* you.

[a] The verb θαυμάζετε is an imperative; the form is the same as an indicative, but did you notice the negative used? What do you remember about the use of οὐ and μή in regard to mood?

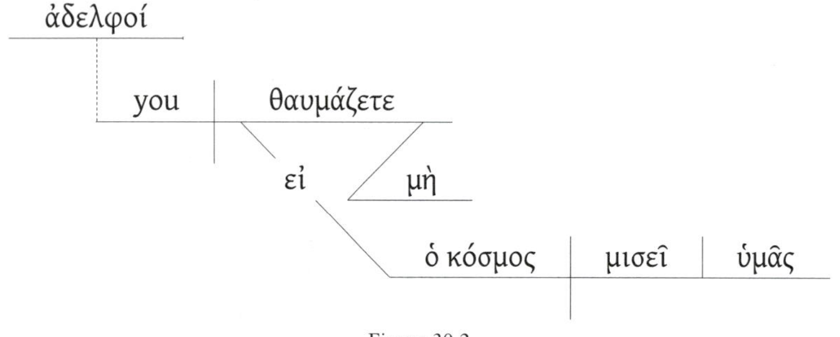

Figure 30.2

Rom. 8:9, ὑμεῖς δὲ οὐκ ἐστὲ ἐν σαρκὶ ἀλλὰ ἐν πνεύματι, **εἴπερ** πνεῦμα θεοῦ **οἰκεῖ** ἐν ὑμῖν.

But you are not in the flesh but in the Spirit *if* indeed the Spirit of God *lives* in you.

Matt. 4:3, **Εἰ** υἱὸς **εἶ** τοῦ θεοῦ, εἰπὲ ἵνα οἱ λίθοι οὗτοι ἄρτοι γένωνται.

If you are the son of God, command that these stones become bread.

This statement should not be used as an instance of understanding the protasis as expressing the idea of "since." Regardless of Jesus' identity, the Tempter is *challenging* Jesus, not assuming that he is, indeed, the Son of God.

Matt. 12:27, **εἰ** ἐγὼ ἐν Βεελζεβοὺλ **ἐκβάλλω** τὰ δαιμόνια, οἱ υἱοὶ ὑμῶν ἐν τίνι ἐκβάλλουσιν;

If I *cast out* demons by Beelzeboul, then by whom do your sons cast [them] out?

This example is a bit different in that it is in the form of a question, but it illustrates a false protasis very well. The speaker (in this instance, Jesus) poses a question in a conditional form that he knows *not to be true in reality*: "If I cast out demons by Beelzeboul"—which Jesus obviously did not do. You can see the problem of insisting that first-class conditions are true and mean "since."

4 Kgdms. (2 Kings) 1:10, ἀπεκρίθη Ἠλίου καὶ εἶπεν πρὸς τὸν πεντηκόνταρχον, Καὶ **εἰ** ἄνθρωπος τοῦ θεοῦ ἐγώ, καταβήσεται πῦρ ἐκ τοῦ οὐρανοῦ καὶ καταφάγεταί σε καὶ τοὺς πεντήκοντά σου· καὶ κατέβη πῦρ ἐκ τοῦ οὐρανοῦ καὶ κατέφαγεν αὐτὸν καὶ τοὺς πεντήκοντα αὐτοῦ.

Elijah answered and said to the captain of fifty [soldiers], "*If I* [*am*] a man of God, fire will come down from heaven and devour you and your fifty [soldiers]"; and fire came down from heaven and devoured him and his fifty [soldiers].

Notice that in this example the indicative verb may be omitted from the protasis. The verbless clause assumes a form of εἰμί.

30.8. *Now You Try It*

Matt. 8:31, οἱ δὲ δαίμονες παρεκάλουν αὐτὸν λέγοντες, **Εἰ ἐκβάλλεις** ἡμᾶς, ἀπόστειλον ἡμᾶς εἰς τὴν ἀγέλην τῶν χοίρων.

Rom. 8:13, **εἰ** γὰρ κατὰ σάρκα **ζῆτε**, μέλλετε ἀποθνῄσκειν· **εἰ** δὲ πνεύματι τὰς πράξεις τοῦ σώματος **θανατοῦτε**, ζήσεσθε.

Gal. 2:21, **εἰ** γὰρ διὰ νόμου δικαιοσύνη, ἄρα Χριστὸς δωρεὰν ἀπέθανεν.

Phil. 3:15, Ὅσοι οὖν τέλειοι, τοῦτο φρονῶμεν· καὶ **εἴ** τι ἑτέρως **φρονεῖτε**, καὶ τοῦτο ὁ θεὸς ὑμῖν ἀποκαλύψει.

Gen. 43:4–5, **εἰ** μὲν οὖν **ἀποστέλλεις** τὸν ἀδελφὸν ἡμῶν μεθ' ἡμῶν, καταβησόμεθα καὶ ἀγοράσωμέν σοι βρώματα· **εἰ** δὲ μὴ **ἀποστέλλεις** τὸν ἀδελφὸν ἡμῶν μεθ' ἡμῶν, οὐ πορευσόμεθα.

Second-Class Conditions

30.9. There are 47 examples of second-class conditions in the NT.[6] In each one the protasis is introduced by εἰ with a verb in a secondary tense-form, indicative mood.[7] The apodosis is linked by the postpositive particle ἄν with a verb in a secondary tense-form, indicative mood.[8] The second class is the most explicit and obvious of all the conditional classes in that it has specific particles that introduce both the protasis and the apodosis. (First-class conditions also introduce the protasis with εἰ, but the apodosis never has ἄν.)

Reversing a Conditional Statement

Caution! Do not assume that you can reverse a conditional statement and still have a valid statement. All you can use as a biblical statement is the explicit form of the text itself. For example, Rom. 8:13, "If you live according to the flesh, you are about to die," cannot be reversed and used to argue that, "If you are about to die, you must have lived according to the flesh."[a] You might, instead, have just been in a serious car accident.

[a] Wallace, *Greek Grammar*, 408–9, discusses several variations of this in greater detail.

6. For further reading on second-class conditions, see Boyer, "Second Class Conditions."

7. Secondary tense-forms, you will remember, are those that have an augment and use the second set of verb endings (B and D): aorist, imperfect, and pluperfect.

8. The particle ἄν is omitted in a few rare instances (e.g., Num. 22:33 and John 15:22). In such instances the second-class condition can be distinguished from the first-class condition only by the sense of the context. See Robertson, *Grammar*, 921; Conybeare and Stock, *Grammar of Septuagint Greek*, §76.

Meaning

30.10. A second-class condition is *stated* as contrary to fact. That is, the speaker *believes* the statement to be contrary to fact, though in two NT examples the speaker is wrong (Luke 7:39; John 18:30). The apodosis states what would have been true *if* the protasis were true: "If x (which I believe to be false) had been true, then y would have been true." Recognizing the meaning of the second-class condition is very important since it tells you something that cannot be determined from an English translation.

30.11. *Examples*

John 8:42, **Εἰ** ὁ θεὸς πατὴρ ὑμῶν **ἦν** **ἠγαπᾶτε ἂν** ἐμέ.

If God *were* your father, *then you would love* me.

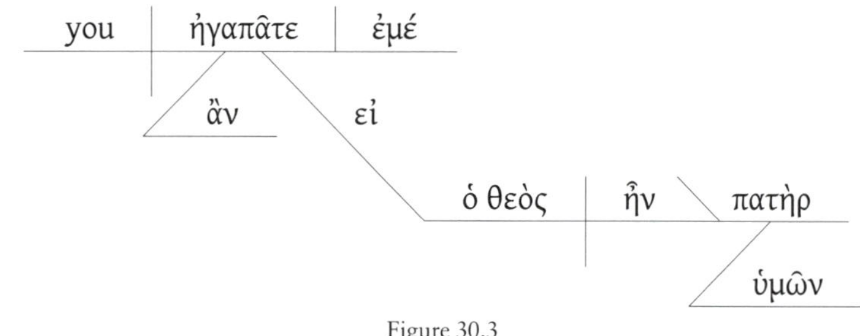

Figure 30.3

John 5:46, **εἰ** γὰρ **ἐπιστεύετε** Μωϋσεῖ, **ἐπιστεύετε ἂν** ἐμοί· περὶ γὰρ ἐμοῦ ἐκεῖνος ἔγραψεν.

For *if you had believed* Moses, *then you would have believed* me, for he wrote concerning me.

Jesus in effect says: If you had believed Moses (which I don't believe that you did), then you would have believed me.[9]

Luke 7:39, ἰδὼν δὲ ὁ Φαρισαῖος ὁ καλέσας αὐτὸν εἶπεν ἐν ἑαυτῷ λέγων,[a] Οὗτος **εἰ ἦν** προφήτης, **ἐγίνωσκεν ἂν** τίς καὶ ποταπὴ ἡ γυνὴ ἥτις ἅπτεται αὐτοῦ, ὅτι ἁμαρτωλός ἐστιν.

But observing [this] the Pharisee who invited him said to himself, "*If* this one *were* a prophet, *then he would know* who and what sort of woman is touching him, that she is a sinner."

[a] It is normal in Greek to have both a finite verb of speaking (εἶπεν) and a participle (λέγων) that refers to the same speaking, but an explicit equivalent of λέγων has been omitted from the translation since it is redundant in English.

The Pharisee thinks to himself: "If this one [= Jesus] were really a prophet [which I don't believe he is], then he would know [and since he permitted

9. If what Jesus "believes" to be true or false is always factual (a theological assumption that was disputed then as well as today), this is a much stronger statement as it stands in the biblical text than Jesus' first hearers would have understood, since they did not accept his claim to truth—the whole point of this episode.

the touch, then I must be right in my assumption: he obviously doesn't know]." Luke's point is delightful irony: it is precisely because Jesus *does* know that he allows the events described.

Judg. 13:23, εἶπεν αὐτῷ ἡ γυνὴ αὐτοῦ, **Εἰ ἐβούλετο** κύριος θανατῶσαι ἡμᾶς, οὐκ **ἂν ἐδέξατο** ἐκ τῶν χειρῶν ἡμῶν ὁλοκαύτωμα καὶ θυσίαν.

His wife said to him, "*If* the Lord *had desired* to kill us, *then he would* not *have accepted* from our hands a burnt offering and a sacrifice."

30.12. *Now You Try It*

1 Cor. 2:8, ἣν οὐδεὶς τῶν ἀρχόντων τοῦ αἰῶνος τούτου ἔγνωκεν· **εἰ** γὰρ **ἔγνωσαν**, οὐκ **ἂν** τὸν κύριον τῆς δόξης **ἐσταύρωσαν**.

John 4:10, ἀπεκρίθη Ἰησοῦς καὶ εἶπεν αὐτῇ, **Εἰ ᾔδεις** τὴν δωρεὰν τοῦ θεοῦ καὶ τίς ἐστιν ὁ λέγων σοι, Δός (give!) μοι πεῖν, σὺ **ἂν ᾔτησας** αὐτὸν καὶ ἔδωκεν ἄν σοι ὕδωρ ζῶν.

Num. 22:29, εἶπεν Βαλαὰμ τῇ ὄνῳ, **εἰ εἶχον** μάχαιραν ἐν τῇ χειρί μου, ἤδη **ἂν ἐξεκέντησά** σε.

Third-Class Conditions

30.13. There are approximately 275 third-class conditions in the NT.[10] In this class of condition the protasis is introduced with ἐάν followed by a subjunctive-mood verb; any kind of verb may be used in the apodosis.

Meaning

A key to the meaning of the third-class condition is the use of the subjunctive mood, which expresses the idea of potentiality. The third-class condition is the condition of potential fulfillment (which is, of necessity, in the future *if* it is fulfilled). It suggests that there is some measure of uncertainty regarding the future fulfillment of the condition. How certain or uncertain that may be is not specified by the condition. There is little difference between the meaning of the first- and third-class conditions. Anything expressed by a third could also have been expressed by a first (the reverse is not true, because first class can refer to past events—third-class conditions do not). Both are simple logical conditions.

10. For further reading on third-class conditions, see Boyer, "Third (and Fourth) Class Conditions."

30.14. *Examples*

John 8:51, **ἐάν** τις τὸν ἐμὸν λόγον **τηρήσῃ**, θάνατον οὐ μὴ θεωρήσῃ.

If anyone *keeps* my word, they[a] will never see death.

[a] "They" is used here as a singular; the back-pocket subject of θεωρήσῃ is a 3rd sg. that refers to τις. Some might prefer to use a generic "he," though that is less common usage in contemporary English.

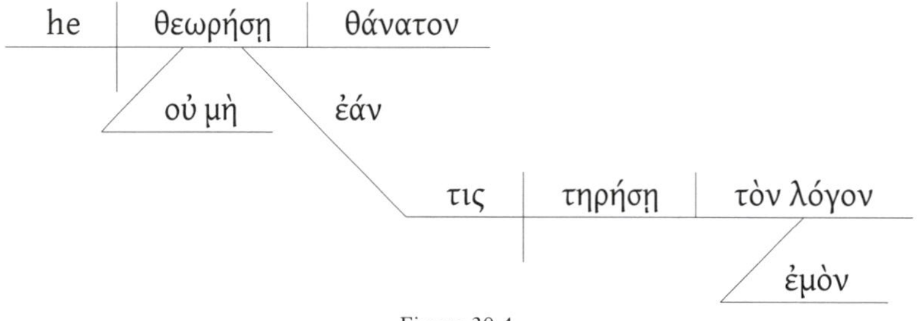

Figure 30.4

John 12:32, κἀγὼ **ἐὰν ὑψωθῶ** ἐκ τῆς γῆς, πάντας ἑλκύσω πρὸς ἐμαυτόν.

And I, *if I am lifted up* from the earth, will draw all people to myself.

John 8:55, οὐκ ἐγνώκατε αὐτόν, ἐγὼ δὲ οἶδα αὐτόν. **κἂν εἴπω** ὅτι οὐκ οἶδα αὐτόν, ἔσομαι ὅμοιος ὑμῖν ψεύστης.

You do not know him, but I know him. And *if I said*, "I do not know him," then I would be like you—a liar.

Note that ἐάν shows up here in the crasis form κἄν = καί + ἐάν.

Gen. 18:26, εἶπεν δὲ κύριος, **Ἐὰν εὕρω** ἐν Σοδόμοις πεντήκοντα δικαίους ἐν τῇ πόλει, ἀφήσω[a] πάντα τὸν τόπον δι' αὐτούς.

[a] ἀφήσω, 1st sg. fut. act. ind. ▶ ἀφίημι, "I forgive"

And the Lord said, *If I find* in Sodom fifty righteous people in the city, then I will forgive all the place because of them.

30.15. *Now You Try It*

1 Cor. 13:1, **Ἐὰν** ταῖς γλώσσαις τῶν ἀνθρώπων **λαλῶ** καὶ τῶν ἀγγέλων, ἀγάπην δὲ μὴ ἔχω, γέγονα χαλκὸς ἠχῶν ἢ κύμβαλον ἀλαλάζον.

Col. 3:13, ἀνεχόμενοι ἀλλήλων καὶ χαριζόμενοι ἑαυτοῖς **ἐάν** τις πρός τινα **ἔχῃ** μομφήν· καθὼς καὶ ὁ κύριος ἐχαρίσατο ὑμῖν, οὕτως καὶ ὑμεῖς.

James 4:15, ἀντὶ τοῦ λέγειν ὑμᾶς, **Ἐὰν** ὁ κύριος **θελήσῃ** καὶ ζήσομεν καὶ ποιήσομεν τοῦτο ἢ ἐκεῖνο.

The apodosis is introduced by καί in this example. This is not a common pattern.

Sir. 6:33, **ἐὰν ἀγαπήσῃς** ἀκούειν, ἐκδέξῃ, καὶ **ἐὰν κλίνῃς** τὸ οὖς σου, σοφὸς ἔσῃ.[a]

[a] ἔσῃ, 2nd sg. fut. mid. ind. ▶ εἰμί, "I am"

Fourth-Class Conditions

30.16. Although we have discussed only three classes of conditions thus far, there are four. The fourth class plays very little role in the NT, but you will encounter it outside the NT. Most of the examples below are from the LXX. A fourth-class condition has a protasis introduced by εἰ followed by a verb in the optative mood; the apodosis may have any kind of verb. There are no complete examples in the NT and only twelve partial ones in which either part or all of the protasis or apodosis is missing.

Meaning

30.17. The fourth-class condition presents the assumption of a possibility for the sake of argument. It is more remote than a first-class or third-class condition, this remoteness coming from the use of the optative mood.[11]

30.18. *Example from the New Testament*

1 Pet. 3:14, ἀλλ' **εἰ** καὶ **πάσχοιτε** διὰ δικαιοσύνην, μακάριοι.	But *if you should suffer* on account of righteousness, [you are] blessed.

This is the most complete example of a fourth-class condition in the NT. It is considered to be incomplete because there is no explicit verb in the apodosis, though as a verbless clause, ἐστέ is assumed.

Here is a complete list of the partial fourth-class conditions in the NT: Acts 17:11, 27; 20:16; 24:19; 25:20; 27:12, 39; 1 Cor. 14:10; 15:37; Gal. 2:17; 1 Pet. 3:14, 17.

11. If you want to read the LXX and other Koine material outside the NT, you may want to review the material on the optative mood at the end of chap. 29, especially if it was skipped in your initial study of that chapter.

30.19. *Examples from the Septuagint*

The English translations given are from NETS.

2 Kgdms. (2 Sam.) 16:12, **εἴ** πως **ἴδοι**[a] κύριος ἐν τῇ ταπεινώσει μου καὶ ἐπιστρέψει μοι ἀγαθὰ ἀντὶ τῆς κατάρας αὐτοῦ τῇ ἡμέρᾳ ταύτῃ.

If somehow the Lord *may look* on my humiliation, then he will return to me good things in place of his curse this day.

[a] ἴδοι, 3rd sg. aor. act. opt. ▶ ὁράω, "I see"

Isa. 49:15, μὴ ἐπιλήσεται γυνὴ τοῦ παιδίου αὐτῆς τοῦ μὴ ἐλεῆσαι τὰ ἔκγονα τῆς κοιλίας αὐτῆς; **εἰ** δὲ καὶ **ἐπιλάθοιτο**[a] ταῦτα γυνή, ἀλλ᾽ ἐγὼ οὐκ ἐπιλήσομαί σου, εἶπεν κύριος.

Will a mother forget her child so as not to have mercy on the descendants of her womb? But even *if* a woman *should forget* these, yet I will not forget you, said the Lord.

[a] ἐπιλάθοιτο, 3rd sg. ²aor. mid. opt. ▶ ἐπιλανθάνομαι, "I forget"

1 Kgdms. 24:20 (1 Sam. 24:19 Eng.), **εἰ εὕροιτό**[a] τις τὸν ἐχθρὸν αὐτοῦ ἐν θλίψει **καὶ ἐκπέμψαι**[b] αὐτὸν ἐν ὁδῷ ἀγαθῇ, καὶ κύριος ἀνταποτείσει αὐτῷ ἀγαθά, καθὼς πεποίηκας σήμερον.

If one *should find* his enemy in distress *and should send* him on a good way, then the Lord will repay him good as you have done today.

[a] εὕροιτο, 3rd sg. aor. mid. opt. ▶ εὑρίσκω, "I find"
[b] ἐκπέμψαι, 3rd sg. aor. act. opt. ▶ ἐκπέμπω, "I send out"

4 Macc. 4:23, ὡς ἐπόρθησεν αὐτούς, δόγμα ἔθετο ὅπως, **εἴ** τινες αὐτῶν **φάνοιεν**[a] τῷ πατρίῳ πολιτευόμενοι νόμῳ, θάνοιεν.

When he had plundered them, he issued a decree that, *if* any of them *were found* living according to the ancestral law, they should die.

[a] φάνοιεν, 3rd pl. ²aor. act. opt. ▶ φαίνω

For additional fourth-class conditions in the LXX, see 4 Macc. 4:17; 5:3, 19; 6:18–19; 8:2, 17; 9:2; 12:4; 14:17; Prov. 25:26; Job 6:2–3; 34:14–15.

Reading Passage: Galatians 1:6–24

30.20. You will find in this passage at least one example of each of the first three classes of conditional statements. They are not marked. Can you identify each one?

The Gospel of Christ and the History of Paul

6 Θαυμάζω ὅτι οὕτως ταχέως μετατίθεσθε (you are deserting) ἀπὸ τοῦ καλέ-
σαντος ὑμᾶς ἐν χάριτι Χριστοῦ εἰς ἕτερον εὐαγγέλιον, 7 ὃ οὐκ ἔστιν ἄλλο, εἰ μή
τινές εἰσιν οἱ ταράσσοντες ὑμᾶς καὶ θέλοντες μεταστρέψαι τὸ εὐαγγέλιον τοῦ
Χριστοῦ. 8 ἀλλὰ καὶ ἐὰν ἡμεῖς ἢ ἄγγελος ἐξ οὐρανοῦ εὐαγγελίζηται ὑμῖν παρ'[a] ὃ
εὐηγγελισάμεθα ὑμῖν, ἀνάθεμα ἔστω. 9 ὡς προειρήκαμεν καὶ ἄρτι πάλιν λέγω,
εἴ τις ὑμᾶς εὐαγγελίζεται παρ' ὃ παρελάβετε, ἀνάθεμα ἔστω.

10 Ἄρτι γὰρ ἀνθρώπους πείθω ἢ τὸν θεόν; ἢ ζητῶ ἀνθρώποις ἀρέσκειν; εἰ ἔτι
ἀνθρώποις ἤρεσκον, Χριστοῦ δοῦλος οὐκ ἂν ἤμην.

11 Γνωρίζω γὰρ ὑμῖν, ἀδελφοί, τὸ εὐαγγέλιον τὸ εὐαγγελισθὲν ὑπ' ἐμοῦ ὅτι
οὐκ ἔστιν κατὰ ἄνθρωπον· 12 οὐδὲ γὰρ ἐγὼ παρὰ ἀνθρώπου παρέλαβον αὐτὸ
οὔτε ἐδιδάχθην ἀλλὰ δι' ἀποκαλύψεως Ἰησοῦ Χριστοῦ.[b]

13 Ἠκούσατε γὰρ τὴν ἐμὴν ἀναστροφήν ποτε ἐν τῷ Ἰουδαϊσμῷ, ὅτι καθ' ὑπερ-
βολὴν ἐδίωκον τὴν ἐκκλησίαν τοῦ θεοῦ καὶ ἐπόρθουν αὐτήν, 14 καὶ προέκοπτον
ἐν τῷ Ἰουδαϊσμῷ ὑπὲρ πολλοὺς συνηλικιώτας ἐν τῷ γένει μου, περισσοτέρως
ζηλωτὴς ὑπάρχων τῶν[c] πατρικῶν μου παραδόσεων. 15 ὅτε δὲ εὐδόκησεν ὁ θεὸς
ὁ ἀφορίσας με ἐκ κοιλίας μητρός μου καὶ καλέσας διὰ τῆς χάριτος αὐτοῦ 16 ἀπο-
καλύψαι τὸν υἱὸν αὐτοῦ ἐν ἐμοί, ἵνα εὐαγγελίζωμαι αὐτὸν ἐν τοῖς ἔθνεσιν,
εὐθέως οὐ προσανεθέμην[d] σαρκὶ καὶ αἵματι 17 οὐδὲ ἀνῆλθον εἰς Ἱεροσόλυμα πρὸς
τοὺς πρὸ ἐμοῦ ἀποστόλους, ἀλλὰ ἀπῆλθον εἰς Ἀραβίαν καὶ πάλιν[e] ὑπέστρεψα
εἰς Δαμασκόν.

18 Ἔπειτα μετὰ ἔτη τρία ἀνῆλθον εἰς Ἱεροσόλυμα ἱστορῆσαι Κηφᾶν καὶ
ἐπέμεινα πρὸς αὐτὸν ἡμέρας δεκαπέντε, 19 ἕτερον δὲ τῶν ἀποστόλων οὐκ εἶδον
εἰ μὴ Ἰάκωβον τὸν ἀδελφὸν τοῦ κυρίου. 20 ἃ δὲ γράφω ὑμῖν, ἰδοὺ ἐνώπιον τοῦ
θεοῦ ὅτι οὐ ψεύδομαι.[f] 21 ἔπειτα ἦλθον εἰς τὰ κλίματα τῆς Συρίας καὶ τῆς Κιλικίας·
22 ἤμην δὲ ἀγνοούμενος[g] τῷ προσώπῳ ταῖς ἐκκλησίαις τῆς Ἰουδαίας ταῖς ἐν
Χριστῷ. 23 μόνον δὲ ἀκούοντες ἦσαν[g] ὅτι[h] Ὁ διώκων ἡμᾶς ποτε νῦν εὐαγγελίζεται
τὴν πίστιν ἥν ποτε ἐπόρθει, 24 καὶ ἐδόξαζον ἐν ἐμοὶ τὸν θεόν.

[a] In vv. 8 and 9 παρά is used with a less common meaning than it often has. Here it governs the accusative case (ὅ). Consult your lexicon: *CL*, 265.3.c; BDAG, 758.6.

[b] You will need to supply a verb in the last clause of v. 12; either of the first two verbs in the first part of the sentence can be used with little difference in meaning. Most English translations repeat the first verb.

[c] The article τῶν does not govern πατρικῶν, but rather it governs παραδόσεων with two genitive modifiers in first attributive position.

[d] προσανεθέμην ▸ προσανατίθημι, "I consulted with." The "consultant" is specified in the dative; here it is an idiomatic expression. How would we normally express σαρκὶ καὶ αἵματι in English?

[e] BDAG explains that πάλιν is used "pleonastically w. verbs that express the component 'back'" (s.v. πάλιν, 752.1.a). That is, you do not need to represent both πάλιν and ὑπέστρεψα in English; together they mean, "I returned."

[f] The word order and syntax of v. 20 is quite different from English. The statement as a whole is somewhat parenthetical to Paul's narrative. He pauses to declare the truthfulness of his account in the form of an oath. The main statement, ἰδοὺ ἐνώπιον τοῦ θεοῦ, does not contain a verb of swearing, though it is implied by ἰδού. A good English equivalent would be, "I assure you that, before God, I am not lying about what I am writing to you!" (NET). BDAG explains that ὅτι is used "after verbs of swearing, affirming and corresponding formulae" (s.v. ὅτι, 731.1.a; here the "corresponding formula" is ἰδοὺ ἐνώπιον τοῦ θεοῦ) to give the content of the oath or affirmation.

[g] What construction is ἤμην ἀγνοούμενος? ἀκούοντες ἦσαν?

[h] Does ὅτι introduce direct or indirect discourse?

30.21. Vocabulary for Chapter 30

Part of Speech	Definition	Possible Glosses	Frequency	
Word			NT	LXX
Adjectives				
ἔρημος, ον	Characterized by being isolated or deserted (either a place or a person); an uninhabited region	isolated, desolate, deserted; wilderness, desert (subst.)	48	386
μικρός, ά, όν	Of limited size, measure, quantity, age, or significance; that which is of such a limited nature (subst.); a little while, a short distance (neut. as adv.)	small, short, unimportant; the little one, what is insignificant; a little while, a short distance	46	165
δεύτερος, α, ον	Next after first in a sequence; for the second time (neut. sg. as adv.)	second; for the second time	43	230
Interjection				
οὐαί	An exclamation of profound grief, pain, or displeasure; a state of intense hardship or distress (subst.)	alas! woe!; woe (subst.)	46	66
Interrogative				
ποῦ	An interrogative adverb of place inquiring as to location [Watch the accent! This is not πού, an enclitic adv., "somewhere."]	where? at which place? to what place?	48	125
Nouns				
ἔτος, ους, τό	A calendar year (in the ancient world calculated on the basis of either lunar or solar cycles consisting of twelve or thirteen months); any period of twelve months	year	49	718
χρεία, ας, ἡ	That which is necessary or needed, but not necessarily possessed; an activity to which one is assigned (LXX)	need, necessity, lack; assignment, mission, (military) action	49	55
κρίσις, εως, ἡ	A scrutiny of conduct for the purpose of evaluation; a legal process of judicial evaluation of a charge; a judicial verdict of guilty and the associated sentence/penalty; the administration of what is right and fair	evaluation; (act of) judging, judgment; condemnation; right (in the sense of justice)	47	280
φόβος, ου, ὁ	A feeling of need to escape from or avoid a threat, anxiety generated by a threatening circumstance; a profound feeling of respect or reverence for an authority, especially for God	fear, terror, fright; reverence, respect, awe	47	199
φυλακή, ῆς, ἡ	A place for detaining a prisoner; a sentry station with its guards; a period of time during which guards are on duty	jail, prison, cell; guard post; watch (of the night) (i.e., a period of time)	47	121
θηρίον, ου, τό	Any living creature other than humans	animal, beast	46	164
Ἰούδας, α, ὁ	A common personal name; when referring to an OT person, the English equivalent is traditionally "Judah," otherwise "Judas" (rarely "Jude")	Judah, Judas	44	901

Part of Speech	Definition	Possible Glosses	Frequency	
Word			NT	LXX
Verbs				
φοβέω	To scare (someone), make (someone) afraid (act.; rare in the LXX, not found in the NT); to be afraid, fear (mid.); to have profound respect for a person or for God due to awe (mid.); to be frightened (by someone or something) (pass.)	I scare, make afraid, frighten (act.); I fear, am afraid (mid.); I reverence, fear, am in awe (mid.); I am frightened (by) (pass.)	95	460
κρατέω	To gain control of, often by seizing with the hands (may or may not imply force); to commit oneself to adhere strongly to someone or something	I seize, control, hold (fast), grasp, take hold of; I hold fast to, keep hold of	47	153
φυλάσσω	To carry out the duties of a sentry/guard; to protect something so that it remains intact; to diligently observe a command/law	I guard, watch; I protect; I observe, follow	31	464

30.22. Key Things to Know for Chapter 30

What is a protasis? What is an apodosis?

Which part of a conditional statement is the main clause?

The significance of conditional statements: what does each of the three major types mean?

The meaning and identification of the three different conditional statements: can you reproduce the "overview chart"? (If your teacher has asked you to learn the fourth-class condition, then there will be four types you should know.)

31

SYNTAX: PART 4

Informal Conditions and Discourse

31.1. In addition to the formal conditions studied in the previous chapter, Greek may also express conditional ideas in less formal ways. They will be our subject in this chapter along with direct and indirect discourse.

Informal Conditions

Informal conditions use various syntactical structures that do not employ an explicit *if . . . then* construction as is found in the four classes of formal conditions. In such instances the conditional factor is implied by the statement as a whole. Some of the more common ways in which this is done use constructions involving adverbial participles, imperatives, indefinite pronouns, or indefinite relative pronouns. In each case there will be a protasis and an apodosis, sometimes explicitly stated, other times only implied. Frequently this will be best represented in English with an *if . . . then* construction, but other times that is either not necessary or too clumsy. In any event, the conditional relationship should be noted. Only some of the more common informal conditions are discussed here; you will encounter other possibilities in future study.

Informal Conditions Involving Adverbial Participles

31.2. Each of the following examples has an adverbial participle that modifies the main verb. The question that must be asked in each instance is, what is the relationship between the action described in the participle and that of the main verb? You will remember from chapters 23 and 24 that there are multiple possibilities for such adverbial relationships. The one that is relevant here is that the participle specifies a condition necessary for the main verb to occur. That is, the participle functions as the protasis, and the main verbal clause is the apodosis.[1]

31.3. Examples

Gal. 6:9, καιρῷ ἰδίῳ θερίσομεν μὴ **ἐκλυόμενοι**.	In due time we will reap *if we do not give up*.
1 Tim. 4:4, πᾶν κτίσμα θεοῦ καλὸν καὶ οὐδὲν ἀπόβλητον μετὰ εὐχαριστίας **λαμβανόμενον**.	Every creation of God is good, and nothing is to be rejected *if it is received* with thanksgiving.
Heb. 7:12, **μετατιθεμένης**[a] γὰρ τῆς ἱερωσύνης[b] ἐξ ἀνάγκης καὶ νόμου μετάθεσις γίνεται.	For *if there is a change* of the priesthood, then of necessity there is also a change of law.

[a] This is a μι verb (see the next chapter): μετατίθημι (μετά + stem θε), "I change"; note the cognate noun in the next clause: μετάθεσις, εως, ἡ, "change."

[b] You will notice that this example is found as part of a genitive absolute. Although most genitive absolutes are temporal, they can express any of the adverbial nuances of an adverbial participle.

Exod. 9:15, νῦν γὰρ **ἀποστείλας** τὴν χεῖρα πατάξω σε καὶ τὸν λαόν σου θανάτῳ, καὶ ἐκτριβήσῃ ἀπὸ τῆς γῆς.	For now *if I had sent* my hand, then I would have struck you and your people with death, and you would have been destroyed from the land.

In this statement, the aorist participle ἀποστείλας appears to be describing a hypothetical past condition. God tells Pharaoh that if he had done something that he had not done (i.e., "sent his hand"), then following that (two future tense-forms, πατάξω and ἐκτριβήσῃ) the consequences would have been dire for Egypt.

31.4. Now You Try It

Luke 9:25, τί γὰρ ὠφελεῖται ἄνθρωπος **κερδήσας** τὸν κόσμον ὅλον ἑαυτὸν δὲ ἀπολέσας.	
Heb. 2:3, πῶς ἡμεῖς ἐκφευξόμεθα τηλικαύτης **ἀμελήσαντες** σωτηρίας.	
Job 35:3, ἢ ἐρεῖς, Τί ποιήσω **ἁμαρτών**;	
Song 8:1, **εὑροῦσά** σε ἔξω φιλήσω σε.	

1. This use of the participle is often discussed in NT grammars, but I am not aware of any similar discussion in LXX grammars, so here are a few additional LXX examples that I have noted: Num. 35:30, πατάξας; 2 Esd. 19:29 (Neh. 9:29 Eng.), ποιήσας; and Prov. 23:2, εἰδώς.

Lev. 18:5, φυλάξεσθε πάντα τὰ προστάγματά[a] μου καὶ πάντα τὰ κρίματά μου καὶ ποιήσετε αὐτά, ἃ **ποιήσας** ἄνθρωπος ζήσεται ἐν αὐτοῖς· ἐγὼ κύριος ὁ θεὸς ὑμῶν.

[a] πρόσταγμα, ατος, τό, "order, command(ment), injunction"

Informal Conditions Involving an Imperative

31.5. Imperatives do not, by themselves, express a condition. They are volitional statements expressing the will of the speaker. There is a construction, however, that includes an imperative functioning in the protasis of an informal condition. The syntactical pattern involved is as follows.

Imperative + καί + future indicative

In most cases where this construction is found in the NT and the LXX, the imperative specifies a command that, if obeyed, will result in the condition described by the future indicative verb. That is, the imperative is part of the protasis, and the future is part of the apodosis.

31.6. Examples

Matt. 11:28, **Δεῦτε** πρός με πάντες οἱ κοπιῶντες καὶ πεφορτισμένοι, κἀγὼ **ἀναπαύσω** ὑμᾶς.

Come to me all who are weary and burdened, and *I will give* you *rest*.

This statement is equivalent to the following condition: "If you come to me, then I will give you rest."[2] The command to come must be obeyed for the rest to be obtained; the imperative is, in essence, a condition that must be met. In this example, δεῦτε is not an imperative form (technically, it is an adverb, "here"), but it functions with the force of a verb (short for "Come here!"). The statement as a whole functions as an informal condition. (The same expression occurs in the example from Mark 1:17 in §31.7.)

James 4:7, **ὑποτάγητε**[a] οὖν τῷ θεῷ, **ἀντίστητε**[b] δὲ τῷ διαβόλῳ καὶ **φεύξεται**[c] ἀφ' ὑμῶν.

Therefore *submit* to God and *resist* the devil, and *he will flee* from you.

[a] ὑποτάγητε, 2nd pl. aor. pass. impv. ▶ ὑποτάσσω
[b] ἀντίστητε, 2nd pl. aor. act. impv. ▶ ἀνθίστημι
[c] φεύξεται, 3rd sg. fut. mid. ind. ▶ φεύγω

This statement is equivalent to the following condition: "*If* you submit to God and resist the devil, *then* he will flee." The commands to submit and

2. Neither here nor in the examples that follow would the imperative be *translated* with an explicit *if* statement. These *are* imperatives. The equivalent *if* statements given in the text are intended to help you understand the meaning of the sentence.

resist must be obeyed so that the devil will flee. The imperatives are, in essence, conditions that must be met. The verb form ὑποτάγητε is still an imperative, but the statement as a whole functions as an informal condition.

Gen. 42:18, Εἶπεν δὲ αὐτοῖς τῇ ἡμέρᾳ τῇ τρίτῃ, Τοῦτο **ποιήσατε καὶ ζήσεσθε.**	So he said to them on the third day, "*Do* this, *and you will live.*"

That is: "*If* you do this, *then* you will live."

31.7. Now You Try It

Mark 1:17, εἶπεν αὐτοῖς ὁ Ἰησοῦς, **Δεῦτε** ὀπίσω μου,[a] καὶ **ποιήσω** ὑμᾶς γενέσθαι ἁλιεῖς ἀνθρώπων.

[a] Δεῦτε ὀπίσω μου, formally, "come behind me"; idiomatically, "follow me"

Ps. 36:3 (37:3 Eng.), **κατασκήνου** τὴν γῆν, καὶ **ποιμανθήσῃ** ἐπὶ τῷ πλούτῳ αὐτῆς.

Informal Conditions Involving Indefinite Relative Pronouns

31.8. Relative pronouns can sometimes introduce a statement that functions as an informal condition. This usually involves an indefinite relative pronoun such as ὅστις or ὃς ἄν. Although these can usually be represented in English with the usual forms for the relative pronoun, it is sometimes helpful to make the intent of the text clear by making the *if . . . then* explicit.

31.9. Examples

Matt. 5:39, ἐγὼ δὲ λέγω ὑμῖν μὴ ἀντιστῆναι τῷ πονηρῷ· ἀλλ' **ὅστις** σε ῥαπίζει εἰς τὴν δεξιὰν σιαγόνα σου, στρέψον αὐτῷ καὶ τὴν ἄλλην.	But I say to you, do not resist the evil person, but *if anyone* slaps you on your right cheek, *then* turn the other to him also.
1 John 3:17, **ὃς δ' ἂν** ἔχῃ τὸν βίον τοῦ κόσμου καὶ θεωρῇ τὸν ἀδελφὸν αὐτοῦ χρείαν ἔχοντα καὶ κλείσῃ τὰ σπλάγχνα αὐτοῦ ἀπ' αὐτοῦ, πῶς ἡ ἀγάπη τοῦ θεοῦ μένει ἐν αὐτῷ;	*But if anyone* has the goods of [this] world and sees his brother who has a need and shuts up his compassion from him, *then* how does the love of God rest in him?
Gen. 44:9, παρ' **ᾧ ἂν** εὑρεθῇ τὸ κόνδυ τῶν παίδων σου, ἀποθνῃσκέτω.	With *whom*, then, should be found the cup among your servants, he must die.[a]

[a] The translation given is very formal. More idiomatically to show the condition: "*If* anyone of your servants should be found to have the cup, *then* he must die."

31.10. Now You Try It

Matt. 5:41, **ὅστις** σε ἀγγαρεύσει μίλιον ἕν, ὕπαγε μετ' αὐτοῦ δύο.

Luke 9:26, **ὃς** γὰρ **ἂν** ἐπαισχυνθῇ με καὶ τοὺς ἐμοὺς λόγους, τοῦτον ὁ υἱὸς τοῦ ἀνθρώπου ἐπαισχυνθήσεται, ὅταν ἔλθῃ ἐν τῇ δόξῃ αὐτοῦ καὶ τοῦ πατρὸς καὶ τῶν ἁγίων ἀγγέλων.

Exod. 12:15, **ὃς ἂν** φάγῃ ζύμην, ἐξολεθρευθήσεται ἡ ψυχὴ ἐκείνη ἐξ Ἰσραήλ.

Informal Conditions Involving Indefinite Pronouns

31.11. The indefinite nuance of the pronoun τις enables it to be used in a statement with an implied condition. English translations have traditionally phrased the following example from James 5 as a question,[3] but the punctuation in the Greek NT uses a comma, not a question mark. Recognizing the informal condition in this verse makes better sense of the comma. The translation given uses a singular "they"; some will prefer to use generic "he" instead. (Notice the use of the third-person imperatives in the apodosis of both sentences.)

31.12. Examples

James 5:13, Κακοπαθεῖ **τις** ἐν ὑμῖν, προσευχέσθω· εὐθυμεῖ **τις**, ψαλλέτω.	*If anyone* among you is suffering, they should pray. *If anyone* is cheerful [giddy?], they should sing psalms.
Gen. 19:12, Εἶπαν δὲ οἱ ἄνδρες πρὸς Λώτ, Ἔστιν **τίς** σοι ὧδε, γαμβροὶ ἢ υἱοὶ ἢ θυγατέρες, ἢ εἴ τίς σοι ἄλλος ἔστιν ἐν τῇ πόλει, ἐξάγαγε ἐκ τοῦ τόπου τούτου.	So the men said to Lot, "*If* you have *anyone* here, sons-in-law or sons or daughters, or if anyone else [is related] to you in the city, then bring [them] out of this place."

The first part of this text is often punctuated as a question ("Have you anyone here . . . ?"), but since that statement is parallel with the explicit **εἴ τίς** in the next clause, it makes better sense to read this as a single statement, recognizing the first part as an informal condition.

3. E.g., NIV, "Is anyone among you in trouble? Let them pray. Is anyone happy? Let them sing songs of praise" (see also NRSV, ESV). For a translation that does not punctuate as a question and that recognizes the condition implied, see CEB, "If any of you are suffering, they should pray. If any of you are happy, they should sing."

31.13. Now You Try It

James 5:14, ἀσθενεῖ **τις** ἐν ὑμῖν, προσκαλεσάσθω τοὺς πρεσβυτέρους τῆς ἐκκλησίας καὶ προσευξάσθωσαν ἐπ' αὐτὸν ἀλείψαντες αὐτὸν ἐλαίῳ ἐν τῷ ὀνόματι τοῦ κυρίου.

James 2:16, εἴπῃ δέ **τις** αὐτοῖς ἐξ ὑμῶν, Ὑπάγετε ἐν εἰρήνῃ, θερμαίνεσθε καὶ χορτάζεσθε, μὴ δῶτε (give) δὲ αὐτοῖς τὰ ἐπιτήδεια τοῦ σώματος, τί τὸ ὄφελος;

Prov. 6:27–28, ἀποδήσει **τις** πῦρ ἐν κόλπῳ, τὰ δὲ ἱμάτια οὐ κατακαύσει; ἢ περιπατήσει **τις** ἐπ' ἀνθράκων πυρός, τοὺς δὲ πόδας οὐ κατακαύσει;

This example need not be translated explicitly as a condition, but the conditions and results (protasis and apodosis) are obvious.

Prov. 3:30, μὴ φιλεχθρήσῃς[a] πρὸς ἄνθρωπον μάτην, μή **τι** εἰς σὲ ἐργάσηται κακόν.

[a] φιλεχθρέω, "I exercise enmity against, quarrel with"

Direct and Indirect Discourse

31.14. The recording of or reference to what people say or think is an important part of narrative texts. You have read many such statements already, but we have not studied such statements as a category of discourse. Here we learn how both direct and indirect discourse are expressed in Greek texts and how that differs from English conventions.

Definitions

Direct discourse is the reporting of someone's statement (or sometimes, thought) with some indication that the words are given as originally spoken. *Indirect discourse* is the reporting of someone's statement or thought in such a way that the content is preserved but the exact words are not recorded.

English Examples

31.15. We will begin with some examples from a popular English epic, *The Lord of the Rings.*

[1]"I wish it need not have happened in my time," said Frodo.

"So do I," said Gandalf, "and so do all we who live to see such times. But that is not for them to decide. All we have to decide is what to do with the time that is given us."

—Tolkien, *Lord of the Rings*, book 1, chap. 2

[2]"That sounds like a bit of old Bilbo's rhyming," said Pippin. "Or is it one of your imitations? It does not sound altogether encouraging."

"I don't know," said Frodo. "It came to me then, as if I were making it up; but I may have heard it long ago. Certainly it reminds me very much of Bilbo in the last years, before he went away. . . . 'It's a dangerous business, Frodo, going out of your door,' he used to say."

—Tolkien, *Lord of the Rings*, book 1, chap. 3

[3]"Well, Sam!" he said. "What about it? I am leaving the Shire as soon as ever I can—in fact I have made up my mind now not even to wait a day at Crickhollow, if it can be helped."

"Very good, sir!"

"You still mean to come with me?"

"I do."

"It is going to be very dangerous, Sam. It is already dangerous. Most likely neither of us will come back."

"If you don't come back, sir, then I shan't, that's certain," said Sam. "'Don't you leave him!' They said to me. 'Leave him!' I said. 'I never mean to. I am going with him, if he climbs to the Moon; and if any of those Black Riders try to stop him, they'll have Sam Gamgee to reckon with,' I said. They laughed."

—Tolkien, *Lord of the Rings*, book 1, chap. 4

[4]So refreshed and encouraged did they feel at the end of their supper (about three quarters of an hour's steady going, not hindered by unnecessary talk) that Frodo, Pippin, and Sam decided to join the company. Merry said it would be too stuffy.

—Tolkien, *Lord of the Rings*, book 1, chap. 9

[5]The Bree-hobbits were, in fact, friendly and inquisitive, and Frodo soon found that some explanation of what he was doing would have to be given. He gave out that he was interested in history and geography (at which there was much wagging of heads, although neither of these words were much used in the Bree-dialect). He said that he was thinking of writing a book (at which there was silent astonishment), and that he and his friends wanted to collect information about hobbits living outside the Shire, especially in eastern lands.

—Tolkien, *Lord of the Rings*, book 1, chap. 9

Comments on the English Examples

31.16. We have a regular system of written conventions in English to indicate direct discourse. The examples above illustrate several of these, including paragraph breaks/indents and quotation marks (both single and double). We also have standard means of introducing both direct and indirect discourse.

Evaluate the five examples given above, and mark all direct discourse and all indirect discourse. How has the author communicated the intended nature of each statement? How is the speaker identified? List or mark each relevant typographical feature and each introductory statement.

Greek Discourse

31.17. The conventions of direct discourse in Greek are quite different from English. That is true of both the original texts and our modern printed editions. Greek did not use quotation marks or even capitalization during the Koine period. There were only limited indications of direct discourse, such as common introductory phrasing; most occurrences were identified by context. Our modern printed editions have updated these practices slightly, but they are still much more limited than English. Printed texts have no quotation marks and no paragraphing system that is related to discourse. The only addition to the ancient system is the use of an initial capital letter to mark direct discourse—and not all editions are consistent in the use of this convention.

Direct Discourse

31.18. Direct discourse is usually easy to identify, since it is almost always introduced with a verb of speaking[4] that may be supplemented with a participle either before or after the main verb—for example, εἶπεν λέγων or ἀποκριθεὶς εἶπεν. This sounds redundant in English but was normal Greek style. It is also common (more so in some writers than others—Mark, for example) to use a conjunction following the verb of speaking, typically ὅτι. The technical name for this is a *recitative* ὅτι. In this situation the ὅτι clause functions as the complement of the verb of speaking (some would call this the *direct object* of the verb). In English the ὅτι is represented by quotation marks (do not translate it as "that"). Do not assume that every ὅτι following a verb of speaking is direct discourse, because it can also introduce indirect discourse. Direct discourse gives the statement as an independent clause embedded in the larger sentence.

4. Technically these are verbs of perception and include words that refer to speaking, thinking, seeing, hearing, knowing, remembering, believing, and so on.

Indirect Discourse

31.19. Indirect discourse is not always as easy to identify, in part because it can be constructed somewhat differently from the equivalent construction in English. Compare the indirect statement with the original in the following table.

Example	Indirect Discourse	Original Statement
4	Merry said it would be too stuffy.	"It will be too stuffy."
5	He gave out that he was interested in history and geography.	"I am interested in history and geography."
	He said that he was thinking of writing a book	"I am thinking of writing a book."
	and that he and his friends wanted to collect information about hobbits living outside the Shire, especially in eastern lands.	"My friends and I want to collect information about hobbits living outside the Shire, especially in eastern lands."

By comparing the English examples of indirect discourse given above, you can observe two types of changes. First, the tense of the verb is changed when a statement is placed in indirect discourse: the tense is backshifted, pushed back one step in time.[5] This is necessary in English because English tense is a time term. Second, the grammatical person of the pronouns is often adjusted to reflect the fact that it is now no longer the speaker making the statement, but it is being reported by someone else. For example, in 5a, "I am" becomes "he was" (first person to third, and present tense to past).

In Greek there are also several differences between direct and indirect statements, but these differences are not all the same as in English. The person of the pronoun often changes in a fashion similar to English. The verb, however, usually does not change tense. This is because the Greek tense-form is primarily aspectual, not temporal; therefore there is no need to adjust the time for a later reference point. The context makes such things clear, though when it is translated into English, the *English tense* must be changed to reflect English usage.

31.20. The Greek verb *may* also be changed in other ways. The most common change is for a finite form to be replaced by an infinitive in the same tense-form.[6] For example, in Mark 6:45 (see the full text below), **ἠνάγκασεν** τοὺς μαθητὰς αὐτοῦ **ἐμβῆναι εἰς τὸ πλοῖον** ("he urged his disciples to embark in the boat") probably reflects an original statement something like ἐμβῆτε εἰς τὸ πλοῖον ("Get into the boat")—a second plural second aorist active imperative becoming a second aorist active infinitive.

5. Technically this is true only if the introductory verb of speaking is an English past tense (as is most commonly the case since discourse normally recounts previous statements). In some contexts, however, the English statement of indirect discourse may be phrased in a present or future tense (e.g., "He says that . . ." or "He will say that . . ."), in which case the tense of the original statement is retained.

6. Less commonly a participle may be used (e.g., 1 John 4:2); that situation is not developed here. In Classical Greek, the optative mood was sometimes used in indirect discourse as a substitute for a secondary tense indicative verb in the direct statement. This occasionally is seen in Koine as well (e.g., Luke 8:9).

The change in pronoun is one of the surest ways to identify indirect discourse. Though not every statement can be identified this way, if a first- or second-person pronoun is changed to third person, it is almost surely indirect discourse. For example, in Mark 1:37, λέγουσιν αὐτῷ ὅτι Πάντες ζητοῦσίν σε ("They said to him, 'Everyone is seeking you'") is direct discourse; if it were indirect, the pronoun σε would have been changed to αὐτόν (λέγουσιν αὐτῷ ὅτι πάντες ζητοῦσιν αὐτόν, "They said to him that everyone was seeking him").

When indirect discourse is introduced by ὅτι (or sometimes by εἰ), the ὅτι is represented in English as *that*. Quotation marks are never used in indirect discourse. Notice also that the statement in indirect discourse is always a subordinate clause that is incorporated into the syntax of the main sentence; it does not stand as its own independent clause, as does direct discourse.

Indirect Questions

31.21. Related to indirect discourse is the indirect question. In this instance the indirect statement refers to and gives the content of a question. This may refer to an actual question that has already been asked directly, or it may be an indirect or polite means of asking a question. This has some difference from an indirect quotation in that it is introduced not by ὅτι but by εἰ or by an interrogative (e.g., τίς or ὅσος).[7] The other matters related to indirect discourse also apply (adjustment of pronouns, retained tense-form, etc.). For example, in Mark 15:44, ὁ δὲ Πιλᾶτος ἐθαύμασεν εἰ ἤδη τέθνηκεν ("Pilate was surprised [to hear] that he was already dead"), the statement was originally, "He is already dead?!" Or, in Acts 10:29, πυνθάνομαι οὖν τίνι λόγῳ μετεπέμψασθέ με; ("I ask, then, why you sent for me"), the question reflected would be "Why did you send for me?" Another possibility is to use ποῖος to introduce an indirect question—for example, in Matt. 24:42, οὐκ οἴδατε ποίᾳ ἡμέρᾳ ὁ κύριος ὑμῶν ἔρχεται ("You do not know what day your Lord will come"), the original would have been "When will our Lord come?" (note the shift in pronouns).

Greek Examples

Direct Discourse

31.22. Read the following passages in your Greek NT: Mark 1:14–18 and 2:5–12. Identify each instance of direct discourse, and explain how you know it is direct rather than indirect discourse.

Indirect Discourse

The following passages include instances of both direct and indirect discourse. The indirect statements have been marked with bold (Greek) and italics

7. Direct questions may also be introduced with the same interrogatives. You are familiar with the use of τίς in this way. For an example of εἰ in a direct question, see Matt. 12:10, ἐπηρώτησαν αὐτὸν λέγοντες, Εἰ ἔξεστιν τοῖς σάββασιν θεραπεῦσαι; ("They asked him, 'Is it lawful to heal on the Sabbath?'").

(English); the direct statements may be identified by the quotation marks in the parallel English translation.

Mark 6:45–50

[45]Καὶ εὐθὺς **ἠνάγκασεν** τοὺς μαθητὰς αὐτοῦ **ἐμβῆναι εἰς τὸ πλοῖον καὶ προάγειν εἰς τὸ πέραν πρὸς Βηθσαϊδάν, ἕως αὐτὸς ἀπολύει τὸν ὄχλον.** [46]καὶ ἀποταξάμενος αὐτοῖς ἀπῆλθεν εἰς τὸ ὄρος προσεύξασθαι. [47]καὶ ὀψίας γενομένης ἦν τὸ πλοῖον ἐν μέσῳ τῆς θαλάσσης, καὶ αὐτὸς μόνος ἐπὶ τῆς γῆς. [48]καὶ ἰδὼν αὐτοὺς βασανιζομένους ἐν τῷ ἐλαύνειν, ἦν γὰρ ὁ ἄνεμος ἐναντίος αὐτοῖς, περὶ τετάρτην φυλακὴν τῆς νυκτὸς ἔρχεται πρὸς αὐτοὺς περιπατῶν ἐπὶ τῆς θαλάσσης καὶ ἤθελεν παρελθεῖν αὐτούς. [49]οἱ δὲ ἰδόντες αὐτὸν ἐπὶ τῆς θαλάσσης περιπατοῦντα **ἔδοξαν ὅτι φάντασμά ἐστιν,** καὶ ἀνέκραξαν· [50]πάντες γὰρ αὐτὸν εἶδον καὶ ἐταράχθησαν. ὁ δὲ εὐθὺς ἐλάλησεν μετ᾽ αὐτῶν, καὶ λέγει αὐτοῖς, Θαρσεῖτε, ἐγώ εἰμι· μὴ φοβεῖσθε.

[45]Then *he urged* his disciples *to embark in the boat and to go ahead of [him] to the other side to Bethsaida, while he was sending the crowd away.* [46]After taking leave of them he went into the hills to pray. [47]When it was evening the boat was in the middle of the lake, and he was alone on the land. [48]Seeing them straining as they rowed—for the wind was against them—about the fourth watch of the night he went to them, walking on the lake. He was about to pass by them, [49]but they, seeing him walking on the lake, *thought that it was a ghost,* and they cried out, [50]for they all saw him and were terrified. But quickly he spoke with them and said to them, "Have courage, it is I;[a] don't be afraid."

[a] "It is I" is technically correct, though it sounds very stilted in ordinary English usage in this context. More colloquially (though it makes English teachers shudder!), we would usually say, "it's me" (cf. NJB, CEB).

Mark 8:14–21

[14]Καὶ ἐπελάθοντο λαβεῖν ἄρτους καὶ εἰ μὴ ἕνα ἄρτον οὐκ εἶχον μεθ᾽ ἑαυτῶν ἐν τῷ πλοίῳ. [15]καὶ διεστέλλετο αὐτοῖς λέγων, Ὁρᾶτε, βλέπετε ἀπὸ τῆς ζύμης τῶν Φαρισαίων καὶ τῆς ζύμης Ἡρῴδου. [16]καὶ **διελογίζοντο** πρὸς ἀλλήλους **ὅτι ἄρτους οὐκ ἔχουσιν.** [17]καὶ γνοὺς λέγει αὐτοῖς, Τί **διαλογίζεσθε ὅτι ἄρτους οὐκ ἔχετε**; οὔπω νοεῖτε οὐδὲ συνίετε; πεπωρωμένην ἔχετε τὴν καρδίαν ὑμῶν; [18]ὀφθαλμοὺς ἔχοντες οὐ βλέπετε καὶ ὦτα ἔχοντες οὐκ ἀκούετε; καὶ οὐ μνημονεύετε, [19]ὅτε τοὺς πέντε ἄρτους ἔκλασα εἰς τοὺς πεντακισχιλίους, πόσους κοφίνους κλασμάτων πλήρεις ἤρατε; λέγουσιν αὐτῷ, Δώδεκα. [20]Ὅτε τοὺς ἑπτὰ εἰς τοὺς τετρακισχιλίους, πόσων σπυρίδων πληρώματα κλασμάτων ἤρατε; καὶ λέγουσιν αὐτῷ, Ἑπτά. [21]καὶ ἔλεγεν αὐτοῖς, Οὔπω συνίετε;

[14]Now they had forgotten to take bread, and except for one loaf, they did not have [bread] with them in the boat. [15]He commanded them, "Watch out; beware of the leaven of the Pharisees and of the leaven of Herod." [16]So *they were discussing* with one another *that they didn't have bread.* [17]Knowing this, [Jesus] said to them, "Why *are you discussing about not having bread*? Do you not yet perceive or understand? Do you have a hardened heart? [18]Having eyes, you do see, don't you? And having ears, you do hear, don't you? You do remember, don't you—[19]when I broke the five loaves for the five thousand—how many full baskets of pieces you picked up?" They answered him, "Twelve." [20]"When [I broke] the seven [loaves] for the four thousand, how many basketfuls of pieces did you pick up?" They answered him, "Seven." [21]He said to them, "Do you still not understand?"

31.23. Advanced Information for Reference: Diagramming Discourse

Mark 8:16, καὶ **διελογίζοντο** πρὸς ἀλλήλους **ὅτι ἄρτους οὐκ ἔχουσιν.**

So *they were discussing* with one another *that they did not have bread.*

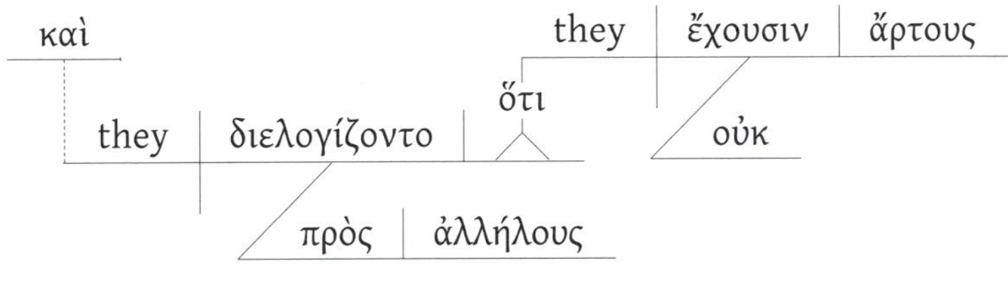

Figure 31.1

Direct and indirect discourse are not distinguished in a grammatical diagram, since they both function the same way: as the object complement (direct object) of a verb of speaking or thinking. The example shown here is indirect discourse, but direct discourse would be diagrammed the same way. If the statement is introduced with a subordinating conjunction such as ὅτι, it is placed on the vertical leg of the stilts.

Reading Passage: Genesis 15:1–18

31.24. This passage from the OT contains a large amount of direct discourse. To enable you to follow the dialogue more easily, it has been paragraphed as we would in English. In Rahlfs's LXX this is all one paragraph. There are some differences from the Hebrew MT and our English translations. The NETS translation has been appended for reference, but you will profit most if you do not read it until you have read the Greek text as best you can. Any vocabulary that is not found in the NT is appended in the notes.

The Covenant with Abram

1 Μετὰ δὲ τὰ ῥήματα ταῦτα ἐγενήθη ῥῆμα κυρίου πρὸς Ἀβρὰμ ἐν ὁράματι λέγων,
Μὴ φοβοῦ, Ἀβράμ· ἐγὼ ὑπερασπίζω[a] σου· ὁ μισθός σου πολὺς ἔσται σφόδρα.
2 Λέγει δὲ Ἀβράμ, Δέσποτα, τί μοι δώσεις (you will give); ἐγὼ δὲ ἀπολύομαι[b]
ἄτεκνος· ὁ δὲ υἱὸς Μάσεκ[c] τῆς οἰκογενοῦς[d] μου, οὗτος Δαμασκὸς Ἐλιέζερ. 3 καὶ
εἶπεν Ἀβράμ, Ἐπειδὴ ἐμοὶ οὐκ ἔδωκας (you gave) σπέρμα, ὁ δὲ οἰκογενής[d] μου
κληρονομήσει[e] με.
4 Καὶ εὐθὺς φωνὴ κυρίου ἐγένετο πρὸς αὐτὸν λέγων, Οὐ κληρονομήσει σε
οὗτος, ἀλλ' ὃς ἐξελεύσεται ἐκ σοῦ, οὗτος κληρονομήσει σε. 5 ἐξήγαγεν δὲ αὐτὸν
ἔξω καὶ εἶπεν αὐτῷ, Ἀνάβλεψον δὴ εἰς τὸν οὐρανὸν καὶ ἀρίθμησον τοὺς ἀστέρας,
εἰ δυνήσῃ ἐξαριθμῆσαι[f] αὐτούς. καὶ εἶπεν, Οὕτως ἔσται τὸ σπέρμα σου.
6 Καὶ ἐπίστευσεν Ἀβρὰμ τῷ θεῷ, καὶ ἐλογίσθη αὐτῷ εἰς δικαιοσύνην.

7Εἶπεν δὲ πρὸς αὐτόν, Ἐγὼ ὁ θεὸς ὁ ἐξαγαγών σε ἐκ χώρας Χαλδαίων ὥστε
δοῦναί (to give) σοι τὴν γῆν ταύτην κληρονομῆσαι.
8Εἶπεν δέ, Δέσποτα κύριε, κατὰ τί[g] γνώσομαι ὅτι κληρονομήσω αὐτήν;
9Εἶπεν δὲ αὐτῷ, Λαβέ μοι δάμαλιν τριετίζουσαν[h] καὶ αἶγα[i] τριετίζουσαν καὶ
κριόν[j] τριετίζοντα καὶ τρυγόνα καὶ περιστεράν.
10Ἔλαβεν δὲ αὐτῷ πάντα ταῦτα καὶ διεῖλεν[k] αὐτὰ μέσα καὶ ἔθηκεν (he placed)
αὐτὰ ἀντιπρόσωπα[l] ἀλλήλοις, τὰ δὲ ὄρνεα οὐ διεῖλεν.[k] 11κατέβη δὲ ὄρνεα ἐπὶ τὰ
σώματα, τὰ διχοτομήματα[m] αὐτῶν, καὶ συνεκάθισεν αὐτοῖς Ἀβράμ.
12Περὶ δὲ ἡλίου δυσμὰς[n] ἔκστασις ἐπέπεσεν τῷ Ἀβράμ, καὶ ἰδοὺ φόβος σκοτεινὸς μέγας ἐπιπίπτει αὐτῷ. 13καὶ ἐρρέθη πρὸς Ἀβράμ, Γινώσκων γνώσῃ[o] ὅτι
πάροικον ἔσται τὸ σπέρμα σου ἐν γῇ οὐκ ἰδίᾳ, καὶ δουλώσουσιν αὐτοὺς καὶ
κακώσουσιν αὐτοὺς καὶ ταπεινώσουσιν αὐτοὺς τετρακόσια ἔτη. 14τὸ δὲ ἔθνος, ᾧ
ἐὰν δουλεύσωσιν, κρινῶ ἐγώ· μετὰ δὲ ταῦτα ἐξελεύσονται ὧδε μετὰ ἀποσκευῆς[p]
πολλῆς. 15σὺ δὲ ἀπελεύσῃ πρὸς τοὺς πατέρας σου μετ᾽ εἰρήνης, ταφεὶς[q] ἐν γήρει[r]
καλῷ. 16τετάρτη[s] δὲ γενεὰ ἀποστραφήσονται ὧδε· οὔπω γὰρ ἀναπεπλήρωνται
αἱ ἁμαρτίαι τῶν Αμορραίων ἕως τοῦ νῦν.
17Ἐπεὶ δὲ ἐγίνετο ὁ ἥλιος πρὸς δυσμαῖς, φλὸξ ἐγένετο, καὶ ἰδοὺ κλίβανος
καπνιζόμενος[t] καὶ λαμπάδες πυρός, αἳ διῆλθον ἀνὰ μέσον τῶν διχοτομημάτων[m]
τούτων. 18ἐν τῇ ἡμέρᾳ ἐκείνῃ διέθετο (made) κύριος τῷ Ἀβρὰμ διαθήκην λέγων,
Τῷ σπέρματί σου δώσω (I will give) τὴν γῆν ταύτην ἀπὸ τοῦ ποταμοῦ Αἰγύπτου
ἕως τοῦ ποταμοῦ τοῦ μεγάλου, ποταμοῦ Εὐφράτου.

[a] ὑπερασπίζω, "I hold a shield over, protect"

[b] In this context ἀπολύω means "I am going away," that is, "I am going to die."

[c] Μάσεκ is a woman's name (indeclinable).

[d] οἰκογενής, -ές (a "two-form" adj., always used substantivally in the LXX), "born in the household, homegrown" (but never refers to one's own children); substantival: "member of the household," can refer to a slave, servant, soldier, etc. (MLS, 488). Since it is feminine in v. 2, it explains who Μάσεκ is, a female slave or servant who belonged to Abram. The full phrase indicates that she is the mother of Δαμασκὸς Ἐλιέζερ. The same word in v. 3 is masculine and refers to Δαμασκὸς Ἐλιέζερ.

[e] When "used with pers. obj. the verb [κληρονομέω] signifies *succeed someone as heir, be someone's heir*" (BDAG, 547.1.b).

[f] ἐξαριθμέω, "I count completely" (MLS, 248)

[g] κατὰ τί, "in accordance with what?" or more idiomatically, "how?"

[h] τριετίζω, "I am three years old"

[i] αἶγα ▸ αἴξ, αἰγός, ὁ, ἡ, "goat"

[j] κριόν ▸ κριός, οῦ, ὁ, "male sheep, ram"

[k] διεῖλεν ▸ διαιρέω

[l] ἀντιπρόσωπος, ον, "facing one another"

[m] διχοτόμημα, ατος, τό, "divided part"

[n] Περὶ δὲ ἡλίου δυσμάς, "but about the going down of the sun" = "about sunset"

[o] Γινώσκων γνώσῃ, "knowing you will know," a formal equivalent translation of the Hebrew construction Qal infinitive absolute + cognate finite verb; used to stress certainty, "know for certain"

[p] ἀποσκευή, ῆς, ἡ, "possessions" (often includes reference to household members; see MLS, 82)

[q] ταφείς ▸ ptc. of θάπτω

[r] γῆρας, gen. γήρως/γήρους, dat. γήρᾳ/γήρει, acc. γῆραν, τό, "old age"

[s] τέταρτος, η, ον, "fourth" ("four" is τέσσαρες)

[t] καπνίζω, "I make smoke"

NETS Translation

[1]Now after these matters the Lord's word came to Abram in a vision, saying, "Do not be afraid, Abram; I am shielding you; your reward shall be very great." [2]But Abram was saying, "O Master, what will you give me? And I, I am going away childless; as for the son of Masek, my female homebred, he is Damascus Eliezer." [3]And Abram said, "Since you have given me no offspring, my male homebred will be my heir." [4]And immediately a divine voice came to him, saying, "This one shall not be your heir, but one who shall come out of you, he shall be your heir." [5]Then he brought him outside and said to him, "Look up to heaven, and number the stars, if you will be able to count them." And he said, "So shall your offspring be." [6]And Abram believed God, and it was reckoned to him as righteousness.

[7]Then he said to him, "I am the God who brought you out of the country of the Chaldeans so as to give you this land to possess." [8]But he said, "O Master, Lord, how shall I know that I shall possess it?" [9]And he said to him, "Take for me a heifer three years old and a female goat three years old and a ram three years old and a turtledove and a dove." [10]And he took for him all these and divided them in the middle and placed them facing one another, but he did not divide the birds. [11]And birds came down on the carcasses, their cut halves, and Abram sat together with them.

[12]Then about sunset a trance fell upon Abram, and look, a great dark fear was falling upon him. [13]And it was said to Abram, "Knowledgeably you shall know that your offspring shall be alien in a land not its own, and they shall enslave them and maltreat them and humble them for four hundred years. [14]But I will judge the nation that they are subject to; then afterward they shall come out here with much baggage. [15]Now as for yourself, you shall depart to your fathers in peace, buried in a good old age. [16]Then in the fourth generation they shall be brought back here, for the sins of the Amorrites are not yet, to the present, filled up."

[17]Now after the sun began to appear in the west, a flame appeared, and look, a smoking oven and torches of fire that passed through between these cut halves. [18]On that day the Lord made a covenant with Abram, saying, "To your offspring I will give this land from the river of Egypt to the great river, the river Euphrates."

31.25. Vocabulary for Chapter 31

Part of Speech	Definition	Possible Glosses	Frequency	
Word			NT	LXX
Adjectives				
ἀκάθαρτος, ον	Contaminated and thus not meeting the requirements for ritual/ceremonial use; in a more general sense, anything characterized by moral impurity	unclean, impure	32	160
φίλος, η, ον	Characterized by having a special interest in and close relationship with another person (i.e., not a casual acquaintance); one who has a close, friendly relationship with another person	friendly, loving, dear; friend (subst., as almost always in the LXX and NT)	29	187

Part of Speech	Definition	Possible Glosses	Frequency	
Word			NT	LXX
Conjunction				
πλήν	An adversative coordinating conjunction that introduces a contrast to the preceding statement	but, however, only, nevertheless	31	248
Nouns				
οἶνος, ου, ὁ	A beverage made from the juice of the grape (usually fermented, but perhaps not necessarily so)	wine, juice (from the grape)	34	253
ἥλιος, ου, ὁ	The star around which the earth orbits	sun	32	211
πλῆθος, ους, τό	A large quantity or number of anything, whether people (most commonly) or things	multitude, throng, large number	31	288
σκότος, ους, τό	The absence of light; ignorance in moral or spiritual matters (metaphorical)	darkness	31	120
χώρα, ας, ἡ	Dry land (in contrast to the sea); the territory of a nation or a smaller geographical area; open country (in contrast to the city); land used for agriculture	land; country, region, place; countryside; field	28	247
ἀδικία, ας, ἡ	The quality of violating a standard of right	unrighteousness, wickedness, injustice	26	228
Verbs				
κράζω	To utter a loud cry, speak vigorously	I cry/call out	56	111
προσφέρω	To bring someone/something to someone; to present an offering or gift to someone	I bring (to); I offer, present	47	161
καθίζω	(1) Transitive: to cause to sit down; (2) intransitive: to take a seated position	(1) I seat, set; (2) I sit down	46	255
διώκω	To engage in pursuit, follow hastily (may be either positive or negative in intent); to harass, organize a systematic program of harassment	I pursue, run after; I persecute	45	104
ἐπιστρέφω	To return to a place where one has previously been; to change direction or turn around in a space; to change one's mind, mode of thinking, belief, or course of action	I return, go back; I turn (around); I turn (back/from), repent	36	534
ἁγιάζω	To set aside for sacred use/purposes; to treat as holy	I set apart, sanctify, dedicate; I revere	28	196

31.26. Key Things to Know for Chapter 31

How might you make a conditional statement in Greek *without* using one of the formal conditional statements?

Do you understand the difference between direct and indirect discourse?

What sort of changes can take place in Greek when indirect discourse is used?

32

μι VERBS: PART 1

INDICATIVE MOOD

32.1. All the verbs you have learned thus far are part of the ω conjugation, in which the lexical form ends with ω.[1] The ω verbs are the most common verb forms in Koine Greek, but there is another, older group of verbs known as the **μι** *conjugation*. In this conjugation, the lexical form ends, not with ω, but with μι.[2]

Textbooks (and instructors) differ as to how much weight to place on the μι verbs. Some spend a lot of time on the subject and try to cover the μι verbs as completely as the ω verbs. Others are content with a more general survey to enable the first-year student to identify most of them, and then leave the others for future study. I have come to prefer the latter approach. I have, however, tried to give fairly complete listings of these forms to provide a reference source when these forms are encountered later.

μι Verb Basics

32.2. By far the most common μι verbs in the NT and the LXX are these three:

		Frequency	
		NT	LXX
δίδωμι	I give	415×	1,991×
ἵστημι	I stand	154×	698×
τίθημι	I put/place	100×	527×

1. Actually that is not quite true. You have already met two μι verbs: εἰμί and οἶδα (formerly spelled ἴδοιμι), but they do not follow the usual μι verb patterns. We learned them early because they occur so often in the NT.

2. Some grammars call these two conjugations the *thematic* (= ω) and *athematic* (= μι) conjugations. The terms come from the fact that the ω verb system uses connecting vowels, also known as theme vowels, whereas μι verbs do not use them, thus *athematic*.

Although they may have once been the standard conjugation, the μι verbs were disappearing even in Classical Greek, being replaced by the ω forms. This process has continued in the Koine. Some of the remaining μι verbs have also begun to use ω verb endings. For example, the verb ἵστημι (the μι verb form) also occurs in the NT as ἱστάνω (an ω form). This trend continues in the later Koine and Byzantine periods so that there are no μι verbs left: δίδωμι, "I give," becomes διδῶ; ἵστημι, "I stand," becomes ἱστάνω; and τίθημι, "I put/place," becomes τιθέω.[3]

There is no difference in meaning between a μι verb and an ω verb. This is just a different way to form the endings. Some of them will seem to have drastically different forms compared to what you have already learned, but that is only a few forms. Most of the conjugation will look very similar to what you know if you remember a few simple changes.

What You Need to Know

32.3. Here is a summary of everything you need to know about the μι verbs. If you can remember these five things, the μι verbs will not cause you trouble. Almost all of the principles that you have already learned for the ω verb will still apply.[4] It is only in present, imperfect, and second aorist tense-forms that there are differences; the other tense-forms will look just like the ω verbs so long as you remember the first principle: the stem.

1. *You must know the stems of the three most common* μι *verbs*. This is *very* important.

μι Verb	Gloss	Stem
δίδωμι	I give	δο-
ἵστημι	I stand	στα-
τίθημι	I put/place	θε-

Since these three verbs also occur in many compound forms, the value of knowing these three stems is multiplied in actual use.

2. *The* μι *verbs use "iota reduplication" in the present tense-form* (and in the imperfect, which is built on the present stem). This looks just like the reduplication you already know from the perfect tense-form in the ω verbs except that it uses an iota instead of an epsilon. For example, the verb δίδωμι, whose stem is δο-, reduplicates in the present as διδο-. Likewise τίθημι, with a stem of θε-, forms τιθε-, and for ἵστημι, στα- becomes ἱστα- in the present.[5]

3. In Modern Greek, δίδωμι appears as δίδω, ἵστημι is now στήνω, and τίθημι has become θέτω. A few middle/passive forms of τίθημι and some compound forms of ἵστημι have been reintroduced in Standard Modern Greek since 1976, though they disappeared from the Demotic form of Modern Greek long before (Horrocks, *Greek*, 463).

4. For example, the stem vowel may undergo ablaut in μι verbs just as it sometimes did in ω verbs. The stem δο- lengthens the stem vowel (omicron) to omega in the first singular form δίδωμι.

5. The variation in the reduplication is also similar to what you have seen in the perfect tense-form. Since the stem of τίθημι begins with the compound sound theta (θε-), it reduplicates with a tau (τιθε-). For ἵστημι, the stem, στα-, begins with a sigma—a known trouble maker—so it reduplicates with a rough breathing mark, thus ἱστα-.

3. *There are (usually) no connecting vowels in the μι verbs.* For example, in the form δίδομεν, the stem is δο- and the personal ending is -μεν. There is no connecting vowel. (The omicron is part of the stem, not a connecting vowel.) In the few places where there *is* a connecting vowel, the verb will look just like an ω verb form, so that will not be a problem.

4. *The aorist normally uses* **κα** *as the form marker instead of* **σα**. The use of κα is why these forms are sometimes called *kappa aorists*. Though this might seem easy to confuse with the perfect marker, the presence of an augment and lack of reduplication will make it clear that it is an aorist, not a perfect. Thus you will see ἐδώκαμεν as the first plural aorist active indicative form rather than the pattern ἐλύσαμεν to which you are accustomed.

Although κα is the normal form marker in the μι verbs, some verbs in this conjugation retain the usual σα form marker found in the ω verbs. The most common verb that does this is ἵστημι. (See the table of these forms in app. A.) This should not pose a problem, since you will recognize it as an aorist form marker.

5. *The A set of personal endings used in the present are slightly different from the A endings in the* ω *verb.* These forms are shown in the tables below. All the other endings are the same as those of ω verbs. These variant forms are used only in the present active indicative; other forms with A endings (e.g., future) use the same set of A endings you already know.

An Example

32.4. With just the information above can you parse this form?

δώσω

Just remember what you have already learned about ω verbs. If you do, I am sure that you will parse this as 1st sg. fut. act. ind. ▸ δίδωμι, "I give." The stem is δο-, sigma is the form marker for future, the first omega is the stem vowel omicron lengthened when a form marker is added, and the final omega is the standard A ending for first-person singular.

Forms of the μι Verbs

32.5. The following chart shows what μι verbs look like. The left side of the chart gives the familiar ω verb forms for comparison.

Present Active Indicative of μι Verbs

	ω Verbs			μι Verbs	
	form	c.v.	A p.e.	form	p.e.
1S	λύω	ο	—	δίδωμι	μι[a]
2S	λύεις	ε	ς	δίδως	ς
3S	λύει	ε	ι	δίδωσι(ν)	σι[a]

	ω Verbs			μι Verbs	
	form	c.v.	A p.e.	form	p.e.
1P	λύομεν	ο	μεν	δίδομεν	μεν
2P	λύετε	ε	τε	δίδοτε	τε
3P	λύουσι(ν)	ο	νσι	διδόασι(ν)	ασι[a]

Note the three forms marked with a superscript letter. These are the only ones that are different from the ω forms. Only the third singular will be troublesome. You know the first singular form just by the name μι *verb*, and the third plural is very similar to the ω forms you know (-ασιν instead of -ουσιν). With this information you can parse just about any present active indicative μι verb. Here are a few simple examples to get you started. You will notice that several of these presents have future time reference in the context.

John 10:28, κἀγὼ **δίδωμι** αὐτοῖς ζωὴν αἰώνιον. [1st sg. pres. act. ind.]

And I *will give* them eternal life.

John 6:32, ὁ πατήρ μου **δίδωσιν** ὑμῖν τὸν ἄρτον ἐκ τοῦ οὐρανοῦ τὸν ἀληθινόν. [3rd sg. pres. act. ind.]

My Father *will give* you the true bread from heaven.

Rev. 17:13, τὴν δύναμιν καὶ ἐξουσίαν αὐτῶν τῷ θηρίῳ **διδόασιν**. [3rd pl. pres. act. ind.]

They will give their power and authority to the beast.

Ps. 144:15 (145:15 Eng.), οἱ ὀφθαλμοὶ πάντων εἰς σὲ ἐλπίζουσιν, καὶ σὺ **δίδως** τὴν τροφὴν αὐτῶν ἐν εὐκαιρίᾳ. [2nd sg. pres. act. ind.]

The eyes of all hope in you, and *you give* their food at the right moment.

The following figures will give you some idea of what μι verb forms you will encounter.

δίδωμι	NT	LXX
Indicative	259	1,447
Participle	48	96
Imperative	35[a]	147
Infinitive	44[b]	175
Subjunctive[c]	25	102
Optative	4	31
Total	**415**	**1,998**

[a] 34 are second person.

[b] 33 are the aorist active infinitive, δοῦναι.

[c] There is one present subjunctive of δίδωμι in the NT and one in the LXX. They are very rare elsewhere in Koine as well; there are none in Josephus or the Apostolic Fathers, only one in the Pseudepigrapha, and three in Philo.

In order of frequency of tense-form, the most common indicative forms of δίδωμι are as follows. The frequency distribution in the NT and in the LXX is very similar.

NT		LXX	
Aorist	119[a]	Aorist	742[c]
Future	66[b]	Future	479[d]
Perfect	35	Present	108
Present	24	Perfect	97
Imperfect	12	Imperfect	19
Pluperfect	3	Pluperfect	2

[a] 64 of these are ἔδωκεν, 3rd sg. aor. act. ind.
[b] 16 of these are δοθήσεται, 3rd sg. fut. pass. ind.
[c] 440 of these are ἔδωκεν, 3rd sg. aor. act. ind.
[d] 205 of these are δώσω, 1st sg. fut. act. ind.

At this point, you need to browse through the following charts to get a feel for these verbs. You do not need to memorize these charts. They are just for reference. Once you have done that, then try parsing the μι verb forms in the examples below.

32.6. *Active Indicative μι Verbs*

Active Indicative Forms of δίδωμι (Stem δο-)

	Present	Imperfect	Future	First Aorist	Second Aorist[a]	Perfect
1S	δίδωμι	ἐδίδουν	δώσω	ἔδωκα	ἔδων	δέδωκα
2S	δίδως	ἐδίδους	δώσεις	ἔδωκας	ἔδως	δέδωκας
3S	δίδωσι(ν)	ἐδίδου	δώσει	ἔδωκε(ν)	ἔδω	δέδωκε(ν)
1P	δίδομεν	ἐδίδομεν	δώσομεν	ἐδώκαμεν	ἔδομεν	δεδώκαμεν
2P	δίδοτε	ἐδίδοτε	δώσετε	ἐδώκατε	ἔδοτε	δεδώκατε
3P	διδόασι(ν)	ἐδίδοσαν or ἐδίδουν	δώσουσι(ν)	ἔδωκαν	ἔδοσαν	δέδωκαν

[a] The second aorist forms of the μι verbs are sometimes called *root aorists* since they attach the personal endings directly to the root rather than use a connecting vowel or a form marker.

Only about half of the forms of δίδωμι on the chart above occur in the NT, but you will see the others when you are reading outside the NT. Of course, other μι verbs may use these endings in the NT as well. None of the second aorist forms of δίδωμι shown above occur in the NT or LXX, but if you read Josephus or Philo, for example, you will encounter them.

32.7. Examples of Active Indicative μι Verbs

Matt. 10:1, προσκαλεσάμενος τοὺς δώδεκα μαθητὰς αὐτοῦ **ἔδωκεν** αὐτοῖς ἐξουσίαν πνευμάτων ἀκαθάρτων.	Summoning his twelve disciples, *he gave* them authority over unclean spirits.
Mark 14:22, ἐσθιόντων αὐτῶν λαβὼν ἄρτον εὐλογήσας ἔκλασεν καὶ **ἔδωκεν** αὐτοῖς καὶ εἶπεν, Λάβετε, τοῦτό ἐστιν τὸ σῶμά μου.	While they were eating, he [i.e., Jesus], taking bread [and] having blessed [it], broke [it] and *gave* [it] to them and said, "Take [it], this is my body."
2 Cor. 8:5, ἑαυτοὺς **ἔδωκαν** πρῶτον τῷ κυρίῳ καὶ ἡμῖν διὰ θελήματος θεοῦ.	*They gave* themselves first to the Lord and [then] to us by the will of God.
Gen. 3:12, εἶπεν ὁ Ἀδάμ, Ἡ γυνή, ἣν **ἔδωκας** μετ' ἐμοῦ, αὕτη μοι **ἔδωκεν** ἀπὸ τοῦ ξύλου, καὶ ἔφαγον.	Adam said, "The woman whom *you gave* [to be] with me, she *gave* me [fruit] from the tree, and I ate."
Gen. 26:4, πληθυνῶ τὸ σπέρμα σου ὡς τοὺς ἀστέρας τοῦ οὐρανοῦ καὶ **δώσω** τῷ σπέρματί σου πᾶσαν τὴν γῆν ταύτην, καὶ ἐνευλογηθήσονται ἐν τῷ σπέρματί σου πάντα τὰ ἔθνη τῆς γῆς.	I will multiply your offspring as the stars of heaven and *will give* to your offspring all this land, and all the nations of the earth will be blessed by your offspring.
2 Chron. 1:12, τὴν σοφίαν καὶ τὴν σύνεσιν **δίδωμί** σοι καὶ πλοῦτον καὶ χρήματα καὶ δόξαν **δώσω** σοι, ὡς οὐκ ἐγενήθη ὅμοιός σοι ἐν τοῖς βασιλεῦσι τοῖς ἔμπροσθέ σου καὶ μετὰ σὲ οὐκ ἔσται οὕτως.	*I am giving* you wisdom and understanding, and *I will give* you riches, possessions, and glory, as there has not been [for anyone] like you among the kings who were before you and will not be so after you.

32.8. Now You Try It

Matt. 15:36, ἔλαβεν τοὺς ἑπτὰ ἄρτους καὶ τοὺς ἰχθύας καὶ εὐχαριστήσας ἔκλασεν καὶ **ἐδίδου** τοῖς μαθηταῖς, οἱ δὲ μαθηταὶ τοῖς ὄχλοις.	
Matt. 7:11, ὁ πατὴρ ὑμῶν ὁ ἐν τοῖς οὐρανοῖς **δώσει** ἀγαθὰ τοῖς αἰτοῦσιν αὐτόν.	
John 7:19, οὐ Μωϋσῆς **δέδωκεν** ὑμῖν τὸν νόμον; (Watch the punctuation.)	
John 17:14, ἐγὼ **δέδωκα** αὐτοῖς τὸν λόγον σου.	

Gen. 3:6, λαβοῦσα τοῦ καρποῦ αὐτοῦ ἔφαγεν· καὶ **ἔδωκεν** καὶ τῷ ἀνδρὶ αὐτῆς μετ' αὐτῆς, καὶ ἔφαγον.

Exod. 20:12, τίμα[a] τὸν πατέρα σου καὶ τὴν μητέρα, ἵνα εὖ σοι γένηται, καὶ ἵνα μακροχρόνιος γένῃ ἐπὶ τῆς γῆς τῆς ἀγαθῆς, ἧς κύριος ὁ θεός σου **δίδωσίν** σοι.

[a] This is an alpha contract form: 2nd sg. pres. act. impv. ▶ τιμάω, "I honor."

Ezek. 3:17, Υἱὲ ἀνθρώπου, σκοπὸν **δέδωκά** σε τῷ οἴκῳ Ἰσραήλ, καὶ ἀκούσῃ ἐκ στόματός μου λόγον καὶ διαπειλήσῃ[a] αὐτοῖς παρ' ἐμοῦ.

[a] διαπειλέω, "I warn"

32.9. *Middle and Passive Indicative μι Verbs*

Middle Indicative Forms of δίδωμι (Stem δο-)

	Present[a]	Imperfect[a]	Second Aorist	Future	Perfect[a]
1S	δίδομαι	ἐδιδόμην	ἐδόμην	δώσομαι	δέδομαι
2S	δίδοσαι	ἐδίδοσο	ἔδου	δώσῃ	δέδοσαι
3S	δίδοται	ἐδίδοτο	ἔδοτο	δώσεται	δέδοται
1P	διδόμεθα	ἐδιδόμεθα	ἐδόμεθα	δωσόμεθα	δεδόμεθα
2P	δίδοσθε	ἐδίδοσθε	ἔδοσθε	δώσεσθε	δέδοσθε
3P	δίδονται	ἐδίδοντο	ἔδοντο	δώσονται	δέδονται

[a] The forms in these columns can also be passive if there is a passive indication in the context.

Passive Indicative Forms of δίδωμι (Stem δο-)

	Aorist	Future
1S	ἐδόθην	δοθήσομαι
2S	ἐδόθης	δοθήσῃ
3S	ἐδόθη	δοθήσεται
1P	ἐδόθημεν	δοθησόμεθα
2P	ἐδόθητε	δοθήσεσθε
3P	ἐδόθησαν	δοθήσονται

Of all the forms of δίδωμι shown here, δοθήσεται is by far the most common in the NT (58×); in the LXX the two most common are ἐδόθη (31×) and δοθήσεται (23×). Many of the forms in the chart above do not occur in the NT or the LXX, though they may occur in other Koine texts.

32.10. Examples of Middle and Passive Indicative μι Verbs

1 Cor. 12:7, ἑκάστῳ δὲ **δίδοται** ἡ φανέρωσις τοῦ πνεύματος πρὸς τὸ συμφέρον.

But to each one *is given* the manifestation of the Spirit for the common good.

Matt. 28:18, **Ἐδόθη** μοι πᾶσα ἐξουσία ἐν οὐρανῷ καὶ ἐπὶ τῆς γῆς.

All authority in heaven and on earth *has been given* to me.

Rev. 6:2, εἶδον, καὶ ἰδοὺ ἵππος λευκός, καὶ ὁ καθήμενος ἐπ' αὐτὸν ἔχων τόξον καὶ **ἐδόθη** αὐτῷ στέφανος καὶ ἐξῆλθεν νικῶν καὶ ἵνα νικήσῃ.

I looked, and behold, a white horse and the one who sat on it having a bow, and a crown *was given* to him, and he went out conquering and to conquer.

Exod. 5:18, νῦν οὖν πορευθέντες[a] ἐργάζεσθε· τὸ γὰρ ἄχυρον[b] οὐ **δοθήσεται** ὑμῖν, καὶ τὴν σύνταξιν[c] τῆς πλινθείας[d] ἀποδώσετε.

Now, then, go, work! For straw *will* not *be given* to you, and the brickmaking levy you will produce.

[a] This is an attendant circumstance participle, which reflects the mood of the adjacent imperative form.

[b] In the NT ἄχυρον always refers to chaff (it occurs only twice there), but the word can refer to either chaff or straw.

[c] σύνταξις, εως, ἡ, "an organized account or arrangement," which may be used to refer to many different sorts of things. Here "levy" fits the context well.

[d] πλινθεία, ας, ἡ, "brickmaking"

Ps. 71:15 (72:15 Eng.), ζήσεται, καὶ **δοθήσεται** αὐτῷ ἐκ τοῦ χρυσίου τῆς Ἀραβίας, καὶ προσεύξονται περὶ αὐτοῦ διὰ παντός, ὅλην τὴν ἡμέραν εὐλογήσουσιν αὐτόν.

He [i.e., the king] will live, and *it will be given* to him from the gold of Arabia, and they will pray for him always; all the day they will bless him.

1 Clem. 30.3, κολληθῶμεν οὖν ἐκείνοις οἷς ἡ χάρις ἀπὸ τοῦ θεοῦ **δέδοται**.

Therefore let us join together with those to whom grace *is given* by God.

32.11. Now You Try It

John 1:17, ὁ νόμος διὰ Μωϋσέως **ἐδόθη**, ἡ χάρις καὶ ἡ ἀλήθεια διὰ Ἰησοῦ Χριστοῦ ἐγένετο.

Luke 11:9, κἀγὼ ὑμῖν λέγω, αἰτεῖτε καὶ **δοθήσεται** ὑμῖν, ζητεῖτε καὶ εὑρήσετε, κρούετε καὶ ἀνοιγήσεται ὑμῖν.

Acts 24:26, ἅμα καὶ ἐλπίζων ὅτι χρήματα **δοθήσεται** αὐτῷ ὑπὸ τοῦ Παύλου.

Luke 8:10, Ὑμῖν **δέδοται** γνῶναι τὰ μυστήρια τῆς βασιλείας τοῦ θεοῦ.

2 Chron. 18:14, ἦλθεν πρὸς τὸν βασιλέα, καὶ εἶπεν αὐτῷ ὁ βασιλεύς, Μιχαία, εἰ[a] πορευθῶ εἰς Ῥαμὼθ Γαλαὰδ εἰς πόλεμον ἢ ἐπίσχω;[b] καὶ εἶπεν, Ἀνάβαινε καὶ εὐοδώσεις, καὶ **δοθήσονται** εἰς χεῖρας ὑμῶν.

[a] Questions may be introduced by εἰ. It is not reflected explicitly in an English equivalent. Here the king addresses a question to the prophet Micaiah (Μιχαία).

[b] ἐπίσχω, 1st. sg. aor. act. subj. ▶ ἐπέχω, "I hold, hold back"

1 En. 104.12, πάλιν ἐγὼ γινώσκω μυστήριον δεύτερον, ὅτι δικαίοις καὶ ὁσίοις καὶ φρονίμοις **δοθήσονται** αἱ βίβλοι μου εἰς χαρὰν ἀληθείας.

T. Levi 4.5, διὰ τοῦτο **δέδοταί** σοι βουλὴ καὶ σύνεσις, τοῦ συνετίσαι τοὺς υἱούς σου περὶ αὐτοῦ.

Parsing Practice

32.12. Thus far in this chapter you have been parsing in context. To enable you to test your parsing skills with μι verbs, try covering the right-hand column below and see if you can parse each of these forms of δίδωμι, then check your answer on the right.

δώσετε	2nd pl. fut. act. ind.
ἔδωκα	1st. sg. aor. act. ind.
δίδωσιν	3rd sg. pres. act. ind.
δέδωκεν	3rd sg. pf. act. ind.
ἔδωκαν	3rd pl. aor. act. ind.
ἐδίδου	3rd sg. impf. act. ind.
διδόασι	3rd pl. pres. act. ind.
δώσω	1st sg. fut. act. ind.
ἐδώκαμεν	1st pl. aor. act. ind.

Additional μι Verbs

32.13. Now that you are familiar with the most common of the μι verbs, δίδωμι, we will add the other two listed at the beginning of the chapter, which are also quite common: ἵστημι ("I stand"; stem στα-) and τίθημι ("I put/place"; stem θε-). The forms of each of these verbs follow the same patterns as δίδωμι. A complete listing of these forms may be found in appendix A, §§A.30–35.

There is a conventional usage pattern with ἵστημι. The meaning varies slightly, depending on the tense. When ἵστημι is intransitive (i.e., without a direct object), it means "I am in a standing position," but when ἵστημι is transitive (with a direct object), it takes a causative meaning: "I cause (someone or thing) to stand." By convention, transitive instances are in the present, imperfect, future active, or first aorist form, but intransitive uses are future middle and passive, second aorist, perfect, or pluperfect. Thus when Jesus "stands" a child in the midst of the disciples (Mark 9:36), the form is ἔστησεν (first aorist), but when John tells us that Jesus "stood" in their midst (John 20:19), the form is ἔστη (second aorist). See the vocabulary list at the end of the chapter and your lexicon for more information.

Examples of ἵστημι

32.14. The most common form of ἵστημι in both the NT and LXX is ἔστη, 3rd sg. ²aor. act. ind. There is also a first aorist form ἔστησεν. Both forms are almost equally common (NT 9× ἔστη, 7× ἔστησεν; LXX 97× ἔστη, 79× ἔστησεν).[6] The first aorist forms of ἵστημι differ from most μι verbs in that they use the same aorist form marker as do ω verbs: σα instead of κα. (See examples in Mark 9:36 and Rev. 11:11 below.)

Mark 9:36, λαβὼν παιδίον **ἔστησεν** αὐτὸ ἐν μέσῳ αὐτῶν.	Taking a little child *he stood* him in their midst.
John 20:19, ἦλθεν ὁ Ἰησοῦς καὶ **ἔστη** εἰς τὸ μέσον καὶ λέγει αὐτοῖς, Εἰρήνη ὑμῖν.	Jesus came and *stood* in the midst and said to them, "Peace to you."
Gen. 41:46, Ἰωσὴφ δὲ ἦν ἐτῶν τριάκοντα, ὅτε **ἔστη** ἐναντίον Φαραὼ βασιλέως Αἰγύπτου.	Now Joseph was thirty years old when *he stood* before Pharaoh, king of Egypt.
Gen. 6:18, **στήσω** τὴν διαθήκην μου πρὸς σέ· εἰσελεύσῃ δὲ εἰς τὴν κιβωτόν, σὺ καὶ οἱ υἱοί σου καὶ ἡ γυνή σου καὶ αἱ γυναῖκες τῶν υἱῶν σου μετὰ σοῦ.	*I will establish* my covenant with you; and you will enter the ark, you and your sons and your wife and the wives of your sons with you.

In this passage ἵστημι has a slightly different sense. See the entry in *CL*, 178.1.b or BDAG, 482.3.

6. The figures for the most common forms of ἵστημι in the NT may not seem very high (only 16 forms), but all forms of ἵστημι occur 154 times in the NT. There are also about 20 compound forms, such as ἀνίστημι and παρίστημι, which occur about 300 times; altogether there are about 450 forms of ἵστημι in the NT. In the LXX there are about 700 instances of ἵστημι, plus nearly 30 compound forms, for a total of 2,165 occurrences.

32.15. *Now You Try It*

Rev. 11:11, μετὰ τὰς τρεῖς ἡμέρας καὶ ἥμισυ πνεῦμα ζωῆς ἐκ τοῦ θεοῦ εἰσῆλθεν ἐν αὐτοῖς, καὶ **ἔστησαν** ἐπὶ τοὺς πόδας αὐτῶν, καὶ φόβος μέγας ἐπέπεσεν ἐπὶ τοὺς θεωροῦντας αὐτούς.

John 1:26, ἀπεκρίθη αὐτοῖς ὁ Ἰωάννης λέγων, Ἐγὼ βαπτίζω ἐν ὕδατι· μέσος ὑμῶν **ἕστηκεν** ὃν ὑμεῖς οὐκ οἴδατε.

Acts 1:11, Ἄνδρες Γαλιλαῖοι, τί **ἑστήκατε** ἐμβλέποντες εἰς τὸν οὐρανόν;

Gen. 24:31, εἶπεν αὐτῷ, Δεῦρο εἴσελθε, εὐλογητὸς κύριος, ἵνα τί **ἕστηκας** ἔξω; ἐγὼ δὲ ἡτοίμακα τὴν οἰκίαν καὶ τόπον ταῖς καμήλοις.

Deut. 31:15, κατέβη κύριος ἐν νεφέλῃ καὶ **ἔστη** παρὰ τὰς θύρας τῆς σκηνῆς τοῦ μαρτυρίου, καὶ **ἔστη** ὁ στῦλος τῆς νεφέλης παρὰ τὰς θύρας τῆς σκηνῆς.

Examples of τίθημι

32.16. You will notice in some of these examples that τίθημι has a fairly wide semantic range. Check your lexicon when the default gloss of "I put/place" does not seem to make good sense in English.

Mark 6:29, ἀκούσαντες οἱ μαθηταὶ αὐτοῦ ἦλθον καὶ ἦραν τὸ πτῶμα αὐτοῦ καὶ **ἔθηκαν** αὐτὸ ἐν μνημείῳ.	Hearing [this], his disciples went and took his corpse and *placed* it in a grave.
John 2:10, λέγει αὐτῷ, Πᾶς ἄνθρωπος πρῶτον τὸν καλὸν οἶνον **τίθησιν** καὶ ὅταν μεθυσθῶσιν τὸν ἐλάσσω· σὺ τετήρηκας τὸν καλὸν οἶνον ἕως ἄρτι.	He said to them, "Everyone *serves* the good wine first, and when they [i.e., the guests] are drunk, [then he serves] the cheaper wine; you have kept the good wine until now!"
John 10:11, Ἐγώ εἰμι ὁ ποιμὴν ὁ καλός. ὁ ποιμὴν ὁ καλὸς τὴν ψυχὴν αὐτοῦ **τίθησιν** ὑπὲρ τῶν προβάτων.	I am the good shepherd. The good shepherd *gives* his life for the sheep.

John 10:17, διὰ τοῦτό με ὁ πατὴρ ἀγαπᾷ ὅτι ἐγὼ **τίθημι** τὴν ψυχήν μου, ἵνα πάλιν λάβω αὐτήν.

For this reason the Father loves me, because I *lay down* my life in order that I may receive it again.

Gen. 2:15, ἔλαβεν κύριος ὁ θεὸς τὸν ἄνθρωπον, ὃν ἔπλασεν, καὶ **ἔθετο** αὐτὸν ἐν τῷ παραδείσῳ ἐργάζεσθαι αὐτὸν καὶ φυλάσσειν.

The Lord God took the man whom he had formed and *placed* him in the garden to work it and guard [it].

Gen. 17:6, αὐξανῶ σε σφόδρα σφόδρα καὶ **θήσω** σε εἰς ἔθνη, καὶ βασιλεῖς ἐκ σοῦ ἐξελεύσονται.

I will increase you very greatly, and *I will make* you into a nation, and kings will come from you.

32.17. *Now You Try It*

John 13:37–38, λέγει αὐτῷ ὁ Πέτρος, Κύριε, διὰ τί οὐ δύναμαί σοι ἀκολουθῆσαι ἄρτι; τὴν ψυχήν μου ὑπὲρ σοῦ **θήσω**. ἀποκρίνεται Ἰησοῦς, Τὴν ψυχήν σου ὑπὲρ ἐμοῦ **θήσεις**; ἀμὴν ἀμὴν λέγω σοι, οὐ μὴ ἀλέκτωρ φωνήσῃ ἕως οὗ ἀρνήσῃ με τρίς.

John 19:19, ἔγραψεν δὲ καὶ τίτλον ὁ Πιλᾶτος καὶ **ἔθηκεν** ἐπὶ τοῦ σταυροῦ· ἦν δὲ γεγραμμένον, Ἰησοῦς ὁ Ναζωραῖος ὁ βασιλεὺς τῶν Ἰουδαίων.

Rom. 4:17, καθὼς γέγραπται ὅτι Πατέρα πολλῶν ἐθνῶν **τέθεικά** σε.

Acts 1:7, εἶπεν δὲ πρὸς αὐτούς, Οὐχ ὑμῶν ἐστιν γνῶναι χρόνους ἢ καιροὺς οὓς ὁ πατὴρ **ἔθετο** ἐν τῇ ἰδίᾳ ἐξουσίᾳ.

2 Tim. 1:11, [τοῦ εὐαγγελίου] εἰς ὃ **ἐτέθην** ἐγὼ κῆρυξ καὶ ἀπόστολος καὶ διδάσκαλος.

Gen. 42:30, Λελάληκεν ὁ ἄνθρωπος ὁ κύριος τῆς γῆς πρὸς ἡμᾶς σκληρὰ καὶ **ἔθετο** ἡμᾶς ἐν φυλακῇ ὡς κατασκοπεύοντας τὴν γῆν.

Deut. 26:4, λήμψεται ὁ ἱερεὺς τὸν κάρταλλον[a] ἐκ τῶν χειρῶν σου καὶ **θήσει** αὐτὸν ἀπέναντι τοῦ θυσιαστηρίου κυρίου τοῦ θεοῦ σου.

[a] κάρταλλος, ου, ὁ, "basket"

Other μι Verbs

32.18. There are quite a few other μι verbs, but they do not occur frequently. Many of them are compound forms of the three major verbs that you are learning in this chapter, so they will be easily recognizable. The lists below are not intended for memorization. Read through them so that you have an idea of what to expect as you read the NT or LXX.

The other μι verbs that occur more than 10 times in the NT include the following compound forms of the three major μι verbs:

	Compound Form	Frequency NT	LXX
δίδωμι	ἀποδίδωμι	48	208
	παραδίδωμι	119	248
ἵστημι	ἀνθίστημι	14	71
	ἀνίστημι	108	473
	ἀφίστημι	14	218
	ἐξίστημι	17	68
	ἐφίστημι	21	72
	καθίστημι	21	205
	παρίστημι	41	90
	συνίστημι	16	42
τίθημι	ἐπιτίθημι	39	264
	παρατίθημι	19	37
	προστίθημι	18	285

If we were to add the most frequent forms from the LXX (50+), the list would increase by only two more compound verbs: ἀνταποδίδωμι (7 NT/87 LXX) and διατίθημι (7/86). The only other μι verbs that occur more than 10 times in the NT are the following:

	NT	LXX
ἀπόλλυμι	90	366
ἀφίημι	143	125
δείκνυμι	30	121
ἐνδείκνυμι	11	—
πάρειμι	24	57
πίμπλημι	24	116
συνίημι	26	97
φημί	66	74

Other frequent μι verbs in the LXX include ὄμνυμι (0/179), ἐμπίπλημι (5/146), and δια(ρ)ρήγνυμι (5/85).

32.19. Only one of the above forms needs further comment. Δείκνυμι has characteristics of both ω verbs and μι verbs. It uses the μι verb endings (except for second singular) without a connecting vowel, but it does not have iota reduplication in the present tense-form.

Present Active Indicative of δείκνυμι

1S	δείκνυμι
2S	δεικνύεις
3S	δείκνυσι(ν)
1P	δείκνυμεν
2P	δείκνυτε
3P	δεικνύασι(ν)

Reading Passage: Genesis 24:1–20

32.20. This reading passage from the LXX is not difficult, though the vocabulary will keep you busy with your lexicon. Words that are not used in the NT (and thus not in *CL*—and often not in BDAG either) are identified in the notes along with some idiomatic expressions and a few obscure forms. The selection is a good story, and it is a fun read. You will find each of the three main μι verbs included. The paragraphing reflects English style to make it easier for you to follow the story.

Isaac and Rebekah

1 Ἀβραὰμ ἦν πρεσβύτερος προβεβηκὼς ἡμερῶν, καὶ κύριος εὐλόγησεν τὸν
Ἀβραὰμ κατὰ πάντα. 2 καὶ εἶπεν Ἀβραὰμ τῷ παιδὶ αὐτοῦ τῷ πρεσβυτέρῳ τῆς
οἰκίας αὐτοῦ τῷ ἄρχοντι πάντων τῶν αὐτοῦ, Θὲς[a] (place!) τὴν χεῖρά σου ὑπὸ
τὸν μηρόν μου, 3 καὶ ἐξορκιῶ[b] σε κύριον τὸν θεὸν τοῦ οὐρανοῦ καὶ τὸν θεὸν
τῆς γῆς, ἵνα μὴ λάβῃς γυναῖκα τῷ υἱῷ μου Ἰσαὰκ ἀπὸ τῶν θυγατέρων τῶν
Χαναναίων, μεθ᾽ ὧν ἐγὼ οἰκῶ ἐν αὐτοῖς, 4 ἀλλὰ εἰς τὴν γῆν μου, οὗ ἐγενόμην,
πορεύσῃ καὶ εἰς τὴν φυλήν μου καὶ λήμψῃ γυναῖκα τῷ υἱῷ μου Ἰσαὰκ ἐκεῖθεν.

5 Εἶπεν δὲ πρὸς αὐτὸν ὁ παῖς, Μήποτε οὐ βούλεται ἡ γυνὴ πορευθῆναι μετ᾽
ἐμοῦ ὀπίσω εἰς τὴν γῆν ταύτην· ἀποστρέψω[c] τὸν υἱόν σου εἰς τὴν γῆν, ὅθεν
ἐξῆλθες ἐκεῖθεν;

6 Εἶπεν δὲ πρὸς αὐτὸν Ἀβραάμ, Πρόσεχε σεαυτῷ, μὴ ἀποστρέψῃς[c] τὸν υἱόν
μου ἐκεῖ. 7 κύριος ὁ θεὸς τοῦ οὐρανοῦ καὶ ὁ θεὸς τῆς γῆς, ὃς ἔλαβέν με ἐκ τοῦ
οἴκου τοῦ πατρός μου καὶ ἐκ τῆς γῆς, ἧς ἐγενήθην, ὃς ἐλάλησέν μοι καὶ ὤμοσέν
μοι λέγων, Σοὶ **δώσω** τὴν γῆν ταύτην καὶ τῷ σπέρματί σου, αὐτὸς ἀποστελεῖ τὸν
ἄγγελον αὐτοῦ ἔμπροσθέν σου, καὶ λήμψῃ γυναῖκα τῷ υἱῷ μου Ἰσαὰκ ἐκεῖθεν.
8 ἐὰν δὲ μὴ θέλῃ ἡ γυνὴ πορευθῆναι μετὰ σοῦ εἰς τὴν γῆν ταύτην, καθαρὸς[d] ἔσῃ
ἀπὸ τοῦ ὅρκου τούτου· μόνον τὸν υἱόν μου μὴ ἀποστρέψῃς[c] ἐκεῖ. 9 καὶ **ἔθηκεν**
ὁ παῖς τὴν χεῖρα αὐτοῦ ὑπὸ τὸν μηρὸν Ἀβραὰμ τοῦ κυρίου αὐτοῦ καὶ ὤμοσεν
αὐτῷ περὶ τοῦ ῥήματος τούτου.

[10]Καὶ ἔλαβεν ὁ παῖς δέκα καμήλους ἀπὸ τῶν καμήλων τοῦ κυρίου αὐτοῦ καὶ ἀπὸ πάντων τῶν ἀγαθῶν[e] τοῦ κυρίου αὐτοῦ μεθ' ἑαυτοῦ καὶ ἀναστὰς ἐπορεύθη εἰς τὴν Μεσοποταμίαν εἰς τὴν πόλιν Ναχώρ. [11]καὶ ἐκοίμισεν[f] τὰς καμήλους ἔξω τῆς πόλεως παρὰ τὸ φρέαρ τοῦ ὕδατος τὸ πρὸς ὀψέ, ἡνίκα ἐκπορεύονται αἱ ὑδρευόμεναι.[g]

[12]Καὶ εἶπεν, Κύριε ὁ θεὸς τοῦ κυρίου μου Ἀβραάμ, εὐόδωσον ἐναντίον ἐμοῦ σήμερον[h] καὶ ποίησον ἔλεος μετὰ τοῦ κυρίου μου Ἀβραάμ.[i] [13]ἰδοὺ ἐγὼ **ἕστηκα** ἐπὶ τῆς πηγῆς τοῦ ὕδατος, αἱ δὲ θυγατέρες τῶν οἰκούντων τὴν πόλιν ἐκπορεύονται ἀντλῆσαι ὕδωρ, [14]καὶ ἔσται ἡ παρθένος, ᾗ ἂν ἐγὼ εἴπω, Ἐπίκλινον[j] τὴν ὑδρίαν σου, ἵνα πίω, καὶ εἴπῃ μοι, Πίε, καὶ τὰς καμήλους σου ποτιῶ, ἕως ἂν παύσωνται πίνουσαι, ταύτην ἡτοίμασας τῷ παιδί σου Ἰσαάκ, καὶ ἐν τούτῳ γνώσομαι ὅτι ἐποίησας ἔλεος τῷ κυρίῳ μου Ἀβραάμ.

[15]Καὶ ἐγένετο πρὸ τοῦ συντελέσαι αὐτὸν λαλοῦντα ἐν τῇ διανοίᾳ, καὶ ἰδοὺ Ῥεβέκκα ἐξεπορεύετο ἡ τεχθεῖσα[k] Βαθουὴλ υἱῷ Μελχὰς τῆς γυναικὸς Ναχὼρ ἀδελφοῦ δὲ Ἀβραὰμ[l] ἔχουσα τὴν ὑδρίαν ἐπὶ τῶν ὤμων αὐτῆς. [16]ἡ δὲ παρθένος ἦν καλὴ τῇ ὄψει σφόδρα· παρθένος ἦν, ἀνὴρ οὐκ ἔγνω αὐτήν. καταβᾶσα δὲ ἐπὶ τὴν πηγὴν ἔπλησεν τὴν ὑδρίαν καὶ ἀνέβη. [17]ἐπέδραμεν[m] δὲ ὁ παῖς εἰς συνάντησιν αὐτῆς καὶ εἶπεν, Πότισόν με μικρὸν ὕδωρ ἐκ τῆς ὑδρίας σου.

[18]Ἡ δὲ εἶπεν, Πίε, κύριε. καὶ ἔσπευσεν καὶ καθεῖλεν τὴν ὑδρίαν ἐπὶ τὸν βραχίονα αὐτῆς καὶ ἐπότισεν αὐτόν, [19]ἕως ἐπαύσατο πίνων. καὶ εἶπεν, Καὶ ταῖς καμήλοις σου ὑδρεύσομαι,[n] ἕως ἂν πᾶσαι πίωσιν. [20]καὶ ἔσπευσεν καὶ ἐξεκένωσεν[o] τὴν ὑδρίαν εἰς τὸ ποτιστήριον[p] καὶ ἔδραμεν ἔτι ἐπὶ τὸ φρέαρ ἀντλῆσαι καὶ ὑδρεύσατο[n] πάσαις ταῖς καμήλοις.

a Θές is an imperative form of τίθημι that you will meet in the next chapter.

b Check this word in your lexicon; it has a causative sense, and here it is followed by a double accusative. The first indicates who is caused to do something, the second the basis on which it is done.

c ἀποστρέφω here means "I return, take back."

d καθαρός does not mean "pure, clean" in this context. Check your lexicon. (*CL* is adequate to figure it out, but if you have access to BDAG, this passage is cited by reference.)

e This is a substantival use of ἀγαθός that is not common in the NT (but see perhaps Luke 16:25). BDAG points out that this adjective can be "used as a pure subst.: . . . pl. ἀγαθά, ῶν, τά *good things, possessions*" (s.v. ἀγαθός, 3.1.b). In *CL*, note the very last clause of the entry.

f κοιμίζω, "I rest, sleep"

g ὑδρεύω, "I carry water"; the form in the text is a participle—pay particular attention to the article, case, and gender.

h "εὐόδωσον ἐναντίον ἐμοῦ σήμερον, guide me happily forwards today, let me prosper today, let me succeed today Gn 24:12" (LEH, s.v. εὐοδόω, 188).

i Formally this phrase is straightforward: ποίησον ἔλεος μετὰ τοῦ κυρίου μου Ἀβραάμ = "do mercy to my master Abraham," but that does not communicate the meaning and does not use natural English. We would say, "show mercy to," or perhaps, "show kindness to." (See also a very similar expression at the end of v. 14.)

j 2nd sg. aor. act. impv. ▸ ἐπικλίνω, "I incline, tip"

k τεχθεῖσα, aor. pass. ptc. fem. sg. nom. ▸ τίκτω, "I bring forth"

l Everything from ἡ τεχθεῖσα to Ἀβραάμ is parenthetical, explaining who Rebekah was. The syntax picks up after this: ἰδοὺ Ῥεβέκκα ἐξεπορεύετο ἔχουσα τὴν ὑδρίαν.

m ἐπέδραμεν ▸ ἐπιτρέχω, "I run to." You may remember from chap. 18 that the simplex form, τρέχω, has a second aorist from a totally different root, ἔδραμον ▸ *δραμ. You will also find ἔδραμεν in v. 20.

n ὑδρεύω, "I draw/carry water"

o ἐκκενόω, "I empty out"

p ποτιστήριον, -ου, τό, "watering trough"

32.21. Vocabulary for Chapter 32

Part of Speech / Word	Definition	Possible Glosses	Frequency NT	Frequency LXX
Adjectives				
ὅμοιος, οία, οιον	Characterized by having some commonality with another object or entity, resembling something	similar, like	45	91
ἐχθρός, ά, όν	Characterized by hostility, hatred, or unfriendliness toward another; characterized by experiencing hostility, hatred, or unfriendliness from others; one who expresses these attitudes toward another, enemy (subst.)	hostile, hating; hated; enemy (subst.)	32	456
Adverb				
ὀπίσω	An adverb describing the verb as taking place behind some object, as reverting direction, or as happening subsequently; more commonly in the NT and LXX as a preposition used with the genitive with the same meaning	behind, backward, afterward (adv.); after, behind (prep. + gen.)	35	461
Nouns				
χαρά, ᾶς, ἡ	The emotion of gladness that comes as a result of circumstances; a deep-seated contentment based on faith in God's promises despite circumstances	joy, delight	59	44
σωτηρία, ας, ἡ	Deliverance/rescue from harm, whether from physical danger or from spiritual death and condemnation	deliverance, rescue, salvation	46	160
θλῖψις, εως, ἡ	Distress that is caused by either outward circumstances or inner anguish	distress, suffering, affliction, oppression, tribulation, trouble	45	134
ἄρχων, οντος, ὁ	One who rules (though with less authority than a βασιλεύς); an administrative official	ruler, prince; leader, official, administrator	37	645
Verbs				
δίδωμι	To cause another person to receive or have (roughly equivalent to the English word "give" with a wide range of glosses possible, depending on the context and referent; LXX even more diverse than NT)	I give	415	2,131
παραδίδωμι	To hand over to legal custody (legal technical term); to transmit something to another (with a variety of English glosses possible, depending on the referent)	I deliver, hand over; I pass on, transmit	119	277
ἀποδίδωμι	To engage in a reciprocal action by repaying money, fulfilling an obligation, transferring something to another; to give a product in exchange for payment or trade (mid.); to yield fruit/produce	I repay, give/pay back; I pay; I give over, give back, restore; I sell, trade; I yield (fruit)	48	220

Part of Speech	Definition	Possible Glosses	Frequency	
Word			NT	LXX
ἵστημι	(1) Intransitive (pf., plpf.): to be in a standing position; to be at a place; to maintain one's belief or one's position (physically); (2) intransitive ([2]aor., fut.): to be in an upright position, desist from movement; (3) transitive (pres., impf., [1]aor.): to cause to be in a place or position; to place in the balance and weigh (LXX); to establish a condition, institute legally	(1) I stand; I stand firm, hold out; (2) I stand still, stop; (3) I put, place, set; I weigh; I establish	154	773
ἀνίστημι	(1) Transitive (fut., [1]aor. act.): to cause to rise up (of an object or of a dead person); (2) intransitive (mid., [2]aor. act.): to stand up from lying or sitting; to come back from the dead; to appear to carry out a function; to initiate an action specified by another verb	(1) I raise, erect, bring to life; (2) I stand up, rise; I come back from the dead; I arise; I set out, get ready	108	539
παρίστημι	(1) Transitive (pres., fut., impf., [1]aor.): to place beside or at one's disposal; to represent/present someone to someone; to offer sacrifice (act.); (2) intransitive (pres., fut., pf., plpf., [2]aor. act.): to be present, stand by; to come to the aid of (mid.)	(1) I place beside; I present; I offer, bring; (2) I am present, stand by; bystander, spectator (subst. pf. ptc.); I help	41	93
τίθημι	To put or place something in a particular location; to assign someone to a task or position; to cause someone or something to undergo a change in condition	I put, place; I appoint, assign; I make, consign	100	558
δείκνυμι (also δεικνύω)	To show so as to be apprehended by the senses; to prove or make clear by evidence, reasoning, or demonstration	I show, point out, make known; I explain, prove, demonstrate	33	124

32.22. Key Things to Know for Chapter 32

What are the three most common μι verbs, and what are their stems?

The μι verbs use "iota reduplication" in the present tense-form. (Remember that the imperfect is built on the present stem, so it also uses iota reduplication.)

There are usually no connecting vowels in the μι verbs.

The aorist uses κα as the form marker instead of σα.

In the μι verbs the A set of personal endings used in the present is slightly different from the A endings in the ω verbs.

33

μι VERBS: PART 2

NON-INDICATIVE FORMS

33.1. In the previous chapter we learned the indicative forms of the μι verbs. Now we will study the non-indicative forms: subjunctives, imperatives, participles, and infinitives. You already understand how these forms function; all we need to do is see what they look like in the μι conjugation. You do not need to memorize these long lists of forms. They are simply for reference so that you can see what they look like in comparison to the ω forms that you already know. The majority of these non-indicative forms are easily identifiable so long as you remember the distinctive features noted at the beginning of the previous chapter, especially their stems. These forms are limited almost entirely to present and aorist. Many of the forms shown do not occur in the NT or LXX, but they do in other Koine literature; they also show up in some of the compound forms in the NT and LXX. Even if your primary interest is in reading the NT or LXX, seeing the full set of forms is helpful so that you can see the pattern of endings used and identify other μι verbs that may occur in these forms.

Subjunctive Mood

33.2. The subjunctive forms of the μι verbs use the regular A and C set of ω verb endings—*even for aorist subjunctives.* They do not use secondary endings (there is no augment) or the different set of A endings used in the present active indicative μι verbs. In the ω verb system, you learned to identify subjunctives by the lengthened connecting vowel. But in the present and second aorist forms of the μι verbs (which are more common than the first aorist in the NT and the only form used in the LXX) it is the *stem vowel* that lengthens, since there is no connecting vowel.[1] For example, in δίδωμι the stem is δο-, which lengthens to δω- throughout the subjunctive. Likewise θε- lengthens to θη- or θω-, and στα- lengthens to στη- or στω-.

Active Subjunctive Forms of δίδωμι

	Present	First Aorist	Second Aorist
1S	διδῶ	δώσω	δῶ
2S	διδῷς	δώσῃς	δῷς
3S	διδῷ	δώσῃ	δῷ[a]
1P	διδῶμεν	δώσωμεν	δῶμεν
2P	διδῶτε	δώσητε	δῶτε
3P	διδῶσι(ν)	δώσωσι(ν)	δῶσι(ν)

[a] There are two alternate third singular forms of the aorist active subjunctive of δίδωμι: δοῖ and δώῃ.

Many of the forms in the chart above do not occur in the NT or the LXX, though they may occur in compound forms or in other Koine texts. There is one example of the present active subjunctive of δίδωμι in the NT and one in the LXX (διδῶ in Rev. 3:9; διδῶσιν in 1 Esd. 8:19) and one instance of ἵστημι (ἱστῶσιν in 1 Macc 8:1). There are no examples of the present active subjunctive of τίθημι. Only three middle subjunctives occur, all aorist forms of τίθημι and all in the LXX. See appendix A for tables showing the full set of subjunctive forms of ἵστημι and τίθημι.

33.3. *Examples*

Mark 7:9, ἔλεγεν αὐτοῖς, Καλῶς ἀθετεῖτε τὴν ἐντολὴν τοῦ θεοῦ, ἵνα τὴν παράδοσιν ὑμῶν **στήσητε**.	He said to them, "You nicely lay aside the commandment of God in order that *you may establish* your tradition."
John 15:13, μείζονα ταύτης ἀγάπην οὐδεὶς ἔχει, ἵνα τις τὴν ψυχὴν αὐτοῦ **θῇ** ὑπὲρ τῶν φίλων αὐτοῦ.	Greater love than this no one has, that someone *would lay down* their life for their friends.
Eph. 1:17, ἵνα ὁ θεὸς τοῦ κυρίου ἡμῶν Ἰησοῦ Χριστοῦ, ὁ πατὴρ τῆς δόξης, **δώῃ** ὑμῖν πνεῦμα σοφίας καὶ ἀποκαλύψεως ἐν ἐπιγνώσει αὐτοῦ.	In order that the God of our Lord Jesus Christ, the Father of glory, *may give* you a spirit of wisdom and revelation in the knowledge of him.
Gen. 38:17, ὁ δὲ εἶπεν, Ἐγώ σοι ἀποστελῶ ἔριφον αἰγῶν ἐκ τῶν προβάτων. ἡ δὲ εἶπεν, Ἐὰν **δῷς** ἀρραβῶνα ἕως τοῦ ἀποστεῖλαί[a] σε.	So he said, "I will send you a kid goat from the flocks." But she said, "If *you give* a pledge until you send [it]."

[a] Did you recognize the aorist infinitive of the liquid verb ἀποστέλλω?

1. The first aorist forms of δίδωμι use a form marker and connecting vowel, so they follow the same pattern as the ω verbs.

Num. 35:12, οὐ μὴ ἀποθάνῃ ὁ φονεύων, ἕως ἂν **στῇ** ἔναντι τῆς συναγωγῆς εἰς κρίσιν.

The murderer will not die until *he stands* before the congregation for judgment.

4 Kgdms. (2 Kings) 4:10, ποιήσωμεν δὴ αὐτῷ ὑπερῷον τόπον μικρὸν καὶ **θῶμεν** αὐτῷ ἐκεῖ κλίνην καὶ τράπεζαν καὶ δίφρον καὶ λυχνίαν.

Now let us make for him an upstairs room, a small place, and *let us place* there for him a bed and a table and a seat and a lampstand.

33.4. *Now You Try It*

John 17:2, καθὼς ἔδωκας αὐτῷ ἐξουσίαν πάσης σαρκός, ἵνα πᾶν ὃ δέδωκας αὐτῷ **δώσῃ** αὐτοῖς ζωὴν αἰώνιον.

Rev. 19:7, χαίρωμεν καὶ ἀγαλλιῶμεν καὶ **δώσωμεν** τὴν δόξαν αὐτῷ, ὅτι ἦλθεν ὁ γάμος τοῦ ἀρνίου καὶ ἡ γυνὴ αὐτοῦ ἡτοίμασεν ἑαυτήν.

1 Cor. 15:25, δεῖ γὰρ αὐτὸν βασιλεύειν ἄχρι οὗ **θῇ** πάντας τοὺς ἐχθροὺς ὑπὸ τοὺς πόδας αὐτοῦ.

Heb. 10:9, τότε εἴρηκεν, Ἰδοὺ ἥκω τοῦ ποιῆσαι τὸ θέλημά σου. ἀναιρεῖ τὸ πρῶτον ἵνα τὸ δεύτερον **στήσῃ**.

3 Kgdms. (1 Kings) 15:4, ὅτι διὰ Δαυὶδ ἔδωκεν αὐτῷ κύριος κατάλειμμα, ἵνα **στήσῃ** τέκνα αὐτοῦ μετ' αὐτὸν καὶ **στήσῃ** τὴν Ἰερουσαλήμ.

2 Chron. 1:7, ἐν τῇ νυκτὶ ἐκείνῃ ὤφθη ὁ θεὸς τῷ Σαλωμὼν καὶ εἶπεν αὐτῷ, Αἴτησαι τί σοι **δῶ**.

Ps. 109:1 (110:1 Eng.), Εἶπεν ὁ κύριος τῷ κυρίῳ μου, Κάθου ἐκ δεξιῶν μου, ἕως ἂν **θῶ** τοὺς ἐχθρούς σου ὑποπόδιον τῶν ποδῶν σου.

Imperative Mood

33.5. The μι verb imperatives are as follows. They are nearly identical to the ω conjugation except for the second singular forms. These do not occur often in the NT, though they are much more frequent in the LXX. The second singular form δός is the most common form in both testaments.

Present Active Imperative of μι Verbs

	δίδωμι	ἵστημι	τίθημι
2S	δίδου	ἵστη	τίθει
3S	διδότω	ἱστάτω	τιθέτω
2P	δίδοτε	ἵστατε	τίθετε
3P	διδότωσαν	ἱστάτωσαν	τιθέτωσαν

Aorist Active Imperative of μι Verbs

	δίδωμι	ἵστημι	τίθημι
2S	δός	στῆθι or στῆσον	θές
3S	δότω	στήτω	θέτω
2P	δότε	στῆτε or στήσατε	θέτε
3P	δότωσαν	στήτωσαν	θέτωσαν

See appendix A for middle imperative forms; there are none of δίδωμι or ἵστημι and only a few of τίθημι in the LXX (none in the NT).

33.6. *Examples*

Matt. 6:11, τὸν ἄρτον ἡμῶν τὸν ἐπιούσιον **δὸς** ἡμῖν σήμερον.

Give us today our daily bread.

Matt. 14:16, ὁ δὲ Ἰησοῦς εἶπεν αὐτοῖς, Οὐ χρείαν ἔχουσιν ἀπελθεῖν, **δότε** αὐτοῖς ὑμεῖς φαγεῖν.

So Jesus said to them, "They do not need to depart; you *give* them [something] to eat."

Exod. 8:16, Εἶπεν δὲ κύριος πρὸς Μωϋσῆν, Ὄρθρισον τὸ πρωὶ καὶ **στῆθι** ἐναντίον Φαραώ.

Now the Lord said to Moses, "Get up early in the morning, and *stand* before Pharaoh."

Num. 21:8, εἶπεν κύριος πρὸς Μωϋσῆν, Ποίησον σεαυτῷ ὄφιν καὶ **θὲς** αὐτὸν ἐπὶ σημείου, καὶ ἔσται ἐὰν δάκῃ[a] ὄφις ἄνθρωπον, πᾶς ὁ δεδηγμένος ἰδὼν αὐτὸν ζήσεται.

The Lord said to Moses, "Make for yourself a snake, and *place* it for a sign, and it will be if a snake bites a person, everyone who is bitten, seeing it will live.

[a] δάκνω, "I bite"

33.7. *Now You Try It*

1 Pet. 5:12, ταύτην εἶναι ἀληθῆ χάριν τοῦ θεοῦ εἰς ἣν **στῆτε**.

Rev. 14:7, Φοβήθητε τὸν θεὸν καὶ **δότε** αὐτῷ δόξαν, ὅτι ἦλθεν ἡ ὥρα τῆς κρίσεως αὐτοῦ, καὶ προσκυνήσατε τῷ ποιήσαντι τὸν οὐρανὸν καὶ τὴν γῆν καὶ θάλασσαν καὶ πηγὰς ὑδάτων.

Judg. 6:20, εἶπεν πρὸς αὐτὸν ὁ ἄγγελος κυρίου, Λαβὲ τὰ κρέα καὶ τοὺς ἄρτους τοὺς ἀζύμους καὶ **θὲς** πρὸς τὴν πέτραν ἐκείνην καὶ τὸν ζωμὸν (broth) ἔκχεον· καὶ ἐποίησεν οὕτως.

3 Kgdms. (1 Kings) 18:23, **δότωσαν** ἡμῖν δύο βόας,[a] καὶ ἐκλεξάσθωσαν ἑαυτοῖς τὸν ἕνα καὶ μελισάτωσαν[b] καὶ **ἐπιθέτωσαν**[c] ἐπὶ τῶν ξύλων καὶ πῦρ μὴ **ἐπιθέτωσαν**,[c] καὶ ἐγὼ ποιήσω τὸν βοῦν τὸν ἄλλον καὶ πῦρ οὐ μὴ ἐπιθῶ.

[a] βοῦς, βοός, ὁ or ἡ (accusative plural, βόας), "head of cattle, cow; cattle (plural)"; masculine forms may be "bull" or "ox" if the context justifies it.

[b] μελίζω, "I cut in pieces"

[c] This is a compound form of one of the common μι verbs.

This verse provides a good review of imperatives. It includes both ω and μι verb imperatives. There is also another μι verb in the indicative mood.

Optative Mood

33.8. The only optative μι verbs that occur in the NT are δῴη (4×), 3rd sg. aor. act. opt. ▸ δίδωμι, "I give"; ὀναίμην (1×), 1st sg. aor. mid. opt. ▸ ὀνίνημι, "I benefit"; and εἴη (12×), 3rd sg. pres. act. opt. ▸ εἰμί, "I am."

In the LXX the only optative forms of common μι verbs that occur more than once are δῴη (29×), 3rd sg. aor. act. opt. ▸ δίδωμι, "I give"; and προσθείη (16×), 3rd sg. aor. act. opt. ▸ προστίθημι, "I add."

33.9. *Examples*

2 Thess. 3:16, Αὐτὸς δὲ ὁ κύριος τῆς εἰρήνης **δῴη** ὑμῖν τὴν εἰρήνην διὰ παντὸς ἐν παντὶ τρόπῳ. ὁ κύριος μετὰ πάντων ὑμῶν.

Now *may* the Lord of peace himself *grant* to you peace at all times in every way. The Lord [be] with all of you.

Gen. 27:28, **δῴη** σοι ὁ θεὸς ἀπὸ τῆς δρόσου τοῦ οὐρανοῦ καὶ ἀπὸ τῆς πιότητος τῆς γῆς καὶ πλῆθος σίτου καὶ οἴνου.

May God *give* you of the dew of heaven and of the fatness of the earth and an abundance of grain and wine.

Deut. 1:11, κύριος ὁ θεὸς τῶν πατέρων ὑμῶν **προσθείη** ὑμῖν χιλιοπλασίως[a] καὶ εὐλογήσαι ὑμᾶς, καθότι ἐλάλησεν ὑμῖν.

May the Lord, the God of your ancestors, *add* to you a thousand times over and bless you, as he said to you.

[a] χιλιοπλασίως, "a thousandfold more, a thousand times over"

Infinitives

33.10. The following forms of the μι verb infinitives occur in the NT and LXX. The infinitive ending -ναι is used where you would have found -ειν in the ω forms. (You should remember seeing this -ναι ending as the aorist passive infinitive ending in the ω conjugation; it is used much more extensively in the μι verbs.) The form δοῦναι is the most common in both Testaments.

Active Infinitive of μι Verbs

	δίδωμι	ἵστημι	τίθημι
Present	διδόναι	ἱστάναι	τιθέναι
First Aorist	—	στῆσαι	—
Second Aorist	δοῦναι	στῆναι	θεῖναι
Perfect	—	ἑστάναι or ἑστηκέναι/ ἑστακέναι	—
Future	δώσειν	στήσειν	θήσειν

33.11. *Examples*

Matt. 7:11, εἰ οὖν ὑμεῖς πονηροὶ ὄντες οἴδατε δόματα ἀγαθὰ **διδόναι** τοῖς τέκνοις ὑμῶν, πόσῳ μᾶλλον ὁ πατὴρ ὑμῶν ὁ ἐν τοῖς οὐρανοῖς δώσει ἀγαθὰ τοῖς αἰτοῦσιν αὐτόν.

Therefore if you, being evil, know [how] *to give* good gifts to your children, how much more rather your Father in heaven will give good [gifts] to those who ask him.

Mark 10:45, γὰρ ὁ υἱὸς τοῦ ἀνθρώπου οὐκ ἦλθεν διακονηθῆναι ἀλλὰ διακονῆσαι καὶ **δοῦναι** τὴν ψυχὴν αὐτοῦ λύτρον ἀντὶ πολλῶν.

For the Son of Man did not come to be served but to serve and *to give* his life a ransom for many.

Rev. 17:17, ὁ γὰρ θεὸς ἔδωκεν εἰς τὰς καρδίας αὐτῶν ποιῆσαι τὴν γνώμην αὐτοῦ καὶ ποιῆσαι μίαν γνώμην καὶ **δοῦναι** τὴν βασιλείαν αὐτῶν τῷ θηρίῳ ἄχρι τελεσθήσονται οἱ λόγοι τοῦ θεοῦ.

For God placed in their hearts to accomplish his purpose and to make one purpose [i.e., by making a joint decision] and *to give* their royal power to the beast until the words of God are fulfilled.

1 Kgdms. (1 Sam.) 22:13, εἶπεν αὐτῷ Σαούλ, Ἵνα τί συνέθου[a] κατ᾽ ἐμοῦ, σὺ καὶ ὁ υἱὸς Ἰεσσαί, **δοῦναί** σε αὐτῷ ἄρτον καὶ ῥομφαίαν καὶ ἐρωτᾶν[b] αὐτῷ διὰ τοῦ θεοῦ **θέσθαι** αὐτὸν ἐπ᾽ ἐμὲ εἰς ἐχθρὸν ὡς ἡ ἡμέρα αὕτη;

Saul said to him, "Why have you conspired against me, you and the son of Jesse, that you *gave* him bread and a sword and asked for him through God *to set* him against me as an enemy as [he is] this day?"

[a] συνέθου, 2nd sg. aor. mid. ind. ▶ συντίθημι, "I put together, to agree, to conspire"
[b] ἐρωτᾶν, pres. act. inf. ▶ ἐρωτάω, "I ask" (a tricky alpha contract)

33.12. *Now You Try It*

Rev. 6:17, ἦλθεν ἡ ἡμέρα ἡ μεγάλη τῆς ὀργῆς αὐτῶν, καὶ τίς δύναται **σταθῆναι**;

John 10:18, οὐδεὶς αἴρει αὐτὴν[a] ἀπ᾽ ἐμοῦ, ἀλλ᾽ ἐγὼ τίθημι αὐτὴν ἀπ᾽ ἐμαυτοῦ. ἐξουσίαν ἔχω **θεῖναι** αὐτήν, καὶ ἐξουσίαν ἔχω πάλιν λαβεῖν αὐτήν.

[a] αὐτήν refers to τὴν ψυχήν μου ("my life") in v. 17.

John 6:52, Ἐμάχοντο οὖν πρὸς ἀλλήλους οἱ Ἰουδαῖοι λέγοντες, Πῶς δύναται οὗτος ἡμῖν **δοῦναι** τὴν σάρκα αὐτοῦ φαγεῖν;

Rom. 14:13, Μηκέτι οὖν ἀλλήλους κρίνωμεν· ἀλλὰ τοῦτο κρίνατε μᾶλλον, τὸ μὴ **τιθέναι** πρόσκομμα τῷ ἀδελφῷ ἢ σκάνδαλον.

1 Cor. 10:12, ὥστε ὁ δοκῶν **ἑστάναι** βλεπέτω μὴ πέσῃ.

Acts 20:35, πάντα ὑπέδειξα ὑμῖν ὅτι οὕτως κοπιῶντας δεῖ ἀντιλαμβάνεσθαι τῶν ἀσθενούντων, μνημονεύειν τε τῶν λόγων τοῦ κυρίου Ἰησοῦ ὅτι αὐτὸς εἶπεν, Μακάριόν ἐστιν μᾶλλον **διδόναι** ἢ λαμβάνειν.

Mal. 2:2, ἐὰν μὴ ἀκούσητε, καὶ ἐὰν μὴ θῆσθε[a] εἰς τὴν καρδίαν ὑμῶν **τοῦ δοῦναι** δόξαν τῷ ὀνόματί μου, λέγει κύριος παντοκράτωρ, καὶ ἐξαποστελῶ ἐφ᾽ ὑμᾶς τὴν κατάραν καὶ ἐπικαταράσομαι[b] τὴν εὐλογίαν ὑμῶν.

[a] Do you recognize this μι verb? It is a form you saw earlier in this chapter.
[b] ἐπικαταράομαι, "I curse, bring curses, call down curses upon"

Participles

33.13. A nearly full set of μι verb participle forms is given in appendix A. There are relatively few of these that occur in the NT. The entire chart is given in each case so that you can see the pattern of endings that are being used. There are no present active participles of ἵστημι in the NT and only one in the LXX (ἱστῶν, pres. act. ptc. masc. sg. nom.), so that chart is omitted.

Present Participles

The μι verb present participle is regular in its formation, with the usual participle markers (ντ and ουσ) and case endings.

Present Active Participle of δίδωμι

	Masc.	Fem.	Neut.
NS	διδούς	διδοῦσα	διδόν
GS	διδόντος	διδούσης	διδόντος
DS	διδόντι	διδούσῃ	διδόντι
AS	διδόντα	διδοῦσαν	διδόν
NP	διδόντες	διδοῦσαι	διδόντα
GP	διδόντων	διδουσῶν	διδόντων
DP	διδοῦσι(ν)	διδούσαις	διδοῦσι(ν)
AP	διδόντας	διδούσας	διδόντα

In the nominative singular and dative plural forms, the ντ participle marker has dropped out due to the sigma in the ending. As a result the stem vowel undergoes ablaut; thus the nominative masculine singular is διδούς instead of διδόντς.

33.14. Examples

John 6:33, ὁ γὰρ ἄρτος τοῦ θεοῦ ἐστιν ὁ καταβαίνων ἐκ τοῦ οὐρανοῦ καὶ ζωὴν **διδοὺς** τῷ κόσμῳ.

For the bread of God is the one who came down out of heaven and *who gives* life to the world.

3 Kgdms. (1 Kings) 5:24, **ἦν** Χιρὰμ **διδοὺς** τῷ Σαλωμὼν κέδρους καὶ πᾶν θέλημα αὐτοῦ.

Hiram *was giving* Solomon cedars [i.e., cedar logs] and all his desires.

2 Clem. 9.7, ὡς ἔχομεν καιρὸν τοῦ ἰαθῆναι, ἐπιδῶμεν ἑαυτοὺς τῷ θεραπεύοντι θεῷ, ἀντιμισθίαν αὐτῷ **διδόντες**.

As we have time to be healed, let us surrender ourselves to God, who heals, *giving* what is due to him.

33.15. Now You Try It

1 Cor. 15:57, τῷ δὲ θεῷ χάρις τῷ **διδόντι** ἡμῖν τὸ νῖκος διὰ τοῦ κυρίου ἡμῶν Ἰησοῦ Χριστοῦ.

James 1:5, Εἰ δέ τις ὑμῶν λείπεται σοφίας, αἰτείτω παρὰ τοῦ **διδόντος** θεοῦ πᾶσιν ἁπλῶς καὶ μὴ ὀνειδίζοντος καὶ δοθήσεται αὐτῷ.

Isa. 43:16, οὕτως λέγει κύριος ὁ **διδοὺς** ὁδὸν ἐν θαλάσσῃ καὶ ἐν ὕδατι ἰσχυρῷ τρίβον.

Did. 1.5, παντὶ τῷ αἰτοῦντί σε δίδου, καὶ μὴ ἀπαίτει· πᾶσι γὰρ θέλει δίδοσθαι ὁ πατὴρ ἐκ τῶν ἰδίων χαρισμάτων. μακάριος ὁ **διδοὺς** κατὰ τὴν ἐντολήν, ἀθῷος γάρ ἐστιν.

Aorist Participles

33.16. The aorist participles are identical to the present forms except that iota reduplication is not used. Notice that there is no form marker used as in the ω verbs (which had σα before the participle marker); the omission of the iota reduplication is sufficient to identify these as non-present participles—and since the aorist is the only other non-reduplicated choice in the participle, it therefore marks them as aorist. Thus διδόντες is present, but δόντες is aorist.

Aorist Active Participle of δίδωμι

	Masc.	Fem.	Neut.
NS	δούς	δοῦσα	δόν
GS	δόντος	δούσης	δόντος
DS	δόντι	δούσῃ	δόντι
AS	δόντα	δοῦσαν	δόν
NP	δόντες	δοῦσαι	δόντα
GP	δόντων	δουσῶν	δόντων
DP	δοῦσι(ν)	δούσαις	δοῦσι(ν)
AP	δόντας	δούσας	δόντα

Aorist Passive Participle of δίδωμι

	Masc.	Fem.	Neut.
NS	δοθείς	δοθεῖσα	δοθέν
GS	δοθέντος	δοθείσης	δοθέντος
DS	δοθέντι	δοθείσῃ	δοθέντι
AS	δοθέντα	δοθεῖσαν	δοθέν
NP	δοθέντες	δοθεῖσαι	δοθέντα
GP	δοθέντων	δοθεισῶν	δοθέντων
DP	δοθεῖσιν	δοθείσαις	δοθεῖσιν
AP	δοθέντας	δοθείσας	δοθέντα

Many of the forms shown above do not occur in the NT or the LXX. There are no aorist middle participles in either corpus, but they are readily recognizable if you should encounter them in other Koine texts, since they are very regular (e.g., δόμενος, aor. mid. ptc. masc. sg. nom. ▸ δίδωμι).

The aorist active participle of ἵστημι is a second aorist form in which the stem στα- has the participle marker ντ and case endings appended; for example, the masculine singular genitive form would be στάντος (there are only four such aorist forms in the NT).[2] There is also an even rarer first aorist active participle form that uses the aorist form marker σα, which causes the stem vowel to lengthen (στη-); for example, the masculine plural nominative form is στήσαντες. For the aorist passive participle of ἵστημι, replace the stem δο- as shown above in the aorist passive participle of δίδωμι with στα-. See appendix A for a complete set of these forms.

For the aorist active participle of τίθημι, replace the stem δο- as shown above with θε-. There are no aorist passive forms of τίθημι in the NT or LXX, though they do occur in other Koine texts (e.g., the Pseudepigrapha, Josephus, Philo, and the Apostolic Fathers). The stem τε- is used (instead of the usual θε-) in the aorist passive participle: τεθείς, τεθέντος, and so on. There are very few of these forms in either the NT or the LXX.

33.17. Examples of Aorist Active Participles of δίδωμι

Luke 20:2, τίς ἐστιν ὁ **δούς** σοι τὴν ἐξουσίαν ταύτην;

Who is *the one who gives* you this authority?

Acts 9:41, **δοὺς** δὲ αὐτῇ χεῖρα ἀνέστησεν αὐτήν.

So *giving* her a hand, he lifted her.

2 Cor. 5:18, τὰ δὲ πάντα ἐκ τοῦ θεοῦ **τοῦ** καταλλάξαντος ἡμᾶς ἑαυτῷ διὰ Χριστοῦ καὶ **δόντος** ἡμῖν τὴν διακονίαν τῆς καταλλαγῆς.

But all things are from God, who reconciled us to himself through Christ and *who gives* to us the ministry of reconciliation.

2. The proportion between first and second aorist forms in the LXX is more evenly divided, but the second aorist is still the most frequent, accounting for 13 of 23 forms.

1 Macc. 11:10, μεταμεμέλημαι γὰρ **δοὺς** αὐτῷ τὴν θυγατέρα μου, ἐζήτησεν γὰρ ἀποκτεῖναί με.

For I have changed my mind [about] *giving* him my daughter, for he sought to kill me.

33.18. Now You Try It

Gal. 1:3–4, χάρις ὑμῖν καὶ εἰρήνη ἀπὸ θεοῦ πατρὸς ἡμῶν καὶ κυρίου Ἰησοῦ Χριστοῦ τοῦ **δόντος** ἑαυτὸν ὑπὲρ τῶν ἁμαρτιῶν ἡμῶν.

Mark 6:2, καὶ γενομένου σαββάτου ἤρξατο διδάσκειν ἐν τῇ συναγωγῇ, καὶ πολλοὶ ἀκούοντες ἐξεπλήσσοντο λέγοντες, Πόθεν τούτῳ ταῦτα, καὶ τίς ἡ σοφία ἡ **δοθεῖσα** τούτῳ, καὶ αἱ δυνάμεις τοιαῦται διὰ τῶν χειρῶν αὐτοῦ γινόμεναι;

Jer. 38:36 (31:35 Eng.), οὕτως εἶπεν κύριος ὁ **δοὺς** τὸν ἥλιον εἰς φῶς τῆς ἡμέρας, σελήνην καὶ ἀστέρας εἰς φῶς τῆς νυκτός.

33.19. Examples of Aorist Active Participles of ἵστημι

Matt. 20:32, **στὰς** ὁ Ἰησοῦς ἐφώνησεν αὐτοὺς καὶ εἶπεν, Τί θέλετε ποιήσω ὑμῖν;

Standing up, Jesus called them and said, "What do you wish that I should do for you?"

Luke 7:38, **στᾶσα** ὀπίσω παρὰ τοὺς πόδας αὐτοῦ κλαίουσα τοῖς δάκρυσιν ἤρξατο βρέχειν τοὺς πόδας αὐτοῦ.

While standing behind [him] by his feet weeping, she began to wet his feet with tears.

Acts 4:7, **στήσαντες** αὐτοὺς ἐν τῷ μέσῳ ἐπυνθάνοντο, Ἐν ποίᾳ δυνάμει ἢ ἐν ποίῳ ὀνόματι ἐποιήσατε τοῦτο ὑμεῖς;

Having stood them in the midst, they inquired, "By what power or what name did you do this?"

Isa. 40:22, ὁ κατέχων τὸν γῦρον[a] τῆς γῆς, καὶ οἱ ἐνοικοῦντες ἐν αὐτῇ ὡς ἀκρίδες, **ὁ στήσας** ὡς καμάραν[b] τὸν οὐρανὸν καὶ διατείνας[c] ὡς σκηνὴν κατοικεῖν.

[He is] the one who stretches out the circle of the earth—and those who live in it [are] like grasshoppers—*the one who set* the sky as a vault and who stretched [it] out as a tent to live in.

[a] γῦρος, ου, τό, "ring, circle"
[b] καμάρα, ας, ἡ, "arch, vault"
[c] διατείνω, "I extend, stretch out"

33.20. Now You Try It

Luke 18:11, ὁ Φαρισαῖος **σταθεὶς** πρὸς ἑαυτὸν ταῦτα προσηύχετο, Ὁ θεός, εὐχαριστῶ σοι ὅτι οὐκ εἰμὶ ὥσπερ οἱ λοιποὶ τῶν ἀνθρώπων.

Acts 5:20, Πορεύεσθε καὶ **σταθέντες** λαλεῖτε ἐν τῷ ἱερῷ τῷ λαῷ πάντα τὰ ῥήματα τῆς ζωῆς ταύτης.

Jdt. 13:4, **στᾶσα** Ἰουδὶθ παρὰ τὴν κλίνην αὐτοῦ εἶπεν ἐν τῇ καρδίᾳ αὐτῆς, Κύριε ὁ θεὸς πάσης δυνάμεως, ἐπίβλεψον ἐν τῇ ὥρᾳ ταύτῃ ἐπὶ τὰ ἔργα τῶν χειρῶν μου εἰς ὕψωμα Ἰερουσαλήμ.

33.21. Examples of Aorist Active Participles of τίθημι

Acts 20:36, ταῦτα εἰπὼν **θεὶς** τὰ γόνατα[a] αὐτοῦ σὺν πᾶσιν αὐτοῖς προσηύξατο.	After saying these things, *kneeling* with all of them, he prayed.[b]

[a] θεὶς τὰ γόνατα: very formally and ignoring the idiom, this says, "to place the knees," but it means simply "kneeling."

[b] This could also be understood to say "*kneeling*, he prayed with all of them." It depends on whether the prepositional phrase modifies the participle or the main verb.

Job 21:5, εἰσβλέψαντες εἰς ἐμὲ θαυμάσατε χεῖρα **θέντες** ἐπὶ σιαγόνι.	Having looked at me, be amazed, *having placed* [your] hand on [your] cheek.[a]

[a] In English idiom we would say, "put/clap your hand over your mouth," as a matter not of etiquette but of shock.

33.22. Now You Try It

Acts 21:5–6, **θέντες** τὰ γόνατα[a] ἐπὶ τὸν αἰγιαλὸν προσευξάμενοι ἀπησπασάμεθα ἀλλήλους καὶ ἀνέβημεν εἰς τὸ πλοῖον.

[a] θέντες τὰ γόνατα: see the example for Acts 20:36 above and the note there.

Isa. 63:11, ποῦ ἐστιν ὁ **θεὶς** ἐν αὐτοῖς τὸ πνεῦμα τὸ ἅγιον;

Perfect Participles

33.23. Of the μι verbs, only ἵστημι has many perfect participles, which are normally found with second perfect (κ-less) forms, though some first perfect participles also occur.

Stative (Perfect) Active Participles

Perfect Active Participle of ἵστημι

	First Perfect		Second Perfect		
	Masc.	Neut.	Masc.	Fem.	Neut.
NS	ἑστηκώς	ἑστηκός	ἑστώς	ἑστῶσα	ἑστός
GS	ἑστηκότος	ἑστηκότος	ἑστῶτος	ἑστώσης	ἑστῶτος
DS	ἑστηκότι	ἑστηκότι	ἑστῶτι	ἑστώσῃ	ἑστῶτι
AS	ἑστηκότα	ἑστηκός	ἑστῶτα	ἑστῶσαν	ἑστός
NP	ἑστηκότες	ἑστηκότα	ἑστῶτες	ἑστῶσαι	ἑστῶτα
GP	ἑστηκότων	ἑστηκότων	ἑστώτων	ἑστωσῶν	ἑστώτων
DP	ἑστηκόσιν	ἑστηκόσιν	ἑστῶσι(ν)	ἑστώσαις	ἑστῶσι(ν)
AP	ἑστηκότας	ἑστηκότα	ἑστῶτας	ἑστώσας	ἑστῶτα

Notice that perfect participles use regular epsilon reduplication. As in the perfect indicative, ἵστημι reduplicates with a rough breathing mark over an epsilon. There are only a few perfect active participle forms of the other μι verbs in the NT and LXX; these forms are not shown in the table above. There is one first perfect feminine participle: ἑστηκυῖα, pf. act. ptc. fem. sg. nom. For δίδωμι, the pf. act. ptc. masc. pl. nom. form δεδωκότες and the pf. act. ptc. masc. pl. acc. form δεδωκότας occur. The only participle form of τίθημι is τεθεικώς, pf. act. ptc. masc. sg. nom.

Stative (Perfect) Middle (or Passive) Participles

33.24. The perfect middle (or passive) participles are easy to identify, though they are scarce in both the NT and LXX; the pattern is very regular: reduplication + stem + middle participle marker μεν + case ending, thus, δε + δο + μέν + ος. Second-declension endings are used for the masculine and neuter, first-declension for feminine. In the NT there are only two such forms of δίδωμι: δεδομένον (4×), pf. pass. ptc. neut. sg. nom., and δεδομένην (1×), pf. pass. ptc. fem. sg. acc. The variety in the LXX is slightly greater, but there are still only fifteen instances. For τίθημι there is only one such form in the NT (τεθειμένος, pf. pass. ptc. masc. sg. nom.), and there are none in the LXX. Likewise, there is only one form of ἵστημι in the LXX (none in the NT): ἑσταμένους, pf. mid. ptc. masc. pl. acc.

33.25. Examples of Perfect Participles of ἵστημι

John 3:29, ὁ ἔχων τὴν νύμφην νυμφίος ἐστίν· ὁ δὲ φίλος τοῦ νυμφίου ὁ **ἑστηκὼς** καὶ ἀκούων αὐτοῦ χαρᾷ χαίρει διὰ τὴν φωνὴν τοῦ νυμφίου. αὕτη οὖν ἡ χαρὰ ἡ ἐμὴ πεπλήρωται.

The one who has the bride is the bridegroom; the friend of the bridegroom *who stands* and listens for him rejoices with joy [when he hears] the bridegroom's voice. Therefore this, my joy, is complete.

Mark 11:5, τινὲς **τῶν** ἐκεῖ **ἑστηκότων** ἔλεγον αὐτοῖς, Τί ποιεῖτε λύοντες τὸν πῶλον;

Some of *those standing* there said to them, "What are you doing, untying the colt?"

Rev. 7:1, Μετὰ τοῦτο εἶδον τέσσαρας ἀγγέλους **ἑστῶτας** ἐπὶ τὰς τέσσαρας γωνίας τῆς γῆς.

After this I saw four angels *standing* at the four corners of the earth.

Josh. 5:13, Καὶ ἐγένετο ὡς ἦν Ἰησοῦς ἐν Ἰεριχώ, καὶ ἀναβλέψας τοῖς ὀφθαλμοῖς εἶδεν ἄνθρωπον **ἑστηκότα** ἐναντίον αὐτοῦ, καὶ ἡ ῥομφαία ἐσπασμένη ἐν τῇ χειρὶ αὐτοῦ. καὶ προσελθὼν Ἰησοῦς εἶπεν αὐτῷ, Ἡμέτερος εἶ ἢ τῶν ὑπεναντίων;

Now it happened as Joshua was at Jericho, that looking up with his eyes, he saw a man *standing* before him and a drawn sword in his hand. Approaching, Joshua said to him, "Are you ours or of those who oppose [us]?"

33.26. Now You Try It

Rev. 7:9, Μετὰ ταῦτα εἶδον, καὶ ἰδοὺ ὄχλος πολύς, ἐκ παντὸς ἔθνους καὶ φυλῶν καὶ λαῶν καὶ γλωσσῶν **ἑστῶτες** ἐνώπιον τοῦ θρόνου καὶ ἐνώπιον τοῦ ἀρνίου.

Rev. 10:5, Καὶ ὁ ἄγγελος, ὃν εἶδον **ἑστῶτα** ἐπὶ τῆς θαλάσσης καὶ ἐπὶ τῆς γῆς, ἦρεν τὴν χεῖρα αὐτοῦ τὴν δεξιὰν εἰς τὸν οὐρανόν.

Luke 5:1, αὐτὸς **ἦν ἑστὼς** παρὰ τὴν λίμνην Γεννησαρέτ.

Gen. 18:22, ἀποστρέψαντες ἐκεῖθεν οἱ ἄνδρες ἦλθον εἰς Σόδομα, Ἀβραὰμ δὲ **ἦν ἑστηκὼς** ἐναντίον κυρίου.

1 Chron. 21:15, ἀπέστειλεν ὁ θεὸς ἄγγελον εἰς Ἰερουσαλὴμ τοῦ ἐξολεθρεῦσαι αὐτήν. καὶ ὡς ἐξωλέθρευσεν, εἶδεν κύριος καὶ μετεμελήθη ἐπὶ τῇ κακίᾳ καὶ εἶπεν τῷ ἀγγέλῳ τῷ ἐξολεθρεύοντι, Ἱκανούσθω σοι, ἄνες τὴν χεῖρά σου· καὶ ὁ ἄγγελος κυρίου **ἑστὼς** ἐν τῷ ἅλῳ Ὀρνὰ τοῦ Ἰεβουσαίου.

Reading Passage: Letter of Jeremiah 1–3, 23–39

33.27. For the final reading passage, you will explore an unfamiliar passage. The choice is deliberate. Not only does it contain numerous μι verbs (many of which are non-indicative forms), but the passage comes from the Apocrypha. It is not likely that you have memorized this passage, and many may not even be familiar with it in English. That makes it an ideal passage with which to determine whether you have learned Greek after completing your study of this textbook, or whether you just have a really good memory of familiar English verses. The passage is not difficult, and notes have been provided where needed, especially for words that do not occur in the NT. There is also an English translation appended so that you can check your work.

The Letter (or Epistle) of Jeremiah, sometimes known as Baruch 6, is a pseudepigraphal work that was probably composed originally in Hebrew, perhaps during the early years of the Babylonian captivity. Our only copies are in Greek, but there is evidence that it is a translation.

A Polemic against Idolatry

Ἀντίγραφον[a] ἐπιστολῆς, ἧς ἀπέστειλεν Ἰερεμίας πρὸς τοὺς ἀχθησομένους[b] αἰχμαλώτους εἰς Βαβυλῶνα ὑπὸ τοῦ βασιλέως τῶν Βαβυλωνίων ἀναγγεῖλαι[c] αὐτοῖς καθότι ἐπετάγη αὐτῷ ὑπὸ τοῦ θεοῦ.

[1]Διὰ τὰς ἁμαρτίας, ἃς ἡμαρτήκατε ἐναντίον τοῦ θεοῦ, ἀχθήσεσθε[b] εἰς Βαβυλῶνα αἰχμάλωτοι ὑπὸ Ναβουχοδονοσὸρ βασιλέως τῶν Βαβυλωνίων. [2]εἰσελθόντες οὖν εἰς Βαβυλῶνα ἔσεσθε ἐκεῖ ἔτη πλείονα καὶ χρόνον μακρὸν ἕως γενεῶν ἑπτά, μετὰ τοῦτο δὲ ἐξάξω ὑμᾶς ἐκεῖθεν μετ᾽ εἰρήνης. [3]νυνὶ δὲ ὄψεσθε ἐν Βαβυλῶνι θεοὺς ἀργυροῦς καὶ χρυσοῦς καὶ ξυλίνους ἐπ᾽ ὤμοις αἱρομένους **δεικνύντας**[d] φόβον τοῖς ἔθνεσιν.

[23]Τὸ γὰρ χρυσίον, ὃ περίκειται[e] εἰς κάλλος,[f] ἐὰν μή τις ἐκμάξῃ τὸν ἰόν, οὐ μὴ στίλψωσιν·[g] οὐδὲ γάρ, ὅτε ἐχωνεύοντο,[h] ᾐσθάνοντο. [24]ἐκ πάσης τιμῆς ἠγορασμένα ἐστίν, ἐν οἷς οὐκ ἔστιν πνεῦμα. [25]ἄνευ ποδῶν ἐπ᾽ ὤμοις φέρονται **ἐνδεικνύμενοι** τὴν ἑαυτῶν ἀτιμίαν τοῖς ἀνθρώποις, αἰσχύνονταί τε καὶ οἱ θεραπεύοντες[i] αὐτὰ διὰ τό,[j] μήποτε ἐπὶ τὴν γῆν πέσῃ, δι᾽ αὐτῶν **ἀνίστασθαι**·[j] [26]μήτε ἐάν τις αὐτὸ ὀρθὸν **στήσῃ**, δι᾽ ἑαυτοῦ κινηθήσεται, μήτε ἐὰν κλιθῇ, οὐ μὴ ὀρθωθῇ,[k] ἀλλ᾽ ὥσπερ νεκροῖς τὰ δῶρα αὐτοῖς **παρατίθεται**.[l] [27]τὰς δὲ θυσίας αὐτῶν **ἀποδόμενοι** οἱ ἱερεῖς αὐτῶν καταχρῶνται·[m] ὡσαύτως δὲ καὶ αἱ γυναῖκες αὐτῶν ἀπ᾽ αὐτῶν ταριχεύουσαι[n] οὔτε[o] πτωχῷ οὔτε ἀδυνάτῳ **μεταδιδόασιν**· τῶν θυσιῶν αὐτῶν ἀποκαθημένη καὶ λεχὼ[p] ἅπτονται. [28]γνόντες οὖν ἀπὸ τούτων ὅτι οὔκ εἰσιν θεοί, μὴ φοβηθῆτε αὐτούς.

[29]Πόθεν γὰρ κληθείησαν[q] θεοί; ὅτι γυναῖκες **παρατιθέασιν** θεοῖς ἀργυροῖς καὶ χρυσοῖς καὶ ξυλίνοις· [30]καὶ ἐν τοῖς οἴκοις αὐτῶν οἱ ἱερεῖς διφρεύουσιν[r] ἔχοντες τοὺς χιτῶνας **διερρωγότας**[s] καὶ τὰς κεφαλὰς καὶ τοὺς πώγωνας[t] ἐξυρημένους, ὧν αἱ κεφαλαὶ ἀκάλυπτοί[u] εἰσιν, [31]ὠρύονται δὲ βοῶντες ἐναντίον τῶν θεῶν αὐτῶν ὥσπερ τινὲς ἐν περιδείπνῳ[v] νεκροῦ. [32]ἀπὸ τοῦ ἱματισμοῦ αὐτῶν[w] ἀφελόμενοι[x] οἱ ἱερεῖς ἐνδύουσιν τὰς γυναῖκας αὐτῶν καὶ τὰ παιδία. [33]οὔτε ἐὰν κακὸν πάθωσιν ὑπό τινος οὔτε ἐὰν ἀγαθόν, δυνήσονται **ἀνταποδοῦναι**· οὔτε **καταστῆσαι** βασιλέα δύνανται οὔτε ἀφελέσθαι. [34]ὡσαύτως οὔτε πλοῦτον οὔτε χαλκὸν οὐ μὴ δύνωνται **διδόναι**· ἐάν τις αὐτοῖς εὐχὴν εὐξάμενος μὴ **ἀποδῷ**, οὐ μὴ ἐπιζητήσωσιν. [35]ἐκ

θανάτου ἄνθρωπον οὐ μὴ ῥύσωνται οὔτε ἥττονα ἀπὸ ἰσχυροῦ οὐ μὴ ἐξέλωνται.
36ἄνθρωπον τυφλὸν εἰς ὅρασιν οὐ μὴ **περιστήσωσιν**,[y] ἐν ἀνάγκῃ ἄνθρωπον ὄντα
οὐ μὴ ἐξέλωνται. 37χήραν οὐ μὴ ἐλεήσωσιν οὔτε ὀρφανὸν εὖ ποιήσουσιν. 38τοῖς
ἀπὸ τοῦ ὄρους λίθοις ὡμοιωμένοι εἰσὶν[z] τὰ ξύλινα καὶ τὰ περίχρυσα καὶ τὰ περι-
άργυρα,[aa] οἱ δὲ θεραπεύοντες αὐτὰ καταισχυνθήσονται. 39πῶς οὖν νομιστέον[bb]
ἢ κλητέον[cc] αὐτοὺς ὑπάρχειν θεούς;

a ἀντίγραφον, ου, τό, "copy (of a book or other writing)"

b ἄγω, square-of-stops form

c This is a liquid verb, *not* a nominative plural noun.

d This is a μι verb, δείκνυμι, so remember that there is no connecting vowel. (There is also an ω form of this word, δεικνύω.) Here it expresses a causative idea: the pagan gods do not show/manifest fear of/to the Gentiles; rather, they cause the nations to be afraid.

e ὃ περίκεινται, "[with] which they are surrounded" or "which they wear"

f κάλλος, ους, τό, "beauty" (≠ adj. καλός)

g Square-of-stops form, β + σ = ψ

h χωνεύω, "I cast in a mold"

i You are most accustomed to seeing θεραπεύω used in the NT with the meaning "I heal," but there is a more general use that is relevant here; see your lexicon.

j The syntax is a bit unusual here; the preposition and the infinitive that it governs are separated by an entire clause, but διὰ τό ἀνίστασθαι should be read together as a causal statement.

k ὀρθόω, "I set upright, straighten myself"

l Do you remember why some singular verbs have a plural subject?

m This statement may seem odd at first, but when you figure out that αὐτῶν refers to the idols, it will make better sense. Make sure you correctly identify subject, verb, and object. How is the adverbial participle (ἀποδόμενοι) being used?

n ταριχεύω, "I salt, preserve"

o οὔτε . . . οὔτε introduces two groups: "neither to the poor nor to the helpless."

p ἀποκαθημένη καὶ λεχώ, "A woman who sits apart and one who has just given birth." The participle is adjectival, used substantivally (ἀποκάθημαι, "I sit apart"), used in parallel with a *noun* (λεχώ, οῦς, ἡ, "woman in childbirth"). The plural verb tells us that two different representative women are in view; both are ceremonially unclean, one due to her monthly uncleanness, the other due to the ceremonial uncleanness that comes from giving birth (Lev. 12; 15). The point being made is that they touch (ἅπτονται) the pagan sacrifices with impunity—the supposed god cannot protect his own sacrifices from defilement.

q κληθείησαν, 3rd pl. aor. pass. opt. ▸ καλέω, "I call"; the aorist stem is κλη-, followed by the aorist passive form marker θε and the optative mood marker ει, which form θει.

r διφρεύω, "I sit"

s διερρωγότας, pf. act. ptc. masc. pl. acc. ▸ διαρρήγνυμι, "I rend"

t πώγων, ωνος, ὁ, "beard"

u ἀκάλυπτος, ος, ον, "uncovered"

v περίδειπνον, ου, τό, "(funeral) feast"

w The pronoun refers to the pagan idols.

x ἀφελόμενοι ▸ ἀφαιρέω

y περιίστημι normally means "I stand around," but here it must mean "I restore."

z Did you recognize the construction ὡμοιωμένοι εἰσίν? There is an explicit nominative subject as well as a dative that specifies the item to which the comparison (ὁμοιόω) is made.

aa περίχρυσος, ος, ον, "gold-plated"; περιάργυρος, ος, ον, "silver-plated"

bb νομιστέος, -α, -ον, "to be thought, to be supposed"

cc κλητέος, -α, -ον, "to be called, to be said"

Translation

A copy of a letter which Jeremiah sent to those who would be led captive to Babylon by the king of the Babylonians to announce to them as it was commanded to him by God.

[1]On account of the sins which you sinned before God you will be led to Babylon as captives by Nebuchadnezzar, king of Babylon. [2]Therefore when you come to Babylon you will be there many years, even a long time, as long as seven generations, but after this I will bring you out from there with peace. [3]But now you will see in Babylon silver, gold, and wooden gods, which cause the Gentiles to fear, carried on shoulders.

[23]For the gold, which they wear for beauty, unless someone wipes off the corrosion, they will not make it shine, for they were not sentient, [even] when they were cast. [24]Those things in which there is no breath are bought at all cost. [25]Without feet they are carried on shoulders, showing their disgrace to the people, so even those who serve them are ashamed because it [i.e., the pagan idol] is caused to stand by them [i.e., by the attendants], lest it fall to the ground. [26]Not even if someone makes it stand upright will it move by itself, nor if it leans over will it straighten itself up, but gifts are placed before them as [before] the dead. [27]But their priests use them by selling their sacrifices. And likewise also their wives preserve some of them [i.e., the sacrifices], [but] they do not share any with the poor or the helpless. A woman who sits apart and one who has just given birth touch their sacrifices. [28]Since you know, therefore, from these things that they are not gods, do not fear them.

[29]For on what basis can they be called gods? [They cannot], because women place [offerings] before silver, gold, and wooden gods! [30]And in their houses the priests sit with their tunics torn and their heads and beards shaved, whose heads are uncovered. [31]They roar and shout before their gods as some [do] at a funeral feast for the dead. [32]Taking from their [i.e., the idols'] clothing, the priests clothe their wives and children. [33]Whether they [i.e., the idols] suffer evil from someone or good, they will not be able to repay. They are not able to put a king in charge, nor can they remove [him] [from power]. [34]Likewise, they can give neither wealth nor money. If anyone who vows a vow to them does not keep it, they will not demand it. [35]They will not deliver a person from death nor rescue a weak person from a strong one. [36]They will not restore a blind person to sight; they will not rescue a person who is in anguish. [37]They will not show mercy to a widow nor do good to an orphan. [38]The things that are wooden and gold- and silver-plated are like the stones from a mountain, and those who serve them will be put to shame. [39]So why should they be thought to be or be called gods?

33.28. Vocabulary for Chapter 33

Part of Speech	Definition	Possible Glosses	Frequency	
Word			NT	LXX
Nouns				
ἱερεύς, έως, ὁ	A person appointed to perform religious duties, particularly (though not exclusively) to offer sacrifice on behalf of others	priest	31	900
φυλή, ῆς, ἡ	A community of people, either a large group, such as a sociopolitical entity, or more commonly a subgroup with a common ethnic heritage	nation, people; tribe	31	444
θυγάτηρ, τρός, ἡ	A female offspring described in relation to the parents (in the NT only of humans, in the LXX also rarely of animals)	daughter	28	641
θυσία, ας, ἡ	Sacrifice offered to deity as part of a priestly system of worship	sacrifice, offering	28	395
θυσιαστήριον, ου, τό	An object on which a θυσία ("sacrifice") is placed when it is offered to deity	altar	23	437
ἔλεος, ους, τό	Kindness expressed to someone in need	mercy, compassion, pity	27	338
παῖς, παιδός, ὁ/ἡ	A person of minor status in terms of either family or age ("child") or social status ("servant")	child, boy, girl; servant, slave, attendant	24	470
Verbs				
ἀφίημι	To release from one's presence; to divorce a spouse; to release from legal or moral obligation, especially from the guilt of sin; to allow to remain behind; to allow someone the freedom to do something	I let go, send away; I divorce; I pardon, forgive; I leave, abandon; I allow, tolerate	143	138
ἀπόλλυμι	(1) Transitive: to cause destruction, put to death; to lose something (act.); (2) intransitive: to experience destruction; to be unavailable; to not be found (mid.)	(1) I ruin, destroy, kill; I lose (act.); (2) I die, perish; I am deprived of; I have gone missing (mid.)	90	378
φημί	To convey one's thinking through speech or writing; to clarify or explain what one means [In the LXX and NT this word occurs almost entirely as ἔφη (3rd sg. aor. act. ind.) or φησίν (3rd sg. pres. act. ind.).]	I say, affirm; I mean	66	74
σταυρόω	To cause to undergo crucifixion; to execute by fastening to a cross	I crucify	46	2
οἰκοδομέω	To erect a structure, construct a building or other structure; to improve someone's ability to live more responsibly and effectively (metaphorically)	I build, erect, construct; I strengthen, build up, edify	40	460
ἐπιτίθημι	To place something on someone/something; to set upon, attack	I lay/put upon, place on; I attack	39	270

Part of Speech	Definition	Possible Glosses	Frequency	
Word			NT	LXX
ἥκω	To be in a place as a result of movement to that place (focuses on the result of movement; ctr. ἔρχομαι, which focuses on the movement itself)	I have come, am present	26	244
συνίημι	To grasp the significance of something	I understand, comprehend	26	117

33.29. Key Things to Know for Chapter 33

What is the distinguishing mark for subjunctive forms of the μι verbs in the present and second aorist forms? How is that different from the same forms in the indicative?

Familiarize yourself with all the non-indicative forms of the μι verbs.

What is the most common infinitive ending in the μι verbs?

What distinguishes present from aorist participles in the μι verbs?

EPILOGUE

Congratulations! When you began studying Greek with this textbook, you were not sure you could really learn to read Greek. But now you have. The question now is, Can I continue to develop my Greek skills into a workable tool for understanding Scripture? The answer is, yes, of course you can—but you will not if you let your hard-won skills sit idle.

Before I make a few simple suggestions for doing that, let me warn you that you now know, as the proverbial saying goes, just enough Greek to be dangerous. *Do* use your Greek, but do so cautiously. If you suddenly discover something brand new in your Greek NT that no one else has ever seen before, be assured that it is almost certainly wrong! Do not abuse or overuse your knowledge. Do plan to continue your study of Greek. If you do not have an option for a formal, academic course that builds on an introductory Greek course, then plan your own course of study.[1] For most students, the language begins to come together in a second year of study. Keep at it!

If you have several months before you can continue formal study, then at a minimum review the entire textbook and read more of the example sentences and all the reading passages at the end of each chapter. Keep your vocabulary fresh; it makes for faster reading and less time with your lexicon. Or perhaps you would find it helpful to read all the way through one of the easier books of the NT, perhaps the Gospels of John or Mark. For a short book, 1 John is a good choice. One of the readers' editions of the NT could be helpful for this, since they give you the less-common vocabulary at the bottom of the page. Or use *two* English translations as you read: one more formal (maybe ESV or NRSV) and one a bit more functional (maybe NIV, NET, or HCSB). Read your Greek NT first, and then compare it with the English versions to see how close your understanding was.

You will need to add a large lexicon in the near future. Bauer, Danker, Arndt, and Gingrich's *Greek-English Lexicon of the New Testament and Other Early*

1. You might find it helpful to use my *Koine Greek Reader: Selections from the New Testament, Septuagint, and Early Christian Writers* (Grand Rapids: Kregel, 2007). It picks up where this book leaves off and allows you to develop your reading skills while also extending your vocabulary in context, reviewing basic grammar, and inductively expanding your understanding of grammar and syntax beyond the level of this book.

Christian Literature (BDAG) is the standard, and there is no other comparable work. You can purchase either a digital copy in Accordance, BibleWorks, or Logos format or the print edition. If you are buying the printed version, be sure to get the newest edition, not a used copy of an older edition; the differences are significant. BDAG is not inexpensive, but it is worth every penny. If you want more detail regarding BDAG and how to use it, see my webpage devoted to this tool: http://ntresources.com/blog/?page_id=2526. There is also an appendix in my *Koine Greek Reader* that discusses the background and use of this lexicon.

You may also want to pick up an analytical lexicon. Ideally you should not use one, but the real world says you ought to have one for those times when you are totally perplexed by an odd form. Do not use an analytical lexicon except for those really tough words. If you do purchase one, I recommend William Mounce, *The Analytical Lexicon to the Greek New Testament* (Grand Rapids: Zondervan, 1993). There are a few others, but this is the best, most complete, and most accurate. It also uses terminology similar (though not identical) to what you have learned in this textbook. A grammatically tagged Greek text in one of the major Bible study programs can serve the same function as an analytical lexicon. If you do not have such a tool yet, I recommend Accordance for language study. This is a Mac program of long standing and has recently come to the Windows platform. (See http://www.accordancebible.com for details.)

Although software programs are invaluable for language study, do not become dependent on them for reading Greek. If you can read a Greek text only by identifying most of the Greek words through use of the program tools, then you do not know Greek. Likewise, some people recommend that you use an interlinear Greek Testament, but *I strongly advise against that!* You will never learn Greek, and it will never be a useful tool, if you use an interlinear. Period. Don't do it!

For those who are interested in working in the LXX, here are the equivalent tools: For a lexicon, see Takamitsu Muraoka, *A Greek-English Lexicon of the Septuagint* (Louvain: Peeters, 2009). A smaller work that is also usable is Johan Lust, Erik Eynikel, and Katrin Hauspie, *Greek-English Lexicon of the Septuagint*, rev. ed. (Stuttgart: Deutsche Bibelgesellschaft, 2003). The best analytical lexicon for the LXX is Bernard Taylor, *Analytical Lexicon to the Septuagint*, 2nd ed. (Peabody, MA: Hendrickson, 2009).

If you want to read some very helpful discussion about the purpose of learning Greek and (most important) how to use it correctly, you will want to master *God, Language and Scripture* by Moisés Silva (Grand Rapids: Zondervan, 1990). This is easily the most significant book on a philosophy of using Greek that you will find. It contains a wealth of good, sane advice to help you avoid misusing Greek. Another equally important book is D. A. Carson's *Exegetical Fallacies*, 2nd ed. (Grand Rapids: Baker, 1996).

Whatever you do, do not stop now. Figure out some way to maintain and develop your budding language skills so that you can continue to read Scripture (and other Koine texts) in Greek. Why settle for secondhand translations when you could read the original for yourself?

Happy reading!

Appendixes

Appendix A

Reference Charts

Nominal System

A.1. *The Article*

	Masc.	Fem.	Neut.
NS	ὁ	ἡ	τό
GS	τοῦ	τῆς	τοῦ
DS	τῷ	τῇ	τῷ
AS	τόν	τήν	τό
NP	οἱ	αἱ	τά
GP	τῶν	τῶν	τῶν
DP	τοῖς	ταῖς	τοῖς
AP	τούς	τάς	τά

A.2. *Nouns*

Complete Case Ending Chart

Decl.	2		1		2		3	
Gend.	(M/f)		(F/m)		Neut.		M/F	Neut.
NS	ος	ς	α/η	–	ον	ν	ς	–
GS	ου	υ	ας/ης	ς	ου	υ	ος	ος
DS	ῳ	ι	ᾳ/ῃ	ι	ῳ	ι	ι	ι
AS	ον	ν	αν/ην	ν	ον	ν	α/ν	–
NP	οι	ι	αι	ι	α	α	ες	α
GP	ων	ν	ων	ν	ων	ν	ων	ων
DP	οις	ις	αις	ις	οις	ις	σι(ν)	σι(ν)
AP	ους	υς	ας	ς	α	α	ας	α

Shaded columns give the technical case endings for first and second declensions without the connecting vowels. The labels "(M/f)" and "(F/m)" indicate the *most common* and *less common* gender for a particular declension.

A.3. First- and Second-Declension Nouns

	Second Declension		First Declension		
	Masc.	Fem.	Fem.		
NS	λόγος	ὁδός	ὥρα	γραφή	δόξα
GS	λόγου	ὁδοῦ	ὥρας	γραφῆς	δόξης
DS	λόγῳ	ὁδῷ	ὥρᾳ	γραφῇ	δόξῃ
AS	λόγον	ὁδόν	ὥραν	γραφήν	δόξαν
NP	λόγοι	ὁδοί	ὧραι	γραφαί	δόξαι
GP	λόγων	ὁδῶν	ὡρῶν	γραφῶν	δοξῶν
DP	λόγοις	ὁδοῖς	ὥραις	γραφαῖς	δόξαις
AP	λόγους	ὁδούς	ὥρας	γραφάς	δόξας

	First Declension (Masc.)	Second Declension Neut.
NS	μαθητής	ἔργον
GS	μαθητοῦ	ἔργου
DS	μαθητῇ	ἔργῳ
AS	μαθητήν	ἔργον
NP	μαθηταί	ἔργα
GP	μαθητῶν	ἔργων
DP	μαθηταῖς	ἔργοις
AP	μαθητάς	ἔργα

A.4. Third-Declension Nouns

For an explanation for the many changes seen in these forms, see *MBG*, 190–213, or Smyth, *Greek Grammar*, 56–71, §§240–80. Each word given here represents a particular morphological pattern.

Six Key, Representative Paradigms

NS	σάρξ, ἡ	ὄνομα, τό	ἄρχων, ὁ	ἔθνος, τό	βασιλεύς, ὁ	πόλις, ἡ
GS	σαρκός	ὀνόματος	ἄρχοντος	ἔθνους	βασιλέως	πόλεως
DS	σαρκί	ὀνόματι	ἄρχοντι	ἔθνει	βασιλεῖ	πόλει
AS	σάρκα	ὄνομα	ἄρχοντα	ἔθνος	βασιλέα	πόλιν
NP	σάρκες	ὀνόματα	ἄρχοντες	ἔθνη	βασιλεῖς	πόλεις
GP	σαρκῶν	ὀνομάτων	ἀρχόντων	ἐθνῶν	βασιλέων	πόλεων
DP	σαρξί(ν)	ὀνόμασι(ν)	ἄρχουσι(ν)	ἔθνεσι(ν)	βασιλεῦσι(ν)	πόλεσι(ν)
AP	σάρκας	ὀνόματα	ἄρχοντας	ἔθνη	βασιλεῖς	πόλεις

Other Third-Declension Paradigms

NS	λαῖλαψ, ἡ	σάλπιγξ, ἡ	θρίξ, ἡ	χάρις, ἡ	ἐλπίς, ἡ	ὄρνις, ὁ/ἡ
GS	λαίλαπος	σάλπιγγος	τριχός	χάριτος	ἐλπίδος	ὄρνιθος
DS	λαίλαπι	σάλπιγγι	τριχί	χάριτι	ἐλπίδι	ὄρνιθι
AS	λαίλαπα	σάλπιγγα	τρίχα	χάριν	ἐλπίδα	ὄρνιθα
NP	λαίλαπες	σάλπιγγες	τρίχες	χάριτες	ἐλπίδες	ὄρνιθες
GP	λαιλάπων	σαλπίγγων	τριχῶν	χαρίτων	ἐλπίδων	ὀρνίθων
DP	λαίλαψι(ν)	σάλπιγξι(ν)	θριξί(ν)	χάρισι(ν)	ἐλπίσι(ν)	ὄρνισι(ν)
AP	λαίλαπας	σάλπιγγας	τρίχας	χάριτας	ἐλπίδας	ὄρνιθας

NS	ὀδούς, ὁ	τέρας, τό	ὕδωρ, τό	φῶς, τό	οὖς, τό	γένος, τό
GS	ὀδόντος	τέρατος	ὕδατος	φωτός	ὠτός	γένους
DS	ὀδόντι	τέρατι	ὕδατι	φωτί	ὠτί	γένει
AS	ὀδόντα	τέρας	ὕδωρ	φῶς	οὖς	γένος
NP	ὀδόντες	τέρατα	ὕδατα	φῶτα	ὦτα	γένη
GP	ὀδόντων	τεράτων	ὑδάτων	φώτων	ὤτων	γενῶν
DP	ὀδοῦσι(ν)	τέρασι(ν)	ὕδασι(ν)	φωσί(ν)	ὠσί(ν)	γένεσι(ν)
AP	ὀδόντας	τέρατα	ὕδατα	φῶτα	ὦτα	γένη

NS	ἰχθύς, ὁ	ναῦς, ὁ	νοῦς, ὁ	αἰών, ὁ	ἡγεμών, ὁ	ποιμήν, ὁ
GS	ἰχθύος	νεώς	νοός	αἰῶνος	ἡγεμόνος	ποιμένος
DS	ἰχθύϊ	νηΐ	νοΐ	αἰῶνι	ἡγεμόνι	ποιμένι
AS	ἰχθύν	ναῦν	νοῦν	αἰῶνα	ἡγεμόνα	ποιμένα
NP	ἰχθύες	νῆες	νόες	αἰῶνες	ἡγεμόνες	ποιμένες
GP	ἰχθύων	νεῶν	νοῶν	αἰώνων	ἡγεμόνων	ποιμένων
DP	ἰχθύσι(ν)	ναυσί(ν)	νουσί(ν)	αἰῶσι(ν)	ἡγεμόσι(ν)	ποιμέσι(ν)
AP	ἰχθύας	ναῦς	νόας	αἰῶνας	ἡγεμόνας	ποιμένας

NS	κύων, ὁ	σωτήρ, ὁ	ἀλέκτωρ, ὁ	ἀστήρ, ὁ	ἀνήρ, ὁ	πατήρ, ὁ
GS	κυνός	σωτῆρος	ἀλέκτορος	ἀστέρος	ἀνδρός	πατρός
DS	κυνί	σωτῆρι	ἀλέκτορι	ἀστέρι	ἀνδρί	πατρί
AS	κύνα	σωτῆρα	ἀλέκτορα	ἀστέρα	ἄνδρα	πατέρα
NP	κύνες	σωτῆρες	ἀλέκτορες	ἀστέρες	ἄνδρες	πατέρες
GP	κυνῶν	σωτήρων	ἀλεκτόρων	ἀστέρων	ἀνδρῶν	πατέρων
DP	κυσίν	σωτῆρσι(ν)	ἀλέκτορσι(ν)	ἀστράσι(ν)	ἀνδράσι(ν)	πατράσι(ν)
AP	κύνας	σωτῆρας	ἀλέκτορας	ἀστέρας	ἄνδρας	πατέρας

Adjectives

A.5. First- and Second-Declension Adjectives

	Masc.	Fem.		Neut.
NS	ἀγαθός	ἀγαθή	πονηρά	ἀγαθόν
GS	ἀγαθοῦ	ἀγαθῆς	πονηρᾶς	ἀγαθοῦ
DS	ἀγαθῷ	ἀγαθῇ	πονηρᾷ	ἀγαθῷ
AS	ἀγαθόν	ἀγαθήν	πονηράν	ἀγαθόν
NP	ἀγαθοί	ἀγαθαί	πονηραί	ἀγαθά
GP	ἀγαθῶν	ἀγαθῶν	πονηρῶν	ἀγαθῶν
DP	ἀγαθοῖς	ἀγαθαῖς	πονηραῖς	ἀγαθοῖς
AP	ἀγαθούς	ἀγαθάς	πονηράς	ἀγαθά

A.6. Two-Form Adjectives

The usual pattern uses second-declension endings, as in ἔρημος. The less common alternate forms use third-declension endings (of which ἀληθής is more common).

	Masc./Fem.	Neut.	Masc./Fem.	Neut.	Masc./Fem.	Neut.
NS	ἔρημος	ἔρημον	ἀληθής	ἀληθές	ἄφρων	ἄφρον
GS	ἐρήμου	ἐρήμου	ἀληθοῦς	ἀληθοῦς	ἄφρονος	ἄφρονος
DS	ἐρήμῳ	ἐρήμῳ	ἀληθεῖ	ἀληθεῖ	ἄφρονι	ἄφρονι
AS	ἔρημον	ἔρημον	ἀληθῆ	ἀληθές	ἄφρονα	ἄφρον
NP	ἔρημοι	ἔρημα	ἀληθεῖς	ἀληθῆ	ἄφρονες	ἄφρονα
GP	ἐρήμων	ἐρήμων	ἀληθῶν	ἀληθῶν	ἀφρόνων	ἀφρόνων
DP	ἐρήμοις	ἐρήμοις	ἀληθέσι(ν)	ἀληθέσι(ν)	ἄφροσι(ν)	ἄφροσι(ν)
AP	ἐρήμους	ἔρημα	ἀληθεῖς	ἀληθῆ	ἄφρονας	ἄφρονα

A.7. Forms of the Adjectives πολύς and μέγας

	Masc.	Fem.	Neut.	Masc.	Fem.	Neut.
NS	πολύς	πολλή	πολύ	μέγας	μεγάλη	μέγα
GS	πολλοῦ	πολλῆς	πολλοῦ	μεγάλου	μεγάλης	μεγάλου
DS	πολλῷ	πολλῇ	πολλῷ	μεγάλῳ	μεγάλῃ	μεγάλῳ
AS	πολύν	πολλήν	πολύ	μέγαν	μεγάλην	μέγα
NP	πολλοί	πολλαί	πολλά	μεγάλοι	μεγάλαι	μεγάλα
GP	πολλῶν	πολλῶν	πολλῶν	μεγάλων	μεγάλων	μεγάλων
DP	πολλοῖς	πολλαῖς	πολλοῖς	μεγάλοις	μεγάλαις	μεγάλοις
AP	πολλούς	πολλάς	πολλά	μεγάλους	μεγάλας	μεγάλα

A.8. Contract Adjectives

A few adjectives have stems ending in epsilon or omicron. Nominative and accusative forms are affected. Some of the feminine forms will use alpha endings in the singular instead of the eta endings shown here.

	Masc.	Fem.	Neut.
NS	διπλοῦς	διπλῆ	διπλοῦν
GS	διπλοῦ	διπλῆς	διπλοῦ
DS	διπλῷ	διπλῇ	διπλῷ
AS	διπλοῦν	διπλῆν	διπλοῦν
NP	διπλοῖ	διπλαῖ	διπλᾶ
GP	διπλῶν	διπλῶν	διπλῶν
DP	διπλοῖς	διπλαῖς	διπλοῖς
AP	διπλοῦς	διπλᾶς	διπλᾶ

A.9. Comparative and Superlative Adjectives

	μέγας	ἄξιος	
	Comparative	Comparative	Superlative
NS	μείζων	ἀξιώτερος	ἀξιώτατος
GS	μείζονος	ἀξιωτέρου	ἀξιωτάτου
DS	μείζονι	ἀξιωτέρῳ	ἀξιωτάτῳ
AS	μείζονα	ἀξιώτερον	ἀξιώτατον
NP	μείζονες	ἀξιώτεροι	ἀξιώτατοι
GP	μειζόνων	ἀξιωτέρων	ἀξιωτάτων
DP	μείζοσι(ν)	ἀξιωτέροις	ἀξιωτάτοις
AP	μείζονας	ἀξιωτέρους	ἀξιωτάτους

A.10. Comparative Forms of πολύς

The comparative form of πολύς is a two-form adjective (masc. and fem. having the same form) using third-declension endings, but there are a few variations that use second-declension endings. The spelling is not totally consistent, with the diphthong ει sometimes appearing as simply an epsilon (an older, contracted spelling). Also πλέον and πλείω (and sometimes πλείονα) are occasionally treated as indeclinable forms and used where a masculine or feminine form would be expected.

	Masc./Fem.	Neut.
NS	πλείων	πλεῖον
GS	πλείονος	πλείονος
DS	πλείονι	πλείονι
AS	πλείονα	πλεῖον
NP	πλείονες[a]	πλείονα
GP	πλειόνων	πλειόνων
DP	πλείοσι(ν)[b]	πλείοσι(ν)
AP	πλείονας[a]	πλείονα

[a] or πλείους

[b] or πλεόνεσσι(ν) or πλείστοις

A.11. Third-Declension Adjectives

These are 3/1/3 adjectives, third declension in masculine and neuter, first declension in feminine.

	πᾶς, πᾶσα, πᾶν			μέλας, αινα, αν[a]		
	Masc.	Fem.	Neut.	Masc.	Fem.	Neut.
NS	πᾶς	πᾶσα	πᾶν	μέλας	μέλαινα	μέλαν
GS	παντός	πάσης	παντός	μέλανος	μελαίνης	μέλανος
DS	παντί	πάσῃ	παντί	μέλανι	μελαίνῃ	μέλανι
AS	πάντα	πᾶσαν	πᾶν	μέλανα	μέλαιναν	μέλαν
NP	πάντες	πᾶσαι	πάντα	μέλανες	μέλαιναι	μέλανα
GP	πάντων	πασῶν	πάντων	μελάνων	μελαινῶν	μελάνων
DP	πᾶσι(ν)	πάσαις	πᾶσι(ν)	μέλασι(ν)	μελαίναις	μέλασι(ν)
AP	πάντας	πάσας	πάντα	μέλανας	μελαίνας	μέλανα

[a] "black"; the neuter, μέλαν, ος, τό, is used substantivally to mean "ink."

A.12. The Adjectives εἷς, δύο, τρεῖς, and τέσσαρες

	εἷς				δύο	τρεῖς		τέσσαρες	
	M	F	N		M/F/N	M/F	N	M/F	N
NS	εἷς	μία	ἕν	NP	δύο	τρεῖς	τρία	τέσσαρες	τέσσαρα (or τέσσερα)
GS	ἑνός	μιᾶς	ἑνός	GP	δύο	τριῶν	τριῶν	τεσσάρων	τεσσάρων
DS	ἑνί	μιᾷ	ἑνί	DP	δυσί	τρισί(ν)	τρισί(ν)	τέσσαρσιν	τέσσαρσιν
AS	ἕνα	μίαν	ἕν	AP	δύο	τρεῖς	τρία	τέσσαρας (or τέσσαρες)	τέσσαρα (or τέσσερα)

A.13. Possessive Adjectives

	First-Person Singular			Second-Person Singular		
	Masc.	Fem.	Neut.	Masc.	Fem.	Neut.
NS	ἐμός	ἐμή	ἐμόν	σός	σή	σόν
GS	ἐμοῦ	ἐμῆς	ἐμοῦ	σοῦ	σῆς	σοῦ
DS	ἐμῷ	ἐμῇ	ἐμῷ	σῷ	σῇ	σῷ
AS	ἐμόν	ἐμήν	ἐμόν	σόν	σήν	σόν
NP	ἐμοί	ἐμαί	ἐμά	σοί	σαί	σά
GP	ἐμῶν	ἐμῶν	ἐμῶν	σῶν	σῶν	σῶν
DP	ἐμοῖς	ἐμαῖς	ἐμοῖς	σοῖς	σαῖς	σοῖς
AP	ἐμούς	ἐμάς	ἐμά	σούς	σάς	σά

	First-Person Plural			Second-Person Plural		
	Masc.	Fem.	Neut.	Masc.	Fem.	Neut.
NS	ἡμέτερος	ἡμετέρα	ἡμέτερον	ὑμέτερος	ὑμετέρα	ὑμέτερον
GS	ἡμετέρου	ἡμετέρας	ἡμετέρου	ὑμετέρου	ὑμετέρας	ὑμετέρου
DS	ἡμετέρῳ	ἡμετέρᾳ	ἡμετέρῳ	ὑμετέρῳ	ὑμετέρᾳ	ὑμετέρῳ
AS	ἡμέτερον	ἡμετέραν	ἡμέτερον	ὑμέτερον	ὑμετέραν	ὑμέτερον
NP	ἡμέτεροι	ἡμέτεραι	ἡμέτερα	ὑμέτεροι	ὑμέτεραι	ὑμέτερα
GP	ἡμετέρων	ἡμετέρων	ἡμετέρων	ὑμετέρων	ὑμετέρων	ὑμετέρων
DP	ἡμετέροις	ἡμετέραις	ἡμετέροις	ὑμετέροις	ὑμετέραις	ὑμετέροις
AP	ἡμετέρους	ἡμετέρας	ἡμέτερα	ὑμετέρους	ὑμετέρας	ὑμέτερα

Pronouns

A.14. First-, Second-, and Third-Person Pronouns

	1st Person	2nd Person	3rd Person		
			Masc.	Fem.	Neut.
NS	ἐγώ	σύ	αὐτός	αὐτή	αὐτό
GS	ἐμοῦ (μου)	σοῦ (σου)	αὐτοῦ	αὐτῆς	αὐτοῦ
DS	ἐμοί (μοι)	σοί (σοι)	αὐτῷ	αὐτῇ	αὐτῷ
AS	ἐμέ (με)	σέ (σε)	αὐτόν	αὐτήν	αὐτό
NP	ἡμεῖς	ὑμεῖς	αὐτοί	αὐταί	αὐτά
GP	ἡμῶν	ὑμῶν	αὐτῶν	αὐτῶν	αὐτῶν
DP	ἡμῖν	ὑμῖν	αὐτοῖς	αὐταῖς	αὐτοῖς
AP	ἡμᾶς	ὑμᾶς	αυτούς	αὐτάς	αὐτά

A.15. Indefinite and Interrogative Pronouns (Third Declension)

	Indefinite[a]		Interrogative	
	M/F	N	M/F	N
NS	τις	τι	τίς	τί
GS	τινός	τινός	τίνος	τίνος
DS	τινί	τινί	τίνι	τίνι
AS	τινά	τι	τίνα	τί
NP	τινές	τινά	τίνες	τίνα
GP	τινῶν	τινῶν	τίνων	τίνων
DP	τισί(ν)	τισί(ν)	τίσι(ν)	τίσι(ν)
AP	τινάς	τινά	τίνας	τίνα

[a] The indefinite pronoun is an enclitic.

A.16. Demonstrative Pronouns

	Near Demonstratives			Far Demonstratives		
	Masc.	Fem.	Neut.	Masc.	Fem.	Neut.
NS	οὗτος	αὕτη	τοῦτο	ἐκεῖνος	ἐκείνη	ἐκεῖνο
GS	τούτου	ταύτης	τούτου	ἐκείνου	ἐκείνης	ἐκείνου
DS	τούτῳ	ταύτῃ	τούτῳ	ἐκείνῳ	ἐκείνῃ	ἐκείνῳ
AS	τοῦτον	ταύτην	τοῦτο	ἐκεῖνον	ἐκείνην	ἐκεῖνο
NP	οὗτοι	αὗται	ταῦτα	ἐκεῖνοι	ἐκεῖναι	ἐκεῖνα
GP	τούτων	τούτων	τούτων	ἐκείνων	ἐκείνων	ἐκείνων
DP	τούτοις	ταύταις	τούτοις	ἐκείνοις	ἐκείναις	ἐκείνοις
AP	τούτους	ταύτας	ταῦτα	ἐκείνους	ἐκείνας	ἐκεῖνα

A.17. Relative and Indefinite Relative Pronouns

	Relative			Indefinite Relative		
	Masc.	Fem.	Neut.	Masc.	Fem.	Neut.
NS	ὅς	ἥ	ὅ	ὅστις	ἥτις	ὅτι
GS	οὗ	ἧς	οὗ	οὗτινος	ἧστινος	ὅτου
DS	ᾧ	ᾗ	ᾧ	ᾧτινι	ᾗτινι	ᾧτινι
AS	ὅν	ἥν	ὅ	ὅντινα	ἥντινα	ὅτι
NP	οἵ	αἵ	ἅ	οἵτινες	αἵτινες	ἅτινα
GP	ὧν	ὧν	ὧν	ὧντινων	ὧντινων	ὧντινων
DP	οἷς	αἷς	οἷς	οἷστισι(ν)	αἷστισι(ν)	οἷστισι(ν)
AP	οὕς	ἅς	ἅ	οὕστινας	ἅστινας	ἅτινα

A.18. Reflexive Pronouns

	1st Person		2nd Person		3rd Person		
	Masc.	Fem.	Masc.	Fem.	Masc.	Fem.	Neut.
NS	—	—	—	—	—	—	—
GS	ἐμαυτοῦ	ἐμαυτῆς	σεαυτοῦ	σεαυτῆς	ἑαυτοῦ	ἑαυτῆς	ἑαυτοῦ
DS	ἐμαυτῷ	ἐμαυτῇ	σεαυτῷ	σεαυτῇ	ἑαυτῷ	ἑαυτῇ	ἑαυτῷ
AS	ἐμαυτόν	ἐμαυτήν	σεαυτόν	σεαυτήν	ἑαυτόν	ἑαυτήν	ἑαυτό
NP					—	—	—
GP					ἑαυτῶν[a]	ἑαυτῶν	ἑαυτῶν
DP					ἑαυτοῖς	ἑαυταῖς	ἑαυτοῖς
AP					ἑαυτούς	ἑαυτάς	ἑαυτά

[a] The third-person plural forms may also function as plurals for first and second person.

A.19. Reciprocal Pronouns

	Masc.	Fem.	Neut.
NP	—	—	—
GP	ἀλλήλων	ἀλλήλων	ἀλλήλων
DP	ἀλλήλοις	ἀλλήλαις	ἀλλήλοις
AP	ἀλλήλους	ἀλλήλας	ἄλληλα

Verbal System

ω Verbs

A.20. Simplified Verb Charts for ω Verbs

Morphological Formulas for Indicative Verbs

Present Active		stem	+ c.v. +	A p.e.
Present Middle		stem	+ c.v. +	C p.e.
Future Active		stem	+ f.m. σ + c.v. +	A p.e.
Future Middle		stem	+ f.m. σ + c.v. +	C p.e.
Future Passive		stem[a]	+ f.m. θησ + c.v. +	C p.e.
Imperfect Active	aug. +	stem	+ c.v. +	B p.e.
Imperfect Middle	aug. +	stem	+ c.v. +	D p.e.
Aorist Active	aug. +	stem	+ f.m. σα +	B p.e.
Aorist Middle	aug. +	stem	+ f.m. σα +	D p.e.
Aorist Passive	aug. +	stem[b]	+ f.m. θη +	B p.e.
Second Aorist Active	aug. +	*aor. stem*	+ c.v. +	B p.e.

Morphological Formulas for Indicative Verbs

Second Aorist Middle	aug. +	*aor. stem*	+ c.v. +	D p.e.
Perfect Active	redup. +	stem[b]	+ f.m. κα +	A p.e.
Perfect Middle	redup. +	stem[b]	+	C p.e.

[a] Follows the same pattern as the aorist passive stem.

[b] *Usually* the same as the present active stem (lexical form), but it may change.

Remember: Liquid (λ, μ, ν, ρ) aorists and liquid futures drop the σ. Second aorist passives and second future passives drop the θ.

Verb Endings Four-Quad Chart

			Primary			Secondary			
			λύω Form	With c.v.	Without c.v.	**λύω** Form	With c.v.	Without c.v.	
Active	Pres. Act. Fut. Act. Pf. Act.	A 1S	λύω	ω	–	ἔλυον	ον	ν[b] B	Aor. Act. Aor. Pass.[c] Impf. Act.
		2S	λύεις	εις	ς	ἔλυες	ες	ς	
		3S	λύει	ει	ι[b]	ἔλυε(ν)	ε(ν)	(ν)	
		1P	λύομεν	ομεν	μεν	ἐλύομεν	ομεν	μεν	
		2P	λύετε	ετε	τε	ἐλύετε	ετε	τε	
		3P	λύουσι(ν)	ουσι(ν)	νσι(ν)	ἔλυον	ον	ν[b]	
Middle	Pres. Mid.[a] Fut. Mid. Fut. Pass. Pf. Mid.[a]	C 1S	λύομαι	ομαι	μαι	ἐλυόμην	ομην	μην D	Aor. Mid. Impf. Mid.[a]
		2S	λύῃ	ῃ[b]	σαι	ἐλύου	ου	σο[b]	
		3S	λύεται	εται	ται	ἐλύετο	ετο	το	
		1P	λυόμεθα	ομεθα	μεθα	ἐλυόμεθα	ομεθα	μεθα	
		2P	λύεσθε	εσθε	σθε	ἐλύεσθε	εσθε	σθε	
		3P	λύονται	ονται	νται	ἐλύοντο	οντο	ντο	

[a] Can also be passive if there is an agent marker in the context.

[b] These forms may have minor variations in endings; see next table below.

[c] Can also be middle if context suggests (θη-middle forms).

Minor Variations in Endings

Four-Quad Chart Variations

	Perfect	Aorist	
A	Active 1S: —	Active 1S: —	B
	Active 3S: ε(ν)	Passive 3P: σαν	
C	Middle 2S: σαι	Middle 2S: σω	D

Square of Stops

				+ σ	+ θ
Labials	π	β	φ	ψ	φθ
Velars	κ	γ	χ	ξ	χθ
Dentals	τ	δ	θ	σ	σθ

Verbs terminating in -ιζω and -αζω often have a stem ending in δ, so they may act like square-of-stops forms.

A.21. Indicatives of the ω Verbs

Present and Imperfect Indicative

	Present		Imperfect	
	Active	Middle[a]	Active	Middle[a]
1S	λύω	λύομαι	ἔλυον	ἐλυόμην
2S	λύεις	λύῃ	ἔλυες	ἐλύου
3S	λύει	λύεται	ἔλυε(ν)	ἐλύετο
1P	λύομεν	λυόμεθα	ἐλύομεν	ἐλυόμεθα
2P	λύετε	λύεσθε	ἐλύετε	ἐλύεσθε
3P	λύουσι(ν)	λύονται	ἔλυον	ἐλύοντο

[a] Can be passive if there is an agent marker in the context.

First Aorist Indicative

	Active	Middle	Passive
1S	ἔλυσα	ἐλυσάμην	ἐλύθην
2S	ἔλυσας	ἐλύσω	ἐλύθης
3S	ἔλυσε(ν)	ἐλύσατο	ἐλύθη
1P	ἐλύσαμεν	ἐλυσάμεθα	ἐλύθημεν
2P	ἐλύσατε	ἐλύσασθε	ἐλύθητε
3P	ἔλυσαν	ἐλύσαντο	ἐλύθησαν

Second Aorist Indicative

	Active	Middle	Passive
	λαμβάνω	γίνομαι	χαίρω
1S	ἔλαβον	ἐγενόμην	ἐχάρην
2S	ἔλαβες	ἐγένου	ἐχάρης
3S	ἔλαβε(ν)	ἐγένετο	ἐχάρη
1P	ἐλάβομεν	ἐγενόμεθα	ἐχάρημεν
2P	ἐλάβετε	ἐγένεσθε	ἐχάρητε
3P	ἔλαβον	ἐγένοντο	ἐχάρησαν

Future Indicative

	Active	Middle	Passive
1S	λύσω	λύσομαι	λυθήσομαι
2S	λύσεις	λύσῃ	λυθήσῃ
3S	λύσει	λύσεται	λυθήσεται
1P	λύσομεν	λυσόμεθα	λυθησόμεθα
2P	λύσετε	λύσεσθε	λυθήσεσθε
3P	λύσουσι(ν)	λύσονται	λυθήσονται

Perfect and Pluperfect Indicative

	Perfect		Pluperfect	
	Active	Middle[a]	Active	Middle[a]
1S	λέλυκα	λέλυμαι	ἐλελύκειν	ἐλελύμην
2S	λέλυκας	λέλυσαι	ἐλελύκεις	ἐλέλυσο
3S	λέλυκε(ν)	λέλυται	ἐλελύκει(ν)	ἐλέλυτο
1P	λελύκαμεν	λελύμεθα	ἐλελύκειμεν	ἐλελύμεθα
2P	λελύκατε	λέλυσθε	ἐλελύκειτε	ἐλέλυσθε
3P	λελύκασι(ν)	λέλυνται	ἐλελύκεισαν	ἐλέλυντο

[a] Can also be passive if there is an agent marker in the context.

A.22. Indicative Contracts of the ω Verbs

Present Active Indicative

	Non-contract	ε Contract	ο Contract	α Contract
	λύω	ποιέω	πληρόω	ἀγαπάω
1S	λύω	ποιῶ	πληρῶ	ἀγαπῶ
2S	λύεις	ποιεῖς	πληροῖς	ἀγαπᾷς
3S	λύει	ποιεῖ	πληροῖ	ἀγαπᾷ
1P	λύομεν	ποιοῦμεν	πληροῦμεν	ἀγαπῶμεν
2P	λύετε	ποιεῖτε	πληροῦτε	ἀγαπᾶτε
3P	λύουσι(ν)	ποιοῦσι(ν)	πληροῦσι(ν)	ἀγαπῶσι(ν)
Inf	λύειν	ποιεῖν	πληροῦν	ἀγαπᾶν

Present Middle Indicative

	Non-contract	ε Contract	ο Contract	α Contract
	λύω	ποιέω	πληρόω	ἀγαπάω
1S	λύομαι	ποιοῦμαι	πληροῦμαι	ἀγαπῶμαι
2S	λύῃ	ποιῇ	πληροῖ	ἀγαπᾷ
3S	λύεται	ποιεῖται	πληροῦται	ἀγαπᾶται

	Non-contract	ε Contract	ο Contract	α Contract
	λύω	ποιέω	πληρόω	ἀγαπάω
1P	λυόμεθα	ποιούμεθα	πληρούμεθα	ἀγαπώμεθα
2P	λύεσθε	ποιεῖσθε	πληροῦσθε	ἀγαπᾶσθε
3P	λύονται	ποιοῦνται	πληροῦνται	ἀγαπῶνται
Inf	λύεσθαι	ποιεῖσθαι	πληροῦσθαι	ἀγαπᾶσθαι

Imperfect Active Indicative

	Non-contract	ε Contract	ο Contract	α Contract
	λύω	ποιέω	πληρόω	ἀγαπάω
1S	ἔλυον	ἐποίουν	ἐπλήρουν	ἠγάπων
2S	ἔλυες	ἐποίεις	ἐπλήρους	ἠγάπας
3S	ἔλυε(ν)	ἐποίει	ἐπλήρου	ἠγάπα
1P	ἐλύομεν	ἐποιοῦμεν	ἐπληροῦμεν	ἠγαπῶμεν
2P	ἐλύετε	ἐποιεῖτε	ἐπληροῦτε	ἠγαπᾶτε
3P	ἔλυον	ἐποίουν	ἐπλήρουν	ἠγάπων

Imperfect Middle Indicative

	Non-contract	ε Contract	ο Contract	α Contract
	λύω	ποιέω	πληρόω	ἀγαπάω
1S	ἐλυόμην	ἐποιούμην	ἐπληρούμην	ἠγαπώμην
2S	ἐλύου	ἐποιοῦ	ἐπληροῦ	ἠγαπῶ
3S	ἐλύετο	ἐποιεῖτο	ἐπληροῦτο	ἠγαπᾶτο
1P	ἐλυόμεθα	ἐποιούμεθα	ἐπληρούμεθα	ἠγαπώμεθα
2P	ἐλύεσθε	ἐποιεῖσθε	ἐπληροῦσθε	ἠγαπᾶσθε
3P	ἐλύοντο	ἐποιοῦντο	ἐπληροῦντο	ἠγαπῶντο

Perfect Middle Indicative

	Non-contract	ε Contract	ο Contract	α Contract
	λύω	ποιέω	πληρόω	γεννάω
1S	λέλυμαι	πεποίημαι	πεπλήρωμαι	γεγέννημαι
2S	λέλυσαι	πεποίησαι	πεπλήρωσαι	γεγέννησαι
3S	λέλυται	πεποίηται	πεπλήρωται	γεγέννηται
1P	λελύμεθα	πεποιήμεθα	πεπληρώμεθα	γεγεννήμεθα
2P	λέλυσθε	πεποίησθε	πεπλήρωσθε	γεγέννησθε
3P	λέλυνται	πεποίηνται	πεπλήρωνται	γεγέννηνται

A.23. Indicative Liquids of the ω Verbs

Liquid Future and Aorist Active Indicative

	Liquid Future	(Liquid) Present[a]	Contract Present[a]	Liquid Aorist
	κρίνω	κρίνω	ποιέω	μένω
1S	κρινῶ	κρίνω	ποιῶ	ἔμεινα
2S	κρινεῖς	κρίνεις	ποιεῖς	ἔμεινας
3S	κρινεῖ	κρίνει	ποιεῖ	ἔμεινε(ν)
1P	κρινοῦμεν	κρίνομεν	ποιοῦμεν	ἐμείναμεν
2P	κρινεῖτε	κρίνετε	ποιεῖτε	ἐμείνατε
3P	κρινοῦσι(ν)	κρίνουσι(ν)	ποιοῦσι(ν)	ἔμειναν

[a] Columns 2 and 3 are provided for comparison.

Liquid Future and Aorist Middle Indicative

	Liquid Future	(Liquid) Present[a]	Contract Present[a]	Liquid Aorist
	κρίνω	κρίνω	ποιέω	μένω
1S	κρινοῦμαι	κρίνομαι	ποιοῦμαι	ἐμεινάμην
2S	κρινῇ	κρίνῃ	ποιῇ	ἐμείνω
3S	κρινεῖται	κρίνεται	ποιεῖται	ἐμείνατο
1P	κρινούμεθα	κρινόμεθα	ποιούμεθα	ἐμεινάμεθα
2P	κρινεῖσθε	κρίνεσθε	ποιεῖσθε	ἐμείνασθε
3P	κρινοῦνται	κρίνονται	ποιοῦνται	ἐμείναντο

[a] Columns 2 and 3 are provided for comparison.

A.24. Subjunctives of the ω Verbs

Present and Aorist Active Subjunctives

	Pres. Act. Subj.	Pres. Act. Ind.[a]	[1]Aor. Act. Subj.	[2]Aor. Act. Subj.
	λύω	λύω	λύω	λαμβάνω
1S	λύω	λύω	λύσω	λάβω
2S	λύῃς	λύεις	λύσῃς	λάβῃς
3S	λύῃ	λύει	λύσῃ	λάβῃ
1P	λύωμεν	λύομεν	λύσωμεν	λάβωμεν
2P	λύητε	λύετε	λύσητε	λάβητε
3P	λύωσι(ν)	λύουσι(ν)	λύσωσι(ν)	λάβωσι(ν)

[a] Indicative column is provided for comparison.

Present and Aorist Middle Subjunctives

	Pres. Mid. Subj.	Pres. Mid. Ind.[a]	[1]Aor. Mid. Subj.	[2]Aor. Mid. Subj.
	λύω	λύω	λύω	γίνομαι
1S	λύωμαι	λύομαι	λύσωμαι	γένωμαι
2S	λύῃ	λύῃ	λύσῃ	γένῃ
3S	λύηται	λύεται	λύσηται	γένηται
1P	λυώμεθα	λυόμεθα	λυσώμεθα	γενώμεθα
2P	λύησθε	λύεσθε	λύσησθε	γένησθε
3P	λύωνται	λύονται	λύσωνται	γένωνται

[a] Indicative column is provided for comparison.

Aorist Passive and Perfect Middle and Passive Subjunctives

	Aor. Pass. Subj. of λύω	Pf. Mid./Pass. Subj. of λύω[a]	Pf. Pass. Subj. of οἶδα
1S	λυθῶ	ὦ + λελυμένος	εἰδῶ
2S	λυθῇς	ᾖς + λελυμένος	εἰδῇς
3S	λυθῇ	ᾖ + λελυμένος	εἰδῇ
1P	λυθῶμεν	ὦμεν + λελυμένοι	εἰδῶμεν
2P	λυθῆτε	ἦτε + λελυμένοι	εἰδῆτε
3P	λυθῶσι(ν)	ὦσι(ν) + λελυμένοι	εἰδῶσι(ν)

[a] All perfect middle and passive subjunctives are formed periphrastically.

Present Active and Middle Subjunctive Contracts

	Present Active			Present Middle		
	ε Contract	ο Contract	α Contract	ε Contract	ο Contract	α Contract
	ποιέω	πληρόω	ἀγαπάω	αἰτέω	λυτρόω	χαλάω
1S	ποιῶ	πληρῶ	ἀγαπῶ	αἰτῶμαι	λυτρῶμαι	χαλῶμαι
2S	ποιῇς	πληροῖς	ἀγαπᾷς	αἰτῇ	λυτροῖ	χαλᾷ
3S	ποιῇ	πληροῖ	ἀγαπᾷ	αἰτῆται	λυτρῶται	χαλᾶται
1P	ποιῶμεν	πληρῶμεν	ἀγαπῶμεν	αἰτώμεθα	λυτρώμεθα	χαλώμεθα
2P	ποιῆτε	πληρῶτε	ἀγαπᾶτε	αἰτῆσθε	λυτρῶσθε	χαλᾶσθε
3P	ποιῶσι(ν)	πληρῶσι(ν)	ἀγαπῶσι(ν)	αἰτῶνται	λυτρῶνται	χαλῶνται

Aorist Active and Middle Subjunctive Contracts

	Aorist Active			Aorist Middle		
	ε Contract	ο Contract	α Contract	ε Contract	ο Contract	α Contract
	ποιέω	πληρόω	ἀγαπάω	αἰτέω	λυτρόω	χράω
1S	ποιήσω	πληρώσω	ἀγαπήσω	αἰτήσωμαι	λυτρώσωμαι	χρήσωμαι
2S	ποιήσῃς	πληρώσῃς	ἀγαπήσῃς	αἰτήσῃ	λυτρώσῃ	χρήσῃ

	Aorist Active			Aorist Middle		
	ε Contract	ο Contract	α Contract	ε Contract	ο Contract	α Contract
	ποιέω	πληρόω	ἀγαπάω	αἰτέω	λυτρόω	χράω
3S	ποιήσῃ	πληρώσῃ	ἀγαπήσῃ	αἰτήσηται	λυτρώσηται	χρήσηται
1P	ποιήσωμεν	πληρώσωμεν	ἀγαπήσωμεν	αἰτησώμεθα	λυτρωσώμεθα	χρησώμεθα
2P	ποιήσητε	πληρώσητε	ἀγαπήσητε	αἰτήσησθε	λυτρώσησθε	χρήσησθε
3P	ποιήσωσι(ν)	πληρώσωσι(ν)	ἀγαπήσωσι(ν)	αἰτήσωνται	λυτρώσωνται	χρήσωνται

Aorist Passive Subjunctive Contracts

	ε Contract	ο Contract	α Contract
	φοβέω	πληρόω	πλανάω
1S	φοβηθῶ	πληρωθῶ	πλανηθῶ
2S	φοβηθῇς	πληρωθῇς	πλανηθῇς
3S	φοβηθῇ	πληρωθῇ	πλανηθῇ
1P	φοβηθῶμεν	πληρωθῶμεν	πλανηθῶμεν
2P	φοβηθῆτε	πληρωθῆτε	πλανηθῆτε
3P	φοβηθῶσι(ν)	πληρωθῶσι(ν)	πλανηθῶσι(ν)

A.25. Imperatives of the ω Verbs

Present and First Aorist Imperatives

	Present Active	Present Middle	Aorist Active	Aorist Middle	Aorist Passive
2S	λῦε	λύου[b]	λῦσον[a]	λῦσαι[a]	λύθητι
3S	λυέτω	λυέσθω	λυσάτω	λυσάσθω	λυθήτω
2P	λύετε[a]	λύεσθε[a]	λύσατε[b]	λύσασθε[b]	λύθητε[b]
3P	λυέτωσαν	λυέσθωσαν	λυσάτωσαν	λυσάσθωσαν	λυθήτωσαν

[a] Identical to another form (indicative, infinitive, or participle).

[b] Similar to the indicative (but no augment).

Second Aorist Imperatives

	Second Aorist Active	Second Aorist Middle	Second Aorist Passive
	ἔρχομαι	λαμβάνω	γίνομαι
2S	ἐλθέ	λαβοῦ	γενήθητι
3S	ἐλθέτω	λαβέσθω	γενηθήτω
2P	ἔλθετε	λάβεσθε	γενήθητε
3P	ἐλθέτωσαν	λαβέσθωσαν	γενηθήτωσαν

The second aorist forms sometimes use first aorist endings with an alpha instead of the normal epsilon (e.g., ἐλθάτω instead of ἐλθέτω).

Present Active Imperative Contracts

	ποιέω	ζηλόω	ὁράω
2S	ποίει	ζήλου	ὅρα
3S	ποιείτω	ζηλούτω	ὁράτω
2P	ποιεῖτε	ζηλοῦτε	ὁρᾶτε
3P	ποιείτωσαν	ζηλούτωσαν	ὁράτωσαν

A.26. Optatives of the ω Verbs

Present and Second Aorist Optatives

	Present Active	Present Middle	Second Aorist Active	Second Aorist Middle
	λύω	λύω	βάλλω	βάλλω
1S	λύοιμι	λυοίμην	βάλοιμι	βαλοίμην
2S	λύοις	λύοιο	βάλοις	βάλοιο
3S	λύοι	λύοιτο	βάλοι	βάλοιτο
1P	λύοιμεν	λυοίμεθα	βάλοιμεν	βαλοίμεθα
2P	λύοιτε	λύοισθε	βάλοιτε	βάλοισθε
3P	λύοιεν	λύοιντο	βάλοιεν	βάλοιντο

First Aorist Optatives

	Active	Middle	Passive
1S	λύσαιμι	λυσαίμην	λυθείην
2S	λύσαις	λύσαιο	λυθείης
3S	λύσαι	λύσαιτο	λυθείη
1P	λύσαιμεν	λυσαίμεθα	λυθεῖμεν
2P	λύσαιτε	λύσαισθε	λυθεῖτε
3P	λύσαιεν	λύσαιντο	λυθεῖεν

A.27. Infinitives of the ω Verbs

	Active	Middle	Passive
Present	λύειν	λύεσθαι	
First Aorist	λῦσαι	λύσασθαι	λυθῆναι
Second Aorist[a]	βαλεῖν	βαλέσθαι	βληθῆναι[b]
Future	λύσειν	λύσεσθαι	—
Perfect	λελυκέναι	λελύσθαι	

[a] The second aorist forms are from βάλλω.

[b] A few verbs drop the theta from the aorist passive form marker so the ending is just -ηναι; these forms are not common.

Contract and Liquid Infinitives

	Present Active	Present Middle	Aorist Active
ποιέω	ποιεῖν	ποιεῖσθαι	ποιῆσαι
πληρόω	πληροῦν	πληροῦσθαι	πληρῶσαι
ἀγαπάω	ἀγαπᾶν	ἀγαπᾶσθαι	ἀγαπῆσαι
μένω	μένειν	μένεσθαι	μεῖναι

A.28. Participles of the ω Verbs

Imperfective (Present) Active and Middle Participles

	Active			Middle		
	Masc.	Fem.	Neut.	Masc.	Fem.	Neut.
NS	λύων	λύουσα	λῦον	λυόμενος	λυομένη	λυόμενον
GS	λύοντος	λυούσης	λύοντος	λυομένου	λυομένης	λυομένου
DS	λύοντι	λυούσῃ	λύοντι	λυομένῳ	λυομένῃ	λυομένῳ
AS	λύοντα	λύουσαν	λῦον	λυόμενον	λυομένην	λυόμενον
NP	λύοντες	λύουσαι	λύοντα	λυόμενοι	λυόμεναι	λυόμενα
GP	λυόντων	λυουσῶν	λυόντων	λυομένων	λυομένων	λυομένων
DP	λύουσι(ν)	λυούσαις	λύουσι(ν)	λυομένοις	λυομέναις	λυομένοις
AP	λύοντας	λυούσας	λύοντα	λυομένους	λυομένας	λυόμενα

Contract Present Active and Middle Participles of ποιέω

	Active			Middle		
	Masc.	Fem.	Neut.	Masc.	Fem.	Neut.
NS	ποιῶν	ποιοῦσα	ποιοῦν	ποιούμενος	ποιουμένη	ποιούμενον
GS	ποιοῦντος	ποιούσης	ποιοῦντος	ποιουμένου	ποιουμένης	ποιουμένου
DS	ποιοῦντι	ποιούσῃ	ποιοῦντι	ποιουμένῳ	ποιουμένῃ	ποιουμένῳ
AS	ποιοῦντα	ποιοῦσαν	ποιοῦν	ποιούμενον	ποιουμένην	ποιούμενον
NP	ποιοῦντες	ποιοῦσαι	ποιοῦντα	ποιούμενοι	ποιούμεναι	ποιούμενα
GP	ποιούντων	ποιουσῶν	ποιούντων	ποιουμένων	ποιουμένων	ποιουμένων
DP	ποιοῦσι(ν)	ποιούσαις	ποιοῦσι(ν)	ποιουμένοις	ποιουμέναις	ποιουμένοις
AP	ποιοῦντας	ποιούσας	ποιοῦντα	ποιουμένους	ποιουμένας	ποιούμενα

Contract Present Active and Middle Participles of πληρόω

	Active			Middle		
	Masc.	Fem.	Neut.	Masc.	Fem.	Neut.
NS	πληρῶν	πληροῦσα	πληροῦν	πληρούμενος	πληρουμένη	πληρούμενον
GS	πληροῦντος	πληρούσης	πληροῦντος	πληρουμένου	πληρουμένης	πληρουμένου
DS	πληροῦντι	πληρούσῃ	πληροῦντι	πληρουμένῳ	πληρουμένῃ	πληρουμένῳ
AS	πληροῦντα	πληροῦσαν	πληροῦν	πληρούμενον	πληρουμένην	πληρούμενον
NP	πληροῦντες	πληροῦσαι	πληροῦντα	πληρούμενοι	πληρούμεναι	πληρούμενα
GP	πληρούντων	πληρουσῶν	πληρούντων	πληρουμένων	πληρουμένων	πληρουμένων
DP	πληροῦσι(ν)	πληρούσαις	πληροῦσι(ν)	πληρουμένοις	πληρουμέναις	πληρουμένοις
AP	πληροῦντας	πληρούσας	πληροῦντα	πληρουμένους	πληρουμένας	πληρούμενα

Contract Present Active and Middle Participles of ἀγαπάω

	Active			Middle		
	Masc.	Fem.	Neut.	Masc.	Fem.	Neut.
NS	ἀγαπῶν	ἀγαπῶσα	ἀγαπῶν	ἀγαπώμενος	ἀγαπωμένη	ἀγαπώμενον
GS	ἀγαπῶντος	ἀγαπώσης	ἀγαπῶντος	ἀγαπωμένου	ἀγαπωμένης	ἀγαπωμένου
DS	ἀγαπῶντι	ἀγαπώσῃ	ἀγαπῶντι	ἀγαπωμένῳ	ἀγαπωμένῃ	ἀγαπωμένῳ
AS	ἀγαπῶντα	ἀγαπῶσαν	ἀγαπῶν	ἀγαπώμενον	ἀγαπωμένην	ἀγαπώμενον
NP	ἀγαπῶντες	ἀγαπῶσαι	ἀγαπῶντα	ἀγαπώμενοι	ἀγαπώμεναι	ἀγαπώμενα
GP	ἀγαπώντων	ἀγαπωσῶν	ἀγαπώντων	ἀγαπωμένων	ἀγαπωμένων	ἀγαπωμένων
DP	ἀγαπῶσι(ν)	ἀγαπώσαις	ἀγαπῶσι(ν)	ἀγαπωμένοις	ἀγαπωμέναις	ἀγαπωμένοις
AP	ἀγαπῶντας	ἀγαπώσας	ἀγαπῶντα	ἀγαπωμένους	ἀγαπωμένας	ἀγαπώμενα

Perfective (Aorist) Active and Middle Participles

	Active			Middle		
	Masc.	Fem.	Neut.	Masc.	Fem.	Neut.
NS	λύσας	λύσασα	λῦσαν	λυσάμενος	λυσαμένη	λυσάμενον
GS	λύσαντος	λυσάσης	λύσαντος	λυσαμένου	λυσαμένης	λυσαμένου
DS	λύσαντι	λυσάσῃ	λύσαντι	λυσαμένῳ	λυσαμένῃ	λυσαμένῳ
AS	λύσαντα	λύσασαν	λῦσαν	λυσάμενον	λυσαμένην	λυσάμενον
NP	λύσαντες	λύσασαι	λύσαντα	λυσάμενοι	λυσάμεναι	λυσάμενα
GP	λυσάντων	λυσασῶν	λυσάντων	λυσαμένων	λυσαμένων	λυσαμένων
DP	λύσασι(ν)	λυσάσαις	λύσασι(ν)	λυσαμένοις	λυσαμέναις	λυσαμένοις
AP	λύσαντας	λυσάσας	λύσαντα	λυσαμένους	λυσαμένας	λυσάμενα

Perfective (Aorist) Passive Participle

	Masc.	Fem.	Neut.
NS	λυθείς	λυθεῖσα	λυθέν
GS	λυθέντος	λυθείσης	λυθέντος
DS	λυθέντι	λυθείσῃ	λυθέντι
AS	λυθέντα	λυθεῖσαν	λυθέν
NP	λυθέντες	λυθεῖσαι	λυθέντα
GP	λυθέντων	λυθεισῶν	λυθέντων
DP	λυθεῖσι(ν)	λυθείσαις	λυθεῖσι(ν)
AP	λυθέντας	λυθείσας	λυθέντα

Perfective (Second Aorist) Active Participle of ἔρχομαι

	Masc.	Fem.	Neut.
NS	ἐλθών	ἐλθοῦσα	ἐλθόν
GS	ἐλθόντος	ἐλθούσης	ἐλθόντος
DS	ἐλθόντι	ἐλθούσῃ	ἐλθόντι
AS	ἐλθόντα	ἐλθοῦσαν	ἐλθόν
NP	ἐλθόντες	ἐλθοῦσαι	ἐλθόντα
GP	ἐλθόντων	ἐλθουσῶν	ἐλθόντων
DP	ἐλθοῦσι(ν)	ἐλθούσαις	ἐλθοῦσι(ν)
AP	ἐλθόντας	ἐλθούσας	ἐλθόντα

Perfective (Second Aorist) Middle Participle of γίνομαι

	Masc.	Fem.	Neut.
NS	γενόμενος	γενομένη	γενόμενον
GS	γενομένου	γενομένης	γενομένου
DS	γενομένῳ	γενομένῃ	γενομένῳ
AS	γενόμενον	γενομένην	γενόμενον
NP	γενόμενοι	γενόμεναι	γενόμενα
GP	γενομένων	γενομένων	γενομένων
DP	γενομένοις	γενομέναις	γενομένοις
AP	γενομένους	γενομένας	γενόμενα

Perfective (Second Aorist) Passive Participle of στρέφω

	Masc.	Fem.	Neut.
NS	στραφείς	στραφεῖσα	στραφέν
GS	στραφέντος	στραφείσης	στραφέντος
DS	στραφέντι	στραφείσῃ	στραφέντι
AS	στραφέντα	στραφεῖσαν	στραφέν
NP	στραφέντες	στραφεῖσαι	στραφέντα
GP	στραφέντων	στραφεισῶν	στραφέντων
DP	στραφεῖσι(ν)	στραφείσαις	στραφεῖσι(ν)
AP	στραφέντας	στραφείσας	στραφέντα

Stative (Perfect) Active and Middle Participles

	Active			Middle		
	Masc.	Fem.	Neut.	Masc.	Fem.	Neut.
NS	λελυκώς	λελυκυῖα	λελυκός	λελυμένος	λελυμένη	λελυμένον
GS	λελυκότος	λελυκυίας	λελυκότος	λελυμένου	λελυμένης	λελυμένου
DS	λελυκότι	λελυκυίᾳ	λελυκότι	λελυμένῳ	λελυμένῃ	λελυμένῳ
AS	λελυκότα	λελυκυῖαν	λελυκός	λελυμένον	λελυμένην	λελυμένον
NP	λελυκότες	λελυκυῖαι	λελυκότα	λελυμένοι	λελυμέναι	λελυμένα
GP	λελυκότων	λελυκυιῶν	λελυκότων	λελυμένων	λελυμένων	λελυμένων
DP	λελυκόσι(ν)	λελυκυίαις	λελυκόσι(ν)	λελυμένοις	λελυμέναις	λελυμένοις
AP	λελυκότας	λελυκυίας	λελυκότα	λελυμένους	λελυμένας	λελυμένα

A.29. *Forms of εἰμί*

The verb εἰμί is defective in that it does not occur in many forms that might be expected; for example, there is no aorist form. The forms given below are the only ones that occur. They are labeled according to their morphology. That is, ἔσομαι is labeled as a future middle indicative even though it represents the only set of future forms; there are no future active indicative forms of this verb. Some grammars list them simply as "future" with no voice designation.

Indicative

	Present [Active]	Imperfect [Middle]	Future [Middle]
1S	εἰμί	ἤμην	ἔσομαι
2S	εἶ	ἦς or ἦσθα	ἔσῃ
3S	ἐστί(ν)	ἦν	ἔσται
1P	ἐσμέν	ἦμεν or ἤμεθα	ἐσόμεθα
2P	ἐστέ	ἦτε	ἔσεσθε
3P	εἰσί(ν)	ἦσαν	ἔσονται

Non-indicative

	Present [Active] Subjunctive	Present [Active] Imperative	Present [Middle] Optative
1S	ὦ	—	εἴην
2S	ᾖς	ἴσθι	εἴης
3S	ᾖ	ἔστω	εἴη
1P	ὦμεν	—	εἶμεν or εἴημεν
2P	ἦτε	ἔστε	εἶτε or εἴητε
3P	ὦσι(ν)	ἔστωσαν	εἶεν or εἴησαν

Present [Active] Infinitive

εἶναι

Present [Active] Participle

	Masc.	Fem.	Neut.
NS	ὤν	οὖσα	ὄν
GS	ὄντος	οὔσης	ὄντος
DS	ὄντι	οὔσῃ	ὄντι
AS	ὄντα	οὖσαν	ὄν
NP	ὄντες	οὖσαι	ὄντα
GP	ὄντων	οὐσῶν	ὄντων
DP	οὖσι(ν)	οὔσαις	οὖσι(ν)
AP	ὄντας	οὔσας	ὄντα

μι Verbs

A.30. Indicatives of the μι Verbs

Active Indicative of δίδωμι (Stem δο-)

	Present	Imperfect	Future	First Aorist	Second Aorist	Perfect
1S	δίδωμι[a]	ἐδίδουν	δώσω	ἔδωκα	ἔδων	δέδωκα
2S	δίδως	ἐδίδους	δώσεις	ἔδωκας	ἔδως	δέδωκας
3S	δίδωσι(ν)	ἐδίδου	δώσει	ἔδωκε(ν)	ἔδω	δέδωκε(ν)
1P	δίδομεν	ἐδίδομεν	δώσομεν	ἐδώκαμεν	ἔδομεν	δεδώκαμεν
2P	δίδοτε	ἐδίδοτε	δώσετε	ἐδώκατε	ἔδοτε	δεδώκατε
3P	διδόασι(ν)	ἐδίδοσαν or ἐδίδουν	δώσουσι(ν)	ἔδωκαν	ἔδοσαν	δέδωκαν

[a] The 1SPAS occurs once in the NT (Rev. 3:9) as διδῶ.

Middle Indicative of δίδωμι (Stem δο-)

	Present[a]	Imperfect[a]	Aorist	Future	Perfect[a]
1S	δίδομαι	ἐδιδόμην	ἐδόμην	δώσομαι	δέδομαι
2S	δίδοσαι	ἐδίδοσο	ἔδου	δώσῃ	δέδοσαι
3S	δίδοται	ἐδίδοτο	ἔδοτο	δώσεται	δέδοται
1P	διδόμεθα	ἐδιδόμεθα	ἐδόμεθα	δωσόμεθα	δεδόμεθα
2P	δίδοσθε	ἐδίδοσθε	ἔδοσθε	δώσεσθε	δέδοσθε
3P	δίδονται	ἐδίδοντο	ἔδοντο	δώσονται	δέδονται

[a] May be passive if there is an agent marker in the context.

Passive Indicative of δίδωμι (Stem δο-)

	Aorist	Future
1S	ἐδόθην	δοθήσομαι
2S	ἐδόθης	δοθήσῃ
3S	ἐδόθη	δοθήσεται
1P	ἐδόθημεν	δοθησόμεθα
2P	ἐδόθητε	δοθήσεσθε
3P	ἐδόθησαν	δοθήσονται

Active Indicative of ἵστημι (Stem στα-)

	Present	Imperfect	Future	First Aorist	Second Aorist	Perfect
1S	ἵστημι	ἵστην	στήσω	ἔστησα	ἔστην	ἕστηκα[b]
2S	ἵστης	ἵστης	στήσεις	ἔστησας	ἔστης	ἕστηκας
3S	ἵστησι(ν)	ἵστη	στήσει	ἔστησε(ν)	ἔστη	ἕστηκε(ν)
1P	ἵσταμεν[a]	ἵσταμεν	στήσομεν	ἐστήσαμεν	ἔστημεν	ἑστήκαμεν
2P	ἵστατε	ἵστατε	στήσετε	ἐστήσατε	ἔστητε	ἑστήκατε
3P	ἱστᾶσι(ν)	ἵστασαν	στήσουσι(ν)	ἔστησαν	ἔστησαν	ἑστήκασι(ν)

[a] In the NT the 1PPAI form occurs only once (Rom. 3:31), and it is an ω form: ἱστάνομεν.
[b] ἑ (rough breathing) = reduplication; contrast ἐ (smooth breathing) = augment in aorist

Several present and imperfect forms are identical; only context can determine the probable tense.

Future Middle of ἵστημι

1S	στήσομαι
2S	στήσῃ
3S	στήσεται
1P	στησόμεθα
2P	στήσεσθε
3P	στήσονται

Active Indicative of τίθημι (Stem θε-)

	Present	Imperfect	Future	Aorist	Perfect
1S	τίθημι	ἐτίθην	θήσω	ἔθηκα	τέθεικα
2S	τίθης	ἐτίθεις	θήσεις	ἔθηκας	τέθεικας
3S	τίθησι(ν)	ἐτίθει	θήσει	ἔθηκε(ν)	τέθεικε(ν)
1P	τίθεμεν	ἐτίθεμεν	θήσομεν	ἐθήκαμεν	τεθείκαμεν
2P	τίθετε	ἐτίθετε	θήσετε	ἐθήκατε	τεθείκατε
3P	τιθέασι(ν)	ἐτίθεσαν or ἐτίθουν	θήσουσι(ν)	ἔθηκαν	τεθείκασι(ν)

Middle and Passive Indicative of τίθημι (Stem θε-)

	Present Middle	Imperfect Middle	Future Middle	Aorist Middle
1S	τίθεμαι	ἐτιθέμην	θήσομαι	ἐθέμην
2S	τίθεσαι	ἐτίθεσο	θήσῃ	ἔθου
3S	τίθεται	ἐτίθετο	θήσεται	ἔθετο
1P	τιθέμεθα	ἐτιθέμεθα	θησόμεθα	ἐθέμεθα
2P	τίθεσθε	ἐτίθεσθε	θήσεσθε	ἔθεσθε
3P	τίθενται	ἐτίθεντο	θήσονται	ἔθεντο

	Perfect Middle	Aorist Passive	Future Passive
1S	τέθειμαι	ἐτέθην	τεθήσομαι
2S	τέθεισαι	ἐτέθης	τεθήσῃ
3S	τέθειται	ἐτέθη	τεθήσεται
1P	τεθείμεθα	ἐτέθημεν	τεθησόμεθα
2P	τέθεισθε	ἐτέθητε	τεθήσεσθε
3P	τέθεινται	ἐτέθησαν	τεθήσονται

Pluperfect Active Indicative

There are a few pluperfect forms of δίδωμι and ἵστημι in the NT and LXX but none of τίθημι:

Word	Parsing Abbreviation	Frequency	
		NT	LXX
δεδώκειν	1SLAI		1
δεδώκει	3SLAI	2	1
δεδώκεισαν	3PLAI	1	
εἱστήκειν	1SLAI		2
εἱστήκεις	2SLAI		1
εἱστήκει	3SLAI	7	27 (+ once as ἑστήκει)
εἱστήκειμεν	1PLAI		1
εἱστήκεισαν	3PLAI	7	10

Present Active Indicative of Other μι Verbs

	δείκνυμι	φημί	ἀφίημι	ἀπόλλυμι	συνίημι
1S	δείκνυμι	φημί	ἀφίημι	ἀπόλλυμι	συνίημι
2S	δεικνύεις[a]	φῄς	ἀφεῖς	ἀπόλλεις	—
3S	δείκνυσι(ν)	φησί(ν)	ἀφίησι(ν)	ἀπολλύει[b]	συνίει
1P	δείκνυμεν	φαμέν	ἀφίομεν	ἀπόλλυμεν	—
2P	δείκνυτε	φατέ	ἀφίετε	ἀπόλλυτε	συνίετε
3P	δεικνύασι(ν)	φασί(ν)	ἀφίουσι(ν)	—	συνιᾶσι(ν)[c]

[a] Alt. form, δείκνυς

[b] Alt. form, ἀπόλλυσι(ν)

[c] Alt. form, συνίουσι(ν)

— = not attested in Koine texts related to the Bible

A.31. Subjunctives of the μι Verbs

Active Subjunctives

	δίδωμι			ἵστημι		τίθημι	
	Present	First Aorist	Second Aorist	Present	First Aorist	Present	Second Aorist
1S	διδῶ	δώσω	δῶ	ἱστῶ	στήσω	τιθῶ	θῶ
2S	διδῷς	δώσῃς	δῷς	ἱστῇς	στήσῃς	τιθῇς	θῇς
3S	διδῷ	δώσῃ	δῷ[a]	ἱστῇ	στήσῃ	τιθῇ	θῇ
1P	διδῶμεν	δώσωμεν	δῶμεν	ἱστῶμεν	στήσωμεν	τιθῶμεν	θῶμεν
2P	διδῶτε	δώσητε	δῶτε	ἱστῆτε	στήσητε	τιθῆτε	θῆτε
3P	διδῶσι(ν)	δώσωσι(ν)	δῶσι(ν)	ἱστῶσι(ν)	στήσωσι(ν)	τιθῶσι(ν)	θῶσι(ν)

[a] There are two alternate third singular forms of the aorist active subjunctive of δίδωμι: δοῖ and δώῃ.

Middle Subjunctives

	Present[a]			Second Aorist		
	δίδωμι	ἵστημι	τίθημι	δίδωμι	ἵστημι	τίθημι
1S	διδῶμαι	ἱστῶμαι	τιθῶμαι	δῶμαι	στῶμαι	θῶμαι
2S	διδῷ	ἱστῇ	τιθῇ	δῷ	στῇ	θῇ
3S	διδῶται	ἱστῆται	τιθῆται	δῶται	στῆται	θῆται
1P	διδώμεθα	ἱστώμεθα	τιθώμεθα	δώμεθα	στώμεθα	θώμεθα
2P	διδῶσθε	ἱστῆσθε	τιθῆσθε	δῶσθε	στῆσθε	θῆσθε
3P	διδῶνται	ἱστῶνται	τιθῶνται	δῶνται	στῶνται	θῶνται

[a] May be passive if there is an agent marker in the context.

Aorist Passive Subjunctives

	δίδωμι	ἵστημι	τίθημι
1S	δοθῶ	σταθῶ	τεθῶ
2S	δοθῇς	σταθῇς	τεθῇς
3S	δοθῇ	σταθῇ	τεθῇ
1P	δοθῶμεν	σταθῶμεν	τεθῶμεν
2P	δοθῆτε	σταθῆτε	τεθῆτε
3P	δοθῶσι(ν)	σταθῶσι(ν)	τεθῶσι(ν)

A.32. Imperatives of the μι Verbs

Present and Aorist Active Imperatives

	Present			Aorist		
	δίδωμι	ἵστημι	τίθημι	δίδωμι	ἵστημι	τίθημι
2S	δίδου	ἵστη	τίθει	δός	στῆθι or στῆσον	θές
3S	διδότω	ἱστάτω	τιθέτω	δότω	στήτω	θέτω
2P	δίδοτε	ἵστατε	τίθετε	δότε	στῆτε or στήσατε	θέτε
3P	διδότωσαν	ἱστάτωσαν	τιθέτωσαν	δότωσαν	στήτωσαν	θέτωσαν

Present and Aorist Middle Imperatives

	Present			Aorist	
	δίδωμι	ἵστημι	τίθημι	δίδωμι	τίθημι
2S	δίδοσο	ἵστασο	τίθεσο	δοῦ	θοῦ
3S	διδόσθω	ἱστάσθω	τιθέσθω	δόσθω	θέσθω
2P	δίδοσθε	ἵστασθε	τίθεσθε	δόσθε	θέσθε
3P	διδόσθωσαν	ἱστάσθωσαν	τιθέσθωσαν	δόσθωσαν	θέσθωσαν

Note: There are no aor. mid. imperatives of ἵστημι in the NT or LXX.

A.33. Optatives of the μι Verbs

The only optative μι verbs that occur in the NT are δῴη, 3SAAO ▸ δίδωμι; ὀναίμην, 1SAMO ▸ ὀνίνημι; and εἴη, 3SPAO ▸ εἰμί. In the LXX the only optative forms of common μι verbs that occur more than once are δῴη, 3SAAO ▸ δίδωμι; and προσθείη, 3SAAO ▸ προστίθημι.

A.34. Infinitives of the μι Verbs

The infinitive forms of only the three major μι verbs and their compounds occurring in the NT and LXX are given here.

Active Infinitives

	δίδωμι	ἵστημι	τίθημι
Present	διδόναι	ἱστάναι	τιθέναι
First Aorist	—	στῆσαι	—
Second Aorist	δοῦναι	στῆναι	θεῖναι
Perfect	—	ἑστάναι or ἑστηκέναι/ ἑστακέναι	—
Future	δώσειν	στήσειν	θήσειν

Middle and Passive Infinitives

	δίδωμι	ἵστημι	τίθημι
Present Middle	δίδοσθαι	ἵστασθαι	τίθεσθαι
Second Aorist Middle	δόσθαι	στήσασθαι	θέσθαι
Perfect Middle	δεδόσθαι	—	—
Aorist Passive	δοθῆναι	σταθῆναι	τεθῆναι
Future Passive	—	σταθήσεσθαι	—
Future Middle	—	στήσεσθαι	—

A.35. Participles of the μι Verbs

Imperfective (Present) Active Participle of δίδωμι and ἵστημι

	δίδωμι			ἵστημι		
	Masc.	Fem.	Neut.	Masc.	Fem.	Neut.
NS	διδούς	διδοῦσα	διδόν	ἱστάς	ἱστᾶσα	ἱστάν
GS	διδόντος	διδούσης	διδόντος	ἱστάντος	ἱστάσης	ἱστάντος
DS	διδόντι	διδούσῃ	διδόντι	ἱστάντι	ἱστάσῃ	ἱστάντι
AS	διδόντα	διδοῦσαν	διδόν	ἱστάντα	ἱστᾶσαν	ἱστάν
NP	διδόντες	διδοῦσαι	διδόντα	ἱστάντες	ἱστᾶσαι	ἱστάντα
GP	διδόντων	διδουσῶν	διδόντων	ἱστάντων	ἱστασῶν	ἱστάντων
DP	διδοῦσι(ν)	διδούσαις	διδοῦσι(ν)	ἱστᾶσι(ν)	ἱστάσαις	ἱστᾶσι(ν)
AP	διδόντας	διδούσας	διδόντα	ἱστάντας	ἱστάσας	ἱστάντα

Only the form ἱστῶν (PAPMSN) occurs as a participle in the LXX; this is a developing ω formation ▶ ἱστάνω.

Imperfective (Present) Active Participle of τίθημι

	Masc.	Fem.	Neut.
NS	τιθείς	τιθεῖσα	τιθέν
GS	τιθέντος	τιθείσης	τιθέντος
DS	τιθέντι	τιθείσῃ	τιθέντι
AS	τιθέντα	τιθεῖσαν	τιθέν
NP	τιθέντες	τιθεῖσαι	τιθέντα
GP	τιθέντων	τιθεισῶν	τιθέντων
DP	τιθεῖσι(ν)	τιθείσαις	τιθεῖσι(ν)
AP	τιθέντας	τιθείσας	τιθέντα

Perfective (Aorist) Active Participle of δίδωμι

	Masc.	Fem.	Neut.
NS	δούς	δοῦσα	δόν
GS	δόντος	δούσης	δόντος
DS	δόντι	δούσῃ	δόντι
AS	δόντα	δοῦσαν	δόν
NP	δόντες	δοῦσαι	δόντα
GP	δόντων	δουσῶν	δόντων
DP	δοῦσι(ν)	δούσαις	δοῦσι(ν)
AP	δόντας	δούσας	δόντα

Perfective (First and Second Aorist) Active and Passive Participles of ἵστημι

	First Aorist Active			Second Aorist Active			Passive
	Masc.	Fem.	Neut.	Masc.	Fem.	Neut.	Masc.
NS	στήσας	στήσασα	στῆσαν	στάς	στᾶσα	στάν	σταθείς
GS	στήσαντος	στησάσης	στήσαντος	στάντος	στάσης	στάντος	σταθέντος
DS	στήσαντι	στησάσῃ	στήσαντι	στάντι	στάσῃ	στάντι	σταθέντι
AS	στήσαντα	στήσασαν	στῆσαν	στάντα	στᾶσαν	στάν	σταθέντα
NP	στήσαντες	στήσασαι	στήσαντα	στάντες	στᾶσαι	στάντα	σταθέντες
GP	στησάντων	στησασῶν	στησάντων	στάντων	στασῶν	στάντων	σταθέντων
DP	στήσασι(ν)	στησάσαις	στήσασι(ν)	στάσι(ν)	στάσαις	στάσι(ν)	σταθεῖσι(ν)
AP	στήσαντας	στησάσας	στήσαντα	στάντας	στάσας	στάντα	σταθέντας

Perfective (Aorist) Active Participle of τίθημι

	Masc.	Fem.	Neut.
NS	θείς	θεῖσα	θέν
GS	θέντος	θείσης	θέντος
DS	θέντι	θείσῃ	θέντι
AS	θέντα	θεῖσαν	θέν
NP	θέντες	θεῖσαι	θέντα
GP	θέντων	θεισῶν	θέντων
DP	θεῖσι(ν)	θείσαις	θεῖσι(ν)
AP	θέντας	θείσας	θέντα

There is also one aorist middle participle of τίθημι in the NT, the MNS θέμενος.

Stative (Perfect) Active Participle of ἵστημι

	[1]Pf. Masc.	[1]Pf. Neut.	[2]Pf. Masc.	[2]Pf. Fem.	[2]Pf. Neut.
NS	ἑστηκώς	ἑστηκός	ἑστώς	ἑστῶσα	ἑστός
GS	ἑστηκότος	ἑστηκότος	ἑστῶτος	ἑστώσης	ἑστῶτος
DS	ἑστηκότι	ἑστηκότι	ἑστῶτι	ἑστώσῃ	ἑστῶτι
AS	ἑστηκότα	ἑστηκός	ἑστῶτα	ἑστῶσαν	ἑστός
NP	ἑστηκότες	ἑστηκότα	ἑστῶτες	ἑστῶσαι	ἑστῶτα
GP	ἑστηκότων	ἑστηκότων	ἑστώτων	ἑστωσῶν	ἑστώτων
DP	ἑστηκόσιν	ἑστηκόσιν	ἑστῶσι(ν)	ἑστώσαις	ἑστῶσι(ν)
AP	ἑστηκότας	ἑστηκότα	ἑστῶτας	ἑστώσας	ἑστῶτα

There is one [1]RAPFSN in the LXX: ἑστηκυῖα. There are only a few perfect active participle forms of the other μι verbs in the NT and LXX—δίδωμι: δεδωκότες, RAPMPN; δεδωκότας, RAPMPA; and τίθημι: τεθεικώς, RAPMSN.

Perfective (Aorist) Passive Participle of δίδωμι

	Masc.	Fem.	Neut.
NS	δοθείς	δοθεῖσα	δοθέν
GS	δοθέντος	δοθείσης	δοθέντος
DS	δοθέντι	δοθείσῃ	δοθέντι
AS	δοθέντα	δοθεῖσαν	δοθέν
NP	δοθέντες	δοθεῖσαι	δοθέντα
GP	δοθέντων	δοθεισῶν	δοθέντων
DP	δοθεῖσιν	δοθείσαις	δοθεῖσιν
AP	δοθέντας	δοθείσας	δοθέντα

Perfective (Aorist) Passive Participles of ἵστημι and τίθημι

For the forms of ἵστημι, simply replace the stem δο- above with στα-. There are no aorist passive forms of τίθημι in the NT or LXX, though they do occur in other Koine texts (e.g., the Pseudepigrapha, Josephus, Philo, and the Apostolic Fathers). The stem τε- is used (instead of the usual θε-): τεθείς, τεθέντος, and so forth.

Stative (Perfect) Middle (or Passive) Participles

The perfect middle (or passive) participles are easy to identify, though they are scarce in both the NT and LXX; the pattern is δε + δο + μέν + ος. Second-declension endings are used for the masculine and neuter, first-declension for feminine. The pattern is very regular and easy to identify. In the NT there are only two such forms of δίδωμι: δεδομένον, RPPNSN; and δεδομένην, RPPFSA. The variety in the LXX is slightly greater, but there are still only fifteen total instances. For τίθημι there is only one such form in the NT (τεθειμένος, RPPMSN), and there are none in the LXX. Likewise, there is only one form of ἵστημι in the LXX (none in the NT): ἑσταμένους, RMPMPA.

Appendix B

Morphology Catalog of Common Koine Verbs

B.1. The following catalog provides two lists. The first list gives selected forms of the most common verbs in the NT and LXX (all those occurring 25+ times in the NT or 100+ in LXX, with a few additional forms, especially some that occur in the reading exercises). Many forms for other Koine texts related to the Bible are also included (OT Pseudepigrapha, Josephus, Philo, Apostolic Fathers), though not as completely. This is not a principal-parts chart, which lists the regular forms in each of the six categories.[1] Although it includes many of those forms in the alphabetical listing, it also gives numerous other forms for the benefit of beginning students.

The second list consists of some odd forms that have various sorts of morphological changes. Most are completely regular in that they follow well-understood rules of morphology and inflection. They are odd only from the perspective of the beginning student, who has not yet learned to recognize all these seemingly complex changes. Some are encountered sufficiently infrequently that even experienced readers are sometimes puzzled. These forms are listed alphabetically with enough information to point the student to the correct entry. Some have complete parsings, but most have only enough to identify the lexical form. This second list is not restricted by the frequency parameters of the first list.

B.2. The catalog is intended as a supplement to Danker's *Concise Lexicon* (*CL*), which has a fairly extensive listing of these forms alphabetically but does not provide the more complete morphological information found in BDAG in the lexical entry for each verb. Although *CL* does have a much more extensive alphabetical listing of the odd forms than many lexicons, there are other forms

1. "Principal Parts" is a traditional system for identifying the various inflected forms of the verb. The system typically lists verbs in six columns in a fixed sequence: pres. act. ind., fut. act. ind., aor. act. ind., pf. act. ind., pf. mid. ind., aor. pass. ind. Reference is then made to these by their position in the list: for example, the "fourth principal part" is the pf. act. ind.

that are not included. Most forms listed alphabetically in *CL* are not repeated in the second list here.

The need for this sort of catalog may not seem obvious, since most people studying Greek these days have a computer program that provides full parsing for any word (usually Accordance, BibleWorks, or Logos). But there are useful purposes despite the availability of such software. First, you may not have access to a computer or the software (power outages are still part of life). Second, most software gives parsing for only individual words, and studying related forms is not as easy or at least as intuitive. Third, you may well have opportunity to read Greek texts that are not morphologically tagged (or you might not own a copy of that tagged text).

Not all forms listed occur in both the Old and New Testament, and some forms listed have, in addition to the ones here, other standard forms that follow the regular paradigm charts. Those that are listed, adapted from BDAG and supplemented from a number of other sources, have various changes from the lexical form that may puzzle beginners. These include not only different stems in the various tense-forms but other spelling changes (e.g., vowel contractions, square-of-stops forms) and morphological variants. A beginning student would not normally recognize many of these variant forms, and some of them occur only outside the NT.

B.3. All the finite forms listed are first singular unless noted otherwise (imperative forms are usually second singular; participles are masculine singular nominative). Where a form other than first singular is listed, either it is due to an anomaly of some sort or it may be the only form attested in Koine texts related to the NT. Aorist forms are first aorist unless marked as second aorist (^{2}A)—likewise with future or perfect forms. Often additional information for compound verbs may be found under the simple form. The sequence of forms is not rigid but generally follows voice order (active, middle, then passive), within which finite indicative forms are followed by non-indicatives, and lastly by non-finite forms.

Forms that have shared middle/passive morphology (sometimes referenced as *mediopassive*) are all cited here as middle, since contextual adjuncts are necessary to identify passive function. This differs from BDAG, which lists such forms as passive. This applies to present, imperfect, perfect, and pluperfect forms. Likewise θη forms are usually listed as passive, though they may well be middle depending on lexis and context.

Liquids identified below include both the technical liquids (stems endings in lambda or rho) and the nasals (mu and nu). For full explanations of the following categories, see the section noted in *MBG*: root aorist (§44.2c), Attic future (§43.7), Doric future (§43.8a), Attic reduplication (§32.6), and liquids (§§43.3, 44.1c).

B.4. Most Common Verbs in the New Testament and Septuagint

*αγαγ: root and aorist stem of ἄγω

ἀγαπάω (LXX 271; NT 143): IAI ἠγάπων; FAI ἀγαπήσω; AAI ἠγάπησα; RAI ἠγάπηκα; RAP ἠγαπηκώς; 3SLAI ἠγαπήκει; FPI ἀγαπηθήσομαι; 2SAPI ἠγαπήθης; RMP ἠγαπημένος

ἁγιάζω (LXX 192; NT 28): AAI ἡγίασα; AAM ἁγίασον; RAI ἡγίακα; FPI ἁγιασθήσομαι; API ἡγιάσθην; APM ἁγιασθήτω; RMI ἡγίασμαι; RMP ἡγιασμένος

ἀγοράζω (NT 30): IAI ἠγόραζον; 1PFAI ἀγοράσομεν; AAI ἠγόρασα; API ἠγοράσθην

ἄγω (LXX 254; NT 67): FAI ἄξω; ²AAI ἤγαγον; 3P²AAI ἤγαγαν or ἠγάγοσαν [AAI reduplicates instead of augments]; RAI ἀγήοχα; IMI ἠγόμην; RMI ἦγμαι; FPI ἀχθήσομαι; API ἤχθην; 3SRMI ἦκται; PAM ἄγε as interjection

ἀδικέω (NT 28): FAI ἀδικήσω; AAI ἠδίκησα; RAI ἠδίκηκα; 3SFPI ἀδικηθήσεται; API ἠδικήθην; RMP ἠδικημένος

αἰνέω (LXX 137): FAI αἰνέσω; AAI ᾔνεσα

αἴρω (LXX 280; NT 101) [liquid]: FAI ἀρῶ; AAI ᾖρα; RAI ἦρκα; RMI ἦρμαι; FPI ἀρθήσομαι; API ἤρθην

αἰτέω (NT 70): 2SPAM αἴτει; FAI αἰτήσω; AAI ᾔτησα; RAI ᾔτηκα; IMI ᾐτούμην; FMI αἰτήσομαι; AMI ᾐτησάμην; RMI ᾔτημαι; PMM αἰτοῦ; AMM αἴτησαι

ἀκολουθέω (NT 90): PAM ἀκολούθει; IAI ἠκολούθουν; FAI ἀκολουθήσω; AAI ἠκολούθησα; RAI ἠκολούθηκα

ἀκούω (LXX 1,014; NT 428): FAI ἀκούσω; FMI ἀκούσομαι; AAI ἤκουσα; ²RAI ἀκήκοα [Attic reduplication]; RAP ἠκουκώς; 3SRMI ἤκουσται; FPI ἀκουσθήσομαι; API ἠκούσθην

ἁμαρτάνω (LXX 258; NT 43): FAI ἁμαρτήσω; ²AAI ἥμαρτον, ²AAS ἁμάρτω; ¹AAI ἡμάρτησα; ¹AAS ἁμαρτήσω; ¹AAP ἁμαρτήσας; RAI ἡμάρτηκα; 1PRAI ἡμαρτήκαμεν; RMP neut. ἡμαρτημένα

ἀναβαίνω (LXX 614; NT 82): FMI ἀναβήσομαι; ²AAI ἀνέβην; RAI ἀναβέβηκα; ²AAM ἀνάβα; 2P²AAM ἀνάβατε or ἀνάβητε (see also **βαίνω**)

ἀναβλέπω (NT 25): FAI ἀναβλέψω; AAI ἀνέβλεψα; AAM ἀνάβλεψον

ἀναγγέλλω (LXX 230) [liquid]: FAI ἀναγγελῶ; AAI ἀνήγγειλα; AAN ἀναγγεῖλαι; RAI ἀνήγγελκα; 3SFPI ἀναγγελήσεται; ²API ἀνηγγέλην

ἀναγινώσκω (NT 32): FAI ἀναγνώσομαι; ²AAI ἀνέγνων; ²AAN ἀναγνῶναι; ²AAP ἀναγνούς; 3PFPI ἀναγνωσθήσονται; API ἀνεγνώσθην; 3SRMI ἀνέγνωσται; RMP ἀνεγνωσμένος

ἀνάγω (LXX 111): FAI ἀνάξω; ²AAI ἀνήγαγον; ¹API ἀνήχθην

ἀναστρέφω (LXX 106): FAI ἀναστρέψω; AAI ἀνέστρεψα; 3SFPI ἀναστραφήσεται; ²API ἀνεστράφην; ²APP ἀναστραφείς; 3SRMI ἀνέστραπται

ἀναφέρω (LXX 155): FAI ἀνοίσω; ²AAI ἀνήνεγκα or ἀνήνεγκον; RAI ἀνενήνοχα; FPI ἀνενεχθήσομαι; API ἀνηνέχθην

ἀνίστημι (LXX 473; NT 108): FAI ἀναστήσω; AAI ἀνέστησα; RAI ἀνέστακα; ²AAI ἀνέστην; ²AAM ἀνάστηθι or ἀνάστα; ²AAP ἀναστάς; FMI ἀναστήσομαι; API ἀνεστάθην; 3SAPS ἀνασταθῇ; APP neut. ἀνασταθέντα

ἀνοίγω (LXX 165; NT 77): FAI ἀνοίξω; AAI ἀνέῳξα, ἠνέῳξα, or ἤνοιξα; ^{2}RAI ἀνέῳγα; RMI ἀνέῳγμαι or ἠνέῳγμαι [R forms beginning ἠνεῳ- have double reduplication]; RMP ἀνεῳγμένος, ἠνεῳγμένος, or ἠνοιγμένος; AAN ἀνοῖξαι; RMN ἀνεῴχθαι; ^{1}API ἠνεῴχθην, ἀνεῴχθην, or ἠνοίχθην; ^{1}APN ἀνεῳχθῆναι or ἀνοιχθῆναι; FPI ἀνοιχθήσομαι; ^{2}API ἠνοίγην, ἠνοίχθησαν, or ἠνοίχθη; ^{2}FPI ἀνοιγήσομαι

ἀνταποδο-: stem of ἀνταποδίδωμι

ἀπαγγέλλω (LXX 232; NT 45) [liquid]: IAI ἀπήγγελλον; FAI ἀπαγγελῶ; ^{1}AAI ἀπήγγειλα; RAI ἀπήγγελκα; RAP ἀπηγγελκότες; 3S^{1}API ἀπηγγέλθη; ^{2}API ἀπηγγέλην

ἀπαίρω (LXX 118) [liquid]: FAI ἀπαρῶ; AAI ἀπῆρα; RAI ἀπῆρκα; API ἀπήρθην

ἀπέρχομαι (LXX 217; NT 117): FMI ἀπελεύσομαι; ^{2}AAI ἀπῆλθον; 3P^{2}AAI ἀπῆλθαν, ἀπήλθασιν, or ἀπήλθοσαν; RAI ἀπελήλυθα [Attic reduplication]; RAP ἀπεληλυθώς; LAP ἀπεληλύθειν

ἀποδίδωμι (LXX 206; NT 48): PAP ἀποδιδοῦν; IAI ἀπεδίδουν; FAI ἀποδώσω; ^{1}AAI ἀπέδωκα; 2S^{2}AAS ἀποδῷς; 3S^{2}AAS ἀποδῷ or ἀποδοῖ; ^{2}AAM ἀπόδος or ἀπόδοτε; ^{2}AMI ἀπεδόμην; 3S^{2}AMI ἀπέδετο; FPI ἀποδοθήσομαι; ^{1}API ἀπεδόθην; ^{1}APN ἀποδοθῆναι; PPP ἀποδεδομένος

ἀποδο-: stem of ἀποδίδωμι

ἀποθνῄσκω (LXX 546; NT 111) [liquid stem in future]: IAI ἀπέθνησκον; FMI ἀποθανοῦμαι; ^{2}AAI ἀπέθανον; 3SRAI ἀποτέθνηκεν

ἀποκαλύπτω (LXX 100; NT 26): FAI ἀποκαλύψω; AAI ἀπεκάλυψα; FPI ἀποκαλυφθήσομαι; API ἀπεκαλύφθην; RMP pl. ἀποκεκαλυμμένοι

ἀποκρίνομαι (LXX 246; NT 231) [liquid]: AMI ἀπεκρινάμην; FPI ἀποκριθήσομαι; AMI ἀπεκρίθην (a θη-middle form)

ἀποκτείνω (LXX 212; NT 74) [liquid]: FAI ἀποκτενῶ; AAI ἀπέκτεινα; API ἀπεκτάνθην; RMP ἀπεκταμμένων; RMN ἀπεκτάνθαι or ἀπεκτονῆσθαι

ἀποκυλίω: (LXX 4; NT 4) 3SRMI ἀποκεκύλισμαι (the σ reflects an old Attic spelling)

ἀπόλλυμι (LXX 366; NT 90): FAI ἀπολέσω; Attic future ἀπολῶ; ^{1}AAI ἀπώλεσα; ^{1}RAI ἀπολώλεκα; ^{2}RAI ἀπόλωλα; FMI ἀπολοῦμαι; ^{2}AMI ἀπωλόμην; ^{2}RAI ἀπόλωλα; ^{2}RAP ἀπολωλώς

ἀπολύω (NT 66): IAI ἀπέλυον; FAI ἀπολύσω; AAI ἀπέλυσα; AAN ἀπολῦσαι; 1PRAI ἀπολελύκαμεν; RMI ἀπολέλυμαι; FPI ἀπολυθήσομαι; API ἀπελύθην

ἀποστέλλω (LXX 651; NT 132) [liquid]: FAI ἀποστελῶ; ^{1}AAI ἀπέστειλα; RAI ἀπέσταλκα; RMI ἀπέσταλμαι; ^{2}API ἀπεστάλην

ἀποστρέφω (LXX 450): FAI ἀποστρέψω; ^{1}AAI ἀπέστρεψα; FPI ἀποστραφήσομαι LXX; ^{2}API ἀπεστράφην; RMI ἀπέστραμμαι

ἅπτω (LXX 122; NT 39): AAI ἧψα; AAP ἅψας; FMI ἅψομαι; AMI ἡψάμην; 3SRMI ἧπται; RMP ἡμμένος; 3SFPI ἀφθήσεται

ἀρνέομαι (NT 33): FMI ἀρνήσομαι; AMI ἠρνησάμην; RMI ἤρνημαι

ἄρχω (NT 86): FAI ἄρξω; AAI ἦρξα; FMI ἄρξομαι; AMI ἠρξάμην; RMI ἦργμαι

ἀσθενέω (NT 33): FAI ἀσθενήσω; AAI ἠσθένησα; RAP ἠσθενικός

ἀσπάζομαι (NT 59): FMP ἀσπασομένους; AMI ἠσπασάμην

ἀφαιρέω (LXX 165): ^{2}FAI ἀφελῶ; ^{2}AAI ἀφεῖλον; ^{2}AAN ἀφελεῖν; ^{2}AMI ἀφειλόμην [ἀφειλάμην in LXX, usually 3P ἀφείλαντο]; ^{1}FPI ἀφαιρεθήσομαι; ^{1}API ἀφῃρέθην; RMI ἀφῄρημαι

ἀφίημι (LXX 125; NT 143): 2SPAI ἀφεῖς or ἀφίεις; 3SPAI ἀφίησιν or ἀφίει; 1PPAI ἀφίομεν or ἀφίεμεν; 3PPAI ἀφίουσιν; 2SIAI ἠφίεις; 3SIAI ἤφιε; FAI ἀφήσω; AAI ἀφῆκα; 2SAAI ἀφῆκες; AAM ἄφησον; 2S^{2}AAM ἄφες; 2P^{2}AAM ἄφετε; AAS ἀφῶ; 2PAAS ἀφῆτε; AAN ἀφεῖναι; PAP ἀφίοντες; AAP ἀφείς; 3PRMI ἀφέωνται; 2SAMM ἄφησαι; 3SRMM ἀφείσθω; FPI ἀφεθήσομαι; ^{1}API ἀφέθην; 3S^{1}API ἀφείθη

ἀφίστημι (LXX 218): 3SPAI ἀφιστᾷ; 3PPAI ἀφιστῶσι; PAP fem. ἀφιστῶσα; FAI ἀποστήσω; ^{1}AAI ἀπέστησα; ^{2}AAI ἀπέστην; AAM ἀπόστα; RAI ἀφέστηκα; RAP ἀφεστηκώς; RAPMPN ἀφεστῶτες; FMI ἀποστήσομαι; RMI ἀφίσταμαι; RMM ἀφίστασο; RMP ἀφέστακα

ἀχθη-: See **ἄγω**

βαίνω [liquid in present stem only]: only compounds in NT and mostly compound forms elsewhere (ἀνα-, ἀπο-, δια-, ἐκ-, ἐμ-, ἐπι-, κατα-, μετα-, παρα-, προ-, προσ-, προσανα-, συνκατα-, συμ-, συνανα-, ὑπερ-); see forms s.v. **ἀναβαίνω**, **διαβαίνω**, and **καταβαίνω**. Root and aorist/future/perfect stem βα-; second aorist forms of βαίνω use μι verb patterns (Smyth, *Greek Grammar*, §687), may be called a *root aorist* since personal endings attach directly to stem (as μι verbs do).

***βαλ**: root and aorist stem of βάλλω

βάλλω (NT 122) [liquid]: FAI βαλῶ; ^{2}AAI ἔβαλον; 3P^{2}AAI ἔβαλον or ἔβαλαν; RAI βέβληκα; FPI βληθήσομαι; API ἐβλήθην; RMI βέβλημαι; LMI ἐβεβλήμην

βαπτίζω (NT 77): FAI βαπτίσω; AAI ἐβάπτισα; AMI ἐβαπτισάμην; IMI ἐβαπτιζόμην; FPI βαπτισθήσομαι; API ἐβαπτίσθην; RMP βεβαπτισμένος

βασιλεύω (LXX 389): FAI βασιλεύσω; AAI ἐβασίλευσα; 3SRAI βεβασίλευκεν

βαστάζω (NT 27): FAI βαστάσω; AAI ἐβάστασα or ἐβάσταξα

βλασφημέω (NT 34): IAI ἐβλασφήμουν; AAI ἐβλασφήμησα; FPI βλασφημηθήσομαι; API ἐβλασφημήθην

βλέπω (LXX 123; NT 132): FAI βλέψω; 3PFMI βλέψονται; AAI ἔβλεψα

βλη-: perfect and aorist passive stem of βάλλω (technically a modified form of *βαλ)

βοάω (LXX 134): IAI ἐβόων; FAI βοήσω; AAI ἐβόησα; AAM βόησον

βοηθέω (LXX 105): FAI βοηθήσω; AAI ἐβοήθησα; AAM βοήθησον; FPI βοηθηθήσομαι; API ἐβοηθήθην

βούλομαι (LXX 121; NT 37): 2SPMI βούλῃ or βούλει; IMI ἐβουλόμην or ἠβουλόμην; 3SFMI βουλήσεται; API ἐβουλήθην or ἠβουλήθην; RMN βεβουλῆσθαι

γαμέω (NT 28): IAI ἐγάμουν; AAI ἔγημα or ἐγάμησα; AAN γῆμαι; AAS γήμω; 3SAAS γαμήσῃ; AAP γήμας; RAI γεγάμηκα; 3SLMI γεγάμητο or ἐγεγάμητο; AMN γήμασθαι; API ἐγαμήθην

***γεν**: root and aorist stem of γίνομαι (≠ γεννάω)

γεννάω (LXX 251; NT 97): FAI γεννήσω; AAI ἐγέννησα; RAI γεγέννηκα; 2PFPI γεννηθήσεσθε; API ἐγεννήθην; RMI γεγέννημαι

γίνομαι (LXX 2,077; NT 669): IMI ἐγινόμην; FMI γενήσομαι; ^{2}AMI ἐγενόμην; ^{2}RAI γέγονα; 3P^{2}RAI γέγοναν or γεγόνασιν; ^{2}RAP γεγονώς; 3SLAI ἐγεγόνει or without augment γεγόνει; 3SAAO γένοιτο; RMI γεγένημαι; AMP γενόμενος;

FPP γενηθησομένων; ^{1}API ἐγενήθην; APM γενηθήτω (This verb is technically a liquid, but it follows regular formation for future and aorist.)

γινώσκω (LXX 690; NT 222): IAI ἐγίνωσκον; FMI γνώσομαι; 1S^{2}AAI ἔγνων; RAI ἔγνωκα; 3PRAI ἔγνωκαν; 2PLAI ἐγνώκειτε; ^{2}AAM γνῶθι, γνώτω; 1&3 ^{2}AAS γνῷ [3S alt. γνοῖ]; 2S^{2}AAS γνώσῃς; 1S^{2}AAO γνῴην; 3S^{2}AAO γνοίη; ^{2}AAN γνῶναι; ^{2}AAP γνούς; RMI ἔγνωσμαι; FPI γνωσθήσομαι; API ἐγνώσθην (This verb is technically a root aorist; it is conventionally listed as second aorist.)

***γνω**: root and future, aorist, and perfect stem of γινώσκω

γνωρίζω (NT 25): FAI γνωρίσω or γνωριῶ; AAI ἐγνώρισα; AMI ἐγνωρισάμην; FPI γνωρισθήσομαι; API ἐγνωρίσθην; 3SRMI ἐγνώρισται

γράφω (LXX 291; NT 191): IAI ἔγραφον; FAI γράψω; ^{1}AAI ἔγραψα; ^{2}RAI γέγραφα; 1PRAI γεγραφήκαμεν; RMI γέγραμμαι; 3SLMI ἐγέγραπτο; ^{2}API ἐγράφην

δεῖ (NT 101): IAI ἔδει; FAI δεήσει; PAS δέῃ; PAN δεῖν

δειγ-: See **δείκνυμι**

δείκνυμι/δεικνύω (LXX 121; NT 30): FAI δείξω; AAI ἔδειξα; AAM δεῖξον; ^{2}RAI δέδειχα; 3SFPI δειχθήσεται; 2PAPI ἐδείχθητε; APN δειχθῆναι; APP δειχθείς; 3SRMI δέδεικται; RMP δεδειγμένον

δειξ- or **δειχ-**: See **δείκνυμι**

δέχομαι (NT 56): FMI δέξομαι; 3SFPI δεχθήσεται; AMI ἐδεξάμην; RMI δέδεγμαι; API ἐδέχθην

δέω (NT 43): 3SPMI δεῖται; FAI δήσω; AAI ἔδησα; AAS δήσω; RAP δεδεκώς; APN δεθῆναι; RMI δέδεμαι

διαβαίνω (LXX 123) [liquid]: FMI διαβήσομαι; ^{2}AAI διέβην; AAP διαβάς (see also **βαίνω**)

διακονέω (NT 37): IAI διηκόνουν; FAI διακονήσω; AAI διηκόνησα; RAN δεδιηκονηκέναι; API διηκονήθην

διδάσκω (LXX 103; NT 97): IAI ἐδίδασκον; FAI διδάξω; AAI ἐδίδαξα; 3SRAI δεδίδαχεν; 1PRMI δεδιδάγμεθα; RMP δεδιδαγμένος; API ἐδιδάχθην

δίδωμι (LXX 1,991; NT 415); stem *δο: 3SPAI διδοῖ; 3PPAI διδόασιν; 3SIAI ἐδίδου or ἐδίδει; 3PIAI ἐδίδουν or ἐδίδοσαν; PAP διδῶν; FAI δώσω; ^{1}AAI ἔδωκα; 3S^{1}AAS δώσῃ; 1P^{1}AAS δώσωμεν; 3P^{1}AAS δώσωσιν; RAI δέδωκα; LAI ἐδεδώκειν or without augment δεδώκειν; 3S^{2}AAS δῷ, δώῃ, or δοῖ; ^{2}AAS 2S δῷς; 3S δῷ, δοῖ, or δώῃ; 1P δῶμεν; 3S^{2}AAO δῴη or δοίη; ^{2}AAM δός; 2P^{2}AAM δότε; ^{2}AAN δοῦναι; ^{2}AAP δούς; FPI δοθήσομαι; ^{1}API ἐδόθην; RMI δέδομαι

διέρχομαι (LXX 146; NT 43): IMI διηρχόμην; FMI διελεύσομαι; ^{2}AAI διῆλθον; RAI διελήλυθα [Attic reduplication]; RAN διεληλυθέναι; RAP διεληλυθώς

δικαιόω (NT 39): FAI δικαιώσω; AAI ἐδικαίωσα; RMI δεδικαίωμαι; RMP δεδικαιωμένος; FPI δικαιωθήσομαι; API ἐδικαιώθην; APS δικαιωθῶ; APP δικαιωθείς

διώκω (LXX 104; NT 45): IAI ἐδίωκον; FAI διώξω; AAI ἐδίωξα; RMP δεδιωγμένος; API ἐδιώχθην

***δο**: root of δίδωμι

δοκέω (NT 62): IAI ἐδόκουν; 3PIAI ἐδοκοῦσαν; FAI δόξω; AAI ἔδοξα; 3SRMI δέδοκται; RMP δεδογμένον

δοξάζω (LXX 136; NT 61): IAI ἐδόξαζον; FAI δοξάσω; AAI ἐδόξασα; AAM δόξασον; 1PRAI δεδοξάκαμεν; RMI δεδόξασμαι; API ἐδοξάσθην

δουλεύω (LXX 143; NT 25): FAI δουλεύσω; AAI ἐδούλευσα; RAI δεδούλευκα; RAP δεδουλευκώς

δύναμαι (LXX 305; NT 210): 2SPAI δύνῃ or δύνασαι; IMI ἠδυνάμην or ἐδυνάμην; FMI δυνήσομαι; API ἠδυνήθην, ἠδυνάσθην, or ἐδυνάσθην; 2PAPI ἐδυνήθητε; 3PAPI ἐδυνήθησαν; RMI δεδύνημαι

ἐγγίζω (LXX 148; NT 42): FAI ἐγγιῶ [Attic future]; AAI ἤγγισα, or with Attic reduplication ἐνήγγισα or ἠνήγγισα; 3PRAI ἠγγίκασιν

ἐγείρω (NT 144) [liquid]: FAI ἐγερῶ; AAI ἤγειρα; PMI ἐγείρομαι; RMI ἐγήγερμαι [Attic reduplication]; 2SPMM ἐγείρου; 2PPMM ἐγείρεσθε; FPI ἐγερθήσομαι; API ἠγέρθην

ἐγκαταλείπω (LXX 179): IAI ἐγκατέλειπον; FAI ἐγκαταλείψω; 3P^{1}AAI ἐγκατέλειψαν; ^{2}AAI ἐγκατέλιπον; ^{2}AAS ἐγκαταλίπω; RAI ἐγκαταλέλοιπα; FPI ἐγκαταλειφθήσομαι; ^{1}API ἐγκατελείφθην; 3SRMI ἐγκαταλέλειπται; RMP ἐγκαταλελειμμένος; RMN ἐγκαταλελεῖφθαι

ἐγνω-: augmented aorist *or* reduplicated perfect stem of γινώσκω

εἶδον [stem, unaugmented, ἰδ-]: functions as second aorist of ὁράω; mixed forms (second aorist stem with first aorist endings) are frequent along with other spelling variations: AAI εἶδα, εἴδαμεν, εἴδατε, εἶδαν; or ἴδον, ἴδες, ἴδεν, ἴδομεν, ἴδατε, ἴδετε; oblique moods: AAS ἴδω; AAO ἴδοιμι; AAM ἴδε; AAN ἰδεῖν; AAP ἰδών; AMN ἰδέσθαι

εἰμί (LXX 6,467; NT 2,462): 2SPMM ἴσθι or ἔσο; 3SPMM ἔστω or ἤτω; 3PPMM ἔστωσαν; PAN εἶναι; 1SIMI ἤμην; 2SIMI ἦσθα or ἦς; 3SIMI ἦν; 1PIMI ἤμεθα or ἦμεν; FMI ἔσομαι; FMP ἐσόμενος

εἶπον (LXX 4,190; NT 928): used as second aorist of λέγω; ^{2}AAS εἴπω; ^{2}AAM εἶπον; ^{2}AAN εἰπεῖν; ^{2}AAP εἰπών; sometimes takes first aorist endings: εἶπα, εἶπας, εἶπαν; ^{2}AAM εἰπόν or εἶπον; 3S^{2}AAM εἰπάτω; 2P^{2}AAM εἴπατε; 3P^{2}AAM εἰπάτωσαν; ^{2}AAP εἴπας; ^{2}AAP fem. εἴπασα; FAI ἐρῶ; RAI εἴρηκα; 3PRAI εἰρήκασιν or εἴρηκαν; RAN εἰρηκέναι; LAI εἰρήκειν; API ἐρρέθην or ἐρρήθην; APP ῥηθείς; RMI εἴρηται; RMP εἰρημένος

εἴρηκα: RAI of λέγω

εἰσάγω (LXX 153): FAI εἰσάξω; ^{2}AAI εἰσήγαγον; 2PRAI εἰσαγειόχατε; ^{2}API εἰσήχθην

εἰσακούω (LXX 238): FMI εἰσακούσομαι; AAI εἰσήκουσα; RAI εἰσακήκοα [Attic reduplication]; FPI εἰσακουσθήσομαι; API εἰσηκούσθην

εἰσέρχομαι (LXX 653; NT 194): FMI εἰσελεύσομαι; ^{2}AAI εἰσῆλθον or εἰσῆλθα; ^{2}AAM εἰσελθάτω; ^{2}RAI εἰσελήλυθα [Attic reduplication]; ^{2}RAP εἰσεληλυθώς; ^{2}LAI εἰσεληλύθει

εἰσπορεύομαι (LXX 157): IMI εἰσεπορευόμην; 1PFMI εἰσεπορευσόμεθα; 3SAMI εἰσεπορεύθη (a θη-middle form); RMI εἰσπεπόρευμαι

ἐκβάλλω (NT 81) [liquid]: FAI ἐκβαλῶ; ^{2}AAI ἐξέβαλον; RAI ἐκβέβληκα; LAI ἐκβεβλήκειν; 3SRMI ἐκβέβληται; RMP ἐκβεβλημένος; 1SFPI ἐκβληθήσομαι; API ἐξεβλήθην

ἐκζητέω (LXX 131): FAI ἐκζητήσω; AAI ἐξεζήτησα; RMP ἐξεζητημένα; FPI ἐκζητηθήσομαι; API ἐξεζητήθην

ἐκκλίνω (LXX 146) [liquid]: FAI ἐκκλινῶ; AAI ἐξέκλινα; 3SRAI ἐκκέκλικεν

ἐκλείπω (LXX 187): FAI ἐκλείψω; ^{2}AAI ἐξέλιπον; RAI ἐκλέλοιπα; RMP ἐκλελειμμένος

ἐκπορεύομαι (LXX 161; NT 33): IMI ἐξεπορευόμην; FMI ἐκπορεύσομαι; RMI ἐκπεπόρευμαι

ἐκτείνω (LXX 137) [liquid]: FAI ἐκτενῶ; AAI ἐξέτεινα; RAI ἐκτέτακα; RMP ἐκτεταμένος; 3SFPI ἐκταθήσεται; 3SAPI ἐξετάθη

ἐκχέω (LXX 140): FAI ἐκχεῶ [Attic future]; AAI ἐξέχεα; RAI ἐκκέχυκα; see also the related form ἐκχύν(ν)ω: FMI ἐκχυθήσομαι; API ἐξεχύθην; RMI ἐκκέχυμαι

ἐλεέω (LXX 132; NT 28): FAI ἐλεήσω; AAI ἠλέησα; AAM ἐλέησον; RMP ἠλεημένος; FPI ἐλεηθήσομαι; API ἠλεήθην

***ελευθ**: root and future and perfect stem of ἔρχομαι

ελθ-: derived aorist stem of ἔρχομαι (*ελευθ with ευ dropped); appears as ηλθ- with augment in indicative

ἐλπίζω (LXX 114; NT 31): FAI ἐλπιῶ [Attic future]; AAI ἤλπισα; RAI ἤλπικα

ἐμπίπλημι/ἐμπίμπλημι (LXX 146): FAI ἐμπλήσω; AAI ἐνέπλησα; 3SIMI ἐνεπίμπλατο; FPI ἐμπλησθήσομαι; API ἐνεπλήσθην; RMI ἐμπέπλησμαι; RMP ἐμπεπλησμένος; alt. form (from ἐμπιμπλάω) for PAP: ἐμπιπλῶν

ἐνδύω (LXX 113; NT 27): FAI ἐνδύσω; AAI ἐνέδυσα; RAP ἐνδεδυκώς; LAN ἐνδεδύκειν; FMI ἐνδύσομαι; AMI ἐνεδυσάμην; RMP ἐνδεδυμένος

ἐντέλλω (LXX 412) [liquid]: in Koine a middle-only verb; FMI ἐντελοῦμαι; AMI ἐνετειλάμην; RMI ἐντέταλμαι; 2SRMI ἐντέταλσαι; 3SLMI ἐνετέταλτο

ἐξάγω (LXX 216): FAI ἐξάξω; ²AAI ἐξήγαγον; 3S²FPI ἐξαχθήσεται; API ἐξήχθην

ἐξαιρέω (LXX 140): FAI ἐξελῶ; ²AAI ἐξεῖλον; ²AAM ἔξελε; FMI ἐξελοῦμαι; ²AMI ἐξειλάμην [rarely ἐξειλόμην]; ²AAN ἐξελέσθαι; 2SRMI ἐξῄρησαι; RMP ἐξῃρημένης; RMN ἐξῃρῆσθαι; 3SFPI ἐξαιρεθήσεται; 3PFPI ἐξαιρεθήσονται

ἐξαίρω (LXX 213) [liquid]: FAI ἐξαρῶ; AAI ἐξῆρα; 2PAAM ἐξάρατε; FPI ἐξαρθήσομαι; 3SAPI ἐξήρθη; 3SRMI ἐξῆρται; RMPMPA ἐξηρμένους

ἐξαποστέλλω (LXX 268) [liquid]: FAI ἐξαποστελῶ; AAI ἐξαπέστειλα; RAI ἐξαπέσταλκα; 3S²FPI ἐξαποσταλήσεται; ²APPNSN ἐξαποσταλέν; RMI ἐξαπέσταλμαι; RMP neut. pl. ἐξαπεσταλμένα

ἐξέρχομαι (LXX 669; NT 218): FMI ἐξελεύσομαι; ²AAI ἐξῆλθον or ἐξῆλθα; 3P²AAI ἐξήλθοσαν; RAI ἐξελήλυθα [Attic reduplication]

ἔξεστιν (NT 31): 3SPAI impersonal ἔξεστιν; 3SFMI ἐξέσται

ἐξιλάσκομαι (LXX 105): FMI ἐξιλάσομαι; AMI ἐξιλασάμην; 3SFPI ἐξιλασθήσεται

ἐξολεθρεύω (LXX 214): FAI ἐξολεθρεύσω; AAI ἐξωλέθρευσα; FPI ἐξολεθρευθήσομαι; API ἐξωλεθρεύθην

ἐξομολογέω (LXX 121): AAI ἐξωμολόγησα; FMI ἐξομολογήσομαι; AMI ἐξωμολογησάμην

ἐπάγω (LXX 143): FAI ἐπάξω; ¹AAP ἐπάξας; ²AAI ἐπήγαγον; RMP ἐπηγμένην; 3S¹APS ἐπάχθῃ; ¹APM ἐπάχθητι; ¹APP ἐπαχθείς

ἐπακούω (LXX 102): FMI ἐπακούσομαι; AAI ἐπήκουσα; 3SRAI ἐπακήκοε [Attic reduplication]; RAN ἐπακηκοέναι; 3SAPI ἐπηκούσθη

ἐπέρχομαι (LXX 108): FMI ἐπελεύσομαι; ²AAI ἐπῆλθον; 3P²AAI ἐπῆλθαν; 3SLAI ἐπεληλύθει

ἐπερωτάω (NT 56): IAI ἐπηρώτων; FAI ἐπερωτήσω; AAI ἐπηρώτησα; 2SAPS ἐπερωτηθῇς; APP ἐπερωτηθείς

ἐπιβλέπω (LXX 108): FAI ἐπιβλέψω; FMI ἐπιβλέψομαι; AAI ἐπέβλεψα; 3S[1]AAI ἐπέβλεψεν

ἐπιγινώσκω (LXX 144; NT 44): FMI ἐπιγνώσομαι; [2]AAI ἐπέγνων; RAI ἐπέγνωκα; [1]API ἐπεγνώσθην

ἐπικαλέω (LXX 184; NT 30): AAI ἐπεκάλεσα; FMI ἐπικαλέσομαι; AMI ἐπεκαλεσάμην; RMI ἐπικέκλημαι; 3SLMI ἐπεκέκλητο; RMP ἐπικεκλημένος; 3SFPI ἐπικληθήσεται; API ἐπεκλήθην

ἐπιλανθάνομαι (LXX 120): FMI ἐπιλήσομαι; [2]AMI ἐπελαθόμην; RMI ἐπιλέλησμαι; FPI ἐπιλησθήσομαι

ἐπισκέπτομαι (LXX 164): FMI ἐπισκέψομαι; AMI ἐπεσκεψάμην; RMI ἐπέσκεμμαι; 3SFPI ἐπισκεπήσεται or ἐπισκεφθήσεται; API ἐπεσκέπην; 3SAPS ἐπισκεφθῇ

ἐπιστρέφω (LXX 497; NT 36): FAI ἐπιστρέψω; [1]AAI ἐπέστρεψα; FPI ἐπιστραφήσομαι; [2]API ἐπεστράφην

ἐπιτίθημι (LXX 264; NT 39): 3PPAI ἐπιτιθέασιν; PAM ἐπιτίθει; 3PIAI ἐπετίθεσαν; FAI ἐπιθήσω; [1]AAI ἐπέθηκα; [2]AAI ἐπέθην; [2]AAM ἐπίθες; [1]AAP ἐπιθείς; FMI ἐπιθήσομαι; [2]AMI ἐπεθέμην

ἐπιτιμάω (NT 29): 3SIAI ἐπετίμα; 3PIAI ἐπετίμων; 2PFAI ἐπιτιμήσετε; AAI ἐπετίμησα; APP ἐπιτιμηθείς

ἐργάζομαι (LXX 120; NT 41): IMI ἠργαζόμην; 2SFMI ἐργᾷ; 3SFMI ἐργᾶται; 3PFMI ἐργῶνται; AMI εἰργασάμην; 3SRMI εἴργασται; RMP εἰργασμένος; 3SFPI ἐργασθήσεται

ἔρχομαι (LXX 978; NT 632): [2]AAI ἦλθον; "mixed" forms ([2]A stem with [1]A endings): 1S ἦλθα, 3P ἤλθοσαν; RAI ἐλήλυθα [Attic reduplication]; 3SLAI ἐληλύθει; IMI ἠρχόμην; FMI ἐλεύσομαι; PMM ἔρχου; 2PPMM ἔρχεσθε

ἐρωτάω (NT 63): FAI ἐρωτήσω; [1]AAI ἠρώτησα; [2]AMI ἠρόμην; RMP ἠρωτημένος; 3S[1]API ἠρωτήθη; APN ἐρωτηθῆναι, APP ἐρωτηθείς

ἐσθίω (LXX 607; NT 158): IAI ἤσθιον; [2]AAI ἔφαγον, sometimes with [1]A endings: 3P ἐφάγοσαν, 1P ἐφάγαμεν; PAP ἐσθίων; FMI ἔδομαι or φάγομαι; 2SFMI φάγεσαι; also spelled ἔσθω: 3SPMI ἔσθεται; 2PPAM ἔσθετε; 2PPAS ἔσθητε; PAP ἔσθων

ἑτοιμάζω (LXX 173; NT 40): FAI ἑτοιμάσω; AAI ἡτοίμασα; RAI ἡτοίμακα; RMI ἡτοίμασμαι; FPI ἑτοιμασθήσομαι; API ἡτοιμάσθην

εὐαγγελίζω (NT 54): FAI εὐαγγελιῶ; AAI εὐηγγέλισα; AAN εὐαγγελίσαι; PMI εὐαγγελίζομαι; IMI εὐηγγελιζόμην; FMI εὐαγγελιοῦμαι; AMI εὐηγγελισάμην; RMI εὐηγγέλισμαι; API εὐηγγελίσθην; APP neut. sg. εὐαγγελισθέν

εὐλογέω (LXX 442; NT 41): IAI ηὐλόγουν or εὐλόγουν; FAI εὐλογήσω; AAI εὐλόγησα or ηὐλόγησα; RAI εὐλόγηκα; FPI εὐλογηθήσομαι; RMP εὐλογημένος (rarely ηὐλογημένος)

εὑρίσκω (LXX 572; NT 176): IAI εὕρισκον or ηὕρισκον; FAI εὑρήσω; [2]AAI εὗρον, sometimes with [1]A endings: 1P εὕραμεν, 3P εὕροσαν, εὕρωσαν, or εὕρησαν; RAI εὕρηκα;[2]AMI εὑράμην; PMI εὑρίσκομαι; 3SIMI ηὑρίσκετο; RMI εὕρημαι; FPI εὑρεθήσομαι; API εὑρέθην or ηὑρέθην

εὐφραίνω (LXX 246) [liquid]: FAI εὐφρανῶ; AAI εὔφρανα or ηὔφρανα; AAN εὐφρᾶναι; FPI εὐφρανθήσομαι; API ηὐφράνθην or εὐφράνθην

εὐχαριστέω (NT 38): AAI εὐχαρίστησα or ηὐχαρίστησα; 3SAPS εὐχαριστηθῇ; APP εὐχαριστηθείς

ἔφαγον: AAI of ἐσθίω

ἐφοράω (LXX 36; NT 2) [see *CL*, s.v. ἐπεῖδον]: [2]FMI ἐπόψομαι; [2]AAI ἐπεῖδον; [2]AAM ἔπιδε

ἔχω (LXX 459; NT 708) [*σεχ]: IAI εἶχον; 1PIAI εἴχαμεν; 3PIAI εἶχαν or εἴχοσαν; FAI ἕξω (note the breathing mark); [2]AAI ἔσχον, sometimes with [1]A endings: 3P ἔσχαν or ἔσχοσαν; RAI ἔσχηκα; LAI ἐσχήκειν; AAS σχῶ

***ϝελ**: root and aor. act. stem for aorist active of αἱρέω (εἱλόμην or εἱλάμην)

***ϝὲρ**: root for future, perfect, aorist passive form of λέγω (ἐρῶ, εἴρηκα, ἐρρέθην)

***ϝιδ**: root for aorist active of ὁράω (εἶδον) and for the aorist active infinitive, pluperfect, and future of οἶδα (εἰδῆσαι, ᾔδειν, εἰδησῶ)

***ϝῖπ**: root for aorist active of λέγω (εἶπον; technically, εἶδον is the second aorist form of εἴδω [a word not used in the NT], but it is used as the aorist of ὁράω.)

***ϝορα**: root for present, perfect for ὁράω (ὁράω, ἑώρακα)

ζάω: see **ζῶ**

ζητέω (LXX 302; NT 117): IAI ἐζήτουν; FAI ζητήσω; AAI ἐζήτησα; 3SIMI ἐζητεῖτο; FPI ζητηθήσομαι; API ἐζητήθην

ζῶ (LXX 528; NT 140) [usually listed as ζάω, but not an alpha contract verb; see the sidebar in chap. 21]: IAI ἔζων; FAI ζήσω; AAI ἔζησα; FMI ζήσομαι

ἡγέομαι (LXX 160; NT 28): FMI ἡγήσομαι; AMI ἡγησάμην; RMI ἥγημαι

ἥκω (LXX 242; NT 26): 3PPAI ἥκασιν; IAI ἧκον; FAI ἥξω; AAI ἧξα; 3PRAI ἥκασιν; PAM ἧκε; FAP ἥξων

ηλθ-: see **ελθ-**

θανατόω (LXX 151): FAI θανατώσω; AAI ἐθανάτωσα; RMI τεθανάτωμαι; FPI θανατωθήσομαι; API ἐθανατώθην

θάπτω (LXX 151): IAI ἔθαπτον; FAI θάψω; AAI ἔθαψα; 3SRMI τέθαπται; [2]FPI ταφήσομαι; [2]API ἐτάφην

θαυμάζω (NT 43): IAI ἐθαύμαζον; FAI θαυμάσω; AAI ἐθαύμασα; 2SRAI τεθαύμακας; FMI θαυμάσομαι; FPI θαυμασθήσομαι; API ἐθαυμάσθην

***θε**: root of τίθημι

θέλω (LXX 153; NT 208) [orig. stem εθελε-, Attic ἐθέλω]: IAI ἤθελον; FAI θελήσω; AAI ἠθέλησα or ἤθελα; 2SRAI τεθέληκας; APS θεληθῶ

θεραπεύω (NT 43): IAI ἐθεράπευον; FAI θεραπεύσω; AAI ἐθεράπευσα; IMI ἐθεραπευόμην; RMP τεθεραπευμένος; API ἐθεραπεύθην

θεωρέω (NT 58): IAI ἐθεώρουν; FAI θεωρήσω; AAI ἐθεώρησα; API ἐθεωρήθην

θνῄσκω: See **ἀποθνῄσκω**

θύω (LXX 134): IAI ἔθυον; FAI θύσω; AAI ἔθυσα; RAI τέθυκα; RMP τεθυμένος; API ἐτύθην; APP τυθείς or θυθείς

ἰάομαι (NT 26): IMI ἰώμην; FMI ἰάσομαι; AMI ἰασάμην; RMI ἴαμαι; FPI ἰαθήσομαι; API ἰάθην; APM ἰαθήτω

***ἰδ**: root and aorist stem (unaugmented) of εἶδον

ἵστημι/ἱστάνω (LXX 705; NT 154); stem *στα: FAI στήσω; [1]AAI ἔστησα; [2]AAI ἔστην; RAI ἕστηκα; LAI εἱστήκειν or ἱστήκειν; 3PLAI εἱστήκεισαν; AAM στῆθι; [1]AAN στῆσαι; [2]AAN στῆναι; AAP στάς; [1]RAP ἑστηκώς; [2]RAP ἑστώς; RAN ἑστάναι; FMI στήσομαι; FPI σταθήσομαι; API ἐστάθην

ἰσχύω (LXX 100; NT 28): FAI ἰσχύσω; AAI ἴσχυσα; RAP neut. sg. ἰσχυκός

καθαρίζω (LXX 124; NT 31): FAI καθαριῶ [Attic future]; 3SFAI καθαρίσει; AAI ἐκαθάρισα; AAM καθάρισον; 3SRMI κεκαθάρισται; RMP κεκαθαρισμένος; FPI καθαρισθήσομαι; API ἐκαθαρίσθην; APM καθαρίσθητι

κάθημαι (LXX 192; NT 91): 2SPMI κάθῃ; 2PPMI κάθησθε; IMI ἐκαθήμην; FMI καθήσομαι; 2PFMI καθήσεσθε; PMM κάθου; PMN καθῆσθαι

καθίζω (LXX 209; NT 46): FAI καθίσω or καθιῶ; AAI ἐκάθισα; AAM κάθισον; 3SRAI κεκάθικεν; 1PRAI κεκαθίκαμεν; FMI καθίσομαι or καθιοῦμαι

καθίστημι/καθιστάνω (LXX 205): 3SPAI καθιστᾷ; IAI καθίστα; PAP καθιστῶν; FAI καταστήσω; AAI κατέστησα; RAI καθέστακα or καθέστηκα; 3PLAI καθειστήκεισαν; RMP καθεσταμένος; FPI κατασταθήσομαι; API καθεστάθην

καλέω (LXX 467; NT 148): IAI ἐκάλουν; FAI καλέσω; AAI ἐκάλεσα; RAI κέκληκα; 3SFMI καλέσεται; RMI κέκλημαι; [1]FPI κληθῆσομαι; 3S[2]FPI κεκλήσεται; API ἐκλήθην

καλύπτω (LXX 89; NT 8): FAI καλύψω; AAI ἐκάλυψα; RMP κεκαλυμμένος

καταβαίνω (LXX 318; NT 81): IAI κατέβαινον; FAI καταβήσομαι; [2]AAI κατέβην; AAM κατάβηθι; RAI καταβέβηκα (see also **βαίνω**)

καταλαμβάνω (LXX 118): [2]AAI κατέλαβον; RAI κατείληφα; FMI καταλήψομαι; [2]AMI κατελαβόμην; 3SRMI κατείληπται; RMP κατειλημμένος; 3PFPI καταλη(μ)θήσονται; [1]API κατελήμφθην

καταλείπω (LXX 279): IAI κατέλειπον; FAI καταλείψω; [1]AAI κατέλειψα; [2]AAI κατέλιπον; RAI καταλέλοιπα; 3SRMI καταλέλειπται; RMN καταλελεῖφθαι; RMP καταλελειμμένος; FPI καταλειφθήσομαι; [1]API κατελείφθην

καταλλάσσω: All NT & LXX forms (each occurs only once): 3SAAI κατήλλαξεν; 1PAPI κατηλλάγημεν; 3SFMI καταλλαγήσεται; AAN καταλλαγῆναι; PAPMSN καταλλάσσων; AAPMSG καταλλάξαντος; AAPMPN καταλλαγέντες; 3SAPM καταλλαγήτω; 2PAPM καταλλάγητε; 3SAAO καταλλαγείη

καταργέω (NT 27): FAI καταργήσω; AAI κατήργησα; RAI κατήργηκα; FPI καταργηθήσομαι; API κατηργήθην; RMI κατήργημαι

κατεσθίω/κατέσθω (LXX 147): [2]AAI κατέφαγον; FMI καταφάγομαι; [2]FMI κατέδομαι

κατοικέω (LXX 641; NT 44): FAI κατοικήσω; AAI κατῴκησα; RAN κατῳκηκέναι; APS κατοικηθῶ

καυχάομαι (NT 37): 2SPMI καυχᾶσαι; FMI καυχήσομαι; AMI ἐκαυχησάμην; RMI κεκαύχημαι

κελεύω (NT 25): IAI ἐκέλευον; FAI κελεύσω; AAI ἐκέλευσα; 3SLAI ἐκεκελεύκει; 1PRMI κεκελεύσμεθα; API ἐκελεύσθην; APPMPN κελευσθέντες

κηρύσσω (NT 61): IAI ἐκήρυσσον; FAI κηρύξω; AAI ἐκήρυξα; AAN κηρύξαι; RAN κεκηρυχέναι; RMI κεκήρυγμαι; FPI κηρυχθήσομαι; API ἐκηρύχθην

κλαίω (LXX 138; NT 40): IAI ἔκλαιον; FAI κλαύσω; FMI κλαύσομαι; AAI ἔκλαυσα; FPI κλαυσθήσομαι; API ἐκλαύσθην

κληρονομέω (LXX 161): FAI κληρονομήσω; AAI ἐκληρονόμησα; RAI κεκληρονόμηκα

κοιμάω (LXX 194): 3SPMI κοιμᾶται; 2SAMM κοιμήσαι; FPI κοιμηθήσομαι; API ἐκοιμήθην; RMI κεκοίμημαι; PMPMPG κοιμωμένων

κράζω (LXX 104; NT 55): IAI ἔκραζον; FAI κράξω; AAI ἔκραξα or ἐκέκραξα; RAI κέκραγα; 3SLAI ἐκεκράγει; FMI κεκράξομαι; PAPNSA κρᾶζον

κρατέω (LXX 140; NT 47): IAI ἐκράτουν; FAI κρατήσω; AAI ἐκράτησα; RAI κεκράτηκα; RAN κεκρατηκέναι; 3SLAI κεκρατήκει; IMI ἐκρατούμην; RMI κεκράτημαι; 3PRMI κεκράτηνται; 3PFPI κρατηθήσονται; API ἐκρατήθην

κρίνω (LXX 248; NT 114) [liquid]: FAI κρινῶ; AAI ἔκρινα; RAI κέκρικα; 3SLAI κεκρίκει or ἐκεκρίκει; IMI ἐκρινόμην; RMI κέκριμαι; FPI κριθήσομαι; API ἐκρίθην

κρύπτω (LXX 143): FAI κρύψω; [1]AAI ἔκρυψα; 3SRMI κέκρυπται; RMP κεκρυμμένος; [2]FPI κρυβήσομαι; [2]API ἐκρύβην

κτάομαι (LXX 101): FMI κτήσομαι; AMI ἐκτησάμην; RMI κέκτημαι; 3SF-RMI κεκτήσεται; 3PFPI κτηθήσοναι

***λαβ**: root and aorist stem of λαμβάνω

λαλέω (LXX 1,127; NT 296): IAI ἐλάλουν; FAI λαλήσω; AAI ἐλάλησα; RAI λελάληκα; RMI λελάλημαι; FPI λαληθήσομαι; API ἐλαλήθην

λαμβάνω (LXX 1,260; NT 258): IAI ἐλάμβανον; FMI λήμψομαι; [2]AAI ἔλαβον; [2]AAM λάβε; 3P[2]AAM λαβέτωσαν; [2]RAI εἴληφα; 2S[2]RAI εἴληφας or εἴληφες; [2]RAP εἰληφώς; 3S[2]RMI εἴληπται; 3SLMI εἴληπτο; FPI ληφθήσομαι; API εἰλήφθην or ἐλήμφθην

λέγω (LXX 2,078; NT 2,353): IAI ἔλεγον; 3PIAI ἔλεγαν; FAI ἐρῶ; RAI εἴρηκα; RMI εἴρημαι; alt. 3SRMI λέλεκται; LMI ἐλέλεκτο; RMP λελεγμένος; 3SFPI λεχθήσεται; 3SAPI ἐλέχθη; 3PAPI ἐλέχθησαν; APPFSN λεχθεῖσα, neut. pl. λεχθέντα (For most aorist forms, see **εἶπον**.)

λογίζομαι (LXX 115; NT 40): IMI ἐλογιζόμην; FMI λογιοῦμαι; AMI ἐλογισάμην; RMI λελόγιμαι; API ἐλογίσθην; FPI λογισθήσομαι

λυπέω (NT 26): AAI ἐλύπησα; RAI λελύπηκα; RMI λελύπημαι; FPI λυπηθήσομαι; API ἐλυπήθην

λυτρόω (LXX 108): FMI λυτρώσομαι; AMI ἐλυτρωσάμην; AMM λύτρωσαι; FPI λυτρωθήσομαι; API ἐλυτρώθην; 3SRMI λελύτρωται; RMP λελυτρωμένος

λύω (NT 42): IAI ἔλυον; FAI λύσω; AAI ἔλυσα; IMI ἐλυόμην; RMI λέλυμαι; 2SRMI λέλυσαι; RMP λελυμένος; FPI λυθήσομαι; API ἐλύθην

μανθάνω (NT 25): FMI μαθήσομαι; [2]AAI ἔμαθον; 2P[2]AAM μάθετε; [2]AAP μαθών; 3SRAI μεμάθηκεν; RAPMPN μεμαθηκότες; RAN μεμαθηκέναι

μαρτυρέω (NT 76): IAI ἐμαρτύρουν; FAI μαρτυρήσω; AAI ἐμαρτύρησα; RAI μεμαρτύρηκα; IMI ἐμαρτυρούμην; RMI μεμαρτύρημαι; API ἐμαρτυρήθην

μέλλω (NT 109) [orig. root *μελλε]: FAI μελλήσω; IAI ἔμελλον or ἤμελλον

μένω (NT 118) [liquid]: IAI ἔμενον; FAI μενῶ; AAI ἔμεινα; RAI μεμένηκα; AAM μεῖνον; RAPMPA μεμενηκότας; LAI μεμενήκειν

μετανοέω (NT 34): FAI μετανοήσω; AAI μετενόησα (or sometimes ἐμετενόησαν with double augment)

μιαίνω (LXX 128) [liquid]: FAI μιανῶ; AAI ἐμίανα; AAP μιάνας; RMI μεμίαμμαι; RMP μεμιαμμένος; 3SFPI μιανθήσεται; API ἐμιάνθην

μιμνήσκομαι (LXX 262): FPI μνησθήσομαι; API ἐμνήσθην; RMI μέμνημαι; RPS μνησθῶ

μισέω (LXX 177; NT 40): IAI ἐμίσουν; FAI μισήσω; AAI ἐμίσησα; RAI μεμίσηκα; 3SRMI μεμίσηται; RMP μεμισημένος; 3SFPI μισηθήσεται; API ἐμισήθην

νικάω (NT 28): FAI νικήσω; AAI ἐνίκησα; RAI νενίκηκα; PAP νικῶν; PAP dat. sg. νικῶντι or νικοῦντι; RMN νενικῆσθαι; API ἐνικήθην; FPN νικηθήσεσθαι; APP νικηθείς

οἶδα (LXX 285; NT 318): FAI εἰδήσω; 2SRAI οἶδας or οἶσθα; 1PRAI οἴδαμεν; 2PRAI οἴδατε; 3PRAI οἴδασιν or ἴσασιν; 2PRAI or 2PRAM ἴστε; RAS εἰδῶ; RAN εἰδέναι or εἰδῆσαι; RAP masc. εἰδώς, fem. εἰδυῖα; LAI ᾔδειν; 2SLAI ᾔδεις; 3PLAI ᾔδεισαν; FMI εἴσομαι

οἰκοδομέω (LXX 449; NT 40): IAI ᾠκοδόμουν; FAI οἰκοδομήσω; AAI ᾠκοδόμησα or without augment οἰκοδόμησα; RAI ᾠκοδόμηκα; 3SLAI ᾠκοδομήκει; 3SIMI ᾠκοδομεῖτο; 3SLMI ᾠκοδόμητο; RMN ᾠκοδομῆσθαι or οἰκοδομῆσθαι; RMP οἰκοδομημένος or ᾠκοδομημένος; FPI οἰκοδομηθήσομαι; API ᾠκοδομήθην or οἰκοδομήθην

ὀμνύω/ὄμνυμι (LXX 179; NT 26): FAI ὀμόσω; AAI ὤμοσα; RAI ὀμώμοκα [Attic reduplication]; 2SAAS ὀμόσῃς; 3SAAS ὀμόσῃ; AAN ὀμνύναι or ὀμόσαι; AAP ὀμόσας; FMI ὀμοῦμαι; 2SFMI ὀμῇ

ὁμολογέω (NT 26): IAI ὡμολόγουν; FAI ὁμολογήσω; AAI ὡμολόγησα; RMI ὡμολόγηται; 3SAPI ὡμολογήθη

ὁράω (LXX 1,394; NT 454): 3PIAI ἑώρων; ^{2}AAI εἶδον; RAI ἑώρακα or ἑόρακα [R forms beginning ἑω- have double reduplication]; 3PRAI ἑώρακαν or ἑόρακαν or ἑωράκασιν; LAI ἑωράκειν; alt. 3SLAI ὦπτο; FMI ὄψομαι; 2SFMI ὄψῃ; AMI ὠψάμην; 3SRMI ὦπται; ^{2}AMS ὄψησθε; RMN ὦφθαι or ἑωρᾶσθαι; FPI ὀφθήσομαι; API ὤφθην, alt. ὡράθην (For most aorist forms, see **εἶδον**.)

ὀφείλω (NT 35): IAI ὤφειλον; FAI ὀφειλήσω [*οφελ; fut. stem οφελε-]

παραγγέλλω (NT 32) [liquid]: IAI παρήγγελλον; AAI παρήγγειλα; RMP παρηγγελμένος

παραγίνομαι (LXX 174; NT 37): 3PIMI παρεγίνοντο; ^{2}AMI παρεγενόμην; RAI παραγέγονα; 3SLAI παραγεγόνει; 3S^{2}API παρεγενήθη

παραδίδωμι (LXX 249; NT 119): 3SPAI παραδίδει; 3SIAI παρεδίδου; 3PIAI παρεδίδουν or παρεδίδοσαν; FAI παραδώσω; AAI παρέδωκα; 3P^{2}AAI παρέδοσαν; RAI παραδέδωκα; 3PLAI παραδεδώκεισαν; 3SPAS παραδιδῷ or παραδιδοῖ; 3S^{2}AAS παραδῷ or παραδοῖ; AAM παράδος; PAP παραδιδούς; AAP παραδούς; RAP παραδεδωκώς; 3SIMI παρεδίδετο or παρεδίδοτο; 3SRMI παραδέδοται; RMP παραδεδομένος; FPI παραδοθήσομαι; API παρεδόθην

παρακαλέω (LXX 137; NT 109): IAI παρεκάλουν; FAI παρακαλέσω; AAI παρεκάλεσα; RAI παρακέκληκα; RMI παρακέκλημαι; FPI παρακληθήσομαι; API παρεκλήθην

παραλαμβάνω (NT 49): ^{2}AAI παρέλαβον; 1P^{2}AAI παρελάβαμεν; RAN παρειληφέναι; FMI παραλήμψομαι; RMI παρείλημμαι; FPI παραλημφθήσομαι; ^{1}APPFSA παραλημφθεῖσαν

παρεμβάλλω (LXX 186) [liquid]: FAI παρεμβαλῶ; ^{2}AAI παρενέβαλον; RAP παρεμβεβληκώς; 3PLAI παρεμβεβλήκεισαν

παρέρχομαι (LXX 137; NT 29): FMI παρελεύσομαι; ^{2}AAI παρῆλθον; RAI παρελήλυθα; ^{2}AAM παρελθάτω

παρίστημι/παριστάνω (NT 41): FAI παραστήσω; ^{1}AAI παρέστησα; ^{2}AAI παρέστην; RAI παρέστηκα; LAI παρειστήκειν; PAP neut. sg. παραστάν [Philo; in later texts, PAN παραστᾶν]; PAPMPN παριστῶντες; RAP παρεστηκώς or παρεστώς; RAN παρεστάναι; FMI παραστήσομαι; ^{1}API παρεστάθην

πάσχω (NT 42): 3SFAI παθεῖται; 3PFMI παθοῦνται; ²AAI ἔπαθον; ²RAI πέπονθα; 3PLAI ἐπεπόνθεισαν; ²RAP πεπονθώς

πατάσσω (LXX 404): FAI πατάξω; AAI ἐπάταξα; 3SFPI παταχθήσεται; APN παταχθῆναι; APP neut. παταχθέν

πείθω (LXX 175; NT 52): IAI ἔπειθον; FAI πείσω; AAI ἔπεισα; AAM πεῖσον; 3S¹RAI πέπεικε(ν); ²RAI πέποιθα; ²LAI ἐπεποίθειν and ἐπεποίθησα; 1P²LAI (ἐ)πεπείσμεθα; IMI ἐπειθόμην; RMI πέπεισμαι; FPI πεισθήσομαι; API ἐπείσθην

πειράζω (NT 38): IAI ἐπείραζον; FAI πειράσω; AAI ἐπείρασα; 2SAMI ἐπειράσω; RMP πεπειρασμένος; API ἐπειράσθην

πέμπω (NT 79): FAI πέμψω; AAI ἔπεμψα; RAI πέπομφα; FPN πεμφθήσεσθαι; API ἐπέμφθην; RMP πεπεμμένος

περιπατέω (NT 95): IAI περιεπάτουν; FAI περιπατήσω; AAI περιεπάτησα or ἐπεριπάτησα

περισσεύω (NT 39): IAI ἐπερίσσευον; FAI περισσεύσω; AAI ἐπερίσσευσα; FPI περισσευθήσομαι

πίμπλημι (LXX 116): FAI πλήσω; AAI ἔπλησα; RMP πεπλησμένα; FPI πλησθήσομαι; API ἐπλήσθην; APP πλησθείς

πίνω (LXX 270; NT 73) [liquid]: IAI ἔπινον; FAI πίομαι; 2SFMI πίεσαι; ²AAI ἔπιον; RAI πέπωκα; 3SLAI πεπώκει; AAM πίε; 3SAAM πιέτω; AAN πιεῖν; API ἐπόθην

πίπτω (LXX 390; NT 90): IAI ἔπιπτον; ²AAI ἔπεσον or ἔπεσα; RAI πέπτωκα; FMI πεσοῦμαι [Doric future]

πιστεύω (NT 241): IAI ἐπίστευον; FAI πιστεύσω; AAI ἐπίστευσα; RAI πεπίστευκα; LAI πεπιστεύκειν; RMI πεπίστευμαι; 3PFPI πιστευθήσονται; API ἐπιστεύθην

πλανάω (LXX 119; NT 39): FAI πλανήσω; AAI ἐπλάνησα; PMI πεπλάνημαι; API ἐπλανήθην

πληθύνω (LXX 199) [liquid]: FAI πληθυνῶ; 3SAAO πληθύναι; IMI ἐπληθυνόμην; 3SRMI πεπλήθυνται; RMP πεπληθυμμένος; 3SFPI πληθυνθήσεται; 3PFPI πληθυνθήσονται; API ἐπληθύνθην

πληρόω (LXX 106; NT 86): 3SIAI ἐπλήρου; FAI πληρώσω; AAI ἐπλήρωσα; RAI πεπλήρωκα; 3SLAI πεπληρώκει; IMI ἐπληρούμην; RMI πεπλήρωμαι; 3SLMI πεπλήρωτο; FPI πληρωθήσομαι; API ἐπληρώθην

ποιέω (LXX 3,204; NT 568): IAI ἐποίουν; FAI ποιήσω; AAI ἐποίησα; RAI πεποίηκα; LAI πεποιήκειν; IMI ἐποιούμην; AMI ἐποιησάμην; RMI πεποίημαι; 3SRMI πεποίηται; RMP πεποιημένος; FPI ποιηθήσομαι; API ἐποιήθην

πολεμέω (LXX 221): FAI πολεμήσω; AAI ἐπολέμησα; FPI πολεμηθήσομαι; 3PAPI ἐπολεμήθησαν

πορεύομαι (LXX 1,116; NT 153): IMI ἐπορευόμην; FMI πορεύσομαι; RMP πεπορευομένος; API ἐπορεύθην

πράσσω (NT 39): IAI ἔπρασσον; FAI πράξω; AAI ἔπραξα; RAI πέπραχα; RMP πεπραγμένος; API ἐπράχθην

προσάγω (LXX 172): ²AAI προσήγαγον; ²AAM προσάγαγε; ²AAN προσαγαγεῖν; 3PRAI προσαγειόχασιν; IMI προσηγόμην; 3SFPI προσαχθήσεται; API προσήχθην

προσέρχομαι (LXX 111; NT 86): [2]AAI προσῆλθον or προσῆλθα; [2]RAI προσελήλυθα [Attic reduplication]; 1PLAI προσεληλύθειμεν; IMI προσηρχόμην; FMI προσελεύσομαι

προσεύχομαι (LXX 100; NT 85): IMI προσηυχόμην; FMI προσεύξομαι; AMI προσηυξάμην

προσέχω (LXX 120): IAI προσεῖχον; FAI προσέξω; [2]AAI προσέσχον; RAI προσέσχηκα; 2PLAI προσεσχήκειτε

προσκαλέω (NT 29): 3SFMI προσκαλέσεται; AMI προσεκαλεσάμην; RMI προσκέκλημαι; 3SAPI προσεκλήθη

προσκυνέω (LXX 206; NT 60): IAI προσεκύνουν; FAI προσκυνήσω; AAI προσεκύνησα

προστίθημι (LXX 285): 3SIAI προσετίθει; FAI προσθήσω; AAI προσέθηκα; [2]AAS προσθῶ; [2]AAM πρόσθες; [2]AAN προσθεῖναι; [2]AAP προσθείς; 2SRAI προστέθεικας; 3PIMI προσετίθεντο; FMI προσθήσομαι; [2]AMI προσεθέμην; FPI προστεθήσομαι; API προσετέθην

προσφέρω (LXX 161; NT 47): IAI προσέφερον; FAI προσοίσω; AAI προσήνεγκον or προσήνεγκα; RAI προσενήνοχα [Attic reduplication]; API προσηνέχθην

προφητεύω (LXX 117; NT 28): IAI ἐπροφήτευον; FAI προφητεύσω; AAI ἐπροφήτευσα or προεφήτευσα; 3SRMI πεπροφήτευται; 3SAPI προεφητεύθη

ῥίπτω/ῥιπτέω (LXX 103): IAI ἐ(ρ)ρίπτουν; 3SFAI ῥίψει; AAI ἔ(ρ)ριψα; 3SRMI ἔρριπται; 3SLAI ἔρριπτο; AAM ῥῖψον; AAP neut. ῥῖψαν; RMP ἐ(ρ)ριμμένος; FPI ῥιφήσομαι; 3SAPI ἐρρίφη; 3PAPI ἐρρίφσαν; APP ῥιφείς; APN ῥιφῆναι

ῥύομαι (LXX 180): FMI ῥύσομαι; AMI ἐ(ρ)ρυσάμην; AMM ῥῦσαι; 3SRMI ἔρυσται [= εἴρυσται]; FPI ῥυσθήσομαι; API ἐ(ρ)ρύσθην

σκανδαλίζω (NT 29): AAI ἐσκανδάλισα; RMP ἐσκανδαλισμένος; FPI σκανδαλισθήσομαι; API ἐσκανδαλίσθην

σπείρω (NT 52) [liquid]: FAI σπερῶ; [1]AAI ἔσπειρα; 2SRAI ἔσπαρκας; 3SFMI σπαρήσεται; RMP ἐσπαρμένος; [2]API ἐσπάρην

***στα**: root of ἵστημι

σταυρόω (NT 46): FAI σταυρώσω; AAI ἐσταύρωσα; RMI ἐσταύρωμαι; API ἐσταυρώθην

συλλαμβάνω (LXX 111): FMI συλλήμψομαι; [2]AAI συνέλαβον; RAI συνείληφα; [2]AMI συνελαβόμην; FPI συλληφθήσομαι; [1]API συνελήμφθην

συνάγω (LXX 360; NT 59): FAI συνάξω; AAI συνῆξα; [2]AAI συνήγαγον; AAN συνάξαι; RMI συνῆγμαι; 3SRMI συνῆκται; FPI συναχθήσομαι; [1]API συνήχθην, 3P συνήχθησαν

συνέρχομαι (NT 30): [2]AAI συνῆλθον; 3PLAI συνεληλύθεισαν [Attic reduplication]; RAP συνεληλυθώς; IMI συνηρχόμην; FMI συνελεύσομαι

συνέχω (LXX 49; NT 12): FAI συνέξω; [2]AAI συνέσχον; IPI συνειχόμην; 3PFPI συσχεθήσονται (LXX); 1SAPI συνεσχέθη, 3PAPI συνεσχέθησαν

συνίημι/συνίω (NT 26): 3PPAI συνιᾶσιν or συνίουσιν; FAI συνήσω; 2SFAI συνιεῖς; [1]AAI συνῆκα; 2P PAI or PAM συνίετε; PAM σύνιε; 3SPAM συνιέτω; 2S[2]AAM σύνες; 2P[2]AAM σύνετε; [2]AAS συνῶ; 2P[2]AAS συνῆτε; 3P[2]AAS συνῶσιν; PAN συνίειν or συνιέναι; [2]AAN συνεῖναι; PAP συνίων or συνιείς; PAPMSG συνιέντος; [2]AAP συνείς

συντάσσω (LXX 124): 3SFAI συντάξει; ^{1}AAI συνέταξα; RAI συντέταχα; ^{2}AMI συνεταξάμην; 3SRMI συντέτακται; ^{2}APP gen. συνταγέντος

συντελέω (LXX 198): FAI συντελέσω; AAI συνετέλεσα; 2PRMI συντετέλεσθε; 3SRMI συντετέλεσται; RMP συντετελεσμένος; RMN συντετελέσθαι; FPI συντελεσθήσομαι; API συνετελέσθην

συντρίβω (LXX 219): FAI συντρίψω; AAI συνέτριψα; RMI συντετρῖφθαι; RMP συντετριμμένος; ^{2}FPI συντριβήσομαι; ^{2}API συνετρίβην

σῴζω (LXX 340; NT 106): FAI σώσω; AAI ἔσωσα; RAI σέσωκα; IMI ἐσῳζόμην; 3SRMI σέσῳσται or σέσωται; RMP σεσῳσμένος; FPI σωθήσομαι; API ἐσώθην

ταπεινόω (LXX 167): FAI ταπεινώσω; AAI ἐταπείνωσα; RMP τεταπεινωμένος; FPI ταπεινωθήσομαι; API ἐταπεινώθην

ταράσσω (LXX 114): IAI ἐτάρασσον; 3SFAI ταράξει; AAI ἐτάραξα; IMI ἐταρασσόμην; RMI τετάραγμαι; RMP τεταραγμένος; 3SFPI ταραχθήσεται; API ἐταράχθην

τελέω (NT 28): FAI τελέσω; AAI ἐτέλεσα; RAI τετέλεκα; RMI τετέλεσμαι; FPI τελεσθήσομαι; API ἐτελέσθην

τηρέω (NT 70): IAI ἐτήρουν; 3PIAI ἐτήρουν or ἐτήρουσαν; FAI τηρήσω; AAI ἐτήρησα; RAI τετήρηκα; 3PRAI τετήρηκαν; IMI ἐτηρούμην; RMI τετήρημαι; API ἐτηρήθην

τίθημι (LXX 527; NT 100); stem *θε: 3SIAI ἐτίθει; 3PIAI ἐτίθεσαν or ἐτίθουν; FAI θήσω; AAI ἔθηκα; RAI τέθεικα; LAI ἐτεθείκει; ^{2}AAS θῶ; 2P^{2}AAM θέτε; ^{2}AAN θεῖναι; ^{2}AAP θείς; FMI θήσομαι; ^{2}AMI ἐθέμην; RMI τέθειμαι; RMP τεθειμένος; 3PFPI τεθήσονται; ^{1}API ἐτέθην

τίκτω (LXX 236): FAI τέξομαι; ^{2}AAI ἔτεκον; RAI τέτοκα; LAI ἐτετόκει; ^{1}API ἐτέχθην; 3SFPI τεχθήσεται; FPP τεχθησόμενος

ὑπάγω (NT 79): IAI ὑπῆγον; FAI ὑπάξω; AAI ὑπήγαγον; RMI ὑπῆγμαι; API ὑπήχθην; APPMSN ὑπαχθείς; RMPMPG ὑπηγμένων

ὑπάρχω (LXX 143; NT 60): IAI ὑπῆρχον; FAI ὑπάρξω; 3SAAI ὑπῆρξεν (This is *not* a middle-only form in the future and aorist, as sometimes listed.)

ὑποστρέφω (NT 35): IAI ὑπέστρεφον; FAI ὑποστρέψω; AAI ὑπέστρεψα

ὑποτάσσω (NT 38): ^{1}AAI ὑπέταξα; RMI ὑποτέταγμαι; ^{2}FPI ὑποταγήσομαι; ^{2}API ὑπετάγην

ὑψόω (LXX 192): FAI ὑψώσω; AAI ὕψωσα; RMP ὑψωμένος; FPI ὑψωθήσομαι; API ὑψώθην

***φαγ**: root used to form future and aorist stem of ἐσθίω

φαίνω (NT 31) [liquid]: 3PFAI φανοῦσιν; AAI ἔφανα; ^{2}RAI πέφηνα; 3SAAS φάνῃ; IMI ἐφαινόμην; FMI φανοῦμαι; 3SRMI πέφανται; 3SAMS φάνηται; RMN πέφανθαι; ^{2}FPI φανήσομαι; ^{2}API ἐφάνην

φανερόω (NT 49): FAI φανερώσω; AAI ἐφανέρωσα; RAI πεφανέρωκα [Attic reduplication]; RMI πεφανέρωμαι; FPI φανερωθήσομαι; API ἐφανερώθην

φέρω (LXX 273; NT 66): IAI ἔφερον; ^{2}FAI οἴσω; ^{2}AAI ἤνεγκα; ^{2}RAI ἐνήνοχα; ^{2}AAP ἐνέγκας; ^{2}AAN ἐνεγκεῖν; ^{2}API ἠνέχθην; 3P^{2}API ἐνέχθησαν (The aorist indicative often reduplicates instead of augments.)

φεύγω (LXX 230; NT 29): FAI φεύξομαι; ^{2}AAI ἔφυγον; RAI πέφυγα

φημί (NT 66): 2SPAI φῄς; 3SPAI φησίν; 3PPAI φασίν; FAI φήσω; 3S IAI or ^{2}AAI ἔφη; 3P IAI or ^{2}AAI ἔφασαν; 3S^{1}AAI ἔφησεν

φιλέω (NT 25): IAI ἐφίλουν; FAI φιλήσω; AAI ἐφίλησα; RAI πεφίληκα

φοβέω (LXX 435; NT 95): 3SIAI ἐφόβει; 3SAAI ἐφόβησεν; FAN φοβήσειν; AAN φοβῆσαι; PAPMPN φοβοῦντες; IMI ἐφοβούμην; FPI φοβηθήσομαι; API ἐφοβήθην (This is *not* a middle-only form, as sometimes listed.)

φρονέω (NT 26): IAI ἐφρόνουν; FAI φρονήσω; AAI ἐφρόνησα; 1PRAI πεφρονήκαμεν

φυλάσσω (LXX 457; NT 31): FAI φυλάξω; AAI ἐφύλαξα; RAI πεφύλαχα; 3SRMI πεφύλακται; RMP πεφυλαγμένος; 3PFPI φυλαχθήσονται; API ἐφυλάχθην

φωνέω (NT 43): IAI ἐφώνουν; FAI φωνήσω; AAI ἐφώνησα; API ἐφωνήθην

χαίρω (NT 74): IAI ἔχαιρον; ^{2}FPI χαρήσομαι; ^{2}AMI ἐχάρην [intransitive θη-middle; ^{2}A omits the θ]; 2P^{2}APS χαρῆτε; ^{2}APN χαρῆναι (This verb is technically a liquid, but it follows regular formation for future and aorist.)

B.5. Odd Forms

See *CL* for other such forms. If found there alphabetically, they are not usually listed here unless they appear in one of the examples cited in the main body of this book. Dual-voice (mid./pass.) forms are listed as middle in form; context may suggest passive in some cases, and some such words may be used only with passive meaning. All finite forms are first singular unless listed otherwise.

***αγαγ**: root and aor. stem of ἄγω

ἀγαπᾶν: PAN ἀγαπάω

ἀκήκοα/ἀκηκόαμεν: 1S^{2}RAI/1P ἀκούω

ἀλλαγήσομαι: ^{2}FPI ἀλλάσσω

ἀλλάξει: 3SFAI ἀλλάσσω

ἀναγγελῶ: FAI ἀναγγέλλω

ἀναδούς: AAP ἀναδίδωμι

ἀναζωσάμενος: AMP ἀναζώννυμι

ἀναφάναντες: AAPMPN ἀναφαίνω (liquid)

ἀνέλω: AAS ἀναιρέω

ἀνελῶ: FAI ἀναιρέω

ἀνεστράφην: ^{2}API ἀναστρέφω

ἀνέστρεψα: AAI ἀναστρέφω

ἀνεῦρον: ^{2}AAI ἀνευρίσκω

ἀνέῳγα: ^{2}RAI ἀνοίγω

ἀνέῳξα: AAI ἀνοίγω

ἀνήγγειλα: AAI ἀναγγέλλω

ἀνοῖξαι: AAN ἀνοίγω

ἀνταποδο-: stem of ἀνταποδίδωμι

ἀντελαβόμην: ^{2}AMI ἀντιλαμβάνω

ἀντέστην: ^{2}AAI ἀνθίστημι

ἀντικατέστην: ^{2}AAI ἀντικαθίστημι

ἀπέθανον: ^{2}AAI ἀποθνῄσκω

ἀπεκρίθην: API ἀποκρίνομαι

ἀπήγγειλα: AAI ἀπαγγέλλω

ἀπηγξάμην: AMI ἀπάγχω

ἀπῄεσαν: 3PIAI ἄπειμι

ἀπόβλητον: adj. (not a verb!)

ἀποδο-: stem of ἀποδίδωμι

ἀποθανοῦμαι: FMI ἀποθνῄσκω (liquid stem)

ἀποκεκύλισται: 3SRMI ἀποκυλίω

ἀπολέσω: FAI ἀπόλλυμι (alt. fut.: ἀπολῶ)

ἀπόλωλα: ^{2}RAI ἀπόλλυμι

ἀπολωλώς: ^{2}RAP ἀπόλλυμι

ἀπώλεσα: AAI ἀπόλλυμι

ἀπωλόμην: 1S^{2}AMI ἀπόλλυμι (3S, -ετο)

ἀπών: PAP ἄπειμι

ἀφίλετο: 3SAMI ἀφαιρέω

ἀφίουσιν: 3PPAI ἀφίημι

ἀφῶ: AAS ἀφίημι

ἀχθη-: see ἄγω

ἅψομαι: FMI ἅπτω

βαίνειν: PAN βαίνω

***βαλ**: root and aor. stem of βάλλω
βᾶσαν: ²AAPFSA βαίνω
βέβηκε: 3SRAI βαίνω
βεβηκέναι: RAN βαίνω
βεβηκότες: RAPMPN βαίνω
βέβληκα: RAI βάλλω
***βη**: ²aor. and pf. stem of βαίνω (root *βα with stem vowel lengthened)
βῆ: 3S²AAI βαίνω
βῇ: 3S²AAS βαίνω
βλη-: pf. and aor. pass. stem of βάλλω (technically a modified form of *βαλ)
γέγονα/γέγονεν: 1S²RAI/3S γίνομαι
γέγραφα: 1S²RAI γράφω
***γεν**: root and aor. stem of γίνομαι (≠ γεννάω)
γνούς: ²AAP γινώσκω (root aor.)
***γνω**: root and fut., aor., and pf. stem of γινώσκω
γνῶναι: ²AAN γινώσκω
γνώτω: 3S²AAM γινώσκω
δέδωκα: 1SRAI δίδωμι
δεδώκει: 3SLAI δίδωμι (augment and movable nu elided)
δειγ-, **δειξ-**, or **δειχ-**: see δείκνυμι
δήσω: AAS δέω
διδούς: PAPMSN δίδωμι
διεθέμην: ²AMI διατίθημαι
διεστείλατο: 3SAMI διαστέλλω
διέστη: 3S²AAI διΐστημι
διεφθάρη/-ησαν: 3S/3P ²API διαφθείρω
διορυχθῆναι: APN διορύσσω
***δο**: root of δίδωμι
δούς: AAPMSN δίδωμι
***δραμ/*δρομ**: root for fut., aor., and pf. of τρέχω (δραμοῦμαι, ἔδραμον, δεδράμηκα)
δύνασε: 2SPAI δύναμαι
ἔβαλον: ²AAI βάλλω
ἐβλήθην: API βάλλω
ἐγενόμην: ²AMI γίνομαι
ἐγήγερμαι: RMI ἐγείρω
ἐγνω-: augmented aor. or reduplicated pf. stem of γινώσκω
ἐγνώκειτε: 2PLAI γινώσκω
ἔγνων: 1S²AAI γινώσκω (root aor.)
ἐδίδοσαν: 3PIAI δίδωμι
ἐδίδοτο: 3SIMI δίδωμι
ἐδίδου: 3SIAI δίδωμι
ἐδίδουν: 1S/3P IAI δίδωμι
ἔθανον: ²AAI θνῄσκω
ἔθεντο: 3PAMI τίθημι
ἔθρεψα: AAI τρέφω
εἶδα: 1S²AAI εἶδον/ὁράω
εἰδήσω: FAI οἶδα
εἶδον: functions as ²aor. of ὁράω
εἰδῶ: RAS οἶδα
εἱλάμην: ²AMI (alt. εἱλόμην) αἱρέω
εἰλευθέρωσεν: alt. 3SAAI ἐλευθερόω
εἴλημμαι: ²RMI λαμβάνω
εἴληφα: ²RAI λαμβάνω
εἱλόμην: ²AMI (alt. εἱλάμην) αἱρέω
εἴπῃ: ²AAS λέγω/εἶπον
εἴργασμαι: RMI ἐργάζομαι
εἴρηκα: RAI λέγω/εἶπον
εἰρήκει: 3SLAI λέγω/εἶπον
ἐκάλυψα: AAI καλύπτω
ἐκδώσομαι: FMI ἐκδίδωμι
ἐκηρύξαμεν: 1PAAI κηρύσσω
ἐκλήθην: API καλέω
ἐκρίθην: API κρίνω
ἐκχύν(ν)ω: see ἐκχέω
ἔλαβον: ²AAI λαμβάνω
ἔλαχον: ²AAI λαγχάνω
***ελευθ**: fut. and pf. stem of ἔρχομαι
ἐλεύσομαι: FMI ἔρχομαι
ἐλήλυθα: 1SRAI of ἔρχομαι
ἐλήλυθεν: 3S²RAI ἔρχομαι
ἐλήμφθη: 3S²API λαμβάνω
ἐλήμφθης: 2S²API λαμβάνω
ελθ-: derived aor. stem of ἔρχομαι (*ελευθ with ευ dropped); appears as ηλθ- with augment in indicative
ἐμνήσθην: API μιμνῄσκομαι
ἐνέγκας: ²AAP φέρω

ἐνεγκεῖν or **ἐνέγκαι**: ^{2}AAN φέρω
***ἐνεκ**: root for aor. and pf. of φέρω (ἤνεγκα, ἐνήνοχα)
ἐνέστηκα: RAI ἐνίστημι
ἐνεχθείς: ^{2}APP φέρω
ἐνήνοχα: ^{2}RAI φέρω
ἔνυξα: AAI νύσσω
ἐνών: PAP ἔνειμι
ἐξαγαγών: AAP ἐξάγω
ἐξεδόμην: ^{2}AMI ἐκδίδωμι
ἐξεῖλον: ^{2}AAI ἐξαιρέω
ἐξεκρεμάμην: IMI ἐκκρέμαμαι
ἔξελε: 2S^{2}AAM ἐξαιρέω
ἐξέλθατε: 2P^{2}AAM ἐξέρχομαι
ἐξελῶ: FAI ἐξαιρέω
ἐξενεγκεῖν: AAN ἐκφέρω
ἐξέπεσον: ^{2}AAI ἐκπίπτω
ἐξεστακέναι: RAN ἐξίστημι
ἐξέστην: 1S^{2}AAI ἐξίστημι
ἐξέστησα: 1S^{1}AAI ἐξίστημι
ἐξέστραμμαι: RMI ἐκστρέφω
ἐξήγειρα: AAI ἐξεγείρω
ἐξήνεγκα: AAI ἐκφέρω
ἐξήραμμαι: RPI ξηραίνω
ἐξηραμμένην: RMP ξηραίνω
ἐξήρανα: AAI ξηραίνω
ἐξηράνθην: API ξηραίνω
ἐξηρῆσθαι: RMN ἐξαιρέω
ἐξητησάμην: AMI ἐξαιτέομαι
ἐξιών: PAP ἔξειμι
ἐξοίσω: FAI ἐκφέρω
ἐξόν: PAP ἔξεστιν
ἕξω: FAI ἔχω (note breathing mark)
ἑόρακα: alt. RAI ὁράω
ἔπαθον: ^{2}AAI πάσχω
ἐπεῖδον: ^{2}AAI ἐφοράω
ἐπέκειλα: AAI ἐπικέλλω
ἐπεκεκλήμην: LPI ἐπικαλέω
ἐπεποίθει: 3S^{2}LAI πείθω
ἔπεσον or **ἔπεσα**: ^{2}AAI πίπτω
ἐπεστράπην: ^{2}API ἐπιστρέφω
ἐπετάγη: API ἐπιτάσσω
ἐπέτυχον: ^{2}AAI ἐπιτυγχάνω
ἔπιδε: ^{2}AAM ἐφοράω/ἐπεῖδον
ἐπιλαθέσθαι: ^{2}AMN ἐπιλανθάνομαι
ἐπισκοπεύω: alt. form of ἐπισκοπέω
ἐπόθην: ^{2}API πίνω
ἐπόψομαι: FMI ἐφοράω/ἐπεῖδον
ἐπρήσθησαν: alt. 3PAPI πρίζω
ἐπρίσθησαν: 3PAPI πρίζω
ἐπυθόμην: ^{2}AMI πυνθάνομαι
ἐρρέθην: API εἶπον
ἐσθήσεσι: FPD ἐσθής (*not* a verb!)
ἔσκυλμαι: RPI σκύλλω
ἐσμέν: 1PPAI εἰμί
ἔσομαι: FMI εἰμί
ἐσόμενος: FMP εἰμί
ἔστω: 3SPAM εἰμί
ἔσχηκα: RAI ἔχω
ἔσχον: ^{2}AAI ἔχω
ἐτύθη: 3SAPI θύω
εὗρον: ^{2}AAI εὑρίσκω
ἐφέστηκα: RAI ἐφίστημι
ἐφεστώς: RAP ἐφίστημι
ἔφη: 3SAAI φημί
ἐφοράω (see ἐπεῖδον in *CL*): FMI ἐπόψομαι; ^{2}AAI ἐπεῖδον; ^{2}AAM ἔπιδε
ἐφύην: ^{2}API φύω
ϝελ**/ϝαλ**: root and aor. act. stem for aor. active of αἱρέω (εἱλόμην or εἱλάμην)
ϝεπ**/ϝοπ**: root for aor. act. of λέγω/εἶπον
***ϝερ**: root for fut., pf., aor. pass. of λέγω (ἐρῶ, εἴρηκα, ἐρρέθην)
***ϝιδ**: root for aor. act. of εἶδον/ὁράω and for aor. act. inf., plpf., and fut. of οἶδα (εἰδῆσαι, ᾔδειν, εἰδησῶ) (Technically, εἶδον is the ^{2}aor. form of εἴδω [a word not used in the NT], but it is used as the aor. of ὁράω.)
***ϝορα**: root for pres. and pf. of ὁράω (ὁράω, ἑώρακα)
ἤγαγον: ^{2}AAI ἄγω
ἠγάπομεν: alt. 1PIAI ἀγαπάω
ἤγγικεν: 3SRAI ἐγγίζω

ἠγορασμένα: RMPNPN ἀγοράζω
ᾔδειν: 1SLAI οἶδα
ἠθέλησα: AAI θέλω (= Classical Greek ἐθέλω)
ἥκασιν: 3PPAI or 3PRAI ἥκω
ἧκον: IAI ἥκω
ἤλλαξαν: 3PAAI ἀλλάσσω
ἡμάρτηκα: RAI ἁμαρτάνω
ἤμελλεν: 3SIAI μέλλω
ἤμην: IMI εἰμί
ἠμφίεσμαι: RMI ἀμφιέννυμι
ἠμφιεσμένος: RMPMSN ἀμφιέννυμι
ἤνεγκα: [2]AAI φέρω
ἠνέχθην: API φέρω
ἠνέῳξα, ἤνοιξα: AAI ἀνοίγω, alt. forms
ἠνοίγην: [2]API ἀνοίγω
ἤνοιξα: AAI ἀνοίγω
ἦξα: AAI ἥκω
ἥξω: FAI ἥκω
ἤρεσα: AAI ἀρέσκω
ἦρκα: RAI αἴρω
ᾖς: 2SPAS εἰμί
ἡσσάομαι: alt. spelling of ἡττάομαι
ἤφιεν: 3SIAI ἀφίημι
ἤχθην: API ἄγω
***θε**: root of τίθημι
θεῖναι: AAN τίθημι
θείς: AAP τίθημι
θέτε: 2PAAM τίθημι
θνῄσκω: see ἀποθνῄσκω
***θρεχ**: root for pres. of τρέχω (No forms with the θ appear in Koine; all have τρεχ-. See *MBG*, 262n9.)
***ἰδ**: root and aor. stem (unaugmented) of εἶδον; the next few forms are attested
ἴδε: 2S[2]AAM εἶδον/ὁράω (but usually used as an interjection in stereotyped form with both sg. and pl.)
ἰδεῖν: [2]AAN εἶδον/ὁράω
ἴδοιμι: [2]AAO εἶδον/ὁράω
ἴδον/-ες/-εν/-ομεν/-ατε: phonetic spellings of εἶδον, etc. (usually *v.l.*)
ἴδω: [2]AAS εἶδον/ὁράω
ἰδών: AAP εἶδον/ὁράω
ἴσθι: 2SPAM εἰμί
ἴστε: 2PRAI or 2PRAM οἶδα
καθελῶ: FAI καθαιρέω
καθῆκα: AAI καθίημι
καλύψω: FAI καλύπτω
καταγεινώσκω: alt. spelling of καταγινώσκω
καταλλαγ-: see καταλλάσσω
κατείλημμαι: RMI καταλαμβάνω
κατέφθαρμαι: RMI καταφθείρω
κατήραμαι: RMI καταράομαι
κεκαλυμμένον: RMPNSN (or acc.) καλύπτω
κεκατήρανται: 3PRMI καταράομαι (LXX; double reduplication)
κέκαυμαι: RMI καίω
κέκληκα: RAI καλέω
κεκόρεσμαι: RMI κορέννυμι
κέκρικα: RAI κρίνω
κηρυχθήσεται: 3SFPI κηρύσσω
κομιοῦμαι: FMI κομίζω (Attic future; see §21.25)
κόψονται: 3PFMI κόπτω
***λαβ**: root and aor. stem of λαμβάνω
λήμψομαι: FMI λαμβάνω
μέμνημαι: RMI μιμνῄσκομαι
μετασταθῶ: APS μεθίστημι
μεταστήσας: AAP μεθίστημι
μετέστησα: AAI μεθίστημι
μνησθῶ: RPS μιμνῄσκομαι
νίψαι: AMM νίπτω
***οι**: root for fut. of φέρω
οἴσω: FAI φέρω
ὄντος: PAPMSG εἰμί
***οπ**: root for fut., aor. mid., and aor. pass. of ὁράω (ὄψομαι, ὠψάμην, ὤφθην)
ὄψομαι: FMI ὁράω
***παθ**: root for pres. and aor. of πάσχω (πάσχω, ἔπαθον)
παθών, παθοῦσα: aor. ptc., masc. and fem., πάσχω

παρῃτούμην: IMI παραιτέομαι

παρών, παροῦσα, παρόν: PAP, M/F/N πάρειμι

πεῖν: ^{2}AAN πίνω

***πενθ**: root for pf. of πάσχω (πέπονθα)

πέπεισμαι: 1SRMI πείθω

πέποιθα: 1S^{2}RAI πείθω

πεπόνθασιν: 3P^{2}RAI πάσχω

πέπραγμαι: RPI πράσσω

πέπραμαι: RPI πιπράσκω

πεπρησμένος: RMP πίμπραμαι

πέπτωκα: RAI πίπτω

πέπωκα: RAI πίνω

περιελών: ^{2}AAP περιαιρέω

πεσοῦμαι: FMI πίπτω

πίννω: alt. form of πίνω

πίομαι: FMI πίνω

πληροῦν: PAN πληρόω

πραθέν: APPNSN πιπράσκω

πρέπον: PAPNS (nom. or acc.) πρέπω

προβάς: ^{2}AAPMSN προβαίνω (see βαίνω under B.4 above)

προβέβηκα: RAI προβαίνω

προέδραμον: ^{2}AAI προτρέχω

προειλόμην: ^{2}AMI προαιρέω

προείρηκα: RAI προλέγω/προεῖπον

προημάρτηκα: RAI προαμαρτάνω

προῄρημαι: RMI προαιρέω

προσεκλίθην: API προσκλίνω

προσεληλύθατε: 2P^{2}RAI προσέρχομαι

πρόσελθε: ^{2}AAM προσέρχομαι

προσήχθην: API προσάγω

***στα**: root of ἵστημι

στάς: ^{2}AAP ἵστημι

στήσω: FAI ἵστημι

συγκέχυμαι: RPI συγχέω

συναχθήσομαι: FPI συνάγω

συνέβη: 3S^{2}AAI συμβαίνω

συνέσταλμαι: RPI συστέλλω

συνεχύθην: API συγχέω

συνῆκται: 3SRMI συνάγω

συνηρπάκει: 3SLAI συναρπάζω

συνήσω: FAI συνίημι

συνήχθησαν: 3PAPI συνάγω

συνκεκέραμμαι, συνκεκέρασμαι, συνκεκέραμαι: alt. forms of συγκεκέρασμαι

σχῶ: ^{2}AAS ἔχω

ταγ-: see τάσσω in *CL* (e.g., τεταγμέναι; cf. ὑποτάσσω under B.4 above)

τέθραμμαι: RPI τρέφω

τέταγμαι: RPI τάσσω

τέτακται: 3SRPI τάσσω

τετάραγμαι: RPI ταράσσω

τετάρακται: 3SRPI ταράσσω

τετέλεσμαι: RMI τελέω

τέτυχα: RAI τυγχάνω

τυθῇ: 3SAPS θύω

***φαγ**: root for fut. and aor. of ἐσθίω

φανήσεται: 3SFPI φαίνω

φυέν: ^{2}APPNSN φύω

φυήσουσι(ν): 3PFAI φύω

ὦ: PAS εἰμί

ὤν: PAPMSN εἰμί

ὠνειδίζομαι: alt. form 1SPPI ὀνειδίζω

ὦπται: 3SRMI ὁράω

ὠσί(ν): dat. sg. of οὖς, ὠτός, τό (*not* a verb!)

ὤφθην: alt. ὡράθην, API ὁράω

ὠψάμην: AMI ὁράω

Appendix C

Participle Chart

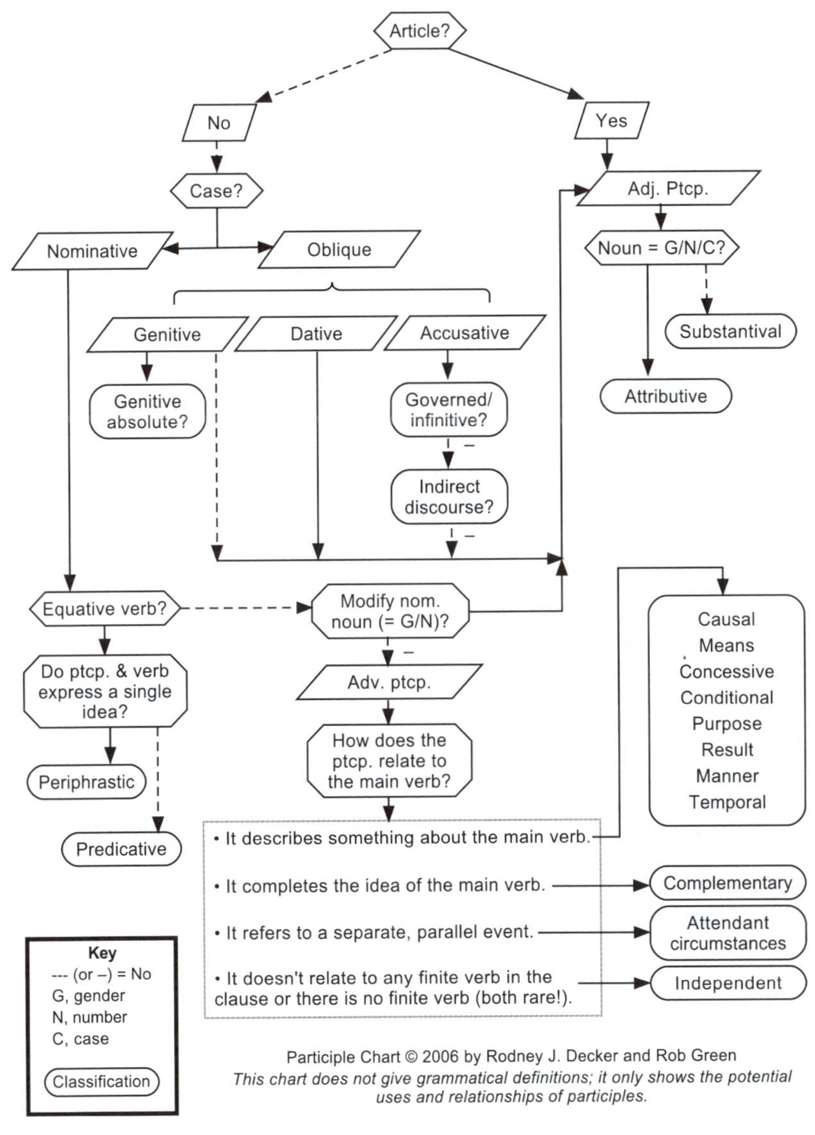

Figure C.1

Appendix D

Vocatives: The Fifth Case

D.1. There are actually five cases, not just four.[1] The textbook chapters have focused on the four major cases that account for the vast majority of case forms in the NT and LXX (and in any other Greek literature of the Classical and Koine periods). But you do need to know the vocative as well. The five cases are nominative, genitive, dative, accusative, and *vocative*. There are 878 vocatives in the NT and 1,587 in the LXX. That sounds like a lot, but it is only a small fraction of the total noun forms: 3 percent of the 27,958 nouns in the NT and only 1 percent of the 153,739 nouns in the LXX are vocatives.

Vocative is the case of direct address, as in the English (yes, we have them here as well): "*Dave*, wake up!" English does not use any special form; that is, the word is spelled the same as the subjective (nominative) or objective (accusative) case. English (and Greek) usually sets the vocative off from the rest of the sentence with a comma. Greek *sometimes* has a special case ending for the vocative; other times it is the same as the nominative. Here is a simple example.

1. There is an old debate regarding the number of cases. Some older grammarians argue for eight cases, and some even think that it is impossible to understand Greek with only five cases. (The other three that some add are the ablative, locative, and instrumental cases.) This has been pretty well settled nowadays. I know of no major Greek scholar today who uses eight cases and no recent intermediate or reference grammars that do either. In some ways you can simply ignore this debate, but if you are interested, here is the basic issue. There are only five sets of case endings that have distinct forms (i.e., that are spelled differently). But it is thought that in older Greek (and it would have to be very old Greek, since it never occurs in any known Greek literature) there used to be three additional cases. The evidence for this comes, not from Greek, but from Sanskrit—a related language that is also descended from Indo-European. Sanskrit does, indeed, have eight cases. To make an eight-case system work in Greek, these older grammarians divided the genitive endings into genitive and ablative, and the dative into dative, locative, and instrumental. Of course the Greek forms are all spelled exactly the same, so this division must be on the basis of function rather than form. As a number of scholars have pointed out, however, if the basis for this distinction is function, then we ought not to stop with eight but ought to have twenty or more cases to describe the ways in which the five case forms actually function. If you want to read about this discussion, see Silva, *God, Language and Scripture*, 102–11; and Wallace, *Greek Grammar*, 32–35.

Matt. 7:21, Οὐ πᾶς ὁ λέγων μοι, **Κύριε κύριε**, εἰσελεύσεται εἰς τὴν βασιλείαν τῶν οὐρανῶν.

Not everyone who says to me, "*Lord, Lord*," will enter the kingdom of heaven.

As shown in this example, κύριος is one of the words that use a special case ending for the vocative: the epsilon (ε) at the end of κύριε.

Forms of the Vocative

D.2. Plural vocatives always have the same form as the nominative plural, as do all neuter nouns (singular or plural). Thus ἄνθρωποι and τέκνον could be nominative or vocative. For the singular, the forms are as follows. First-declension words usually have a vocative with the same form as the nominative; first-declension feminine nouns are always the same, while masculine words sometimes have just an alpha.

Nominative	Vocative
ἀδελφή	ἀδελφή
σατανᾶς	σατανᾶ
τέκνον	τέκνον

The second-declension vocative ending is usually epsilon. Note that the connecting vowel drops out.

Nominative	Vocative
ἄνθρωπος	ἄνθρωπε
θεός	θεέ
κύριος	κύριε

In the third declension either there is no ending (the vocative consists of just the stem) or the vocative form is the same as the nominative. Sometimes the stem vowel undergoes ablaut.

Nominative	Vocative
πόλις	πόλι
πατήρ	πάτερ
γραμματεύς	γραμματεύς

There is *no vocative article*, so if a word has an article, the form is *not* a vocative. The vocative is usually set off from the rest of the sentence by commas (see the Matt. 7:21 example above).

D.3. There are other vocative forms (that is, different case endings other than epsilon) that are best identified by context and learned through reading rather than by trying to memorize more forms. For example: δέσποτα ▸ δεσπότης;

γύναι ▸ γυνή. The following table lists all vocative forms occurring more than three times in the NT, arranged according to frequency.[2] As you can tell, they do not account for a large portion of the vocabulary of the NT—and just two words account for a very large share of them. Knowing the five most common will account for about 40 percent of all the vocatives in the NT.

Nominative	Vocative	Gloss	NT Frequency
κύριος	κύριε	lord	124
ἀδελφός	ἀδελφέ	brother	112
πατήρ	πάτερ	father	35
ἀνήρ	ἄνερ	man	33
διδάσκαλος	διδάσκαλε	teacher	31
γυνή	γύναι (sg.)	woman	13
θεός	θεέ	God	13
ῥαββί	**ῥαββί**	Rabbi	13
τέκνον	**τέκνον**	child	12
ὑποκριτής	ὑποκριτά	hypocrite	12
βασιλεύς	βασιλεῦ	king	11
υἱός	υἱέ	son	11
Ἰησοῦς	Ἰησοῦ	Jesus	10
ἄνθρωπος	ἄνθρωπε	man	9
δοῦλος	δοῦλε	slave	9
Σίμων	**Σίμων**	Simon	9
Σαούλ	**Σαούλ**	Saul	8
τεκνίον	τεκνία (pl.)	little child	8
ἐπιστάτης	ἐπιστάτα	master	7
Φαρισαῖος	Φαρισαῖε	Pharisee	7
γραμματεύς	γραμματεῖς (pl.)	scribes	6
Ἀγρίππας	Ἀγρίππα	Agrippa	5
θυγάτηρ	θύγατερ	daughter	5
Ἰσραηλίτης	Ἰσραηλῖται (pl.)	Israelites	5
γέννημα	γεννήματα (pl.)	brood	4
Ἰερουσαλήμ	**Ἰερουσαλήμ**	Jerusalem	4
παιδίον	**παιδίον**	child	4
ἀββᾶ	**ἀββᾶ**	father	3
γενεά	**γενεά**	generation	3
δεσπότης	δέσποτα	master	3
ἑταῖρος	ἑταῖρε	friend	3

2. The frequency figure includes both singular and plural forms, though only the singular is indicated. (You will remember that the vocative plural is always the same as the nominative plural.)

Nominative	Vocative	Gloss	NT Frequency
νεανίσκος	νεανίσκε	young man	3
Πέτρος	Πέτρε	Peter	3
σατανᾶς	σατανᾶ	Satan	3

Note: Words in bold have the same form in both nominative and vocative. The notation "pl." indicates that the vocative singular of that word does not occur in Koine texts related to the Bible.

The vocative functions the same in the LXX as it does in the NT. The following table lists all the vocatives that occur more than twenty times in the LXX.

Nominative	Vocative	Gloss	LXX Frequency
κύριος	κύριε	lord	695
υἱός	υἱέ	son	148
βασιλεύς	βασιλεῦ	king	77
τέκνον	τέκνον	child	57
θυγάτηρ	θύγατερ	daughter	47
Ἰσραήλ	Ἰσραήλ	Israel	37
ἀδελφός	ἀδελφέ	brother	32
δεσπότης	δέσποτα	master	31
πατήρ	πάτερ	father	21

Vocative Adjectives

D.4. Since adjectives must agree with nouns they modify in gender, number, and case, there is also a vocative-case adjective. In all NT instances the vocative ending on the adjective either is identical to the nominative or is an epsilon. In the LXX the same pattern is generally found, though there are a few vocative adjectives with alpha or eta endings.[3]

Vocative Adjectives Modifying Nouns in Vocative Case (NT)

Matt. 18:32, Δοῦλε **πονηρέ**, wicked slave
Matt. 23:26, Φαρισαῖε **τυφλέ**, blind Pharisee
Matt. 25:21, 23, δοῦλε **ἀγαθὲ** καὶ **πιστέ**, good and faithful slave
Matt. 25:26, **Πονηρὲ** δοῦλε καὶ **ὀκνηρέ**, wicked and lazy slave
Mark 1:24; Luke 4:34, Ἰησοῦ **Ναζαρηνέ**, Jesus Nazarene
Mark 10:17; Luke 18:18, Διδάσκαλε **ἀγαθέ**, good teacher
Luke 1:3, **κράτιστε** Θεόφιλε, most excellent Theophilus
Luke 19:17, **ἀγαθὲ** δοῦλε, good slave

3. LXX vocative adjectives with alpha or eta endings (nominative, vocative): ἀδάμαστος, ἀδάμαστα; ἐμός, ἐμή; ἱερός, ἱερά; μονογενής, μονογενή; μόνος, μόνη; ποθεινός, ποθεινοτέρα; τέλειος, τελεία; τίμιος, τιμία; φίλος, φίλη; ψευδής, ψευδής.

Luke 19:22, **πονηρὲ** δοῦλε, wicked slave
John 17:11, Πάτερ **ἅγιε**, holy Father
Acts 24:3, **κράτιστε** Φῆλιξ, most excellent Felix
Acts 26:25, **κράτιστε** Φῆστε, most excellent Festus
Phil. 4:3, **γνήσιε** σύζυγε, loyal yokefellow (or, loyal Syzygos)
James 2:20, ὦ ἄνθρωπε **κενέ**, O empty fellow

Vocatives of Adjectives Used Substantivally (NT)

Matt. 5:22, Μωρέ, fool
Matt. 14:31, Ὀλιγόπιστε, you of little faith
Luke 11:5; 14:10, Φίλε, friend
Acts 13:10, ἐχθρέ, enemy
3 John 2, 5, 11, Ἀγαπητέ, Beloved

Appendix E

Greek Numbers and Archaic Letters

E.1. Some alphabetic matters are not common in Koine texts related to the Bible but do crop up from time to time. For reference purposes, here is the information you may need someday to solve a puzzle involving an odd-looking letter or Greek numeral.

Greek Numbers

Greek numerals are alphabetic characters with a "hash" mark (ʹ). These are not used in modern printed Greek Testaments or LXX texts other than in the titles of paired books such as ΠΡΟΣ ΚΟΡΙΝΘΙΟΥΣ Αʹ and Βʹ or ΒΑΣΙΛΕΙΩΝ Αʹ, Βʹ, Γʹ, and Δʹ and to number the Psalms,[1] but they do show up in some NT manuscripts as textual variants. You will also find them used elsewhere in various reference works.[2]

Trivia

In Rev. 13:18 the "number of the beast" is normally written out in Greek manuscripts: ἑξακόσιοι ἑξήκοντα ἕξ (six-hundred sixty-six). However, in 𝔓115 (P.Oxy. 4499; third/fourth cent.) and two minuscule manuscripts (5 and 11, no longer extant), it is written in Greek numerals: χιϛ—which is 616.[a]

[a] See the discussion in Metzger, *Textual Commentary*, 676, for an interesting explanation as to why this might be.

1. The UBS text omits the number mark; the NA text includes it. These numerals are used for chapter and verse numbers in Greek Testaments printed in Greece (Modern Greek or Koine) as well as some from the Eastern tradition, but the scholarly editions used in the West do not use Greek numerals.

2. The archaic letters used for 6, 90, and 900 are explained in the next section (§E.2). For further information on Greek numbers and numerals, see Goetchius, *Language of the New Testament*, §§289–92; or for an even more detailed discussion see Smyth, *Greek Grammar*, §§347–54.

		10	ι´	20	κ´
1	α´	11	ια´	21	κα´
2	β´	12	ιβ´	22	κβ´
3	γ´	13	ιγ´	23	κγ´
4	δ´	14	ιδ´	24	κδ´
5	ε´	15	ιε´	25	κε´
6	ς´	16	ις´	26	κς´
7	ζ´	17	ιζ´	27	κζ´
8	η´	18	ιη´	28	κη´
9	θ´	19	ιθ´	29	κθ´

10	ι´	100	ρ´
20	κ´	200	σ´
30	λ´	300	τ´
40	μ´	400	υ´
50	ν´	500	φ´
60	ξ´	600	χ´
70	ο´	700	ψ´
80	π´	800	ω´
90	ϙ´	900	ϡ´
		1000	͵α

Archaic Letters

E.2. There are several characters in Greek that you have not seen yet. The following characters are all obsolete in Koine Greek writing; they did exist in earlier stages of the language. They do not appear in the NT at all, though some were still used in Koine for numerals (see the preceding section). They occasionally appear as textual variants in some NT manuscripts, but they are not in our modern printed texts.

Vau (ϝαῦ), also known as digamma: ϝ. This character affects the forms and spelling of some NT words that still reflect changes that took place when the digamma was in use. It was last used about 200 BC in the Boethian dialect of Greek.[3]

Sampi: ϡ (= the obsolete letter san + π) This symbol was sometimes used for the number 900.

Koppa: ϙ was sometimes used for the number 90.

3. For more details about the digamma, see Smyth, *Greek Grammar*, §3; and *MBG*, §27.

Stigma: ϛ (ctr. ς) is an abbreviation of στ. Watch the spelling. This is not *sigma*. Note that the top of the stigma projects further to the right than does the letter sigma, though this is more pronounced in some digital fonts than others. It is sometimes used for the numeral 6.

There is also a consonantal iota worth noting. This is not another letter but an older use of the letter iota as a consonant. In Koine texts it sometimes still acts that way, or more often affects the spelling of some words. If distinguished in printed form, it is written as an inverted breve *below* the letter iota: ι̯.[4]

4. See further *MBG*, §11.22, §26.

Appendix F

Glossary

The following glossary includes only those words assigned as vocabulary in this textbook. It is not a complete lexicon, nor are the entries complete. (See the explanations in the preface and in chap. 1.) The format of each entry is uniform as shown in figure F.1.

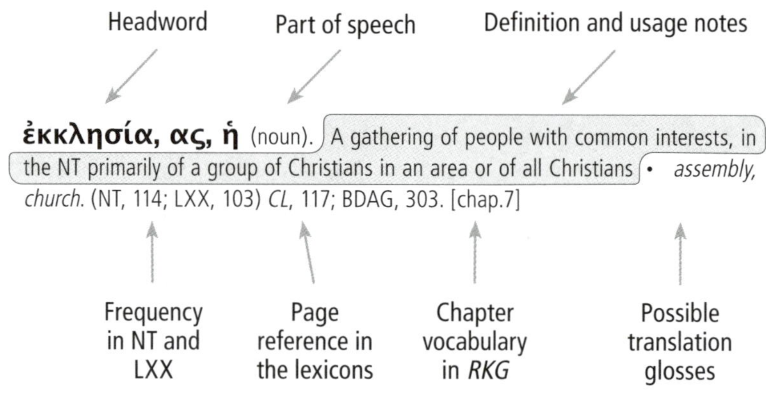

Figure F.1

Ἀβραάμ, ὁ (noun). An indeclinable personal name, in the LXX and NT the father of the Jewish nation through Isaac (and other people groups through Ishmael), formerly named Ἀβράμ • *Abraham*. (NT 73; LXX 210) *CL*, 1; BDAG, 2. [chap. 24]

ἀγαθός, ή, όν (adj.). Achieving a high standard of excellence, positive moral qualities • *good, useful, beneficial, helpful*. (NT 102; LXX 599) *CL*, 2; BDAG, 3. [chap. 9]

ἀγαπάω (verb). To have an interest in another person to the extent that one determines to contribute to that person's well-being [often synonymous with φιλέω; see LN §25.43] • *I love*. (NT 143; LXX 283) *CL*, 2; BDAG, 5. [chap. 7]

ἀγάπη, ης, ἡ (noun). High interest in and regard for the well-being of another, love, affection • *love*. (NT 116; LXX 19) *CL*, 2; BDAG, 6. [chap. 4]

ἀγαπητός, ή, όν (adj.). To be in a special relationship with another, to be loved/esteemed • *beloved, dear, esteemed*. (NT 61; LXX 24) *CL*, 3; BDAG, 7. [chap. 16]

ἄγγελος, ου, ὁ (noun). A personal being (human or supernatural) who transmits a message on behalf of another • *messenger, angel.* (NT 175; LXX 350) *CL*, 3; BDAG, 8. [chap. 3]

ἁγιάζω (verb). To set aside for sacred use/purposes; to treat as holy • *I set apart, sanctify, dedicate; I revere.* (NT 28; LXX 196) *CL*, 3; BDAG, 9. [chap. 31]

ἅγιος, α, ον (adj.). Set apart for deity • *holy* (adj.); *God's people, saints* (subst.). (NT 233; LXX 832) *CL*, 3; BDAG, 10. [chap. 6]

ἀγρός, οῦ, ὁ (noun). An area of land outside settled/residential areas, typically for agricultural use • *field, land, countryside, open country.* (NT 36; LXX 246) *CL*, 5; BDAG, 15. [chap. 26]

ἄγω (verb). To direct the movement of an object from one position to another; metaphorically, to direct the intellectual or moral life of another • *I lead, bring.* (NT 67; LXX 274) *CL*, 6; BDAG, 16. [chap. 14]

ἀδελφός, οῦ, ὁ (noun). Male sibling (i.e., "brother"); in an extended sense, one with common interests, community fellow • *brother; compatriot, "brother(s) and/or sister(s)."* (NT 343; LXX 924) *CL*, 6; BDAG, 18. [chap. 2]

ἀδικέω (verb). To act in an unjust manner by violating law; to do wrong to someone, treat unjustly; to cause damage to, mistreat • *I do wrong, act unjustly; I wrong (someone); I injure, harm, mistreat.* (NT 25; LXX 70) *CL*, 7; BDAG, 20. [chap. 27]

ἀδικία, ας, ἡ (noun). The quality of violating a standard of right • *unrighteousness, wickedness, injustice.* (NT 26; LXX 228) *CL*, 7; BDAG, 20. [chap. 31]

αἷμα, ατος, τό (noun). The red, oxygen-bearing liquid circulating in the bodies of humans and animals; any dark-red liquid; descent, parentage; metaphorically, a person's life (to take, shed, or give blood is to kill/die) • *blood; descent, parentage; lifeblood; murder, killing, death.* (NT 97; LXX 401) *CL*, 9; BDAG, 26. [chap. 22]

αἴρω (verb). To raise something to a higher position; to move from one place to another • *I lift/take/pick up; I remove, take/carry away.* (NT 101; LXX 289) *CL*, 10; BDAG, 28. [chap. 21]

αἰτέω (verb). To ask for something; to ask that something be given or that an action be performed; to present a petition to deity, make a request in prayer; to demand [This is a somewhat stronger word for asking than ἐρωτάω, sometimes implying a claim or expectation; though it can be used anyplace that ἐρωτάω is used, the reverse is not necessarily true.] • *I ask, request; I petition, pray; I demand, insist on.* (NT 70; LXX 94) *CL*, 11; BDAG, 30. [chap. 26]

αἰών, ῶνος, ὁ (noun). A long period of time, in either the past or the future; a segment of time as a particular unit of history; eternity (if context suggests no end) • *age, eternity.* (NT 122; LXX 750) *CL*, 12; BDAG, 32. [chap. 11]

αἰώνιος, ον (adj.). Describing a period of time as being a long time ago or as being without boundaries or interruption or as of unending duration • *long ago; eternal.* (NT 71; LXX 153) *CL*, 12; BDAG, 33. [chap. 15]

ἀκάθαρτος, ον (adj.). Contaminated and thus not meeting the requirements for ritual/ceremonial use; in a more general sense, anything characterized by moral impurity • *unclean, impure.* (NT 32; LXX 160) *CL*, 12; BDAG, 34. [chap. 31]

ἀκολουθέω (verb). To follow in the footsteps of someone; to follow as a disciple • *I follow, accompany, go along with.* (NT 90; LXX 13) *CL*, 13; BDAG, 36. [chap. 25]

ἀκούω (verb). To receive information via the ear; to heed or understand what is said • *I hear; I obey, understand.* (NT 428; LXX 1,069) *CL*, 13; BDAG, 37. [chap. 5]

ἀλήθεια, ας, ἡ (noun). That which is really so or what actually happened • *truth.* (NT 109; LXX 206) *CL*, 15; BDAG, 42. [chap. 7]

ἀλλά (conj.). An adversative coordinating conjunction most often used following a negative statement to suggest a contrasting statement or view or to explain • *but, yet, except.* (NT 638; LXX 557) *CL*, 16; BDAG, 44. [chap. 3]

ἀλλήλων (pron.). A pronoun that refers to a reciprocal relationship between two or more people (or rarely, things); never occurs in nominative or in singular, so genitive plural is used for lexical form • *one another.* (NT 100; LXX 42) *CL*, 17; BDAG, 46. [chap. 10]

ἄλλος, η, ο (adj.). That which is distinct from another entity • *other, another.* (NT 155; LXX 108) *CL*, 17; BDAG, 46. [chap. 6]

ἁμαρτάνω (verb). To commit a wrong by violating the standards established by God (almost always so in the NT), custom, or (human) law • *I sin.* (NT 43; LXX 270) *CL*, 19; BDAG, 49. [chap. 29]

ἁμαρτία, ας, ἡ (noun). A volitional choice or act contrary to (usually God's) standards of uprightness, which results in liability/guilt • *sin.* (NT 173; LXX 545) *CL*, 19; BDAG, 50. [chap. 3]

ἁμαρτωλός, όν (adj.). Characterized by failure to meet or neglect of moral, religious, cultural, or legal expectations; given to ἁμαρτία (usually in relation to God in the LXX and NT, but also of human expectations) • *sinful, irreligious; sinner, outsider* (subst.). (NT 47; LXX 178) *CL*, 19; BDAG, 51. [chap. 29]

ἀμήν (foreign word). A transliterated Hebrew word expressing strong affirmation of what is stated, often used by Jesus and later by Christians in a worshipful context • *amen, truly, verily, "so let it be."* (NT 129; LXX 10) *CL*, 20; BDAG, 53. [chap. 16]

ἄν (particle). A particle with diverse uses, most of which nuance the verb with some element of contingency or generalization, often translated as a part of the verbal phrase rather than as a discrete element • *then, would, ever, might.* (NT 167; LXX 619) *CL*, 21; BDAG, 56. [chap. 17]

ἀναβαίνω (verb). To be in motion, usually upward; to get into a boat; to emerge, make an appearance; "to enter the heart" (idiom = "to think about") • *I go up, ascend, come up; I embark; I appear; I think.* (NT 82; LXX 614) *CL*, 22; BDAG, 58. [chap. 25]

ἀνήρ, ἀνδρός, ὁ (noun). An adult human male; a specific man as related to a woman, i.e., a husband • *man, male; husband.* (NT 216; LXX 1,918) *CL*, 32; BDAG, 79. [chap. 11]

ἄνθρωπος, ου, ὁ (noun). Human being, often used generically of men or women, either in distinction from God or in reference to a specific person. • *man, person, human being, mankind, humankind.* (NT 550; LXX 1,430) *CL*, 33; BDAG, 81. [chap. 2]

ἀνίστημι (verb). (1) Transitive (fut., [1]aor. act.): to cause to rise up (of an object or of a dead person); (2) intransitive (mid., [2]aor. act.): to stand up from lying or sitting; to come back from the dead; to appear to carry out a function; to initiate an action specified by another verb • (1) *I raise, erect, bring to life;* (2) *I stand up, rise; I come back from the dead; I arise; I set out, get ready.* (NT 108; LXX 539) *CL*, 34; BDAG, 83. [chap. 32]

ἀνοίγω (verb). To move or change something from a shut or closed position to enable access or function • *I open.* (NT 77; LXX 182) *CL*, 34; BDAG, 84. [chap. 14]

ἀντί (prep.). A preposition used with the genitive case indicating correspondence in which one thing is to be replaced by or substituted with or for another • (prep. + gen.) *instead of, for, in behalf of.* (NT 21; LXX 391) *CL*, 36; BDAG, 87. [chap. 19]

ἄξιος, ία, ον (adj.). Deemed to correspond to an expectation of worth; deserving, worthy of (reward or punishment) • *worthy, fit, deserving.* (NT 41; LXX 40) *CL*, 38; BDAG, 93. [chap. 20]

ἀπαγγέλλω (verb). To give an account of something (usually oral); to make something known publicly • *I announce, report, tell; I proclaim.* (NT 45; LXX 254) *CL*, 39; BDAG, 95. [chap. 21]

ἅπας, ασα, αν (adj.). The totality of something (intensive form of the adj. πᾶς) • *all, the whole* (with articular noun); *all, everybody, everything* (subst.). (NT 34; LXX 78) *CL*, 40; BDAG, 98. [chap. 12]

ἀπεκρίθη (verb). Very common inflected verb form (a θη-middle form): 3rd sg. aor. pass. ind. of ἀποκρίνω; to make a response, to either a specific question, a statement, or a situation • *he/she/it answered.* (NT 82; LXX 95) *CL*, 46; BDAG, 113. [chap. 18]

ἀπέρχομαι (verb). To depart from a place • *I go away, depart.* (NT 117; LXX 229) *CL*, 42; BDAG, 102. [chap. 15]

ἀπό (prep.). A preposition used with the genitive case that generally indicates separation or source, sometimes temporal or causal • (prep. + gen.) *from.* (NT 646; LXX 4,150) *CL*, 44; BDAG, 105. [chap. 9]

ἀποδίδωμι (verb). To engage in a reciprocal action by repaying money, fulfilling an obligation, transferring something to another; to give a product in exchange for payment or trade (mid.); to yield fruit/produce • *I repay, give/pay back; I pay; I give over, give back, restore; I sell, trade; I yield (fruit).* (NT 48; LXX 220) *CL*, 45; BDAG, 109. [chap. 32]

ἀποθνῄσκω (verb). To stop living • *I die.* (NT 111; LXX 600) *CL*, 46; BDAG, 111. [chap. 25]

ἀποκρίνω (verb). To make a response, to either a specific question, a statement, or a situation (never act. in NT, once in LXX; act. appears more often in other Koine literature; often listed as ἀποκρίνομαι) • *I answer, reply, say in response/reaction to.* (NT 231; LXX 277) *CL*, 46; BDAG, 113. [chap. 21]

ἀποκτείνω (verb). To forcibly end the life of someone or something • *I kill.* (NT 74; LXX 212) *CL*, 47; BDAG, 114. [chap. 25]

ἀπόλλυμι (verb). (1) Transitive: to cause destruction, put to death; to lose something (act.); (2) intransitive: to experience destruction; to be unavailable; to not be found (mid.) • (1) *I ruin, destroy, kill; I lose* (act.); (2) *I die, perish; I am deprived of; I have gone missing* (mid.). (NT 90; LXX 378) *CL*, 47; BDAG, 115. [chap. 33]

ἀπολύω (verb). To set free from a condition or obligation (legal or medical, etc.); to cause to depart from a place; to terminate a marriage • *I release, set free, deliver; I dismiss, send away; I divorce.* (NT 66; LXX 27) *CL*, 48; BDAG, 117. [chap. 14]

ἀποστέλλω (verb). To send someone or something from one place to another • *I send, send away.* (NT 132; LXX 691) *CL*, 49; BDAG, 120. [chap. 21]

ἀπόστολος, ου, ὁ (noun). One who is sent on a mission; in the NT, usually the Twelve, who were Jesus' official messengers • *apostle, envoy, messenger.* (NT 80; LXX 0) *CL*, 50; BDAG, 122. [chap. 8]

ἅπτω (1); **ἅπτομαι** (2) (verb). (1) To cause to burn or give light (act.); (2) to make contact with something (for various purposes) [2 is a middle-only verb; 1 and 2 are homonyms] • (1) *I kindle, ignite* (act.); (2) *I touch, take hold of, cling to* (mid.). (NT 39; LXX 134) *CL*, 51; BDAG, 126. [chap. 19]

ἄρα (particle). A postpositive particle that introduces an inference or result from what precedes; may also add a sense of tentativeness to a statement (ctr. ἀρά, "curse"; and the interrogative ἆρα) • *then, so, consequently, as a result; perhaps, conceivably.* (NT 49; LXX 77) *CL*, 52; BDAG, 127. [chap. 20]

ἄρτος, ου, ὁ (noun). A baked cake or loaf made from a cereal grain (barley, wheat, etc.); food in general • *bread, loaf; food.* (NT 97; LXX 307) *CL*, 56; BDAG, 136. [chap. 8]

ἀρχή, ῆς, ἡ (noun). The commencement or derivation of something; an authority figure who is preeminent [See also ἄρχω.] • *beginning, start, origin; ruler, authority.* (NT 55; LXX 239) *CL*, 56; BDAG, 137. [chap. 28]

ἀρχιερεύς, έως, ὁ (noun). The person who serves as the head priest in a religious system; in plural, collective for priests of high rank • *high priest; chief priests.* (NT 122; LXX 44) *CL*, 56; BDAG, 139. [chap. 22]

ἄρχω (verb). (1) To rule or govern (act.; only twice in the NT, more common in the LXX); (2) to initiate an action, process, or state (mid.) [probably homonyms] • (1) *I rule* (act.); (2) I *begin* (mid.). (NT 86; LXX 231) *CL*, 57; BDAG, 140. [chap. 17]

ἄρχων, οντος, ὁ (noun). One who rules (though with less authority than a βασιλεύς); an administrative official • *ruler, prince; leader, official, administrator.* (NT 37; LXX 645) *CL*, 57; BDAG, 140. [chap. 32]

ἀσθενέω (verb). To experience physical weakness as a result of sickness or some other incapacity; to lack capacity for something whether physical or otherwise • *I am weak/sick; I am deficient.* (NT 33; LXX 77) *CL*, 58; BDAG, 142. [chap. 19]

ἀσπάζομαι (verb). To address someone hospitably, either in person (whether arriving or departing) or in correspondence • *I greet, welcome, say good-bye.* (NT 59; LXX 10) *CL*, 58; BDAG, 144. [chap. 15]

αὐτός, ή, ό (pron.). Pronoun: personal, third person ("he, she, it, they"); adjective [see chap. 6]: intensive ("-self") or identifying ("[the] same") • (1) *he, she, it, they;* (2) *him-, her-, itself;* (3) *same.* (NT 5,595; LXX 29,416) *CL*, 62; BDAG, 152. [chap. 4]

ἀφίημι (verb). To release from one's presence; to divorce a spouse; to release from legal or moral obligation, especially from the guilt of sin; to allow to remain behind; to allow someone the freedom to do something • *I let go, send away; I divorce; I pardon, forgive; I leave, abandon; I allow, tolerate.* (NT 143; LXX 138) *CL*, 64; BDAG, 156. [chap. 33]

ἄχρι, ἄχρις (prep.). A preposition used with the genitive (sometimes as a conjunction) to indicate an extent of time up to a specified event, mostly used of time, occasionally of situations [The spelling ἄχρις is not common; it is sometimes used before words beginning with a vowel.] • *until* (prep. + gen., or conj.); *as far as.* (NT 49; LXX 3) *CL*, 65; BDAG, 160. [chap. 22]

βάλλω (verb). To cause to move from one location to another, with either a forceful or more subdued motion (English equivalents will depend largely on the object moved and other contextual factors.) • *I throw, hurl; I put, place, lay.* (NT 122; LXX 59) *CL*, 67; BDAG, 163. [chap. 25]

βαπτίζω (verb). To dip, plunge, or immerse in water or another liquid, to drown [see LSJ and M-M]; in the LXX, to dip in water, to wash; in the NT it designates one of several actions, including a Jewish cleansing ritual using water, John's ceremony for confession of sin in the Jordan River, a similar ceremony authorized by Jesus, the Christian water ceremony of confession of faith, a metaphorical reference to a work involving the Spirit uniting people with Christ and his Body at conversion, and various other metaphorical uses. [Christians differ as to the mode of the confessional ceremony; some think the unmarked meaning is to be preserved (i.e., baptism by immersion); others allow other modes (pouring, sprinkling), so they transliterate the word as "I baptize."] • *I dip, immerse, baptize.* (NT 77; LXX 4) *CL*, 67; BDAG, 164. [chap. 14]

βασιλεία, ας, ἡ (noun). The act of ruling; the realm over which that rule is exercised; especially God's reign in fulfillment of promises to Israel • *kingdom, kingship.* (NT 162; LXX 447) *CL*, 69; BDAG, 168. [chap. 3]

βασιλεύς, έως, ὁ (noun). A man who is the supreme ruler in a country by right of succession to the throne; God as the supreme ruler of everything that exists by right of being the Creator • *king.* (NT 115; LXX 3,476) *CL*, 69; BDAG, 169. [chap. 11]

βασιλεύω (verb). To exercise royal authority as king; to become king • *I am king, I rule/reign as king; I become king.* (NT 21; LXX 402) *CL*, 69; BDAG, 170. [chap. 19]

βιβλίον, ου, τό (noun). Written document regardless of size (one or multiple sheets or pages) or format (loose sheet, scroll, or codex form) • *book, scroll; document.* (NT 34; LXX 186) *CL*, 71; BDAG, 176. [chap. 9]

βλέπω (verb). To use one's eyes for sensory perception (various metaphorical uses are also common) • *I see, look at.* (NT 133; LXX 133) *CL*, 72; BDAG, 178. [chap. 5]

βούλομαι (verb). To desire to have/experience something; to plan a course of action on the basis of deliberation • *I wish, desire; I intend, plan, determine.* (NT 37; LXX 128) *CL*, 74; BDAG, 182. [chap. 26]

Γαλιλαία, ας, ἡ (noun). A postexilic geographical area constituting the northern part of Palestine • *Galilee.* (NT 61; LXX 25) *CL*, 76; BDAG, 187. [chap. 27]

γάρ (conj.). A multipurpose, postpositive marker that may function as a narrative connector or as an expression of reaction or perspective, "for" (usually a subordinating conjunction): (1) explanatory; (2) astonishment; (3) causal; or (4) inferential. • *for.* (NT 1,041; LXX 1,529) *CL*, 76; BDAG, 189. [chap. 2]

γενεά, ᾶς, ἡ (noun). A group of people born about the same time; a period of time in which a group of people born about the same time live; those people having common characteristics or interests; an undefined period of time • *generation, contemporaries; kind (of people), race; age.* (NT 43; LXX 238) *CL*, 77; BDAG, 191. [chap. 29]

γεννάω (verb). To cause something to come into existence, usually of the human father's role in the conception of a child, but also of childbirth by the mother or occasionally of animal procreation; to cause something to happen • *I beget,* *father, procreate; I bear (a child), give birth to; I bring forth, produce.* (NT 97; LXX 253) *CL*, 78; BDAG, 193. [chap. 25]

γῆ, γῆς, ἡ (noun). The earth (i.e., the planet on which we live) or figuratively of the people who live there; some part of the earth, whether a region/land, or the soil • *land, earth, region, soil.* (NT 250; LXX 3,154) *CL*, 79; BDAG, 196. [chap. 3]

γίνομαι (verb). Generally, to transfer from one state or condition to another; to come into being by birth, production, or manufacture; to occur; to enter a new condition; to change location; etc. [Read the summary in *CL*!] • *I become, I am/exist; I am born/produced; I come about, take place.* (NT 669; LXX 2,174) *CL*, 79; BDAG, 196. [chap. 18]

γινώσκω (verb). To be in receipt of information that results in understanding; to form a judgment • *I know, learn; I understand.* (NT 222; LXX 746) *CL*, 79; BDAG, 199. [chap. 5]

γλῶσσα, ης, ἡ (noun). The muscular organ in the mouth used for tasting, licking, swallowing, and making sounds (in humans, for speaking; "tongue"); a system of words used in communication ("language") • *tongue; language.* (NT 50; LXX 169) *CL*, 80; BDAG, 201. [chap. 28]

γραμματεύς, έως, ὁ (noun). A government official charged with record keeping; a specialist in the law of Moses • *secretary (of state), clerk; scribe, legal scholar.* (NT 63; LXX 85) *CL*, 81; BDAG, 206. [chap. 23]

γραφή, ῆς, ἡ (noun). That which is written; in the NT used exclusively as a designation of the OT, "Scripture"; outside the NT it can refer to other written documents • *writing, Scripture.* (NT 50; LXX 50) *CL*, 82; BDAG, 206. [chap. 3]

γράφω (verb). To inscribe letters or symbols on a writing surface; to compose a written text; to write • *I write.* (NT 191; LXX 304) *CL*, 82; BDAG, 207. [chap. 5]

γυνή, αικός, ἡ (noun). An adult human female; a specific woman as related to a man, i.e., a wife • *woman; wife.* (NT 215; LXX 1,074) *CL*, 83; BDAG, 208. [chap. 11]

δαιμόνιον, ου, τό (noun). An evil, incorporeal, supernatural being often identified as a fallen/sinful angel • *demon.* (NT 63; LXX 17) *CL*, 83; BDAG, 210. [chap. 24]

Δαυίδ, ὁ (noun). An indeclinable personal name, in the LXX and NT refers to Israel's great king • *David.* (NT 59; LXX 1,090) *CL*, 84; BDAG, 212. [chap. 24]

δέ (conj.). A multipurpose coordinating, postpositive conjunction or narrative marker linking two grammatically equal items that have some difference in referent (subject, participant, time, place, etc.) • *but, now, and.* (NT 2,792; LXX 4,887) *CL*, 84; BDAG, 213. [chap. 2]

δεῖ (verb). An impersonal verb expressing what is necessary, compulsory, or fitting • *it is necessary; one must; it had to be.* (NT 101; LXX 50) *CL*, 85; BDAG, 213. [chap. 16]

δείκνυμι (also **δεικνύω**) (verb). To show so as to be apprehended by the senses; to prove or make clear by evidence, reasoning, or demonstration • *I show, point out, make known; I explain, prove, demonstrate.* (NT 33; LXX 124) *CL*, 85; BDAG, 214. [chap. 32]

δέκα (adj.). The number ten (indeclinable) • *ten, 10.* (NT 25; LXX 326) *CL*, 86; BDAG, 216. [chap. 12]

δεξιός, ά, όν (adj.). On the right-hand side as opposed to the left in a particular frame of reference; the right hand, the right-hand side (subst.) • *right* (opposite of "left"; ≠ "correct"); *the right hand/side.* (NT 54; LXX 228) *CL*, 86; BDAG, 217. [chap. 28]

δεύτερος, α, ον (adj.). Next after first in a sequence; for the second time (neut. sg. as adv.) • *second; for the second time.* (NT 43; LXX 230) *CL*, 88; BDAG, 220. [chap. 30]

δέχομαι (verb). To accept the presence of a person or the arrival of a thing, often with connotations of enthusiasm or joy; to readily receive information and to regard it as true • *I receive, welcome, take; I accept, receive readily.* (NT 56; LXX 62) *CL*, 88; BDAG, 221. [chap. 15]

δέω (verb). To restrain someone or something (usually) by physical means (may also be metaphorical, e.g., a legal restraint); to fasten objects together • *I bind; I tie.* (NT 43; LXX 69) *CL*, 88; BDAG, 221. [chap. 7]

διά (prep.). A preposition used with the genitive (spatial, temporal, instrumental) and accusative cases (spatial or causal) • (prep. + gen.) *through, during;* (prep. + acc.) *because of, on account of.* (NT 667; LXX 1,427) *CL*, 88; BDAG, 223. [chap. 9]

διάβολος, ον (adj.). Characterized by intent to slander, oppose, or otherwise harm someone's reputation or interests; in the NT usually substantival, διάβολος, ου, ὁ, referring to the devil • *slanderous, accusing falsely; devil, adversary* (subst.). (NT 37; LXX 22) *CL*, 89; BDAG, 226. [chap. 26]

διδάσκαλος, ου, ὁ (noun). A person who provides instruction by giving information or by showing or explaining how to do something • *teacher, instructor, tutor.* (NT 59; LXX 2) *CL*, 95; BDAG, 241. [chap. 24]

διδάσκω (verb). To provide instruction in a formal or informal setting; to tell someone what to do • *I teach, instruct; I tell (what to do).* (NT 97; LXX 107) *CL*, 95; BDAG, 241. [chap. 14]

δίδωμι (verb). To cause another person to receive or have (roughly equivalent to the English word "give" with a wide range of glosses possible, depending on the context and referent; LXX even more diverse than NT) • *I give.* (NT 415; LXX 2,131) *CL*, 95; BDAG, 242. [chap. 32]

διέρχομαι (verb). To travel/move in or through an area • *I go/pass (through); I come, arrive.* (NT 43; LXX 146) *CL*, 96; BDAG, 244. [chap. 15]

δίκαιος, α, ον (adj.). In accord with standards for acceptable behavior, that which is obligatory in view of certain requirements of justice; conforming to the laws of God, being in a right relationship with God; substantivally, one who has been declared right before God • *upright, fair; righteous, just.* (NT 79; LXX 435) *CL*, 97; BDAG, 246. [chap. 6]

δικαιοσύνη, ης, ἡ (noun). A state that is in accord with standards for acceptable behavior; being in a right relationship with God, either declaratively (the result of justification) or practically (living in such a way as to reflect the judicial reality) • *uprightness, righteousness.* (NT 92; LXX 351) *CL*, 97; BDAG, 247. [chap. 16]

δικαιόω (verb). To render a favorable verdict, pronounce innocent; in Pauline theology, a judicial act in which God declares the believing sinner righteous • *I justify, vindicate.* (NT 39; LXX 51) *CL*, 97; BDAG, 249. [chap. 19]

διό (conj.). A subordinating conjunction that introduces an inference from the preceding statement • *wherefore, therefore, for this reason.* (NT 53; LXX 24) *CL*, 98; BDAG, 250. [chap. 8]

διότι (conj.). A subordinating conjunction that gives a reason for the preceding statement or that draws an inference from it • *because, for; therefore.* (NT 24; LXX 341) *CL*, 98; BDAG, 251. [chap. 18]

διώκω (verb). To engage in pursuit, follow hastily (may be either positive or negative in intent); to harass, organize a systematic program of harassment • *I pursue, run after; I persecute.* (NT 45; LXX 104) *CL*, 99; BDAG, 254. [chap. 31]

δοκέω (verb). To consider an idea as probable; to entertain an opinion • *I think, suppose, believe, regard, decide; I seem, have the appearance, think.* (NT 62; LXX 64) *CL*, 99; BDAG, 254. [chap. 27]

δόξα, ης, ἡ (noun). Esteem, either an intrinsic characteristic or an attribution of it; a splendid/magnificent display, seen as a visible brightness/radiance or, metaphorically, as worthy character • *glory, majesty, fame, brightness.* (NT 166; LXX 453) *CL*, 100; BDAG, 257. [chap. 3]

δοξάζω (verb). To enhance or exalt the esteem or reputation of another by word or action; to attribute high status to someone • *I glorify, praise, honor.* (NT 61; LXX 143) *CL*, 101; BDAG, 258. [chap. 14]

δοῦλος, ου, ὁ (noun). A male slave, a person who is the legal property of another whom he must obey (pl. may be generic) • *slave.* (NT 124; LXX 383) *CL*, 101; BDAG, 259. [chap. 4]

δύναμαι (verb). To be capable of doing something (used with an infinitive to specify what is done) • *I am able.* (NT 210; LXX 332) *CL*, 102; BDAG, 262. [chap. 15]

δύναμις, εως, ἡ (noun). The capacity to function adequately in a particular situation; a deed that demonstrates this capacity [This word often refers to a miracle in the NT, but it should not be translated as such; cf. σημεῖον and τέρας.] • *ability, capability, strength, power; deed of power* (NT); *armed military force* (LXX). (NT 119; LXX 590) *CL*, 102; BDAG, 262. [chap. 22]

δυνατός, ή, όν (adj.). Having power or competence; capable of being realized, to be possible • *able, capable, powerful; it is possible* (neut.). (NT 32; LXX 185) *CL*, 103; BDAG, 264. [chap. 6]

δύο (adj.). The number two • *two, 2.* (NT 135; LXX 645) *CL*, 103; BDAG, 264. [chap. 12]

δώδεκα (adj.). The number twelve (indeclinable); when used as a noun in the NT, this word refers to the group of Jesus' disciples (even if not all twelve are present) • *twelve, 12; the Twelve.* (NT 75; LXX 100) *CL*, 103; BDAG, 266. [chap. 18]

ἐάν (conj.). Conditional particle that introduces the "if" part of a conditional statement; sometimes used as a subordinating temporal conjunction, "when" (governs subjunctive mood) • *if; when.* (NT 351; LXX 1,343) *CL*, 104; BDAG, 267. [chap. 8]

ἑαυτοῦ, ῆς, οῦ (pron.). A pronoun that makes a reflexive reference to a person or thing (third person; never occurs in nominative case, so lexical form is genitive; cf. first person, ἐμαυτοῦ; second person, σεαυτοῦ) • *himself, herself, itself; themselves.* (NT 319; LXX 662) *CL*, 104; BDAG, 269. [chap. 10]

ἐγγίζω (verb). To draw closer to a reference point (either spatially or temporally) • *I come/draw near, approach.* (NT 42; LXX 158) *CL*, 105; BDAG, 270. [chap. 29]

ἐγείρω (verb). To move from an inert state or position, the nature of which depends on the context, whether from sitting, lying, sleeping, sickness, death, inertia, or obscurity • *I rise, get/raise/lift up; I awake, rouse.* (NT 144; LXX 57) *CL*, 106; BDAG, 271. [chap. 21]

ἐγώ (pron.). Personal pronoun, first-person singular nominative. • *I.* (NT 1,725; LXX 12,529) *CL*, 107; BDAG, 275. [chap. 4]

ἔθνος, ους, τό (noun). A group of people viewed as an entity on the basis of kinship, geography, or custom; in the plural often refers to non-Jews, i.e., Gentiles • *nation; Gentiles* (pl.). (NT 162; LXX 1,003) *CL*, 108; BDAG, 276. [chap. 11]

εἰ (particle). A conditional particle that marks a contingency of some sort (mostly used with the indicative mood) • *if, whether.* (NT 503; LXX 805) *CL*, 108; BDAG, 277. [chap. 17]

εἶ (verb). An inflected verb form: 2nd sg. pres. (act.) ind. of εἰμί • *you are.* (NT 92; LXX 255) *CL*, 110; BDAG, 282. [chap. 7]

εἶδον (verb). To perceive by seeing with the eyes; to become aware of or notice something (used as ²aor. of ὁράω) [see chap. 21] • *I saw, perceived; I noticed.* (NT 76; LXX 207) *CL*, 109; BDAG, 279. [chap. 18]

εἰ μή (idiom). An idiomatic expression specifying an exception • *except.* (NT 86; LXX 93) *CL*, 109, s.v. εἰ; BDAG, 278.6.i., s.v. εἰ. [chap. 18]

εἰμί (verb). The Greek "being/linking/copula/auxiliary" verb, roughly equivalent to the English "to be" (English requires a broad range of translations) • *I am, exist, live, am present.* (NT 2,460; LXX 6,947) *CL*, 110; BDAG, 282. [chap. 5]

εἶπεν (verb). Very common inflected verb form: 3rd sg. ²aor. act. ind. of εἶπον (λέγω) • *he/she/it said/told.* (NT 613; LXX 2,758) *CL*, 111; BDAG, 286. [chap. 18]

εἶπον (verb). To express a thought, opinion, or idea in spoken words (used as the ²aor. of λέγω) • *I said, told.* (NT 62; LXX 4,608) *CL*, 111; BDAG, 286. [chap. 18]

εἰρήνη, ης, ἡ (noun). A state of concord or harmony in personal or political relationships; a state of well-being (used as a greeting) • *peace.* (NT 92; LXX 294) *CL*, 111; BDAG, 287. [chap. 16]

εἰς (prep.). A preposition used with the accusative case that generally refers to entrance into, direction, or limit (these can be spatial or temporal), but usage is quite varied with many possible English equivalents, depending on the context; in Koine, often overlaps with ἐν in meaning [Note the smooth breathing: this is not εἷς.] • (prep. + acc.) *into, in, among; until.* (NT 1,768; LXX 7,438) *CL*, 112; BDAG, 288. [chap. 9]

εἷς, μία, ἕν (adj.). The number one [rough breathing, not εἰς] • *one, 1.* (NT 344; LXX 1,052) *CL*, 112; BDAG, 291. [chap. 12]

εἰσέρχομαι (verb). To enter into a space or into an event or state • *I come/go in(to), enter.* (NT 194; LXX 700) *CL*, 113; BDAG, 293. [chap. 15]

εἰσί(ν) (verb). An inflected verb form: 3rd pl. pres. (act.) ind. of εἰμί • *they are.* (NT 157; LXX 261) *CL*, 110; BDAG, 282. [chap. 5]

εἴτε (particle). A function word indicating a direct or indirect question suggesting alternatives, usually paired (εἴτε . . . εἴτε) [crasis form: εἰ + τέ] • *if, whether (if x or if y; whether x or y).* (NT 65; LXX 9) *CL*, 114; BDAG, 279, s.v. εἰ, 6.o. [chap. 24]

ἐκ, ἐξ (prep.). A preposition used with the genitive case that generally refers to separation or derivation, but usage is quite varied with many possible English equivalents, depending on the context • (prep. + gen.) *out of, from.* (NT 914; LXX 3,823) *CL*, 114; BDAG, 295. [chap. 9]

ἕκαστος, η, ον (adj.). An individual person or thing, each one of an aggregate in an individual sense; can also be used as a substantive • *each, every; each one, everyone.* (NT 82; LXX 356) *CL*, 114; BDAG, 298. [chap. 16]

ἐκβάλλω (verb). To cause to move away from a place or condition (English idiom varies considerably, depending on various contextual factors.) • *I put out, cast out, throw out, take out, send out.* (NT 81; LXX 101) *CL*, 114; BDAG, 299. [chap. 25]

ἐκεῖ (adv.). An adverb of place indicating a location in contrast to "here" • *there, in that place.* (NT 105; LXX 798) *CL*, 116; BDAG, 301. [chap. 6]

ἐκεῖθεν (adv.). An adverb of place indicating source as from a particular place • *from there.* (NT 37; LXX 150) *CL*, 116; BDAG, 301. [chap. 26]

ἐκεῖνος, η, ο (pron.). Far demonstrative pronoun referring to the person or thing that is comparatively remote ("that" as opposed to οὗτος/"this") • *that, that one/man/woman/thing; those.* (NT 265; LXX 739) *CL*, 116; BDAG, 301. [chap. 10]

ἐκκλησία, ας, ἡ (noun). A gathering of people with common interests, in the LXX with reference to the assembled nation of Israel, in the NT primarily of a group of Christians in an area or of all Christians • *assembly, church.* (NT 114; LXX 103) *CL*, 117; BDAG, 303. [chap. 7]

ἐκπορεύομαι (verb). To move from one place to another, usually of people, but various other uses such as water flowing from a place • *I come/go (out), proceed.* (NT 33; LXX 172) *CL*, 119; BDAG, 308. [chap. 22]

ἔλεος, ους, τό (noun). Kindness expressed to someone in need • *mercy, compassion, pity.* (NT 27; LXX 338) *CL*, 122; BDAG, 316. [chap. 33]

ἐλπίζω (verb). To have confidence of something positive coming to pass • *I hope, hope for; I expect.* (NT 31; LXX 117) *CL*, 123; BDAG, 319. [chap. 19]

ἐλπίς, ίδος, ἡ (noun). The state of looking forward to something with confidence regarding its realization; that which is the basis for such a hope; that for which one hopes • *hope, expectation.* (NT 53; LXX 116) *CL*, 123; BDAG, 319. [chap. 23]

ἐμαυτοῦ, ῆς (pron.). A pronoun that makes a reflexive, first-person reference to the speaker; a reflexive pronoun (first person; never occurs in nominative case, in plural, or in neuter, so lexical form is genitive; cf. second person, σεαυτοῦ; third person, ἑαυτοῦ) • *myself.* (NT 37; LXX 59) *CL*, 124; BDAG, 320. [chap. 10]

ἐμός, ἐμή, ἐμόν (pl. ἡμέτερος) (pron.). A pronoun that refers to something pertaining to the speaker, often a possessive or responsible relationship • *my, mine; our.* (NT 76; LXX 112) *CL*, 124; BDAG, 323. [chap. 10]

ἔμπροσθεν (prep.). A preposition used with the genitive to indicate position in front of something; occasionally used in its older adverbial sense of place in front • *before, in front of* (prep. + gen.); *in front, ahead* (adv.). (NT 48; LXX 162) *CL*, 125; BDAG, 325. [chap. 22]

ἐν (prep.). A preposition used with the dative case that generally refers to position within, but usage is quite varied with many possible English equivalents, depending on the context • (prep. + dat.) *in, on, among.* (NT 2,752; LXX 14,275) *CL*, 126; BDAG, 326. [chap. 9]

ἐνδύω (verb). To provide covering, to put clothing on someone (act.); to clothe oneself, put on, wear (mid.) • *I dress, clothe* (act.); *I put on, wear* (mid.). (NT 27; LXX 118) *CL*, 128; BDAG, 333. [chap. 14]

ἐντέλλω (verb). To give authoritative instructions • *I command, order.* (NT 15; LXX 424) *CL*, 130; BDAG, 339. [chap. 19]

ἐντολή, ῆς, ἡ (noun). An authoritative directive for action; the Mosaic covenant as a whole, the law • *command, commandment, law; the law (of Moses).* (NT 67; LXX 240) *CL*, 131; BDAG, 340. [chap. 24]

ἐνώπιον (prep.). A preposition used with the genitive to indicate being in the sight of someone • (prep. + gen.) *before, in front of, in the sight of.* (NT 94; LXX 558) *CL*, 131; BDAG, 342. [chap. 10]

ἕξ (adj.). The number six (indeclinable) • *six, 6.* (NT 13; LXX 134) *CL*, 132; BDAG, 343. [chap. 12]

ἐξέρχομαι (verb). To move away from a location • *I go/come out/away.* (NT 218; LXX 742) *CL*, 133; BDAG, 347. [chap. 15]

ἐξουσία, ας, ἡ (noun). The right to speak or act without first obtaining approval, freedom of choice or action; the right to control or govern, power exercised by rulers or others in high position by virtue of their office • *authority, right, power, control.* (NT 102; LXX 79) *CL*, 135; BDAG, 352. [chap. 8]

ἔξω (adv.). Formally, an adverb of place indicating a position beyond a limit or boundary, but it can also be used as an adjective, that which does not belong; a preposition used with the genitive to indicate movement away from; a substantive (with the article), those who are not part of the referenced group • *without* (adv.); *outer, foreign* (adj.); *outside* (prep. + gen.); *outsiders* (subst. with article). (NT 63; LXX 104) *CL*, 136; BDAG, 354. [chap. 17]

ἐπαγγελία, ας, ἡ (noun). That which one has committed to do for another • *promise.* (NT 52; LXX 8) *CL*, 136; BDAG, 355. [chap. 28]

ἐπερωτάω (verb). To ask a question [not distinguishable from ἐρωτάω] • *I ask, inquire; I ask for, request.* (NT 56; LXX 75) *CL*, 139; BDAG, 362. [chap. 26]

ἐπί (prep.). A preposition used with any of three cases that generally refers to location ("on" or "over") or time ("at" or "in"); some English equivalents are usable with all three cases, others are appropriate for only one of the cases [see *CL* or BDAG] • (prep. + gen.) *on, over, when;* (prep. + dat.) *on the basis of, at;* (prep. + acc.) *on, to, against.* (NT 890; LXX 7,297) *CL*, 139; BDAG, 363. [chap. 9]

ἐπιγινώσκω (verb). To be in receipt of information that results in understanding; sometimes the context suggests the contribution of the prefixed preposition: to understand/know well/exactly/completely; to recognize based on previous knowledge [often indistinguishable from γινώσκω] • *I know, understand, learn, find out; I understand/know well/exactly/completely; I recognize, acknowledge.* (NT 44; LXX 145) *CL*, 141; BDAG, 369. [chap. 29]

ἐπιθυμία, ας, ἡ (noun). A strong desire for something, whether good or bad • *desire, longing, craving, lust.* (NT 38; LXX 85) *CL*, 142; BDAG, 372. [chap. 26]

ἐπικαλέω (verb). To give a name to someone or address someone by a name; to call upon someone, to invoke; legal term: to appeal (a ruling), to call a witness • *I name, give a name; I call upon, call out; I appeal to* (mid.). (NT 30; LXX 188) *CL*, 142; BDAG, 373. [chap. 7]

ἐπιστρέφω (verb). To return to a place where one has previously been; to change direction or turn around in a space; to change one's mind, mode of thinking, belief, or course of action • *I return, go back; I turn (around); I turn (back/from), repent.* (NT 36; LXX 534) *CL*, 145; BDAG, 382. [chap. 31]

ἐπιτίθημι (verb). To place something on someone/something; to set upon, attack • *I lay/put upon, place on; I attack.* (NT 39; LXX 270) *CL*, 146; BDAG, 384. [chap. 33]

ἑπτά (adj.). The number seven (indeclinable) • *seven, 7.* (NT 88; LXX 377) *CL*, 148; BDAG, 388. [chap. 12]

ἐργάζομαι (verb). To engage in activity that involves effort; to do or accomplish something through work (the result of the activity) • *I work; I do, accomplish, carry out.* (NT 41; LXX 122) *CL*, 148; BDAG, 389. [chap. 15]

ἔργον, ου, τό (noun). That which is done, an activity ("work") or the result of activity ("product"); more generally, "thing, matter" • *work, deed, action, task; thing, matter.* (NT 169; LXX 590) *CL*, 148; BDAG, 390. [chap. 3]

ἔρημος, ον (adj.). Characterized by being isolated or deserted (either a place or a person); an uninhabited region • *isolated, desolate, deserted; wilderness, desert* (subst.). (NT 48; LXX 386) *CL*, 149; BDAG, 391. [chap. 30]

ἔρχομαι (verb). To move from one point to another (geographical or temporal), which may be described from the perspective of either the origin or destination ("come" is the usual equivalent; "go" is less common in Koine). • *I come, arrive; I go.* (NT 634; LXX 1,054) *CL*, 150; BDAG, 393. [chap. 15]

ἐρωτάω (verb). To ask for/seek information, ask a question; to ask that something be given or that an action be performed; to invite [This is a more generic word for asking, in contrast to αἰτέω.] • *I ask, inquire; I ask for, request; I invite.* (NT 63; LXX 70) *CL*, 150; BDAG, 395. [chap. 26]

ἐσθίω (verb). To consume food (various metaphorical uses are also common) • *I eat.* (NT 158; LXX 686) *CL*, 150; BDAG, 396. [chap. 5]

ἐσμέν (verb). An inflected verb form: 1st pl. pres. (act.) ind. of εἰμί • *we are.* (NT 52; LXX 46) *CL*, 110; BDAG, 282. [chap. 7]

ἐστέ (verb). An inflected verb form: 2nd pl. pres. (act.) ind. of εἰμί • *you are.* (NT 92; LXX 41) *CL*, 110; BDAG, 282. [chap. 7]

ἐστί(ν) (verb). An inflected verb form: 3rd sg. pres. (act.) ind. of εἰμί • *he/she/it is.* (NT 896; LXX 1,863) *CL*, 110; BDAG, 282. [chap. 5]

ἔσχατος, η, ον (adj.). Coming at the end or after all others, either spatially, temporally, or in rank • *last, farthest; later; least, most insignificant.* (NT 52; LXX 154) *CL*, 150; BDAG, 397. [chap. 28]

ἕτερος, α, ον (adj.). Distinct from another item, sometimes indicating dissimilarity [often synonymous with ἄλλος]; one's neighbor • *other, another, different; neighbor.* (NT 98; LXX 258) *CL*, 151; BDAG, 399. [chap. 9]

ἔτι (adv.). A function word indicating continuation (or with a negative, lack of it) or addition (ctr. ἤδη, "already") • *still, yet; (not) anymore, any longer.* (NT 93; LXX 549) *CL*, 151; BDAG, 400. [chap. 16]

ἑτοιμάζω (verb). To put in a state of readiness • *I prepare, make ready.* (NT 40; LXX 173) *CL*, 152; BDAG, 400. [chap. 20]

ἔτος, ους, τό (noun). A calendar year (in the ancient world calculated on the basis of either lunar or solar cycles consisting of twelve or thirteen months); any period of twelve months • *year.* (NT 49; LXX 718) *CL*, 152; BDAG, 401. [chap. 30]

εὐαγγελίζω (verb). To pass on information that is good news to the recipient; to spread the good news of God's provision of salvation in Jesus Christ (usually mid., sometimes pass.; rarely act.) • *I announce/bring good news/the gospel.* (NT 54; LXX 23) *CL*, 152; BDAG, 402. [chap. 17]

εὐαγγέλιον, ου, τό (noun). An announcement or message containing good news; the content of the NT message of God's good news—the provision of salvation in Jesus Christ; reward for good news (LXX) [The later use as a title of a written work about Jesus' life and teaching is not found in the NT text.] • *good news, gospel; reward for good news* (LXX). (NT 76; LXX 1) *CL*, 152; BDAG, 402. [chap. 23]

εὐθύς (adv.). A temporal adverb referring to a short period of time, either the time before something takes place or the rapidity with which it happens; in a few instances the context makes it clear that there is little if any time interval; a "weakened" sense occurs with καί εὐθύς in Mark, where it functions as a conjunction, "then, next" [The more common word is εὐθέως, "immediately"; do not confuse with the adj. εὐθύς, εῖα, ύ, "straight."] • *quickly, promptly, at once; immediately; then, next.* (NT 51; LXX 66) *CL*, 153; BDAG, 406. [chap. 23]

εὐλογέω (verb). To say something commendatory of someone, express high praise; to invoke God's favor on someone, ask for the granting of special favor; to bestow favor or benefit • *I speak well of, praise, extol; I bless; I provide with benefits.* (NT 42; LXX 516) *CL*, 154; BDAG, 407. [chap. 29]

εὑρίσκω (verb). To find or locate something (intentionally or coincidentally) • *I find.* (NT 176; LXX 613) *CL*, 155; BDAG, 411. [chap. 5]

εὐχαριστέω (verb). To express appreciation for benefit received, express gratitude to • *I give thanks; I thank.* (NT 38; LXX 6) *CL*, 156; BDAG, 415. [chap. 25]

ἔφη (verb). An inflected verb form: 3rd sg. (impf. or ²aor.) act. ind. of φημί • *he/she/it was saying* (or *said*). (NT 43; LXX 23) *CL*, 157; BDAG, 1053. [chap. 29]

ἐχθρός, ά, όν (adj.). Characterized by hostility, hatred, or unfriendliness toward another; characterized by experiencing hostility, hatred, or unfriendliness from others; one who expresses these attitudes toward another, enemy (subst.) • *hostile, hating; hated; enemy* (subst.). (NT 32; LXX 456) *CL*, 157; BDAG, 419. [chap. 32]

ἔχω (verb). To possess; to bear/carry on one's person; to be in a position to do something; etc. (a very diverse semantic range) • *I have, hold.* (NT 708; LXX 497) *CL*, 158; BDAG, 420. [chap. 5]

ἕως (conj.). Subordinating conjunction indicating a temporal limit ("until"); or used as a preposition with the genitive, either spatially or temporally ("as far as" or "until") • *until* (conj.); *as far as, until* (prep. + gen.). (NT 146; LXX 1,565) *CL*, 158; BDAG, 422. [chap. 8]

ζάω. See **ζῶ**.

ζητέω (verb). To search for something (not necessarily something lost), whether an object, information, or some action • *I seek, look for; I investigate, deliberate.* (NT 117; LXX 320) *CL*, 161; BDAG, 428. [chap. 21]

ζῶ (usually listed as ζάω; see the sidebar in chap. 21) (verb). To be alive physically or spiritually; to conduct oneself in a certain manner • *I live, am alive; I live.* (NT 140; LXX 554) *CL*, 160, 161; BDAG, 424. [chap. 21]

ζωή, ῆς, ἡ (noun). Life, that which distinguishes plants and animals from inanimate things; the period between birth and death • *life.* (NT 135; LXX 289) *CL*, 161; BDAG, 430. [chap. 7]

ἤ (particle). A particle indicating either an alternative or a series of alternatives (disjunctive, "or"), or a comparison ("than") • *or, either . . . or; than, rather than.* (NT 343; LXX 934) *CL*, 162; BDAG, 432. [chap. 17]

ἤδη (adv.). A temporal adverb most commonly expressing completion or referring to a previous situation (ctr. ἔτι, "still") • *already, now.* (NT 61; LXX 64) *CL*, 163; BDAG, 434. [chap. 18]

ἥκω (verb). To be in a place as a result of movement to that place (focuses on the result of movement; ctr. ἔρχομαι, which focuses on the movement itself) • *I have come, am present.* (NT 26; LXX 244) *CL*, 163; BDAG, 435. [chap. 33]

ἥλιος, ου, ὁ (noun). The star around which the earth orbits • *sun.* (NT 32; LXX 211) *CL*, 163; BDAG, 436. [chap. 31]

ἡμεῖς (pron.). Personal pronoun, first-person plural nominative of ἐγώ • *we.* (NT 864; LXX 176) *CL*, 164; BDAG, 275 (ἐγώ). [chap. 4]

ἡμέρα, ας, ἡ (noun). A period of time of varying length, whether a twenty-four-hour day, the period from sunrise to sunset, or a longer period of time during which something happens • *day.* (NT 389; LXX 2,567) *CL*, 164; BDAG, 436. [chap. 3]

ἦν (verb). An inflected verb form: 3rd sg. impf. (act.) ind. of εἰμί • *he/she/it was.* (NT 413; LXX 1,297) *CL*, 110; BDAG, 282. [chap. 16]

θάλασσα, ης, ἡ (noun). A large body of salt water; a large inland body of fresh water • *sea; lake.* (NT 91; LXX 450) *CL*, 166; BDAG, 442. [chap. 16]

θάνατος, ου, ὁ (noun). Death, either natural/physical or spiritual • *death.* (NT 120; LXX 362) *CL*, 166; BDAG, 442. [chap. 4]

θαυμάζω (verb). To be extraordinarily impressed or disturbed/shocked by something • *I marvel, wonder (at), am amazed, astonished, shocked.* (NT 43; LXX 57) *CL*, 167; BDAG, 444. [chap. 29]

θέλημα, ατος, τό (noun). That which one wishes to happen [≠ legal "last will and testament"] • *will, desire, what is willed or desired.* (NT 62; LXX 51) *CL*, 167; BDAG, 447. [chap. 23]

θέλω (verb). To have a desire for something • *I wish, desire, will.* (NT 208; LXX 148) *CL*, 167; BDAG, 447. [chap. 5]

θεός, οῦ, ὁ (noun). An immortal entity/deity, whether in a monotheistic or polytheistic context, may refer to a supreme being in any religion, or in a lesser sense to the devil, or even to human beings who have some special status • *god, God.* (NT 1,317; LXX 3,984) *CL*, 168; BDAG, 450. [chap. 2]

θεραπεύω (verb). Generally, to offer helpful service; specifically, to care for or treat medically, thus to cause someone to recover health • *I heal, restore; I help out, serve.* (NT 43; LXX 24) *CL*, 169; BDAG, 453. [chap. 14]

θεωρέω (verb). To observe attentively; to conclude on the basis of personal experience • *I look at, observe, take notice of; I infer, perceive.* (NT 58; LXX 53) *CL*, 169; BDAG, 454. [chap. 27]

θηρίον, ου, τό (noun). Any living creature other than humans • *animal, beast.* (NT 46; LXX 164) *CL*, 170; BDAG, 455. [chap. 30]

θλῖψις, εως, ἡ (noun). Distress that is caused by either outward circumstances or inner anguish • *distress, suffering, affliction, oppression, tribulation, trouble.* (NT 45; LXX 134) *CL*, 170; BDAG, 457. [chap. 32]

θρόνος, ου, ὁ (noun). A special chair set aside for someone of high status (e.g., a king) • *throne.* (NT 62; LXX 163) *CL*, 171; BDAG, 460. [chap. 27]

θυγάτηρ, τρός, ἡ (noun). A female offspring described in relation to the parents (in the NT only of humans, in the LXX also rarely of animals) • *daughter.* (NT 28; LXX 641) *CL*, 171; BDAG, 460. [chap. 33]

θύρα, ας, ἡ (noun). An object used to open or close an entranceway; a passageway providing entrance to a place • *door; entrance, gateway, doorway.* (NT 39; LXX 239) *CL*, 172; BDAG, 462. [chap. 20]

θυσία, ας, ἡ (noun). Sacrifice offered to deity as part of a priestly system of worship • *sacrifice, offering.* (NT 28; LXX 395) *CL*, 172; BDAG, 462. [chap. 33]

θυσιαστήριον, ου, τό (noun). An object on which a θυσία ("sacrifice") is placed when it is offered to deity • *altar.* (NT 23; LXX 437) *CL*, 172; BDAG, 463. [chap. 33]

ἴδιος, α, ον (adj.). Belonging to oneself • *one's own.* (NT 114; LXX 79) *CL*, 173; BDAG, 466. [chap. 6]

ἰδού (interj.). A demonstrative particle that draws attention to what follows or marks strong emphasis • *behold! see! look!* (or just "*!*"). (NT 200; LXX 1,145) *CL*, 173; BDAG, 468. [chap. 16]

ἱερεύς, έως, ὁ (noun). A person appointed to perform religious duties, particularly (though not exclusively) to offer sacrifice on behalf of others • *priest.* (NT 31; LXX 900) *CL*, 174; BDAG, 469. [chap. 33]

ἱερόν, οῦ, τό (noun). A building dedicated to the service and worship of a god or gods, in the LXX and NT usually of the temple in Jerusalem, including the entire complex with its various courts • *temple.* (NT 71; LXX 116) *CL*, 174; BDAG, 470. [chap. 24]

Ἱεροσόλυμα, ἡ (noun); also spelled Ἰερουσαλήμ (either spelling may have smooth or rough breathing). Usually the proper name of the main city in Israel or its inhabitants • *Jerusalem.* (NT 139; LXX 881) *CL*, 174; BDAG, 470. [chap. 20]

Ἰησοῦς, οῦ, ὁ (noun). Personal name used of various individuals, in the NT most commonly Jesus Christ • *Jesus, Joshua.* (NT 917; LXX 272) *CL*, 175; BDAG, 472. [chap. 3]

ἱκανός, ή, όν (adj.). Characterized by sufficient extent, quantity, or degree; extensive in extent or degree (with no reference to sufficiency) • *sufficient, adequate, competent, qualified, able; considerable, many, quite a few.* (NT 39; LXX 46) *CL*, 175; BDAG, 472. [chap. 26]

ἱμάτιον, ου, τό (noun). Clothing in general; the outer garment worn over a χιτών • *garment, clothing; cloak, coat, robe.* (NT 60; LXX 221) *CL*, 176; BDAG, 475. [chap. 27]

ἵνα (conj.). A conjunction that normally introduces a subordinate clause indicating purpose, result, content, or explanation (governs subjunctive mood) • *in order that, that.* (NT 663; LXX 615) *CL*, 176; BDAG, 475. [chap. 4]

Ἰουδαῖος, αία, αῖον (adj.). Jewish/Judean either by birth/ethnicity or by practice (adj.); Jew/Judean (subst.) • *Jewish/Judean* (adj.); *Jew/Judean* (subst.). (NT 195; LXX 207) *CL*, 176; BDAG, 478. [chap. 6]

Ἰούδας, α, ὁ (noun). A common personal name; when referring to an OT person the English equivalent is traditionally "Judah," otherwise "Judas" (rarely "Jude") • *Judah, Judas.* (NT 44; LXX 901) *CL*, 177; BDAG, 479. [chap. 30]

Ἰσραήλ, ὁ (noun). An indeclinable personal name, in Scripture the patriarch Jacob; Jacob/Israel's descendants, the twelve tribes composing the nation of Israel • *Israel.* (NT 68; LXX 2,748) *CL*, 178; BDAG, 481. [chap. 23]

ἵστημι (verb). (1) Intransitive (pf., plpf.): to be in a standing position; to be at a place; to maintain one's belief or one's position (physically); (2) intransitive ([2]aor., fut.): to be in an upright position, desist from movement; (3) transitive (pres., impf., [1]aor.): to cause to be in a place or position; to place in the balance and weigh (LXX); to establish a condition, institute legally • (1) *I stand; I stand firm, hold out;* (2) *I stand still, stop;* (3) *I put, place, set; I weigh; I establish.* (NT 154; LXX 773) *CL*, 178; BDAG, 482. [chap. 32]

ἰσχύω (verb). To have the necessary resources and capacity to accomplish something; to be in control • *I am able/strong, have power, am competent.* (NT 28; LXX 106) *CL*, 179; BDAG, 484. [chap. 7]

Ἰωάννης, ου, ὁ (noun). Personal name of a number of people in the NT and Apocrypha, in the NT most frequently John the Baptizer or John the apostle • *John.* (NT 135; LXX 16) *CL*, 179; BDAG, 485. [chap. 7]

κἀγώ (crasis). A crasis form of καί + ἐγώ (κἀμοί, dat.; κἀμέ, acc.); a personal affirmation adding to or confirming a previous statement • *and I, but I; I also; I in particular.* (NT 84; LXX 94) *CL*, 180; BDAG, 487. [chap. 14]

καθαρίζω (verb). To make clean by removing dirt or impure substance; to cleanse ritually by meeting ceremonial requirements; to heal someone of disease; to cleanse from sin • *I make clean, cleanse; I heal; I purify.* (NT 31; LXX 125) *CL*, 181; BDAG, 488. [chap. 22]

καθαρός, ά, όν (adj.). Free from contamination, whether ceremonial or physical; free from guilt or moral impurity • *clean, cleansed, pure; innocent.* (NT 27; LXX 160) *CL*, 181; BDAG, 489. [chap. 10]

κάθημαι (verb). To be in a seated position; to take a seated position; metaphorically, to be a resident in a place • *I sit; I sit down, take a seat; I live, reside* (metaphorical). (NT 91; LXX 180) *CL*, 182; BDAG, 491. [chap. 15]

καθίζω (verb). (1) Transitive: to cause to sit down; (2) intransitive: to take a seated position • (1) *I seat, set;* (2) *I sit down.* (NT 46; LXX 255) *CL*, 182; BDAG, 491. [chap. 31]

καθώς (adv.). A marker of similarity or manner • *as, even as, just as.* (NT 182; LXX 279) *CL*, 183; BDAG, 493. [chap. 6]

καί (conj.). A function word that marks connection or addition: (1) connective (copula), "and," joining equal words, clauses, etc.; (2) additive (adjunctive/adverbial), "also, even." • *and* (conj.); *even, also* (adv.). (NT 9,153; LXX 62,240) *CL*, 183; BDAG, 494. [chap. 2]

καινός, ή, όν (adj.). Characterized by having been in existence for only a short time, of recent origin; being new and therefore superior; not being well known previously [not distinguishable from νέος in most instances] • *new, recent; unfamiliar, previously unknown.* (NT 42; LXX 58) *CL*, 183; BDAG, 496. [chap. 29]

καιρός, οῦ, ὁ (noun). A point of time or a period of time, general or specific (wide variety of uses, depending on contextual adjuncts) • *time, period.* (NT 85; LXX 487) *CL*, 184; BDAG, 497. [chap. 18]

κακός, ή, όν (adj.). Having a harmful or injurious effect, causing harm; morally or socially reprehensible, contrary to custom or law; that which is bad/evil, one who does what is bad/evil (subst.) • *harmful, dangerous; bad, evil; misfortune, a wrong, an evil deed/person.* (NT 50; LXX 384) *CL*, 185; BDAG, 501. [chap. 28]

καλέω (verb). To express something aloud; to request the presence or response of someone ("invite," social or soteric); to call authoritatively ("summon"); to assign a name • *I call, say; I invite; I summon, call; I name.* (NT 148; LXX 512) *CL*, 185; BDAG, 502. [chap. 14]

καλός, ή, όν (adj.). Of high quality and therefore satisfying; a positive moral quality that is favorably valued; attractive in outward form; fitting • *good, beautiful.* (NT 100; LXX 235) *CL*, 186; BDAG, 504. [chap. 9]

καρδία, ας, ἡ (noun). The physical organ that pumps blood in the body; metaphorically (always so in the NT), the person/personhood, often with cognitive, affective, volitional, or moral overtones; middle, center • *heart, mind* (wide range [see lexicon]). (NT 156; LXX 963) *CL*, 187; BDAG, 508. [chap. 4]

καρπός, οῦ, ὁ (noun). The product of a plant (whether tree, vine, bush, vegetable, etc.), agricultural produce; the offspring of a person; metaphorically of the result or outcome of an action or attitude • *fruit, produce* (subst.), *crop, harvest; offspring; result, product* (metaphorical). (NT 66; LXX 125) *CL*, 187; BDAG, 509. [chap. 24]

κατά (prep.). A preposition used most commonly with the accusative case (sometimes with the genitive), expressing measure in terms of extension or correspondence • (prep. + acc.) *according to, throughout, during;* (prep. + gen.) *down, against.* (NT 473; LXX 2,140) *CL*, 188; BDAG, 511. [chap. 9]

καταβαίνω (verb). To be in motion downward, descend from a higher to a lower place • *I go down, come down.* (NT 81; LXX 349) *CL*, 189; BDAG, 513. [chap. 25]

καταλείπω (verb). To leave someone or something behind by departure or death; to depart from a place • *I leave behind, leave alone; I leave, depart.* (NT 24; LXX 289) *CL*, 191; BDAG, 520. [chap. 19]

κατοικέω (verb). To live or stay as a resident • *I live, dwell, inhabit, reside.* (NT 44; LXX 685) *CL*, 197; BDAG, 534. [chap. 29]

κεφαλή, ῆς, ἡ (noun). The part of the body that contains the brain (human or animal); authority due to rank; the uppermost part, extremity of something • *head; extremity.* (NT 75; LXX 433) *CL*, 199; BDAG, 541. [chap. 23]

κηρύσσω (verb). To make a public pronouncement as a herald • *I preach, proclaim.* (NT 61; LXX 31) *CL*, 200; BDAG, 543. [chap. 29]

κλαίω (verb). To express grief or sorrow aloud (ctr. δακρύω, which may refer to a more silent expression of grief) • *I weep, cry, sob.* (NT 40; LXX 168) *CL*, 201; BDAG, 545. [chap. 20]

κόσμος, ου, ὁ (noun). An orderly arrangement of things, whether the entire cosmos ("universe"), our planet ("world"), society/culture, or the human beings who live in or compose one of the above • *world, universe, people.* (NT 186; LXX 72) *CL*, 206; BDAG, 561. [chap. 2]

κράζω (verb). To utter a loud cry, speak vigorously • *I cry/call out.* (NT 56; LXX 111) *CL*, 206; BDAG, 563. [chap. 31]

κρατέω (verb). To gain control of, often by seizing with the hands (may or may not imply force); to commit oneself to adhere strongly to someone or something • *I seize, control, hold (fast), grasp, take hold of; I hold fast to, keep hold of.* (NT 47; LXX 153) *CL*, 207; BDAG, 564. [chap. 30]

κρίμα, ατος, τό (noun). The evaluation of conduct by a court of law; the legal decision as a result of such evaluation; the process of bringing a legal claim before a court of law • *judging, judgment; decision, verdict; lawsuit.* (NT 27; LXX 255) *CL*, 207; BDAG, 567. [chap. 11]

κρίνω (verb). To make a distinction between items or situations so as to come to a conclusion; may be used in a variety of contexts, both positive and negative, whether of a legal judgment or sentence, of pressing legal charges, or seeing that justice is done (esp. LXX); or of personal matters in which a decision is made • *I prefer, select; I judge, condemn, press charges; I judge justly, see that justice is done; I decide, think, consider.* (NT 114; LXX 271) *CL*, 208; BDAG, 567. [chap. 21]

κρίσις, εως, ἡ (noun). A scrutiny of conduct for the purpose of evaluation; a legal process of judicial evaluation of a charge; a judicial verdict of guilty and the associated sentence/penalty; the administration of what is right and fair • *evaluation; (act of) judging, judgment; condemnation; right* (in the sense of justice). (NT 47; LXX 280) *CL*, 208; BDAG, 569. [chap. 30]

κύριος, ου, ὁ (noun). Person who is in control due to possession, ownership, or position; or who is esteemed for authority or high status, whether human or divine • *lord, master, sir.* (NT 717; LXX 8,591) *CL*, 210; BDAG, 576. [chap. 2]

λαλέω (verb). To make a sound; to utter words so as to make a statement • *I make sounds; I speak, say, tell.* (NT 296; LXX 1,189) *CL*, 212; BDAG, 582. [chap. 21]

λαμβάνω (verb). To get hold of something; to take possession of; to take away; to receive a person or thing; to be a receiver (in a passive sense) • *I take, grasp; I acquire; I take away, remove; I accept; I receive.* (NT 258; LXX 1,335) *CL*, 212; BDAG, 583. [chap. 18]

λαός, οῦ, ὁ (noun). A group of humans either gathered together or identified geographically, ethnically, or with reference to their relationship to God • *people.* (NT 142; LXX 2,064) *CL*, 213; BDAG, 586. [chap. 4]

λέγω (verb). To make a statement or utterance, either oral or written, for which English often has specific words appropriate to various contexts ("say, speak, tell, declare, report, call," etc.) • *I say, speak.* (NT 2,354; LXX 4,610) *CL*, 213; BDAG, 588. [chap. 5]

λίθος, ου, ὁ (noun). A piece of rock, whether naturally formed or in a fabricated shape; a precious stone, jewel • *stone.* (NT 59; LXX 306) *CL*, 216; BDAG, 595. [chap. 24]

λογίζομαι (verb). To engage in numerical calculation, determine by mathematical process; metaphorically of mental activity in general: to give careful thought to a matter • *I reckon, account, calculate; I think about, consider, ponder.* (NT 40; LXX 121) *CL*, 216; BDAG, 597. [chap. 15]

λόγος, ου, ὁ (noun). An expression of the content of thought, whether an individual term ("word") or longer expressions (written or oral; widely varied English glosses may be used, e.g., "statement," "question," or "report"); the personified expression of God, "the Logos" • *word, statement, message; Logos.* (NT 330; LXX 1,238) *CL*, 217; BDAG, 598. [chap. 2]

λοιπός, ή, όν (adj.). Left and remaining out of a larger quantity; not previously included; that which/the one who remains (subst.); from now on, finally (adv.) •

remaining; rest of; the rest, the other (subst.); *from now on, finally* (adv.). (NT 55; LXX 120) *CL*, 218; BDAG, 602. [chap. 28]

λύω (verb). To undo something that is used to tie up or constrain something; to do away with; to reduce something to ruin by tearing down or breaking to pieces • *I loose, set free, untie; I bring to an end, abolish; I destroy, tear down, break up.* (NT 42; LXX 29) *CL*, 219; BDAG, 606. [chap. 5]

μαθητής, οῦ, ὁ (noun). One who learns under the instruction of a teacher, whether with committed attachment ("disciple") or less formally ("student, pupil") • *disciple; student, pupil.* (NT 261; LXX 0) *CL*, 220; BDAG, 609. [chap. 3]

μακάριος, ία, ιον (adj.). Being in a desirable, agreeable condition, enjoying special advantage or favor • *blessed, happy, fortunate, privileged.* (NT 50; LXX 73) *CL*, 220; BDAG, 610. [chap. 28]

μᾶλλον (adv.). A comparative adverb indicating increase or addition, or marking a change in procedure • *(much) more, all the more; rather, instead.* (NT 81; LXX 52) *CL*, 221; BDAG, 613. [chap. 17]

μαρτυρέω (verb). To attest to something based on personal knowledge, bear witness • *I bear witness, testify.* (NT 76; LXX 13) *CL*, 222; BDAG, 617. [chap. 25]

μέγας, μεγάλη, μέγα (adj.). A large quantity in terms of extent, scale, space, measure, number, time, status, importance, intensity, etc.; comparative form: μείζων; superlative: μέγιστος (many possible equivalents in English, depending on referent and context) • *great, large, big, long.* (NT 243; LXX 916) *CL*, 224; BDAG, 623. [chap. 22]

μέλλω (verb). To take place in the future, whether an expected event or one intended or determined, whether imminent or distant • *I am about to; I intend, propose; I have determined.* (NT 109; LXX 43) *CL*, 225; BDAG, 627. [chap. 21]

μέν (particle). A postpositive particle marking emphasis, typically used with other particles or conjunctions (e.g., μέν . . . δέ) to contrast opposing statements or sometimes to emphasize a parallel • *on the one hand, indeed.* (NT 179; LXX 222) *CL*, 226; BDAG, 629. [chap. 17]

μένω (verb). To remain in a place, condition, or position for a period of time • *I remain, stay, continue; I live* (in a place). (NT 118; LXX 89) *CL*, 227; BDAG, 630. [chap. 21]

μέρος, ους, τό (noun). A piece or part of a whole (wide usage depending on context: body part, geographical area, party, etc.) • *part, member; region; party.* (NT 42; LXX 139) *CL*, 227; BDAG, 633. [chap. 19]

μέσος, η, ον (adj.). A middle position (either spatial or temporal); position within or between; "the middle" (subst., τὸ μέσον) • *middle, in the midst, among.* (NT 58; LXX 872) *CL*, 228; BDAG, 634. [chap. 27]

μετά (prep.). A preposition used with the genitive case to indicate association or accompaniment, or with the accusative case to indicate position or sequence (either temporal or spatial) • (prep. + gen.) *with;* (prep. + acc.) *after.* (NT 469; LXX 2,534) *CL*, 228; BDAG, 636. [chap. 9]

μή (adv.). Particle of negation, usually used adverbially to negate a non-indicative verb or non-finite verbal • *no, not, lest.* (NT 1,042; LXX 3,179) *CL*, 231; BDAG, 644. [chap. 5]

μηδέ, μήτε (particle). A negative particle indicating disjunction as part of a series • *and not, but not, nor, not even, don't even.* (NT 56; LXX 139) *CL*, 232; BDAG, 647. [chap. 24]

μηδείς, μηδεμία, μηδέν (adj.). A marker of negation typically used with non-indicative-mood verbs • *no one, nothing.* (NT 114; LXX 67) *CL*, 232; BDAG, 647. [chap. 12]

μήτηρ, μητρός, ἡ (noun). A female parent; numerous metaphorical uses with an analogical meaning • *mother.* (NT 83; LXX 338) *CL*, 233; BDAG, 649. [chap. 22]

μικρός, ά, όν (adj.). Of limited size, measure, quantity, age, or significance; that which is of such a limited nature (subst.); a little while, a short distance (neut. as adv.) • *small, short, unimportant; the little one, what is insignificant; a little while, a short distance.* (NT 46; LXX 165) *CL*, 234; BDAG, 651. [chap. 30]

μιμνῄσκω (verb). To remind someone of something (act.); to recall information from one's own memory (mid.); to be reminded (pass.) (never act. in the NT or LXX; often listed as μιμνῄσκομαι) • *I remind* (act.); *I remember, mention* (mid.); *I am reminded* (pass.). (NT 23; LXX 262) *CL*, 234; BDAG, 652. [chap. 19]

μισέω (verb). To have a strong aversion to or dislike for someone or something; to consider unworthy of notice [The English word "hate" is sometimes too strong and may have wrong connotations.] • *I hate; I disregard, disdain.* (NT 40; LXX 182) *CL*, 234; BDAG, 652. [chap. 21]

μνημεῖον, ου, τό (noun). A memorial structure to recall a past event; a place for depositing the remains of a deceased person • *monument, memorial; grave, tomb.* (NT 40; LXX 16) *CL*, 235; BDAG, 654. [chap. 20]

μόνος, η, ον (adj.). The only entity in a class or the only such entity that is present • *only, alone.* (NT 114; LXX 164) *CL*, 237; BDAG, 658. [chap. 6]

μου & ἐμοῦ (pron.). Personal pronoun, first-person singular genitive of ἐγώ • *my.* (NT 677; LXX 4,834) *CL*, 237; BDAG, 275 (ἐγώ). [chap. 4]

Μωϋσῆς, έως, ὁ (noun). A personal name, in the LXX and NT the name of Israel's leader at the time of the exodus; the books of the OT written by him • *Moses.* (NT 80; LXX 819) *CL*, 238; BDAG, 663. [chap. 22]

ναός, οῦ, ὁ (noun). A building dedicated to the service and worship of a god or gods, in the LXX and NT usually of the temple proper in Jerusalem composed of the Holy Place and the Most Holy Place, located at the center of the larger temple complex (ἱερόν), though sometimes referring to the entire complex • *temple.* (NT 45; LXX 118) *CL*, 239; BDAG, 665. [chap. 24]

νεκρός, ά, όν (adj.). Without life, "dead" (adj.); one who is dead, "corpse" (subst.) (both adj. and noun may refer to physical or spiritual/moral death) • *dead* (adj.); *dead body, corpse* (subst.). (NT 128; LXX 83) *CL*, 240; BDAG, 667. [chap. 6]

νέος, α, ον (adj.). Characterized by having been in existence for only a short time; being new and therefore superior; a living being who is relatively young, often the younger of two [not distinguishable from καινός in most instances] • *new, recent; young, younger.* (NT 23; LXX 125) *CL*, 240; BDAG, 669. [chap. 29]

νόμος, ου, ὁ (noun). A principle or standard relating to behavior, whether traditional and unwritten ("custom, norm") or written as legislation ("law") in general or a specific legal corpus ("the law," e.g., the Mosaic law) • *law, principle.* (NT 194; LXX 427) *CL*, 242; BDAG, 677. [chap. 2]

νῦν (adv.). A temporal adverb that indicates present time • *now* (adv.); *the present* (subst.). (NT 147; LXX 701) *CL*, 244; BDAG, 681. [chap. 6]

νύξ, νυκτός, ἡ (noun). The chronological span from sunset to sunrise; a symbol of intellectual, moral, and spiritual ignorance and darkness • *night*. (NT 61; LXX 294) *CL*, 244; BDAG, 682. [chap. 23]

ὁ, ἡ, τό (article). A diverse, multipurpose marker: (1) a defining marker, the Greek article, "the"; (2) as a demonstrative, "this one, that one." • *the; this/that one*. (NT 19,870; LXX 88,439) *CL*, 245; BDAG, 686. [chap. 2]

ὁδός, οῦ, ἡ (noun). A route for traveling; metaphorically, way of life; the lifestyle and beliefs of Christianity ("the Way") • *road, way, highway; the Way*. (NT 101; LXX 891) *CL*, 246; BDAG, 691. [chap. 8]

οἶδα (verb). To find out, have information about; to grasp the meaning of something • *I know, understand*. (NT 318; LXX 283) *CL*, 247; BDAG, 693. [chap. 20]

οἰκία, ας, ἡ (noun). A physical structure in which people live; a group of people who live in that structure • *house, home*; *household, family*. (NT 93; LXX 268) *CL*, 247; BDAG, 695. [chap. 8]

οἰκοδομέω (verb). To erect a structure, construct a building or other structure; to improve someone's ability to live more responsibly and effectively (metaphorically) • *I build, erect, construct; I strengthen, build up, edify*. (NT 40; LXX 460) *CL*, 248; BDAG, 696. [chap. 33]

οἶκος, ου, ὁ (noun). A physical structure for habitation ("house") or a place where people live ("home"); the people who live in a house ("household, family") • *house, home; household*. (NT 114; LXX 2,062) *CL*, 248; BDAG, 698. [chap. 4]

οἶνος, ου, ὁ (noun). A beverage made from the juice of the grape (usually fermented, but perhaps not necessarily so) • *wine, juice* (from the grape). (NT 34; LXX 253) *CL*, 249; BDAG, 701. [chap. 31]

ὀλίγος, η, ον (adj.). Being relatively small in number or extent; quickly, a little (neut. used as adv.) • *few; little, small, short; quickly, a little*. (NT 40; LXX 101) *CL*, 249; BDAG, 702. [chap. 20]

ὅλος, η, ον (adj.). Being complete in extent • *whole, complete* (adj.); *entirely* (adv.). (NT 109; LXX 272) *CL*, 250; BDAG, 704. [chap. 9]

ὀμνύω (verb). To take an oath affirming the truthfulness of what one says • *I swear, take an oath*. (NT 26; LXX 188) *CL*, 250; BDAG, 705. [chap. 14]

ὅμοιος, οία, οιον (adj.). Characterized by having some commonality with another object or entity, resembling something • *similar, like*. (NT 45; LXX 91) *CL*, 251; BDAG, 706. [chap. 32]

ὄνομα, ατος, τό (noun). A designation used to identify, either specifically (i.e., a proper name) or generally (referring to a category) • *name, reputation*. (NT 231; LXX 1,045) *CL*, 252; BDAG, 712. [chap. 11]

ὀπίσω (adv.). An adverb describing the verb as taking place behind some object, as reverting direction, or as happening subsequently; more commonly in the NT and LXX as a preposition used with the genitive with the same meaning • *behind, backward, afterward* (adv.); *after, behind* (prep. + gen.). (NT 35; LXX 461) *CL*, 253; BDAG, 716. [chap. 32]

ὅπου (adv.). An adverb of place indicating location • *where; wherever* (with subjunctive). (NT 82; LXX 22) *CL*, 253; BDAG, 717. [chap. 17]

ὅπως (conj.). A subordinating conjunction indicating purpose (governs subjunctive mood) • *in order that, that, how.* (NT 53; LXX 264) *CL*, 254; BDAG, 718. [chap. 8]

ὁράω (verb). To perceive with the eye or the mind; to understand; to be alert or to accept responsibility for something (hortatory or imperatival) • *I see, notice; I perceive; See to it!* (impv.). (NT 454; LXX 1,539) *CL*, 254; BDAG, 719. [chap. 21]

ὀργή, ῆς, ἡ (noun). Strong displeasure with the conduct of another; strong displeasure directed toward retribution for offensive behavior • *wrath, anger.* (NT 36; LXX 305) *CL*, 254; BDAG, 720. [chap. 26]

ὄρος, ὄρους, τό (noun). A geographical elevation that is higher than a βοῦνος ("small hill"); a region characterized by this feature [As in English, "hill" and "mountain" are relative terms and locale specific.] • *mountain, hill; mountainous region, hilly area.* (NT 63; LXX 680) *CL*, 255; BDAG, 724. [chap. 23]

ὅς, ἥ, ὅ (pron.). Relative pronoun that usually refers to another noun earlier in the sentence or discourse, introducing a clause that further describes that noun • *who, which, that.* (NT 1,365; LXX 4,886) *CL*, 255; BDAG, 725. [chap. 10]

ὅσος, η, ον (pron.). A relative pronoun indicating quantity or number (in the LXX never a correlative as in Classical Greek; NT only rarely correlative) • *all who, all that, as many as, as much as.* (NT 110; LXX 615) *CL*, 256; BDAG, 729. [chap. 22]

ὅστις, ἥτις, ὅτι (pron.). Relative pronoun that usually refers to another noun earlier in the sentence or discourse, introducing a clause that further describes that noun (originally an indefinite relative pronoun, but not usually distinguished from ὅς in Koine Greek) • *who, which* (sometimes indefinite: *whoever, whatever, whichever*). (NT 153; LXX 135) *CL*, 257; BDAG, 729. [chap. 12]

ὅταν (particle). A temporal conjunction (or particle) that refers to a conditional or possible action, one that is sometimes repeated ("whenever"); usually used with the subjunctive mood • *when, at the time that; whenever.* (NT 123; LXX 210) *CL*, 257; BDAG, 730. [chap. 17]

ὅτε (particle). A temporal conjunction (or particle) that links two events either in terms of when they both occur or in terms of the temporal extent of both • *when; as long as, while.* (NT 103; LXX 173) *CL*, 257; BDAG, 731. [chap. 17]

ὅτι (conj.). A conjunction that links two clauses by (1) defining, "that"; (2) introducing a subordinate clause or indirect statement; (3) introducing a direct statement = quotation marks; (4) indicating cause, "because," inference, "for," or a query, "why?" • *because, that, since.* (NT 1,296; LXX 4,041) *CL*, 257; BDAG, 731. [chap. 2]

οὐ, οὐκ, οὐχ, οὐχί (adv.). Particle of negation, usually used adverbially to negate an indicative-mood verb (spelling variations depend on the next word; meaning is unchanged) [See "The Negatives" in chap. 6.] • *no, not.* (NT 1,606; LXX 6,077) *CL*, 257; BDAG, 733. [chap. 5]

οὐαί (interj.). An exclamation of profound grief, pain, or displeasure; a state of intense hardship or distress (subst.) • *alas! woe!; woe* (subst.). (NT 46; LXX 66) *CL*, 258; BDAG, 734. [chap. 30]

οὐδέ, οὔτε (conj.). A coordinating conjunction that negates a clause and links it to a preceding negative clause • *and not, not even, neither, nor.* (NT 143; LXX 614) *CL*, 258; BDAG, 734. [chap. 8]

οὐδείς, οὐδεμία, οὐδέν (adj.). A marker of negation typically used with indicative-mood verbs • *no one, nothing.* (NT 234; LXX 270) *CL*, 258; BDAG, 735. [chap. 12]

οὐκέτι (adv.). Up to a point, but not beyond (temporal); a negative inference (logical) • *no longer, no more; not, then not.* (NT 47; LXX 112) *CL*, 259; BDAG, 736. [chap. 29]

οὖν (conj.). An inferential or sequence marker (postpositive, coordinating conjunction) used to indicate a conclusion drawn from preceding information or to mark a stage of narrative development • *then, therefore.* (NT 499; LXX 260) *CL*, 259; BDAG, 736. [chap. 3]

οὐρανός, οῦ, ὁ (noun). That part of the universe surrounding the earth including the atmosphere ("sky") and/or the place where other cosmic bodies are located ("the heavens"); the place where God's presence is manifested ("heaven") • *sky, the heavens; heaven.* (NT 273; LXX 682) *CL*, 259; BDAG, 737. [chap. 2]

οὖς, ὠτός, τό (noun). The organ of hearing (ctr. ὠτάριον, which refers to the outer ear); the mental ability to understand or perceive • *ear; hearing.* (NT 36; LXX 190) *CL*, 260; BDAG, 739. [chap. 26]

οὔτε (adv.). A negative adverbial particle (actually οὐ τέ) that dismisses an activity or thing that follows, most often occurring in multiples • *and not, neither . . . nor.* (NT 87; LXX 123) *CL*, 260; BDAG, 740. [chap. 17]

οὗτος, αὕτη, τοῦτο (pron.). A near demonstrative pronoun referring to the person or thing comparatively near at hand ("this" as opposed to ἐκεῖνος/"that") • *this, this one, these; he, she, it, they.* (NT 1,388; LXX 4,411) *CL*, 260; BDAG, 740. [chap. 10]

οὕτως (adv.). A particle that introduces a description of the manner or way in which something is done • *in this manner, thus, so.* (NT 208; LXX 852) *CL*, 260; BDAG, 741. [chap. 6]

ὀφθαλμός, οῦ, ὁ (noun). Sensory organ of sight; metaphorically of moral/spiritual understanding • *eye, sight.* (NT 100; LXX 678) *CL*, 261; BDAG, 744. [chap. 8]

ὄχλος, ου, ὁ (noun). A group of people, usually consisting of a large number of such • *crowd, multitude.* (NT 175; LXX 55) *CL*, 262; BDAG, 745. [chap. 3]

παιδίον, ου, τό (noun). A young human being, normally one who has not yet reached puberty, though sometimes (esp. in the LXX) used of older people (teens and young adults) • *child.* (NT 52; LXX 169) *CL*, 263; BDAG, 749. [chap. 28]

παῖς, παιδός, ὁ/ἡ (noun). A person of minor status in terms of either family or age ("child") or social status ("servant") • *child, boy, girl; servant, slave, attendant.* (NT 24; LXX 470) *CL*, 263; BDAG, 750. [chap. 33]

πάλιν (adv.). An adverb that indicates repetition or additional occurrence • *again, once more.* (NT 141; LXX 88) *CL*, 264; BDAG, 752. [chap. 6]

πάντοτε (adv.). A temporal adverb expressing continuation • *always, at all times.* (NT 41; LXX 2) *CL*, 265; BDAG, 755. [chap. 20]

παρά (prep.). A preposition used with three cases, all referring to some sort of association: with the genitive, a point of origin or source; with the dative, a close connection; and with the accusative, nearness • (prep. + gen.) *from;* (prep. + dat.) *with, beside, near, in the presence of;* (prep. + acc.) *alongside, by.* (NT 194; LXX 879) *CL*, 265; BDAG, 756. [chap. 10]

παραβολή, ῆς, ἡ (noun). A story or pithy saying designed to illustrate a truth through comparison; something that serves as an example pointing beyond itself to a future realization • *parable, illustration; type, symbol.* (NT 50; LXX 45) *CL*, 266; BDAG, 759. [chap. 28]

παραγίνομαι (verb). To come to be in a place (either generally or with focus on the public nature of the place) • *I arrive, come, draw near, am present; I appear.* (NT 37; LXX 178) *CL*, 266; BDAG, 760. [chap. 26]

παραδίδωμι (verb). To hand over to legal custody (legal technical term); to transmit something to another (with a variety of English glosses possible, depending on the referent) • *I deliver, hand over; I pass on, transmit.* (NT 119; LXX 277) *CL*, 266; BDAG, 761. [chap. 32]

παρακαλέω (verb). To summon someone into one's presence; to urge or request strongly; to exhort someone to have courage or joy • *I invite, call; I exhort, urge; I encourage, comfort.* (NT 109; LXX 139) *CL*, 267; BDAG, 764. [chap. 21]

παραλαμβάνω (verb). To take into close association; to gain control of • *I take (to myself), take with/along; I take over; I accept.* (NT 49; LXX 38) *CL*, 268; BDAG, 767. [chap. 18]

παρίστημι (verb). (1) Transitive (pres., fut., impf., [1]aor.): to place beside or at one's disposal; to represent/present someone to someone; to offer sacrifice (act.); (2) intransitive (pres., fut., pf., plpf., [2]aor. act.): to be present, stand by; to come to the aid of (mid.) • (1) *I place beside; I present; I offer, bring;* (2) *I am present, stand by; bystander, spectator* (subst. pf. ptc.); *I help.* (NT 41; LXX 93) *CL*, 272; BDAG, 778. [chap. 32]

πᾶς, πᾶσα, πᾶν (adj.). An adjective denoting comprehensiveness, either as an aggregate ("all, whole") or with reference to the components of the whole ("each, every") • *all, whole; each, every.* (NT 1,244; LXX 6,833) *CL*, 273; BDAG, 782. [chap. 12]

πάσχω (verb). Generally to experience something, whether positive or negative, but in the NT almost always negative, to undergo a painful experience, to be subject to difficult circumstances; also in the LXX, to grieve over • *I suffer, endure/undergo (something).* (NT 42; LXX 19) *CL*, 274; BDAG, 785. [chap. 14]

πατήρ, πατρός, ὁ (noun). A male parent or ancestor; metaphorically of someone esteemed; God as Father (of Jesus or a believer) • *father.* (NT 413; LXX 1,451) *CL*, 275; BDAG, 786. [chap. 11]

Παῦλος, ου, ὁ (noun). A personal name; in the NT usually of the apostle Paul • *Paul.* (NT 158; LXX 0) *CL*, 276; BDAG, 789. [chap. 3]

πείθω (verb). Generally, to persuade, but this verb evidences the affects of voice and tense-form on meaning more than many verbs and may consist of conflated homonyms: to cause someone to come to a particular point of view or course of action (act.); to submit to, comply, conform to, follow, obey (mid.); to be persuaded or convinced by someone else (focus on the process) (pass.); to believe/trust, be confident, having been convinced (focus on the state of confidence) (pf. act. and mid.) • *I persuade, appeal to, urge* (act.); *I submit* (mid.); *I am persuaded* (pass.); *I believe* (pf. act./mid.). (NT 52; LXX 184) *CL*, 276; BDAG, 791. [chap. 17]

πειράζω (verb). To make an effort to determine the nature or character of someone or something; to entice to commit sin; to attempt to trap someone by a malicious query or offer • *I test, try, make trial of, put to the test; I tempt.* (NT 38; LXX 62) *CL*, 277; BDAG, 792. [chap. 25]

πέμπω (verb). To cause someone or something to depart for a particular purpose • *I send.* (NT 79; LXX 22) *CL*, 277; BDAG, 794. [chap. 14]

πέντε (adj.). The number five (indeclinable) • *five, 5.* (NT 38; LXX 278) *CL*, 277; BDAG, 796. [chap. 12]

περί (prep.). A preposition used with the genitive and accusative cases that describes various aspects of being near or related to something (spatial, temporal, logical) • (prep. + gen.) *about, concerning;* (prep. + acc.) *around.* (NT 333; LXX 852) *CL*, 278; BDAG, 797. [chap. 9]

περιπατέω (verb). To move about by walking, be a pedestrian; metaphorically, to engage in a course of action, conduct one's life • *I walk, walk/go about; I live, behave* (metaphorical). (NT 95; LXX 34) *CL*, 280; BDAG, 803. [chap. 25]

περισσεύω (verb). (1) Intransitive: to be in abundance (number, amount, quality, etc.); to be wealthy; (2) transitive: to cause something to exist in abundance • (1) *I abound, am rich, have an abundance;* (2) *I cause to abound.* (NT 39; LXX 9) *CL*, 281; BDAG, 805. [chap. 19]

Πέτρος, ου, ὁ (noun). Personal name, in the NT the apostle Peter; stone (LXX, but not so used in the NT) • *Peter, stone.* (NT 156; LXX 13) *CL*, 282; BDAG, 810. [chap. 4]

Πιλᾶτος, ου, ὁ (noun). A personal name; in the NT, the Roman prefect (πραίφεκτος/*praefectus*, Roman administrator) of Judea AD 26–36 • *Pilate.* (NT 55; LXX 0) *CL*, 283; BDAG, 813. [chap. 28]

πίνω (verb). To swallow a liquid; to take in or absorb a liquid • *I drink.* (NT 73; LXX 297) *CL*, 284; BDAG, 814. [chap. 26]

πίπτω (verb). To move downward from a higher to a lower level, typically rapidly and freely without control; to drop deliberately to the ground as a sign of humility before a high-ranking person or before God; metaphorically, to experience destruction or ruin, either physically or morally • *I fall (down); I am destroyed.* (NT 90; LXX 424) *CL*, 284; BDAG, 815. [chap. 14]

πιστεύω (verb). To have confidence in the reliability of something or that something will be granted • *I believe, trust, have faith in.* (NT 241; LXX 88) *CL*, 284; BDAG, 816. [chap. 7]

πίστις, εως, ἡ (noun). Confidence based on the reliability of the one trusted; that which is believed; a characteristic of someone in whom confidence can be placed • *faith, belief; the faith; faithfulness.* (NT 243; LXX 59) *CL*, 284; BDAG, 818. [chap. 11]

πιστός, ή, όν (adj.). Worthy of trust, of dependable character; characterized by trust, "believing"; one who confesses the Christian faith, "believer" (subst.) [cf. the noun πίστις] • *faithful, dependable, trustworthy; believing; believer.* (NT 67; LXX 75) *CL*, 285; BDAG, 820. [chap. 16]

πλανάω (verb). To cause someone to go astray, lead them from the right path (act.); to depart from the right path (mid.); to be misled, deceived (pass.) • *I lead astray, deceive* (act.); *I go astray* (mid.); *I am misled, deceived* (pass.). (NT 39; LXX 126) *CL*, 285; BDAG, 821. [chap. 19]

πλείων (adj.). The comparative adjective form of πολύς ("much, large"), a quantity greater in scope than another • *larger, more, greater, bigger.* (NT 55; LXX 86) *CL*, 286; BDAG, 824. [chap. 28]

πλῆθος, ους, τό (noun). A large quantity or number of anything, whether people (most commonly) or things • *multitude, throng, large number.* (NT 31; LXX 288) *CL*, 287; BDAG, 825. [chap. 31]

πλήν (conj.). An adversative coordinating conjunction that introduces a contrast to the preceding statement • *but, however, only, nevertheless.* (NT 31; LXX 248) *CL*, 287; BDAG, 826. [chap. 31]

πληρόω (verb). To increase the contents of something to maximum capacity; to bring an event, period of time, or prophecy to completion • *I fill, fill up; I fulfill, complete, finish.* (NT 86; LXX 112) *CL*, 287; BDAG, 827. [chap. 25]

πλοῖον, ου, τό (noun). A vessel for traveling on water, ranging in size from a small fishing boat to a large seagoing ship • *boat, ship.* (NT 68; LXX 41) *CL*, 288; BDAG, 830. [chap. 24]

πνεῦμα, ατος, τό (noun). Air in motion ("wind"); one aspect of a human's immaterial being (ctr. σῶμα, "body"); an attitude or disposition; a divine person, the third member of the godhead (in orthodox Christian theology); an incorporeal, supernatural being (e.g., an angel) • *wind, breeze; spirit; Spirit.* (NT 379; LXX 382) *CL*, 289; BDAG, 832. [chap. 11]

ποιέω (verb). To produce something material; to bring about a state or condition • *I make, create; I do, perform.* (NT 568; LXX 3,390) *CL*, 290; BDAG, 839. [chap. 7]

πόλις, εως, ἡ (noun). A population center of varying size and population; by metonymy it may refer to the people who live in that place • *city, town.* (NT 162; LXX 1,576) *CL*, 291; BDAG, 844. [chap. 11]

πολύς, πολλή, πολύ (adj.). Extensive in scope, whether with reference to number, quantity, measure, or quality; comparative form: πλείων; superlative: πλεῖστος (many possible equivalents in English, depending on referent and context) • *much* (sg.), *many* (pl.); *large, great, big.* (NT 416; LXX 822) *CL*, 292; BDAG, 847. [chap. 22]

πονηρός, ά, όν (adj.). Morally or socially worthless, by either social or divine standards; deficient in quality so as to be worthless (of physical goods); unhealthy • *evil, wicked, bad; worthless; sick.* (NT 78; LXX 381) *CL*, 293; BDAG, 851. [chap. 15]

πορεύω (verb). To cause to go, to carry (act.; not in the NT or LXX); to move or travel from one place to another (mid. and pass.) • *I go, proceed* (mid. and pass.). (NT 153; LXX 1,263) *CL*, 293; BDAG, 853. [chap. 18]

ποῦ (interrog.). An interrogative adverb of place inquiring as to location [Watch the accent! This is not πού, an enclitic adv., "somewhere."] • *where? at which place? to what place?* (NT 48; LXX 125) *CL*, 295; BDAG, 857. [chap. 30]

πούς, ποδός, ὁ (noun). The body part at the end of the leg (sometimes the reference is to the entire leg); the equivalent part of an animal; the supporting piece of an object (e.g., the bottom part of a table leg, or sometimes the entire leg); a measure of distance • *foot.* (NT 93; LXX 301) *CL*, 295; BDAG, 858. [chap. 22]

πράσσω (verb). To engage in activity so as to accomplish something (often equivalent to ποιέω); to behave in a certain way • *I do, accomplish; I act, behave.* (NT 39; LXX 37) *CL*, 296; BDAG, 860. [chap. 25]

πρεσβύτερος, α, ον (adj.). Older in age; usually substantival: older person (relatively); an old person (absolutely); a recognized leader in either Jewish or Christian contexts; used temporally of one's progenitors, either individually or corporately • *older, elder; ancestors.* (NT 66; LXX 206) *CL*, 297; BDAG, 862. [chap. 24]

πρό (prep.). A preposition used with the genitive case that indicates either a spatial position in front of something or a temporal location earlier than another point

• (prep. + gen.) *before, in front of; earlier than, before.* (NT 47; LXX 251) *CL*, 297; BDAG, 864. [chap. 24]

πρόβατον, ου, τό (noun). A grass-eating animal with a thick, wool coat and cared for by a shepherd (i.e., a sheep); metaphorically, people under the care of a leader, such as a king or pastor • *sheep.* (NT 39; LXX 296) *CL*, 298; BDAG, 866. [chap. 20]

πρός (prep.). A preposition most commonly used with the accusative case to indicate destination or goal ("to, toward"), but occasionally with the genitive ("in the interest of") or dative ("at, near") case • (prep. + acc.) *to, toward, with;* (prep. + gen.) *in the interest of;* (prep. + dat.) *at, near.* (NT 700; LXX 3,338) *CL*, 301; BDAG, 873. [chap. 9]

προσέρχομαι (verb). To approach a person, move toward someone/something; to approach a deity in worship, fellowship, or prayer • *I come/go to, approach.* (NT 86; LXX 113) *CL*, 303; BDAG, 878. [chap. 15]

προσευχή, ῆς, ἡ (noun). A petition addressed to deity; a place where such petitions are regularly offered (in the NT usually a synagogue, though also informal locations) • *prayer; place of prayer.* (NT 36; LXX 115) *CL*, 303; BDAG, 878. [chap. 26]

προσεύχομαι (verb). To address a deity in prayer (a general term for presenting requests, worship, etc.) • *I pray.* (NT 85; LXX 107) *CL*, 303; BDAG, 879. [chap. 15]

προσκυνέω (verb). To do obeisance to, prostrate oneself before; to express in attitude or gesture one's complete dependence on, submission to, or reverence of a high authority figure (human or divine) • *I do obeisance to, prostrate myself before, welcome respectfully; I worship.* (NT 60; LXX 229) *CL*, 305; BDAG, 882. [chap. 27]

προσφέρω (verb). To bring someone/something to someone; to present an offering or gift to someone • *I bring (to); I offer, present.* (NT 47; LXX 161) *CL*, 306; BDAG, 886. [chap. 31]

πρόσωπον, ου, τό (noun). The front part of the head; personal presence (many idiomatic uses, especially with prepositions; see the lexicon); the outer surface of something • *face, appearance; person; surface, countenance.* (NT 76; LXX 1,297) *CL*, 307; BDAG, 887. [chap. 23]

προφητεύω (verb). To reveal hidden information (in Scripture this is typically through divine revelation, but it can refer to other agency); to foretell the future • *I prophesy, foretell.* (NT 28; LXX 117) *CL*, 308; BDAG, 890. [chap. 7]

προφήτης, ου, ὁ (noun). A person who expounds matters transcending normal insight or awareness, known only by special revelation (in the NT almost always an OT or Christian prophet, rarely a non-Christian, polytheist; in the LXX usually a "true" prophet, but also used of "false" prophets); by metonymy, the writing of a prophet or sometimes the OT as a whole • *prophet; the Prophets* (NT 144; LXX 328) *CL*, 308; BDAG, 890. [chap. 4]

πρῶτος, η, ον (adj.). Having primary position in a sequence, either temporally, numerically, or in prominence • *first, earlier.* (NT 155; LXX 223) *CL*, 309; BDAG, 892. [chap. 6]

πτωχός, ή, όν (adj.). In a needy, impoverished condition; deficient in quality or worn out • *poor; shabby; beggar* (subst.). (NT 34; LXX 124) *CL*, 310; BDAG, 896. [chap. 10]

πῦρ, πυρός, τό (noun). Combustion that produces light and heat • *fire.* (NT 71; LXX 540) *CL*, 311; BDAG, 898. [chap. 23]

πῶς (adv.). An interrogative adverb that inquires as to the manner or way in which something is by requesting information or clarification, expressing surprise, criticism, or deliberation; an exclamatory marker • *how? how!* (NT 103; LXX 129) *CL*, 312; BDAG, 900. [chap. 16]

ῥῆμα, ατος, τό (noun). That which is said (typically oral instead of written, ctr. λόγος; many English variations possible due to context); that which can be spoken about • *word, saying; a matter, thing, event.* (NT 68; LXX 548) *CL*, 314; BDAG, 905. [chap. 23]

σάββατον, ου, τό (noun). The seventh day of the week in Israel's calendar ("Sabbath"); the period of seven days divided by the Sabbath (usually pl.) ("week") • *Sabbath; week.* (NT 68; LXX 130) *CL*, 316; BDAG, 909. [chap. 24]

σάρξ, σαρκός, ἡ (noun). The material that covers the bones of a human or animal body ("flesh"); the physical body; a living being with a physical body; humans as physical beings; an immaterial aspect of a person viewed as a source of or subject to sinful desires (ethical use) • *flesh, body; sinful nature.* (NT 147; LXX 215) *CL*, 318; BDAG, 914. [chap. 11]

σεαυτοῦ, ῆς (pron.). A pronoun that makes a reflexive, second-person reference to a person; a reflexive pronoun (second person; never occurs in nominative case or in neuter, so lexical form is genitive; cf. first person, ἐμαυτοῦ; third person, ἑαυτοῦ) • *yourself.* (NT 43; LXX 218) *CL*, 318; BDAG, 917. [chap. 10]

σημεῖον, ου, τό (noun). A distinctive indication or confirmation by which something is known (in the NT this word often refers to a miracle, but it should not usually be translated as such; cf. δύναμις and τέρας) • *sign, indication; (miraculous) sign, portent.* (NT 77; LXX 120) *CL*, 319; BDAG, 920. [chap. 18]

σήμερον (adv.). A temporal adverb indicating reference to the present day (though day is not necessarily defined in strict, twenty-four-hour terms) • *today.* (NT 41; LXX 290) *CL*, 320; BDAG, 921. [chap. 20]

Σίμων, ωνος, ὁ (noun). A personal name of multiple people in both the OT and NT, most commonly in the NT of the apostle Simon Peter • *Simon.* (NT 75; LXX 80) *CL*, 321; BDAG, 924. [chap. 23]

σκηνή, ῆς, ἡ (noun). A temporary, movable shelter • *tent, hut, booth, tabernacle.* (NT 20; LXX 434) *CL*, 322; BDAG, 928. [chap. 19]

σκότος, ους, τό (noun). The absence of light; ignorance in moral or spiritual matters (metaphorical) • *darkness.* (NT 31; LXX 120) *CL*, 323; BDAG, 932. [chap. 31]

σοφία, ας, ἡ (noun). Knowledge that makes possible skillful activity or performance, the capacity to understand and to act prudently as a result • *wisdom, skill.* (NT 51; LXX 254) *CL*, 324; BDAG, 934. [chap. 28]

σπείρω (verb). To sow seeds, plant a field by sowing; to scatter abroad (LXX) • *I sow (seeds), plant; I scatter, disperse.* (NT 52; LXX 62) *CL*, 325; BDAG, 936. [chap. 27]

σπέρμα, ατος, τό (noun). The source from which something is propagated, both plants (seed) and animals or humans (semen); the product of propagation collectively (of animals or humans) • *seed, semen; offspring, children, posterity, descendants.* (NT 43; LXX 280) *CL*, 325; BDAG, 937. [chap. 29]

σταυρόω (verb). To cause to undergo crucifixion; to execute by fastening to a cross • *I crucify.* (NT 46; LXX 2) *CL*, 327; BDAG, 941. [chap. 33]

στόμα, ατος, τό (noun). The body part used for eating and speaking/creating sounds (either human or animal); the opening (or edge) of an object analogous to the body part • *mouth, jaws; edge.* (NT 78; LXX 489) *CL*, 329; BDAG, 946. [chap. 22]

σύ (pron.). Personal pronoun, second-person singular nominative • *you* (sg.). (NT 1,069; LXX 10,692) *CL*, 330; BDAG, 949. [chap. 4]

σύν (prep.). A preposition used with the dative to indicate association or connection • (prep. + dat.) *with.* (NT 128; LXX 233) *CL*, 336; BDAG, 961. [chap. 10]

συνάγω (verb). To bring together as a group (either people or things) • *I gather/call together, assemble.* (NT 59; LXX 377) *CL*, 336; BDAG, 962. [chap. 16]

συναγωγή, ῆς, ἡ (noun). An assembly or collection of things or people; a place where people assemble; in the NT, the Jewish synagogue (where Jews assembled for worship) or a place where Christians assembled; the people who gathered in such a place (Jews or Christians) • *assembly, collection; synagogue, meeting/assembly place; congregation.* (NT 56; LXX 228) *CL*, 336; BDAG, 963. [chap. 27]

συνίημι (verb). To grasp the significance of something • *I understand, comprehend.* (NT 26; LXX 117) *CL*, 341; BDAG, 972. [chap. 33]

σῴζω (verb). To rescue from a hazardous situation, from sickness, or from spiritual/eternal death • *I save, deliver, heal.* (NT 106; LXX 363) *CL*, 345; BDAG, 982. [chap. 22]

σῶμα, ατος, τό (noun). A structured physical unit viewed as a whole, whether human, animal, plant, etc.; a unified group of people, in the NT often Christian believers as a whole, both living, dead, and yet to be • *body.* (NT 142; LXX 136) *CL*, 345; BDAG, 983. [chap. 11]

σωτηρία, ας, ἡ (noun). Deliverance/rescue from harm, whether from physical danger or from spiritual death and condemnation • *deliverance, rescue, salvation.* (NT 46; LXX 160) *CL*, 346; BDAG, 985. [chap. 32]

τέ (particle). An enclitic particle that marks a close relationship between sequential states or events, or between coordinate nonsequential items (often combined with other particles or conjunctions) [see *CL*] • *and (so), so, and likewise.* (NT 215; LXX 277) *CL*, 348; BDAG, 993. [chap. 17]

τέκνον, ου, τό (noun). The offspring of human parents without specific reference to sex or age; plural may refer collectively to descendants from a common ancestor; one who is dear to another (not related genetically) • *child, descendant.* (NT 99; LXX 314) *CL*, 349; BDAG, 994. [chap. 8]

τέλος, ους, τό (noun). A point of time that marks the end of a period or process; the goal toward which something is being directed; the name for an indirect revenue tax, either a toll or customs duties • *end, termination; goal, outcome; tax, (customs) duty.* (NT 40; LXX 165) *CL*, 350; BDAG, 998. [chap. 20]

τέσσαρες, α (adj.). The number four • *four, 4.* (NT 41; LXX 224) *CL*, 350; BDAG, 1000. [chap. 12]

τηρέω (verb). To maintain in a secure state by maintaining custody or by perpetuating a state or activity; to conduct oneself in obedience to instruction or law • *I keep watch over, guard, preserve; I observe, keep.* (NT 70; LXX 37) *CL*, 352; BDAG, 1002. [chap. 27]

τίθημι (verb). To put or place something in a particular location; to assign someone to a task or position; to cause someone or something to undergo a change in condition • *I put, place; I appoint, assign; I make, consign.* (NT 100; LXX 558) *CL*, 352; BDAG, 1003. [chap. 32]

τιμή, ῆς, ἡ (noun). The amount at which something is valued; a high level of respect • *price, value; honor, esteem.* (NT 41; LXX 77) *CL*, 352; BDAG, 1005. [chap. 20]

τις, τι (pron.). A pronoun that refers to an unspecified person or thing (an indefinite pronoun, enclitic) • *someone, anyone; something, anything* (neut.). (NT 525; LXX 319) *CL*, 353; BDAG, 1007. [chap. 12]

τίς, τί (pron.). A pronoun that introduces a question (an interrogative pronoun) • *who? what? which? why?* (NT 555; LXX 1,530) *CL*, 353; BDAG, 1006. [chap. 12]

τοιοῦτος, αύτη, οῦτον (adj.). Similar to some person or thing already mentioned in a context (used either as an adj., pron., or subst. and may be correlative with ὅστις, οἷος, or ὥσπερ) • *such, of such a kind, such as this; such a person/thing* (subst.). (NT 57; LXX 82) *CL*, 354; BDAG, 1009. [chap. 27]

τόπος, ου, ὁ (noun). A spatial area, whether a specific named locality or a general reference; the location for an object or activity, etc. • *place, location, space.* (NT 94; LXX 613) *CL*, 355; BDAG, 1011. [chap. 16]

τότε (adv.). A temporal adverb that specifies sequence (A then B) or refers to a specific time (either past or future) • *then, at that time, when.* (NT 160; LXX 293) *CL*, 355; BDAG, 1012. [chap. 6]

τρεῖς, τρία (adj.). The number three • *three, 3.* (NT 68; LXX 376) *CL*, 356; BDAG, 1014. [chap. 12]

τρίτος, η, ον (adj.). Third in a series; a third part of something (subst.); for the third time (adv.) • *third; third part* (subst.); *third time, thrice* (adv.). (NT 56; LXX 179) *CL*, 356; BDAG, 1016. [chap. 27]

τυφλός, ή, όν (adj.). Unable to see; lacking understanding (metaphorical); a person who cannot see or understand (subst.) • *blind; blind person.* (NT 50; LXX 25) *CL*, 358; BDAG, 1021. [chap. 28]

ὕδωρ, ὕδατος, τό (noun). The liquid we know as water; a body of water; metaphorically of life-giving salvation • *water.* (NT 76; LXX 675) *CL*, 360; BDAG, 1023. [chap. 23]

υἱός, οῦ, ὁ (noun). Male offspring (human or animal), or by extension, someone closely related (not necessarily by birth) or characterized by some quality • *son, descendant, offspring, child,* or (if context allows) *person.* (NT 377; LXX 5,190) *CL*, 360; BDAG, 1024. [chap. 2]

ὑμεῖς (pron.). Personal pronoun, second-person plural nominative of σύ • *you* (pl.). (NT 1,840; LXX 3,335) *CL*, 360; BDAG, 949 (σύ). [chap. 4]

ὑπάγω (verb). To proceed from a position, be on the move in a particular direction; to leave someone's presence • *I go; I depart, go away, leave.* (NT 79; LXX 2) *CL*, 361; BDAG, 1028. [chap. 14]

ὑπάρχω (verb). To be present; to come into being; what belongs to someone (subst. neut. ptc.) • *I am, exist; property, holdings, possessions* (subst.). (NT 60; LXX 157) *CL*, 361; BDAG, 1029. [chap. 16]

ὑπέρ (prep.). A preposition used with either the genitive (benefit, replacement, cause, or interest) or accusative (extent beyond) cases • (prep. + gen.) *in behalf of, for, in place of, because of, about;* (prep. + acc.) *above, beyond, over.* (NT 150; LXX 427) *CL*, 362; BDAG, 1030. [chap. 10]

ὑπό (prep.). A preposition used with the genitive to indicate agent or cause, or with the accusative to indicate a lower position • (prep. + gen.) *by;* (prep. + acc.) *under, below.* (NT 220; LXX 498) *CL*, 364; BDAG, 1035. [chap. 10]

ὑποτάσσω (verb). To place under/below, either under the authority of or appended in a document (LXX) (act.); to become subject to (pass.); to subject oneself to, obey (mid.) • *I subject, subordinate (someone else)* (act.); *I append, attach* (LXX) (act.); *I become subject to* (pass.); *I submit, obey* (mid.). (NT 38; LXX 28) *CL*, 367; BDAG, 1042. [chap. 27]

φανερόω (verb). To cause to be in a condition that makes observation or knowledge possible • *I reveal, disclose, make known/visible.* (NT 49; LXX 1) *CL*, 369; BDAG, 1048. [chap. 25]

Φαρισαῖος, ου, ὁ (noun). A member of a religious and political Jewish party at the time of Jesus characterized by strict observance of the Mosaic law as understood by the scribes • *Pharisee.* (NT 98; LXX 0) *CL*, 370; BDAG, 1049. [chap. 8]

φέρω (verb). To move something from one place to another by either carrying it or otherwise causing it to move; metaphorically, to carry something (positive or negative); to bring about a yield, be productive (of plants) [numerous other less common uses; see BDAG and MLS] • *I carry, transport, lead, bring; I endure; I produce, yield, bear.* (NT 66; LXX 290) *CL*, 370; BDAG, 1051. [chap. 27]

φεύγω (verb). To seek safety by fleeing from a place or situation; to avoid something due to danger • *I flee, escape; I avoid, shun.* (NT 29; LXX 250) *CL*, 370; BDAG, 1052. [chap. 19]

φημί (verb). To convey one's thinking through speech or writing; to clarify or explain what one means [In the LXX and NT this word occurs almost entirely as ἔφη (3rd sg. aor. act. ind.) or φησίν (3rd sg. pres. act. ind.).] • *I say, affirm; I mean.* (NT 66; LXX 74) *CL*, 371; BDAG, 1053. [chap. 33]

φιλέω (verb). To have a special interest in and high regard and affection for someone or something; to indicate that affection by a kiss [Originally the more common word in older forms of Greek, but in Koine is often replaced by and synonymous with ἀγαπάω; see LN §25.43; BDAG, 1056.] • *I love, like; I kiss.* (NT 25; LXX 32) *CL*, 372; BDAG, 1056. [chap. 21]

φίλος, η, ον (adj.). Characterized by having a special interest in and close relationship with another person (i.e., not a casual acquaintance); one who has a close, friendly relationship with another person • *friendly, loving, dear; friend* (subst., as almost always in the LXX and NT). (NT 29; LXX 187) *CL*, 373; BDAG, 1058. [chap. 31]

φοβέω (verb). To scare (someone), make (someone) afraid (act.; rare in the LXX, not found in the NT); to be afraid, fear (mid.); to have profound respect for a person or for God due to awe (mid.); to be frightened (by someone or something) (pass.) • *I scare, make afraid, frighten* (act.); *I fear, am afraid* (mid.); *I reverence, fear, am in awe* (mid.); *I am frightened (by)* (pass.). (NT 95; LXX 460) *CL*, 374; BDAG, 1060. [chap. 30]

φόβος, ου, ὁ (noun). A feeling of need to escape from or avoid a threat, anxiety generated by a threatening circumstance; a profound feeling of respect or reverence for an authority, especially for God • *fear, terror, fright; reverence, respect, awe.* (NT 47; LXX 199) *CL*, 374; BDAG, 1062. [chap. 30]

φυλακή, ῆς, ἡ (noun). A place for detaining a prisoner; a sentry station with its guards; a period of time during which guards are on duty • *jail, prison, cell; guard post; watch (of the night)* (i.e., a period of time). (NT 47; LXX 121) *CL*, 377; BDAG, 1067. [chap. 30]

φυλάσσω (verb). To carry out the duties of a sentry/guard; to protect something so that it remains intact; to diligently observe a command/law • *I guard, watch; I protect; I observe, follow.* (NT 31; LXX 464) *CL*, 377; BDAG, 1068. [chap. 30]

φυλή, ῆς, ἡ (noun). A community of people, either a large group, such as a socio-political entity, or more commonly a subgroup with a common ethnic heritage • *nation, people; tribe.* (NT 31; LXX 444) *CL*, 377; BDAG, 1069. [chap. 33]

φωνέω (verb). To utter or give out a sound intended to attract attention (human or otherwise); to summon someone to come • *I call/cry (out), speak loudly; I summon, invite.* (NT 43; LXX 24) *CL*, 378; BDAG, 1071. [chap. 29]

φωνή, ῆς, ἡ (noun). Any type of sound or auditory effect; the ability to produce a sound • *sound, noise, voice.* (NT 139; LXX 633) *CL*, 378; BDAG, 1071. [chap. 7]

φῶς, φωτός, τό (noun). The physical agent that stimulates the sense of sight to make things visible ("light"); a source of light; metaphorically of various situations that can be illustrated with illumination • *light.* (NT 73; LXX 176) *CL*, 378; BDAG, 1072. [chap. 23]

χαίρω (verb). To experience joy or contentment in a particular circumstance or event; to express a polite social greeting upon meeting someone or at the beginning of a letter (impv. or inf.) • *I rejoice, am glad/cheerful; Greetings! Hello!* (NT 74; LXX 87) *CL*, 379; BDAG, 1074. [chap. 26]

χαρά, ᾶς, ἡ (noun). The emotion of gladness that comes as a result of circumstances; a deep-seated contentment based on faith in God's promises despite circumstances • *joy, delight.* (NT 59; LXX 44) *CL*, 380; BDAG, 1077. [chap. 32]

χάρις, ιτος, ἡ (noun). A disposition marked by generosity, frequently unmotivated by the worth of the recipient; a response to such generosity; with reference to God, divine favor or work for the benefit of others at no cost to them • *grace, favor, kindness; thanks, gratitude.* (NT 155; LXX 164) *CL*, 381; BDAG, 1079. [chap. 11]

χείρ, χειρός, ἡ (noun). The body part at the end of the arm containing fingers ("hand"; occasionally of an animal, e.g., a dog's paw); one component of that part (i.e., "finger") or occasionally the entire member, arm as a whole; that which may be produced with the hand ("handwriting") (numerous metaphorical uses, esp. in the LXX) • *hand, finger; handwriting.* (NT 177; LXX 1,943) *CL*, 382; BDAG, 1082. [chap. 11]

χιλιάς, άδος, ἡ (noun). A group of one thousand (collective noun) • *(group of) a thousand.* (NT 23; LXX 340) *CL*, 382; BDAG, 1084. [chap. 19]

χρεία, ας, ἡ (noun). That which is necessary or needed, but not necessarily possessed; an activity to which one is assigned (LXX) • *need, necessity, lack; assignment, mission, (military) action.* (NT 49; LXX 55) *CL*, 383; BDAG, 1088. [chap. 30]

Χριστός, οῦ, ὁ (noun). Expected fulfiller of the hopes of Israel for an end-time deliverer; also sometimes used almost as a personal name for Jesus • *Messiah, Christ.* (NT 529; LXX 51) *CL*, 384; BDAG, 1091. [chap. 2]

χρόνος, ου, ὁ (noun). A period/span of time (time during which); a particular point of time (time at which) • *period of time, time; occasion.* (NT 54; LXX 141) *CL*, 385; BDAG, 1092. [chap. 28]

χώρα, ας, ἡ (noun). Dry land (in contrast to the sea); the territory of a nation or a smaller geographical area; open country (in contrast to the city); land used for agriculture • *land; country, region, place; countryside; field.* (NT 28; LXX 247) *CL*, 386; BDAG, 1093. [chap. 31]

χωρίς (adv.). An adverb that indicates a situation occurs by itself, separately from other factors; also used as a preposition with the genitive • *separately, apart, by itself* (adv.); *without, apart from* (prep. + gen.). (NT 41; LXX 20) *CL*, 386; BDAG, 1095. [chap. 20]

ψυχή, ῆς, ἡ (noun). The quality of physical life without which a body cannot function, that which animates a body; that which is integral to being a person, the seat and center of the inner human life • *life; soul, (inner) self.* (NT 103; LXX 976) *CL*, 388; BDAG, 1098. [chap. 8]

ὧδε (adv.). Adverb of place with reference to relative nearness; can also have temporal implications referring to a present circumstance • *here, in this place; in this case.* (NT 61; LXX 89) *CL*, 388; BDAG, 1101. [chap. 18]

ὥρα, ας, ἡ (noun). Period of time as one division of a day, a term used roughly as our "hour" (both having various degrees of precision); an undefined time reference that may be relatively short; a particular time when something is to happen • *hour, occasion, moment, time.* (NT 106; LXX 74) *CL*, 389; BDAG, 1102. [chap. 3]

ὡς (particle). A particle used in very diverse ways (adverb, conjunction, comparative particle), typically indicating some similarity or comparison [see BDAG or *CL* for details] • *as, like; when, after, while; (so) that, how; in order to; about, approximately* (with numerals). (NT 504; LXX 1,965) *CL*, 389; BDAG, 1103. [chap. 17]

ὥστε (conj.). A conjunction that introduces a result clause, either coordinate or subordinate; sometimes "intended result" = purpose • *for this reason, therefore; so that, that; in order that.* (NT 83; LXX 182) *CL*, 390; BDAG, 1107. [chap. 8]

Bibliography

Abbott-Smith, George. *A Manual Greek Lexicon of the New Testament*. 3rd ed. Edinburgh: T&T Clark, 1936.

Aland, B., et al. *The Greek New Testament*. 4th rev. ed. New York: United Bible Societies, 1994.

Aland, Kurt, and Barbara Aland. *The Text of the New Testament*. Grand Rapids: Eerdmans, 1987.

Bakker, Egbert. "Voice, Aspect and Aktionsart: Middle and Passive in Ancient Greek." In *Voice: Form and Function*, ed. B. Fox and P. Hopper, 23–47. Amsterdam: John Benjamins, 1994.

Bauer, W., F. W. Danker, W. F. Arndt, and F. W. Gingrich. *A Greek-English Lexicon of the New Testament and Other Early Christian Literature*. 3rd ed. Chicago: University of Chicago Press, 2000.

Blass, F., A. Debrunner, and R. Funk. *A Greek Grammar of the New Testament and Other Early Christian Literature*. Chicago: University of Chicago Press, 1961.

Boyer, James. "First Class Conditions: What Do They Mean?" *Grace Theological Journal* 2 (1981): 75–114.

———. "Second Class Conditions in the New Testament." *Grace Theological Journal* 3 (1982): 81–88.

———. "Third (and Fourth) Class Conditions." *Grace Theological Journal* 3 (1982): 163–75.

Buck, Carl D. *The Greek Dialects*. 2nd ed. Chicago: University of Chicago Press, 1955.

Buckler, William, and William McAvoy. *American College Handbook of English Fundamentals*. New York: American Book, 1965.

Campbell, Constantine R. *Basics of Verbal Aspect in Biblical Greek*. Grand Rapids: Zondervan, 2008.

———. *Verbal Aspect, the Indicative Mood, and Narrative: Soundings in the Greek of the New Testament*. Studies in Biblical Greek 13. New York: Peter Lang, 2007.

Carson, D. A. *Exegetical Fallacies*. 2nd ed. Grand Rapids: Baker, 1996.

———. *The Gospel according to John*. Pillar New Testament Commentary. Grand Rapids: Eerdmans, 1991.

———. *Greek Accents: A Student's Manual*. Grand Rapids: Baker, 1985.

Chamberlain, Gary Alan. *The Greek of the Septuagint: A Supplemental Lexicon*. Peabody, MA: Hendrickson, 2011.

Conrad, Carl. "New Observations on Voice in the Ancient Greek Verb." November 19, 2002. http://www.artsci.wustl.edu/~cwconrad/docs/NewObsAncGrkVc.pdf.

Conybeare, F. C., and George Stock. *Grammar of Septuagint Greek*. Boston: Ginn, 1905.

Culy, Martin. "The Clue Is in the Case: Distinguishing Adjectival and Adverbial Participles." *Perspectives in Religious Studies* 30.4 (2003): 441–53.

Danker, Frederick William, with Kathryn Krug. *The Concise Greek-English Lexicon of the New Testament*. Chicago: University of Chicago Press, 2009.

Decker, Rodney J. "Adapting Technology to Teach Koine Greek." In Porter and O'Donnell, *Linguist as Pedagogue*, 25–42.

———. *Koine Greek Reader: Selections from the New Testament, Septuagint, and Early Christian Writers*. Grand Rapids: Kregel, 2007.

———. *Mark: A Handbook on the Greek Text*. Baylor Handbook on the Greek New Testament. Waco: Baylor University Press, 2014.

———. *Temporal Deixis of the Greek Verb in the Gospel of Mark with Reference to Verbal Aspect*. Studies in Biblical Greek 10. New York: Peter Lang, 2001.

———. "The Use of εὐθύς ('immediately') in Mark." *Journal of Ministry and Theology* 1 (1997): 90–121.

Fairbairn, Donald. *Understanding Language: A Guide for Beginning Students of Greek and Latin*. Washington, DC: Catholic University of America Press, 2011.

Fanning, Buist M. *Verbal Aspect in New Testament Greek*. Oxford Theological Monographs. Oxford: Clarendon, 1990.

Farrar, Frederic W. *A Brief Greek Syntax and Hints on Greek Accidence*. 8th ed. London: Longmans, Green, 1876.

Funk, Robert W. *Beginning-Intermediate Grammar of Hellenistic Greek*. 2nd ed. 3 vols. Missoula, MT: Scholars Press/SBL, 1973.

Gesenius, F. H. W., E. Kautzsch, and A. E. Cowley. *Hebrew Grammar*. 2nd English ed. Oxford: Clarendon, 1909.

Goetchius, Eugene Van Ness. *The Language of the New Testament*. New York: Scribner's, 1965.

Goodwin, William. *Syntax of the Moods and Tenses of the Greek Verb*. Boston: Ginn, 1890.

Green, Robert E. "Understanding EIMI Periphrastics in the Greek of the New Testament." PhD diss., Baptist Bible Seminary, 2012.

Greenbaum, Sidney. *The Oxford English Grammar*. Oxford: Oxford University Press, 1996.

Holmes, Michael W. *The Apostolic Fathers: Greek Texts and English Translations*. 3rd ed. Grand Rapids: Baker Academic, 2007.

Horrocks, Geoffrey. *Greek: A History of the Language and Its Speakers*. 2nd ed. Chichester, West Sussex: Wiley-Blackwell, 2010.

Huddleston, Rodney. *Introduction to the Grammar of English*. Cambridge Textbooks in Linguistics. Cambridge: Cambridge University Press, 1984.

Huddleston, Rodney, and Geoffrey K. Pullum. *The Cambridge Grammar of the English Language*. Cambridge: Cambridge University Press, 2002.

———. *A Student's Introduction to English Grammar*. Cambridge: Cambridge University Press, 2005.

Kaplan, Jeffrey P. *English Grammar: Principles and Facts*. 2nd ed. Englewood Cliffs, NJ: Prentice Hall, 1995.

Kühner, Raphael. *Grammar of the Greek Language*. Translated by B. Edwards and S. Taylor. New York: Appleton, 1852.

Lee, J. A. L. "Some Features of the Speech of Jesus in Mark's Gospel." *Novum Testamentum* 27 (1985): 1–26.

Liddell, Henry George, Robert Scott, and Henry Stuart Jones. *A Greek-English Lexicon*. 9th ed. with rev. supplement. Oxford: Clarendon, 1968.

Louw, Johannes P., and Eugene A. Nida. *Greek-English Lexicon of the New Testament Based on Semantic Domains*. 2nd ed. 2 vols. New York: United Bible Societies, 1989.

Lust, Johan, Erik Eynikel, and Katrin Hauspie. *Greek-English Lexicon of the Septuagint*. Rev. ed. Stuttgart: Deutsche Bibelgesellschaft, 2003.

McGaughy, Lane C. *A Descriptive Analysis of Εἶναι as a Linking Verb in New Testament Greek*. Society of Biblical Literature Dissertation Series 6. Missoula, MT: Society of Biblical Literature, 1972.

McKay, K. L. "The Use of the Ancient Greek Perfect Down to the End of the Second Century." *Bulletin of the Institute of Classical Studies* 12 (1965): 1–21.

Metzger, Bruce M. *Reminiscences of an Octogenarian*. Peabody, MA: Hendrickson, 1997.

———. *A Textual Commentary on the Greek New Testament*. 2nd ed. New York: United Bible Societies, 1994.

Moo, Douglas. *The Epistle to the Romans*. New International Commentary on the New Testament. Grand Rapids: Eerdmans, 1996.

Moule, C. F. D. *An Idiom Book of New Testament Greek*. 2nd ed. London: Cambridge University Press, 1960.

Moulton, James H., and G. Milligan. *Vocabulary of the Greek New Testament*. 1930. Reprint, Peabody, MA: Hendrickson, 1997.

Moulton, James H., W. F. Howard, and N. Turner. *A Grammar of New Testament Greek*. 4 vols. Edinburgh: T&T Clark, 1908–76.

Mounce, William D. *The Analytical Lexicon to the Greek New Testament*. Grand Rapids: Zondervan, 1993.

———. *The Morphology of Biblical Greek*. Grand Rapids: Zondervan, 1994.

Muraoka, Takamitsu. *A Greek-English Lexicon of the Septuagint*. Louvain: Peeters, 2009.

Nestle, E., B. Aland, and K. Aland. *Novum Testamentum Graece*. 27th ed. Stuttgart: Deutsche Bibelgesellschaft, 1993.

Palmer, Leonard R. *The Greek Language*. The Great Languages. 1980. Reprint, Norman, OK: University of Oklahoma Press, 1996.

Pence, R., and D. Emery. *Grammar of Present-Day English*. 2nd ed. New York: Macmillan, 1963.

Porter, Stanley E. *Idioms of the Greek New Testament*. 2nd ed. Biblical Languages: Greek 2. Sheffield: JSOT Press, 1994.

———, ed. *The Language of the New Testament: Classic Essays*. Journal for the Study of the New Testament Supplement Series 60. Sheffield: JSOT Press, 1991.

———. *Verbal Aspect in the Greek of the New Testament, with Reference to Tense and Mood*. 2nd ed. Studies in Biblical Greek 1. New York: Peter Lang, 1993.

Porter, Stanley E., and Matthew Brook O'Donnell, eds. *The Linguist as Pedagogue*. New Testament Monographs 11. Sheffield: Sheffield Phoenix, 2009.

Preisendanz, K., ed. *Papyri graecae magicae: Die griechischen Zauberpapyri*. 3 vols. Leipzig and Berlin: Teubner, 1928–41.

Rahlfs, Alfred, ed. *Septuaginta*. Rev. Robert Hanhart. Stuttgart: Deutsche Bibelgesellschaft, 2006.

Robertson, A. T. *A Grammar of the Greek New Testament in the Light of Historical Research*. 4th ed. Nashville: Broadman, 1923.

Rydbeck, Lars. *Fachprosa, vermeintliche Volkssprache und Neues Testament: Zur Beurteilung der sprachlichen Niveauunterschiede im nachklassischen Griechisch*. Stockholm: Almqvist & Wiksell, 1967. One of the concluding chapters is available in English: "On the Question of Linguistic Levels and the Place of the New Testament in the Contemporary Language Milieu." In *The Language of the New Testament: Classic Essays*, edited by Stanley E. Porter, 191–204. Journal for the Study of the New Testament: Supplement Series 60. Sheffield: JSOT Press, 1991.

Silva, Moisés. *God, Language and Scripture: Reading the Bible in the Light of General Linguistics*. Grand Rapids: Zondervan, 1990.

Smyth, Henry Weir. *Greek Grammar*. Revised by G. M. Messing. Cambridge, MA: Harvard University Press, 1956.

Taylor, Bernard. *Analytical Lexicon to the Septuagint*. 2nd ed. Peabody, MA: Hendrickson, 2009.

Thackery, Henry St. John. *A Grammar of the Old Testament in Greek according to the Septuagint*. Vol. 1, *Introduction, Orthography and Accidence*. Cambridge: Cambridge University Press, 1909.

Tolkien, J. R. R. *The Lord of the Rings*. 50th Anniversary Edition. Boston: Houghton Mifflin, 2004.

Trenchard, Warren C. *A Concise Dictionary of New Testament Greek*. Cambridge: Cambridge University Press, 2003.

Voelz, James. *Fundamental Greek Grammar*. 3rd rev. ed. St. Louis: Concordia, 2011.

Wallace, Daniel B. *Greek Grammar beyond the Basics: An Exegetical Syntax of the New Testament*. Grand Rapids: Zondervan, 1996.

Waltke, Bruce K., and M. O'Connor. *An Introduction to Biblical Hebrew Syntax*. Winona Lake, IN: Eisenbrauns, 1990.

Index

All numbers refer to sections unless preceded by p. (page) or n. (note). Sections in the introduction are preceded by I, and in the appendixes by A–F. See the glossary (app. F) for a list of all the Greek vocabulary and the chapter where each word is first introduced.